Providing Sound Foundations for Cryptography

ACM Books

Editor in Chief

M. Tamer Özsu, *University of Waterloo*

ACM Books is a new series of high-quality books for the computer science community, published by ACM in collaboration with Morgan & Claypool Publishers. ACM Books publications are widely distributed in both print and digital formats through booksellers and to libraries (and library consortia) and individual ACM members via the ACM Digital Library platform.

Providing Sound Foundations for Cryptography: On the work of Shafi Goldwasser and Silvio Micali
Oded Goldreich, *Weizmann Institute of Science*
2019

Concurrency: The Works of Leslie Lamport
Dahlia Malkhi, *VMware Research* and *Calibra*
2019

The Essentials of Modern Software Engineering: Free the Practices from the Method Prisons!
Ivar Jacobson, *Ivar Jacobson International*
Harold "Bud" Lawson, *Lawson Konsult AB (deceased)*
Pan-Wei Ng, *DBS Singapore*
Paul E. McMahon, *PEM Systems*
Michael Goedicke, *Universität Duisburg–Essen*
2019

Data Cleaning
Ihab F. Ilyas, *University of Waterloo*
Xu Chu, *Georgia Institute of Technology*
2019

Conversational UX Design: A Practitioner's Guide to the Natural Conversation Framework
Robert J. Moore, *IBM Research–Almaden*
Raphael Arar, *IBM Research–Almaden*
2019

Heterogeneous Computing: Hardware and Software Perspectives
Mohamed Zahran, *New York University*
2019

Providing Sound Foundations for Cryptography

On the work of Shafi Goldwasser and Silvio Micali

Oded Goldreich, editor

Weizmann Institute of Science

ACM Books #30

Providing Sound Foundations for Cryptography: On the work of Shafi Goldwasser and Silvio Micali
Oded Goldreich, editor

books.acm.org
http://books.acm.org

ISBN: 978-1-4503-7266-4   hardcover
ISBN: 978-1-4503-7267-1   paperback
ISBN: 978-1-4503-7268-8   EPUB
ISBN: 978-1-4503-7269-5   eBook

Series ISSN: 2374-6769 print   2374-6777 electronic

DOIs:

10.1145/3335741	Book	10.1145/3335741.3335756	Chapter 14
10.1145/3335741.3335742	Preface	10.1145/3335741.3335757	Chapter 15
10.1145/3335741.3335743	Chapter 1	10.1145/3335741.3335758	Chapter 16
10.1145/3335741.3335744	Chapter 2	10.1145/3335741.3335759	Chapter 17
10.1145/3335741.3335745	Chapter 3	10.1145/3335741.3335760	Chapter 18
10.1145/3335741.3335746	Chapter 4	10.1145/3335741.3335761	Chapter 19
10.1145/3335741.3335747	Chapter 5	10.1145/3335741.3335762	Chapter 20
10.1145/3335741.3335748	Chapter 6	10.1145/3335741.3335763	Chapter 21
10.1145/3335741.3335749	Chapter 7	10.1145/3335741.3335764	Chapter 22
10.1145/3335741.3335750	Chapter 8	10.1145/3335741.3335765	Chapter 23
10.1145/3335741.3335751	Chapter 9	10.1145/3335741.3335766	Chapter 24
10.1145/3335741.3335752	Chapter 10	10.1145/3335741.3335767	Chapter 25
10.1145/3335741.3335753	Chapter 11	10.1145/3335741.3335768	Chapter 26
10.1145/3335741.3335754	Chapter 12	10.1145/3335741.3335769	Index/Bios
10.1145/3335741.3335755	Chapter 13		

A publication in the ACM Books series, #30
Editor in Chief: M. Tamer Özsu, *University of Waterloo*

This book was typeset in Arnhem Pro 10/14 and Flama using ZzTEX.

First Edition

10 9 8 7 6 5 4 3 2 1

Contents

Chapter 20   **Fundamentals of Fully Homomorphic Encryption**   543

Zvika Brakerski

Chapter 21   **Interactive Proofs for Lattice Problems**   565

Daniele Micciancio

Chapter 22   **Following a Tangent of Proofs**   599

Johan Håstad

Preface

There are no privileges without duties.

—Advocate Klara Goldreich-Ingwer (1912–2004)

Cryptography is concerned with the construction of schemes that withstand any abuse: A cryptographic scheme is constructed so as to maintain a desired functionality, even under malicious attempts aimed at making it deviate from its prescribed behavior. The design of cryptographic systems must be based on firm foundations, whereas ad hoc approaches and heuristics are a very dangerous way to go. These foundations were developed mostly in the 1980s, in works that are all co-authored by Shafi Goldwasser and/or Silvio Micali. These works have transformed cryptography from an engineering discipline, lacking sound theoretical foundations, into a scientific field possessing a well-founded theory, which influences practice as well as contributes to other areas of theoretical computer science. The current book celebrates these works, which were the basis for bestowing the 2012 Turing Award upon Shafi Goldwasser and Silvio Micali.

◇ ◇ ◇

Cryptography as we know it today is based entirely on concepts, definitions, techniques, and feasibility results put forward and developed in the works of Goldwasser and/or Micali. A significant portion of this book reproduces some of these works, whose contents is briefly outlined next.

"Probabilistic Encryption" (Chapter 7). The pivot of the aforementioned body of work is the pioneering work "Probabilistic Encryption," whose title reflects the realization that a robust notion of secure encryption requires the use of randomization in the process of encrypting each message (and not only in the process of generating cryptographic keys). This work of Goldwasser and Micali defined the mind-set of the field by establishing conceptual frameworks and demonstrating their usefulness. In particular:

- This work suggested viewing computationally indistinguishable objects as equivalent. This revolutionary suggestion has played a key role in all standard cryptographic definitions and has served as the pivot of the acclaimed theory of pseudorandomness (to be briefly reviewed below).

- This work suggested interpreting security as the ability to emulate an ideal setting. This suggestion, further clarified by Goldwasser and Micali in early versions of "The Knowledge Complexity of Interactive Proof Systems" (briefly reviewed below), has been adopted as the basic approach to defining security in almost all cryptographic settings. This approach, known as the **simulation paradigm**, *resolves the Gordian knot that has frustrated previous attempts to define security by trying to enumerate all desired properties.* The simulation paradigm bypasses this enumeration by asserting that security means that anything that can be efficiently obtained by an attack on the cryptographic system can be essentially obtained (as efficiently) without attacking the system. Thus, any gain that an attacker claims is actually not due to the use of the cryptographic system.

- This work demonstrated the fruitfulness of the aforementioned paradigm shift by providing robust definitions for the most basic cryptographic primitive (i.e., encryption schemes) and by constructing a secure encryption scheme based on a standard complexity assumption. In addition to demonstrating the viability of the new-at-the-time approach, this paper set the standard for the two-step process to be followed by all subsequent works:
  - First, a robust definition is developed, based on the aforementioned approach.
  - Next, schemes satisfying this definition are proven to exist (and actually explicitly constructed) based on much better understood assumptions.

  For example, once defined, it was not a priori clear whether zero-knowledge proofs exist at all, and thus relating this question to well-known conjectures demonstrated the viability of zero-knowledge.

- This work also introduced important techniques, one being later termed *the hybrid argument*, which found numerous applications in cryptography and in the theory of pseudorandomness. Notably, this work also heralded worst-case to average-case reductions (also known as random self-reducibility).

"The Knowledge Complexity of Interactive Proof Systems" (Chapter 8). The second most influential work of Goldwasser and Micali is their joint work on zero-knowledge, which after not being understood by most researchers for three years, and being revised several times, appeared in the "formal verification" session of STOC '85 (indicating that it was misunderstood even by the program committee that accepted it for presentation). I can testify to the fact that the lack of understanding has not been due to a poor presentation of the ideas, but rather to their revolutionary nature. (By the way, their earlier work "Probabilistic Encryption" also faced lack of understanding for a couple of years.)

Nowadays, it is well-understood that this work introduced two fascinating and highly influential concepts: the concept of interactive proofs and the concept of zero-knowledge. The concept of interactive proofs had a vast impact on complexity theory, to be briefly reviewed below. The concept of zero-knowledge, on top of being very intriguing (once one stops being confused by it), became a central tool in cryptography and led to fundamental discoveries regarding general secure multi-party computation. Initial indications to the vast potential impact of these concepts were provided by the results and discussions in the conference version of this work (reproduced in Chapter 8).

"How to Generate Cryptographically Strong Sequences of Pseudo-Random Bits" (Chapter 9). This work defined pseudorandom generators as producing a sequence of unpredictable bits. This definition was later shown to be equivalent to being computationally indistinguishable from the uniform distribution over bit-strings of adequate length. The notion of computational indistinguishably used here is the same as the notion introduced in "Probabilistic Encryption," but subsequent works introduced a variety of alternative definitions yielding a host of notions of pseudo-random generators. This work also defined the notion of a hard-core predicate of a one-way function, and established its existence for the modular exponentiation function.

"How to Construct Random Functions" (Chapter 10). This work extended the theory of pseudorandomness to functions, and showed how to construct pseudorandom functions based on any pseudorandom generator. The notion of a pseudorandom function found numerous applications in cryptography, starting from the construction of message authentication codes and private-key encryption schemes that withstand chosen ciphertext attacks.

"A Digital Signature Scheme Secure Against Adaptive Chosen-Message Attacks" (Chapter 11). The result proved by this paper was considered impossible or at least "paradoxical" at the time, because it was (falsely) believed that a "constructive proof of unforgeability" (under passive attacks) implies a successful chosen-message attack.

"Proofs that Yield Nothing but their Validity or All Languages in NP Have Zero-Knowledge Proof Systems" (Chapter 12). This work demonstrated the generality and wide applicability of zero-knowledge proofs. In particular, assuming the existence of secure commitment schemes, it showed how to construct zero-knowledge interactive proof systems for any set in NP, yielding a powerful tool for the design of various cryptographic schemes. Loosely speaking, zero-knowledge proofs offer a way for a party to prove that it has behaved according to a predetermined protocol, *without revealing its own secrets*, and so they can be used to force parties to behave in "honest-but-curious" manner.

"How to Play any Mental Game—A Completeness Theorem for Protocols with Honest Majority" (Chapter 13). This work presented constructions of secure protocols for any multi-party computation problem. In other words, it shows how a trusted party can be emulated by a set of mutually distrustful parties. This result combines the construction of "privacy-preserving" protocols for the "honest-but-curious" model with a method (presented in Chapter 12) of forcing parties to behave in an honest-but-curious manner. The privacy-preserving protocols rely on the existence of a public-key encryption scheme and an Oblivious Transfer protocol, which can both be based on the existence of trapdoor permutations.

"Non-Interactive Zero-Knowledge (NIZK) Proof Systems" (Chapter 14). The model of noninteractive proof systems introduced in this work includes a common random string provided from the outside and available to both the prover and the verifier. The work showed how to provide zero-knowledge (noninteractive) proofs for any NP-assertion. Such NIZKs have been used as a building blocks in many subsequent works (e.g., in constructing public-key encryption schemes that withstand chosen-ciphertext attacks).

"Completeness Theorems for Non-Cryptographic Fault-Tolerant Distributed Computation" (Chapter 15). This work obtained general results similar to those of the work presented in Chapter 13, except that it uses no intractability assumptions. Instead, this work presumes the existence of private channels between each pair of parties (and a larger percentage of honest parties).

"Multi-Prover Interactive Proofs: How to Remove Intractability Assumptions" (Chapter 16). Motivated by the desire to construct zero-knowledge proof systems without relying on intractability assumptions, this work presented a model of multi-prover interactive proofs in which the provers cannot interact with one another during their interaction with the verifier. This model, denoted MIP, turned out to be closely related to the PCP model, which was introduced later and is briefly reviewed below.

Part II of this book reproduces the conference versions of the ten foregoing works (while using the titles of their journal versions, which are different in a few of the cases). These conference versions are extended abstracts that lack many of the details that support the claims made in them, but they best portray the spirit of innovation, boldness, and freshness that is characteristic of Shafi Goldwasser and Silvio Micali.

♣ ♣ ♣

Part III of this book presents scientific surveys of the works of Shafi Goldwasser and Silvio Micali and of works that were directly inspired by their work. This part starts with a survey of the foundations of cryptography.

On the Foundations of Cryptography. Before spelling out what these foundations are, let us briefly reflect on the significance of such theoretical foundations to cryptographic practice. While the following argument is widely accepted nowadays, it required a convincing advocation in the 1980s. Needless to say, Shafi Goldwasser and Silvio Micali provided such advocation when presenting their pioneering work.

Surely, providing sound theoretical foundations is of great importance for any discipline, but more so for cryptography, since cryptography is concerned with the construction of schemes that should be robust against malicious attempts to make these schemes deviate from their prescribed functionality. A heuristic may make sense when the designer has a very good idea about the environment in which a scheme is to operate, yet a cryptographic scheme has to operate in a maliciously selected environment that typically transcends the designer's view. In fact, the adversary is likely to take the very actions that were dismissed or ignored by the designer. Thus, the design of cryptographic systems has to be based on *firm foundations*, as provided by the research project lead by Goldwasser and Micali in the 1980s.

The foundations of cryptography are the main paradigms, approaches and techniques used to conceptualize, define and provide solutions to natural cryptographic problems. These foundations will be reviewed in Chapter 17, starting with a presentation of some of the central tools used in cryptography; that is, computational difficulty (in the form of one-way functions), pseudorandomness, and zero-knowledge proofs. Based on these tools, the survey treats basic cryptographic applications such as encryption and signature schemes as well as the design of general secure cryptographic protocols. It is striking to note that the entire exposition is rooted directly or indirecting in works of Goldwasser and Micali. Indeed, the history of laying the foundations of cryptography is the story of the works of Goldwasser and Micali.

Impact on Complexity Theory.   The revolutionary evolution of cryptography in the 1980s had a great impact on other areas of computer science, most notably on complexity theory. Some of this impact will be reviewed in Chapter 18. Among the direct contributions of the cryptographic evolution to Computer Science, I wish to highlight the theory of pseudorandomness and the study of probabilistic proof systems. Notably, Goldwasser and Micali played a key role also in the development of these specific areas.

A fresh view at the "question of randomness" was taken in the theory of computing: It has been postulated that a distribution is *pseudorandom* if it cannot be told apart from the uniform distribution by any efficient procedure. This paradigm, which was introduced in cryptography where efficient procedures were associated with polynomial-time algorithms that may be stronger than the (purported pseudorandom) generator, has been applied also with respect to a variety of limited classes of such distinguishing procedures, including polynomial-size circuits that are smaller than the running time of the generator, constant-depth circuits, space-bounded machines, local tests (cf., limited independence generators), linear tests (cf., small bias generators), nondeterministic polynomial-time machines, and more. Indeed, this paradigm has been the basis of a vast body of intriguing research concerned with the role of randomness in computation. Also worth noting are the application of pseudorandom functions (e.g., to hardness of *PAC learning* and to "Natural Proofs").

Various types of *probabilistic* proof systems have played a central role in the development of computer science in the last decades. Such nontraditional formulations of proof systems, which allow for a bounded probability of error and view the proof as a dynamic process rather than as a static object, have many advantages over the classical formulation of proof systems (which underlies NP). These advantages are demonstrated by the known results regarding interactive proofs, zero-knowledge proofs, and probabilistically checkable proofs (PCP). The fruitful connection between PCPs and the complexity of natural approximation problems was also discovered in such a work. This connection has provided a breakthrough in the study of approximation algorithms, which has been almost literally stuck for two decades.

On Some Other Works of Goldwasser and Micali. Although the main topic of this book is the contributions of Goldwasser and Micali to the foundations of cryptography, it would be inappropriate not to mention their direct contributions to other areas within the theory of computation. Some of these contributions are surveyed in Chapter 18, where the perspective is of the impact of cryptography on complexity theory. In addition, Chapter 19 surveys a few other contributions, without mentioning the relations of some of them to cryptography. The selection of titles includes:

- "An $O(\sqrt{|V|} \cdot |E|)$-Time Algorithm for Finding Maximum Matching in General Graphs," which still holds the record for the fastest algorithm for this central computational problem.

- "Certifying Almost All Primes Using Elliptic Curves," which presented a randomized polynomial-time algorithm that produces (absolute) certificates of primality for almost all primes.

- "Private Coins versus Public Coins in Interactive Proof Systems," which provided a transformation of general interactive proof systems into ones in which the verifier only poses totally random challenges.

- "An Optimal Randomized Protocol for Synchronous Byzantine Agreement," which provided a constant-round protocol for this central problem.

- "PCPs and the Hardness of Approximating the Size of Maximum Cliques," which provided a PCP system of almost logarithmic randomness and query complexity for NP, and linked such systems to the complexity of a central approximation problem.

- "Computationally Sound Proofs," which presented natural notions of computationally-sound proof systems.

- "Property Testing and Its Connection to Learning and Approximation," which initiated a general study of approximate decision problems that can be solved in sublinear time, while focusing on testing properties of (dense) graphs.

- "Pseudo-Deterministic Algorithms," which initiated the study of probabilistic algorithms for solving search problems in a consistent manner (i.e., almost always return the same canonical solution).

For each of these selected works, the original abstract is reproduced, and a few additional comments about the work are made. It should be stressed that although Chapters 17–19 review many of the most influential works of Goldwasser and Micali, they are far from exhausting this list, as illustrated by Chapters 21, 24 and 26.

Scientific Vignettes by Some of Their Former Students. A few of Goldwasser's and Micali's former students were asked to write chapters about topics of their choice. Most of them agreed, and some of them delivered. Certainly, Shafi and Silvio do not educate their students to be timely. In their defense, one may say that they don't preach what they don't practice.

Zvika Brakerski's survey (Chapter 20), "Fundamentals of Fully Homomorphic Encryption," reviews a topic that was not pioneered by Goldwasser and Micali. In fact, the partial homomorphic property of the Goldwasser–Micali encryption scheme was considered more as a bug than as a feature, which led them to suggest using it only for the establishing of a key for a symmetric encryption scheme (see their "Why and How to Establish a Private Code on a Public Network," with Po Tong in FOCS 1982). Nevertheless, perspectives have changed, and the potential benefits of fully homomorphic encryption, envisioned by Rivest et al. (in 1978), have been materialized by the surprising discovery of fully homomorphic encryption schemes whose security are based on computational problems regarding lattices.

Computational problems regarding lattices are also the pivot of Daniele Micciancio's survey (Chapter 21), "Interactive Proofs for Lattice Problems." The starting point of this survey is a work of Goldreich and Goldwasser that presented perfect zero-knowledge interactive proof systems for central problems regarding lattices (in order to demonstrate that they are unlikely to be NP-hard). The survey provides the basic background for the computational aspects of lattices, and focuses on several interactive proof systems for various claims regarding lattices, while exposing their underlying ideas.

Johan Håstad's survey (Chapter 22), "Following a Tangent of Proofs," also starts with interactive proof systems, but its actual focus is on the non-approximability results that can be derived from *probabilistically checkable proofs* (PCPs), which in turn arised from multi-prover interactive proof systems. Håstad confesses that, at the time, he considered the multi-prover model to be "artificial" and doubted the justification of introducing an esoteric complexity class that corresponds to it. His past reaction was reminiscent of the reactions that other notions introduced previously by Goldwasser and Micali have received (e.g., probabilistic encryption and zero-knowledge). Needless to say, in all cases, these skeptic reactions were proved wrong.

Rafael Pass's "Tutorial on Concurrent Zero-Knowledge" (Chapter 23) addresses the issue of preserving the zero-knowledge feature under "concurrent composition." The point is that the original definition of zero-knowledge refers to a stand-alone execution, and the preservation of security under sequential, parallel, and even concurrent executions is far from clear. While augmenting the original definition with auxiliary inputs suffices for sequential composition, preservation of security under parallel and concurrent executions requires some work. Dealing with concurrent executions is most challenging, and the tutorial presents the simplest known solution, which did not appear is isolation before.

Guy Rothblum's survey (Chapter 24), "Doubly-Efficient Interactive Proofs," revisits the notion of interactive proof systems with a focus on more strict complexity requirements. In particular, the (honest) prover strategy is required to run in polynomial time, and the verifier strategy is required to run in almost linear time. Such interactive proof systems, later termed *doubly efficient*, were first defined and constructed by Goldwasser, Kalai, and Rothblum. Interestingly, this notion was considered by Shafi, Silvio, and myself in the mid-1980s, but we failed to find any appealing example (i.e., one in which interaction speeds up verification).

The starting point of Salil Vadhan's survey (Chapter 25), "Computational Entropy," is the notion of computational indistinguishability, put forward by Goldwasser and Micali (see Chapter 7), as applied in the theory of pseudorandomness. This starting point leads to the introduction of computational analogues of other statistical notions such as entropy, min-entropy, KL-divergence, and more. These notions play a major role in the constructions of pseudorandom generators and statistically hiding commitment schemes, which are surveyed in this chapter.

Deviating for the framework that underlies all the foregoing, Yael Tauman Kalai and Leonid Reyzin's "Survey of Leakage-Resilient Cryptography" (Chapter 26) considers cases in which the computing devices used by the honest parties may leak partial information about the their computation or storage. That is, whereas the foregoing views algorithms and strategies as functions (which, once feed with inputs, return adequate outputs), the leakage models attempt to account for the fact that computation is taking place on a physical device that may be subject to various physical measurements, and leakage-resilient schemes attempt to protect against corresponding physical attacks. As noted in the survey, Goldwasser and Micali have contributed significantly also to this research direction.

♠ ♠ ♠

In contrast to this preface, which started with a review of the works of Goldwasser and Micali, the book starts with their lives and voices. Specifically, Part I contains a brief personal biography of each of them, an interview with each of them, which touches on both the personal and the professional, and revised transcripts of their Turing Award lectures.

Brief Biographies.   Given the timidness of the theory of computation community, writing personal biographies of its pioneers seems quite challenging. On top of this, I was quite curious to see how a professional writer, who has no background in computer science, will view and portray Shafi and Silvio. I feel that both challenges were well addressed by Michelle Waitzman. It is quite remarkable that Michelle was able to identify key features of their personalities and link these features to characteristics of their scientific research. Her success is well reflected in the titles she choose for the personal biographies: "A Story Behind Every Problem: A Brief Biography of Shafi Goldwasser" and "One Obsession at a Time: A Brief Biography of Silvio Micali."

Interviews.   Given that both Shafi and Silvio are very interactive personalities, interviewing them must have been a pleasure. The pleasure was shared among Alon Rosen, who interviewed Shafi Goldwasser, while building on his expertise in cryptography, and Stephen Ibaraki, who interviewed Silvio Micali (as part of an interview series with outstanding computer professionals). The interviews refer both to the personal life and professional work of Goldwasser and Micali, and the former aspects have some overlap with the biographies, where a common theme is indeed the relation of the personal and the professional. Lightly edited extracts from the two interviews are included in this volume.

The Turing Lectures.   Finally, this volume includes lightly edited versions of the Turing lectures given by Shafi Goldwasser and Silvio Micali during the *46th Annual Symposium on the Theory of Computing*, which took place in New York, in June 2014. Shafi's lecture focused on the influence of cryptographic research on the rest of computer science, whereas Silvio's lecture focused on the evolution of the notion of proofs.

♡ ♡ ♡

I believe that the work of Shafi Goldwasser and Silvio Micali is of historical dimension. Its impact on the development of cryptography and related areas in complexity theory has the flavor of a scientific revolution (in Kuhn's sense). Hence, whoever performs research in these areas is living in a world created and shaped by their work. In light of the above, it is our professional and personal duty to acknowledge our debt to these works. This assertion definitely holds about myself, having had also the privilege of benefiting from numerous interactions with Shafi and Silvio.

Oded Goldreich
Tel-Aviv, July 2019

Postscript: The ACM production of this book included re-typing the original papers (for Part II), rather than using facsimiles of these papers, and changing various aspects of the texts of Part III (e.g., the bibliographic conventions and the numbering of theorem-like environments). These production decisions were forced upon the editor, who strongly objected them both per merits and due to the likelihood of errors caused by implementing them.

Acknowledgments

The original papers reproduced in Chapters 8–16 were co-authored also by researchers other than Shafi Goldwasser and Silvio Micali. The list, in chronological order, includes Manuel Blum (Chapter 9), Charles Rackoff (Chapter 8), myself (Chapters 10 and 12–13), Ronald Rivest (Chapter 11), Avi Wigderson (Chapters 12–13 and 15–16), Paul Feldman (Chapter 14), Michael Ben-Or (Chapters 15–16), and Joe Kilian (Chapter 16). Indeed, it is fitting to start the acknowledgments by thanking these researchers. Needless to say, thanks are also due to the many researchers who made contributions that served as a basis and starting point for these works.

Next, I would like to thank the colleagues who have contributed scientific chapters to this book. The list includes Zvika Brakerski (Chapter 20), Daniele Micciancio (Chapter 21), Johan Håstad (Chapter 22), Rafael Pass (Chapter 23), Guy Rothblum (Chapter 24), Salil Vadhan (Chapter 25), and Yael Tauman Kalai and Leonid Reyzin (Chapter 26).

Special thanks to Michelle Waitzman, who wrote the two biographies (appearing as Chapters 1–2), and to Alon Rosen and Stephen Ibaraki for conducting the two interviews (appearing as Chapters 3 and 4, respectively).

Last, I wish to thank Tamer Özsu, the editor-in-chief of ACM Books, for monitoring and assisting the writing and production of this volume. I also thank Paul Anagnostopoulos of Windfall Software for supervising the production while trying to accommodate my various requests as much as allowed by the ACM.

Photo and Text Credits

Photos

Text

Page 157   © 2014 Silvio Micali

Page 176   Shafi Goldwasser and Silvio Micali. 1982. Probabilistic encryption & how to play mental poker keeping secret all partial information. In *Proceedings of the fourteenth annual ACM symposium on Theory of computing (STOC '82)*. ACM, New York, NY, USA, 365–377. DOI: http://dx.doi.org/10.1145/800070.802212

Page 204   S. Goldwasser, S. Micali, and C. Rackoff. 1985. The knowledge complexity of interactive proof-systems. In *Proceedings of the seventeenth annual ACM symposium on Theory of computing (STOC '85)*. ACM, New York, NY, USA, 291–304. DOI: http://dx.doi.org/10.1145/22145.22178

Page 228   M. Blum and S. Micali, "How to generate cryptographically strong sequences of pseudo random bits," in *23rd Annual Symposium on Foundations of Computer Science*, Chicago, IL, USA, 1982 pp. 112–117. DOI: http://dx.doi.org/10.1109/SFCS.1982.72

Page 242   Oded Goldreich, Shafi Goldwasser and Silvio Micali. "How to Construct Random Functions (Extended Abstract)," 25th Annual Symposium on Foundations of Computer Science, 1984, Singer Island, FL, USA, 1984, pp. 464–479. © 1984 IEEE. DOI: http://dx.doi.org/10.1145/6490.6503

Page 266   S. Goldwasser, S. Micali and R. L. Rivest, "A 'Paradoxical' Solution To The Signature Problem," 25th Annual Symposium on Foundations of Computer Science, 1984, Singer Island, FL, USA, 1984, pp. 441–448. DOI: http://dx.doi.org/10.1109/SFCS.1984.715946

Page 285   O. Goldreich, S. Micali, and A. Wigderson, "Proofs that yield nothing but their validity and a methodology of cryptographic protocol design," 27th Annual Symposium on Foundations of Computer Science, 1986, Singer Island, FL, USA, 1986, pp. 174–187. DOI: http://dx.doi.org/10.1109/SFCS.1986.47

Page 308   O. Goldreich, S. Micali, and A. Wigderson. 1987. How to play ANY mental game. In *Proceedings of the nineteenth annual ACM symposium on Theory of computing (STOC '87)*, Alfred V. Aho (Ed.). ACM, New York, NY, USA, 218–229. DOI: http://dx.doi.org/10.1145/28395.28420

Page 330   Manuel Blum, Paul Feldman, and Silvio Micali. 1988. Non-interactive zero-knowledge and its applications. In *Proceedings of the twentieth annual ACM symposium on Theory of computing (STOC '88)*. ACM, New York, NY, USA, 103–112. DOI: https://doi.org/10.1145/62212.62222

Page 352   Michael Ben-Or, Shafi Goldwasser, and Avi Wigderson. 1988. Completeness theorems for non-cryptographic fault-tolerant distributed computation. In *Proceedings of the twentieth annual ACM symposium on Theory of computing (STOC '88)*. ACM, New York, NY, USA, 1–10. DOI: https://doi.org/10.1145/62212.62213

Page 374   Michael Ben-Or, Shafi Goldwasser, Joe Kilian, and Avi Wigderson. 1988. Multi-prover interactive proofs: how to remove intractability assumptions. In *Proceedings of the twentieth annual ACM symposium on Theory of computing (STOC '88)*. ACM, New York, NY, USA, 113–131. DOI: https://doi.org/10.1145/62212.62223

Page 413   "On the foundations of cryptgraphy," by Oded Goldreich. Copyright © 2019 by Oded Goldreich. Reprinted by permission of Oded Goldreich

Page 497   "On the impact of crytography on complexity theory," by Oded Goldreich. Copyright © 2019 by Oded Goldreich. Reprinted by permission of Oded Goldreich

BIOGRAPHIES, INTERVIEWS, AND AWARD LECTURES

A Story Behind Every Problem: A Brief Biography of Shafi Goldwasser

Shafi Goldwasser has always loved a good story. As a little girl, she couldn't get enough of them and sometimes returned to the library several times a day to exchange one book for another. Early on, she expected that this would lead her to become a writer, but life had other plans for her.

Discovering that mathematics was even more exciting than literature, Shafi's path changed direction and she became a leading theoretical computer scientist. Her way of seeing the world—connecting ideas that may seem unconnected to most people—has led to a career full of accomplishments, awards, and admiration. But the storyteller in Shafi never left. Instead, it has given her a creative approach to working on mathematical problems. Shafi sees the "story" behind each problem that she researches. Where some might see a verifier checking a proof, she can picture a detective questioning a suspect.

Shafi says, "I usually find a problem interesting if there's a story associated with it. If I can think of the story of why a problem is interesting, not necessarily an application—something I could grab onto: a model, a story. I think my love of stories is kind of the way I think of these models."

One of Shafi's former students, Guy Rothblum, summarizes her talents this way: "Shafi is both incredibly brilliant and creative as a researcher. She makes things that used to be impossible—or that you would think were impossible—possible. She makes these incredible leaps between fields and finds these connections and you think, 'How in the world did she come up with this?'"

Fellow researcher Oded Goldreich agrees that Shafi's ideas can seem so unusual at first that it's tempting to dismiss them as impossible. "When Shafi suggests anything, one should resist the immediate reaction of saying 'this cannot work' and examine the core idea carefully," he says. "Carefully think about the core of what she said, rather than dismissing it on the spot as being 'odd.'"

Shafi recognizes that she sees things differently than some of her peers, as she explained in an interview with technology journalist Stephen Ibaraki. "I don't think in narrow ways, I try to see things from a larger perspective. I try to think of a problem from different perspectives and I see connections to problems I've thought about in the past, or maybe something that other people are working on."

When Shafi was invited to present an AMS/MRSI congressional briefing on the topic of data protection in 2017, she explained how theoretical research like hers can have surprising applications many years later. After all, her early work on cryptography took place long before we lived in a world of online commerce and big data. She told the briefing attendees, "A problem that seems unsolvable actually often has technical solutions that are based on some basic research that was done 30 or 40 years ago by people who didn't know about the problem—or care about it."

In a field where the value of creativity is often not recognized, Shafi is a living example of what can be accomplished when a precise mathematical mind and a creative outlook are combined in one dedicated researcher.

1.1 Beaches and Books: An International Childhood

Shafi's parents grew up in very different circumstances. Her father, Zvi, was a young man studying law in Poland when the Second World War interrupted his plans. He fled to Russia, and eventually returned to Poland to help drive the German army out. Not knowing whether any of his relatives had survived the war, Zvi moved to Israel to get a fresh start. He would eventually reconnect with his mother and sister and bring them to Israel, too.

Rachael, Shafi's mother, was born in Israel and raised in an agricultural community. She was a student during the late 1940s, and returned home from her studies to find Zvi renting a room in her parents' house. She began teaching him Hebrew, and soon he asked her to be his wife. They married in 1948.

Zvi never completed his legal studies, but instead found work with the new Israeli health service. The young country lacked everything: doctors, hospitals, and of course funds. Zvi and his family were sent to New York City to try to entice Jewish Americans to help. Young doctors were encouraged to move to Israel, and wealthy members of the community were asked to donate to the health service. The couple already had a young son, Nathan, when they moved overseas. In 1958, while they were living in New York, they had a baby girl and named her Shafrira, but she would be called Shafi by everyone she knew.

From her first day, Shafi had two nationalities. She was American-born to Israeli parents. She spent her earliest years in a coastal community just outside New York City, called Seagate. The community is surrounded by beaches and very close to the famous Coney Island beach and boardwalk. Shafi has fond memories of daily trips to the beach with her mother. She attended a local kindergarten in New York. In true urban fashion, the school's playground was on the roof of the building.

When Shafi was about six years old, her father was transferred back to Israel, and the family moved to Tel Aviv. They settled in an area known as the "Old North" of the city, and brought with them a Dodge Dart that they had bought in New York. It was a common car in the United States at the time, but a real novelty in Israel. "At that time in Israel they didn't exist," says Shafi. "In the United States we had this car, and it was just a small car. Then it arrived on the ship to Israel and it was huge—it was like the biggest car ever in the streets."

She had moved across the world, but Shafi still continued to have a strong connection to the sea. "My parents used to go to the beach every day in Tel Aviv, because my father loved swimming, and so did my mother since she grew up in Kfar Vitkin, which was near the beach. And we used to go every day—six o'clock in the morning," Shafi recalls. Her parents' love of swimming rubbed off on Shafi, who cherished their daily swims throughout her childhood.

She also had the opportunity to learn about rural life by going to visit her grandparents. Growing up in the urban surroundings of New York and Tel Aviv, this rural experience was a precious opportunity. "My grandparents from my mother's side, they lived in Kfar Vitkin. They had an agricultural farm or unit—they had cows and chickens—and I had cousins there. Every weekend we would go there to spend time with them, have lunch, go to the beach. Sometimes I would spend weeks there in the summer. So this connection with this farming place, or *moshav*, is very strong in my mind. That is really childhood, that and the beach."

Her family had arrived in Tel Aviv well after the beginning of the school year, so Shafi had to quickly adapt to a new type of schooling in a new language. She was a novelty to her fellow students, who were not used to people immigrating from the United States. "I think that for the rest of my duration at school, which was eight years—and even today, they remember me as the girl who came from America. Which shows you how Israel was at that time, that that was such a rare occurrence. And because I didn't know Hebrew for the first few weeks, I think they sort of remembered me as someone who didn't know how to speak Hebrew in the beginning," she says.

The school was far from her home and she had to take a bus there, but it was recommended to Shafi's parents because it was affiliated with the ruling political party in Israel at the time, and it had long hours and provided a good education with strong fundamentals. However, not everything there was good, according to Shafi. "I kind of hated the food. I remember that one day they wanted me to stay and eat everything, because you're supposed to clean your plate, especially at that time in Israel. My mother happened to pass by and she told the teacher that there's no need to force me to eat anything. That's a very strong, protective memory of my mother, that I knew that I could really do whatever I want, which was always true."

It was during these school days that Shafi developed her love of reading and stories. She read novels, historical dramas, short stories—anything that would feed her imagination. Her mother was also a great lover of literature and history. Although writing stories of her own seemed like a natural progression for her, she was not prolific. "I liked to write essays and short stories, but I didn't write that much. With all my fantasies about being a writer, I don't have a bunch of manuscripts hidden in my drawers," she says.

She did team up with one of her friends to create a newspaper. Shafi wrote the articles and her friend was the business manager. But sales of the first issue were disappointing (she thinks they sold one or two copies) and the venture didn't last.

As for those short stories, Shafi was a shy author and didn't share her creative endeavors. "I think they were so full of my own desires and fantasies for the future that I would have considered them extremely personal and I don't think I would have shown them to anyone," she says.

Shafi's childhood took another turn when at age 11 she became a big sister to a new baby girl, Ricky. "I remember when she was born. I was in the sixth grade or something like that. In fact, I remember that I'd made a deal with my parents. I really wanted a dog, and they said that the dog, I won't get. So then I said, 'Okay, so either a dog or a sister,' and we wrote this contract. And I have it actually. I found it a few years ago, when I was cleaning my parents' apartment. In any case, I got a sister."

Given her reluctance to share her writing with the world, it is perhaps fortunate that she found a new area of interest in high school: mathematics and science. It became clear to Shafi that she was good at these subjects, and in Israel at that time they were considered to be very important areas of study. "And that's still true in Israel," she says. "Those in math and science, those are the people who are respected. I think it was the combination of finding it interesting, being good at it, and realizing that this is what was expected of me."

"I think that growing up in Israel during those times—and it's maybe not so much growing up in Israel as growing up as children to a generation of parents who either came to Israel after the (Second World) War, or grew up during the war for independence in Israel—there's a great deal of pragmatism in the education system and what they teach you, and in terms of your approach to life. There's always a goal; you always have the future in mind. There's a goal you're working toward."

The 1960s and early '70s was a difficult time to grow up in Israel. The country was at war at times during Shafi's childhood, and the threat of war was never far away. During the Six-Day War, which took place in June 1967, Shafi was in fourth grade and remembers hiding in a bunker when sirens sounded. Years later, her brother Nathan was doing his compulsory military service when the Yom Kippur War began in October 1973, and Shafi recalls that he came home briefly before heading off to war. "He told us that there's going to be a war. And my father said to him, 'What are you speaking nonsense for?' Because for Jews that came from the (Second World) War, the whole idea of talking about death and war—it was something that you just don't talk about because it's just bad luck or you just don't say things like that. Then he was called and he left, because he had to go back to the army, and we didn't see him for a few weeks."

Shafi's parents were worried about their son's safety. Zvi had lived through the horrors of the Second World War, and both parents were in Israel during the country's war of independence. That war lasted from 1947 to 1949, and a large number of the young soldiers lost their lives.

The Yom Kippur War also took its toll on Nathan. "I remember when he came back home the first time, he had a lot less hair. It was amazing that this kind of traumatic experience can do that. So he went with a full head of hair, and it receded."

After the war, Nathan had planned to study mathematics at Hebrew University in Israel. But Shafi's parents feared that he might be involved in another war and wanted him to leave Israel. "My father just wanted him out of Israel as fast as possible. He was so afraid for his safety that he wanted him to go to school in the States. And he got accepted to Carnegie Mellon and he left. That affected me because that started some sort of chain reaction in the family," says Shafi. In fact, all three siblings eventually ended up living in the United States as adults.

Shafi would not join her brother at Carnegie Mellon for several more years. In the meantime, she was exploring her interest in math and science. At Shafi's high school, students specialized for their final two years. "When we went into the specializations, there was a class that specialized in math and physics. There were a few girls, not too many. But they were very strong, the ones who were there were very strong." Despite being in the minority, Shafi never felt that her teachers treated her differently because she was a girl. "I was a good student always. And I felt that the teachers respected me."

"I enjoyed math, because there's always a right answer. At least in high school it seems like there's always a right answer. But I loved physics even more." Shafi was particularly attracted to physics because it gave her the tools to find solutions. "The understanding from axiomatic or first principles, how you get to a conclusion." She also felt that the problems associated with physics had stories associated with them. Physics was not just about manipulating numbers, it was about understanding how things in the real world affect one another.

Even at this early age, Shafi was looking at problems differently from her peers. Not many teenagers would describe the derivation from principles as "beautiful," but that's how Shafi felt about it. Her approach to problems was not tied to rote learning. On exams, she would consider the problems in more creative ways and come up with answers that took her teachers by surprise. Shafi's high school physics teacher may have been the first person to get a glimpse of the talent for making unexpected connections that has been the hallmark of her research.

Shafi credits her high school math and science teachers for encouraging her love of these subjects and igniting her curiosity. They sparked an interest in her that continued to build throughout her studies. What began as a general curiosity about these subjects in high school had opened her eyes to the excitement of studying and the pursuit of knowledge, which would lead her to explore fundamental questions throughout her career. She feels that she was lucky to have had those teachers early on who fed her curiosity and sent her down that path of investigating problems that excited her.

Shafi's parents also had a big influence on her decisions. Throughout her childhood, Shafi was encouraged to pursue great things in her life. Her father did not let traditional gender roles alter his expectations. "You know, there was no difference between men and women here, and he thought we could do anything. That was very unusual, and that was true all along. This whole idea that women should behave a certain way, they should get married, they should have families, that was completely beside the point for him. And he was very vocal about that. And he thought I was bigger than life. That was a good thing, to grow up having that image of yourself—that empowerment."

Although Shafi's mother was a homemaker, she also encouraged her daughters to be strong and not depend on anyone else to take care of them. "She would say to us, both me and my sister throughout growing up, that a woman has to take care of herself and she has to be independent, it's extremely important. And I think that probably was because she wasn't. My father was the one who was the breadwinner. And I think in her mind, anything that was a step toward accomplishing that was a good step."

At the time, Shafi's thoughts had not yet turned to the next stage in her education. In Israel, compulsory military service normally takes place between graduating high school and going to university. Students will take their exams at the end of high school, but applying to universities still seems a long time off. However, Shafi found herself in an unusual situation. Having her birthday late in the year meant that she was younger than most of her classmates. So even though she had completed high school, it would be almost a year before she was due to report for her military service. She had a substantial amount time on her hands.

"My father wanted me to go to the U.S. to study so that I didn't waste any time. This idea of wasting time is something very problematic, or was very problematic when I was growing up. Now it seems like everybody's just taking trips around the world as soon as they finish the army, or before the army, and wasting time is not called 'wasting time' any more but 'gaining life experience.' In any case, my father wanted me to go to the States, and as usual I did what he recommended."

1.2 The Mind-Blowing World of Computer Science

Sending their 17-year-old daughter overseas did not seem to worry Shafi's parents. Not only was she a bright, hard-working student, she was going to be studying at Carnegie Mellon University, where her older brother Nathan was a graduate student, and he would be nearby if she needed him.

Her flight landed in New York City and Shafi had her first opportunity to revisit the home of her early childhood. "I wasn't there for 11 years, but when I took the taxi from the airport to the city it seemed extremely familiar." Her brother met her in New York and traveled with her to Pittsburgh, where she would move into the student dorms at Carnegie Mellon and wait for the new academic year to begin.

Her brother knew the math professors at the university, and told them that his sister was spending a year there and that she was good at math. Based on his word alone, Shafi was able to start classes as an undergraduate student in the math program without ever officially applying to the program.

Shafi's plan was to spend the year studying and then return to Israel in time for her military service. However, things didn't go according to plan. During that first year, Shafi decided that she'd rather not interrupt her studies, and she applied to the Israeli government to defer her military service. That deferral took several months to secure, and in time it became a permanent deferral and Shafi was able to focus on her education with no interruptions.

Shafi's first lecture was difficult for her to understand, and she thought perhaps she'd made a mistake and wasn't ready for these university-level math courses. But after telling her brother about her struggles, he realized that her problem was not with understanding the math, it was simply that she hadn't learned the mathematical terminology in English. After she got a rundown of how the Hebrew words translated into English, everything made much more sense, and Shafi had no more problems understanding the lectures. But the courses were still a big change from what she'd been used to at high school.

"When you get to math in college after high school, it's very abstract. There's this gap between the beautiful abstractions and this field (of computer science) that seems to capture things about life." Although Shafi felt that these abstract concepts were interesting, she was not sure that this was the field she wanted to pursue. She thought that this approach to mathematics was going to take too long to come to fruition, and that perhaps she should try studying computer science instead. The undergraduate mathematics program had a computer science specialization that students could select, and that was what Shafi chose to do.

That turned out to be a life-changing decision for Shafi. Soon, she had her first computer science classes and her first experience with computers. She recalls, "I was fascinated by their potential; I was fascinated by the first courses I took on computer programming, which had a lot of algorithm design. You design a program to resolve an algorithmic problem and there are many ways to do it and there are efficiency constraints and technical constraints and then—the program just did it! Now it's taken for granted, but that idea that you can use a computer to solve a mathematical task was sort of mind-blowing to me."

She had decided to study mathematics at Carnegie Mellon simply because her brother was there, but that decision was one that likely affected the rest of her career. She arrived in 1976, when there were few computer science departments at universities anywhere in the world. Carnegie Mellon was one of the pioneering institutions in the field and had attracted some of the top academics of the time. In fact, computer science was already well established at the university by the time

Shafi arrived. They had introduced their first computer science course in 1958, the year of Shafi's birth. By 1961, they had added a Ph.D. in the field, and in 1965 they established a computer science department.

"I think being at Carnegie Mellon was a godsend," she told Stephen Ibaraki. "It was a very exciting time. There were all these greats in the field: I took artificial intelligence with Raj Reddy, and I took my first algorithms course with Jon Bentley, and I took a course in software engineering from Anita Jones. All these people were tremendous lecturers and they taught me a tremendous amount. That made me realize how exciting computer science was."

Turing Award–winner Raj Reddy was a leading artificial intelligence researcher and one of the first academics to explore speech recognition. He sparked a strong interest in AI for Shafi. "I loved the idea of doing artificial intelligence. I thought that's maybe what I would do—understand the brain, understand how people think and how machines can mimic our thought process."

Shafi drew on her love of literature to help create a program that could generate poetry using artificial intelligence. "Compared to what they do today, it's probably totally childish," she said in an interview with the Heidelberg Laureate Forum. "But at the time, the whole possibility of writing down a sort of linguistic map of how language can be derived was fascinating."

The computer programming professors at Carnegie Mellon included Anita Jones and Mary Shaw. Jones would later become Director of Defense Research and Engineering for the U.S. Department of Defense and Vice-Chair of the National Science Board, which advises the President on science, engineering, and education. Shaw has been a faculty member at Carnegie Mellon since completing her Ph.D. there in 1972. She is considered one of the founders of the field of software architecture. Studying in a faculty with female professors who were "figures of importance" in computer science was empowering for Shafi. Women were far outnumbered by men in her classes, but Shafi had no trouble demonstrating to her professors that she was a very capable student. Professor Jones was working at the time with the university's 50-processor computer on a project called Cm*. She brought Shafi onto the project, making her one of the first people to work with a multiprocessor computer.

Shafi was excited about her newly discovered love of computer science, but she was still a teenager away from her friends and family for the first time. Most of her high school friends were doing their military service, and Shafi wrote letters back and forth with some of them, but they eventually drifted apart. At the same time, her fellow students in Pittsburgh were very welcoming. "The people I met were very curious about the world, and they were curious about me."

When she'd moved from the United States to Israel at the age of six, she'd grown up as the girl from America. Now, her American peers thought of her as the girl from Israel. It seemed as though Shafi was destined to be "exotic" no matter where she went. She found that her fellow students were more adventurous than she was. "I'd lived a very sheltered life, I think. At that time kids (in the United States) were much more adventurous in high school than I was. So that was surprising, to be in this place where everybody's exploring different aspects of life."

During her first year in the United States, Shafi's only contact with her parents was through writing letters. "I think in their minds I was capable of this journey. But really, internally, I was just a kid. I missed my parents very much. At that time, in Israel, somehow the idea of a phone call to the U.S.—it was like an impossibility. It wasn't really an impossibility, but it seemed *so* expensive, nobody called."

Her family did come to the United States for a visit during summer break, reuniting with Shafi and her brother. Her father would later return to attend her graduation. However, it would be several years before Shafi would have an opportunity to travel back to Israel. She spent her summers at Carnegie Mellon taking courses that didn't fit into her regular studies. Computer science was her passion, but she hadn't abandoned her love of a great story. "I found the literature courses that I took in the summer incredible—of course I was exposed to literature in school, but all these wonderful English-language plays and writers—I loved it, it was fabulous."

1.3   Blue Skies and Green Hills

After completing her bachelor's degree, Shafi had to decide whether to get a job in the industry, return to Israel, or further her education in the United States. She decided the third option was the most appealing and that she should apply to graduate school. Despite having gone through her undergraduate education entirely in the United States, however, nobody had informed Shafi about the required entrance exam for U.S. graduate schools. "I decided to apply to grad school and then I found out you're supposed to take this exam, the GRE. It's like the day before. I never opened a book. I'm not going to say what I got." Despite her lack of preparation and the feeling that she hadn't done well on the test, Shafi was accepted into the engineering program at Carnegie Mellon and the computer science program at the University of California, Berkeley.

She decided that she would continue her studies at Carnegie Mellon, but first Shafi needed to earn some tuition money. Her AI professor, Raj Reddy, recommended her for a job at RAND Corporation and she was offered a position for the summer. Spending the summer in Santa Monica, California, was appealing, but the job itself opened up Shafi's eyes to the corporate world.

"Being at RAND and seeing that all these Ph.D.s were really running the show, it became very clear to me that I wanted be able to be in charge and define my own projects, rather than do what I'm told. I never really had any interest in business or being on the corporate side," she says.

During that summer, she met up with a friend who was also working in Southern California, and the pair took a road trip up the coast to Berkeley. Shafi was struck by the beauty of the California coastline, and her arrival at Berkeley for the first time quickly changed her plans for the future. The clear blue skies, the rolling green hills, and the charming buildings of the Berkeley campus were irresistible. Shafi decided to attend the university for her graduate studies.

"The computer science department—I loved the building where it was. There were big windows with a view of the campanile. I thought I was going back to Carnegie Mellon, but I had a look [at Berkeley] and I fell in love," she says.

This decision would change more than the scenery and weather for Shafi. She'd had every intention of pursuing artificial intelligence on her return to Carnegie Mellon. Once she was at Berkeley, however, she found herself moving in a different direction.

Shafi told the Heidelberg Laureate Forum, "On Mondays they'd have these seminars and three professors would get up and talk about their research. And based on that I decided to go into a master's with Dave Patterson on the RISC (restricted instruction set computer) project. The project was to collect statistics for the Pascal programming language—how often different commands were being used—because he was trying to optimize the instruction set, and those instructions would be included in the hardware. So I wrote this very large system and that's my master's."

It was her first big project and she threw herself into it. The idea of being so engaged in a project that she would continue working on it day and night was new to Shafi. As an undergraduate she had done a lot of reading and studying for exams, but this was different. She was in charge of her own project and deadlines, although expected to accomplish things and deliver results to her supervisor. It was her first taste of life as a researcher.

After completing her master's, Shafi finally returned to Israel for the summer to visit her family. Her family had come to the United States to see her, but Shafi had not been back to the country she had called home for most of her life since her departure after high school. Her sister was growing up quickly, and it had also been several years since she'd seen her mother. But the reunion was temporary since Shafi had already decided to return to Berkeley to get her Ph.D.

1.4   Theory and the Cryptography Revolution

Although her master's project had been programming based, once she returned for her Ph.D. Shafi was won over by the theory students and professors. "I meet all these theory students. And they're telling me, this Manuel Blum, he's great, and Dick Karp, and I should really go and talk to them. So I talked to Manuel Blum, and we hit it off and he says, 'Yeah, if you want to work with me, you can work with me.' The next year he teaches a course on computational number theory and I love it. It's clear to me that I've found something that I really like. Somehow it's extremely appealing to me," she told the Heidelberg Laureate Forum. "And then in the last few lectures he talks about RSA (Rivest–Shamir–Adleman) and cryptosystems and it's fabulous!" Shafi was fascinated by the combination of algorithms and number theory, the use of randomization in algorithmic design, and the connection to cryptography.

It was during that course in computational number theory taught by Manuel Blum that Shafi and Silvio Micali started down their shared path toward revolutionizing the field of cryptography—the work that would eventually earn them the Turing Award. Shafi was inspired by Blum's discussion of a theoretical problem in one of his lectures. "He presents this problem at the end," she says, and describes the story of a couple who are fighting over custody of their dog. One of them lives in San Francisco and the other in Los Angeles. They decide that flipping a coin would be a fair way to decide, but they can't do it in person, and neither one trusts the other to do it fairly. Can they do it over a distance and be sure of the result? Shafi was intrigued, as she told the Heidelberg Laureate Forum. "How would they do it using computational number theory ideas? Silvio Micali's also taking this class and I'm telling him this is really *the* problem. We should work on this. It's clear—I want to work on this."

The question was fascinating mathematically, and there was an added appeal for Shafi because Manuel Blum had presented the problem as a story, with characters who needed to resolve their situation. The story behind the problem was easy to see here, and the same could be said when Shafi and Silvio went on to work on the problem of playing "mental poker." The problem could easily be pictured by imagining someone shuffling nonexistent decks of cards, and having to encrypt 52 different potential cards without letting their opponents know anything about which cards they've been dealt.

When it came to those early research projects at Berkeley, Shafi claims that she and her peers simply "followed our excitement." It was not important to find real-world problems that needed to be solved, or to see commercial applications for their work. Intellectual curiosity and a challenging problem were enough to inspire their work. She has always felt that it is important for researchers to ignore the current trends or popular problems that other researchers are working on. Only by getting past the dogma of the time is it possible to do truly innovative work.

Shafi found her place in the areas of cryptography and complexity theory, and also made some wonderful new friends. The theory students at Berkeley would become constant companions for the next several years. They would work together, eat together, relax together, and spend vast amounts of time talking to each other about theoretical computer science with endless enthusiasm.

This close group of friends included Silvio Micali, who would co-write Shafi's first paper with her and remain her close friend throughout their careers. She also became good friends with Vijay Vazirani, Faith Fich, Joan Plumstead, Mike Luby, Eric Bach, and Jeff Shallit. The students were also friendly with their professors and spent a lot of time with them. "The professors like Dick Karp and Manuel Blum and Eugene Lawler—all three of them were such open personalities and so perceptive and so wise, and they would go to a coffee shop with a group of graduate students and we would ask questions and talk about research. It was such a marvelous intellectual and dynamic and inspiring place," Shafi says. "Their enthusiasm for what they were doing and their clarity of thinking were priceless for me."

While Shafi might have seemed exotic to her American peers, she was equally fascinated by the other members of her multicultural group of friends, each of whom was a wonderful new source of stories. Silvio could share his stories about Italy, and Vijay had stories about India. Her new friends were worldly and colorful, and they helped to expand her experience of the world. Most were a bit older than Shafi, and she enjoyed talking about life and work with them when they hung out on campus and in local restaurants. Shafi also had good friends at Carnegie Mellon, but at undergraduate school there was a different atmosphere. People came to graduate school at Berkeley from all around the world and they had very different backgrounds and stories, which was an ideal atmosphere for Shafi.

Shafi and Silvio submitted their paper on playing mental poker to a conference held by STOC (Symposium on the Theory of Computing), which was attended by members of the theoretical computer science community. Their paper was accepted, and it was Shafi's first opportunity to talk about her research to her peers outside of Berkeley. STOC is one of the two main conferences for theoretical computer science. In those days there were no parallel sessions; only one presentation was given at a time, so all of the attendees could see every presentation. Other students might have been intimidated in this situation, but Shafi remembers feeling good about it. "Somehow I had confidence as a presenter, maybe unjustified to begin with."

According to former MIT graduate student Guy Rothblum, her confidence was not misplaced. "Both Silvio and Shafi have this sort of magnetic field where, when you're listening to what they're thinking about, it's clear that it's the most interesting thing in the world."

For Shafi, it was an eye-opening experience as a graduate student to attend and give presentations at conferences during her studies. "I realized that there was a community of theoretical computer science at large that was very excited about research we were doing. And I realized that there was this whole world out there of people who were really intensely dedicated to this, and that I was part of it as a graduate student and as a researcher; being able to present at these things, being able to be respected and listened to, to realize that my work was important."

This enlightening experience came just two years into Shafi's Ph.D. studies. She would continue down this research path until she completed her thesis, "Probabilistic Encryption: Theory and Applications," in 1983.

1.5   A Mecca for Cryptography

With her studies complete, Shafi headed to the east coast to take up a postdoctoral position at the Massachusetts Institute of Technology (MIT). She felt that there as no better place for a cryptography researcher, describing it as a "Mecca for cryptography," in particular because pioneering cryptography researcher Ron Rivest was on the MIT faculty, and because the RSA cryptographic system, invented by Rivest, Adi Shamir, and Leonard Adleman, was associated with MIT, since all three were members of the MIT community at the time. But MIT's commitment to the field of cryptography would soon become even more apparent. Within months of arriving as a postdoc, Shafi would be offered a staff position in the computer science department, and within a year, they would add Silvio Micali to their staff. In addition, Adi Shamir and Michael Ben-Or were visiting professors for a year, and Oded Goldreich started his postdoc there and eventually stayed for three years. In a brief period, MIT built one of the leading cryptography groups in the world. "When I came to MIT from Berkeley, it was just an explosion of research and research freedom. There was a very active group of researchers who I collaborated with and who made everything very exciting," she told Stephen Ibaraki.

This atmosphere enabled Shafi and Silvio to enjoy more of the productive collaboration that had begun between them back at Berkeley, and they continued to work on papers together, sometimes with other collaborators. Silvio reflected on what makes Shafi such an interesting research partner. "I sometimes joke that she has multiple personalities! So it's great to interact with her because it's like interacting with more than one person. For example, she will advocate A, then the opposite of A, then B, then C. I find her unpredictable. I think unpredictability is a good thing in research," he says. "With some people, you talk to them and you get what you're going to get from them, but with Shafi you keep on going because she changes, and that's crucial."

Shafi agrees that one of the reasons she and Silvio are such productive collaborators is the differences in how they approach problems. "We don't have the same kind of mind. I think that collaboration between people with the same kind of mind is sort of useless. Silvio is very 'extrematic,' he's very abstract, and I'm much more intuitive."

Other colleagues at MIT can confirm Silvio's description of Shafi's unpredictable nature, and it's one of the things they enjoy most about spending time with her. According to Ronitt Rubinfeld, a professor in MIT's computer science department since 2004, Shafi's spontaneity extends beyond the research realm into her social life. Nights out with Shafi are such an adventure that her friends never turn down the chance to see what will happen next.

"They drop anything to be with her," Ronitt says, "knowing that if she suggested to go to a movie, once arriving at the theatre, the plan may change to going for a walk, but as soon as the walk starts, it changes to going to a cafe, and after five minutes at the cafe, who knows what would be next. But they don't really care what exactly they are doing when they are with her, they just care about being in her presence, because there is something about being with her that makes life exciting."

Shafi's tendency to act on her intuition can also be seen in the seemingly random ways that she finds problems she'd like to work on. Oded Goldreich has seen this in practice. "I believe that in most cases, she hears an idea (mostly in a talk) and takes it to a totally different place, which would make little sense to the person who communicated the idea but makes sense to her," he explains. "I think one should think of the ideas she hears and processes as raw material for her spontaneous imaginative processes." Oded also feels that Shafi's creative nature plays a huge role in her abilities as a researcher. "What is stunning with Shafi is her intuitive creativity—her spontaneous nature. She just sees things that nobody does. Her insights are totally out of the box."

Shafi and her peers continued to produce research that would change the study of cryptography going forward. They hadn't necessarily set out on a mission to revolutionize the field, but their approach to solving theoretical problems led to just such a revolution and laid the groundwork for many eventual applications. She told the Heidelberg Laureate Forum, "Nobody aims for revolutionary impact. I believe that basic research is the only way that this type of impact will come about. I don't believe that there's anything that can be done that will have such fundamental implications if you already know the applications, because everybody else can do it. It can be interesting and good, but it's not revolutionary."

In addition to her research, Shafi was now teaching courses at MIT. During her first experiences, she had the support of more experienced professors. "Nobody really teaches you how to teach. At least in my time they didn't. The lucky part was that when they were teaching big undergraduate courses there were other people teaching with me."

Her teaching evolved over time, and she has developed her own courses over the years that cover her research topics. "I used to really go through the process of how you get to a result, especially if I was talking about my own research."

As a former graduate student who was supervised by Shafi, Guy Rothblum found Shafi's lectures on her own work very compelling. "She has a grasp of the big picture and she always knows how to explain what's revolutionary about the work. She's good at explaining the conceptual aspects of the work, and not just the technical part. In her talks, what she really homes in on and what she really gets across are what the big, new, important ideas are: what's exciting about this problem," he recalls. "It's unbelievably exciting to be talking with someone like that, who's sort of fearless, not only in terms of the kinds of problems she approaches, but who has also shown the right way, or the right direction to take in order to make progress on these sorts of very basic, big problems."

Creativity has continued to be a big part of Shafi's motivation, whether applied to her own work or to the students she is supervising. "The best part about being at a university is you meet new students and people are so talented and you never know where their talents lie," she says. "This creativity or this ability, it never ceases to amaze you. And that's one thing that I love about mentoring graduate students. Some people are very creative mathematically. And some people are creative in terms of finding problems. And some people are creative in seeing connections between different kinds of mathematics. And some people understand the connections between mathematics and other fields of science."

Because she puts so much value on creativity and individual talents, Shafi's students don't all follow in her footsteps or work closely with her on her current area of research. She has collaborated with several of her students on research projects, but with others she has provided more hands-off guidance. Guy Rothblum observed the range of research that has been produced by her students. "You look at her students and every student has done something different. She's an extraordinary mentor in that way—she teaches you a lot about how to think. And she's fearless about what kinds of problems to approach. It's a type of environment where any problem is fair game if you're intellectually curious. Shafi was really good at guiding, but also letting students determine how to follow their own taste, their own curiosity."

Guy says that Shafi has a natural talent for seeking out the right problems to work on. "Shafi has this thing that can't really be taught—but it seems to rub off on some of her students—which is having this intuition or taste for problems. Just intuitively knowing what's a good problem to think about and being able to make a connection between two different areas."

The field of cryptography has developed beyond what Shafi might have imagined in the early 1980s, and she is now considering questions that were not on anyone's mind, perhaps even ten years ago. For example, how can a society balance the power of big data to create solutions that improve people's lives with the threats to personal privacy that can come from the use of that data? And should governments or law enforcement be able to override encryption protections in name of law and order?

The ethical questions may remain for a long time to come, but according to Shafi some technical solutions in the area of privacy already exist, they just need to become more widely available. She told the BBVA Foundation that she feels it is vital that people learn to value their personal data, and stop giving them away for free. She believes that using the cryptographic tools that are available today, privacy and security are compatible concepts. "We have effective cryptographic methods that are still not being used," she says, encouraging IT firms to "do more to build systems to make use of the beautiful ideas we have come up with in the cryptographic field that have never been implemented."

1.6 The Traveling Professor

While Shafi was very happy to be part of the faculty at MIT, she still had a strong attachment to Israel and her parents were still living there. In 1987 she became a visiting professor at Hebrew University. It was an opportunity to spend time back in the country of her childhood. Her stay there would also have a profound influence on the rest of her life because it was during this visit that she met the man who would become her husband: fellow computer scientist Nir Shavit. From that point on, Shafi would have a foot in two worlds.

The added complexity of her renewed attachment to Israel didn't slow down Shafi's progress as a respected researcher. She received the NSF (National Scientific Foundation) Presidential Young Investigator Award from 1987 to 1996, and the NSF

Award for Women in Science from 1991 to 1996. In 1993, she received her first Gödel Prize for outstanding papers in the area of theoretical computer science (which was the first one ever awarded) along with Silvio Micali and their collaborators in the field of interactive proof systems. She would win the prize again in 2001 with a group of researchers who worked on the PCP theorem in the area of complexity theory. The Gödel Prize is presented jointly by the ACM Special Interest Group on Algorithms and Computation Theory (SIGACT) and the European Association for Theoretical Computer Science (EATCS).

When Shafi and Nir decided to get married, Shafi sought out a position at a university in Israel in order to put down more enduring roots there. She received several offers, and decided to join the prestigious Weizmann Institute in 1993. "Shimon Ullman was there and Adi Shamir and David Harel," she recalls. "Every single person there was very interesting—the top of their field—and that's still true about them. They hire the best and the brightest."

As a professor at two universities, Shafi split her time between Cambridge and Tel Aviv. Her family, which would eventually include her two children, Yonadav and Lior, moved from one place to the other every few years. Raising children is always a big adjustment, and raising them in two countries added to the challenge. "Being a parent is different than being a scientist. It's all-consuming and the well-being of these children is everything. It becomes everything. But having children and having these sort of dual homes academically meant that we lived our life in a certain way where we all spend a few years in Israel, then a few years in Boston, and then in Israel, and then in Boston. The good side was that we always went to the same place and the kids had the same schools. But the fact that it was kind of a predestined departure gave an alternative structure to our life which I think is unique. But you know what, they came out pretty good!"

It's not a lifestyle that all academics would seek out, but Shafi believes that working in two respected institutions gave her the best of both worlds in terms of her career. "Both at Weizmann and at MIT there's a very strong group for cryptography and complexity theory. There's probably more focus on complexity theory at Weizmann and maybe more focus on applications at MIT. But both places are among the best in the world," Shafi told the Heidelberg Laureate Forum.

The two universities are quite different when it comes to the overall environment. The Weizmann Institute is a more intimate campus with only graduate-level students, and a smaller number of them than MIT. (Weizmann currently has around 1000 graduate students enrolled, while MIT has almost 7000, plus an undergraduate program.) Most of the students at the Weizmann Institute are Israeli, although they do attract some students from overseas. MIT, on the other hand, is a large, bustling campus. The students there, especially those pursuing postgraduate degrees, come from all over the world. It's a very stimulating and energetic environment, but also one that can be distracting for a researcher.

"MIT is very intense. There's a lot of people, a lot of graduate students. And there's continuous seminars and meetings, and you really feel like you're in the midst of it," Shafi explains. "Weizmann has fantastic faculty members, very, very good graduate students, but fewer. So there's more time to think, but there's less intensity, and I think that they're very different that way. So I think that after a few years in Weizmann, I was very eager to go back to MIT, and after a few years at MIT, I was very eager to rest a little bit and just kind of be able to think [at Weizmann]."

As her career has progressed, Shafi's contribution to computer science has been recognized in several ways. In 1996, she won the ACM Grace Murray Hopper Award, which is awarded to the outstanding young computer professional of the year, for her early work relating computation, randomness, knowledge, and proofs.

In 2006, she was named a distinguished alumna at the University of California, Berkeley. Shafi's position as a woman in a leading computer science role was recognized by ACM's Committee on Women in Computing with their Athena Lecturer Award in 2008.

In 2010, Shafi received the Benjamin Franklin Medal from the Franklin Institute. The Franklin Institute's Awards date back to 1824 and provide public recognition and encouragement of excellence in science and technology. As one of their honorees, she is in the company of some of the biggest names in science, including Nikola Tesla, Pierre and Marie Curie, Albert Einstein, Jane Goodall, and Stephen Hawking.

Shafi was one of the final recipients of the IEEE (Institute of Electrical and Electronics Engineers) Emanuel R. Piore Award for outstanding contributions in the field of information processing in relation to computer science. The award was established in 1977 and discontinued in 2012; Shafi received the award in 2011.

Shafi and her longtime friend and collaborator Silvio Micali won the ACM Turing Award in 2012 for their work together. She joins a very exclusive list: Only three women have received the Turing Award in its history of more than 50 years. The award is considered to be the pinnacle of achievement in the field of computer science, and she told Stephen Ibaraki that her peers were very supportive when they found out about it. "The reaction from my colleagues was really overwhelming. As soon as it was announced I heard from people who were graduate students with me at the time—many, many years ago—my own ex-students, my colleagues around the world, my friends, and everyone was extremely well-wishing. It seemed like they were truly happy for us. It's a wonderful feeling." This recognition also confirmed to Shafi that her wide-ranging approach to research can pay off. "I certainly will feel more confident giving my students the kind of advice I've always given them: that they should work on risky projects, they should work on more general problems rather than trying to solve a specific problem that was posed by other people. Because in a sense that's what the award is for—that's the kind of work we did that has been awarded."

Her awards are not just recognition of her past achievements; they also help Shafi to establish her authority as a researcher. "I'm not sure that they have a direct impact on how I do research. I assume that they will affect my influence on the directions of computer science. Maybe in some sense it does allow one to work on more open-ended research."

All of this recognition puts Shafi in the position of many famous scientists who came before her: as someone who will inspire future generations of researchers. However, Shafi did not draw inspiration from these kinds of legendary scientists and mathematicians for her own career. She told Stephen Ibaraki, "I was inspired by my mentors, my colleagues, and my students. If you're looking for historical figures—that speaks less to me. Those who inspire me are people I was in contact with, not people I read about in books."

1.7   New Perspectives

Despite her many years of commitment to her research and her students, Shafi still sees the value in removing herself from her day-to-day routines to work in a new environment and get a fresh perspective. During the 2017–18 academic year, she was a fellow at the Radcliffe Institute for Advanced Study, which is part of Harvard University. The goal of the institute is to create an interdisciplinary, international community of 50 fellows each year across the arts, humanities, sciences, and social sciences. During her Radcliffe fellowship, Shafi turned her attention to applying encrypted computation methods to the analysis of social science data. She also took advantage of the time to work on a couple of projects that allowed her to flex her creative muscles in a completely different way: a book on pasta and protocols and a photography series on the women of New England.

Even when she's working in more familiar surroundings, Shafi finds unique approaches to expanding her way of looking at the world and to discovering new connections to explore. She explains, "A few years ago I was on sabbatical at Weizmann and I took this course about the connection between dance and science. It sounds like an unlikely connection, but there was a dance group, and a bunch of scientists who loved them, who were meeting once a week. Each scientist would describe their research and a dance was choreographed about it."

Shafi's love of creative expression attracted her to this unconventional method of bringing scientific research to life. She even found inspiration in it for her own research. "There was a scientist whose research was about clocks and biological processes; how every cell has a clock. It intrigued me, this issue about clocks and individual cells. And after that I went on to start this research on how to model biological cells as computer cells, maybe having a little memory, maybe having an internal clock. How would they be communicating with each other?"

While biology and computer science are fields that have not had much interaction in the past, this is beginning to change. It's thanks to researchers like Shafi, who can make these creative connections between the two fields, that new areas of research are able to gain momentum.

In 2018, Shafi took her career in a new direction when she became the director of the Simons Institute for the Theory of Computing at Berkeley, returning to her alma mater (and the beautiful California campus) after more than three decades away.

The Simons Institute was founded in 2012 as a venue for collaborative research in theoretical computer science. Its founding director was Richard Karp, one of Shafi's former professors from her graduate school days at Berkeley. She felt compelled to move into this new leadership role that would put her wide experience in the field to use by making her a guiding force in the current and future directions of theoretical computer science research.

"I want to have impact, and the kind of impact that I'm talking about now is impact as the director of the Simons Institute or someone who directs—someone who has some influence about where the field is going in the sense of what's important and what's not important. I feel I have an intuition to serve me, and also a lot of experience."

Shafi believes that theoretical computer science is a field of fundamental importance in human society at this point, on equal footing with chemistry, physics, and biology. When Shafi's appointment to the Simons Institute was announced in 2017 she told the *Berkeley News*, "Algorithms govern our computing-based world in the same way that the laws of nature govern the physical one. Their mathematical underpinnings are thus as important to modern society as the periodic table, relativity or the genome."

As she told Stephen Ibaraki, the fact that she has already accomplished so much in her field does not mean that she is planning to slow down. "I've achieved some of my life goals already, but this is not going to change my passion for science and the kind of problems I've been working on. I still hope that I have some important work to do."

As computers become a part of more and more human endeavors and interactions, it is crucial to have researchers like Shafi involved in the ongoing evolution of computer science. Seeing the connections between computer science and other important fields of knowledge may take society in unexpected directions, or prevent potential disasters. Her ability to identify ideas that others dismiss as impossible, and to see how to make them possible, is a unique gift with the potential to contribute to the advancement of society for years, and possibly generations, to come.

Shafi's sphere of influence continues to grow, and there is no doubt that she is creating a valuable legacy in the fields of cryptography and complexity theory, and perhaps many others.

One Obsession at a Time: A Brief Biography of Silvio Micali

Obsession can be a debilitating problem for some people, but for Silvio Micali it's his modus operandi. "I'm a monomaniac," he explains. "I pursue one thing at a time, for a long time." In Silvio's world, a long time generally equates to about five years. That's how long he tends to spend investigating a subject and working on a problem. Of course, some problems are solved more quickly than others, but for the most part a field of research will hold his attention for about five years. Rather than delving deeper and deeper into the same topic, or finding related problems that still need resolving, Silvio prefers to walk away and find something new to obsess over. "I'm leaving behind beautiful problems that ought to be solved. And they will be solved—they are being solved—but not by me."

Silvio's tendency to become obsessed with a problem can be traced back to his childhood anxieties. The first huge, theoretical problem he tried to tackle was whether the world in which he lives exists at all, or whether it is just a construct of his mind. This question plagued him, at times making it difficult to carry on with the everyday activities and interact with people who suddenly were possibly just figments of his imagination. It's actually a condition known commonly as solipsism syndrome, which calls into question whether reality is objective or subjective. Clearly, staring into the unknown and looking for provable answers is something that has intrigued Silvio throughout his life. This was the starting point for a career spent asking, and attempting to answer, some of the biggest questions in cryptography and beyond.

Natural curiosity is a big part of any great researcher's personality. Looking back, it may seem obvious that Silvio was born to be a researcher. But pursuing a career in theoretical computer science was far from a given for a young Sicilian man who would not even encounter his first computer until graduate school. His journey has involved a mixture of purposeful focus and serendipity. He has had the good fortune to sometimes be in the right place at the right time, and the wherewithal to realize it.

Silvio Micali the researcher is well known in the computer science community. Less well known is Silvio Micali the devoted son and big brother, the husband and father, the mentor and teacher to many, and the colleague and treasured friend to a fortunate few.

2.1 A Childhood Among the Ruins

Sicily is a large island that lies just to the west of Italy's southern "toe." It is rich in history and culture, having been alternately occupied by the Phoenicians, Greeks, Carthaginians, Romans, Byzantines, Arabs, Normans, Germans, Spaniards, French and others before uniting with Italy in the 19th century. In the 1950s, however, Sicily was economically poor and underdeveloped. In October 1954, Silvio was born in the island's largest city, Palermo. It was his father's hometown, while his mother hailed from a nearby area.

His family soon relocated to Agrigento, a town perched on a hilltop near the island's southern coast. Silvio's father, Giovanni, was a judge, following in the footsteps of his own father, who'd been a lawyer and a judge as well. Silvio's mother, Franca, was a homemaker who looked after Silvio and his sister, Aurea, who was born one-and-a-half years after Silvio.

Agrigento is best known for its historical importance as home to the "valley of the temples"—a collection of ancient Greek temple ruins. In the 1950s, there was no real industry in the town apart from some agriculture and a small but important tourist trade. The town's tourists gave Silvio a strong sense of place, as he watched people from around the world who came to his town to see the temples. "You cannot appreciate history if you're Sicilian," he says, "because you are smack in the middle of it with so many cultures all around you." The present cannot be separated from the past there.

To this day, Sicily's population reflects its diverse history. Its people are descended from the large number of different ethnicities that each dominated the island at times. This was certainly true in Agrigento, where remnants of the past could be seen everywhere. This immersion in his town's multifaceted culture helped Silvio to forge a strong identity as a Sicilian, which has remained with him even after he adopted additional identities as an Italian and eventually as an American. Agrigento's much-admired ruins also instilled in him the idea that if you create something beautiful, it will be recognized and appreciated for a long time. He began to understand the concept of leaving a legacy.

Silvio spent his early years attending the local primary school, and fighting with his sister the way only siblings can fight. "We're very close now, but we fought like cats and dogs until we were eighteen," he says.

His education was taken very seriously from the beginning. The teachers in Agrigento were very dedicated, and with little industry in the town, education was a high priority. "It's hard for people to understand, because we now live in a society which is much more diversified in achievements. But I lived in a society where [education] was the only possible level of achievement—perhaps to study the past, or to do something cultural or scientific—there were no other venues available," Silvio says. Although the town was economically depressed, its residents had an appreciation for education and culture that he has not experienced anywhere else—not even in Rome, where he spent the later part of his youth.

A good education was considered to be not just the first step to a better life, but the most noble pursuit. Education for the sake of education, and culture for the sake of culture, were valued in Silvio's upbringing. This idea, that the pursuit of knowledge for its own sake was a noble endeavor, would certainly influence his decisions later in life. "Education is the only thing that you can always keep with you," he says. "It's completely portable. I had a sense of its intrinsic value. Your own understanding of the world, your appreciation for research, nobody can take that away from you." In a town where there was little to do, discussion and debate were favorite pastimes, and great training for anyone going into groundbreaking fields of research where new ideas and theories must be fiercely defended.

Teachers were Silvio's early role models for his future career in academia. In fact, Silvio considers some of his middle school teachers to be among the most influential mentors in his life. They instilled in him an appreciation of the past and tradition, while preparing him for the road ahead. From an early age, he was attracted to mathematics and science, and also to the idea of having a job where he could discuss scholarly, important things. He felt that would be the best job in the world! At an age where many young people are still hoping to become sports stars or superheroes, Silvio was already dreaming of a career as a researcher.

Silvio's father also played a large role in his education. Silvio describes him as a "force of nature"—an influential man who liked to philosophize and debate. Silvio, however, grew tired of philosophy and felt he should focus on something else. Following the family tradition and becoming a lawyer was not something that appealed to him, and his father did not push him in that direction. It was only when Silvio was ready to enter university that his father urged him to consider law as a more practical choice than becoming a mathematician, fearing that his son would find himself without a job. Having no experience with academic careers and research himself, Giovanni Micali was understandably nervous about Silvio's prospects. By that time, however, Silvio has fallen in love with mathematics and the legal profession was simply not an option for him.

While his mother was not as outwardly forceful as his father, she was at least as influential in Silvio's upbringing. Perhaps embodying a stereotype of Italian mothers, she held "heroic" expectations of her children. So while his father set a high bar in terms of educational achievement, his mother set a far higher bar, "in another dimension" according to Silvio, in terms of what her children should achieve in their lives. Since no child wants to disappoint his mother, Silvio took these expectations to heart, realistic or not, and felt compelled to do something great with his life.

It wasn't all work and no play during Silvio's childhood. During the summer breaks, he would spend his time playing sports and doing other outdoor activities. But during the school year his attention was on his schoolwork, and so he didn't really mix his summer activities into the rest of the year. Work time and play time were kept separate from an early age, perhaps indicating that Silvio was already developing the intense focus that would eventually make him such a dedicated researcher.

2.2   Rome: The World as a Museum

At the age of twelve, Silvio was thrown into an entirely new environment. His father was transferred to Rome to work for the *Tribunale di Rome*. He would be moved up later to Rome's Court of Appeals before eventually being offered a position at the *Corte Suprema di Cassazione* (Supreme Court of Cassation), Italy's highest court.

For a young boy from a Sicilian town with a population of around 50,000, Rome was another world—a large, cosmopolitan city where school was no longer just down the road and the sheer size of the city and the number of people were almost incomprehensible to him. The family lived in an area called Nuovo Salario, north of the city center.

Once he was in Rome, Silvio began to appreciate the legacy of the Romans in a way he hadn't in Sicily. Agrigento's ruins are mainly Greek, so although the Romans had ruled Sicily for a time, they hadn't left their mark on Silvio's childhood the way the Greeks had. In addition to adapting to a new, larger city, he was absorbing the new culture and history that it represented.

Silvio began attending high school in Rome, which involved traveling into the city center. High schools in Italy at that time took a classical approach to education. Students did not specialize according to their interests or abilities; they all focused on the same basic areas of study to give them the fundamentals of learning. "If you wanted to become a scientist, that's fine," Silvio says, "but you started by studying Latin, Greek, philosophy, history . . . and a *little* bit of Euclidean geometry." Despite the lack of focus on science and mathematics, that bit of continued exposure was enough to keep the flame lit under Silvio in his pursuit of a career in math and science.

Learning about the classics wasn't limited to the classroom. Living in Rome, the classics were all around him on the streets—in the architecture, the ruins, the fountains. "You're walking down the street and you see the place where Galileo's trial was held," he recalls. "It was really a fabulous time and it had a very, very big impact on me."

Silvio's father was also a big influence when it came to appreciating the historical treasures of Rome. "My father was an absolute maniac when it came to museums," he says. "I was fourteen or fifteen and we were living in Rome—all of a sudden it's like you're a kid in a candy store. There are museums everywhere!"

Every Sunday the pair would wake up early in order to be the first visitors to arrive at their museum of choice. They loved having the museum to themselves for a little while, when most people lingered in bed. They would stay all day, forgoing lunch (since museum cafes and snack shops were not common at the time), and clutching a book with descriptions of each piece in the collection. "Painting, painting, painting—stone, stone, stone—statue, statue, statue, until your legs would crumble under you," he recalls. At the end of the day they would leave exhausted.

This activity continued even beyond the city's many museums as Silvio's seemingly insatiable appetite for art and history drew him into Rome's churches to see famous works on display in their original settings. Masterpieces that appeared in his art history books could be seen up close. He loved the idea of touring the city on foot and enjoying art where it was meant to be displayed.

At the same time, Silvio was cultivating his mental capacity by trying to come up with theories. The fact that he did not have the necessary data or skills to prove any of his theories at the time was not an issue for him. Influenced by the study of classical philosophers, he would devote much of his time to an attempt to extract meaning from things and answer the most basic questions about life. "These basic questions never left me," he says.

When he was introduced to basic proofs for geometric concepts like the congruence of triangles in his classes at school, he would wonder how the proof was created. He was very intrigued by statements like "two triangles are equal." What does that mean? How can you deduce more by starting with less? It seemed almost magical to him. He felt like, as with the conservation of energy, you could not create something (a meaning) that wasn't already there. "Questions like 'What is a proof?' and these sorts of things fascinated me even when I was very young." It would be a while before Silvio had the mathematical and intellectual tools to start properly addressing these problems, but his awareness of them can be traced back to his teen years, when he began to question things that other students were willing to accept as axiomatic.

This questioning of the world around him could be quite challenging for Silvio's teachers. Now and then he would present them with some incomprehensible pages outlining his physical theory of the universe or other equally ambitious theories. His teachers were very patient and took his ambitions seriously, rather than dismissing them out of hand. It seems they had the foresight to understand that encouraging a curious young mind, even if he was attempting things far beyond his current abilities, was worthwhile and could build his confidence. If his early theories had been mocked or dismissed by his teachers, it is possible that Silvio would have become more cautious about attempting to answer those big questions he loves so much, and that have been such an important part of his career.

2.3   Preparing for a Nobel Prize . . . Or Not

When it came time to begin his college education, Silvio was already quite sure that his future would involve research. Silvio chose to attend La Sapienza University of Rome. It was the early 1970s, and at the time it was common for Italian students to attend a nearby university (if they lived in a major center) and continue living with their parents. The campus culture of the United States had not caught on in Europe, so the fully immersive student lifestyle that some of his future colleagues were already experiencing at that time was unknown to Silvio. Because he was still living in the family home, it was easy for Silvio to devote his time completely to study and not have to worry about the burdensome details of living on his own, like making his own food, doing laundry, or paying rent.

Despite his strong interest in mathematics, Silvio enrolled in the college's physics program. Why physics? He was swayed by the fact that there was a Nobel Prize for physics but none for mathematics. An ironic line of reasoning for a man who would eventually enter the field of computer science—in which it is also impossible to win a Nobel Prize—and who would go on to win a number of prestigious prizes in his field. These would include the Turing Award, which has earned the nickname "the Nobel Prize of computer science."

Silvio experienced his first research-oriented courses at the age of nineteen. His classical high school education had perhaps left him behind some of his peers in terms of this type of study. He was starting from scratch on his understanding of advanced mathematics. But his enthusiasm for the subject made up for his lack of knowledge, and he felt strongly that this was what he wanted to do with his life. He wanted to become an academic and do theoretical research.

Although he was enrolled as a physics student, the Italian universities had discovered that the students emerging from the typical high schools of the time, where only the basics of mathematics were taught, were ill-equipped to understand advanced physics; they simply couldn't follow the calculations involved. So during his first semester at college, before his physics education began in earnest, Silvio spent his time learning about calculus and geometry. The following semester they began to learn physics. This was a departure from the normal course structure at the university, which generally involved full-year courses.

What was meant to be preparatory work for Silvio's study of physics ended up changing the direction of his education. "After six months of learning about mathematics I began to think, who cares about physics?" he says. He had decided that mathematics was a more interesting field and there was no looking back. Silvio changed his course of study and pursued a degree in mathematics, abandoning his dream of one day winning a Nobel Prize in physics.

Once he was learning math a higher level, Silvio was better equipped to explore some of the questions that had begun to dog him during high school. This first emerged when he began to study calculus during that fateful first semester of his degree. The rigorous reasoning and impressive information architecture left an impression on him.

Silvio considers his first calculus teacher, Luciano De Vito, a real gift and a big influence on his love of mathematics. He did all of his teaching using problems. He would come up with a sequence of problems that would push his students to reconstruct the definitions to use in the theorems, helping them to arrive at the definitions themselves rather than just presenting them to the students. This was much more work than simply learning the curriculum out of a textbook.

For some of his classmates, studying calculus was simply a means to an end, and they may not have valued a deeper understanding of it. But for someone with an inclination toward research, this type of learning was quite inspiring. It was a totally different approach to teaching than Silvio had experienced in the past, and it gave him a much greater appreciation for the subject. It also helped him to see how having the right tools could help him to prove what he wanted to prove. Since Silvio already had a long history of exploring difficult questions, it was a revelation to understand that through his education he could obtain the tools to finally start discovering the answers. Silvio would later use a similar approach to teaching course material to his own graduate students.

During his mathematical studies, Silvio anticipated using the education he received in this area to undertake mathematical analysis. Professor De Vito was disappointed that Silvio had abandoned the idea of pursuing a career in physics, but felt that if was determined to pursue mathematics instead, the most interesting field was theoretical computer science. He thought that analysis was not a good pursuit for someone young and ambitious, despite the fact that he was a mathematical analyst himself. De Vito told Silvio about the work of Alan Turing and others, and as far as he was concerned, this was the only worthwhile area of research in mathematics.

At first, Silvio rejected this advice and pursued his interest in mathematical analysis. But in his final year of undergraduate study, he got his first glimpse into his future. He took a course in logic and one in lambda calculus, which functions as a kind of abstract programming, with Professor Corrado Böhm. Silvio enjoyed these courses more than many of the others he'd taken to date.

After those courses, he was convinced that he should pursue further studies in computer science. For his undergraduate thesis, he worked under Professor Böhm, who was one of the fathers of computer science in Italy and whom Silvio credits with "discovering" him and seeing his potential. He gave Silvio a lot of encouragement to pursue his interest in computer science, and they two wrote an article together, marking Silvio's first academic publication. Böhm advised Silvio to leave Italy for his graduate studies. In the 1970s there was no Ph.D. program in computer science available in Italy.

The Italian college system was quite different from the system he later experienced in the United States. Part of this contrast was due to the difference in campus culture. Many American students lived on campus in student residences or fraternities, while in Italy most students continued to live with their families. But the college itself took a different approach—less structured than the American system. Most courses were year-long courses, four per year, and exams could be taken whenever he felt he was ready for them. He didn't have to deal with the pressure of exam week or sitting in a lecture hall full of his classmates while everyone wrote the exam together. Instead, he could prepare at his own pace, and spread out his exams over several months if he wanted to. For someone who prefers to focus on one problem at a time, this was an ideal arrangement. Sometimes he would learn new concepts very quickly and progress through the curriculum at a fast pace once he was "on the scent" of things. In other situations, he'd have the opportunity to kick ideas around for longer and to make sure he was confident about his understanding of a problem before moving on. For Silvio, the absence of time pressure was fundamental to absorbing material and to thinking deeply about a topic. Throughout his education and career, he has continued to consider unstructured time an absolute necessity.

Now that he has the benefit of his experience with students at MIT, he can see that the Italian system suited him very well. The American classes involve assigning problem sets one after the other, each of which is graded, and culminating in a final exam. For students who fall behind at the beginning, it can be very difficult to catch up. The more self-paced Italian system allowed him to study at his own natural rhythm. The notion of learning on a schedule was quite foreign to him when he eventually arrived in the United States, and quite terrifying as well.

Silvio completed his undergraduate program in 1978. Despite his enthusiasm to continue his studies, Silvio's timing was off. He missed the application deadline for the following year's academic intake and found himself forced to wait.

To keep himself busy and productive, he took a course in computer science over the summer. During this course, Silvio studied under another wonderful mentor who introduced him to the use of algorithms. Silvio had never seen an algorithm before (or a computer, for that matter). The teacher was Shimon Even, who hailed from Israel. Silvio became fascinated with algorithms, which cemented his decision to do a Ph.D. in theoretical computer science. Shimon Even would later refer to Silvio as "the brightest student I ever met."

If he'd wanted to remain in Italy and become an academic there, Silvio would have entered a system with three levels: He would have started as a researcher, then become an assistant professor, and eventually reached the level of full professor. By this point he had a couple of publications on lambda calculus under his belt and was considered a bit of an expert in this area. He did, in fact, take up a researcher position for a while after completing his undergraduate degree. But this did not seem like the right path for him, and he ended up resigning his position before long in order to become a student again. He would leave behind lambda calculus and forge ahead with algorithms.

Silvio applied to the University of California at Berkeley, and was accepted conditionally. His English was not at an acceptable level, and he needed to raise his score on the TOEFL (test of English as a foreign language) before he could be admitted to the Ph.D. program. The test was only administered once every six months, so if he failed again it would lead to another long delay in his plans. This was a challenge quite different from those Silvio was used to. He is not a natural when it comes to languages. He studied French in middle school, and was able to make himself understood in that language years later when he presented one of his lambda calculus papers at a conference in France. However, French is closely related to Italian. English is a different story.

Silvio was not starting from scratch when it came to learning English. His father had had the foresight to decide that his children should learn English, long before it was considered the "universal language." They attended an English school in Rome to learn the language. It was far from where they lived and required a one-hour bus trip in each direction to attend the one-hour lesson. But half a day of sacrifice seemed worthwhile to Mr. Micali, who wanted to give his children the opportunity to embrace the world beyond Italy. However, it was not enough to prepare Silvio for graduate studies in the United States, and he had to work hard on this English in order to improve his test scores.

2.4 California, Here I Come!

Moving to America was a big decision, but it was one that Silvio was ready for. He'd always planned on leaving Italy at some point. Not because he disliked Italy, or wanted to leave it behind—in fact he still considers himself to be a "quintessential Italian" who loves his home country and his culture, and he has always visited regularly. He felt strongly, however, that leaving behind what he knew was essential to being innovative. He had to shake off the past in order to move forward.

He felt that this was especially important for someone who grew up in Italy, which is so steeped in history, tradition, and culture. The responsibility for preserving the past, this great history of Western civilization, weighs heavily on the Italian population—especially in Rome. Silvio likens it to living in a house full of expensive and delicate artwork. You aren't allowed to run around because you might break something. You have to show great respect for what is around you, and so your freedom is limited. It's easy to fall in with a uniform way of thinking in such an environment, which makes it difficult to do something truly new. "You cannot be disruptive and respectful at the same time," he says. Great research, Silvio believes, is disruptive. He confesses that his literary hero was Ulysses. He explores the world, taking years to return to his family. Silvio needed to find his own path, and to go on his own heroic journey of sorts, so that he could move beyond his roots.

Silvio arrived in Berkeley in March 1979. Despite his improved English scores on the TOEFL, he soon discovered that his language skills were going to make life in America difficult for him. Landing at the airport in San Francisco, he tried asking people how to find the shuttle that would take him to Berkeley. Nobody could understand what he was trying to say.

He felt completely isolated in his new home. The language barrier was a major setback, but that was only part of the problem. Compared with the American students, Silvio had no real background in computer science. His undergraduate work had been in mathematics, while his American peers had been learning about the basics of computer science. Silvio's experience was limited to the one summer course he'd taken, so he found that he did not have the prerequisites for the courses he wanted to take. In fact, he found himself enrolled in "CS1"—the introductory course in computer science. Silvio, at 24 years old, was surrounded by 18-year-old students, and some as young as 16, with whom he had little in common. With no friends and a limited ability to have conversations in English, Silvio had practically no social life outside of his lectures. Not long after embarking on his great adventure, Silvio felt ready to pack up and go home. He spent a lot of time coming up with reasons that he should leave, convincing himself that this wasn't what he was meant to be doing. He wanted to create a narrative that justified his decision without admitting that he was doing it for purely emotional reasons.

When it looked like Silvio was ready to give up on Berkeley, it took just one person to change his mind, and to redirect the remainder of his education and possibly his career. He met a graduate student named David Lichtenstein, who was almost finished his Ph.D., and who was much closer in age to Silvio than his classmates in CS1. His new friend started to give him the helpful advice he needed in order to break out of his downward spiral and take control of his situation. The two remained friends for many years after David completed his doctorate.

David's first recommendation to Silvio was to forget about the rules and enroll in advanced courses even though he didn't have the prerequisites. He figured it was better to beg forgiveness later than to ask for permission. This one piece of advice changed everything for Silvio. When he returned to Berkeley after the summer break, he took courses with his graduate-level peers and began to make friends who had similar interests. It was the turning point in what could otherwise have been a very short career in computer science.

During that challenging first year at Berkeley, Silvio was on a fellowship provided by the Italian National Council of Research. He was given in advance half the money for the year; the other half he would receive in travelers checks that he collected at the Italian consulate, the preferred method in the days before electronic money transfers.

It was Silvio's first time living away from home, and so it was the first time he'd had to pay his own way and budget for himself. It was also the first time he had to eat on his own, without his mother's delicious cooking. He hated the food at the university cafeteria, calling it "cruel and unusual punishment," and decided he could not eat it. Instead he found a local restaurant that served very good food and proceeded to eat there practically every night.

Soon enough, he ran out of money, having spent far too much on food. Rather than return to the school cafeteria, Silvio decided to try cooking for himself. Although he had sometimes helped his mother out in the kitchen, he hadn't really absorbed what she was doing in detail. He could remember many of the dishes she'd made but was unsure how to cook them, so he was forced to experiment. He made occasional (expensive) long distance calls home, sometimes waking his mother in the middle of the night, to find out what ingredients went into his favorite recipes. Even with her help, cooking Sicilian specialties was not easy since many of the ingredients were simply not available in California in the late 1970s.

Necessity became the mother of invention as Silvio struggled to creatively substitute ingredients in the recipes from home. Even mozzarella cheese, a staple in today's American supermarkets, was not to be found. In the end, the recipes ended up being his own, since if you keep substituting one ingredient after another you eventually end up with a different dish altogether. His substitutions were hit and miss, and some of Silvio's friends were subject to failed experiments where the recipes didn't turn out as planned. But he developed a love of cooking, believing it to be a "great aggregator" to bring his friends together. Silvio still enjoys having people over to share a home-cooked meal. He also still believes that there's no reason to eat badly, food being one of the necessities of life. Later on, Silvio's parties would become a highlight for his friends and colleagues, and his cooking always featured prominently.

It was also at Berkeley that Silvio finally had his first interaction with a computer. Even then, he never actually saw the computer. After all, this was before the era of desktop computing. He was able to use a console with a keyboard and a monitor, but the computer itself was located in another part of the building, hardwired to his console and those of other users. The one computer had to be shared among the students and faculty at Berkeley.

2.5 The "Perfect Storm" of Cryptography

After spending the summer in Italy with his family, Silvio returned to Berkeley in the fall and began to take the research courses he'd been missing out on during his first year. He took an algorithm course under Professor Richard Karp, and along with Vijay Vazirani, who was a classmate, he developed an algorithm for maximum matching. This would be presented at the 21st Foundations of Computer Science (FOCS) conference in 1980. And so, in less than a year, he had evolved from taking introductory computer science classes to doing research that he would present in front of his academic peers in the field.

Vijay also would go on to a highly respected career as a researcher in the design of algorithms, as well as computational complexity theory, cryptography, and algorithmic game theory. The two would spend a lot of time together during their studies at Berkeley, along with a tight-knit group of their peers that included Shafi Goldwasser and Mike Luby. He also got to know Michael Sipser, who would eventually become the Dean of Science at MIT. It was an exciting and inspiring time for Silvio as he realized that he had found his "tribe" and was not alone in his love of research and his fascination with mathematics. The group became friends and supported one another. It finally seemed like enrolling at Berkeley had been the right choice after all. Any doubts about his choice disappeared during his second year on campus.

Silvio and his friends were a diverse group who had come together through a love of problem solving and a keen interest in computer science. Silvio had come from Italy, of course, while Shafi was from Israel, Vijay from India, and Mike from the United States. They all had different experiences and perspectives to share. There was much to discuss about each other's backgrounds and views on the world, but in the end most conversations would eventually steer themselves toward computer science, such was their enthusiasm for the subject.

This led to an atmosphere of complete immersion in computer science for Silvio. Whether he was attending lectures, doing research, or just hanging out with his friends, his whole life revolved around computer science and the problems that fascinated this group of budding researchers. They would strategize about the direction their careers should take, what problems they ought to work on, and what fields would be the most rewarding. Like students in every field of study, they were anxious about the future and concerned about making the right choices. They felt, even thought they were young and still learning, that they had important things to say, and that they carried a big responsibility.

Perhaps the atmosphere at Berkeley exacerbated these feelings of responsibility. Their studies during the early 1980s took place not long after the tumultuous student protest movements that were triggered by the war in Vietnam, the civil rights movement, and the free speech movement. Berkeley had been at the center of American counterculture and social reform during the 1960s and 70s. Although less famous, there were protests at Berkeley in response to earlier political issues as well. In 1950, students rallied in support of their professors, who were being forced to take a McCarthy-era anti-communist loyalty oath.

The students of Berkeley had always felt that they could make a difference in the world and should speak out about injustice. It was a legacy of youth empowerment that would have been palpable to Silvio and his classmates. Perhaps computer science was not a political hot topic at the time, but since the field was still young and establishing itself, the sense of being responsible for its future direction was not misplaced. But the excitement of the seemingly endless possibilities in the field outweighed any anxiety on Silvio's part. In fact, he believes that if you're not a bit anxious about your decisions, you're not pushing yourself hard enough. Beginning with his early research at Berkeley, Silvio has always done his best work outside his comfort zone.

One of the courses Silvio took at Berkeley was in computational number theory, taught by Professor Manuel Blum. The course included a few lectures on cryptography, since it was not yet offered as a course of its own. Silvio was fascinated with cryptography right away. For him, it created a "perfect storm" because he had discovered an emerging field where there were a lot of things still to be done, and at Berkeley nobody had really embraced this area yet. There was a need for notions, for definitions, for tools. It fed his desire to theorize about a field and to start things from scratch, rather than simply applying the work of others. At last he found the field of study he'd been searching for. Blum would become Silvio's thesis advisor, supervising his work on cryptographically strong pseudorandom generation.

Manuel Blum's lectures were also the inspiration for Silvio and Shafi Goldwasser to begin collaborating on research projects. They were both very interested in a problem that Blum had described to the class: How do you toss a coin over the phone? The two found themselves compelled to solve this problem—obsessed, as Silvio would say. They would eventually move on from flipping coins over the phone to playing mental poker.

Although it was the first problem they explored together, the coin problem would be far from the last. The pair have worked together on and off for decades, and since they are both professors at the same university, they have the opportunity to discuss their research with one another even when they are not collaborating. Silvio enjoys the fact that Shafi is unpredictable and can approach a problem from very different, perhaps even conflicting, points of view.

In those early days, when doing something completely new was a big risk, teamwork was essential to Silvio. "You need the companionship and, particularly if you want to do something unusual, somebody else must believe in it too. It was very important to have her on my side."

The pair's paper "Probabilistic Encryption" was presented at a STOC (Symposium on Theory of Computing) conference in 1982, just as their time at Berkeley was coming to an end. It would prove to be a landmark paper in the field of cryptography. The Association for Computing Machinery (ACM) describes it as "one of the most influential papers in the history of computer science. It set the foundations on which thousands of researchers base their work."

The friendship that was born at Berkeley has stood the test of time. In fact, when Silvio got the call that he and Shafi were to receive the 2012 ACM Turing award, the two already had plans for their families to spend the day together skiing.

"She is my best friend, and that's really a gift," he says. The fact that they have a shared interest in the same field of research has contributed to their friendship, because it can be difficult to find friends who can truly understand you, but Shafi has an in-depth understanding of Silvio's work as well as supporting him as a friend.

The field of computer science was exciting to Silvio during his studies because it was so nascent at the time, and there seemed to be so much fundamental work to be accomplished. To advance science, he felt, one needs a portfolio of different approaches and different people putting ideas forward. Silvio admits that it is very difficult to do great research in a field that looks like a desert, "with no structure and everything looking the same in every direction." It's hard to know where to go. And yet this was exactly the type of research landscape that appealed to him—he aspired to tame the desert and unearth the structure on which future researchers could build their innovations. Anything less would not keep his interest.

Although Silvio's time at Berkeley was very focused on computer science once he surrounded himself with his fellow graduate students, the summers were a time to completely disconnect from this intense focus and return to his family and his Italian home. This break was much needed in order to refresh his mind and allow him to go back and be innovative. In his three months of leisure time, he would not just relax, but also have a chance to mull over what to work on next.

Silvio spent every summer break in Italy, partly in Rome, and partly at a flat that his parents rented on a quiet beach the Agrigento region of Sicily, in a town called Siculiana Marina. There were miles of protected beach along the harbor, in pristine natural condition. During the winter, the tiny fishing village was home to only twenty people or so; in the summer it was a little busier, but far from crowded. It was a perfect place to get away from it all, and certainly a contrast to the hot, busy streets of Rome. His father had a small fishing boat, and for one month of the year this respected judge would transform into an avid fisherman. Silvio would wake up long before dawn to help him set the nets. Silvio remembers that when he was younger these duties would keep him from socializing with the other kids his age, since he'd have to go to bed early just as the others were heading out to have fun. As a graduate student who lived overseas for most of the year, he was able to appreciate this precious time with his father. As his father grew older and Silvio was rarely around to help, Mr. Micali eventually gave up fishing because it was too dangerous to go out alone. Instead, he took up mushroom hunting in the Alps as a new obsession. But Silvio still visits Sicily once in a while to see a childhood friend who owns a farm near Palermo.

Siculiana Marina was certainly a world away from the academic world, and this unstructured time was indispensable to Silvio. Perhaps because of his Italian upbringing, he maintained this very "European" attitude toward vacations while his American peers and professors seemed to feel more pressure to put their summers to productive use. But Silvio did sometimes convince a friend or two to join him in Italy. Silvio maintained these three-month breaks for as long as he could, until the demands of his work, and his assimilation into the American schedule, gradually reduced the time he was able to get away. Nonetheless, Silvio continues to visit Italy regularly, twice per year if he can, to see his parents. Both of Silvio's parents are still enjoying life in their nineties, but they are no longer able to make the journey to the United States for visits, so it's up to Silvio and his family to make the trip to Italy.

2.6   I Have a Ph.D., Now What?

After completing his Ph.D. in 1982, Silvio found himself heading to another new country—Canada. He decided to do a post-doctoral fellowship at the University of Toronto. The university had a strong theory group at that time, and Silvio would find new mentors in Steve Cook, Charlie Rackoff, and Allan Borodin. Silvio had already met both Steve and Allan, and it was Allan who had invited Silvio to pay them a visit in Toronto and convinced him to join their research group. It turned out to be a momentous decision for Silvio, and one that would have a great influence on his career. He began working with Charlie Rackoff, "a first-class researcher—very creative and also very obsessed about definitions," Silvio recalls. The two would go on to work together on many research collaborations over the years.

Thanks to the encouragement he received from the members of this group, Silvio felt that the environment was perfect for someone like him who was just beginning his career, and therefore had reason to be a bit nervous about putting forward his theories. "If you really want to do something that is always at the point of failure, you need support all the time," he says. In Toronto, he found the kind of kinship and support that enabled him to undertake risky and uncertain work that would attempt to break new ground. The more he pushed himself, the more important it became to have this kind of support. From Steve Cook especially, Silvio found intellectual support in addition to emotional support.

This intellectual support was invaluable in boosting Silvio's confidence to pursue his ideas. He had so much regard for Steve's judgment that if Steve thought he was onto something, he felt he could move forward with much less worry. The result of all this was Silvio's early work on zero-knowledge proofs, including his explorations of how to define a proof. Once again, it appeared that Silvio had found himself in the right place, surrounded by the right people. While he considered Manuel Blum to have been very influential when he undertook his first forays into encryption at Berkeley, when Silvio moved onto this next phase of his research, Steve Cook and Charlie Rackoff proved to be equally influential.

Intellectual support has been a key factor in Silvio's success, but it was not always a given. Any researcher looking to push the boundaries of his field will meet with resistance, and Silvio was no exception. He calls the rejection of his theories "devastating," but at the same time rejection can be the impetus to commit to a high standard of research and fight for what he believes to be true. In fact, he feels that if a theorem is worth proving, it should be difficult to convince people of its importance. Otherwise, you are dealing with a widely accepted concept already, not something truly innovative. Silvio's paper on zero-knowledge proofs, for example, was rejected several times. But in the end, this made it a more thorough paper. If you struggle because your peers don't agree with you when you first argue your theory, you need to have the stamina to keep yourself on target until you have convinced them.

According to Silvio, great research requires the conviction to keep on your path when everyone else seems to be heading in the opposite direction. When it comes to being a researcher, Silvio believes that being stubborn is a prerequisite, but if you are too stubborn you can end up committed to something that ends up being wrong—it's a delicate balance. There were times when Silvio feared that he had taken an incorrect path in his research, and he had to make contingency plans in case his theory turned out to be incorrect or he was unable to solve the problem he had decided to tackle. He has had several occasions where he was close to admitting defeat, but has been able (and stubborn enough) to keep trying until he worked through the problem that was holding him back.

Along with being stubborn, Silvio is extremely focused when he's involved in a research project. He's the sort of researcher who will work day and night on an interesting problem unless someone is there to make him stop. And even when he is compelled to put his work on hold by family or friends, it remains at the back of his mind while he is doing other things. He finds it very hard to step back from a problem he's trying to solve.

This is a tendency that was easier to indulge in his early days as a graduate student, and as a young researcher at the beginning of his career at the Massachusetts Institute of Technology (MIT). However, it became harder and harder as his life filled with other priorities, like a wife and children.

And MIT was in fact Silvio's next stop. In 1983, after his year in Toronto, a position opened up at MIT, where his friend Shafi Goldwasser was already doing post-doctoral work. It was a bold strategic move on the part of MIT. They already employed cryptographer Ronald Rivest, and decided to hire on Shafi, who was also doing research in cryptography. Creating an additional position for Silvio may have seemed like a large commitment to what was a relatively minor field of computer science—at the time, there were almost no cryptography courses offered at any university other than MIT, and to some degree at Berkeley. But MIT was willing to bet on cryptography becoming an important field, and they were setting their university up to be the leader in this research area. Little did they know that it would be essential to the security of the internet one day, making possible many of the online activities that people now take for granted.

When Silvio was offered the position, he took a road trip with his mother to make his way to his new home. Mrs. Micali had made the trip from Italy to Toronto (Mr. Micali was not able to get away from his work at the time) and the two traveled through Quebec and Maine, eventually arriving in Cambridge. It was a rare opportunity to spend time together without the distractions of work or the other members of the family.

2.7 Professor Micali of MIT

On arrival at MIT in 1983, Silvio became part of their growing cryptography group. At that time, fellow cryptographer Oded Goldreich also arrived to do postdoctoral work, and he would remain there until 1986. Oded had already been introduced to Silvio and Shafi's work on probabilistic encryption through Richard Karp. He had immediately realized that the pair were redefining the field, and that their work would form the basis of all future work in cryptography. Oded was even more captivated once he had the opportunity to get to know Silvio personally at MIT. "He was extremely charming and outstandingly inspiring and empowering," Oded recalls. The pair have worked together many times, and they also remain good friends.

Thanks to this team of enthusiastic and dedicated researchers, the atmosphere in the cryptography group was friendly and lively. Silvio, Shafi, and Oded were all young and single, and they spent much of their time together even outside of work—dining together, going to movies, and chatting for hours. At work, Silvio and Shafi had neighboring offices, and the whole department was an "open-door" environment where discussions with a student or visitor would end up involving multiple people. Research discussions would also bounce around the offices, which made for an open and enthusiastic exchange of ideas.

In 1990, when he was well settled in his role at MIT and his life in Cambridge, Silvio's life took a new turn: Silvio met Daniela, the woman who would eventually become his wife. The two met at a party in Cambridge. She is also Italian born, but she spoke English so well that Silvio believed her to be British when they first met. In his first attempts to engage this interesting woman in conversation, he found himself tripping over his words and sounding less than impressive. Finally, after an hour of difficult conversation, she interrupted him to tell him that it was fine if he wanted to speak Italian. It was the beginning of a beautiful and enduring relationship.

Daniela is a legal scholar and law professor at Boston University. When she and Silvio first met, she had completed her master's in law at Harvard and was attending university in Florence to complete her Ph.D. This made for a very long-distance relationship for the two at first. Nonetheless, after about a year and a half they married.

Having a law professor as a daughter-in-law was, of course, welcome news to Silvio's father, the respected judge who'd reluctantly accepted that his son would not be following in his footsteps. And to add to the irony, Daniela's parents were mathematicians, so they were equally pleased to find their daughter marrying someone with a love of mathematics that she did not have herself.

The couple now have two adult sons, Stefano and Enrico. Enrico is currently studying at MIT, with a keen interest in both biology and computer science. He's tackling computer science first, which is a brave decision considering the large shoes he may be expected to fill.

The children are well acquainted with their Italian roots. Until the age of five, they spoke only Italian at home. This has enabled them to have a stronger relationship with their grandparents back in Italy, who don't speak much English. In fact, the boys have a facility with languages that Silvio finds very impressive. Apart from fluent English and Italian, they can also speak French and Spanish.

Long before he had sons to think about, Silvio had to deal with other young minds—his students. Taking on an assistant professor position (which would lead to a full professorship in 1991) meant that Silvio was responsible for teaching and supervising both undergraduate and graduate students, along with doing his own research. For someone who prefers to focus completely on one task at a time, this was rather inconvenient. He was expected to teach one course per semester, so at least he did not have to divide his attention between multiple courses. He typically teaches undergraduates during one semester, and graduate students during the other.

Silvio believes that his strength is teaching research courses because the material is all in his head and he simply has to share it with his students. His theory is that in order to understand a topic, one has to completely exhaust all of the possible ways to misunderstand it. He therefore examines all of the detours that can be taken, and that the students would perhaps be tempted to take. He has great empathy for the students who are exploring a new subject for the first time, because it's a journey he has already taken. Rather than just feeding the students his own results and conclusions, he invites them to experience the entire process that was required for him to reach those results. They see how he changed his mind at certain points and arrived at his conclusions, and he feels that it gives them a more complete understanding of the topic. As a side effect, it may also make them feel that their own doubts and struggles are not unusual, or a sign that failure is imminent, as they undertake their own original research. Surely if their eminent professor experiences these struggles, it should not be surprising that they are going through similar struggles themselves.

Leo Reyzin was a graduate student at MIT in the 1990s, and he took Silvio's course "Cryptography and Cryptoanalysis" during his first year at the university. He recalls Silvio's lectures with great admiration. "He's very inspiring. He treats every lecture as a performance. There's drama, there's tension—every lecture has to tell a story and draw the audience in. You don't give away the plot at first, you hold the audience in suspense," Leo says. "There's the bad way to do things and the right way to do things. And he deliberately misleads you and then says, 'Aha! That's what's wrong!' and you really have to stay on top of it to follow him. He does it to keep you thinking, to keep you on your toes."

Courses on basic topics outside his field of expertise are a different matter. These are the courses that Silvio is less confident about teaching. The textbooks explain how things should be done, but they don't reflect on the genesis of the ideas behind the lessons. The subjects he feels he teaches best are the ones he has struggled with himself, because then he understands how to explain them to students who may be struggling as well. To make up for this, he prepares more for the courses that are outside his expertise. He's also a terrible procrastinator when it comes to doing this because he's usually involved in some research at the same time that is his main focus. Yet somehow it all comes together.

Because Silvio's path to understanding a topic involves an in-depth examination of the process that was taken to reach a particular conclusion, he likes to undertake this type of examination with his students so that the knowledge becomes an integral part of their psyche—they own it. To Silvio's dismay, the course curricula are not designed with this kind of detailed analysis in mind. So Silvio struggles to get through everything he is supposed to be teaching, and would much rather cover less material in greater depth. His students are sometimes expected to cover certain topics on their own using the course books, while they learn others in impressive detail during Silvio's lectures. In a system that relies on prerequisite courses as the students progress, covering everything in the course outline is taken for granted. Silvio must find a way to make that happen and to teach at a pace that does not always come naturally.

As a supervisor, Silvio sees his students not as young minds to be molded but as research peers. He will only take on a student who has taken a research course with him, so that he has a good idea of that student's understanding of his research and the field in general. This prevents students from coming to him with preconceived ideas about his research that aren't necessarily accurate. It also helps students to self-select as people who are fond of Silvio's style and his personality.

Leo Reyzin was one of those students who wanted to work under Silvio even before he arrived at MIT. He'd seen Silvio present at a seminar and a conference and was very interested in what Silvio had to say. "He seemed creative and energetic," Leo recalls.

Since the relationship will be a close one, and will last for several years, personal and professional compatibility are important. Together Silvio and his student will find a subject that they are really interested in and then jointly "obsess" over the research. He doesn't look for topics that are specifically "suitable" for a first major research project; he expects his students to take on the same kinds of big questions and innovative research that have always attracted him. Silvio won't hand off a piece of research to a student that he doesn't have the patience to look at himself, as a sort of outsourcing project. He takes an all-or-nothing approach, and the research takes as long as it takes until they solve the problem. Because he doesn't advocate lower-level research, there's a greater chance that his students may experience failure, but Silvio feels that the lessons learned from this process are valuable and will help his students to succeed going forward. Although they may have less experience, Silvio believes his students to be just as intelligent as any colleague he works with.

Because of this fully immersive approach to working with his students, Silvio generally only supervises one student at a time. He doesn't believe that he has the capacity to properly participate in the research of more than one student. "If you are obsessed about two different things," he says, "you are not really obsessed." They work together until the thesis is almost complete, and then Silvio will begin to look at another student to begin a new round of research with. This is another reason that it's so important that the pair find a topic they are both truly excited about. For the duration of the project, this will be Silvio's only research focus. He does not undertake his own individual research at the same time.

Leo Reyzin says, "He's very much goal and project oriented. It's not like there's a weekly hour-long meeting. If we're working on something then it's very intense. Silvio is all-consumed by things. When he's consumed by something he's really consumed by it."

During their time working together, both he and Silvio were at one point each expecting a child (Leo's first and Silvio's second). Knowing that fatherhood would soon be making more demands on their time, Silvio wanted to get as much work done as possible before that happened. "He said, 'I'm about to have a kid, you're about to have a kid, let's get to work *now*!'"

Leo says that during the times the two worked on separate projects, it was a challenge to get Silvio's attention, since he'd be focused on something else. "When he had time for you, he really did. He had hours and hours and hours. But when he didn't, he didn't. The only way to communicate with him at the time was to leave physical notes on his office door. He didn't do email; calling him was pointless."

Leo recalls the long hours spent working together on a research project. "We'd pace the halls and work on the whiteboard, and when the time came to write up the results we'd actually sit at the computer together and write, which is a very rare treat—to work with someone at one keyboard and just take over who's driving. We kind of completed each other's sentences."

This type of approach fits in well with Silvio's preference for collaborative research. Collaboration has been Silvio's preferred research method since his early work with Vijay Vazirani and Shafi Goldwasser at Berkeley. Of the more than 100 papers listed on Silvio's curriculum vitae, only a handful were written alone. Whether he was working with his fellow students during his graduate school days, with professional colleagues, or with his own graduate students as a supervisor, Silvio has almost always taken a team-based approach to research.

In fact, he traces his preference for working with others all the way back to his childhood anxiety about whether the outside world really existed, or whether he was simply imagining it. Interacting with his parents and schoolmates helped him to overcome his doubts at the time. As a researcher, his collaborators play a similar role; they help to assure him that he's not making things up and that the research they're undertaking is rooted in reality.

Silvio also feels that when you are coming up with a new theory, you're going out on a limb and could be there for quite a long time as you work to confirm it. It can be a very uncomfortable place to remain alone, and it's easy to start doubting yourself. Talking things out is an important part of the process for Silvio, and he prefers to learn about new subjects through discussion rather than by reading about them. When working with a partner (or several), there is thoughtful discussion about the theory right from the beginning, and he believes that this makes the chances of heading down the wrong path much lower. It is no accident that Silvio's Turing Award honors his collaborative work with Shafi Goldwasser.

Although the collaborative process involves a lot of mutual support, that doesn't mean that it's all about agreement. "Argument is the essence of life!" Silvio proclaims. Perhaps this is another way in which his Italian upbringing comes through in his work. He grew up with a very forceful father, who was skilled in the art of argument through his legal training. Silvio describes their arguments as "incendiary," although there was great love and respect between them. His sister Aurea is also skilled at arguing, likely for the same reasons. As a result, Silvio grew up learning that he would have to be persuasive in order to get his way, and that argument is not antithetical to friendship or respect. Instead, he feels that opposing forces and clashes of opinions are required if you want to forge something new and great. When it comes to his research, he has at times felt that opinions were so divided that perhaps he and his partner should stop collaborating, but somehow they always end up on the same page in the end.

Oded Goldreich, who has collaborated extensively with Silvio, feels that "Silvio's collaborators are presented with such forceful and beautiful arguments that they do not feel bad when arguing with him. So tension does not arise, because one is compelled by his arguments and captured by his charm. Later, one may find a flaw in Silvio's arguments, but one finds it hard to be annoyed at him even then, since the charm stays and the beauty of the arguments stays too." Oded can also attest to Silvio's steadfastness in defending his point of view. "As to changing Silvio's mind or making him do anything he does not want to do—this is definitely impossible."

Oded offers support for the idea that Silvio's facility for argument has its roots in his earlier learning about philosophy. "I think that what Silvio talks about is not arguing, but rather the articulation of views. Indeed, the articulation of views is a key ingredient in interaction with him. Silvio does not just say 'let's do X,' but rather articulates why it is a good idea to do *X*. Silvio's articulations are always grounded in philosophical considerations, and are richly framed in a wide context."

In addition to collaborating on research, Silvio mentors his graduate students in a variety of ways. One of his specialties is teaching his students how to present their work at conferences and seminars. Silvio is well known for his compelling "performances" when he lectures, and he tries to help his students to master "the Silvio method."

Leo Reyzin explains the process he went through with Silvio before his first big presentation. "He makes you prepare your slides, and you give the talk, and by slide five I can see he's just not there, he's tuning out. I say 'This is not working, is it?' and he says 'No, it's not, do you know why?'" The student then needs to go off and figure out what's wrong, fix it, and present to Silvio again and again until all of the problems are fixed and they are finally able to get through the whole presentation. If a student needs more specific feedback about what's not working, Silvio will provide it, but he prefers to let his students find the problems themselves. "I don't know how many times we rehearsed my first talk," says Leo. "It was over and over and over and every time we'd get a little farther into it. A lot of his former students are now faculty at various universities and I know them pretty well, and they're all good presenters—so it works."

Silvio also develops a strong personal relationship with his students. "He's a wonderful mentor," says Leo. "The number of conversations we had about life and career, and balancing what one wants out of an academic and nonacademic career, and how to balance having kids and your family obligations. He was so generous with his time and advice." He was also generous in other ways. "He never let me pay for our lunch while I was a student. Until you get your Ph.D. you can't pay for lunch. I guess I owe him a lot of lunches!"

Silvio's time at MIT is divided between teaching and research, making for a full schedule. Schedules and Silvio simply do not get along well. "If you don't get bored and spend time figuring out what to do, you cannot do original work," he says. During the month of January, he has no scheduled classes to teach. This gives Silvio time to think about things more deeply, with no distractions. He thinks that this time is crucial if you want to do something different; idleness and creativity go together. Nothing happens for a while and then something clicks. For Silvio, it is necessary to have unstructured time on your hands that you can shape any way you want.

In addition to his work at MIT, Silvio's career has taken him around the globe, presenting his research at conferences and universities. It's an inevitable part of being a researcher, and the more successful one is, the more requests are made for this type of presentation. Silvio enjoys the opportunities to talk with his peers, although the fact that he describes these pleasant talks as "confrontations" is perhaps indicative of his argumentative conversational style. Rather than attending scheduled sessions at conferences, he prefers to sit down with people to have a discussion about a topic of interest.

While Silvio is never one to back away from an argument, his interactions with his peers in his own field and others are always gracious. According to Oded Goldreich, "Silvio is very generous. One may forget this when seeing him fight for some cause or interest of his; when he is doing anything, he does it full-heartedly. But when the fight is over, he is the most generous winner one can imagine. In the rare cases that he loses, he is also graceful about it."

When he is putting together a conference presentation about his research, Silvio tries to imagine himself in the audience, because he considers himself to be the worst kind of person to present to. When he attends another researcher's presentation, he often gets lost by the second slide. A complex illustration will draw his focus, causing him to stop listening to the presenter and get completely off track. He figures if he can understand a presentation, anyone can understand it. For his own talks, he tries to distill everything down to the simplest terms, which takes a lot of time and preparation. He uses his own hand-drawn cartoons to illustrate concepts because he finds them less distracting than more complex representations. He claims that he will use any trick in the book to make things easier to understand. In a field like theoretical computer science, as many scholars and interested laypersons can attest, this is no easy task.

2.8 Kudos and Companies

Another sign of his long and distinguished research career is the number of awards and honors that Silvio has received. In 1993, work on interactive proof systems that he did with Shafi Goldwasser and Charlie Rackoff was awarded the inaugural Gödel Prize. This prize is given jointly by European Association for Theoretical Computer Science (EATCS) and the Association for Computing Machinery for outstanding papers in the area of theoretical computer science.

In 2003, Silvio was elected to the American Academy of Arts and Science's Computer Science section. The Academy's members include more than 250 Nobel Prize laureates. Silvio was also elected to the National Academy of Sciences and the National Academy of Engineering in 2007. Both of these honors illustrate the high regard in which Silvio's peers hold him. These academies only bestow membership on leaders in their fields and to be recognized by three such organizations shows an exceptional level of achievement.

Silvio was also the winner of the RSA Conference Award in Mathematics in 2003. His 2004 paper, co-written with his student Leo Reyzin, "Physically Observable Cryptography" won the inaugural TCC Test-of-Time Award in 2015. This award is presented at the Theory of Cryptography Conference (TCC) for a paper published at TCC at least eight years earlier that made a significant contribution to the theory of cryptography, preferably with influence in other areas of cryptography, theory, and beyond. Silvio was also named Berkeley Distinguished Alumnus of the Year in 2006 by the Electrical Engineering and Computer Science department of his alma mater.

Adding to this already impressive list of achievements, Silvio received the ACM Turing Award with Shafi Goldwasser in 2012, in recognition of their "transformative work that laid the complexity-theoretic foundations for the science of cryptography, and in the process pioneered new methods for efficient verification of mathematical proofs in complexity theory."

It is true that Silvio abandoned the hope of winning a Nobel Prize one day when he changed his undergraduate major from physics to mathematics, but perhaps his collection of other prestigious prizes has made up for that loss, at least in part. While recognition from his peers is always welcome, Silvio believes that winning major awards has additional benefits, both to himself and to computer science in general. He feels that the awards bring more attention to certain fields of research that might otherwise go unnoticed in the mainstream, and they invite outside observations on the work.

This type of judgment from outside one's field, although it might make some researchers uncomfortable, is necessary according to Silvio. He thinks that there is a danger to conducting research in a "bubble" where there is no outside judgment of what you are doing. Diverse opinions provide the necessary perspective to help researchers decide which paths to pursue.

Awards also help to introduce researchers in other fields to one's work. Certainly, Silvio was well known among the cryptography community long before he won the Turing Award, but afterward, researchers in other fields learned about him and his work. It has given him an opportunity to become a sort of ambassador in his areas of expertise, to answer questions, and to facilitate connections between scholars in different areas.

Another benefit he sees in winning awards is the permission it gives him to explore new areas of research that are not currently well recognized. These awards give him the credibility he needs in order to take on more risk, because there is an implicit recognition that he is a top researcher and unlikely to be pursuing a frivolous idea. The idea of taking bigger risks is also easier from his own perspective, because the confidence boost of a major award makes him feel more energized about doing something new and innovative.

Groundbreaking research can lead to awards, certainly, but it can also find its way into the commercial realm. Silvio and Shafi's early work in cryptography has laid the groundwork for a number of online security features that are widely used today.

While you might expect that this in-depth knowledge of online security would make Silvio extremely cautious when it comes to his own online life, he does not actually practise what he preaches. "I'm extremely suspicious as a cryptographer when I'm doing research," he explains, "but then I don't even lock my door!" He doesn't use the best practices for creating passwords or lock his front door because he's more concerned about locking himself out than keeping his property safe. The work itself, however, he takes very seriously.

The practical applications of Silvio's work have continued throughout his career. He often sets out to solve a purely theoretical question—to change the way that an entire field is viewed or approached—but in the end the solutions usually have practical implications. Silvio believes that technology transfer is crucial, whether he is involved in the transfer himself or whether it is left to others who pick up where he has left off and develop applications for his research. "Knowledge has to be transferred to society," he says. "I really believe that this is important." Silvio owns dozens of patents covering several different areas of his research.

Silvio finds that actually achieving technology transfer is a challenge. The types of technologies he develops, such as digital signatures and simultaneous electronic transactions, require a shift in the way large numbers of people do business. The benefits of the technology must be so compelling that everybody is convinced to make the change in a short period of time. He uses fax machines as an example of this type of challenge. If you thought fax technology was interesting when it first emerged and purchased a fax machine, it was useless unless everyone you wanted to send faxes to also had one. The technology could only succeed if a certain level of market penetration took place. The timing can be as important as the technology itself. Introduce your technology to society before they're ready for it, and it will be passed by. Introduce it too late, and there will be a large number of competing technologies on the market. So while the chances of coming up with the next big thing are small, Silvio believes that in some cases, the benefit to society of a technological shift are so great that it's worth the risk.

Despite these challenges, Silvio has delved into the commercial side of research. He worked with a team in 2003 to develop CoreStreet, a credential validation technology, while on sabbatical from MIT. He also worked with Ronald Rivest on a micropayment system called Peppercoin. This type of endeavor is quite different from academic research, and Silvio is well aware of his limitations. He tries to bring in the best possible developers and engineers, plus those who can handle the fundraising and other business aspects of a startup.

Among other challenges, Silvio had to present the products to venture capitalists. Accustomed to audiences of computer scientists, Silvio needed to find nontechnical ways to explain the products—a true test of Silvio's dramatic presentation style. Both of these companies were later acquired, and Silvio returned to his position at MIT. Silvio recently took another sabbatical from MIT to focus on a business called Algorand, which has created a new type of distributed ledger. Although the field is already competitive, he thinks his product is superior and is optimistic about convincing others that it is the right choice. It seems that his powers of persuasion are strong, since in early 2018 he convinced venture capitalists to invest $4 million in the company.

2.9   The Road Ahead

Now in his sixties, Silvio has no plans to take it easy. When asked about retirement, he reacts as though it was the most absurd idea he's ever heard. "Retire from what?" he asks. "From life? It makes no sense to me." He believes that if there comes a time that he can no longer indulge his research obsessions, he will find something else that he can do well and he will become obsessed with that instead. He thinks that we all have an obligation to continue to contribute in our own way for as long as we are able, and to be fully engaged in life.

Although he is certain that many more projects lie in his future, Silvio has no idea what they might be. It's part of his obsessive, in-the-moment nature that he does not make long-term plans. Whatever comes up when his current project winds down, he'll decide on a direction at that time. Retrospectively, he can see that every five years or so he tends to switch to a new project, but it's not a timeline that he plans in advance, and the next project is never intentionally lined up and waiting in the wings.

What is clear is that Silvio will continue to commit himself completely to his undertakings, to enjoy time with his friends and family, to cook his mother's wonderful recipes, and to live his life one obsession at a time.

An Interview with Shafi Goldwasser

This is a partial transcript of an interview of Shafi Goldasser by Alon Rosen. The interview took place on November 23, 2017. The transcript was lightly edited for clarity.

Rosen: Hi. My name is Alon Rosen. I am a professor of computer science at the Herzliya Interdisciplinary Center in Israel. Today is the 23rd of November 2017 and I'm here in Rehovot at the Weizmann Institute of Science together with Shafi Goldwasser, who is being interviewed as part of the ACM Turing Award Winners project.

Hi, Shafi. We are here to conduct an interview about your life, about your achievements. Generally speaking, we will go chronologically and we will talk at two levels. The first level will be a general audience type of level and the second level will be more specific, more oriented towards people that specialize in the subject and are interested in the details. So let's begin with your high school experience.

Goldwasser: Okay. Well, first of all, thank you Alon for taking this opportunity to interview me.

High school. Right. Those years I remember quite vividly. The orientation changed a bit for me from sort of being interested in the sort of more humanity subjects to more the mathematical subjects. You know, mathematics, and the sciences. I remember I loved physics. I didn't really like life sciences, but physics and math I liked quite a bit. And I had a great math teacher from eleventh and twelfth grade. Somehow I did well and I think that was part of why I wanted to do it. I also had a great teacher for physics, and physics in my mind was just fantastic. You know, things made sense, you could derive things. I think early on that's what I wanted to study.

Rosen: What about mathematics?

Goldwasser: In mathematics, again I was good at it, but mathematics itself at that time was not described as mathematics with some sort of motivation. It was more the method, you know? So taking derivatives, integrals, and it was in trigonometry and all that. And I could perform it well, but it didn't have the stories associated with them that physics did.

Rosen: So it was more about the technique and less about . . . ?

Goldwasser: About technique rather than about motivation.

Rosen: And did you already then have the sense that you missed the concepts and the . . . ?

Goldwasser: I had no idea that there were concepts, you know? All I knew was that I liked the concepts in physics. The whole derivation from principles was beautiful in my eyes. And I remember questions on the exam and then you would have to think. And I have the impression of some memory where my [laughs] answer was different than others and he was surprised, the professor. But I cannot, for the life of me, remember what the question was or what the derivation was.

Rosen: So it sort of sounds like this professor, he had an encouraging influence on you.

Goldwasser: Yes, both of them. Yes.

Rosen: Okay. How significant do you think it is to have a good professor? To have someone who influences you that early?

Goldwasser: Extremely significant. I think if you're very lucky, there is someone early on—and that could be high school, it could be maybe college, but better in high school—that awakens something in you, a spark, an interest, so that maybe later you're not going to do exactly that but you know there's something about studying and about pursuing knowledge that is exciting. I think it's fundamental, and I don't think that it has to be more than one.

I had other good teachers there, you know. The literature, I remember the teacher. The history teacher. I remember learning Shakespeare in English class. But something about . . . there was some spark there in the science classes and in the math classes that I recall.

Rosen: So by then, your self-image was sort of that you were set towards studying scientifically oriented subject?

Goldwasser: No, not at all. [laughs] I loved to write, and I think that my inner image was that I was going to be a writer. But I guess—you're right—by the time we got to the eleventh and twelfth grade, my parents, or especially my father was very kind of insistent that I should follow the realistic . . . this is what we call in Hebrew "realistic studies," or mathematics and physics studies. Because as people of his generation, and maybe people of the current generation in Israel as well, there was a real emphasis on pragmatism and the exact sciences, and that everything else is a bit less . . . It might be enjoyable, but it's not as real as what one must do in life.

Rosen: I'd be interested to hear now about your view on the global experience of Israel at the time.

Goldwasser: Sure. Yeah, I do have the tendency to talk about the personal stuff, but it's what I know best. But let me tell you a little bit about my memories about Israel. First of all, I lived here through a few wars, right? I remember the Six-Days War [of June 1967]. I think I was in fourth grade. I remember that. And I remember we went down to the bunker. I remember the sirens. And I remember right after the war, my family and I, we drove to Jerusalem. I remember still seeing the Wailing Wall before they kind of opened up the huge square. It was somewhat of a euphoria. Who knew that this would be a "tragedy forever."

But in any case, this is fourth grade. Then I remember Yom Kippur [October 1973] War. Yom Kippur War is a different story. Then I'm already in tenth grade I think and my brother was a soldier. I remember the first phone call that he made. My father asked him how was his commander, who was someone that my father felt that was going to protect him. And he said, "He is no longer." And I remember my father just burst out crying. He was just so worried about him. Then I remember when he came back home the first time . . . I don't know how long it was really, because he stayed in the army for about six months afterward. He was supposed to be released but he stayed longer because of the war. But I remember that he had a lot less hair. He had like those two sides of his forehead, his hair receded quite a bit. It was amazing that this kind of traumatic experience can do that.

Rosen: Do you think any of this had any effect on you in the long term, on your personality, outlook?

Goldwasser: I think it had an effect on my father. I think that when my brother came back from the army, he joined the Hebrew University, because he was going to go and study mathematics, and he went right away. They postponed the semester because of all these soldiers. They started a new semester in January, like a new school year. But my father just wanted him out of Israel as fast as possible. He was so afraid for his safety that he wanted him to go to school in the States. And within a year, like the second year he just sort . . . he somehow arranged . . . he kind of made him apply abroad. And he got accepted to Carnegie Mellon and left. That affected me because that started some sort of chain reaction in the family.

Rosen: And okay, you said your brother wanted to study mathematics. What did he end up doing and how did it all affect you?

Goldwasser: He studied mathematics as his first degree, and then he went to business school at Carnegie Mellon. It's called GSIA, Graduate School of Industrial Administration. And then he went to work.

And I, when I arrived at Carnegie Mellon, I had like a year or so before my military service, since my father wanted me to go to the U.S. to study so that I don't waste any time. This idea of wasting time is something very problematic, or was very problematic when I was growing up. Now it seems like everybody in Israel is taking trips around the world as soon as they finished the army, or before the army, and wasting time is not called "wasting time" anymore but "gaining life experience." In any case, my father wanted me to go to the States, and as usual I did what he recommended and went to Carnegie Mellon, and I went to study mathematics.

So I arrive to the U.S., it's summer 1976. I land in the U.S. and my brother comes and picks me up in New York, and we spend a few days in New York. Then we took a bus to Pittsburgh. I knew nothing about Pittsburgh. I spent the summer in the dorms waiting for the school year to start. I actually never applied to the school. Just my brother told his professors that his sister is coming for a year and she's good at math. And since he was good at math and they knew that he was a talent, they said, "Does she want to come and study here?" and he said, "Yes," and they said, "Okay." And that was it. I became an undergraduate in mathematics, in applied mathematics.

But then it was applied mathematics and computer science. Now there's a undergraduate computer science program at Carnegie Mellon. At the time, there wasn't. And the truth is that I actually loved studying. This was a revelation. When you go to high school, you sort of do what you're told, right? But I found it really interesting. I found the math interesting, I found the computer science interesting. I took this introduction class in FORTRAN programming. In the beginning, I had no idea. There were these cards where you put an instruction on every card and it goes through a machine and then it executes each instruction. I've never seen a computer before, I haven't really heard about computers before, but it was fascinating. It was really marvelous.

Rosen: Okay, I have two questions now about the admissions, you said the admissions process was unorthodox in your case?

Goldwasser: I would say. [laughs]

Rosen: Now, I want to ask what would have happened today with admissions?

Goldwasser: Ah, today. Today, no, the whole college admissions in the U.S. is something bordering on insane. You know, there are standardized tests, there's grades, there's extracurricular activities, there are huge committees that sit and deal with every case. They accept legacy and people with talents that supplement whatever the needs of the school are, and who knows what else. And there's also a big mystery about this. All, in my opinion, geared toward making money on the admissions process. So, is the outcome any better? I believe serendipity is a big part of one's life trajectory, and maybe some of the serendipity is lost with this whole process that is very meticulous. But they're talking these days about having machine learning take over the admissions process, so we are in for a whole new era if that's going to be the case.

Rosen: Okay, so undergrad years?

Goldwasser: Right. Undergrad years I'm in Carnegie Mellon. I start in mathematics. There is even this program called Math Studies, which only a few kids go to, where there are these two professors who teach a handful of kids. It's supposed to go through all mathematics, you know, topology, geometry, algebra of course, logic, and everything in two years. And they spend essentially the first semester arguing with each other how to define each concept, definition, back and forth, back and forth. It's abstract beyond anything that I've ever seen because in Israeli high school, things are very method-oriented. They are teaching you how to perform, how to solve exercises. They don't really teach you . . . at least at that time, they didn't teach you about the concept of a limit or why are you taking derivatives and why you're integrating. Here, we are completely . . . it's all axiomatic.

So I go through this semester, maybe a year, and the whole thing is a two-year program, and after a year I quit. And I think to myself, "This is going to take too much time and I'm not the best at the class," and I decided I'm going to go and do computer science, sort of the computer science specialty within the math. So I take this class on—I think—combinatorics or data structures or algorithms, whatever, and it's trivial because my mind of course was so sharpened by this one year of dealing with abstractions and dealing with definitions that even if you don't think you're understanding them, you're completely in a different level. Then when you go back to something of a lower level, it's a triviality.

This is an interesting experience that I have seen time and again with myself, with my kids. You push yourself to a place which is much more abstract and much more formal than maybe you care to be, and inevitably you start thinking more clearly, and you are able to sort of verbalize and conceptualize and define and understand. It's a fabulous discovery. Somebody has to prove a theorem about it explaining why is it that being able to verbalize, being able to define, and using precise concepts and precise thinking makes everything else simpler.

Rosen: So now you defend the very same thing that caused you to quit, like the abstraction?

Goldwasser: I know, I know. I mean in retrospect, maybe I should have stuck it out for another year, but that's what I did.

Rosen: Okay, so then you moved to computer science?

Goldwasser: I moved to computer science. I remember a lot of my professors at Carnegie Mellon. I remember Raj Reddy, who taught AI. He was the founder of real speech recognition. At the time, it was the Harpy project. And I remember Anita Jones. She taught software engineering. She was one of my recommenders to graduate school later. So was Raj Reddy. And I remember there was another professor, Nico Habermann, who taught us compilers and I had a compiler project that I did with a friend. I remember we wrote this compiler which never compiled. [laughs] I remember writing this program for generating poetry. Today, they talk in machine learning about GANs, these things that can generate let's say poetry in a way that's indistinguishable from let's say poetry of a particular poet. But at the time, the way these programs generating poetry would work is that you would have some sort of a notion of a verb and a noun and how a sentence is structured, then you would have a dictionary and you would form a poem. I loved that.

Rosen: How large were the classes back then?

Goldwasser: The classes were small. I would say there were like about twenty kids. Again, very few women. That I do remember, that I was one of two and the professor also treated us a little bit with, you know, half . . . I was going to say "forgiveness," but "forgiveness" might not be the right word. A little bit, you know, like we were silly, even though we weren't really. And that, after I start doing very well in the class, he realized that. But that was my feeling. It didn't matter to me much because I didn't think of myself that way, but I do remember that.

I remember coming from Israel, my command of English was not perfect to say the least, and on every program that I wrote there always were these comments where he says, "Indent, indent, indent." I didn't know what word "indent" meant until the end of the term, but then I realized that "indent" meant that I was supposed to like, you know, indent the "for loops" and the different commands. So now I know what that means. But it was these silly things.

It was like. I remember the first lesson of calculus when you come from Israel to America, and I remember telling my brother, who was in school at that time, I said, "I can't do this. It's too difficult." So he sat down with me. This is the first class ever in calculus, and he said, "Okay, so what didn't you understand?" and then it turned out that I didn't know the words "multiply" and "divide" and "integrated" and "differentiate." Then he told me what they all meant in Hebrew and I said "Ah." That was it. Then it wasn't difficult.

Then I had to make a decision at the end of that year whether to go back to Israel to my army service or ask for a deferral. I asked for a deferral, because I actually kind of liked studying and I kind of wanted to continue.

Rosen: Happy moments?

Goldwasser: Oh, lots of happy moments. I made lots of new friends and also I became a young woman, so there's also like personal relationships that you develop which happen when you are a young woman, and that regardless of where you're at is very exciting, right? You're coming of age. And I came of age in Carnegie Mellon during those years, between the age of 17 and 20.

Rosen: Okay. Just to be a bit more specific about those years, any particular topics that you related to, specific ones, beyond the aspect of . . . ?

Goldwasser: Yeah. I was very interested in artificial intelligence at the time, I think because of the class that I took, because of this poetry generation, because of the whole concept of speech understanding and so forth, and also I think because this whole idea of understanding the brain and how we think and how we dream and why we dream, what we dream. That was fascinating to me.

So it was very clear to me when I finished that I would like to study this further. That's why I applied to graduate school. And I applied to graduate school at the same time that I applied for jobs, because I wasn't very clear about what I was going to do. There were sort of three options. In fact, this is the story of my life—there's always at least three options, sometimes four, but never one. And the options then were to go back to Israel or to go to graduate school or to get a job. The idea of going back to Israel was complex: I wanted to go back to Israel, but I was very afraid. Because at this point I was kind of distanced from it, and furthermore, I felt that I would like to go back to Israel, but at least I'd like to show something for all these years that I was away.

And I felt like I think a lot of people feel when they finish undergraduate school. At least I think they feel. That I knew nothing. Even though I studied for . . . I did my degree in three years in the States, although usually it's four. I studied during the year and I studied during the summers because I wanted to finish quickly so I could go back to Israel. At the end, you feel like, "What do I know more than anybody else? I want to own something. It'll be something that I'll understand better than anybody." It's not even so much the idea of understanding better than anybody, but actually going into some subject in depth. At that point, it could have been related to artificial intelligence or algorithms. I remember also an algorithms course that was taught by Jon Bentley, and it was fascinating. I loved that as well.

So I wanted to know, understand something really well. I was told that there is this thing called graduate school. You have to understand, I didn't come from an academic family, it wasn't something that was standard, but . . .

In any case, I was told that there was this thing called graduate school. I think that like a day or two before, they said that I'm supposed to take this exam called the GRE. I didn't prepare at all, but I signed up and I went to the GRE. I didn't even know you were supposed to prepare, you know? It seems ridiculous how naive I was. So I took the GRE. I don't think I did very well. But in any case, I applied to graduate school and I got accepted to Carnegie Mellon in engineering and Berkeley in computer science. First, I said to Carnegie Mellon that I'm going to go there, and I went for the summer to the RAND Corporation, where Raj Reddy actually recommended me as an intern. This was in Santa Monica, in California on the beach. And I remember this California. Wow. The beach. Fantastic, you know? I lived in Venice Beach and there's the roller skaters and the bikers and . . .

Rosen: Mellon . . . ?

Goldwasser: So I was admitted to Carnegie Mellon, which was the place I spent my undergraduate, and I was debating between the two, and I also had a bunch of job offers, but it was clear that I wasn't going to get a job. I was going to go to graduate school. And I decided I'll go to Carnegie Mellon. I mean I wasn't sure, but I decided I'll go to Carnegie Mellon, because I had friends there. You know, I had a boyfriend, whatever, you know the kind of things that people have, and friends.

But I had the summer job at RAND. And I remember that summer. I cannot tell you what I worked on, but I do remember that I was thinking to myself that the supervisors were all Ph.D.s, and they were telling me what to do. It was some sort of AI-related project. I remember thinking to myself, "Why should they tell me what to do? I should get a Ph.D. and I should tell somebody else what to do." [laughs]

In any case, so that summer was a fabulous summer. First of all, there was research and it was interesting, although I can't tell you what it was about because I really have no recollection whatsoever. And second of all, all of a sudden it was, you know, I had an apartment of my own on the beach, it was California as I said before. You know, there were the roller skaters and the bikes. And then one day me and [a friend of mine from CMU], we decided to take a drive up the coast, up the California coast and go and see Berkeley, and go visit somebody that she knew in Palo Alto. Anyway, we drove up the coast. And I remember driving into the Berkeley exit on University Avenue, and it was just blue skies that like you've never seen and the green hills in the background. I'm just sort of driving to campus. It's such a glorious image. I can't tell you . . . This is something you don't forget. And it was "Wow, California, Berkeley." Then I told CMU that I'm not coming and I told Berkeley that I'm coming, because it was just captivating.

Rosen: What year was that?

Goldwasser: This was 1979. So I arrived at Berkeley. I had to find an apartment, the usual things that graduate students do. I lived with a bunch of astronomer graduate students. In any case, I wanted to do artificial intelligence. At the time, there were few people at Berkeley doing artificial intelligence, but as I told you, serendipity is the name of the game. I was a TA, I had to support myself, so I had a teaching assistantship. Then I actually somehow got to work with Dave Patterson on the RISC project, reduced instruction set computer.

Rosen: Maybe you can tell a bit about that.

Goldwasser: About the RISC project? At the time, the RISC project was this idea of Patterson and other people at Intel at the time that the thing to do is to figure out which of the instructions are used most often, let's say programs in Pascal and C, and those are the instructions that should be put in hardware in order to speed up computation. My part of the project was to figure out which instructions in fact are being used most often in Pascal programs. So I was quite the programmer at the time. And I worked on this very large system, which I think adapted an existing Pascal compiler, a sort of thing that collects dynamic statistics, and I modified it sort of extensively to figure out which instructions should really be optimized or put in hardware. And that was my master's thesis, which I got at the end of that year.

Rosen: Did you enjoy it?

Goldwasser: Actually, it was Professor Powell and Professor Patterson. Did I enjoy it? Yeah, it was interesting. You know, it was a lot of work. It was very intense. This whole idea of being incredibly focused on a project and being in the office from day to night was born at that time. I mean as an undergraduate, you spend a lot of time in libraries and studying for exams, but this idea that you have your own project and you set your own deadlines, although you know the professors expect things of you, it really comes from that time.

But at that time also, all of a sudden I wanted to go back . . . after I had the master's, I wanted to go back to Israel. I wanted to see Israel again. It's been four years. And I went for the summer. That was one of the highest . . . After four years not being in Israel, just being around here and with my mother and my sister. My sister was already a big girl. I remember taking a bus to Yamit. This was a time when they were actually withdrawing from the Sinai Desert. So I was in Israel then for three weeks, and then I came back to Berkeley and I continued to my Ph.D.

Rosen: Is there something about the initial time in Berkeley that you recall that is worthy of mentioning?

Goldwasser: I remember the professors. There were the theory professors. There was Manuel Blum and Dick Karp and Gene Lawler. And I remember meeting theory students, the theory graduate students. There was Silvio, which later on became a very close friend and a close colleague of mine. There was Vijay Vazirani. There was Faith Fich. There was Joan Plumstead. There was Mike Luby. They were all contemporaries of mine and I liked them. You know, I liked some of them more than others [laughs] as things are, and they're interesting characters. I took a class I think from Gene Lawler on scheduling, and there was a TA there called Chip Martel. Anyway, and I did some projects on scheduling with Vijay and Silvio. I remember that.

Rosen: That was your first collaboration with Silvio?

Goldwasser: It was a project—right—in class. Yeah, that was the first collaboration. Then I met . . . I took a . . . I met Manuel Blum, and Manuel offered me to be his student. I spent the summer working with him, and that was fantastic because he was such an unusual thinker, and he wanted to work with me, or he suggested that I would be his graduate student. It was a huge compliment.

Rosen: You felt like it's a compliment at the time?

Goldwasser: Yeah, sure. It was a huge compliment.

Rosen: Who were his other graduate students at the time?

Goldwasser: I think that Vijay and Silvio were his graduate students. I think before that it was Mike Sipser and Dana Angluin, and we were sort of the new wave. There was the three of us, maybe Joan too, Plumstead.

Rosen: What was it about them that you liked at the time, do you remember?

Goldwasser: They were extremely intense. They really loved what they were doing. They would talk about this incessantly, but they were a lot of fun too. You know, Silvio was from Italy and Vijay was from India, and they were so colorful and they had fabulous sense of humor. And they went out to restaurants all the time and talked about work and told stories. It was really just somehow these were people of the world. So as much as I liked Carnegie Mellon and had a lot of good friends, this was like a different dimension of personalities. If you think about it, people come to graduate school from foreign countries. They have lived a different life, each of them. They're older, they're sort of more worldly, and I was taken by it.

Rosen: Any particular memories, events from that or before . . . ?

Goldwasser: Yeah. There is actually a memory or an event . . . I think it was after about maybe like six months in or almost close to a year in Berkeley, I'm like a graduate student, I had a down period. It was like it's too hard and I don't have any original ideas and I'm never going to get through this, and I'm lonely, I don't know anybody, because I didn't have friends yet, close friends. And who do I think I am? And I was torturing myself continuously. What do I think about going to graduate school? Who do I think I am that I can just do this?

You know, I decided to leave Carnegie Mellon where I had lots of friends and just kind of conquer this new place totally on my own. I remember going through this cycle again and again and again, and then I had this realization that okay, maybe it's all true. Maybe I will amount to nothing and maybe I know nothing, and maybe I'm a failure. But if I'm going to be against myself and I'm not going to be my own friend, then who else? I'm going to have to like myself whatever I am. I got to accept that. And some of that was like a very kind of deep, decisive moment, that from then on, everything became better.

Because I think it's very important to realize that, for graduate students especially, which have moments like this, I'm sure it's universal, where you go, you've decided on this big adventure, and then it's very unclear, right? Are you going to succeed? Are you not going to succeed? There's a lot of competition. Everybody seems better than you. And there's a—I think—tendency for self-beating, at least for some people, and it's very important to realize that it is what it is, you know you got to like yourself, because at the end of the day, this is what you've got.

Rosen: Okay. Grad school, research, Manuel Blum.

Goldwasser: Research, grad school, right. Manuel Blum. Okay. Manuel Blum took me as a student, but as things go, it takes time to find a research project. Then

Manuel taught this class on algorithmic number theory. In this class, he taught us about, first of all, the basic elements of number theory, primes and composite numbers and quadratic residues and quadratic nonresidues and generators and cyclic groups and all these things, and all from an algorithmic point of view. That is, how to test that a number is prime, how to generate a prime, how to find the quadratic residue, how to test that something is a quadratic residue, modular arithmetic, and so forth, and always from an algorithmic perspective and analyzing running times. I found it fascinating. I really loved it. You know, it's very basic. I like this stuff.

Rosen: I remember you teaching me this.

Goldwasser: That's right. So I really love this material. And at the end, he had a few lectures where he talked about cryptography. At that point, there was essentially [only] RSA encryption scheme, a public-key encryption scheme, which is a way to send messages between people who have never met before, secret messages. It all is based on the fact that it's hard to factor composite numbers which are a product of let's say of two primes, but it's easy to generate prime numbers. And that was nice. Then there was another lecture on another method by Merkle–Hellman which Adi Shamir broke. And he did some cryptanalysis. That was interesting as well.

And then he asked the question, which was I think really defining for the rest of my career. He said there is an Alice and Bob, and they are deciding to get a divorce. Alice is in Boston and Bob is in San Francisco, or vice versa, and they have to decide who gets the dog. And they want to be fair, so they decide to toss a coin, except they're not in the same place and they have to toss a coin over the phone, except neither one wants a dog. Or both want the dog, whichever is the case. And the idea that Alice just tosses the coin and then she says to Bob "It's heads" doesn't exactly work because they don't trust each other. So he asked, "How would you do that? Can you use number theory to do that?"

So what's the connection? You know, why number theory? And that was sort of fascinating. Can you use sort of number theory? The idea that let's say factoring numbers is a hard problem, is there a way to toss coins over the telephone?

And I start thinking about it, and I had an idea. The idea was . . . that there was this function, which is a modular exponentiation function, like $g^x \bmod p$. The idea was to essentially hide . . . for Alice to pick like a random x and send $g^x \bmod$ prime p to Bob and have him guess what x is. This is a function which is hard to invert: From $g^x \bmod p$ (and g) it's hard to find x. And Bob tries to guess x, or actually to be more precise, he tries to guess something about x, like whether x is odd or even or greater than p over 2 or smaller than p over 2. And he makes a guess, then she tells him what x is and both can check if the guess is correct or not. If the guess is correct, it's like heads has been tossed, and if the guess is incorrect, it's like tails.

And Silvio and I talked about it. I told Silvio about this. Then you needed to prove something, right? You needed to prove that this is like a coin toss, that really it's impossible for Bob to guess better than 50–50 whether x was greater than p over 2 or smaller than p over 2. And we had some proof, but there was a bug in it. And that was sort of the beginning of a lot of cryptography.

Rosen: And I want to ask at this point how much context about cryptography did you have at the time beyond what Manuel [taught in the class]?

Goldwasser: Nothing. Zero. Uh . . . Zero.

Rosen: Did you know about Shannon's work?

Goldwasser: Nothing. That was not part of the class. The class was about number theory and applications of number theory. I think that's what interested Manuel.

Rosen: Yeah, so why did Manuel Blum teach that class at that time?

Goldwasser: Because we're talking about 1980. Was it 1980 or 1981? And the invention of public-key cryptography was 1976 and then the RSA . . .

Rosen: Maybe you can give some context to the general . . . ?

Goldwasser: Right. So 1976, there was this incredible paper by Diffie and Hellman which suggested this idea that we are having this possibility of digital communication, that eventually everybody's going to be communicating with everybody else over the digital network. This is the case today. It wasn't the case in '76, but the possibility was there. And they were asking, "How can we utilize this in order to kind of shift the world into this mode of electronic commerce?" I think they even talked about these things explicitly in this paper. And they brought up these two suggestions.

One is what they call public-key encryption, which is a way for let's say an Alice and a Bob who've never met before to communicate secretly. Somehow there would be a directory where Alice would publish something that they called a public key, and Bob could read Alice's public key and use that in order to send her coded messages that only she, who knew also a corresponding private key, would be able to read, but no one else could. This was one thing.

Another thing that they suggested is this idea of a digital signature, which is that people could sign documents so that everybody can verify that, say, Shafi signed it, but only Shafi could sign it. As you know, a handwritten signature, if I have a signature, it looks the same no matter which document I put it on. Here the case was that you would take a document and you would do a transformation to a new document which is called a signed document, and the ability to perform the transformation would be something that each user in the system, Shafi or Alon, could do in a way unique to them, because they knew some information or some private key that enabled them to do so and yet there was a matching verification key that would be able to verify that this was signed by Shafi or alternatively something was signed by Alon. In any case, they proposed these two things. They didn't give ways to do it.

A year later, there was a paper by Rivest, Shamir, and Adleman where they showed how to do it using number theory. Around the same time, there was also a paper by Michael Rabin who showed yet a different way to do it also based on number theory.

And Manuel taught those three papers, because they were just mind-boggling. This whole idea, very tantalizing. Not only that; I think that Len Adleman was a student of Manuel's, so there was some affinity there as well. But one would have to ask Manuel why he taught that class. I think it was the first time he did teach that class, in any case. I think. You know what, maybe not. Maybe he has taught it before. Maybe, because there are these notes, these lecture notes on number theory by Dana Angluin. So he must have taught it before when Dana was a student, but I don't think he taught the public-key cryptography part of it.

Rosen: Who else was in the class besides you and Silvio?

Goldwasser: Me, Silvio, Vijay, Mike Luby. You know, the usual suspects. I mean all of the crowd at Berkeley was there. Jeff Shallit was another good friend at Berkeley, and Eric Bach.

Rosen: They went on to do computational number theory.

Goldwasser: That's right. You know, that's right. Eric has this very famous paper about how to generate primes in factored form, which is an important paper for generating generators for the multiplicative group mod a prime. Jeff Shallit also had very interesting work, and they later wrote a book together on computational number theory. And we were all colleagues, and friends. And we're still friends.

Rosen: Okay, so now it begins?

Goldwasser: Now it begins. Right, so okay. So Silvio and I decided to work on the following problem, and the problem was how to play mental poker. Because there was one other paper that Manuel mentioned, and that was a paper by Shamir, Rivest, and Adleman where they used their encryption scheme in order to show how to play mental poker.

What is mental poker? People probably know what poker is, although I didn't because my parents didn't play cards and the whole idea of card playing was supposed to be this thing that you did not do, somehow there was something improper about it. Anyway, so this mental poker protocol by Shamir, Rivest, and Adleman, the idea is again, we are two players, we don't have a physical deck, we want to play poker over the phone, over the computer line, and how are we going to do that? How are we going to deal cards in such a way that you're going to get a random hand, I'll get a random hand, and once we get the cards they're not in the deck anymore without knowing what each other's decks are? They had an ingenious idea where there was a way to deal cards in such a way . . . I mean it seemed like you don't know what my cards are, that I did choose random cards, and same for you.

But Lipton noticed that this protocol, there was a problem with it, that there was something about the implementation of this protocol that they proposed where it's true that you couldn't tell what my cards were, but you could possibly tell some information about my cards. For example, let's say that you could identify something was a high card versus a low card. So there was something about the encoding of the cards that did not hide all information about the card. Now for a card game, that's detrimental, right? If you know that I have a high versus a low card, then this changes your strategy completely.

So the problem we set out to solve was how are you going to play mental poker hiding all partial information about the cards? I remember that we're thinking about this problem and what do we need, and Silvio had this idea that we need to have some encryption scheme that . . . Not encryption scheme. We didn't talk about encryption. I think it was Silvio's idea that we needed a decision question, like a yes/no question, where it's hard to tell whether it's a "yes" or a "no" better than 50–50. But this was like an abstraction, right? And a little bit like the Diffie–Hellman.

Because I loved the number theory, I remember sitting in a seminar where some people were talking about something else . . . and in fact I must say that this repeats in my career over and over again. I get ideas while I sit in seminars when people talk about something else, which is probably a good reason to go to seminars. [laughs] And all of a sudden, I had this idea about quadratic residues. I said, "You know what . . . " I think to myself that the way to encode the zero and one, the decision question would be to decide whether the number is a quadratic residue or quadratic nonresidue modulo a composite number n, and this was a hard problem. I mean Manuel told us this was a hard problem, a hard problem in the sense that there were no efficient algorithms to solve it. And the reason why I thought it was a good idea is because it seemed to be a problem which is hard on the average. In fact, not only that you cannot tell whether something is a quadratic residue or nonresidue, but you couldn't really do better than 50–50. And one would have to prove that, right?

But there was something about this problem, which is a notion . . . later on defined formally, which is called random self-reducibility. It was sort of a way of showing that if you had one number, if it was a quadratic residue you can generate lots of [random] quadratic residues, or if it was a quadratic nonresidue you could generate lots of [random] quadratic non-residues. And then that means that if you could sort of distinguish one sample from the other even a little bit, then you will be able to distinguish whether your original number was a quadratic residue or a quadratic nonresidue.

Rosen: How did you feel at that moment, or . . . ?

Goldwasser: That moment of thinking about the quadratic residuosity being the right problem and then telling Silvio? God, excitement. It's just incredible. Because pretty quickly, we could sort of come up with a proof.

And then, just to come back to the mental poker, the idea was that this would be a way to write down a card. Let's say the card is five of diamonds, okay. Then you write this down in binary, the five of diamonds—so that's in zero/ones—and now you want to encrypt the zero, encrypt the one, encrypt a zero, encrypt a one, each time encoding it by a different quadratic or nonquadratic residue. Quadratic residue for zeros let's say, nonresidues for one. You choose them at random. And now you have an encoding of the card, which is what we would call later probabilistic encryption.

Rosen: At the time, did you realize it's public-key encryption, or . . . ?

Goldwasser: We didn't even realize it was encryption. We had a card. We had a way to encode cards so that we could prove that there is no way you can distinguish one card from any other, because you couldn't distinguish zeros from ones better than 50–50.

Then, we went to Dick Karp, I think because Manuel was on leave at MIT for a semester, and we told him about this. He asked us, "What about other partial information, not just with a zero/one?" These questions professors ask you are incredibly significant, because you don't think this way, right? I mean now it's an immediate question, but at the time it was a very fundamental question. And then we went away and proved that if you could tell any partial information regarding (the sequence of bits that encodes) the card—and you had to define what partial information is—then you could actually reconstruct the individual bits of the card.

Which implied that you could tell whether a number was a quadratic residue versus a quadratic nonresidue, which was a hard problem.

Rosen: Can you tell something about the process of figuring out the right definition?

Goldwasser: The way I'm telling it to you, it's really derived from the goal. The goal was to play mental poker in such a way that it hides all partial information. In order to do that, it was clear that you had to encode every bit individually, and furthermore it was clear that you would have to encode them in a probabilistic manner, because otherwise you couldn't hide all partial information. Then there was that question of Karp's, so we arrived to the question "What is partial information?" It should be any function that kind of divides the world of cards into two parts. So any function that partitions the cards into sort of the left and the right, you know?

The process was just . . . it was like being in some kind of a mad state of creativity. And working with Silvio was just a very intense experience, as anybody who's worked with him knows. I mean there's no day and no night. And I think he's still that way. I'm not, but at the time I was. He was very intense, it was very exciting. And of course we didn't do it completely in isolation. There were these questions that Karp asked us, and then I think maybe it was him or maybe we understood already there was a way to encrypt here, that it doesn't have to do with card games. There's a way to encrypt the zero and encrypt the one.

That's something that was not known, because the public-key encryption of Rivest, Shamir, and Adleman or even the Diffie–Hellman concept, it really was intended for encrypting long messages which are unknown. And here zero and one, you know that everybody knows you're either encrypting a zero or a one, but they can't tell which is which. So this was a completely new way to encrypt information. We understood this is much bigger than our original goal, but . . .

And we went to consult people in number theory, you know, in the math department. There was Lehmer and he was the expert. We were supposed to talk to him and ask him, "Is it really the case that you cannot tell apart quadratic residues from nonresidues? Maybe not just perfectly, but better than 50–50?" And I remember this quote. He said . . . We told him the whole story and we asked him what would he do if he needed to distinguish whether a number was a square or a nonsquare mod n. He said that if it was less than n over 2, he would bet it was a square. We asked him why, and he said, "Because there's a lot of small perfect squares." But he said he's not a betting man. Then it turned out that this is okay because this doesn't give much of an advantage.

Rosen: When you came to him, did you feel the stakes are high?

Goldwasser: No. We came to him as two young graduate students and he was very accepting. A little bit maybe I thought he was a little humorous, because it's such a frivolous question, right? Playing cards, using quadratic residues. But I think the whole attitude of mathematicians to computer science has changed radically. Not to say that he wasn't helpful. He was extremely helpful. But in general I think, at the time, mathematics was this hard science and it was serious, right? And the whole computer scientists and the algorithm aspects and using it for cryptography was considered more of—I think—a toy activity. I think this is very, very different now. If I look at the mathematicians at MIT, and I'm sure it's true all over the world, they have respect because we are studying hard questions, we are studying important questions, we've made impact on the world. Cryptography certainly has made a lot of impact. It's making a lot of impact today. And only more so, as you well know as well.

Rosen: And I'm asking again about the stakes because I am curious to know, when did you realize how big your discovery is at the time?

Goldwasser: Right. So we realized that we have actually a scheme for encrypting single bits, something that was an open question that nobody addressed. And when you encrypt a single bit, obviously it's going to have to be a randomized method, because it is a public-key encryption, so everybody can encrypt a zero and a one. If all encryptions of zero were the same, when you see the encryption, you can just yourself try to encrypt zero or try to encrypt one, and if it's the same as what was sent, you know what was sent. So it has to be the case that there's lot of encryptions of zero and lots of encryptions of one, and an adversary shouldn't be able to distinguish whether we're encrypting zeros or ones. You cannot actually have any better than 50–50 plus negligible probability of success in guessing which random bit was encrypted.

Now, in the context of a protocol, if you think about this mental poker example, not only that you're encrypting the cards but there's a lot of other information going around. There's the dealing of the cards where many cards that are being encrypted. You could ask the question whether, having been part of this game, playing the cards, maybe you gain more and more knowledge as you go along so that now you are able to guess something about the unrevealed cards better than what can be inferred from the revealed cards. The definition, which we called semantic security, covers this too.

In order to prove semantic security, we came up with this idea of a proof by reduction, the idea being that you say . . . well, let's suppose that your goal in the world really, you have no interest in mental poker, but what you want to distinguish is quadratic residues, quadratic nonresidues. Okay? And somebody tells you that there is this mental poker game that's built on encoding cards with quadratic residue and quadratic nonresidues, and they know how to cheat in this game. So what you say to yourself, "Okay, I'm going to show a reduction now. I'm going to show that if in fact there is this person"—or this adversary, which we usually call them—"who is able to cheat in the mental poker game, even by slightly better than he should, then there is a way to use this strategy and turn it into an algorithm that can distinguish quadratic residues from nonresidues."

Since you believe that quadratic residues and nonresidues cannot be distinguished in polynomial time, it means that such strategy does not exist. But how do you show such a reduction? In a sense you need to simulate everything, the entire view of the adversary—that is, the encoding of the cards and the dealing and everything that went on and was available to him to enable his cheating strategy. This is what's called proof by simulation, which later has become a big paradigm in cryptography, in how to actually give security proofs. You can prove security if you can sort of recreate the real world in which cryptography is used and its security is supposedly violated. And if you can simulate it although distinguishing quadratic residues from nonresidues is hard, then it means that this violation must have not been that useful, because you could have simulated this violation anyway.

Rosen: In hindsight, you can view Shannon's security as being the information-theoretic sort of analogue of semantic security. Did you see that at the time, or you came up . . . ?

Goldwasser: No, we didn't really know about Shannon's paper, because we were ignoramuses, [chuckles] which helped us actually. Shannon's information theory in fact, if you look at the definition, essentially says that the probability of two messages is the same given the ciphertext. That's one way to think of Shannon's security. An equivalent definition is the *a posteriori* and *a priori* probability of a message is the same, where the *a priori* is without given the ciphertext, and the *a posteriori* is given the ciphertext. In other words, the ciphertext gives no information about the message. Or, if you think about the first definition, given ciphertext for the bit zero or ciphertext for the bit one, there is no information in there that can tell you whether it was a zero or one.

If you think about semantic security, it's the computational analogue of it. That is, in principle, information theoretically you actually do have enough information to tell whether you're seeing an encryption of a zero or a one, because it's a public-key encryption scheme. But computationally within polynomial time, you don't, if distinguishing quadratic residues from nonresidues is a hard problem, or if factoring integers is hard.

Of course, it could be that factoring integers is easy. We know that for quantum algorithms, factoring integers is easy. So if quantum computers can be built, then this whole tower of cards collapses. But this is only for the first probabilistic encryption scheme. Today we have a lot of other problems, not just quadratic residues versus quadratic nonresidues, not just the factoring problem, but also problems on integer lattices, which are problems essentially from geometry. Now, we can apply this idea of a decision question which is hard to solve in the sense that it is infeasible to decide better than 50–50, and encode zero by this decision question where the answer is yes and one by a decision question where the answer is no. And these lattice problems, I mention them because they are quantum-resilient. In other words, we don't know any quantum algorithms that can solve them efficiently. They are what we call post-quantum cryptographic candidates.

Rosen: Okay, so at the time, the idea of basing something on an unproven assumption, it was in the air, or was it kind of a bold move?

Goldwasser: Right. Well, if you think about RSA, they're also basing it on an unproven assumption. They are the first. They are assuming that factoring integers is a hard problem. We took another problem, which was distinguishing squares from nonsquares. But obviously that's an assumption, and you know mathematics prides itself by having proofs, and proofs are proofs and not conjectures. So there's an underlying conjecture here, and that is that there's a problem which we don't know how to solve efficiently. But if you think about it, all of complexity theory is predicated on the conjecture that the class P of polynomial-time problems and the class NP of problems which you can verify the correctness of the solution in polynomial time are different. So to give meat to the entire field, there is an underlying conjecture which is widely believed but not proven, and then one builds on that conjecture.

Rosen: And at the time, what was the atmosphere? Did you experience any resistance to this idea?

Goldwasser: To this probabilistic encryption? We submitted it to a conference and it got in the first time. This was a conference in San Francisco, in 1982. I think it was a STOC conference and I gave the paper, and the name of the paper was "How to Play Poker Hiding All Partial Information and Probabilistic Encryption." It was a long title. And I think that people were genuinely very positive, but speaking with people afterwards, I think they had no idea what I was talking about. [laughs] But certainly in the cryptographic crowd, there was excitement.

Rosen: Was it your first talk in the conference?

Goldwasser: Yes.

Rosen: And how did you feel?

Goldwasser: I felt on the top of the world.

Rosen: How well attended was it, just . . . ?

Goldwasser: Oh. In that time, the conferences were very well attended. There were no parallel sessions and people came to the entire conference, and it was a fairly small community.

Rosen: Can you tell us a bit more about the atmosphere at the conferences back then?

Goldwasser: I think that, you know, very intimate, very informed people. They were already people who were working on different fields—you know, algorithms and complexity theory, here's a cryptography example, and distributed computing. People started talking then about Byzantine Agreement. A lot of these big ideas that are still around as sort of fundamental problems were being discovered at the time.

Rosen: Were you attending all talks?

Goldwasser: Yeah, I was. Everybody was.

Rosen: And was it accessible to everybody, to a wider audience than it is today? How do you compare?

Goldwasser: I think so. But it's natural. When a field is young and not overburdened by definitions and history and background, it's easier to understand. On the other hand, people give much better talks today. People have learned how to simplify their talks—PowerPoint has helped quite a bit—and people have more respect to distilling the essence rather than giving all details.

Rosen: And what happened next? How did things evolve?

Goldwasser: Then, I had been to Berkeley at that point for three and a half years, and I had a very strong urge to get a job and leave. Somehow, I think about it now, I don't know why it was so urgent to leave, but Berkeley seemed to me then like this small place and it's time to go. I applied for a postdoc and I got a postdoc with Ron Rivest at MIT. I was there for half a year actually. Then, they were looking for faculty members and I started interviewing for faculty positions all over the country and also at MIT, and I got an offer for a faculty position and I started on the faculty in '83.

Rosen: After having published what results at that time?

Goldwasser: There was this probabilistic encryption paper. Then there was another paper which we start realizing that it's not just this particular quadratic residues versus nonresidue, but you can take actually any function which is what we call a one-way function. That is a function which is easy to compute but hard to invert. And in particular the RSA function. We asked what bit about it is well-hidden . . . The RSA function is you take an x and you take it to some power modulo a composite number n, like x^3 or x^5 mod n. The question is "What about x is really well-hidden?"—well-hidden in the sense that you can guess better than 50–50. So the paper was on that, looking at the bits of x and showing, proving that they are as hard to guess as it is to invert.

Rosen: And this was still at Berkeley, or . . . ?

Goldwasser: This was still at Berkeley, yeah.

Rosen: With who was the paper, do you remember?

Goldwasser: This was Silvio and Po Tong, who was another graduate student. I think that those were the two papers that I had, yeah.

[Editor: Actually, there were another couple of papers on signatures, both with Silvio Micali and Andy Yao. So, at that time, there were four conference publications altogether, and no journal publications at all.]

Rosen: Okay, so you start as faculty at MIT?

Goldwasser: I started as faculty at MIT and Silvio came a semester later. He was at University of Toronto and he also got a faculty position at MIT. It was like an incredibly intellectually exciting time. Oded Goldreich, who is now at Weizmann, came as a postdoc. There was Benny Chor, who was a graduate student there. Later also Yoram Moses came. I think Michael Ben-Or was there for some period of time. And all these people, they were young, they were brilliant, they were enthusiastic. We would work from day to night and then we would have dinners and talk about work and go to movies. And cryptography was starting to march along.

So I think that the next thing that I did was this paper on pseudorandom functions. There was an early paper by Manuel Blum and Silvio Micali on how to generate pseudorandom numbers in a way that you cannot distinguish these pseudorandom numbers from truly random. And the next question was how do you actually generate not just a polynomial-sized list of numbers but a very, very long list of numbers, an exponentially long list of numbers, in a way that you could sort jump in the middle. Another way to think of it is a function. So . . .

Rosen: And what was the motivation for this specific question, given that you can generate a polynomially long?

Goldwasser: The motivation was that there are a lot of applications where you want to sort of random access. For example—I think this is one of the original motivations we had in the paper—is what we called an "identify friend or foe" system. We were saying, let's say that we are in a group, and we want to identify ourselves to each other, but there are some enemies that come along, and we don't want to use this password system where they ask, "What's the password?" I tell them what the password is, and now they know. Instead, I want them to ask me a random sort of question, which I can answer. And if we are from the same group, they can verify my answer is correct, but anybody else, really as far as they're concerned it's a random answer. So if you had what we call a pseudorandom function, there is a way for all of us who'll know the secret of this function—or what we call the seed of this function—to be able to compute this function f on any x, and then the random challenge would be x and I will tell you what f of x is. But being pseudorandom means that for anybody else, they can't tell it apart from a random function, so when they are asked x, to them f of x is like totally random. That's an application.

Rosen: So on that thread, I'm curious to hear how much of a role did practical motivation play in coming up with these notions?

Goldwasser: With these notions? That's a very good question, because it's not clear what you mean by practical. When you say "practical" today, you mean there's going to be a startup that's going to implement it. No such thing, no startups. Nobody implementing. So the level of practical that made any sense at that time was to say that there is a story, like identify friend-or-foe or people sending encrypted messages or people trying to authenticate themselves. And somehow I think those stories were important for narrative, because I've always liked stories, like the biblical stories. And in general I think people have an easier time to read, especially in a new field where there it isn't a mathematical problem that's been defined for many years and that people are interested in and they don't need any motivation. In a new field, you need to compel people, and stories are helpful.

But for us, it was really more of an intellectual story. The pseudorandom-number generator was just a polynomial sequence of numbers. Then the question about being able to kind of have an exponential sequence where you can sort of jump in the middle and just generate a polynomial number of them or this abstraction of a pseudorandom function is what interested us. And once you had it, you could tell a story, many stories.

Rosen: So you didn't feel any pressure to practically motivate any of your . . . ?

Goldwasser: No, no. None.

Rosen: And what do you think about this versus the alternative? The need to find practical motivation.

Goldwasser: I think that every once in a while I have graduate students, and they come up with a question. For example, I have these two students now, they asked about pseudorandom functions, what happens if somebody knows the secret of how to generate these pseudorandom values? Does it still possess some cryptographic hardness? This is a very technical question. But some of the reactions they got is that "What is the application?" And they came to me and they asked me if they should work on it or stop, what's my opinion, is it interesting? I said, "It's very interesting." It's intellectually interesting. They had a beautiful sort of approach to it. They had a beautiful proof. And at the end, that's the nugget, right? It's sort of something that captivates you, you have to use some ingenuity to solve it, and you have insight. And if it's important, even for applications, it will emerge, but it's not necessarily obvious in the moment that you start. And sometimes if it is very obvious, first of all, lots of people work on it, and you know competition is good but only to a certain extent. If everybody's working on the same problem, there's some kind of . . . I don't know. I don't like to be in a space that's very crowded.

Rosen: How did it feel back then in the early MIT days in terms of competition?

Goldwasser: Right. As I said, we were a big, happy family, but [laughs] a big, happy family of a lot of people who wanted to do well. So we worked collaboratively, we've got a lot of joint papers, also with Benny on this thing called verifiable secret sharing and with Oded on pseudorandom function. But we each started, within a couple of years everybody started going in their own way as well, because you are in an academic system, they compare you, they promote you at different times, they tell you that you should kind of shine individually.

And I personally . . . You asked how I felt. Remember we talked about the crisis of becoming a graduate student. That was again a time which was extremely difficult, because you're trying to do something new, you're trying to do it on your own, you are always comparing yourself to the people around you who are always brilliant, and more brilliant than you are, and you don't know that they're all feeling the same thing. You know this imposter feeling? Apparently they're all feeling it.

Some admit it, some don't admit it. [laughs] But once you realize that this is the name of the game, I think again it's these moments of realization.

Rosen: So did you have such a moment?

Goldwasser: Yes, yes.

Rosen: When was that?

Goldwasser: I think I was talking to somebody . . . and I told them about how I feel and they told me about the imposter syndrome. Now everybody knows it, but then I never . . . I asked what it was and they explained, and it was like, "Ah, okay."

Rosen: That was a person external to the . . . ?

Goldwasser: Yeah. Like a friend, yeah.

Rosen: Okay. What about teaching? Do you have any memories?

Goldwasser: Yeah. Teaching we really started . . . I started and then Silvio also together teaching this class on cryptography. It was the course of Manuel Blum but with a lot more, because at this point the cryptography was a big part of it. There was the definition of bit security and the semantic security of an encryption and the mental poker, and the partial information, pseudorandom functions, pseudorandom number generator. It started being a field. And we haven't talked about zero-knowledge yet.

Rosen: That was before zero-knowledge?

Goldwasser: Around the same time. It was before it got in, but . . .

Rosen: Before we get to zero-knowledge, who were the students in this class that you remember?

Goldwasser: The students, yeah. There was Johan Håstad, there was Joe Kilian, there was Bill Aiello. I think in the early years there was Yishay Mansour, but I think he was a little bit later. Those are the students . . . there's Paul Feldman, who was a student of Silvio's. The others were student of mine. And they're all big names, fantastic researchers in their own right.

Rosen: How did the other MIT faculty treat the young field of cryptography? How did they perceive it?

Goldwasser: MIT is an incredible place. I think that they really have had the foresight of hiring people who were not necessarily in the mainstream of theoretical computing, but sort of doing something with the tools of theoretical computing which is a little bit on the fringes. Rivest was like that. Public-key cryptography after all was exciting, but it was unusual, right? And Silvio and I certainly, and

Charles Leiserson was doing also things which were, you know, with applications. At that time, I think it was data structures and stuff like that. Nancy Lynch was doing distributed computing and Byzantine Agreement and lower-bounds on Byzantine Agreement.

So I felt that they were incredibly proud of all achievements, and especially Ron Rivest, who was a major mentor. Because now that I think of it, he wasn't really much older than we were. Maybe 5, maybe 10 years, no more. And he was extremely supportive of us. We have a paper joined with him, digital signatures. But by and large, we each did our own thing, and I think Ron started working on computational learning fairly quickly, so he kind of left the cryptography field, except for its commercial aspects, for a few years.

Rosen: What other faculty do you remember from the time being supportive?

Goldwasser: Albert Meyer was very supportive. I think he was really a very significant mentor in his own way, sort of in the background. I mean Ron was in my field, so it was sort of more of a daily advice or monthly advice. But Albert was at the head of the theory group and he saw something in me and put me up for the Grace Murray Hopper Award, which made me feel good, made me be recognized.

Rosen: Okay. Is it time for zero-knowledge?

Goldwasser: Yeah, I think so. So zero-knowledge. Alright. So this whole idea of having a protocol where let's say two people are sending messages back and forth and there's a goal for the protocol usually. The goal might be to . . . In the context of going back to that mental poker, say you want to prove that the cards that you encoded were encoded properly, but you don't want to say what the encoding was. So there's a statement here, and that is that all 32 . . . sorry, all 52 cards have been encrypted and no two cards are the same, but you're not going to tell me which card is which. Then there is apparently a way to do it. Apparently. We showed a way to do this, which amounts to actually showing whether something is a quadratic residue or a quadratic nonresidue, so that I can prove to you that something is a quadratic residue or that something is an encryption of zero, or let's say the two things are encrypting different bits, in such a way that you will have learned nothing else.

Rosen: So you had a protocol?

Goldwasser: So we had a protocol. And now we had to have a definition. What does it mean, "prove so that you learn nothing else"? The definition went back to the simulation paradigm and it is called zero-knowledge. Let me explain what it means. So I'm a prover. I know something and I'm proving it to you. I'm proving you some mathematical statement without actually giving you the proof, which seems a bit weird, so at the end you'll be convinced that the statement is correct. But what do I want? I want you not to be able to prove it to a third party. In fact, I want you to learn nothing from it. So how do you define it? The way you define it is that whatever you can compute after you interacted with me, that's no different than what you could have computed before you interact with me. And an equivalent definition to that is that you could essentially simulate the entire interaction between us. And if you could indeed do so, it means that interacting with me was useless to you, assuming the theorem statement is correct.

Rosen: And the name "simulator," when did it come about?

Goldwasser: Who remembers?

Rosen: At what stage? There's a story about multiple rejections?

Goldwasser: Ah, okay. Right. So this paper, we started. We didn't actually call it "simulation," I don't think. I think it had some other definition. They were many names for this paper. It started, it was "Participatory proofs . . . " "Interactive proofs such that they hide all partial information." There were many, many names until we got to the final name, which was "Interactive proofs and zero knowledge" or "The Knowledge Complexity of Interactive Proof." And the paper was rejected three times. God knows. But we were very persistent, you know?

Rosen: How did you feel with each rejection? What's the . . .

Goldwasser: Well, you know there were three of us. I mean in the beginning there were two of us actually on this paper, Silvio and I. And then Charlie Rackoff joined. He improved the paper, but it also got rejected. Because there were three of us, we could sort of build each other up. And how did we feel? We felt like everybody else was an idiot. [laughs]

Rosen: You had this confidence back then that you're onto something?

Goldwasser: But this concept was so interesting and we liked them, and it was clear that this is a great paper.

Rosen: And Charlie Rackoff was at the time where?

Goldwasser: He was in Toronto.

Rosen: In Toronto, so how did the interaction work back then?

Goldwasser: I think Silvio and Charlie interacted when Silvio was in Toronto. They had some paper on coin tossing or something. Then Silvio came to MIT and we continued working on the interactive proofs, but I think there must have been some interaction between them. I wasn't . . . It really wasn't a three-way interaction.

Rosen: But how was communication with people from other institutions working in general?

Goldwasser: Well, there was email, but there certainly wasn't the World Wide Web, or it wasn't immediate. There were phone calls, a lot of phone calls. There were visits.

Rosen: Do you remember any notable visits, visitors and/or visits from the time or from . . . ?

Goldwasser: Adi Shamir used to come to work with Ron. Again, I told you that Oded Goldreich was around. And that's about it.

Rosen: Okay. So zero-knowledge was rejected and you said the manuscript improved over time with the rejection?

Goldwasser: It did improve over time. Sort of in the beginning, I think the simulation was under computational assumption, then it became without an assumption. Finally, it got in. We were mighty happy. And we went to the conference. I'm trying to remember who gave that talk, if it was me or Silvio. I don't remember.

[Editor: Silvio gave the talk.]

But in any case, at the same time, at the same conference there was another paper, which was called "Arthur–Merlin Games." This was a paper by Babai, who introduced this concept where there was a prover and a verifier like we had, except the prover's name was Merlin and the verifier's name was Arthur. And the difference between a verifier and Arthur was that Arthur was just tossing coins, he was very naïve, and Merlin then, based on Arthur's coins, he would kind of teach him things or prove to him things, such that if he was proving a correct statement, Arthur would believe it, which we call completeness, and if he was proving an incorrect statement, it doesn't matter what strategy Merlin would employ, Arthur would not believe it. That was the same as interactive proofs, except our verifier didn't just toss coins. He tossed coins and did computations, and based on these computations would send messages.

Rosen: And his motivation was totally . . .

Goldwasser: His motivation, there was some group-theoretic problems that he wanted to show were in NP, but he couldn't, so he allowed this extension . . . In NP, you also can think of it as a proof system where there is an all-powerful prover and he writes down a string which is a short proof that can be checked in polynomial time. An interactive proof, it can go back and forth, back and forth, so the prover can send the string, the verifier asks the question based on some coin tosses, the prover sends another string, go back and forth, back and forth, and in the end the verifier says, "I'm convinced."

Rosen: So essentially in your paper, there are two main topics . . .

Goldwasser: Yes, there were the interactive proof systems and the zero-knowledge ones, which are an important special case.

But, just to finish the previous thought: As I was saying, what Babai was trying to show, some problem, some group-theoretic problem was in NP, but he couldn't, so what he did is he added this Arthur that was able to toss coins. And for an Arthur that could toss coins, there was a short interaction by which you could show some group membership problem.

Rosen: And when did you realize that it's a similar related concept? At the conference? Was it at the time of the conference?

Goldwasser: I think it was at the conference.

Rosen: And did you already realize back then, view it as a generalization of proof systems?

Goldwasser: Yeah, we did. I don't know if he did, because for him it was really a way to show a complexity bound, the complexity of certain problems. He defined a complexity class and showed that these problems are in this complexity class. For us, it was always a proof system, because we were coming from the cryptographic setting. So there were parties. There were these Alice and Bob, where Alice was the prover, say, and Bob was the verifier.

Rosen: To what extent did you understand the important open problems that emerged from this new concept at the time?

Goldwasser: Yeah, they were abundant. One question was whether this system of Babai and interactive proofs were the same. He had this system of Arthur–Merlin. We had this verifier–prover. Arthur could only toss coins, the verifier could actually toss coins and compute on them, and that seemed to be a very important feature that enabled you to prove things you couldn't do just with coin tossing. So that was a clear question. Then Mike Sipser and I, we proved that those two classes were the same.

Interestingly, it all started again from the quadratic residue question, which was a question that kind of followed my career, because it seemed like to prove that something was a quadratic nonresidue required, without sort of revealing information, required a verifier's power to hide the results of his coin tosses. And I was talking to Mike about this, and then he had this idea that we could look at the set of all quadratic residues and the set of quadratic nonresidues, and talk about what are the union of those sets. Anyway, we talk about size of sets and relate that to the question of whether a number was a quadratic residue or quadratic nonresidue, which is related in turn to the question whether Arthur–Merlin games and interactive proofs are the same class or not.

Rosen: Did you have any applications in mind beyond the original mental poker application?

Goldwasser: Not really. It was again a concept. How do you prove a theorem in such a way that you will believe the statement but you will learn nothing else, with the definition that I gave you, and that you won't be able to prove the theorem to a third party?

But very quickly after, as soon as the paper came out, Adi Shamir pointed out the application for preventing identity theft. Here in this situation, you would think about me. What identifies me is the fact that I know how to prove some theorem and nobody else knows, because it's a difficult theorem to prove. But I have the proof. How do I have the proof? Maybe the proof is something like I know the factorization of some number. How do I know it? Because I took two primes and I multiplied them, so of course I know how to factor it. Now I want to prove to you that I know this factorization or something about this factorization that only I will know. That would identify Shafi: that there's this composite number and she knows how to factor it. He realized that this is an identification method, and he took actually a protocol that we have for proving that something is a quadratic residue and made it more efficient in terms of how many rounds you need to accomplish it, and it . . . This is the work of Fiat and Shamir, and this became an identification scheme.

But the interesting thing about zero-knowledge is that is really the tip of the iceberg. Really, "the tip of the iceberg" is the wrong analogy. In any case, that's just scratching the surface, because it turned out that even though we showed the applications of zero-knowledge in the sense of particular number-theoretic questions you could do in zero-knowledge, like whether something is a square or a nonsquare, it had a much wider applicability.

There's a follow-up paper by Silvio Micali, Oded Goldreich, and Avi Wigderson where they showed how a prover can prove to a verifier that a graph is three-colorable, and that's an NP-complete problem, and what follows from this is that you can actually show any NP statement in zero-knowledge. So I can prove to you any statement that has a short proof in such a way that at the end, you'll believe the statement but you will have no idea of the proof. In order to do that, they used computational assumptions, so this was under the assumption that one-way functions exist.

What this means—okay, going a little bit into the field—is that essentially we can take any protocol, any protocol between let's say multiple people, not just two, where there's a program say that specifies what messages I'm supposed to send to Alon and what messages Alon has sent to a third party and so forth. The thing is that the messages that I'm supposed to send are based, let's say, on my passwords or some private information I have. The messages you have, you're supposed to send are based on what you have received from me and your private information . . . So I do my computation, I send the message. If we're all honest, everything's fine.

But suppose I'm a liar. I'm an adversary. We're in a cryptographic setting. We're all liars in some sense, or we have to protect ourselves in any case. How do you know I'm sending the right message? How do you know I did the computation correctly, based on my private information and all the messages I receive? Well, that's an NP statement, right? So there's a statement to prove, and that is that I am sending the correct message. If I can prove that in zero-knowledge, it means that I can actually transform all protocols that work when people behave properly to protocols that work when people behave improperly, because essentially every message I send is accompanied with the proof that it is the correct message, and it's a zero-knowledge proof so I'm not revealing anything about my secrets.

Rosen: What about other applications?

Goldwasser: Lots of other applications. The next application is something called multi-party computation, which is a little related to what I just said, but it's actually much more relevant to today. So let's talk about the fact that we are now living in this data-driven society and different parties, it might be different hospitals or different national agencies, and they have a lot of data. If you think about hospitals, it could be one hospital has my genomic information and another hospital has my blood type, my blood test over the years. Another hospital might know something about illnesses that I have experienced. And they would like to compute something based on this data, but they don't want to reveal to each other the data. Another example might be that I am the tax authorities and you are the immigration office and somebody else is, I don't know, another governmental agency. And because of regulations, they're not allowed to share their information. Still, they would like to compute some function that's based on all of the data together.

That's what we call multi-party computation. There's multiple parties, each one has data which is confidential, and they want to compute some function that depends on all the data without revealing it to each other. It turns out that it can be done. And it can be done partially . . . there's a little bit of algebra involved, it's beautiful theory, but what does zero-knowledge have to do with it? If everybody's honest, it can be done. It's an interesting method of how. But what if somebody's not honest? Maybe they're not following the protocol. Well, you just tag on zero-knowledge proofs to each one of their messages, and then even if they are potentially dishonest, you will be guaranteed correctness because they will be caught if they deviate from the protocol.

Rosen: Did you foresee the generality of the method at the time?

Goldwasser: No, no. It's way . . . way ahead of its time.

Rosen: And again, what was the reaction back then?

Goldwasser: About multi-party computation?

Rosen: Yeah, to these new revolutionary ideas.

Goldwasser: First, there was a paper by Goldreich, Micali, and Wigderson, who did this multi-party computation based on the existence of Oblivious Transfer. That got in. I think it had strong reaction. I mean good reaction. But then there was a follow-up paper that is by myself, Miki Ben-Or, and Avi Wigderson which happened at a time that I was visiting Hebrew University on sabbatical, and that did not have computational assumptions.

So there was a sort of a partition, within theoretical computer science, maybe less so these days. Some of them are so intrigued by the concepts and they're willing to make assumptions like the existence of one-way functions or that it's hard to factor integers and so forth. Others, such assumptions discount results for them, so when you can prove an information-theoretic result without assumptions, they're happier. So I think that the fact that there were information-theoretic analogues was very helpful for this whole theory to be adopted.

Rosen: Okay. Before we move on, I'd like to ask more about applications.

Goldwasser: Actually, I want to say something more about zero-knowledge.

First, it was intellectual curiosity. Then Fiat and Shamir realized this is important for preventing identity theft. Next step was that this enabled a conversion of protocols from honest parties to potentially misbehaving parties. But then all of a sudden in recent years, it had some very unusual usages.

One of them was by some researchers in Princeton together with Boaz Barak where they talked about the use of zero-knowledge for nuclear disarmament. Now it sounds like, you know, out of nowhere. The idea there is that you want to be able . . . let's say the Russians and the Americans want to make sure that they are disarming nuclear warheads, but they don't want to show each other the technology. How do you prove that a nuclear warhead is in fact a nuclear warhead without looking inside? It sounds like you want to prove a statement but give zero-knowledge. And it's not just by association. There's actually a concrete method that they use which uses a lot of underlying principles from the mathematics of zero-knowledge.

Another example, which Moni Naor from Weizmann came up with, is suppose you are a suspect in a crime and you want to prove that you did not commit it, so they are asking you to give some DNA so that they can compare it to the forensic. The point is you don't want to give it because maybe you are planning on doing a crime in the future or your children are. So how do you prove that you were not in the crime scene, or your DNA does not match without actually giving the DNA? Again, zero-knowledge is the answer.

So there's all these applications all over the place. The last application is the blockchains. Today, as you know, there's this whole idea of Bitcoin, blockchains, how do we put transactions out on a blockchain so that they are serialized in time? And some of the questions are, okay, so you want to put transactions, or transactions meaning things you've done, you want to have records that everybody can see. But sometimes you don't want everybody to know the details of the records. You might want to prove that two records are the same, or other properties of the records, and you want to do that in zero-knowledge. So it has actually become very well known to people in the trade these days and there are even companies that specialize in zero-knowledge.

Rosen: And also digital signatures?

Goldwasser: Yes, also digital signatures. Yes. So what are you asking about that?

Rosen: Fiat–Shamir, the standards digital signatures over the Web is based on ideas going back to zero-knowledge, the ones that started in the late '80s.

Goldwasser: So digital signatures were invented, as I said, in Diffie–Hellman's paper. Then RSA had implementation, but there was really no definition of security. So obviously . . . it shouldn't be forgeable. But what would that mean exactly? Let's say someone's a notary public, so they're able to sign. You want to make sure that even though I can go to the notary public and give him documents at will for them to sign, that I am not able to learn how they sign and be able to sign any other document in the future. This is what we call digital signature secure against chosen message attack. In other words, I can choose the documents that I feed the notary public to sign and yet, even though I see polynomial number of signatures, I'm not able to produce yet one more document for which I sign it without the help of the notary public.

Rosen: And you came up with the first definition of what this means.

Goldwasser: Definition and construction, we had a way to do it.

[Editor: At the time, this notion of "existential forgery" was considered paradoxical and it was not clear if it could be achieved. Indeed, as in the case of encryption and zero-knowledge, the utmost robust notion of security was coupled by a proof of feasibility under better understood assumptions. That is, robust definitions were coupled with constructions that achieve them under widely believed assumptions such as the infeasibility of factoring.]

Rosen: And then eventually it became crucial to the development of electronic commerce over the Internet.

Goldwasser: Absolutely.

Rosen: Okay, so moving onto information-theoretic and unconditional results. Maybe first we talk about geographically, where are you located now, your area?

Goldwasser: Yeah, so this is 1986 and I . . . Actually, we should talk about primality then before.

Rosen: Right. So let's talk first about primality?

Goldwasser: Yeah. Okay, so as I told you, interactive proofs, or maybe I didn't mention it, but we were talking about the fact there's a prover and there's a verifier. The verifier is tossing coins. They go back and forth. The big distinction of interactive proofs from classical proofs is that there is a probability of error. I proved to you something and with very, very high probability you know it's correct. Or another way to say that, there's a very small probability that I managed to cheat and prove an incorrect statement. That's what enables zero-knowledge.

So, as I told you, I was always interested in number theory, and there was this problem around, which was how do you test numbers for being prime? And a beautiful old result by Solovay and Strassen and Rabin are algorithms for testing numbers whether they're primes or not, fast algorithms that have a probability of error. So at the end, you run this algorithm, you know with very good probability that your number is prime. In fact, what it is, is that if it's composite, you're likely to detect that it's composite, and if you don't detect that it's composite, you say, "It's probably prime." So an interesting question was can you have a primality test that doesn't have any probability of error? Can we test that a number is prime or composite and be 100% correct? And can you do that without actually factoring the number? That was work that I really enjoyed tremendously and did with my graduate student Joe Kilian at the time.

Rosen: And do you want to tell us more a bit about it . . . the story?

Goldwasser: Yeah. I was in a conference again. As I told you, sitting in lectures really works well for me. I was in a conference, and René Schoof gave a talk about some algorithm he had for taking square roots mod p for small numbers. It had something to do with elliptic curves over finite fields, which was something I knew nothing about, but he described what an elliptic curve was and he had some algorithm for counting how many points are on a curve. And this whole elliptic curve was defined with respect to a prime. So there was some equation, you know, like y^2 is equal to x^3 plus ax plus b mod p, and you could count the number of solutions (y, x) in this defined group, and he was doing some operations on the group.

In any case, he had an algorithm. And when I was sitting in this lecture, I started thinking to myself, "What if you'd run this algorithm mod p, except you didn't know whether p was a prime or composite? How would the algorithm perform? Would it work? Would it not work?" And I asked him that question. I think it sounded like a really weird question and he was like, "Well, it probably would be garbage if you ran it mod p where p was composite."

So then I went back to Cambridge and I think I invited Schoof to come and give the talk at MIT. And he came and gave the talk again, so I understood a bit more. Then I start talking to Joe about the question of what if this prime was a composite, and we start talking about how to use these elliptic curves working mod a modulus which we're trying to tell whether it's a prime or composite, and then the rest is history. We had a primality test based on elliptic curves that was randomized but there was no error probability.

Rosen: That was in '86?

Goldwasser: That was in '86, yeah.

Rosen: Okay. And then what?

Goldwasser: Then what? So then just, you know, it was '86 or '87 and I haven't been in Israel for many years. I used to come visit, but I was really pining away in some sense to being in Israel for some extended period of time. And I had a sabbatical and I decided to spend it in Israel. And I came to the Hebrew University and there, there was Avi Wigderson and Nati Linial and Michael Ben-Or. I didn't know what I was going to work on. I was teaching a course about primality and elliptic curves, and they were very excited because elliptic curves were creatures that they didn't use in computer science. They haven't been used that much either since, but in any case, I was teaching this class.

Then I remember that I was in Avi's office and he asked me this question. He says, "What else is there to do in cryptography? Because we've already done encryption and we had like good definitions and signatures and identification schemes and zero-knowledge, and what else is there?" So this is a question for some reason people ask many times, many years later. At that time sort of under the pressure of the moment, which was always very good for me to be asked questions under the pressure of the moment, [laughs] I answered like, "Well, you know, we make assumptions, and maybe we could make some sort of physical assumptions rather than computational assumptions like that factoring is hard, and we could prove results absolutely."

Somehow that conversation led to two different papers. One of them was, when I told you about interactive proofs, I told you that there was that result that said that you can actually prove any statement in zero-knowledge using an interactive proof if one-way functions exist. If you like, if factoring is hard. And that's a conditional result, right? So one question is, can you do it without any assumptions? Well, what we came up with at the time, and this was with Joe Kilian also, was this model where there wasn't a single prover and a single verifier, but there were two provers. Now that sounds weird. Like, why two? You know, anyway this prover is supposedly very powerful. Why does he need another powerful friend?

So there was this idea that these two provers, they are like committing a crime. What's the crime? The crime is that they are trying to convince you of an incorrect theorem. And just like the police, the police is like the verifier, it's interrogating these provers. In order to check that their alibi holds up, they put them in separate rooms. They ask some questions from one, you know, potential criminal, and then they go and they ask the other, and they compare the answers. Now, this defines a model. What's the model? We have two provers. We have one verifier. The verifier can ask questions from each one depending on the question he asked the other, and the restriction on the two of them is they can't speak to each other.

That's a new definition of a proof system. We still want there should be proofs for correct statements, and there shouldn't be proofs for incorrect statements no matter what these two guys. But now we have an assumption, except it's not that factoring is hard but that these two guys are isolated from each other. And of course I had some idea that it's not so bizarre, because we can think of an ID card, because I was thinking about Adi's motivation—that instead of having one ID card, you would have two of them and you put them into a bank machine. There were already bank machines at that point. Which might not sound interesting to you, but ATMs are also an invention that occurred during that time. [laughs]

Rosen: I'm not that young.

Goldwasser: You're not that young. [laughs] Okay. Neither one of us. In any case, so there are two cards, and you think about there's two cards, there's two provers, they're proving that they are Shafi. And the ATM is the verifier and it could make noise so they can't talk to each other, they can't see what questions are being asked. We had a patent on this.

Rosen: Okay, so I think maybe now maybe we can actually go down the line with this line of research and then I'll go back to the other area later.

Goldwasser: Right, right. In any case, we had this model, the two provers. Why did we invent this model? Because it turned out that you could prove that every theorem that has a short proof, can be proved in this model in zero-knowledge. That is, there is a two-prover interactive proof, where these two provers are in separate rooms, and they're going to convince the verifier of the correctness of the statement without giving him the proof in zero-knowledge, no assumptions. Okay, so there was a system. We did it for zero-knowledge in order to remove the assumptions like factoring is hard.

Then there was a paper by I think Fortnow, Rompel, and Sipser where they asked how many rounds you needed for this two-prover system. Then a whole bunch of results started to follow.

And then there was this incredible, incredible result by Noam Nisan, who was a postdoc at the time at MIT. What he showed was you can, with a two-prover system, prove the value of a permanent to a verifier. Now I don't want to get into the technical definition, but this is a very, very hard problem. It is extremely . . . It's beyond NP. And all of a sudden it seemed like. . . . And additionally it's a complete problem for counting sharp-P class and it seems like the two provers were extremely powerful. And what followed after that is that using the techniques that Noam used, within sort of a whirlwind of results it has been shown that this class of interactive proofs with a single prover was as powerful as polynomial space. And then again, within months or weeks, it was shown that this class of two-prover interactive proofs was as powerful as non-deterministic exponential time. All of a sudden, these weird creatures that we've introduced with provers and verifiers and interactions and people locked in different rooms were sort of grounded in the traditional complexity theory with classes like polynomial space and nondeterministic exponential time and equivalences were shown.

Rosen: And how did you feel at that time?

Goldwasser: I thought it was . . . first of all, the mathematics was fantastic. It was really new matter . . . It was arithmetization, expressing decision problems using polynomials. So the math was fascinating and I thought that . . .

Rosen: You were pleased?

Goldwasser: I was pleased. Yes, I was very pleased.

Rosen: Okay. Let's continue on that line and then we'll rewind back.

Goldwasser: Yeah, then I had a couple of years later, I think it was like 1990, I was in Princeton for a sabbatical and I think Joe Kilian gave a talk there about something about . . . I can't remember anymore. Some two-prover proof system in nondeterministic exponential time. And there was something about his talk that made me think that you could sort of simulate nondeterministic . . . you could do all nondeterministic exponential time in exponential time. Which like you would show collapse of these deterministic and nondeterministic classes. And I told Muli Safra about that, who was actually my postdoc at the time I think, and he was also in Princeton.

We started talking about it and then it turned out that that would be true if—now it seems like a rabbit out of a hat—if some graph-theoretic problem was easy to approximate. The graph-theoretic problem is called the clique problem. It's like you have a graph and you would like to find a subset of the graph where all vertices have edges between them. It turned out that if you could approximate the size of the largest clique in a graph, then you could have showed that nondeterministic exponential time was equal to exponential time. Turning this on its head, it says that it's hard to approximate the size of the largest clique in a graph if nondeterministic exponential time is not equal to exponential time. Then when you sort of downsize this, you get essentially a result that says that it's hard to approximate clique if P is different than NP. So there's an NP-hardness result hiding in there.

Rosen: So you sort of started with complexity, went to cryptography, and came back?

Goldwasser: And came back, yeah. And this whole idea of using multi-prover inter-active proofs, something that then morphed to something called probabilistically checkable proofs, PCPs, started with that work, and how to use that in order to prove hardness of approximation started with that work. That's become a complete field, which I'm very proud of.

Rosen: Rightfully so. So, okay. So now you want to continue a bit on this thread or go back to the other paper with the . . . ?

Goldwasser: Let me just say a few more things about this. We've talked about interactive proofs, right? Single prover and verifier. We've talked about this multi-prover interactive proof. What is this probabilistically checkable proof? So far, everything was just very general, right? There are these two provers, there's a verifier, they exchange messages, at the end the verifier accepts the proof, doesn't accept the proof, there's some probability of error. But now we start quantifying things a bit. So you can talk about how much randomness is the verifier using? How many coins does it have to toss? You can talk about the length of the messages that are being sent. You can talk about how many questions are being asked and you can talk about the probability of error. And once you start quantifying this, I mean these are parameters, and if you change these parameters, they can be sort of very tightly coupled to the problems that you can either approximate or nonapproximate.

But let me say it in a different way. There's this third creature, which I mentioned, probabilistically checkable proof. What is that? There the idea is much easier to understand. In a sense, it doesn't require the stories of provers and verifiers and so forth, even though I love stories and I would never have got into any of this without stories. So probabilistically checkable proof, the idea is the following. Usually people think of proofs, mathematicians think a proof is a string that you can read in a book, right? It starts from statement one, statements follow, and then QED. Probabilistically checkable proof is a way to write a proof in such a way that you can actually . . . you don't have to read the entire proof. You can probe it at some locations, not in all of them, and you should think of it as if I'm choosing these locations at random, and make some check on those locations you've probed, some local checks, and if there is a mistake in the original proof, there's a very good chance you'll find a mistake in the local check.

So it's these proofs which are probabilistically checkable because you're sort of choosing the locations at random, and furthermore you have to read a lot less than reading the entire proof. Of course, you don't get certainty. You get probability of error. And now the kind of parameters that I talked about a minute ago come into play. How many places in the proof do you have to look at? What is the probability of error? What are the sizes of the questions and answers? And these are parameters that, in the original paper that I had with Muli, and then with Lovasz and Feige who joined . . . , we joined forces, these parameters were improved, and subsequently more by work by Arora and Safra and then by the well-known paper by Arora, Lund, Motwani, Sudan, and Szegedy to be sort of optimal, where you really need just log n randomness and look at constant number of bits of the proof and you will catch a mistake if it exists.

Rosen: Now let's rewind back to the late '80s to the second result you were alluding to.

Goldwasser: Right. That's a result with Ben-Or and Avi, and that's about how to do multi-party computation, the same problem I told you about with the different hospitals that want to compute some function of their data without sharing it. What we showed was how to turn this problem into an algebraic problem where the data that you have is represented as essentially shares of a polynomial. This is called secret sharing that was invented by Adi Shamir. It is a way to take a piece of data and share it among n people so that only looking at some of the shares you have no idea what the data is, but if you have sufficient number of shares you can reconstruct it.

But Adi's secret sharing was just a way to share data. What we were asking is how do you compute on data? So now we have these three hospitals. Let's say each one of them has shared their data, secret-shared among all three. But that's not enough. They want to do a computation on it, like they want to do maybe some linear regression or they want to find out how many patients are there whose DNA is of a specific type and it had infections in the past and their blood test is in a certain range. So they want to do maybe set intersection or something like that. You can write any such function as essentially a sequence of operations on the data, which essentially looks like summing and multiplying.

What we realized is how you can take these shares of secrets, which were essentially values of polynomials, and compute with them. How can we add them and multiply them where each of us only has their shares? I have the shares of your data, I have shares of everybody else's data, and using these shares I can essentially compute a share of the sum of the data, a share of the product of the data. I can keep doing this iteratively, so essentially any program that we want to run on this data can be run in such a way that at the end I will only have a share of the result and I will have learned nothing about the data except for that share of the result. And since all of us have shares of the result, now we can reconstruct the result. That means that I knew my input, I'm going to know the result, and I can tell whatever is implied by knowing my input and the result, but nothing else. And this is . . . It's important. [laughs] Yeah.

Rosen: Why is it important?

Goldwasser: Again, for lots and lots of applications these days. If you want to connect it, if we kind of zoom to 2017, you know all the rave now is machine learning, right? Everybody's talking about these neural nets and logistic regression and how it is going to change our lives, for medical, for actual medicine, precision medicine, for targeting consumers, for making decisions on who to set on bail and so forth.

But there is a question, and that is a lot of this is driven by the fact that we have tons and tons of data about people, and this data sometimes should not be shared. And it's held let's say by either individuals or by entities that even are bound by regulation not to share it. So how are you going to get them to use their data for running a machine learning algorithm without sharing it; that is, in a way that respects the privacy of individuals?

The technique of multi-party computation is essential for that, because you may think of coming up with a machine learning algorithm, let's say in the training phase, taking the data, training on it and figuring out a model that can do predictions as a protocol that has access to data toward the end of coming up with a prediction algorithm, but not for seeing the data explicitly. And multi-party computation because of its generality can be used.

Now there's a difference here between theory and practice. On paper all is good. That is, we wrote papers and we proved theorems. But in order to use it in practice in a way that's efficient enough, you need to do a lot of optimization, you need to improve, you need to implement. Only time will tell if these methods will be used as they are or they will be modified, and hopefully not modified to such an extent that they will be insecure.

Rosen: Well, they are already being deployed in a commercial context.

Goldwasser: Yes.

Rosen: Okay. Now I'd like to ask you about some retrospective about advising students throughout the years. You'd had many great students, well known, very successful, and in several ways, in several generations.

Goldwasser: Alright. First of all, I have had incredible students, and these students, I am thankful for that every day. Early in my career I worked with my colleagues. You know, I worked with Silvio and Oded and Avi and others, so I did not write papers with my students. But now I do. In any case, then the students were really more doing their own thing and I was advising them in the sense that they would tell me about their stuff, and sometimes questions came from me, sometimes questions came from them. Now it's more that I'm in an advisory role, that most of the questions come from me, but the students do a lot of the work. I think that my advising style must have changed because it became much more working together with the students than it was before.

I'm always in awe at the fact that there's a new student and there's a new talent and that they really make something out of nothing. Not in the sense that they are nothing. In the sense that they come up with new ideas and new questions, and where does it come from? That's the incredible thing of working in university. There's this young generation one after the other, and they are so excited about what they do and they are remarkable. So that's really a gift of being able to be in university.

Rosen: Okay. Can you mention different styles of students, of researchers that you encountered? Different characters?

Goldwasser: Different characters. I've met lots of characters. [laughs] I remember Joe Kilian was really into limericks and a great sense of humor and a very creative, unusual researcher. Then there are people who are very like technically extremely sharp, right? Like Johan, but so was Joe too. I'm mentioning them in the beginning, because at my advanced age [laughs] it's easy to remember the past rather than the present. No, but I've had amazing students really all along. Some of my students are faculty members at Weizmann where we're sitting right now, like Zvika Brakerski and Guy Rothblum, who've both done amazing things. Then some of my students are faculty members at MIT, like Vinod Vaikuntanathan. Then there's Yael Kalai. And I have former students all over Israel, like Yishay Mansour and Adi Akavia, and many others all over the world.

Rosen: So now let's talk about the property testing and delegation?

Goldwasser: Sure. Okay, so property testing.

Rosen: How did it all start?

Goldwasser: How did it all start? I actually think that my first thoughts in the direction of property testing come again to a talk that I attended in Hebrew University, of Michael Kearns' actually, where he talked about learning. He had some model of statistical query learning. In any case, and then I drove back with him to Tel Aviv and we had some conversation in the car that made me start thinking about the question of not learning where you have examples and you're trying to predict a label of a future example, but more about being able to tell a property of whether the examples you are seeing belong to one distribution or another distribution.

Or another way to say about it . . . What do I mean by examples? Let's say that you have a function and you can't look at the function table. You actually don't have a description of the function, but you can query the function in different places. And what you would like to find out is a property of this function. So what could be an example of a function? An example could be . . . let's say there's a graph and I actually can't look at the whole graph because the graph might be extremely large, but what I could apply a function to two vertices and the function will say one if there's an edge between them and zero otherwise.

So that's a description of the graph. It's a function. So there's sort of an indirect description. Now I'd like to ask questions about this graph. Does this graph have a large clique? Is this graph connected? Can this graph be partitioned into two sets of vertices that there's only edges going between the sets and not between vertices within the two sets? It's called a bipartite graph. So that's a property. And obviously some of these questions you have to look at the entire graph. You have to sort of ask the function, the entire function table for every pair of vertices, what the edge is and then solve the problem.

Then property testing paradigm says, "You know what, let's relax the question, because we really cannot write down the whole graph, we cannot query the function in all places. We'd like to tell whether the graph that's being described by this function which I can sort of query is close to a graph that has that property." So if we think . . . Let's look at a specific graph property that's say bipartite. This graph that the function is describing, is it bipartite or is it far from being bipartite? But what do I mean by far from being bipartite? It means that if you look at the closest graph to it by removing edges or adding edges, let's say it's epsilon apart, you have to add epsilon or subtract epsilon fraction of the edges. So there's a fraction of edges that you have to insert or delete, and I'd like to tell which is the case. Is it a bipartite graph or is it far from any bipartite graph? And I'd like to do that by querying the function in very few places.

So for the layman, let's think of it this way. We are not living in the age of dinosaurs anymore, right? We find bones of dinosaurs. Can we just by looking at bones of dinosaurs tell whether the entire dinosaurs was a tyrannosaurus? Was it a meat-eater or herbivore? Apparently people make conjectures based on very little data. So the question here is if I can only look at very little places in the graph, either given or I can query the graph at places of my choice, can I tell something about the graph more globally, like being bipartite or being far from bipartite?

This is the way I like to describe property testing, and that's a field that was kind of started in a paper together with Oded Goldreich and Dana Ron. We wrote on testing properties of graphs and more generally testing properties of natural structures. You know, graphs as a natural structure or other functions are possible too, not just to describe graphs. And we would like to find out whether a function let's say is monotone and we can't write down the whole function table. We can just query the function in a few places. Can you tell if it's monotone or far from monotone? This is a direction that's become a whole field. I mean that paper, I think, was fairly influential.

And then you asked me about delegation?

Rosen: And lattices, if you want to mention some more about lattices.

Goldwasser: So time moves on and people start talking about different models of computation like cloud computing. And the idea of cloud computing is that there are these computers out there and I'm a client, and I'd like to use the computers and they will do all the computation for me and then give me the results. So the clear question is how do I know they are even computing it correctly? I am delegating my computation to an outside computer. I want to get some proof that the result has been correctly computed. We call this a delegation problem, and that's a problem that is a little bit similar to interactive proofs because this computer proves a statement to me. The statement is that it did the computation correctly. That's been a problem that I've been very interested in.

And the delegation paradigm isn't just delegating computation, but you can think about it in other contexts, like you want to delegate in the context of error-correcting codes. Let's say I want to code a message in such a way that even if there's noise on the line, you can detect it. Then there's the question of how much work you have to invest in order to encode and how much work do you have to invest to decode, and you can talk about delegating work of the encoder to the decoder or vice versa. So this whole delegation paradigm is something that I've been interested in in the last, I don't know, 15 years already. And that's been fascinating. This is work with my students Yael Kalai and Guy Rothblum. So that's something that I'm still interested in. I think that this delegation paradigm is very powerful in today's sort of modern computational world.

And you asked about lattices. As I mentioned, the theory of lattices has become a source of hard computational problems. Like if you define some sort of integer lattice via basis, find the short vector in the lattice . . . This theory and these hard problems have become the basis of what we call post-quantum cryptography. And implementing sort of essentially cryptographic primitive based on these type of problems is a fascinating field which I've been involved in.

Rosen: And you were very early on.

Goldwasser: Yeah. This was work with Oded Goldreich, where we sort of asked this question of interactive proofs to show that a shortest vector in a lattice is not so short and we introduced some new methods in this field.

Rosen: You actually, yeah, introduced a method to show that it's unlikely to be as hard to approximate as other approximations.

Goldwasser: Yeah. But in any case, the method is more important than actually the result, because the method is essentially what underlies a lot of proofs of security in modern cryptographic systems that are the basis of this post-quantum cryptography.

And I want to mention actually one more student, Daniele Micciancio, who was one of my students, which I love very much. He started working on logic actually with Albert Meyer, this was his master thesis, then he came and worked with me about digital signatures. And for his exam . . . There are these exams at MIT which don't exist anymore where you're supposed to give a student a few papers and then they are supposed to read it and do some original contribution within three weeks. So I gave him some papers on lattices and he came up with some beautiful new result proving the hardness of approximation of shortest vector in a lattice, and that became his field of research. I feel privileged to have suggested the problem to him, or the papers to him. I think he's one of the sort of guiding lights in the field of lattice-based cryptography.

Rosen: Okay. You want to mention something more about students?

Goldwasser: I think that I have a new crop of students which are wonderful, and they're doing . . . Today it's actually interesting. A lot of the students are not only interested in sort of the science, but they're actually interested also in impact on society. So this is sort of a modern wave. I mean as you see people, you know there is this generation that's just interested in going to startups and the generation that's just interested in doing complexity theory and then doing cryptography. And the new generation that I have at least, they're very interested in the impact of the methods on today's world. And when I say impact, I don't mean just implementing systems that are run efficiently, but really questions of like how is this going to change the world from a society point of view?

Rosen: So for them, the application might be more of a guideline?

Goldwasser: The application might be more of a guideline but it's not an application that is necessarily only having to do with utility. It actually also has to do with doing good. I mean privacy anyway is doing good, in my book, but it's beyond that.

Rosen: And what's your take on privacy, whether it's doing good, whether it helps?

Goldwasser: Of course it's doing good. I mean, you know the line that I think they attribute to Judge Brandeis, but I think it was Brandeis and another lawyer that they were in a law firm together. This is after the original cameras were invented, the kind of cameras, portable cameras that you could take out of the camera shop. And they wrote this paper about "What about the right to be left alone?" You know, it's very nice that you can take photographs, but now I could have my pbotograph taken without my permission. Now imagine where we are at. Right? Everything we do on our iPhone, every Google query we make, every email we send is being recorded by these giant companies and they are deriving conclusions from it, like giving us advertising for us. So the right to be left alone is something nobody imagines anymore, you know with all these sensors and the cameras. It really alters our reality and I think we need to think about it.

Rosen: And you don't think it's too late by now to do anything about it?

Goldwasser: You know, it's just like talking about the environment, right? So with the environment, we have a lot of pollution, but somehow it's self-regulating. Not as well as it should be, but there are climate agreements and people don't sell the kind of cars they used to. There's emission controls. So my feeling is that every revolution has at some point people realize that there are some things to fix. And I don't see why the lack of privacy is not going to be the same, because the methods exist. And we can develop more methods. But people have to be aware, people have to kind of pull back, people have to implement these methods on top of the existing ability to spy or to have sensors and . . .

Rosen: And what about the negative implications of the ability to encrypt data and hide it from others?

Goldwasser: I guess the negative implications is that we could go dark, right? This idea that now that the encryption methods are being developed and they're so strong and they're so well known, that we won't be able to pursue criminals, right? So being able to read messages, being able to wiretap, being able to listen to digital communication is a police tool. It is a national security tool. We all know there's more and more threats. So by enabling this encryption for the public, you are in a sense making it more difficult for law enforcement to behave. I buy it, but it's a very thin line, right?

On one hand, privacy has so many good outcomes. It's enabled electronic commerce. It's enabled a use of remote computers for delegating computation. It's going to enable doing machine learning on data while keeping it private. On the other hand, there are these criminals who should be caught and we should enable law enforcement to catch them.

How do you reconcile the two? One opinion is that you just say, "Well, tough. Let the law enforcement figure out other methods to catch criminals and don't give up on privacy." And another point of view, which is the other extreme, is let the law enforcement have all the keys to all the encryption algorithms out there. And maybe there's a third sort of economic model where you sort of think of cost–benefit analysis and you're able to trade it off, so you can sort of trade off privacy in policing. I don't think people have looked at it, but just again, if we go back to the example of environmental science, there is sort of a cost–benefit analysis of putting regulations, and there are resources that are renewable, resources that are not renewable, and there's measures. So this is not really my expertise, but I can imagine a world where that kind of theory is developed also with respect to privacy.

Rosen: What about the future?

Goldwasser: That's the thing about the future, you don't know do you? As we say in Israel, "all will be well." [laughs] No, you're asking about the scientific future.

Rosen: Not necessarily.

Goldwasser: Not necessarily. The future is that I'd love to continue doing research. I love interacting with young people, with postdocs, with graduate students. I'm still inventing new questions. We haven't talked about them, but that might be in another interview. And I still get excited from new questions and new answers.

I'm looking at what has happened to cryptography. It's kind of amazing in terms of the number of people and the impact and the excitement, so this is sort of a future which is inevitable. There's no question that cryptography has a future. And personally I hope to do more. I hope the field will do more. I'm very optimistic.

Rosen: Where do you see yourself five years from now?

Goldwasser: You know what, I think that's the one question I can't answer. [laughs] I don't know.

Rosen: In terms of aspirations, just . . . ?

Goldwasser: I want to keep on working. I want to keep on creating. I want to have ideas. I want to have impact, and the kind of impact that I'm talking about now is also impact as let's say the director of the Simons Institute or someone who directs . . . someone who has some influence about where the field is going in the sense of what's important and what's not important. I think that I've had a good hunch and I feel I have an intuition to serve me and also a lot of experience. So if I have made impact in the next five years both in terms of research and in terms of leadership, if my kids do well and they're happy, then I will be very happy in five years.

Rosen: Okay. Thank you very much, Shafi.

Goldwasser: Okay. Thank you.

An Interview with Silvio Micali

This is a full transcript of an interview of Silvio Micali by Stephen Ibarkaki. The interview took place on October 15, 2013. The transcript was lightly edited for clarity.

Ibaraki: Welcome today to our interview series with outstanding professionals. I'm Stephen Ibaraki, and I'm conducting an exclusive interview with Professor Silvio Micali, ACM Turing Award recipient in 2012. The Turing Award is widely considered the Nobel Prize of computing. Professor Silvio Micali is also a world-renowned, distinguished researcher, and a professor at MIT.

Now, Silvio, you have a lifetime of outstanding research contribution with lasting significant global impact. Thank you for coming in today and sharing your considerable expertise, deep accumulated insights, and wisdom with our audience.

Micali: Thank you, Stephen. It is a pleasure talking to you and your audience.

Ibaraki: Now, Silvio, you have this extraordinary honor now. When did you hear about this, and how did you feel at the time? What was the reaction of your colleagues and your family?

Micali: Well, I heard about it on a Friday afternoon. We were planning to leave for a family ski trip with my colleague Shafi, my co-recipient of the Turing Award. And then the telephone rang . . . So it was quite a coincidence, you might say.

How did I feel about winning the Turing award? What can I say? I felt good. I felt good in particular to have won it with Shafi. You must know that we were graduate students together. We worked for many years and overcame many difficulties, even multiple rejections of our work, before we got an award. And so I was very happy to get the award together with her. Shafi and I had good interaction. You know, we were trying to develop a theory of interaction, it takes two to interact, and when you interacted with Shafi you were actually interacting with at least seven people, (laughter) depending on which of her multiple personalities were in charge on that day. So that was how I personally felt.

About the feelings of my colleagues, I actually was very happy to see that there was a very large, positive reaction. You must know that we are a very interactive community. We collaborate a lot across institutions, so, what can I say? I put a premium on their opinion and I'm glad to see that it was positive. Some of my colleagues were actually so kind, almost happier than we were. Of course, some of them did not react at all. So, some may have disagreed on the importance of our results, or taken them for granted. Whatever the case, it's important to have dissenting opinions, right?

In sum, I felt that the overall response was very positive. And my family was ecstatic.

Ibaraki: Well, I can see how your family would be very pleased, because you're a legend, you're an icon in the industry, and, of course, you're part of the historical record forever. [laughter]

Micali: Well, maybe not forever. But it's good enough for us, right?

Ibaraki: Now, Silvio, how will the ACM Turing Award impact your work, your influence, and your thinking?

Micali: Oh well, to tell you the truth, on the one side we should strive for absolute truth and novelty. But on the other side, you know, we should strive, or at least I do strive, also for universal recognition. Somehow, the coexistence of these two goals is good, in my opinion. If the pursuit of absolute truth required disregarding social judgment, then we would have a lot of trouble on our hands. OK, greater recognition and strife for truth can be antagonistic. In the short term, somehow, if you choose universal recognition, then you have to work on problems everybody perceives to be important. In other words, that choice requires pursuing a more established and conservative line of research. So: What do I hope from the Turing Award? That, taking care of some of my desire for recognition, it leaves me free to go on a limb and take some more scientific risk, to go and explore new wildernesses, so to speak. This is the impact that, I hope, the Turing Award will have on my work.

As for my influence, let's see . . . First of all, you know, I have nothing against recognition or having some influence. After all, we work very hard to increase our reputation. This said, my peers [laughter] will continue to judge my work according to strict standards, as they should. However, I do see that the Turing Award can actually give me some additional influence on researchers outside my field. So, I hope I can use this additional influence wisely when interacting with scientists from other disciplines.

Finally, if I may add another thing, awards tend to make us feel good. And if we feel good, we can do more things, have more energy. So I hope to put this extra energy to work in my thinking, my teaching, and everything else.

Ibaraki: Now, again, you have this amazing body of work, and you've got this significant achievement in the ACM Turing Award. From that, then, what are your life goals that you want to achieve, and how will you achieve them?

Micali: Oh, wow, life goals? . . . This is a hefty and difficult question, Stephen. In fact, it's so personal that if I answer it truthfully I will be a little bit enigmatic, OK?

My goals essentially are to understand the world and to be understood. And these, in my mind, actually are quite the same goal. So how to achieve understanding myself and understanding others? By really getting into the minds of others, and letting them into mine, if I can. And through a combination of supreme confidence and supreme doubt.

Ibaraki: OK, we're now going to talk about your work that led to the Turing Award. And the first question is: What led you to co-write one of the most influential papers in computing science as a graduate student in 1983?

Micali: All right, if you want me to outline [laughter] the story of that work, I'll tell you, it is a tale of fearlessness and shamelessness, luck and ignorance, everything combined, OK?

Let me start with luck. You know, I'm not ashamed to start with luck, because nothing substantial can be accomplished without it. My good luck was to be in Berkeley, in a wonderful atmosphere, with fantastic teachers and great fellow students. In particular, I was lucky to be in a course taught by Manuel Blum on computational number theory, whose last three lectures—maybe four, no more, actually—were on public-key cryptography. Cryptography at that point was not that developed, at least in academia. Manuel was an absolutely inspiring teacher, and cryptography was an incendiary material. So it was a match made in heaven. [Laughter] If you'll allow me the pun, the match lit.

So that was how we started. A problem mentioned in class was that of mental poker. In other words, can you and I play cards over the phone, or by email? There was an approach to this problem proposed in the past, but it did not quite work. So Shafi and I decided to solve it. That's where fearless and shameless come in, right? Because the problem was actually very hefty, and a satisfactory solution would've taken years of further development and many more techniques than we had at the time. And we ultimately built those techniques, but at the time our youth and inability to properly size the problem were a big help in taking on this challenge. Simplifying things, we essentially thought first about encrypting the cards, and then about implementing the *dealing*, the random shuffling of the cards. The first step was actually challenging enough to make us understand that we needed a new encryption scheme and a new notion of security.

OK, without getting into too many details, encryption at that time was deterministic. This means that every encryption method used to have a single ciphertext corresponding to a given message. What made a ciphertext hard to understand was the "length" (technically speaking, I should say the "entropy," but never mind) of its corresponding message. In fact, you can imagine that it is hard to guess a long message in its entirety, right? Yet, with deterministic encryption, if you were lucky, if you guessed the message in its entirety, then, being encryption deterministic, you could actually verify the correctness of your guess. What makes mental poker really challenging is that the possible "messages" are only 52, because there are only 52 cards. So, in this application, it's easy to guess the intended message, because it is easy to cycle through all 52 of them, right? In other words, in this application, the message space, so to speak, is very, very sparse. And so we decided that if we wanted to encrypt such few messages, then we had to encrypt them probabilistically. That is, we had to flip coins to choose a ciphertext of a given message.

Think of it like this. I have not just one way to encrypt a message, but I have many, many, many, many, many ways, exponentially many ways (in the number of coins you toss), and I flip coins to choose which one to use and then send you the corresponding ciphertext. Now, a fundamental property should be that, even though every message can be ciphered in so many ways, from every single one of its ciphertexts, you can actually retrieve the original message that I send you. That, essentially, is the idea.

Actually, we decided to further generalize the problem at hand and considered a worse situation. How about having only two possible messages: say, 0 and 1? That is, if you want to encrypt a single, randomly selected, bit? What should we want from encryption in such a case? We should want to make sure that, from a ciphertext, one should not be able to guess the corresponding bit with probability better than 50–50. Mind you, that everybody can always get the bit correctly with probability 50%, right? Indeed, even if you don't know anything about encryption at all, when you see a ciphertext, you flip a coin and say, "If heads, I predict zero; if tails, I predict one." You flip the coin, and you'll be right with probability one-half. So to claim that you are "breaking" the encryption scheme, you must at least do a tiny, teeny better—"epsilon better", as we say—than 50%. Perhaps, you must be able to correctly guess the bit with probability 51%, or 50.1%, or 50.001%, or something like this. A one-bit encryption scheme should be considered secure only when it is practically impossible to have even such small advantages over random guessing. (This essentially started our development of the notion of *computational indistinguishability*, as we called it later on.)

We then proved the following theorem: Namely, if we can encrypt a single bit in this way, then we can as securely encrypt arbitrarily many multi-bit messages. The underlying proof technique came to be known as *the hybrid argument*. Thanks to this theorem, to the hybrid argument, all that remained was finding a candidate scheme for encrypting a single bit. The ability to securely encrypt arbitrary message spaces would automatically follow.

Here is where ignorance actually came to the rescue. And not only ignorance, but luck again, of course, because knowing a lot of things is tantamount to having a haystack in your mind, right? And among so many, many, many, many pieces of straw, you look for a special one, "the needle." This means trouble because you might never find the needle among so many pieces of straw, or you may find it when it's too late. Shafi and I were lucky, because we wanted to construct a candidate one-bit cryptosystem based on computational number theory, and we didn't know much computational number theory. So, if some facts at all could be put together to construct our cryptosystem, we had to choose them from the very few facts we knew. We got lucky, because the needle was possible to find in our small stack. The needle we zeroed in was the *quadratic residuosity* problem.

Essentially the problem is distinguishing squares from nonsquares modulo N, where N is a large integer whose prime factorization you do not know. I will not bother you with the details, but you can easily disregard some numbers from being squares modulo N, but for another half of the numbers modulo N, when N is of a certain form, it is not at all clear how to distinguish squares from nonsquares. Thus, we thought that the difficulty of making such a distinction might be useful to encrypt a single bit. But: Was the quadratic residuosity problem really computationally difficult?

We started by asking our advisor, then we started asking our other authorities, and somehow nobody knew how to solve the quadratic residuosity problem. So we said, what the heck? Let's assume it is computationally hard and build on it our candidate cryptosystem. We took a risk. The danger was that, after publishing our system, somebody could come up the next day and say, "What are you talking about, quadratic residuosity? Here is how to solve it." But we took the risk. Again, we were young, so we didn't have a reputation to maintain yet, or perhaps we disregarded our reputations, or whatever. So, with ignorance, luck, and risk taking, things worked out.

By the way, today we know much more, and if quadratic residuosity were to become easy tomorrow, it would not be a problem, because at this point we have enough candidates to base our cryptosystem on (in fact, we have a way to distill them). So, in some sense, timing was crucial, and timing is another form of luck, right? Again, I think I made it abundantly clear, I strongly believe that, never mind all our good deeds and whatever we do to deserve our successes, luck has a major part. I am Italian, right? My ancestors, the Romans—I mean, were very determined people. They conquered a lot of the then-known world, but at the end they really knew whom to thank, and they built a monumental temple to luck, to Fortune. If you go to Rome, take a trip to nearby Palestrina. There is an entire mountain transformed into a temple, the temple of the *Fortuna Primigenia*. In the end, luck matters.

But then, you know, you have to work for your luck. So, Shafi and I developed various techniques, in particular *random self-reducibility*, to help us prove that quadratic residuosity, the problem we selected, really had all the properties we wanted. We came up with the hybrid argument and with computational indistinguishability. These actually were techniques that we introduced in our work on probabilistic encryption for a particular context, but that also proved crucial in subsequent and harder contexts. So in some sense, we were wise, or lucky again, to use them in a simpler problem to begin with.

Ibaraki: Well, it's a particularly amazing piece of work. It reflects an inflection point in history, the work that you did. And when you talk about luck, I guess that's where preparation and opportunity meet, so . . . [laughter]

Micali: Absolutely. Luck favors the prepared, [laughter] but luck is needed anyway.

Ibaraki: Now, can you provide added details behind your approach, *the simulation paradigm*?

Micali: Sure. I actually find the simulation paradigm the most natural thing. Let me forget mathematics for a minute and put you in the right mood. It's a simple concept, really. It's a very human concept. So let me recall a personal episode, which I'm sure is actually common to all of us, and yet is very personal to all of us. Here we go.

I remember, when I was a kid, of somehow getting an acute attack of classic solipsism, which is a fancy way to say that I started being fearful that there was no outside reality, that it was all in my head, that I was alone, that the world was a product of my imagination, etc., etc. You know, it could very well have been a power trip. I'm sure it was. But somehow, at the time, I recall the feeling to be one of loneliness and despair. So my mother got to work: You know, it lasted a few days . . . She sat next to me on my bed and said, "I listen to what you say, but I'm here. I do exist. Let me help you." And I said, "No! You're not here! I place you next to me on my bed, I'm letting you say these things," and so on and so forth. I eventually got out of it, but somehow I was able to positively turn all these feelings into science.

What impressed me at the time—I remember this distinctly—was how impossible it was to break that symmetry, I mean, to decide which was virtual and which was real. And, if I cannot distinguish the real from the virtual, then in what sense could they be considered different? Somehow that thought stuck with me. Fast-forward a few decades, and we have the simulation paradigm.

So what is the simulation paradigm? Essentially, it is the technique that ensures that no information, or not much information, is leaked in a cryptographic interaction. In cryptography, there is no you, Stephen, or me, Silvio. What distinguishes you from anybody else is a secret that only you have. It's called a secret *key* in cryptographic lingo. It is a secret number that only you know, and you use it to send your messages in a cryptographic transaction. Of course, nobody's going to be so dumb to send his own secret key along with his messages in a cryptographic protocol. But you use your secret key to generate the messages you send. In some sense, somebody who sees the messages you send essentially sees a kind of shadow of your secret, projected on an imaginary wall, a hypothetical wall. And perhaps, if an adversary sees enough shadows of your secret key—say, from many angles—then he could reconstruct it.

Indeed, I may not know the shape of an object, but after seeing its projection onto one wall, other projections onto other walls, I start getting the zest of it and become able to reconstruct the unknown shape. So, when you're taking part in a cryptographic protocol you are in a bind. If you never use your secret key, the secrecy of your key is guaranteed, but you are not doing anything that's cryptographically relevant either. On the other hand, if you use your secret key, which you must do to accomplish anything of interest, you actually reveal shadowed images of your secret key. So, will it remain secret at the end?

The solution of the riddle is to send messages using your secret key in a way that the adversary, without knowing your secret key, can simulate you, can reproduce what you say in essentially the exact same way in which you say things. So by watching you, the adversary watches your reality, but you ensure that he, without knowledge of your secret key, is able to generate a virtual reality that is actually identical to the one you generate for him. And if you succeed in acting in a simulatable way, then your secret is secure. Why? Because if the adversary could imitate what you say without knowing your secret key, then what you say cannot inadvertently betray your secret key. So that's the whole idea of how to ensure that the amount of secret information you reveal is "contained." This containment is what the simulation paradigm gives you.

So if you go back now to solipsism, I could not decide whether [laughter] the world is real or I am making my own virtual reality, but at least I could put this impossibility to good use. Because the impossibility of distinguishing reality from a creation of our mind is our best way to guarantee the security of a cryptographic protocol.

May I abuse your patience a little bit more to give you a concrete example of how to apply the simulation paradigm? Consider public-key encryption. What do you do in this setting? Assume that you select a specific secret message to send me. You probabilistically encrypt it in my key, and then you send me the resulting ciphertext. Call it C. C is a good acronym for a ciphertext. Assume now that there is an adversary in between us. Then, what is his real view? His real view (besides my public encryption key) is this string, C, the ciphertext that you actually so produced, OK? However, nothing stops the adversary, without ever seeing C, from choosing a random message, a creature of his own mind without any objective reality; then, from encrypting it probabilistically using my public key, so as to obtain a virtual ciphertext D that nobody sent; and, finally, from looking at D. So now the adversary has actually two worlds: one, C, that you created by encrypting your specific message—M, call it; and another one, D, that the adversary himself created probabilistically by encrypting a random message. And if a cryptosystem guarantees that his real view—the ciphertext C that you sent—and his virtual view—the D that he himself created—are essentially indistinguishable, then the secrecy of your specific message is safe, right?

Simplifying a bit, this is what the simulation paradigm means in encryption, but the principle is the same across other applications. It may actually become a little bit harder to implement and to grasp in these other applications, but the idea is the same.

Ibaraki: Now, can you further describe your notions of encryption security—for example, *semantic security* and *indistinguishability*—and how these measures must be met for schemes to provide security across a wide range of cryptographic applications?

Micali: All right, so we are going from technical to more technical. OK, let me try.

Semantic security is essentially what you intuitively want from an encryption scheme. In some sense, it extends Shannon's notion of perfect secrecy, which was applicable only to a very constrained scenario; namely, when a sender and a receiver share beforehand a string of random bits, and only need to encrypt messages whose total bit length does not exceed that of their shared random string.

When somebody is going to transmit a message, we have, from context, a probability distribution—we call it a message space—of what he is going to say, right? Consider all messages that are a thousand letters long. Then, some messages actually have probability zero—for instance, those that contain five consonants in a row, just because one cannot even pronounce them. Of the remaining messages, some have higher probability than others, depending again on the contexts we are in. In sum, there is an *a priori* probability distribution from which the message sender is going to choose his message. In this setting, you want to guarantee not only the secrecy of the chosen message in its entirety, but also that of partial information about the message.

So, what should this partial information be? You can think that it's a function from the message space to some other, perhaps smaller, space. For instance, you may be satisfied to figure out whether the sender's message is about attacking or retreating, or whether it expresses worry, and things like this. (Indeed, you would like to understand that your enemy is worried, even though you cannot quite understand what he is saying.) For simplicity, assume that this "partial information" function F you are interested in maps any message into a number between one and 1,000, say, OK? Even if you're not able to decrypt the message sent, you may be satisfied to learn the value of F on the message sent.

Now consider the following situation. Assume that somebody tells you that the sender has selected a message m from the message space, and has sent it by magic, by teleportation, to its destination. So, what is the value of $F(m)$? If you would like to win this game, what would you answer? You would say: "Well, if I try to be as right as I can be, what is the most popular value, the most probable value this F can take?" Since F maps every possible message to a number between one and 1000, and since you know from context what is the probability distribution over all possible message, you figure out that, say, maybe 727 is the most popular value of F, and it occurs with probability 2%. So, if you answer 727 you'll be automatically correct with probability 2%, right? You don't need any cryptoanalysis. You don't need to know anything. You just know what the message space is, what the distribution is, and you choose the most popular value for F, given this distribution.

OK, now consider a dramatically different situation. The sender not only has chosen the message m from the given probability distribution, but also encrypts it, transmits an encryption of it, and so you also see the encryption of this message. Not only do you know that the message m has been selected according to the given probability distribution, but, lo and behold, you have an encryption of m. Now, can you guess what $F(m)$ is better than before? Remember, before seeing the encryption of m, without any cryptanalysis, you could be right 2% of the time. Now, by cryptanalyzing the encryption of m, can you improve your probability of correctly guessing $F(m)$? If you cannot improve it to more than 2%, that is, not 2.01%, not 2.001%, not 2 plus epsilon percent, then we call the encryption semantically secure. OK, that is the whole idea. Now it's computational complexity, rather than information theory à la Shannon, that is being used to drive the notion of semantic security.

Actually, we developed computational indistinguishability as a tool to prove semantic security, and we proved that if we had a system which was computationally indistinguishable, then it was also semantic secure. We actually proved that also the opposite was true, that is, that semantic security implies computational indistinguishability, and that other notions of security are all equivalent to each other. And this is the most reassuring thing there can be in science, when you try to approach a new object. You use one avenue, then another one, then a third one, and suddenly you realize that all these avenues are absolutely equivalent.

Going back to Turing, at the time in which the notion of computation was up for grabs, people were trying to figure it out. "OK, I understand poetry. I understand other human endeavors. But how should I define computation?" Turing defined it using Turing machines. Church used lambda calculus. Another definition was recursive functions. And then, at some point, it was figured out that all these definitions were provably equivalent to one another. So one did not have to pick and choose which definition was the right one, because they were one and the same. It is this identity of different looking notions that reassures us that the right notion has been achieved.

So the equivalence of semantic security and computation indistinguishability, and other notions as well, tell us that a robust notion of secure encryption has been reached. Being equivalent, you might prefer to use semantic security to best convey what secure encryption means. But you may want to stick to computational indistinguishability when you want to prove that a particular encryption scheme is secure, because proofs are simpler when you use computational indistinguishability.

Ibaraki: It's just so amazing, [laughter] the level of thinking. And I can see now the profound impact of your work. And speaking about that, how do you see your work revolutionizing the study of cryptography, and laying the foundation for the theory of cryptographic security?

Micali: Well, cryptography has existed since time immemorial. For thousands of years people wanted to encrypt their messages. But they did not design a cryptosystem so as to achieve a predefined rigorous goal of security. They simply designed a cryptosystem which "achieved whatever it achieved." They tried the best they could. They tried to poke their system as best as they could. There were no notions of security, no proofs, only heuristics. They essentially considered a laundry list of possible attacks, and then checked that each attack that they knew of failed. There was no guarantee that a new, yet known, attack would fail too.

So, later, even when the encryption was based on a mathematical problem like in the RSA, there was only a loose connection between the human problem of decryption, that is, between breaking the system and the difficulty of the purely mathematical problem that was chosen as the basis of a cryptosystem. Solving the underlying purely mathematical problem is one thing, and may be very difficult. But decrypting messages exchanged in a cryptosystem loosely based on that mathematical problem is a totally different thing, because you are helped by grammar constraints, by logical constraints, by context, by a lot of other things. Right? So these two problems are not quite the same.

Let me give you an example. Assume that the problem you have chosen as the basis of your cryptosystem is factoring integers. This is actually a great problem. Some numbers are primes, like two, three, five, seven. It turns out that you can randomly pick two large primes—say, a thousand digits each. Then, you can easily multiply them—in fact, you can still do it by pen and paper. But then, if you give their product to someone else and say, "I multiplied two random primes to get to this number; which primes did I use?" then nobody knows how to factor your product and retrieve the two primes you started with. Gauss and plenty of other mathematicians have looked at this problem without being able to solve it. So factoring integers is a very difficult pure mathematical problem. But it has nothing to do with decrypting.

When building a cryptosystem loosely based on factoring, we built it so that, if you knew how to factor, then you knew how to decrypt. But this is not a very interesting direction, right? The interesting direction is the opposite one. What we really want is that nobody could decrypt our messages, or even gain partial information about them, without being able to factor, so that, if factoring is hard, then the system is absolutely unbreakable. And if somebody somehow decrypts what I encrypted because he's able to solve the factoring problem, thus succeeding where Gauss and company failed, you know what? He deserves to know what I was saying. [laughter] OK?

So, the main contribution of Shafi and me was building cryptosystems for which one could rigorously prove that the purely mathematical underlying problem is absolutely identical to the very human problem of decrypting or even getting partial information about encrypted messages. In a sense, we found a way to rigorously reduce apples to oranges! By now, one routinely designs cryptosystems with this notion of security embedded and with this type of reduction. In sum, I believe that replacing heuristics with proofs, and introducing these sophisticated apples-to-oranges reductions was our contribution to the field.

Ibaraki: And what a contribution! Again, an historical inflection point, [laughter] which really marks a huge shift, in my opinion, so . . .

Micali: Thanks!

Ibaraki: Now, Silvio, can you talk more about your work with knowledge complexity and *zero-knowledge proofs*?

Micali: Yes. Proofs are supposed to convey knowledge, right? There is a theorem statement. You don't know if it is true at all, so you ask somebody to prove it to you. He or she provides you a proof, and at this point, at the end of the proof, if the proof checks, after you verify it, you know not only that the statement as claimed is true, but you also know a lot of other things. You know *why* the statement is true. You must get a lot of details to get convinced that the theorem statement is true.

Assume instead that we want to reduce to a minimum the amount of knowledge necessary to convince somebody that the theorem is true. What should this minimum be? Well, at the end of the day, the minimum should be that you learned that the statement is true, which you didn't know beforehand, right? That is the minimum I really need to reveal in any proof. Now, a zero-knowledge proof is a proof that reveals only that minimum: that the statement is true, without adding any other piece of knowledge.

But the question is how can you tell that no other knowledge has leaked from the proof? This is another application of a simulation paradigm, which we were discussing before. Essentially, you want to prove a theorem in a way that ensures that if somebody knew beforehand that the statement of a theorem was true, then he could reconstruct the proof you give to him in exactly the same way in which you provide it. In other words, how do I know that from this proof, from this big interaction, I don't learn much more than the statement of a theorem being true? Indeed, from this interaction you learn that the theorem is true, and I wanted to give you this. But if you could simulate my proof in its entirety if you knew beforehand that this theorem was true, then there is no other further information in my proof. This is what a zero-knowledge proof is.

Sometimes you may want to reveal a little bit more. For example, think of an election. There is no theorem here, but there may still be a "zero-knowledge interaction." Assume that you have a hundred people in a room, and they want to carry out a very simple election, the simplest election: a referendum. OK? So what do we want to do? We want to tally our yeas and nays. Each one votes yea or nay, and we want to tally how many yeas there are. Assume there actually are 60 yeas and 40 nays. So you want to compute that there are 60 yeas and 40 nays, but you don't want to reveal who voted for what. You want to keep *private* the votes, but you want to compute the tally *correctly*. So you want to have correctness and privacy at the same time.

Now, correctness without privacy, that's not a problem, because I can just say, "OK, ladies and gentlemen, whoever votes yes raises their hands. I count 60 hands, so there are 60 yeas in this referendum." On the other hand, if I want to have privacy alone, without the correctness of the tally at all, I can say, "Everybody writes a yea or a nay on a piece of paper, and throws the paper to the fireplace." By so doing, total secrecy is easily guaranteed. But then, what is the tally? So what we want, instead, is that, without trusting anybody, we can compute the tally of 60 yeas in a way that we have no idea who voted yes and who voted no.

Of course, if we trust somebody, she can just say, "Oh, just whisper in my ear what your vote is and I promise not to tell anybody, and further, I promise to announce the correct tally." Sure! I mean, this is not going to fly with anybody, and with cryptographers in particular. So, the idea is that we replace this trust in some individual, in order to guarantee correctness and privacy simultaneously, by just talking to each other, and trust that the majority of us are honest. Essentially, the idea is a *blending* of correctness and privacy. And because correctness matters in all human enterprises, and privacy matters to all humans, I believe that this blending is a good building block for a theory of human interaction.

Ibaraki: That's very interesting. So what do you see as the implications of this work, and how does the work extend to other domains?

Micali: All right. The implications. First of all, you can imagine that in a general cryptographic protocol, or in an economic transaction, you want to have both correctness and secrecy. Let me give you an example. Assume that you go to a carpet store, right? And you see a carpet there. As it happens, in such stores, carpets are not tagged with their prices. So you say, "I'm interested in this carpet. How much does it cost?" And the other guy says, "Well, wait a second. How much are you willing to offer?" "No, no, no, you go first," right?

The situation is very complicated, and we could benefit from a new transaction, one that we didn't quite have available before, such as the following. We engage in a cryptographic protocol in which I, as the buyer, choose my input to the protocol to be the maximum buying price I am willing to pay, and you, as the seller, choose as your input the minimum selling price you may consider. And now, through our protocol, without telling each other these two values, we just compare them. If there is no overlap, that is, if my maximum buying price is below your minimum selling price, we only learn, "Sorry, guys, the two of you cannot transact. No carpet sale today." On the other hand, if there is an overlap, we end up with a contract, digitally signed by both of us, stating that the carpet is sold and is now mine at the price that, say, sits in the middle between my minimum buying price and your maximum buying price, or whatever price formula we want to choose. So, this transaction is something that somehow enlarges the realm of the possibilities we have in our "paper world," our ordinary-world transactions.

But in my opinion the implications of this theory go beyond business transactions. Because enabling secure transactions enables more interaction. Let me give you another example. Assume now we have a dating game, OK? There are two individuals, and I go first and say, "Hey, on a scale of one to ten, I like you ten. How much do you like me?" And the answer comes back: "Two." [laughter] With such an answer, I know I will never interact with anybody in the near future, because I need to recover psychologically, right? But assume now that you can actually interact in another way, in which you can somehow compare these two numbers but only figure out whether both of you like each other ten, or whether both of you don't like each other ten. In such an interaction, I've much less to lose in self-image, and thus I can safely interact much more in this fashion. In other words, if I can control the amount of privacy I might lose, I can confidently enter into many more transactions than before. So this is another implication of correctness and privacy. It enables not only business transactions, but also personal transactions.

You ask about other domains. There are plenty of other domains. Because essentially, at this point, from just encryption, cryptography has become *the science of adversarial computing*. And adversaries are everywhere, [laughter] as everybody knows, not only cryptographers. In a proof, the adversary is whoever wants to convince you of false statement. In encryption, the adversary is somebody who wants to understand information about your messages. In pseudorandom number generation, the adversary is somebody who wants you to generate biased rather than unbiased coin flips, etc., etc. More generally, the best way to model a very complex system is to model it *adversarially*. Because the more complex a system is, the more it looks like there is really an evil guy there trying to wreck it apart, to make sure that nothing works.

So, essentially, this theory is becoming more and more hand in glove with fault-tolerant computing, where you really want to make sure that, you know, a network of computers continues to work properly together, even though some of them fail, and fail in a way that is seemingly controlled by an adversary. In a different domain, this theory has by now encompassed all pseudorandom number generation. It has also provided bounds for what is learnable. Valiant and Kearns have somehow used Shafi's and my results together with Oded Goldreich on pseudorandom functions to figure out what cannot be efficiently learned. In sum, because adversarial computing is so pervasive, and allows us to model so many things, there are many, many domains to which this work may apply.

Ibaraki: I see. I mean, that's fascinating, I can see this now and in ten years' time a Nobel Prize.

Micali: [laughter] Thanks. I don't know about this, but thanks.

Ibaraki: Now, you've somewhat addressed this in all the different kinds of answers you've provided, and the dialogue we've had so far, but how does your work address important practical problems, such as the protection of data from being viewed or modified, and providing a secure means of communication and transactions over the Internet?

Micali: All right, yes, sure. You know, encryption is not the only thing you want to do on the Internet. Protection of data from being viewed, we have discussed, but from being modified we have not yet discussed, right? About protection against data modification, Shafi and Ron Rivest, my colleague at MIT and a prior Turing Award winner, and I developed a *digital signature scheme* that actually has set the standard for subsequent digital signatures. Can I describe briefly what this involves? Let me go on a limb and take another five minutes.

Essentially, what is a digital scheme? A digital signature scheme involves a pair of matching keys, a *secret key* that allows me to sign messages and a *public key* that enables everyone to verify the messages I sign using my secret key. The crucial property is that the public verification key does not betray the secret signing key. That is, knowledge of the verification key should not enable one to compute the signing key in any remotely feasible time, such as a few millions years, even with the fastest computer. So to prove that a given message, M, comes from me, I use my secret signing key to compute a short string S, my digital signature of M. Such digital signature S depends on M, because different M's would have different digital signatures from me. But then you can use my signature S and M and my public verification key to see whether S is indeed the correct signature of mine for the message M. If this is the case, you can rest assured that I consented to the message M, right?

Now, for this to work, it is necessary that these signatures are unforgeable by somebody else. OK, but what does this mean? In the past, it used to mean that an adversary could not come in, look at my public verification key, and forge my signature of his favorite message, such as, you know, "Silvio owes me a million dollars." But, we need more security than that. So what do we need? We also need that somebody cannot modify a prior signature of mine so as to forge my signature on a modified message. So, for instance, if I did sign, "I, Silvio, owe you, Stephen, $1000," somebody should not be able to change it "I, Silvio, owe Stephen (or somebody else) $2000," right?

Even more, you want that somebody cannot ask me to sign a few things, and then, assuming that I do agree and sign them, learn to sign other messages. Think of a notary public, who essentially is somebody who signs messages chosen by other people. And of course, he could use digital signatures to digitally sign messages. So you don't know how to forge the digital signatures of this notary public, but you can ask him to sign a given message, and he does. Then you say, "Ah, that's interesting. I just learned something that I didn't know before. I think I start getting the idea how the signatures of this notary public look like, but I'm not quite sure, so let me ask him for a second one. Could you please sign this second message?" And the notary public signs it again. You say, "Oh, gee, now I'm getting the gist of it." And so you go on with this process a bunch of times. You request signatures. The guy agrees and sends them back. So what one should really want is that, at the end, you cannot sign any new message at all. In other words, forging someone else's signatures should not only be hard from scratch, but also *unlearnable*.

When I arrived in this country, you know, English was a cryptosystem for me. More or less, I could not really be understood by anybody. But then I was able to ask questions, "How do you say this? How do you say that?" And slowly slowly, I learned enough to get by. So we don't want this to happen in a secure digital signature scheme. We want a more stringent notion of security. We want signatures that are unlearnable. I believe that this requirement is crucial if you really want to prevent data from being tampered with over the Internet. And signature schemes guaranteeing this stronger property have already been developed.

Ibaraki: Now, what is the impact of your work on computational complexity?

Micali: Well, *interactive proofs* were crucial to complexity theory, because they let us understand which class of problems have an efficient proof. Remember, proving a theorem is the most frustrating thing. Proofs are very frustrating to write down, and it is very frustrating to read them. Interactive proofs actually transform this frustrating thing into a game between the *prover* and the *verifier*. Somehow, if the theorem is true, and I act as a prover, then I should win a very simple game between you and me. Say that the game has five moves: I move, you move, I move, you move, and one of us wins, and then we can determine who wins. If the theorem is true, then I should win all the time. If the theorem is false, I should win at most half of the time. So if we play this game, say, 100 times, and you see that I win 100 times in a row, you conclude, "Well, you know what? The best explanation is that the theorem is actually true."

Figuring out which theorems are easily provable is important in complexity theory. As for another impact in complexity theory, my work on *pseudorandomness*, with Manuel Blum first and with Shafi later, essentially has helped us understand which problems can be solved deterministically. Thanks to Solovay and Strassen, and Rabin, by now we know that there are plenty of problems that can be efficiently solved probabilistically. But then what happens if your computer cannot flip coins? Somehow the theory of pseudorandom number generation allows us to understand what problems can be solved efficiently and deterministically.

More generally, a lot of my work depends on a *one-way function*, OK? A one-way function F is a function that has two crucial ingredients, very antagonistic to each other. The first is that the function F is easy to evaluate, which means on input x, you can compute $F(x)$ very, very quickly. The second is that the function is hard to invert, meaning that given $F(x)$, you have no idea how to retrieve one such x. Essentially that is the mathematical analogue of the one-way phenomena that we so commonly experience in the real world.

For instance, if I take a glass, and I smash it on the floor, that is very easy, but to reconstitute the original glass from its pieces is much harder. So this a one-way phenomenon. As for another example, it is easy to scramble an egg, yes? But to unscramble it is a totally different (and in fact much harder) story. So a one-way function essentially incorporates in itself both easy and hard computation. Thus, it's not surprising that understanding one-way functions increases our understanding of complexity theory, which is the field devoted to figure out which problems are easy to solve and which ones are not.

Ibaraki: Yeah, that's fascinating. What are your thoughts about things like in quantum mechanics and the twin particle effect, and sort of the impact that's going to have perhaps on your field? Or do you see sort of the work of Judea Pearl in causality and counterfactuals and external validity and artificial intelligence—do you see some kind of connection between some of this research you've done and those areas, at all?

Micali: Well, certainly let me address the field that [laughter] is more dangerous to mine, quantum computing. We need hard problems to base cryptography on. As we said, we want to take a purely computational problem, a purely mathematical problem, and massage it around and transform it by magic into a very human problem, like proving "This message comes from Stephen," right? Of course what is easy computation and what is hard computation depends a lot on the available computational model. If you have an abacus, what is hard and what is easy is one thing. If you have now a modern computer, but still a classical computer, it's something else. The jury is still out on whether quantum effects can practically and dramatically speed up computation or not, but they might. In this case, first of all, we have to redefine what is easy and what is hard, and then define functions that are one-way for quantum computers, rather than for digital ones. So some specific candidates for one-way functions, such as factoring, may disappear, but that does not mean that we cannot generate other candidates, because we now have a more general theory of one-way computation.

Ibaraki: You know, amongst our listeners there's people who are not necessarily heavily involved in all the technical aspects, and in some ways they could be consumers, because they're in senior management now, and their technical years are long past. So what are the practical implications and applications of your work influencing all of our daily lives?

Micali: All right, the simple practical example is that of a password. I'm sure everybody has dealt with passwords, right? For thousands of years, a password has been some secret phrase, such as "Abracadabra," that I use to enter, say, a castle. If I'm a medieval knight, and I'm on the other side of a moat, and I see the bridge is drawn, and I want it to be lowered, I say to the guard upstairs, "Abracadabra," and recognizing the password, the guard lowers the bridge and I can come in. You can use your mother's maiden name as a password. I can use the name of my favorite uncle. Either way, it is a secret that we actually need to communicate. This password system, of course, has some drawbacks. Essentially, if in the moat of the castle, in the water there, there is somebody, he can hear that the knight whispers "Abracadabra" before getting into the castle. Thus, at a later time, he can impersonate the knight with no problems. He puts on helmet and armor, says "Abracadabra," and the bridge will be lowered for him too.

In addition, a classical password system has another drawback: The gatekeeper himself knows know the password, so if I use the same password for other systems, say, not only to enter the castle but also to log in at MIT and to log into my bank site and wire money out of it, I am in danger, because I actually am enabling any verifier of one of these systems to impersonate me to any other system. So, what am I going to do?

I generate somehow a theorem whose proof only I know. For instance, I take two large random primes and I multiply them together to generate an integer N, and then I tell MIT, the castle, and my bank, "This number N here is Silvio's number. Anybody who proves to you that it is product of exactly two primes, let him enter my castle, let him wire money on my behalf, let him access my files at MIT. With my consent."

But how do I prove that N is the product of two primes? Do I send over the two primes I originally multiplied? Absolutely not: such a proof could be copied and used to impersonate me to another system. I use instead a zero-knowledge proof. That is, when, say, I want to log in at MIT, I engage its server with a zero-knowledge proof that N is the product of two primes. Such a proof can be verified by everybody, and thus by MIT's server. But it's a zero-knowledge proof, so nobody having verified that N is indeed the product of two primes is able to prove this to anybody else. Because, after a zero-knowledge proof, you don't learn how to prove the statement—you only learn that the statement is true.

So suddenly you essentially a have an ideal password system. It lets you safely use the same passwords with multiple systems, it is very efficient, and it is implementable via a smart card. It is the most practical application that I can think of.

Ibaraki: Silvio, you're this giant in industry and education and research and so on, and your work resonates throughout the world, and so I know our audience would be interested if you can additionally profile your extensive research history, its lasting impact, and some valuable lessons you wish to share from each of your top research areas that we haven't talked about yet.

Micali: [laughter] All right. First of all, let me just mention, without any details, that, in addition to whatever else we just discussed, I've been working on distributed computing, on private information retrieval, etc. But perhaps, you know, we should move from the technical work to the lessons learned.

The most valuable lesson that has worked for me (and many others) is to really generalize and simplify the concrete examples that motivate you. Concrete examples are wonderful. They really drive us. But they are also typically messy, right? They contain an abundance of details that may blind us. So my lesson would be just, you know, get rid of as many details possible. Generalize your problem as much as possible. Back up, and back further up until you see the whole picture in its simplicity. Generalize a problem until it becomes either impossible to solve or very simple to solve. Back up to get the full view and drive yourself to a corner. And once you have no escape you may lose, but you may also find additional strength and win big. At the end of the day, who needs partial victories? So my lesson would be drive yourself to a corner and go from there.

Ibaraki: That's an interesting concept. So how many times have you done that?

Micali: Oh, I've done it as a graduate student. I've done it as an undergraduate student. I've done it as an assistant professor. [laughter] I've done it a few times. The amazing thing is that it often works. So I'm not advocating without practicing, let's put it this way.

Ibaraki: It seems to me that concept could be applied to so many other areas, perhaps friends and family and business deals, as well.

Micali: Why not? Never sit at a negotiating table if you cannot get up and leave at any time, and never shoot for "just friendship." You know, sometimes I think it's worth it to risk it all.

Ibaraki: I see, Silvio. So this could be a book beyond your research [laughter] that the general public will read.

Micali: [laughter] I'm sure I'm not alone, right? I'm sure many people would agree with me.

Ibaraki: Now, Silvio, you talked about your past research, and you also talked about some of the other areas that you have researched. Can you get into more detail about your current research interests?

Micali: Yes. Somehow, at a late age, unfortunately, I encountered a beautiful notion that was put forward some half a century ago by economists, *mechanism design*. Essentially, this is a way to choose an optimal outcome without data. Optimizing is never easy, even if you have the data, but if you don't have the data it is actually much harder. And so why don't you have that data? Because other people, the so-called *players*, have the data. You may say, "Why can't you just ask them?" Well, because they may have a stake in the outcome you choose, and therefore, when you ask them for the data, they may lie so as to manipulate in their favor the outcome you choose. And so you must engineer a game so that, when everybody plays it so as to maximize his own utility, you learn, as a side product, which outcome you should choose. It's a fascinating field, and that's what I'm currently working on, from my own special perspective, of course.

Ibaraki: And then what are the broad implications and applications of this work?

Micali: Well, in principle, any decision-maker, in particular any politician, would stand to benefit from mechanism design. If you really want to go one step farther, mechanism design may be the best way to engineer a system, like the Internet, that is very decentralized, in which no one is in charge. And because no one is in charge, you can put all the rules and laws that you want, but unless you design the system so that everybody is incentivized to stick to the rules, the system will never quite work. So mechanism design may actually be used in engineering large decentralized systems. And finally, you know, I'll not be surprised if mechanism design were to provide us with key insights for understanding successful biological systems. Perhaps our complex organisms are not the visible product of some unlikely kind of equilibrium, a very fragile thing, but actually are the robust outcomes of properly and slowly designed mechanisms.

Ibaraki: Oh, fascinating. And again I mention, gee, maybe a Nobel Prize, as well.

Micali: [laughter] Ahi Ahi Ahi!

Ibaraki: What are your future research interests?

Micali: If you stress *future*, the answer is the brain. Yes, the brain might be my future interest, and not only mine. [laughter] In fact, other computer scientists before me—in particular, Les Valiant—started working on it. I think that I'm considering working on it.

Ibaraki: Oh, that's fascinating. In terms of that work, you're thinking of applying sort of a mathematical model to it, or getting more sort of into the engineering side, or getting into sort of the works like external validity or causation and some of that area? Sort of what's the approach?

Micali: Remember that I truthfully answered your question by stressing *future*. So, right now we don't know, at least I don't know which angle it's going to be, but certainly it's going to be a computational angle. At the end, I believe that a big part of the brain's function, and memory in particular, should be modeled as a computer, and you want to put things in memory, and retrieve them efficiently, and with some redundancy. And we know a lot about how to store, retrieve, and manipulate information when we have total liberty to decide the components. Here, the components are decided beforehand, but perhaps some of the lessons we learn from distributed computing may be applicable to the brain, too. More than this, I do not know. Right now I'm working on mechanism design, as I was saying.

Ibaraki: It's interesting, the whole concept of that kind of research, and I'm thinking of Daniel Dennett and *Consciousness Explained*, or Descartes and this sort of mind/body connection, or Penrose and some of the work that he's done in thinking about the brain, but from a model of a philosophical sense, or Kurzweil, and this idea of a singularity, which in some circles is controversial. Do you have any feelings about that sort of idea about a soul and a brain, and is there something more that we don't understand?

Micali: We don't understand *a lot*. But [laughter], if you ask me, remember whatever I said about the simulation paradigm? Never mind the mind and the body. Really, the question is whether the whole universe can fit in the brain, right? [laughter] I mean, I'm a little bit of an extremist here. But again, there are tremendous possibilities, but I have not given them the rigorous thought that I've given to some other fields yet.

Ibaraki: Silvio, I could just see those roots of this kind of thinking going back to when you were a child, and talking to your mother. [laughter] Now, what are your most difficult challenges in research, and what valuable lessons do you wish to share?

Micali: Well, my challenges, if I can be frank, are inability to work alone and lack of knowledge. And so the lessons I wish to share are the same ones that I used to cope with my challenges: collaboration and imagination. So what if you cannot work alone? You can always collaborate, provided that you hold on to your own individual obsessions, no matter how extensively you collaborate. And again, who cares if your arsenal is quite small? Be imaginative, forge your own tool, and march ahead.

Ibaraki: Every time you get researchers together, or you get, I guess, any group or cohort together, you're going to get a lot of discussion. You're going to get debate. You're going to get some controversy. You're going to get different points of view. So what would you describe as additional areas of controversy in the areas that you research?

Micali: [laughter] Well, controversy is . . . Everything is controversial. Actually, I think that the main controversy, not only in my research area but in any area, is the very definition of an area. This is the most contentious item in research. To be clear, defining an area is both necessary and useful to focus the effort of future work, to flesh out the problems, to attract fresh minds, etc., etc. But it's also a constraint. It's a boundary, right? And boundaries may always incarcerate us. So we have to be very, very, very careful.

Our theoretical community is just amazing. I really love my community. It has invaded new territories with determination, ferocity, and cleverness, like a bunch of conquistadores, but fortunately [laughter] no physical bloodshed. But even we, a progressive and ready-to-abandon-all-boundaries society, risk to transform ourselves into 'the guardians of the sacred fire'. And at a very great speed. We start fighting to protect the purity of our field against outside contamination. It is mind-boggling to me.

Suddenly, the game is not to find solutions to problems that do not yet exist, but to solve *older* problems. And the older the better, because you get more credit for solving, you know, a 50-year-old problem, than you get for solving a 10-year-old problem, etc., etc. Of course, you need both to pose and solve new problems and to solve old problems. But I don't understand the emphasis on old problems, right? That is really a disease.

If you chair a prestigious conference, or you are the editor in chief of a flagship journal, somehow you start feeling that you are expected to become a businessman, to satisfy the customers who put you there. So if you publish outlandish material, the number of subscribers may drop in droves. How would you look? Can you accept this damage to your reputation? Publishing such material may cost you further advancement. On the other hand, refusing to publish dangerous new material is hidden from the public eye, so you may actually harm the growth of your field, but no one will ever know. I'm actually saddened by the fact that journals and conferences publish a disproportionate amount of small—but declared big—advances on the status quo. I believe that the incentives are misplaced, and we can and must do better and never define in too strict a way any area.

Ibaraki: Hmm, that's quite fascinating what you just stated there. I mean, it kind of reminds me of this idea of disruptive innovation or research, and this concept of innovators being a platform where they sort of model what creates breakthrough innovation, what creates breakthrough disruptive innovation. They find sort of these five qualities, one of which is always actively questioning everybody, everything and everybody, always actively observing everything and everybody, always actively experimenting in diverse areas, even across areas that are outside of your domain, to get a different perspective. And the final two elements are associating, and that is synthesizing all the kind of different concepts in all the different areas, and integrating that information as you sort of proceed day to day. And then finally networking. Networking with others, but particularly with those who hold diverse views, and perhaps contradictory views, or even to the point where it could break the system, or close to sort of your collaborative team. It sounds like you're sort of speaking to that, not to get into this sort of groupthink idea.

Micali: Oh, absolutely. Of course there is the risk that, if everything is innovating so fast, then we cannot discern anything anymore. We need some rigidity, I don't know, it's an old question whether geometry could have been invented if we were water animals. I mean, [laughter] we need some solid terrain, perhaps, to hypothesize a triangle, and so on and so forth. Or maybe not. But what I'm saying is that we must do better than just barring this. It would be nice if every journal or conference actually accepted, say, every ten articles, two oddball articles, if people actually expected two such articles. And I bet they would be read with interest. Even simple policies like this would go a long way to incentivize us to question ourselves and our own fields and to make progress.

Ibaraki: I see. So, actively embrace outliers. [laughter]

Micali: Yes, yes, bring them into the fold. We need outliers. But we also need, you know, to make progress on very established questions. My problem is that I perceive a disproportionate emphasis on traditional work. Of course innovation will break through once in a while, but not at the right rate. We can actually control and optimize the rate a bit. Actually, quite a bit.

Ibaraki: Now, Silvio, can you describe the types of research being created or updated that will drive our experiences in five or ten years, and what will these experiences be like? Can you paint a picture for our audience?

Micali: Well, frankly, my prediction for future research can only be based on what I know, so I expect more and better of the same. I don't know how interesting that may be. All expert predictions matter less than the developments we cannot predict. I mean, if our predictions were exact, our future would be doomed to boredom and missed opportunity. I personally look forward to major surprises, [laughter] and I must confess that those I cannot anticipate.

Ibaraki: Now, you have this remarkable background—your educational background, that is—at the University of Rome and in Berkeley. So what specific challenges in your education at these two famous institutions were catalysts to inflection points in your lifetime of contributions, and how and why did this happen?

Micali: Oh, wow! Thanks for asking. [laughter] I really would like to give credit to both great educational systems, in Rome and in Berkeley, and the actual people behind them, who really shaped me . . . So let me have a crack at explaining. First of all, both universities, and in particular the specific teachers I met, have been very *flexible*. This really shaped my attitude towards research.

In the United States, to tell you the truth, a course is run more tightly than in Italy. As a student, you are continuously monitored with problem sets, and the exam coincides, so to speak, with the last day of the course. There is not much room for negotiations [laughter] of alternative dates. In the Italian system, instead, you are much more in charge of yourself. There are lectures, of course, there are sessions of exercises, but it's totally up to you to attend or not to attend. And the exam, you can actually take it when you feel ready: after a month, after a few months, after a year, even. That for me was really ideal, because I would have not functioned otherwise. Typically, I took four yearlong courses, where yearlong [laughter] meant from November to May. Then I took, say, one exam in June, another in July, one in September, and one in October. And then courses started again. It was crucial for me to be able to take an exam when I felt ready. I absorb things slowly, and that flexibility was extremely important to me.

People-wise, I really, really admire and I owe a lot to Professor Luciano DeVito. He taught us mathematical analysis. You must know that, in the typical Italian fashion of the time, I took a classical high school: lots of humanities, history, philosophy, and very little math. In fact, the only math that I was exposed to was Euclidian geometry, maybe because it was Greek. [laughter] Yet, I was fascinated by it enough to decide to enroll in physics, and thus I was exposed for the first time to mathematical analysis. A marvelous field. You started talking about infinity in rigorous terms. It was wonderful. But whatever made this course unique, as I realized later, was that this guy, DeVito, organized the entire course around problems. He never engaged in a classical definition-theorem-proof sequence. He would ask, "How might 'area' be defined?" And then a big debate started. Sometimes, he posed problems that we could not solve right away, but we solved them very much later. The problems were really center stage, and we were obliged, actually, to define things if we wanted to make progress. And somehow this necessity to define things became an ability, and helped me tremendously in my career.

So, in essence, his course was entirely devoted to research and that was the first course that I ever took, OK? I loved it so much to conclude, "Who cares about physics? Actually, what I care about is mathematics." I understood mathematics to be analysis. So I told him, "Professor DeVito, I really want to switch to mathematics." To my surprise, the guy says no: "You cannot switch." I said, "Why not?" Because, he says, he's proud to have been an analyst himself, but analysis was for older people like him, and a young person like me would be better off staying in physics. OK! [laughter]

I followed his advice, thinking that perhaps I could change his mind if I actually proved something. At some point, he mentioned the general axioms of measurability according to Lebegue and the existence of a set non-Lebegue-measurable. Somehow I decided to find such a set. But I was unprepared for the problem, and could not solve it, at least not right away. So I totally obsessed about it, to the point that I actually neglected to follow his lectures. I was behind in the course. In fact, I dropped all the other courses as well. But eventually, I managed to solve the problem, and I presented a solution to him. He was very happy and gave me an A+ at the first exam opportunity, while I was intending to take the exam much later. For me, that was really a transformative experience. Somehow I got the notion that it was OK to carve a path on my own, and that somehow research has to be center stage. I really felt empowered. More importantly, he now gave me permission to switch to mathematics, but he added, "If you really want to do mathematics, then you should focus on . . . " —he didn't use the word, but he essentially described theoretical computer science. He told me about Gödel and Turing. But then he says [laughter] "You really watch out, because to do this stuff you need a big stomach."

I switched to mathematics, but I neglected his advice and followed instead courses in analysis. But, in the fourth year, I paid attention to what he said enough to follow informally as a listener two courses, one on lambda calculus with Corrado Böhm, which was and is the father of Italian computer science, and one in logic with Giuseppe Iacopini. Corrado has always been very enthusiastic. He sought me out. He convinced me to leave analysis, to actually formally enroll in his class, and also he gave me a challenge. He said, you know, "Why don't you take the class, and why don't you try to prove that?" That challenge then became my undergraduate thesis and our first paper.

So now at this point, to tell you the truth, I was convinced that I wanted to do computer science, but I was totally unprepared. At the time there was no CS graduate program in Italy. So Corrado quite unselfishly suggested that I pursue a doctoral degree in CS abroad. Before applying, I followed a one-month summer school in computer science. The idea was to choose four courses out of some eight. I chose my four, but then dropped two. Since no degrees were awarded, why not? The course I liked the most was on *graph algorithms*, and it was taught by Shimon Even. Shimon was a wonderful teacher from the Technion, in Israel. He really introduced me to algorithmic thinking, and he became a beloved friend and mentor. The other course was also on algorithms, but more general, and it was taught by Fabrizio Luccio, from Pisa. At the end, they both gave me the same advice as Corrado: "I think you have to go abroad."

Somehow all three of them suggested Berkeley as the more suitable place for me to study. So I applied, I actually was admitted, and eventually went. I must tell you that was another lesson for me: Receiving caring advice on how to complete my studies from people who were not my advisers and had no formal responsibilities towards me, somehow gave me the impression that research really was an enterprise without borders, that I was helped by people who owed me nothing and who really encouraged me to go far, [laughter] in a way. I realized I was entering a community of the mind without borders, and that the people out there actually cared to advance Science with a capital S. It was an amazing message, right?

I was saying that I was studying history in high school, but my history books were de facto centered on the history of nation states. Or at least I read them that way. So somehow I didn't take notice of the fact that there was a parallel, in fact, a transversal universe. I mean, I knew, on paper, that science was a big enterprise. You know, Archimedes and Eratosthenes exchanged letters, Pythagoras traveled all over the Mediterranean, medieval scholars moved from Bologna, to Prague, Paris, etc., etc. Artists were born in one city, lived in another, worked in another, and died in another yet. Really, all this I knew, but somehow I never *registered* it. So, from that point on I must tell you that geopolitical boundaries faded in the background forever. And so that's it. Gotten this mythical view of what science ought to be, I decided that, yes, I would go to Berkeley.

Now, Berkeley: I was admitted, but not right away. My score in the test of English as a foreign language was actually abysmally low, so I had to take it again. Finally, I got a barely decent score, and I could begin at Berkeley in, I think, March 1979. And I was utterly miserable. First of all, I realized that my English was really poor, that I could not communicate with anyone, that I knew no one, and that I had no prerequisites in computer science, while Berkeley had a very tough prerequisite tree. So the only course I could take was CS1—the name says it all—an entry programming course attended by 18-year-old people, and even precocious younger people. I was 25, so there was very little mingling there. The other courses were equally elementary. So, bottom line, I decided I'd finish the trimester, I'd pack up, and I'd go back home. Accordingly, I also decided I might as well enjoy the city.

Just when I lowered my guard—perhaps because I was a bit more open—I actually met David Lichtenstein, who at that time was a Ph.D. student about to graduate. He took me under his wing, really, and was another marvelous example of the generous help that had been showered on me over the years. He showed me around San Francisco. He told me: "Forget about prerequisites. I think you need to do research. Why don't you pick up along the knowledge you need?" He told me that Professor Blum was actually finishing chairing the department of CS at Berkeley that summer, and said, "He's a great advisor, and you're lucky, because he has not taken new students during his chairmanship, so in the fall when he steps down he needs new students, so why don't you propose yourself?" I said, "I will try." He actually had [laughter] another reason in favor of Manuel: Being from Caracas, Manuel spoke Spanish. So, you know, "He can understand your Italian." [laughter] Because apparently my English wasn't good enough.

So I went to see Manuel. He was very kind, but he said that his hands were full, that we should reconsider everything in the fall, that we should wait. But David didn't give up. He was determined that I started doing research and stay motivated. And so he told me about a problem posed by another graduate student, who had just graduated with a superb thesis, Mike Sipser, now a leading complexity theorist, and the chair of MIT Math Department. In his thesis, Mike had left an open problem, and David suggested that I should try to solve it. The problem was in automata theory, which, of course, I knew nothing about it. So, he said, "No problem, so I'll give you a crash course in it." The "course" took two hours, or maybe three, at a coffee shop in Berkeley. We were sitting there, sipping cappuccinos, and he was telling me one definition, then giving a small exercise. He was patient and understanding, and so on and so forth. And at the end, with the last cappuccino— I call it the four-cappuccino course; that's how many cappuccinos [laughter] I was able to drink in one session—he says, "OK, now, here is the problem you should try to solve."

A few days later, I was actually able to solve it, and told David, and he says, "That's wonderful. Now you have to go back to Manuel and explain it to him too." I said, "But Manuel said his hands are full." He said, "Never mind, Manuel knows the problem. In fact, he was the advisor of Mike, so he would like to see the solution." So I went to Manuel, and David was right: Manuel wanted to hear the problem right away. He cleared his schedule, cleared the board, and let me explain the solution. And at that point, he agreed to pick me up as a student, and from that point on we only spoke of research. I mean, *I've never seen anybody so research-oriented as Manuel*. He really was wonderful.

So, at this point, you know, I decided to stay in Berkeley, and I showed up again in the fall. By then, David actually was no longer there—he already went off to his job—but that's when I met Shafi, and actually Vijay Vazirani, too, and Mike Luby, a group of extraordinary researchers and great people, as they turned out to be. We formed a gang of sorts. We dined out with modest finances, but still enjoyed the food, working together, and actually trying to solve the problem sets together. It was really wonderful. We took a course of Dick Karp, which was to test the flexibility of Berkeley [laughter] despite being a U.S. university.

Dick Karp is a fabulous teacher, too, and he ran a famous algorithm class. And he mentioned a problem, fortunately or unfortunately, kind of early on in the course. It was a problem in algorithmic graph theory, the same subject that Shimon made me enthusiastic about. The problem was extending the running time of the best-known algorithm for *matching* from bipartite graphs, which are special types of graphs, to general graphs. So Vijay and I decided to work together to try to solve the problem. We spent hours and hours together. Vijay was capable of satisfying all the other courses and taking care of the other problem sets. As for me, I, again, dropped out from all courses, including the one with Dick Karp. I only spoke to Vijay. But at the end, by our good fortune, by the end of the course we found a solution, right? (That solution, by the way, continues to be to this very day the most efficient solution for general graphs.)

So now what do I do? Dick, I must say, to his honor, let me pass the course, which by any standard I should have failed, with a B-minus. I mean, Dick is a very generous and fair person. I'm sure I must have tested his patience, [laughter] but he had to give me a B-minus. And now I was a little bit in trouble, because surviving as a Ph.D. student with only one course with a B-minus on my transcript was no joke. And to make things worse, I had to pass a barrier to continue the Ph.D. program, the *prelim exam*, and having not taken any hardware classes, I failed the hardware portion of this exam. So Dick and Manuel had to personally testify in front of the relevant committee so that I could continue my doctorate. Somehow, they were very persuasive, so I was allowed to continue.

And then our gang attended Manuel's course on computational number theory, and we all had a great time, we cemented our friendship, and at that point Shafi and I joined forces on cryptography for many, many years. And she actually had a tremendous influence on me in many ways. In particular, she convinced me that, given that nothing came easy to me, I might as well focus on hard things only. I must say that her insights, personal and scientific, really spurred me on in decades of joint work. I was indeed very fortunate to join forces with such a scientist and a friend and a colleague. So at this point I had a course that I loved, taken from Manuel, and the companionship from great friends and researchers. The people were much more flexible than the system, and I really felt, you know, that I really was in the proper crowd.

Manuel, I don't know if you know him, but he's a permanent revolutionary. We already spoke about Dick Karp. And then there was also another faculty member at the time, Andrew Yao, who started also as a physicist but, unlike me, a real one, with a Ph.D., a post-doctorate, etc., but then he got fascinated by computation and switched to computer science, and was then a professor at Berkeley, too. And I'm glad he was, because Shafi and I and he actually had a marvelous and fruitful interaction.

All these guys were actually marvelous teachers, but in very different ways. I mean, I have the fondest memories. Such a high standard to live by. It's scary, really. Manuel, I don't know, he was a magician. He did not explain a theorem. He actually forced you, actually all of his students, to prove the theorem on the spot: the trials, errors, anxiety, heartbeat accelerations, the whole shebang when you try to solve a problem. Dick was most clear, organized, a perfect sense of timing. I mean, I have a terrible memory, but whatever he explained I still remember. And Andy, he was not formally one of my professors, but I attended all of the lectures that he gave, and two of them really changed my life. You know, one was on *Shamir's secret sharing*, when I was a student, and another one when I was an assistant professor at MIT. The latter was a lecture on what came to be known as Yao's *garbled circuit*, which had also tremendous influence, not only on the field but on me in particular.

At Berkeley, I really think that the flexibility, the focus on research, and the ability to pardon cutting corners—provided that you actually strive forward at least in one direction—was really what made me what I really am. I really felt I was in a magical place. Remember, I had a very Europe-centered point of view, right? I thought of Berkeley as the far edge of a civilized universe, in front of the Pacific Ocean, that mythical barrier to mankind, right? I felt I was in heaven, but, keeping with the metaphor, [laughter] I also felt, "Who could live in such a small city, except, you know, monks?" I saw them as monks, Manuel and Dick and Andy, living in this remote hermitage at the confine of Earth. Really, it's hard to communicate such a personal experience, you know. I learned so much. And I learned what I really wanted to learn: that finally I was not alone. I learned that Science really had the power to understand anything, even things that seem to be impenetrable to quantification or rational analysis altogether. I learned the power of interaction. I've never forgotten it. And really, I learned that experiences that cannot be written down or repeated in any way, like these I just described, really are the most permanent and precious. Ever since, I became a very big fan of the oral tradition. We should go back to this oral tradition, the strongest and most effective tradition we ever had.

Ibaraki: Silvio, that's just an amazing history, in terms of the mentors that you've had, and continue to have, the collaboration with so many people, as you indicated, the flexibility that you were given, and I guess now that's generated [laughter] some questions in my mind. You had this very unique kind of program, both at University of Rome and at Berkeley, where people have given you some agility and some, as you indicated, some flexibility. Now, do you pass that on in terms of your interaction with your students, and so on, your graduate students? Has that influenced your interactions with potential researchers?

Micali: Oh, absolutely it has influenced. The extent to which I actually succeed at giving back what I received, that I don't know. But I certainly try. [laughter] I have my own rigidity to worry about, of course, but you bet I try to be as flexible to others as my teachers have been to me.

Ibaraki: You know, it's interesting: in this dialogue I can feel and sense your energy and your passion for the research that you do and the things that excite you, and I know that your collaborators, and those students that you influence, as well, would feel that same passion, so they'd be very excited [laughter] to work with you, I think.

Micali: Oh, these are very passionate people. You're right.

Ibaraki: Another question is that, you know, you worked with your colleague Shafi for some time, starting at Berkeley, and that collaboration has continued. You know, any time you collaborate with somebody, sometimes there's tension, and how do you manage that tension? Or, you know, let's say if you disagree on a point of view, how do you manage that?

Micali: Well, the best thing is not to manage. Somehow, tension gets resolved. Tension is good, right? Somehow you are pulled in two directions, but I think you generate energy. I think that as long as there is goodwill, this energy gets released in a positive direction. I've never tried to be, quote, "polite," in an interaction. It doesn't work for me. And other people have been very genuine when interacting with me. Sometimes, we start "polite," but then as we become more and more friendly with one another [laughter] and we become more and more direct, tension rises. And to tell you the truth, I think it's good. I don't think we should manage tension. If the tension becomes too high, and you have to say "Go to hell" for a day, and "I'll never work with you anymore," you can always restart on the next day. But if you try to keep everything at a quiet or moderate tension level, I'm not sure . . . It may work for others, by the way. I don't want to dampen it. But it just doesn't work with me, and with the people with whom I've had the pleasure or the honor of working.

Ibaraki: In the past your supervisors and collaborators, but also your mentors in the past, have given you a lot of flexibility, sort of allowing this sort of oral tradition in terms of you proving that you had the expertise or the knowledge, or you've done the required research in your problem solving. You know, there's this new idea that came out of Stanford—oh, I guess it's not new, but it sort of got more attention back in 2011. That's this idea of massive, open, online courses, you know, where they had the artificial intelligence course, 160,000 students enrolled from 190 countries, volunteers translating in 44 languages, and MIT and Harvard had started something called edX, and it's sort of in that same area, or Coursera, you know, is all about MOOCs. What's your opinion of MOOCs, and do you see that in conflict with sort of the traditional side of teaching, or do you see it sort of aligned with how you were kind of mentored, and the kind of support that you've received in your life?

Micali: So, we have to distinguish here the personal, what is good for me, from what may be good for others. Tell you the truth, I really believe that enabling a very large audience to get educated is something extremely beautiful and extremely useful. Ideally, we'd like to do this one-on-one, but if we cannot, then these online courses are perhaps, you know, a very good alternative. For me, actually, personally, it does not work, but that does not mean that it's not good. Just I'll be a very poor e-teacher. Remember that I continue to struggle with the doubt of whether there is somebody "on the other side," right? So, I hate writing letters, because who knows if the other one will ever receive it. And if it is received, in what state or mood he or she is. So I prefer a phone call to a letter anytime. Actually, if it's something that is very important, I really insist on physical presence. And so the notion that I, personally, could go in front of a microphone and a camera and deliver an e-course gives me . . . [laughter] I shudder at the thought.

But, however, that does not mean that it's not good. Actually it may be a way. But I really believe that there has got to be room for an old-fashioned way, for, as you say, oral tradition, personal interaction within a small group of people. I believe that you can actually subliminally transmit so much more this way. It's just a way that does not scale. So I don't want that in order to guarantee scale we suppress this other mode, but we can certainly augment it with e-learning and remote learning. I think that it is, again, a beautiful project that I certainly applaud. I'm not sure that I'll be successful in this particular mode. But that's just me.

Ibaraki: Again illustrating your continuing leadership, one of the things you did was you cofounded the information and security group, and because you're one of the cofounders of this very important group, can you detail your objectives in both the short and long term?

Micali: Those are actually quite simple, really: to foster interest, education, and research in cryptography. Pure and simple. I think that's the goal of any research group that has been founded, and ours is no different. It just focuses on cryptography, that I still like [laughter] despite my recent adventures in mechanism design.

Ibaraki: Now, throughout this interview it's clear that you have a lot of energy that you put to different areas, and one of them is *Advances in Computing Research*, that five-volume textbook series. Why are you so supportive of that series? You know, what motivates you? What generates all of that passion?

Micali: All right. First of all, about this specific series, let me tell you right away that I'm very proud of that volume. I mean, the volume I edited was dedicated to randomness in computation, and I believe that the interplay of *randomness and computation* is crucial to our field, and I'm proud, actually, of the confidence bestowed upon me by the many contributors—who, by the way, are all great leaders in our field—and by the editor of entire series, Franco Preparata. So, I'm very proud of that volume. I liked it, and I still like it.

But let me generalize your question a little bit. I believe that this volume, like other volumes, in whatever form—because the form changes—are occasions of common and focused reflection on what we try to understand, and are very important. To advance a given field, we need original technical contributions. But, somehow, I also find that it's important that, from time to time, we take a little bit of time to record our coordinates in our journey, right? As the saying goes, *how* we got to know things is at least as important as what we know. And I could not agree more. Unfortunately, it's much more efficient to communicate only the sleek proof of whatever we found, ignoring the torturous path that usually leads to it. The path is forgotten, and that is a pity. And those with any experience of scientific discovery know only too well that such a path is very far [laughter] from sleek and linear. No one could exactly guess in advance the conceptual barriers that preceded a solution. "Where were we, conceptually, beforehand?" I find this to be a fascinating aspect of science, too. And it's one which is very hard to reconstruct afterwards.

Personally, I do not subscribe to the theory that history helps us avoid the mistakes of the past. If it does, it may do so only in part, in a very indirect way. But I believe in the history of ideas *for its own sake*. Period. I mean, knowing humanity's past journey may actually make us better men, and, if we are better men, then we can actually do better science. And all this may be true. But if it's not true, I don't care. I still want to know the *history* of our ideas. And this is because, at the end, I really believe that, we develop *one* reality, but I don't believe that there is a *single* reality for us to discover over time, that we just, you know, peel off *the* reality. I think science is a variegated process. We always choose what to discover, and, in that sense, we continually define our own scientific reality. Most people like stories. I think that scientific development is really a fascinating story. So I really believe that once in a while we should really find the time to document the stage of the path we are in. I think that's important. It may slow us down a little bit, but it may also motivate us, right?

Hopefully, it will not stifle us. Because if you start staring at your own navel, pretty much you don't look further up anymore. Nevertheless, I think it's a risk worth taking. Ultimately, if we don't care about how we got here, we may also not consider it important to decide where we want to go.

Ibaraki: Silvio, when I look at your profile of all the things you've done in the past, it's just an incredible profile, just an inspiring list of contributions over so many years. And as a result, you've also won some awards and recognitions. So can you share some valuable experiences and lessons from your prior awards and recognitions?

Micali: Well, OK, valuable or not, you know, my experience seems to follow the following track: First I'm happy, then I'm depressed, then I meet other awardees and I feel better again. That's the trajectory. Somehow I meet these other awardees for the first time, like, let's say, in the induction to an academy. Sometimes I actually have first and very different discussions with these people I always wanted to know, and because these are very motivated people, they tell me about their own goals. These are their goals, not mine. But somehow I realize how worthy and clear their very personal and very different goals are. We live in an era of extreme specialization in science, right? Most of the time, you know, I don't even walk to another floor, and even less to another department. So these I find very special and very motivating moments.

Ibaraki: Silvio, you laid many of the foundational pillars in your pioneering work, and distilling from your experiences, what are the greater burning challenges and research problems for today's youth to solve, to inspire them to go into computing?

Micali: Get into computing! Because computation is everywhere. Perhaps computation is a mental construct that we superimpose to the world, but then we only experience the world via ourselves. So computation is everywhere, in one way or another. So the real questions that I'd like to know and try to induce others to solve is to what extent can we use computation to understand physical, biological, and social laws, and can we perhaps use computation to influence some of these laws? I think these are very big questions, and we need all the manpower we can get to answer them, or even to scratch at their answers.

Ibaraki: It's interesting, your answer kind of reminds me of this folded game where there's these sort of problems of how proteins fold into enzymes, and now they use computers, and just people. They crowdsource it. It's a solution, where they throw it out to math as a people, including middle-schoolers, and they solve problems in this area that couldn't be solved by supercomputers and experienced researchers. Or there's this other online game which they're using to model economic behavior. So it's kind of interesting, this idea that computing is everywhere, and how can it influence some of the other domains that are out there. Or perhaps it is very important, all the other domains out there, and how can we maybe further that work in some way?

Micali: Yeah, I agree, but not only because somehow we can use humans to solve computational problems. Certainly development, embryo development, is an unfolding computation in one way or another, right? But even if you want to look at a particle . . . [laughter] Maybe, a particle follows "the laws." But, also maybe, it actually *computes* where it should go. I wouldn't be surprised of that. We really don't know. I really believe that computation is the development of something. We ourselves in the universe, and anything else are the development of something. I think there ought to be a bit more explanation to gain by understanding computations. For sure in biological systems, but almost also everywhere else.

Ibaraki: Now, again, because of the position that you hold in history, and also in the computing field, but also many other domains, again, this question is directed regarding our youth, to our youth, with an interest in the future of computing, but without the educational foundation, how would you explain your work?

Micali: All right. I said that computation is everywhere, but perhaps I was not able to study much of it. I chose to use computation to model, to study, and to augment our ability to interact with others. I really used computation to cooperate with others while retaining our individuality, our secrets, and to efficiently convince others of what we laboriously found to be true. That's my chosen aspect of computation. That's the one I cherish. That's the one I'd develop. And my hope, for every single one of you, is that you find what is your own aspect and develop that.

Ibaraki: Now, what specific qualities make you excel, and why?

Micali: Oh! I'm going to be very direct and therefore I'm going to be very brief, OK? So, I'd say: the ability to convert emotions into science, creativity, admiration for the past, willingness to gamble the present, and yearning for the future.

Ibaraki: Hey, I like those answers. [laughter]

Micali: Well, like them or not, these are my answers.

Ibaraki: Now, past, present, or future—and you've already discussed this, in a way, when you discussed your journey at the University of Rome and then Berkeley, all these sort of collaborators and people who've mentored you and so on, but can you name three or more who inspire you, and why is this so?

Micali: Well, certainly I'll mention a few names, Stephen. [laughter] But actually let it be known that we'd not have this conversation without the tremendous influence of many other minds and friends, right? Ultimately, we are the people who inspired us. So I've got a few other people I've not yet mentioned but really should be mentioned. One of them is Charlie Rackoff, who was the co-author with Shafi and me of zero-knowledge proofs. Oded Goldreich, with whom we co-authored pseudorandom functions. Independent of that, you know, he just had a great influence, in fact a crucial influence in transforming a set of theorems to a new theory. And Avi Wigderson, without whom zero-knowledge might have remained a quite limited intellectual enterprise. And Ron Rivest was the one, actually, who attracted Shafi and me at MIT and nurtured our career and our intellectual development in innumerable ways. The list could, of course, go on.

But, that said, let me highlight three researchers whose research *style* really most impressed me, right? And these are Alan Turing, Manuel Blum, and Michael Rabin. And what I see in them is an innate ability of solving problems by *conceptualization*. That is, these guys internalize the problem so well, and they metabolize it so thoroughly, that at the end all they have to do is to pick flowers in a sunny field. It is like magic. The problem solves itself. This naturalness, of course, is very hard, [laughter] and maybe a little bit artificial. You have to work very hard for it. But we should always strive towards it.

Ibaraki: Silvio, we're down to our last two questions, and this is pretty open-ended. And I'm telling you, you choose the topic area, and then what do you see as the three top challenges facing us today, and how do you propose they be solved?

Micali: Three top challenges . . . Well, you know, one top challenge should be enough for each one of us, right? Fortunately, there is many of us, [laughter] so we ended up with many challenges. But let me try to multiply mine. The top challenge I see today is, as I mentioned before, really solving the mystery of the brain. How do I propose to solve it? I don't have an exact recipe, but somehow I really believe that, to go after the opportunity, education is going to be crucial. So now we have two challenges: the brain and education.

So why I think they are correlated? Because perhaps the brain puzzle could be solved via one breakthrough, or a cascade of great insights in very rapid succession. But we cannot sit down and wait for one of these events to occur, right? That is hardly a proposal. I'm not the only one to believe that computation would be crucial, as well as biology, for reaching a satisfactory understanding of the brain. I was telling you that Les Valiant has certainly given this a lot of thought. In fact, actually, he's maybe a main motivator for me to think about this idea. But the role of computation in this endeavor is still unclear. We need many more biologists with an *intuitive* understanding of computation. Intuitive doesn't mean simplistic, by the way, but that you know something so well that it comes second nature to you. And we need plenty of computer scientists with an intuitive understanding of biology. I must admit that, at least currently, I'm not one of them. But we don't need one person only, because we cannot put all the bets on one person. If we know who the right one is, so be it. But we need to bring up many and hope to actually nurture the one who really is going to solve the problem, right? So education is crucial, because we need to foster the synergy between biology and computation.

Synergies at some point should really become the norm in science. Right now we are scattering. We are going deeper and deeper in subfields. It's scary. So we need to come together. Certainly for the brain this will be crucial. So an attack maximizing success should include a strong interdisciplinary educational component. And education, I must say, is a challenge, was a challenge, and will always remain a challenge. I actually repeat myself here, because I cannot stress education too much, right? People, at the end, only use—and are motivated by—what they know. So we must continually revise what we know and how we teach what we know. And by understanding the world better, we are able to push knowledge and ideas earlier and earlier in our educational system, and more intuitively, up to, say, middle school. And even before, why not? When, as a society, we care a lot about a problem we must accelerate its solution. We cannot just wait for just this natural percolation in the earlier educational years. We may have to be creative here. And I think one way to be creative—who knows—is allowing faculty members to teach only one course: You teach a course and you take someone else's course, in another discipline. In any case, to enable further and deeper advances, I think we should always find ways to generate shared knowledge more efficiently.

Now, let me go on a limb and mention something else that I think is really a challenge. More a psychological challenge, perhaps, but why not? A main challenge, as I see it, is living outside our planet *very soon*. I view this as a psychological necessity. I think that there is great psychological harm in feeling trapped on the surface of a small physical sphere. And our sphere used to be much bigger not long ago. Of course, there are going to be other "infinities" for us to explore. But, somehow, *physical* exploration, I believe, is in our DNA. I'm sure that if you go back to what I said, I must have used "journey" as a metaphor several times. So I don't know if we can really survive this loss of, quote, "infinite," end quote, physical journeys. I think we are going to be suffering a lot unless we find a solution.

Ibaraki: Just very fascinating, your take on that question. And now we're down to our last question. You've had this very long and distinguished career. What are your top lessons that you want to share with a broad audience?

Micali: All right, if it is the last one, I'm going to revert to my cryptographic roots and be a little bit cryptic, if I may, but hopefully not too obscure. So I think that power is really the symbiosis of opposites. I believe that our emotions are our ultimate power. And that nothing boils down to one thing.

Ibaraki: That's a great closing set of lessons to pass on to our audience, and it reflects the individual that you are, the professional that you are, the remarkable scientist and researcher that you are. And I know your schedule is demanding. You've spent considerable time sharing your deep wisdom with our audience, and we are indeed fortunate, and thank you for coming in today.

Micali: Thank you, Stephen. It's been a great pleasure. [laughter] Thank you for your provocative questions.

Ibaraki: I'm Stephen Ibaraki, and this concludes our exclusive interview with Professor Silvio Micali, ACM Turing Award winner, recipient in 2012, and the Turing Award is widely considered the Nobel Prize of computing. Professor Silvio Micali is also a world-renowned, distinguished researcher and professor at MIT.

The Cryptographic Lens: Shafi Goldwasser's Turing Lecture

I'm very happy to give the talk here at STOC 2014, because the first conference I attended in Computer Science was a STOC conference. It was in 1982 in San Francisco. It was also the first conference that I ever had a paper in, which was on probabilistic encryption. We titled it "Probabilistic Encryption and How to Play Mental Poker Keeping Secret all Partial Information" and it is mentioned in the Turing Award citation. It was the first public talk I ever gave.

The deal with Silvio was that, because he had a STOC paper before, I was going to give the talk. In exchange, I let him speak first this time, and I think it was a mistake. Had I known better, maybe I would have done it differently.[1] But seriously, I'm incredibly thankful to Silvio for all the years of collaboration and friendship and inspiration and advice.

Okay, so today we are in 2014 and it is evident that theoretical computer science has gone a tremendous journey, starting from the 1970s to today. Many fundamental ideas on the nature of computation have been discovered, including nondeterminism, randomness, synchronization, parallelism, fault tolerance, interaction, locality, and more. Back in 1982, a lot of the things that we take as granted today were not known. For example, we didn't know that linear programming, or primality testing, can be done in polynomial time, and so forth. All these grand theorems were proved later.

---

1. Editor's note: But eventually, Shafi's got her way, at least in the sense that her lecture appears before Silvio's (see Chapter 6). A few additional references to that lecture appear in the rest of this text (see, e.g., "Silvio said").

Not only that we as a theoretical field have made amazing algorithmic advances and explored fundamental notions, we've also made a lot of impact on the technology. When started out, theory may have been viewed as the ivory tower esoteric side of computer science, whereas now it's the backbone of search algorithms and secure electronic commerce, routing and load balancing, and much more. We've also had an impact on science. Indeed, many times you hear physicists talk about getting interested in quantum computation due to Shor's algorithm and so forth. So much so that people have coined the phrase *the Computational Lens* to talk about how you can view science, engineering, and technology through the prism of computation, thinking about a computer as an abstract process that happens in biology, physics, the brain, and so forth.

Today, I'm going to talk about a different lens, which I call *the Cryptographic Lens*. I'm going to tell you how looking through this Cryptographic Lens you can view theoretical computer science according to Shafi.

5.1   Historical and Social Perspective

Before we begin the story, let me add that it's interesting historically to notice that two of the grandfathers of the field, Shannon and Turing, the inventor of information theory and the inventor of the Universal computer, were both also known for their work in cryptography. In fact, probably for the popular public, Turing is notable as someone who broke the Enigma machine, the German code, rather than the inventor of the universal Turing machine.

Interestingly, Shannon, worked on two papers at the same time, one was "The Mathematical Theory of Communication," where he introduces information theory. The other one was titled "A Communication Theory of Secrecy Systems," where he defined what it is that you should want from a perfectly private system, how would you achieve it, and what are some bounds on what can be achieved. Apparently, Shannon's own testimony is that these two results were linked to each other. They motivated each other, although one was published before the other, on account of being classified.

My main point here is not so much the love of history—I know very little of it—but that those two guys were motivated in their interest in cryptography by wartime research. The impetus for their work—in fact, I think they met in Princeton at some point during the War—was their interest to win the War. And this is exactly where we depart when we talk about modern cryptography. When we think about modern cryptography, we don't think just about fighting some bad guys, an enemy, a wartime effort. Modern cryptography was born at a time when computers and communication using computers were becoming available beyond the military, and when people were trying to think of how this progress could be used for economic growth. Furthermore, the bulk of the work in the theory of cryptography in the last 30 years concentrates on the correctness and privacy of computation. Not just dedicated to protecting communication over enemy lines.

There are sort of three bullets that I'd like to hit on in this talk. One is that modern cryptography has enabled a lot of—in my opinion—fascinating computational phenomena, which seem paradoxical in nature. The second is that it has been a catalyst for many notions and techniques that led to a series of intellectual leaps—new paradigms of thought—in theoretical computer science. And third, I believe that cryptographic research has not only enabled these paradoxical and beautiful abilities in the past, as well as led to progress in theory at large, it has a promising future in front of it. This is because today we have a tremendous amount of data out there and tremendous connectivity, which present a truly pressing question: *Now what? It's all out there, can we still keep some basic rights for privacy in this world?*

Judge Brandeis said, in 1890, that "we have a basic right to be left alone." That is a great quote. Can we still be "left alone" in some sense in this day and age? I think that cryptography and its tools—some of which I'll tell you about—provides our best chance to somewhat be left alone. So, I know that Silvio says we should interact all the time, but sometimes we want to just be left alone. I mean there's some merit, also, to that.

5.2 A List of Wonders

Let me start with a list of some catalytic, paradoxical abilities that crypto makes possible. Obviously, I'm not going to talk about all of them, but let me just mention them in brief. Many people here are familiar with this list, mainly because cryptography is very accessible—there's something very sexy about it. Possibly, some of you, even when you were in grade school, have tried to come up with codes and break codes.

First and foremost, I would put public key cryptography, the fact that people can exchange secret information without ever meeting, an amazing concept. You now all take it for granted, but to start with, it seems absolutely impossible.

The second one is the fact that it is possible for two people sitting in remote places around the world to actually sign a contract simultaneously. Obviously, they cannot do it simultaneously. Information must travel from one to the other before it travels back, but yet we can emulate the simultaneity using cryptographic means.

A third one is that starting from very little true randomness, we can generate deterministically very long strings that will behave, for all practical purposes, like long random strings.

Next is that we can prove theorems without revealing anything about the proof; that is, zero-knowledge proofs, which I'll talk more about. Furthermore, we can play games, digital games virtually around the world with each other, without access to physical card games or boards, and without referees, and actually be able to trust the result when somebody is declared a winner. Again, this is due to underlying cryptographic ideas.

We can retrieve information from databases, where the database doesn't know what information we are after. These days, we can even compute on encrypted data without decrypting it, and much more.

A Common Theme.   This looks like a laundry list. You could give a course on each one of them. What's in common among all these inventions? The unifying theme, among all of this—generating some random numbers, proving theorems in zero-knowledge, and so forth—is the presence of an adversary, which is an integral part of the definition of the problem.

Note that also in an introduction to algorithms class, we talk about adversaries. When we prove that an algorithm runs in a certain amount of time, we can do so by proving that even for an adversarially chosen input, the worst input, the algorithm runs quickly. This talk of an adversary, however, is different in cryptography because we're not talking about analysis, but really about the definition of the problem in itself—there wouldn't be a problem to solve if there was no adversary.

For example, if two people communicate, and there is no curious adversary in the world, why the heck would they encrypt? It only makes sense if somebody is trying to listen. And if there's a mathematical statement, which I claim I proved to be true, why should I provide the proof unless you suspect that the claim is false and my proof is wrong. In other words, the proof is needed only because an adversarial claim and a false argument is a possibility. And when you talk about randomness, I would ask randomness with respect to whom?

Adversaries are an integral part of the definition of problems in cryptography, and as such, the quality of the adversary is going to determine also the quality of the solution. We will say that a solution is good or bad for a problem, depending on who the adversary is. Finally, as Silvio said, this approach is the key to how we can analyze any complex system because if we could show that such a system works in the presence of an adversary, then the system would work under all eventualities.

What is the power of this adversary? We're going to make no assumption on its strategy. We're not going to say that we know how he behaves and prove a system secure with respect to this particular adversary. The adversary is going to be worst case. However, we will make the assumption, through almost all that I'll talk about, although not everything, that the adversary cannot work for as much time as he wants, he doesn't have an infinite amount of space or time. He has only a polynomial amount of resources. We choose this limitation because it's realistic, and because it gives us great power. Once we think of the adversary as computationally bounded, we can achieve the paradoxical seeming abilities above. If he wasn't computationally bounded, many of these tasks can be shown to be impossible, but when we have computational limitations on the power of the adversary, we can achieve the amazing abilities of cryptography.

5.3 Two Axioms

I'd like to give you two axioms that we use, in cryptography, when we prove our results. The first is called "computational indistinguishability."

Computational Indistinguishability.   Look at this picture. There is the adversary sitting on one side of a wall and on the other side there is one of two probability distributions. We can view them as distributions over k-bit strings, D1 and D2. The adversary wants to know whether he's interacting with Distribution 1 or Distribution 2. He presses a button, and gets a sample. He can ask for a polynomial number of samples, and at the end will declare a verdict. We will say that the distributions are indistinguishable (by him) if he cannot tell from looking at a polynomial number of samples whether he was getting samples from D1 or getting samples from D2. In that case, we say that, to the cryptographic adversary, these two distributions are effectively the same.

This will enable us to talk about D1 being the same as D2, D2 as D3, D3 as D4, and so on. We can start manipulating these probability distributions and reach interesting conclusions at the end about what is and isn't indistinguishable from each other. This type of definition or axiom has been applied to encryption, to pseudorandomness, to simultaneity, and verifying correctness. Let me show you how through a couple of examples.

So, the first example, is how to define secure encryption, at least in that original paper from 1982. The idea is the following. What would be the two distributions? The first distribution might be the encryption of one message. Since the encryption algorithm can be probabilistic, many ciphertexts may exist for the same message.

So, one distribution are the ciphertexts for one message, and the other distribution are the ciphertexts for another message. And the requirement is that the adversary cannot tell them apart; that is, the adversary cannot tell whether an encryption is of one message or the other. The adversary cannot tell this in polynomial time, no matter how many examples he sees of encryptions of message M1 versus message M2. He can't tell which is which. If so, then the encryption system is called secure. If a scheme satisfies such security, then it can be shown that ciphertexts will hide all partial information about the underlying messages.

What's another place you could apply this type of definition? How about randomness? I think Avi talked earlier today about pseudo-random generators. Lets think about randomness. What are the distributions now? One is the distribution over say all k-bit strings, which is a totally random k-bit string. And the other distribution is over a smaller set of pseudorandom strings. Now, an adversary would like to know whether he's looking at truly random strings or at pseudorandom ones. So he asks for samples and after awhile he declares, "I think I know which is which." But if he can't tell them apart, that is cannot tell whether he is getting random strings or pseudorandom strings, then we say that these pseudorandom strings were generated by a good pseudorandom generator.

What does this mean? It means that you can use these pseudorandom bits in any application that runs in polynomial time and it will be as good as using random bits. For example, you could use these pseudorandom bits for choosing which patient to give a placebo versus the real drug to. You could use these bits in any application that needs randomness as long as it runs in polynomial time. The application should perform just as well when using pseudorandom sequences as it will perform using truly random sequences. Clearly, this is the right definition. Furthermore, one can show that pseudorandom number generators and pseudorandom functions exist, if one-way functions exist.

One more example is in the context of obfuscation, and this is very timely, as there's a lot of research now in cryptography on obfuscation. I don't know if some of you have heard of it. What does obfuscation mean? Say there is a program which we want to scramble or hide its internals so that an adversary will not know how to reverse engineer it. How would you define this goal formally? One way to define it, using computational indistinguishability, would be to take two programs with the same input–output relation and let one distribution be all of the obfuscated versions of one program and the second distribution all of the obfuscated versions of the second program. Then demand that you should not be able to distinguish whether you are getting an obfuscation of the first program or of the second one. That's the definition of indistinguishable obfuscation. You can—it turns out—construct programs, which satisfy this definition under some computational assumptions. This seems a very strong definition, which enables a lot of applications that you may want from the intuitive obfuscation of programs. That's it for the first axiom.

The Simulation Paradigm.   Sometimes, the adversary does not just sit behind a curtain, pressing buttons and looking at samples. Sometimes the adversary is part of the system itself. He may be one of the parties within the system. He's not sitting on the outside looking in. How would we talk about being secure in the presence of such an adversary? What we say then is that the insider's view, being an insider, should give him zero extra knowledge. But how would we define that? Essentially, we say that if he could have simulated the conversation, on his own, sitting at home, it gives zero extra knowledge to be an insider.

This is what's called the simulation paradigm; again, it essentially says that if the adversary could simulate the execution on his own, he might as well stay at home. He gains nothing from actually being in a protocol. So the protocol does not introduce any vulnerability. Of course, he might gain something, which is the stated goal of the system, say buying something on Amazon. But the issue is that he doesn't learn anything beyond the stated goal of the system. If you can show protocols that have this kind of strength, then you can show that they can be composed maintaining security.

To summarize, these two notions are useful to the way we think as cryptographers: Computational indistinguishability and simulation. Let's now move on to the catalytic developments—that I was referring to earlier—in theoretical computer science.

5.4 Impact on Theory of Computation at Large

I'm going to have a few threads here, starting with the one that's probably most well known. I'll elaborate on the *zero-knowledge proofs* thread, which led to the notion of probabilistically checkable proofs, which morphed into many other probabilistic verification systems, and down the line to surprising results on the hardness of approximation problems. I've listed it first, both because it's well known, and because of implications of this development for research today on how to delegate computations to the Cloud.

Another development thread is that of *pseudorandomness*. Pseudorandom number generators and functions were also a very early cryptographic goal, because we wanted to generate lots of randomness to use in our randomized cryptographic algorithms. And it turned out that there was an interesting duality between computational hardness and randomness, and you could generate randomness based on hardness. But they had other very surprising applications. The first application is that if you have a pseudorandom number generator, you can use it to derandomize complexity classes. That makes sense. Maybe what makes less sense is that it works so well. Next, using pseudorandom functions, we can present "concept classes" that are not PAC learnable. So, it yields examples of the impossibility of representation independent learning for concepts that are in low level complexity classes. Finally, pseudorandom functions are behind some impossibility of lower bound using natural proofs, as shown by Razborov and Rudich.

Let's go on. This is one of my favorites threads, as it is an unusual development. In cryptography, we want one-way functions whose pre-images have parts that are "really hard" to compute, called hard-core bits. Hard-core bits should be essentially impossible to guess better than 50–50. The first result about hard-core bits for general functions was proved by Goldreich and Levin, with a very interesting proof, which although set out to establish a cryptographic goal, ended up showing how to come up with a polynomial-time *list-decoding* algorithm for Hadamard Codes. Now, Hadamard is a well-known error-correcting code. This was the beginning of an incredible development in error correction, where list-decoding became almost the rule rather than the exception, whereas before its existence for natural codes was an open question in information theory, in the error-correcting code research community. All of a sudden there was list-decoding of Reed–Solomon codes, by Madhu's famous work, followed by a long list of works till today, where work of Guruswami et al. gives list-decoding of explicit codes that meet the list-decoding bound. This is an truly surprising development, going from a proof technique that shows you how the inversion of a function is equivalent to predicting a single bit about its pre-image, to fundamental progress in list-decoding.

The next one is regarding *oblivious transfer*. Oblivious transfer is a seemingly strange mechanism that Michael Rabin invented when he visited Berkeley one summer. For cryptographers this is a natural mechanism; for others it may seem bizarre. The idea of oblivious transfer is that there are two parties, one of which intends to send the other party some information, but instead of just sending it, we want the information to be transmitted obliviously, without the sender knowing whether it was successfully delivered or not. Although this may seem of dubious merit, it turns out to be incredibly fundamental for cryptography, and has led to—among other things—the concept of private information retrieval (PIR). With a PIR you can search a remote database, say lookup keywords in a patent database, without enabling the database to know which keyword you were looking for. Of course, I can't show you the reduction, but there's a direct connection from oblivious transfer. And PIR, in turn, has led to other research, on locally decodable codes. These are error-correcting codes where you can recover partial information about the encoded data without looking at the entire corrupted codeword but only looking at a small number of places in the corrupted codeword. This is of incredible significance, also practical significance. These days we already have linear-rate codes with sublinear decoding time.

Finally, my last thread, although not the last development, is about techniques. So far, we've talked about results, models, and questions that led to other questions. What about techniques? At the heart of cryptographic security proofs, the goal is to force the adversary to solve impossibly difficult computational problems. In a cryptographic setting, it's not good enough for these difficult problems to be hard on a worst-case instance. They must be hard on an average-case instance. Thus, we need techniques for mapping worst case instances to average case instances, such as *random self-reducibility techniques*. When you can reduce solving any worst-case instance to solving an average-case instance, the conclusion is that if the problem is hard at all, then it is hard on the average. Equivalently, if a problem is easy on an average instance, then it's easy everywhere.

Through further work on program checking and so forth, the next idea was to show how this mapping can work between different problems and not just different instances of the same problem. Say that, in order to check a global property of a combinatorial object, you would *translate checking the global property to checking average local properties*. This is the fundamental technique of property testing. We want to test global properties by making a few local random tests, and therefore be able to work in sublinear time rather than linear or more.

Finally, I'm not going to recount the impact of trying to break RSA on improvements in integer factoring and on Quantum computation. Those are sort of obvious.

5.5 Following One Thread

What I'd like to do now is to follow one of these threads in more detail, to give you an idea of how the development took place. As Silvio said, classical proofs are attributed to very famous mathematicians, well some more, some less. But they all have the same blueprint. There is a theorem to prove, you start from some axioms, follow intermediate reductive steps, and at the end, QED. That's how classical proofs work. However, one component is omitted: the verifier, who has to read these proofs.

I would like now to give the *verifier* his proper place and separate it out. Whereas the prover may work very hard and solve computationally hard problems, we want to make sure that the verifier can check the proof in polynomial time. These are the kind of proofs we're going to be interested in.

What's an example? Take an equation in n Boolean variables, which is difficult to solve, and a prover who claims there exists a solution to the equation. One way to convince the verifier that the equation can be solved is for the prover to come up with a solution to the equation and send it to the verifier. All the verifier has to do is plug the solution into the equation and see if it solvable. If so, the verifier says, yes, I believe there exists a solution to the equation. And if not, the verifier says I don't believe it, I reject it, this is an unconvincing proof.

The Knowledge Communicated by Proofs.   Notice however that the verifier did not only learn that there is a solution to the equation, he also learned a particular solution. We ask "Is there any other way? Is it possible that the verifier will be convinced there is a solution, but won't get any idea of what the solution is?"

This is a cryptographer's concern. Rather than learning from a proof, we want to show that the theorem is true and reveal nothing else. And the answer is, that it is possible. And the crux of the idea is for the prover to say, "I am not going to give you the solution, but will prove to you that I could if I felt like it." If the verifier is convinced that the prover could provide a solution if she felt like it, he knows there is a solution.

How do you do it? How do you convince one that there exists a solution by proving that you could show it if you felt like it? You use randomness and interaction. Here is an example—it's really the first example, in that original paper, with Silvio—and indeed we're looking at a particular equation. The equation is a very simple equation. It is $Q = X^2 \pmod{N}$, where Q and N are part of the description of the equation.

If N is hard to factor, then it is a hard equation to solve. If N is easy to factor, it's easy to solve. As the prover is powerful, she can factor N and solve the equation, and compute X. However, she wants to convince the verifier, that naive guy, that there exists a solution without giving it. So how does she do it? The idea here is that she essentially comes up with two other equations, one is a random equation, $S = R^2 \pmod{N}$, the other one is the product of the random equation and the original one, $QS = (XR)^2 \pmod{N}$. If both are solvable, then the original one is as well.

The prover says, "Look at these two equations $S = Y^2 \pmod{N}$ and $QS = Z^2 \pmod{N}$. I will solve one of them for you—the first one or the second one. You choose which one." The verifier then chooses at random whether he wants to see a solution of the first equation or the second. The point is that if the original equation has no solution, then at least one of the two equations has no solution, and there is at least a 50–50 chance that the verifier will ask for that one and catch the prover at a mistake. And if we repeat this again and again, and the prover provides each time new random equations, the chance she can actually satisfy the verifier's questions when there isn't a solution to the original one, is extremely small. On the other hand, the verifier gets nothing from this interaction, except for being convinced of the validity of the original claim, since he could generate the interaction by himself. We call this zero-knowledge because he never sees both solutions, and therefore can never derive the original.

This is just an example, but to some degree, all zero-knowledge proofs work this way. We take a classical proof, somehow transform it into another one that is split into pieces such that only if all of them are true the original proof exists. Then the prover only exposes few of the pieces, which the verifier chooses at random. Goldreich, Micali, and Wigderson's theorem showing 3-colorability, and therefore any NP language, has a zero-knowledge interactive membership proof, works in the same fashion.

Interactive Proofs. Embedded here is *a new notion of a proof, an interactive proof*. The parties interact for some time, and the required property is that if the theorem is correct, then the verifier will accept, and if the theorem is incorrect, the verifier will reject with extremely high probability. There is some small quantifiable chance that the verifier will be convinced of an incorrect theorem.

Although zero-knowledge was very influential for cryptography and so forth, perhaps even more importantly it was a catalyst. It was really the first time that we decoupled verifying correctness of the theorem, from knowledge of the proof. And once we've done this mental separation, we were now willing to accept these kind of mechanisms as proofs, or "interactive proofs," could start asking new questions about what is a proof. For example:

- Can this kind of proof be used to prove harder theorems than those you could prove by writing a proof in a book?
- Can it be more efficient to prove this way?
- Are there other forms of probabilistic verification?

These are the type of questions that have been asked and answered in the last 25 years.

Indeed, we may ask what's interactively provable. With classical polynomial-size proofs, we can verify membership in NP languages. How about coNP? That is, can we prove that an equation has no solutions? Can we verify how many solutions the equation has? An amazing result by Fortnow, Karloff, Lund, Nissan and then Shamir showed that you can verify more with interaction and randomness than with classical proofs. You can, in fact, not only show that there exists a solution to the equation, but that there are no solutions, exactly K solutions, and most generally verify correctness of any polynomial space computation.

Multi-Prover Interactive Proofs.   Fabulous. Amazing! But we were not satisfied yet. We asked, how about other ways to define proofs? The next step was what I call "the arrival of the second prover." This is joint work with Avi, Ben-Or, and Kilian. We asked the following: What if we added another prover? To begin with, it seems like it's a frivolous idea, because we allowed the first prover to take as much time as she wants. Why would another prover be of any use? Because what we do is to separate the two provers, and allow the verifier to ask questions and interact with each one separately but adaptively. Namely, each prover will not see the questions the verifier is asking of the other prover, but these questions may be related or even depend on the answers that the verifier obtained from the other prover, akin to two suspects in a crime interrogated by the police (the verifier) while sitting in separate jail cells.

Why would you expect this mechanism to be powerful? The idea is that by comparing their answers, you might be able to catch them in an inconsistency if there was no real proof of the statement at hand that they both claim to know. And if the statement at hand is correct and a classical proof does exist, then the two provers can always be consistent. Back to the analogy of interrogating suspects, by asking them the right carefully chosen questions, chosen via a random process, which they couldn't have predicted in advance, we will be able to catch them and disprove their alibi, or disprove the correctness of their proof.

Going back to cryptography being a catalyst, when we introduced the second prover, we thought that it was useful for removing assumptions from cryptographic constructions. As I mentioned, GMW proved that NP is in Zero-Knowledge. That's actually under the assumption that one-way functions exist. We instead wanted to prove an unconditional result, and in fact, we showed that, with these two provers, you can convince a verifier of membership in an NP language, unconditionally, maintaining zero knowledge, soundness and completeness.

However, we were unprepared for the fact that this second prover seemed to be kind of a game-changer in terms of recognizing more languages, which was shown shortly after by Babai, Fortnow, and Lund. What they showed is that—actually— two provers, guys, can convince the verifier of even harder statements than ones in PSPACE. That is, statements that require nondeterministic exponential time to verify. Now this is an exponential gap in power from NP proofs. Classically, in a textbook, noninteractive NP-type proof, you can verify membership in NP languages. With two provers, interactively, you can verify membership in NEXPTIME languages. To prove this, a key concept that was used was linearity testing, developed in the work on program self-testing and self-correcting by Blum, Luby, and Rubinfeld.

As beautiful as it is, one may dismiss this latter development as merely building towers of abstractions in the air, using the language of probabilistically verifiable proofs to capture previously defined complexity classes such as #P, PSPACE, and nondeterministic exponential time. Does this teach us anything of significance for "down to earth" questions beyond intellectual beauty?

Indeed it does. We can scale down this result on two provers capturing NEXPTIME problems, and address the verifiability of classical NP problems more efficiently. The intuition is that since the verifier could verify NEXPTIME problems in polynomial time, receiving polynomial size messages from the provers, it is possible that he could verify simpler NP statements with even less resources.

This was established in a sequence of works, starting with Babai, Fortnow, Levin, and Szegedy, followed by Feige, Goldwasser, Lovasz, Safra, and Szegedy, who also made a connection to hardness of approximation for NP-Hard problems. Whereas in these two works the hope was to get shorter proof, perhaps logarithmic in size, it turned out—in follow-up work by Arora–Safra and Arora–Lund–Motwani–Sudan–Szegedy—that you can in fact verify NP statements in polynomial time by interacting with a constant number of provers. The verifier uses only logarithmic amount of randomness and reads a constant number of bits in the proof to be assured that, with constant probability, he can find a mistake in a fallacious proof.

As people know this has led to much insight on the hardness of approximation problems. I won't get into that. I do want to give you an idea of why these two provers enable more succinct proofs than possible interacting with a single prover. Let's look at an example.

Say the verifier is given a set of linear equations mod 2, each equation here is a function of 3 Boolean variables. And he is promised that one of two cases holds. Either almost all these equations are satisfiable—say, 99% of them—or at most 50% are satisfiable. The prover claims that in fact the first case holds; that is, more than 99% of the equations are satisfiable. A single prover could convince the verifier of this fact by solving 99% of them, and sending over to the verifier—to check—the solution that satisfies 99% of the equations. The length of this proof is essentially

n, the size of the assignment. Not too bad, but it's still as big as the size of the problem. What can two provers do to improve on this?

In the case of two provers, the verifier does the following: Choose a random equation, go to one prover and ask "Hey, could you tell me the value of the 3 variables that appear in this equation, for the solution that satisfies 99% of the equations?" The prover gives the value of the requested 3 variables, 3 bits. Then the verifier turns to the second prover, who doesn't know which equation was chosen, chooses one of the 3 variables at random, and asks its value from the second prover. If the value of the variable in question is the same in both answers, the verifier will accept, else he will reject.

Now if there is a 99% satisfying solution, the first prover gives the verifier the values for that equation, and the second prover always gives the corresponding value of the requested variable. The verifier gets a consistent answer, he accepts. However, if there is no assignment satisfying more than 50% of these equations, then there is no strategy for the two provers to not be caught in inconsistent answers with probability at least half.

What I'm claiming is that we have a new proof system for an NP-complete problem, shown by Hastad, in which the verifier receives 4 bits and will catch a mistake with probability at least half. This should give you an idea of why verifying inconsistency is so powerful, and allows you to communicate so much less and yet catch a mistake in a proof.

I want to say that this method of using two provers in order to check the correctness of a statement has been shown in a completely different arena recently; specifically, to enable two quantum polynomial-time machines to convince a classical verifier of the correctness of the computation.

5.6 The Future

I promised that there are three bullets. One was paradoxical abilities, two was catalytic, and three was the future. And for the future, as usual, we only have five minutes.

Let us talk a little bit about the future. As we know, the world of computation has evolved, and these days we have a big Cloud and a small computer, whereas before we had a big computer and a small Cloud. The whole paradigm of computation is changing, with a migration of data, photographs, DNA information, our documents, our financial information—everything is migrating to the Cloud, because we put it there, because someone has collected information about us.

It's not only migration of data but there's migration of computation. In the future, all computation will be done in the Cloud. We will only have a device that sends inputs and receives outputs. This globalization of knowledge and connectivity is quite impressive as well as what we can gain in terms of saving on local storage and computation. It can help us in medical research, energy usage, traffic rerouting, and much more. It is hard to summarize all the beautiful things that can be done by being able to know so much.

However, there's also enormous risk in this globalization of knowledge. And some of the risks are that we lose control. Whereas before, the computation was done at home, now it's been done somewhere else. And what do I know if the computation is done correctly? We lose privacy as well. We lose the "right to be left alone." We lose fairness. They know so much about me, they might profile me, they might charge me more than I should be charged, they might not accept me to graduate school, and so forth.

The question is: Can we essentially advance as a society without losing these rights to the extent we have them today? Can we not relinquish individual control entirely? I think that cryptography's magic offers us a hope.

Even in what I've shown, verification in zero-knowledge means that you don't have to see the proof to verify the correctness of a computation, and in a similar way, computation on data doesn't necessarily mean that you have to see the data. There is indeed a host of techniques that have been developed since the '80s, and matured remarkably in the last 5, 6 years, to this end. We should do exactly that. These techniques show how you can compute on data without actually seeing it.

Let me just sort of very quickly breeze through the kind of problems that people are working on these days, on Cloud computing, using cryptography. First thing is verifying correctness of computation in the cloud: *Trust but check*.

Instead of trusting the Cloud, what we'd like to do is tell the Cloud, "Hey, listen, why don't you compute and then prove the results?" Of course, I would like to take much less time than the cloud did, as the whole point is that I (the verifier) is much weaker. So, I want the kind of proofs, which are extremely efficient to verify. What would be the proof, interactive proof, the Cloud would say, "I actually ran the program for this F, and that's the result." As we said IP is equal to PSPACE. Are we done?

The problem is that these original results were about the complexity classes. They didn't care about specific computation. And they went through complete problems. So, if you link up these results, the work that the Cloud is going to have to do, in order to do the proofs, is going to be more than polynomial time. The modern challenge is that you want to make sure that the Cloud, when it gives you a proof, doesn't have to work much harder to come up with that efficient proof. We want both to verify superefficiently, but also the Cloud should not lose too much time in overhead.

This is an area of extremely active research. The results change depending on whether you use interactive proof, which doesn't make any assumptions on the computational power of the cheating Cloud, or you want a computationally sound proof like Silvio discussed in his talk. There's incredible progress there. There's a paper in this conference, by Kalai, Raz, and Rothblum, who show how to take any time T computation, and add only linear time overhead on top of what the prover has to do.

Now, what's nice about these results is, again, that they have also this catalytic flavor to them, in that people are now aiming to go from theory to practice, applying a lot of these techniques to real-life programs. Writing compilers, designing hardware, to take real programs and attach a proof to them quickly.

What's the second challenge? The second challenge concerns privacy in the Cloud. Do I really want to give the Cloud all my data? I could encrypt everything that I put in the Cloud, but once I encrypt it, how is the Cloud going to do computations on it now that it's encrypted? *Can we maintain privacy, and get utility?*

That is a beautiful question posed by Rivest, Adelman, and Dertouzos many years ago, and there have been an amazing trailblazing progress in the last few years, in how to compute on encrypted data. New forms of encryption have been invented to do exactly that. The most famous one is the *Fully Homomorphic Encryption* scheme by Gentry, presented in 2009, where he shows an encryption scheme, where you could evaluate arbitrary polynomial-time functions on the encrypted domain.

When this was first shown, it was very slow, and it used assumptions we were unfamiliar with. There has been incredibly rapid progress since. At this point, the best assumption—as far as I know—is as good as the best nonhomomorphic cryptographic scheme based on lattices. Furthermore, a tremendous amount of money was poured in by DARPA and other agencies to go from theory to practice.

Third challenge: Okay, so we can encrypt our data in the Cloud, we can get proofs that everything is correct. We can utilize the Cloud as computation engine. What else? What else do we want? Well, we don't necessarily always want to go back to the client with encrypted data and say, "Hey, here is your answer, you can decrypt it." We want to do more than that. We want to aggregate information in the Cloud and be able to compute on it and get the result. And this is the third challenge: Can we encrypt data in the Cloud and allow the server to extract partial information on this encrypted data and nothing else, without explicitly coming back to the client who would decrypt the result of the computation each time?

This would be useful for medical research, for traffic information, and so forth, where can each server extract the information relevant to them and only that. The answer in principal is, yes. But before I give you the *how*, I want to give you two beautiful applications.

Suppose you are a hospital, with loads of medical records. They're all encrypted. The hospital is not allowed to reveal to the drug company, let's say, these medical records because the patients didn't give them the authority to do so. But the drug company wants to run an algorithm that checks for a gene presence in a cohort of patients. They don't really care about looking at the entire medical file. Can it be done and if so, how?

Another example is surveillance searching for suspects in photographs. Imagine surveillance cameras would produce only encrypted photographs. Yet to make these photos useful, you want to evaluate a comparison to a suspect database. Could you do that? Could you just find out if there's a suspect in the picture, and if so, get the picture decrypted. Can I just extract that information and nothing else?

Surprisingly, this seems possible in principle. A new type of encryption called *functional encryption* was introduced in 2005 by Sahai and Waters, to do just that. It is a special encryption scheme, where for every program that you want to run on data, there will be a special key that enables you to do just that, given the encryption of the data, and nothing else. One program, one key. Another program, another key. And so forth. Where are these keys coming from? There is a master key that not only enables to decrypt, but also to come up with these auxiliary keys, which enable someone just to compute specific functions. It's a beautiful concept. And raises beautiful questions. The progress has been to first address some interesting functions, then for any polynomial time computation in a way that increases the cipher-text size, then for multiple keys, and so forth.

5.7 Concluding Remarks

My talk has been long. There are two takeaway messages, before I express my thanks.

First of all, our physical intuition today shouldn't constrict our expectations from the digital privacy of tomorrow. Often, even if a goal may seem paradoxical in nature, once you define it the right way, find the right model, and add the cryptographic toolbox, you can achieve it.

Second, given how much progress we made in complexity theory in the past by thinking cryptographically, it may be worthwhile exploring how today's new methods such as Fully Homomorphic, Functional Encryption, and so on, would affect the complexity theory of tomorrow.

Finally, I want to thank my co-authors everywhere, but specifically the ones I mentioned in the talk. I've co-authored with lots of people whose results I mentioned, but there's always the Unknown Soldier out there.

I also want to thank my mentors in Berkeley and at MIT: Manuel Blum, Dick Karp, and Ron Rivest, and my fabulous students, which are phenomenal. More than all, I am forever grateful to my family for tolerating me so very well all this time, thank you.

Proofs, According to Silvio: Silvio Micali's Turing Lecture

Good afternoon, everybody!

It's an honor and a pleasure to be here, and it's even more of an honor and more of a pleasure to be here together with Shafi. When the two of us strategized on what to talk about in our Turing lectures, we decided to talk about proofs and agreed on how to carve this huge topic between us. Shafi and I work together quite well. But I'm not sure we coordinate that well. . . . Hence, the qualification "According to Silvio" makes sure that my lecture represents my own take about proofs. I hope Shafi covers the rest.

My lecture is articulated in three sections: Thanks, Science, and Advice. If you get lost, just wait for the next section.

6.1 Thanks

If I am before you today, it's because I have many thanks to give. But I'll be brief.

I'd like to thank my family (including my original one): my parents Giovanni and Franca; my sister Aurea; my wife Daniela; and our kids Stefano and Enrico.

I'd like to thank my teachers: Corrado Böhm, for lovingly luring me from mathematics to computer science; Shimon Even, for introducing me to algorithms; and Dick Karp, Manuel Blum, and Andy Yao, for providing me a lifetime of inspiration. In particular, I'd like to thank Manuel for introducing me to cryptography, and for simply being the best advisor one can hope to have. At the time of my arrival, Berkeley was, to computer science, what Göttingen must have been for mathematics at the beginning of the last century. With Dick, Manuel, and Andy, I found myself at a place and time of revolutionary progress. And I was terrified.

Thankfully, I was helped by my fellow students. In this picture, David Lichtenstein appears in his traditional *rhetorical* pose, Vijay Vazirani in his traditional *defiant* pose, Michael Sipser in his traditional *cool* pose. The picture was taken by Michael Luby, appearing in here in his traditional *pensive* pose. I really could not have survived the big stress, conceptual and otherwise, that Berkeley was for me, without their scientific and human help. In particular, I'd like to thank them for smartly decoding my Italian, and kindly ignoring my English.

Most of all, I'd really like to thank my best friend, Shafi, shown here in our Berkeley days. As you know, Shafi is a very interactive person. In fact, thanks to her multiple personalities, we could pack more interaction in a single day of joint work than less fortunate souls could pack in a year. And interact we did, for many years. We produced many works we are both proud of. We were fortunate in our scientific quest. Fortune, they say, favors the prepared. If this is so, then it must have made a huge exception, because in our case it favored the naïve and the shameless, but also the fearless. In fact, I must admit, we were totally *unprepared* to achieve the goals that we set forward for ourselves. I thus feel doubly fortunate that we actually managed to achieve them! But, work aside, the best thing for me is that, after so many years, Shafi and I remain best friends. Given the personalities involved, this really is a sort of miracle. So, thank you Shafi!

I'd like to thank that special place that is MIT, and my two guardian angels there, Ron Rivest and Barbara Liskov. In particular, many thanks to Ron for continuing to be a scientific and human mentor to me. I'd like to thank my other wonderful colleagues—indeed, the best colleagues one can hope for.

My deep thanks to my stupendous Ph.D. students, Paul Feldman, Claude Crépau, Bonnie Berger, Mihir Bellare, Phil Rogaway, Rafail Ostrovsky, Shai Halevi, Ray Sidney, Rosario Gennaro, Moses Liskov, Leo Reyzin, Abhi Shelat, Matt Lepinski, Chris Paikert, Rafael Pass, Paul Valiant, Jing Chen, Pablo Azar, Alessandro Chiesa, and Zeyuan Zhu, for injecting so many ideas in my mind and so much warmth in my heart.

Special thanks to my wonderful neighbors, Michael Rabin, Les Valiant, and Leonid Levin; and my neighbors in spirit, Charlie Rackoff, Oded Goldreich, and Avi Wigderson for so many years of fun and science together, a truly heavenly combination.

Finally, I'd like to thank our magnificent field. Last century, as it was said, was meant to be the Century of the Atom, and it was instead the Century of the Computer. The introduction of the computer in human history has been almost as momentous as the invention of fire. Computation has really revolutionized the world and us. Even more, since I am a theoretician, it has revolutionized the way we think about the world and ourselves.

The charge of the light brigade at Balaclava, vividly recalled here in the painting of Richard Canton Woodville Jr., admittedly was a low-tech affair. But it may be the best way to convey the impetus, the courage, and the intellectual ferocity with which we are contributing not only to our own field, but also to other great fields like biology, economics, quantum mechanics—you name it. I am mighty proud to belong to such a generous and insatiable community. So, thank you all for being such a community.

I would have more thanks to give, but wish instead to leave you with two suggestions: (1) We really are those who have influenced us, and (2) Science is a collective adventure.

6.2 Science

The evolution of the notion of a proof has taken more than two thousand years. But I will summarize it in just 30 minutes: a real bargain! So, a better title for this section would be "History of Proofs (Abridged)."

Classical Proofs. In my tradition, the classical notion of a proof started in ancient Greece and ended up with Gödel and Turing. The traditional iconography of these two extraordinary individuals shows them older and marked by the hardships of life. But I love to recall them in the glory of their student days, as we all should be recalled, young and invincible. Here are their photos. Even though they had very different approaches—very formalistic the first, very intuitive the second—they agreed on one thing: Proofs are strings satisfying special syntactic properties. In one formalization, a proof consists of a sequence of lines of text. In a line, you can invoke an axiom. In another line, you may invoke a derivation rule. And so on. If, in the last line, you manage to write down the statement of the theorem you care about, the theorem is proven.

The Need for Efficiency. Classical proofs ignore efficiency. But, in my opinion, efficiency is really crucial to differentiate the notions of "truth" and "proof." Truth is something that you can achieve *on your own*, in isolation. Proof is a *social* process, involving, at least implicitly, two different actors: a "prover" and a "verifier." This social process is truly meaningful only if the prover helps the verifier to ascertain more efficiently the truthfulness of a given statement. Indeed, should the time required to verify a proof be (essentially) equal to that required to find the proof, there wouldn't be much use for mathematicians!

So, which proofs are efficient?

NP. In the '70s, Steve Cook, Dick Karp, and Leonid Levin proposed the notion of NP, short for *nondeterministic polynomial time*. (Too "techy," right? We should hire a good PR firm!) Colloquially speaking, NP proofs are strings that are short (i.e., polynomially long in the length of a statement) and easily (i.e., polynomial-time) verifiable.

Interactive Proofs. About a decade later, Shafi, Charlie (Rackoff), and I, and independently Babai and Moran, somehow stopped looking at proofs as purely syntactic objects, and started looking at them as interactive processes. Very much like those we remember from our good old school days, when proofs were Q&A sessions in a classroom. To keep things simple, interactive proofs can be formalized as special games. Let me be the prover, you the verifier, and S a statement we care about. We both know (e.g., via a classical proof) that, corresponding to each such S, there is a game G_S satisfying the following property. I can win G_S all the time, if S is true; else I can win G_S at most half of the time. Assume now that we play G_S a hundred times and that I win every single time. Then, you may conclude that either (a) "Statement S is true, and this is why Silvio has always won," or (b) "S is false and Silvio has won a hundred times in a row only because I have been extremely unlucky." If I were you I would conclude (a).

When interactive proofs were introduced, their power was far from clear. Oded (Goldreich), Avi (Wigderson), and I showed that graph nonisomorphism, a famous problem for which no NP proofs are known to exist, possesses very simple interactive proofs. This result boded well for the power of the new notion.

But it was with Fortnow, Karloff, Lund, and Nisan that the power of interactive proofs really started to take off. They indeed showed that all problems in #P have interactive proofs. And then Adi Shamir actually showed that the set of problems having an interactive proof coincides with PSPACE. This amazing achievement exactly captures how much interaction helps in a proof.

(By the way, interaction has actually proved helpful in a lot of other things. For example, Noam Nisan has recently shown that it helps the communication complexity of game-theoretic mechanisms. Interaction is a wonderful thing!)

Zero-Knowledge Proofs. From interactive proofs, we were able to develop zero-knowledge proofs. Essentially, the latter proofs enable one to prove something hiding all possible details. After the zero-knowledge proof of a given statement, you know that the statement is true, but nothing else. Shafi, Charlie, and I introduced the notion of a zero-knowledge proof and provided its first example. But Oded, Avi, and I actually proved the power of zero-knowledge proofs. That is, we proved that not just some theorems but actually all theorems in NP can be proved interactively in a zero-knowledge manner. Actually, through a combination of other results, the same holds for PSPACE.

By the way: Who cares about proofs that hide knowledge? Well, if you are in cryptography, you care, because zero-knowledge is clearly crucial to guarantee *security*. In particular, zero knowledge has enabled *general multiparty computation*. Let $P_1, \ldots, P_n$ be parties, where each P_i has a secret input x_i; let f be an efficient function on n inputs; and let $(y_1, \ldots, y_n) = f(x_1, \ldots, x_n)$. Then, secure computation guarantees that there is an efficient way for the n parties to talk back and forth with each other so that, at the end, each P_i correctly learns his own output y_i, but does not learn any other information about the inputs of the other parties that is not deducible from y_i itself. This result was first proved by Oded, Avi, and me based on public-key cryptography (following an earlier two-party result of Andy in a slightly weaker model). Soon after, Ben-Or, Shafi, and Avi, showed a noncryptographic proof of the result, assuming instead that each pair of parties is connected by a separate secure channel.

In addition, zero-knowldge is important to achieve *reliability*. For example, zero-knowledge has played a central role in Byzantine agreement, as defined by Pease, Shostak and Lamport. Assume that we have a group of players, each of which starts with his own initial bit. Then, informally, at the end of a Byzantine agreement protocol, two properties must be satisfied. First, all honest players (i.e., all those who follow all the instructions of the protocol) output the same bit. Second, the bit output by all honest players must be 0, if the initial bit of every player was 0; and 1, if the initial bit of every player was 1. Crucially, the above two properties must hold even if, during the execution of the protocol, 1/3 of the players can be corrupted by an Adversary, who can force them to deviate from their protocol instructions in any way she wants.

As defined, Byzantyne agreement has no privacy constraint whatsoever. Its only constraint is an elaborate and delicate form of (reliable) correctness. Yet, somehow, privacy—in fact, zero knowledge—really helps to enforce correctness, in Byzantine agreement and in countless other protocols. Why? Because the best way to model a sufficiently complex system is to assume that it is controlled by an Adversary. Indeed, if a system is large enough and operates for long enough, then you can count that it will eventually start to behave adversarially. So, how to defeat an adversary? In any strategic setting, an adversary has little power if she knows little about what you intend to do. Thus, although you only want to protect the correctness of your system from the evil influence of an adversary, you may want to artificially inject privacy in your system, so as to curb the power of your adversary. It is thus no surprise that zero knowledge has proved crucial to efficiently reach Byzantine agreement.

Probabilistically Checkable Proofs. Probabilistically checkable proofs (PCPs) started with the works of Feige, Goldwasser, Lovasz, and Szegedy and Babai, Fortnow, Levin, and Szegedy, and culminated with that of Arora, Lund, Motwuani, Sudan, and Szegedy. PCPs are a remarkable achievement. As we all know, when we verify a proof we must carefully read all its bits; otherwise, we may overlook a fatal mistake. (If one assumes $0 = 1$ somewhere in his proof, then he can prove anything!) It is thus incredible that we can encode a proof so as to actually ascertain its correctness by just sampling a few of its bits. Really amazing. These possibilities were not at all on our radar screens just a few years ago.

Multiprover Interactive Proofs.. PCPs have found lots of applications, but, strictly speaking, are not efficient. This is so, because they essentially transform a classical proof into a longer, but "samplable" proof. Since receiving a string must have a cost proportional to its length, the verifier may prefer receiving from the prover a classical proof and read it in its entirety to receiving a longer proof that he can later just read in a few places.

This problem cannot be avoided by having the prover ship to the verifier a piece of random-access memory containing the longer, samplable proof. Indeed, I have never heard that shipping a piece of hardware containing a string s is cheaper than sending s! Nor can it be avoided by (1) having the prover compute and keep the longer and samplable proof and (2) having the verifier simply ask the prover for the portions he wants to read. In this way, in fact, it becomes trivial for the prover to cheat without being caught.

The problem is instead elegantly addressed by multiprover interactive proofs (MIPs), proposed by Michael Ben-Or, Shafi, Joe Kilian, and Avi. Informally, in their model, the longer and samplable proof is known to each of two distinct provers, who are assumed to be unable of communicating to each other during the proving process. By separately and cleverly interrogating them, the verifier can reconstruct any piece of the proof he wants to read, without fear of being undetectably cheated. Importantly, this property continues to hold even if, before their interaction with the verifier starts, the provers have met and agreed on a joint strategy for answering the verifier's questions.

However, it is not trivial to guarantee that two provers cannot communicate with each other during the proving process. Verbal communication may be prevented by thick walls. Cell-phone communication by Faraday cages. But there may be many other forms of communication . . .

CS Proofs. Computationally sound proofs (CS proofs for short) have been formalized by me based on the work of Kilian. Such proofs envisage a single prover and a single verifier (and do properly "charge" for any bit sent). Essentially, they are super-efficient "proofs" for all statements. Did I say "all theorems?" No. I said "all statements." In fact, every statement is guaranteed to have a CS proof that is both super short and super easy to verify. Thus, a CS proof system is both *complete* (i.e., all true statements are provable) and *inconsistent* (i.e., all false statements are provable).

To be sure, inconsistency has been the big scarecrow of mathematics. Non-Euclidian geometries have been developed out of the fear that the 5th postulate could lead to some contradiction. In a CS proof system, however, the ability of proving true and false statements alike is de facto rendered harmless by a crucial asymmetry: Very roughly, proving a true statement is always feasible, while proving a false one is always extremely hard.

The joining of two opposites is rarely inconsequential. The gods and goddesses who combine opposite forces typically enjoy great powers themselves. In complexity theory, the notion of a one-way function also combines two opposites. Informally, a function is one-way if it is easy to evaluate and hard to invert. The power of such functions is almost inconceivable. Most of cryptography originates from this power. By enjoying both completeness and consistency, CS proof systems are extremely powerful too. Indeed, they finally succeed in simultaneously simplifying the job of the prover and that of the verifier. All prior notions of an efficient proof only aimed at simplifying the job of the verifier. But this simplification may not be very useful if the work of the prover is made astronomically more complex. In such a case, in fact, no one in the real world will be able to play the role of the prover. Finding the proofs of some theorems required a life-time of work. But if we further demanded that such proofs should be checkable by verifiers with the attention span of a three-year old, finding them might require an astronomical (rather than a human) amount of time.

A CS proof, instead, allows you to convince a most impatient verifier that a given true statement S is true in roughly the same time it took you to convince yourself that S is indeed true. But, if S is false, then convincing the verifier that S is true is hopelessly hard.

Two-Message Delegation. Let me continue our abridged history of efficient proofs with two-message delegation, as just discovered by Kalai, Raz, and Rothblum. What is this? It is an efficient way to prove mathematical statements via a detour through quantum mechanics. (Do not worry: The visit to physics is a round trip. At the end, what is produced is a purely mathematical proof!) It's a wonderful and unusual result. It shows that fields are often artificially separate. There is one humanity and one human knowledge.

SNARKS. SNARKS is short for Succinct Noninteractive ARguments of Knowledge. Their essential bibliography includes the works of Valiant; Bitansky, Chiesa, Ishai, Ostrovsky, and Paneth; Gennaro, Gentry, Parno, Raykova; Parno, Gentry, Howell, Raykova; Ben-Sasson, Chiesa, Genkin, Tromer, and Virza; Lipmaa; and Bitansky, Canetti, Chiesa, Tromer. An amazing sequence of works. Conceptually, a SNARK can be constructed by starting with a CS proof. Then, by adding a nondeterministic compiler. (Compilers are optimized to work for ordinary programs. But this time you want to optimize things for the prover, who is indeed a nondeterministic program.) And, finally, by adding some zero-knowledge. The end result is a proof so compact as to consist of just 256 bytes. Thus, you can use a bar code to encode your proof. Anyone can scan it with her phone and easily verify it.

In sum, even disregarding zero-knowledge, SNARKS enable one to use proofs anytime and anywhere. SNARKS have a tremendous potential.

Rational Proofs. Last chapter in our abridged history are *rational proofs*. Such proofs, introduced by Pablo Azar and me, are indeed the new kid on the block. They include some ingredients that have been neglected so far. So, I'll take a bit more time to discuss them.

Let me start with a story: Call it a "CS Tale." Merlin and Arthur, as you know, have been living a happy life. Once in a while, Arthur asks, "Is X true?"; Merlin replies "Yes" or "No," whatever the case may be; and then they quickly interact, until Arthur is convinced. Their arrangement has lasted for a long time. Suddenly, Arthur asks "Is X true?" and Merlin replies "Go to hell!" Arthur: "What happened?" Merlin: "Simple. Dumbledore works for Goldman Sachs; Gandolf for Citi; Potter for J.P. Morgan. They are making money hands over fist. How about me? Now that I have money on my mind, I don't want to hear about proving your stupid theorems any more." Somehow, Arthur is practical. "You know what? If money is what you want, okay, I'll pay." The smile comes back on Merlin's face.

The purpose of this tale raises a very serious question: *How to pay a math expert?* The answer better be a lot, but there are various options. The first is the "fixed price" one: \$1 for a correct proof and \$0 for an incorrect one. This option simply mimics the standard interactive-proof setting and does not enlarge the range of what is efficiently provable. So, *can we, with more flexible monetary incentives, be able to prove efficiently more theorems?* In particular, can we prove them with fewer rounds of communication? Communication rounds matter a lot. They actually are the most expensive resource. General interactive proofs in principle require polynomially many elementary computational steps (such as increasing a counter by 1) and polynomially many rounds. Now assume that an interactive proof requires n^3 computational steps and n^2 rounds of communication, where $n = 1000$. Then, the first constraint is not a problem: The laptop I am using right now can easily perform a billion elementary operations. However, we cannot feasibly exchange e-mails back and forth a million times!

Rational proofs are very round-savvy. Currently, they are a theoretical model, to be sure, but they address a real concern and may become practically relevant at least in some applications. To be more intuitive, I will discuss *Rational Merlin Arthur* (RMA for short) as a set of *functions*, rather than languages. Moreover, I will *informally* describe only $RMA[k]$, where k is the number of rounds of communication utilized by Arthur and Merlin.

A function F belongs to $RMA[k]$ if there exist two polynomial-time functions, a *conclusion function* C and a *reward function* R, that, for any input x, enable Arthur to learn $F(x)$ as follows. Arthur and Merlin talk back and forth for k rounds. Like in the classical Merlin–Arthur system, Arthur is a dumb interacting algorithm that sends messages r_i consisting of polynomially many (in the length of x) random bits. Merlin, on the other hand, is an arbitrary interactive algorithm (thus capable of performing an unbounded amount of computation) that sends polynomially long messages s_i. Merlin goes first. So the transcript of their conversation about x is of the form $T = s_1, r_1, \ldots, s_k, r_k$.

At the end of their conversation, two things happen:

(a) The reward function R is evaluated, on the input x and the transcript T, to determine the amount of money that Arthur pays to Merlin.

(b) The conclusion function C is evaluated on x and T to determine a value y, which Arthur concludes to be $F(x)$.

That is, Merlin wanted to be paid and now he is paid. Namely, he is paid $R(x, T)$ dollars. Arthur wanted to know about the value of $F(x)$ and now takes it to be $y = C(x, T)$.

Thus a natural question arises: How about verifying that $C(x, T) = F(x)$? The answer is surprisingly simple: There is no such verification! However, the proof system $RMA[k]$ offers some guarantee. Assume you're Merlin. Finally, you get paid. OK, but: How much? As we have just discussed, according to rule R. Again, whatever strings $s_1, s_2, \ldots$ you may choose, if Arthur chooses the random string r_i as his own ith message, then you will receive the amount of money $R(x, (s_1, r_1, \ldots, s_k, r_k))$. And if you had said $s_1', s_2', \ldots$ instead, then you would have received the amount of money $R(x, (s_1', r_1, \ldots, s_k', r_k))$. In other words, it is your lucky day: you get money no matter what you say. It's a bonanza! True. But, *what is best for you to say?* If you are rational, your optimal strategy for choosing your ith string is as follows. Given the transcript generated so far, $s_1^\star, r_1, \ldots, s_{i-1}^\star, r_{i-1}$, find the string $s_i^\star$ that maximizes your expected reward. This reward, of course, is computed over the possible continuations of the transcript (knowing that Arthur's future strings will continue to be chosen at random, and yours will be chosen by your optimal strategy). Let $T^\star$ denote a transcript so generated. Then the guarantee offered is that, when you maximize your expected money, Arthur correctly learns $F(x)$. That is, $C(x, T^\star) = F(x)$ for all inputs x.

To check our understanding, let us focus on $RMA[1]$. In this proof system, Merlin sends a single random string, s_1, Arthur replies with a single string, r_1, and a transcript has the form $T = s_1, r_1$. To show that a given function F is in $RMA[1]$ we must choose a reward function R and a proof function C so that Merlin maximizes his money if and only if Arthur learns the truth about $F(x)$. The first idea that comes to mind is to choose R and C as follows: For any string s that Merlin may choose, any random string r that Arthur may choose, and any input x for F,

- $C(x, (r, s)) = s$ and
- $R(x, (r, s)) = 1$ if $s = F(x)$, and 0 otherwise.

Indeed, with such choices of R and C, to maximize his reward, Merlin must send Arthur the string $s = F(x)$. Thus, whenever Merlin so chooses s, Arthur correctly learns $F(x)$.

Of course, a problem with the above choice of C and R is that R cannot be polynomial-time unless so is F. However, this problem does not exclude the possibility, for some hard-to-evaluate function F, to find two efficient functions C and R showing that F is in $RMA[1]$.

Consider SAT, the NP-complete language of satisfiability, which can be equivalently defined as a function as follows: for all Boolean formulas f,

$SAT(f) = YES$ if there exists x such that $f(x) = TRUE$, and *NO* otherwise.

This function should be hard to evaluate. Yet let me argue that SAT belongs to $RMA[1]$ by informally and trivially constructing the required functions C and R as follows. Arthur pays Merlin \$2 if Merlin gives him a satisfying assignment of f, and \$1 in all other cases (e.g., if Merlin tells him that f is not satisfiable). Consider first the case that f is satisfiable. In this case, Merlin maximizes his money by giving Arthur a satisfying assignment, z, of f. Indeed, Arthur can easily verify that $f(z) = TRUE$, and thus that Merlin should receive \$2. But, in so doing, Arthur of course correctly concludes that f is satisfiable! Consider now the case that f is not satisfiable. In this case, Merlin maximizes his money no matter what he tells Arthur, because he can only receive \$1. At the same time, Arthur correctly deduces that f is not satisfiable, because, no matter what Merlin can tell him, he cannot tell him a satisfying assignment of f, if none exists. QED. What could be simpler?

On the basis of the above example, we might believe that trivial rational proofs exist any function of interest. But not so fast. Consider the following two functions.

1. #: *for any Boolean formula* f, $\#(f) \overset{\text{def}}{=} |x : f(x) = TRUE|$.

    That is, # tells us the number of satisfying assignments of every possible Boolean formula.

2. $MinMax_k$: *for any (2k-input) finite function* g, *denoting by* $\bar{g}$ *a compact encoding of* g,

$$MinMax_k(\bar{g}) \overset{\text{def}}{=} \min_{x_1} \max_{y_1} \ldots \min_{x_k} \max_{y_k} g(x_1, y_1, \ldots, x_k, g_k).$$

    That is, $MinMax_k$ tells us the value of any k-round game.

Hmm . . . OK, rational proof may not be as trivial for the above two functions, but they still exist—and are not too hard to find either! Indeed, $\# \in RMA[1]$ and $MinMax_k \in RMA[k]$. The first of the above two results may be surprising, because it trivially implies that there exist single-round rational proofs for $\#P$. By contrast, in the traditional Arthur–Merlin model, one round does not suffice for $\#P$, unless the polynomial-time hierarchy collapses—something disbelieved by most researchers. Thus, proving that $\#P$ can be decided one-round rational proofs (without any unproven assumptions!) shows the power of rational proofs.

The rational proof model may be made more realistic by extending it to experts who cannot perform arbitrary amounts of computation. A more robust model actually envisages that both parties incur monetary costs for the amount of computation they perform, but that Merlin's cost for computation is less than Arthur's.

Rational proofs point out that efficiently conveying the truth can sometimes be viewed as the maximization of an easy to evaluate function. Forget interpreting the reward function as "money": The truth you are looking for is the value that maximizes a given function R. This perspective enlarges the applicability of rational proofs. In the extreme, in a living organism, cells may not care about money or produce written reports. However, some cells may care about receiving—say—some proteins, and the production of these proteins may be strongly correlated to those cells' reports about the status of some vital aspect of the organism!

Efficient Proofs and the Computation Market. Computation is the new Atlas that keeps the world up. OK, the world can stand on its own, but pretty much anything else in the world needs computation. Computation may be more valuable than oil, water, and lots of other resources. It is a good thing that those with more computation power use it to solve the computational needs of those who have less computational power. But we need good ways of selling computation. And proofs will play a crucial role in ensuring that computation is correctly bought. This was one of my original motivations behind interactive proofs. And this motivation has never waned. Rather, the ability of proofs to power a vibrant and meaningful computation market has increased.

Final and Personal Considerations. In mere 30 years, we have brought forward NP, interactive proofs, zero-knowledge proofs, probabilistically checkable proofs, multi-prover interactive proofs, computationally sound proofs, 2-message delegation, SNARKS, rational proofs .... Cathedrals and other splendid architectures of the past have been erected to the skies over multiple generations. It is thus amazing that the notion of an efficient proof, this formidable conceptual architecture, has been erected in a single generation. I cannot tell you how fortunate I feel to have witnessed and participated to such a momentous development.

Everything is fair in love, war, and proofs. But with proofs we have abandoned all restraints. Proofs used to be syntactic objects; now they are interactive processes.

They used to be deterministic; now they are probabilistic. They had to be verified by full reading, and now can be verified by spot reading. Proof systems had to be consistent to be useful; and now some proof systems are more useful because they are properly inconsistent. Like love and war, proofs demand total commitment. For them, we must certainly summon our intellect, but also emotions, personal history, and sense of aesthetics. All of these make us figure out which of the infinitely many theorems out there we should try to prove and how.

Proofs are going to become more and more useful as the complexity of our world increases. Our survival as a species will depend on proving that some very complex mechanism, which will keep us alive, actually works.

Proofs are our past, our present, and our future.

6.3   Advice

I have always loved to give advice. And, at this point, I feel a little bit legitimized to give it. . . . My advice, of course, is to the students among you. Here we go.

1. *Collaboration.* Collaboration wins over competition anytime. And on top of it, it's much more fun. Don't ever believe that research is a zero-sum game.
    Collaborate as much as you can!

2. *Confidence and Doubt.* Confidence and doubt are both crucial. If you're not confident, you're not going to attempt doing anything worth doing. But if you have no doubts about succeeding in what you are trying to do, then you are not pushing yourself hard enough.
    Be confident, until you doubt yourself!

3. *Fortune.* Never be ashamed of luck. I'm not. Nothing of importance is ever accomplished without a good dose of luck. My ancestors, the Romans, defined luck as "that without which nothing." And, in Palestrina, they dedicated a monumental temple—better a mountain turned into a temple—to Fortune. And fortune has many forms. Particularly in Science.
    One form of luck is *timing*. Working on the right problem, with the right collaborators, at the right time.
    Another form of luck is *ignorance*. Finding a needle in a haystack is very hard. But if your haystack is very, very small, you'll find the damned needle. A long time ago, when we were graduate students, Shafi and I wanted to find a candidate encryption scheme satisfying our new and demanding notion of security. In part, we succeeded to find it thanks to our limited knowledge of

computational number theory, because this feasibly restricted a potentially enormous search space. Ignorance may occasionally help.

Yet another form of luck is *myopia*. Because, if we could really see what you are up against, rather than charging forward we would run away. Failure to grasp the magnitude of the task ahead gives us the courage to get going.

In sum, be lucky!

4. *Stubbornness.* I'm stubborn as a mule, and I'm proud of it. Stubbornness is believing in yourself when nobody else does. Consider zero-knowledge proofs. Shafi and I started calling them "Proofs with Untrusted Oracles." And we were so proud of them, so confident. "This stuff will catch fire; everybody will love it." To make the deadline of the next conference, we wrote our paper furiously: day after night, after day, after night . . . Rejected! Okay. It cannot happen again. Let's re-write it and re-submit it. We changed the title to "Interactive and Minimal Computation." To better convey the nature of the beast, and to better hide the prior rejection from the next committee . . . New rejection! Next conference, next title: "The Information Content of Proof Systems." Way more respectable. It should have worked. It didn't! Next, we got ourself a wonderful collaborator: Charlie. He told us: "You guys! The way you write! Leave the introduction to me." We did. Let me read to you the opening paragraph. "Communication is a tool for transferring or exchanging knowledge. In traditional computational complexity or communication complexity, the goal is to communicate as much knowledge as possible as efficiently as possible. Since all participants are considered good friends, no one cares if more knowledge than necessary is communicated. The situation with respect to cryptographic protocols is very different." Ah! Such a beautiful prose . . . Canned! But, finally, some 30 years ago, "The Knowledge Complexity of Interactive Proof Systems" was accepted by the 17th Symposium of Theory of Computing.

Be stubborn!

5. *Limitations.* How can I do research, limited as I am? Actually, if you are limited you can think about a different approach to the problem. An approach that less limited people will miss. Limitations can be strengths. In fact, it is a powerful trick to artificially limit ourselves, so as to make ourselves stronger. In 1519, Hernán Cortes, with a few hundred men, disembarked in what is now Mexico. He was facing an unchartered territory and a huge enemy army. He was in a pretty weak position. So, what did he do? He decided to fortify his stance. He sank his own ships, thus depriving his men of any possible

escape and ultimately securing victory. If you use the same strategy toward peaceful ends, you'll make a better world.

Enjoy your limitations!

6. *Inspiration.* Where do we find it? Leo Tolstoy had it right: "If you want to be universal, start by painting your own village." Actually, you do not have to leave your house and roam around your village. Stay inside and look inside. Speak about the deepest part of your heart and you'll be universal. In any artistic endeavor as well as in any scientific endeavor, what motivates us is an emotional problem that has been bothering us since we were kids. And we'll never tire and we'll never rest. Because we want to solve the damned problem that has bothered us for so long. In my case: "Is there someone out there with whom I can interact? And if there is, should I fear the interaction?" And in your case?

Find the true source of your inspiration!

I know it is hard. The path of self- discovery is long and tortuous. But then: Do we have anything better to do in this world than figuring out who we really are and what we really want? I don't think so. So, let's embrace our destiny;,let's pack our belongings, and let's start our journey. Step after step, with hope, with joy, with confidence, and most of all, with

GOOD LUCK!

ORIGINAL PAPERS

Probabilistic Encryption &
How To Play Mental Poker Keeping Secret All Partial Information

Shafi Goldwasser * and Silvio Micali **
Computer Science Department
University of California - Berkeley

1. Introduction

This paper proposes an Encryption Scheme that possess the following property:

> An adversary, who knows the encryption algorithm and is given the cyphertext, cannot obtain any information about the cleartext.

Any implementation of a Public Key Cryptosystem, as proposed by Diffie and Hellman in [8], should possess this property.

Our Encryption Scheme follows the ideas in the number theoretic implementations of a Public Key Cryptosystem due to Rivest, Shamir and Adleman [13], and Rabin [12].

Security is based on Complexity Theory and the intractability of some problems in number theory such as factoring, index finding and deciding whether numbers are quadratic residues with respect to composite moduli is assumed. In this context, impossibility means computational infeasibility and proving that a problem is hard means to show it equivalent to one of the above mentioned problems.

The key idea in both the RSA scheme and the Rabin scheme is the selection of an appropriate trapdoor function; an easy to evaluate function f such that x is not easily computable from $f(x)$, unless some extra information is known. To encrypt a message m, one simply evaluates $f(m)$.

We would like to point out two basic weaknesses of this approach:

1) The fact that f is a trapdoor function does not rule out the possibility of computing x from $f(x)$ when x is of a special form. Usually messages do not consist of numbers chosen at random but possess more structure. Such structural information may help in decoding. For example, a function f, which is hard to invert on a generic input, could conceivably be easy to invert on the ASCII representations of English sentences.

2) **The fact that f is a trapdoor function does not rule out the possibility of easily computing some partial information about x (even every other bit of x) from $f(x)$.** The danger in the case that x is the ASCII representation of an English sentence is self evident. Encrypting messages in a way that ensures the secrecy of all partial information is an extremely important goal in Cryptography. The importance of this point of view is particularly apparent if we want to use encryption to play card games over the telephone. If the suit or color of a card could be compromised the whole game could be invalid.

Though no one knows how to break the RSA or the Rabin scheme, in none of these schemes is it **proved** that decoding is hard without any assumptions made on the message space. Rabin shows that, in his scheme, decoding is hard for an adversary if the set of possible messages has some density property.

The novelty of our contribution consists of

1. The notion of Trapdoor Functions is replaced by **Probabilistic Encryption**. To encrypt each message we make use of a fair coin. The encoding of each message will depend on the message plus the result of a sequence of coin tosses. Consequently, there are many possible encodings for each message. However, messages are always uniquely decodable![1]

This research was supported by
* NSF Grant MCS-79-037667
** fellowship from Consiglio Nazionale delle Ricerche - Italy and in part by NSF Grant MCS-79-037667

---

[1] Probabilistic Encryption is completely different from the technique of appending random bits to a message as suggested in [12] and [16].

Probabilistic Encryption

This chapter reproduces the contents of the paper "Probabilistic Encryption and How to Play Mental Poker Keeping Secret All Partial Information," which appeared in the proceedings of the *14th Annual ACM Symposium on Theory of Computing*, pages 365-377, 1982.

This pioneering work of Shafi Goldwasser and Silvio Micali defined the mindset of the field by establishing conceptual frameworks and demonstrating their usefulness. In particular, it advocated rigorous and robust definitions of security as well as reducing the security of complex systems to better understood complexity assumptions; it presented computational indistinguishability as a proxy for equivalence; it heralded viewing security as an emulation of an ideal setting (via the simulation paradigm); and introduced techniques such as the hybrid argument. The term "probabilistic encryption" reflects the realization that a robust notion of secure encryption requires the use of randomization in the process of encrypting each message (and not only in the process of generating cryptographic keys).

Probabilistic Encryption & How To Play Mental Poker Keeping Secret All Partial Information

Shafi Goldwasser* (University of California - Berkeley),
Silvio Micali** (University of California - Berkeley)

1 Introduction

This paper proposes an Encryption Scheme that possess the following property:

> An adversary, who knows the encryption algorithm and is given the cyphertext, cannot obtain any information about the cleartext.

Any implementation of a Public Key Cryptosystem, as proposed by Diffie and Hellman in [8], should possess this property.

Our Encryption Scheme follows the ideas in the number theoretic implementations of a Public Key Cryptosystem due to Rivest, Shamir and Adleman [13], and Rabin [12].

This research was supported by
*NSF Grant MCS-79-037667
** fellowship from Consiglio Nazionale delle Ricerche - Italy and in part by NSF Grant MCS-79-037667

Security is based on Complexity Theory and the intractability of some problems in number theory such as factoring, index finding and deciding whether numbers are quadratic residues with respect to composite moduli is assumed. In this context, impossibility means computational infeasibility and proving that a problem is hard means to show it equivalent to one of the above mentioned problems.

The key idea in both the RSA scheme and the Rabin scheme is the selection of an appropriate trapdoor function; an easy to evaluate function f such that x is not easily computable from $f(x)$, unless some extra information is known. To encrypt a message m, one simply evaluates $f(m)$.

We would like to point out two basic weaknesses of this approach:

1. The fact that f is a trapdoor function does not rule out the possibility of computing x from $f(x)$ when x is of a special form. Usually messages do not consist of numbers chosen at random but possess more structure. Such structural information may help in decoding. For example, a function f, which is hard to invert on a generic input, could conceivably be easy to invert on the ASCII representations of English sentences.

2. The fact that f is a trapdoor function does not rule out the possibility of easily computing some partial information about z (even every other bit of x) from $f(z)$. The danger in the case that z is the ASCII representation of an English sentence is self evident. Encrypting messages in a way that ensures the secrecy of all partial information is an extremely important goal in Cryptography. The importance of this point of view is particularly apparent if we want to use encryption to play card games over the telephone. If the suit or color of a card could be compromised the whole game could be invalid.

Though no one knows how to break the RSA or the Rabin scheme, in none of these schemes is it **proved** that decoding is hard without any assumptions made on the message space. Rabin shows that, in his scheme, decoding is hard for an adversary if the set of possible messages has some density property.

The novelty of our contribution consists of

1. The notion of Trapdoor Functions is replaced by **Probabilistic Encryption**. To encrypt each message we make use of a fair coin. The encoding of each message will depend on the message plus the result of a sequence of coin tosses. Consequently, there are many possible encodings for each message. However, messages are always uniquely decodable.[1]

---

1. Probabilistic Encryption is completely different from the technique of appending random bits to a message as suggested in [12] and [16].

2. Decoding is easy for the legal receiver of a message, but **provably** hard for an adversary. Therefore the spirit of a trapdoor function is maintained. In addition, in our scheme, without imposing any restrictions on the message space, we can prove that decoding is equivalent to deciding quadratic residuosity modulo composite numbers.

3. No Partial Information about an encrypted message could be obtained by an adversary. Assume that the message space has an associated probability distribution and that, with respect to this distribution, an easy to compute predicate P (such as "the exclusive or of all the bits in the message is 1") has probability p to be true. Let $p \geq .5$ without any loss of generality. Then, without any special ability, an adversary, given the cyphertext, can always guess that P is true for the cleartext, and be correct with probability p.

   Based on the assumption that deciding quadratic residuosity modulo composite numbers is hard, we prove that an adversary cannot guess correctly with probability $p + \varepsilon$, from the cyphertext, whether the cleartext satisfies the predicate P, where ε is a non negligible positive real number.

Probabilistic Encryption has been useful for the solution of Mental Poker. The problem whether it is possible to play a "fair" game of Mental Poker has been raised by Robert Floyd. Shamir, Rivest and Adleman proposed an elegant solution to this problem in [14] using commutative encryption functions, but they could not prove that partial information could not be compromised using their scheme. Indeed, several problems in the implementation of their scheme have been pointed out by Lipton in [10].

We present a solution for Mental Poker, for which we can prove, based on the assumption that factoring and deciding quadratic residuosity modulo composite numbers is hard, that not a single bit of information about a card which should remain hidden can be discovered. Our solution does not use commutative encryption functions.

2 The Security of a Public Key Cryptosystem

All the number theoretic notation used in this section will be defined in Section 3.1.

2.1 What is a Public Key Cryptosystem?

The concept of a Public Key Cryptosystem was introduced by Diffie and Hellman in their ingenious paper [8]. Let M be a finite message space, $A, B, \ldots$ be users, and let $m \in M$ denote a message. Let $E_A: M \to M$ be A's encryption function, which is ideally bijective, and D_A be A's decryption function such that $D_A(E_A(m)) = m$ for all $m \in M$. In a Public Key Cryptosystem E_A is placed in a public file, and user A keeps D_A private. D_A should be difficult to compute knowing only E_A. To send message m to A, B takes E_A from the public file, computes $E_A(m)$ and sends this message to A. A easily computes $D_A(E_A(m))$ to obtain m.

2.2 The RSA Scheme and the Rabin Scheme

The two implementations of a Public Key Cryptosystem most relevant and inspiring for this paper are the RSA scheme [13], due to Rivest, Shamir and Adleman, and its particularization suggested by Rabin [12].

The key idea in both the RSA scheme and the Rabin scheme consists in the selection of an appropriate number theoretic trapdoor function. In the RSA scheme, user A selects N, the product of two large primes p_1 and p_2 and a number s such that s and $\phi(N)$ are relatively prime, where ϕ is the Euler totient function. A puts N and s in a public file and keeps the factorization of N private. Let $Z_N^* = \{x \mid 1 \le x \le N - 1$ and x and N are relatively prime$\}$. For every message $m \in Z_N^*$, $E_A(m) = m^s \bmod N$. Clearly, the ability to take sth roots mod N implies the ability to decode. A, who knows the factorization of N, can easily take sth mod N. No efficient way to take sth roots mod N is known when the factorization of N is unknown.

About the RSA scheme Rabin remarks that, for all we know, inverting the function $x^s \bmod N$ may be a hard problem in general, and yet easy for a large percentage of the x's.

He suggests to modify the RSA scheme by choosing $s = 2$. Thus, for all users A, $E_A(x) = x^2 \bmod N$. Notice that E_A is a 4-1 function because our N is the product of two primes. In fact, every quadratic residue mod N, i.e every q such that $q = x^2 \bmod N$ for some $x \in Z_N^*$, has four square roots mod N: $\pm x \bmod N$ and $\pm y \bmod N$. As A knows the factorization of N, upon receiving the encrypted message $m^2 \bmod N$, he could compute its four square roots and get the message m. The ambiguity in decoding could be eliminated, for example, by sending the first 20 digits of m in addition to $m^2 \bmod N$. Such extra information cannot effectively help in decoding: we could always guess the first 20 digits of m.

The following theorem shows how hard is it to invert Rabin's function $x^2 \bmod N$.

Theorem (Rabin): If for 1% of the q's quadratic residues mod N one could find one square root of q, then one could factor N in Random Polynomial Time.

The theorem follows from the following lemma that we state without proof.

Lemma 1   Given $x, y \in Z_N^*$ such that $x^2 = y^2 \bmod N$ and $x \neq \pm y \bmod N$, there is a polynomial time algorithm to factor N. (In fact the greatest common divisor of N and $x \pm y$ is a factor of N).

Proof   **Informal proof of Rabin's theorem:**   Assume that we have a magic box B such that given q, a quadratic residue mod N, for 1% of the q's it outputs one square root of q mod N. Then we could factor N by iterating the following step:

> Pick i at random in Z_N^* and compute $q = i^2 \bmod N$. Feed the magic box B with q. If M outputs a square root of q different from i or $-i$ mod N, then (by the above lemma) factor N.

The expected number of iterations is low, as at each step, we have a 0.5% chance to factor N.

2.3   Objections to Cryptosystems based on Trapdoor Functions

Covering ones face with a handkerchief certainly helps to hide personal identity. However:

1. It will not hide from me the identity of a special subset of people: my mother, my sister, close friends.

2. I can gather a lot of information about the people I cannot identify: their height, their hair color, and so on.

Essentially, the same kind of problems may arise in the RSA scheme and in the Rabin scheme and, more generally, in any other Public Key Cryptosystem based on Trapdoor Functions:

1. The fact that f is a trapdoor function does not rule out the possibility of computing x from $f(x)$ when x is of special form.

2. The fact that f is trapdoor function does not rule out the possibility of easily computing some partial information about x from $f(x)$.

2.4   Discussion of Objection 1

One may argue that Rabin's Public Key Cryptosystem is as hard to break as factoring in the following way; whoever can get a message m from their encryptions $m^2 \bmod N$ 1% of the time, is actually realizing the magic box of Rabin's theorem and thus could efficiently factor n.

We would like to point out the following fact.

Claim If M, the set of messages, is "sparse" in $Z_N{}^*$, the ability to decode 1% of all messages does not yield a random polynomial time algorithm for factoring.

By "sparse" we mean that for a randomly chosen $x \in Z_N{}^*$, the probability that x is a message is virtually 0.

Let $f(x) = x^2 \bmod N$. Assume that we are able to invert the function f only on $f(M)$. Then we would have a magic box MB which, fed $m^2 \bmod N$, would output m whenever $m \in M$; and fed q, outputs nothing whenever $q \notin \{m^2 \bmod N \mid m \in M\}$, except, at most, for a negligible portion of the q's. With the use of such a magic box we could decode, but not factor N efficiently. Using such MB, let us look at the above informal proof of Rabin's theorem. If we pick $m \in M$ and feed $m^2 \bmod N$ into MB, then we get back m and we cannot factor. If we pick $i \notin M$ and feed $i^2 \bmod N$ to MB, then the probability that one square root of $i^2 \bmod N$ different from i, belongs to M is practically 0 and we get no answer.

2.5 Discussion of Objection 2

We would like to define a Public Key Cryptosystem to be secure if an adversary, given the cyphertext, cannot obtain any partial information about the cleartext. This latter notion needs to be formalized:

Let P be any easy to evaluate, non constant, boolean predicate defined on the message space M. Let $m \in M$. If, given the encryption of m, an adversary can efficiently compute the value of $P(m)$, then **partial information** about m can be obtained from the encryption of m.

Notice that, according to the above definition, no Public Key Cryptosystem *based on trapdoor functions* is secure. In fact, if E_A is a trapdoor function, the following predicate P, defined on the cleartext, is easy to evaluate from the cyphertext: $P(x)$ is true if and only if $E_A(x)$ is even. We can avoid such problems using Probabitistic Encryption.

We know that some decision problems may be hard to solve for particular inputs, but easy to solve for most of the inputs. In view of the special purpose of Cryptography, the requirement that obtaining partial information should be difficult needs to be strengthened.

Assume that the message space has an associated probability distribution and that, with respect to this distribution, a predicate P has a probability p to be true. Without loss of generality, let $p \geq 0.5$.

Definition An adversary has an ε advantage in evaluating the predicate P, if he can correctly guess the value of P relative to the cleartext with probability greater than $p + \varepsilon$.

We are now able to restate the previous partial information definition.

Definition A Public Key Cryptosystem is ε secure if an adversary does not have an ε advantage in evaluating, given the cyphertext, any easy to compute predicate relative to the cleartext.

Based on the assumption that deciding quadratic residuosity modulo composite numbers is hard, we introduce an ε-secure Public Key Cryptosystem, for every non negligible, positive, real number ε. Let us first deal with the question of sending securely a single bit in a Public Key Cryptosystern. This question, closely related to the security of Partial Information, has been raised by Brassard in [7].

2.6 Attempts to Send a Single Bit Securely in Public Key Cryptosystems based on TrapDoor Functions

Suppose that user B wants to send a single bit message to user A in great secrecy. The bit is equally likely to be a 0 or a 1. B wants no adversary to have a 1% advantage in guessing correctly his message. B knows that E_A is hard to invert and tries to make use of this fact in the following way.

Idea 1: All users in the system agree on an integer i. User B selects $r \in M$ at random, except for the ith bit of r, which will be his message. B sends $E_A(r)$ to A.

A can decode and thus get the desired bit. But what can an adversary do?

Danger: let $y = E_A(x)$, where E_A is a one way function. Then, given y, it could be difficult to compute x but not a specific bit of x.

Example Let p be a large prime such that $p - 1$ has at least one large prime factor. Let g be a generator for $Z_p{}^*$. Then $y = g^x \bmod p$ is a well known one-way function. But, even though it is difficult to compute x from $g^x \bmod p$ (the index finding problem), it is easy to get the last bit of x. In fact, x ends in 0 if and only if y is a quadratic residue mod p. For p prime we have fast random polynomial time algorithms to test quadratic residuosity, see [10].

The following idea was suggested by Donald Johnson.

Idea 2: B selects $8 \leq i \leq 100$ at random, and sets the ith bit of x to the bit he wants to communicate. The remaining 93 bits of x are chosen at random, except for the first 7 bits of x, which specify location i. B sends $E_A(x)$ to A.

Danger: If, given $E_A(x)$, we can easily compute the first 7 bits of x and one of the last 93 bits of x, then we could guess B's message with a 1/93 advantage.

Summarizing: There are many ways in which a single bit could be "embedded" in a binary number x. Taking the "exclusive or" of all the digits of x is just one more example. However, given $y = E_A(x)$, being able to discover some particular bits embedded in x DOES NOT CONTRADICT the fact that it is hard to compute x. Then, what is a secure way to send a single bit? The answer to this problem is discussed in the next section.

3 Deciding Quadratic Residuosity Is Hard on the Average

The symbol (x, N) will denote the greatest common divisor of x and N. We use $\Pr(X)$ to denote the probability of the event X. We let $Z_N^* = \{x \mid 1 \le x \; N - 1$ and $(x, N) = 1\}$.

3.1 Background and Notation

Given $q \in Z_N^*$, is $q = x^2 \bmod N$ solvable? If N is prime, then the answer to this question is easily computed. If a solution exists, q is said to be a quadratic residue mod N. Otherwise q is said to be a quadratic non-residue mod N. From now on let P_1, and P_2 be odd, distinct primes and $N = P_1 P_2$. Then, $q = x^2 \bmod N$ is solvable if and only if both $q = -x^2 \bmod P_1$ and $q = x^2 \bmod p_2$ are solvable. If this is the case, q is said to be a quadratic residue mod N, otherwise q is said to be a quadratic non-residue mod N. We will call the problem of determining whether an element $q \in Z_N^*$ is a quadratic residue, the quadratic residuosity problem.

Let p be an odd prime and $q \in Z_p^*$, then the Jacobi symbol (q/p) equals i if q is a quadratic residue mod p and -1 otherwise. The Jacobi symbol (q/N), is defined as $(q/N) = (q/p_1)(q/p_2)$. Despite the fact that the Jacobi symbol (q/N) is defined through the factorization of N, (q/N) is computable in polynomial time even when the factorization of N is not known!

It is easy to see, from the above definitions that if $(q/N) = -1$ then q must be a quadratic non-residue mod N. In fact, q must be a quadratic non-residue either mod P_1 or mod P_2. However, if $(q/N) = +1$, then either q is a quadratic residue mod N or q is a quadratic non-residue for both the prime factors of N.

Let us count how many of the q's, such that $(q/N) = 1$, are actually quadratic residues.

Theorem Let p be an odd prime. Then Z_p^* is a cyclic group.

Theorem Let 9 be a generator for Z_p^*, then $g^s \bmod p$ is a quadratic residue if and only if s is even.

Corollary Half of the numbers in Z_p^* are quadratic residues and half are quadratic non-residues.

Theorem Let $N = P_1 P_2$ where p_1 and p_2 are distinct odd primes. Then half of the numbers in Z_N^* have Jacobi symbol equal to -1 and thus are quadratic non-residues. The

Jacobi symbol of the rest of the numbers is 1. Exactly half of these latter ones are quadratic residues.

3.2 A Difficult Problem in Number Theory

If the factorization of N is not known and $(q/N) = 1$, then there is no known procedure for deciding whether q is a quadratic residue mod N. This decision problem is well known to be hard in Number Theory. It is one of the main four algorithmic problems discussed by Gauss in his "Disquisitiones Arithmeticae" (1801). A polynomial solution for it would imply a polynomial solution to other open problems in Number Theory, such as deciding whether a composite n, whose factorization is not known, is the product of 2 or 3 primes, see open problems 9 and 15 in Adleman [3]. Recently, Adleman [1] showed that a generalization of quadratic residuosity is equivalent to factoring. Using this generalized notion in our protocol, we could base the security of our cryptosystem on factoring. At present, we await the final version of Adelman's paper.

Assumption   Let $0 < \varepsilon < 1$. For each positive integer k, let $C_{k,\varepsilon}$ be the minimum size of circuits C that decide correctly quadratic residuosity mod n for a fraction ε of the k bit integers n. Then, for every $0 < \varepsilon < 1$ and every polynomial Q, there exists $\delta_{\varepsilon,Q}$ such that $k > \delta_{\varepsilon,Q}$ implies $C_{\varepsilon,k} > Q(k)$.

3.4 A Number Theoretic Result

We want to show that deciding whether q is a quadratic residue mod N, is not hard in some special cases, but is hard on the average in a very strong sense. In order to do so, let us recall the weak law of large numbers:

If $y_1, y_2 \ldots y_k$ are k independent Bernoulli variables such that $y_i = 1$ with probability p, and $S_k = y_1 + \cdots + y_k$, then for real numbers $\psi, \delta > 0$, $k \geq \frac{1}{4\delta\psi^2}$ implies that

$$\Pr\left(\left|\frac{Sk}{k} - p\right| > \psi\right) < \delta.$$

Notice that k is bounded by a polynomial in ψ^{-1} and ψ^{-1}.

Let $A_N{}^* = \{x \mid x \in Z_N{}^* \text{ and } (x/N) = 1\}$.

Definition   For a composite number N, and for real number $0 < \varepsilon \leq \frac{1}{2}$, we say that we can guess with ε advantage whether q drawn at random from $A_N{}^*$ is a quadratic residue mod N if we can, in polynomial ($\mid N \mid$) time, guess quadratic residuosity mod N correctly for at least $\frac{1}{2} + \varepsilon$ of the elements of $A_N{}^*$.

Theorem 1   Let $0 < \varepsilon \leq \frac{1}{2}, 0 < \delta \leq 1$ be nonnegligible numbers. Suppose we could guess, with an ε advantage whether q, drawn at random from $A_N{}^*$, is a quadratic residue mod N. Then we could decide quadratic residuosity of any integer mod N with probability $1 - \delta$ by means of a polynomial in $\mid N \mid, \varepsilon^{-1}$ and δ^{-1} time probabilistic algorithm.

Proof   Assume, to the contrary, that we have a polynomial time magic box MB which guesses correctly whether $q \in A_N{}^*$ is a quadratic residue mod N, for $\frac{1}{2} + \varepsilon$ of the elements of $A_N{}^*$.

Let,

$\alpha = $ Pr (MB answers "q is a quadratic residue" $\mid q$ is a quadratic residue mod n)
$\beta = $ Pr (MB answers "q is a quadratic residue" $\mid q$ is a quadratic non-residue mod N, $q \in A_N{}^*$).

The fraction of $A_N{}^*$ on which MB is correct equals $\frac{1}{2}\alpha + \frac{1}{2}(1 - \beta)$. In order for MB to have a ε advantage, it must be that $\alpha - \beta \geq 2\varepsilon$. However, α need not be equal to $\varepsilon + \frac{1}{2}$. We will now show how to get a good estimate for α.

Construct a sample of k quadratic residues chosen at random in $Z_N{}^*$ (the value of k will be defined later on). This can be easily done by picking $s + 1. \ldots .s_k$ at random in $Z_N{}^*$ and squaring them mod N.

Initialize two counters R and NR to 0.

Feed each s_i^2 to MB. Every time that MB answers "quadratic residue," increment the R counter. Every time that MB answer "quadratic non residue," increment the NR counter.

Let $\psi = \frac{2\varepsilon}{4}$. If k is chosen to be suitably large, $k \geq \frac{1}{\delta\psi^2}$, the weak law of large numbers assures that

$$Pr\left(\left| \alpha - \frac{R}{k} \right| > \psi \right) < \frac{\delta}{4},$$

i.e. R/k is a very good approximation to how well MB guesses if the inputs are only quadratic residues.

We are now ready to determine the quadratic residuosity of elements in A_N^*.

Let q be an element of A_N^* that we want to test for quadratic residuosity. Randomly generate k quadratic residues, $x_1, \ldots, x_k$, elements of $Z_N{}^*$ and compute $y_i \equiv qx_i \bmod N$ for $i = 1, \ldots, k$. Notice that

(a) if q is a quadratic residue, then the y_i's are random quadratic residues in $Z_N{}^*$

(b) if q is a quadratic non-residue in $A_N{}^*$, then the y_i's are random quadratic non-residues in $A_N{}^*$.

Let us postpone the proof of (a) and (b) and assume, for the time being, that they are true. Initialize two counters R^* and NR^* to 0. Feed the sample $\{Y_i\}$ into MB. Increment R^* every time that MB answers "quadratic residue," and NR^* every time that MB answers "quadratic non-residue." We know, that if q is a quadratic residue, then the

$$Pr\left(\left|\frac{R^*}{k}-\frac{R}{k}\right|\leq 2\psi\right)\geq\left(1-\frac{\delta}{4}\right)^2,$$

and if q is a quadratic non-residue then

$$Pr\left(\left|\frac{R^*}{k}-\frac{R}{k}\right|\leq 2\psi\right)< 1-\left(1-\frac{\delta}{4}\right)^2.$$

Thus if $\left|\frac{R^*}{k}-\frac{R}{k}\right|\leq 2\psi$ then with probability greater than $1-\delta$, q is a quadratic residue mod N, otherwise, again with probability greater than $1-\delta$, q was a quadratic non-residue mod N.

We still need to prove (a) and (b). We will only prove (a) as the proof for (b) is similar. It will suffice to prove that, given any quadratic residue q, any other quadratic residue y in Z_N^* can be uniquely written as $y=qx$ where x is a quadratic residue mod N. It is a well known theorem in algebra that $Z_N^*=Z_{p_1}^*\times Z_{p_2}^*$. Thus let a and b be generators for $Z_{p_1}^*$ and $Z_{p_2}^*$ such that $(a,p_2)=1$ and $(b,p_1)=1$. Then any element of Z_N^* can be written uniquely as a^ib^j where $1\leq i\leq p_1-1$ and $l\leq j\leq p_2-1$. Moreover, q is a quadratic residue mod N if and only if it can be written as $q=a^{2i}b^{2j}$ where $1\leq 2i\leq p_1-1$ and $1\leq 2j\leq p_2-1$. Thus if $y=a^{2s}b^{2t}$ is any quadratic residue and $x=a^{2(s-i)}b^{2(t-j)}$, then $y=qx$ part (a) is proved. ∎

Theorem 2   Let $r\in A_N^*$ be a publicized quadratic non-residue mod N. Let $0<\varepsilon\leq\frac{1}{2}0<\delta\leq 1$ be non-negligible numbers. Suppose we could guess with an ε advantage whether q, drawn at random from A_N^*, is a quadratic residue mod N. Then we could decide quadratic residuosity of any integer mod N with probability $1-\delta$ by means of a polynomial in $I|N|$, ε^{-1} and δ^{-1} time probabilistic algorithm.

Proof   Assume first that given any r quadratic non-residue mod N, $r\in A_N^*$, someone could build a polynomial time magic box MB_r that has a ε advantage in distinguishing between quadratic residues and non-residues mod N. We will show that even if one is not given such an r, quadratic residuosity can still be decided.

Construct a set T consisting of 20 elements chosen at random from A_N^*. With probability $1-(1/2)^{20}$ one of the elements in T will be a quadratic non-residue mod N. For each $x\in T$ do the following:

Choose k as in Theorem 1. Construct MB_x and test its performance on k random quadratic residues, $S = \{s_1, \ldots, s_k\}$, as we did in Theorem 1. Also pick $y_1, \ldots, y_{20}$ at random from $A_N{}^*$. Again, with very high probability, at least one of the y_i's will be a quadratic non-residue. Now, construct samples $H_i = \{y_i s \mid s \in S\}$, and feed them into MB_x.

(a) If MB_x performs on all the H_i's as it performed on S, then go to the next element in T. Halt if all elements in T have been used.

(b) If MB_x performs "significantly" differently on, say H_i, than it did on S, halt.

If case (b) occurs then y_i is a quadratic non-residue and, most importantly, we obtain a magic box, MB_x, which distinguishes between quadratic residues and non-residues in random polynomial time.

Case (b) occurs when there is an $x \in T$ which is a quadratic non-residue mod N, and at least one of its corresponding y_i's is a quadratic non-residue mod N. Thus case (b) occurs with probability $\left(1 - \frac{1}{2}^{20}\right)^2$. This contradicts our assumption that deciding quadratic residuosity is hard.

In the above, we assumed that given any quadratic non residue $r \in A_N{}^*$, one could construct a magic box MB_r, having a ε advantage in deciding quadratic residuosity, and we derived a contradiction.

Suppose one is able to build a MB_r, having a ε advantage in deciding quadratic residuosity, only for 1% of the quadratic non-residues, $r \in A_N{}^*$. Then all that would be changed in the above proof would be the size of the set T, so that T will include a suitable r. ∎

4 How to Send Messages in a Public Key Cryptosystem in a Provably Secure Way

Every user in the system publicizes a large composite number N whose factorization, $N = p_1 p_2$, he alone knows, and $y \in A_N^*$ such that y is a quadratic non-residue mod N.

Let N be the public key of user A. Suppose user B wants to send A a binary message $m = (m_1, \ldots, m_k)$. Then, for each m_i, B randomly picks an $x_i \in Z_N{}^*$, and sets

$$e_i \leftarrow \begin{cases} x_i^2 \bmod N \text{ if } m_i \text{ is a 0} \\ yx_i^2 \bmod N \text{ if } m_i \text{ is a 1} \end{cases}$$

B sends $(e_1, \ldots, e_k)$ to A.

To decode m, user A, who knows the factors of N, reconstructs m by letting

$$m_i \leftarrow \begin{cases} 1 \text{ if } e_i \text{ is a quadratic residue mod } N \\ 0 \text{ if } e_i \text{ is a quadratic non-residue mod } N \end{cases}$$

Testing whether $q \in A_N^*$ is a quadratic residue mod N, when the factorization of N is known, is easy by the following lemma.

Lemma 2   If the factorization of N is known, we can test whether there exists an x such that $q \equiv x^2 \bmod N$ in polynomial time.

Proof q is a quadratic residue mod N if and only if q is a quadratic residue mod p_1 AND p_2. For a prime p, q is a quadratic residue mod p if and only if $q^{(p-1)/2} = 1 \bmod p$. Thus, to test whether q is a quadratic residue mod N we need only compute $q^{(p_1-1)/2} \bmod p_1$ and $q^{(p_2-1)/2} \bmod p_2$.

We now address the question of the security of the newly proposed Public Key Cryptosystern. Let $E(x)$ stand for our new encryption function and let M be the set of all possible messages.

The definition of security in a Public Key Cryptosystem is very difficult. It depends on the model assumed of the possible behavior of an adversary. At present, we assume that an adversary may intercept $E(m)$ and try to extract information about m. He can make use only of a computer, the cyphertext and the a priori knowledge of the message space M. No restrictions on M are assumed.

Notice that in our scheme, differently from the RSA, an adversary, given $E(m)$, may be lucky in guessing correctly m and yet not able to prove the correctness of his guess. However, the possibility of understanding a message, without being able to prove what it is, is still dangerous for the security of the Public Key Cryptosystem.

We show that, given $E(m)$ for $m \in M$, if an adversary can do better than guessing m at random, then deciding quadratic residuosity of any integer mod N, is easy.

Recall that $A_N^* = \{x \in Z_N^* \mid (x/N) = 1\}$.

Definition   Let $x \in A_N^*$. The **signature** of x, $\sigma_N(x)$ is defined as

$$\sigma_N(x) \leftarrow \begin{cases} 1 \text{ if } x \text{ is a quadratic residue mod } N \\ 0 \text{ if } e_i \text{ is a quadratic non-residue mod } N \end{cases}$$

Let S_N^n be the set of all sequences of n elements from A_N^*.

Definition   Let $s = (x_1, \ldots, x_n) \in S_N^n$. The n-signature of s, $\Sigma_N(s)$, is defined to be the string $\Sigma_N(s) = \sigma_N(x_1)\sigma_N(x_2) \cdots \sigma_N(x_n)$.

Definition   A **decision** function is a function $d \colon S_N^n \to \{0, 1\}$.

Let $a = (a_1, \ldots, a_n)$ and $b = (b_1, \ldots, b_n)$ be n-signatures.

Definition   The **distance** between a and b is defined to be the number of positions in which a and b differ. We say that a and b are **adjacent** if the distance between them is 1.

For any decision function d and n-signature l, let $P_d(l): \{0, 1\}^n \to [0, 1]$ be defined as

$$P_d(l) = \Pr(d(x) = l \mid \Sigma_N(x) = l \text{ for } x \in S_N{}^n)$$

Theorem 3   Let $0 < \varepsilon \le \frac{1}{2}$ and $0 < \delta \le 1$ be non-negligible numbers. If there exists a decision function d which is easy to compute and two n-signatures, u and v, have been found such that $\mid P_d(u) - P_d(v) \mid > \varepsilon$, then we can decide quadratic residuosity of any integer mod N with probability $1 - \sigma$ by means of a polynomial (in $\mid N \mid, \varepsilon^{-1}$, and σ^{-1}) time probabilistic algorithm.

Proof   Suppose there exists a decision function d and two n-signatures u and v such that $\mid P_d(u) - P_d(v) \mid > \varepsilon$. Let Δ be the distance between u and v. Let $a_0, a_1, \ldots, a_\Delta$ be a sequence of n-signatures such that $a_0 = u$, $a_\Delta = v$ and a_i is adjacent to a_{i+1} for $\le i < m$. As $\mid P_d(u) - P_d(v) \mid > \varepsilon$, there must exist $i, 0 \le i \le \Delta - 1$, such that $\mid P_d(a_i) - P_d(a_{i+1}) \mid \varepsilon/n$. For convenience, let $s = a_i$ and $t = a_{i+1}$.

Let us choose $\psi = \frac{\varepsilon}{4n}$. Also, let $k \ge \frac{1}{\delta\psi^2}$. Choose k elements, $x_1, \ldots, x_k$ at random from $\Omega_s = \{x \in S_N^n \mid \Sigma_N(x) = s\}$ and k elements, $y_1, \ldots, y_k$ at random from $\Omega_t = \{x \in S_N^n \mid \Sigma_N(x) = t\}$. Then, by the weak law of large numbers,

$$Pr\left(\left\mid P_d(s) - \frac{d(x_1) + \cdots + d(x_k)}{k} \right\mid > \psi\right) < \frac{\delta}{4}$$

and

$$Pr\left(\left\mid P_d(t) - \frac{d(y_1) + \cdots + d(y_k)}{k} \right\mid > \psi\right) < \frac{\delta}{4}$$

Set,

$$\alpha = \frac{d(x_1) + \cdots + d(x_k)}{k}, \beta = \frac{d(y_1) + \cdots + d(y_k)}{k}$$

As $s = (s_1, \ldots, s_n)$ and $t = (t_1, \ldots, t_n)$ are adjacent, they differ in exactly one location. Call this location r. Let us assume, without loss of generality, that $s_r = 1$ and $t_r = 0$.

We will now show that we can decide quadratic residuosity mod N with probability greater than $1 - \delta$. Let q be an element of A_N^* that we want to test for residuosity. Choose k random quadratic residues in $A_N{}^*: x_1^2, \ldots, x_k^2$ and compute $y_j = q \cdot x_j^2 \bmod N$ for $1 \le j \le k$. By Theorem 1, the y_j's are all quadratic residues if q is a quadratic residue and all quadratic non-residues in A_N^*, otherwise.

In Theorem 2 we showed that knowing a non-residue in A_N^* does not help in deciding quadratic residuosity. Therefore we can assume that such a non-residue, h, is known. This allows us to pick quadratic non-residues at random from A_N^* (by computing hx^2).

We are now ready to decide whether q is a quadratic residue.

(* Construct a random sample of k elements $(y_{1,1}, \ldots, y_{1,n}), \ldots, (y_{k,1}, \ldots, y_{k,n}) \in S_N^*$ such that for all $1 \le i \le n$, $i \ne r$, $1 \le j \le k$, $\sigma_N(y_{j,i}) = s_i$, and for all $1 \le j \le k$, $y_{j,r} = y_j$.*)

For $i = 1, \ldots, r - 1, r + 1, \ldots, n$ do

begin
For $j = 1, \ldots, k$ do
  draw $x \in A_N^*$ at random.
  if $s_i = 1$ then $y_{j,i} := x^2 \bmod N$
  else if $s_i = 0$ then $y_{j,i} := hx^2 \bmod N$
end.

(* Evaluate the decision function d on each member of the sample *)
For $j = 1, \ldots, k$ do
$X_j = d(y_{j,1}, \ldots, y_{j,r-1}, y_j, y_{j,r+1}, \ldots, y_{j,n})$

Notice that the entire sample $\{y_{j,1}, \ldots, y_{j,r-1}, y_j, y_{j,r+1}, \ldots, Y_{j,n} \mid 1 \le j \le k\}$ is either a subset of Ω_s or a subset of Ω_t. Thus with probability greater than $1 - \delta$ one of the following two mutually exclusive events will occur:

$$(1) \quad \left| \frac{(X_1 + \cdots + X_k)}{k} - \alpha \right| < \frac{\varepsilon}{2n}$$

or

$$(2) \quad \left| \frac{(X_1 + \cdots + X_k)}{k} - \beta \right| < \frac{\varepsilon}{2n}.$$

If case (1) occurs, we conclude, with probability greater than $1 - \delta$, that q is a quadratic residue. Otherwise, we conclude, again with probability greater than $1 - \delta$ that q is a quadratic non-residue. ∎

The notion of a decision function is immediately generalized to that of a discriminating function. This is a decision function which can take on more than 2 values. For any non empty set Ω, let $D: S_N^n \to \Omega$. Let $a \in \Omega$, then $P_{D,a}(l) = Pr(D(x) = a \mid \Sigma_N(x) = l$ for $x \in S_N^n)$. The following theorem is an easy extension of Theorem 3 and we will state it without proof.

Theorem 4 Let $0 < \varepsilon \leq \frac{1}{2}$ and $0 < \delta \leq 1$ be non-negligible numbers. If there exists a discriminating function $D: S_N^n \rightarrow A$, which is easy to compute and two n-signatures, u and v, have been found such that $| P_{D,a}(u) - P_{D,a}(v) |> \varepsilon$, then we can decide quadratic residuosity of any integer mod N with probability $1 - \delta$ by means of a polynomial (in $| N |$, ε^{-1}, and $\delta - 1$) time probabilistic algorithm.

Let us introduce some more notation. Let, $M^n = \{m_l, m + 2, \ldots, \}$ be the set of messages whose length is n, where n is bounded by a polynomial function in $| N |$. Set $k =| M^n |$. Let M_i be the set of all possible encodings of message $m_i \in M^n$, using the scheme described at the beginning of this section. Clearly, $M_i \subset S_N^n$ and for all i and j, $| M_i |=| M_j |$. Set $X \chi =| M_i |$.

4.1 The Security of Partial Information

In the present version of the paper, we assume that all messages in M^n are equally likely. Let P be an easy to evaluate predicate, defined on M^n. Let p be the probability that $P(x)$ is true for a random $x \in M^n$. Since M^n is uniformly distributed, and $| M^n |= k$, P must evaluate to 1 on pk messages in M^n.

Let MB be a magic box that receives as input the cyphertext $E(m) \in_N^n$, where $m \in M^n$, and outputs 0 or 1, its guess for the value of $P(m)$. Let 0_j be the number of 0's and let 1_j be the number of 1's that MB guesses on encodings of m_j. Clearly, $0_j + 1_j = X$. Let

$$C_j = \begin{cases} 1_j \text{ if } P(m_j) = 1 \\ 0_j \text{ if } P(m_j) = 0 \end{cases}$$

C_j represents the number of encodings of message m_j on which MB correctly guesses the value of $P(m_j)$.

Theorem 5 Let $0 < \delta < 1$ be a non negligible real number. If $\frac{1}{k_\chi} \sum_{j=1}^{k} C_j \geq p + \varepsilon$, for some non-negligible real $\varepsilon > 0$, then we could decide quadratic residuosity of any integer mod N with probability $1 - \delta$ by means of a polynomial in $| N |$, ε^{-1}, and δ^{-1} time probabilistic algorithm.

Proof Let us partition M^n into $10/\varepsilon$ buckets, $M^n = \bigcup_{i=1}^{10/\varepsilon} B_i$, such that $m \in B_i$ if and only if $(i - 1)\frac{\varepsilon}{10} \leq \frac{1m}{(10\varepsilon^{-1})^2}k$. $(i - 1)\frac{\varepsilon}{10} \leq \frac{1_m}{\chi} < i\frac{\varepsilon}{10}$. We show that there exist two non-adjacent buckets, each containing a non-negligible portion of the messages. More formally, we show there exist g, h where $1 < h + 1 < g \leq 10/\varepsilon$ such that $| B_g |$, $| B_h |> \frac{1}{(10\varepsilon^{-1})^2}k$. Say, that B_i is big if $| B_i |> \frac{1}{(10\varepsilon^{-1})^2}k$ and small otherwise. Then we want to show that there are two non adjacent big buckets. Assume, for contradiction, that this is not the case. Then one of the following cases must apply:

1. There are no big buckets.

2. There is only one big bucket: B_i

3. There are exactly two adjacent big buckets: B_i and B_{i-1}.

Note that case 1 can never be true; otherwise $k = \sum_{i=1}^{10\varepsilon^{-1}} |B_i| \le \frac{k}{10\varepsilon^{-1}} < k$. In case 2, $\sum_{m_j \in B_i} C_j$ is maximum for $i = \frac{\varepsilon}{10}$, and if all messages m_j for which $P(m_j) = 1$ belong to $B_{\frac{\varepsilon}{10}}$, i.e. when MB guesses 1 for all the encodings of all the messages for which the predicate is true.

Thus,

$$p + \varepsilon \le \frac{1}{k\chi} \sum_{m_j \in M^n} C_j = \frac{1}{k\chi} \left(\sum_{m_j \in B_i} C_j + \sum_{m_j \in B_k, k \ne i} C_j \right) \le p + \frac{\varepsilon}{10} < p + \varepsilon$$

In case 3, $\sum_{m_j \in B_i} C_j + \sum_{m_j \in B_{i-1}} C_j$ is maximum when $i = \frac{\varepsilon}{10}$ and all the messages for which P is true belong to $B_{\frac{\varepsilon}{10}}$ and all the messages for which P is false belong to $B_{\frac{\varepsilon}{10}-1}$.

Thus,

$$p + \varepsilon \le \frac{1}{k\chi} \sum_{m_j \in M^n} C_j = \frac{1}{k\chi} \left\{ \left(\sum_{m_j \in B_i} C_j + \sum_{m_j \in B_{i-1}} C_j \right) + \sum_{m_j \varepsilon B_k k \ne i, i+1} C_j \right\}$$

$$\le \frac{1}{k\chi} \left\{ \left[pk\chi + (1-p)2\varepsilon 10^{-1} k\chi \right] + k\chi\varepsilon 10^{-1} \right\}$$

$$\le \frac{2}{k\chi} (pk\chi + 3\varepsilon 10^{-1} k\chi) < p + \frac{\varepsilon}{2}$$

In all three cases we reach a contradiction.

Thus there exist two non adjacent buckets B_g and B_h each containing at least $\frac{\varepsilon}{10}k$ messages. By sampling, we can find, in a small expected time, two messages u and v in B_g and B_h, respectively. We view MB as a decision function $D: S_N^n \to [0, 1]$. Then, $P_D(u) - P_D(v) > \frac{\varepsilon}{10}$ and Theorem 3 applies.   ∎

Next, we will see that an adversary cannot decode more than a negligible fraction of the encodings of all messages.

4.2   An Adversary Cannot Decode

Let MB be a magic box that receives as input $E(m)$ for $m \in M^n$, and outputs m_i. MB's output can be interpreted as MB's guess of what m is.

Let $r_{j,i}$ denote the number of encodings of message m_j, on which MB answers m_i. Clearly, $r_{i,i}$ will denote the number of times, over all possible encodings of m_i, that MB answers correctly.

Theorem 6 Let $0 < \delta < 1$ be a non negligible real number. If $\sum_{i=1}^{k} \frac{r_{i,i}}{k\chi} > \varepsilon + \frac{1}{k}$ for some non-negligible $\varepsilon < 1 - \frac{1}{k}$, then we can decide quadratic residuosity mod N with probability $1 - \delta$ by means of a polynomial in $|N|$, ε^{-1} and δ^{-1} time probabilistic algorithm.

Proof Say that a message m_i is well decoded if $r_{i,i} > \left(\frac{1}{2}\varepsilon\right)\chi$. Let, W be the set of well-decoded messages and $W' = M^n - W$.

Claim 1: There exist at least $\frac{\varepsilon k}{2}$ well-decoded messages.

Proof:

$$\varepsilon k \chi < \varepsilon k + \chi < \sum_{i=1}^{k} r_{i,i} = \sum_{i \in W} r_{i,i} + \sum_{i \in W} r_{i,i}$$

$$\leq \chi \mid W \mid + (k - \mid W \mid)\frac{1}{2}\varepsilon\chi = \chi\left[\left(1 - \frac{1}{2}\varepsilon\right)\mid W \mid + k\frac{1}{2}\varepsilon\right]$$

Hence, $\frac{|W|}{k} > \frac{\varepsilon/2}{(1-\varepsilon/2)} > \frac{\varepsilon}{2}$. (claim 1) ∎

Clearly, if we pick messages at random from M^n, we expect to find a well-decoded message in $2\varepsilon^{-1}$ trials. Let $\Omega \subset W$ such that $\mid \Omega \mid > 2\varepsilon^{-1}$ and let $p > \frac{1}{2\varepsilon^{-1}(2\varepsilon^{-1}+1)}$.

Claim 2: There exists two well-decoded messages $m_i, m_j \in \Omega$ such that $\left| \frac{r_{i,i}}{\chi} - \frac{r_{j,i}}{\chi} \right| > \rho$.

Proof: Fix $m_j \in \Omega$. How many messages $m_i \in \Omega$ can be such that $\left| \frac{r_{i,i}}{\chi} - \frac{r_{j,i}}{\chi} \right| \leq \rho$? There are at most $\frac{1}{\left(\frac{1}{2}\varepsilon - \rho\right)} < 2\varepsilon^{-1} + 1$ such messages. Thus there exists an $m_i \in \Omega$ that satisfies the claim. (claim 2) ∎

Let us transform MB into a discriminating function $D: S_N^n \to M^n \cup \{\gamma\}$. If $x \in S_N^n$ and MB, on input x, outputs m_j, then set $D(x) = m_j$. If y is not the encoding of any message, then one of 3 cases must occur:

1. MB outputs m_i for $1 \leq i \leq t$. Set $D(y) = m_i$.

2. MB outputs m_i for $i < 1$ or $i > t$. Set $D(y) = \gamma$.

3. MB does not answer within a certain time limit. Set $D(y) = \gamma$.

Now, note that in claims 1 and 2 just proved above, we showed that we can quickly find two well-decoded messages m_i and m_j such that $\mid P_{D,m_i}(m_i) -$

$P_{D,m_i}(m_j) \mid > \rho$. Thus the hypothesis of Theorem 4 holds and deciding quadratic residuosity mod N is polynomial in $\mid N \mid$, ε^{-1} and δ^{-1}.

Theorem 6 shows that inverting the function E on the encrypted messages is as hard as deciding quadratic residuosity, independently of the sparsity of M^n.

5   Mental Poker

Mental Poker is played like regular poker except that there are no cards and no deck The game is played over the telephone lines, or over a computer network. Since we can not send physical cards over the phone lines, dealing and playing must be simulated by exchanging messages between the players. The players do not trust each other more than ordinary players do. A **fair game on the telephone** should ensure that:

1. Neither player can have any partial information about the cards in his opponent's hand or in the deck,

2. There is no overlap in the cards dealt to players,

3. All possible hands are equally probable for both players,

4. At the end of the game each player can verify that the game was played according to the rules and no cheating occurred.

Note that in a fair game of Mental Poker it is not enough to show that it is computationally difficult to get the exact value of a card. We must also show that no partial information about the card can fall into the hands of an adversary.

We present a protocol for two people to play a fair game of Mental Poker, using eneryption. We prove that there is no way a player can get any information about cards not in his hand under the assumption that deciding quadratic residuosity is hard.

There are two main tools used in our implementation of Mental Poker. One is a method for coin-flipping over the telephone [5] and the other is the method for sending a single bit securely in a Public Key Cryptosystem presented here.

A different solution to the problem of Mental Poker has been obtained independently by Manuel Blum in [6]. His solution is based on the assumption that factoring is hard and that completely secure one way functions exist.

5.1   Background For Coin Flipping

To *flip a coin in the well*—A and B stand far apart from each other. B is standing next to a deep well. A throws a coin into the well from a distance. Now, B knows the outcome of the flip (by looking into the well) but can not change it, and A has no way of knowing the outcome. Later on when B would like to prove to A that he won (or lost), he lets A come closer and look into the well.

Essentially, if we can simulate a flip in the well by exchanging messages over the telephone, A can send a random bit to B, where A does not know what he sent, but B can, if necessary, prove to A what the bit was. This is especially applicable to cryptographical games.

The notion of coin flipping in the well has been introduced by Blum and Micali in [5], in which, based on the assumption that index finding is hard, they show how to flip a coin in the well over the telephone lines. Another method based on the assumption that factorization is hard has been found by Blum in [4]. We sketch a third method, based on the difficulty of distinguishing quadratic residues from non-residues with respect to composite moduli.

> A and B want to flip a coin. A generates two large odd primes at random, P and Q and sets $N = P * Q$. A publicizes N and $y \in A_N^*$ such that y is a quadratic non-residue mod N. A picks a number q at random from A_N^* and asks B, who does not know the factorization of N, whether q is a quadratic residue mod N or not. B tells A what his guess is. A now knows whether B won (lost), and can later prove to B that he indeed won(lost) by releasing the factorization of N.

To avoid adding new assumptions to the ones that we already have, we propose to use one of these latter two coin flipping methods in our protocol for Mental Poker.

The next section will list some known results that will be used in the proof of the protocol.

5.2 Useful Results

Let p_1, p_2 be odd primes and $N = p_1 p_2$.

Lemma 3 If the factorization of N is known, we can find $q \in Z_N^*$ such that $(q/N) = 1$ and q is a quadratic non-residue, in random polynomial time.

Proof Pick $a \in$ This can be done in 2 expected trials. Similarly, pick $b \in Z_{p_2}$ such that $(b/p_2) = -1$. Using the Chinese Remainder theorem compute the Z_{p_1} such that $(a/p_1) = -1$. unique $q \in Z_N^*$ such that $q \equiv a \pmod{p_1}$ and $q \equiv b \pmod{p_2}$. Now, q is a quadratic non-residue and $(q/N) = (q/p_1 p_2) = (q/p_1) \cdot (q/p_2) = (a/p_1) \cdot (b/p_2) = 1$. ∎

Lemma 4 Let $N = p_1 p_2$ such that $p_1 \equiv p_2 \equiv 3 \bmod 4$. For all x, $y \in Z_N^*$, if $x^2 \equiv y^2 \bmod N$ and $x \neq \pm y \bmod N$ then $(x/N) = -(y/N)$.

Proof Let

$$c \leftarrow \begin{cases} 1(\bmod\ p_1) \\ 0(\bmod\ p_2) \end{cases}$$

$$d \leftarrow \begin{cases} 1(\bmod\ p_2) \\ 0(\bmod\ p_1) \end{cases}$$

We can find c and d through the Chinese Remainder Theorem. Let $a^2 \equiv x^2(\bmod\ p_1)$ and $b^2 \equiv x^2(\bmod\ p_2)$. Then the four square roots $(\bmod\ N)$ are given by $ac + db$, $-ac + db$, $-(ac + db)$ and $(ac - db)$. Let $x = ac + db$, and $y = -ac + bd$. Since $N \equiv 1 \bmod 4$ implies $(x/N) = (-x/N)$, we need only prove that $(+x/N) = -(+y/N)$. Thus, $(x/N) = (ac + bd/N) = (ac + bd/p_1)(ac + bd/p_2) = (ac/p_1)(bd/p_2)$. And $(y/N) = (-ac + bd/N) = (-ac + bd/p_1)(-ac + bd/p_2) = (-ac/p_1)(bd/p_2) = (-1/p_1)(x/N)$. Since $p_1 = 3(\bmod 4)$, $(-i/p_1) = -1$. ■

By a theorem of de la Vallee Poussin [15], approximately half of all primes of a given length are congruent to 3 mod 4. Thus, composite numbers of the form $N = p_1 p_2$ where $p_1 \equiv p_2 \equiv 3 \bmod 4$ constitute approximately 1/4 of all composite numbers which are a product of two odd primes of a given length. Thus factoring and deciding quadratic residuosity modulos such special N's remains a hard problem. Another method, which does not use special composite numbers, but increases the number of messages exchanged in the protocol, will appear in the final paper.

5.3 The Protocol

To represent 52 cards in binary we must use at least 6 bits per card. Thus at first A and B agree on 52 different bit patterns which correspond to the 52 cards.

From now on, when we say that A flips k to B, we mean that B receives a number k at random from A, and A has no information whatsoever about k. k is actually sent bit by bit through a sequence of *coin flips into a well*.

5.3.1 The Algorithm

STEP 1: B chooses at random 52 pairs of large prime numbers: (p_1, q_l), (p_2, q_2), $(p_3, q_3), \ldots, (p_{52}, q_{52})$ such that $p_i \equiv q_i \equiv 3 \bmod 4$ for $1 \leq i \leq 52$, and produces 52 large composite numbers whose factorization she knows, i.e. $N_l := p_1 \cdot q_l$, $N_2 := p_2 \cdot q_2, \ldots, N_{52} := p_{52} \cdot q_{52}$. Next, she shuffles the deck of cards in her hands and assigns $N_1, \ldots, N_{52}$ to the shuffled deck, an N_i per the ith card. She publicizes the ordered 52 tuple $< N_1, N_2, \ldots, N_{52} >$.

STEP 2: A does the same. Let us denote the primes chosen by him as (s_1, t_1), (s_2, t_2), $(s_3, t_3), \ldots, (s_{52}, t_{52})$ such that $s_i \equiv t_i \equiv 3 \bmod 4$ for $1 \le i \le 52$, and his 52 composite numbers by $M_1 := s_1 \cdot t_1$, $M_2 := s_2 \cdot t_2, \ldots, M_{52} := s_{52} \cdot t_{52}$. He shuffles the deck of cards and assigns $M_1, \ldots, M_{52}$ to the shuffled deck, an M_i, per the ith card. He publicizes the ordered 52 tuple $< M_1, M_2, \ldots, M_{52} >$.

STEP 3: B publicizes his entire deck. The deck is encrypted in the following way. For every card C_i (with public key N_i), B publicizes an ordered list of 6 numbers in $A^*_{N_i}$, $(q_l, \ldots, q_6)$ such that for $1 \le j \le 6$, q_j is a quadratic residue if and only if the jth bit of C_i is a 1.

For example, let the first card in B's deck be 010010. Then B publicizes $(q_l, q_2, q_3, q_4, q_5, q_6)$ where q_l, q_3, q_4 and q_6 are quadratic non-residues mod N_i, and q_2, q_5 are quadratic residues mod N_i with Jacobi symbol 1. The q_i's are chosen at random among the elements of $A^*_{N_i}$ with the desired properties. This can be done in random polynomial time, by Lemma 3.

NOTE that, by Lemma 2, if A can factor N_i, he can also determine whether the numbers that B posed as corresponding to the bits in the encoding of C_i are quadratic residues or not and therefore determine what the card is. If A can not factor N_i, he can not tell whether the numbers corresponding to bits in the cards encoding are quadratic residues or not, and therefore can not tell what the remaining cards are.

STEP 4: A publicizes his deck in the exact same way that B did.

STEP 5 [B deals a Card to A]: Suppose A decided to pick the K-th card from B's deck. Repeat the following procedure for each card in B's encrypted deck. We describe it for the i-th card, to which N_i corresponds. B flips $x \in Z^*_{N_i}$, to A. A computes $x^2 \bmod N_i$ and (x/N_i). At this point A must follow one of two procedures: P1 if $i = K$ and P2 otherwise.

> **P1:** A sends $x^2 \bmod N_i$ and $-(x/N_i)$ to B.
> **P2:** A sends $x^2 \bmod N_i$ and (x/N_i) to B.

B computes the square roots of $x^2 \bmod N_i$. Let the square roots be $x, n - x, y$ and $n - y$. Next, B sends the root whose Jacobi symbol she received from A : y if she received $-(x/N_i)$ from A, and x otherwise. By Lemma 4, (x/N_i) uniquely identifies x, and $-(x/N_i)$ uniquely identifies y. Thus if A followed P1 then he will receive 4 square roots of $x^2 \bmod N_i$, and by Lemma 1 can factor. If A followed P2, he will get no new information as to the value of C_i. B from her side has no information as to which card A selected. Later, B can verify what he flipped to A, and hence verify that B has only found out the factorization of a single card.

STEP 6: At this point A knows the factorization of N_K. To reconstruct the actual card C_K, A applies the polynomial time test of Lemma 2 to the encrypted representation of C_K, $(q_1, \ldots, q_6)$. Next, A must delete C_K from his encrypted deck. B can see which encrypted element in A's deck is being erased, but this does not enable her to decrypt it.

STEP 7 [A deals a card to B]: Clearly, the same procedure as in Step 5 and 6 is done with the roles of A and B reversed. Now B will discover the factorization of one of $M_1, \ldots, M_{52}$.

STEP 8: If any more cards need to be dealt throughout the game, a similar protocol takes place. Whenever A needs a card, he will pick a card from B's deck, by following the procedure in step 5 and 6. And similarly whenever B needs a card, she will pick it from A's deck.

STEP 9 [after game verification]: After the game is over, A can prove to B that everything he claims she flipped him, was indeed flipped by her and in what order. B can do the same. A releases the factorization of each of the M, for all $1 \leq i \leq 52$, and B releases the factorization of each of the N_i for all $1 \leq i \leq 52$. They can both prove to each other whatever claim they made in the game such as "N is a product of two primes," "all cards where present at the deck at all times," "these are the quadratic residues you flipped to me," or "I won."

5.3.2 Proof Of Correctness

Claim 1 All hands are equally probable.

Proof In step 9, A and B verify that both encrypted decks contained all 52 cards. In step 5, A himself chooses which encrypted value from B's deck he wants, thus he is equally likely to get any card in the deck. Similar reasoning holds for B. ∎

Claim 2 No overlapping or repeating hands.

Proof When A is dealt a card, he erases that card from his encrypted deck. Thus B can never be dealt the same card. A knows which cards he picked from B's deck, and thus will never pick the same card twice. ∎

Claim 3 If player A knows the factorization of N_i he can reconstruct C_i in $0(|N|^3)$ time.

Proof We are given $N_i = p_1 p_2$, and $(q_1, \ldots, q_6)$ such that for all j, $q_i \in Z_N^*$ and $(q_j/N_i) = 1$. To reconstruct, C_i, we must test whether q_j is a quadratic residue mod N_i for all j. That can be done in $0(|N|^3)$ steps by Lemma 2.

It still remains to be shown that neither player can have, at any stage of the game, any partial information, about a single encrypted card not in his hand, or any subset of encrypted cards not in his hand. A complete proof will be found in the final paper. Here we restrict ourselves to proving that when two players A and B publicize their respective encrypted decks, neither A nor B can answer quickly with 1% advantage a 1 bit question about a single card in the opponents deck. Examples of such 1 bit questions are: is the i-th card in the deck black? Are the first and third bit of the i-th card equal? Is the mod 2 sum of the bits in the i-th card 0 or 1?

Theorem 7   If A, when B publicizes her encrypted deck, can answer, in polynomial time, a 1-bit question Q about a single card in B's deck with 1% advantage, then he can decide quadratic residuosity modulo a random composite N with probability 1, by means of a polynomial $(|N|)$ time probabilistic algorithm.

Proof   Suppose A can answer a 1-bit question Q about card i, to which composite N_i corresponds. A's ability to answer Q with a 1% advantage can be viewed as a decision function $d: S^6 \rightarrow 0, 1$ (S^6 = all 6-1ong sequences of elements from $A^*_{N_i}$). Since A answers Q correctly 51 times out of a 100, we can efficiently find two 6-signatures u and v such that $|P_d(u) - P_d(v)| \geq 1/100$. Thus we can apply Theorem 3 and decide quadratic residuosity modulo N_i in polynomial time. Contradiction!

5.3.3   Implementation Details

In order to perform the protocol we must be able to do the following:

1. Generate large prime numbers, This can be done using Gary Miller's test for primality [11] .

2. Find square roots of x^2 mod N when the factorization of N is known. Use Adleman, Manders and Miller's polynomial time algorithm [2] for finding square roots.

6   Remarks and Further Improvements

In this paper we showed that it is possible to encrypt messages in such a way, that an adversary, given the cyphertext, cannot extract information about the cleartext. This is sufficient for protocols such as Mental Poker or for encrypting one's private files. An adversary can read these files but cannot understand them.

We also showed that Probabilistic Encryption can be used in a Public Key Environment. However, in a Public Key Cryptosystem, getting hold of the cyphertext and trying to understand it is the most obvious attack to the security of the scheme.

- An adversary could, as a user, try to break the scheme by communicating.

- He could try to break the scheme by intercepting some other user's messages and changing them.

- Finally, he may try to break the scheme by making use of the decoding equipment !

The Public Key Cryptosystem presented in this paper is not secure against these possible attacks. However, by forcing the users to follow a particular protocol for exchanging messages, we have built a Public Key Cryptosystem which is provably secure against the above mentioned attacks. These results will appear in a future paper.

Acknowledgements

Our most sincere thanks go to Richard Karp, who supervised this research, for his contributions, encouragement and great patience, and to Manuel Blum for a wonderful course in Number Theory, many insightful discussions and for having found a way to reduce the numbers of messages exchanged in the protocol.

We are particularly indebted to Faith Fich, Mike Luby, Jeff Shallit and Po Tong. Without their generous help this paper would have never been written.

Andrew Yao pointed out to us some general difficulties arising with commutative encryption functions. The claim in Section 2.4 was obtained with Vijay Vazirani. We thank them both.

We are grateful to Ron Rivest and Mike Sipser for a very inspiring discussion. It improved this paper a great deal.

References

[1] Adleman, L. *Private Communication*. 1981.

[2] Adleman, L., Manders, and Miller, G. *On taking roots in finite fields*. Proceedings of the 18th Annual IEEE Symposium on Foundations of Computer Science (FOCS), 1977, 175–177.

[3] Adleman, L. *On distinguishing prime numbers from composite numbers*. *Proceedings of the 21st IEEE Symposium on the Foundations of Computer Science (FOCS)*, Syracuse, N.Y., 1980, 387–408.

[4] Blum, M., *Three Applications of The Oblivious Transfer*, to appear, 1981.

[5] Blum, M., and Micali, S. *How to Flip A Coin Through the Telephone*, to appear, 1982.

[6] Blum, M. Mental Poker, to appear, 1982.

[7] Brassard, G. *Relativized Cryptography*. Proceedings of the 20st IEEE Symposium on the Foundations of Computer Science (FOCS), San Juan, Puerto Rico, 1979, 383–391.

[8] Diffie, W. and M. E. Hellman, *New Direction in Cryptography*. IEEE Trans. on Inform. Th. IT-22, 6 (1976), 644–654.

[9] Coldwasser, S., and Micali S. *A Bit by Bit Secure Public Key Cryptosystem*, Memorandum NO. UCB/ERL M81/88, University of California, Berkeley, December 1981.

[10] Lipton, R. *How to Cheat at Mental Poker*. Proceedings of the AMS Short Course on Cryptology, January 1981.

[11] Miller, G. *Riemann's Hypothesis and Tests for Primality*. Ph.D. Thesis, U.C. Berkeley, 1975.

[12] Rabin, M. *Digitalized Signatures and Public Key Functions As Intractable As Factorization*. MIT/LCS/TR-212, Technical Memo MIT, 1979.

[13] Rivest, R., Shamir, A., Adleman, L. *A Method for Obtaining Digital Signatures and Public Key Cryptosystems*. Communications of the ACM, February 1978.

[14] Shamir, Rivest, and Adleman. *Mental Poker*. MIT Technical Report, 1978.

[15] Shanks, D. *Solved and Unsolved Problems in Number Theory*, Chelsea Publishing Co. (1978).

Added in proof:

[16] Chaum, D. L. *Untraceable Electronic Mail, Return Addresses, and Digital Pseudonymus*. Communications of the ACM, 24,2 (1981) 84–88.

The Knowledge Complexity of Interactive Proof Systems

This chapter reproduces the contents of the paper "The Knowledge Complexity of Interactive Proof-Systems," which appeared in the proceedings of the *17th Annual ACM Symposium on Theory of Computing*, pp. 291–304, 1985.

This seminal work of Shafi Goldwasser, Silvio Micali, and Charles Rackoff introduced two fascinating and highly influential concepts: the concept of interactive proofs and the concept of zero-knowledge. The concept of interactive proofs had a vast impact on complexity theory, to be illustrated in numerous chapters of this volume. The concept of zero-knowledge, on top of being very intriguing, became a central tool in cryptography (see Chapter 12), and led to fundamental discoveries regarding general secure multi-party computation (see Chapters 13 and 15). Initial indications of the vast potential impact of these concepts were provided by the results and discussions in this work.

The Knowledge Complexity of Interactive Proof-Systems (Extended Abstract)

Shafi Goldwasser (MIT)**, Silvio Micali** (MIT),
Chales Rackoff (University of Toronto)

1 Introduction

In the first part of the paper we introduce a new theorem-proving procedure, that is a new *efficient method of communicating a proof*. Any such method implies, directly or indirectly, a definition of proof. Our "proofs" are probabilistic in nature. On input an n-bits long statement, we may erroneously be convinced of its correctness with very small probability, say, $\frac{1}{2^n}$, and rightfully be convinced of its correctness with very high probability, say, $1 - \frac{1}{2^n}$.

Our proofs are *interactive*. To efficiently verify the correctness of a statement, the "recipient" of the proof must actively ask questions and receive answers from the "prover."

This research was supported in part by 1BM Young Faculty Development Award dated September 1983. IBM Young Faculty Development Award dated September 1984, and NSF grant DCR-8413577.

In the second part of the paper, we address the following question:

How much knowledge should be communicated for proving a theorem T?

Certainly enough to see that T is true, but usually much more. For instance, to prove that a graph is Hamiltonian it suffices to exhibit an Hamiltonian tour. This appears, however, to contain, much additional knowledge than the single bit "Hamiltonian/non-Hamiltonian."

We give a computational complexity measure of knowledge and measure the amount of <u>additional</u> knowledge contained in proofs.

We propose to classify languages according to the amount of additional knowledge that must be released for proving membership in them.

Of particular interest is the case where this additional knowledge is essentially 0 and we show that is possible to interactively prove that a number is quadratic non residue mod m releasing 0 additional knowledge. This is surprising as no efficient algorithm for deciding quadratic residuosity mod m is known when m's factorization is not given. Moreover, all known NP proofs for this problem exhibit the prime factorization of m. This indicates that adding interaction to the proving process, may decrease the amount of knowledge that must be communicated in order to prove a theorem.

2   Interactive Proof Systems

Much effort has been previously devoted to make precise the notion of a theorem-proving procedure, NP constitutes a very successfull formalization of this notion. Loosely speaking, a theorem is in provable in NP if its proof is easy to verify once it has been found. Let us recall Cook's [C] (and independently Levin's [L]) influential definition of NP in this light.

> The NP proof-system consists of two communicating Turing machines A and B: respectively, the *prover* and the *verifier*. The prover is exponential-time, the verifier is polynomial-time. Both A and B are deterministic, read a common input and interact in a very elementary way. On input a string x, belonging to an NP language L, A computes a string y (whose length is bounded by a polynomial in the length of x) and writes y on a special tape that B can read. B then checks that $f_L(y) = x$ (where f_1 is a polynomial-time computable function relative to the language L) and, if so, halts and accepts. This process is illusuated in Figure 1.

What is intuitively required from a theorem-proving procedure? First, that it is possible to "prove" a true theorem. Second, that it is impossible to "prove" a false theorem. Third, that communicating a proof should be <u>efficient</u> in the following

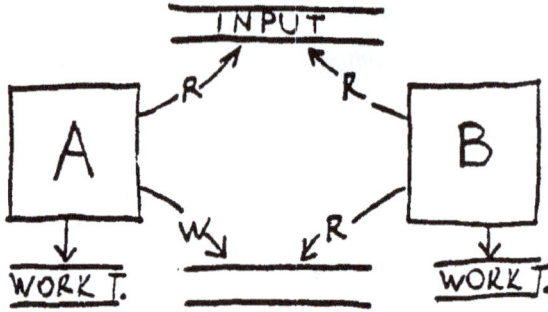

Figure 1   The *NP* proof-system[(*)].

sense. It does not matter how long must the prover compute during the proving process, but it is essential that the computation required from the verifier is easy.

Theorem-proving procedures differ in the underlying definition of a proof. The notion of a proof, like the notion of a computation, is an intuitive one. Intuition, however, may and must be formalized. Computability by (deterministic) Turing machines is an elegant example of formalization of the intuitive concept of a computation. Each formalization, however, cannot entirely capture our original and intuitive notions, exactly because they are intuitive. Following our intuition, probabilistic algorithms [R] [SS] are means of computing, though they are not in the previous formal model. Similarly, *NP* is an elegant formalization of the intuitive notion of a theorem-proving procedure. However, *NP* only captures a particular way of communicating a proof. It deals with those proofs that can be "written down in a book". In this paper we introduce interactive proof-systems to capture a more general way of communicating a proof. We deal with those proofs that can be "explained in class". Informally, in a classroom, the lecturer can take full advantage of the possibility of interacting with the "recipients" of the proof. They may ask questions at crucial points of the argument and receive answers. This makes life much easier. Writing down a proof that can be checked by everybody without interaction is a much harder task. In some sense, because one has to answer in advance all possible questions. Let us now formally set up the proper computational model.

[(*)] (By $\longrightarrow$ we denote a read/write head. By $\longrightarrow$R a read-only head and by $\longrightarrow$W a write-only head).

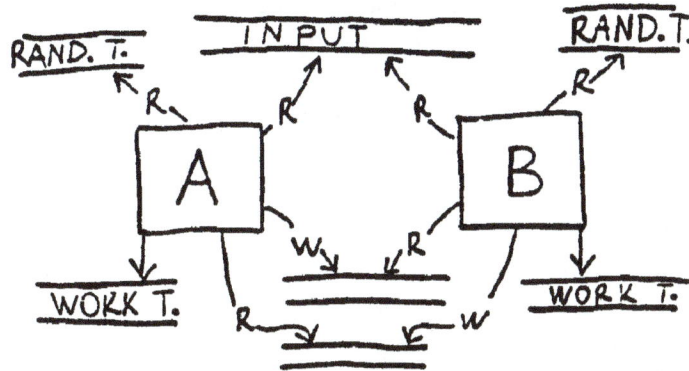

Figure 2 An interactive pair of Turing machines.

2.1 Interactive Turing Machines and Interactive Pairs of Turing Machines

An interactive Turing machine (ITM) is a Turing machine with a read-only input tape, a work tape and a random tape. The random tape contains an infinite sequence of random bits. The random tape can be scanned only from left to right. When we say that an interactive machine flips a coin we mean that it reads next bit in its own random tape. This tape is the only source of randomness for the machine. In addition an interactive machine has a read-only communication tape and a write-only communication tape. The head writing on the latter tape moves only from left to right, writes only on a blank cell and cannot move to the right without writing.

Two ITM's A and B form an *interactive pair of Turing machines* (A, B) by

1. letting A and B share the same input tape and

2. letting B's write-only communication tape be A's read-only communication tape and vice versa.

The interactive pair (A, B) is ordered and machine B starts the computation. The machines take turns in being active. When, say, A is active, it can perform internal computation, read and write on the proper tapes and send a message to B by writing on the appropriate communication tape. The ith message of A is the entire string that A writes on the communication tape during its ith turn. The ith message of B is similarly defined. Either machine can, during its turn, terminate the computation of the pair. Consider a computation of (A, B) on input x. Let the computation consist of n turns and let a_i be A's ith message and b_i be B's ith message. Then the text of the computation is defined to be the sequence $\{b_1, a_1, \ldots, b_n, a_n\}$. ($a_n$ is empty if it is B that halts the computation of (A, B) in its nth turn). The text of all possible computations of A and B on input x will be of relevance to our analysis and it will bc denoted by $(A, B)[x]$. This set has the structure of a probability space in the natural way. The probability of each computation in $(A, B)[x]$ is taken over the coin tosses of both machines.

2.2 Interactive Proof-Systems

Let $L \subseteq \{0.1\}^*$ be a language and (A, B) an interactive pair of Turing machines. We say that (A, B) is an *interactive proof-sysrem* for L if A (the prover) has infinite power, B (the *verifer*) is polynomial time and they satisfy the following properties.

1. For any $x \in L$ given as input to (A, B), B halts and accepts with probability at least $1 - \frac{1}{n^k}$ for each k and sufficiently large n.

2. For any ITM A^* and for any x not in L given as input to (A^*, B), B accepts with probability at most $\frac{1}{n^k}$ for each k and sufficiently large n.

Here n denotes the length of the input and the probabilities are taken <u>only over B's own coin tosses</u>.

Condition 1 essentially says that. if $x \in L$, there exist a way to easily prove this fact to B that succeeds with overwhelming probability. This way is A's algorithm. In other words, it is possible to prove a true theorem so that the proofs are easily verified (B is polynomial-time). Condition 2 says that, if x not in L, there exist no strategy, for convincing B of the contrary, that succeeds with non negligible probability. In other words, no one can prove a false theorem. In fact, B needs not to trust (or to know) the machine with which it is interacting. It is enough for B to trust the randomness of its own coin tosses. Notice that, as for NP, the emphasis is on the "yes-instances": if a string is in the language we want to show it, if it is not we do not care. Let us consider an example of an interactive proof-system.

Example 1   Let Z_m^* denote the set of integers between 1 and m that are relatively prime with m. An element $a \in Z_m^*$ is a *quadratic residue* mod n if $a = x^2 \bmod m$ for some $a \in Z_m^*$, else it is a *quadruric nonresidue*. Now let $L = \{(m, x) \mid x \in Z_m^* \text{ is a quadratic nonresidue}\}$. Notice that $L \in NP$: a prover needs only to compute the factorization of m and send it to the verifier without any further interaction. But looking ahead to zero knowledge proof-systems, we will consider a more interesting interactive proof-system for L. The verifier B begins by choosing $n = \mid m \mid$ random members of Z_m^*, $\{r_1, r_2, \ldots, r_n\}$. For each i, $1 \leq i \leq n$, he flips a coin, and if it comes up heads he forms $t_t = r_1^2 \bmod m$, and if it comes up tails he forms $t_t = x \cdot r_1^2 \bmod m$. Then B sends $t_1, t_2, \ldots, t_n$ to A. The prover, having unrestricted computing power, finds which of the t_t, are quadratic residues, and uses this information to tell B the results of his last n coin tosses. If this information is correct, B accepts.

Why does this work? If $(m, x) \in L$, then A correctly predicts all last n coin tosses of B who will definitely accept. If (m, x) not in L, then the $\{t_i\}$ are just random quadratic residues, and the prover will respond correctly in the last part of the computation with probability $\frac{1}{2^n}$. In fact, for each of the last n coin tosses of B, A has probability exactly $1/2$ of guessing it correctly.

A more complex interactive proof-system for L, that releases essentially 0 additional knowledge, can be found in Section 4.2.

2.3 Interactive Complexity Classes

We define *IP*, *Interactive Polynomial-time*, to be the class of languages possessing an interactive proof-system. In this case we may also say that L, is interactively provable. To emphasize that the prover has unlimited power, we may write IP_∞ for *IP*. To closer analyze the role of the prover, we define $IP_{T(n)}$ to be the class of languages having an interactive proof-system whose prover runs in time $T(n)$. To focus on the role of interaction, we let $IP[f(n)]$ denote the class of languages having a proof-system that, on input a string x of length n, halts within $f(n)$ turns. Here f is a non decreasing function from natural numbers to natural numbers.

Interactive proof-systems should be contrasted with the "Arthur-Merlin" games of Babai [B]. In those games Merlin plays the role of A and Arthur the role of B. The big difference is that Merlin sees all results of Arthur's coin tosses. This allows Babai to prove that arbitrary interaction is not necessary in his framework: it is sufficient to allow Arthur to talk to Merlin and have Merlin respond; at least as long they alternate a constant number of times. Actually Arthur's message to Merlin consists exactly of the sequence of its own coin tosses. (See Figure 3).

If membership in a language L can be proved by an Arthur-Merlin game ($L \in AM$) then, for any random oracle O, $L \in NP^O$ with probability 1. It is apparent that $AM \subseteq IP$ (actually, $AM \subseteq IP[1]$) and we believe that the inclusion is a strict one. We also believe that our "interactive hierarchy" does not collapse, i.e. that $IP[k]$ is strictly contained in $IP[k+1]$. In any case, interactive proof-systems are the right proof model to both analyze and reduce the knowledge complexity of a language. Next section is devoted to the discussion of this more subtle notion. Let us also mention Papadimitriou [P] "games against nature". This is an elegant characterization of **PSPACE**, though not an efficient method of communicating a proof.

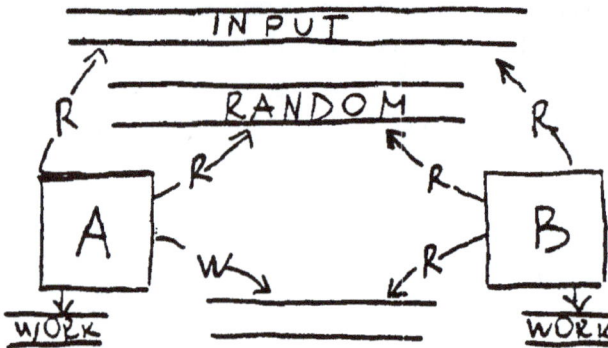

Figure 3   The Arthur-Merlin proof-system.

3 Knowledge Complexity

Communication is a tool for transferring or exchanging knowledge. Knowledge has received a lot of attention in a model-theoretic framework [FHV], [HM]. In this context, roughly speaking,

1. *All participanrs are considered to have infinite computing power*. (E.g. each participant "knows" <u>all</u> logical consequences of the information in his hands) and

2. *The object they try to "know better" is not an available public input.* (Rather some event occurs that is witnessed or noticed by <u>some</u> but not <u>all</u> participants. To give an elementary example, one participant flips a coin and tells the outcome to a few others who now "know" it. The remaining participants do not "know" what the outcome was and they have to decide between two possible worlds: one in which "heads" came up and one in which "tails" came up).

This scenario may not be realistic in many practical contexts. In physics. for example, scientists have *bounded resources* and the object they try to know better is a *public input*: nature. Our point of view is that

1. *Knowledge is a notion relative to a specfic model of computation with specified computing resources and*

2. *One studies and gains knowledge about available objects.*

In this paper we mcasure the amount of knowledge that can be gained from a communication by a participant with polynomially bounded resources and investigate how much knowledge must bc communicated for proving a theorem.[1] Our computational complexity measure of knowledge is, howcvcr, of wider applicability. For example, as sketched in Section 6, it constitutes a powerful tool for developing a mathematical theory of cryptographic protocols. The following concept will be crucial to our analysis.

3.1 Degrees of Distinguishability for Probability Distributions

Let I be an infinite set of strings and c a positive constant. For each $x \in I$ with length n, let Π_x be a probability distribution over the n^c-bit strings. Then we say that $\Pi = \{\Pi_x \mid x \in I\}$ is a *I-c-ensemble*. By saying that Π is an *ensemble* or a *I-ensemble* we mean, respectively, that there exist I and c or simply c such that Π is a I-c-ensemble.

A *distinguisher* is a probabilistic polynomial-time algorithm D that on input a string s outputs a bit b. Let $\Pi_1 = \{\Pi_{1,x} \mid x \in I\}$ and $\Pi_2 = \{\Pi_{2,x} \mid x \in I\}$ be two I-c-ensembles. Let $p^D_{x,1}$ denote the probability that D outputs 1 on input a $\mid x \mid^e$-bit long string randomly selected with probability distribution $\Pi_{1,x}$. Symmetrically, $p^D_{x,2}$ denotes the probability that D outputs 1 on input a $\mid x \mid^e$-bit long string randomly selected with probability distribution $\Pi_{2,x}$. Let $p: N \to [0, 1]$. We say that the ensembles Π_1 and Π_2 are *atl most p-distinguishable* if for all distinguishers D, $\mid p^D_{x,1} - a^D_{x,2} \mid < p(\mid x \mid) + \frac{1}{|x|^k}$ for all k and sufficiently long x.

Of particular interest will be the notion of at most 0-distinguishability (or indistinguishability). In this case the two ensembles are "equal" with respect to any polynomial-time computation. In Section 4.2 we will present an interesting example of indistinguishable ensembles. In this example. the $\Pi_{1,x}$ and $\Pi_{2,x}$ are indistinguishable in a stronger sense. In fact the probability that they assign to each $\mid x \mid^c$-bit string is identical except for a set of strings strings whose total probability does not exceed $\frac{1}{2^{d|x|}}$ for some constant d between 0 and 1. Such strong indistinguishability is a luxury not always available and, in any case, is not necessary to develop our theory.

Notice that our distinguishers are fed with a single $\mid x \mid^c$-bit string at a time. One may consider distinguishers that are fed with more strings of length $\mid x \mid^c$ at the same time. In this case, if two ensemble are 0-distinguishable, they will remain undistinguishable (as long "more" $< poly(\mid x \mid)$). If the two ensembles are at most p-distinguishable, they may remain at most p-distinguishable or the probability of "distinguishing" them may become much higher. (This plays a role for deciding

---

1. Our definitions may be given with respect to any time bound, but we restrict our attention to polynomial-time both to simplify the matter a bit and because we believe that it constitutes the most important case.

whether a certain cryptographic protocol may be played securely more than once using the same secret key).

Related notions of indistinguishability have been previously considered in [GM] in the context of probabilistic encryption and then in [Y] and [GGM] in the context of pseudo-random number generation.

3.2   The Knowledge Computable from a Communication

Which communications convey knowledge? Informally, those that transmit the output of an unfeasible computation, a computation that we cannot perform ourselves. For example, if A sends to B n random bits, this will be n bits of information. We would say this contains no knowledge, however, because B could generate random bits by himself. Similarly, the result of any probabilistic polynomial-time computation will not contain any knowledge. With this in mind we would like to derive an upper bound (expressed in bits) for the *amount* of knowledge that a polynomially bounded B can extract from a communication.

First a bit of notation. Notice that any probabilistic Turing machine M generates the ensemble $M[\cdot] = \{M[x]\}_{x \in I}$, where $M[x]$ denotes the set of possible outputs of M (on input $x \in I$) taken with the probability distribution induced by M's coin tosses. Similarly, we will denote by $(A, B)[\cdot]$ the ensemble associated to an interactive pair of Turing machines (A, B). We are now ready to introduce our definition.

Definition   Let (A, B) be an interactive pair of Turing machines and I the set of its inputs. Let B be polynomial-time and $f: N \to N$ be non decreasing. We say that A *communicates atl most $f(n)$ bits of knowledge to B* if there exists a probabilistic polynomial-time machine M such that the I-ensembles $M[\cdot]$ and $(A, B)[\cdot]$ are at most $1 - \frac{1}{2^{f(n)}}$-distinguishable. We say that A *conmmicates at most $f(n)$ bits of know1edge* if for all polynomial-time ITM's B' A communicates at most $f(n)$ bits of knowledge to B'.

Remark 1   Assume M, on input x, tries to select a string "as undistinguishable as possible" from a computation randomly selected in $(A, B)[x]$. Note that in this attempt no information is hidden from M: A's program, B's program and x are all inputs of M. M may have "built in" the description of A. This, however, is not of great help, as A's algorithm may be absolutely inefficient.

A non mathematical discussion: Let us try to illustrate the above definitions. Assume that a crime x has happened, B is a reporter and A a police officer. A understands the rights of the press but, for obvious reasons, also tries not to communicate too much knowledge. Should reporter B call the police officer A to know more about x? It depends. If he has probability essentially equal to 1 of generating at home, in front of his typewriter, the "same" conversations about this <u>specific</u> x that he might have with A, he should not bother to call. A will give him essentially 0 knowledge about x. If, instead, say, he may generate an honest conversation about x with probability 1/4 (i.e. what he generates is at most 3/4-distinguishable from the "real" conversations), then the officer may tell him something that he does not know. This knowledge however, will not exceed two bits and may not be of the "useful" kind! Still, it may pay off to call. If, finally, B has only chance 1 in 2^{100} of generating the possible conversations about x with the police officer, then A is a real gossiper and B should rush to the telephone! Assume now that B is so news-hungry that is ready to become dishonest during the phone conversation, i.e. he is ready to transform himself to B'. Despite this, if the officer is so skillful to be one who communicates, say, at most 2 bits of knowledge, no matter how tricky questions B' asks and how much he cheats, he will not get out of him more than two bits about x. (Here we are implicitly assuming that a cheating reporter still remains a polynomial-time one!)

Example 2 Consider the ITM (A, B) of Example 1. Restrict its inputs only to the strings in L. Then A communicates at most 0 bits of knowledge to B. In fact, there exists a probabilistic polynomial-time machine M such that (for those inputs) generates exactly the same ensemble that (A, B) does. Essentially, M can simulate B, as B is polynomial-time, and simulates A <u>by looking at B's coin tosses</u> as follows. When B sends t_i computed by squaring r_t, M will answer "quadratic residue". When B sends t_i computed by squaring r_t and then multiplying it by x, M answers "quadratic nonresidue".

Notice, however, that, if the problem of deciding quadratic residuosity is not in probabilistic polynomial-time, A <u>does not</u> communicate at most 0 bits of knowledge. In fact, some machine B', interacting with A, may decide to create the t_i's in a different way. For instance, such a B may send the, sequence of integers $t_i = i$ and therefore receive an answer about their quadratic residuosity that it may not be able to compute by itself.

An interesting ITM A that communicates at most 0 bits of knowledge may be found in section 4.2.

3.3 The Knowledge Complexity of a Language

How much knowledge should be communicated to provide a proof of a theorem T? Certainly enough to verify that T is true. Usually, much more. For example, to prove that a certain $a \in Z_m^*$ is a quadratic residue, it is sufficient to communicate an x such that $a \equiv x^2 \bmod m$. This communication, however, contains more knowledge than just the fact that a is a quadratic residue. It communicates a <u>square root</u> of a. We intend to measure the additional knowledge that a prover gives to a verifier during a proof, and investigate whether this additional knowledge may be essentially 0.

Definition Let L be a language possessing an interactive proof-system (A, B). Let $f: N \to N$ be non decreasing. We say that L has *knowledge complexity* $f(n)$ if, <u>when restricting</u> the inputs of (A, B) to the strings in L A communicates at most $f(n)$ bits of knowledge. We denote this fact by $L \in KC(f(n))$.

An informal discussion. Let us recall that we are concentrating on the "yes-instances." When a string x is not in the language the prover "gives up" and we do not measure knowledge. When, instead, $x \in L$, what is the verifier's point of view at the end of an interactlve proof? First, it is "convinced" (correctly with overwhelming probability) that $x \in L$. This was the goal of the proof-system in the first place. Second, it possesses the text of the entire computation with the prover on input X. This text, has been used to verify that $x \in L$, but does not contain more than $f(n)$ bits of additional knowledge. In fact, on input $x \in L$, we are guaranteed to be able to easily generate such texts with probability distribution at most $(l - \frac{1}{2^{f(n)}})$-distinguishable from the "real" texts, no matter with which machine B' A is interacting. The special case $L \in KC(0)$ is of particular interest. In this case, by interacting with A and from the text of the computation, B can verify that $x \in L$, but, with respect to polynomial-time computation, the text is irrelevant for any other purpose, no matter with which B' A is interacting. In fact, on input a guaranteed $x \in L$, such texts can be easily selected with essentially the right probability distribution and without A.

We believe that knowledge complexity is one of the fundamental parameters of a language or, equivalently, of a theorem-proving procedure. Theorem-proving procedures are intended to communicate knowledge and it is very natural to classify them according to the amount of knowledge they communicate.

Note that knowledge complexity is also defined for NP proof-systems as they are a special type of interactive proof-system. However, their knowledge complexity tends to be very high.

A very important application of knowledge complexity is that it enables proving correctness of cryptographic protocols in a *modular way* (see section 6).

4 Languages in KC(0)

Every language in P or RP or BPP has trivially knowledge complexity 0. If L is not in probabilistic polynomial-time, no *NP* proof-system for L can release 0 additional knowledge. However, there may be a more interactive proof-system for L that <u>does</u>

release 0 additional knowledge. A natural question arises. Do meaningful examples of languages in $KC(0)$ exist or is $KC(0)$-BPP a fancy way to define the empty set? A similar question could bc asked for, say, RP. Namely, is RP-P a fancy name for the empty set? The best sign of a possible negative answer to the latter question is constituted by the fact that primality testing is in RP [SS] [R] and, while the problem of deterministically deciding primality has received a lot of attention for centuries, no polynomial-time algorithm is currently known. Similarly, it is of great interest to find candidates for languages in $KC(0)$ but not in, say, *BPP*. This is the best one can do, given our current knowledge about proving lower-bounds.

We know of two interesting languages that have knowledge complexity 0. Both are algebraic. The first one is the following language BL proposed by Blum in [Bl1] where he gives all the essential ingredients to prove $BL \in KC(0)$. Let n be an integer with prime factorization $n = p_1^h \cdots p_k^{h_k}$. Then $n \in BL$ if the number of different p_is congruent to 3 mod 4 is even. The other language that is known to belong to $KC(0)$ is the well known quadratic non-residuosity language. We give a proof of this fact in this section.

For $y \in Z_m^*$ we define

$$Q_{(y)} = \begin{cases} 0 & \text{if } y \text{ is a quadratic residue mod } m \\ 1 & \text{otherwise} \end{cases}$$

Then $L = \{(Y, m) \mid Q_m(y) = 1\}$ is the quadratic non-residuosity language.

Our proof that $L \in KC(0)$ does not depend on <u>any unproved computational complexity assumptions</u>. We first review what is known about the complexity of deciding membership in this language.

4.1 The Quadratic Residuosity Problem

The quadratic residuosity problem with parameters $m \in N$ and $x \in Z_m^*$ consists of computing $Q_m(x)$. If the factorization of m is known, it is trivial to compute Q_m. If the factorization of m is unknown, then there is no known efficient procedure for computing Q_m. This decision problem is one of the four main problems discussed by Gauss in "Disquisitiones Arithmeticae" (1801) (along with primality testing, integer factorization and Solvability of Diophantine Equations). A polynomial time solution for it would imply a probabilistic polynomial time solution for other open problems in Number Theory such as deciding whether a composite integer m is a product of 2 or 3 primes.

The Jacobi symbol $\left(\frac{x}{m}\right)$ for $m \in N$ and $x \in Z_m^*$ is a polynomial time computable function that evaluates to 1 and -1 and provides some information about $Q_m(x)$. Namely, if $\left(\frac{x}{m}\right) = -1$ then $Q_m(x) = 1$. However, when $\left(\frac{x}{m}\right) = 1$ then computing $Q_m(x)$

is a hard problem. n fact, it is not even known how to efficiently produce a single "guaranteed" quadratic nonresidue mod m with Jacobi symbol 1.

4.2   A "0" Knowledge Interactive Proof System for *L*

In the proof system, (A, B), that we exhibit for $(y, m) \in L$ the prover A is only required to be a probabilistic polynomial time Turing machine with the additional power of being able to evaluate Q_m. (Of course, it remains true that no infinitely powerful A' can convince B that y is a quadratic non-residue mod m if that is not the case).

For simplicity, we only consider proving that $(y, m) \in L$, when the Jacobi symbol $\left(\frac{y}{m}\right) = 1$. The case where $\left(\frac{y}{m}\right) = -1$ is uninteresting. We specify A and B by giving their explicit program at each step of the interaction.

The basic idea is that B generates numbers of two types: $x = r^2 \bmod m$ (type 1) and $x = y \cdot r^2 \bmod m$ (type 2) where r is randomly chosen, and quizzes A about them. If indeed (y, m) is in L, then A can tell the types of these numbers. If (y, m) is not in L, they look all the same to A and it will fail the quizzes with very high probabiilty. The danger with this basic idea arises when indeed $(y, m) \in Z_n^*$ is in L as A, when answering the quizzes, may release some knowledge other than $(y, m) \in Z_n^*$ (e.g. the quadratic residuosity of specific other $x \in Z_n^*$ chosen by a cheating B'). We overcome this danger, by having A make sure that the machine with which it is interacting "knows" what are the types of the numbers it quizzes A about.

A and B's Interactive Program

Input: $(y, m) \in L$ such that $\left(\frac{y}{m}\right) = 1$ and $n = \log_2 m$.

Initialize *iteration* $= 0$.

Step 1:.

B first chooses a random r_0 from Z_m^*, and then tosses a coin C_x. If $C_x = 0$, then B sets $x = r_0^2 \bmod n$, else if $C_x = 1$, B sets $x = y \cdot r_0^2 \bmod n$. B sends x to A.

Then, B chooses two random sets, each of size n,

$$T = \{t_1, t_2, \ldots, t_n \mid t_i = r_i^2 \bmod m\}$$

and,

$$S = \{t_{n+1}, t_{n+2}, \ldots, t_{2n} \mid t_i = y \cdot t_{n+1}, t_{n+2}, \ldots, t_{2n} \mid t_i = \bmod m\}$$

B sends to A the elements in $T \cup S$ in random order.

Step 2:.

A picks a random subset $Z \subseteq T \cup S$ of size n and sends it back to B.

Step 3:.

For each $z \in Z$, B sends to A r such that $z = r^2 \bmod m$ or $z = y \cdot r^2 \bmod m$.
Suppose that the sizes of $T - Z$ and $S - Z$ differ by d. Then. B chooses d
random elements from the larger set, $t_{i_1}, \ldots, t_{i_d}$ and sends their respective
$r_{i_1}, \ldots, r_{i_d}$ to A. (i.e. $t_{i_j} = r_{i_j}^2$ or $t_{i_j} = y \cdot r_{i_j} \bmod m$ for some $1 \leq i_j \leq 2n$)). B sets
$X = T - Z - \{t_{i_1}, \ldots, t_{i_d}\}$, and $Y = S - z - \{t_{i_1}, \ldots, t_{i_d}\}$.
If $x = r_0^2 \bmod m$, B lets:

$$X' = \{r_0 \cdot r_i = \sqrt{x \cdot t_i} \bmod n \mid t_i \in X\}$$

$$Y' = \{y \cdot r_0 \cdot r_1 = \sqrt{y \cdot x \cdot t_i} \bmod n \mid t_i \in Y\}.$$

else if $x = y \cdot r_0^2 \bmod m$, B lets:

$$X' = \{y \cdot r_0 \cdot r_i = \sqrt{y \cdot x \cdot t_i} \bmod n \mid t_i \in X\}$$

$$Y' = \{y \cdot r_0 \cdot r_1 = \sqrt{x \cdot t_i} \bmod n \mid t_i \in Y\}.$$

B then sends the elements in $X' \cup Y'$ to A in random order.

Step 4:.

A checks that $X' \cup Y'$ is of the form specified in step 3 (i.e for all $w \in X' \cup Y'$,
$w^2 = t_i x \bmod m$ or $w^2 = t_i \cdot x \cdot y \bmod m$ for some $t_i \in X \cup Y$) and that $\mid X' \cup Y' \mid > \frac{n}{3}$. If this is not the case, A halts detecting cheating. Otherwise, A sends
B the value $v = Q_m(x)$.

Step 5:.

If $v \neq C_x$, then B halts detecting cheating, otherwise *iteration = iteration + 1*
(this is the end of an iteration).
If *iteration $\geq n$*, then B accepts $(y, m) \in L$, otherwise B goes back to step 1.

Let us first prove that (A,B) constitutes an interactive proof-system for L.

Remark 2   Note that if A, B both operate according to specification, then each iteration of the
program will be completed with probability $> 1 - \frac{1}{2^{cn}}$ for $0 < c \leq 1$.

The following claims 1 & 2 hold for each completed iteration.

Claim 1   If (y, m) is not in L, then A (or any other A') correctly guessed C_x (i.e sends $v = C_x$),
with probability exactly $\frac{1}{2}$.

Proof The proof follows from the fact that $C_x = 0$ with probability exactly $\frac{1}{2}$ and that even with infinite computation power A' can't distinguish between a computation with B in which $C_x = 0$ from one in which $C_x = 1$. The latter can be seen as follows. ∎

Suppose $C_x = 0$.

Then, in step 3 for all $t_i \in X$, A receives $r_0 r_1 = \sqrt{t_i x} = \sqrt{r_1^2 r_0^2} \bmod m$. Note that $e_i = t_i \cdot x \bmod m$ is a random square, (as t_i is) and $r_0 r_i$ is a random square root of $e_1 \bmod m$. for all $t_i \in Y$, A receives $y \cdot r_0 \cdot r_i = \sqrt{y \cdot t_i \cdot x} = \sqrt{y^2 r_i^2 r_0^2} \bmod m$. Note that $f_i = y \cdot t_i \cdot x = y^2 \cdot r_i^2 \cdot x \bmod m$ is a random square, (as r_i^2 is) and $y \cdot r_0 \cdot r_0 \cdot r_i$ is a random square root of $f_i \bmod m$.

Suppose $C_x = 1$.

Then, in step 3, for all $t_i \in X$, A receives $y \cdot r_0 \cdot r_i = \sqrt{y \cdot t_i \cdot x} = \sqrt{y^2 r_i^2 \cdot r_0^2} \bmod m$. Note that $e_i = y \cdot t_i \cdot x \bmod m$ is a random square, (as both y and t_i are now squares and t_i is a random square) and $y \cdot r_0 \cdot r_i$, is a random square root of $f_i \bmod m$.

for all $t_i \in Y$, A receives $y \cdot r_0 \cdot r_i = \sqrt{t_i \cdot x} \bmod m$. Note that $f_i = t_i \cdot x = y^2 \cdot r_i^2 \cdot r_0^2 \bmod m$ is a random square, (as r_i^2 is) and $y \cdot r_0 \cdot r_i$ is a random square root of $f_i \bmod m$.

Thus, for both $C_x = 0$ and $C_x = 1$ A will still receive random square roots of random squares. Therefore A can't have any advantage in predicting C_x.

Claim 2 If (y, m) in L, then A correctly computed C_x in step 4.

Theorem 1 (A,B) is an interactive proof-system for L.

Proof For every $(y, m) \in L$ given as input to (A,B), B halts and accepts with probability greater than $\left(1 - \frac{1}{2^{cn}}\right)$ for all constants $0 < c \leq 1$ and sufficiently large n. This follows by claim 2. For any machine A' and for any (y, m) not in L. given as input to (A', B), B accepts with probability at most $\frac{1}{2}$ by claim 1 and remark 3. ∎

We now proceed to show that L has knowledge complexity 0.

Theorem 2 L has knowledge complexity 0.

Proof To show that (A, B) constitutes a 0 knowledge proof-system for L we must show that for each polynomial-time ITM B', there exists a probabilistic polynomial-time Turing Machine M, such that the two ensembles $M[\cdot]$ and $(A, B')[\cdot]$ are indistinguishable. The basic idea is that M can easily simulate B', as B' runs in polynomial time. On the other hand, M will succeed in simulating A, by running B' twice with the same coin tosses.

A more precise description of M is the following: On input $(y, m) \in L$, M randomly fills the random tape of B' with a sufficiently long string R, and makes B' perform "its own version" of step 1. (B' may in fact execute a different algorithm than B during step 1.) Simulating A in step 2 is easy for M, as all A does here is picking a random subset. Next, M makes B' perform its own version of step 3. Now, M must simulate A in step 4. Notice that it is easy to check whether A will halt in step 4. Therefore it will be easy for M to simulate A in a computation with B' in which A halts in step 4. Difficulties arise if A won't halt but continue. This implies that M must compute $Q_m(x)$ correctly as A does. This is easy to do for A who has enough power to decide the quadratic residuosity of x. Notice that this would also be easy for M if B', either generated x by squaring mod m an r_0 that M may observe (in which case M knows that $Q_m(x) = 0$), or if B' generated x by squaring mod m an r_0 and multiplying by y (in which case M knows that $Q_m(x) = 1$). However, life may be not so easy. B' might have generated x in some other way (e.g. at random) which would make it hard for M to compute $Q_m(x)$. We overcome this difficulty as follows. By $c_1, c_2, c_3, \ldots$ we denote fixed, positive constants depending on A and B'. Without loss of generality, we may assume that on input (y, m) A will halt in step 4 with probability less than $1 - \frac{1}{2^{c_1 n}}$. (Otherwise by simulating A and B' for steps 1, 2 and 3, as above, and having A halt in step 4, we trivially generate computations which are indistinguishable from $(A, B')[(y, m)]$.

At the end of step 3, M saves all messages sent so far by B' and the "virtual" A. M now runs B' again with the same input (y, m) and the same content R in the random tape of B'. For this second compuation, M simulates A anew, by flipping new coins. Four things will happen in this second computation.

1. B' sends in step 1 the same sets S and T, as in its first computation.

2. In step 2, A will select a random subset $\tilde{Z} \subseteq T \cup S$. With probability greater than $1 - \frac{1}{2^{c_2 n}}$, $\tilde{Z} \neq Z$ (where Z denotes the set chosen in the first computation).

3. In step 3, B sends the sets $\tilde{X}$ and $\tilde{Y}$. (The respective sets in the first compuation were X' and Y'). With probability $> 1 - \frac{1}{2^{c_3 n}}$, X and Y are of the right form (i.e could not cause the legal A to halt).

4. With probability $1 - \frac{1}{2^{c_4 n}}$, $\tilde{X} \neq X'$ and $\tilde{Y} \neq Y'$.

M now selects an element $t_i \in (T - X') \cap \tilde{X}$. As $t_i \in T - X'$, in the first compuation B' sent its corresponding r_i. As $t_i \in \tilde{X}$, in the second computation B' sends $\sqrt{xt_i}$ mod m or $\sqrt{xt_i y}$ mod m. Now, in whatever case, it is just a matter of algebra for

M to easily compute r_0 such that $r_0^2 = x \bmod m$ or $r_0^2 \cdot y = x \bmod m$. If $(y, m) \in L$, exactly one of these cases may occur. Therefore M, having computed r_0, can simulate A by sending a $v = Q_m(x)$.). ■

5 A Parenthetical Section

Remark 3   A stronger way of saying that A communicates at most $f(n)$ bits of knowledge with respect to polynomial-time computation, is the following.

> For all ITM B' there exist a polynomial-time ITM M that by interacting with B' (but also reading the random tape of B'!) produces an ensemble at most $\left(1 - \frac{1}{s^{f(n)}}\right)$-distinguishable from $(A, B')[\cdot]$.

This notion is stronger as it allows B' not to be bound to polynomial-time computation while A needs not to know what the computing power of B' is. Full details will be given in the final paper. Interestingly, the interactive proof-system for quadratic non-residuosity of section 4.2 releases 0 additional knowledge even with respect to this stronger definition.

An informal definition: One advantage of the point of view of Remark 3 is that it allows one to express in a clean way notions like "the polynomial-time machine B knew x at some point of its computation". Let us consider a particular example. Assume that machine B started computing on input k and outputs a k-bit integer m. B may have randomly selected two primes p_1 and p_2, multiplied them together to produce m, then "erased" p_1 and p_2 and output m. What could one mean by saying that B knew the factorization of m? A natural choice is that B is able to compute it. In a narrow sense, this may mean that, in performing next instruction, B will output m's factorization or that it was written, say, at the beginning of B's work-tape at some point in time. In a broader sense it may mean that if a probabilistic polynomial-time machine M "monitors" the sequence of istantaneous descriptions of B's computation, then M outputs m's factorization with very high probability in poly(k) time. This, however, may not be general enough. In fact, "extracting" m's factorization may not be easy for M, and still B had enough "potential" to efficiently compute it (though B's program may never explicitly do so). We believe that the following (informal) definition achieves the right level of generality. Let M be a probabilistic polynomial-time machine that monitors B's computation from the start till it outputs m. In particular, M reads all the inputs (random and not) of B and all its outputs. Informally we say that B *knew m's factorization* if M can now use B to compute m's factorization. This use of B may be very general. For example, M

may run B more than once after altering the content of its tapes. An example of this is implicit in section 4.2. Full details will be given in the final paper.

6 Applications to Cryptographic Protocols

Given our current state of knowledge about lower bounds, the security of a cryptographic protocol must be proved based on the intractability assumption of some candidate hard problem. Thus one must accept that further analysis may reveal some candidate hard problems to be efficiently solvable. What is not acceptable is that a protocol may be broken <u>without violating the relative intractability assumption</u>.

In traditional computational complexity or communication complexity, the goal is to communicate as much knowledge as possible as efficiently as possible. Since all participants are considered good friends, no one cares if more knowledge than necessary is communicated. The situation with respect to cryptographic protocols is very different. In this case there is generally no problem at all communicating the knowledge efficiently, but the whole problem is making sure not *too much* knowledge has been communicated.

Model theoretic knowledge has been used to analyze protocols. For example, in [HR] it has been used to prove Rabin's "Oblivious Transfer" correct in some setting. However, as pointed out in [FMR], Rabin's oblivious transfer still lacks a proof of correctness in a complexity theoretic framework.

We believe that knowledge complexity provides the right framework to discuss the correctness of crytographic protocols. Applying these ideas, [FMR] modified Rabin's oblivious transfer so that it can be proved correct. A sketch of this can be found in section 6.1.

Knowledge complexity helps in proving or disproving the correctness of cryptographic protocols as these are based on the secrecy of some private information and should preserve this secrecy. The privacy of some information is what gives us an advantage over our adversaries. Let A(lice) possess the prime factorization of an integer n (say $n = p_1 \cdot p_2$), while B(ob) only knows n. During a protocol with B, A must protect the privacy of her information. Assume that A can perform each step of the protocol without having even to look at the value of $p - 1$ and p_2. Then it is easy to show that the protocol did not compromise the privacy of n's factorization. It is also easy to see, however, that the protocol could not have accomplished any interesting task. In fact A has not made use of her "advantage"! The protocol may accomplish a non-trivial task if, in at least one step of it, A performs a computation c that depends on p_1 and p_2. This raises the question:

Will $c(p_1 p_2)$ betray to much information about p_1 and p_2?

Classical information theory does not provide an answer to this question. Knowledge complexity can. In particular,

1. We can quantify the amount of knowledge about p_1 and p_2 that c conveys and

2. We can design protocols so to minimize this amount of knowledge.

If (A, B) is a 0 knowledge interactive proof-system for L, we already saw that, on input $x \in L$, A gives B at most *one* bit of knowledge, namely $x \in L$. (That is 0 additional knowledge). More generally however, we define an upper bound, measured in bits, on the amount of knowledge A gives to B in a particular protocol (to appear in the final paper).

We use this to give an upper bound on the number of times a single protocol or a combination of protocols can be played, using a common secret key, without giving away too much information about the secret key. In addition, trying to measure the amount of knowledge revealed during the execution of a protocol about the secret, may pin point weaknesses in the design of the protocol. For example the amount of knowledge revealed in a protocol of [BD] appeared to be unreasonably large. Further analysis by [H] showed that this protocol could be broken if the encryption function used in the protocol is RSA with low exponents or Rabin's function.

A most important application of these ideas is that it allows us to prove correctness of protocols in a *modular way*. Complex protocols are usually composed of sub-protocols. For instance, many protocols use a sub-protocol for "coin tossing over a telephone" (Blum [Bl1]). However, it is not clear how to use a "normal" definition of correctness of "coin tossing" to prove the correctness of the main protocol. In general, it appears that much stronger definitions for these sub-protocols are needed in order to fit them modularly and cleanly inside larger protocols. Full details will be given in the final paper.

6.1   A Modification of the Oblivious Transfer That Is Provably Equivalent to Factoring

This section is joint work of [FMR]. The notion of an Oblivious Transfer (OT) has been introduced by Rabin [HR] who also proposed the first protocol implementing it. OT appears useful as a design tool. See for example Blum [Bl2] and Even Goldreich and Lempel [EGL]. Rabin introduced OT (to be described below) in a number theoretic setting. More generally tbc OT can bc viewed as a protocol for transfering a large amount of knowledge with probability 1/2 [EGL]. Berger, Peralta and Tedrick

[BPT] present a correct protocol for "obliviously transferring" a random number. Different from OT, this protocol transfers no knowledge.

The notion of an OT involves two parties A and B and an integer n (product of two large distinct primes) whose factorization is only known to A. A would like to send the factorization of n to B with the following constraints:

1. B must have 50% chance of receiving the factorization of n and the other half of the time B should not know any information at all about the factors of n.

2. A should not have any idea whether or not B received the factorization of n.

Rabin's protocol relies on the computational difficulty of factoring. However, as described below, there is a potential flow in his protocol: it is *possible* that B can cheat and factor n with probability much higher than 1/2 even if the intractability assumption of factoring holds. Although we cannot prove that B can really cheat, no one has yet been able to prove that B cannot. Before proceeding any further, let us describe Rabin's proposed protocol. We assume that A and B both know n and that A knows its factorization.

Step 1: B chooses a random x, $1 \leq x \leq n$, relatively prime with n. Then B computes $y \equiv x^2 \bmod n$ and sends y to A.

Step 2: A computes a random square root $(\bmod\, n)$ z of y and sends z to B. (If no square root exists, A does nothing).

Step 3: B checks that $z^2 \equiv y \bmod n$. (If not, B halts detecting cheating). Let us assume that $z^2 \equiv y \bmod n$. It is well known that y has four square roots mod n that can be written as $\{x, -x, w, -w\}$, where B knows x. With probability 50% z will be x or $-x$ and B receives no knowledge. With probability 50%, however, z will be w or $-w$, in which case $gcd(n, x + z)$ will be a factor of n, allowing B to compute the factorization of n.

Party A cannot cheat by sending back some cleverly chosen square root z of of n: no matter what n does, $z \in \{x, -x\}$ with probability 50% and $z \in \{w, -w\}$ with probability again 50% and A cannot know which is the case.

Is it clear, however, that B cannot cheat? We wish it to be the case that at the end of the protocol B cannot factor with probability (much) bigger than 1/2, even if B cheats, and we wish to prove this assuming only that factoring is hard. What happens if B does not square any x at all, but instead picks a particular cleverly chosen square mod n y to send? Perhaps knowing any square root mod n of y will allow B to factor n. That is, perhaps there is a polynomial time algorithm that given n produces a "special" square mod n y, and another polynomial time algorithm that given y, n and any square root of y mod n factors n. The point is not that we have such algorithms, but that no one has proved that the existence of such algorithms contradicts the assumption that factoring is hard. Hence, the proof that Rabin's protocol is correct relies not only on the assumption that factoring is hard, but on an additional complicated and unnatural assumption, essentially that the above algorithms do not exist.

We have been able to prove that a modified version of Rabin's OT is correct. I.e. the probability (taken over the possible choices of n and all possible random choices of B) that B can factor n in k steps at the end of the protocol, equals $1/2 +$ the probability that B can factor n in k steps before the protocol starts. The heart of the modified protocol is that in addition to y, B gives A a minimum knowledge interactive proof that he possesses a square root of y following the ideas in section 4.2. In particular, such interactive proof will not reveal any information about which square root B knows. Now that we have made sure that B knows one square root of y, when A will give him one of them at random, it is easy to prove that B's probability of factoring n at the end of the protocol equals $1/2 +$ the probability that he had of factoring n before the start of the protocol.

7 Open Problems

Many open problems arise. We only list a few of them.

1. Is *NP* strictly contained in *IP*?

2. Is KC(0) contained in NP?

3. Is KC(0) contained in $IP[1]$?

4. Is *IP*[k] strictly contained in *IP*[$k + 1$]?

5. Are there NP Complete languages in $KC(\Omega(n))$?

6. For what time-bound $T(n)$, if any, $IP_{infinite} \subseteq IP_{T(n)}$?

Acknowlededgements

Mike Sipser greatly helped in focusing on this problem.

We highly benefited from the encouragement and the ideas of Dena Angluin, Manuel Blum, Steve Cook, Mike Fischer, Oded Goldreich. Ravi Kannan, Dick Karp, David Lichtenstein, Albert Meyer, Gary Miller, Ron Rivest and Paul Weiss.

To all our most sincere thanks.

References

[B]   Babai L., *Trading Group Theory for Randomness*

[Bl1]   M. Blum, *Coin flipping by relephone*, IEEE COMPCON 1982.

[Bl2]   M. Blum. *Three applications of the oblivious transfer*, Unpublished manuscript, 1981

[BPT]   Berger, Peralta, Tedrick, *On fixing the Oblivious Transfer*, Presented in Eurocrypt 1983. These Proceedings

[C]   S. Cook, *The Complexity of Theorem-Proving Procedures, Proc. of 3rd STOC, 1971.*

[DB]   D. Dolev, A. Broder, *Flipping Coins in Many Pockets*, Proc. of 25th FOCS, 1984.

[EGL]   Even, Goldreich Lempel, *A randomized profocol for Signing Contracts*, Advances in Cryptology: proceedings of Crypto 1982, Plenum press, 1983, 205–210.

[FHV]   R. Fagin, J. Halpem, M. Vardi, A model-theoretic analysis of knowledge, Proc. of 25th FOCS, 1984.

[FMR]   M. Fischer, S. Micali and C. Rackoff, *A Secure Protocol for the Oblivious Transfer*, Eurocrypt 1984.

[HM]   J. Halpern, Y. Moses, *Knowledge and Common Knowledge in a Distributed Environment*, Proc. of 3rd PODC, 1984.

[H]   J. Hastad, *On Solving A System of Simultaneous Modular Polynomial Equations of Low Degree*, In preparation.

[HR]   J. Halpcrn and M.O. Rabin, *A Logic to reason about likehood*, Proc. of 15th. STOC, 1983.

[HS]   J. Hastad, A. Shamir, *On the Security of Linearly Truncated Sequences*, this proceedings.

[GM]   S. Goldwasser, and S. Micali, *Probabilistic Encryprion*, JCSS Vol. 28, No. 2, April 1984.

[GM]   S. Goldwasser, and S. Mlcali, *Proofs with Untrusted Oracles*, Unpublished Manuscript 1983.

[GGM]   O. Goldreich, S. Goldwasser, and S. Micali, *How to Construct Random Function*, 25th FOCS, 1984.

[L]   L.A. Levin, *Universal Sequential Search Problems*, Probl. Inform. Transm. 9/3 (1973), pp. 265–266.

[P]   C. Papadimitriou, *Games against nature*, Proc. 24th ann. Symp. on Foundations of Computer Science, 1983, pp 446–450.

[PS]   Papadimitriou and Sipser, *Communication Complexity*, 14th STOC, 1982.

[y]   A.C. Yao, *Some Complexity Questions Related to Distributive Computing*, Proc. of 11th STOC, 1979.

[Y]   A.C. Yao, *They and Applications of Trapdoor Functions*, Proc. of 23rd FOCS, 1982.

How to Generate Cryptographically Strong Sequences of Pseudorandom Bits

This chapter reproduces the contents of the paper "How to Generate Cryptographically Strong Sequences of Pseudo Random Bits," which appeared in the proceedings of the *23rd Annual Symposium on Foundations of Computer Science*, pp. 112–117, 1982.

This pioneering work of Manuel Blum and Silvio Micali defined pseudorandom generators as producing a sequence of unpredictable bits. This definition was later shown by Yao to be equivalent to being computationally indistinguishable from the uniform distribution over bit-strings of adequate length. This work also defined the notion of a hard-core predicate of a one-way function and established its existence for the modular exponentiation function.

How To Generate Cryptographically Strong Sequences Of Pseudo Random Bits*

Manuel Blum (University of California - Berkeley),
Silvio Micali (University of California - Berkeley)

1 Introduction

1.1 Randomness and Complexity Theory

We introduce a new method of generating sequences of Pseudo Random Bits. Any such method implies, directly or indirectly, a definition of Randomness.

Much effort has been devoted in the second half of this century to make precise the notion of Randomness. Let us informally recall one of these definitions due to Kolmogorov [ ].

> A sequence of bits $A = a_1, a_2, \ldots, a_k$ is random if the length of the minimal program outputting A is at least k.

We remark that the above definition is highly non constructive and rules out the possibility of pseudo random number generators. Also, the length of a program, from a Complexity Theory point of view, is a rather unnatural measure. A more operative definition of Randomness should be pursued in the light of modern Complexity Theory.

Let us consider the following example.

* Supported in part by NSF grant MCS 82-04506.

Example   A and B want to play head and tail in 4 different ways. In all of them A "fairly" flips a "fair" coin. In the first way. A asks B to bet and then flips the coin. In such a case we expect B to win with a 50% frequency. In the second way, A flips the coin and, while it is spinning in the air, she asks B to bet. We are still expecting B to win with a 50% frequency. However, in the second case the outcome of the toss is determined when B bets: in principle, he could solve the equation of the motion and win !

The third way is similar to the second one: B is allowed to bet when the coin is spinning in the air, but he is also given a pocket calculator. Nobody will doubt that in this case B is going to win with 50% frequency, as while he is still initializing any computation the coin will have come up head or tail.

The fourth way is similar to the third, except that now B is given a very powerful computer, able to take pictures of the spinning coin, and quickly compute its speed, momentum etc. In such a case we will not say that B will always win, but we may suspect he may win 51% of the time !

The purpose of the above example is to suggest that

The Randomness of an event is relative to a specific Model of Computation with a specified amount of computing resources.

The links between randomness and the computation model were first pointed out by Michael Sipser in [ ]. where he shows that certain sequences appear random to a finite automaton. In his very nice paper [ ], Shamir considers also the factor of the computing resources, presents significant progress in this direction and points out some open problems as well.

In this paper we investigate the Randomness of k bit long sequences with respect to the computation model of **Boolean circuits with only Poly (k) gates.**

1.2 Our Generator

We show under which conditions it is possible to construct Generators of Cryptographically Strong Sequences of Pseudo Random Bits. Such a Generator is a program G that, upon receiving as input a random number s (hereafter referred to as "the seed"), outputs a sequence of Pseudo Random Bits $b_l, b_2, b_s, \ldots$

Our Generators have three main properties:

1. **The bits b_i's are polynomially many in the length of the seed.**

2. **The bits b_i's are easy to generate.** Each b_i is output in time polynomial in the length of the seed.

3. **The bits b_i's are unpredictable.** Given the Generator G and $b_1, \ldots, b_k$, the first k output bits, **but not** the seed s, it is computationally infeasible to predict the k+1st bit in the sequence with better than 50-50 chance.

1.3 Related Results and Applications

Our Generator is an improvement of Shamir's pseudo random number generator. In [ ]. Shamir presents programs that from a short secret random seed, output a sequence of "unpredictable" numbers x_i's. The main differences between ours and Shamir's generators are:

(a) **Shamir's notion of unpredictability is more restricted.** He proves that not all the generated x_i's can be computed from knowledge of the program and the preceding outputs, permitting that some of the x_i's **could** be so computed.

(b) **Shamir's generator outputs numbers and not bits.** Such numbers could be unpredictable and yet of very special form. In particular every bit of (information about) the next number in the sequence could be heavily biased or predictable with high probability.

The classical sequence $x_{i+l} = ax_i + b \bmod n$, provides a fast way of generating pseudo random numbers. Such sequence is known to pass many statistical tests (see Knuth [ ]), however it is not Cryptographically Strong. Plumstead [ ], shows that the sequence can be inferred even when a, b and n are all unknown.

On the other hand, Yao [ ] proves a very interesting result about Cryptographically Strong Sequences of Pseudo Random Bits: they pass all Polynomial Time statistical tests. As a consequence, under the intractability assumption of the Discrete Logarithm Problem, Random Polynomial Time is contained in Deterministic Time $(2^{n \, \varepsilon})$ for all $\varepsilon > 0$.

We finally point out the relevance of Cryptographically Strong Pseudo Random Bit Sequences to Cryptography. In **Private Key Cryptography**, one time pads constitute the simplest and safest type of Cryptosystem. Two partners who have exchanged one of our Generators and have secretly exchanged a random seed, are actually sharing a long bit sequence that can be used as a one time pad.

Our Generators also find applications in **Public Key Cryptography.** In [ ], Goldwasser and Micali show that, under the assumption that deciding quadratic residuosity modulo composite numbers is hard, there exist Encryption Schemes possessing the following property:

An adversary, who knows the encryption algorithm and is given the cyphertext, cannot obtain any information about the cleartext.

Such Encryption Shemes are Probabilistic: the encoding of a message m depends on m and a sequence of coin tosses known only to the transmitter. In this context, Cryptographically Strong Pseudo Random Bits Generators are needed as an adversary might be able to decode not because he is able to efficiently decide quadratic residuosity, but because he is able to predict the random numbers used to encrypt! Such a worry is not an abstract one as shown by Plumstead.

An analysis of a particular simple pseudo random sequence generator appears in Blum, Blum, and Shub [ ]. They point out that *well-mixed sequences* in which *hard problems are embedded* can nevertheless be poor pseudo-random sequences. Something more is needed to construct good generators of pseudo random sequences; what that is is pointed out below.

2 The Generator Model

1n this section we present a set of conditions that allow one to generate Cryptographically Strong Sequences of Pseudo Random Bits. In the next section we show that under the intractability assumptlon of the Discrete Logarithm Problem, it is possible to find a concrete implementation for the Generator Model.

Definitions $N = \{0.1, 2, \ldots\}$. B is said to be a *set of predicates* if $B = \{B_i : D_i \to \{0.1\}/i \in S_n, n \in N\}$, where S_n is a subset of the n-bit integers and D_i is a subset of the integers with at most n bits.

B is an *accessible set of predicates* if for all $n \in N$ it is possible in Probabilistic Poly(n) Time to select any element in $I_n = \{(i, x)/i \in S_n, X \in D_i\}$ with probability $\frac{1}{|I_n|}$.

Let B be a set of predicates. For any $e > 0$, let $C_{n,\varepsilon}$ denote the size (number of gates) of a minimum size circuit $C = C[i, x]$ that computes $B_i(x)$ correctly for at least a fraction $\frac{1}{2} + \varepsilon$ of the inputs $(i, x) \in I_n$. B is *input hard* if for any $\varepsilon > 0$ and any given polynomial Q, $C_{n,\varepsilon} > Q(n)$ for all sufficiently large n.

For example, suppose S_n = set of all n-bit composite integers that are products of two equal-length primes; $D_i = Z_i^*(+1)$, the set of all integers x relatively prime to i such that the Jacobi symbol $(x/i) = +1$; and $B_i : x \to 1$ if x is a quadratic residue mod i, 0 otherwise. Then it is easy to show that B is accessible. Furthermore, under the reasonable assumption that deciding quadratic residuosity modulo composite numbers is hard, B is input-hard.

Theorem 1 Let B be an input hard and accessible set of predicates. Let $\varepsilon > 0$, let Q and P be given polynomials. Let $n \in N$ and $i \in S_n$, and suppose

1. the function f: i $\to$ f_i is Poly(n) Time computable

2. $f_i : D_i \rightarrow D_i$ is a. permutation computable in Poly(n) Time

3. the function $h : x \in D_i \rightarrow B_i(f_i(x)$ is Poly(n) Time computable.

Then it is possible in Poly(n) Time to compute, from initial random seeds $(i, x) \in I_n$, sequences $S_{i,x}$, each $Q(n) + 1$ bits long such that:
for each integer $k \in [1, Q(n)]$, for any circuit C of size less than P(n) with k Boolean inputs and one Boolean output y: if C is fed the first k bits of an $S_{i,x}$ sequence S, then Prob {y is equal to the k+1st bit of S} $< \frac{1}{2} + \varepsilon$ for all sufficiently large n. I.e. for all sufficiently large n $|\{(i, x) \in I_n / y = \text{the k+lst bit of } S_{i,x}\}| < (\frac{1}{2} + \varepsilon)|I_n|$.

Proof Let n be a natural number. As B is an accessible set of predicates, select (i,x) at random in I_n. (i,x) will be the seed of the Pseudo Random Bit Sequence. Set $c = Q(n) + 1$, the desired length of the sequence.

> Generate the sequence $T_{i,x} = x, f_i(x), f_i^2(x), \ldots, f_i^c(x)$.
> **From right to left** (!), extract one bit from each element in $T_{i,x}$ in the following way: for $j = c$ to 1, output the bit $B_i(f_i^j(x))$. (We note below that $B_i(f_i^j(x))$ is easy to compute because x is known, by (3)).

The above procedure constitutes the Generator that takes the random seed (i,x) and stretches it into the sequence $S_{i,x} = (s_j | 1 \le j \le c, s_j = B_i(f_i^{c-f+1}(x)))$.

We first prove that the Generator operates in Poly(n) Time. The sequence $T_{i,x}$ can be constructed in Poly(n) time as the two functions f : i $\rightarrow$ f_i and $f_i : D_i \rightarrow D_i$ are both Poly(n) Time computable (hypothesis (1) and (2)).

Once the sequence $T_{i,x}$ is computed and stored, it is easy, by virtue of hypothesis (3), to compute each bit s_j of the $S_{i,x}$ sequence for $1 \le j \le c$.

We now prove that, when n is large enough, for any k between 1 and c, a circuit C with less than P(n) gates, cannot "predict" s_{k+1} with probability greater than $\frac{1}{2} + \varepsilon$. The proof is by contradiction. Assume that there is a "small" circuit C predicting s_{k+1} with probability at least $\frac{1}{2} + \varepsilon$. Then we will show that the set of predicates B is not input hard. We will do this by showing that there is another "small" circuit that computes $B_i(x)$ for a fraction bigger than $\frac{1}{2} + \varepsilon$ of the $(i, x) \in I_n$. Such a small circuit is derived by the following Poly(n) Time algorithm that makes calls to the circuit C.

> For each $(i, x) \in I_n$, generate the sequence of bits $(b_1, \ldots, b_{k-1}, b_k) = (B_i(f_i^k(x)), \ldots, B_i(f_i^2(x)), B_i(f_i(x)))$. Input these k bits to the circuit C to compute a bit y.

We reach a contradiction if we show that y equals $B_i(x)$ for a fraction at least $\frac{1}{2} + \varepsilon$ of the $(i, x) \in I_n$. Notice that the bits $b_1, \ldots, b_k$ are the first k bits of the Pseudo

Random Bit Sequence $S_{i,f_i^{k-c}(x)}$. Thus $y = B_i(x)$ if and only if C correctly predicts the k+1st bit of $S_{i,f_i^{k-c}(x)}$. But this will happen for a fraction at least $\frac{1}{2} + \varepsilon$ of the $(i,x) \in I_n$ as the function f_i^{k-c} is bijective (as f_i is a permutation) and we are now assuming that C correctly predicts the k+1st bit of the $S_{i,x}$ sequences for at least a fraction $\frac{1}{2} + \varepsilon$ of the $(i,x) \in I_n$.

Qed

3   The Discrete Logarithm Problem

Let p be a prime. The set of integers $[1, p-l]$ forms a cyclic group under multiplication mod p. Such group is denoted by Z_p^*. Let g be a generator for Z_p^*. The function $f_{p,g} : x \in Z_p^* \to g \bmod p$, defines a permutation in Z_p^* computable in Poly(|p|) Time. The *Discrete Logarithm Problem* (DLP) with parameters p,g and y consists in finding the $x \in Z_p^*$ such that $g^x \bmod p = y$. A circuit C[., ., .] *solves* the DLP mod a prime p if for any g generator for Z_p^* and any $y \in Z_p^*$, C[p, g, y] = x such that $x \in Z_p^*$ and $g^x \bmod p = y$. x will be simply denoted by $index_g(y)$ whenever no ambiguity may arise about p.

3.1   Actual knowledge about the DLP

$g^x \bmod p$ seems to be a one-way function. The fastest algorithm known for the DLP is due to Adleman and runs in time $O(2^{c\sqrt{\log p \ \log \log p}})$. It is easy to see that the difficulty of the DLP does not depend on the generator g or y. By this we mean that if for a non negligible fraction $(l/\text{Poly}(|p|))$ of pairs (g,y), g a generator and $y \in Z_p^*$, the DLP with parameters p,g and y could be efficiently solved, then it could be solved in Random Poly(|p|) Time for any g and any y. Thus our intractability assumption for the DLP will depend only on the prime p.

Pohlig and Hellman [ ] show that the DLP mod a prime p such that $p-1$ contains only small prime factors can be efficiently solved. However such primes constitute a negligible portion of all primes. We expect that for (nearly all) randomly selected primes p, $p-1$ has a large prime factor. No "small" circuits are known that solve the DLP mod a single prime p, for the primes p such that $p-1$ has a large prime factor (thus the DLP seems to have a higher circuit complexity than factoring: for any composite integer k there is a small circuit storing its factorization). In this paper we show how to generate Pseudo Random Bit Sequences under either one of the following assumptions.

Definition   A prime p is *hard* if p = P x + 1, where P is prime and $1 \leq x \leq \text{Poly}(|P|)$.

It is known (De la Vallee Poussin [ ]) that asymptotically $\frac{1}{|P|}$ of the integers of the sequence P x + 1, x = 1, 2.3, . . . , are primes.

Using efficient primality tests, there is an efficient procedure to decide if an integer, p, is a hard prime; and if so, to factor p − 1.

First intractability assumption for the DLP. Let $\varepsilon > 0$ be a fixed constant and Q be a fixed polynomial. Then for all sufficiently large n, the size of any circuit that solves the DLP mod p for at least a fraction ε of the n-bits-long hard primes p, is greater than Q(n).

Second intractability assumption for the DIP. Let $\varepsilon > 0$ be a fixed constant and Q be a fixed polynomial. Then for all sufficiently large n, the size of any circuit that solves the DLP for at least a fraction ε of the n-bit primes p, is greater than Q(n).

3.2 The DLP and the Principal Square Root Problem

We recall some known results about Z_p^*.

An element T of Z_p^* is called a quadratic residue if and only if $T = x^2 \bmod p$ for some $x \in Z_p^*$; such an x is called a square root mod p of T.

Fact 1. Given any generator g for Z_p^*, an element T of Z_p^* is a quadratic residue mod p if and only if $T = g^{2s} \bmod p$ for some $s \in [1, \frac{p-1}{2}]$. We recall that such a representation of T is unique. Moreover T has two square roots mod p: $g^s \bmod p$ and $g^{s+((p-l)/2)} \bmod p$. (see [ ])

Fact 2. There exists a polynomial time algorithm for testing whether an element T of Z_p^* is a quadratic residue mod p (See [ ]).

Fact 3. (Miller [ ], Adleman and Manders [ ], Berlekamp [ ]) Given any T, a quadratic residue mod p, there exists a random polynomial time algorithm to compute both square roots of T mod p.

We introduce the following basic definition.

Definition Let g be a generator for Z_p^*, T a quadratic residue mod p and 2s the unique index of T such that $2s \in [1, p - 1]$. Then $g^s \bmod p$ will be called the *principal square root* of T, and $g^{s+((p-l)/2)} \bmod p$ the non principal square root of T.

Let g be a generator for Z_p^*. Notice that given T, a quadratic residue mod p, but not the index of T in base g, one can still test efficiently that T is indeed a quadratic residue and can effectively extract its two square roots mod p, say X and Y. However the next theorem shows that deciding which square root of T is the principal one is a much harder problem. In fact, even allowing a **weak oracle** for the Principal Square Root Problem, the DLP becomes easy.

Definition   Let g be a generator for Z_p^* and $x \in Z_p^*$. The predicate $B_{p,g}(x)$ is defined to be equal to 1 if x is the principal square root of x^2 mod p and 0 otherwise.

Remark 1   Notice that, given x, it is easy to evaluate $B_{p,g}(g^x \bmod p)$: just check whether $x < \frac{p-1}{2}$ or $x > \frac{p-1}{2}$, and output a 1 or a 0 respectively.

Theorem 2   Let $\varepsilon > O$, p prime and g generator for Z_p^*. Then, given an oracle ME (Magic Box) such that $MB[x] = B_{p,g}(x)$ for a fraction $\geq \frac{1}{2} + \varepsilon$ of the $x \in Z_p^*$, one can construct an algorithm with oracle MB that solves the DLP mod p in Probabilistic Poly($|p|$) Time.

We first establish some intermediate results.

Lemma 1   Let $\varepsilon > 0$, P prime and g generator for Z_p^*. Then, given an oracle ME such that $MB[x] = B_{p,g}(x)$ **for all** the $x \in Z_p^*$, there exist a Poly($|p|$) Time Algorithm (with oracle MB) for the DLP mod p.

Proof   We will exhibit a Poly($|p|$) Algorithm, making calls to MB, that finds indices mod p in base g. Such an algorithm will solve the DLP mod p as, for each generator h for Z_p^* and each $y \in Z_p^*$, $index_h(y) index_g(h) \bmod p - 1 = index_g(y)$. The algorithm, given $y \in Z_p^*$, finds $x = index_g(y)$ bit by bit from right to left. In the middle of the execution, the variable *index* will contain the right half of the bits of x and the variable *element* is such that $index_g(element)$ equals the left half of x. Think of $index_g(element)$ and *index* as lists of 0's and 1's. The algorithm, abstractly, transfers the last bit of $index_g(element)$ in front of *index* until $index_g(element)$ vanishes (i.e. $element = g^0 = 1$) and thus all of x has been reconstructed in *index*. " " denotes the concatenation operator.

    Step 0. (Initialization)
      element := y; *index* := empty word.

    Step 1. (Check for termination condition)
      If *element* = 1   HALT.   *index* equals x.

    Step 2. (find one more bit of x)
      Test whether *element* is a quadratic residue mod p. If yes *index* := 0 *index* and go to step 4 else *index* := 1 *index* and go to step 3.

    Step 3. (*element* is a quadratic non residue, i.e. $index_g(element)$ is odd. Change the last bit of $index_g(element)$ from 1 to 0)
      element := $g^{-1}element$ mod p

    Step 4. (Erase 0 from the tail of $index_g(element)$)
      element is a quadratic residue. Compute both square roots of *element* mod p.

Have MB select the principal one. *element* := principal square root of element and go to Step 1.

Qed

The algorithm in lemma 1 needs, for |p| times, to select the Principal Square Root of a quadratic residue mod p. It does so by making |p| calls to the oracle MB that computes $B_{p,g}$ correctly 100% of the time.

We should ask what happens to the algorithm if it is allowed to make calls only to an oracle MB_ε that evaluates $B_{p,g}$ only slightly better than guessing at random, i.e. correctly for a fraction $\frac{1}{2} + \varepsilon$ of the $x \in Z_p^*$.

The following lemma, making use of the algebraic structure of Z_p^*, shows how to "concentrate a stochastic advantage", i.e. how to turn an oracle that answers **most** of the instances of a decision problem correctly into an oracle answering a **particular instance** correctly with arbitrarily high probability. Let us first recall the Weak Law of Large Numbers.

If $y_1, \ldots, y_k$ are k independent 0-1 variables such that $y_i = 1$ with probability α, and $S_k = y_1 + \cdots + y_k$, then for real numbers ψ and $\phi > 0$,

$$k > \frac{2}{4\phi\psi^2} \text{ implies that } \Pr\left(\left|\frac{S_k}{k} - \alpha\right| > \psi\right) < \phi.$$

Let us define trials$(\psi, \phi) = \frac{1}{4\phi\psi^2}$. Notice that trials$(\psi, \phi)$ is a polynomial in ψ^{-1} and ϕ^{-1}.

Lemma 2   Let $\varepsilon \in (0, \frac{1}{2})$, $\delta \in (0, 1)$, p a prime and g a generator for Z_p^*. Set n = trials(ε, δ) and define IS, the *initial segment* of Z_p^* as follows: IS = $\{g^x \bmod p \ 1 \le x \le \frac{p-1}{n}\}$. Then, given an oracle MB_ε such that $MB_\varepsilon[x] = B_{p,g}(x)$ for at least a fraction $\frac{1}{2} + \varepsilon$ of the $x \in Z_p^*$, there is a Probabilistic Poly($|p|, \varepsilon^{-1}, \delta^{-1}$) Algorithm with oracle MB_ε that, with Probability $1 - \delta$, correctly selects the Principal Square Root of **any** quadratic residue e mod p belonging to IS.

Proof   Select $r_1, \ldots, r_n$ at random in $[1, \frac{p-1}{2}]$. Compute $2r_1, \ldots, 2r_n$. Compute $e_1 = e_g^{2r_1} \bmod p, \ldots, e_n = e_g^{2r_n} \bmod p$. All the e_i's are quadratic residues mod p as $index_g(e_i)$ is even for all i's. In fact $index_g(e_i) = (index_g(e) + 2r_i) \bmod$ p-1 and both $index_g$ (e) and p-1 are even. Compute the two square roots X_i and Y_i of each e_i. (Note that while these can be computed, it is not (yet) clear which of X_i and Y_i is principal.) For each e_i select $PSQR_i$, your guess for the principal square root of e_i, in the following way: if $MB_\varepsilon[X_i] = MB_\varepsilon[Y_i]$, set $PSQR_i$ = one of $MB_\varepsilon[X_i], MB_\varepsilon[Y_i]$ selected at random with probability 1/2. Otherwise, if $MB_\varepsilon[X_i] = 1$, set $PSQR_i = X_i$; else set

$PSQR_i = Y_i$. Notice that the e_i's have been drawn at random with uniform probability among the quadratic residues mod p: in fact every even index between 1 and p-1 can be uniquely written in the form $(index_g(e) + 2r)$ mod p-l, for $1 \le 2r \le p - 1$. Thus, even if an **adversary** had chosen the x's for which $MB_\varepsilon[x] = B_g(x)$, the Weak Law of Large Numbers guarantees that with Probability $1 - \delta$, $|\frac{S_n}{n} - (\frac{1}{2} + \varepsilon)| < \frac{\varepsilon}{2}$. I.e., with probability $1 - \delta$, we have selected the principal square root of the e_i's more correctly than incorrectly. We exploit this fact in the following way.

Initialize to 0 two counters C_X and C_Y. Compute a square root of e, call it X. For each r_i compute $S_i = Xg^{r_i}$ mod p. If $S_i = PSQR_i$ then increment the counter C_X, else increment the counter C_Y.

Notice the following fact:

> Let $e = g^{2s}$ mod p ($2s \in [1, p - 1]$) be a quadratic residue mod p and let X and Y be its square roots mod p. Let $2s + 2r < p - 1$. Then Xg^r mod p is the principal square root of eg^{2r} mod p if and only if X is the principal square root of e.

Without loss of generality, let $C_X > C_Y$ and let 2s be the index of *e* in base *g*. If **for all** the r_i's, $2s + 2r_i < p - l$; then with probability $1 - \delta$, X will be the Principal Square Root of *e*.

2s is unknown, but we know that $2s \in [1, \frac{p-1}{n}]$. Thus all r_i's for which $2s + 2r_i > p - 1$ must belong to the interval $[(n - 1)\frac{p-1}{n}, p - 1]]$. But the $2r_i$'s are n even integers drawn at random with uniform probability in [l,p-1]; thus each $2r_i$ has the same probability to belong to each of the n sub intervals $[k\frac{p-1}{n}, (k + 1)\frac{p-1}{n}]$. Let t be the number of r_i's belonging to the dangerous interval $[(n - 1)\frac{p-1}{n}, p - 1]$. This t will be so small that also $C_X - t$ will be greater than C_y. Thus still with probability $1 - \delta$, X will be the Principal Square Root of e.

Qed

Lemma 3 Let $\varepsilon \in (0, \frac{1}{2})$ and $\phi \in (0, 1)$, p prime and g generator for Z_p^*. Set n = trials$(\varepsilon, \frac{1}{2|p|})$ and define IS $= \{g^x \text{ mod p} | x \in [1, \frac{p-1}{n}]\}$. Then, given an oracle MB_ε such that $MB_\varepsilon[x] = B_{p,g}(x)$ for at least a fraction $\frac{1}{2} + \varepsilon$ of the $x \in Z_p^*$, there is a Probabilistic Algorithm that finds indices of **any** $y \in IS$ in Expected Poly($|p|$) Time.

Proof Let y be any element in IS. Apply the algorithm in lemma 1 to find the index of y, In Step 4, to select the principal square root of a quadratic residue in IS, instead of calling MB, apply the algorithm in lemma 2 with $\delta = \frac{1}{2|p|}$. In view of lemma 2, Step 4 will be performed correctly with **independent** probability equal to $1 - \frac{1}{2|p|}$. Notice that if x belongs to IS, so does xg^{-1} mod p; and that if x is a quadratic residue mod p belonging to IS, also its principal square root will belong to IS. Therefore. if in Step 4 the algorithm correctly selects the principal square root, the total computation will be done in the initial segment IS. As Step 4 is executed at most $|p|$ times, the probability that the index of y will be found correctly is greater than $(1 - \frac{1}{2|p|})^{|p|} > \frac{1}{2}$. It is easy to see that the whole computation is polynomial in ε^{-1} and $|p|$, thus polynomial in $|p|$ for sufficiently large p.

    Qed

Proof of Theorem 2   The following Probabilistic Poly($|p|$) Time Algoriihm finds $index_g(y)$ for any $y \in Z_p^*$. Set $n = \text{trials}(\varepsilon, \frac{1}{2|p|})$ and define IS $= \{g^z \bmod p | x \in [1, \frac{p-1}{n}]\}$.

    Step 0. (Initialization)
      i:=l

    Step 1. (guess that $y \in [i\frac{p-1}{k}, (i+1)\frac{p-1}{k}]$ and map y into IS)
      $w := yg^{-i\frac{p-1}{k}} \bmod p$

    Step 2. (find the index of w)
      Apply the algorithm in Lemma 3 to find the index of w. index(w) := the index of w.

    Step 3. (check whether the index of y has been found)
      $candidate := \text{index(w)} + i\frac{p-1}{k}$: if $g^{candidate} \bmod p = y$ then HALT: *candidate* is the index of y in base g. Else continue.

    Step 4. (keep on guessing)
      $i := i + l$. If $i > k$ then i := l and go to Step 0; else go to Step 1.

    Qed

4   A Concrete Implementation of the General Model

We merely sketch the proofs that will appear in the final paper.

4.1 First Implementation

This implementation is more efficient than the second one. It assumes the first intractability assumption for the DLP and the constructability of the hard primes (suggested, but not implied, by the De La Vallee Poussin Theorem, which is an asymptotic result).

    Let $n \in N$. Let S_{2n}, be the set of 2n-bit long integers i such that the first n bits of i constitute a hard prime p, and the next n bits a generator g for Z_p^*. For $i \in S_{2n}$, $i = pg$, set $D_i = Z_p^*$ and, for x an n-bit integer, set $B_i(x) = B_{p,g}(x)$. Then the set of predicates $B = B_i | i \in S_{2n}$ is an accessible, input hard set of predicates.

    B is accessible : Flip 3n coins. An element $(i, x) \in I_{2n}$ has been obtained if

1. The first n bits constitute a hard prime p. This will happen in n^2 expected trials (Prime theorem & De La Vallee Poussin Theorem). Moreover, success can be easily detected by means of fast primality tests.

2. The next n bits constitute a generator for Z_p^*. This will happen in a low expected number of trials as the fraction of generators for Z_p^* is asymptotically greater than $\frac{1}{6 \log \log(p)}$. Also notice that as we easily have the complete factorization of p-l, it is easy to check whether g is a generator for Z_p^*.

3. The last n bits constitute an integer $x \in [l, p - 1]$.

If the 3n flips have not generated a complete element of I_{2n}, flip 3n coins again.

B is input hard : If there were a circuit C, of size less than Q(n) for some fixed polynomial Q, that evaluates correctly $B_{p,g}(x)$ for a fraction of at least $\frac{1}{2} + \varepsilon$ of the n-bit inputs p, g, and x, then a counting argument shows that there would be a fraction of pairs (p,g) for which the circuit guesses $B_{p,g}(x)$ correctly for at least a fraction $\frac{1}{2} + \varepsilon$ of the $x \in Z_p^*$. By the results in the previous section, using C as an oracle, there would be a Probabilistic Poly(n) Time Algorithm, for solving the DLP for a fixed fraction of the hard primes of n bits. As the size of C is bounded by Q(n) and any Probabilistic Poly Algorithm is easily seen to admit small circuits, the first intractability assumption for the DLP has been violated.

B satisfies the hypothesis of Theorem 1 : Define $f_i(x) = g^x \bmod p$.

4.2   Second Implementation

Assume that we can pick a prime p with uniform probability, among those of a given size, so that the factorization of p-1 is known. Then, set S_{2n} equal to the set of 2n bit integers i such that the first n bits of i constitute a prime p and the second n bits a generator g for Z_p^*. Set $D_i = Z_p^*$. $f_i(x) = g^x \bmod p$. Then as in the previous section, $\{B_i : x \to B_{p,g}(x) | i \in S_{2n}\}$ is an accessible set of predicates satisfying hypothesis (1), (2) and (3) of Theorem 1. However we do not know how to pick at random a prime p so that the factorization of p-l is known. So, after having picked a prime p we would have trouble picking a generator for Z_p^*, as no way is known of proving that $x \in Z_p^*$ is a generator without having the factorization of p-l. However there is an "abundance" of generators in Z_p^*: one out of 6 log log (p) elements is a generator. Thus having picked at random k = log(p) elements $x_1, \ldots, X_k$ in Z_p^*, with probability greater than any fixed ε one of the x_i's will be a generator. Consider each x_i to be a generator for Z_p^* and implement k Pseudo Random Bit Generators $G_1, \ldots G_k$ as above. We now make use of the "exclusive or" function in a way similar to Yao [ ]. Construct the following new Pseudo Random Bit Generator G: generate the ith bit by outputting the ith bit for $G_1, G_2, \ldots, G_k$ and take their "exclusive or". It is easy to see that, if at least one of the G_i's is Cryptographically Strong so is G.

Acknowledgements

We are proud to thank many friends.

We are grateful to Shafi Goldwasser for numerous valuable discussions, to Richard Karp for his precious gift of setting the context and making vague ideas precise, and to Andy Yao for having brought to light hidden potentials.

This work has benefitted highly from the insightful comments of Erich Bach. Lenore Blum, Faith Fich, Donald Johnson, Donald Knuth, Leonid Levin, David Lichtenstein, Mike Luby, Gary Miller, Joan Plumstead, Ron Rivest, Jeff Shallit, Mike Sipser, Po Tong, Umesh Vazirani, Vijay Vazirani and Frances Yao.

References

[1] L. Adleman, "A Subexponential Algorithm for the Discrete Logarithm Problem with Applications to Cryptography," 20th FOCS (1979), 55-60.

[2] L. Blum., M. Blum, and M. Shub, "A Simple Secure Pseudo-Random Number Generator," in Proc. CRYPTO-82, ed. Allen Gersho.

[3] S. Goldwasser and S. Micali, "Probabilistic Encryption and How to Play Mental Poker Keeping Secret all Partial Information," 14th STOC (1982). 365-377.

[4] D. Knuth, "The Art of Computer Programming: Seminumerical Algorithms," Vol. 2, Addison-Wesley Pub. Co., 1981.

[5] J. Plumstead, "Inferring a Sequence Generated by a Linear Congruence," submitted to FOCS 1982.

[6] S. Pohlig and M. Hellman, "An Improved Algorithm for Computing Logarithms over GF(p) and Its Cryptographic Significance," IEEE Trans. on Info. Theory, Vol. It-24, No. 1, (1978), 106-110.

[7] R. Rivest, A. Shamir, and L. Adleman, "On Digital Signatures and Public Key Cryptosystems," Commun. ACM, vol. 21 (Feb. 1978), 120-126.

[8] A. Shamir, "On the Generation of Cryptographically Strong Pseudo-random Sequences," ICALP 1981.

[9] M. Sipser, "Three Approaches to a Definition of Finite State Randomness," unpublished manuscript.

[10] A. Yao, "A Relation Between Random Polynomial Time and Deterministic Polynomial Time," submitted to FOCS 1982.

How to Construct Random Functions

This chapter reproduces the contents of the paper "How to Construct Random Functions," which appeared in the proceedings of the *25th Annual Symposium on Foundations of Computer Science*, pp. 464–479, 1984.

This influential work of Oded Goldreich, Shafi Goldwasser, and Silvio Micali extended the theory of pseudorandomness to functions, and showed how to construct pseudorandom functions based on any pseudorandom generator. The notion of a pseudorandom function found numerous applications in cryptography, starting from the construction of message authentication codes and private-key encryption schemes that withstand chosen ciphertext attacks.

How to Construct Random Functions (Extended Abstract)

Oded Coldreich (Massachusetts Institute of Technology),
Shafi Goldwasser (Massachusetts Institute of Technology),
Silvio Micali (Massachusetts Institute of Technology)

Abstract

This paper develops a constructive theory of randomness for functions based on computational complexity.

We present a deterministic polynomial-time algorithm that transforms pairs (g, r), where g is any one-way (in a very weak sense) function and r is a random k-bit string, to polynomial-time computable functions $f_r : \{1, \ldots, 2^k\} \to \{1, \ldots, 2^k\}$. These f_f's cannot be distinguished from random functions by any probabilistic polynomial time algorithm that asks and receives the value of a function at arguments of its choice.

The result has applications in cryptography, random constructions and complexity theory.

1 Introduction

Measuring randomness has attracted much attention in the second half of this century. However most of the previous work focused on measuring the randomness of strings.

The first author was supported in part by a Weizmann Postdoctoral fellowship. The second author was supported in part by the International Business Machines Corporation under the IBM/MIT Joint Research Program, Faculty Development Award agreement dated August 9, 1983.

In Kolmogorov Complexity ([Kol], [Sol], [ZL], [Ch], [L2], [L3], [L4], [ML], [Sch] and [Ga]) the measure of randomness of a string is the length of its *shortest description*: randomness is an inherent property of *individual* strings. This approach is nonconstructive and far from being applicable to pseudo-random string generation. (Interesting generalizations of Kolmogorov Complexity have been considered in [A], [Si], [HI] and [W].)

In [BM] and [Y] (following a result of [Sh]) a constructive approach to the randomness of strings is introduced based on computational complexity. In this approach a *set* of strings is *random* if elements randomly selected in it retain, with respect to polynomial-time computation, properties of elements randomly selected in the set of all strings.

In this paper we further develop this latter approach by introducing a constructive theory of randomness for functions. In particular,

1. We introduce a computational complexity measure of the randomness of functions.

   (Loosely speaking, we call a function random if no polynomial time algorithm, asking for the values of the function at arguments of its choice, can distinguish a computation during which it receives the true values of the function, from a computation during which it receives the outcome of independent coin flips. Notice the analogy with the Turing Test for intelligence.)

2. Assuming the existence of one-way functions, we present an algorithm for constructing functions that achieve maximum randomness with respect to the above measure.

Our result solves, and was motivated by, an open problem of [BBS].

Organization of the Paper

In the rest of this section we informally discuss the notion of a poly-random collection: a set of easy to select and to evaluate functions that achieve randomness with respect to polynomial-time computation. We compare this new notion with the previously considered notions of one-way functions and Cryptographically Strong Pseudo-Random Bit generators (CSPRB generators). In section 2 we briefly recall the basic definitions and results about CSPRB generators and the Blum Blum Shub open problem. In section 3 we formally define poly-random collections and show how to construct a poly-random collection given any one-way function. In section 4 we characterize poly-random collections as extremely hard prediction problems. In section 5 we briefly discuss various applications of poly-random collections. We conclude this paper with some reflections on the internal coherence of polynomial-randomness: the approach that constructively bases randomness on computational complexity.

1.1 Poly-Random Collections

Let I_k denote the set of all k-bit strings. Consider the set, H_k, of all functions from I_k into I_k. Note that the cardinality of H_k is 2^{k2^k}. Thus to specify a function in H_k we would need $k2^k$ bits: an impractical task even for a moderately large k. Even more, assume that one randomly selects subsets $H'_k \subseteq H_k$ of cardinality 2^k so that each function in H_k has a unique k-bit index; then there is no polynomial time algorithm that, given the index of a function $f \in H'_k$ and $x \in I_k$, will evaluate $f(x)$.

Our goal is to make "random functions" accessible for applications. I.e. to construct functions that can be easily specified and evaluated and yet cannot be distinguished from functions chosen at random in H_k. Thus we restrict ourselves to choose functions from a subset $F_k \subseteq H_k$ where the collection $F = (F_k)$ has the following properties:

1. **Indexing:** Each function in F_k has a unique k-bit index associated with it. (Thus picking randomly a function $f \in F_k$ is easy.)

2. **Poly-time Evaluation:** There exists a polynomial algorithm that given as input an index of a function $f \in F_k$ and an argument x, computes $f(x)$.

3. **Pseudo-Randomness:** No probabilistic algorithm that runs in time polynomial in k can distinguish the functions in F_k from the functions in H_k. (see section 3.1 for a precise definition).

Such a collection of functions F will be called a *poly-random collection.* Loosely speaking, despite the fact that the functions in F are easy to select and easy to evaluate, they will exhibit, to an examiner with polynomially bounded resources, all the properties of randomly selected functions.

The above definition is highly constructive. We transform *any* one-to-one one-way function (formally defined in section 2.3) to a poly-random collection. The construction is in two steps: first, we use a construction due to Yao [Y] to transform a one-to-one one-way function into a high quality pseudo-random bit generator, called a CSPRB-generator; next, we use any CSPRB-generator to construct a poly-random collection.

1.2 Comparison with One-way Functions

We construct random functions from any one-way permutation. This confirms the great potential present in the notion of a one-way computation. However, this power needs to be carefully brought out.

Although the inverse of a one-way function is somewhat unpredictable, this does not mean that it is random. In fact, all permutations that are believed to be one-way satisfy various algebraic identities (e.g., the RSA function [RSA] is multiplicative, thus given its inverse on x and y, one can easily infer its inverse at $x \cdot y$. This clearly does not happen with truly random functions, and in fact will not happen with a function randomly selected from a poly-random collection $\{F_k\}$. In particular, our construction hides all the identities of the one-way function upon which it is based from any observer with polynomially bounded resources:

> Choose and fix $f \in F_k$. Let a probabilistic poly(k) time algorithm A ask for the value of f on polynomially many (in k) arguments of its choice: $y_1 y_2, \ldots, y_{k^i}$. Then let A choose an argument x ($x \neq y_i$, for all i's) as an exam. If A is now given two numbers in random order, one of which is $f(x)$ and the other a random k-bit number, it cannot guess which of the two is $f(x)$ with probability greater than $1/2$.

Not only that $f(x)$ cannot be computed from the values of f at other arguments, but it cannot even be recognized when given! The above test is a complete characterization of poly-random collections (see section 4).

1.3 Comparison with CSPRB Generators

CSPRB generators are deterministic programs that stretch a (random) k-bit long seed to a k^t-bit long (pseudo-random) sequence that is indistinguishable from a k^t-bit long truly random sequence for some constant $t > 0$ (see section 2.1). Their existence has interesting implications with respect to probabilistic computation.

Performing a probabilistic polynomial-time computation that requires k^t random bits is trivial if we are willing to flip k^t coins. Interestingly, CSPRB generators guarantee the same result of the computation by flipping only k coins.

We now address the problem of efficiently simulating more complex probabilistic computations: computations with a random oracle.

A random oracle (see Bennet and Gill [BG]) is a special case of a random function: it associates the result of a single coin toss to each string. Notice that computing with a random oracle has advantages over computing with a coin. The bit associated with each string x, not only is random, but does not change in time. That is, if one asks twice for the bit associated with string x, then he gets the same (random) result. The advantages of computing with a random oracle are clarified by all the applications listed in section 5.

It is trivial to simulate a random oracle that is queried on k^t strings if one is willing to use $O(k^{t+l})$ bits of storage:

For each query q, generate a random (or pseudo-random) bit b and store some encoding of the pair (q, b) so to be able to recognize whether a query occurred before and give the same answer.

Clearly, if the queries cannot be compressed (as for random queries) then this simple simulation would require at least k^{t+1} bits of storage. An interesting feature of poly-random collections is that they guarantee the same result of any computation with a random oracle for k-bit strings (by using only k coin flips and) by storing only k bits! This can be done by randomly selecting and storing a k-bit index specifying a function in a poly-random collection.

Poly-Random Collections Allow to Share Randomness in a Distributed Environment

An additional advantage of poly-random collections is that they enable many parties to *efficiently share* a random function f in a distributed environment. By *sharing f* we mean that if f is evaluated at different times by different parties on the same argument x, the same value $f(x)$ will be obtained. Such sharing is *efficient* as it can be achieved by only flipping k coins, using k bits of storage (per party) and *without exchanging any messages at all*. Again, each party (processor) will simply have in memory a common, randomly selected k-bit string specifying a function f in a poly-random collection.

1.4 Conventions

All definitions and results in this paper are stated with respect to the Turing Machine computational model. The results can also be stated and proved in terms of circuit complexity.

Also, all definitions and results are stated with respect to the uniform probability distribution. The results can be stated and proved with respect to more general probability distributions.

The parameter k, when given as input to any algorithm discussed in this paper, will be presented in unary.

Let A be a multiset with distinct elements $a_l, \ldots, a_n$ occurring with multiplicities $m_1, \ldots, m_n$, respectively. Then $|A| = \sum_{i=1}^{n} m_i$. By writing $a \in_R A$ we mean that the element a has been randomly selected from the multiset A. I.e. an element occurring in A with multiplicity m is chosen with probabilility $\frac{m}{|A|}$.

2 CSPRB Generators

In this section we recall some of the basic definitions and results concerning Cryptographically Strong Pseudo-Random Bit generators (CSPRB generator).

2.1 The Notion of a CSPRB Generator

Improving a result of Shamir [Sh], Blum and Micali [BM] introduced the notion of a Cryptographically Strong Pseudo-Random Bit generator (CSPRB generator). Let P be a polynomial. A CSPRB generator, G, is a deterministic *poly(k)*-time program that stretches a k-bit long randomly selected seed into a $P(k)$-bit long sequence (called a CSPRB sequence) that passes all *next-bit-tests*:

Let P be a polynomial, S_k is a multiset consisting of $P(k)$-bit sequences and $S = \cup_k S_k$. A *next-bit-test* for S is a probabilistic polynomial-time algorithm T that on input k and the first i bits in a srting $s \in_R S_k$ outputs a bit b. Let P_k denote the probability that b equals the $i + 1$st bit of s.

We say that S passes the next-bit-test T if for all $\epsilon > O$, for all sufficiently large k: $|p_k - \frac{1}{2}| < \varepsilon$.

A more general definition of string randomness has been suggested by Yao [Y] and is formally stated below.

2.2 Polynomial-Time Statistical Tests for Strings

Let P and $S = \cup_k S_k$ be as above. A *polynomial time statistical test for strings* is a probabilistic polynomial-time algorithm T that, on input a $P(k)$-bit string, outputs only 0 or 1.

The multiset *S passes the test T* if for any polynomial Q, for all sufficiently large k:

$$|p_k^S - p_k^R| < \frac{1}{Q(k)}$$

where p_k^S denotes the probability that T outputs 1 on $s \in_R S_k$ and p_k^R the probability that T outputs 1 on a randomly selected $P(k)$-long bit sequence.

Yao [Y] shows that by substituting ε by $\frac{1}{poly(k)}$ in the definition of the next-bit-test the following theorem can be proved.

Theorem 1 (Yao [Y]): A multiset $S = \cup_k S_k$, of bit-sequences passes the next-bit-test if and only if it passes all polynomial-time statistical tests for strings.

Thus, CSPRB sequences pass all polynomial-time statistical tests for strings. Theorem 4 generalizes the above theorem. The reader can derive a proof of Theorem 1 from the proof of Theorem 4.

2.3 Implementations of CSPRB Generators

Blum and MiCali [BM] presented an algorithmic scheme for constructing CSPRB generators based on a general complexity theoretic assumption (a sketch can be found in the Appendix). They also presented the first instance of their scheme based on a specific assumption: the intractability assumption of the discrete logarithm problem (DLP). Namely, if the next bit in the sequences produced by their generator could be predicted with probability greater than $\frac{1}{2} + \varepsilon$, then there would exist a $poly(k, \varepsilon^{-1})$ algorithm for solving the DLP for a fraction ε of all primes of length k.

Other instances of CSPRB generators based on various number theoretic assumptions appeared in [Y] [BBS] [GMT] [BCS] [VV1] [LW] [ACGS].

More generally, Yao [Y] showed how to obtain CSPRB generators if any (weak) one-way permutation is given. Let us be more formal.

Definition   (Yao)   Let $D_k \subseteq I_k$. Let $f_k : D_k \to D_k$ be a sequence of permutations and let the function f be defined as follows: $f(x) = f_k(x)$ if $X \in D_k$. f is said to be a *one-to-one one-way function* if

1. f is polynomial-time computable.

2. f is (moderately) hard to invert: there exists a polynomial Q such that for every polynomial-time algorithm A and for all sufficiently large k, $A(x) \neq f_k^{-1}(x)$ for at least a fraction $\frac{1}{Q(k)}$ of the $x \in D_k$.

3. There exists a probabilistic polynomial-time algorithm that, on input k, select an $X \in D_k$ with uniform probability distribution.

Theorem 2   (Yao [Y])   Given a weak one-to-one one-way function, it is possible to construct CSPRB generators.

A sketch of the construction used by Yao is given in the Appendix.

Levin [L5] pointed out that Theorem 2 still holds with respect to "locally one-way" functions, a notion weaker than the above defined notion of a one-way permutation. Moreover he exhibits a function that is locally one-way if any locally one-way function exists. An informal sketch of Levin's definition is given in the Appendix.

2.4   CSPRB Generators with Direct Access

Blum, Blum and Shub [BBS] present an interesting CSPRB generator whose sequences pass all polynomial time statistical tests if and only if *squaring modulo a Blum-integer*[1] is a weak one-to-one one-way function.[2]

---

1. A Blum integer is an integer of the form $p_1 p_2$ where p_l and p_2 are distinct primes both congruent to 3 mod 4.

2. This generator has been proved [BBS] to be cryptographically strong based on the intractability of deciding Quadratic Residuosity modulo a Blum-integer. Recently, it has been pointed out [VV2] that the results in [ACGS] imply that this generator is cryptographically strong based on a weaker assumption: the intractability of factoring Blum-integers.

Notice that, even though a CSPRB sequence generated with a k-bit long seed consists of polynomially many (in k) bits, a CSPRB generator and a seed s define an infinite (ultimately periodic) bit-sequence $b_0, b_1, \ldots$ An interesting feature first present in Blum Blum Shub's generator is that knowledge of the seed and of the factorization of the modulus allows direct access to each of the first 2^k bits. I.e. if $\log i < k$, the ith bit in the string, b_i, can be computed in poly(k) time. This is due to the special weak one-way permutation on which the security of their generator is based. However, this directly-accessible exponentially-long bit-string may not appear "random." Blum, Blum and Shub only prove that any **single** polynomially long interval of consecutive bits in the string passes all polynomial time statistical tests for strings. Indeed, it may be the case that, given $b_1, \ldots, b_k$ and $b_{2^{\sqrt{k}}+1}, \ldots, b_{2^{\sqrt{k}}+k}$ it is easy to compute any other bit in the string.

The Blum Blum Shub open problem consists of whether direct access to exponentially far away bits in their pseudo-random pad is a "randomness preserving" operation. This problem has also been discussed by Angluin and Lichtenstein [AL].

Notice that there is a natural one-to-one correspondence between "randomness preserving" directly-accessible $k \cdot 2^k$-bit long strings and random functions from I_k to I_k. By constructing a poly-random collection $F = \{F_k\}$, we virtually construct $k \cdot 2^k$-bit strings $\{s_f = f(1)f(2) \cdots f(2^k)\}_{f F_k}$ which can be directly accessed in a "randomness preserving" manner. This practically solves the Blum Blum Shub problem in a strong sense since we construct poly-random collections not only if squaring modulo a Blum-integer is a one-way permutation, but given any one-way permutation.

3 Constructing Poly-Random Collections

In this section we show how to construct functions that pass all "polynomially bounded" statistical tests.

A *collection of functions*, F, is a collection $\{F_k\}$, such that for all k and all $f \in F_k$, $f : I_k \to I_k$.

3.1 Polynomial Time Statistical Tests for Functions

A *polynomial time statistical test for functions* is a probabilistic polynomial time algorithm T that, given k as input and access to an oracle O_f for a function $f : I_k \to I_k$, outputs either 0 or 1. Algorithm T can query the oracle O_f only by writing on a special query-tape some $y \in I_k$ and will read the oracle answer, $f(y)$, on a separate answer-tape. As usual, O_f prints its answer in one step.

Let $F = \{F_k\}$ be a collection of functions. We say that F passes the test T if for any polynomial Q, for all sufficiently large k:

$$| p_k^F - p_k^H | < \frac{1}{Q(k)}$$

where p_k^F denotes the probability that T outputs 1 on input k and access to an oracle for a function $f \in_R F_k$. p_k^H is the probability that T outputs 1 when given the input k and access to an oracle O_f for a function $f \in_R H_k$ (i.e. a random function).

The above definition can be interpreted as follows. A function f is "judged" to be random depending on its input-output relation. The test T consists of two phases. First it gathers information about f by getting f's values at arguments of its choice. Then it outputs its "verdict": 0 (if it "thinks" that $f \in_R F_k$) or 1 (if it "thinks" that $f \in_R H_k$). If the collection F passes the test T, then the output of T given oracle 0_f gives no information on whether $f \in_R F_k$ or $f \in_R H_k$. In either case T will output 1 with essentially the same probability.

Passing all polynomial-time statistical tests for functions is an extremely general randomness criterion. This can be intuitively argued as follows. Should some efficient algorithm A find any dependencies among the selected input-output pairs of $f \in_R F_k$, it can be converted to a statistical test T_A that will halt outputting 0 (i.e. judging that $f \in_R F_k$) when detecting these dependencies. Since such dependencies cannot be found when $f \in_R H_k$, the collection $F = \{F_k\}$ will not pass the test T_A.

We now exhibit a collection F that passes all polynomial time statistical tests, under the assumption that there exisis a weak one-to-one one-way function.

3.2 The Construction of *F*

We construct poly-random collections given any CSPRB generator G that stretches a seed $x \in I_k$ into a 2k-bit long sequence, $G(x) = b_1^x \ldots b_{2k}^x$. By Theorem 2, such generator G can be constructed given any one-way permutation.

Let S_k be the multiset of the 2k-bit sequences output by G on seeds of' length k. Recall that $S = \cup_k S_k$ passes all polynomial-time statistical tests for strings.

Let $x \in I_k$. By $G_0(x)$ we denote the first k bits output by G on input x. I.e. $G_0(x) = b_1^x \ldots b_k^x$. By $G_1(x)$ we denote the next k bits output by G. I.e. $G_1(x) = b_{k+1}^x \ldots b_{2k}^x$. Let $a = a_1 a_2 \ldots a_t$ be a binary string. We define $G_{a_1 a_2 \ldots a_t}(x) = G_{a_t}(\cdots (G_{a_2}(G_{a_1}(x))) \cdots)$.

Let $x \in I_k$. The function $f_x : I_k \rightarrow I_k$ is defined as follows:

$$\text{For } y = y_1 y_2 \ldots y_k, \ f_x(y) = G_{y_1 y_2 \ldots y_k}(x).$$

$$\text{Set } F_k = \{f_x\}_{x \in I_k} \quad \text{and} \quad F = \{F_k\}.$$

Note that a function in F_k needs not be one-to-one.

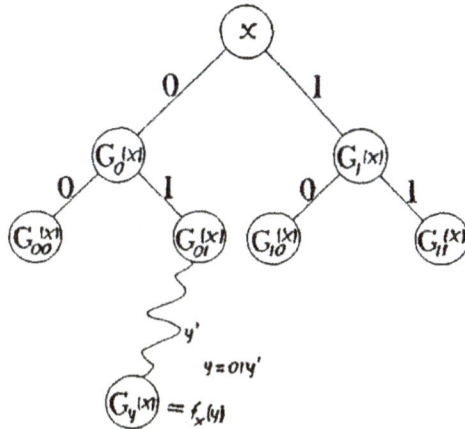

The reader may find it useful to picture a function $f_x : I_k \to I_k$ as a full binary tree of depth k with k-bit strings stored in the nodes and edges labelled 0 or 1. The k-bit string x will be stored in the root. If a k-bit string s is stored in an internal node, v, then $G_0(s)$ is stored in v's left-son, v_l , and $G_1(s)$ is stored in v's right-son, v_r. The edge (v, v_l) is labelled 0 and the edge (v, v_r) is labelled 1. The string $f_x(y)$ is then stored in the leaf reachable from the root following the edge-path labelled y. See figure 1.

Efficiency Consideration

Let T_k denote the (worst case) number of steps used in the computation of the CSPRB sequence $G(x)$ on input $x \in I_k$. Clearly, computing $f_x(y)$ on inputs x and y can be done in at most $k \cdot T_k$ steps. Thus, the efficiency of the evaluation of a function in our poly-random collection is reduced to the efficiency of the underlying CSPRB generator. The latter question is referred to in the Appendix.

3.3   The Poly-Randomness of F

Note that the collection F just defined satisfies conditions 1 (indexing) and 2 (poly-time evaluation) of a poly-random collection. The main theorem shows that condition 3 (pseudo-randomness) is also satisfied. We prove the main theorem using a (new) variant of Yao's statistical test.

Definition   (population test)   Let P and P_1 be polynomials and $S = \cup_k S_k$ be a set of sequences, where S_k consists of $P(k)$-bit sequences. A *polynomial-time population test for strings* is a probabilistic polynomial-time algorithm T that, on input $P_1(k)$ strings each

$P(k)$-bit long, outputs either 0 or 1. We say that S *passes the test* T if for any polynomial Q, for all sufficiently large k:

$$| p_k^S - p_k^R | < \frac{1}{Q(k)}$$

where p_k^S denotes the probability that T outputs 1 on $P_1(k)$ randomly selected strings in S_k and p_k^R denotes the probability that T outputs 1 on $P_1(k)$ random bit-strings each of length $P(k)$.

Lemma   A set of bit-sequences $S = \cup_k S_k$ passes all polynomial-time statistical tests if and only if it passes all polynomial-time population tests.

The proof of the Lemma can be easily obtained by techniques similar to the ones used for proving Theorem 4.

Main Theorem   (Theorem 3)   The collection of functions F passes all polynomial time statistical tests for functions.

Proof   Let T be a polynomial time test for functions. Let $p_k^F (p_k^H)$ be the probability that T outputs 1 when given the input parameter k and access to an oracle O_f for a function $f \in_R F_k (f \in_R H_k)$.

Assume, for contradiction, that for some polynomial Q and for infinitely many k, $|p_k^F - p_k^H| > \frac{1}{Q(k)}$.

Let us consider computations of T in which, instead of an oracle O_f, an algorithm A_i answers T's queries. For $0 \le i \le k$ and for each computation of T with oracle A_i, A_i is defined as follows.

Let y$= y_1 y_2 \ldots y_k$ be a query to A_i. Then A_i responds as follows:

If y is the first query with prefix $y_1 \ldots y_i$, A_i selects a string $r \in I_k$ at random, stores the pair $(y_1 \ldots y_i, r)$, and answers $G_{y_{i+1} \ldots y_k}(r)$.

Else, A_i retrieves the pair $(y_1 \ldots y_i, v)$ and answers $G_{y_{i+1}} \ldots y_k(v)$.

(In terms of the tree representation of f_x, A_i stores random k-bit strings in the nodes of level i. The nodes of higher level will contain k-bit strings deterministically computed as in the previous subsection based on the actual values in level i).

For $0 \le i \le k$, p_k^i is defined to be the probability that T outputs 1 when given k as input and access to the oracle A_i.

Note that $p_k^0 = p_k^F$ and that $p_k^k = p_k^H$.

We will reach a contradiction by exhibiting a polynomial-time population test for strings, A, so that S will not pass A.

Let k be such that $|p_k^0 - p_k^k| > \frac{1}{Q(k)}$, without loss of generality let $p_k^0 - p_k^k > \frac{1}{Q(k)}$. On input k, with probability greater than $1 - \frac{1}{8k \cdot Q(k)}$, A finds an i ($0 \le i < k$) such that $p_k^i - p_k^{i+1} > \frac{1}{2k \cdot Q(k)}$. Algorithm A does so by running a polynomial-time Monte-Carlo experiment using T as a subroutine.

Let now R_k be the set of all $2k$-bit long strings and S_k be as in section 3.2.

Algorithm A gives k as input to algorithm T and answers T's oracle queries consistently using the set U_k as follows. (U_k is either R_k or S_k).

Assume T writes $y = y_1 \ldots y_k$ on the oracle tape.

If y is the first query with prefix $y_1 \ldots y_i$, A picks at random, in the set U_k, $u = u_0 u_1$ ($u_0 u_1$ is the concatenation of u_o and u_1, and $|u_0| = |u_1| = k$). A stores the pairs $(y_1 \ldots y_i 0, u_o)$ and $(y_1 \ldots y_i 1, u_i)$. A answers

$$Gy_{y_{i+2}\ldots y_k}(u_0) \quad \text{if } y_{i+l} = 0 \text{ and}$$

$$Gy_{y_{i+2}\ldots y_k}(u_1) \quad \text{if } y_{i+l} = 1.$$

Else A retrieves the pair $(y_1 \ldots y_{i+1}, v)$ and answers $Gy_{y_{i+2}} \ldots y_k(v)$ if $i \le k - 2$ and v if $i = k - 1$.

Note that, when $U_k = S_k$, A simulates the computation of T with oracle A_i. When instead $U_k = R_k$, A simulates the computation of T with oracle A_{i+l}. Since T's output differs, in a measurable way, on these two computations for infinitely many k, letting A output the same bit that subroutine T does, we have reached a contradiction. ∎

3.4   Generalized Poly-Random Collections

Let P_1 and P_2 be polynomials. In some applications, we would like to have random functions from $I_{p_1(k)} \to I_{p_2(k)}$ (e.g. in hashing we might want functions from I_{1000} into I_{10}). We meet this need by constructing a generalized poly-random collection $\{F_k^{P_1, P_2}\}$. The modified construction can be simply described in terms of two different CSPRB generators: G as above and G' mapping k random input bits to $P_2(k)$ pseudo-random bits. For $x \in I_k$ the function $f_x \in F_k^{P_1, P_2}$ is defined as follows: on input $y \in I_{p_l(k)} f_x(y) = G'(G_y(x))$. By a proof similar to the one of the Main Theorem one can prove that the collection $\{F_k^{P_1, P_2}\}$ possesses properties (l), (2) and (3) of poly-random collections.

3.5   A Universal StatisticalTest

Our definition of a poly-random collection consists of passing all polynomial-time statistical tests for functions. In fact it is enough to consider one universal polynomial-time statistical test for functions (a collection will pass this universal test if and only if it passes all tests). Essentially, this universal test will guess a program of a statistical test and then execute it. Further details will be given in the full version of this paper. Similarly, universal tests exist also for all the other classes of tests mentioned in this paper.

4   Prediction Problems and Poly-Random Collections

Physics may be viewed as a prediction problem. This problem may seem to be tractable if

1. There is an a priori guarantee that the "laws of nature" are "simple" (the functions one needs to predict can be computed in polynomial time once some trapdoor information is given).

2. It is possible to conduct selected experiments (one is given temporary access to an oracle for the function).

3. The goal is only to approximately predict the "laws of nature" (the function).

Note that the ability to perform *selected* experiments (query the function) is a much more powerful tool than learning from given examples. The power of this tool is hereafter demonstrated.

An Example   Consider the set C of all integers product of two primes of equal length. No efficient algorithm is known for factoring the integers $n \in C$: furthermore, the question whether such an efficient algorithm exists constitutes one of the oldest computational problems. For $n \in C \cap I_k$, we define the following functions $f_n : I_k \to I_k$ as follows: $f_n(x) =$ the smallest square root of $x^2 \bmod n$ if $gcd(x, n) = 1$, and 0 otherwise. These functions are "simple," i.e. are polynomial-time computable if the trapdoor information (the factorization of n) is given. If the factorization of n is not part of the input then these f_n's may be hard to compute: Rabin [Ra] proved that factoring $n \in C$ is probabilistic polynomial-time reducible to computing $f_n(y)$ on input n and y. However, a simple extension of Rabin's proof shows that (even when the index n is not a part of the input), these "simple" functions can be computed after being given temporary access to an oracle (O_n) which on query q returns the value of the function at argument q (i.e. $f_n(q)$). In fact, after asking the oracle a few questions, n can be easily computed and factored.

One might therefore wonder whether for all "simple" functions f, temporary access to an oracle for f may enable one to hereafter easily compute f. We answer this question negatively in a strong sense, under the assumption that one-way permutations exist. Given any one-way permutation g, we construct "simple" functions $f^{(g)}$ that cannot be predicated (even in a weaker sense than discussed above).

Remark The $f^{(g)}$'s we construct cannot be weakly predicted after temporary access to an oracle for them, even if the one-way permutation g at the base of the construction can be easily computed after temporary access to an oracle for g.

Formal Setting

Let F be a collection of functions satisfying conditions 1 (indexing) and 2 (poly-time evaluation) of a poly-random collection. Let A be a probabilistic polynomial-time algorithm capable of oracle calls as in section 3.1. On input k and access to an oracle O_f for a function $f \in F_k$, algorithm A carries out a computation during which it queries O_f about $x_1, \ldots, x_j$. Then, algorithm A outputs $x \in I_k$ such that $x \neq x_1, \ldots, x_j$. This x will be called the *chosen exam*. At this point A is disconnected from O_j, and is presented $f(x)$ and $y \in_R I_k$ in random order. A is asked to guess which of the two is $f(x)$.

Let Q be a polynomial. We say that A Q–*Queries-and-Learns* F if on input k the probability that A guesses correctly which-is-which is greater than $\frac{1}{2} + \frac{1}{Q(k)}$.

We say that F cannot be *polynomially-inferred* if there exists no probabilistic polynomial time algorithm A and polynomial Q such that A can Q–query-and-learn F.

Note that polynomially-inferring the collection F is a much more easy task than predicting $f \in_R F_k$ in the sense discussed in the beginning of this section.

Theorem 4 F cannot be polynomially-inferred if and only if F passes all polynomial-time statistical tests for functions.

Proof Assume, on one hand, that F can be polynomially-inferred. Let Q be a polynomial and A be a probabilistic algorithm that Q–queries-and-learns F. Clearly, A cannot Q–queries-and-learns $H = \{H_k\}$. Thus A can be used to construct a statistical test T_A which distinguishes F from H as follows:
On input k, T_A initiates A with input k and answers A's queries by forwarding them to the oracle O_f ($f \in_R F_k$ or $f \in_R H_k$). When A asks to be examined on the exam x, T_A queries O_f on x, picks randomly $y \in I_k$ and returns y and $f(x)$ to A in random order. If A guess right the identity of $f(x)$ then T_A outputs 1; otherwise T_A outputs 0. Note that the probability that T_A outputs 1 is exactly $\frac{1}{2}$ when ($f \in_R H - k$; while it (the probability T_A outputs 1) is greater then $\frac{1}{2} + \frac{1}{Q(k)}$ when $f \in_R F_k$.

Assume, on the other hand, that F does not pass the statistical test T. Then there exist a polynomial, Q, such that $|p_k^F - p_k^H| > \frac{1}{Q(k)}$, where p_k^F and p_k^H are defined, as in section 3.1, relative to T. Let P be a polynomial. Without loss of generality, given k as input, T always asks $P(k)$ oracle queries and all queries are different. Without loss of generality assume that $|p_k^H - p_k^F| > \frac{1}{Q(k)}$. We will construct a probabilistic polynomial time algorithm, A_T, that $2 \cdot P(k) \cdot Q(k)$–queries-and-learns F.

For $f \in F_k$, the pseudo-oracle O_f^i is formally defined as follows:

Let x_j be the j-th query presented to O_f^i.
> **If** $j \leq i$, then O_f^1 answers with $f(x_j)$,
> **Else** O_f^i answers with a random k-bit string.

Define p_k^i to be the probability that T outputs 1 when given access to the oracle O_f^i. Here the probability is taken over all $f \in F_k$ and all possible computations of T. Note that $p_K^0 = p_k^H$ and $p_k^{P(k)} = P_k^F$.

On input k with probability $1 - \frac{1}{8P(k)Q(k)}$, A_T, finds an i $(0 \leq i < P(k))$, such that $p_k^i - p_k^{i+1} > \frac{1}{2 \cdot P(k) \cdot Q(k)}$ by running a Monte-Carlo experiment.

A_T uses T as follows: A_T starts T on the same input k it receives. A_T answers the first i queries of T using the oracle O_f. When T asks for its $i + 1$st query, x_{i+1}, A_T outputs x_{i+1} as its (A_T's) chosen exam. Upon receiving $f(x_{i+1})$ and y where $y \in_R I_k$, A_T chooses randomly $z \in \{f(x_{i+1}), y\}$ and writes z on T's answer tape (i.e. as the $i + 1$st oracle answer). A_T answers all subsequent queries of T by randomly selecting k-bit strings. If T outputs 1 then A_T guesses that $z \in_R I_k$; otherwise then A_T guesses that $z = f(x_{i+1})$. ∎

5 Applications

In this section we briefly discuss some of the problems which can be solved using a poly-random collection. Our solutions are the first which are proved secure under the general assumption that one-way permutations exist. A detailed discussion of these applications is presented in [CGM2]. Brassard [B] has pointed out that application 5.2 could be possible if the BBS open problem had a positive solution.

5.1 Storageless Distribution of Secret Identification Numbers

Consider a distributed system with one or more *servers* and many *users* each having a distinct name. The problem is to distribute, to each user, a secret user-identification number (ID) such that the ID is verifiable by the servers but infeasible to compute by any other user. An example of such a problem is assigning calling card numbers to telephone customers.

Our solution uses the poly-random collection $F = \{F_k\}$ in order to assign random secret IDs to the users. First, the servers jointly pick a $f \in_R F_k$ in secrecy, and each server stores the k-bit index of f. (This is all the servers need to store!) Then, every user X in the system is assigned as an ID $f(X)$.

Note that each server can verify whether a given number is the ID of *Alice*, by computing $f(Alice)$. However, it is infeasible for any set of users to compute the ID of any user not in the set.

5.2 Message Authentication and Time-Stamping

Using poly-random collections it is possible, for the first time, to construct deterministic, memoryless, authentication schemes which are highly robust, as discussed in the following concrete setting.

Assume that all the employees of a large bank communicate through a public network. As an adversary may be able to inject messages, the employees need to authenticate the messages they sent to each other (e.g. "transfer sum S from account A to account B"). A solution may consist of appending to the message in an authentication tag which is hard to compute by an adversary. In particular, we propose the following. Let all employees have access to authentication machines which compute a function f_s in a poly-random collection. The tag associated with a message m is $f_s(m)$. We can tradeoff security for the length of the tag. For example, if one uses only the first 20 bits of $f_s(m)$ as an authentication tag, then the chance that an adversary could successfully authenticate a message is about 1 in a million.

To avoid playback of previously authenticated messages, it is common practice to use time-stamps. Namely, authenticate m concatenated with date it was sent. So far, time-stamping was only a heuristic as an adversary who sees the message m authenticated with date D could conceivably authenticate m with another date (say $D+1$). Using our solution for message authentication, time-stamping makes playback provably hard. This is the case as for a random function $f(x)$ is totally unrelated to $f(x+1)$, and therefore the same holds (with respect to polynomial-time adversaries) for poly-random collections.

Another threat to the Bank's security is the loyalty of its own employees. They have the authenticating computer at their disposal and can use it to launch a chosen message attack against the scheme, so that when they are fired they can forge transactions. Our message authentication scheme remains secure even when the employees are not trustworthy, if each message to be authenticated is automatically time stamped by the computer. An employee who leaves the bank, after having widely experimented with the machine, will not be able to authenticate even one new message.

5.3 An Identify Friend or Foe System

The members of an exclusive society are well known for their brotherhood spirit. Upon meeting each other, anywhere in the world, they extend hospitality, favors, advice, money etc. Naturely, they face the danger of imposters trying to take advantage of their generosity. Thus, upon meeting each other, they must execute a protocol for establishing membership. As they meet in public places (busses, trains, theatre), they must be careful not to yield information that can lead to future successful impersonations. They go around carrying pocket computers on which they may make calculations.

Clearly a password scheme will not suffice in this context, as the conversations are public. An interactive identification scheme is needed where the ability to ask questions does not enable future successful impersonations. Note that that the questions that A may ask member B, *must be picked from an exponential range* to prevent an active imposter from asking all possible questions, receiving all possible answers and thereafter successfully impersonating as a member (or to prevent a passive imposter from having a non-negligible probability of being asked a question that he overheard the answer to).

Using our poly-random collection, we can fully solve this problem. Let the president of the society choose a k-bit random string s, specifying a function f_s in a poly-random collection. Each member receives a computer which calculates f_s. When member A meets B, he asks z? where $z \in_R I_k$. Only if B answers $f_s(z)$, will member A be convinced that B is a member. In addition, if the computers that calculate f_s can be manufactured so that they cannot be duplicated, then losing a computer does not compromise the security of the entire scheme; it just allows one non-member to enjoy the privileges of the society.

Note that using any of the "known" one-way functions in the role of f_s may not work here, since ability to ask questions may compromise the security of the entire society as for the case of Rabin's function (see section 4).

5.4 Dynamic Hashing

Poly-random collections from long bit-strings to short bit-strings constitute very good hash functions. Note that such hash functions have advantages, with respect to polynomial-time computation, over the Universal Hashing scheme suggested by Carter and Wegman [CW]. In their scheme the hash functions perform well with respect to a fixed a priori probability distribution for the keys. Our scheme performs well even if an adversary does not fix his key distribution a priori, but can dynamically change the key distribution during the hashing process upon seeing the hash function values on previous keys.

Such a scheme may be useful in applications where accessing memory is more expensive than evaluating the hash functions.

5.5 Speeding-up CSPRB Generation

Assume that G is an "inherently-sequential" CSPRB generator. That is, on input a k-bit seed, computing the i-th bit in the output sequence of G takes time $i \cdot T(k)$. Assume that our application (see example below) requires to compute the bits in the $poly(k)$-bit long sequence output by G in arbitrary order, and that only $O(k)$ bits of storage are available. Then it would be desirable to access the bits in the pseudo-random sequence "directly" rather than "sequentially."

Using G to construct a function in a poly-random collection, we effectively construct an exponentially (in k) long pad each bit of which can be accessed in time $k \cdot 2k \cdot T(k)$.

Example Protecting a data base.   Suppose that one would like to store a huge data base on a public computer while maintaining the information contained in it private. To achieve this one may encrypt each of the records of the data base, place the encrypted records on the public computer and store only a relatively small secret key on his home computer. Suppose that encryption has been done by using the sequence output by a CSPRB generator as a one-time pad. In this case the private key consists of the input seed to the generator. To retrieve the information on a record one has to access the segment of the pseudo-random pad used for encrypting it.

6 Concluding Remarks

The Notion of Polynomial Pseudo-Randomness

A CSPRB generator can be viewed as a tool for simulating a source of truly random coin tosses. Consider the following source of randomness: a probabilistic polynoinial-time Turing Machine (TM) that, on input the security parameter k, outputs polynomially many bits. Using a CSPBR generator, one can construct a probabilistic polynomial-time TM that, on input k, simulates the source using only k internal coin tosses. The simulation is perfect with respect to all polynomially bounded observers.

Let its now consider interactive sources. An *Interactive Source* is an interactive, probabilistic, polynomial-time TM which answers queries presented to it by an inspection machine (another interactive, probabilistic, polynomial-time TM). The interaction consists of a sequence of interleaved queries and answers. In this extended abstract, we considered a special case of interaction and showed how such interactive sources can be perfectly simulated by a poly-random collection, using only k internal coin tosses and k^C bits of storage (for some fixed C). We believe that this case captures the notion of polynomial pseudo-randomness.

A Tool for Cryptographic Protocol Design

As shown in the applications mentioned in section 5.1, 5.2 and 5.3, the poly-random collections are a powerful tool in cryptographic protocol design. The following methodology for protocol design appears fruitful. First, design a protocol which uses truly random functions, and prove it correct. Then, replace the truly random functions by functions randomly selected from a poly-random collection. This implementation will provably maintain all properties of the original protocol with respect to polynomially bounded adversaries. Also note that if two independent random functions are substituted by two functions randomly selected from a poly-random collection, then the latter will be totally uncorrelated (as the former ones). This provable independence is very useful in protocol design.

Recently, Luby and Rackoff [LR] used polyrandom collections to construct collections of polyrandom permutations. This result leads to the construction of ideal private key cryptosystems.

Acknowledgements

Our greatest thanks go to Benny Chor for sharing with us much of the labor involved in this research.

Leonid Levin relentlessly encouraged us to get this result and, once obtained, helped us to better understand it in the course of so many inspiring discussions. Thank you Lenia!

We are particularly grateful to Ron Rivest who assisted us all along with many insights and precious criticism.

We are very grateful to Albert Mayer for quickly rescuing us from a fearful dead end.

Many thanks to Michael Ben-Or, Steve Cook, Tom Leighton, Gary Miller, Charles Rackoff and Mike Sipser for several helpful discussions.

Oded Goldreich would like to thank Dassi Levi for her existence.

Appendix
Sufficient Conditions for Constructing CSPRB Generators

Let $D_k \subseteq I_k$ and $B_k : D_k \to \{0,1\}$. Let g_k be a permutation over D_k. Let $D = \cup_k D_k$, $B = \{B_k\}$ and $g = \{g_k\}$. Blum and Micali [BM] showed that CSPRB generators can be constructed under the following conditions:

1. The Domain is accessible: there exists a *probabilistic* polynomial-time algorithm that on input k, chooses $x \in D_k$ with uniform probability distribution.

2. There exists a polynomial-time algorithm that on input k and $x \in D_k$, computes $g_k(x)$.

3. Let A be a *probabilistic* polynomial-time algorithm and Q be a polynomial. Then for all sufficiently large k:

   $A(x) \neq B_k(x)$ for at least for a fraction $\frac{1}{2} - \frac{1}{Q(k)}$ of the $x \in D_k$.

4. There exists a polynomial-time algorithm that on input k and $x \in D_k$, computes $B_k(g_k(x))$.

Note that the above conditions imply that g is a one-way permutation as defined in section 2.3. Yao [Y] showed that the existence of a one-way permutation (over an accessible domain) is a sufficient condition for constructing CSPRB generators.

A Sketch of Yao's Construction

Yao's construction [Y] can be viewed as a method to construct B and g as above, when given any one-way permutation $h = \{h_k\}$ over the accessible domain $E = \cup_k E_k$. Recall that no polynomial algorithm can invert h without being mistaken on a $\frac{1}{k^c}$ fraction of the domain, for some constant c, when k is sufficiently large.

Set D_k to be the Cartesian product of k^{2q} copies of E_k.

Set $g_k(x_1 x_2 \ldots x_{k^{2q}}) = h_k(x_1) h_k(x_2) \ldots h_k(x_{k^{2q}})$, where $x_j \in E_k$.

Set $B_k^{(i,j)}(x)$ to be the ith bit of $h_k^{-1}(x)$, where $x \in E_k$ and

$$B_k(x_1 x_2 \ldots x_{k^{2q}}) = \bigoplus_{i=1}^{k} \bigoplus_{j-1}^{k^{2q-1}} B_k^{(i,j)}(x_{k^{2q-1}(i-1)+j})$$

Then $\cup_k D_k$, $\{g_k\}$, and $\{B_k\}$ defined above satisfy all 4 conditions of the Blum-Micali scheme (a proof of this appears in [G]).

A Sketch of Levin's Definition

A function (algorithm) A is (t, e)–*one-way on an input* $x \in I_k$ if

1. There exists an i such that $A^i(x) = x$.

2. The computation of A on input x takes time at most $t(k)$.

3. An *optimal inverting algorithm* (for A) requires at least time $e(k)$ in order to compute and verify x on input $A(x)$. (The existence of an optimal inverting algorithm for NP-search problems was pointed out in [L6].)

A function (algorithm), A, is *locally one-way* if there exist a polynomial t and a function e which grows faster than any polynomial such that A is (t, e)–one-way on at least a $\frac{1}{t(k)}$ fraction of the inputs in I_k.

Levin has pointed out a universal algorithm, u, (with k^2 time bound) which is locally one-way, unless no function is locally one-way. Furthermore, in case u is locally one-way it is (t_u, e_u)–locally one-way, where $t_u(k) = k^2$ and e_u grows faster than any polynomial. Note that, u can be used in Yao's construction (of a CSPRB generator) instead of the given one-way permutation.

On the Running Time of the Known CSPRB Generators

The running time of CSPRB generators should be compared with respect to the intractability assumption on which they are based. Basing a generator on any weak one-way permutation, though very appealing from a theoretical point of view, seems to have a practical drawback: slow running time (see Yao's construction above). It seems that in order to get fast generators, one would have to rely on stronger assumptions (i.e. on the intractability of specific problems). Let us consider the following two assumptions:

1. The *Intractability Assumption for the Discrete Logarithm Problem (DLA)*: It is infeasible to compute discrete logarithms modulos all but a negligible fraction of the primes. (For a precise formulation of DLA see [BM].)

2. The *Intractabilily Assurnplion for the Inleger Factorization Problem (FA)*: It is infeasible to factor all but a negligible fraction of the Blum Integers. (For a precise formulation of FA see [GMT].)

The fastest CSPRB generator known under DLA is presented in [LW]. It produces $O(\log k)$ bits of output at the cost of one modular exponentiation of k-bit integers.

The fastest CSPRB generators known under FA can be obtained by the results in [ACGS]. In particular, $O(\log k)$ bits of output can be produced at the cost of one modular multiplication of k-bit integers.

References

[A]   L. Adleman, *Time, Space and Randomness*, MIT/LCS/TM-131, 1979

[ACGS]   W. Alexi, B. Chor, 0. Goldreich and C.P. Schnorr, *RSA/Rabin Least Significant Bits Are $\frac{1}{2} + \frac{1}{poly(\log N)}$-Secure*, this proceedings.

[AL]   D. Angluin and D. Lichtenstein, *Provable Security of Cryptosystems: a Survey*, YaleU/DCS/TR-288, 1983

[BG]   C.H. Bennet and J. Gill, *Relative to a Random Oracle A, $P^A \neq NP^A \neq co - NP^A$ with Probabilily 1*, SIAM Jour. on Computing, 10 (1981), pp. 96–113.

[BCS] M. Ben-Or, B. Chor and A. Shamir, *On the Cryptographic Security of Single RSA Bits*, Proc. 15th ACM Symp. on Theory of Computing, 1983, pp. 421–430.

[BBS] L. Blum, M. Blum and M. Shub, *A Simple Secure Pseudo-Random Number Generator*, Advances in Cryptology: Proc. of CRYPTO-82, ed. D. Chaum, R.L. Rivest and A.T. Sherman, Plenum press, 1983, pp. 61–78.

[BM] M. Blum and S. Micali, *How to Generate Cryptographically Strong Sequences of Pseudo-Random Bits*, Proc. 23rd IEEE Symp. on Foundations of Computer Science, 1982, pp. 112–117. To appear in SIAM Jour. on Computing

[B] G. Brassard, *On Computationally Secure Authentication Tags Requiritig Short Secret Shared Keys*, Advances in Cryptology: Proc. of CRYPTO-82, ed. D. Chaum, R.L. Rivest and A.T. Sherman, Plenum press, 1983, pp. 79–86.

[CW] J.L. Carter and M.N. Wegman, *Universal Classes of Hash Functions*, Proc. 9th ACM Symp. on Theory of Computing, 1977, pp. 106–112.

[Ch] G.J. Chaitin, *On the Length of Programs for Computing Finite Binary Sequences*, JACM 13 (1966), pp. 547–570.

[DH] W. Diffie, and M. E. Hellman, *New Directions in Cryptography*, IEEE Transactions on Info. Theory, IT-22 (Nov. 1976), pp. 644–654.

[Ga] P. Gacs, *On the Symmetry of Algorithmic Information*, Soviet Math. Dokl. 15, 1974 p 1477

[GGMl] O. Goldreich, S. Goldwasser and S. Micali, *How to Construct Random Functions*, MIT/LCS/TM-244, November 1983

[GGM2] O. Goldreich, S. Goldwasser and S. Micali, *On the Cryptographic Applications of Random Functions*, to appear in the proceedings of Crypto84, 1984

[G] S. Goldwasser, *Probnbilistic Encryption: Theory and Applications*, Ph.D. Thesis, Berkeley, 1984

[GMR] S. Goldwasser, S. Micali and R.L. Rivest, *A "Paradoxical" Signature Scheme*, these proceedings

[GMT] S. Goldwasser, S. Micali and P. Tong, *Why and How to Establish a Private Code on a Public Network*, Proc. 23rd IEEE Symp. on Foundations of Computer Science, 1982, pp. 134–144.

[H] J. Hartmanis, *Generalized Kolmogorov Complexity and the Structure of Feasible Computations*, Proc. 24th IEEE Symp. on Foundation of Computer Science, 1983, pp. 439–445.

[Kol] A. Kolmogorov, *Three Approaches to the Concept of "The Amount Of Infomation,"* Probl. of Inform. Transm. 1/1, 1965

[ZL] A.K. Zvonkin and L.A. Levin, *The Complexity of Finite Objects and the Algorithmic Concepts of Randomness and Information*, UMN (Russian Math. Surveys), 25/6, 1970, pp. 83–124.

[L2] L.A. Levin, *On the Notion of a Random Sequence*, Soviet Math. Dokl. 14/5 (1973), p. 1413

[L3] L.A. Levin, *Various measures of complexity for finite objects (axiomatic descriptions)*, Soviet Math. Dokl. 17/2 (1976) pp. 522–526.

[L4] L.A. Levin, *Randomness Conservation Inequalities: Information and Independence in Mathematical Theories*, to appear in Inform. and Control.

[L5] L.A. Levin, private communication, 1984

[L6] L.A. Levin, *Universal Sequential Search Problems*, Probl. Inform. Transm. 9/3 (1973), pp. 265–266.

[LW] D.L. Long and A. Wigderson, *How Discreet is Discrete Log?*, in preparation. A preliminary version appeared in Proc. 15th ACM Symp. on Theory of Computing, 1983, pp. 413–420.

[LR] M. Luby and C. Rackoff, in preparation

[ML] P. Martin-Lof, *The Definition of Random Sequences*, Inform. and Control, 9, 1966, pp. 602–619.

[Ra] M.O. Rabin, *Digitalized Signatures and Public Key Functions as Intractable as Factoring*, MIT/LCS/TR-212, 1979.

[RSA] R. Rivest, A. Shamir, and L. Adleman, *A Method for Obtaining Digital Signatures and Public Key Cryptosystems*, Comm. ACM, Vol. 21, Feb. 1978, pp. 120–126.

[Sch] C.P. Schnorr, *Zufaelligkeit und Wahrscheinlichkeit*, Springer Verlag, Lecture Notes in Math., Vol. 218, 1971.

[Sh] A. Shamir, *On the Generation of Cryptographically Strong Pseudo-random Sequences*, 8th International Colloquium on Automata, Languages, and Programming, Lect. Notes in Comp. Sci. 62, Springer Verlag, 1981, pp. 544–550.

[Si] M. Sipser, *A Complexity Theoretic Approach to Randomness*, Proc. 15th ACM Symp. on Theory of Computing, 1983, pp. 330-335.

[Sol] R.J. Solomonoff, *A Formal Theory of Inductive Inference*, Inform. and Control, 7/1, 1964, pp. 1–22.

[W] R.E. Wilber, *Randomness and the Density of Hard Problems*, Proc. 24th IEEE Symp. on Foundation of Computer Science, 1983 pp. 335–342.

[VV1] U.V. Vazirani and V.V. Vazirani, *RSA Bits are .732+e Secure*, Advances in Cryptology: Proc. of CRYPTO-83, ed. D. Chaum, Plenum press, 1984, pp. 369–375.

[VV2] U.V. Vazirani and V.V. Vazirani, *Efficient and Secure Pseudo-Random Number Generation*, these proceedings.

[Y] A.C. Yao, *Theory and Applications of Trapdoor Functions*, Proc. 23rd IEEE Symp. on Foundations of Computer Science, 1982, pp. 80-91.

A Digital Signature Scheme Secure Against Adaptive Chosen-Message Attacks

This chapter reproduces the contents of the paper "A 'Paradoxical' Solution to the Signature Problem," which appeared in the proceedings of the *25th Annual Symposium on Foundations of Computer Science*, pp. 441–448, 1984.

Assuming the intractability of factoring integers, this surprising (at the time) work of Shafi Goldwasser, Silvio Micali, and Ronald Rivest provided a signature scheme that is unforgeable under chosen-message attacks. Such a result was considered impossible at the time, because it was (falsely) believed that a "constructive proof of unforgeability (under passive attacks)" implies a successful chosen-message attack.

A "Paradoxical" Solution to the Signature Problem*

Shafi Goldwasser (MIT Laboratory for Computer Science),
Silvio Micali (MIT Laboratory for Computer Science),
Ronald L. Rivest (MIT Laboratory for Computer Science)

Brief Abstract

We present a general signature scheme which uses any pair of trap-door permutations (f_0, f_1) for which it is infeasible to find any x, y with $f_0(x) = f_1(y)$. The scheme possesses the novel property of being robust against an adaptive chosen message attack: no adversary who first asks for and then receives signatures for messages of his choice (which may depend on previous signatures seen) can later forge the signature of even a single additional message.

For a specific instance of our general scheme, we prove that

1. forging signatures is provably equivalent to factoring, while

2. adaptive chosen message attacks are of no help to an "enemy" who wishes to forge a signature.

Such a scheme is "paradoxical" since the above two properties were believed (and even "proven" in the folklore) to be contradictory.

The new scheme is potentially practical: signing and verifying signatures are reasonably fast, and signatures are not too long.

---

* This research was supported by NSF grant MCS-80-06038, an IBM/MIT Faculty Development Award, and DARPA contract N00014-85-K-0125.

Keywords: Cryptography, digital signatures, factoring, chosen message attacks, authentication, claw-free pairs of functions, randomization.

Introduction

The idea of a "digital signature" first appeared in Diffie and Hellman's seminal papers, "New Direction in Cryptography" [DH76]. They propose that a user A's signature for a message M should be a value which depends on M and on information held secret by A such that anyone can verify the validity of A's signature (using information published by A) but no one can forge A's signature on any messages. They also proposed a way of implementing signatures based on "trap-door functions" (see section II.A).

While the notion of a digital signature is robust, useful, and even legal [LM78, Ma79], a number of technical problems arise if they are implemented as suggested using trap-door functions; these problems have been addressed in part elsewhere. For example, [GMY83] showed how to handle arbitrary or sparse messages sets and how to ensure that if an enemy sees previous signatures it does not help him to forge new signatures (this is a so-called "non-adaptive chosen message attack"). For further discussion see section IV.

One difficult problem with simple trap-door signature schemes is proving they are secure agains *adaptive* chosen message attackes, where the enemy can request signatures of messages which depend on previously obtained signatures.

We present a new digital signature scheme that is seemingly "paradoxical", in that we prove that forgery is equivalent to factoring, even if the enemy uses an *adaptive* chosen message attack.

We can restate the paradox as follows:

- Any general technique for forging signatures can be used as a "black box" in a construction that enables the enemy to factor one of the signer's public moduli (he has two in our scheme),

but

- The technique of "forging" signatures by getting the real signer to play the role of the "black box" (i.e. getting the real signer to produce some desired genuine signatures) does not help the enemy to factor either of the signer's moduli.

Resolving this paradox was previously believed to be impossible and contradictory [Wi80, misled by Rivest].

From a cryptographer's viewpoint, the following points might be judged to be even more significant than resolving the apparent paradox:

- What we prove to be difficult is *forgery*, and not merely obtaining the secret trap-door information embedded in the signing algorithm (or obtaining an efficient equivalent algorithm).

- Forgery is proven to be difficult for a "most general" enemy who can mount an "adaptive chosen message attack": an enemy who can use the real signer as "an oracle" can not in time polynomial in the size of the public keys forge a signature for any message whose signature was not obtained from the oracle. In contrast to all previous published work on this problem, we prove the scheme invulnerable against such an "adaptive" attack (where each message whose signature is requested may depend on all the signatures previously obtained from the oracle). We believe that such an "adaptive chosen message attack" to be the most powerful attack possible for an enemy who is restricted during his attach to using the signature scheme in a natural manner.

- The properties we prove about the new signature scheme do not depend in any way on the set of messages which can be signed or on any assumptions about an input probability distribution on the message set.

- Our scheme can be generalized so that it can be based on "hard" problems other than factoring whenever one can create (so-called "claw-free") pairs of trap-door permutations (f_0, f_1) such that the hard problem is equivalent to find x, y with $f_0(x) = f_1(y)$ (a "claw"—see Figure 1). The paradoxical nature of the signature scheme remains.

The scheme as a "pumping" nature: using any family of pairs of trap-door permutations we can produce a signature scheme that is *invulnerable* to a chosen message attack, even if the trap-door permutations are *vulnerable* to a chosen message attack when used to make a trap-door signature scheme (see section II).

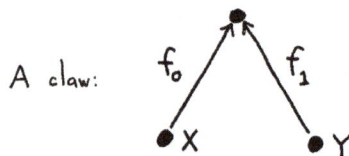

Figure 1

Fundamental ideas in the construction are the use of randomization, signing by using two authentication steps (the first step authenticates a random value which is used in the second step to authenticate the message), and the use of a tree-like branching authentication structure to produce short signatures.

We note that because our signature scheme is randomized it is not of the simple Diffie-Hellman "trap-door" type. (For example, a given message can have many signatures.)

The rest of the paper is organized as follows. In section II we review the fundamental notions of what it means to "break" a signature scheme and what it means to "attack" a signature scheme. In section III we review more closely the nature of the "paradox", and present the folklore "proof" that it is impossible to have a signature scheme for which forgery is provably equivalent to factoring and which is simultaneously invulnerable to an adaptive chosen message attack. In section IV we review previously proposed signature schemes. In section V we give the details of our proposed signature scheme, and in section VI we prove that it has the desired properties.

Fundamental Notions

To properly characterize the results of this paper, it is helpful to answer the following questions:

- What is a digital signature scheme?
- What kinds of attacks can the enemy mount against a digital signature scheme?
- What is meant by "breaking" the signature scheme?

II.A   What Is a Digital Signature Scheme?

A *digital signature scheme* contains the following components:

- A *key generation algorithm* $\kappa(R, k)$ which any user A can use to produce a pair (P_A^k, S_A^k) of matching *public* and *secret* keys from inputs k and (random) input R. (The secret key is sometimes called the *trap-door information*. The parameter k is called the *security parameter*; a number of quantities (e.g. the length of signatures, overall security) may depend on k.

- A *message space* $\mathcal{M}$ which is the set of messages to which the signature algorithm may be applied. We assume here that the messages are represented in some encoding suitable for the signature algorithm.

- A *signature algorithm* which produces a signature $\sigma(M, S_A, R)$ for a message M using the secret key S_A and random input R. (This is the *memoryless* model; it is also permissible to have the signature algorithm depend on the number of messages previously signed and even how they were signed. The scheme proposed in this paper is not memoryless.)

- A *verification predicate* $\tau(S, M, P_A)$ which tests whether S is valid signature for message M using the public key P_A.

We note that there are other kinds of "signature" problems which are not dealt with here; the most notable being the "contract signing problem" where two parties wish to exchange their signatures to an agreed-up contract *simultaneously* (for example, see [EGL82]).

II.A.1   Trap-Door Signatures

To create a signature scheme Diffie and Hellman proposed that A use a "trap-door function" f: a function for which it is easy to evaluate $f(x)$ for any argument x but for which, given only $f(x)$, it is computationally infeasible to find *any* y with $f(y) = f(x)$ without the secret "trap-door" information. Then A publishes f and anyone can validate a signature by checking that $f(signature) = message$. Only A possesses the "trap-door" information allowing her to invert f: $f^{-1}(message) = signature$. A *trap-door permutation* is a trap-door function which is one-to-one and onto; then any message can be signed since the domain of f^{-1} is the entire message space. We call any signature scheme that fits into this model (i.e. uses trap-door functions and signs by apply f^{-1} to the message) a *trap-door signature scheme*.

We note that not all signature schemes are trap-door schemes, although most of the proposals in the literature are of this type.

II.B   Kinds of Attacks

The enemy may mount an attack knowing only the real signer's public key—what we call a *direct attack*. Of more concern, however, are what we call *known* or *chosen message attacks* where the enemy is able to examine some signatures corresponding to either known or chosen messages before his attempt to break the scheme. (These are analogous to "chose ciphertext attacks" for encryption schemes.)

We identify the following four kinds of message attacks, which are characterized by how the messages who signatures the enemy sees are constructed. (Here we let A denote the user whose signature method is being attacked.)

- **Known Message Attack:** The enemy sees signatures for a set of messages $M_1, \ldots, M_k$. The messages are known to the enemy but are not in any way chosen by him.

- **Generic Chosen Message Attack:** Here the enemy is allowed to obtain from A valid signatures for a chosen list of message $M_1, \ldots, M_k$ before he attempts to break A's signature scheme. These messages are *chosen* by the enemy, but they are *fixed* and *independent* of A's public key (for example the M_i's may be chosen at random). This attack is *nonadaptive:* the entire message list is constructed before any signatures are seen. This attack is "generic" since it does not depend on the A's public key; the same attack is used against everyone.

- **Directed Chosen Message Attack:** This is similar to the generic chosen message attack, except that the list of messages to be signed may depend on A's public key. However, it is still nonadaptive as before. This attack is "directed" against a particular user A.

- **Adaptive Chosen Message Attack:** This is more general yet: here the enemy is also allowed to use A as an "oracle"; not only may he request from A signatures of messages which depend on A's public key but he may also request signatures of messages which depend additionally on previously obtained signatures.

We use the term "non-adaptive message attack" to mean a know, generic chosen, or directed chosen message attack.

II.C What Does It Mean to "Break" a Signature Scheme?

One might say that the enemy has "broken" user A's signature scheme if this attack allows him to do any of the following with a non-negligible probability:

- **A Total Break:** Compute A's secret trap-door information.

- **Universal Forgery:** Find an efficient signing algorithm functionally equivalent to A's signing algorithm (based on possibly different but equivalent trap-door information).

- **Selective Forgery:** Forge a signature for a particular message chosen *a priori* by the enemy.

- **Existential Forgery:** Forge a signature for at least one message. The enemy has no control over the message whose signature he obtains, so it may be random or nonsensical. Consequently this forgery may only be a minor nuisance to A.

We say that a scheme is respectively *totally breakable, universally forgeable, selectively forgeable,* or *existentially forgeable* if it is breakable in one of the above senses. Note that is it more desirable to prove that a scheme is not even existentially forgeable than to prove that it is not totally breakable. The above list is not exhaustive; there may be other ways of "breaking" a signature scheme which fit in between those listed, or are somehow different in characer.

Our notion of *forgery* means that the enemy must produce a signature for a message whose signature he was not given by A during his attack; it is not forgery to obtain from A a valid signature for a message and then claim that he has now "forged" that signature, any more than photocopying a signed document is an instance of forgery.

To say that the scheme is "broken", we insist that it be broken with a non-negligible probability—for at least some positive fraction ϵ of all possible public keys.

We note here that the characteristics of the signature scheme may depend on its message space in subtle ways. For example a scheme may be existentially forgeable for a message space $\mathcal{M}_1$ but not existentially forgeable if restricted to a message space which is a sparse subset of $\mathcal{M}_1$.

For examples of the notions, see section IV (where we review previously proposed signature schemes).

The Paradoxical Problem of Proving Signature Schemes Secure

The paradoxical nature of signature schemes which are provably secure against chose message attacks made its first appearance in Rabin's paper, "Digitalized Signatures as Intractable as Factorization". The signature scheme he proposed there works as follows. User A publishes a number n which is the product of two large primes. To sign a message M, A computes as M's signature one of M's square roots modulo n. (When M is not a square modulo n, A modifies a few bits of M to find a nearby square.) Here signing is essentially just extracting square roots modulo n. Using the fact that extracting square roots modulo n enables one to factor n, it follows that selective forgery in Rabin's scheme is equivalent to factoring if the enemy is restricted to at most a known message attack.

However, it is true (and was noticed by Rabin) that an enemy might totally break the scheme using a directed chosen message attack. By asking A to sign a value x^2 (mod n) (where x was picked at random), the enemy would obtain with probability $\frac{1}{2}$ another square root y of x^2 such that $\gcd(x + y, n)$ was a prime factor of n.

Rabin suggested that one could overcome this problem by, for example, having the signer concatenate a fairly long randomly chosen pad U to the message before signing it. In this way the enemy can not force A to extract a square root of any particular number.

However, the reader may now observe that the proof of the equivalence of selective forgery to factoring no longer works for the modified scheme. That is, being able to selectively forge no longer enables the enemy to directly extract square roots and thus to factor. Of course, breaking this equivalence was really the whole point of making the modification.

III.A The Paradox

We now "prove" that it is impossible to have a signature scheme for which it is both true that forgery is provably equivalent to factoring, and yet the scheme is invulnerable to adaptive chosen message attacks. (This is essentially the argument given in [Wi80].) By *forgery* we mean in this section any of universal, selective, or existential forgery—we assume that we are given a proof that forgery of the specified type is equivalent to factoring.

Let us begin by considering this given proof. The main part of the proof presumably goes as follows: given a subroutine for forging signatures, a construction method is specified for factoring. (The other part of the equivalence, showing that factoring enables forgery, is usually easy, since factoring usually enables the enemy to totally break the scheme.)

But it is trivial then to show that an adaptive chosen message attack enables an enemy to totally break the scheme. The enemy merely executes the constructive method given in the proof. Whenever he needs to execute the forgery subroutine, he merely performs an "adaptive chosen message attack" step—getting the real user to sign a message. In the end the unwary user has enabled the enemy to factor his modulus! (If the proof relates to universal or selective forgery, we have to get real user to sign a particular message. If the proof relates to existential forgery, we can get him to sign anything at all.)

III.B Breaking the Paradox

How can one hope to get around the apparent contradictory natures of equivalence to factoring and invulnerability to an adaptive chosen message attack?

A major idea in both the construction and the proof is the notion of "random rooting". Each user publishes not only his two composite moduli $n1$ and $n2$, but also a "random root" R_0. This value R_0 is used when validating the user's signatures. The paradox is resolved using this notion as follows:

- It is provably equivalent to factoring for an enemy to have a *uniform* algorithm for forging; uniform in the sense that for each pair of composite numbers $n1$ and $n2$, if the enemy can randomly forge signatures for a significant fraction of the possible random roots R_0, then he can factor either $n1$ or $n2$.

- The above proof *requires* that the enemy be able to pick R_0 himself—the forgery subroutine is fed triples $(n1, n2, R_0)$ where the R_0 part is chosen by the enemy according the procedure specified in the constructive proof. *However*, the user has picked a fixed R_0 at random to put in his public file, so an adaptive chosen message attack will not enable the enemy to "forge" signatures corresponding to any other values of R_0. Thus the constructive method given in the proof can not be applied!

IV Previous Signature Schemes

In this section we list a number of previously proposed signature schemes and briefly review some facts about their security.

Trap-Door Signatures Schemes [DH76]. Any trap-door signature scheme is existentially forgeable with a direct attack since a valid (message, signature) pair can be created by beginning with a random "signature" and applying the public verification algorithm to obtain the corresponding message. A common heuristic for handling this problem in practice is to require that the message space be sparse (e.g. by having each message contain a reasonably long checksum); in this case the proposed attack is not likely to result in a successful existential forgery.

Rivest-Shamir-Adleman [RSA78]. The RSA scheme is selectively forgeable using a directed chosen message attack, since RSA is *multiplicative:* the signature of a product is the product of the signatures. (This can be handled in practice as above using a sparse message space.)

Merkle-Hellman [MH78]. Shamir showed the basic Merkle-Hallman "knapsack" sehem to be universally forgeable using just a direct attack [Sh82]. (This scheme was perhaps more an encryption scheme than a signature scheme, but had been proposed for use as a signature scheme as well.)

Rabin [Ra79]. As noted earlier, Rabin's signature scheme is totally breakable if the enemy uses a directed chosen message attack. However, for non-sparse message spaces selective forgery is as hard as factoring if the enemy is restricted to a known message attack.

Williams [Wi80]. This scheme is similar to Rabin's. The proof that selective forgery is as hard as factoring is slightly stronger, since here only a single instance of selective forgery guarantees factoring (Rabin needed a probabilistic argument). Williams uses effectively (as we do) the properties of numbers which are the product of a prime $p \equiv 3 \pmod 8$ and prime $q \equiv 7 \pmod 8$.

Lieberherr [Li81]. This scheme is similar to Rabin's and Williams'.

Shamir [Sh78]. This knapsack-type signature scheme has recently been shown by Tulpan [Tu84] to be universally forgeable with a direct attack for any practical values of the security parameter.

Goldwasser-Micali-Yao [GMY83]. This paper presents two signature schemes, which are not of the trap-door type. These schemes have the interesting property that their characteristics hold for *any* message space (even a sparse one). The first signature scheme presented in [GMY83] was proven not to be even existentially forgeable against a *generic* chosen message attack unless factoring is easy. However, it is not known to what extent *directed* chosen message attacks or adaptive chosen message attacks might aid an enemy in "breaking" the scheme.

The second scheme presented there (based on the RSA function) was also proven not to be even existentially forgeable against a generic chosen message attack. This scheme may also resist existentially forgery against an adaptive chosen message attack, although this has not been proven. (A proof would probably require showing certain properties about the distribution of prime numbers and making a stronger intractability assumption about inverting RSA.)

By comparison, the scheme presented here is much faster, produces much more compact signatures, and is based on the much simpler assumptions (only the difficulty of factoring or more generally the existence of sets of claw-free pairs of functions).

Several of the ideas and techniques presented in [GMY83], such as bit-by-bit authentication, are used in the present paper.

Ong-Schnorr-Shamir [OSS84]. Totally breaking this scheme using an adaptive chosen message attack has been show to be as hard as factoring. However, Pollard [Po84] has recently been able to show that the "OSS" signature scheme is universally forgeable in practice using just a direct attack; he developed an algorithm to forge a signature for any given message without obtaining the secret trap-door information. A more recent "cubic" version has recently been show to be universally forgeable in practice using just a direct attack (also by Pollard).

El Gamal [EG84].   This scheme, based on the difficulty of computing discrete logarithms, is existentially forgeable with a generic message attack and selectively forgeable using a directed chosen message attack.

V Description of the Scheme

A General Scheme.   It is convenient to present our scheme in a general manner that is divorced from any particular assumptions, such as that factoring is hard. This clarifies the exposition, and helps to establish the true generality of the proposed scheme.

Definition   We define a *claw-free family* to be a set of pairs of trap-door permutations such that:

- It is easy, given a security parameter k, to select members of the family at random which have the given security parameter together with the trap-door information allowing inversion of the permutations chosen. We note that the family may contain many pairs of permutations associated with a given security parameter, just as there are many composite numbers of a given length.

- For each such pair (f_0, f_1) we have $domain(f_0) = domain(f_1)$.

- Given a pair (f_0, f_1) of permutations from the family it is computationally infeasible (even by a probabilistic algorithm) given just a description of the pair to find any (x, y) with $f_0(x) = f_1(y)$ (a "claw"—specifically, an "f-claw") with a non-negligible probability.

We also call each pair of permutations in the family "claw-free".

Remark   Note that if it is infeasible to find claws, then it is infeasible to invert either permutation, since an inversion algorithm enables one to create claws easily. It is thus a *stronger* requirement that the pair of functions be claw-free than that they merely be one-way in the sense that inversion is infeasible. Note, for example, that the RSA functions $f_0(x) = x^s \pmod{n}$ and $f_1(x) = x^t \pmod{n}$ are not easily invertible but are also not claw-free, since their commutativity allows one to create claws easily.

Remark   This is a slight generalization of the notion of a "claw-free" function f (one for which both inversion is hard and finding x, y with $f(x) = f(y)$ is hard). This latter notion has previously been proposed in the literature, and has been proposed as the proper notion of a one-way function. (See [Yu79, Li81], for example.)

Notation If (f_0, f_1) and (g_0, g_1) are claw-free pairs of functions, we extend the notation f_i and g_i to handle the case $i > 1$ by:

$$f_i(x) = f_{i_d}(f_{i_{d-1}}(f_{i_{d-2}}(\dots(f_{i_1}(f_{i_0}(x))\dots))))$$

if $i = i_d i_{d-1} \dots i_1 i_0$ in binary.

Notation f_i^{-1} is interpreted as $(f_i)^{-1}$ so that $f_i^{-1}(f_i(x)) = x$.

Prefix-Free Encodings.
We will be using the mapping from i to $f_i^{-1}(x)$ as a one-way function, where the pair (f_0, f_1) and the value x were previously known or proven to have been produced by the real signer. Anyone will be able to check this result, since $f_i(f_i^{-1}(x)) = x$.

It is important for this use that the value i be chosen from a set whose elements have a prefix-free binary encoding. (An encoding scheme is prefix-free if no encoding of an element of the set is a prefix of the encoding of any other element of the set.) If a prefix-free encoding scheme were not used, an enemy could "forge" $f_j^{-1}(x)$ from $f_i^{-1}(x)$ if the encoding for j is a prefix of the encoding for i.

We do not care to fix a particular prefix-free encoding for use here, but note that such encodings are simple to devise (e.g. code each 0 as 00, each 1 as 11, and terminate the encoding with 01).

We do, however, introduce the notation $[x]$ to denote the chosen prefix-free encoding of the integer x. Thus, our basic one-way function can be represented as $f_{[i]}(x)$.

Message Space. The new signature scheme can use any countable set as a message space, as long as a prefix-free encoding is used. Like the schemes presented in [GMY83], the properties of the new scheme do not depend on the message space used (even if it is, say, sparse).

An Atomic Authentication Step. Given an "authenticated" quantity Q, we can authenticate *two* new quantities L and R if $f_{[R]}^{-1}(Q) = L$. This is done is a *bit by bit* manner: by examining the bits of $[R]$ one-by-one, we can easily compute L. Only someone who knowns how to invert the f_i's could have produced a valid (L, R) pair from Q. (In [GM82] and [GMY83] very similar ideas appeared.)

Randomization. The signer flips coins; there are many valid signatures for any one message.

Signing by Two-Step Authentication. Signing the i-th message M_i consists of first authenticating a random message R_i, and then authenticating the given message M from the random starting point R_i. (This is reminiscent of the routing scheme for the boolean n-cube proposed by Reif and Valiant [RV83].)

Tree Authentication. We begin with an authenticated root R_0 (authenticated by being in the public file), and from each authenticated point R_i (resp. L_i) we authenticate two new values (L_{2i+1}, R_{2i+1}) (resp. (L_{2i}, R_{2i})). Each R_i is randomly chosen and the L_i values are determined from them. This defines a tree structure on the L_i and R_i values. (This tree can either be grown as new signatures are needed or can have a suitably large size defined initially.) A path from any node to the root is an "authentication chain" which authenticates the node, assuming the root has been authenticated.

Random Rooting. The initial value R_0, which is placed in the public directory, is randomly chosen.

Signatures. The signature for the j-th message M_j consists of

- The message M_j itself.
- A random quantity R_j and an authentication chain for it.
- An atomic authentication for M_j beginning at R_j.

Thus, each message M_i is authenticated by producing a pair (S_i, M_i) authenticated from R_i (which in turn is authenticated in the tree structure defined above).

V.A   How to Generate Keys

Each user publishes his public key, consisting of:

- two claw-free pairs of permutations (f_0, f_1) and (g_0, g_1), and
- a random number R_0 in the range of f_0 and f_1.

V.B   How to Sign

Implicit. User Alice has an infinite list $R_0, R_1, R_2, \ldots$ of random numbers in the range of f_0, f_1. She will use one such number per signature, begining with R_1. In practice, Alice will create these as needed rather than all at the beginning.

Authenticators. Alice will include R_j as part of her j-th signature, and provide an "authenticator" that it is valid (really created by Alice). Define

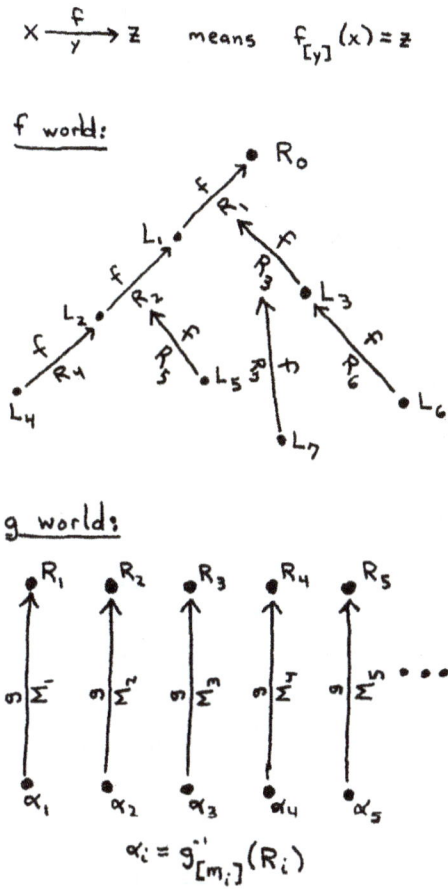

$$X \xrightarrow[y]{f} z \quad \text{means} \quad f_{[y]}(x) = z$$

f world:

g worlds:

$$\alpha_i = g^{-1}_{[m_i]}(R_i)$$

Figure 2

$$L_j = \begin{cases} f^{-1}_{[R_j]}(L_{j/2}), & \text{if } j \text{ is even;} \\ f^{-1}_{[R_j]}(R_{j-1/2}), & \text{if } j \text{ is odd.} \end{cases}$$

and

$$A_j = \begin{cases} (1, R_1, L_1), & \text{if } j = 1; \\ (j, R_j, L_j, A_{\lfloor j/2 \rfloor}), & \text{if } j > 1. \end{cases}$$

Here "A_j" is the "authenticator" for R_j; only Alice could have created it but anyone can check for it. The authenticators form a "tree-like" structure (see Figure 2).

Signature.   Alice's signature for the j-th message M_j is $(M_j, A_j, g_{[M_j]}^{-1}(R_j))$.

V.C   How to Verify a Signature

First, authenticate R_j using the published f_i's.

Then, authenticate M_j using the published g_i's.

V.D   Efficiency of the Proposed Signature Scheme

Let us assume that all numbers and messages have length $O(k)$, where k is the "security parameter" for the system. Then the time to compute a signature is $O(k)$ function inversions (i.e. inversions of f_0 or f_1).

Then length of the j-th signature is

$$O(\log(j) \cdot k).$$

VI   Proof of Security

We recall that a signature scheme is existentially forgeable if the enemy is able to forget any valid message/signature pairs at all. We also recall that in an adaptive chosen message attack the enemy can use the real signer as an "oracle" for a while before attempting to forge a new signature.

Theorem   The proposed signature scheme is not existentially forgeable, even if the enemy uses an adaptive chosen message attack.

Proof   Assume that there exists an adaptive chosen message attack which enables the enemy to later forge valid signatures. We prove that this would enable an enemy to create an f-claw or a g-claw, or to invert one of the f_i's or the g_i's.

We assume that the security parameter k is given.

Choose at random a claw-free pair of functions f_0, f_1 with the correct security parameter from the given family of pairs of claw-free functions, so we don't know f_i^{-1} ($i = 0, 1$). We will show that the existence of the effective attack by the enemy would violate the claw-freeness assumption for the f_i's.

We choose g_i at random with corresponding trapdoor information ($i = 0, 1$). We can therefore invert each g_i.

We consider two cases and apply the presumed attack to each:

Case 1.   Apply the attack to the (f, g) signature scheme—(i.e. as described above). Note that we can "simulate" the attack (i.e. play the role of the actual signer when asked to sign messages) even though we don't know f_i^{-1}, since we can *a priori* create the necessary tree in the "f-world" using f in the forward direction only (since all nodes in the "f-world" are randomly chosen). So the attack can be executed resulting in the forgery of a new message.

Case 2. Apply the attack as in case 1, but switching the roles of f and g (but not their names). Here it is easy to simulate the attack by simulating the signing of messages as needed, without using f_i^{-1}. To do this, given a message M_j to sign, we can compute $f_{[M_j]}(S)$ where S is randomly chosen, resulting in a a value R_j. We can then "authenticate" R_j in the "g-world" by using g^{-1} as needed.

Lemma A successful attack will, when it forges its signature, either create an f-claw, a g-claw.

Proof Sketch We can view the authentication structure produced by the legitimate signer during a chosen message attack as a collection of atomic authentication steps, each of which authenticate two values from one previously authenticated value. (Some of these steps are in g-world and some in f-world, but it doesn't matter here.) To forge a new signature means to produce new atomic authentication steps (otherwise nothing new has been signed) which "link in" to values previously authenticated by the real signer. If it "links in" in g-world we get a g-claw and if it "links in" in f-world we get an f-claw. ∎

By assumption about the ways in which the f_i's and the g_i's were chosen, the attack could not tell if it was in case 1 or case 2. Therefore the attack will with probability at least 1/2 (if it succeeds) "break" the given f_i's by creating an f-claw. By assumption, however, (f_0, f_1) was a claw-free pair for which we did not know the trap-door information. This contradiction proves that it is impossible to have a uniform method of forging signatures with an adaptive chosen signature attack. ∎

VI.A An Implementation of Our Scheme as Intractable as Factoring

The assumption of the existence of "claw-free" pairs was made in a general manner, and not based on any particular number theoretic assumptions. Thus, the above proof of security holds even if factoring turns out to be in polynomial time. However for concretely implementing our scheme the following is suggested.

We first make an assumption about the intractability of factoring, and then exhibit a family of claw free pairs whose existence is thereby implied.

Notation Let $H_k = \{n = p \cdot q \mid |p| = |q| = k\}$ (the set of composite numbers which are the product of two k-bit primes), and let $H = \cup_k H_k$.

Remark   Randomly selected members of H seem to be among the "hardest" inputs for all known factoring algorithms.

The following assumption about the intractability of factoring is made throughout this section.

The Intractability Assumption for Factoring (IAF).   Let $0 < \epsilon < 1$, let Q be an arbitrary polynomial, and let $C_{\epsilon,k}$ denote the minimum size of a boolean circuit that can factor at least a fraction ϵ of the numbers in H_k. Then $C_{\epsilon,k} > Q(k)$ for all sufficiently large k.

Consider the subset B of H whose elements are the product of a prime $p \equiv 3$ (mod 8) and prime $q \equiv 7$ (mod 8). (These numbers were used in [Wi80, Bl82].) We note that for $n \in B_n$:

−1 has Jacobi symbol +1 but is not a quadratic residue (mod n).

2 has Jacobi symbol −1 (and is not a quadratic residue (mod n)).

Let Q_n denote the set of quadratic residues (modulo n). Define f_0^n and f_1^n as permutations of Q_n as follows:

$$f_0^n(x) = x^2 \ (\text{mod } n)$$

$$f_1^n(x) = 4x^2 \ (\text{mod } n)$$

(It is not too difficult to prove that f_0^n and f_1^n are permutations of Q_n when $n \in B_n$. See [Bl82] for example.)

Claim   Under the IAF, $F = \{(f_0^n, f_1^n) \mid n \in B\}$ is a claw-free family of permutations.

Proof   Every $x \in Q_n$ has exactly one square root $y \in Q_n$, but has four square roots $y, -y, w, -w$ altogether. Roots w and $-w$ have Jacobi symbol −1, while y and $-y$ have Jacobi symbol +1.

Let $n \in B$ and $(f_0^n, f_1^n) \in F$. First f_0 and f_1 are permutations. Second they are trapdoor under IAF, by Rabin's proof. Finally, we show if there exists a fast algorithm that finds x and y in Q_n such that $y^2 \equiv 4x^2$ (mod n) then factoring is easy. Suppose such an x and y have been found. Then, $x^2 \equiv (2y)^2$ (mod n). Since $x \in Q_n, y \in Q_n, 2 \notin Q_n$, we have $2y \notin Q_n$ so that $x \not\equiv \pm 2y$ (mod n). Thus $gcd(x \pm 2y, n)$ will produce a nontrivial factor of n.   ∎

VII   Conclusions and Open Problems

- Can a signature scheme be developed with the properties of the new scheme proposed here, except that it is "memoryless" in the sense that the signature algorithm does not depend on the number of messages previously signed or how they were signed?

- It is an open question whether the RSA scheme is universally forgeable under an adaptive chosen message attack.

- Can an encryption scheme be developed for which decryption is provably equivalent to factoring yet for which an adaptive chosen ciphertext attack is of no help to the enemy?

VIII   References

[Bl82] Blum, M. "Coin Flipping by Telephone," *Proc. IEEE Spring COMPCOM* (1982), 133-137.

[DH76] Diffie, W. and M. E. Hellman, "New Directions in Cryptography", *IEEE Trans. Info. Theory* **IT-22** (Nov. 1976), 644-654.

[EG84] "A Public Key Cryptosystem and a Signature Scheme Based on Discrete Logarithms", To appear in *Proceedings of Crypto 84*. (by El Gamal, Taher).

[EGL82] Even, S., O. Goldreich, and A. Lempel, "A Randomized Protocol for Signing Contracts", *Advances in Cryptology – Proceedings of Crypto 82*, (Plenum Press, New York, 1983), 205-210.

[GM82] Goldwasser, S., and S. Micali, "Probabilistic Encryption," *JCSS* **28** (April 1984), 270-299.

[GMY83] Goldwasser, S., S. Micali, and A. Yao, "Strong Signature Schemes," *Proc. 15th Annual ACM Symposium on Theory of Computing*, (Boston Massachusetts, April 1983), 431-439.

[La79] Lamport, Leslie, "Constructing Digital Signatures from a One-Way Function," SRI Intl. CSL-98. (Oct. 1979)

[Li79] Lieberherr, K. "Uniform Complexity and Digital Signatures," *Theoretical Computer Science* **16**,1 (Oct. 1981), 99-110.

[LM78] Lipton, S., and S. Matyas, "Making the Digital Signature Legal — and Safeguarded," *Data Communications* (Feb. 1978), 41-52.

[Ma79] Matyas, S. "Digital Signatures — An Overview," *Computer Networks* **3** (April 1979(87-94.

[MH78] Merkle, R., and M. Hellman, "Hiding Information and Signatures in Trap-Door Knapsacks," *IEEE Trans. Infor. Theory* **IT-24** (Sept. 1978), 525-530.

[OSS84] Ong, H., C. Schnorr, and A. Shamir, "An Efficient Signature Scheme Based on Quadratic Equations," *Proc. 16th Annual ACM Symposium on Theory of Computing,* (Washington, D.C., April 1984), 208-217.

[Po84] Pollard, J. "How to Break the 'OSS' Signature Scheme", Private Communication (1984).

[Ra78] Rabin, Michael, "Digitalized Signatures," In FOUNDATIONS OF SECURE COMPU-TATION, (Edited by R. A. DeMillo, D. Dobkin, A. Jones, and R. Lipton), (Academic Press, New York, 1978), 133-153.

[Ra79] Rabin, Michael, "Digitalized Signatures as Intractable as Factorizations," MIT Laboratory for Computer Science Technical Report MIT/LCS/TR-212 (Jan. 1979).

[RV83] Reif, J. and L. Valiant, "A logarithmic time sort for linear size networks," *Proceedings 15th Annual ACM Symposium on Theory of Computing,* (Boston Massachusetts, April 1983), 10-16.

[RSA78] Rivest, R., A. Shamir, and L. Adleman, "A Method for Obtaining Digital Signatures and Public-Key Cryptosystems," *Comm. of the ACM* (Feb. 1978), 120-126.

[Sh78] Shamir, A., "A Fast Signature Scheme," MIT Laboratory for Computer Science Technical Memo MIT/LCS/TM-107 (July 1978).

[Sh82] Shamir, A., "A Polynomial Time Algorithm for Breaking the Basic Merkle-Hellman Cryptosystem," *Proc 23rd Annual IEEE FOCS Conference* (Nov. 1982), 145-152.

[Tu84] Tulpan, Y., "Fast Cryptanalysis of a Fast Signature System," Master's Thesis in Applied Mathematics, Weizmann Institute. (1984)

[Wi80] Williams, H. C., "A Modification of the RSA Public-Key Cryptosystem," *IEEE Trans. Info. Theory* **IT-26** (Nov. 1980), 726-729.

[Yu79] Yuval, G., "How to Swindle Rabin," *Cryptologia* **3** (July 1979), 187-189.

Proofs that Yield Nothing but Their Validity or All Languages in NP Have Zero-Knowledge Proof Systems

This chapter reproduces the contents of the paper "Proofs that Yield Nothing But their Validity and a Methodology of Cryptographic Protocol Design," which appeared in the proceedings of the *27th Annual Symposium on Foundations of Computer Science*, pp. 174–187, 1986.

This influenial work of Oded Goldreich, Silvio Micali, and Avi Wigderson demonstrated the generality and wide applicability of zero-knowledge proofs. In particular, assuming the existence of secure commitment schemes, it showed how to construct zero-knowledge interactive proof systems for any set in NP, yielding a powerful tool for the design of various cryptographic schemes. Loosely speaking, zero-knowledge proofs offer a way for a party to prove that it has behaved according to a predetermined protocol *without revealing its own secrets*, and so they can be used to force parties to behave in "honest-but-curious" manner.

Proofs that Yield Nothing but Their Validity and a Methodology of Cryptographic Protocol Design (Extended Abstract)

Oded Goldreich (Dept. of Computer Sc., Technion),

Silvio Micali (Lab. for Computer Sc., MIT),

Avi Wigderson (Inst. of Math. and CS, Hebrew University)

In this paper we demonstrate the generality and wide applicability of *zero-knowledge proofs*, a notion introduced by Goldwasser, Micali and Rackoff. These are probabilistic and interactive proofs that, for the members x of a language L, efficiently demonstrate membership in the language without conveying any additional knowledge. So far, zero-knowledge proofs were known only for some number theoretic languages in $NP \cap Co\text{-}NP$.

Summary of Our Results

Under the assumption that encryption functions exist, we show that all languages in NP have zero-knowledge proofs. That is, it is possible to demonstrate that a

Work done while first author was at the Laboratory for Computer Science, MIT; and the third author was at the Mathematical Sciences Research Institute, UC-Berkeley. Work was partially supported by an IBM Postdoctoral Fellowship, NSF Grants DCR-8509905 and DCR-8413577, and an IBM Faculty Development Award.

CNF formula is satisfiable without revealing any other property of the formula. In particular, without yielding neither a satisfying assignment nor properties such as whether there is a satisfying assignment in which $x_1 = x_3$ etc.

The above result allows us to prove two fundamental theorems in the field of (two-party and multi-party) cryptographic protocols. These theorems consist of automatic and efficient transformations that, given a protocol that is correct with respect to an extremely weak adversary, output a protocol correct in the most adversarial scenario. Thus, these theorems imply a powerful methodology for developing secure two-party and multi-party protocols.

We also demonstrate that zero-knowledge proofs exist "independently of cryptography and number theory". Using no unproved assumptions, we show that both graph isomorphism and graph nonisomorphism possess zero-knowledge interactive proofs. The mere existence of an interactive proof for graph non-isomorphism is interesting, since graph non-isomorphism is not known to be in NP and thus did not possess so far any efficient proofs.

1 Introduction

It is traditional to view NP as the class of languages whose elements posses short proofs of membership. A "proof that $x \in L$" is a witness w_x such that $P_L(x, w_z) = 1$ where P_L is a polynomially computable Boolean predicate associated to the language L such that $P_L(x, y) = 0$ for all y if x is not in L. The witness must have length polynomial in the length of the input x, but needs not be computable from x in polynomial-time. A slightly different point of view is to consider NP as the class of languages L for which a powerful prover may prove membership in L to a polynomial-time deterministic verifier. The interaction between the prover and the verifier, in this case, is trivial: the prover sends a witness (proof) and the verifier computes for polynomial time to verify that it is indeed a proof.

This formalism was recently generalized by allowing more complex interaction between the prover and the verifier and by allowing the verifier to toss coins and to be convinced by overwhelming statistical evidence [GMR, B]. The prover has some computational advantage over the verifier and for the definition to be interesting one should assume that this advantage is crucial for proving membership in the language (otherwise the verifier can do this by itself). In other words, we will implicitly assume that there exist interesting languages (say in *PSPACE*) which are not in *BPP*, and be interested in proof systems for such languages.

A fundamental measure proposed by Goldwasser, Micali and Rackoff [GMR] is that of the amount of knowledge released during an interactive proof. Informally, a proof system was called zero-knowledge if whatever the verifier could generate in probabilistic polynomial-time after "seeing" a proof of membership, he could also generate in probabilistic polynomial-time when just told by a trusted oracle that the input is indeed in the language. In other words, zero-knowledge proofs have the remarkable property of being both convincing and yielding nothing except that the assertion is indeed valid.

Besides being a very intriguing notion, zero-knowledge proofs promise to be a very powerful tool for the design of secure cryptographic protocol. Typically these protocols must cope with the problem of distrustful parties convincing each other that the messages they are sending are indeed computed according to their pre-determined local program. Such proofs should be carried out without yielding any secret knowledge. In particular cases, zero-knowledge proofs were used to design secure protocols [FMRW, GMR, CF]. However, in order to demonstrate the general-ity of this tool (and to utilize its full potential) one should have come with general results concerning the existence of zero-knowledge proof systems. Until now, no such general results were obtained.

In this paper, we present general results concerning zero-knowledge proof systems. In particular, we show how to give zero-knowledge proofs to every NP-statement. A general methodology for designing secure cryptographic protocols follows. Its core is a compiler which, making primary use of the above result, trans-lates protocols correct in a weak adversary model to protocols correct in the most adversarial environment.

1.1   What Is an Interactive Proof

An interactive proof system for a language L is a protocol (i.e. a pair of local pro-grams) for two probabilistic interactive machines called the prover and the verifier. Initially both machine have access to a common input tape. The two machines send messages to one another through two communication tapes. Each machine only sees its own tapes, the common input tape and the communication tapes. In par-ticular, it follows that one machine cannot monitor the internal computation of the other machine nor read the other's coin tosses, current state, program etc. The verifier is bounded to a number of steps which is polynomial in the length of the common input, after which he stops either in an accept state or in a reject state. At this point we put no restrictions on the local computation conducted by the prover.

We require that, whenever the verifier is following his predetermined program, V, the following two conditions hold:

1. *Completeness of the interactive proof system*: If the common input x is in L and the prover runs his predetermined program, P, then the verifier accepts

x with probability $\geq 1- |\,x\,|^{-c}$, for every constant $c > 0$. In other words, the prover can convince the verifier of $x \in L$.

2. *Validity of the interactive proof system:* If the common input x is NOT in L, then for every program P^*, run by the prover, the verifier rejects x with probability $\geq 1- |\,x\,|^{-c}$ (for every constant $c > 0$). In other words, the prover cannot fool the verifier.

An important example of an interactive proof system is presented in section 2.1.

Remark 1 Note that it does not suffice to require that the verifier cannot be fooled by the predetermined prover (such a mild condition would have presupposed that the "prover" is a trusted oracle).

Remark 2 As is the case with NP, the conditions imposed on acceptance and rejection are not symmetric. Thus the existence of an interactive proof for the language L *does not* imply its existence for the complement of L.

Remark 3 The above "definition" follows the one of Goldwasser, Micali and Rackoff [GMR]. A different definition due to Babai [B], restricts the verifier to generate random strings, send them to the prover, and evaluate a deterministic polynomial-time predicate at the end of the interaction. Demonstrating the existence of proof systems is easier when allowing the verifier to flip private coins (i.e. [GMR] model), while relating interactive proof systems to traditional complexity classes seems easier if one restricts oneself to Babai's model. Surprisingly, these two models are equivalent, as far as language recognition is concerned [GS] (see Sec. 1.3).

Remark 4 The ability to toss coins is crucial to the non-triviality of the notion of an interactive proof system. If the verifier is deterministic then interactive proof systems coincide with *NP*.

Remark 5 Without loss of generality, we assume that the last message sent during an interactive proof is sent by the prover. (A last message sent by the verifier has absolutely no effect.)

1.2 What Is a Zero-Knowledge Proof

Intuitively, a zero-knowledge proof is a proof which yields nothing but its validity. This means that for all practical purposes, "whatever" can be done after interacting with a zero-knowledge prover, can be done when just believing that the assertion he claims is indeed valid. (In "whatever" we mean not only the computation of functions but also the generation of probability distributions.) Thus, zero-knowledge is a property of the predetermined prover. It is the robustness of the prover against attempts of the verifier to extract knowledge via interaction. Note that the verifier may deviate arbitrarily (but in polynomial-time) from the predetermined program. This is captured by the formulation appearing in [GMR] and sketched below.

Denote by $V^*(x)$ the probability distribution generated by a machine V^* which interacts with (the prover) P on input $x \in L$. We say that the proof system is *zero-knowledge* if for all probabilistic polynomial-time machines V^*, there exists a probabilistic polynomial-time algorithm M_V^* that on input x produces a probability distribution $M_{V^*}(x)$ such that $M_{V^*}(\cdot)$ and $V^*(\cdot)$ are polynomially-indistinguishable.

(For every algorithm A, let $p_A(x)$ denote the probability that A outputs 1 on input x and an element chosen according to the probability distribution $D(x)$. Similarly, $P'_A(x)$ is defined (w.r.t. D'). The distribution ensembles $D(\cdot)$ and $D'(\cdot)$ are *polynomially-indistinguishable* if for every probabilistic polynomial-time algorithm A, $p_A(x) - p'_A(x) \leq |x|^{-c}$, for every constant $c > 0$ and sufficiently long x. This notion appeared in [GM] and in [Y1].)

Remark 6 It is not difficult to see that if a language L has a zero-knowledge proof system in which only one message is sent, then $L \in BPP$. Thus, the non-triviality of the interaction is a necessary condition for the non-triviality or the notion of zero-knowledge.

1.3   Previous Results Concerning Interactive Proof Systems

Let Q be a polynomial. Denote by $IP(Q)$ the class of languages L such that membership of $x \in L$ can be proved through a general interaction consisting of $Q(|x|)$ message exchanges. Similarly, let $AM(Q)$ denote languages proven through the restricted type interaction in which the verifier only tosses "public coins" (i.e. Babai's Arthur-Merlin framework). Babai [B] showed that for every polynomial Q, $AM(Q + 1) = AM(Q)$. This means that his finite level hierarchy collapses. (Note that this does not imply the collapse of the unbounded level hierarchy! For more details see [AGH].) Goldwasser and Sipser [GS] showed that, for every polynomial Q, $IP(Q) \subseteq AM(Q + 2)$. This means that from a complexity theoretic point of view, the $IP(\cdot)$ hierarchy and the $AM(\cdot)$ hierarchy essentially coincide. Both the above results say nothing about the preservation of zero-knowledge by the transformations.

The bounded level IP hierarchy is related to the polynomial-time hierarchy by Babai's proof that $AM(2) \subseteq \prod_2^P$ and that $AM(2) \subseteq NP^B$ for almost all oracles B.

Several Number Theoretic languages, not known to be in BPP, have been previously shown to have zero-knowledge proof systems. The first language for which such a proof system has been demonstrated is Quadratic Non-Residuosity [GMR].

Other zero-knowledge proof systems were presented in [GMR], [GHY], [CF] and [G]. All these languages are known to lie in $NP \cap C_0 - NP$.

1.4 Organization of the Paper

In Section 2 we present zero-knowledge interactive proofs for graph isomorphism and graph non-isomorphism. We also discuss complexity theoretic implications of the existence of an interactive proof for graph nonisomorphism. In Section 3 we show how to use any one-way permutation in order to construct a zero-knowledge interactive proof for any language in NP. This result is extended to any language in *IP*.

In Section 4, we outline the methodological theorems for two-party and multi-party cryptographic protocols.

2 Proofs of Graph Isomorphism and Graph Non-Isomorphism

We start by presenting a (probably nonzero- knowledge) interactive proof for graph non-isomorphism. Next we present a zero-knowledge interactive proof for graph isomorphism, and for graph non-isomorphism. Let us set some common notations.

Let A be a set. Then $Sym(A)$ denote the set of permutations over A. When writing $a \in_R A$, we mean an element chosen at random with uniform probability distribution from the set A.

We will consider undirected graphs, $G(V, E)$. V will denote the vertex set, and E the edge set of the graph G. n will denote the size of the vertex set, and m the size of the edge set (i.e. $n = |V|$, $m = |E|$). The graph $G(V, E)$ will be represented by the set E, in an arbitrary fixed order (e.g. lexicographic).

Two graphs $G(V, E)$ and $H(V, F)$ are *isomorphic* if and only if there exist a permutation $\pi \in Sym(V)$ such that

$$(u, v) \in E \text{ iff } (\pi(u), \pi(v)) \in F.$$

The *graph isomorphism problem consists* of two graphs as input, and one has to determine whether they are isomorphic. The graph isomorphism problem is trivially in NP, is not known to be in Co-NP, and is believed not to be NP-complete.

We say that the graph $H(V, F)$ is a *random isomorphic copy* of the graph $G(V, E)$ if H is obtained from G by picking $\pi \in_R Sym(V)$ and letting

$$F = \{(\pi(u), \pi(v)) : (u, v) \in E\}.$$

2.1   An Interactive Proof of Graph Non-Isomorphism

In this subsection we examplify the notion of an interactive proof system by presenting an interactive proof for graph non-isomorphism. The fact that graph non-isomorphism has interactive proofs is interesting as it is not know to be in NP, and thus has not been know previously to have any efficient proofs. Moreover, the existence of an interactive proof for graph non-isomorphism has interesting complexity theoretic consequences.

In the following protocol the prover needs only to be a probabilistic polynomial-time machine with access to an oracle for graph isomorphism.

common input: Two graphs $G_l(V, E_1)$ and $G_2(V, E_2)$.

1. The verifier chooses at random n integers $\alpha_i \in_R \{1, 2\}$, $1 \leq i \leq n$. The verifier computes n graphs $H_i(V, F_i)$ such that H_i is a random isomorphic copy of G_{a_i}. The verifier sends the H_i's to the prover.

2. The prover answers with a string of β_i's (each in $\{1, 2\}$), such that $H_i(V, F_i)$ is isomorphic to $G_{\beta_i}(V, E_{\beta_i})$.

3. The verifier tests whether $\alpha_i = \beta_i$, for every $1 \leq i \leq n$. If the condition is violated then the verifier *rejects*; otherwise he *accepts*.

Theorem 1   The above protocol constitutes a (two-move) interactive proof system for Graph Non-Isomorphism.

Proof   If the graphs G_1 and G_2 are not isomorphic, and both prover and verifier follow the protocol, then the verifier always accepts. If on the other hand, G_l and G_2 are isomorphic then, for each i, we have $\alpha_i \neq \beta_i$ with probability at least 1/2, even if the prover does not follow the protocol. The reason being that in case G_1 and G_2 are isomorphic,

$$Prob(\alpha_i = 1 \mid \text{verifier sent } H_i) = 1/2.$$

The probability that the verifier does not reject two isomorphic graphs is thus at most 2^{-n}.

The above Theorem has interesting implications on the traditional complexity of the graph isomorphism problem. Namely,

Corollary 1   Graph Isomorphism is in $(NP \cap Co\text{-}NP)^A$, for a random oracle A. Also, Graph Non-Isomorphism can be recognized by a (non-uniform) family of non-deterministic polynomial-size circuits (i. e. non-uniform NP).

Proof   By the Theorem 1, Graph Non-Isomorphism (*GNI*) is in $IP(2)$. Using Goldwasser and Sipser's transformation of $IP(k)$ protocols to $AM(k+2)$ protocols, $GNI \in AM(4)$. By Babai's proof of the finite $AM(\cdot)$ collapse, $GNI \in AM(2) \subseteq NP^A$ for a random oracle A. Finally, it has been pointed out by Mike Sipser that $AM(2)$ is contained in non-uniform NP.

Another interesting corollary concerning graph isomorphism is due to Boppana and Hastad [BH].

Corollary 2 [BH]   If Graph Isomorphism is NP-Complete then the polynomial-time hierarchy collapses to its second level.

Proof   Boppana and Hastad showed that if *Co-NP* $\subseteq IP(k)$ (for some fixed k) then the entire polynomial-time hierarchy collapses to $AM(2) \subseteq \prod_2^P$. Since Theorem 1 states that graph non-isomorphism is in $IP(2)$, the Corollary follows.

Corollary 2 may be viewed as providing additional support to the belief that Graph Isomorphism is not NP-Complete.

2.2   A Zero-Knowledge Proof for Graph Isomorphism

In this section we examplify the notion of zero-knowledge proof systems by presenting a zero-knowledge proof for graph isomorphism. The fact that graph isomorphism has efficient proofs is apparent, since it is in NP. However, the fact that graph isomorphism can be proved in zero-knowledge, and in particular without demonstrating the isomorphism is interesting.

In the following protocol, the prover needs only to be a probabilistic polynomial-time machine which gets, as an auxiliary input, the isomorphism between the input graphs.

common input: Two graphs $G_1(V, E_1)$ and $G_2(V, E_2)$.

Let ϕ denote the isomorphism between G_1 and G_2. The following four steps are executed n times, each time using independent random coin tosses.

1. The prover generates a graph H, a random isomorphic copy of G_1. This is done by selecting a permutation $\pi \in_R Sym(V)$, and computing $H(V, F)$ such that $(\pi(u), \pi(v)) \in F$ iff $(u, v) \in E_1$. The prover sends the graph $H(V, F)$ to the verifier.

2. The verifier chooses at random $\alpha \in_R \{1, 2\}$, and sends α to the prover. (Intuitively, the verifier asks the prover to prove to him that H and G_α are indeed isomorphic.)

3. If $\alpha \notin 1, 2$ then the prover halts. If $\alpha = 1$ then the prover sends π to the verifier, else the prover sends $\pi\phi^{-1}$.

4. If the permutation received from the prover is not an isomorphism between G_α and H then the verifier stops and *rejects*; otherwise he continues.

If the verifier has completed n iterations of the above steps then he *accepts*.

The reader can easily verify that the above constitutes an interactive proof system for graph isomorphism. Intuitively, this proof is zero-knowledge since whatever the verifier receives is "useless", as he can generate random isomorphic copies of the input graphs by himself. This is easy to see in case the verifier follows the protocol. In case the verifier deviates from the protocol, the situation is much more complex. The verifier may set the α's depending on the graphs presented to him. In such a case it can not be argued that the verifier only receives random isomorphic copies of the input graph. The issue is fairly involved, as we have to defeat a universal quantifier which is not well understood (i.e. all possible deviations from the protocol). We cannot really trust our intuition in such matters, so a formal proof is indeed required.

Theorem 2   The above protocol constitutes a zero-knowledge interactive proof system for Graph Isomorphism.

Proof's Sketch   It is clear that the above prover conveys no knowledge to the *specified* verifier. We need however to show that our prover conveys no knowledge to all possible verifiers, including cheating ones that deviate arbitrarily from the protocol.

Let V^* be an arbitrary fixed program of a probabilistic polynomial-time machine interacting with the prover, specified by the protocol. We will present a probabilistic polynomial-time machine M_{V^*} that generates a probability distribution which is identical to the probability distribution induced on V^*'s tapes during its interaction with the prover. In fact it suffices to generate the distribution on the random tape and the communication tape of V^*.

Our demonstration of the existence of such V^* is constructive: given an interactive program V^*, we use it in order to construct the machine V^*. The way we use V^* in this construction does not correspond to the traditional notion of (a subroutine) reduction [K, C], but rather to a more general notion of reduction suggested in [AHU, pp. 373–374]. Typically, we will try to guess which isomorphism the machine V^* will ask to check. We will construct the graph H such that we can answer V^* in case we were lucky. The cases in which we failed will be ignored. It is crucial that from the point of view of V^* the case which leads to our success and the case which leads to our failure look identical. By throwing away the instances where we failed, we only slow down our construction, but we do not change the probability distribution that V^* "sees".

Following is a more detailed description of M_{V^*}. On input G_1 and G_2, the machine M_{V^*} will monitor the execution of the program V^* on this input and will "simulate" the prover to V^*. M_{V^*} will start by choosing and fixing random coin tosses r (random tape) for V^*, and placing r on a special record tape. All subsequent coin tosses are for M_{V^*}. (The random tape of V^*, denoted r, will remain fix and V^* is "deterministic" given its random tape r.) Machine M_{V^*} proceeds in n rounds as follows.

1. M_{V^*} chooses at random $\beta \in_R \{1, 2\}$ and a permutation $\pi \in_R Sym(V)$. It computes $H(V, F)$ such that $(\pi(u), \pi(v)) \in F$ if and only if $(u, v) \in E_\beta$. M_{V^*} places H on the communication tape of V^*. (Note that H is an isomorphic copy of G_β.)

2. M_{V^*} reads V^* answer from the communication tape of V^*. When V^* answers with $\alpha = \beta$ (lucky for M_{V^*}), machine M_{V^*} places π on the communication tape of V^*, appends (H, α, π) to its record tape, and proceeds to the next round. If $\alpha \notin \{1, 2\}$ (V^* is obviously cheating) then the machine M_{V^*} appends (H, α) to its record tape and stops outputting its record tape. If $\alpha + \beta = 3$ (unlucky for M_{V^*}) then M_{V^*} is going to repeat the current round. This is done by "rewinding" V^* to its configuration at the beginning of the current round, and by repeating Steps 1 and 2 with new random choices. (V^* configuration consists of the contents of its tapes, the positions of its heads and its internal state.)

If all rounds are completed then M_{V^*} outputs its record and halts. It should be noted that, for each repetition of the ith round, $Pr(\beta = 1| \mid H^{(i)}) = 1/2$, where $H^{(i)}$ is the list of graphs send to V^* so far (this includes the graph sent in the current repetition of round i, but does not include graphs after which V^* was rewound). Therefore, $Pr(\beta = \alpha(r, H^{(i)}|H^{(i)}) = 1/2$, where $\alpha(r, H^{(i)}$ is V^*'s answer on random tape r and communication tape $H^{(i)}$. It is left to the reader to verify that the ith round is repeated j times with probability at most 2^{-j}. Machine M_{V^*} stops and outputs its record tape after n rounds were completed or after encountering an improper $\alpha \notin \{1, 2\}$. In the first case the machine outputs a sequence of n triples of the form (H, α, π), where π is an isomorphism between H and G_α. It is left to the reader to verify that in both cases, M_{V^*} outputs the right probability distribution.

∎

Remark 7 In the above proof, the probability distribution output by the simulator M_{V^*} is *identical* to the distribution during an interaction between V^* and the prover. This is more than required by the definition of zero-knowledge, which only requires that these distributions be polynomially-indistinguishable. We call a proof system for which such a result (i.e. identical distributions) is demonstrated a *perfect zero-knowledge* proof system.

Remark 8 *Serial execution v. parallel execution: the case where the intuition fails?* Although one's intuition may insist that the above zero-knowledge protocol, remains zero-knowledge even when executed in parallel instead than serially, we do not know how to prove this statement. We even doubt this intuition, and will explain why in the full version of this paper.

2.3 Zero-Knowledge Proof of Graph Non-Isomorphism

The interactive proof for graph nonisomorphism presented in section 2.1 is probably not zero-knowledge: a user interacting with the prover may use the prover in order to test to which of the given graphs (G_1 and G_2) is a third graph G_3 isomorphic. The way to fix this flaw, is to let the verifier first "prove" to the prover that he "knows" an isomorphism between his query graph H and one of the input graphs. The modified protocol and the proof that it constitutes a zero-knowledge interactive-proof system, are omitted from this extended abstract. We get

Theorem 3 There exist a zero-knowledge interactive proof system for Graph Non-Isomorphism.

3 All Languages in NP Have Zero-Knowledge Proof Systems

In this section we assume the existence of secure encryption schemes (in the sense of Goldwasser and Micali [GM]). Such schemes exist if unapproximable predicates exist [GM]. The existence of unapproximable predicates has been shown by Yao to be a weaker assumption than the existence of one-way permutations [Y1].

An encryption scheme secure as in [GM] is a probabilistic polynomial-time algorithm f that on input x and internal coin tosses r, outputs an encryption $f(x, r)$. Decryption is unique: that is $f(x, r) = f(y, s)$ implies $x = y$.

We begin by presenting a zero-knowledge interactive proof for graph 3-colourability. Using this interactive proof and the power of NP-Completeness, we present zero-knowledge proofs for every language in NP. Finally, we show that "everything that is efficiently provable" can be proved in zero-knowledge.

3.1 A Zero-Knowledge Proof for Graph 3-Colourability

The common input to the following protocol is a graph $G(V, E)$. In the following protocol, the prover needs only to be a probabilistic polynomial-time machine which gets a proper 3-colouring of G as an auxiliary input. Let us denote this colouring by ϕ ($\phi: V \to \{1, 2, 3\}$). Let $n = |V|$, $m = |E|$. For simplicity, let $V = \{1, 2, \ldots, n\}$. The following four steps are executed m^2 times, each time using independent coin tosses.

1. The prover chooses a random permutation of the 3-colouring, encrypts it, and sends it to the verifier. More specifically, the prover chooses a permutation $\pi \in_R Sym(\{1, 2, 3\})$, and random r_v's, computes $R_v = f(\pi(\phi(v)), r_v)$ (for every $v \in V$), and sends the sequence $R_1, R_2, \ldots, R_n$ to the verifier.

2. The verifier chooses at random an edge $e \in_R E$ and sends it to the prover. (Intuitively, the verifier asks to examine the colouring of the endpoints of $e \in E$.)

3. If $e = (u, v) \in E$ then the prover reveals the colouring of u and v and "proves" that they correspond to their encryptions. More specifically, the prover sends $(\pi(\phi(u)), r_u)$ and $(\pi(\phi(v)), r_v)$ to the verifier. If $e \notin E$ then the prover stops.

4. The verifier checks the "proof" provided in step (3). Namely, the verifier checks whether $R_u = f(\pi(\phi(u)), r_u)$, $R_v = f(\pi(\phi(v)), r_v)$, $\pi(\phi(u)) \neq \pi(\phi(v))$, and $\pi(\phi(u)), \pi(\phi(v)) \in \{1, 2, 3\}$. If either condition is violated the verifier rejects and stops. Otherwise the verifier continues to the next iteration.

If the verifier has completed all m^2 iterations then it accepts.

The reader can easily verify the following facts: When the graph is 3-colourable and both prover and verifier follow the protocol then the verifier accepts. When the graph is not 3-colourable and the verifier follows the protocol then no matter how the prover plays, the verifier will reject with probability at least $(1 - m^{-l})^{m^2} = \exp(-m)$. Thus, the above protocol constitutes an interactive proof system for 3-colourability. Proving that the above protocol is zero-knowledge is even more involved that the proof of Theorem 2.

Proposition 4 If $f(\cdot, \cdot)$ is a secure probabilistic encryption, then the above protocol constitutes a zero-knowledge interactive proof system for 3-colourability.

Proof's Sketch As in the proof of Theorem 2, we will present a machine M_{V*} for every interactive machine V^*. Typically, we will try to guess which edge the machine V^* will ask to check. We will encrypt an illegal colouring of G such that we can answer V^* in case we were lucky. The cases in which we failed will be ignored. It is crucial that from the point of view of V^* the case which leads to our success and the case which leads to our failure are polynomially indistinguishable.

The machine M_{V^*} monitoring V^*, starts by choosing a random tape r for V^*. M_{V^*} places r on its record tape and proceeds in m^2 rounds as follows.

1. M_{V^*} picks an edge $(u, v) \in_R E$ and a pair of integers $(a, b) \in_R \{(i, j) : 1 \leq i \neq j \leq 3\}$ at random. M_{V^*} chooses random r_i's and computes $R_i = f(c_i, r_i)$, where c_i is 0 for $i \in V - \{u, v\}$, $c_u = a$ and $c_v = b$. M_{V^*} places the sequence of R_i's on the communication tape of V^*.

2. M_{V^*} reads e from the communication tape of V^*. If $e \notin E(V^*$ obviously cheats) then M_{V^*} appends the R_i's and e to its record tape, outputs the record tape, and stops. If $e \neq (u, v)$ (unlucky for M_{V^*}) then M_{V^*} rewinds V^* to the configuration at the beginning of the current round, and repeats the current round with new random choices. If $e = (u, v)$ (lucky for M_{V^*}) then M_{V^*} proceeds as follows: First, it places (a, r_u) and (b, r_v) on the communication tape of V^*. Second, it appends the R_i's, e, (a, r_u) and (b, r_v) to its record tape; and finally, it proceeds to the next round.

If all rounds are completed then M_{V^*} outputs its record and halts. A technical lemma (to be stated and proved in the final paper) guarantees that the three possible "answers" of the verifier (i.e. $e \in E$, $e \in E - \{(u, v)\}$ and $e = (u, v)$) occur with essentially the same probability as in the interaction of V^* and the real prover. Thus, the probability that the simulation of a particular round requires more than $k \cdot m$ rewinds is smaller than 2^{-k}, and M_{V^*} terminates in polynomial time. The only difference between the probability distribution of the true interactions and the distribution generated by M_{V^*} is that the first contain probabilistic encryptions of colourings while the second contains probabilistic encryptions of mostly 0's. However, a second technical lemma (postponed to the final paper) asserts that this difference is indistinguishable in probabilistic polynomial-time.

Remark 9 The above protocol needs m^2 rounds. In the final version of our paper we will present two alternative ways of modifying the above protocol so to get a four-round zero-knowledge protocol for graph 3-colorability. In both modifications the idea is to have the verifier commit himself to all his queries (i.e. which edge he wants to check for each copy of the coloured graph) before the prover sends to the verifier the corresponding coloured graphs. The two modifications differ by the manner in which the verifier commits to his queries. One modification is based on the intractability of factoring. The second modification is based on a relaxation of the definition of a proof system so that the prover is also restricted to polynomial-time (and his "computational advantage" over the verifier consists of an auxiliary input). This relaxation is natural in the cryptographic applications.

3.2 Zero-Knowledge Proofs for all NP

Incorporating the standard reductions into the protocol for graph 3-colourability, we get

Theorem 5 If $f(\cdot, \cdot)$ is a secure probabilistic encryption, then every NP language has a zero-knowledge interactive proof system.

Slightly less obvious is the proof of the following Theorem 6 that adapts Theorem 5 to a cryptographic scenario in which all players are bounded to efficient computation. What is needed is to notice that the standard reductions transform *efficiently* also the solution to the instances.

Theorem 6 If there exists a secure probabilistic encryption, then every language in NP has a zero-knowledge interactive proof system in which the prover is a probabilistic polynomial-time machine that gets an NP proof as an auxiliary input.

(Namely, in case the common input x is in the language L, the polynomial-time prover gets an NP proof that $x \in L$ as an auxiliary input.)

Remark 10 The number of computational steps required by both parties in the above interactive proof is bounded by $O(T^2(n) \cdot F(n) \cdot \log^4 n)$, where $n = |x|$ is the length of the common input x, $T(n)$ is the number of steps required by a non-deterministic machine to accept x, and $F(n)$ is the number of steps require to encrypt a bit when the security parameter is n.

A Positive Use of NP-Completeness

So far NP-completeness have mostly had a "negative" utility: it was (and is) the most practical way to give evidence to the infeasibility of a problem. Here we want to point out a "positive" use of NP-completeness: its primary role in deriving the general results of Theorems 5 and 6 (i.e. zero-knowledge proofs of every NP statement) from Proposition 4 (i.e. a zero-knowledge proof of a particular NP-Complete problem).

An Example: Verifiable Secret Sharing

Due to its generality, Theorem 6 has a dramatic effect on the design of cryptographic protocols. Let us first demonstrate this point by using Theorem 6 to present a simple solution to a problem which until recently was considered very complex: *Verifiable Secret Sharing*. The more general implications of Theorem 6, are outlined in Section 4.

The notion of a verifiable secret sharing was presented by Chor, Goldwasser, Micali and Awerbuch [CGMA], and constitutes a powerful tool for multi-party protocol design. Loosely speaking, a *verifiable secret sharing* is a $n + 1$-party protocol through which a *sender* (S) can distribute to the *receivers* (R_i's) *pieces* of a secret s recognizable through an a-priori known "encryption" $g(s)$. The n pieces should satisfy the following three conditions (with respect to $1 \leq l < u \leq n$):

1. It is infeasible to obtain any knowledge about the secret from any l pieces;

2. Given any u messages the entire secret can be easily computed;

3. Given a piece it is easy to verify that it belongs to a set satisfying condition (2).

The notion of a verifiable secret sharing differs from Shamir's secret sharing [Sha], in that the secret is recognizable and that *the pieces should be verifiable as authentic* (i.e. condition (3)).

Following the first implementation presented in [CGMA], improvements in efficiency and "tolerance" appeared in [FM, AGY, F]. These solutions are conceptually complicated, and rely on specific properties of particular encryption functions.

Assuming the existence of arbitrary one-way permutations, we present a conceptually simple solution allowing $u = l + 1 \leq n$. Our scheme combines Theorem 6 with Shamir's (non-verifiable) secret sharing [Sha]. To share a secret $s \in Z_p$ recognizable through $r = g(s)$, the sender proceeds as follows: First, the sender chooses at random a l-degree polynomial over Z_p^* and evaluates it in n fixed points (these are the pieces in Shamir's scheme). Next, the sender encrypts the ith piece using the Public encryption algorithm of the ith receiver, and sends all encrypted secrets to all receivers. Finally, the sender provides each receiver with a zero-knowledge proof that the encrypted messages correspond to the evaluation of a single polynomial over Z_p^*, and that applying g to the free term of this polynomial yields r (note that this is a NP statement).

3.3 Everything Efficiently Provable Can Be Proven in Zero-Knowledge

We now generalize Theorem 5 to show that not only NP is in zero-knowledge, but also "probabilistic NP" is. Namely,

Theorem 7 If there exists a secure probabilistic encryption, then for every fixed k every language in $IP(k)$ has zero-knowledge proof systems.

Proof's Sketch Using the results of [GS] and [B], it suffices to demonstrate zero-knowledge proof systems for languages in $AM(2)$. The intuitive idea is to let the verifier send random coins and then let the prover prove that "he could have convinced the verifier with respect to these coins", which is an NP statement! To oblige the verifier to send random coins and not strings of his choice, coin flipping into the well [Blu] is used. It has to be proven however, that the substitution of certified random coins by coin flips into the well preserves zero-knowledge. ■

Recently, Ben-Or extended Theorem 7 and showed that every language which has an interactive proof system, has a zero-knowledge one [Ben]. As above, the result of Goldwasser and Sipser [GS] is used to restrict attention to languages in *AM*. This time we can not use Babai's result [B], since the number of interactions is unbounded. The idea is to first execute the *AM* protocol in an encrypted form (only the messages of the prover need to be encrypted and this does not disturb the verifier who only toss coins), and next have the prover convince the verifier in zero-knowledge that the encrypted interaction corresponds to an accepting interaction in the original *AM* protocol.

The following question was raised by Leonid Levin: Let M be a probabilistic polynomial-time interactive machine having access to a machine P_1 which is able to prove that $x \in L$ via an arbitrary predetermined interactive proof system. Can M prove that $x \in L$ to another machine V_2 in a zero-knowledge manner? Clearly the answer is negative if M first interact with P_1 and only later interact with V_2 (hint: P_1 may use a zero-knowledge proof system). However, M is allowed to interleave its interactions in an arbitrary manner. Theorem 6 answers Levin's question positively for the case that P_1 sends M an NP-proof. (In fact this was the motivation for his question.) It is easy to answer Levin's question positively for the case that P_1 interacts with M via an *AM* protocol. Recently, using a result of Yao [Y2], we have answered this question positively also for the general case (of *IP* protocols).

3.4 Related Results

Using the intractability assumption of *quadratic residuosity*, Brassard and Crepeau have discovered independently (but subsequently) zero-knowledge proof systems to all languages in NP [BC1]. These proof systems heavily rely on *particular properties of quadratic residues* and do not seem to extend to arbitrary encryption functions.

Recently, Brassard and Crepeau showed that if factoring is intractable then every NP language has a perfect zero-knowledge interactive proof system [BC2]. It should be stressed that the protocol they proposed constitutes an interactive proof provided that factoring is intractable. In other words, the validity of the interactive proofs depends on an intractability assumption; while in this paper and in [BCI] the validity of the proofs do not rely on such an assumption.

Independently, Chaum [Cha] discovered a protocol which is very similar to the one in [BC2]. Chaum also proposed an interesting application of such "perfect zero-knowledge proofs". His application is to a setting in which the verifier may have infinite computing power while the prover is restricted to polynomial-time computations (see also [CEGP]). In such a setting it makes no sense to have the prover demonstrate properties (as membership in a language) to the verifier. However, the prover may wish to demonstrate to the verifier that he "knows" something without revealing what he "knows". More specifically, given a CNF formulae, the prover wishes to convince the verifier that he "knows" a satisfying assignment in a manner that would yield no information which of the satisfying assignments he knows. A definition of the notion of "a program knowing a satisfying assignment" can be derived from [GMR].

4   A Methodology of Cryptographic Protocol Design

Assuming the existence of arbitrary encryption functions, we will present extremely powerful methodologies for developing secure two-party and multi-party protocols. These methodology consists of efficient "correctness and privacy preserving" transformations of protocols from a weak adversary model to the most adversarial model. These (explicit) transformations are informally summarized as follows

Informal Theorem A   There exist an efficient compiler transforming a protocol P designed for $n = 2t + 1$ honest players, to a cryptographic protocol P' that achieves the same goals even if t of its n players are faulty. Faulty players are allowed to deviate from P' in any arbitrary but polynomial-time way.

In the formal statement of the corresponding Theorem, we avoid talking about "achieving goals". The "goal of a protocol" is a semantic object that is not well understood. Instead, we make statements about well understood syntactic objects: the probability distribution on the tapes of interactive machines. In the final version of this paper we will *define* the notions of a "correctness preserving compiler" and a "privacy preserving compiler". Both notions will be defined as relations between the probability distribution on the tapes of interactive machines during the execution of protocol P (in a weak adversarial environment) and the distribution on these tapes during the execution of P' (in a strong adversarial environment). Loosely speaking, "preserving correctness" means that whatever a party could compute after participating in the original protocol P, he could also compute when following the transformed protocol P', properly. "Preserving privacy" means that whatever a set of dishonest players can compute after participating in P', the corresponding players in P can compute from their joint local "histories" after participating in P. Similarly we formalize the following

There exist an efficient compiler transforming a two-party protocol P that is correct in a fail-stop model, to a cryptographic two-party-protocol P' that achieves the same goals even if one of the players deviates from P' in any arbitrary but polynomial-time way.

The proofs of the above Theorems make primary use of Theorem 6 to allow a machine to "prove" to other machines that a message it sent is computed according to the protocol. In addition, these proofs make innovative use of most of the cryptographic techniques developed in the recent years. Essential ingredients in the proof of Theorem A are the notions of verifiable secret sharing and simultaneous broadcast proposed and first implemented by Chor, Goldwasser, Micali and Awerbuch [CGMA]. An essential ingredient in the proof of Theorem B is Blum's "coin flipping into the well" [Blu].

Further Improvement

Theorem A constitutes a procedure for automatically constructing fault-tolerant protocols, the goal of which is to compute a predetermine function of the private inputs scattered among the players. This procedure takes as input a distributed specification of the function (i.e. a protocol for honest players), not the function itself. It is guaranteed that this procedure will output a fault-tolerant protocol for computing this very function (i.e. the "correctness" condition) and that the "privacy" present in the specification will be preserved. Thus, the degree of privacy offered by the output fault-tolerance protocol depends on the specification, and not on the function to be computed. Furthermore, for some functions f it seems to be difficult to write a distributed specification (protocol for honest players) which offers the maximum degree of privacy. Recently, assuming the exist of an arbitrary secure encryption scheme, we found a polynominal-time algorithm which on input a *Turing machine* specification of a n-ary function f, outputs a protocol for n honest players which offers the maximum possible privacy. Namely, at the termination of the protocol, each subset of players can compute from their joint local history only whatever they could have computed from their corresponding local inputs and the value of the function. Essential ingredients in the algorithm are the "circuit encoding" of Barrington [Bar], a modification of the two-party protocol of Yao [Y2], and a general implementation of a variant of Oblivious Transfer using any encryption function. Details will appear in a forthcoming paper [GMW].

The algorithm claimed above can also be applied to any Turing machine specification of a probability distribution (depending on n variables). Equivalently, one can view the algorithm as a compiler that on input a n-party protocol (for honest players) outputs a fault tolerant n-party protocol, for computing the same distributed input-output relation, which offers the maximum degree of privacy. This compiler, which may increase the privacy present in the input protocol, improves on and uses as a subroutine the compiler of Theorem A (which only preserves the privacy present in the input). The compiler of Theorem A, in turn, improves on and uses as subroutine the compiler of Chor, Goldwasser, Micali and Awerbuch [CGMA].

Acknowledgements

We are very grateful to Benny Chor and Shafi Goldwasser for many discussions concerning methodologies for Cryptographic Protocol Design. We also wish to thank Baruch Awerbuch, Manuel Blum, Mike Fischer, Leonid Levin, Albert Meyer, Yoram Moses, Michael Rabin, Charlie Rackoff, Ron Rivest, and Mike Sipser for many helpful discussions concerning this work.

References

[ABU] Abo, A.V., J.E. Hopcroft, and J.D. Ullman, *The Design and Analysis of Computer Algorithms*, Addison-Wesley Publ. Co., 1974.

[AGH] Aiello, W., S. Goldwasser, and J. Hastad, "On the Power of Interaction", these proceedings.

[AGY] Alon, N., Z. Galil, and M. Yung, "A Fully Polynomial Simultaneous Broadcast in the Presence of Faults", manuscript, 1985.

[B] Babai, L., "Trading Group Theory for Randomness", *Proc. 17th STOC*, 1985, pp. 421-429.

[Bar] Barrington, D.A., "Bounded-Width Polynomial-Size Branching Programs Recognize Exactly Those Languages in NC^1", *Proc. 18th STOC*, 1986, pp. 1-5.

[Ben] Ben-Or, M., private communication, 1986.

[Blu] Blum, M., "Coin Flipping by Phone", *IEEE Spring COMPCOM*, pp. 133-137, February 1982.

[BH] Boppana, R., and J. Hastad, "Does Co-NP Have Short Interactive Proofs?", in preparation, 1986.

[BC1] Brassard, G., and C. Crepeau, "Zero-Knowledge Simulation of Boolean Circuits", manuscript, presented in *Crypto86*, 1986.

[BC2] Brassard, G., and C. Crepeau, "Non-Transitive Transfer of Confidence: A Perfect Zero-Knowledge Interactive Protocol for SAT and Beyond", these proceedings.

[BD] Broder, A.Z., and D. Dolev, "Flipping Coins in Many Pockets (Byzantine Agreement on Uniformly Random Values", *Proc. 25th FOCS*, 1984, pp. 157-170.

[Cha] Chaum, D., "Demonstrating that a Public Predicate can be Satisfied Without Revealing Any Information About How", manuscript, presented in *Crypto86*, 1986.

[CEGP] Chaum, D., J.H. Evertse, J. van de Graaf, and R. Peralta, "Demonstrating Possession of a Discrete Logarithm without Revealing It", manuscript, presented in *Crypto86*, 1986.

[CGMA] Chor, B., S. Goldwasser, S. Micali, and B. Awerbuch, "Verifiable Secret Sharing and Achieving Simultaneity in the Presence of Faults", *Proc. 26th FOCS*, 1985, pp. 383-395.

[Coh] Cohen, J.D., "Secret Sharing Homomorphisms: Keeping Shares of a Secret Secret", technical report YALEU/DCS/TR-453, Yale University, Dept. of Computer Science, Feb. 1986. Presented in *Crypto86*, 1986.

[CF] Cohen, J.D., and M.J. Fischer, "A Robust and Verifiable Cryptographically Secure Election Scheme", *Proc. 26th FOCS*, pp. 372-382, 1985.

[C] Cook, S.A., "The Complexity of Theorem Proving Procedures", *Proc. 3rd STOC*, pp. 151-158, 1971.

[F] Feldman, P., "A Practical Scheme for Verifiable Secret Sharing", manuscript, 1986.

[FM] Feldman, P., and S., Micali, in preparation, 1985.

[FMRW] Fischer, M., S. Micali, C. Rackoff, and D.K. Wittenberg, "An Oblivious Transfer Protocol Equivalent to Factoring", in preparation. Preliminary versions were presented in *EuroCrypt84* (1984), and in the *NSF Workshop on Mathematical Theory of Security*, Endicott House (1985).

[GRY] Galil, Z., S. Haber, and M. Yung, "A Private Interactive Test of a Boolean Predicate and Minimum-Knowledge Public-Key Cryptosystems", *Proc. 26th FOCS*, 1985, pp. 360-371.

[GJ] Garey, M.R., and D.S. Johnson, *Computers and Intractability: A Guide to the Theory of NP-Completeness*, W.H. Freeman and Company, New York, 1979.

[G] Goldreich, O., "A Zero-Knowledge Proof that a Two-Prime Moduli Is Not a Blum Integer", unpublished manuscript, 1985.

[GMW] Goldreich, O., S. Micali, and A. Wigderson, "How to Automatically Generate Correct and Private Fault-Tolerant Protocols", in preparations.

[GM] Goldwasser, S., and S. Micali, "Probabilistic Encryption", *JCSS*, Vol. 28, No. 2, 1984, pp. 270-299.

[GMR] Goldwasser, S., S. Micali, and C. Rackoff, "Knowledge Complexity of Interactive Proofs", *Proc. 17th STOC*, 1985, pp. 291-304.

[GS] Goldwasser, S., and M. Sipser, "Arthur Merlin Games versus Interactive Proof Systems", *Proc. 18th STOC*, 1986, pp. 59-68.

[K] Karp, R.M., "Reducibility among Combinatorial Problems", *Complexity of Computer Computations*, R.E. Miller and J.W. Thatcher (eds.), Plenum Press, pp. 85-103, 1972.

[L] Levin, L.A., "Universal Search Problems", *Problemy Peredaci Informacii 9*, pp. 115-116, 1973. *Translated in problems of Information Transmission 9*, pp. 265-266.

[Sha] Shamir, A., "How to Share a Secret", *CACM*, Vol. 22, 1979, pp. 612-613.

[Y1] Yao, A.C., "Theory and Applications of Trapdoor Functions", *Proc. of the 23rd IEEE Symp. on Foundation of Computer Science*, 1982, pp. 80-91.

[Y2] Yao, A.C., "How to Generate and Exchange Secrets", these proceedings.

How to Play Any Mental Game: A Completeness Theorem for Protocols with Honest Majority

This chapter reproduces the contents of the paper "How to Play Any Mental Game, or A Completeness Theorem for Protocols with Honest Majority," which appeared in the proceedings of the *19th Annual ACM Symposium on Theory of Computing*, pp. 218–229, 1987.

This influenial work of Oded Goldreich, Silvio Micali, and Avi Wigderson presented constructions of secure protocols for any multi-party computation problem. In other words, it shows how a trusted party can be emulated by a set of mutually distrustful parties. This result combines the construction of "privacy-preserving" protocols for the "honest-but-curious" model with a method (presented in Chapter 12) of forcing parties to behave in an honest-but-curious manner. The privacy-preserving protocols rely on the existence of a public-key encryption scheme and an Oblivious Transfer protocol, which can both be based on the existence of trapdoor permutations.

How to Play Any Mental Game, or A Completeness Theorem for Protocols with Honest Majority (Extended Abstract)

Oded Goldreich (Dept. of Computer Sc., Technion),
Silvio Micali (Lab. for Computer Sc., MIT),
Avi Wigderson (Inst. of Math. and CS, Hebrew University)

Abstract

We present a polynomial-time algorithm that, given as a input the description of a game with incomplete information and any number of players, produces a protocol for playing the game that leaks no partial information, provided the majority of the players is honest.

Our algorithm automatically solves all the multi-party protocol problems addressed in complexity-based cryptography during the last 10 years. It actually is a *completeness theorem* for the class of distributed protocols with honest majority.

Work partially supported by NSF grants DCR-8509905 and DCR-8413577, an IBM post-doctoral fellowship and an IBM faculty development award. The work was done when the first author was at the Laboratory for Computer Science at MIT; and the second author at the mathematical Sciences Research Institute at UC-Berkeley.

Such completeness theorem is optimal in the sense that, if the majority of the players is not honest, some protocol problems have no efficient solution [c].

1 Introduction

Before discussing how to "make playable" a general game with incomplete information (which we do in section 6) let us address the problem of making playable a special class of games, the *Turing machine games* (*Tm-games* for short).

Informally, n parties, respectively and individually owning secret inputs $x_1, \ldots, x_n$, would like to *correctly* run a given Turing machine M on these x_i's while keeping the maximum possible *privacy* about them. That is, they want to compute $y = M(x_1, \ldots, x_n)$ without revealing more about the x_i's than it is already contained in the value y itself. For instance, if M computes the sum of the x_i's, every single player should not be able to learn more than the sum of the inputs of the other parties. Here M may very well be a probabilistic Turing machine. In this case, all players want to agree on a single string y, selected with the right probability distribution, as M's output.

The correctness and privacy constraint of a Tm-game can be easily met with the help of an extra, trusted party P. Each player i simply gives his secret input x_i to P. P will privately run the prescribed Turing machine, M, on these inputs and publically announce M's output. Making a Tm-game playable essentially means that the correctness and privacy constraints can be satisfied by the n players themselves, without invoking any extra party. Proving that Tm-games are playable retains most of the flavor and dificulties of our general theorem.

2 Preliminary Definitions

2.1 Notation and Conventions for Probabilistic Algorithms

We emphasize the number of inputs received by an algorithm as follows. If algorithm A receives only one input we write "$A(\cdot)$", if it receives two inputs we write $A(\cdot, \cdot)$ and so on.

RV will stand for "random variable"; in this paper we only consider RVs that assume values in $\{0, 1\}*$. In fact, we deal almost exclusively with random variables arising from probabilistic algorithms. (We make the natural assumption that all parties may make use of probabilistic methods.)

If $A(\cdot)$ is a probabilistic algorithm, then for any input x the notation $A(x)$ refers to the RV which assigns to the string σ the probability that A, on input x outputs σ. If S is a RV that assigns positive probability only to a single element e, we denote the value e by S. (For instance, if $A(\cdot)$ is an algorithm that, on input x outputs x^3, then we may write $A(2) = 8$.) This is in agreement with traditional notation.

If $f(\cdot)$ and $g(\cdot, \cdots)$ are probabilistic algorithms then $f(g(\cdot, \cdots))$ is the probabilistic algorithm obtained by composing f and g (i.e. running f on g's output). For any inputs $x, y, \cdots$ the associated RV is denoted $f(g(x, y, \cdots))$.

Let *PA* denote the set of probabilistic polynomial-time algorithms. We assume that a natural representation of these algorithms as binary strings is used.

By 1^k we denote the unary representation of integer k.

2.2   Game Networks and Distributed Algorithms

Let us start by briefly describing the communication networks in which games will be played. This is the standard network supporting the execution of multi-party protocols.

Informally, a *game network* of size n is a collection of (interacting) probabilistic polynomial-time Turing machines. Each machine has a private read-only input tape, a private write-only output tape and a private read-write work tape. All machines share a common read-only input tape and a common write-only output tape. The n machines communicate by means of $n \cdot (n-1)$ special tapes. Machine i publicly sends messages (strings) to machine j by means of a special tape $i \rightarrow j$ on which only i can write and that all other machines can read. There is a common clock whose pulses define time intervals $1, 2, \ldots$. Messages are sent at the beginning of a time interval and are received within the same time interval. We stress, though, that our result is largely independent from the specific communication mechanism, and also holds for "less equipped" communication networks.[1]

A probabilistic distributed algorithm S running in a game network of size n is a sequence of programs $S = (S_i, \ldots, S_n)$, where S_i is the program of the ith Turing machine in the network. We denote by PDA the class of all probabilistic polynomial-time distributed algorithms.

Let $S \in PDA$ run in a game network of size n with common input CI and (respective) private inputs $x_1, \ldots, x_n$. Then $HS(x_1, \ldots, x_n, CI)$ denotes the RV consisting of the *public history*, that is the sequence of all messages sent in an execution of

1. For instance, there may be only one communication tape. In this case, digital signatures can be used to authenticate the sender. In case that not all machines may read all communication tapes, Byzantine agreement can be used to simulate the fact that all processors agree on what message machine i has sent to machine j at time t. The common clock may be replaced by local clocks that don't drift "too much". The quite tight synchrony of the message delivery can be replaced by a feasible upper bound on the time it takes a message to be delivered, and so on.

S; $HS_i(x_1, \ldots, x_n, CI)$ denotes the RV consisting of the *private history* of machine i, that is the sequence of the internal configurations of machine i in an execution of S; for $T \subset \{1, \ldots, n\}$, $HS_T(x_1, \ldots, x_n)$ denotes the vector of the private histories of the members of T in an execution of S; and $OS(x_i, \ldots, x_n, CI)$ denotes the RV consisting of the private output of machine i in an execution of S.

2.3 Adversaries

We consider two interesting types of adversaries (faulty machines) in a game network: passive ones (a new notion) and malicious ones (a more standard notion).

A *passive adversary* is a machine that may compute more than required by its prescribed program, but the messages it sends and what it outputs are in accordance to its original program. (Passive adversaries may be thought as machines who only try to violate the privacy constraint. They keep on running their prescribed programs correctly, but also run, "on the side", their favorite polynomial-time program to try to compute more than their due share of knowledge. In an election protocol, a passive adversary may be someone who respects the majority's opinion -and thus does not want to corrupt the tally- and yet wants to discover who voted for whom.)

A *malicious adversary* is, instead, a machine that deviates from its prescribed program in any possible action. That is, we allow the program of such a machine to be replaced by any fixed probbilistic polynomial-time program. (Malicious adversary not only have a better chance of disrupting the privacy constraint, but could also make the outcome of a Tm-game vastly different than in an ideal run with a trusted party.)

We allow machines in a game network to become adversarial in a *dynamic fashion*, during the execution of a protocol. We also allow adversarial machines (of either type) to undetectedly cooperate. Adversarial machines are not allowed, however, to monitor the private tapes or the internal state of good machines.

We believe the malicious-adversary scenario to be the most adversarial among all the natural scenarios in which cryptography may help.

Jumping haed, we will show that all Tm-games are playable with any number of passive adversaries or with $< n/2$ malicious adversaries.

2.4 Indistinguishability of Random Variables

Throughout this paper, we will only consider families of RVs $U = \{U_k\}$ where the parameter k ranges in the natural numbers. Let $U = \{U_k\}$ and $V = \{V_k\}$ be two families of RVs. The following notion of computational indistinguishability expresses the fact that, when the length of k increases, U_k becomes "replaceable" by V_k in the following sense. A random sample is selected either from U_k or from V_k and it is handed to a "judge". After studying the sample, the judge will proclaim his verdict: 0 or 1. (We may interpret 0 as the judge's desicion that that the sample came from U_k; 1 as the desicion that the sample came from V_k.) It is then natural to say that V_k becomes "replaceable" by V_k for k large enough if, when k increases, the verdict of any computationally bounded judge becomes "meaningless", that is essentially uncorrelated to which of the two distributions the sample came from.

To formalize the notion of computational indistinguishablity we make use of nonuniformity. Thus, our "judge", rather than polynomial time Turing machine, will be a poly-size family of circuits. That is a family $C = \{C_k\}$ of Boolean circuits C_k with one Boolean output such that, for some constants $c, d > 0$, all $C_k \in C$ have at most k^c gates and k^d Boolean inputs. In order to feed samples from our probability distributions to such circuits, we will consider only *poly-bounded* families of RVs. That is families $U = \{U_k\}$ such that, for some constant $e > 0$, all RV $U_k \in U$ assigns positive probability only to strings whose length is exac:tly k^e. If $U = \{U_k\}$ is a poly-bounded family of RVs and $C = \{C_k\}$ a poly-size sequence of circuits, we denote by $P(U, C, k)$ the probability that C_k outputs 1 on input a random strings from U_k. (Here we assume that the length of the strings that are assigned positive probability by U_k equals the number of Boolean inputs of C_k.)

Definition (Computational indistinguishability): Two poly-bounded families of RVs U and V are *computationally indistinguishable* if for all poly-size family of circuits C, for all constants $f > 0$ and all sufficiently large $k \in N$,

$$|P(U, C, k) - P(V, C, k)| < k^{-1}.$$

This notion was already used by Goldwasser and Micali [GM] in the context of encryption and by Yao [Y] in the context of pseudo-random generation. For other notions of indistinguishability and further discussion see [GMR].

Remark 1 Let us point out the robustness of the above definition. In this definition, we are handing our computationally bounded "judge" only samples of size 1. This, however, is not restrictive. It should be noticed that two families of RVs $\{U_k\}$ and $\{V_k\}$ are computationally indistinguishable with respect to samples of size 1 if and only if they are computationally indistinguishable with respect to samples whose size is bounded by a fixed polynomial in k.

3 Tm-games With Passive Adversaries

An *Tm-game problem* consists of a pair $(\bar{M}, 1^k)$, that is, the description of a Turing machine M and an integer k, the security parameter, presented in unary.

Let us now make some simplifications that will expedite our exposition. Without loss of generality in our scenario, we assume that, when $(\bar{M}, 1^k)$ is the common input in a game network, all private inputs have the same length l and that $T(l)$, the running time of M on inputs of size l, is less than k.

Let $S \in PDA$. We say that S is a *Tm-game Solver for passive adversaries* if, for all *Tm-game problems* $(\bar{M}, 1^k)$ given as common input and for all (respective) private inputs $x_1, \ldots, x_n$,

1. (*Agreement constraint*)

    At the end of each execution of S, for all machines i and j, i's private output equals j's private output.

2. (*Correctness constraint*)

    $OS_1(x, \ldots, x_n, (\bar{M}1^k)) = M(x_1, \ldots, x_n)$ and

3. (*Privacy constraint*)

    $\forall T \subset \{1, \ldots, n\}$ and $\forall A \in PPT$, $\exists B \in PPT$ such that $\{A_k\}$ and $\{B_k\}$ are computationally undistinguishable RVs.

Here

$$A_k = A((\bar{M}, 1^k), HS((\bar{M}, 1^k)), HS_T((\bar{M}1^k)))$$

and

$$B_k = B((\bar{M}, 1^k), M(x_1, \ldots, x_n), \{(i, x_i) : i \in T\}).$$

Let us now interpret the above definition.

The Agreement Constraint

This constraint essentially says that all machines agree on a single, common string as the output of S.

The Correctness Constraint

This constraint ensures that the output of a game solver S coincides with the one of M. As M may be probabilistic, the equality of the correctness constraint must interpreted ss equality between RVs.

The Privacy Constraint

Notice that passive adversaries appear in the above definition in an implicit way. Algorithm A can be thought as all the members of T being passive adversaries computing after an execution of S. In fact passive adversaries are obliged to send messages according to S and their private history, in an execution of S, is an explicit input to A. Let us stress that the private history of a machine i contains the name i, the private input x_i and M's output as well. Thus the privacy constraint essentially says that whatever the passive adversaries may compute after executing S, they could also easily deduce from the desired M's output, y, and their own private inputs (which they are entitled to have!). In fact, if they are given y by running S, the passive adversaries will see, in addition to y, only the public history and their own private history. However, whatever they could efficiently compute with this additional input, they could also have computed without it. In other words, S keeps whatever privacy of the inputs of the good parties is not "betrayed" by the value y itself. For instance, if M computes the sum of the x_i's, then the privacy constraint will allow the adversarial players to compute (at the end of S) essentially only the sum of the inputs of the good parties. As for another example, if M is the identity function, then the privacy constraint holds vacuously. Same if the set T is the set of all players.

4 Hints on How to Play Tm-games With Passive Adversaries

At a first glance enforcing both correctness and privacy constraints of a Tm-game appears easy only for special cases of M, say the ones computing a constant function. None-the-less,

Theorem If trapdoor functions exist, there exists a Tm-game solver for passive adversaries.

In this extended abstract we limit ourselves to give a few indications, in an informal manner, about the proof of the above theorem. Moreover, not to get into further complications, we do not let the set of adversarial machines to be chosen dynamically, during the execution of the protocol, but at its start. (We stress, though, that the adversarial set is still unknown to the good machines). This restriction will be removed in the final paper.

4.1 A New and General Oblivious Transfer Protocol

In [HR], Rabin proposes the beautiful notion of an *Oblivious Transfer* (OT). This is a probabilistic polynomial-time algorithm that allows A(lice), who knows the prime factorization of an integer n, to send it to B(ob), who knows just n, so that B will receive n's factorization with probability $l/2$ and A does not know whether or not B received it. Clearly, Rabin's notion of an OT, supposes that factoring is computationally hard. Under this assumption, he proposed a protocol that, if A and B are allowed to be at most passive adversaries, correctly implements an OT. This protocol, however, may not work (i.e. no longer possesses a proof of correctness) if A and B are allowed to be malicious. Using the interactive proof-systems of [GMR], Fischer, Micali, Rackoff and Wittenberg [FMRW] found a protocol that correctly implements OT under the simple (and in this context minimal) assumption that factoring is hard. Rabin's OT has proved to be a very fruitful notion, as exemplified by various applications proposed by Blum [B].

A more general and useful notion of OT has been proposed by Even, Goldreich and Lempel [EGL], the *one-out-of-two* OT. In their framework, A has two messages m_0 and m_1. By using a cryptosystem E, she computes $\sigma_0 = E(m_0)$ and $\sigma_1 = E(m_1)$ and sends σ_1 and σ_2 to B. B chooses one of these encryption, σ_i. A one-out-of-two OT allows B to read the corresponding message m_i, while A will not know which message B has read (whenever m_0 and m_1 are different). This notion achieves the right level of generality and is crucial to what follows. Even, Goldreich and Lempel also proposed the first implementation of a one-out-of-two OT using public-key cryptosystems. Their protocol has the merit of having freed the implementation of an oblivious transfer from the algebraic setting to which it appeared to be confined. Their protocol, though, requires a quite strong set of assumptions even when the adversaries are only passive.

Below, we contribute a new protocol that correctly implements a one-out-of-two OT in presence of passive advarsaries. The existence of trapdoor permutations suffices to prove the correctness of our protocol.

Trapdoor and One-Way Functions

A satisfactory definition of a trap-door permutation is given in [GoMiRi]. Here let us informally say that a family of trapdoor permutations f possesses the following properties:

- It is easy, given an integer k, to randomly select permutations f in the family which have k as their security parameter, together with some extra "trapdoor" information allowing easy inversion of the permutations chosen.

- It is easy to randomly select a point in f's domain.

- It is hard to invert f without knowing f's trap-door on a random element in f's domain.

We can interpret the above by saying that a party A can randomly select a pair of permutations, (f, f^{-1}), inverses of each other. This will enable A to easily evaluate and invert f; if now A publicizes f and keeps secret f^{-1}, then inverting f will be hard for any other party. We may write f_k, to enphasize that k is the security parameter of our permutation.

Trap-door permutations are a special case of one-way permutations. These are permutations enjoying the three properties above, except that we do not insist that the trap-door information exists.

Random Bits in One-Way Permutations

Our one-out-of-two OT protocol makes use of trap-door functions f hiding a random bit B_f. Here B_f is a polynomial-time computable Boolean function; the word "bit" is appropriate as B_f evaluates to 1 for half of the :'s in f's domain.

We say that $\{B_f\}$ is a *random bit* in a family $\{f\}$ of trap-door permutations if $\forall$ predicting algorithm *Alg* that, on inputs $f = f_k$ and $f(x)$, outputs, in $T(k)$ steps, a guess for $B_f((x))$ that is correct with probability ε, $\exists Alg'$ that, on inputs f and $f(x)$, outputs x in poly$(T(k), \varepsilon^{-1})$ expected time.

Thus, being f trap-door, no probabilistic, polynomial-time algorithm given $f_k(x)$, can correctly predict $B_{f_k}(x)$ with probability $> 1/2 + 1/poly(k)$. We might as well flip a coin. Thus, for a one-way permutation f, given $f(x)$ the value of $B_f(x)$ cannot be guessed in polynomial time essentially better than at random.

The notion of a random bit in a one-way permutation was introduced by Blum and Micali [BM] who showed a random bit in the Discrete Logarithm Problem, a well known candidate one-way permutation. Chor and Goldreich show random bits in the RSA function. Do all one-way functions have a random bit? We do not know the answer to this question, but Yao [Y] has shown the next best thing. Namely, that given a one-way (trap-door) permutation f, one can construct a one-way (trap-door) permutation F with a random bit BF (for a detailed proof of this theorem see [BH]). Levin [L] has actually proved a more general version of this theorem.

Our Protocol

Without loss of generality, we assume that the two messages in the one-out-of-two OT both consist of a single bit.

In our protocol, both A and $B \in PA$. A's inputs are a pair of bits (b_0, b_1) and their corresponding pair of encryptions $(E(b_0), E(b_1))$ where E is a probabilistic encryption algorithm [GM]. The pair $(E(b_0), E(b_1))$ is also an input to B who has an additional private input bit α. It is desired that even if some party is a passive adversary the following two properties hold:

(i) B will read the bit b_0, but will not be able to predict the other bit, $b_{\bar{\alpha}}$, essentially better than at random.

(ii) *A cannot predict α essentially better than at random.*

We achieve this by means of the following protocol.

Step 1

A randomly selects (f, f^{-1}), a trap-door function of size k (having a random bit B_j) together with its inverse. She keeps f^{-1} secret and sends f to B.

Step 2

B randomly selects x_0 and x_1 in f's domain and computes $z = f(x_0)$ and sends A the pair

$$(u, v) = \begin{cases} (f(x_0), x_1) & \text{if } \alpha = 0 \\ (x_0, f(x_1)) & \text{if } \alpha = 1 \end{cases}$$

Step 3

A computes $(c_0, c_1) = (B_f(f^{-1}(u)), B_f(f^{-1}(v)))$. She sets $d_0 = b_0 \; xor \; c_0$ and $d_1 = b_1 \; xor \; c_1$ and sends (d_0, d_1) to B.

Step 4

B computes $b_\alpha = d_\alpha \; xor \; B_j(x_\alpha)$.

First notice that $A, B \in PA$ and that B correctly reads b_α. Property i) is satisfied as B only sees $b_{\bar\alpha}$, exclusived-ored with a bit essentially 50-50 unpredictable to him. Thus he cannot correctly guess $b_{\bar\alpha}$ essentially better than at random. Let us now show that ii) holds. As f is a permutation, randomly selecting x in f's domain and computing $f(x)$ yealds a randomly selected element in f's domain. Thus (u, v) is a pair of randomly selected elements in f's domain both if $\alpha = 0$ or $\alpha = 1$. As (u, v) is the only message B sends A, not even with infinite computing power A will find out whether B has read b_0 or b_1.

Notice that the protocol makes use that the adversaries are at most passive in a crucial way. Should in fact B send $(u, v) = (f(x_0), f(x_1))$ in step 2, he will easily read both bits. Thus, we will make use of additional ideas to handle malicious adversaries.

Notice also that we never made use of the encryptions $E(b_0)$ and $E(b_1)$. b_0 and b_1 could have been bits in "A's mind." We have added these encryptions for uniformity with the next protocol in which the two messages must appear encrypted. Another reason is that, when we will handle malicious adversaries, we will need these encryptions to define the problem.

It is easy to see that, having solved the single-bit messages case, we have also solved the case of arbitrary messages m_0 and m_1 of equal, known length l. In fact, we can repeat the above protocol l times, so that, if α is 0(1), B is required at the ith time to learn the ith bit of $m_0(m_1)$.

4.2 4.2 Strengthening Yao's Combined Oblivious Transfer

In [Y2], Yao presented a protocol that we call combined oblivious transfer (COT). The protocol involves two parties A and B, respectively owning private inputs a and b and any chosen function g. It possesses the following property: upon termination, A computes $g(a, b)$, while B has no idea of what A has computed. If we think of a ad b as secrets, B appears to obliviously transfering a prescribed combination of his and A's secret to A. Yao implemented COT based on the assumption that factoring is hard, (which yelds, as shown by Blum [B]) a particular trap-door permutation. We strengthen his result by showing that COT can be correctly implemented based on any trap-door permutation. We do this by using the one-out-of-two OT of section 4.1 in Yao's scheme. Let us consider first the case where a and b are bits and g is the Boolean *AND*. Consider figure 1. Here $E_1, \ldots, E_6$ are independently selected encryption algorithms, respectively having decryption keys $D_1, \ldots, D_6$. E_1 and E_2 label the first input-wire, E_3 and E_4 the second input-wire, and E_5 and E_6 the output-wire. Each row in the gate is formed by the encryption of two strings. m and n are two randomly selected strings whose bit-by-bit exclusive-or equals D_5. p and q are two randomly selected strings whose xor equals D_6; so are x and t; so are u and v. The 4 rows have been put in the gate in random order. E_1, E_2 and E_5, E_6 are publically labelled by complementary bits. E_3 and E_4 are each secretely labelled by a bit; more precisely, E_3 is SECRETELY labelled 0 with probability 1/2 and E_4 is labelled with the complement of E_3's bit. (This secrecy is pictorially indicated by drawing E_3 and E_4's bits by a dotted line.) Define the value of a wire to be 0 (1) if one ONLY possesses the decoding algorithm of encryption algorithm labelled 0 (1). Then figure 1 is a or-gate. For instance, assume that both input-wires have value 0. That is, one possesses only D_1 and D_4. Then one is able to decrypt both entries only in the third row. By taking the *xor* of u and v, one easily obtains D_6, but has no idea what D_5 may be. Thus the output-wire has value $0 = AND(0, 0)$.

To COTransfer $AND(a, b)$, B generates a COT *AND*-gate like in figure 1, keeping for himself all decoding algorithms and all the strings in the rows. Then, he gives A the decoding algorithm of the second input-wire that corresponds to the value of b, his own input. Notice that as the association between E_3, E_4 and 0, 1 is secret (and E_1, E_2, E_3, E_4 enter symmetrically in the gate rows), this will not betray b at all. Now A will get either D_1 or D_2, according to the value of a, by means of our one-

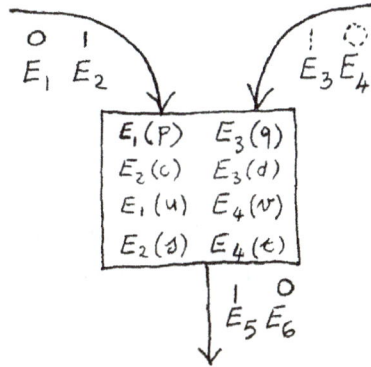

Figure 1   A COT *AND*-gate

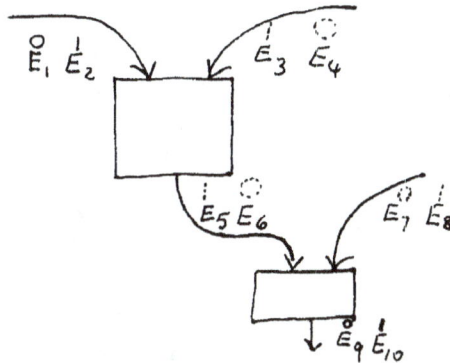

Figure 2

out-of-two OT. Thus, *B* will not know which algorithm she got. At this point *A* can easily compute the value of the output-wire. Thus she will be the only one to know $AND(a, b)$.

It is trivial to build a COT *NOT*-gate. Notice that *B* may also keep secret the corresponding between $0, l$ and E_5, E_6. This allows the out-put wire to become an input-wire of another gate. If the encryption algorithms of this second gate are publically labelled 0/1 (see fig. 2), we see that *A* may evaluate any 2-gates function on her and *B*'s inputs, without knowing intermediate results. Better said, *B* can "COTransfer" the value of any 2-gates function. By cascading this way COT *AND*-gates and COT *NOT*-gates (which are trivial to design), we can see that B can COTransfer the value of any function, provided that there is an upper bound to the length of A's and B's inputs, (else, the length of the inputs will be betrayed).

4.3   The Tm-game Solver for Passive Adversaries

Recall that a Tm-game solver wants to compute $M(x_1, \ldots, x_n)$ while respecting the privacy constraint. We want to use COT as a subroutine to construct a Tm-solver. This does not appear to be straightforward. For instance, if two parties i and j use COT so that i will compute $g(x_i, x_j)$ for some function g, this would already be a violation of the privacy constraint. Recall also that the Tm-game solver has to be polynomial not only in M's running time, but also in n, the number of players.

We find a way out by making special use of a lemma of Barrington's [Ba] that simulates computation by composing permutations in S_5, the symmetric group on 5 elements. The general picture is the following. First transform the Turing machine M of a Tm-game to an equivalent circuit C in a standard way. The Boolean inputs of C will be $b_1^1, \ldots, b_l^1, \ldots, b_1^n, \ldots, b_l^n$, the bits of the n, l-bit long, inputs of tour parties. This circuit C is then transformed to straight-line program as in [Ba]. This straight-line program is essentially as long as C is big. In it,

- 0,1 are encoded by two (specially selected) 5-permutations

- the variables range in S_5 and

- each instruction consists of multiplying (composing) two 5-permutations σ and τ, whre $\sigma(\tau)$ is either a constant, or a variable, or the inverse (in S_5) of a variable.

At the start, each party takes each of his private bits and encodes it by a 5-permutation σ as in [Ba]. Then he divides σ. That is, he selects at random n-1 5-permutations $\sigma_1, \ldots, \sigma_{n-1}$ and gives the pair (i, σ_i) to party i (possibly himself). He then sets $\sigma_n = (\sigma_1 \cdot \cdots \cdot \sigma_{n-1})^{-1} \cdot \sigma$ and gives (n, σ_n) to party n. Now, inductively, assume that each variable is divided among the parties. That is, for each variable σ, each player i possesses an index permutation pair (x, σ_z) so that $\Pi_{x=1}^x \sigma_z = \sigma$ and, given only $n-1$ pieces, σ cannot be guessed better than at random. We now want to show that each instruction can be performed (i.e., each party can compute his individual piece of the result) respecting the privacy constraint. There are essentially 3 cases.

Case 1: The instruction is of the form $\sigma \cdot c$, where σ is a variable and c a constant. By induction, each party has a piece of the form (x, σ_x). Then the party owning the piece (n, σ_n) sets his new piece to be $(n, \sigma_n \cdot c)$ and all each party leaves his piece untouched. It is immediately checked that the ordered product of the new pieces is $\sigma \cdot c$ and that privacy has been preserved against $n - 1$ passive adversaries.

Case 2: The instruction is of the form $\sigma^{-1} \cdot c$ where, again, σ is a variable and c a constant. It will be enough to show how to compute pieces for σ^{-1} respecting the privacy constraint. To do this, if a party has a piece (x, σ_x), he sets his new piece to be $(n - x + 1, \sigma_x^{-1})$.

Case 3: The instruction is of the form $\sigma \cdot \tau$, where both u and τ are variables. Then $\sigma \cdot \tau = \sigma_1 \cdots \sigma_n \cdot \tau_1 \cdots \tau_n$, and assume for simplicity that party i possesses piece σ_i and τ_i. Unfortunately, party 1 cannot compute his piece of $\sigma \cdot \tau$ by multiplying his own two pieces. In fact, they are n positions apart in the product and S_6 is not commutative (a fact crucial in Barrington's argument). The idea will then consist of making "partial progress". That is, moving party 1's pieces closer together by "swapping" σ_n and τ_1. This can be correctly accomplished by giving party 1 a piece τ_1' and party n a piece σ_n' so that $\tau_i' \cdot \sigma_n' = \sigma_n \cdot \tau_1$. This way the product of the new (and newly ordered pieces) would remain $\sigma \cdot \tau$. One way of doing this would be of having party 1 and party n tell each other σ_n and τ_1. However this would violate the privacy constraint with respect to a set of $n - 1$ passive adversaries. Instead, we use COT in the following way. Party n randomly selects a 5-permutation p. Consider now the function g such that, for 5-permutations x,y, and z, $g(x, (y, z)) = w$ where $w \cdot z = y \cdot x$. Let now party 1 (with the role of A and input $a = \tau_1$) and party n (with the role of B and input $b = (\sigma_n, \rho)$) play COT with function g. Set $\tau_1' = g(a, b)$ and $\sigma_n = \rho$. Then we have made the desired partial progress. In fact, not only the product of the new pieces is unaltered, but we have also respected the privacy constraint. Informally, party n's new piece is a random 5-permutation selected by party n himself and thus cannot give him any information neither about party 1's old piece nor the new one; moreover the transference of $g(a, b)$ is oblivious and thus cannot give party n any knowledge either. On the other side, party 1 is dealt a new piece $g(r_1, (\sigma_n, \rho))$ and he knows τ_1. However, as for all z and y, $g(x, (y_1 \cdot))$ is injective on S_δ, and ρ has been randomly and secretely selected by party n, also party 1 does not get any knowledge that he did not possess before! Notice also that during this "swap" we did not create any other pieces. Thus after n "swaps" the only two pieces of party 1 will be in the first two positions in the product and he can thus multiply them together. This product will be party 1's piece for the variable $\sigma \cdot \tau$. It should be verified that the entire walk of party 1 τ-piece towards the left preserves correctness and does not violate the privacy constraint. Essentially because a new, random piece is created at each step. This way, after $O(n^2)$ "swaps", and in polynomial time, all parties receive their piece of $\sigma \cdot \tau$.

At the end of the straight-line program, for each output variable γ, each party publicizes his own piece (x, γ_x), the ordered product of these pieces is computed and the output bit recovered so to satisfy both the correctness and the privacy constraint. (A more formal argument will be given in the final paper.)

5 Malicious Adversaries

The complexity of our Tm-game solver greatly increases when up to half of the players is allowed to be malicious and can more powerfully collaborate to try to disrupt the correctness and the privacy constraints. We use essentially all the cryptographic tools developed in the last ten years in the (correct) hope that they would make possible protocol design. Also, the proof of its correctness is rather delicate and unsuitable for an abstract. We will give it in the final paper. Here we only indicate what making playable a Tm-game with malicious advesaries may *mean* and which general ideas are involved in our solution.

As in this case some of the parties may not follow their prescribed programs at all, it is necessary to clarify what a private input is. After all, what stops someone from pretending that his private input is different from what it actually is? To avoid this, we assume that the parties have established their private inputs by announcing correct encodings of them. Their inputs are by definition the unique decryption of their respective encodings. Moreover, it shoud be clear that seeking a solution to a Tm-game problem makes sense only if the parties are "willing to play". If, say, one of them "commits suicide", carrying with himself what his private input was, there is very little one can do besides investing exponential time and break his encryption. However we can, loosely speaking, prove that

> Given n players willing to play, less than half of which malicious, all Tm-games are playable.

The above term "willing to play", indicates a technical condition rather than a psychological one. Namely, having successfully completed the *engagement protocol*. After completing this protocol, all players can be forced to play any desired game. The engagement protocol consists of two phases.

1. For each player i, a protocol is performed at the end of which no minority of the players can even predict a bit of i's private input with chances essentially better than $1/2$. However, *it is guaranteed* that any subset of cardinality $> n/2$ can, without the cooperation or even against the actions of other players, easily compute i's private input.

2. The community deals to each player a sequence of encrypted "random" bits so that a) the recipient knows their decryption, b) they appear unpredictable

to any minority of the players, but c) they are easily computable by any majority of the players.

We stress that while no one can be forced to complete the engagement protocol (so to become "willing to play"), no one can decide not to complete it because he received a better idea of what the result of the subsequent game may be. Completing the engagement protocol will not give any player (or any small enough group of players) any knowledge about the others' private inputs.

Phase 1 of the engagement protocol consists of a verifiable secret sharing in the sense of Awerbuch, Chor, Goldwasser and Micali [CGMA]. However, we contribute a new protocol both tolerating up to $n/2$ malicious adversaries and using any trapdoor function whatsoever. Phase 2 of the engagement protocol is the multy-party version of Blum's coin flipping by telephone. Despite the (deceivingly) similarity with the verifiable secret sharing of phase 1, to implement phase 2 we must make use of a yet unpublished theorem (and algorithm) of ACGM.

We now give a bird's eye view of how to make any Tm-game g playable despite malicious adversaries. On input M, 1^k, we first run the engagement protocol, then the passive-adversary playable version of the Tm-game. Here we require all parties to use, as their private inputs, the strings they shared in phase 1 of the engagement protocol and, as a source of randomness, the encrypted random bits each was dealt in phase 2. The key point is that, now, no malicious adversary can deviate from his prescribed program, and thus he becomes a simple passive adversary. In fact, he is required to prove, in zero-knowledge (in the sense of Goldwasser, Micali and Rackoff [GoMiRa]), that each message he sends is what he should have sent being honest, given his private input, his random choices and the messages he received so far. (Here, an essential tool is our recent result that all *NP* languages possess zero-knowledge proofs [GMW].) If a malicious party, frustrated at not being able to send messages according to a different program, decides to stop, his input and random bits will be reconstructed by the community who will compute his messages when necessary, without skewing the probability distribution of the final outcome.

We would like to stress our new use of *NP*-completeness. From being our most effective way to prove lower-bounds, it now becomes our most effective tool to construct correct protocols.

6   General Games

Many actions in life, like negotiating a contract, casting a vote in a ballot, playing cards, bargaining in the market, submitting a STOC abstract, driving a car and simply living, may be viewed as participating with others in a game with payoffs/penalties associated with its results. This is not only true for individuals, but also for companies, governments, armies etc. that are engaged in financial, political and physical struggles. Despite the diversity of these games, all of them can be described in the elegant mathematical framework laid out by Von Neumann and Morgenstern earlier in this century. *Game theory*, however, exhibits a "gap", in that it neglected to study whether, or how, or under which conditions, games can be *implemented*. That is, it never addressed the question of whether, given the description of a game, a method exists for physically or mentally playing it. We do fill this gap by showing that, in a complexity theoretic sense, all games can be played.

In this extended abstract we will only informally clarify what and how this is. We start by briefly recalling the ingredients used by game theory to model a n-players game with *incomplete information*.

6.1   Games

Essentially, a game consists of a set S of possible *states*, representing all possible instantaneous descriptions of the game, a set M of possible *moves*, describing all possible ways to change the current state of the game, a set $\{K_1, K_2, \ldots, K_n\}$ of *knowledge functions*, where $K_i(\sigma)$ represents the partial information about state σ possessed by player i, and a function p, the *payoff junction*, that, evaluated on the final state, tells the outcome of the game. Without loss of generality, the players make moves in cyclic order and the set of possible moves in any state are the same for all states. Also, WLOG, the game goes on for a fixed number of moves m. With little restriction we do assume that the players make use of recursive strategies for selecting their moves. (The classical model does not rule out selecting moves according to an infinite table.)

Let us now see how a game evolves using, in parenthesis, poker as an example. The game starts by having "NATURE" select an initial state σ_1. (For poker, σ_1 is a randomly selected permutation of the 52 cards; the first $5n$ cards of the permutation representing the players initial hands and the remaining ones the deck.) Player 1 moves first. He does not know σ_1 -nor does anybody else-, he only knows $K_1(\sigma_1)$, his own hand: the first 5 elements of permutation σ_1). Based solely on $K_1(\sigma_1)$, he will select a move p (e.g. he changes 3 of his cards with the first 3 cards of the deck). This move automatically updates the -unknown!- current state to σ_2. (The new state consists of the cards currently possessed by each player, the sequence of cards in the deck and which cards were discarded by player 1. $K_1(\sigma_2)$ consists of the new hand of player 1 and the cards he just discarded.) Now it is the turn of player 2. He also does not know the current state σ_2, he only knows $K_2(\sigma_2)$. Based solely on this information, he selects his move, which updates the current state, and so on. After the prescribed number of moves, the payoff function p is evaluated at the final state to compute the result of the game. (In poker the result consists of who has won, how much he has won and how much everyone else has individually lost.)

Note that a Tm-game is indeed a game in which the initial state is empty and each player moves only once. State σ_i consists of the sequence of the first i moves. Each player has no knowledge about the current state and chooses his move to be the string x_i, his own private input. The payoff function M is then run on σ_n. (Having probabilistic machines running on the final state, rather than deterministic ones, is a quite natural generalization.)

From this brief description it is immediately apparent that, by properly selecting the knowledge functions, one can enforce any desired "privacy" constraints in a game.

6.2 Playable Games

Game theory, besides an elegant formulation, also suggests to the players strategies satisfying some desired property (e.g. optimality). That is, game theory's primary concern is how TO SELECT MOVES WELL. However, and ironically!, it never addressed the question of how TO PLAY WELL. For a general n-player game, all we can say is that we need $n + 1$ parties to properly play it; the extra party being the "trusted party". The trusted party communicates privately with all players. At step t, he knows the current state σ_t of the game. He kindly computes $\alpha = k_{t \bmod n}(\sigma_t)$, communicates α to player $t \bmod n$, receives from him a move μ, secretly computes the new state $S_{t+1} = \mu(S_t)$, and so on. At the end, the trusted party will evaluate the payoff function on the final state and declare the outcome of the game. Clearly, playing with the trusted party achieves exactly the privacy constraints of the game description, and at the end each player will get the correct outcome.

Now, the fact that, in general, a n-person game requires $n + 1$ people to be played, not only is grotesque, but it also diminuishes the otherwise wide applicability of game theory! In fact, in real life situations, we may simply not have any trusted parties, whether men or public computers. Recently, complaints have been raised about finantial transactions in the stock market. The complaints were about the fact that some parties were enjoying knowledge that was considered "extra" before choosing their move, i.e. before buying stocks. Just another game, the stock market, but one in which you may desire trusting no one!

We are thus led to consider the notion of a *(purely) playable* game. This is a n-person game that can be implemented by the n players without invoking any trusted parties. In general, however, given the specification of a game with complicated knowledge functions, it is not at all easy to decide whether it is playable in some meaningful way. Here, among the "meaningful way", we also include non-mathematical methods. Yet, the decision may still not be easy.

Poker, for instance, has simple enough knowledge functions (i.e. privacy constraints) that makes it playable in a "physical" way. In it we use cards with equal "back" and "opaque", tables whose top does not reflect light too much, we shuffle the deck "a lot", and we hand cards "facing down". All this is satisfactory as in our physical model (world) we only see along straight lines. However, assume we define NEWPOKER as follows. A player may select his move not only based on his own hand, but also on the knowledge of whether, combining the current hands of all players, one may form a royal flush. NEWPOKER is certainly a game in the Von Neumann's framework but it, is no longer apparent whether any physical realization of the game exists, particularly if some of the players may be cheaters.

This is what we perceive lacking in game theory: the attention to the notion of playability. At this point a variety of good questions naturally arises:

Is there a model (physical or mathematical) which makes all games playable?

Or at least,

Does every game have a model in which: it is playable?

And if not,

Should we restrict our attention to the class of playable games?

We show that the first question can be affirmatively answered in a computational complexity model.

6.3 A General Result

Theorem If any trap-door function exists, any game is playable if more than half of the players are honest.

Essentially our result consists of a protocol for simulating the trusted party of an ideal game. That is, if more than half of the players follow our protocol, whatever a player (or a set of players of size less than $n/2$) knows at any step of the game, he would have also known in an *ideal execution* of the game with a trusted party. In our context the knowledge constants are satisfied in a computational complexity sense. Namely, any player (or collection of dishonest players) in order to compute anything more than his due share of the current state, should perform an exponential-time computation. Unfortunaly, we cannot, in this extended abstract, elaborate on the relationship between general games and Tm-games, nor how to pass from solving the latter ones to solve the general case. We'll do this in the final paper.

6.4 A Completeness Theorem for Fault-Tolerant Computation

Our main theorem has direct impact to the field of fault-tolerant computation. This is so as protocols, when properly formalized (which we will do in the final paper), are games with partial information. Thus, as long as the majority of the players is honest, all protocols may be correctly played. Actually, slightly more strongly, the correct way to play a game can be found in a uniform manner. Namely, we exhibit a specific, efficient algorithm that, on input a protocol problem, outputs an efficient, distributed protocol for solving it.

It should be noticed that, before this, only an handful of multi-party protocol problems were given a satisfactory solution (e.g. collective coin flipping and poker over the telephone, secret exchange, voting, and a few others). Moreover the security of some of these solutions crucially depended on the "trap-doorness" of specific functions satisfying some additional, convenient property (e.g. multiplicativity). By contrast, our completeness theorem is proved based on any trap-door function (multiplicative or not, associative or not, etc.). That is, we prove that, if public-key cryptography is possible at all, then all protocols problems are (automatically!) solvable if more than half of the players are honest.

7 Recent Developments

Recently, Haber and Micali found a Tm-game solver that is algorithmically much simpler (for instance it does not use Barrington's straight-line programs) but more difficult to prove correct. Also, Goldreich and Vainish found a simpler solution based on a specific assumption, the computational difficulty of quadratic residuosity.

8 Acknowledgements

We are very grateful to Shimon Even, Dick Karp, Mike Merritt, Albert Meyer, Yoram Moses for having doubted the generality of some of our intermediate solutions and having encouraged us to reach the right level of generality. In particular, Albert Meyer contributed the beautiful notion of a Turing-machine game, and Dick Karp steered us toward games with incomplete information as the best avenue to our completeness theorem for protocols.

We also would like to thank Benny Chor, Mike Fischer and Shafi Goldwssser for helpful discussions concerning the issues of this paper.

9   References

[Ba]   D. Barrington , *Bounded-Width Branching Programs Recognize Exactly Those Languages in NC¹*, Proc. 18th STOC, 1986 pp 1-5

[B1]   M. Blum, *Coin Flipping by Telephone*, IEEE COMPCON 1982, pp. 133-137.

[BH]   R. Boppana and R. Hirschfeld, *Pseudo-Random Generatora and Complexity Classes*, To appear in Randomness and Computation, 5th volume of Advances in Computing Research, ed. S. Micali

[BM]   M. Blum and S. Micali, *How To Generate Sequences Of Cryptographically Strong Pseudo-Random Bits*, SIAM J. on Computing, Vol. 13, Nov 1984, pp. 850-864

[CG]   B. Chor and 0. Goldreich, *RSA/Rabin Bits Are 1/2 + 1/poly(log N) Secure*, To appear SIAM J. on Computing. Earlier version in Proc. FOCS 1984, pp. 449-463

[CGMA]   B. Chor, S. Goldwasser, S. Micali, and B. Awerbuch, *Verifiable Secret Sharing and Achieving Simultaneity in the Presence of Faults'*, Proc. 26th FOCS, 1985, pp. 383-395

[EGL]   S. Even, O. Goldreich, and A. Lempel, *A Randomized Protocol for Signing Contracts*, CACM, vol. 28, No. 6, 1985, pp. 637-647

[FMRW]   M.Fischer, S. Micali, C. Rackoff and D. Witenberg, *A Secure Protocol for the Oblivious Transfer*, In preperation 1986.

[GM]   S. Goldwasser, and S. Micali, *Probabilistic Encryption*, JCSS Vol. 28, No. 2, April 1984. An earlier version (containing other results) was titled *Probabilistic Encryption and How to Play Mental Poker Hideing Ail Partial Injormation*,

[GMR]   S. Goldwasser, S. Micali and C. Rackoff, *The Knowledge Complexity of Interactive Proof-Systems*, To appear SIAM J. on Computing (manuscript available from authors). Earlier version in Proc. 17th Annual ACM Symp. on Theory of Computing, pp 291-304.

[GoMiRi]   S. Goldwasser, S. Micali, and R. Rivest, *A Digital Signature Scheme Secure Against Adaptive, Chosen Cyphertezt Attack* To appear in SLAM J. on Computing (available from authors)
Earlier version, titled "*A Paradoxical Solution to the Signature Problem*, in Proc. 25th FOCS, 1984, pp. 441-448

[GMW]   O. Goldreich, S. Micali and A. Wigderson, *Proofs that Yield Nothing but their Validity and a Methodology of Cryptographic Design*, Proc. of FOCS 1986.

[HR]   J. Halpern and M.O. Rabin, *A Logic to reason about likelihood*, Proc. of 15th STOC, 1983.

[L]   L. Leonid, *One-Way Functions and Pseud0-Random Generators*, Proc. 17th STOC, 1985, pp. 363-365

[Y]   A.Yao, *Theory and Application of Trapdoor Functions*, Proc. of 23rd FOCS, IEEE, Nov., 1982, pp. 80-91.

[Y2]   A.Yao, *How to Generate and Exchange Secrets*, Proc. 27th STOC, 1986, pp. 162-167

Non-Interactive Zero-Knowledge (NIZK) Proof Systems

This chapter reproduces the contents of the paper "Non-Interactive Zero-Knowledge and its Applications," which appeared in the proceedings of the *20th Annual ACM Symposium on Theory of Computing*, pp. 103–112, 1988.

This influential work of Manuel Blum, Paul Feldman, and Silvio Micali introduced a model that includes a common random string provided from the outside and available to both the prover and the verifier. It then showed how to provide zero-knowledge (non-interactive) proofs for any NP-assertion. Such NIZKs have been used as a building blocks in many subsequent works (e.g., in constructing public-key encryption schemes that withstand chosen-ciphertext attacks).

Non-Interactive Zero-Knowledge and Its Applications (Extended Abstract)

Manuel Blum* (Computer Science Dept., Univ. of Calif., Berkely, CA),
Paul Feldman (MIT Lab. for Computer Sci, Cambridge, MA),
Silvio Micali† (MIT Lab. for Computer Sci, Cambridge, MA)

Abstract

We show that interaction in any zero-knowledge proof can be replaced by sharing a common, short, random string. We use this result to construct the *first* public-key cryptosystem secure against chosen ciphertext attack.

1 Introduction

Recently [GMR] have shown that it is possible to prove that some theorems are true without giving the slightest hint of why this is so. This is rigorously formalized in the somewhat paradoxical notion of a *zero-knowledge proof system*

* Supported by NSF Grant # DCR85-13926
† Supported by ARO Grant # DAAL03-86-K-0171

If secure encryption schemes exist, though, these proof systems are far from being a rare and bizar event. In fact, under this assumption, [GMW] demonstrate that any language in NP possesses zero-knowledge proof systems.

Actually, as recently pointed out by Ben-Or, Goldreich, Goldwasser, Hastad, Micali and Rogaway [BGGHMR], the same is true for all languages in IP; also, as pointed out by Blum [B2], any theorem at all admits a proof that conveys zero-knowledge other than betraying its own length.

Zero-knowledge proofs have proven very useful both in complexity theory and in cryptography. For instance, in complexity theory, via results of fortnow [F] and Boppana and Hastad [BH], zero-knowledge provides us an avenue to convince ourselves that certain languages are not NP-complete. In cryptography, zero-knowledge proofs have played a major role in the recently proven completeness theorem for protocols with honest majority [GMW2]. They also have inspired rigorously-analyzed identification schemes [FFS] that are as efficient as folklore ones.

Despite its wide applicability, zero-knowledge remains an intriguing notion: What makes zero-knowledge proofs work?

Three main features differentiate all known zero-knowledge proof systems from more traditional ones:

1. *Interaction:* The prover and the verifier talk back and forth

2. *Hidden Randomization:* The verifier tosses coins that are hidden from the prover and thus unpredictable to him.

3. Computational Difficulty: The prover imbeds in his proofs the computational difficulty of some other problem.

At a first glance, all of these ingredients appear to be necessary. This paper makes a first, important step in distilling what is essential in a zero-knowledge proof. We show that computational difficulty alone (for instance the hardness of distinguishing products of 2 primes from products of 3 primes) may make *inessential* the first resource (interaction) and and *eliminate the secrecy* of the second resource (randomness). That is, if the prover and the verifier share a common random string, the prover can non-interactively and yet in zero-knowledge convince the verifier of the validity of any theorem he may discover. A bit more precisely, for any constants c and d, sharing a k-bit long random string allows a prover p to prove in zero-knowledge to a poly(k)-time verifier V any k^c theorems of k^d size non-interactively; that is, without ever reading any message from V.

A Conceptual Scenario: Think of P and V as two mathematicians. After having played "heads and tails" for a while, or having both witnessed the same random event, P leaves for a long trip along the world, during which he continues his mathematical investigations. whenever he discovers a theorem, he writes a postcard to v proving the validity of his new theorem in zero-knowledge. Notice that this is necessarily a non-interactive process; better said, it is a mono-directional interaction: From P to V only. in fact, even if V would like to answer or talk to P, he couldn't: P has no fixed (or predictable) address and will move away before any mail can reach him.

1.1   Our Model Versus the Old One

While the definition of zero-knowledge remains unchanged, the mechanics of the computation of the prover and verifier changes dramatically.

Notice that sharing a random string σ is a weaker requirement than being able to interact. In fact, if P and V could interact they would be able to construct a common random string by coin tossing over the phone [B1]; the converse, however, is not true.

Also notice that sharing a common random string is a requirement even weaker than having both parties access a random beacon in the rabin's sense (e.g., the same geiger counter). In this latter case, in fact, all made coin tosses would be seen by the prover, but the future ones would still be unpredictable to him. by contrast, our model allows the prover to see in advance all the coin tosses of the verifier. That is the zero-knowledgeness of our proofs does not depend on the secrecy, or unpredictability of 7, but on the "well mixedness" of its bits! This curious property makes our result potentially applicable. For instance, all libraries in the country possess identical copies of the random tables prepared by the rand corporation. Thus, we may think of ourselves as being already in the scenario needed for non-interactive zero-knowledge proofs.

1.2   The Robustness of Our Result

As we have already said, we guaranltee that all theorems proved in our proof systems are correct and zero-knowledge if the string σ is a truly random one. We may rightly ask what would happen if σ was not, in fact, truly randomly selected. fortunately, the poor randomness of σ may upset the zero-knowledgeness of our theorems, but not their correctness. That is, for almost all (poorly random) σ's, there is no wrong statement that can be accepted by the verifier. This is indeed an important property as we can never be sure of the quality of our natural sources of randomness. Unfortunately, due to the limitations of an extended abstract, we cannot further elaborate on this and similar points. We wish, however, to point out the following important corollary of our result.

1.3 Applications of our Result

A very noticeable application of non-interactive zero-knowledge is the construction of encryption schemes á la diffie and hellman that are secure against chosen ciphertext attacks. Whether such schemes existed has been a fundamenatal open problem ever since the appearence of complexity-based cryptography. We will discuss this application in Section 3.

1.4 What's Coming

The next section is devoted to set up our notation, recall some elementary facts from Number Theory and state the complexity assumption which suffices to show the existence of non-interactive, zero-knowledge proofs.

In Section 3, we show that if a k^4-bit string is randomly selected and given to both the proven and the verifier, then the first can prove in zero-knowledge, for any single string x (of length k) belonging, to a NP-language L, that indeed $x \in L$.

Only in Section 4 we show that, for each fixed polynomial $Q(\cdot)$, using the *same* randomly chosen k^4-bit string, the prover can show in zero-knowledge membership in NP languages for any $Q(k)$ strings of length $Q(k)$.

2 Preliminaries

2.1 Notations and Conventions

Let us quickly recall the standard notation of [GoMiRi].

We emphasize the number of inputs received by an algorithm as follows. If algorithm a receives only one input we write "$A(\cdot)$", if it receives two inputs we write "$A(\cdot, \cdot)$" and so on.

If $A(\cdot)$ is a probabilistic atgorithm, then for any input x, the notation $A(x)$ refers to the probability space that assigns to the string σ the probability that A, on input x, outputs σ. If S is a probability space, then $PR_S(e)$ denotes the probability that S associates with the element e.

If $f(\cdot)$ and $g(\cdot, \ldots, \cdot)$ are probabilistic algorithms then $f(g(\cdot, \ldots, \cdot))$ is the probabilistic algorithm obtained by composing f and g (i.e. running f on g's output). For any inputs $x, y, \ldots$ the associated probability space is denoted by $f(g(x, y, \ldots))$.

If s is any probability space, then $z \leftarrow S$ denotes the algorithm which assigns to x an element randomly selected according to S. If f is a finite set, then the notation $x \leftarrow f$ denotes the algorithm which assigns to x an element selected according to the probability space whose sample space is f and uniform probability distribution on the sample points.

The notation $Pr(z \leftarrow S; y \leftarrow T; \ldots : p(x, y, ..))$ denotes the probability that the predicate $p(x, y, \ldots)$ will be true after the ordered execution of the algorithms $x \leftarrow S, y \leftarrow T, \ldots$

The notation $\{z \leftarrow S; y \leftarrow T; \ldots : (x, y, ...)\}$ denotes the probability space over $\{(x, y, \ldots)\}$ generated by the ordered execution of the algorithms $x \leftarrow S, y \leftarrow T, \ldots$.

Let us recall the basic definitions of [GMR]. We address the reader to the original paper for motivation, interpretation and justification of these definitions.

Let $U = \{U/(x)\}$ be a family of random variables taking values in $\{0, 1\}^*$, with the parameter x ranging in $\{0, 1\}^*$. $U = \{U(x)\}$ is called poly-bounded family of random variables, if, for some constant $e \in \backslash$, all random variables $U(z) \in u$ assign positive probability only to strings whose length is exactly $|x|^e$.

Let $C = \{C_x\}$ be a poly-size family of boolean circuits, that is, for some constants $c, d > 0$, all C_x, have one boolean output and at most $|x|^e$ gates and $|x|^d$ inputs. In the following, when we say that a random string, chosen according to $U(x)$, where $\{U(x)\}$ is a poly-bounded family of random variables, is given as input to C_x, we assume that the length of the strings that are assigned positive probability by $U(x)$ equals the number of boolean inputs of $C|x$.

Definition 2.1 (Indistinguishability) Let $L \subset \{0, 1\}^*$ be a language. Two poly-bounded families of random variables $U = \{U(z)\}$ and $V = \{V(x)\}$ are indistinguishable on L if for all poly-size families of circuits $C = \{C_x\}$,

$$\left| Pr(A \leftarrow U(x) : C_x(a) = 1) - Pr(a \leftarrow V(x) : C_x(a) = 1) \right| < |x|^c$$

For all positive constants c and sufficiently large $x \in L$.

Definition 2.2 (Approximability) Let $L \subset \{0, 1\}^*$ be a language. a family of random variables $U = \{U(x)\}$ is approximable on L if there exists a probabilistic turing machine M, running in expected polynomial time, such that the families $\{U(x)\}$ and $\{M(x)\}$ are indistinguishable on L.

2.2 Number Theory

Let $Z_s(k)$ denote the set of integers product of $s > 1$ distinct primes of length k.

Let N be the set of the natural numbers, $x \in N$, $Z_x^* = \{y \mid 1 \leq y < x, gcd(x, y) = 1\}$ and $Z_x^{+1} = \{y \in Z_x^* \mid (y \mid x) = +1\}$, where $(y \mid x)$ is the jacobi symbol. We say that $y \in Z_x^*$ is a quadratic residue modulo x iff there is $w \in Z_x^*$ such that $w^2 \equiv y \bmod x$. If this is not the case we call w a quadratic non residue modulo x.

Define the quadratic residuosity predicate to be

$$Q_x(y) = \begin{cases} 0, & \text{if } y \text{ is a quadratic residue modulo } x; \\ 1, & \text{otherwise;} \end{cases}$$

and the languages QR and QNR as

$$QR = \{(y, x) \mid Q_x(y) = 0\}$$

$$QNR = \{(y, x) \mid (y \in Z_x^{+1} \text{ and } Q_x(y) = 1\}.$$

Fact 1 Let $\sim$ be the relation so defined: $y_1 \sim y_2$ iff $Q + x(y_1y_2) = 0$. Then $\sim$ is an equivalence relation in Z_x^{+1}. Two elements are equivalents if they have the same quadratic character modulo each of the prime divisors of x. Thus, if $x \in Z_2(k)$ there are 2 equivalence classes, if $x \in Z_3(k)$ there are 4; in general if $x = p_i^{h_1} \cdots, p_n^{h_n}$ where each p_i is a prime > 2 and $p_i \neq p_i$ if $i \neq j$, then there are 2^n equivalence classes.

Fact 2 For each $y_1, y_2 \in Z_x^{+1}$ one has

$$Q_x(y_1y_2) = Q_x(y_1) \oplus Q_x(y_2).$$

Fact 3 Where "$\oplus$" denotes the *exclusive or* operator. the jacobi symbol function $x|n$ is polynomial-time computable.

We now formalize the complexity assumption that is sufficient for non-interactive zero-knowledge. Namely, that it is computationally hard to distinguish the integers product of 2 primes leftarrow the ones product of 3 primes.

2.3 A Complexity Assumption

2OR3A: for each poly-size family of circuits $\{C_k | k \in N$

$$|P_{Z_3(k)} - P_{Z_3(k)}| < k^{-c}$$

for all positive constants c and sufficiently large k; where

$$P_{Z_2(k)} = P_R(X \leftarrow Z_2(k) : C_k(x) = 1) \text{ and}$$

$$P_{Z_3(k)} = P_R(x \leftarrow Z_3(k) : C_k(x) = 1).$$

2OR3A is a stronger assumption than assuming that deciding quadratic residuosity is hard. (Having an oracle for $Q_n(\cdot)$, allows one to prbabilistically count the number of $\sim$ equivalence in Z_x^{+1} and thus, by fact 1, to distinguish whether $n \in Z_2(k)$ or $n \in Z_3(k)$). Thus we can freely use that quadratic residuosity is computationally hard (as formalized below) without increasing our assumption set.

Quadratic Residuosity Assumption (QRA)

For each poiy-size family of circuits $\{C_k | k \in \mathcal{N}\}$,

$$Pr\left(x \leftarrow Z_2(k); y \leftarrow Z_x^{+1} : C_k(x, y) = Q_x(y)\right) < 1/2 + 1/k^{-O(1)}.$$

The QRA was introduced in [GM] and is now widely used in Cryptography. The current fastest algorithm to compute $Q_x(y)$ is to first factor x and then compute $Q_x(y)$, while it is well known that, given the factorization of x, $Q_x(y)$ can be computed in $O(|x|^3)$ steps. In what follows, we choose $x \in Z_2(k)$ since these integers constitute the hardest input for any known factoring algorithm.

3 Single-Theorem Non-Interactive Zero-Knowledge Proofs

To prove the existence of single-theorem Non-Interactive Zero-Knowledge Proof Systems (single-theorem non-interactive ZKPS) for all NP languages, it is enough to prove it for *3COL* the NP-complete language of the 3-colorable graphs [GJ]. For $k > 0$, we define the language $3COL_k = \{x \in 3COL | |x| \leq k\}$.

Definition 3.1 A Single-Theorem Non-Interactive ZKPS is a pair (A, B) where A is a Probabilistic Turing Machine and $B(\cdot, \cdot, \cdot)$ is a deterministic algorithm running in time polynomial in the length of its first input, such that:

1. **Completeness.** (The probability of succeeding in proving a true theorem is overwhelming.)

$$\exists c > 0 \text{ such that } \forall x \in 3COL_k$$

$$Pr\left(\sigma \leftarrow \{0, 1\}^{n^c}; y \leftarrow A(\sigma, x) : B(x, y, \sigma) = 1\right) > 1 - n^{-O(1)}.$$

2. **Soundness.** (The probability of succeeding in proving a false theorem is negligible.)

$\exists c > 0$ such that $\forall x \ni 3COL_k$ and for each Probabilistic Turing Machine A'

$$Pr\left(\sigma \leftarrow \{0, 1\}^{n^c}; y \leftarrow A'(\sigma, x) : B(x, y, \sigma) = 1\right) < n^{-O(1)}.$$

3. **Zero-Knowledge.** (The proof gives no information but the validity of the theorem.)

$\exists c > 0$ such that the family of random variables $V = \{V(x)\}$ is approximable over *3COL*. Where

$$V(x) = \{\sigma \leftarrow \{0, l\}^{|x|^c}; y \leftarrow A(\sigma, x) : (\sigma, y)\}),$$

Remark   Notice that, as usual, the zero-knowledge condition guarantees that the verifier's *view* can be well simulated; that is, all the verifier may see can be reconstructed with essentially the same odds. In our scenario, what the verifier sees is only the common random string and the proof, i.e., the string, received by A. Notice that in our scenario, the definition of zero-knowledge is simpler. As there is no interaction between B and A, we do not have to worry about possible cheating by the verifier to obtain a "more interesting view." That is, we can eliminate the quantification "$\forall B'$" from the original definition of [GMR].

Theorem 3.1   Under the QRA, there exists a Single-Theorem Non-Interactive $ZKPS$ for 3-*COL*.

This theorem will be rigorously proven in the final paper. Here we restrict ourselves to informally describe the programs P and V of a single-theorem non-interactive ZKPS (P,V) and, even more informally, to argue that they posses the desired properties.

3.1   The Proof-System (P,V)

Instructions for P

1. Randomly select $n_1, n_2, n_3 \in Z_2(k)$

2. For $i = 1, 2, 3$ randomly select q_i such that $(q_i | n_i) = 1$ and q_i is a quadratic non-residue mod n_i.

3. Color G with colors 1,2,3.

4. For each node u of G whose color is i, label v with a randomly selected triplet $(v_1, v_2, v_3) \in Z_x^{+1} \times Z_{n_2}^{+1} \times Z_{n_3}^{+1}$ such that $Q_n(v_i) = 0$ and $Q_{n_j}(v_j) = 1$ for $j \neq i$. Call G' the so labeled G
   {**Remark 1:** WLOG (else purge σ in the "right way") let $\sigma = \sigma_1 \circ \sigma_2 \circ \sigma_3 \circ \sigma_4, \cdots$, where all triplets $(\sigma_1, \sigma_2, \sigma_3)(\sigma_4, \sigma_5, \sigma_6), \cdots$ belong to $Z_{n_1}^{+1} \times Z_{n_i}^{+1} \times Z_{n_3}^{+1}$.}
   {**Convention:** The first $8k$ triplets are assigned to the first edge of G (in the lexicographic order), the next $8k$ triplets to the second edge, and so on.}

5. For each edge (a, b) of G' (where node a has label (a_1, a_2, a_3) and node b (b_1, b_2, b_3)) and each of its $8k$ assigned triplets (z_1, z_2, z_3) compute one of the following types of *signature*.
   {**Comment:** Only one is applicable if steps 1-4 are performed correctly)}

$$\left(\sqrt{z_1}, \sqrt{z_2}, \sqrt{z_3}\right) \qquad \text{type 0}$$

$$\left(\sqrt{q_1 z_1}, \sqrt{z_2}, \sqrt{z_3}\right) \qquad \text{type 1}$$

$$\left(\sqrt{z_1}, \sqrt{q_2 z_2}, \sqrt{z_3}\right) \qquad \text{type 2}$$

$$\left(\sqrt{z_1}, \sqrt{z_2}, \sqrt{q_3 z_3}\right) \qquad \text{type 3}$$

$$\left(\sqrt{a_1 z_1}, \sqrt{a_2 z_2}, \sqrt{a_3 z_3}\right) \qquad \text{type 4}$$

$$\left(\sqrt{b_1 z_1}, \sqrt{b_2 z_2}, \sqrt{b_3 z_3}\right) \qquad \text{type 5}$$

$$\left(\sqrt{a_1 b_1 z_1}, \sqrt{a_2 b_2 z_2}, \sqrt{a_3 b_3 z_3}\right) \qquad \text{type 6}$$

$$\left(\sqrt{q_1 z_1}, \sqrt{q_2 z_2}, \sqrt{q_3 z_3}\right) \qquad \text{type 7}$$

{**Notation "by example"**: Let x_1 be a quadratic non residue mod n_1, z_2 a quadratic residue mod n_2, and z_3 is a quadratic residue mod n_2. Then the signature of the triplet (z_1, z_2, z_3) a triplet of type 1: $(\sqrt{q_1 z_1}, \sqrt{z_2}, \sqrt{z_3})$ where $\sqrt{q z_1}$ denotes a randomly selected square root of the quadratic residue $q_1 \cdot z_1 \bmod n_1$; and for $i = 2, 3$ $\sqrt{z_i}$ denotes a randomly selected square root of $z_i \bmod n_i$}

6. Send V $n_1, n_2, n_3, q_1, q_2, q_3, G'$, and the signature of the triplets composing σ.

   {**Comment:** Note that the edges of G' are labelled with triples, not with colors!}

Instructions for V

1. Verify that n_1, n_2, and n_3 are not even and not integer powers. Verify that G' is a proper labelling of G. That is, each node u has assigned a triplet (v_1, v_2, v_3) such that $v_i \in Z_{n_i}^{+1}$ for $i = 1, 2, 3$.

2. Break σ into triplets, verify that for each edge you received a signature of some type for each of its $8k$ triplets.

3. If all the above verifications have been successfully made, accept that G is 3-colorable.

3.2   A Rough Idea of why (P,V) is a Single-Theorem Non-Interactive ZKPS

First notice that, the communication is mono-directional: From P to V. Then let us convince ourselves that the statement of Remark 1 really holds without loss of generality. In our context, WLOG means with overwhelming probability.

If G has a edges, our protocol assumes σ to consist of $8 \cdot k \cdot a$ triplets in $Z_{n_1}^{+1} \times Z_{n_2}^{+1} \times Z_{n_3}^{+1}$. Such a string σ is easily obtainable from a (not too much larger) random string p. Consider p to be the concatentation of k-bit strings grouped into triplets

$$p = (p_1, p_2, p_3)(p_4, p_5, p_6) \cdots$$

Then obtain σ by "purging" p. That is, obtain σ from p by discarding all triplets not in $Z_{n_1}^{+1} \times Z_{n_2}^{+1} \times Z_{n_3}^{+1}$. We now argue that p is not much longer than σ. Let n be either n_1 or n_2 or n_3. Now a random k-bit integer (with possible leading 0's) is less than n with probability $\geq \frac{1}{3}$; a random integer less than n belongs to Z_n^* with probability $\geq \frac{1}{2}$; a random element of Z_n^* belongs to Z_n^{+1} with probability $\geq \frac{1}{2}$. Thus, we expect that at least 1 in 64 of the triplets of p not to be discarded.

Now let us consider the question of V's running time. V can verify in poly-time whether $n_i = x^\alpha$ (where x, α integers; $\alpha > 1$) as only values $1, \cdots, \log n_i$ should be tried for α and binary search can be performed for finding x, if it exists. All other steps of V are even easier.

Now let us give some indication that (P,V) constitute a single-theorem non-interactive ZKPS.

Completeness: Assuming that σ is already consiting of triplets in $Z_{n_1}^{+1} \times Z_{n_2}^{+1} \times Z_{n_3}^{+1}$, if P operates correctly, V will be satisfied with probability 1.

Soundness: If the verification step 1 is successfully passed, by fact 1, there must be $\geq 2 \sim$ equivalence classes in each $Z_{n_i}^{+1}$ (exactly two if P honestly chooses all the n_i's in $Z_2(k)$).

Thus, if we define two of our triplets (z_1, z_2, z_3) (w_1, w_2, w_3) to be equivalent if $z_i w_i \bmod n_i$ is a quadratic residue for $i = 1, 2, 3$, we obtain ≥ 8 equivalence classes among the triplets (exactly 8 if P is honest).

To exhibit a signature of a given type for a triplet, essentially means to put the triplet in one of ≤ 8 possible "drawers". (there are 8 types of signatues, but they may not be mutually exclusive; thus two drawers may be equal). Moreover, it is easy to see that if two triplets are put in the same drawer, they must belong to the same equivalence class.

As σ is randomly selected, each of its triplets in $Z_{n_1}^{+1} \times Z_{n_2}^{+1} \times Z_{n_3}^{+1}$ is equally likely to belong to any of the ≥ 8 equally-numerous equivalence classes. However, since if there were > 8 classes, there would be (by fact 1) at least 16, the fact that all triplets can be fit in ≤ 8 drawers, "probabilistically proves" several facts:

1. There are exactly 8 equivalence classes among the triplets and exactly 8 distinct drawers.

2. The n_i's are product of two distinct prime powers.

3. $Q_{n_1}(q_1) = Q_{n_2}(q_2) = Q_{n_3}(q_3) = 1$

4. $Q_{n_1}(q_1) + Q_{n_2}(q_2) + Q_{n_3}(q_3) = 2$
That is, (a_1, a_2, a_3) is a proper color (i.e., properly encodes a color: Either 1,2, or 3).

5. That (b_1, b_2, b_3) is a proper color.

6. That (a_1, a_2, a_3) and (b_1, b_12, b_3) are different colors. Else drawer 6 and drawer 0 would be the same.

Item 6 being true for all edges in G' implies that G is 3-colorable which is what was to be proven.

Zero-Knowledgeness

Let us specify the simulating machine M that, under the QRA, generates a pair $(\sigma,$ proof) with the "right odds" on input G (without any coloring!)

Instructions for M

1. Randomly select $n_1, n_2, n_3, \in Z_2(k)$ together with their prime factorization.

2. Randomly select q_1, q_2, q_3 so that $Q_{n_1}(q_1) = Q_{n_1}(q_2) = Q_{n_3}(q_3) = 0$

3. For each node v of G, label v with a triplet $(v_1, v_2, v_3) \in Z^*_{n_1} \times Z^*_{n_2} \times Z^*_{n_3}$ such that $Q_{N_1}(v_1) = Q_{n_2}(v_2) = Q_{n_3}(v_3) = 0$. Call G' the so labelled graph.

4. Construct $\sigma = (\sigma_1, \sigma_2, \sigma_3)(\sigma_4, \sigma_5, \sigma_6) \cdots$, such that each triplet $(\sigma_{3j+1}, \sigma_{3j+2}, \sigma_{3j+3})$ is randomly selected so that $Q_{n_i}(\sigma_{3j+i}) = 0$ for $i = 1, 2, 3$.
{**Remark:** Also in the simulation we only deal with already 11purged strings". It is not hard to see that M could also handle generating "unpurged strings".}

5. For each edge (a, b) of G' and each of its assigned $8k$ triplets (z_1, z_2, z_3), choose an integer i at random between 0 and 7, and compute a signature of type i.
{**Comment:** By using the prime factorization of the n_i.}

6. Output $\sigma, n_1, n_2, n_3, q_1, q_2, q_3, G'$, and the computed signatures.

We now informally argue that M is a good simulator for the view of V. Essentially, this is so because efficiently detecting that the triplets of σ are not randomly and independently drawn from the space $Z^{+1}_{n_1} \times Z^{+1}_{n_2} \times Z^{+1}_{n_3}$ is tantamount as violating the QRA (to be explained in the final paper). For the same reason, it cannot be detected efficiently that G' is an illegal labelling or that q_1, q_2, q_3 are squares mod, respectively, n_1, n_2, n_3. Given that, the distribution of the various types of signature looks "perfect".

{**Remark:** the reader is encouraged to verify that if (P,V) uses part of the used σ to show that another graph is 3-colorable, then extra knowledge would leek. For instance that there exists 3-coloring of G and H in which nodes v_1 and v_2 in H respectively have the same clolors as nodes w_1 and w_2 in G.)

4 Non-Interactive ZKPS

The Single-Theorem Non-Interactive ZKPS of Section 3 has a limited applicability. This is best illustrated in terms of our conceptual scenario where the prover P is leaving for a trip. It is unlikely that for each theorem T that P finds, a string σ_T comes from the sky "devoted" to T and is presented to (is read by) both P and V. It is instead more probable, that P and V have witnessed or generated (i.e., by flipping a coin), the same common random event of "size n" when they were together.

However, the Proof System of Section 3 will enable P to subsequently prove in Zero-Knowledge to V only a single theorem of size, smaller than n. He is out of luck should he discover the proofs of many theorems or of a theorem of bigger size.

This drawback is eliminated by the following notion of non-interactive ZKPS.

Our formal definition is slightly oriented towards our solution. Namely, at the beginning, independently of the theorems T_i's we care about, we let the prover choose a *random* theorem T and use the common string σ to compute a string y_o, proving that T is true.

Subsequently, for each *desired* and important theorem T_i, the prover will produce a proof y_i. The correctness of y_i is checked by the verifier, not only on input T_i and σ but also y_o, the proof of the initial, random theorem.

This somewhat awkward mechanics, justified by the technical needs of our proof, does not change the rules of the game of our conceptual scenario in any essential way. In fact, notice in the definition that every important theorem is proven ALONE. That is, P is able to select the zero-knowledge proof of each important theorem INDEPENDENTLY from the proofs or the statements of every other important theorem. In other words, P may have forgotten what important theorems he has already proved, and does not yet know what other important theorems he will discover: A true mathematician!

Only the proof, y_o, of the initial random theorem needs to be remembered. This random theorem and its proof are selected before and independently of every important theorem.

Definition 4.1   A Non-Interactive ZKPS is a pair (P, V) where P is a pair, (P_0, P_1), of Probabilistic Turing Machines and $V(\cdot, \cdot, \cdot, \cdot)$ is a deterministic algorithm running in time polynomial in the length of its first input, such that:

1. **(Completeness)** For all polynomials P, Q, and for all $(x_1, x_2, \ldots, x_{Q(n)}) \in (3COL_{P(n)})^{Q(n)}$

$$
Pr(\, \sigma \leftarrow \{0, 1\}^{n^{O(1)}};
$$
$$
y_O \leftarrow A_0(\sigma);
$$
$$
y_1 \leftarrow A_1(\sigma, x_1, y_0);
$$
$$
\vdots \qquad\qquad \vdots
$$
$$
y_{Q(n)} \leftarrow A_1(\sigma, x_{Q(n)}, y_0):
$$
$$
\bigwedge_{j=1}^{Q(n)} B(x_j, y_j, y_0, \sigma) = 1
$$
$$
) > 1 - n^{-O(1)}.
$$

2. **(Soundness)** For all polynomials P, Q, for all $(x_1, x_2, \ldots x_{Q(n)}) \notin (3COL_{P(n)})^{Q(n)}$ and for each $A' = (A'_0, , A'_1)$

$$
Pr(\, \sigma \leftarrow \{0, 1\}^{n^{O(1)}};
$$
$$
y_O \leftarrow A'_0(\sigma);
$$
$$
y_1 \leftarrow A'_1(\sigma, x_1, y_0);
$$
$$
\vdots \qquad\qquad \vdots
$$
$$
y_{Q(n)} \leftarrow A'_1(\sigma, x_{Q(n)}, y_0):
$$
$$
\bigwedge_{j=1}^{Q(n)} B(x_j, y_j, y_0, \sigma) = 1
$$
$$
) < n^{-O(1)}.
$$

3. **(Zero-Knowledge)** For each polynomial Q, the family of random variables $V = \{V(x_1, \ldots, x_{Q(n)})\}$, where

$$V(x_1, \ldots, x_{Q(n)}) =$$

$$\{ \quad \sigma \leftarrow \{0,1\}^{n^{O(1)}};$$

$$y_O \leftarrow A_0(\sigma);$$

$$y_1 \leftarrow A_1(\sigma, x_1, y_0);$$

$$\vdots \qquad\qquad \vdots$$

$$y_{Q(n)} \leftarrow A_1(\sigma, x_{Q(n)}, y_0):$$

$$(\sigma, y_0, y_1, \ldots, y_{Q(n)}$$

$$\}$$

is approximable over $\bigcup_n (3COL)^{Q(n)}$.

4.1 The Proof System (P,V)

Below *Gen* is a cryptographically strong pseudo-random bits generator [RM] [Yl. (Not to increase our assumptions, *Gen* could be the generator suggested in [BBS] that is based on quadratic residuosity , actually on factoring as shown in [ACGS].)

Common Inputs to P and V

A random string $\sigma \circ p$, a security parameter k, a sequence of 4-colorable graphs $G_1, G_2, \cdots$

Stage 1

P Chooses at random $n \in Z_3(k)$ and non-interactively, in zero-knowledge proves to V that indeed $n \in Z_3(k)$. P does so as in Section 3 by reducing the statement "$n \in Z_3(k)$" to the 3-colorability of an auxiliary graph H. P proves that H is 3-colorable by only using σ, the first segment of the common random string. **Remark:** This is another example of the fact that proving a more general theorem is easier. Here we only needed to prove membership in $Z_3(k)$. However, we were not able to find a direct non-interactive zero-knowledge proof of it. (What is easy by using a guaranteed random string, is proving membership in $Z_2(k)$ by sampling. Namely, by fact 1, to prove that $n \in Z_2(k)$ is enough to show that half of the elements in Z_n^{+1} are quadratic residues mod n). Only when we thought of generalizing the problem of membership in $Z_3(k)$ to the more general 3-colorability problem, we succeeded in proving the desired result.

Stage 2

For each input graph, $G \in 4 - COL_k$, G_1 P's and V's programs are as follows:

Instructions for P

1. Number the equivalence classes of Z_n^{+1} 1 through 4.

2. Find a 4-coloring for G.

3. For any vertex v in G, if v is colored i, randomly choose an element e_v, in class i and label v with e_v. Call G' the so labeled graph.

4. Send G' to V.

5. For each edge (u, v) in G, randomly choose $y_{uv} \in Z_n^{+1}$ so that $e_u \cdot e_v \cdot y_{uv}$ mod+n is a square, compute a random square root of it, x_{uv} and send y_{uv} and x_{uv} to V.

6. for each y_{uv} do: Output the next k^h bits of *Gen* on input p (here h is a constant to be determined later); group these bits into consecutive *blocks* of k bits each; consider all blocks that represent elements in Z_n^{+1}; for each block representing a square mod n, send a random square root of it to V; for each block that is in the same $\sim$ equivalence class as y_{uv}, send V a square root of its product with y_{uv}.

Instructions for V

1. Check that all labels of G are Jacobi symbol 1 elements of Z_n^*.

2. For all edges (u, v), check that x_{uv} is a square root of $e_u \cdot e_v \cdot y_{uv}$ mod n

3. For each y_{uv}, check to have received correcrt square roots for more than $\frac{k^h}{5}$ of its associated blocks and for more than $\frac{k^h}{5}$ other blocks "times" y_{uv}.

4. If all checks are passed "accept" that G is 4-colorable.

4.2   The Zero-Knowledgeness of (P,V)

We now *very informally* argue that (P,V) is a non-interactive ZKPS.

First notice that the communication is mono-directional: from P to V. Second that all of V's computation can be done in probabilistic polynomial time.

Completeness

If G is 4-colorable and P and V follow their instructions, V will accept with probability essentially 1. The reader can easily derive a proof of it. (Reading the ideas of the proof about the soundness property may help.)

Soundness

Since n has passed stage 1 successfully, with probability essentially 1 it is the product of three distinct primes[1]. (All modular operations mentioned are mod n)

Second, with probability essentially equal to 1, the sequence of blocks associated with each y_{uv} contains more than $\frac{k^h}{5}$ elements in each of the 4 equivalence classes. In fact, a random sequence of Jacobi symbol 1 elements mod n would "visit" each class with probability 1/4. This is also true for the output of *Gen* since it is poly-indistinguishable from a truly random sequence[2] If $\frac{k^h}{5}$ blocks "times" y_{uv} have square roots mod n, then they all belong to the same equivalence class as y_{uv}. Moreover, if another $\frac{k^h}{5}$ elements have square roots mod n by themselves, then, with probability essentially 1, y_{uv} is a non-square mod n. (Otherwise $\frac{2 \cdot k^h}{5}$ blocks would be squares mod n rather than the expected $\frac{k^h}{4}$.) Finally, if y_{uv} is a non-square mod n, then the edge (u,v) is properly colored; that, is, e_u and e_v belong to different classes. In fact, since $e_u \cdot e_v \cdot y_{uv}$ has a square root, $(e_u \cdot e_v)$ belongs to the same class as y_{uv}; and if e_u, and e_v, belonged to the same class, their product would be a square and so would y_{uv}. Each edge being correctly colored, so is G.

Zero-Knowledgeness

We must now argue that the above proof system is zero-knowledge. That is, that there exists an efficient simulator that, given any sequence of 4-colorable graphs (but not their colorings!), a probability distribution on the pairs (σ, proof,) that is computationally indistinguishable from the one $V^{prime'}$ would "see" if listening to P. What V' would see is stage 1 and in stage 2, messages from P about each input graph. The proof of zero knowledge is quite delicate. We restrict ourselves to merely outlining its high level steps, without further details. We do point out, though, which parts of the proof are easy and which are hard.

4.2.1 The Simulation of Stage 1

The first message a verifier receives from P is a random member of $Z_3(k)$. The simulating machine M, instead, randomly generates two primes and multiplies

---

1. n is or is not product of 3 primes wheter or not it passed the first stage; but you know what I mean and it is easier to read!

2. A subtle point: this is so even if in our application *Gen*'s seed, p, is not secret. In fact, all efficiently checkable statistical properties hold for *Gen*'s output if the random seed is kept secret, and the particular statistical property of interest to us cannot "disappear" if the seed is made public!

them together to generate a random member of $Z_2(k)$. So far, because of the 2or3A, this will fool any polynomially-bounded judge.

Then M in a standard way constructs a graph H that is S-colorable if and only if $n \in Z_3(k)$.

Since the latter statement is false, H *will not* be 3-colorable. Nonetheless, M follows the protocol described in Section 3 where H is the input graph.

Given the 2or3A, the distribution so obtained is polynomial-time indistinguishable from random a correct execution of Stage 1 (including the choice of σ)!

This may appear paradoxical,. How can M generate such an "indistinguishable" distribution on input $n \in Z_2(k)$, if, after all, P's message (which is an integral part of V's view) was proving that $n \in Z_3(k) \neq Z_2(k)$?

The paradox disappears when we consider that P's message was convincing since the random choice of σ was not under its control. In the simulation, instead, M chooses σ![3]

In fact, in stage 2, the simulator will label all vertices of any graph G by squares mod n ($\in C_2(k)$). That is, to each vertex u he associates a randomly selected square e_u. (No efficient judge may reject this labelling, since the hardness of quadratic residuosity implied by our assumption.) Then, to each edge (u, v), he associates a randomly selected square y_{uv}. Now the simulator correctly runs *Gen* on its random seed to obtain a pseudo-random k^h-long block sequence. Roughly half of the elements of Jacobi symbol 1 of these blocks will be squares mod n, as n is the product of 2 primes. For a randomly selected half of them the simulator will extract a square root, which it can easily done as he chose n in factored form. For each block in the remaining half, he extracts a square root of its product with y_{uv}. Again this will fool the judge as he cannot efficiently decide quadratic residuosity.

Notice that faking the proof of a single theorem (membership in Z_3^k) allowes us to fake the proof of an arbitrary number of other theorems. This is one of the reasons to choose the computational difficulty of distinguishing products of 2 primes from products of 3 primes.

---

3. It should be noted where the 2or3A comes into play. Let L is a poly-time language, $x \notin L$ and G is a graph 3-colorable if and only if $x \in L$. Let M, or input G, follow the protocol in Section 3 to (necessarily) *fake* P's proof that G is 3-colorable.

Such proof will not fool a poly-time judge not because the quadratic-residousity labeling would give away that the graph is not 3-colored; but because he can easily check that $x \notin L$ (and thus that the underlying graph, without any labeling, is not 3-colorable).

The 2or3A guarantees that this easy check is not available to a poly-time judge. In the final paper we essentially show that there are no other easy checks.

5 A No-Longer Long-Standing Open Problem

One of the most beautiful gifts of complexity-based cryptography is the notion of a public-key cryptosystem. As proposed by Diffie and Hellman [DH], each user U publicizes a string P_U and keeps secret an associated string S_U. Another user, to secretely send a message m to U, computes $y = E(P_U, m)$ and sends y; upon receiving y, U retrieves m by computing $D(S_U, y)$; here E and D are polynomial-time algorithms chosen so that it will be infeasible, for any other user, to compute m from y.

Notice that in this set-up any other user is thought to be a "passive" adversary who tries to retrieve m by computing solely on inputs y and P_U. This is indeed a mild type of adversary and other types of attacks have been considered in the literature. It is widely believed that the strongest type of attack among all the natural ones is the *chosen-cipher-text attack*. In such an attack, someone tries to break the system by asking and receiving decryptions of ciphertexts of his choices. Rivest has shown that Rabin's scheme (whose breaking is, for a passive adversary, as hard as factoring if the messages are uniformly selected strings of a given length) is easily vulnerable to such an attack. Indeed, this is an attack feasible to any employee who works at the decoding equipment of, say, a large bank. The power by this attack is very well exemplified by an elegant scheme of Rabin [R] that is as secure as factoring in the passive adversary model but is easily broken by chosen-ciphertext attack. Since observing this phenomenon, people tried to design cryptosystems invulnerable to such attacks, but in vain. A positive answer has been found [GMT] only allowing interaction, during the encryption process, between legal sender and legal receiver. However, for the standard (non-interactive) Diffie-and-Hellman model, the existence of a cryptosystem invulnerable to chosen ciphertext attack has been an open problem since 1978.

Non-interactive zero-knowledge proofs allow us to finally solve this problem. The essence of our solution (instead of its details) is informally described as follows. Instead of sending U an encryption, y, of a message m, one is required to send two strings: y and and σ, where σ is a *zero-knowledge and non-interactive proof that the sender knows the decoding of y*. The "decoding equipment" (read: the decoding function) checks that σ is convincing and, if so, outputs m, the decoding of y; Otherwise, it outputs nothing. Notice that, now, being able to use the decoding equipment provably is of no advantage! In fact, only when we feed it with ciphertexts whose decoding we can prove we know, does the decoding equipment output these decodings! In other words, the decoding equipment can only be used to output what we already know. A detailed discussion of this powerful application will appear in the final paper.

(A formal setting and the proof require some care. For instance, the decoding equipment may be used as an oracle to check whether a given string σ is a "correct proof of knowledge". Thus, in particular, one should prove that such an oracle cannot help. In the final paper we will essentially show that if one can generate a legal (y, σ) pair without having m as an input, then one can easily decrypt all messages on input y and P_U only.)

6 Improvements

It has very often been the case in cryptography that new notions and results have been first obtained under a specific intractability assumption. This is so because one can exploit the additional properties of a specific, candidate intractable problem. Number theory has always played a leading role as a basis of new cryptographic concepts. For instance, cryptographically strong pseudo-random number generators were first exhibited based on the computational difficulty of the discrete logarithm problem [BM]. Only later a construction was presented based on a more general assumption: the existence of one-way permutations [Y]. Finally it has been established that cryptographically strong pseudo-random number generation is possible if and only if one-way functions exist [L].

Non-interactive ZKPS have been introduced and still are based on the intractability of algebraic problems. Very recently, our intractability assumption has been relaxed. DeSantis, Micali, and Persiano have exhibited non-interactive ZKPS based only on the quadriatic residensity assumption.

We hope this new notion will be given a sounder foundation; hopefully by basing it on the existence of any general trap-door or one-way function.

7 References

[ACGS] W. Alexi, B. Chor, O. Goldreich, and C. Schnorr *RSA/Rabin Bits Are* $1/2 + 1/_{poly}(\log N)$ *Secure*, To appear SIAM J. on Computing.

[B1] M. Blum, *Coin Flipping by Telephone*, IEEE COMPCON 1982, pp. 133-137.

[B2] M. Blum, unpublished manuscript

[BBS] M. Blum, L. Blum and M. Shub,*A simple and secure pseudo-randomnumber generator*,SIAM Journal of Computing, 1986

[BGGHMR] M. Ben-Or, O. Goldreich, S. Goldwasser, J. Hastad, S. Micali, and P. Rogaway, to appear

[BH] R. Boppana, J. Hastad and S. Zachos, *Interactive Proofs Systems for CO-NP Imply Polynomial Time Hierarchy Collapse*, In preperation.

[BM] M. Blum and S. Micali, *How To Generate Sequences Of Cryptographically Strong Pseudo-Random Bits*, SIAM J. on Computing, Vol. 13, Nov 1984, pp. 850-864

[DH] Diffie, W., and M.E. Hellman, *New Directions in Cryptography*, IEEE Trans. on Inform. Theory,

[F] L. Fortnow, *The Complecity of Perfect Zero-Knowledge*, Proc. 19th ann. Symp. on Theory of Computing, New York, 1987.

[FFS] Feige, Fiat and A. Shamir, *Zero-knowledge proofs of identity*, Proceedings of the 19th Annual ACM Symp. on Theory of Computing, 1987, pp. 210-217

[GM] S. Goldwasser, and S. Micali, *Probabilistic Encryption*, JCSS Vol. 28, No. 2, April 1984.

[GMR] S. Goldwasser, S. Micali and C. Rackoff, *The Knowledge Complexity of Interactive Proof-Systems*, To appear SIAM J. on Computing (manuscript available from authors).

[GoMiRi] S. Goldwasser, S. Micali, and R. Rivest, *A Digital Signature Scheme Secure Against Adaptive, Chosen Cyphertext Attack* To appear in SIAM J. on Computing (available from authors)

[GMT] S. Goldwasser, S. Micali, and P. Tong, *Why and how to establish a perivate code in a public network*, Proc. 23rd Symp. on Foundations of Computer Science, Chicago, Ill., 1982

[GMW] O. Goldreich, S. Micali and A. Wigderson, *Proofs that Yield Nothing but their Validity and a Methodology of Cryptographic Design*, Proc. of FOCS 1986.

[GMW2] O. Goldreich, S. Micali and A. Wigderson, *How to Play Any Mental Game*, Proceedings of the 19th Annual ACM Symp. on Theory of Computing, 1987, pp. 218-229.

[GS] S. Goldwasser and M. Sipser, *Private Coins versus Public Coins in Interactive Proof Systems*, Proceedings of the 18th Annual ACM Sympl on Theory of Computing, 1986, pp. 59-68.

[R] M. Rabin, *Digitalized signatures and public-key functions as intractable as factorization*, MIT/LCS/TR-212, Technical report MIT, 1978

[Y] A.Yao, *Theory and Application of Trapdoor Functions*, Proc. of 23rd FOCS, IEEE, Nov., 1982, pp. 80-91.

Completeness Theorems for Non-Cryptographic Fault-Tolerant Distributed Computation

This chapter reproduces the contents of the paper "Completeness Theorems for Non-Cryptographic Fault-Tolerant Distributed Computation," which appeared in the proceedings of the *20th Annual ACM Symposium on Theory of Computing*, pp. 1–10, 1988.

This influential work of Michael Ben-Or, Shafi Goldwasser, and Avi Wigderson obtained general results similar to those of Chapter 13, except that it uses no intractability assumptions. Instead this work presumes the existence of private channels between each pair of parties (and a larger percentage of honest parties).

Completeness Theorems for Non-Cryptographic Fault-Tolerant Distributed Computation (Extended Abstract)

Michael Ben-Or[*] (Hebrew University),
Shafi Goldwasser[†] (MIT),
Avi Wigderson[‡] (Hebrew University)

Abstract

Every function of n inputs can be efficiently computed by a complete network of n processors in such a way that:

1. If no faults occur, no set of size $t < n/2$ of players gets any additional information (other than the function value),

*Supported by Alon Fellowship.
†Supported in part by NSF grant 865727-CCR, ARO grant DAAL03-86-K-017, and US-Israel BSF grant 86-00301, Jerusalem, Israel.
‡Supported by Alon Fellowship.

2. Even if Byzantine faults are allowed, no set of size $t < n/3$ can either disrupt the computation or get additional information.

Furthermore, the above bounds on t are tight!

Introduction

The rapid development of distributed systems raised the natural question of what tasks can be performed by them (especially when faults occur). A large body of literature over the past ten years addressed this question. There are two approaches to this question, depending on whether a limit on the computational power of processors is assumed or not.

The cryptographic approach, inaugurated by Difiie and Hellman [DH], assumes the players are computationally bounded, and further assumes the existence of certain (one-way) functions, that can be computed but not inverted by the player.

This simple assumption was postulated in [DH] in order to achieve the basic task of secure message exchange between two of the processors, but turned out to be universal! In subsequent years ingenious protocols based on the same assumption were given for increasingly harder tasks such as contract signing, secret exchange, joint coin flipping, voting and playing Poker. These results culminated, through the definition of zero-knowledge proofs [GMR], their existence for NP-complete problems [GMW1] in completeness theorems for two-party [Y1] and multi-party [GMW2] cryptographic distributed computation. In particular the results of Goldreich, Micali and Wigderson in [GMW2] were the main inspiration to our work. They show, that if (non-uniform) one way functions exist then every (probabilistic) function of n inputs can be computed by n computationally bounded processors in such a way that: (1) If no faults occur, no subset of the players can compute any additional information, and (2) Even if Byzantine faults are allowed, no set of size $t < n/2$ can either disrupt the computation or compute additional information.

The non-Cryptographic (or information-theoretic) approach does not limit the computational power of the processors. Here, the notion of privacy is much stronger - for a piece of data to be unknown to a set of players it does not suffice that they cannot compute it within a certain time bound from what they know, but simply that it cannot be computed at all!

To facilitate the basic primitive of secret message exchange between a pair of players, we have secure channels. (For an excellent source of results and problems in the case no secure channels exist, see [BL]). Unlike the cryptographic case, very little was known about the capabilities of this model. Two main basic problems were studied and solved (in the synchronous case): Byzantine agreement [LPS, DS, . . .] and collective coin flipping [Y2].

This paper provides a full understanding of the power and limits of this model, by proving a few completeness theorems. Comparing these results to the cryptographic case of [GMW2], one gets the impression that one-way functions are "more powerful" than secure channels. This should not be surprising, if one considers the case of $n = 2$. Clearly, here a secure channel is useless, and indeed two (non-faulty) players can compute the OR function of their bits using cryptography, while the reader can convince herself (it will be proven later) that any protocol will leak information in the information-theoretic sense. The lower bounds we provide show that the same phenomenon is true for any value of n. A similar situation arises in the Byzantine case where, using cryptography one can allow $t < n/2$ faulty players, but in the non-Cryptographic case one must have $t < n/3$.

As happened in the cryptographic case, the protocols are based on a new method for computing with shared secrets. Our constructions are based on Algebraic Coding Theory, particularly the use of generalized BCM codes.

It is important to stress here that our main protocols require only a polynomial amount of work from the players. (In fact, they are efficient enough to be practical!). Putting no bound on the computational power serves only to allow the most stringent definition of privacy and the most liberal definition of faultiness, both of which we can handle.

Essentially the same results we obtain here were independently discovered by Chaum, Crepeau and Damgard [CCD]. We briefly point out the small differences of this work from ours. The simple case of no faults is almost identical. Their solution in the case of Byzantine faults is elementary and requires no error correcting codes. The error correction is achieved using a clever scheme of zero knowledge proofs. This has two consequences: They have to allow an exponentially small error probability for both correctness and privacy (we can guarantee them with no errors), and the frequent zero knowledge proofs increase the complexity of their protocols. In the solution of [CCD] the simulation is of Boolean operations while our solution allows direct simulation of arithmetic operations in large finite fields. Thus, for example, computing the product of two n bit numbers using [CCD] calls for $O(\log n)$ communication rounds. This can be done in $O(1)$ rounds using our solution.

We mention that the above results already found application in the new, constant expected number of rounds protocol for Byzantine agreement of Feldman and Micali [FM].

We proceed to define the model, state the results and prove them. In the full paper we mention generalizations and extensions of our results to other tasks (playing games rather than computing functions), to other model parameters (synchrony, communication networks) and other complexity measures (number of rounds).

Definitions and Results

For this abstract, we define the model and state the results on an intuitive level. Since even the formal definition of the notions of privacy and resiliency are non-trivial, we give them explicitly in an appendix.

The model of computation is a complete synchronous network of n processors. The pairwise communication channels between players are secure, i.e. they cannot be read or tempered with by other players. In one round of computation each of the players can do an arbitrary amount of local computation, send a message to each of the players, and read all messages that were sent to it at this round.

We shall be interested in the computational power of this model when imposing privacy and fault tolerance requirements. For simplicity, we restrict ourselves to the computation of (probabilistic) functions f from n inputs to n outputs. We assume that player i holds the i-th input at the start of computation, and should obtain the i-th output at the end, but nothing else.

A protocol for computing a function is a specification of n programs, one for each of the players. We distinguish two kinds of faults: "Gossip" and "Byzantine". In the first, faulty processors send messages according to their predetermined programs, but try to learn as much as they can by sharing the information they received. In the second, they can use totally different programs, collaborating to acquire more information of even sabotage the computation.

A protocol is *t-private* if any set of at most t players cannot compute after the protocol more than they could jointly compute solely from their set of private inputs and outputs.

A protocol is *t-resilient* if no set of t or less players can influence the correctness of the outputs of the remaining players. For this to make sense, the function definition should be extended to specify what it is if some players neglect to give their inputs or are caught cheating (see appendix).

We can now state the main results of this paper.

Theorem 1   For every (probabilistic) function f and $t < n/2$ there exists a t-private protocol.

Theorem 2　There are functions for which there are no $n/2$-private protocols.

Theorem 3　For every probabilistic function and every $t < n/3$ there exists a protocol that is both t-resilient and t-private.

Theorem 4　There are functions for which there is no $n/3$-resilient protocol.

Proof of Theorem 1

Let $P_0, \ldots, P_{n-l}$ be a set of players, and let $n \geq 2t + 1$. Let F be the function which this set of players wants to compute t-privately, where each player holds some input variables to the function F. Let E be some fixed finite field E, with $|E| > n$. Without loss of generality we may assume that all inputs are elements from E and that F is some polynomial (in the input variables) over E, and that we are given some arithmetic circuit computing $|F|$, using the operations $+$, $\times$ and constants from E.

To simplify our explanation we divide the computation into three stages.

Stage I: The input stage, where each player will enter his input variables to the computation using a secret sharing procedure.

Stage II: The computation stage, where the players will simulate the circuit computing F, gate by gate, keeping the value of each computed gate as secret shared by all players.

Stage III: The final stage, where the secret shares of the final value of F are revealed to one or all of the players.

Stages I and III are very simple and we describe them below, and delay the details of the computation stage to the next section.

The Input Stage

Let $(\alpha_0, \ldots, \alpha_{n-1}$ be some n disbinct non zero points in our field E. (This is why we need $|E| > n$.) Each player holding some input $s \in E$, introduces the input to the computation by selecting t random elements $a_i \in E$, for $i = 1, \ldots, t$, setting

$$f(x) = s + a_1 x + \cdots + a_t x^t$$

and sending to each player P_i the value $s_i = f(\alpha_i)$.

As in Shamir's [Sh] secret sharing scheme, the sequence $(s_0, \ldots, s_{n-1})$ is a sequence of t-wise independent random variables uniformly distributed over E, thus the value of the input is completely independent from the shares $\{s_i\}$ that are given to any set of t player that does not include the player holding the secret.

The Final Stage

To keep the t-privacy condition, we will make sure that the set of messages received by any set of t players will be completely independent from all the inputs. During the whole computation each gate which evaluates to some $s \in E$, will be "evaluated" by the players by sharing the secret value of s using a completely independent from all the inputs, random polynomial $f(x)$ of degree t, with the only restriction that $f(0) = s$. In particular at the end of the computation we will have the value of F shared among the players in a similar manner. If we want to let just one player know the output value, all the players send their shares to that particular player. This player can compute the interpolation polynomial $f(x)$ and use its free coefficient as the result.

Note that there is a one-to-one correspondence between the set of all shares and the coefficients of the polynomial $f(x)$. Since all the coefficients of $f(x)$, except for its free coefficient, are uniform random variables that are independent of the inputs, the set of all shares does not contain any information about the inputs that does not follow from the value of $f(0)$.

The Computation Stage

Let $a, b \in E$ be two secrets that are shared using the polynomials $f(x)$, $g(r)$ respectively, and let $c \in E$, $c \neq 0$ be some constant. It is enough to show how one can "compute" $c \cdot a$, $a + b$, and $a \cdot b$.

The two linear operations are simple and for their evaluation we do not need any communication between the players. This is because if $f(x)$ and $g(x)$ encode a and b, then the polynomials $h(x) = c \cdot f(x)$ and $k(x) = f(x) + g(x)$ encode $c \cdot a$, $a + b$ respectively. Thus to compute for example $a + b$, each player P_i holding $f(\alpha_i)$, and $g(\alpha_1)$ can compute $k(\alpha_i) = f(\alpha_i) + g(\alpha_i)$. Likewise, since c is a known constant P_i can compute $h(\alpha_i) = c \cdot f(\alpha_i)$. Furthermore, $h(x)$ is random if only $f(x)$ was, and $k(x)$ is random if only one of $f(x)$ or $g(x)$ was.

As a corollary we immediately have

Lemma (Linear Functional) For any t, $(t \leq n - 1)$, and any linear functional

$$F(x_0, \ldots, x_{n-1}) = a_0 x_0 + \cdots + a_{n-1} x_{n-1}$$

where each P_i has input x_i and the a_i are known constants, can be computed t-privately.

From the lemma we have

Corollary   (Matrix Multiplication) Let A be a constant $n \times n$ matrix, and let each P_i have an input variable x_i. Let $X = (x_0, \ldots, x_{n-1})$ and define $Y = (y_1, \ldots, y_n)$ by

$$Y = X \cdot A,$$

then for any t, $(t \leq n - l)$, we can t-privately compute the vector Y such that the only information given to P_i will be the value of Y_i, for $i = 0, \ldots, n - l$.

Proof   Matrix multiplication is just the evaluation of n linear functionals. By the Lemma, we can compute each linear functional Y_i independently, and reveal the outcome only to P_i.   ■

The Multiplication Step

The multiplication step is only a bit harder. Let a and b be encoded by $f(x)$ and $g(x)$ as above. We now assume that $n \geq 2t + 1$. Note that the free coefficient, of the polynomial $h(x) = f(x)g(x)$ is $a \cdot b$. There are two problems with using $h(x)$ to encode the product of a times b. The first, and obvious one, is that the degree of $h(x)$ is $2t$ instead of t. While this poses no problem with interpolating $h(x)$ from its n pieces since $n \geq 2t + 1$, it is clear that further multiplications will raise the degree, and once the degree passes n we will not have enough points for the interpolation. The second problem is more subtle. $h(x)$ is not a *random* polynomial of degree $2t$ (ignoring of course the free coefficient). For example, $h(x)$, as a product of two polynomials, cannot be irreducible.

To overcome these two problems we will, in one step, randomize the coefficients of $h(x)$, and reduce its degree while keeping the free coefficient unchanged. We first describe the degree reduction procedure and then combine it with the randomization of the coefficients.

The Degree Reduction Step
Let

$$h(x) = h_0 + h_1 x + \cdots + h_{2t} x^{2t}$$

and let

$$s_i = h(\alpha_i) = f(\alpha_i)g(\alpha_i),$$

for $i = 0, \ldots, n - 1$ be the "shares" of $h(x)$. Each P_i holds an s_i. Define the truncation of $h(x)$ to be

$$k(x) = h_0 + h_1 x + \cdots + h_t x^t,$$

and $r_i = k(\alpha_i)$ for $i = 1, \ldots, n - 1$.

Claim Let $S = (s_0, \ldots, s_{n-1})$ and $R = (r_0, \ldots, r_{n-1})$ then there is a constant $n \times n$ matrix A such that

$$R = S \cdot A.$$

Proof Let H be the n-vector

$$H = (h_0, \ldots, h_t, \ldots, h_{2t}, 0, \ldots, 0)$$

and let K be the n-vector

$$K = (h_0, \ldots, h_t, 0, \ldots, 0).$$

Let $B = (b_{i,j})$ be the $n \times n$ (Vandermonde) matrix, where $b_{i,j} = \alpha_j^i$ for $i,j = 0, \ldots, n - 1$. Furthermore, let P be the linear projection

$$P(x_0, \ldots, x_{n-1}) = (x_0, \ldots, x_t, 0, \ldots, 0).$$

We have

$$H \cdot B = S$$
$$H \cdot P = K$$

and

$$K \cdot B = R.$$

Since B is not singular (because the α_i-s are distinct) we have

$$S \cdot (B^{-1}PB) = R$$

but $A = B^{-1}PB$ is some fixed constant matrix, proving our claim. ∎

The Randomization Step

As noted above the coefficients of the product polynomial are not completely random, and likewise the coefficients of its truncation $k(x)$ may not be completely random. To randomize the coefficients, each player P_i randomly selects a polynomial $q_i(x)$ of degree $2t$ with a zero free coefficient, and distributes its shares among the players. By a simple generalization of the argument in Shamir's [Sh] scheme, it is easy to see that knowing t values on this polynomial gives no information on the vector of coefficients of the monomials of $x, x^2, \ldots, x^t$ of $q_i(x)$.

Thus instead of using h(x) in our reduction we can use

$$\tilde{h}(x) = h(x) + \sum_{j=0}^{n-1} q_j(x)$$

which satisfies $\tilde{h}(0) = h(0)$ but the other coefficients of x^i, $1 \leq i \leq t$, are completely random. Since each player can evaluate his point $\tilde{s} = \tilde{h}(\alpha_i)$, we can now apply the truncation procedure using the matrix multiplication lemma to arrive at a completely random polynomial $\tilde{k}(x)$ which satisfies both $\deg \tilde{k}(x) = t$, and $\tilde{k}(0) = a \cdots b$, and $k(x)$ is properly shared among all the players.

Thus (omitting many well known details, see [GMW]) we have proved

Theorem 1   For every (probabilistic) function F and $t < n/2$ there exists a t-private protocol.

Remarks

(1) The complexity of computing F t-privately is bounded by a polynomial (in n) factor times the complexity of computing F.

(2) If F can be computed by an arithmetic circuit over some field using unbounded fan-in linear operation and bounded fan-in multiplication, in depth d, then F can be computed t-privately in $O(d)$ rounds of exchange of information.

(3) In our construction we have to reduce the degree of our polynomial only when its degree is about to pass $n - 1$. Thus if $t = O(n^{1-\epsilon})$, for some fixed $\epsilon > 0$, and we start with polynomials of degree t, the players can simulate many steps of the computation before the degree comes close to n, by doing the computation each on their own shares, without any communication(!). When the degree does get close to n, we reduce the degree back to t in one radomizing, degree reducing step.

Two simple examples are:

(a) Any Boolean function $F : \{0, 1\}^n \rightarrow \{0, 1\}$ can be represented as a multilinear polynomial over the field F. Thus if $t = O(n^{1-\epsilon})$ we can compute t-privately, in parallel, all the monomials of F in $O(1)$ number of rounds and then use a big fan-in addition to evaluate F. This procedure may use exponentially long messages but only constant number of rounds.

(b) The Boolean Majority function has a polynomial size $O(\log n)$ depth circuit, and thus for $t = O(n^{1-\epsilon})$, this function can be computed t-privately using only polynomially long messages in constant number of rounds.

For completeness we state the following simple result

Theorem 2 There are functions for which there are no $n/2$-private protocols.

Proof It is easy to see that two players, each holding one input bit, cannot compute the OR function of their bits, without one of them leaking some information. This immediately generalizes to prove the theorem. ∎

Sharing a Secret with Cheaters

Let $n = 3t + 1$ and let $P_O, \ldots, P_{n-1}$ be a set of n players among which we want to share a secret such that

(A) Any set of at most t players does not have any information about the secret and

(B) It is easy to compute the secret from all its shares even if up to t pieces are wrong or missing.

The following scheme achieves both requirements:

Let E be a (finite) field with a primitive n-th root of unity, $\omega \in E$, $\omega^n = 1$ and for all $1 < j < n$, $\omega^j \neq 1$. Without loss of generality we can assume that our secret s is in E.

Pick a random polynomial $f(x) \in E[x]$, of degree t such that $f(0) = s$. That is, set $a_0 = s$ and pick random $a_i \in E$ for $i = 1 \ldots t$ and set

$$f(x) = a_0 + a_1 x + \cdots + a_t x^2.$$

Define the share of P_i, $i = 0 \ldots n - 1$, to be $s_i = f(\omega^i)$. As in [Sh], the s_i-s are t-wise independent random variables that are uniformly distributed over E, and thus our first requirement (A) is met.

Note that setting $a_i = 0$ for $i > t$ makes our secret shares the Discrete Fourier Transform of the sequence $(a_0, \ldots, a_{n-1})$. Let $\hat{f}(x) = s_0 + s_1 x + \cdots + s_{n-1} x^{n-1}$. By the well known formula for the inverse transform

$$a_i = \frac{1}{n} \hat{f}(\omega^{-i})$$

and in particular $\hat{f}(\omega^{-i}) = 0$ for $i = t + 1, \ldots, n - 1$. Explicitly the s_i satisfy the linear equations

$$\sum_{i=0}^{n-1} \omega^{r \cdot i} \cdot s_i = 0 \quad \text{for} \quad r = 1, \ldots, 2t.$$

Thus the polynomial $g(x) = \prod_{i=t+1}^{n-1}(x - \omega^{-i})$ divides the polynomial $\hat{f}(x)$, which in the language of Error Correcting Codes says that the vector $s = (s_0, \ldots, s_{n-1})$ is a codeword in the Cyclic Code of length n generated by $g(x)$. By our choice of $g(x)$, this cyclic code is the well known Generalized Reed-Miller code. Such codes have a simple error correction procedure to correct $\frac{1}{2} \deg g(x) = t$ errors. See for example [PW, page 283).

Verifying a Secret

Assume that player P has distributed a secret in the manner described above. Before entering this shared secret into a computation we wish to verify that the secret shares we are holding are shares of a real secret and not some n random numbers. We want to do so without revealing any information about the secret or any of its shares. This is easily done using the following Zero Knowledge proof technique. We will later show how to verify a secret using a different technique that has absolutely no probability of error. We present this Zero Knowledge technique because it is simpler, and uses fewer rounds of communication.

Simple Verification of a Secret

Let f_0 be the original polynomial. Let $f_1, \ldots, f_m$, $m = 3n$ be random polynomials of degree t generated by P, and have P send to P_i the values $f_j(\omega^i)$ for $j = 1, \ldots, m$. Each P_i selects a random $\alpha \neq 0$ from E and sends it to all the other players. After reaching agreement on the set of α-s, the dealer broadcasts the set of polynomials $f^a = \sum_{k=0}^{m} \alpha^k f_k$ to all players. Each player P_i checks that at the point ω^i, the shares he received satisfy the required equations, for all the α-s. If some P_i finds an error he broadcasts his complaint. If $t + 1$ or more player file a complaint, we decide that the dealer is faulty and take some default value, say 0, to be the dealers secret, (and pick 0 for all the needed shares).

Claim Let T be a set of good players that did not complain. Let f_i^T be the the the interpolation polynomial through the points in T of the original polynomial f_i. Then with probability at least

$$1 - m 2^n / |E|$$

all the polynomials f_i^T are of degree t.

Proof Omitted. ∎

Keeping in mind the (polynomial) complexity of the players computation, we can certainly allow $|E| \geq 2^{2n}$. This makes the error probability exponentially small.

(The case of small $|E|$ is similar: Using a somewhat larger m, each player, using a different set of random polynomials, asks the dealer to reveal either f_i or $f_0 + f_i$.)

Note that if $n \geq 5t + 1$, then our secret sharing scheme can correct $2t$ errors. If a secret is accepted then at most t good players may have wrong values. This together with at most t more wrong values that may come from the bad players, gives altogether at most $2t$ errors. Thus in this case the secret is uniquely defined and there is a simple procedure to recover its value using the error correcting procedure.

To handle the case of $n = 3t + 1$ we must make sure that all the pieces in the hands of the good players lie on a polynomial of degree t. To achieve this we ask the dealer of the secret to make public all the values that were sent to each player who filed a complaint. We now repeat the test, using new random α-s. Each player now checks at his point and at all the points that were made public, and if there is an error he files a complaint. If by now more than $t + 1$ players have complained we all decide that the secret is bad and take the default zero polynomial. Otherwise,

Claim   With very high probability, all good players are on a polynomial of degree t.

Proof   Omitted.   ■

Note that if the dealer is correct then no good player's value will become public during the verification process. This together with the fact that all the polynomials that the dealer reveals during this verification procedure are completely independent from the secret polynomial f_0, ensures that the bad players will not gain any information about the dealer's secret. (Detailed proof omitted).

Absolute Verification of a Secret

The verification procedure described above leaves an exponentially small probability of error. In this section we describe a secret verification procedure that leaves no probability of errors[1].

Instead of just sending the shares $\{s_i\}$, the dealer of the secret selects n random polynomials $f_0(x), \ldots, f_{n-1}(x)$, with

$$(1) \quad s_i = f_i i(0) \quad \text{for} \quad i = 0, \ldots, n - 1, \quad \text{and}$$

$$(2) \quad \sum_{i=0}^{n-1} \omega^{r \cdot i} f_i(x) = 0 \quad \text{for} \quad r = 1, \ldots, 2t$$

---

1. Our original protocol was simpliied by Paul Feldman who independently observed that the verification procedure can be accomplished in a constant number of communication rounds.

In other words, the dealer selects a random polynomial $f(x, y)$, of degree t in both variables x and y, with the only restriction that $f(0, 0) = s$ (his secret). Then he sends the polynomials $f_i(x) = f(x, \omega^i)$ and $g_i(y) = f(\omega^i, y)$ to player P_i, for $i = 0, \ldots, n - 1$. The real share is just $s_i = f_i(0)$, but for the purpose of its verification, the dealer also sends the polynomials $f_i(x)$ and $g_i(y)$. At this point each player P_i sends the polynomials $s_{i,j} = f_i(\omega^j) = f(\omega^j, \omega^i) = g_j(\omega^i)$ to each player P_j.

Note that if the dealer is correct, then when a good player P_j is looking at the sequence $SS_j = (s_{0,j}, s_{1,j}, \ldots s_{n-1,j})$, then all these points should be on his polynomial $g_j(y)$. Therefore P_j can compare the incoming values with his own computation and find out which values are wrong. Furthermore it is clear that in this case no good player will have to correct any value coming from other good players.

On the other hand we have

Lemma If no correct player has to correct a value given by a correct player, then there is a polynomial of degree t that passes through the interpolation points of all the correct players.

Proof Simple algebra. Omitted. ∎

To make sure that the condition of this lemma is satisfied, each player P_j broadcasts a request to make the coordinates (i, j) he had to correct public. If P_j detects more than t wrong incoming values, or had to correct his own value, the dealer is clearly faulty. In such a case P_j broadcasts a request to make both $f_j(x)$ and $g_j(y)$ public. At this point the dealer broadcasts the (supposedly true) values $s_{i,j}$ at all these points, and the polynomials that were to be made public. Note that making f_j and g_j public makes all the $s_{k,j}$ and $s_{j,k}$ public for $0 \le k < n$, for that particular j.

Now if some player P_i observes that some new public $s_{i,j}$ contradicts the polynomials he is holding, or finds out the the public information already contradicts itself, he broadcasts a request to make all his information public. Here once more, the dealer makes public all the requested information, Finally, each P_i checks all the public and private information he received from the dealer. If P_i finds any inconsistencies he broadcasts a complaint by asking all his private information to be made public.

If at this point $t + 1$ or more players have asked to make their information public, the dealer is clearly faulty and all the players pick the default zero polynomial as the dealer's polynomial. Likewise, if the dealer did not answer all the broadcasted requests he is declared faulty. On the other hand, if t or less players have complaint, then there are at least $t + 1$ good players who are satisfied. These uniquely define the polynomial $f(x, y)$ and they conform with all the information that was made public. In this case the complaining players take the public information as their share.

Note that if the dealer has distributed a correct secret then no piece of information of any good player was revealed during the verification process. If however the dealer was bad, we do not have to protect the privacy of his information, and the verification procedure ensures us that all the good players values lie on some polynomial of degree t.

Some More Tools

Before going into the computation stage, we need two more tools

(1) Generating (and verifying) a random polynomial of degree $2t$, with a zero free coefficient.

(II) Allowing a dealer to distribute three secrets, a, b, and c, and verifying that $c = a \cdot b$.

Both of these are not needed when $n \geq 4t + 1$, but are required to handle the $n = 3t + 1$ case.

(I) Generating Polynomials of Degree $2t$

Let each player P_i distribute t random (including the free coefficient) polynomials $g_{i,k}, k = 1, \ldots, t$, of degree t. Define $f_i(x)$ by

$$f_i(x) = \sum_{k=1}^{t} x^k \cdot g_{i,k}$$

and let the players evaluate from their points on the $g_{i,k}$-s their corresponding point on $f_i(x)$.

After we have verified that indeed deg $g_{i,k} \leq t$, it is clear that $deg\ f_i(x) \leq 2t$, and $f_i(0) = 0$. (It is also clear that the vector of coefficients of the monomials of x^i, $i = 1, \ldots, t$, in $f_i(x)$ are uniformly distributed and are completely independent from the information held by any set of at most t players that does not include P_i.)

Finally, as our random polynomial we take

$$f(x) = sum_{i=0}^{n-1} f_i(x).$$

(II) Verifying that $c = a \cdot b$

Let the player P distribute a and b using the polynomials $A(x)$ and $B(x)$ respectively.

We want P to also distribute a random polynomial encoding $c = a \cdot b$, in such a way that the players can all verify that indeed $c = a \cdot b$. Let

$$D(x) = A(x) \cdot B(x) = c + c_1 x + \ldots + c_{2t} x^{2t}$$

and let

$$D_t(x) \quad = r_{t,0} + r_{t,1} x + \ldots + r_{t,t-1} x^{t-1} + c_{2t} x^t$$

$$D_{t-1}(x) = r_{t-1,0} + \ldots + r_{t-1,t-1} x^{t-1} + \ldots + [c_{2t-1} - r_{t,t-1}] x^t$$

$$\vdots \qquad \vdots$$

$$D_1(x) \quad = r_{1,0} + \ldots + r_{1,t-1} x^{t-1} + \ldots + [c_t - r_{t,1} - r_{t-1,2} - \ldots - r_{2,t-1}] x^t$$

where the $r_{i,j}$ are random elements from E. P selects the $D_i(x)$ and distributes their shares to all the players. After verifying that $A(x)$, $B(x)$ and all the $D_i(x)$ are of degree t, define

$$C(x) = D(x) \sum_{i-1}^{t} x^t \cdot D_i(x).$$

and verify that $C(x)$ is also of degree t. From the construction of $C(x)$ it is clear that $C(x)$ is a random polynomial of degree t with the only restriction that $C(0) = a \cdot b$.

Proof of Theorem 3

We separate again the computation to its Input, Computation and Final stages. At the input stage, we let each player enter his inputs to the computation using our secret sharing scheme, while verifying that each secret shared is indeed some polynomial of degree t. The secret verification assures that the inputs of any Byzantine player is well defined, but does not ensure that it is in the domain of our function. For example, in a 0-1 vote, we must verify that the input is 0 or 1. We defer this type of verification to the computation stage.

The final stage is exactly the same as in the proof of Theorem 1. When we have simulated the circuit, and the players are holding the pieces of a properly shared secret, encoding the final output, they send all the pieces to one or all the players. As at most t pieces are wrong, each player can use the error correcting procedure and recover the result.

The Computation Stage – Byzantine Case

Let a and b be properly encoded by $f(x)$ and $g(x)$ respectively, where by "properly encoded" we mean that all the pieces of the good players are on some polynomial of degree t. Since $f(x)$ and $g(x)$ are properly encoded the polynomials $f(x) + g(x)$, and $c \cdot f(x)$, properly encode $a + b$, and $c \cdot a$, for any constant $c \in E$. The same argument of Theorem 1 implies that we can do the computation of any linear operation with no communication at all.

Here again, the multiplication step is more involved. To repeat the procedure of theorem I, using the degree reduction step, via the Matrix Multiplication Lemma, we must make sure the all the players use, as input to this procedure, their correct point on the product polynomial $h(x) = f(x)g(x)$. To guarantee that this indeed happens, we use the Error Correcting Codes again.

Let $a_i = f(\omega^i)$, $b_i = g(\omega^i)$ and $c_i = h(\omega^i) = a_i \cdot b_i$ be the points of P_i on these polynomials. We ask each P_i to pick a random polynomial of degree t, $A_i(x)$, such that $a_i = A_i(0)$, and use this polynomial to distribute a_i as a secret to all the players. Similarly, P_i distributes b_i using $B_i(x)$. We also ask P_i to distribute c_i using the polynomial $C_i(x)$, while verifying that $A_i(x)$, $B_i(x)$, $C_i(X)$ are all of degree t, and that $C_i(0) = A_i(0)B_i(0)$.

We want to verify that the free coefficients of the polynomials $C_i(x)$ are all points on the product polynomial $h(x)$. It is enough to verify that all the free coefficient of the $A_i(x)$ and $B_i(x)$ are on $f(x)$ and $g(x)$ respectively. We do this as follows.

The free coefficient of the $A_i(x)$-s are a code word with at most t errors. By our assumption, all the $A_i(x)$ are properly distributed. We can therefore use them to compute any linear functional. In particular, using the same $A_i(x)$-s we can compute the polynomials

$$S_r(x) = \sum_{i=0}^{n-1} \omega^{r \cdot i} A_i(x)$$

for $r = 1, \ldots, 2t$. At this point all the players reveal their points on the polynomials $S_r(x)$, enabling all the players to recover the value of $s_r = S_r(0)$, for $r = 1, \ldots, 2t$.

Note that if all the $A_i(0)$ are correct (i.e. on a polynomial of degree t) then $s_r = 0$ for all r. Thus the computed value of the s_r, are just a function of the errors introduced by the Byzantine players. In particular, this implies that the value of the s_r does not reveal any information that is held in the hands of the good players!

Since at most t of the $A_i(0)$ can be wrong, the value of the $s_r - s$, the so called Syndrome Vector, is the only information needed by the error correction procedure to detect which coordinates $A_i(x)$ encode a wrong $A_i(0)$ and give the correct value. Therefore, if some $s_r \neq 0$, all the players compute the wrong coordinates, the correct value of $f(\omega^i)$, and use the constant polynomial with this value, instead of $A_i(x)$.

In a similar way we can check and correct the $B_i(x)$. We can, therefore, also check (and correct) the $C_i(x)$, so we are sure that all the inputs to the linear computation we have to do in the degree reduction procedure are correct.

Note that much of this is not needed when $n \geq 4t + 1$, because then we can still correct up to t errors on polynomials of degree $2t$. In this case we can do the error correction on the points of $h(x)$ directly.

As in the proof of Theorem 1, we have,

Theorem 3   For every probabilistic function and every $t < n/3$ there exists a protocol that is both t-resilient and t-private.

For completeness we state,

Theorem 4   There are functions for which there is no $n/3$-resilient protocol.

Proof   Follows immediately from the lower bound for Byzantine Agreement in this model. We note that even if we allow broadcast as a primitive operation, theorem 4 remains true. This is because we can exhibit functions for three players that cannot be computed resiliently, when one player is bad. This generalizes immediately to $n/3$.

■

Remark   All the remarks following the statement of theorem 1 apply also to theorem 3.

References

[BL]   M. Ben-Or and N. Linial, Collective coin flipping, FOCS86.

[CCD]   D. Chaum, C. Crepeau and I. Damgard, Multiparty unconditionally secure protocols, These proceedings.

[DH]   W. Diffie and M. E. Helman, New directions in cryptography, IEEE Trans. Inform. Theory, Vol.IT-22,pp.644-654, 1976.

[DS]   D. Dolev and R. Strong, Polynomial algorithms for multiple processor agreement. STOC82.

[FM]   P. Feldman and S. Micali, Optimal algorithms for Byzantine agreement, These proceedings.

[GMW1]   O. Goldriech, S. Micali and A. Wigderson, Proofs that yield nothing but the validity of the assertion, and a methodology of cryptographic protocol design, FOCS86, pp. 174-187.

[GMW2]   O. Goldriech, S. Micah and A. Wigderson, How to play any mental game, STOC87, pp. 218-229.

[GMR]   S. Goldwasser, S. Micali and C. Rackoff, The knowledge complexity of interactive proof systems, STOC85, pp. 291-304.

[PSL]   M. Pease, R. Shostak and L. Lamport, Reaching agreement in the presence of faults, JACM Vol. 27, pp. 228-234, (1980).

[PW] W. W. Peterson and E. J. Weldon, Error correcting codes, Second Ed., MIT Press, (1972).

[Sh] A. Shamir, How to share a secret, CACM, 22, pp. 612-613, (1979).

[Y1] A. C. Yao, How to generate and exchange secrets, STOC86.

[Y2] A. C. Yao, On the succession problem for Byzantine Generals, manuscript, (1983).

Appendix

Formal Notation

Let F be a field. Let $U = F^n$ denote the standard n-dimensional vector space over F and $M_n(F)$ the ring of $n \times n$ matrices over F.

Let R be a random variable with distribution D over F. Then R^k (R^*) denotes k (finitely many) independent draws from D.

Comment: Unless otherwise specified, F will be finite, and D the uniform distribution over F.

The Basic Model

Fix $n > 0$ and a field F. Intuitively, an (n, F) - *network* is a complete synchronous network of n probabilistic machines (players) $P_0, P_1, \ldots P_{n-1}$. At every round, each player can send one message (element of F) to each other player, receive a message from each other player, and perform arbitrary computation.

If we assume for convenience that players send messages to themselves too, a round of communication is neatly described by a matrix $M \in M_n(F)$, where each P_i sent the ith row of M, and receives the ith column of M. (This formalizes the security of private channels).

Formally, a T round (n, F) - *network* is a set of players $\{P_0, P_1, \ldots, P_{n-1}\}$. Each P_i is a tuple

$$P_i = <Q_i, q_i^{(0)}, R_i, \delta_i >,$$

where Q_i is a set of states, $q_i^{(0)}$ the initial state, R_i is a random variable over F (distributed like R) and

$$\delta_i : [T] \times Q_i \times F^n \times R_i^* \to Q_i \times F^n$$

is a transition function that given a round number, state, previous round input and private coin tosses computes the next state and this round's output.

A *protocol* is simply $\delta = <\delta_0, \delta_1, \ldots, \delta_{n-1}>$, the transition functions prescribing to each player what to do in each round.

A run M of a protocol δ is a sequence $(M_1, M_2, \ldots, M_T)$, $M_j \in M_n(F)$ of matrices describing the communication in rounds $j = 1, 2, \ldots, T$. Note that M is a random variable, depending on $\{q_i^{(0)}\}$, the initial states, and $\{R_i^*\}$, $(= R^*)$, the random draws from D.

A *(probabilistic) function* is a function f,

$$f : F^n \times R^m \to F^n.$$

Intuitively, a protocol *computes* a function f if for all $v \in F^n$, if P_i is given $v_i \in F$ before round 1, then after round T it knows u_i, such that $u = <u_0, u_1, \ldots, u_{n-1}>$ is distributed exactly like $f(v \times R^m)$. For convenience we denote a vector $<a_0, a_1, \ldots, a + n - 1>$ by $<a_i>$. Also, let $q_i^{(j)}$ denote the state of P_i after round j.

To formally define what it means for a protocol to compute a function, we assume fixed input and output functions, $I_i, O_i : Q_i \to F$ for each player P_i. Now δ computes f, if for every choice of $< q_i^{(0)}) >$, we have $< O_i(q_i^{(T)}) >= f(I_i(q_i^{(0)}) \times R^m)$ (as random variables).

Some Intuition

The bad players in our model can completely coordinate their actions. Hence, for a bad set (coalition) $C \subseteq [n] = \{0, 1, 2, \ldots, n-1\}$, the transition functions $\delta_i, i \in C$ are replaced by arbitrary functions δ_i' that compute the next state and messages of P_i from the joint information of the current states, previously received messages and random choices of all $\{P_i\}$, $i \in C$. We denote any protocol in which a set C is bad (in this sense) by δ_C.

We distinguish two types of bad behavior. The benign (gossip) kind, in which bad players send messages according to the original protocol δ, but try to learn as much as they can from it by joining their forces. The malign (Byzantine) kind puts no restrictions on the bad players, i.e. the δ_i' can really be arbitrary.

To formalize the benign kind of bad behavior we need the following definition: Two protocols δ and δ' *look alike* if their runs have the same distribution, i.e. $M = M'$ as random variables, for every fixed initial state $< q_i^{(0)} >$ of all players.

A bad coalition C is called *gossip* if the protocol δ_C looks like δ, otherwise it is called *Byzantine*.

In the case of gossip, we don't have to worry about the correctness of computing f - this follows from the definition "look alike". Here all we shall have to prevent is leakage of information. In case of Byzantine faults, we will have to guarantee also the correctness of the computation. We proceed now to define the important notions of Privacy and Correctness.

Privacy (Preliminary)

Intuitively, a coalition C did not learn anything from a protocol for computing f, if whatever it can compute after the protocol (from its final states), it could compute only from its inputs (initial states) and its components of the function values.

Let $Q_C = \prod_{i \in C} Q_i$ and A be an arbitrary set. Also, if $u = <u_0, u_1, \ldots, u_{n-1}>$, u_C denotes the sub-vector of u that contains u_i, $i \in C$. Formally, a set C is *ignorant* in a protocol δ (for computing f), if for every set of initial states $< q_i^{(0)}) >$, every protocol δ_C that looks like δ and every function $g' : Q + c \to A$ there exists a funclion $d : Q_C \times F^{|C|} \to A$ satisfying

$$g'(q_C^{(T)}) = g(q_C^{(0)}, f, (< I_i(q_i^{(0)}) >)_C) \qquad (*)$$

A protocol δ (for computing f) is *t-private* if every coalition C with $|C| \le t$ is ignorant.

Correctness

This issue is problematic, since some of the bad players can obliterate their initial inputs, and the function value is not well defined (a simple example is Byzantine agreement). To ignore bad inputs for every set $B \subseteq [n]$, we need a (sub)function of f that depends on the input coordinates of only $[n] \setminus B$. (a special case is assigning default values to input coordinates in B).

So now by f we mean a family of functions $\{f_B : F^{n \setminus B} \times R^M \to F^n\}$, $B \subseteq [n]$, with f_ϕ being the original function f. Typically, (as in Byzantine agreement) this exponential size family is very succinctly described.

So now, a computation is correct, if all good players compute a function f_B, where B is a subset of the bad players.

More formally, a coalition C is harmless if for every set of initial states $< q_i^{(O)} >$ and every protocol δ_C,

$$\{< O_i(q_i^{(T)}) >\}_{[n] \setminus C} = f_B(\{< I_i(q_i^{(0)}) >\}_{[n] \setminus B})_{[n] \setminus C}$$

for some $B \subseteq C$.

A protocol is *t-resilient* if every coalition C with $|C| \le t$ is harmless.

Privacy Revisited

For the case of Byzantine faults, the assumption that δ_C looks like δ is invalid. For any harmless coalition C we can remove this assumption from the definition of ignorance, and replace f in $(*)$ above, by f_B, the function that will actually be computed by the good players.

Now the notion of a protocol that is both *t-resilient* and *t-private* is well defined.

Multi-Prover Interactive Proofs: How to Remove Intractability Assumptions

This chapter reproduces the contents of the paper "Multi-Prover Interactive Proofs: How to Remove Intractability Assumptions," which appeared in the proceedings of the *20th Annual ACM Symposium on Theory of Computing*, pp. 113–131, 1988.

This influential work of Michael Ben-Or, Shafi Goldwasser, Joe Kilian, and Avi Wigderson introduced a model, denoted MIP, that turned out to be closely related to the PCP model, which was introduced later and had a vast impact on complexity theory. Interestingly, the original motivation was constructing zero-knowledge proof systems without relying on intractability assumptions, a goal that was indeed achieved in this work.

Multi-Prover Interactive Proofs: How to Remove Intractability Assumptions

Michael Ben-Or[*] (Hebrew University),
Shafi Goldwasser[†] (MIT),
Joe Kilian[‡] (MIT),
Avi Wigderson[**] (Hebrew University)

Abstract

Quite complex cryptographic machinery has been developed based on the assumption that one-way functions exist, yet we know of only a few possible such candidates. It is important at this time to find alternative foundations to the design of secure cryptography. We introduce a new model of generalized interactive proofs as a step in this direction. We prove that all NP languages have perfect zero-knowledge proof-systems in this model, without making any intractability assumptions.

---

*Supported by Alon Fellowship.

†Supported in part by NSF grant 865727-CCR, ARO grant DAAL03-86-K-017, and US-Israel BSF grant 86-00301. Jerusalem, Israel.

‡Supported by a Fannie and John Hertz Foundation fellowship.

**Supported by Alon Fellowship

The generalized interactive-proof model consists of two computationally unbounded and untrusted provers , rather than one, who jointly agree on a strategy to convince the verifier of the truth of an assertion and then engage in a polynomial number of message exchanges with the verifier in their attempt to do so. To believe the validity of the assertion, the verifier must make sure that the two provers can not communicate with each other during the course of the proof process. Thus, the complexity assumptions made in previous work, have been traded for a physical separation between the two provers.

We call this new model the multi-prover interactive-proof model, and examine its properties and applicability to cryptography.

1 Introduction

The notion of randomized and interactive proof system, extending NP, was introduced in [GMR] and in [B]. An interactive proof-system consists of an all powerful prover who attempts to convince a probabilistic polynomial-time bounded verifier of the truth of a proposition. The prover and verifier receive a common input and can exchange upto a polynomial number of messages, at the end of which the verifier either accepts or rejects the input. Several examples of interactive proof-system for languages not known to be in NP (e.g graph non-isomorphism) are known.

In [GMWl] Goldreich, Micali and Wigderson show the fundamental result that that if "nonuniform" one-way functions exist (i.e no small circuits exist for the function inverse computation), then every NP language has a computationally zero-knowledge interactive proof system. This has far reaching implications concerning the secure design of cryptographic protocols. It also seems to be the strongest result possible. Results in [F] and [BHZ] imply that if perfect zero-knowledge interactive proof-systems for NP exist, (i.e which do not rely on the fact that the verifier is polynomial time bounded) then the polynomial time hierarchy would collapse to its second level. This provides strong evidence that it will be impossible (and at least very hard) to unconditionally show that *NP* has zero-knowledge interactive proofs.

In light of the above negative results, it is interesting to examine whether the definition of interactive proofs can be modified so as to still capture the notion of efficient provability and yet allow perfect zero-knowledge proofs for NP, making no intractability assumptions.

This is particularily important from a cryptographic view point, as the possible one-way functions currently considered are very few and almost exclusive to number theory (e.g. integer factorization, discrete logarithm computation and elliptic logarithm computation.) If these were found to be efficiently solvable, the crypto-graphic consequences of the [GMW] result would be unusable.

1.1   New Model

We extend the definition of an interactive proof for language L as follows: instead of one prover attempting to convince a verifier that x, the input string, is in L, our prover consists of two separate agents (or rather two provers) who jointly attempt to convince a verifier that x is in L. The two provers can cooperate and communicate between them to decide on a common optimal strategy before the interaction with the verifier starts. But, once they start to interact with the verifier, they can no longer send each other messages or see the messages exchanged between the verifier and the "other prover". As in [GMR] the verifier is probabilistic polynomial time, and can exchange upto a polynomial number of messages with either one of the two provers (with no restriction on interleaving the exchanged messages) before deciding to accept or reject string x.[1]

We restrict the verifier to send messages to the prover in a predetrmined order. It can be shown that this is equivalent with respect to language recognition, to a model in which the verifier is free to talk to the provers in any order he wishes. Moreover, the verifier can be forced to send messages to the provers in a predeter-mined order by using a simple password scheme. Thus, we can work in the easier to deal with synchronous model completely without loss of generality.

The main novelty of our model is that the verifier can "check" its interactions with the provers "against each other". One may think of this as the process of checking the alibi of two suspects of a crime (who have worked long and hard to prepare a joint alibi), where the suspects are the provers and the verifier is the interrogator. The interrogators conviction that the alibi is valid, stems from his conviction that once the interrogation starts the suspects can not talk to each other as they are kept in separate rooms, and since they can not anticipate the randomized questions he may ask them, he can trust his findings (i.e receiving a correct proof of the proposition at hand).

Applying this model in a cryptographic scenario, one may think of a bank customer holding two bank-cards rather than one, attempting to prove its identity to the bank machine. The machine makes sure that once the two cards are inserted

---

1. A proof-system for a language in this model is defined in a similar manner to [GMR]. Namely, L has a multi-prover interactive proof-system if there exist a verifier V and provers P1, P2 such Lllat when $x \in L$ the probability that V accepts is greater than 2/3, and when x is not in L then for all P1, P2 the probability that V accepts is less than 1/3.

they can no longer communicate with each other. In this scenario, the provers correspond to the two cards, and the verifier to the bank machine.

1.2   Results

1.2.1   Perfect Zero Knowledge Multi-Prover Interactive Proofs

We show, that in our extended model all NP languages have a perfect zero-knowledge interactive proof-system, making no intractability assumptions.

The protocol for NP languages proposed, requires the two provers to share either a polynomially long random pad or a function which they can compute but the polynomially bounded verifier can not. It is well known that such functions exist by counting arguments. Most of the burden of the proof lies on one predetermined prover. In fact, the "other" prover sole function is to periodically output segments of the random pad he shares with the "primary prover". The protocol is constant (two) round.

Differently then in the case of the graph non-isomorphism and quadratic non-residousity proof-systems in [GMR], [GMW], paralle1 executions of the protocol remain perfect zero-knowledge.

More generally, we show that any lauguage which can be recognized in our extended model, can be recognized in perfect zero-knowledge making no intractability assumptions.

Our construction does not assume that the verifier is polynomial time bounded. The assumption that there is no communication between the two provers while interacting with the verifier, must be made in order for the verifier to believe the validity of the proofs. It need not be made to show that the interaction is perfect zero-knowledge.

1.3   Language Recognition Power of New Model

It is interesting to consider what is the power of this new model solely with respect to language recognition. Clearly, $NP \subseteq IP$ which in turn is a subset of languages accepts by our extended model. We show that adding more provers than two, adds no more power to the model.

We also show for every language possessing a two prover interactive proof there exists another two prover interactive proof which achieves completeness, i.e. the verifier will always accept strings which are in the language.

Fortnow, Rompel and Sipser [FRS] have shown that two provers can accept any language in IP (one-prover model with polynomial number of rounds) using only a constant number of rounds. They also show that three provers can accept in a constant number of rounds all languages recognized by a multi prover model.

Feige, Shamir and Tennenholtz [FST] look at a model they call the k-noisy oracle model, in which the verifier is interacting with k oracles all of which but one may be dishonest. Based on the assumption that one of the oracles is trusted, they show that P-space langauages can be recognized in a 2-noisy oracle model.

1.4   Open Problem

Whether the two-prover proof-system is actually more powerful with respect to language recognition than the original one-prover interactive proof-system of [GMR],[B], remains an open problem.

Even the simplest case of two-round two-prover proof-system in which the verifier sends the result of his coin tosses first (some to prover 1 and some to prover 2), receives responses (from both provers) on the subsequent round, and then evaluates a polynomial time predicate to decide whether to accept or reject, is not known to lie in PSPACE. Hastad and Mansour [HM] show that resolving this question in the positive will imply that $NP \neq poly(\log) \text{ - } SPACE$.

2   Definitions

Definition 1   Let $P_1, P_2, \ldots, P_k$ be Turing machines which are computationally unbounded and V be a probabilistic polynomial time Turing machine. All machines have a read-only input tape, a work tape and a random tape. In addition, $P_1, P_2, \ldots, P_i$ share an infinite read-only random tape of 0's and 1's. Every P_i has one write-only communication tape on which it writes messages for V. V has k write-only communication tapes. On communication tape i, V writes messages to P_i. We call $(P_1, P_2, \ldots, P_k, V)$ a *k-prover interactive protocol*.

Remark 1   Fortnow, Rompel and Sipser [FRS] remark that the above can be modeled as a probabilistic polynomial time Turing machine V and an oracle p such that queries to p are prefixed always by $1 \leq i \leq k$, corresponding to whether the query is directed to prover i. Each query contains the history of the communication thus far.

We note that although this memoryless formulation is equivalent to the i-prover formulation with respect to language recognition, it is not equivalent when zero-knowledge is considered. In this latter case the provers must be able to check that the history is indeed what is claimed by the verifier, before answering the next query. Since the verifier is not untrusted, the provers can not be memoryless.

Definition 2   Let $L \subset \{0, 1\}^*$, We say that L has a *k-prover interactive proof-system*(IPS) if there exists an interactive BPP machine V such that:

1. $\exists P_1 P_2, \ldots, P_k$ such that $(P_1, P_2, \ldots, P_k, V)$ is a k-prover interactive protocol and $\forall x \in L$, prob(V accepts input x) $\geq \frac{2}{3}$.

2. $\forall P_1, P_2, \ldots, P_k$ such that $(P_1, P_2, \ldots, P_k, V)$ is a k-prover interactive protocol, prob(V accepts input x) $\leq \frac{1}{3}$.

Remark 2   if L has an k-prover interative proof-system and condition (1) holds for a particular $\hat{P}_1 \hat{P}_2, \ldots, \hat{P}_k$, then we say that $(\hat{P}_1, \hat{P}_2, \hat{P}_k, V)$ is a k-prover interactive proof-system for L.

Remark 3   if L has an two-prover interative proof-system, then L has a two-prover interactive proof-systems (P_1, P_2, V) such that for $x \in L$, prob(V accepts x) $= 1$. See Theorem 5.

Remark 4   For convenience, without loss of generality, we assume that every verifier V outputs his coin tosses at the end of his interaction with the P_i's.

Definition 3   Let $I P_k = \{L$ which have k-prover interactive proof-system $\}$.

The following definition of perfect zero-kowledge is identical to the Goldwasser-Micali-Rackoff [GMR] definition of perfect zero-knowledge in the 1-prover model.

Definition 4   Let $(P_1, P_2, \ldots, P_k, V)$ be a k-prover interactive proof-system for L. Let $View_{P_1, P_2, \ldots, P_k, V}(x)$ denote the verifier's view during the protocol (namely the sequence of messages exchanged between the verifier and the two provers including the last message of the verifier which contains his coin tosses - see remark 4 above). This is a probability space taken over the coin tosses of V and the joint random tape of $P_1, P_2, \ldots, P_k$. We say that k-prover interactive protocol $(P_1, P_2, \ldots, P_k, V)$ is *perfect zero-knowledge for V* if there existe a BPP machine M such that $M(x) = View_{P_1, P_2, \ldots, P_k, V}(x)$. We say that L has a *k-prover perfect zero-knowledge proof-system* if there exists provers $P_1, P_2, \ldots, P_k$ such that for all BPP verifiers $\hat{V}$, there exists a probabilistic Turing machine M such that for all x in L, $M(x) = View_{P_1, P_2, \ldots, P_k, \hat{V}}(x)$ and $M(x)$ terminates in expected polynomial time.

3   Statement of Our Results

Theorem 1   Every $L \in NP$ has a two-prover perfect zero-knowledge interactive proof-system.

Proposition 1   parallel executions of the perfect zero-knowledge interactive proof-system for NP remain perfect zero-knowledge.

Theorem 2   Every $L \in IP_2$ has a perfect zero-knowledge interactive proof-system.

Theorem 3   Any two party oblivious function computation can be done in this model.

Theorem 4   For all $k \geq 2$, if $L \in IP_k$, then $L \in IP_2$.

Theorem 5   If $L \in IP_2$ then $\exists P_1, P_2, V$ such that (P_1, P_2, V) is a two-prover interactive proof-system for L and for all $x \in L$, Prob(V accepts x) = 1.

3   Key Ideas

A general primitive used in complexity based cryptography (and in particular in the proof that NP is in zero-knowledge under the assumption that one-way functions exist) is the ability to encrypt a bit so that the decryption is unique. In our model, encryption is replaced by a commitment protocol to a bit such that the bit is *equally likely* to be 0 or 1 (information theoretically), and yet the probability that a different bit can be decommited (i.e revealed) is less than $\frac{1}{2}$ (this fraction can then be made arbitrarily small using standard techniques). The idea is that one prover is used to commit the bit, and the other to reveal it.

Another important primitive is that of oblivious circuit evaluation. This primitive allows two parties, A and B, possessing secrets i and j respectively, to compute some agred upon function $f(i, j)$ in such a way that A learns nothing, and B learns only $f(i, j)$. The original implementation of this protocol, due to Yao [Yao86a], requires the existence of trapdoor functions. In fact, oblivious circuit evaluation can not be implemented without cryptographic assumptions in the standard two party scenario. However, we show that oblivious circuit evaluation between verifier and 1 prover can be done without assumptions in the two-prover model. The proof relies on a result of [K] reducing oblivious circuit evaluation to a simpler protocol, known as 1-out-of-2 oblivious transfer, which was reduced by [C] to a still simpler protocol, known as oblivious transfer. This last protocol is implemented in the two-prover model.

4   Proof of Theorem 1: How to Commit Bits

We first show that every language in NP has a perfect zero-knowledge two-prover interactive proof-system.

Theorem 1   Every L in *NP* has a two-prover perfect zero-knowledge interactive proof-system.

Idea of Proof

Let (P_1, P_2, V) denote a multi-prover protocol which receives as input the graph $G = (\mathcal{V}, \mathcal{E})$. Let P_1 and P_2 share an infinite random pad R such that $R = r_2 r_2 \ldots r_k \ldots$ where $r_i \in \{0, 1, 2\}$.[2] Let $n = \mathcal{V}$.

---

2. Alternatively, R can be replaced by the outcome of $f(x)$ where x is the input and $f : \{0, 1\}^* \rightarrow \{0, 1\}^*$ is a function such that for all $x \in \{0, 1\}^*$, for all $i < |f(x)|$, the i-th bit of $f(x)$ is equally

Let us quickly review[3] one of the, by now standard proofs ([GMW1], [Bl]) that NP is in zero-knowledge under the assumption that one-way functions exist.

Review: The prover is attempting to convince the verifier that G is Hamiltonian. The prover publicizes an probabilistic encryption algorithm E (as in [GM], [Yao82a])[4] The prover and verifier repeat the following protocol n times:

STEP 1. prover randomly permutes the vertices of graph G (using permutation π) to obtain graph G and sends to verifier

- an $n \times n$ matrix $\alpha = \{\alpha_{ij}\}$ where α_{ij} in $E(b_{ij})$ and $b_{ij} = 1$ if edge ij is present in the $\hat{G}$ and 0 otherwise.

- $\beta \in E(\pi)$, i.e an encryption of π.

STEP 2. verifier chooses at random *coin* $\in \{0, 1\}$, and sends *coin* to the prover.

STEP 3. If *coin* $= 1$, prover decrypts β and α_{ij} for all $i, j \leq n$ and sends decryptions to verifier. If *coin* $= 0$, prover decrypts those α_{ij} such that edge ij is in the Hamiltonian path in $\hat{G}$.

STEP 4. If prover is unable to preform step 3 correctly, verifier rejects. Otherwise, after n iterations of steps 1 through 4, verifier accept.

End of Review

Returning to the two prover model, prover P_1 replaces the prover in step 1 of above protocol and prover P_2 replaces the prover in step 2 of above protocol. Algorithm E is no longer a probabilistic encryption algorithm based on the existence of one-way functions as in [GM] or [Yao86a], but rather a commitment algorithm computed as follows.

Let $\sigma_0, \sigma_1 : \{0, 1, 2\} -> \{0, 1, 2\}$ be such that

1. for all i, $\sigma_0(i) = i$,

2. $\sigma_1(0) = 0$, $\sigma_1(1) = 2$ and $\sigma_1(2) = 1$.

Let m_k be the k-th bit to be committed to in the protocol.

---

likely to be 0 or 1 with respect to any probabilistic polynomial time machine. Such functions can be shown to exist by standard diagonalization techniques over all probabilistic polynomial time machines.

3. the proof reviewed is from [Bl]

4. The encryption algorithm E is public. We denote $\gamma \in E(m)$ to mean that there exists string r such that algorithm E using r for his coin tosses, on input m, produces γ. Given γ there exists unique m, r such that E, on coin tosses r and input m outputs γ. To decrypt γ both m, r are revealed.

<u>To commit m_k :</u>

- V chooses at random $c_k \in \{O, 1\}$ and sends c_k to P_1.
- P_1 sets $E(c_k, m_k) = \sigma_{c_k}(r_k) + m_k \bmod 3$, where $r_k \in \{0, 1, 2\}$ is read off the random tape P_1 shares with P_2, and sends $E(c_k, m_k)$ to V.

To reveal the k-th bit committed in the protocol, V and P_2 engage in the following protocol.

<u>To reveal the k-th bit:</u>

- V sends k to P_2.
- P_2 sends V the string r_k.
- V computes $\sigma_{c_k}(r_k)$ and sets m_k to $(E(c_k, m_k) - \sigma_{c_k}(r_k)) \bmod 3$.

Note: P_2 does not know c_k and has never seen $E(c_k, m_k)$.

We prove two properties of the above pair of commit-reveal protocols. First, since P_2 sees neither $E(c_k, m_k)$ nor c_k, but knows exactly what P_1's program is, the probability that P_2 successfully reveals a bit value different than the one P_1 committed to is less than $\frac{1}{2}$.

Claim 1.1 $\forall r \in \{0, 1, 2\}, m \in \{0, 1\}$,

$$\text{prob}(\hat{r} \text{ is s.t. } E(c, r, m) = E(c, \hat{r}, \overline{m})) \leq \frac{1}{2}$$

Comment: To decrease the probability of successfuly cheating from $\frac{1}{2}$ to $\frac{1}{2^n}$, P_1 preform n commits to m_k and P_2 preforms n reveals correspondingly.

Knowing k, $E(c_k, m_k)$ and c_k gives the verifier no advantage in guessing m_k.

Claim 1.2 $\forall c \in \{0, 1\}$,

$$\text{prob}(m = 0|E(c, r, m)) = \text{prob}(m = 1|E(c, r, m)) = \frac{1}{2}$$

Proving now that the altered mutli-prover Hamiltonian cycle protocol constitutes a two-prover interactive proof for the Hamiltonian cycle problem follows directly from [Bl]'s proof and claim 1.

Proving that the protocol is perfect-zero-knowledge is more subtle.

To this end, we exhibit a probabilistic Turing machine M such that

- for Hamiltonian graphs G, $M(G)$ terminates in expected polynomial time.

- for all $\hat{V}$ such that $(P_1, P_2, \hat{V})$ is a two-prover protocol, and for all Hamiltonian graphs G, $M(G) = View_{P_1, P_2, \hat{V}}$. (where P_1, P_2 are honest provers as specified above.)

WLOG let the number of coin tosses of verifier and prover on input $G = (\mathcal{V}, \mathcal{E})$ where $|\mathcal{V}| = n$ be be bounded by polynomial $Q(n)$.

Simulator M program: (tailored after steps 1-4 above in [Bl]'s proof)

STEP 1. M chooses $\rho \in \{0, 1\}^{Q(n)}$ at random for the coin tosses to be used by $\hat{V}$. and sets $R = r_1 r_2 \ldots r_k \ldots$, $|R| \in \{0, 1\}^{Q(n)}$ where $r_k \in \{0, 1, 2\}$ are chosen at random. ($\hat{V}(\rho, G)$ will denote the program $\hat{V}$ on input G and coin tosses ρ.) M picks a random permutation π of the vertices of graph G to obtain the permuted graph $\hat{G}$ and an $n \times n$ random binary matrix MAT. Next, M simulates a commitment protocol to π and MAT as follows. To simulate a commitment protocol to the k-th bit m: M runs $\hat{V}(\rho, G)$ to obtain c, computes $E(c, m) = \sigma_{c_k}(r_k) + m \mod 3$ for $r_k \in R$, and writes $E(c, m)$ on $\hat{V}(\rho, G)$'s tape.

STEP 2. M continues running $\hat{V}(\rho, G)$ to obtain *coin*.

STEP 3. if *coin* $= 1$, M reveals π (as P_2 would do in real protocol) by writing the appropriate $r \in R$ on $\hat{V}(\rho, G)$'s tape. Revealing MAT to V is more involved, as follows. Let $MAT = \{m_{ij} | 1 \leq i, j \leq n\}$r and $\alpha = E(c, m_{ij}) = \sigma_c(r) + m_{ij} \mod 3$ where $r \in R$ is the r used in step 1 to commit m_{ij}. Let $\hat{r}$ be such that $\alpha = \sigma_c(\hat{r}) + \overline{m}_{ij} \mod 3$. Note that such $\hat{r}$ always exists and since M knows c (differently from P_2 in the real protocol) M can compute it. Set

$$\check{r} = \begin{cases} r & \text{if } m_{ij} = 1 \text{ and } ij \text{ is an edge of } \hat{G}, \\ & \text{or } m_{ij} = 0 \text{ and } ij \text{ is not an edge of } \hat{G} \\ \hat{r} & \text{if } m_{ij} = 0 \text{ and } ij \text{ is an edge of } \hat{G}, \\ & \text{or } m_{ij} = 1 \text{ and } ij \text{ is not an edge of } \hat{G} \end{cases}$$

Then M reveals $\check{r}$ to $\hat{V}(\rho, G)$.

If *coin* $= 0$, M selects n ij entries at random in MAT such that no two entries are in the same column or in the same row. Set

$$\check{r} = \begin{cases} r & \text{if } m_{ij} = 1 \\ \hat{r} & \text{if } m_{ij} = 0 \end{cases}$$

Where again $r \in R$ from step 1 such that $\alpha = E(c, m_{ij}) = \sigma_c(r) + m_{ij} \mod 3$, and $\hat{r}$ is such that $\alpha_{ij} = \sigma_c(\hat{r}) + \overline{m}_{ij} \mod 3$. Next, M reveals $\check{r}$ to $\hat{V}(\rho, G)$.

Finally, M sets $\check{R}$ to be R with the values of $\check{r}$ substituted for r used to commit the matrix MAT.

STEP 4. M runs $\hat{V}$ to either accept or reject. It then outputs the transcript of its exchanges with $\hat{V}$ followed by $\check{R}$. DONE

It is clear that, M on G operates in polynomial time in the running time of $\hat{V}$. Since $\hat{V}$ is assumed to be probabilistic polynomial time, so is M.

To show that the probability space generated by M is identical to that in $View_{(P_1, P_2, \hat{V})}$, we notice that for fixed ρ (coin tosses of the verifier) and fixed $\check{R}$ (joint random tape of P_1 and P_2) the output of $M(G)$ is identical to $View_{(P_1, P_2, \hat{V})}$. This is so as M actually runs $\hat{V}$ to obtain his moves and therefore $\hat{V}$'s moves are guaranteed to be perfectly simulated, while M itself follows the moves P_1, P_2 would have made on joint random tape $\hat{R}$. Since ρ was picked by M at random at step 1, it remains to argue that the probability that $\check{R}$ was chosen by P_1 and P_2 is the same as the probability that $\check{R}$ was output by M. This is trivially true by claim 1.2. ∎

We claim, without proof here, that independent executions of the above protocol for any language $L \in NP$ can be performed in parallel and the resulting protocol will still be a 2-prover perfect zero-knowledge proof-system for L.

In the 1-prover model the question of whether it is possible in general to preform parallel executions of perfect zero-knowledge protocols maintaining perfect zero-knowledge is unresolved. In particular, it is not known how to parallelize the proof-systems for quadratic residuosity and graph isomorphism.

5 Proof of Theorem 4: $IP_k = IP_2$ for all $k \geq 2$

We now show that any k-prover $(P_1, \ldots, P_k, V)$ interactive proof-system for language L can be converted into a 2-prover $(\hat{P}_1, \hat{P}_2, \hat{V})$ interactive proof-system. The idea is as follows.

Verifier $\hat{V}$ tosses all his coins and sends them to prover $\hat{P}_1$. In return, $\hat{P}_1$ sends $\hat{V}$ the entire history of communication that would have occured for theses coin tosses between the real verifier V and the k real provers P_i's. If this is an accepting conversation for V, $\hat{V}$ now uses $\hat{P}_2$ to check the validity of the conversation. This is done by $\hat{V}$ selecting at random an original prover P_i, and simulating with $\hat{P}_2$ the conversation between V and P_i on these coin tosses. If the conversation does not match the conversation sent by $\hat{P}_1$ then $\hat{V}$ rejects, otherwise the protocol is repeated k times (in series) and finally $\hat{V}$ accepts.

Note that the number of rounds in the simulating protocol is $k^2 t$, where t is the number of rounds in the k-prover interactive proof-system. Fortnow, Rompel and

Sipser in [FRS] show that for each $L \in IP_2$, there exists a 3-prover IPS for L with only a constant number of rounds.

Theorem 4 Let $k \geq 2$. If $L \in IP_k$ then $L \in IP_2$.

Proof Let L have a k-prover interactive proof-system $(P_1, \ldots, P_k, V)$. Let $I_k = \{1, 2, \ldots, k, \$\}$ and r denote the coin tosses made by the verifier. For a $w \in L$, the optimal provers $P_1, \ldots, P_k$ and the verifier V can be thought of as deterministic functions $P_i : \Sigma^* \to \Sigma^*$ and $V : \Sigma^* \times I_k \times \Sigma^* \to \Sigma^* \cup \{(accept, reject\}$ such that $y_j^i = P_i(h_{j-1}^i \# x_j^i)$ denotes the j-th message of the i-th prover to the verifier, $x_j^i = V(r, i, h_{j-1}^1, \ldots, h_{j-1}^k)$ denotes the j-th message of the verifier to the i-th prover, and $h_j^i = \# x_1^i \# y_1^i \# \ldots \# x_j^i \# y_j^i$ denotes the history of communication as prover i sees it at round j. Let t the total number of rounds, then $V(r, \$, h_t^1, \ldots, h_t^k) \in \{accept, reject\}$. Let Q be a polynomial such that $|r|, |x_j^i|, |y_j^i| < Q(|w|)$. ∎

We now define provers $\hat{P}_1$ and $\hat{P}_2$ and verifier $\hat{V}$ in the simulating two-prover protocool $\hat{P}_1, \hat{P}_2, \hat{V}$).

On input w,

STEP 1. $\hat{V}$ chooses $r \in \{0, 1\}^{Q(|w|)}$ at random, sends r to $\hat{P}_1$.

STEP 2. $\hat{P}_1$ sends $h_t^1, \ldots, h_t^k$ to $\hat{V}$ where the h_t^i's are computed according to functions $\hat{P}_1, \ldots, \hat{P}_k$ and V. If $V(r, \$, h_t^1, \ldots, h_t^k) = reject$ then $\hat{V}$ rejects and halts. Otherwise V picks $1 \leq i \leq k$ at random, sets $j = 1$ and continues.

STEP 3. $\hat{V}$ sends $u_j^i = V(r, i, \hat{h}_{j-1}^i)$ to $\hat{P}_2$, where $h_j^i = \# u_1^i \# v_1^i \# \ldots \# u_j^i \# v_j^i$ for $j \leq t$. if $j = t$ and $\hat{h}_t^i = h_t^i$ then $\hat{V}$ accepts and halts , otherwise $\hat{V}$ rejects and halts.

STEP 4. $\hat{P}_2$ sends $u_j^i = P_i(h_{j-1}^i \# u_j^i)$ to $\hat{V}$. Set $j = j + 1$ and GOTO STEP 3.

Claim 5.1 $\forall w \in L$,

$$\text{prob}(\hat{V} \text{ accepts } w) = \text{prob}(V \text{ accepts } w)$$

Proof If $\hat{P}_i$ follow the protocol as described above and compute the h_t^i according to the functions of the corresponding P_i's, then for every sequence of coin tosses r on which V would accept so would $\hat{V}$. ∎

Claim 5.2 if $w \in L$, $\text{prob}(V \text{ accepts } w) \leq (\text{prob}(V \text{ accepts } w) + e^{-k}$.

Proof Assume $w \notin L$. Then, the $\text{prob}(\hat{V} \text{ accepts } w) \leq \text{prob}(\hat{V} \text{ accepts } w | \forall i \leq k \forall j \leq t, y_j^i = \hat{P}_i(h_{j-1}^i)) + \text{prob}(\hat{V} \text{ accepts } w | \exists l, j \text{ s.t. }, y_j^l \neq \hat{P}_l(h_{j-l}^l)) \leq \text{prob}(V \text{ accepts } w)$

$+ \text{prob}(\ V(r, \$, h_t^1, \ldots, h_t^k) = accept,$ and $\exists\ 1 \leq k,$ s.t. $h_t^l, \neq \hat{h}_t^l,$ but i of step 4 is s.t. $h_t^i = \hat{h}_t^i) \leq \text{prob}(\ V \text{ accepts } w) + (1 - \frac{1}{k}).$

If the above protcol is repeated k^2 independent times, the probability of success is reduced to $\text{prob}(\ V \text{ accepts } w) + (1 - \frac{1}{k})^{k^2} \leq \text{prob}(\ V \text{ accepts } w) + e^{-k}.$

This completes the proof, and L is indeed in IP_2. ∎

6 Proof of Theorem 5: Completeness

Goldreich, Mansour and Sisper (GMS) showed that any $L \in IP$ has an interactive proof-system for which strings in L are always accepted. We show the corresponding property for any $L \in IP_2$.

Theorem 5 If $L \in IP_2$, then there exists a 2-prover interactive proof-system (P_1, P_2, V) for L such that for all $x \in L$, $\text{prob}(\ V \text{ accepts }) = 1$.

Proof Suppose (P_1, P_2, V) is a 2-prover interactive proof-system for L such that $\epsilon = \text{prob}(\ V \text{ accepts } |w \text{ not in } L)$ and the number of coin tosses on input w which V makes is a polynomial $Q(|w|)$. We show a simulating 2-prover interactive proof-system $(\hat{P}_1, \hat{P}_2, V)$ for L which also achieves completenes. The simulation is done in two stages. In stage 1, we use the idea of the completeness proof for the l-prover interactive proof-system model by Goldreich, Mansour and Sisper in [MGS] (based on Lautman's Lemma) where $\hat{P}_1$ plays the part of both $\hat{P}_1$ and $\hat{P}_2$. In stage 2, as in the proof of the theorem of section 6, V uses $\hat{P}_2$ to check the validity of stage 1.

Let t denote the number of rounds in $(P_1, P2, V)$. Again, consider P_1, P_2 and V as deterministic functions as in the proof of theorem of section 6.

Let r denote the coin tosses of the verifier. For $i = 1, 2$, let $h_t^i(r) = \#x_1^i\#y_1^i\# \ldots \#x_t^i\#y_t^i$ where $x_j^i = V(r, i, h_{j-1}^i, (r))$, and $y_j^i = P_i(h_{j-1}^i(r)\#x_j^i).$

Define $W = \{r | V(r, \$, h_t^1, h_t^2) = accept\}$. Note that for $w \in L$, $\frac{|W|}{2^{Q(|w|)}} \geq (1 - \epsilon)$ and for w not in L $\frac{|W|}{2^{Q(|w|)}} \leq \epsilon$. Lautman[L] shows that $\forall w \in L \exists s_1, \ldots, s_{Q(|w|)}, |s_i| = Q(|w|),$ s.t. $\forall r, |r| = Q(|w|), \exists l$ s.t. $r \oplus s_l \in W$. We use this in a manner similar to [GMS]. ∎

On input w,

STEP 1. $\hat{P}_1$ sends V $s_1, \ldots, s_(Q|w|)$ such that $s_i \in \{0, 1\}^{Q(|w|)}$

STEP 2. $\hat{V}$ sends r to $\hat{P}_1$ where r is randomly selected in $\{0, 1\}^{(Q|w|)}$

STEP 3. $\hat{P}_1$ sends to $\hat{V}$, $h_t^i(s_j \oplus r)$ for $i = 1, 2$ and $1 \leq j \leq Q(|w|)$. (These are the histories of conversations which would have been exchanged in original protocol (P_1, P_2, V) on coin tosses $r \oplus s_j, 1 \leq j \leq Q(|w|)$.)

STEP 4. if $V(r \oplus s_j, h_t^1(r \oplus s_j), h_t^2(r \oplus s_j)) = reject$ for all $1 \leq j \leq k$, then $\hat{V}$ rejects. If $\exists 1$ s.t. $V(r \oplus s_l, h_t^1(r \oplus s_l), h_t^2(\oplus s_l)) = accept$, then goto STEP 5.

STEP 5. $\hat{V}$ chooses $i \in \{1, 2\}$ at random. It then interacts with prover $\hat{P}_2$ in the same way that V and P_i would have on coin tosses $r \oplus s_1$. If this interaction produces exactly the same history string $h_t^i(r \oplus 1)$ sent by $\hat{P}_1$ in STEP 3 then $\hat{V}$ accepts, otherwise it rejects.

The above protocol is repeated $(Q|w|)s$ times, and the verifier accepts if and only if he accepeted in any of these iterations.

Claim 1 prob(V accepts $|w| \in L$) $= 1$

Proof if $\hat{P}_1$, and $\hat{P}_1$ follow the program outlined above, follows directly from [L] and [GMS]. ∎

Claim 2 prob(V accepts $|w|$ not in L) $\leq \frac{1}{3}$

Proof We now can not assume that $\hat{P}_1$, $\hat{P}_2$ follow the protocol. Let h_{ij}, for $i = 1, 2, 1 \leq j \leq Q(|w|)$ denote the strings sent by $\hat{P}_1$ in STEP 3. ∎

prob(V accepts in one iteration $|w \notin L) \leq \sum_l$ prob($\exists l, V(r \oplus s_l, h_{1l}, h_{2l}) = accept | \hat{P}_1, \hat{P}_2$ honest) $+$prob($\hat{P}_1, \hat{P}_2$ not caught in step 5 but $\exists j, i, h_t^i(r \oplus s_j \neq j_{ij})$ $\leq (Q|w|) \cdot \epsilon + \left(1 - \frac{1}{(Q|w|)}\right) = 1 - \frac{1}{(Q|w|)} + (Q|w|) \cdot \epsilon$ Now, prob(V accepts in $Q(|w|)^3$ iterations $|w \in L) = \left(1 - \frac{1}{(Q|w|)} \cdot \epsilon\right)^{(Q|w|)^3}$ which is less than a 1/3 for ϵ sufficiently small. ∎

7 Proof of Theorem 2: Outline

Overview

The proof of Theorem 2 is very long and complicated. The main idea of the proof is the implementation of a technique we call *encrypted conversations*. This is a general technique for transforming proof systems into zero-knowledge proof systems. A protocol that has been transformed using this technique closely mirrors the original protocol. Indeed, all the questions and answers of the transformed protocol can be mapped to questions and answers in the original protocol. However, these questions and answers are all strongly encrypted, in an information theoretic sense, using keys that are known by the provers, but not by the verifier. Because the conversation is so strongly encrypted, the verifier gets no information, so the protocol is zero-knowledge.

Two concerns such a transformation must deal with are

- How can the verifier, who in a strong sense knows little of what has happened in an encrypted conversation, be convinced that the conversation indeed mirrors a valid conversation from the original protocol? Also, how can the verifier be convinced that the unencrypted conversation would indeed have caused the original verifier to accept?

- How can one insure that a malicious verifier cannot subvert the encrypted protocol in order to acquire information in some way?

We deal with the first concern by showing how the provers and verifier can take an encrypted transcript of the first i rounds of a conversation, and compute an encrypted transcript of the first $i + 1$ rounds of a conversation. This is done in such a way that the verifier can verify with high probability that this is the case. We deal with the second concern by insuring that the encrypted conversation, if generated at all, will mirror a conversation between the prover and an honest verifier. Thus, if the verifier follows the simulation, he will only find out whether the original verifier, on a random set of coin tosses, accepted. Since the original verifier accepts with probability 1, this is no information. Furthermore, we guarentee that if the verifier does not go along with the simulation, he will not get any information.

In order to accomplish these goals, we use a very useful tool called *oblivious circuit computation*. This tool, first developed by Yao [Yao86a], is a protocol by which two parties, A and B, possess secrets i and j respectively, and have agreed upon some circuit f. At the end of the protocol, A learns nothing about j, and B learns $f(i, j)$, but nothing more about i than can be inferred from knowing j and $f(i, j)$. The provers and verifier can compute the next step of an encrypted conversation by obliviously evaluating a circuit. We sketch the reduction from encrypted conversations to oblivious circuit evaluation in appendix A.3.

A large portion of our construction is devoted to implementing oblivious circuit evaluation. Yao's implementation of this protocol relies on complexity theoretic assumptions, and is therefore unsuitable for our purposes. More recently, however, this protocol was implemented using a subprotocol known as *oblivious transfer* in lieu of any cryptographic assumptions[K]. In the standard, two-party scenario, oblivious transfer cannot be implemented without complexity theoretic assumptions. However, we show that oblivious transfer can be implemented in the two-prover scenario without recourse to these assumptions. Our implementation uses a result of Barrington [Ba] that NC^1 languages can be accepted by bounded width branching programs. We sketch our implementation in appendix A.2.

8 Acknowledgements

We are grateful to Oded Goldreich for many helpful discussions during the course of this research and otherwise. His remarks have been instrumental in pointing us to possible future directions of this research.

We would also like to thank Yishai Mansour, Nimrod Megiddo and John Rompel for useful remarks.

References

[AL] Angluin, Dana and David Lichtenstein. "Provable Security of Cryptosystems: a Survey," YALEU/DCS/TR-288,1983. *Proceeding of the 17th STOC*, 1985, pp. 421-429.

[Ba] Barrington, D. "Bounded Width Polynomial Size Branching Programs Recognize Exactly Those Languages in NC^1", *Proceedings of 18th STOC*, 1986, pp. 1-5.

[Bl] Blum, M., Private Communication.

[BC] Brassard, Gilles and Claude Crépeau. "Zero-Knowledge Simulation of Boolean Circuits," *Proceedings of the 27th FOCS*, IEEE, 1986,188-195.

[BHZ] Boppana, Ravi, Johan Hastad, and Stathis Zachos. "Does CoNP Have Short Interactive Proofs?," *IPL*, 25, 1987, 127-132.

[CDvdG] Chaum, David, Ivan Damgard, and Jeroen van de Graaf. "Multiparty Computations Ensuring Secrecy of Each Party's Input and Correctness of the Output," *Proceedings of CRYPTO '87. Proceedinga of CRYPTO '85*, Springer-Verlag, 1986, 477-488.

[CG] Chor, B, Goldreich G, "Unbiased Bits from Sources of Weak Randomness and Probabilistic Communication Complexity", *Proceedings of the 26th FOCS*, 1985.

[Ck] Crápeau C., Kilian J., Private Communication.

[CW] Carter L., Wegman M., "Universal Classes of Hash Functions", JCSS 18, 1979, pp. 143-154.

[C] Crépeau Claude, "On the Equivalence of Two Types of Oblivious Transfer", Crypto87.

[FST] Feige, U., Shamir, A., Tennenholtz, M., "The Noisy Oracle Problem", Private Communication of Manuscript

[F] Fortnow, Lance. "The Complexity of Perfect Zero-Knowledge," *Proceedings of the 19th STOC*, ACM, 1987, 204-209.

[FRS] Fortnow, Lance., Rompel J., Sipser M., "On the Power of Multi-Prover Interactive Proofs" *In preparation*.

[FMR] Fischer M., Micali S., Rackoff C., and Wittenberg S., "An Oblivious Transfer Protocol Equivalent to Factoring", In Preparation.

[GM] Goldwasser S., and Micali S., "Probabilistic Encryption", JCSS, vol. 28, no. 2, 1984, pp. 270-299.

[GHY] Galil Z., Haber S., and Yung M., "A Private Interactive Test of a Boolean Predicate and Minimum-Knowledge Public-Key Cryptosystem", *Proceedinga of the 26th FOCS*, 1985, pp. 360-371.

[EGL] Even S., Goldreich O., and A. Lempel, *A Randomized Protocol for Signing Contracts*, CACM, vol. 28, no. 6, 1985, pp. 637-647.

[GMS] Goldreich O.,, Mansour Y.,, and Sipser M.,, "Interactive Proof Systems: Provers that Never Fail and Random Selection", *Proceedings of the 28th FOCS*, 1987, pp. 449- 462.

[GMW1] Goldreich, Oded, Sitvio Micali, and Avi Wigderson. "Proofs that Yield Nothing but the Validity of the Assertion, and a Methodology of Cryptographic Protocol Design," *Proceedings of the 27th FOCS*, IEEE, 1986, 174-187.

[GMW2] Goldreich, Oded, Silvio Micah, and Avi Wigderson. "How to Play ANY Mental Game," *Proceedings of the 19th STOC*, ACM, 1987, 218-229.

[GV] Goldreich, O., Vainish, R. "How to Solve any Protocol Problem: An Efficiency Improvement", Crypto 87.

[GMR] Goldwasser, Shafi, Silvio Micali, and Charles Rackoff. "The Knowledge Complexity of Interactive Proof-Systems," *Proceedinga of the 17th STOC*, ACM, 1985,291-304.

[HM] Hasted J., Mansour Y., "Private Communication"

[K] Kilian, J. "On the Flower of Oblivious Transfer," *Proceedings of this conference*

[L] Lautemann C., "BPP and the Polynomial Time Hierarchy", IPL, 14, 1983, pp. 215-217.

[R] Rabin, M., "How to exchange secrets by oblivious transfer", Tech. Memo TR-81, Aiken Computation Laboratory, Harvard University, 1981.

[Yao82] Yao, Andrew C. "Protocols for Secure Computations," *Proceedings of the 23rd FOCS*, IEEE, 1982, 160-164.

[Yao86a] Yao, Andrew C. "How to Generate and Exchange Secrets," *Proceedings of the 27th FOCS*, IEEE, 1986, 162-167.

[Yao86b] Yao, Andrew C. "Theory and Applications of Trapdoor Functions", Proc. of the 23rd FOCS, 1982, IEEE, pp.80-91.

A Structure of the Transformed Protocol

Given a 2-prover IPS, we transform it into a zero-knowledge 2-prover IPS that has three distinct phases. These stages will be referred to as the *commital* phase, the *oblivious transfer phase*, and the *encrypted conversation* phase. In the commital phase of the protocol, the two provers commit a set of bits to the verifier. In the oblivious transfer phase of the protocol, the provers and verifier create a random sequence O of oblivious transfer bits. Sequence O has the following three properties.

- All of the bits of O are known to the provers.
- Each bit in O is known to the verifier with probability $\frac{1}{2}$.
- Neither prover knows which bits in O the verifer knows.

The third and final stage actually simulates the original 2 prover IPS. In this stage, sequence O is used to perform oblivious circuit computation, which then allows the use of the encrypted conversation technique. We now describe the three phases in greater detail.

A.1 The Commital Phase

It is necessary for the two provers to be able to commit bits for use in the second, oblivious transfer phase of the protocol. This commital is of the same type as in the proof that any language in NP has a zero-knowledge 2-prover IPS. We use the same commital protocol as is used in Section!5.

The bits committed to in the commital phase may be random. In order to commit a bit b in the oblivious transfer phase, a prover can tell the verifier the value of $b \oplus b_c$, where b_c is a bit committed to in the commital phase. To decommit b, the prover can then simply decommit b_c.

A.2 The Oblivious Transfer Phase

The oblivious transfer phase of the zero-knowledge IPS consists of several parallel evaluations of the oblivious transfer protocol, described below.

Introduction to Oblivious Transfer

We can view oblivious transfer as a protocol between two parties, A and B. Initially, A knows some random bit b, which is unknown to B. At the end of the protocol, the following two conditions hold.

1. (The Transfer Condition) One of the following two events has occured, each with probability $\frac{1}{2}$. Either B learns the value of b, or B learns nothing. Player B knows which of the two events occurred.

2. (The Obliviousness Condition) Player A receives no information about whether or not B learned the value of b.

Oblivious transfer, first introduced by Rabin[R], is a powerful cryptographic primitive. Its applications include contract signing [EGL] and oblivious circuit evaluation ([Y], [GMW2], [GHY], [AF], [GV], [K]). The first implementation of oblivious transfer by Rabin [R] was based on the difficulty of factoring and only worked for honest parties, Fischer, Micali, and Rackoff[FMR] presented the first implementation based on factoring and robust against computationally bounded adversaries. Even-Goldreich-Lempel[EGL] reduced the intractibility assumption to the existence of trapdoor permutations.

Unfortunately, these reductions are all cryptographic in nature, and thus of no use to us. Our implementation, which is not based on any cryptographic assumptions, exploits the lack of direct communication between the two provers.

A Variant of Oblivious Transfer in the 2-Prover Model

We implement an analog to oblivious transfer in the two-prover model. At the beginning of the protocol, the provers know(have chosen) solve random bit b, which the verifier does not know. The provers and the verifier have also agreed on a security parameter K. At the end of the protocol, the following variants of the usual transfer and obliviousness conditions hold.

1. (The Transfer Condition) One of the following events occurs with probability $\frac{1}{2}$. Either the verifier fully learns the value of b (i.e. can predict b with probability 1), or the verifier gains only partial knowledge of b (i.e. can predict b with probability $\frac{3}{4}$). The verifier knows which of the two events occurred.

2. (The Obliviousness Condition) Let K denote the security parameters. For all $c > 0$, and for K sufficiently large, if the two provers communicate less than K bits of information, they cannot predict, with probability $\frac{1}{2} + 1/K^c$, whether the verifier fully learned b.

Our implementation of this oblivious transfer protocol requires a constant number of rounds. The total number of bits of communication between the provers and the verifier will by polynomial in K and the size of the input.

Both the transfer and the obliviousness conditions are relaxed versions of the standard ones. The transfer condition is relaxed purely for ease of implementation. Using the techniques of Crépeau-Kilian[CK], we can show that achieving this weakened transfer condition is equivalent to achieving the ideal transfer condition. The standard obliviousness condition, however, *cannot* be implemented in this model if the two provers are allowed to freely communicate. To get around this difficulty, we show that for interactive proof systems, a set of bits transferred under the non-ideal obliviousness condition may be used in place of a set of bits transferred under the ideal obliviousness condition.

Branching Programs

The main idea behind the oblivious transfer protocol is a simulation of width 5 permutation branching programs(W5PBP), as defined in [B]. Before describing the protocol, we first present a slightly nonstandard way to specify a W5PBP. We then show a way of randomizing this specification. Using this randomized representation, we can then describe our oblivious ransfer protocol.

W5PBP's may be formally thought of as having some polynomial $p(n)$ levels, each with five nodes. On level 1 there is a distinguished start node s; on level $p(n)$ there is a distinguished accept node a. For each level, i, $1 \le i \le p(n)$, there is an input variable, which we denote by v_i, and two 1–1 mappings, f_0^i and f_1^i, that map the nodes at level i to the nodes at level $i + 1$. Intuitively, the mapping f_0^i tells where to go if the input variable v_i is 0, and f_1^i tells where to go if v_i is equal to 1. A branching program may be evaluated by on a set of inputs by computing

$$\text{Branching\_Program}(x_1, \ldots, x_n) = \left(f_{v_{p(n)-1}}^{p(n)-1} \circ f_{v_{p(n)-2}}^{p(n)-2} \circ \cdots \circ f_{v_1}^1 \right)(s). \quad \text{(A.2.1)}$$

If this value if equal to the accept node a, the branching program accepts, otherwise, it is rejects. An example of a program is in fig. 1.

As described above, our branching programs consist of variables, nodes, and functions from nodes to nodes. For our protocol, we need an alternate representation for branching programs. Given a W5PBP, we first pick a random mapping γ, that maps nodes to $\{1, \ldots, 5\}$, subject to the constraint that no two nodes on the same level are mapped to the same number. We then replace each function f_k^i, $k \in \{0, 1\}$, by a permutation h_k^i, subject to the constraint

$$h_k^i(\gamma(N)) = \gamma(f_k^i(N)), \quad \text{(A.2.1)}$$

for all nodes N on level i. From equations (A.2.1) and (A.2.2) we have

$$\gamma(\text{Branching\_Program}(x_1, \ldots, x_n)) = \left(h_{v_{p(n)-1}}^{p(n)-1} \circ h_{v_{p(n)-2}}^{p(n)-2} \circ \cdots \circ h_{v_1}^1 \right)(\gamma(s)). \quad \text{(A.2.3)}$$

This isomorphism between evaluating the permutations h_k^i on $\gamma(s)$ and evaluating the original branching program proves very useful in implementing oblivious transfer, as we will show in the next section. The following simple lemma is useful in analyzing the information transferred by the oblivious transfer protocol we will present.

Lemma A.1 Suppose that for each level, i, of a branching program, exactly one of the functions h_0^i or h_1^i is specified. Suppose also that for some level j, $\gamma(N)$ is specified for all nodes N on level j. Then there is exactly one way of consistently defining γ and the functions h_k^i.

Proof Outline First, we note that specifying γ specifies all the h's. Thus we need only show that there is exactly one way of consistently defining γ. By equation A.2.2, we have

$$\gamma(N) = h_k^{i-1}(\gamma(f_k^i(N)), \quad \text{and} \quad \text{(A.2.4)}$$

$$\gamma(N) = h_k^i(\gamma(f_k^{i-1}(N))). \quad \text{(A.2.5)}$$

If γ is defined on level i, equation(A.2.4) uniquely extends it to level $i-1$, and equation (A.2.5) uniquely extends it to level $i+1$. Inductively, one can uniquely extend γ from row j to the entire branching program. This extension is easily shown to be consistent. ∎

The Oblivious Transfer Protocol

We now outline the oblivious transfer protocol between the two provers and the verifier. For the exposition, we assume that the provers follow the protocol. It is not hard to convert this protocol to one that works with adversarial provers.

Stage 1:.   Let $n = K^2$. Both provers initially start with some canonical W5PBP that, given two vectors $\vec{x} = [x_1 \; x_2 \ldots x_n]$ and $\vec{y} = [y_1 \; y_2 \ldots y_n]$, accepts iff $\vec{x} \cdot \vec{y} = 1$. They then agree on a random mapping γ, and permutations h_k^i. The provers send the verifier the exclusive-or of b and the least significant bit of $\gamma(a)$.

Stage 2:.   The verifier and Prover 1 pick a random vector x. The verifier and Prover 2 pick a random vector y. As a subprotocol, the prover and verifier flip an unbiased coin in the following manner: Prover i chooses as his bit, r_p, one of the bits committed in the commital phase of the protocol. The verifier chooses a bit r_v at random, and announces it to Prover i. Prover i then decommits r_p. The bit r, defined by $r = r_p \oplus r_v$ will be unbiased if either Prover i or the verifier obeys the protocol.

Stage 3:.   Prover 1 sends the verifier the permutations $h_{u_i}^i$, for all i such that $v_i = x_j$, for some j. Likewise, Prover 2 sends the verifier the permutations $h_{v_i}^i$, for all i such that $v_i = y_j$, for some j. For example, if $v_i = y_7$, and $y_7 = 0$, then Prover 2 would send the verifier h_0^i, but not send him h_1^i.

We now show how to convert this protocol to one in which the provers may be adversarial. First, we require that the provers commit their γ and their permutations h_0^i and h_1^i at Stage 1 of the oblivious transfer protocol, using the commital protocol described in section 1. The verifier must be assured that the following two conditions are met.

1. The permutations it receives correspond to those that have been committed, and

2. The permutations and γ correspond to a legitimate randomized branching program.

The first condition is assured by having the provers decommit their permutations in Stage 3 of the protocol. To assure that the second condition is met, we have the verifier perform a "spot-check" with probability $1/n^c$, where n is the size of the input, and c is some positive constant. To perform a spot-check, the verifier halts the oblivious transfer protocol at the beginning of Stage 2. Instead of using the committed W5PBP to implement oblivious transfer, the verifier requests that γ and all the hash functions are revealed. The verifier can then check whether or not the two provers gave a legitimate randomized W5PBP, and reject if they did not. Note that it is only necessary for the verifier to be able to detect cheating by the provers some polynomial fraction of the time. This probability may be amplified by successively running the zero-knowledge proof system sufficiently many times.

Properties of the Oblivious Transfer Protocol

The following theorems state that the above protocol does indeed implement our variant of oblivious transfer.

Theorem (Transfer) After the above protocol has been executed, one of the following two events may occur, each with probability 1/2.

1. The verifier knows the value of b.

2. The verifier can guess the value of b with probability at most 3/4.

Furthermore, the verifier can tell which event occurred.

Proof Outline Suppose, that $\vec{x} \cdot \vec{y} = 1$. Then the verifier can compute $\gamma(a)$, and thus compute b. This corresponds to event (1). Now suppose that $\vec{x} \cdot \vec{y} \neq 1$. The verifier knows, for each level i, exactly one of the functions h_0^i or h_1^i. The verifier can also compute $\gamma(a')$, where a' is also on the last level, and $a' \neq a$. Everything else the verifier knows can be computed from this information. Using Lemma 1, we have that any specification of γ on the top level nodes can be consistently extended in exactly one way. Thus, the verifier has no information about $\gamma(a)$ other than the fact that $\gamma(a) \neq \gamma(a')$. The verifier's predictive ability is maximized when $\gamma(a')$ is even, in which case the conditional probability that $\gamma(a)$ is odd is 3/4. In this situation, the verifier can predict b with probability 3/4. ∎

Theorem (Obliviousness) Let c be a constant, $c > 0$, and K, the security parameter, be sufficiently large (possibly depending on c). If, after the above protocol has been executed, the two provers exchange only K bits of information, they cannot predict, with probnbility $\frac{1}{2} + 1/K^c$, whether the verifier received the bit.

Proof Outline   We again use the observation that the verifier receives a bit iff the dot product of the two randomly chosen vectors is equal to 1. Determining if the verifier received the bit is equivalent to computing the dot product of two random vectors of size n. We now cite a theorem of Chor and Goldreich [CG] concerning the communication complexity of computing dot products.   ■

Theorem[CG]   Let players A and B each receive random n bit boolean vectors, $\vec{x}$ and $\vec{y}$ respectively. If they exchange $o(n)$ bits, they cannot predict $\vec{x} \cdot \vec{y}$ with probability greater than $\frac{1}{2} + 1/n^c$, for any c.

Our theorem follows directly from this result.   ■

Ideal versus Nonideal Oblivious Transfer Bits

As we have meutioned above, the oblivious transfer protocol we implement is nonideal in the obliviousness conditions. The nonideal nature of the obliviousness condition is inherent to our model, if the transfer condition is indeed ideal in the information theoretic sense. If the two infinitely powerful provers are allowed to communicate freely, they can each learn the entire transcript of the oblivious transfer protocol, and thus determine everything the verifier could have learned from the protocol. This violates the obliviousness condition of oblivious transfer, yielding the following observation.

Observation: It in impossible to implement an ideal oblivious transfer protocol between two provers and a verifier if the provers are allowed to communicate freely after the protocol.

The nonideal nature of the oblivious condition does not affect whether a protocol is zero-knowledge; the verifier learns exactly as much from a pseudo-oblivious source as from an oblivous one. However, using a pseudo-oblivious source of bit instead of an ideal source could conceivably cause a protocol to no longer be a proof system. We show that, provided the security parameter for our pseudo-oblivious source is sufficiently high, this will not be the case.

Formalizing Proof Systems with Oblivious Transfer Channels

In order to state our resuIt more precisely, we first augment our definition of two-prover interactive proof systems by adding a fourth party, a transfer source.

Definition   A two-prover interactive protocol with oblivious transfer consists of a four-tuple of parties, $< P_1, P_2, V, T >$. Parties P_1, P_2, V may be formally described as mappings from sequences of Σ^* (informally, the history of that party's conversation so far) to distributions on Σ^* (informally, the next answer/question given/asked by the party).

Player T may be formally described as a mapping from $\{0, 1\}^*$ to a distribution on triples (I_{P_1}, I_{P_2}, I_V). The values I_{P_1}, I_{P_2} may be informally thought of as information leaked back to the provers, P_1 and P_2, by a possibly nonideal oblivious transfer protocol. The possible values of I_V on input $O = O_1, \ldots, O_k$ are elements of $\{(0, 1, \#\}^*$, of the form $O'_1; \ldots, O'_k$, where $O'_i = O_i$ or $O'_i = \#$. Informally, I_V consists of the bits that are tranferred to the verifier, V.

For the rest of the discussion, we will anthromorphize our descriptions of the P_1, P_2, V and T, describing their behavior in terms of actions by players instead of as values of functions.

Protocols with oblivious transfer are evaluated in nearly the same way as standard protocols, but for an initial oblivious transfer phase. At the beginning of the protocol, the provers, P_1 and P_2, agree on a sequence of bits O, which they send to the transfer mechanism, T. The transfer mechanism sends some of these bits to the verifier, and sends additional information back to the two provers. At this point, T no longer plays any part in the protocol, and the players P_1, P_2, and V proceed to interact in the same manner as with standard two-prover protocols. Players P_1, P_2, and V treat their views of the oblivious transfer phase as special inputs.

Modeling Ideal and Nonideal Sources in Our Formalism

We now give a specification for an oblivious transfer mechanism which models the information received by the provers by the actual oblivious transfer mechanism we have implemented in the two-prover model.

Specification: Oblivious transfer mechanism $T_{n,k}$ is specified by its input from the provers and its output to the provers and the verifier. $T_{n,k}$ takes as input a sequence of bits $O = O_1, \ldots, O_k$. It flips k coins, $b_1, \ldots, b_k$. $T_{n,k}$ randomly selects two sequences of n element boolean vectors, $\vec{x}_1, \ldots, \vec{x}_k$ and $\vec{y}_1, \ldots, \vec{y}_k$, subject to $\vec{x} \cdot \vec{y}_i = b_i$. $T_{n,k}$'s output is as follows.

Transfer to V : $T_{n,k}$, sends the verifier sequence $O' = O'_1, \ldots, O'_k$ where $O'_i = O_i$ iff $b_i = 1$. Otherwise, $O'_i = \#$.

Transfer to P_1: $T_{n,k}$ sends P_1 the sequence $\vec{x}_1, \ldots \vec{x}_k$.

Transfer to P_2: $T_{n,k}$ sends P_2 the sequence $\vec{y}_1, \ldots, \vec{y}_k$.

This model for our transfer channel makes the following simplifications. The verifier does not get any partial glimpses at bits that it hasn't completely received, whereas in the actual protocol, it may guess it with probability 3/4. Also, it does not get any record of its interactions with the provers in the oblivious transfer protocol. For instance, in the actual protocol, the verifier would also know the $\vec{x}_i$'s and $\vec{y}_i$'s, whereas in this model it does not. These simplifications turns out to be irrelevant to our analysis, since the valid verifier completely disregards all of this extra information.

More significantly, the provers do not receive any of the extra information they might obtain in the commital and oblivious transfer phases. One can show that any pair of provers which have any chance of fooling the verifier must abide by rules of the commital and oblivious transfer protocols. The extra information they receive from an honest run of these protocols is of no value to them. They may, in a certain technical sense, simulate all of this extra information, once given their respective vector sequences $\vec{x}_1, \ldots, \vec{x}_k$ and $\vec{y}_1, \ldots, \vec{y}_k$. Thus, the provers cannot cheat any more effectively using our simplified channel than they could using the actual commital and oblivious transfer protocols. The details of this argument are ommitted.

Modeling an Ideal Oblivious Transfer Mechanism

It is fairly straightforward to model an ideal oblivious transfer mechanism in our formalism. We denote this transfer channel T_k^{ideal}, which we specify as follows.

Specification: Oblivious transfer mechanism T_k^{ideal} is specified by its input from the provers and its output to the provers and the verifier. T_k^{ideal} takes as input a sequence of bits $O = O_1, \ldots, O_k$. It flips k coins, $b_1, \ldots, b_k$. It randomly selects two sequences of n element boolean vectors, $\vec{x}_1, \ldots, \vec{x}_k$ and $\vec{y}_1, \ldots, \vec{y}_k$. T_k^{ideal}'s output ir as follows.

Transfer to V: T_k^{ideal} sends the verifier sequence $O' = O'_1, \ldots, O'_k$ where $O'_i O_i$ iff $b_i = 1$. Otherwise, $O'_i = \#$.

Transfer to P_1 and P_2: T_k^{ideal}, sends nothing to P_1 or P_2.

A Practical Equivalence Between $T_{n,k}$ and T^{ideal}

We can now state our theorem concerning the the practical equivalence of our oblivious transfer protocol and the ideal one.

Theorem   Let $< P_1, P_2, V, T_{p(n)}^{ideal} >$ be an interactive proof system with oblivious transfer. Here, $p(n)$ denotes some polynomial in the size of the input. Then there exists some some polynomial $q(n)$ such that $< P_1, P_2, V, T_{q(n), p(n)} >$ is also an interactive proof system with oblivious transfer.

Brief Outline of Proof   The proof of this theorem is somewhat involved. We show that if one could cheat more effectively using a $T_{q(n), p(n)}$ transfer channel, for $q(n)$ arbitrarily large, then one could use this fact to create a protocol for computing the dot product of two random $q(n)$ element boolean vectors. The communication complexity for this protocol will depend on V and n, but not on the function q. From this it is possible to use the Chor-Goldreich lower bound on the communication complexity of boolean dot product to reach a contradiction.

In order to constuct the protocol for computing boolean dot products, we first define a sequence of transfer mechanisms that are intermediate between our non-ideal and ideal transfer mechanisms. We show that if the provers can cheat using the nonideal transfer mechanism, then two consecutive transfer mechanisms in our sequence can be distinguished. We then show how to use these transfer mechanisms to generate two very simple and very similar transfer mechanisms whose behavior is distinguishable. Finally, we use the distinguishability of this final pair of transfer mechanisms to create a protocol for boolean dot-product. We proceed to formalize this argument.

Transfer Mechanisms That Are Intermediate Between The Ideal and Nonideal Models

We specify a sequence of oblivious transfer mechanisms as follows.

Specification: Oblivious transfer mechanism $T_{n,k}^i$ is specified by its input from the provers and its output to the provers and the verifier. $T_{n,k}^i$ takes as input a sequence of bits $O = O_1, \ldots, O_k$. It flips k coins, $b_1, \ldots, b_k$. $T_{n,k}^i$ randomly selects two sequences of n element boolean vectors, $\vec{x}_1, \ldots, \vec{x}_k$ and $\vec{y}_1, \ldots, \vec{y}_k$. For $1 \leq j \leq i$, vectors $\vec{x}_j$ and $\vec{y}_j$ are subject to the constraint $\vec{x}_j \cdot \vec{y}_j = b_j$. $T_{n,k}^i$'s output is as follows.

Transfer to V: $T_{n,k}^i$ sends the verifier a sequence $O' = O_1', \ldots, O_k'$ where $O_i' = O_i$, iff $b_i = 1$. Otherwise, $O_i' = \#$.

Transfer to P_1: $T_{n,k}^i$ sends P_1 the sequence $\vec{x}_1, \ldots, \vec{x}_k$.

Transfer to P_2: $T_{n,k}^i$ sends P_2 the sequence $\vec{y}_1, \ldots, \vec{y}_k$.

The only difference between $T_{n,k}$ and $T_{n,k}^i$ is that the vectors sent to the provers by $T_{n,k}$ all have some correlation with whether the bit was sent to the verifier, whereas only the first i vectors sent to the provers by $T_{n,k}^i$ are so correlated. Note that $T_{n,k}^O$ is equivalent to the ideal channel T_k^{ideal}, and $T_{n,k}^i$ is equivalent to $T_{n,k}$.

Analysis of Cheating Probabilities for Different Transfer Mechanisms

The sequence of oblivious transfer mechanisms we defined above is "continuous" in that any two consecutive mechanisms are only incrementally different from each other. Using an argument similar to that of [GM], we show that if the probability of successfully cheating using one transfer mechanism in the sequence is significantly greater than the probability of successfully cheating using a different transfer mechanism in the sequence, then there must be two consecutive mechanisms which differ in the probability of a particular cheating strategy being successful.

Definition Let L be some language, and $< P_1, P_2, V, T^{ideal}_{p(n)} >$ a two-prover IPS for L, with oblivious transfer. For some $x \in L$, $|x| = n$, we define $cheat_{ideal}(x)$ as the probability that V can be tricked into accepting x.

We wish to analyze how frequently the provers can cheat if they use a nonideal transfer mechanism, $T_{q(n),p(n)}$. Let $P_{1,q(n)}, P_{2,q(n)}$ be optimal cheating provers for the protocol $< P_{1,q(n)}, P_{2,q(n)}, V, T_{q(n),p(n)} >$. For $x \in L$, $|x| = n$, we define $cheat^i_{q(n)}(x)$ as the probability that $P_{1,q(n)}, P_{2,q(n)})$ causes V to accept x in protocol $< P_{1,q(n)}, P_{2,q(n)}, V, T_{q(n),p(n)} >$.

Clearly, we have $cheat^0_{q(n)}(x) \leq cheat_{ideal}(x)$. We also have, by definition, that $cheat^{p(n)}_{q(n)}(x)$ is the maximum probability that any provers can trick V into accepting x, using transfer mechanism $T_{q(n),p(n)}$.

Using a simple pigeonhole argument, we can show the following.

Lemma A.2 Let $x \notin L$, and $|x| = n$. For all polynomials $q(n)$, there exists some i, $q(n) \leq i \leq p(n)$, such that

$$cheat^{i+1}_{q(n)}(x) - cheat^i_{q(n)}(x) \geq \frac{cheat^{p(n)}_{q(n)}(x) - cheat^0_{q(n)}(x)}{p(n)}. \tag{A.2.6}$$

We now show that if for for all polynomials $q(n)$, there exists a $c > 0$, such that $cheat^{i+1}_{q(n)}(x) - cheat^i_{q(n)}(x) > 1/|x|^c$ for infinitely many x, then we can create efficient algorithms for computing dot products of random vectors. To do this, we first must introduce the notion of "hardwired" versions of transfer mechanisms $T^i_{q(n),p(n)}$.

Restricted Versions of Oblivious Transfer Mechanisms
Given two easily distinguishable mechanisms $T^i_{q(n),p(n)}$ and $T^{i+1}_{q(n),p(n)}$, we would like to create even simpler pairs of mechanisms that are easily distinguishable, yet preserve the essential differences between $T^i_{q(n),p(n)}$ and $T^{i+1}_{q(n),p(n)}$. We observe that the only difference between these two mechanisms lies in the distibutions imposed on the vectors $\vec{x}_{i+1}$ and $\vec{y}_{i+1}$ which are sent to $P_{1,q(n)}$ and $P_{2,q(n)}$. We would like to be able to fix all the other aspects of these channels. To do this, we make the following definitions.

Definition A transfer restriction $R \in \mathcal{R}^i_{n,k}$ is a 3-tuple (R_b, R_x, R_y), where

- R_b is a sequence of bits, $b_1, \ldots, b_k$.

- R_x is a $k - 1$ element sequence of n element boolean vectors, $\vec{x}_1, \ldots, \vec{x}_{i-1}$, $\ldots, \vec{x}_{i+1}, \ldots, \vec{x}_k$.

- R_y is a $k - 1$ element sequence of n element boolean vectors, $\vec{y}_1, \ldots, \vec{y}_{i-1}$, $\ldots, \vec{y}_{i+1}, \ldots, \vec{y}_k$.

Furthermore, we require that for $1 \leq j < i$, $\vec{x}_j \cdot \vec{y}_j = b_j$

Intuitively, we can think of $R \in \mathcal{R}_{n,k}^i$ as a specification for which bits get through to the verifier, and, except for the ith bit, specifications for which vectors are transmitted back to the provers.

Definition Given a transfer restriction $R \in \mathcal{R}_{n,k}^j$ We specify a restricted version of $T_{n,k}^i$, which we denote by $T_{n,k}^i[R]$, as follows.

Specification: Oblivious transfer mechanism $T_{n,k}^i[R]$ takes as input a sequence of bits $O = O_1, \ldots, O_k$. Let $R_b = b_1, \ldots, b_k$, $R_x = \vec{x}_1, \ldots, \vec{x}_{i-1}, \ldots, \vec{x}_{i+1}, \ldots, \vec{x}_k$, and $R_y = \vec{y}_1, \ldots, \vec{y}_{i-1}, \ldots, \vec{y}_{i+1}, \ldots, \vec{y}_k$. $T_{n,k}^i[R]$ randomly selects two n element boolean vectors, $\vec{x}_j$ and $\vec{y}_j$. If $j \geq i$, $\vec{x}_j$ and $\vec{y}_j$ are chosen s.t $\vec{x}_j \cdot \vec{y}_j = b_j$. $T_{n,k}^i[R]$'s output is as follows.

Transfer to $T_{n,k}^i[R]$ sends the verifier sequence $O_1'; , \ldots, O_k'$; where $O_i' = O_i$ iff $b_i = 1$. Otherwise, $O_i' = \#$.

Transfer to P_1: $T_{n,k}^i[R]$ sends P_1 the sequence $\vec{x}_1, \ldots, \vec{x}_k$.

Transfer to P_2: $T_{n,k}^i[R]$ sends P_2 the sequence $\vec{y}_1, \ldots, \vec{y}_k$.

Analysis of Cheating with Respect to Restricted Transfer Mechanisms

Recall that provers $P_{1,q(n)}$ and $P_{2,q(n)}$ cheat optimally, given oblivious transfer mechanism $T_{q(n),p(n)}^i$. We would like to describe what happens when these provers are run using restricted transfer mechanisms. To this end, we define $cheat_{q(n)}^i[R](x)$ as the probability that $P_{1,q(n)}$, $P_{2,q(n)}$, causes V to accept x in protocol $< P_{1,q(n)}, P_{2,p(n)}, V,$ $T_{q(n),p(n)}^i[R] >$.

Using a simple probabilistic argument, we prove the following important lemma.

Lemma A.3 Let $x \notin L$, and $|x| = n$. Let $1 \leq i < p(n)$. For all polynomials $q(n)$, there exists a restriction $R \in \mathcal{R}_{q(n),p(n)}^{i+1}$) such that

$$cheat_{q(n)}^{i+1}[R](x) - cheat_{q(n)}^i[R](x) \geq cheat_{q(n)}^{i+1}(x) - cheat_{q(n)}^i(x). \quad \text{(A.2.7)}$$

Using $T_{q(n),p(n)}^i[R]$, $T_{q(n),p(n)}^{i+1}[R]$ to compute dot products.

Recall that a restriction $R \in \mathcal{R}^{i+1}_{q(n), p(n)})$ defines the entire input/output properties of a restricted transfer protocol $T^i_{q(n), p(n)}[R]$, but for the output vectors $\vec{x}_i$, $\vec{y}_i$ transmitted back to the provers. If the two provers have a source $M_{q(n)}$, which produces vector pairs $\vec{x}$, $\vec{y}$, of size $q(n)$ and sends them to *Prover1* and *Prover2*, respectively, we can use it to simulate $T^i_{q(n), p(n)}[R]$.

We also note that, if allowed to communicate directly, two provers can "simulate" the verifier in the following way. They can send to each other the messages they would have sent to the verifier. By knowing the set of transfer bits, which bits were received by the verifier, and a transcript of the conversation so far between the verifier and the provers, the provers can determine exactly what the verifier's next question in the conversaton will be.

We now can explicitly write down a protocol for computing the dot product of random boolean vectors. The assume that the two parties P_1 and P_2 have agreed on some $x(x \notin L.|x| = n)$, q, i, and $R = (R_b, R_x, R_y) \in \mathcal{R}^{i+1}_{q(n), p(n)})$. The protocol is specified as follows. Player P_1 receives a random boolean vector $\vec{x}$, and player P_2 receives a random boolean vector $\vec{y}$. At the end of the protocol, player P_1 outputs a 0 or 1, which hopefully corresponds to $\vec{x} \cdot \vec{y}$.

Protocol   Dot-Product($\vec{x}$, $\vec{y}$) /* P_1 knows $\vec{x}$, P_2 knows $\vec{y}$, and $|\vec{x}| = |\vec{y}| = q(n)$ */

P_1 and P_2 simulate the protocol $< P_{1,q(n)}, P_{2q(n)}, V, T^i_{q(n), p(n)}[R] >$, on input x. They treat vectors $\vec{x}$ and $\vec{y}$ as substitutes for $\vec{x}_{i+1}$, $\vec{y}_{i+1}$ (which are not defined by R).

If the simulated verifier accepts, then P_1 outputs b_{i+l}, where $R_b = b_1, \ldots, b_{p(n)}$. Otherwise it outputs the complement of b_{i+l}.

We now analyze the communication complexity of this protocol.

Definition   Given a two-prover protocol $\mathcal{P} < P_1, P_2, V, T >$, and some input x, we define the *leakage* $\mathcal{L}(\mathcal{P}, x)$ as the total number of bits transmitted from the provers to the verifier.

The following lemma follows immediately from the definition of Dot-Product.

Lemma A.4   Let $\mathcal{P} =< P_{1,q(n)}, P_{2,q(n)}, V, T^i_{q(n), p(n)}[R] >$. Then protocol Dot-Product requires $\mathcal{L}(\mathcal{P}, x)$ bits of communication.

Finally, we can bound below Dot–Product's success rate on random vectors by the following lemma.

Lemma A.5   Given $q(n)$ bit vectors $\vec{x}$, $\vec{x}$ distributed uniformly, the probability that Dot-Product $(\vec{x}, \vec{y}) = \vec{x} \cdot \vec{y}$ is at least

$$\frac{1}{2} + \left(cheat^{i+1}_{q(n)}[R](x) - cheat^i_{q(n)}[R](x) \right). \tag{A.2.8}$$

Proof Our proof is by a straightforward calculation of conditional probabilities, which we outline below. We define the variables *good* and *bad* by

$$good = prob(\text{The simulated verifier accepts } |\vec{x} \cdot \vec{y} = b_i), \quad \text{and,}$$

$$bad = prob(\text{The simulated verifier accepts } |\vec{x} \cdot \vec{y} \neq b_i).$$

The probability that IDot-Product yields the correct answer is equal to

$$\frac{1}{2} \cdot good + \frac{1}{2} \cdot (1 - bad) \tag{A.2.9.}$$

We now solve for *good* and *bad* in terms of $cheat^i_{q(n)}[R](x)$ and $cheat^{i+1}_{q(n)}[R](x)$. Using our definitions for $cheat^i_{g(n)}[R](x)$ and $cheat^{i+1}_{g(n)}[R](x)$, we have

$$cheat^{i+1}_{q(n)}[R](x) = good, \quad \text{and,} \tag{A.2.A}$$

$$cheat^i_{q(n)}pR](x) = \frac{1}{2} \cdot good + \frac{1}{2} \cdot bad. \tag{A.2.11}$$

Solving for *good* and *bad*, we have

$$good = cheat^{i+1}_{q(n)}[RJ(x), \quad \text{and,} \tag{A.2.12}$$

$$bad = cheat^{i+1}_{q(n)}[RJ(x) - 2\left(cheat^{i+1}_{q(n)}[R](x) - cheat^i_{q(n)}[R](x)\right). \tag{A.2.13}$$

Substituting equations (A.2.12) and (A.2.13) into equation A.2.9), and simplifying, we get equation (A.2.8).

A.3 Implementing Zero-Knowledge with Circuits

In this section we outline a technique we call *the method of encrypted conversations*. This technique represents a fairly general methodology for converting protocols into zero-knowiedge protocols. Its main requirement is the ability of the parties involved to perform oblivious circuit evaluation.

A Normal Form for Two-Prover IPS's

For ease of exposition, we consider a normal form for two-prover interactive proof systems(IPS's). This normal form consists of three stages, as described below.

Notation: Throughout this section, $q_i(x, r, \cdot, \cdot, \cdot)$ will denote the i-th question of the verifier computed on his random coin tosses r, the input x, and the history of the communication so far. (a_i correspond to the provers answers).

Stage 1:. On input x, where $|x| = n$, the verifier generates a sequence $r = r_1, \ldots, r_{p(n)}$ of random bits. The verifier computes his first question, $q_1 = q_1(x, r)$.

Stage 2:. The verifier sends q_1 to Prover 1. Prover 1 sends its answer, a_1 back to the verifier. The verifier computes his second question, $q_2 = q_2(x, r, a_1)$.

Stage 3:. The verifier sends q_2 to Prover 2. Prover 2 sends its answer, a_2, back to the verifier. The verifier computes its decision predicate, $accept(x, t, a_1, a_2)$, and accepts iff $accept(x, r, a_1, a_2)$ evaluates to "true".

We use the following result.

Theorem (normal form for 2 prover IPS's): Given any two prover IPS $\mathcal{P}$ for a language L, there exists an IPS $\mathcal{P}'$, with the following 2 properties.

1. If $x \in L$ then $prob(\mathcal{P}'(x) \text{ accepts}) = 1$.

2. There exists some $c > 0$ such that if $x \notin L$ then $prob(\mathcal{P}'(x) \text{ accepts}) \leq 1 - 1/|x|^c$.

Remark It is currently open whether the $\leq 1 - 1/|x|^c$ failure probability can be reduced. However, if greater reliability is desired, one may run a normal form protocol several times serially to achieve an exponentially low probability of failure.

We now need to show how to convert an IPS in normal form into a zero-knowledge IPS.

Conceptually, we would like to have the use of a black box into which the verifier inputs an encrypted history of the communication, the prover inputs its answer to the question and the output which is given to the verifier is the encrypted answer of the prover and the encrypted next question of the verifier. See fig. 2.

The encryption scheme used to encrypt the questions and answers should be an information theoretically strong encryption scheme with respect to the verifier, while the provers will be given the ability to decrypt.

We describe how this is achieved in the following section A.3.1. The box is achieved by the technique of oblivious circuit evaluation as described in section A.3.2.

A.3.1 Strong Encryption Using 2-Universal Hash Functions

We need a cryptographic system (call it E for the sake of discussion) which is both unbreakable, and existentially unforgeable. By unbreakable, we mean that if one is given $E(x)$, an encryption of x, but one does not have the decryption key, then one cannot infer anything about x. By existentially unforgeable, we mean that if one is given $E(x)$, an encryption of x, but one does not have the decryption key, then one cannot produce any string *forge* such that *forge* $= E(y)$ for some y. These security requirements are information theoretic, and must apply to someone with arbitrary computational power.

To accomplish this, we use the notion of universal hash functions, first introduced by Carter and Wegman[CW]. In addition, we require the following property of our universal sets.

Definition   A family of 2-universal sets $\mathcal{H}_n$, of functions $h : \{0, 1\}^n \to \{0, 1\}^n$ is *almost self-inverse* iff for all c, and for all n sufficiently large (with respect to c), a function h, picked uniformly from $\mathcal{H}$, will have an inverse $h^{-1} \in \mathcal{H}$ with probability $> 1 - n^{-c}$.

One example of an almost self-inverse 2-universal set of hash functions is the set of linear equations over $GF(2^n)$. As there is a trivial correspondence between $\{0, 1\}^n$ and $GF(2^n)$, we treat all our elements as being in $\{O, 1\}^n$.

For our encryption system, we require that all legal messages m are padded with a number of trailing 0's equal to the length of the original message. We encrypt a message $m \in \{0, 1\}^n$ by applying some uniformly selected function $h \in \mathcal{H}_n$ to it. We can decrypt $h(m)$ by by applying its h^{-1} to it. For our purposes, we can safely ignore the possibility that a uniformly chosen h isn't invertible. The following lemma shows that this encryption scheme is unbreakable and unforgeable.

Lemma   Let h be chosen uniformly from $\mathcal{H}_n$. Then

1. (unbreakability) $(\forall x, y \in \{0, 1\}^n) prob(h(x) = y) = 2^{-n}$.

2. (unforgeability) $(\forall x, y, z \in \{0, 1\}^n))$

$$prob((\exists w \in \{0, 1\}^{n/2} 0^{n/2}) h(w) = z | h(x) = y) = 2^{-n/2}.$$

Proof   Both properties follow immediately from the definition of 2-universal hash functions.   ∎

In the protocol the provers will agree on four random hash functions $h_1, h_2, h_3, h_4 \in \mathcal{H}_{p(n)}$. At the end of the protocol, the verifier will possess the values of $h_1(r)$, $h_2(q_1)$, and $h_3(a_1)$, but will not possess any extra information about which functions h_1, h_2, and h_3 actually are. However, knowing the value of $h(x)$ gives no information, in the information theoretic sense, about the value of x. This is roughly how the zero-knowledge aspect of our protocol is achieved.

A.3.2 Use of Oblivious Circuit Evaluation

We use the reduction of Kilian[K] from oblivious transfer to oblivious circuit computation. This reduction maintains the usual security properties desired of oblivious circuit evaluation, without recourse to any intractibility assumptions.[5] Its sole requirement is a sequence $O = O_1, \ldots, O_{p(n)}$ of bits, all of which are known to A, and haif of which are known to B(a more detailed description of this condition is given in section A.2). This set of bits(or, more technically, a reasonable approximation to such a set) is provided by the oblivious transfer protocol outlined in section A.2. for the rest of this discussion, we treat oblivious circuit evaluation as a primitive operation.

A.3.3 Outline of the Zero-Knowledge Protocol

We can now describe our zero-knowledge transformed protocol For our expositions, we still treat oblivious circuit computation of as a primitive. (A description of circuits C_0, C_1, C_2 and C_3 is given following the protocol.) Note the similaruty between this description and the description of the normal-form for protocols given above.

On input x, where $|1x| = n$.

Step 0:. Provers 1 and 2 agree on random invertible hash functions h_1, h_2, h_3, $h_4 \in \mathcal{H}_{2p(n)}$, and random string $r_1 \in \{0, 1\}^{p(n)}$. The verifier selects a random string $r_2 \in \{0, 1\}^{p(n)}$. The verifier and Prover 1 evaluate $r' = C_0[x](r_1, r_2, h_1)$. (*r* will the random coin tosses to be used by the verifier).

Step 1:. The verifier and Prover 1 then evaluate $q_1' = C_1[x](r', h_1^{-1}, h_2)$, the encrypted version of the verifier's first question.

Step 2:. The verifier sends q_1' to Prover 1. If $h_2^{-1}(q_1')$ does not decrypt to a legitimate message, then Prover 1 halts the conversation. Otherwise, Prover 1 computes his answer, a_1, and sends the verifier $a_1' = h_3(a_1)$. The verifier and Prover 1 evaluate $q_2' = C_2[x](r', a_1', h_1^{-1}, h_3^{-1}, h_4)$, the encrypted version of the verifiers second question.

Step 3:. The verifier sends q_2' to Prover 2. If $h_4^{-1}(q_2')$ does not decrypt to a legitimate message, then Prover 2 halts the conversation. Otherwise, Prover 2 computes his answer, a_2. The verifier and Prover 2 evaluate $decision = C_3[x](r', a_1', a_2, h_1^{-1}, h_3^{-1})$.

---

5. Goldreich-Vainish describe a simple reduction from oblivious circuit evaluation to oblivious transfer, without any intractibility assumptions. However, this reduction only works for honest parties, and is thus unuseable by us.

At the end of this ;protocol, verifier accepts iff *decision* = *true*.

We now describe circuits C_i for $i = 0, 1, 2, 3$.

For each circuit, we give the input from the prover, the input from the verifier, and the output given to the verifier. We adopt the convention that $|x| = n$, and assume without loss of generality that all strings being exchanged in the protocol are of length $p(n)$, for some polynomial p. We use the following simple functions to simplify our exposition. Function $pad_n : \{0, 1\}^n - \{0, 1\}^{2n}$ pads an extra n zeros onto the end of an n-bit string Function $strip_n : \{0, 1\}^{2n} \rightarrow \{0, 1\}^n$, which removes the last n bits from a $2n$-bit string. Predicate $legal_n : \{0, 1\}^{2n} \rightarrow \{true, false\}$ is true iff the last n bits of the input string are equal to 0.

$C_0[x]$:

Input from the prover: A sequence of bits, $b = b_1, \ldots, b_{p(n)}$, and a hash function
  $h \in \mathcal{H}_{2p(n)}$.

Input from the verifier: A sequence of bits $c = c_1, \ldots, c_{p(n)}$.

Output to the Verifier: Output($h(pad_n(b \oplus c))$)

Circuit $C_0 s[x]$ is the initialization circuit that creates the verifiers random bits in Stage 1 of the protocol described above.

$C_1[x]$:

Input from the prover:
  Hash functions $h_1^{-1}, h_2 \in \mathcal{H}_{2p(n)}$.

Input from the verifier:
  String $r' \in \{O, 1\}^{2p(n)}$.

Output to the verifier:
  $r = h_1^{-1}(r')$
  If $legal_{p(n)}(r) = false$
  Then Output($O^{2p(n)}$)
  Else $r = strip_{p(n)}(r)$
    $q_1 = q_1(x, r)$
    Output($h_2(pad_{p(n)}(q_1))$)

Circuit $C_1[x]$ is used to implement Stage 1 of the protocol described above.

$C_2[x]$:

Input from the prover:
  Hash functions $h_1^{-1}, h_3^{-1}, h_4 \in \mathcal{H}_{2p(n)}$

Input from the verifier:
  Strings $r', a_1' \in \{0, 1\}^{2p(n)}$.

Output to the verifier:

$r = h_1^{-1}(r')$

$a_1 = h_3^{-1}(a_1')$

If $(legal_{p(n)}(r)$ and $legal_{p(n)}(a_1)) = false$

Then Output($0^{2p(n)}$)

Else $r = strip_{p(n)}(r)$

　　　$a_1 = strip_{p(n)}(a_1)$

　　　$q_2 = q_2(x, r, a_1)$

　　　Output($h_4(pad_{p(n)}(q_2))$)

Circuit $C_2[x]$ is used to implement Stage 2 of the protocol described above.

$C_3[x]$:

Input from the prover:

　　Hash functions $h_1^{-1}, h_3^{-1} \in \mathcal{H}_{2p(n)}$,

String $a_2 \in \{0, 1\}^{2p(n)}$

Input from the verifier:

Strings $r', a_1' \in \{0, 1\}^{2p(n)}$.

Output to the verifier:

$r = h_1^{-1}(r')$

$a_1 = h_3^{-1}, (a_1')$

If $(legal_{p(n)}(r)$ and $legal_{p(n)}(a_1)) = false$

Then Output($02^{2p(n)}$)

Else $r = strip_{p(n)}(r)$

　　　$a_1 = strip_{p(n)}(a_1)$

　　　Output($accept(z, r, a_1, a_2)$)

Circuit $C_3[x]$ is used to implement Stage 3 of the protocol described above.

The two obvious questions we must deal with are, "Is this protocol still a proof system?", and "Is this protocol zero-knowledge?"

Is This Protocol a Proof System?

If the verifier is honest, and if the provers input the correct hash functions, and their inverses, into the circuits being evaluated, then one can map transcripts of conversations in this protocol into transcripts of the original protocol (with possibly *cheating provers*). In this case, the provers cannot cheat any more effectively they could in the original protocol, and the new protocol will remain a proof system if the original one was.

If the provers do not input consistent sets of hash functions, then nothing can be guarenteed about whether the protocol remains a proof system. However, using

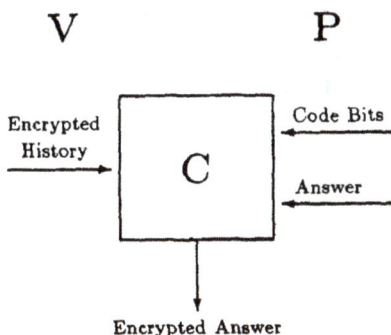

Figure 1 Schematic of encrypted conversation.

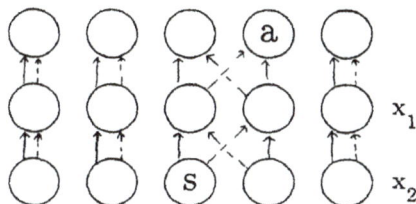

Figure 2 Schematic of a simple W5PBP. Solid lines correspond to functions f_1^i, dashed lines correspond to functions f_0^i. In this program, $v_1 = x_2$ and $v_2 = x_1$. This branching program is equivalent to $x_1 \oplus x_2$.

the machinery developed in [K], it is possible for the provers to commit, at the beginning of the protocol, all the hash functions they input to the circuits, along with a zero-knowledge proof that these inputs are consistent with each other.

Is This Protocol Zero-Knowledge?

The proof that this protocol is zero-knowledge is, while not overly complex or difficult, relies too heavily on machinery from [K] to be concisely presented here. We make the following intuitive argument for why the protocol is zero-knowledge.

First, note that the verifier's actions are severely restricted by the use of circuits and the encryption scheme. Except for its random bits, all the inputs it gives to the provers or the circuits are encrypted with an unforgeable system. If the verifier ever attempts to give an incorrect string to a prover, the prover will detect the forgery will probability exponentially close to 1. Likewise, if the verifier inputs an incorrect string to a circuit, it will almost certainly output either $O^{2p(n)}$ or *false*. This rules out any active attack on the part of the verifier.

Second, we show that passive attacks by the verifier do not yield ay information. The intermediate outputs of circuits $C_1, \ldots, C_3$ are all uniformly distributed, and thus yield no information.

III

PERSPECTIVES

On the Foundations of Cryptography

Oded Goldreich

We survey the main paradigms, approaches, and techniques used to conceptualize, define, and provide solutions to natural cryptographic problems. We start by presenting some of the central tools used in cryptography—that is, computational difficulty (in the form of one-way functions), pseudorandomness, and zero-knowledge proofs. Based on these tools, we turn to the treatment of basic cryptographic applications such as encryption and signature schemes as well as the design of general secure cryptographic protocols. Our presentation assumes basic knowledge of algorithms, probability theory, and complexity theory, but nothing beyond this.[1]

17.1 Introduction and Preliminaries

It is possible to build a cabin with no foundations, but not a lasting building.

—Eng. Isidor Goldreich (1906–1995)

17.1.1 Introduction

The vast expansion and rigorous treatment of cryptography is one of the major achievements of theoretical computer science. In particular, concepts such as computational indistinguishability, pseudorandomness, and zero-knowledge interactive proofs were introduced, classical notions such as secure encryption and unforgeable signatures were placed on sound grounds, and new (unexpected) directions and connections were uncovered. Indeed, modern cryptography is strongly

---

1. This is a revision of the primer [Goldreich 2005].

linked to complexity theory (in contrast to "classical" cryptography, which is strongly related to information theory).

Modern cryptography is concerned with the construction of information systems that are robust against malicious attempts to make these systems deviate from their prescribed functionality. The prescribed functionality may be the private and authenticated communication of information through the Internet, the holding of incoercible and secret electronic voting, or conducting any "fault-resilient" multi-party computation. Indeed, the scope of modern cryptography is very broad, and it stands in contrast to "classical" cryptography (which has focused on the single problem of enabling secret communication over insecure communication media).

The design of cryptographic systems is a very difficult task. One cannot rely on intuitions regarding the "typical" state of the environment in which the system operates. For sure, the ***adversary*** attacking the system will try to manipulate the environment into "untypical" states. Nor can one be content with countermeasures designed to withstand specific attacks, since the adversary (which acts after the design of the system is completed) will try to attack the schemes in ways that are different from the ones the designer had envisioned. The validity of the above assertions seems self-evident, still some people hope that in practice ignoring these tautologies will not result in actual damage. Experience shows that these hopes rarely come true; cryptographic schemes based on make-believe are broken, typically sooner than later.

In view of the foregoing, we believe that it makes little sense to make assumptions regarding the specific *strategy* that the adversary may use. The only assumptions that can be justified refer to the computational *abilities* of the adversary. Furthermore, the design of cryptographic systems has to be based on *firm foundations*; whereas ad hoc approaches and heuristics are a very dangerous way to go. A heuristic may make sense when the designer has a very good idea regarding the environment in which a scheme is to operate, yet a cryptographic scheme has to operate in a maliciously selected environment that typically transcends the designer's view.

This chapter is aimed at providing an introduction to the foundations for cryptography. The foundations of cryptography are the paradigms, approaches and techniques used to conceptualize, define and provide solutions to natural "security concerns." We will present some of these paradigms, approaches, and techniques, as well as some of the fundamental results obtained using them. *It is quite striking that doing so means focusing on research that was conducted either by Goldwasser and Micali or was directly inspired and informed by their work.*

Solving a cryptographic problem (or addressing a security concern) is a two-stage process consisting of a *definitional stage* and a *constructive stage*. First, in the definitional stage, the functionality underlying the natural concern is to be identified, and an adequate cryptographic problem has to be defined. Trying to list all undesired situations is infeasible and prone to error. Instead, one should define the functionality in terms of operation in an imaginary ideal model, and require a candidate solution to emulate this operation in the real, clearly defined model (which specifies the adversary's abilities). Once the definitional stage is completed, one proceeds to construct a system that satisfies the definition. Such a construction may use some simpler tools, and its security is proved relying on the features of these tools. In practice, of course, such a scheme may need to satisfy also some *specific* efficiency requirements.

The emphasis of the chapter is on the clarification of fundamental concepts and on demonstrating the feasibility of solving several central cryptographic problems. It focuses on several archetypical cryptographic problems (e.g., encryption and signature schemes) and on several central tools (e.g., computational difficulty, pseudorandomness, and zero-knowledge proofs). For each of these problems (respectively, tools), we start by presenting the natural concern underlying it (respectively, its intuitive objective), then define the problem (respectively, tool), and finally demonstrate that the problem may be solved (respectively, the tool can be constructed). In the latter step, our focus is on demonstrating the feasibility of solving the problem, not on providing a practical solution. As a secondary concern, we typically discuss the level of practicality (or impracticality) of the given (or known) solution.

Computational Difficulty

The aforementioned tools and applications (e.g., secure encryption) exist only if some sort of computational hardness exists. Specifically, all these problems and tools require (either explicitly or implicitly) the ability to generate instances of hard problems. Such ability is captured in the definition of one-way functions. Thus, one-way functions are the very minimum needed for doing most natural tasks of cryptography (see Impagliazzo and Luby [1989]). (It turns out, as we shall see, that this necessary condition is "morally" sufficient; that is, the existence of one-way functions (or augmentations and extensions of this assumption) suffices for doing most of cryptography.)

Our current state of understanding of efficient computation does not allow us to prove that one-way functions exist. In particular, if $\mathcal{P} = \mathcal{NP}$ then no one-way functions exist. Furthermore, the existence of one-way functions implies that $\mathcal{NP}$

is not contained in $\mathcal{BPP} \supseteq \mathcal{P}$ (not even "on the average"). Thus, proving that one-way functions exist is not easier than proving that $\mathcal{P} \neq \mathcal{NP}$; in fact, the former task seems significantly harder than the latter. Hence, we have no choice (at this stage of history) but to assume that one-way functions exist. As justification to this assumption we may only offer the combined beliefs of hundreds (or thousands) of researchers. Furthermore, these beliefs concern a simply stated assumption, and their validity follows from several widely believed conjectures that are central to various fields (e.g., the conjectured intractability of integer factorization is central to computational number theory).

Since we need assumptions anyhow, why not just assume what we want (i.e., the existence of a solution to some natural cryptographic problem)? Well, first we need to know what we want: as stated above, we must first clarify what exactly we want; that is, go through the typically complex definitional stage. But once this stage is completed, can we just assume that the definition derived can be met? Not really: Once a definition is derived, how can we know that it can at all be met? The way to demonstrate that a definition is viable (and that the corresponding intuitive security concern can be satisfied at all) is to construct a solution based on a *better understood* assumption (i.e., one that is more common and widely believed). For example, looking at the definition of zero-knowledge proofs (introduced by Goldwasser, Micali, and Rackoff [Goldwasser et al. 1989]), it is not a priori clear that such proofs exist at all (in a nontrivial sense). The nontriviality of the notion was first demonstrated (in Goldwasser et al. [1989]) by presenting a zero-knowledge proof system for statements, regarding Quadratic Residuosity, that are believed to be hard to verify (without extra information). Furthermore, contrary to prior beliefs, it was later shown (by Goldreich, Micali, and Wigderson [Goldreich et al. 1991]) that the existence of one-way functions implies that any NP-statement can be proved in zero-knowledge. Thus, facts that were not known at all to hold (and even believed to be false) were shown to hold by reduction to widely believed assumptions (without which most of modern cryptography collapses anyhow). To summarize, not all assumptions are equal, and so reducing a complex, new, and doubtful assumption to a widely believed simple (or even merely simpler) assumption is of great value. Furthermore, reducing the solution of a new task to the assumed security of a well-known primitive typically means providing a construction that, using the known primitive, solves the new task. This means that we do not only know (or assume) that the new task is solvable but we also have a solution based on a primitive that, being well-known, typically has several candidate implementations.

Prerequisites and Structure

Our aim is to present the basic concepts, techniques, and results in cryptography. As stated above, our emphasis is on the clarification of fundamental concepts and the relationship among them. This is done in a way independent of the particularities of some popular number-theoretic examples. These particular examples played a central role in the development of the field and still offer the most practical implementations of all cryptographic primitives, but this does not mean that the presentation has to be linked to them. On the contrary, we believe that concepts are best clarified when presented at an abstract level, decoupled from specific implementations. Thus, the most relevant background for this chapter is provided by basic knowledge of algorithms (including randomized ones), computability, and elementary probability theory.

The chapter is organized in two main parts, which are preceded by preliminaries (regarding efficient and feasible computations). The two parts are "Basic Tools" and "Basic Applications." The basic tools consist of computational difficulty (one-way functions), pseudorandomness, and zero-knowledge proofs. These basic tools are used for the basic applications, which in turn consist of encryption schemes, signature schemes, and general cryptographic protocols.

In order to give some feeling of the flavor of the area, we have included in this chapter a few proof sketches, which some readers may find too terse. We stress that following these proof sketches is *not* essential to understanding the rest of the material. In general, later sections may refer to definitions and results in prior sections, but not to the constructions and proofs that support these results. It may be even possible to understand later sections without reading any prior section, but we believe that the order we chose should be preferred because it proceeds from the simplest notions to the most complex ones.

Suggestions for Further Reading

This chapter is a brief summary of the author's two-volume work on the subject [Goldreich 2001, Goldreich 2004]. Furthermore, Part I corresponds to Goldreich [2001], whereas Part II corresponds to Goldreich [2004]. Needless to say, the reader is referred to these textbooks for further detail.

Two of the topics reviewed by this chapter are zero-knowledge proofs (which are probabilistic) and pseudorandom generators (and functions). A wider perspective on probabilistic proof systems and pseudorandomness is provided in Chapter 18 (of this volume) as well as in Goldreich [2008, Chap. 8–9].

Needless to say, this chapter (as well as Goldreich 2001, 2004) provide only an introduction to the foundations of cryptography, which are still a topic of very active research. As a rule of thumb, developments that deviate from the basic definitions presented in this chapter are not even referenced in this text, and the interested readers will have to look for them elsewhere.

Practice. The aim of this chapter is to introduce the reader to the *theoretical foundations* of cryptography. As argued above, such foundations are necessary for *sound* practice of cryptography. Indeed, practice requires more than theoretical foundations, whereas the current chapter makes no attempt to provide anything beyond the latter. However, given a sound foundation, one can learn and evaluate various practical suggestions that appear elsewhere (e.g., in Menezes et al. [1996]). On the other hand, lack of sound foundations results in inability to critically evaluate practical suggestions, which in turn leads to unsound decisions. Nothing could be more harmful to the design of schemes that need to withstand adversarial attacks than misconceptions about such attacks.

17.1.2 Preliminaries

Modern cryptography, as surveyed here, is concerned with the construction of *efficient* schemes for which it is *infeasible* to violate the security feature. Thus, we need a notion of efficient computations as well as a notion of infeasible ones. The computations of the legitimate users of the scheme ought be efficient, whereas violating the security features (by an adversary) ought to be infeasible. We stress that we do not identify feasible computations with efficient ones, but rather view the former notion as potentially more liberal.

Efficient Computations and Infeasible ones
Efficient computations are commonly modeled by computations that are polynomial time in the security parameter. The polynomial bounding the running time of the legitimate user's strategy is *fixed and typically explicit* (and *small*). Indeed, our aim is to have a notion of efficiency that is as strict as possible (or, equivalently, develop strategies that are as efficient as possible). Here (i.e., when referring to the complexity of the legitimate users) we are in the same situation as in any algorithmic setting. Things are different when referring to our assumptions regarding the computational resources of the adversary, where we refer to the notion of feasible that we wish to be as wide as possible. A common approach is to postulate that *feasible computations* are polynomial time too, but here the polynomial is NOT *a priori*

specified (and is to be thought of as arbitrarily large). In other words, the adversary is restricted to the class of polynomial-time computations and anything beyond this is considered to be *infeasible*.

Although many definitions explicitly refer to the convention of associating feasible computations with polynomial-time ones, this convention is *inessential* to any of the results known in the area. In all cases, a more general statement can be made by referring to a general notion of feasibility, which should be preserved under standard algorithmic composition, yielding theories that refer to adversaries of running time bounded by any specific super-polynomial function (or class of functions). Still, for sake of concreteness and clarity, we shall use the former convention in our formal definitions (but our motivational discussions will refer to an unspecified notion of feasibility that covers at least efficient computations).

Randomized (or Probabilistic) Computations

Randomized computations play a central role in cryptography. One fundamental reason for this fact is that randomness is essential for the existence (or rather the generation) of secrets. Thus, we must allow the legitimate users to employ randomized computations, and certainly (since randomization is feasible) we must consider also adversaries that employ randomized computations. This brings up the issue of success probability: Typically, we require that legitimate users succeed (in fulfilling their legitimate goals) with probability 1 (or negligibly close to this), whereas adversaries succeed (in violating the security features) with negligible probability. Thus, the notion of a *negligible probability* plays an important role in our exposition. One requirement of the definition of negligible probability is to provide a robust notion of rareness: A rare event should occur rarely even if we repeat the experiment for a feasible number of times. That is, in case we consider any polynomial-time computation to be feasible, a function $\mu : \mathbb{N} \to \mathbb{N}$ is called *negligible* if $1 - (1 - \mu(n))^{p(n)} < 0.01$ for every polynomial p and sufficiently big n (i.e., μ is negligible if for every positive polynomial p' the function $\mu(\cdot)$ is upper-bounded by $1/p'(\cdot)$). However, if we consider the function $T(n)$ to provide our notion of infeasible computation then functions bounded above by $1/T(n)$ are considered negligible (in n).

We will also refer to the notion of *noticeable probability*. Here the requirement is that events that occur with noticeable probability, will occur almost surely (i.e., except with negligible probability) if we repeat the experiment for a polynomial number of times. Thus, a function $\nu : \mathbb{N} \to \mathbb{N}$ is called *noticeable* if for some positive polynomial p' the function $\nu(\cdot)$ is lower-bounded by $1/p'(\cdot)$.

Part I   **Basic Tools**

In this part we survey three basic tools used in modern cryptography. The most basic tool is computational difficulty, which in turn is captured by the notion of one-way functions. Next, we survey the notion of computational indistinguishability, which underlies the theory of pseudorandomness as well as much of the rest of cryptography. In particular, pseudorandom generators and functions are important tools that will be used in later sections. Finally, we survey zero-knowledge proofs and their use in the design of cryptographic protocols. For more details regarding the contents of the current part, see our textbook [Goldreich 2001].

17.3   **Computational Difficulty and One-Way Functions**

Modern cryptography is concerned with the construction of systems that are easy to operate (properly) but hard to foil. Thus, a complexity gap (between the ease of proper usage and the difficulty of deviating from the prescribed functionality) lies at the heart of modern cryptography. However, gaps as required for modern cryptography are not known to exist; they are only widely believed to exist. Indeed, almost all of modern cryptography rises or falls with the question of whether one-way functions exist. We mention that the existence of one-way functions implies that $\mathcal{NP}$ contains search problems that are hard to solve *on the average*, which in turn implies that $\mathcal{NP}$ is not contained in $\mathcal{BPP}$ (i.e., a worst-case complexity conjecture).

Loosely speaking, one-way functions are functions that are easy to evaluate but hard (on the average) to invert. Such functions can be thought of as an efficient way of generating "puzzles" that are infeasible to solve (i.e., the puzzle is a random image of the function and a solution is a corresponding preimage). Furthermore, the person generating the puzzle knows a solution to it and can efficiently verify the validity of (possibly other) solutions to the puzzle. Thus, one-way functions have, by definition, a clear cryptographic flavor (i.e., they manifest a gap between the ease of one task and the difficulty of a related one).

17.3.1   **One-Way Functions**

One-way functions are functions that are efficiently computable but infeasible to invert (in an average-case sense). That is, a function $f: \{0, 1\}^* \to \{0, 1\}^*$ is called *one-way* if there is an efficient algorithm that on input x outputs $f(x)$, whereas any feasible algorithm that tries to find a preimage of $f(x)$ under f may succeed only with negligible probability (where the probability is taken uniformly over the choices of x and the algorithm's coin tosses). Associating feasible computations with probabilistic polynomial-time algorithms, we obtain the following definition.

Definition 17.1   (One-way functions)   A function $f\colon \{0, 1\}^* \to \{0, 1\}^*$ is called ***one-way*** if the following two conditions hold:

> **easy to evaluate.**   There exist a polynomial-time algorithm A such that $A(x) = f(x)$ for every $x \in \{0, 1\}^*$.
>
> **hard to invert.**   For every probabilistic polynomial-time algorithm A', every polynomial p, and all sufficiently large n,
>
> $$\Pr[A'(f(x), 1^n) \in f^{-1}(f(x))] < \frac{1}{p(n)},$$
>
> where the probability is taken uniformly over all the possible choices of $x \in \{0, 1\}^n$ and all the possible outcomes of the internal coin tosses of algorithm A'.

Algorithm A' is given the auxiliary input 1^n so to allow it to run in time polynomial in the length of x, which is important in case f drastically shrinks its input (e.g., $|f(x)| = O(\log |x|)$). Typically, f is length preserving, in which case the auxiliary input 1^n is redundant. Note that A' is not required to output a specific preimage of $f(x)$; any preimage (i.e., element in the set $f^{-1}(f(x))$) will do. (Indeed, in case f is one-to-one, the string x is the only preimage of $f(x)$ under f; but in general there may be other preimages.) It is required that algorithm A' fails (to find a preimage) with overwhelming probability, when the probability is also taken over the input distribution. That is, f is "typically" hard to invert, not merely hard to invert in some ("rare") cases.

Some of the most popular candidates for one-way functions are based on the conjectured intractability of computational problems in number theory. One such conjecture is that it is infeasible to factor large integers. Consequently, the function that takes as input two (equal-length) primes and outputs their product is widely believed to be a one-way function. Furthermore, factoring such a composite is infeasible if and only if squaring modulo such a composite is a one-way function (see Rabin [1979]). For certain composites (i.e., products of two primes that are both congruent to 3 mod 4), the latter function induces a permutation over the set of quadratic residues modulo this composite. A related permutation, which is widely believed to be one-way, is the RSA function [Rivest et al. 1978]: $x \mapsto x^e \bmod N$, where $N = P \cdot Q$ is a composite as above, e is relatively prime to $(P - 1) \cdot (Q - 1)$, and $x \in \{0, \ldots, N - 1\}$. The latter examples (as well as other popular suggestions) are better captured by the following formulation of a collection of one-way functions (which is indeed related to Definition 17.1):

Definition 17.2   (Collections of one-way functions)   A collection of functions, $\{f_i: D_i \to \{0, 1\}^*\}_{i \in \overline{I}}$, is called ***one-way*** if there exists three probabilistic polynomial-time algorithms, I, D and F, so that the following two conditions hold

> **easy to sample and compute.**   On input 1^n, the output of (*the index selection*) algorithm I is distributed over the set $\overline{I} \cap \{0, 1\}^n$ (i.e., is an n-bit long index of some function). On input (an index of a function) $i \in \overline{I}$, the output of (*the domain sampling*) algorithm D is distributed over the set D_i (i.e., over the domain of the function). On input $i \in \overline{I}$ and $x \in D_i$, (*the evaluation*) algorithm F *always* outputs $f_i(x)$.

> **hard to invert.**[2]   For every probabilistic polynomial-time algorithm, A', every positive polynomial $p(\cdot)$, and all sufficiently large n's

$$\Pr\left[A'(i, f_i(x)) \in f_i^{-1}(f_i(x))\right] < \frac{1}{p(n)},$$

> where $i \leftarrow I(1^n)$ and $x \leftarrow D(i)$.

The collection is said to be a collection of ***permutations*** if each of the f_i's is a permutation over the corresponding D_i, and $D(i)$ is almost uniformly distributed in D_i.

For example, in case of the RSA, $f_{N,e}: D_{N,e} \to D_{N,e}$ satisfies $f_{N,e}(x) = x^e \bmod N$, where $D_{N,e} = \{0, \ldots, N - 1\}$. Definition 17.2 is also a good starting point for the definition of a trapdoor permutation.[3] Loosely speaking, the latter is a collection of one-way permutations augmented with an efficient algorithm that allows for inverting the permutation when given adequate auxiliary information (called a trapdoor).

Definition 17.3   (Trapdoor permutations)   A collection of permutations as in Definition 17.2 is called a ***trapdoor permutation*** if there are two auxiliary probabilistic polynomial-time algorithms I' and F^{-1} such that (1) the distribution $I'(1^n)$ ranges over pairs of strings so that the first string is distributed as in $I(1^n)$, and (2) for every (i, t) in

---

2. Note that this condition refers to the distributions $I(1^n)$ and $D(i)$, which are merely required to range over $\overline{I} \cap \{0, 1\}^n$ and D_i, respectively. (Typically, the distributions $I(1^n)$ and $D(i)$ are (almost) uniform over $\overline{I} \cap \{0, 1\}^n$ and D_i, respectively.)

3. Indeed, a more adequate term would be a collection of trapdoor permutations, but the shorter (and less precise) term is the commonly used one.

the range of $I'(1^n)$ and every $x \in D_i$ it holds that $F^{-1}(t, f_i(x)) = x$. (That is, t is a trapdoor that allows to invert f_i.)

For example, in case of the RSA, $f_{N,e}$ can be inverted by raising to the power d (modulo $N = P \cdot Q$), where d is the multiplicative inverse of e modulo $(P-1) \cdot (Q-1)$. Indeed, in this case, the trapdoor information is (N, d).

Strong versus Weak One-Way Functions

Recall that the above definitions require that any feasible algorithm *succeeds in inverting* the function *with negligible probability*. A weaker notion only requires that any feasible algorithm *fails to invert* the function *with noticeable probability*. It turns out that the existence of such weak one-way functions implies the existence of strong one-way functions (as defined above). The construction itself is straightforward: The argument to the new function F is parsed into sufficiently many equal-length blocks, and the weak one-way function f on the individual blocks. We warn that the hardness of inverting F is not established by mere "combinatorics" (i.e., considering the relative volume of S^t in U^t, for $S \subset U$, where S represents the set of "easy to invert" images). Specifically, one may *not* assume that the potential inverting algorithm works independently on each block. Indeed, this assumption seems reasonable, but we should not assume that the adversary behaves in a reasonable way (unless we can actually prove that it gains nothing by behaving in other ways—i.e., ways that seem unreasonable to us).

The hardness of inverting the resulting function F is proved via a so called "reducibility argument" (which is used to prove all conditional results in the area). Specifically, we show that any algorithm that inverts F with nonnegligible success probability can be used to construct an algorithm that inverts the original function f with success probability that violates the hypothesis (regarding f). In other words, we reduce the task of "strongly inverting" f (i.e., violating its weak one-wayness) to the task of "weakly inverting" F (i.e., violating its strong one-wayness). We hint that, on input $y = f(x)$, the reduction invokes the F-inverter (polynomially) many times, each time feeding it with a sequence of random f-images that contains y at a random location. (Indeed such a sequence corresponds to a random image of F.) The analysis of this reduction, presented in Goldreich [2001, Sec. 2.3], demonstrates that dealing with computational difficulty is much more involved than the analogous combinatorial question. An alternative demonstration of the difficulty of reasoning about computational difficulty (in comparison to an analogous purely probabilistic situation) is provided in the proof of Theorem 17.1.

17.3.2   **Hard-Core Predicates**

Loosely speaking, saying that a function f is one-way implies that given y (in the range of f) it is infeasible to find a preimage of y under f. This does not mean that it is infeasible to find out partial information about the preimage(s) of y under f. Specifically, it may be easy to retrieve half of the bits of the preimage (e.g., for any one-way function f, consider the function f' defined by $f'(x,r) \stackrel{\text{def}}{=} (f(x), r)$, for every $|x| = |r|$). As will become clear in subsequent sections, hiding partial information (about the function's preimage) plays an important role in more advanced constructs (e.g., secure encryption). Thus, we will first show how to transform any one-way function into a one-way function that hides specific partial information about its preimage, where this partial information is easy to compute from the preimage itself. This partial information can be considered a "hard core" of the difficulty of inverting f. Loosely speaking, a *polynomial-time computable* (Boolean) predicate b, is called a hard-core of a function f if no feasible algorithm, given $f(x)$, can guess $b(x)$ with success probability that is nonnegligibly better than one-half.

Definition 17.4   (Hard-core predicates [Blum and Micali 1984])   A polynomial-time computable predicate $b : \{0, 1\}^* \to \{0, 1\}$ is called a **hard-core** of a function f if for every probabilistic polynomial-time algorithm A', every positive polynomial $p(\cdot)$, and all sufficiently large n's

$$\Pr\left[A'(f(x)) = b(x)\right] < \frac{1}{2} + \frac{1}{p(n)},$$

where the probability is taken uniformly over all the possible choices of $x \in \{0, 1\}^n$ and all the possible outcomes of the internal coin tosses of algorithm A'.

Note that for every $b : \{0, 1\}^* \to \{0, 1\}$ and $f : \{0, 1\}^* \to \{0, 1\}^*$, there exist obvious algorithms that guess $b(x)$ from $f(x)$ with success probability at least one half (e.g., the algorithm that, obliviously of its input, outputs a uniformly chosen bit). Also, if b is a hard-core predicate (for any function), then it follows that b is almost unbiased (i.e., for a uniformly chosen x, the difference $|\Pr[b(x) = 0] - \Pr[b(x) = 1]|$ must be a negligible function in n). Finally, if b is a hard-core of a one-to-one function f that is polynomial-time computable, then f is a one-way function.

Theorem 17.1   (Goldreich and Levin [1989]; see simpler proof in Goldreich [2001, Sec. 2.5.2])   For any one-way function f, the inner-product mod 2 of x and r is a hard-core of $f'(x,r) = (f(x), r)$.

The proof is by a so-called *reducibility argument* (which is used to prove all conditional results in the area). Specifically, we reduce the task of inverting f to the task of predicting the hard-core of f', while making sure that the reduction (when applied to input distributed as in the inverting task) generates a distribution as in the definition of the predicting task. Thus, a contradiction to the claim that b is a hard-core of f' yields a contradiction to the hypothesis that f is hard to invert. We stress that this argument is far more complex than analyzing the corresponding "probabilistic" situation (i.e., the distribution of the inner product mod 2 of X and r, where r is uniformly distributed in $r \in \{0, 1\}^n$, and X is an independent random variable with super-logarithmic min-entropy, which represents the "effective" knowledge of x, when given $f(x)$).[4]

Proof Sketch   The actual proof refers to an arbitrary algorithm B that, when given $(f(x), r)$, tries to guess $b(x, r)$. Suppose that this algorithm succeeds with probability $\frac{1}{2} + \epsilon$, where the probability is taken over the random choices of x and r (as well as the internal coin tosses of B). By an averaging argument, we first identify a $\epsilon/2$ fraction of the possible coin tosses of B such that using any of these coin sequences B succeeds with probability at least $\frac{1}{2} + \epsilon/2$. Similarly, we can identify a $\epsilon/4$ fraction of the x's such that B succeeds (in guessing $b(x, r)$) with probability at least $\frac{1}{2} + \epsilon/4$, where now the probability is taken only over the r's. We will show how to use B in order to invert f, on input $f(x)$, provided that x is in the good set (which has density $\epsilon/4$).

As a warm-up, suppose for a moment that, for the aforementioned x's, algorithm B succeeds with probability $p > \frac{3}{4} + 1/\operatorname{poly}(|x|)$ (rather than $p \geq \frac{1}{2} + \epsilon/4$). In this case, retrieving x from $f(x)$ is quite easy: To retrieve the ith bit of x, denoted x_i, we first randomly select $r \in \{0, 1\}^{|x|}$, and obtain $B(f(x), r)$ and $B(f(x), r \oplus e^i)$, where $e^i = 0^{i-1}10^{|x|-i}$ and $v \oplus u$ denotes the addition mod 2 of the binary vectors v and u. Note that if both $B(f(x), r) = b(x, r)$ and $B(f(x), r \oplus e^i) = b(x, r \oplus e^i)$ hold, then $B(f(x), r) \oplus B(f(x), r \oplus e^i)$ equals $b(x, r) \oplus b(x, r \oplus e^i) = b(x, e^i) = x_i$. The probability that both $B(f(x), r) = b(x, r)$ and $B(f(x), r \oplus e^i) = b(x, r \oplus e^i)$ hold, for a random r, is at least $1 - 2 \cdot (1 - p) > \frac{1}{2} + \frac{1}{\operatorname{poly}(|x|)}$. Hence, repeating the foregoing procedure sufficiently many times (using independent random choices of such r's) and ruling by majority, we retrieve x_i with very high probability. (We note that the same holds if these choices are pairwise independent.) Similarly, we can retrieve

---

4. The ***min-entropy of*** X is defined as $\min_v\{\log_2(1/\Pr[X = v])\}$; that is, if X has min-entropy m then $\max_v\{\Pr[X = v]\} = 2^{-m}$. The Leftover Hashing Lemma [Sipser 1983, Bennett et al. 1988, Impagliazzo et al. 1989] implies that, in this case, $\Pr[b(X, U_n) = 1|U_n] = \frac{1}{2} \pm 2^{-\Omega(m)}$, where U_n denotes the uniform distribution over $\{0, 1\}^n$, and $b(u, v)$ denotes the inner-product mod 2 of u and v.

all the bits of x, and hence invert f on $f(x)$. However, the entire analysis was conducted under (the unjustifiable) assumption that $p > \frac{3}{4} + \frac{1}{\text{poly}(|x|)}$, whereas we only know that $p > \frac{1}{2} + \frac{\epsilon}{4}$ (for $\epsilon > 1/\text{poly}(|x|)$).

The problem with the foregoing procedure is that it doubles the original error probability of algorithm B on inputs of the form $(f(x), \cdot)$. Under the unrealistic assumption (made above), that B's average error on such inputs is nonnegligibly smaller than $\frac{1}{4}$, the "error-doubling" phenomenon raises no problems. However, in general (and even in the special case where B's error is exactly $\frac{1}{4}$) the foregoing procedure is unlikely to invert f. Note that the *average* error probability of B (for a fixed $f(x)$, when the average is taken over a random r) can not be decreased by repeating B several times (e.g., for every x, it may be that B always answer correctly on three quarters of the pairs $(f(x), r)$, and always err on the remaining quarter). What is required is an *alternative way of using* the algorithm B, a way that does not double the original error probability of B.

The key idea is to generate the r's in a way that allows to apply algorithm B only once per each r (and i), instead of twice. Specifically, we will use algorithm B to obtain a "guess" for $b(x, r \oplus e^i)$ and obtain $b(x, r)$ in a different way (which does not use B). The good news is that the error probability is no longer doubled, since we only use B to get a "guess" of $b(x, r \oplus e^i)$. The bad news is that we still need to know $b(x, r)$, and it is not clear how we can know $b(x, r)$ without applying B. The answer is that we can guess $b(x, r)$ by ourselves. This is fine if we only need to guess $b(x, r)$ for one r (or logarithmically in $|x|$ many r's), but the problem is that we need to know (and hence guess) the value of $b(x, r)$ for polynomially many r's. The obvious way of guessing these $b(x, r)$'s yields an exponentially small success probability. Instead, we generate these polynomially many r's such that they are "sufficiently random" on the one hand, whereas, on the other hand, we can guess all the $b(x, r)$'s with noticeable success probability.[5] Specifically, generating the r's in a specific *pairwise-independent* manner will satisfy both (seemingly contradictory) requirements. We stress that in case we are successful (in our guesses for all the $b(x, r)$'s), we can retrieve x with high probability. Hence, we retrieve x with noticeable probability.

A word about the way in which the pairwise-independent r's are generated (and the corresponding $b(x, r)$'s are guessed) is indeed in place. To generate $m = \text{poly}(|x|)$ many r's, we uniformly (and independently) select $\ell \stackrel{\text{def}}{=} \log_2(m + 1)$ strings in $\{0, 1\}^{|x|}$. Let us denote these strings by $s^1, \ldots, s^\ell$. We then guess $b(x, s^1)$ through

---

5. Alternatively, we can try all polynomially many possible guesses.

$b(x, s^\ell)$. Let us denote these guesses, which are uniformly (and independently) chosen in $\{0, 1\}$, by σ^1 through σ^ℓ. Hence, the probability that all our guesses for the $b(x, s^i)$'s are correct is $2^{-\ell} = \frac{1}{\mathrm{poly}(|x|)}$. The different r's correspond to the different *nonempty* subsets of $\{1, 2, \dots, \ell\}$. Specifically, for every such subset J, we let $r^J \stackrel{\mathrm{def}}{=} \oplus_{j \in J} s^j$. The reader can easily verify that the r^J's are pairwise independent and each is uniformly distributed in $\{0, 1\}^{|x|}$. The key observation is that $b(x, r^J) = b(x, \oplus_{j \in J} s^j) = \oplus_{j \in J} b(x, s^j)$. Hence, our guess for $b(x, r^J)$ is $\oplus_{j \in J} \sigma^j$, and with noticeable probability all our guesses are correct. ∎

17.4 Pseudorandomness

In practice "pseudorandom" sequences are often used instead of truly random sequences. The underlying belief is that if an (efficient) application performs well when using a truly random sequence, then it will perform essentially as well when using a "pseudorandom" sequence. However, this belief is not supported by ad hoc notions of "pseudorandomness" such as passing the statistical tests in Knuth [1969] or having large linear-complexity (as in Golomb [1967]). In contrast, the foregoing belief is an easy corollary of defining pseudorandom distributions as ones that are computationally indistinguishable from uniform distributions.

Loosely speaking, pseudorandom generators are efficient procedures for creating long "random-looking" sequences based on few truly random bits (i.e., a short random seed). The relevance of such constructs to cryptography is in the ability of legitimate users who share short random seeds to create large objects that look random to any feasible adversary (who does not know the said seed).

17.4.1 Computational Indistinguishability

Indistinguishable things are identical (or should be considered as identical).

—The Principle of Identity of Indiscernibles, G. W. Leibniz (1646–1714)

(Leibniz admits that counterexamples to this principle are conceivable but will not occur in real life because God is much too benevolent.)

A central notion in modern cryptography is that of "effective similarity" (introduced by Goldwasser, Micali, and Yao [Goldwasser and Micali 1984, Yao 1982]). The underlying thesis is that we do not care whether or not objects are equal, all we care about is whether or not a difference between the objects can be observed by a feasible computation. In the case where the answer is negative, the two objects are equivalent as far as any practical application is concerned. Indeed, in the sequel we will often interchange such (computationally indistinguishable) objects. Let $X = \{X_n\}_{n\in\mathbb{N}}$ and $Y = \{Y_n\}_{n\in\mathbb{N}}$ be probability ensembles such that each X_n and Y_n is a distribution that ranges over strings of length n (or polynomial in n). We say that X and Y are ***computationally indistinguishable*** if for every feasible algorithm A the difference $d_A(n) \stackrel{\text{def}}{=} |\Pr[A(X_n) = 1] - \Pr[A(Y_n) = 1]|$ is a negligible function in n. That is:

Definition 17.5   (Computational indistinguishability [Goldwasser and Micali 1984, Yao 1982])   We say that $X = \{X_n\}_{n\in\mathbb{N}}$ and $Y = \{Y_n\}_{n\in\mathbb{N}}$ are ***computationally indistinguishable*** if for every probabilistic polynomial-time algorithm D every polynomial p, and all sufficiently large n,

$$|\Pr[D(X_n) = 1] - \Pr[D(Y_n) = 1]| < \frac{1}{p(n)},$$

where the probabilities are taken over the relevant distribution (*i.e., either X_n or Y_n*) and over the internal coin tosses of algorithm D.

We can think of D as somebody who wishes to distinguish two distributions (based on a sample given to it), and think of 1 as D's verdict that the sample was drawn according to the first distribution. Saying that the two distributions are computationally indistinguishable means that if D is a feasible procedure, then its verdict is not really meaningful (because the verdict is almost as often 1 when the input is drawn from the first distribution as when the input is drawn from the second distribution).

Indistinguishability by Multiple Samples

We mention that, for "efficiently constructible" distributions, indistinguishability by a single sample (as defined above) implies indistinguishability by multiple samples (see Goldreich [2001, Sec. 3.2.3]). The proof of this fact, which we briefly present next, provides a simple demonstration of a central proof technique, originating in the work Goldwasser and Micali [1984] and known as a *hybrid argument*.

To prove that a sequence of m independently drawn samples of one distribution is indistinguishable from a sequence of independently drawn samples from the other distribution, we consider $m + 1$ *hybrid* sequences such that the ith hybrid consists of $i - 1$ samples taken from the first distribution and the rest taken from the second distribution. The "homogeneous" sequences (which we wish to prove to be computational indistinguishable) are the extreme hybrids (i.e., the first and last hybrids considered above). The key observation is that distinguishing the extreme hybrids (toward the contradiction hypothesis) yields a procedure for distinguishing single samples of the two distributions (contradicting the hypothesis that the two distributions are indistinguishable by a single sample). Specifically, if D distinguishes the extreme hybrids, then it also distinguishes a random pair of neighboring hybrids (i.e., D distinguishes the ith hybrid from the $i + 1$st hybrid, for a randomly selected $i \in [m]$). Using D, we obtain a distinguisher D' of single samples: Given a single sample, D' selects $i \in [m]$ uniformly at random, generates $i - 1$ samples from the first distribution and $m - i$ samples from the second distribution, and invokes D with the corresponding sequence, while placing the input sample in location i of the sequence. We stress that although the original distinguisher D (arising from the contradiction hypothesis) was only "supposed to work" for the extreme hybrids, we may consider D's performance on any distribution that we please, and draw adequate conclusions (as we have done).

17.4.2 Pseudorandom Generators

Loosely speaking, a ***pseudorandom generator*** is an efficient (deterministic) algorithm that on input a short random *seed* outputs a (typically much) longer sequence that is computationally indistinguishable from a uniformly distributed sequence (of the same length). Pseudorandom generators were introduced by Blum, Micali, and Yao [Blum and Micali 1984, Yao 1982], and are formally defined as follows.

Definition 17.6 (Pseudorandom generator [Blum and Micali 1984, Yao 1982])   Let $\ell : \mathbb{N} \to \mathbb{N}$ satisfy $\ell(n) > n$, for all $n \in \mathbb{N}$. A ***pseudorandom generator***, with ***stretch function*** ℓ, is a (*deterministic*) polynomial-time algorithm G satisfying the following:

1. For every $s \in \{0, 1\}^*$, it holds that $|G(s)| = \ell(|s|)$.

2. $\{G(U_n)\}_{n \in \mathbb{N}}$ and $\{U_{\ell(n)}\}_{n \in \mathbb{N}}$ are computationally indistinguishable, where U_m denotes the uniform distribution over $\{0, 1\}^m$.

Indeed, the probability ensemble $\{G(U_n)\}_{n \in \mathbb{N}}$ is called ***pseudorandom***.

Thus, pseudorandom sequences can replace truly random sequences not only in "standard" algorithmic applications but also in cryptographic ones. That is, *any* cryptographic application that is secure when the legitimate parties use truly random sequences, is also secure when the legitimate parties use pseudorandom sequences. The benefit in such a substitution (of random sequences by pseudorandom ones) is that the latter sequences can be efficiently generated using much less true randomness. Furthermore, *in an interactive setting*, it is possible to eliminate all random steps from the on-line execution of a program, by replacing them with the generation of pseudorandom bits based on a random seed selected and fixed off-line (or at set-up time).

Various cryptographic applications of pseudorandom generators will be presented in the sequel, but first let us show a construction of pseudorandom generators based on the simpler notion of a one-way permutation. Using Theorem 17.1, we may actually assume that such a function is accompanied by a hard-core predicate. We start with a simple construction that suffices for the case of one-to-one (and length-preserving) functions.

Theorem 17.2   (Blum and Micali [1984], Yao [1982]; see Goldreich [2001, Sec. 3.4])   Let f be a one-to-one function that is length-preserving and efficiently computable, and b be a hard-core predicate of f. Then $G(s) = b(s) \cdot b(f(s)) \cdots b(f^{\ell(|s|)-1}(s))$ is a pseudorandom generator (with stretch function ℓ), where $f^{i+1}(x) \overset{\text{def}}{=} f(f^i(x))$ and $f^0(x) \overset{\text{def}}{=} x$.

As a concrete example, consider the permutation[6] $x \mapsto x^2 \bmod N$, where N is the product of two primes each congruent to 3 (mod 4) and x is a quadratic residue modulo N. Then we have $G_N(s) = \text{lsb}(s) \cdot \text{lsb}(s^2 \bmod N) \cdots \text{lsb}(s^{2^{\ell(|s|)-1}} \bmod N)$, where $\text{lsb}(x)$ is the least significant bit of x (which is a hard-core of the modular squaring function [Alexi et al. 1988]).

Proof Sketch   (of Theorem 17.2)   We use the fundamental fact that asserts that the following two conditions are equivalent:

1. The distribution X (in our case $\{G(U_n)\}_{n \in \mathbb{N}}$) is pseudorandom (i.e., is computationally indistinguishable from a uniform distribution (on $\{U_{\ell(n)}\}_{n \in \mathbb{N}}$)).

2. The distribution X is unpredictable in polynomial time; that is, no feasible algorithm, given a prefix of the sequence, can guess its next bit with a nonnegligible advantage over $\frac{1}{2}$.

Clearly, pseudorandomness implies polynomial-time unpredictability (i.e., polynomial-time predictability violates pseudorandomness). The converse is shown using a hybrid argument, which refers to hybrids consisting of a prefix of X followed by truly random bits (i.e., a suffix of the uniform distribution). Thus, we focus on proving that $G'(U_n)$ is polynomial-time unpredictable, where $G'(s) = b(f^{\ell(|s|)-1}(s)) \cdots b(f(s)) \cdot b(s)$ is the reverse of $G(s)$.

Suppose toward the contradiction that, for some $j < \ell \overset{\text{def}}{=} \ell(n)$, given the j-bit-long prefix of $G'(U_n)$ an algorithm A' can predict the $j + 1$st bit of $G'(U_n)$. That is, given $b(f^{\ell-1}(s)) \cdots b(f^{\ell-j}(s))$, algorithm A' predicts $b(f^{\ell-(j+1)}(s))$, where s is uniformly distributed in $\{0, 1\}^n$. Then, for x uniformly distributed in $\{0, 1\}^n$,

---

6. It is a well-known fact (see Goldreich [2001, Appendix A.2.4]) that, for such N's, the mapping $x \mapsto x^2 \bmod N$ is a permutation over the set of quadratic residues modulo N.

given $y = f(x)$, one can predict $b(x)$ by invoking A' on input $b(f^{j-1}(y)) \cdots b(y) = b(f^j(x)) \cdots b(f(x))$, which in turn is polynomial-time computable from $y = f(x)$. In the analysis, we use the hypothesis that f induces a permutation over $\{0, 1\}^n$ and associate x with $f^{\ell-(j+1)}(s)$. ∎

We mention that the existence of a pseudorandom generator with any stretch function (including the very minimal stretch function $\ell(n) = n + 1$) implies the existence of pseudorandom generators for any desired stretch function. The construction is similar to the one presented in Theorem 17.2. That is, for a pseudorandom generator G_1, let $F(x)$ (respectively, $B(x)$) denote the first $|x|$ bits of $G_1(x)$ (respectively, the $|x| + 1$st bit of $G_1(x)$), and consider $G(s) = B(s) \cdot B(F(s)) \cdots B(F^{\ell(|s|)-1}(s))$, where ℓ is the desired stretch. Although F is not necessarily one-to-one, it can be shown that G is a pseudorandom generator [Goldreich 2001, Sec. 3.3.2].

We conclude this section by mentioning that pseudorandom generators can be constructed from *any* one-way function (rather than merely from one-way permutations, as above). On the other hand, the existence of one-way functions is a necessary condition for the existence of pseudorandom generators. That is:

Theorem 17.3 ([Håstad et al. 1999])   Pseudorandom generators exist if and only if one-way functions exist.

The necessary condition is easy to establish. Given a pseudorandom generator G that stretches by a factor of 2, consider the function $f(x) = G(x)$ (or, to obtain a length-preserving function, let $f(x, y) = G(x)$, where $|x| = |y|$). An algorithm that inverts f with nonnegligible success probability (on the distribution $f(U_n) = G(U_n)$) yields a distinguisher of $\{G(U_n)\}_{n \in \mathbb{N}}$ from $\{U_{2n}\}_{n \in \mathbb{N}}$, because the probability that U_{2n} is an image of f is negligible.

17.4.3 Pseudorandom Functions

Pseudorandom generators provide a way to efficiently generate long pseudorandom sequences from short random seeds. Pseudorandom functions, introduced and constructed by Goldreich, Goldwasser, and Micali [Goldreich et al. 1986], are even more powerful: They provide efficient direct access to bits of a huge pseudorandom sequence (which is not feasible to scan bit by bit). More precisely, a *pseudorandom function* is an efficient (deterministic) algorithm that given an n-bit *seed*, s, and an n-bit *argument*, x, returns an n-bit string, denoted $f_s(x)$, so that it is infeasible to distinguish the values of f_s, for a uniformly chosen $s \in \{0, 1\}^n$, from the values of a truly random function $F : \{0, 1\}^n \to \{0, 1\}^n$. That is, the (feasible) testing procedure is given oracle access to the function (but not its explicit description), and cannot distinguish the case it is given oracle access to a pseudorandom function from the case it is given oracle access to a truly random function.

One key feature of the foregoing definition is that pseudorandom functions can be generated and shared by merely generating and sharing their seed; that is, a "random-looking" function $f_s : \{0, 1\}^n \rightarrow \{0, 1\}^n$ is determined by its n-bit seed s. Parties wishing to share a random-looking function f_s (determining 2^n-many values) merely need to generate and share among themselves the n-bit seed s. (For example, one party may randomly select the seed s and communicate it, via a secure channel, to all other parties.) Sharing a pseudorandom function allows parties to determine (by themselves and without any further communication) random-looking values depending on their current views of the environment (which need not be known a priori). To appreciate the potential of this tool, one should realize that sharing a pseudorandom function is essentially as good as being able to agree, on the fly, on the association of random values to (on-line) given values, where the latter are taken from a huge set of possible values. We stress that this agreement is achieved without communication and synchronization: Whenever some party needs to associate a random value to a given value, $v \in \{0, 1\}^n$, it will associate to v the (same) random value $r_v \in \{0, 1\}^n$ (by setting $r_v = f_s(v)$, where f_s is a pseudorandom function agreed upon beforehand).

Theorem 17.4   (Goldreich et al. [1986]; see Goldreich [2001, Sec. 3.6.2])   Pseudorandom functions can be constructed using any pseudorandom generator.

Proof Sketch   Let G be a pseudorandom generator that stretches its seed by a factor of 2 (i.e., $\ell(n) = 2n$), and let $G_0(s)$ (respectively, $G_1(s)$) denote the first (respectively, last) $|s|$ bits in $G(s)$. Define

$$G_{\sigma_{|s|} \cdots \sigma_2 \sigma_1}(s) \stackrel{\text{def}}{=} G_{\sigma_{|s|}}(\cdots G_{\sigma_2}(G_{\sigma_1}(s)) \cdots).$$

We consider the function ensemble $\{f_s : \{0, 1\}^{|s|} \rightarrow \{0, 1\}^{|s|}\}_{s \in \{0,1\}^*}$, where $f_s(x) \stackrel{\text{def}}{=} G_x(s)$. Pictorially, the function f_s is defined by n-step walks down a full binary tree of depth n having labels at the vertices. The root of the tree, hereafter referred to as the level 0 vertex of the tree, is labeled by the string s. If an internal vertex is labeled r, then its left child is labeled $G_0(r)$ and its right child is labeled $G_1(r)$. The value of $f_s(x)$ is the string residing in the leaf reachable from the root by a path corresponding to the string x.

We claim that the function ensemble $\{f_s\}_{s \in \{0,1\}^*}$ is pseudorandom. The proof uses the hybrid technique: The ith hybrid, H_n^i, is a function ensemble consisting of

$2^{2^i \cdot n}$ functions $\{0, 1\}^n \rightarrow \{0, 1\}^n$, each defined by 2^i random n-bit strings, denoted $\bar{s} = \langle s_\beta \rangle_{\beta \in \{0,1\}^i}$. The value of such function $h_{\bar{s}}$ at $x = \alpha\beta$, where $|\beta| = i$, is $G_\alpha(s_\beta)$. (Pictorially, the function $h_{\bar{s}}$ is defined by placing the strings in $\bar{s}$ in the corresponding vertices of level i, and labeling vertices of lower levels using the very rule used in the definition of f_s.) The extreme hybrids correspond to our indistinguishability claim (i.e., $H_n^0 \equiv f_{U_n}$ and H_n^n is a truly random function), and neighboring hybrids can be related to our indistinguishability hypothesis (specifically, to the indistinguishability of $G(U_n)$ and U_{2n} under multiple samples). ∎

Useful variants (and generalizations) of the notion of pseudorandom functions include Boolean pseudorandom functions that are defined over all bit strings (i.e., $f_s : \{0, 1\}^* \rightarrow \{0, 1\}$) and pseudorandom functions that are defined for other domains and ranges (i.e., $f_s : \{0, 1\}^{d(|s|)} \rightarrow \{0, 1\}^{r(|s|)}$, for arbitrary polynomially bounded functions $d, r : \mathbb{N} \rightarrow \mathbb{N}$). Various transformations between these variants are known (see Goldreich [2001, Sec. 3.6.4], and Goldreich [2004, Appendix C.2]).

Applications and a generic methodology. Pseudorandom functions are a very useful cryptographic tool: One may first design a cryptographic scheme assuming that the legitimate users have black-box access to a random function, and next implement the random function using a pseudorandom function. The usefulness of this tool stems from the fact that having (black-box) access to a random function gives the legitimate parties a potential advantage over the adversary (which does not have free access to this function).[7] The security of the resulting implementation (which uses a pseudorandom function) is established in two steps: First, one proves the security of an idealized scheme that uses a truly random function, and next one argues that the actual implementation (which uses a pseudorandom function) is secure (because otherwise one obtains an efficient oracle machine that distinguishes a pseudorandom function from a truly random one).

17.5 Zero-Knowledge

Zero-knowledge proofs, introduced by Goldwasser, Micali, and Rackoff [Goldwasser et al. 1989], provide a powerful tool for the design of cryptographic protocols. Loosely speaking, zero-knowledge proofs are proofs that yield nothing

---

7. The foregoing methodology is sound provided that the adversary does not get the description of the pseudorandom function (i.e., the seed) in use, but has only (possibly limited) oracle access to it. This is different from the so-called Random Oracle Methodology formulated in Bellare and Rogaway [1993] and criticized in Canetti et al. [1998].

beyond the validity of the assertion. That is, a verifier obtaining such a proof only gains conviction in the validity of the assertion (as if it was told by a trusted party that the assertion holds). This is formulated by saying that anything that is feasibly computable from a zero-knowledge proof is also feasibly computable from the (valid) assertion itself. The latter formulation follows the simulation paradigm, which is discussed next.

17.5.1   The Simulation Paradigm

A key question regarding the modeling of security concerns is how to express the intuitive requirement that an adversary "gains nothing substantial" by deviating from the prescribed behavior of an honest user. The answer provided by the simulation paradigm is that the adversary *gains nothing* if whatever it can obtain by unrestricted adversarial behavior can also be obtained within essentially the same computational effort by a benign behavior. The definition of the "benign behavior" captures what we want to achieve in terms of security, and is specific to the security concern to be addressed. For example, in the previous paragraph, we said that a proof is zero-knowledge if it yields nothing (to the adversarial verifier) beyond the validity of the assertion; hence the benign behavior in this case is any computation that is based (only) on the assertion itself (while assuming that the latter is valid). Other examples are discussed in Sections 17.7.1 and 17.9.1.

A notable property of the aforementioned simulation paradigm, as well as of the entire approach surveyed in this text, is that this approach is overly liberal with respect to its view of the abilities of the adversary as well as to what might constitute a gain for the adversary. Thus, the approach may be considered overly cautious, because it prohibits also "nonharmful" gains of some "far fetched" adversaries. We warn against this impression. First, there is nothing more dangerous in cryptography than to consider "reasonable" adversaries (a notion which is almost a contradiction in terms): Typically, the adversaries will try exactly what the system designer has discarded as "far fetched." Second, it seems impossible to come up with definitions of security that distinguish "breaking the scheme in a harmful way" from "breaking it in a nonharmful way": What is harmful is application dependent, whereas a good definition of security ought to be application independent (since otherwise using the scheme in any new application will require a full re-evaluation of its security). Furthermore, even with respect to a specific application, it is typically very hard to classify the set of "harmful breakings."

17.5.2 The Actual Definition

A proof is whatever convinces me.

—Shimon Even (1935–2004)

Before defining zero-knowledge proofs, we have to define proofs. The standard notion of a static (i.e., noninteractive) proof will not do, because static zero-knowledge proofs exist only for sets that are easy to decide (i.e, are in $\mathcal{BPP}$) [Goldreich and Oren 1994], whereas we are interested in zero-knowledge proofs for arbitrary NP-sets. Instead, we use the notion of an interactive proof (introduced exactly for that reason by Goldwasser, Micali, and Rackoff [Goldwasser et al. 1989]). That is, here a proof is a (multi-round) randomized protocol for two parties, called **verifier** and **prover**, in which the prover wishes to convince the verifier of the validity of a given assertion. Such an **interactive proof** should allow the prover to convince the verifier of the validity of any true assertion (i.e., **completeness**), whereas NO prover strategy may fool the verifier to accept false assertions (i.e., **soundness**). Both the *completeness* and *soundness* conditions should hold with high probability (i.e., a negligible error probability is allowed). The prescribed verifier strategy is required to be efficient. No such requirement is made with respect to the prover strategy; yet we will be interested in "relatively efficient" prover strategies (see below).[8]

Zero-knowledge is a property of some prover strategies. More generally, we consider interactive machines that yield no knowledge while interacting with an arbitrary feasible adversary on a common input taken from a predetermined set (in our case, the set of valid assertions). A strategy A is **zero-knowledge** on (inputs from) the set S if, for every feasible strategy B^*, there exists a feasible computation C^* such that the following two probability ensembles are computationally indistinguishable:[9]

---

8. We stress that the relative efficiency of the prover strategy refers to the strategy employed in order to prove valid assertions; that is, relative efficiency of the prover strategy is a *strengthening* of the completeness condition (which is indeed *required* for cryptographic applications). This should not be confused with the relaxation (i.e., weakening) of the soundness condition that restricts its scope to feasible adversarial prover strategies (rather than to all possible prover strategies). The resulting notion of "computational soundness" is discussed in Section 17.5.4.1, and indeed *suffices* in most cryptographic applications. Still, we believe that it is simpler to present the material in terms of interactive proofs (rather than in terms of computationally sound proofs).

9. Here we refer to a natural extension of Definition 17.5: Rather than referring to ensembles indexed by $\mathbb{N}$, we refer to ensembles indexed by a set $S \subseteq \{0, 1\}^*$. Typically, for an ensemble

1. $\{(A, B^*)(x)\}_{x \in S} \overset{\text{def}}{=}$ the output of B^* after interacting with A on common input $x \in S$; and

2. $\{C^*(x)\}_{x \in S} \overset{\text{def}}{=}$ the output of C^* on input $x \in S$.

We stress that the first ensemble represents an actual execution of an interactive protocol, whereas the second ensemble represents the computation of a stand-alone procedure (called the "simulator"), which does not interact with anybody.

The foregoing definition does *not* account for auxiliary information that an adversary B^* may have prior to entering the interaction. Accounting for such auxiliary information is essential for using zero-knowledge proofs as subprotocols inside larger protocols (see Goldreich and Krawczyk [1996], Goldreich and Oren [1994]). This is taken care of by a stricter notion called *auxiliary-input zero-knowledge*.

Definition 17.7 (Zero-knowledge [Goldwasser et al. [1989]; revisited in Goldreich and Oren [1994]]) A strategy A is ***auxiliary-input zero-knowledge*** on inputs from S if, for every probabilistic polynomial-time strategy B^* and every polynomial p, there exists a probabilistic polynomial-time algorithm C^* such that the following two probability ensembles are computationally indistinguishable:

1. $\{(A, B^*(z))(x)\}_{x \in S, z \in \{0,1\}^{p(|x|)}} \overset{\text{def}}{=}$ the output of B^* when having auxiliary-input z and interacting with A on common input $x \in S$.

2. $\{C^*(x, z)\}_{x \in S, z \in \{0,1\}^{p(|x|)}} \overset{\text{def}}{=}$ the output of C^* on inputs $x \in S$ and $z \in \{0, 1\}^{p(|x|)}$.

Almost all known zero-knowledge proofs are in fact auxiliary-input zero-knowledge. As hinted above, *auxiliary-input zero-knowledge is preserved under sequential composition* [Goldreich and Oren 1994]. A simulator for the multiple-session protocol can be constructed by iteratively invoking the single-session simulator that refers to the residual strategy of the adversarial verifier in the given session (while feeding this simulator with the transcript of previous sessions). Indeed, the residual single-session verifier gets the transcript of the previous sessions as part of its auxiliary input (i.e., z in Definition 17.7). (For details, see Goldreich [2001, Sec. 4.3.4].)

$\{Z_\alpha\}_{\alpha \in S}$, it holds that Z_α ranges over strings of length that is polynomially related to the length of α. We say that $\{X_\alpha\}_{\alpha \in S}$ and $\{Y_\alpha\}_{\alpha \in S}$ are ***computationally*** indistinguishable if for every probabilistic polynomial-time algorithm D every polynomial p, and all sufficiently long $\alpha \in S$,

$$| \Pr[D(\alpha, X_\alpha) = 1] - \Pr[D(\alpha, Y_\alpha) = 1]| < \frac{1}{p(|\alpha|)},$$

where the probabilities are taken over the relevant distribution (i.e., either X_α or Y_α) and over the internal coin tosses of algorithm D.

17.5.3 Zero-Knowledge Proofs for All NP-Assertions and Their Applications

A question avoided so far is whether zero-knowledge proofs exist at all. Clearly, every set in $\mathcal{P}$ (or rather in $\mathcal{BPP}$) has a "trivial" zero-knowledge proof (in which the verifier determines membership by itself); however, what we seek is zero-knowledge proofs for statements that the verifier cannot decide by itself.

Assuming the existence of "commitment schemes" (see below), which in turn exist if one-way functions exist [Naor 1991, Håstad et al. 1999], *there exist* (auxiliary-input) *zero-knowledge proofs of membership in any NP-set* (i.e., sets having efficiently verifiable static proofs of membership). These zero-knowledge proofs, first constructed by Goldreich, Micali, and Wigderson [Goldreich et al. 1991] and depicted in Figure 17.1, have the following important property: The prescribed prover strategy is efficient, provided it is given as auxiliary-input an NP-witness to the assertion (to be proved).[10] That is:

Theorem 17.5 (Goldreich et al. [1991]; using Håstad et al. [1999], Naor [1991])   If (*nonuniformly hard*) one-way functions exist, then every set $S \in \mathcal{NP}$ has a zero-knowledge interactive proof. Furthermore, the prescribed prover strategy can be implemented in probabilistic polynomial time, provided it is given as auxiliary input an NP-witness for membership of the common input in S.

Theorem 17.5 makes zero-knowledge a very powerful tool in the design of cryptographic schemes and protocols (see below). We comment that the intractability assumption used in Theorem 17.5 seems essential; see Ostrovsky and Wigderson [1993] and Vadhan [2004].

Analyzing the Protocol of Figure 17.1. Let us consider a single execution of the main loop (and rely on the preservation of zero-knowledge under sequential composition). Clearly, the prescribed prover is implemented in probabilistic polynomial time, and always convinces the verifier (provided that it is given a valid 3-coloring of the common input graph). In the case where the graph is not 3-colorable, then, no matter how the prover behaves, the verifier will reject with probability at least $1/|E|$ (because at least one of the edges must be improperly colored by the prover). We stress that the verifier selects uniformly which edge to inspect after the prover

---

10. The auxiliary input given to the prescribed prover (in order to allow for an efficient implementation of its strategy) is not to be confused with the auxiliary-input that is given to malicious verifiers (in the definition of auxiliary-input zero-knowledge). The former is typically an NP-witness for the common input, which is available to the user that invokes the prover strategy (see the generic application discussed below). In contrast, the auxiliary input that is given to malicious verifiers models arbitrary partial information that may be available to the adversary.

Commitment schemes are digital analogs of sealed envelopes (or, better, locked boxes). Sending a commitment means sending a string that binds the sender to a unique value without revealing this value to the receiver (as when getting a locked box). Decommitting to the value means sending some auxiliary information that allows the receiver to read the uniquely committed value (as when sending the key to the lock).

> **Common Input:** A graph $G(V, E)$. Suppose that $V \equiv \{1, \ldots, n\}$ for $n \stackrel{\text{def}}{=} |V|$.
>
> **Auxiliary Input (to the prover):** A 3-coloring $\phi : V \rightarrow \{1, 2, 3\}$.

> The following four steps are repeated $(t \cdot |E|)$ many times so to obtain soundness error $\exp(-t)$.

> **Prover's first step (P1):** Select uniformly a permutation π over $\{1, 2, 3\}$. For $i = 1$ to n, send the verifier a commitment to the value $\pi(\phi(i))$.
>
> **Verifier's first step (V1):** Select uniformly an edge $e \in E$ and send it to the prover.
>
> **Prover's second step (P2):** Upon receiving $e = (i, j) \in E$, decommit to the ith and jth values sent in Step (P1).
>
> **Verifier's second step (V2):** Reject if either the decommitted values are not different elements of $\{1, 2, 3\}$ or the decommitments do not match the commitments received in Step (P1).

> (If the verifier did not reject in any iteration, then it accepts.)

Figure 17.1 The zero-knowledge proof of graph 3-colorability (of Goldreich et al. [1991]). Zero-knowledge proofs for other NP-sets can be obtained using the standard reductions.

has committed to the colors of all vertices. Thus, Figure 17.1 depicts an interactive proof system for graph 3-colorability (with error probability $\exp(-t)$). As the reader might have guessed, the zero-knowledge property is the hardest to establish, and we will confine ourselves to presenting an adequate simulator. We start with three simplifying conventions (which are useful in general):

1. Without loss of generality, we may assume that the cheating verifier strategy is implemented by a *deterministic* polynomial-time algorithm with an auxiliary input. This is justified by fixing any outcome of the verifier's coins (as part of the auxiliary input), and observing that our (uniform) simulation of the various (residual) deterministic strategies yields a simulation of the original probabilistic strategy.

2. Without loss of generality, it suffices to consider cheating verifiers that (only) output their view of the interaction (i.e., their input, coin tosses, and the

messages they received). In other words, it suffices to simulate the view of the cheating verifier rather than its output (which is the result of a polynomial-time post-processing of the view).

3. Without loss of generality, it suffices to construct a "weak simulator" that produces an output with some noticeable probability, provided that (conditioned on producing output) the output is computationally indistinguishable from the desired distribution (i.e., the view of the cheating verifier in a real interaction). This is the case because, by repeatedly invoking this weak simulator (polynomially) many times, we may obtain a simulator that fails to produce an output with negligible probability. Finally, letting the simulator produce an arbitrary output rather than failing, we obtain a simulator that never fails (as required by the definition), while skewing the output distribution by at most a negligible amount.

Our simulator starts by selecting uniformly and independently a random color (i.e., element of $\{1, 2, 3\}$) for each vertex, and feeding the verifier strategy with random commitments to these random colors. Indeed, the simulator feeds the verifier with a distribution that is very different from the distribution that the verifier sees in a real interaction with the prover. However, being computationally restricted, the verifier cannot tell these distributions apart (or else we obtain a contradiction to the security of the commitment scheme in use). Now, if the verifier asks to inspect an edge that is properly colored, then the simulator performs the proper decommitment action and outputs the transcript of this interaction. Otherwise, the simulator halts proclaiming failure. We claim that failure occurs with probability approximately 1/3 (or else we obtain a contradiction to the security of the commitment scheme in use). Furthermore, based on the same hypothesis (but via a more complex proof (see Goldreich [2001, Sec. 4.4.2.3])), conditioned on not failing, the output of the simulator is computationally indistinguishable from the verifier's view of the real interaction.

Commitment schemes. Loosely speaking, commitment schemes are two-stage (two-party) protocols allowing for one party to commit itself (at the first stage) to a value while keeping the value secret. In a (second) later stage, the commitment is "opened" and it is guaranteed that the "opening" can yield only a single value determined in the committing phase. Thus, the (first stage of the) commitment scheme is both *binding* and *hiding*. A simple (unidirectional communication) commitment scheme can be constructed based on any one-way one-to-one function f (with a corresponding hard-core b). To commit to a bit σ, the sender uniformly selects $s \in \{0, 1\}^n$ and sends the pair $(f(s), b(s) \oplus \sigma)$. Note that this is both binding and hiding. An alternative construction, which can be based on any one-way function, uses a pseudorandom generator G that stretches its seed by a factor of 3. A commitment is established, via two-way communication, as follows (see Naor [1991]): The receiver selects uniformly $r \in \{0, 1\}^{3n}$ and sends it to the sender, which selects uniformly $s \in \{0, 1\}^n$ and sends $r \oplus G(s)$ if it wishes to commit to the value 1 and $G(s)$ if it wishes to commit to 0. To see that this is binding, observe that there are at most 2^{2n} "bad" values r that satisfy $G(s_0) = r \oplus G(s_1)$ for some pair (s_0, s_1), and with overwhelmingly high probability the receiver will not pick one of these bad values. The hiding property follows by the pseudorandomness of G.

Zero-knowledge proofs for other NP-sets. By using the standard Karp-reductions to 3-colorability, the protocol of Figure 17.1 can be used for constructing zero-knowledge proofs for any set in $\mathcal{NP}$. We comment that this is probably the first time that an NP-completeness result was used in a "positive" way (i.e., in order to construct something rather than in order to derive a hardness result).[11]

Efficiency considerations. The protocol in Figure 17.1 calls for invoking some constant-round protocol for a nonconstant number of times (and its analysis relies on the preservation of zero-knowledge under sequential composition). At first glance, it seems that one can derive a constant-round zero-knowledge proof system (of negligible soundness error) by performing these invocations in parallel (rather than sequentially). Unfortunately, as indicated in Goldreich and Krawczyk [1996], it is not clear that the resulting interactive proof is zero-knowledge. Still, under standard intractability assumptions (e.g., the intractability of factoring), constant-round zero-knowledge proofs (of negligible soundness error) do exist for every set in $\mathcal{NP}$ (see Goldreich and Kahan [1996]). We comment that the number of rounds in a protocol is commonly considered the most important efficiency criterion (or complexity measure), and typically one desires to have it be a constant.

A generic application. As mentioned above, Theorem 17.5 makes zero-knowledge a very powerful tool in the design of cryptographic schemes and protocols. This wide applicability is due to two important aspects regarding Theorem 17.5: First, Theorem 17.5 provides a zero-knowledge proof for every NP-set, and second the prescribed prover can be implemented in probabilistic polynomial time when given an adequate NP-witness. We now turn to a typical application of zero-knowledge

---

11. Subsequent positive uses of completeness results have appeared in the context of interactive proofs (see the proof of Goldreich [2008, Thm. 9.4]), probabilistically checkable proofs (see the proof of Goldreich [2008, Thm. 9.16]), and statistical zero-knowledge [Sahai and Vadhan 2003].

proofs. In a typical cryptographic setting, a user U has a secret and is supposed to take some action depending on its secret. The question is how can other users verify that U indeed took the correct action (as determined by U's secret and publicly known information). Indeed, if U discloses its secret, then anybody can verify that U took the correct action. However, U does not want to reveal its secret. Using zero-knowledge proofs we can satisfy both conflicting requirements (i.e., having other users verify that U took the correct action without violating U's interest in not revealing its secret). That is, U can prove in zero-knowledge that it took the correct action. Note that U's claim to having taken the correct action is an NP-assertion (since U's legal action is determined as a polynomial-time function of its secret and the public information), and that U has an NP-witness to its validity (i.e., the secret is an NP-witness to the claim that the action fits the public information). Thus, by Theorem 17.5, it is possible for U to efficiently prove the correctness of its action without yielding anything about its secret. Consequently, it is fair to ask U to prove (in zero-knowledge) that it behaves properly, and so to force U to behave properly. Indeed, "forcing proper behavior" is the canonical application of zero-knowledge proofs (see Goldreich et al. [1987], Goldreich [1998]).

This paradigm (i.e., "forcing proper behavior" via zero-knowledge proofs), which in turn is based on the fact that zero-knowledge proofs can be constructed for any NP-set, has been utilized in numerous different settings. Indeed, this paradigm is the basis for the wide applicability of zero-knowledge protocols in cryptography.

17.5.4 Variants and Issues

In this section we consider numerous variants on the notion of zero-knowledge and the underlying model of interactive proofs. These include computational soundness (Section 17.5.4.1), black-box simulation and other variants of zero-knowledge (Section 17.5.4.2), as well as notions such as proofs of knowledge, noninteractive zero-knowledge, and witness indistinguishable proofs (Section 17.5.4.3). We conclude this section by reviewing results regarding the composition of zero-knowledge protocols and the power of non-black-box simulation (Section 17.5.4.4).

17.5.4.1 Computational Soundness

A fundamental variant on the notion of interactive proofs was introduced by Brassard, Chaum, and Crépeau [Brassard et al. 1988], who relaxed the soundness condition so that it only refers to feasible ways of trying to fool the verifier (rather than to all possible ways). Specifically, the soundness condition was replaced by a ***computational soundness*** condition that asserts that it is infeasible to fool the verifier into accepting false statements. We warn that although the computational-soundness error can *always* be reduced by sequential repetitions, it is *not* true that this error can *always* be reduced by parallel repetitions (see Bellare et al. [1997]).

Protocols that satisfy the computational-soundness condition are called ***arguments***.[12] We mention that argument systems may be more efficient than interactive proofs (see Kilian [1992] vs. Goldreich and Håstad [1998], Goldreich et al. [2002]) as well as provide stronger zero-knowledge guarantees (see Brassard et al. [1988], Haitner et al. [2009] vs. Fortnow [1987], Aiello and Håstad [1987]). Specifically, perfect zero-knowledge arguments for $\mathcal{NP}$ can be constructed (based on the same assumption used in Theorem 17.5) [Haitner et al. 2009], where perfect zero-knowledge means that the simulator's output is distributed *identically* to the verifier's view in the real interaction (see discussion in Section 17.5.4.2). Note that stronger security for the prover (as provided by perfect zero-knowledge) comes at the cost of weaker security for the verifier (as provided by computational soundness). The answer to the question of whether or not this trade-off is worthwhile seems to be application dependent, and one should also take into account the complexity of the corresponding protocols and their reliability (i.e., the assumptions that underlie their security).[13]

17.5.4.2   Definitional Variations

We consider several definitional issues regarding the notion of zero-knowledge (as defined in Definition 17.7).

Universal and black-box simulation.   Further strengthening of Definition 17.7 is obtained by requiring the existence of a ***universal simulator***, denoted $\mathcal{C}$, that is given the program of the verifier (i.e., B^*) as an auxiliary input; that is, in terms of Definition 17.7, one should replace $C^*(x, z)$ by $\mathcal{C}(x, z, \langle B^* \rangle)$, where $\langle B^* \rangle$ denotes the description of the program of B^* (which may depend on x and on z). That is, we effectively restrict the simulation by requiring that it be a uniform (feasible) function of the verifier's program (rather than arbitrarily depend on it). This restriction is very natural, because it seems hard to envision an alternative way of establishing the zero-knowledge property of a given protocol. Taking another step, one may argue that since it seems infeasible to reverse-engineer programs, the simulator may as well just use the verifier strategy as an oracle (or as a "black box"). This reasoning gave rise to the notion of ***black-box simulation***, which was introduced

---

12. A related notion (not discussed here) is that of CS-proofs, introduced by Micali [2000].

13. Still, as stated in Footnote 8, we believe that a presentation in terms of proofs should be preferred for expositional purposes.

and advocated in Goldreich and Krawczyk [1996] and further studied in numerous works (see, e.g., Canetti et al. [2001]). The belief was that inherent limitations regarding black-box simulation represent inherent limitations of zero-knowledge itself. For example, it was believed that the *fact* that the parallel version of the interactive proof of Figure 17.1 cannot be simulated in a black-box manner (unless $\mathcal{NP}$ is contained in $\mathcal{BPP}$ [Goldreich and Krawczyk 1996]) *implies* that this version is not zero-knowledge (as per Definition 17.7 itself). However, the (underlying) belief that any zero-knowledge protocol can be simulated in a black-box manner was refuted by Barak [2001]. For further discussion, see Section 17.5.4.4.

Honest verifier versus general cheating verifier. Definition 17.7 refers to all feasible verifier strategies, which is most natural (in the cryptographic setting) because zero-knowledge is supposed to capture the robustness of the prover under *any feasible* (i.e., adversarial) attempt to gain something by interacting with it. A weaker and still interesting notion of zero-knowledge refers to what can be gained by an "honest verifier" (or rather a semi-honest verifier)[14] that interacts with the prover as directed, with the exception that it may maintain (and output) a record of the entire interaction (i.e., even when directed to erase all records of the interaction). Although such a weaker notion is not satisfactory for standard cryptographic applications, it yields a fascinating notion from a conceptual as well as a complexity-theoretic point of view. Furthermore, as shown in Goldreich et al. [1998] and Vadhan [2004], every proof system that is *zero-knowledge with respect to the honest-verifier* can be transformed into a *standard zero-knowledge* proof (without using intractability assumptions and in case of "public-coin" proofs this is done without significantly increasing the prover's computational effort).

Statistical versus computational zero-knowledge. Recall that Definition 17.7 postulates that for every probability ensemble of one type (i.e., representing the verifier's output after interaction with the prover) there exists a "similar" ensemble of a second type (i.e., representing the simulator's output). One key parameter is the interpretation of "similarity." Three interpretations, yielding different notions of zero-knowledge, have been commonly considered in the literature (see Goldwasser et al. [1989], Fortnow [1987]):

---

14. The term "honest verifier" is more appealing when considering an alternative (equivalent) formulation of Definition 17.7. In the alternative definition (see Goldreich [2001, Sec. 4.3.1.3]), the simulator is "only" required to generate the verifier's view of the real interaction, where the verifier's view includes its (common and auxiliary) inputs, the outcome of its coin tosses, and all messages it has received.

- *Perfect zero-knowledge* requires that the two probability ensembles be identical.[15]

- *Statistical zero-knowledge* requires that these probability ensembles be statistically close (i.e., the variation distance between them is negligible).

- *Computational* (or rather, general) *zero-knowledge* requires that these probability ensembles be computationally indistinguishable.

Indeed, computational zero-knowledge is the most liberal notion, and is the notion considered in Definition 17.7. We note that the class of problems having statistical zero-knowledge proofs contains several problems that are considered intractable. The interested reader is referred to Vadhan [1999].

Strict versus expected probabilistic polynomial time. So far, we did not specify what we exactly mean by the term probabilistic polynomial time. Two common interpretations are:

- *Strict probabilistic polynomial time*. That is, there exist a (polynomial in the length of the input) bound on the *number of steps in each possible run* of the machine, regardless of the outcome of its coin tosses.

- *Expected probabilistic polynomial time*. The standard approach is to look at the running-time as a random variable and *bound its expectation* (by a polynomial in the length of the input). As observed by Levin (see Goldreich [2001, Sec. 4.3.1.6], and Barak and Lindell [2004]), this definitional approach is quite problematic (e.g., it is not model independent and is not closed under algorithmic composition), and an alternative treatment of this random variable is preferable.

Since the notion of expected polynomial time raises a variety of conceptual and technical problems, whenever possible, one should prefer the more robust (and restricted) notion of strict (probabilistic) polynomial time. Thus, with the *exception of constant-round* zero-knowledge protocols, whenever we talked of a probabilistic polynomial-time verifier (respectively, simulator) we mean one in the strict sense. In contrast, with the exception of Barak [2001] and Barak and Lindell [2004], all results regarding *constant-round* zero-knowledge protocols refer to a strict polynomial-time verifier and an expected polynomial-time simulator, which is indeed a small

---

15. The actual definition of perfect zero-knowledge allows the simulator to fail (while outputting a special symbol) with negligible probability, and the output distribution of the simulator is conditioned on its not failing.

cheat. For further discussion, the reader is referred to Barak and Lindell [2004] and Goldreich [2010].

17.5.4.3 Related Notions: POK, NIZK, and WI

We briefly discuss the notions of proofs of knowledge (POK), non-interactive zero-knowledge (NIZK), and witness indistinguishable proofs (WI).

Proofs of Knowledge. Loosely speaking, proofs of knowledge (discussed in Goldwasser et al. [1989] and defined in Bellare and Goldreich [1992]) are interactive proofs in which the prover asserts "knowledge" of some object (e.g., a 3-coloring of a graph), and not merely its existence (e.g., the existence of a 3-coloring of the graph, which in turn is equivalent to the assertion that the graph is 3-colorable). Before clarifying what we mean by saying that a machine knows something, we point out that "proofs of knowledge", and in particular zero-knowledge "proofs of knowledge", have many applications to the design of cryptographic schemes and cryptographic protocols. One famous application of zero-knowledge proofs of knowledge is to the construction of identification schemes (e.g., the Fiat–Shamir scheme [Fiat and Shamir 1987]).

What do we mean by saying that a *machine* knows something? Any standard dictionary suggests several meanings for the verb to know, which are typically phrased with reference to *awareness*, a notion which is certainly inapplicable in the context of machines. Instead, we must look for a *behavioristic* interpretation of the verb to know. Indeed, it is reasonable to link knowledge with ability to do something (e.g., the ability to write down whatever one knows). Hence, we will say that a machine knows a string α if it *can* output the string α. But this seems as total nonsense too: A machine has a well-defined output—either the output equals α or it does not. So what can be meant by saying that *a machine can do something?* Loosely speaking, it may mean that the machine can be *easily modified* so that it does whatever is claimed. More precisely, it may mean that there exists an *efficient* machine that, using the original machine as a black box (or given its code as an input), outputs whatever is claimed.

So much for defining the "knowledge of machines." Yet whatever a machine knows or does not know is "its own business." What can be of interest and reference *to the outside* is whatever can be deduced about the knowledge of a machine by interacting with it. Hence, we are interested in proofs of knowledge (rather than in mere knowledge). For sake of simplicity let us consider a concrete question: *How can a machine prove that it knows a 3-coloring of a graph?* An obvious way is just to send the 3-coloring to the verifier. Yet we claim that applying the protocol in

Figure 17.1 (i.e., the zero-knowledge proof system for 3-colorability) is an alternative way of proving knowledge of a 3-coloring of the graph.

The definition of a *verifier of knowledge of 3-coloring* refers to any possible prover strategy. It requires the existence of an efficient universal way of "extracting" a 3-coloring of a given graph by using any prover strategy that convinces the verifier to accept the graph (with noticeable probability). Surely, we should no expect much of prover strategies that convince the verifier to accept the graph with negligible probability. However, a robust definition should allow a smooth passage from noticeable to negligible, and should allow to establish the intuitive zero-knowledge property of a party that sends some information to another party after the other party proved that it knows this information.

Loosely speaking, we may say that an interactive machine, V, constitutes a ***verifier for knowledge*** of 3-coloring if, for any prover strategy P, the complexity of extracting a 3-coloring of G when using machine P as a "black box"[16] is inversely proportional to the probability that the verifier is convinced by P (to accept the graph G)—namely, the extraction of the 3-coloring is done by an oracle machine, called an *extractor*, that is given access to a function specifying the behavior P (i.e., the messages it sends in response to particular messages it may receive). We require that the (expected) running time of the extractor, on input G and access to an oracle specifying P's strategy, be inversely related (by a factor polynomial in $|G|$) to the probability that P convinces V to accept G. In case P always convinces V to accept G, the extractor runs in expected polynomial time. The same holds in case P convinces V to accept with noticeable probability. On the other hand, in case P never convinces V to accept, essentially nothing is required of the extractor. (We stress that the latter special cases do not suffice for a satisfactory definition; see discussion in Goldreich [2001, Sec. 4.7.1].)

Noninteractive zero-knowledge. The model of noninteractive zero-knowledge proof systems, introduced in Blum et al. [1988], consists of three entities: a prover, a verifier, and a uniformly selected ***reference string*** (which can be thought of as being selected by a trusted third party). Both the verifier and prover can read the reference string, and each can toss additional coins. The interaction consists of a single message sent from the prover to the verifier, who then is left with the final decision (whether or not to accept). The (basic) zero-knowledge requirement refers to a simulator that outputs pairs that should be computationally indistinguishable from the distribution (of pairs consisting of a uniformly selected reference string and a

---

16. Indeed, one may consider also non-black-box extractors as done in Barak and Lindell [2004].

random prover message) seen in the real model.[17] Noninteractive zero-knowledge proof systems have numerous applications (e.g., to the construction of public key encryption and signature schemes, where the reference string may be incorporated in the public key). Several different definitions of noninteractive zero-knowledge proofs were considered in the literature:

- In the *basic definition*, one considers proving a single assertion of a priori bounded length, where this length may be smaller than the length of the reference string.

- A natural extension, required in many applications, is the ability to prove multiple assertions of varying length, where the total length of these assertions may exceed the length of the reference string (as long as the total length is polynomial in the length of the reference string). This definition is sometimes referred to as the *unbounded definition*, because the total length of the assertions to be proved is not a priori bounded.

- Other natural extensions refer to the preservation of security (i.e., both soundness and zero-knowledge) when the assertions to be proved are selected *adaptively* (based on the reference string and possibly even based on previous proofs).

- Finally, we mention the notion of *simulation soundness*, which is related to *nonmalleability*. This extension, which mixes the zero-knowledge and soundness conditions, refers to the soundness of proofs presented by an adversary after it obtains proofs of assertions of its own choice (with respect to the same reference string). This notion is important in applications of non-interactive zero-knowledge proofs to the construction of public-key encryption schemes secure against chosen ciphertext attacks (see Goldreich [2004, Sec. 5.4.4.4]).

Constructing noninteractive zero-knowledge proofs seems more difficult than constructing interactive zero-knowledge proofs. Still, based on standard intractability assumptions (e.g., intractability of factoring), it is known how to construct a noninteractive zero-knowledge proof (even in the adaptive and nonmalleable sense) for any NP-set (see Feige et al. [1999], De Santis et al. [2001]).

Witness indistinguishability and the FLS-technique. The notion of witness indistinguishability was suggested in Feige and Shamir [1990] as a meaningful relaxation

---

17. Note that the verifier does not affect the distribution seen in the real model, and so the basic definition of zero-knowledge does not refer to it. The verifier (or rather a process of adaptively selecting assertions to be proved) will be referred to in the adaptive variants of the definition.

of zero-knowledge. Loosely speaking, for any NP-relation R, a proof (or argument) system for the corresponding NP-set is called **witness indistinguishable** if no feasible verifier can distinguish the case in which the prover uses one NP-witness to x (i.e., w_1 such that $(x, w_1) \in R$) from the case in which the prover is using a different NP-witness to the same input x (i.e., w_2 such that $(x, w_2) \in R$). Clearly, any zero-knowledge protocol is witness indistinguishable, but the converse does not necessarily hold. Furthermore, it seems that witness indistinguishable protocols are easier to construct than zero-knowledge ones. Another advantage of witness indistinguishable protocols is that they are closed under arbitrary concurrent composition [Feige and Shamir 1990], whereas in general zero-knowledge protocols are not closed even under parallel composition [Goldreich and Krawczyk 1996]. Witness indistinguishable protocols turned out to be an *important tool in the construction of more complex protocols*, as is demonstrated next.

Feige, Lapidot, and Shamir [Feige et al. 1999] introduced a technique for constructing zero-knowledge proofs (and arguments) based on witness-indistinguishable proofs (respectively, arguments). Following is a sketchy description of a special case of their technique, often referred to as the **FLS-technique**, which has been used in numerous works. On common input $x \in L$, where L is the NP-set defined by the witness relation R, the following two steps are performed:

1. The parties generate an instance x' for an auxiliary NP-set L', where L' is defined by a witness relation R'. Loosely speaking, the *generation protocol* in use should satisfy the following two conditions:

    1. If the verifier follows its prescribed strategy then no matter which strategy is used by the prover, with high probability, the protocol's outcome is a NO-instance of L'.

    2. There exists an efficient (noninteractive) procedure for producing a (random) transcript of the generation protocol such that the corresponding outcome is a YES-instance of L' and yet the produced transcript is computationally indistinguishable from the transcript of a real execution of the protocol. Furthermore, this procedure also outputs an NP-witness for the YES-instance that appears as the protocol's outcome.

    For example, L' may consist of all possible outcomes of a pseudorandom generator that stretches its seed by a factor of 2, and the generation protocol may consist of the two parties iteratively invoking a "coin tossing" protocol to obtain a random string. Note that the outcome of a real execution will be an almost uniformly distributed string, which is most likely a NO-instance of L', whereas it is possible to efficiently generate a (random) transcript corresponding to any desired outcome (provided that the parties use an adequate coin tossing protocol).

2. The parties execute a *witness-indistinguishable* proof for the NP-set L'' defined by the witness relation $R'' = \{((\alpha, \alpha'), (\beta, \beta')) : (\alpha, \beta) \in R \vee (\alpha', \beta') \in R'\}$. The sub-protocol is such that the corresponding prover can be implemented in probabilistic polynomial time given any NP-witness for $(\alpha, \alpha') \in L''$. The sub-protocol is invoked on common input (x, x'), where x' is the outcome of Step 1, and the sub-prover is invoked with the corresponding NP-witness as auxiliary input (i.e., with $(w, 0)$, where w is the NP-witness for x (given to the main prover)).

The soundness of the above protocol follows by Property (a) of the generation protocol (i.e., with high probability $x' \notin L'$, and so $x \in L$ follows by the soundness of the protocol used in Step 2). To demonstrate the zero-knowledge property, we first generate a simulated transcript of Step 1 (with outcome $x' \in L'$) along with an adequate NP-witness (i.e., w' such that $(x', w') \in R'$), and then emulate Step 2 by feeding the sub-prover strategy with the NP-witness $(0, w')$. Combining Property (b) of the generation protocol and the witness indistinguishability property of the protocol used in Step 2, the simulation is indistinguishable from the real execution.

17.5.4.4 Two Basic Problems: Composition and Black-Box Simulation

We conclude this section by considering two basic problems regarding zero-knowledge, which actually arise also with respect to the security of other cryptographic primitives.

Composition of protocols. The first question refers to the *preservation of security* (i.e., zero-knowledge in our case) *under various types of composition operations*. These composition operations represent independent executions of a protocol that are attacked by an adversary (which coordinates its actions in the various executions). The preservation of security under such compositions (which involve only executions of the same protocol) is a first step toward the study of the security of the protocol when executed together with other protocols (see further discussion in Section 17.9.4). Turning back to zero-knowledge, we recall the main facts regarding sequential, parallel, and concurrent execution of (arbitrary and/or specific) zero-knowledge protocols:

Sequential composition:. As stated above, zero-knowledge (with respect to auxiliary inputs) is preserved under sequential composition.

Parallel composition:. In general, zero-knowledge is NOT preserved under parallel composition [Goldreich and Krawczyk 1996]. Yet, some zero-knowledge proofs (for NP) preserve their security when many copies are executed in parallel. Furthermore, some of these protocol use a constant number of rounds (see Goldreich [2006]).

Concurrent composition:.   One may view parallel composition as concurrent composition in a model of strict synchrony. This leads us to consider more general models of concurrent composition. We distinguish between a model of full asynchronicity and a model of naturally limited asynchronicity:

- In the full asynchronous model, some zero-knowledge proofs (for NP) preserve their security when many copies are executed concurrently (see Richardson and Kilian [1999], Kilian and Petrank [2001], Prabhakaran et al. [2002]), but such a result is not known for constant-round protocols.

- In contrast, some constant-round zero-knowledge proofs (for NP) preserve their security in a model of limited asynchronicity (see Dwork et al. [1998], Goldreich [2006]), where each party holds a local clock such that the relative clock rates are bounded by an a priori known constant and the protocols may employ time-driven operations (i.e., time-out in-coming messages and delay out-going messages).

The study of zero-knowledge in the concurrent setting provides a good test case for the study of concurrent security of general protocols. In particular, the results in Goldreich and Krawczyk [1996] and Canetti et al. [2001] point out inherent limitations of the "standard proof methods" (used to establish zero-knowledge) when applied to the concurrent setting, where Goldreich and Krawczyk [1996] treats the synchronous case and Canetti et al. [2001] uncovers much stronger limitations for the asynchronous case. By "standard proof methods" we refer to the establishment of zero-knowledge via a single simulator that obtains only oracle (or "black-box") access to the adversary procedure.

Black-box proofs of security. The second basic question regarding zero-knowledge refers to the usage of the adversary's program within the proof of security (i.e., demonstration of the zero-knowledge property). For 15 years, all known proofs of security used the adversary's program as a black-box (i.e., a universal simulator was presented using the adversary's program as an oracle). Furthermore, it was believed that there was no advantage in having access to the code of the adversary's program (see Goldreich and Krawczyk [1996]). Consequently, it was conjectured that negative results regarding black-box simulation represent an inherent limitation of zero-knowledge. This belief was refuted by Barak [2001], who constructed a zero-knowledge argument (for NP) that has important properties that are impossible to achieve by black-box simulation (unless $\mathcal{NP} \subseteq \mathcal{BPP}$). For example, this zero-knowledge argument uses a constant number of rounds and preserves its security when an a priori fixed (polynomial) number of copies are executed concurrently.[18]

Barak's results (see Barak [2001] and also 2002) call for the re-evaluation of many common beliefs. Most concretely, they say that results regarding black-box simulators do not reflect inherent limitations of zero-knowledge (but rather an inherent limitation of a natural way of demonstrating the zero-knowledge property). Most abstractly, they say that there are meaningful ways of using a program other than merely invoking it as a black-box. Does this mean that a method was found to "reverse engineer" programs or to "understand" them? We believe that the answer is negative. Barak [2001] is using the adversary's program in a significant way (i.e., more significant than just invoking it), without "understanding" it.

The key idea underlying Barak's protocol [Barak 2001] is to have the prover prove that either the original NP-assertion is valid or that he (i.e., the prover) "knows the verifier's residual strategy" (in the sense that it can predict the next verifier message). Indeed, in a real interaction (with the honest verifier), it is infeasible for the prover to predict the next verifier message, since the verifier generates random messages, and so computational soundness of the protocol follows. However, a simulator that is given the code of the verifier's strategy (and not merely oracle access to that code) can produce a valid proof of the foregoing disjunction by properly executing the sub-protocol using its knowledge of an NP-witness for the second disjunctive. The simulation is computationally indistinguishable from the real execution, provided that one cannot distinguish an execution of the sub-protocol in which one NP-witness (i.e., an NP-witness for the original assertion) is used from an execution in which the second NP-witness (i.e., an NP-witness for the auxiliary assertion) is used. That is, the sub-protocol should be a *witness indistinguishable* argument system, and the entire construction uses the *FLS technique* (described in Section 17.5.4.3). We warn the reader that the actual implementation of the foregoing idea requires overcoming several technical difficulties (see Barak [2001], Barak and Goldreich [2002]).

---

18. This result falls short of achieving a fully concurrent zero-knowledge argument, because the number of concurrent copies must be fixed before the protocol is presented. Specifically, the protocol uses messages that are longer than the allowed number of concurrent copies. However, even preservation of security under an a priori bounded number of executions goes beyond the impossibility results of Goldreich and Krawczyk [1996] and Canetti et al. [2001] (which refer to black-box simulations).

Part II

Basic Applications

Encryption and signature schemes are the most basic applications of cryptography. Their main utility is in providing secret and reliable communication over insecure communication media. Loosely speaking, encryption schemes are used to ensure the secrecy (or privacy) of the actual information being communicated, whereas signature schemes are used to ensure its reliability (or authenticity). In this part we survey these basic applications as well as the construction of general secure cryptographic protocols. For more details regarding the contents of the current part, see our textbook [Goldreich 2004].

17.7   Encryption Schemes

The problem of providing *secret communication over insecure media* is the traditional and most basic problem of cryptography. The setting of this problem consists of two parties communicating through a channel that is possibly tapped by an adversary. The parties wish to exchange information with each other but keep the "wiretapper" as ignorant as possible regarding the contents of this information. The canonical solution to the foregoing problem is obtained by the use of encryption schemes. Loosely speaking, an encryption scheme is a protocol allowing these parties to communicate *secretly* with each other. Typically, the encryption scheme consists of a pair of algorithms. One algorithm, called *encryption*, is applied by the sender (i.e., the party sending a message), while the other algorithm, called *decryption*, is applied by the receiver. Hence, in order to send a message, the sender first applies the encryption algorithm to the message, and sends the result, called the *ciphertext*, over the channel. Upon receiving a ciphertext, the other party (i.e., the receiver) applies the decryption algorithm to it, and retrieves the original message (called the *plaintext*).

In order for the foregoing scheme to provide secret communication, the communicating parties (at least the receiver) must know something that is not known to the wiretapper. (Otherwise, the wiretapper can decrypt the ciphertext exactly as done by the receiver.) This extra knowledge may take the form of the decryption algorithm itself, or some parameters and/or auxiliary inputs used by the decryption algorithm. We call this extra knowledge the *decryption key*. Note that, without loss of generality, we may assume that the decryption algorithm is known to the wiretapper, and that the decryption algorithm operates on two inputs: a ciphertext and a decryption key. We stress that the existence of a decryption key, not known to the wiretapper, is merely a necessary condition for secret communication. The foregoing description implicitly presupposes the existence of an efficient algorithm for generating (random) keys.

Evaluating the "security" of an encryption scheme is a very tricky business. A preliminary task is to understand what is "security" (i.e., to properly define what is meant by this intuitive term). Two approaches to defining security are known. The first ("classical") approach, introduced by Shannon [1949], is *information theoretic*. It is concerned with the "information" about the plaintext that is "present" in the ciphertext. Loosely speaking, if the ciphertext contains information about the plaintext, then the encryption scheme is considered insecure. It has been shown that such a high (i.e., "perfect") level of security can be achieved only if the key in use is at least as long as the *total* amount of information sent via the encryption scheme [Shannon 1949]. This fact (i.e., that the key has to be longer than the information exchanged using it) is indeed a drastic limitation on the applicability of such (perfectly secure) encryption schemes.

The second ("modern") approach, followed in the current text, is based on *computational complexity*. This approach is based on the thesis that it *does not matter* whether the ciphertext contains information about the plaintext, but rather whether this information can be *efficiently extracted*. In other words, instead of asking whether it is *possible* for the wiretapper to extract specific information, we ask whether it is *feasible* for the wiretapper to extract this information. It turns out that the new (i.e., "computational complexity") approach can offer security even when the key is much shorter than the total length of the messages sent via the encryption scheme.

The computational complexity approach enables the introduction of concepts and primitives that cannot exist under the information theoretic approach. A typical example is the concept of *public-key encryption schemes*, introduced by Diffie and Hellman [1976]. Recall that in the foregoing discussion we concentrated on the decryption algorithm and its key. It can be shown that the encryption algorithm must get, in addition to the message, an auxiliary input that depends on the decryption-key. This auxiliary input is called the **encryption key**. Traditional encryption schemes, and in particular all the encryption schemes used in the millennia until the 1980s, operate with an encryption key that equals the decryption key. Hence, the wiretapper in these schemes must be ignorant of the encryption key, and consequently the *key distribution* problem arises: how can two parties wishing to communicate over an insecure channel agree on a secret encryption/decryption key? (The traditional solution is to exchange the key through an alternative channel that is secure though (much) more expensive to use.) The computational complexity approach allows the introduction of encryption schemes in which the encryption key may be given to the wiretapper without compromising the security of the scheme. Clearly, the decryption key in such schemes is different from the encryption key, and furthermore infeasible to compute from the encryption key.

Such encryption schemes, called ***public-key*** schemes, have the advantage of trivially resolving the key distribution problem (because the encryption key can be publicized). That is, once some Party X generates a pair of keys and publicizes the encryption key, any party can send encrypted messages to Party X so that Party X can retrieve the actual information (i.e., the plaintext), whereas nobody else can learn anything about the plaintext.

In contrast to public-key schemes, traditional encryption schemes in which the encryption key equals the description key are called ***private-key*** schemes, because in these schemes the encryption key must be kept secret (rather than be public as in public-key encryption schemes). We note that a full specification of either schemes requires the specification of the way in which keys are generated; that is, a (randomized) key-generation algorithm that, given a security parameter, produces a (random) pair of corresponding encryption/decryption keys (which are identical in case of private-key schemes).

Thus, both private-key and public-key encryption schemes consist of three efficient algorithms: A ***key generation*** algorithm denoted G, an ***encryption*** algorithm denoted E, and a ***decryption*** algorithm denoted D. For every pair of encryption and decryption keys (e, d) generated by G, and for every plaintext x, it holds that $D_d(E_e(x)) = x$, where $E_e(x) \stackrel{\text{def}}{=} E(e, x)$ and $D_d(y) \stackrel{\text{def}}{=} D(d, y)$. The difference between the two types of encryption schemes is reflected in the definition of security: The security of a public-key encryption scheme should hold also when the adversary is given the encryption key, whereas this is not required for a private-key encryption scheme. Below we focus on the public-key case (and the private-key case can be obtained by omitting the encryption key from the sequence of inputs given to the adversary).

17.7.1   Definitions

A good disguise should not reveal the person's height.
A good disguise should not allow a mother to distinguish her own children.

—Shafi Goldwasser and Silvio Micali, 1982

For simplicity, we first consider the encryption of a single message (which, for further simplicity, is assumed to be of length n).[19] As implied by the foregoing dis-

---

19. In the case of public-key schemes no generality is lost by these simplifying assumptions, but in the case of private-key schemes one should consider the encryption of polynomially many messages (as we do below).

cussion, a public-key encryption scheme is said to be secure if it is infeasible to gain any information about the plaintext by looking at the ciphertext (and the encryption key). That is, whatever information about the plaintext one may compute from the ciphertext and some a priori information, can be essentially computed as efficiently from the a priori information alone. This fundamental definition of security (called semantic security) turns out to be equivalent to saying that, for any two messages, it is infeasible to distinguish the encryption of the first message from the encryption of the second message, even when given the encryption key. Both definitions were introduced by Goldwasser and Micali [1984].

Definition 17.8 (Semantic security [following Goldwasser and Micali [1984]; revisited in Goldreich [1993]]) A *public-key* encryption scheme (G, E, D) is *semantically secure* if for every probabilistic polynomial-time algorithm, A, there exists a probabilistic polynomial-time algorithm B so that for every two functions $f, h: \{0, 1\}^* \to \{0, 1\}^*$ such that $|h(x)| = \text{poly}(|x|)$, and all probability ensembles $\{X_n\}_{n \in \mathbb{N}}$, where X_n is a random variable ranging over $\{0, 1\}^n$, it holds that

$$\Pr[A(e, E_e(x), h(x)) = f(x)] < \Pr[B(1^n, h(x)) = f(x)] + \mu(n),$$

where the plaintext x is distributed according to X_n, the encryption key e is distributed according to $G(1^n)$, and μ is a negligible function.

That is, it is feasible to predict $f(x)$ from $h(x)$ as successfully as it is to predict $f(x)$ from $h(x)$ and $(e, E_e(x))$, which means that nothing is gained by obtaining $(e, E_e(x))$. Note that no computational restrictions are made regarding the functions h and f. We stress that the foregoing definition (as well as the next one) refers to public-key encryption schemes, and in the case of private-key schemes algorithm A is not given the encryption key e. The following technical interpretation of security states that it is infeasible to distinguish the encryptions of two plaintexts (of the same length).

Definition 17.9 (Indistinguishability of encryptions [following Goldwasser and Micali [1984]]) A *public-key* encryption scheme (G, E, D) has *indistinguishable encryptions* if for every probabilistic polynomial-time algorithm, A, and all sequences of triples, $(x_n, y_n, z_n)_{n \in \mathbb{N}}$, where $|x_n| = |y_n| = n$ and $|z_n| = \text{poly}(n)$, it holds that

$$| \Pr[A(e, E_e(x_n), z_n) = 1] - \Pr[A(e, E_e(y_n), z_n) = 1]| = \mu(n).$$

Again, e is distributed according to $G(1^n)$, and μ is a negligible function.

In particular, z_n may equal (x_n, y_n). Thus, it is infeasible to distinguish the encryptions of any two fixed messages (such as the all-zero message and the all-ones message).

Definition 17.8 is more appealing in most settings where encryption is considered the end goal. Definition 17.9 is used to establish the security of candidate encryption schemes as well as to analyze their application as modules inside larger cryptographic protocols. Thus, their equivalence is of major importance.

Equivalence of Definitions 17.8 and 17.9—proof ideas. Intuitively, indistinguishability of encryptions (i.e., of the encryptions of x_n and y_n) is a special case of semantic security; specifically, it corresponds to the case that X_n is uniform over $\{x_n, y_n\}$, f indicates one of the plaintexts, and h does not distinguish them (i.e., $f(w) = 1$ iff $w = x_n$ and $h(x_n) = h(y_n) = z_n$, where z_n is as in Definition 17.9). The other direction is proved by considering the algorithm B that, on input $(1^n, v)$ where $v = h(x)$, generates $(e, d) \leftarrow G(1^n)$ and outputs $A(e, E_e(1^n), v)$, where A is as in Definition 17.8. Indistinguishability of encryptions is used to prove that B performs as well as A (i.e., for every h, f and $\{X_n\}_{n \in \mathbb{N}}$, it holds that $\Pr[B(1^n, h(X_n)) = f(X_n)] = \Pr[A(e, E_e(1^n), h(X_n)) = f(X_n)]$ approximately equals $\Pr[A(e, E_e(X_n), h(X_n)) = f(X_n)]$).

Probabilistic encryption. It is easy to see that a secure *public-key* encryption scheme must employ a probabilistic (i.e., randomized) encryption algorithm. Otherwise, given the encryption-key as (additional) input, it is easy to distinguish the encryption of the all-zero message from the encryption of the all-ones message.[20] This explains the association of the aforementioned robust security definitions and *probabilistic encryption*, an association that goes back to the title of the pioneering work of Goldwasser and Micali [1984].

Further discussion. We stress that (the equivalent) Definitions 17.8 and 17.9 go way beyond saying that it is infeasible to recover the plaintext from the ciphertext. The latter statement is indeed a minimal requirement from a secure encryption scheme, but is far from being a sufficient requirement. Typically, encryption schemes are used in applications where even obtaining partial information on the plaintext may endanger the security of the application. When designing an application-independent encryption scheme, we do not know which partial information endan-

---

20. The same holds for (stateless) *private-key* encryption schemes, when considering the security of encrypting several messages (rather than a single message as done above). For example, if one uses a deterministic encryption algorithm, then the adversary can distinguish two encryptions of the same message from the encryptions of a pair of different messages.

gers the application and which does not. Furthermore, even if one wants to design an encryption scheme tailored to a specific application, it is rare (to say the least) that one has a precise characterization of all possible partial information that endanger this application. Thus, we need to require that it is infeasible to obtain any information about the plaintext from the ciphertext. Furthermore, in most applications the plaintext may not be uniformly distributed and some a priori information regarding it may be available to the adversary. We require that the secrecy of all partial information is preserved also in such a case. That is, even in presence of a priori information on the plaintext, it is infeasible to obtain any (new) information about the plaintext from the ciphertext (beyond what is feasible to obtain from the a priori information on the plaintext). The definition of semantic security postulates all of this. The equivalent definition of indistinguishability of encryptions is useful in demonstrating the security of candidate constructions as well as for arguing about their effect as part of larger protocols.

Security of multiple messages.   Definitions 17.8 and 17.9 refer to the security of an encryption scheme that is used to encrypt a single plaintext (per generated key). Since the plaintext may be longer than the key,[21] these definitions are already nontrivial, and an encryption scheme satisfying them (even in the private-key model) implies the existence of one-way functions. Still, in many cases, it is desirable to encrypt many plaintexts using the same encryption key. Loosely speaking, an encryption scheme is secure in the multiple-messages setting if analogous definitions (to Definitions 17.8 and 17.9) hold when polynomially many plaintexts are encrypted using the same encryption key (see Goldreich [2004, Sec. 5.2.4]). It is easy to see that *in the public-key model*, security in the single-message setting implies security in the multiple-messages setting. We stress that this is not necessarily true *for the private-key model*.

17.7.2 Constructions

It is common practice to use "pseudorandom generators" as a basis for private-key encryption schemes. We stress that this is a very dangerous practice when the "pseudorandom generator" is easy to predict (such as the linear congruential generator or some modifications of it that output a constant fraction of the bits of each resulting number). However, this common practice becomes sound provided

---

21. Recall that for sake of simplicity we have considered only messages of length n, but the general definitions refer to messages of arbitrary (polynomial in n) length. We comment that, in the general form of Definition 17.8, one should provide the length of the message as an auxiliary input to both algorithms (A and B).

one uses pseudorandom generators (as defined in Section 17.4.2). An alternative and more flexible construction follows.

Private-key encryption schemes based on pseudorandom functions. We present a simple construction that uses pseudorandom functions as defined in Section 17.4.3. The key generation algorithm consists of selecting a seed, denoted s, for a (pseudorandom) function, denoted f_s. To encrypt a message $x \in \{0, 1\}^n$ (using key s), the encryption algorithm uniformly selects a string $r \in \{0, 1\}^n$ and produces the ciphertext $(r, x \oplus f_s(r))$, where $\oplus$ denotes the exclusive-or of bit strings. To decrypt the ciphertext (r, y) (using key s), the decryption algorithm just computes $y \oplus f_s(r)$. The security of this encryption scheme can be proved in two steps (suggested as a general methodology in Section 17.4.3):

1. Prove that an idealized version of the scheme, in which one uses a uniformly selected function $F: \{0, 1\}^n \to \{0, 1\}^n$, rather than the pseudorandom function f_s, is secure.

2. Conclude that the real scheme (as presented above) is secure (because, otherwise one could distinguish a pseudorandom function from a truly random one).

Note that we could have gotten rid of the randomization (in the encryption process) if we had allowed the encryption algorithm to be history dependent (e.g., use a counter in the role of r). This can be done provided that either only one party uses the key for encryption (and maintains a counter) or that all parties that encrypt, using the same key, coordinate their actions (i.e., maintain a joint state (e.g., counter)). Indeed, when using a private-key encryption scheme, a common situation is that the same key is only used for communication between two specific parties, which update a joint counter during their communication. Furthermore, if the encryption scheme is used for FIFO communication between the parties and both parties can reliably maintain the counter value, then there is no need (for the sender) to send the counter value. (The resulting scheme is related to "stream ciphers" that are commonly used in practice.)

We comment that the use of a counter (or any other state) in the encryption process is not reasonable in the case of public-key encryption schemes, because it is incompatible with the canonical usage of such schemes (i.e., allowing all parties to send encrypted messages to the "owner of the encryption-key" without engaging in any type of coordination or communication). Furthermore, as discussed before, probabilistic encryption is essential for a secure public-key encryption scheme *even in the case of encrypting a single message* (unlike in the case of private-key schemes). Following Goldwasser and Micali [1984], we now demonstrate the use of *probabilistic encryption* in the construction of a public-key encryption scheme.

Public-key encryption schemes based on trapdoor permutations. We present two constructions that employ a collection of trapdoor permutations, as defined in Definition 17.3. Let $\{f_i : D_i \rightarrow D_i\}_i$ be such a collection, and let b be a corresponding hard-core predicate. The key generation algorithm consists of selecting a permutation f_i along with a corresponding trapdoor t, and outputting (i, t) as the key pair. To encrypt a (*single*) bit σ (using the encryption key i), the encryption algorithm uniformly selects $r \in D_i$, and produces the ciphertext $(f_i(r), \sigma \oplus b(r))$. To decrypt the ciphertext (y, τ) (using the decryption key t), the decryption algorithm computes $\tau \oplus b(f_i^{-1}(y))$ (using the trapdoor t of f_i). Clearly, $(\sigma \oplus b(r)) \oplus b(f_i^{-1}(f_i(r))) = \sigma$. Indistinguishability of encryptions can be easily proved using the fact that b is a hard-core of f_i. We comment that the foregoing scheme is quite wasteful in bandwidth; however, the paradigm underlying its construction (i.e., applying the trapdoor permutation to a randomized version of the plaintext rather than to the actual plaintext) is valuable in practice.

A more efficient construction of a public-key encryption scheme, which uses the same key-generation algorithm, was suggested in Blum and Goldwasser [1984] and proceeds as follows. To encrypt an ℓ-bit long string x (using the encryption key i), the encryption algorithm uniformly selects $r \in D_i$, computes $s \leftarrow b(r) \cdot b(f_i(r)) \cdots b(f_i^{\ell-1}(r))$ and produces the ciphertext $(f_i^{\ell}(r), x \oplus s)$. To decrypt the ciphertext (y, v) (using the decryption key t), the decryption algorithm first recovers $r = f_i^{-\ell}(y)$ (using the trapdoor t of f_i), and then obtains $v \oplus b(r) \cdot b(f_i(r)) \cdots b(f_i^{\ell-1}(r))$. Note the similarity to the construction in Theorem 17.2, and the fact that the proof can be extended to establish the computational indistinguishability of $(b(r) \cdots b(f_i^{\ell-1}(r)), f_i^{\ell}(r))$ and $(u, f_i^{\ell}(r))$, for random and independent $r \in D_i$ and $u \in \{0, 1\}^{\ell}$. Indistinguishability of encryptions follows, and thus the aforementioned scheme is secure.

17.7.3 Beyond Eavesdropping Security

Our treatment so far has referred only to a "passive" attack in which the adversary merely eavesdrops the line over which ciphertexts are being sent. Stronger types of attacks, culminating in the so-called chosen ciphertext attack, may be possible in various applications. Specifically, in some settings it is feasible for the adversary to make the sender encrypt a message of the adversary's choice, and in some settings the adversary may even make the receiver decrypt a ciphertext of the adversary's choice. This gives rise to *chosen plaintext attacks* and to *chosen ciphertext attacks*, respectively, which are not covered by the security definitions considered in Sections 17.7.1 and 17.7.2. In this section we briefly discuss such "active" attacks, focusing on chosen ciphertext attacks (of the stronger type known as "*a posteriori*" or "CCA2").

Loosely speaking, in a chosen ciphertext attack, the adversary may obtain the decryptions of ciphertexts of its choice, and is deemed successful if it learns something regarding the plaintext that corresponds to some different ciphertext (see Katz and Yung [2000], Bellare et al. [1998b], and Goldreich [2004, Sec. 5.4.4]). That is, the adversary is given oracle access to the decryption function corresponding to the decryption-key in use (and, in the case of private-key schemes, it is also given oracle access to the corresponding encryption function). The adversary is allowed to query the decryption oracle on any ciphertext except for the "test ciphertext" (i.e., the very ciphertext for which it tries to learn something about the corresponding plaintext). It may also make queries that do not correspond to legitimate ciphertexts, and the answer will be accordingly (i.e., a special "failure" symbol). Furthermore, the adversary may effect the selection of the test ciphertext (by specifying a distribution from which the corresponding plaintext is to be drawn).

Private-key and public-key encryption schemes secure against chosen ciphertext attacks can be constructed under (almost) the same assumptions that suffice for the construction of the corresponding passive schemes. Specifically:

Theorem 17.6 (folklore, see Goldreich [2004, Sec. 5.4.4.3]) Assuming the existence of *one-way functions*, there exist *private-key* encryption schemes that are secure against chosen ciphertext attack.

Theorem 17.7 (Naor and Yung [1990] and Dolev et al. [2000], using Blum et al. [1988] and Feige et al. [1999]; see Goldreich [2004, Sec. 5.4.4.4]) Assuming the existence of *suitably enhanced trapdoor permutations*,[22] there exist *public-key* encryption schemes that are secure against chosen ciphertext attack.

Both theorems are proved by constructing encryption schemes in which the adversary's gain from a chosen ciphertext attack is eliminated by making it infeasible (for the adversary) to obtain any useful knowledge via such an attack. In the case of private-key schemes (i.e., Theorem 17.6), this is achieved by making it infeasible (for the adversary) to produce legitimate ciphertexts (other than those explicitly

---

22. The exact definition of the suitable enhancement has been augmented several times (see account in Goldreich and Rothblum [2013], further corrected by Canetti and Lichtenberg [2017]).

given to it, in response to its request to encrypt plaintexts of its choice). This, in turn, is achieved by augmenting the ciphertext with an "authentication tag" that is hard to generate without knowledge of the encryption-key; that is, we use a message-authentication scheme (as defined in Section 17.8). In the case of public-key schemes (i.e., Theorem 17.7), the adversary can certainly generate ciphertexts by itself, and the aim is to make it infeasible (for the adversary) to produce legitimate ciphertexts without "knowing" the corresponding plaintext. This, in turn, will be achieved by augmenting the plaintext with a non-interactive zero-knowledge "proof of knowledge" of the corresponding plaintext.

Security against chosen ciphertext attack is related to the notion of *non-malleability* of the encryption scheme (see [Dolev et al. 2000]). Loosely speaking, in a non-malleable encryption scheme it is infeasible for an adversary, given a ciphertext, to produce a valid ciphertext for a related plaintext (e.g., given a ciphertext of a plaintext $1x$, for an unknown x, it is infeasible to produce a ciphertext to the plaintext $0x$). For further discussion see Dolev et al. [2000], Bellare et al. [1998b], and Katz and Yung [2000].

17.8 Signature and Message Authentication Schemes

Both signature schemes and message authentication schemes are methods for "validating" data; that is, verifying that the data was approved by a certain party (or set of parties). The difference between signature schemes and message authentication schemes is that signatures should be "universally verifiable", whereas authentication tags are required to be verifiable only by parties that are also able to generate them.

Signature schemes. The need to discuss "digital signatures" [Diffie and Hellman 1976, Rabin 1977] has emerged with the introduction of computer communication to the business environment (in which parties need to commit themselves to proposals and/or declarations that they make). Discussions of "unforgeable signatures" did take place also in previous centuries, but the objects of discussion were handwritten signatures (and not digital ones), and the discussion was not perceived as related to "cryptography." Loosely speaking, a ***scheme for unforgeable signatures*** should satisfy the following:

- Each user can *efficiently produce its own signature* on documents of its choice.

- Every user can *efficiently verify* whether a given string is a signature of another (specific) user on a specific document.

- *It is infeasible to produce signatures of other users* to documents they did not sign.

We note that the formulation of unforgeable digital signatures provides also a clear statement of the essential ingredients of handwritten signatures. The ingredients are each person's ability to sign for itself, a universally agreed verification procedure, and the belief (or assertion) that it is infeasible (or at least hard) to forge signatures (i.e., produce some other person's signatures to documents that were not signed by it such that these "unauthentic" signatures are accepted by the verification procedure). It is not clear to what extent handwritten signatures meet these requirements. In contrast, our discussion of digital signatures provides precise statements concerning the extent to which digital signatures meet the foregoing requirements. Furthermore, unforgeable digital signature schemes can be constructed based on some reasonable computational assumptions (i.e., the existence of one-way functions).

Message authentication schemes.   Message authentication is a task related to the setting considered for encryption schemes—that is, communication over an insecure channel. This time, we consider an active adversary that is monitoring the channel and may alter the messages sent over it. The parties communicating through this insecure channel wish to authenticate the messages they send so that their counterpart can tell an original message (sent by the sender) from a modified one (i.e., modified by the adversary). Loosely speaking, a *scheme for message authentication* should satisfy the following:

- Each of the communicating parties can *efficiently produce an authentication tag* to any message of its choice.

- Each of the communicating parties can *efficiently verify* whether a given string is an authentication tag of a given message.

- *It is infeasible for an external adversary* (i.e., a party other than the communicating parties) *to produce authentication tags* to messages not sent by the communicating parties.

Note that, in contrast to the specification of signature schemes, we do not require universal verification: only the designated receiver is required to be able to verify the authentication tags. Furthermore, we do not require that the receiver can not produce authentication tags by itself (i.e., we only require that *external parties* can not do so). Thus, message authentication schemes cannot convince *a third party* that the sender has indeed sent the information (rather than the receiver having generated it by itself). In contrast, signatures can be used to convince third parties; in fact, a signature to a document is typically sent to a second party so that in the future this party may (by merely presenting the signed document) convince third parties that the document was indeed generated (or sent or approved) by the signer.

17.8.1   Definitions

Formally speaking, both signature schemes and message authentication schemes consist of three efficient algorithms: *key generation*, *signing* and *verification*. As in the case of encryption schemes, the key-generation algorithm is used to generate a pair of corresponding keys, one is used for signing and the other is used for verification. The difference between the two types of schemes is reflected in the definition of security. In the case of signature schemes, the adversary is given the verification key, whereas in the case of message authentication schemes the verification key (which may equal the signing key) is not given to the adversary. Thus, schemes for message authentication can be viewed as a private-key version of signature schemes. This difference yields different functionalities (even more than in the case of encryption): In typical use of a signature scheme, each user generates a pair of signing and verification keys, publicizes the verification key and keeps the signing key secret. Subsequently, each user may sign documents using its own signing key, and these signatures are *universally verifiable* with respect to its public verification key. In contrast, message authentication schemes are typically used to authenticate information sent among a set of *mutually trusting* parties that agree on a secret key, which is being used both to produce and verify authentication tags. (Indeed, it is assumed that the mutually trusting parties have generated the key together or have exchanged the key in a secure way, prior to the communication of information that needs to be authenticated.)

We focus on the definition of secure signature schemes. Following Goldwasser, Micali, and Rivest [Goldwasser et al. 1988], we consider very powerful attacks on the signature scheme as well as a very liberal notion of breaking it. Specifically, the attacker is allowed to obtain signatures to any message of its choice. One may argue that in many applications such a general attack is not possible (because messages to be signed must have a specific format). Yet our view is that it is impossible to define a general (i.e., application-independent) notion of admissible messages, and thus a general/robust definition of an attack seems to have to be formulated as suggested here. (Note that at worst, our approach is overly cautious.) Likewise, the adversary is said to be successful if it can produce a valid signature to *any* message for which it has not asked for a signature during its attack. Indeed, this deems the ability to form signatures to possibly "nonsensical" messages as a breaking of the scheme.

Yet, again, we see no way to have a general (i.e., application-independent) notion of "meaningful" messages (so that only forging signatures to them will be considered a breaking of the scheme).

Definition 17.10 (Secure signature schemes—a sketch) A ***chosen message attack*** is a process that, on input a verification-key, can obtain signatures (*relative to the corresponding signing-key*) to messages of its choice. Such an attack is said to ***succeed*** (*in existential forgery*) if it outputs a valid signature to a message for which it has NOT requested a signature during the attack. A signature scheme is ***secure*** (*or unforgeable*) if every *feasible* chosen message attack succeeds with at most negligible probability, where the probability is taken over the initial choice of the key-pair as well as over the adversary's actions.

The private-key version is defined analogously, except that in that case the attacker is given only the security paramter as input. We stress that *plain* RSA (alike plain versions of Rabin's scheme [Rabin 1979] and the DSS [NIST 1991]) is not secure under the foregoing definition. However, it may be secure if the message is "randomized" before RSA (or the other schemes) is applied.

17.8.2 Constructions

Secure *message authentication schemes* can be constructed using pseudorandom functions [Goldreich et al. 1986]. Specifically, the key-generation algorithm consists of selecting a seed $s \in \{0, 1\}^n$ for such a function, denoted $f_s: \{0, 1\}^* \to \{0, 1\}^n$, and the (only valid) tag of message x with respect to the key s is $f_s(x)$. As in the case of our private-key encryption scheme, the proof of security of the current message authentication scheme consists of two steps:

1. Proving that an idealized version of the scheme, in which one uses a uniformly selected function $F: \{0, 1\}^* \to \{0, 1\}^n$, rather than the pseudorandom function f_s, is secure (i.e., unforgeable).

2. Concluding that the real scheme (as presented above) is secure (because, otherwise one could distinguish a pseudorandom function from a truly random one).

Note that the aforementioned message authentication scheme makes an "extensive use of pseudorandom functions" (i.e., the pseudorandom function is applied directly to the message, which requires a generalized notion of pseudorandom functions (see Section 17.4.3)). More efficient schemes may be obtained either based on a more restricted use of a pseudorandom function or based on other cryptographic primitives (see Goldreich [2004, Sec. 6.3]).

Constructing secure *signature schemes* seems more difficult than constructing message authentication schemes. Nevertheless, secure signature schemes can be constructed based on any one-way function. Furthermore:

Theorem 17.8 (Naor and Yung [1989], Rompel [1990]; see Goldreich [2004, Sec. 6.4])   The following three conditions are equivalent:

1. One-way functions exist.

2. Secure signature schemes exist.

3. Secure message authentication schemes exist.

We stress that, unlike in the case of public-key encryption schemes, the construction of signature schemes (which may be viewed as a public-key analogue of message authentication) does not use a trapdoor property.

How to Construct Secure Signature Schemes

Three central paradigms used in the construction of secure *signature schemes* are the "refreshing" of the "effective" signing key, the usage of an "authentication tree," and the "hashing paradigm" (all to be discussed in the sequel). In addition to being used in the proof of Theorem 17.8, all three paradigms are also of independent interest.

The refreshing paradigm.   Introduced in Goldwasser et al. [1988], the *refreshing paradigm* is aimed at limiting the potential dangers of chosen message attacks. This is achieved by signing the actual document using a newly (randomly) generated instance of the signature scheme, and authenticating (the verification key of) this random instance with respect to the fixed public key. That is, consider a basic signature scheme (G, S, V) used as follows. Suppose that the user U has generated a key pair, $(s, v) \leftarrow G(1^n)$, and has placed the verification key v on a public file. When a party asks U to sign some document α, the user U generates a new ("fresh") key pair, $(s', v') \leftarrow G(1^n)$, signs v' using the original signing key s, signs α using the new signing key s', and presents $(S_s(v'), v', S_{s'}(\alpha))$ as a signature to α. An alleged signature, (β_1, v', β_2), is verified by checking whether both $V_v(v', \beta_1) = 1$ and $V_{v'}(\alpha, \beta_2) = 1$ hold. Intuitively, the gain in terms of security is that a full-fledged chosen message attack cannot be launched on a fixed instance of (G, S, V) (i.e., on the fixed verification key that resides in the public file and is known to the attacker). All that an attacker may obtain (via a chosen message attack on the new scheme) is signatures, relative to the original signing key s of (G, S, V), to random strings (distributed according to $G(1^n)$) as well as additional signatures that are each relative to a random and independently distributed signing key.

Authentication trees. The security benefits of the refreshing paradigm are increased when combining it with the use of *authentication trees*, as introduced in Merkle [1980]. The idea is to use the public verification key in order to authenticate several (e.g., two) fresh instances of the signature scheme, use each of these instances to authenticate several additional fresh instances, and so on. We obtain a tree of fresh instances of the basic signature scheme, where each internal node authenticates its children. We can now use the leaves of this tree in order to sign actual documents, where each leaf is used at most once. Thus, a signature to an actual document consists of (1) a signature to this document authenticated with respect to the verification key associated with some leaf, and (2) a sequence of verification keys associated with the nodes along the path from the root to this leaf, where each such verification key is authenticated with respect to the verification key of its parent. We stress that (by suitable implementation)[23] *each instance of the signature scheme is used to sign at most one string* (i.e., a single sequence of verification-keys if the instance resides in an internal node, and an actual document if the instance resides in a leaf). Thus, it suffices to use a signature scheme that is secure as long as it is used to legitimately sign a single string. Such signature schemes, called ***one-time signature schemes*** and introduced in Rabin [1977], are easier to construct than standard signature schemes, especially if one only wishes to sign strings that are significantly shorter than the signing key (respectively, than the verification key). For example, using a one-way function f, we may let the signing key consist of a sequence of n pairs of strings, let the corresponding verification key consist of the corresponding sequence of images of f, and sign an n-bit long message by revealing the adequate pre-images.[24]

The hashing paradigm. Note, however, that in the aforementioned authentication-tree, the instances of the signature scheme (associated with internal nodes) are used to sign a pair of verification keys. Thus, we need a one-time signature scheme

---

23. In order to implement the aforementioned (full-fledged) signature scheme, one needs to store in (secure) memory all the instances of the basic (one-time) signature scheme that are generated throughout the entire signing process (which refers to numerous documents). This can be done by extending the model so to allow for memory-dependent signature schemes. Alternatively, we note that all that we need to store are the random coins used for generating each of these instances, and the former can be determined by a pseudorandom function (applied to the name of the corresponding vertex in the tree). Indeed, the seed of this pseudorandom function will be part of the signing key of the resulting (full-fledged) signature scheme.

24. That is, the signing key consist of a sequence $((s_1^0, s_1^1), \ldots, (s_n^0, s_n^1)) \in \{0, 1\}^{2n^2}$, the corresponding verification key is $(f(s_1^0), f(s_1^1)), \ldots, (f(s_n^0), f(s_n^1)))$, and the signature of the message $\sigma_1 \cdots \sigma_n$ is $(s_1^{\sigma_1}, \ldots, s_n^{\sigma_n})$.

that can be used for signing messages that are longer than the verification key. Here is where the *hashing paradigm* comes into play. This paradigm refers to the common practice of signing documents via a two-stage process: First, the actual document is hashed to a (relatively) short bit string, and next the basic signature scheme is applied to the resulting string. This practice (as well as other usages of the hashing paradigm) is sound provided that the hashing function belongs to a family of *collision-free hashing* functions (i.e., loosely speaking, given a random hash function in the family, it is infeasible to find two different strings that are hashed by this function to the same value; cf. Damgård [1987]). (A variant of the *hashing paradigm* uses the weaker notion of a family of *universal one-way hash functions* (cf. Naor and Yung [1989]), which in turn can be constructed using any one-way function [Naor and Yung 1989, Rompel 1990].)

17.8.3 Public-Key Infrastructure

The standard use of public-key encryption schemes (respectively, signature schemes) in real-life communication requires a mechanism for providing the sender (respectively, signature verifier) with the receiver's authentic encryption key (respectively, signer's authentic verification key). Specifically, this problem arises in large-scale systems, where typically the sender (respectively, verifier) does not have a local record of the receiver's encryption-key (respectively, signer's verification key), and so must obtain this key in a "reliable" way (i.e., typically, certified by some trusted authority). In most theoretical works, one assumes that the keys are posted on and can be retrieved from a public file that is maintained by a trusted party (which makes sure that each user can post only keys bearing its own identity). In practice, maintaining such a public file is a major problem, and mechanisms that implement this abstraction are typically referred to by the generic term *public-key infrastructure (PKI)*. For a discussion of the practical problems regarding PKI deployment see, for example, Menezes et al. [1996, Chap. 13].

17.9 General Cryptographic Protocols

The design of secure protocols that implement arbitrary desired functionalities is a major part of modern cryptography. Taking the opposite perspective, the design of any cryptographic scheme may be viewed as the design of a secure protocol for implementing a suitable functionality. Still, we believe that it makes sense to differentiate between basic cryptographic primitives (which involve little interaction) like encryption and signature schemes on the one hand, and general cryptographic protocols on the other hand.

We survey *general* results concerning secure *multi*-party computations, where the *two*-party case is an important special case. In a nutshell, these results assert that one can construct protocols for securely computing *any* desirable multi-party functionality. Indeed, what is striking about these results is their generality, and we believe that the wonder is not diminished by the (various alternative) conditions under which these results hold.

Our focus on the *general* study of secure multi-party computation (rather than on protocols for solving specific problems) is natural in the context of the theoretical treatment of the subject matter. We wish to highlight the importance of this *general* study to practice. First, this study clarifies fundamental issues regarding security in a multi-party environment. Second, it draws the lines between what is possible in principle and what is not. Third, it develops general techniques for designing secure protocols. And last, sometimes it may even yield schemes (or modules) that may be incorporated in practical systems.

A general framework for casting (*m*-party) cryptographic (protocol) problems consists of specifying a random process[25] that maps m inputs to m outputs. The inputs to the process are to be thought of as the local inputs of m parties, and the m outputs are their corresponding (desired) local outputs. The random process describes the desired functionality. If the m parties were to trust some (possibly external) party, then they could each send their local input to the trusted party, who would compute the outcome of the process, and send to each party the corresponding output. A pivotal question in the area of cryptographic protocols is to what extent can this (imaginary) trusted party be "emulated" by the mutually distrustful parties themselves.

The results surveyed below describe a variety of models in which such an "emulation" is possible. The models vary by the underlying assumptions regarding the communication channels, numerous parameters relating to the extent of adversarial behavior, and the desired level of emulation of the trusted party (i.e., level of "security").

Organization. Section 17.9.1 provides a rather comprehensive survey of the various definitions used in the area of secure multi-party computation, whereas Sec-

---

25. That is, we consider the secure evaluation of randomized functionalities, rather than "only" the secure evaluation of functions. Specifically, we consider an arbitrary (randomized) process F that on input $(x_1, \ldots, x_m)$, first selects at random (depending only on $\ell \stackrel{\text{def}}{=} \sum_{i=1}^{m} |x_i|$) an m-ary function f, and then outputs the m-tuple $f(x_1, \ldots, x_m) = (f_1(x_1, \ldots, x_m), \ldots, f_m(x_1, \ldots, x_m))$. In other words, $F(x_1, \ldots, x_m) = F'(r, x_1, \ldots, x_m)$, where r is uniformly selected in $\{0, 1\}^{\ell'}$ (with $\ell' = \text{poly}(\ell)$), and F' is a function mapping $(m + 1)$-long sequences to m-long sequences.

tion 17.9.2 surveys the main known results. However, some readers may prefer to first consider one concrete case of the definitional approach, as provided in Section 17.9.1.2, and proceed directly to see some constructions (in Section 17.9.3). All the foregoing refers to the security of stand-alone executions, and the preservation of security in an environment in which many executions of many protocols are being attacked is considered in Section 17.9.4.

17.9.1   The Definitional Approach and Some Models

Before describing the aforementioned results, we further discuss the notion of "emulating a trusted party," which underlies the definitional approach to secure multi-party computation (as initiated and developed in Goldwasser and Levin [1990], Micali and Rogaway [1991], Beaver [1991a], [1991b], Canetti [1995], [2000]). The approach can be traced back to the definition of zero-knowledge (see Goldwasser et al. [1989]), and even to the definition of secure encryption (see Goldreich [1993]; rephrasing, Goldwasser and Micali [1984]). The underlying paradigm (called the simulation paradigm (see Section 17.5.1)) is that a scheme is secure if whatever a feasible adversary can obtain after attacking it, is also feasibly attainable "from scratch." In the case of zero-knowledge this amounts to saying that whatever a (feasible) verifier can obtain after interacting with the prover on a prescribed valid assertion, can be (feasibly) computed from the assertion itself. In the case of multi-party computation we compare the effect of adversaries that participate in the execution of the actual protocol to the effect of adversaries that participate in an imaginary execution of a trivial (ideal) protocol for computing the desired functionality with the help of a trusted party. If whatever the adversaries can feasibly obtain in the former real setting can also be feasibly obtained in the latter ideal setting then the protocol "emulates the ideal setting" (i.e., "emulates a trusted party"), and so is deemed secure. This basic approach can be applied in a variety of models, and is used to define the goals of security in these models.[26] We first discuss some of the parameters used in defining various models, and next demonstrate the application

---

26. A few technical comments: First, we assume that the inputs of all parties are of the same length. We comment that as long as the lengths of the inputs are polynomially related, the foregoing convention can be enforced by padding. On the other hand, some length restriction is essential for the security results, because in general it is impossible to hide all information regarding the length of the inputs to a protocol. Second, we assume that the desired functionality is computable in probabilistic polynomial time, because we wish the secure protocol to run in probabilistic polynomial time (and a protocol cannot be more efficient than the corresponding centralized algorithm). Clearly, the results can be extended to functionalities that are computable within any given (time-constructible) time bound, using adequate padding.

of this approach in two important models. For further details, see Canetti [2000] or Goldreich [2004, Sec. 7.2 and 7.5.1].

17.9.1.1 Some Parameters Used in Defining Security Models

The following parameters are described in terms of the actual (or real) computation. In *some cases*, the corresponding definition of security is obtained by imposing some restrictions or provisions on the ideal model. For example, in the case of two-party computation (see below), secure computation is possible only if premature termination is *not* considered a breach of security. In that case, the suitable security definition is obtained (via the simulation paradigm) by allowing (an analogue of) premature termination in the ideal model. In *all cases*, the desired notion of security is defined by requiring that for any adequate adversary in the real model, there exist a corresponding adversary in the corresponding ideal model that obtains essentially the same impact (as the real-model adversary).

The communication channels:. The parameters of the model include questions like whether or not the channels may be tapped by an adversary, whether or not they are tamper-free, and questions referring to the network behavior (in the case of multi-party protocols).

- *Wire-tapping versus the private-channel model*: The standard assumption in cryptography is that the adversary may tap all communication channels (between honest parties). In contrast, one may *postulate* that the adversary cannot obtain messages sent between a pair of honest parties, yielding the so-called *private-channel model* (cf. Ben-Or et al. [1988], Chaum et al. [1988]). The latter postulate may be justified in some settings. Furthermore, it may be viewed as a useful abstraction that provides a clean model for the study and development of secure protocols. In this respect, it is important to mention that, in a variety of settings of the other parameters, private channels can be easily emulated by ordinary "tapped channels."

- *Broadcast channel*: In the multi-party context, one may postulate the existence of a *broadcast channel* (cf. Rabin and Ben-Or [1989]), and the motivation and justifications are as in the case of the private-channel model.

- The *tamper-free assumption*: The standard assumption in the area is that the adversary cannot modify, duplicate, or generate messages sent over the communication channels (between honest parties).

Again, this assumption can be justified in some settings and can be emulated in others (cf. Bellare et al. [1998a], Canetti [2001]).

■ *Network behavior*: Most works in the area assume that communication is *synchronous* and that point-to-point channels exist between every pair of processors (i.e., a *complete network*). However, one may also consider *asynchronous communication* (cf. Ben-Or et al. [1993]) and *arbitrary networks* of point-to-point channels (cf. Dolev et al. [1993]).

Set-up assumptions:. Unless stated differently, we make no set-up assumptions (except for the obvious assumption that all parties have identical copies of the protocol's program). However, in some cases it is assumed that each party knows a verification key corresponding to each of the other parties (or that a public-key infrastructure is available). Another assumption, made more rarely, is that all parties have access to some common (trusted) random string.

Computational limitations:. Typically, we consider computationally bounded adversaries (e.g., probabilistic polynomial-time adversaries). However, the private-channel model allows for the (meaningful) consideration of computationally unbounded adversaries.

We stress that, also in the case of computationally unbounded adversaries, security should be defined by requiring that for every real adversary, whatever the adversary can compute after participating in the execution of the actual protocol is computable *within comparable time* by an imaginary adversary participating in an imaginary execution of the trivial ideal protocol (for computing the desired functionality with the help of a trusted party). That is, although no computational restrictions are made on the real-model adversary, it is required that the ideal-model adversary that obtains the same impact does so within comparable time (i.e., within time that is polynomially related to the running time of the real-model adversary being simulated). Thus, any construction proven secure in the computationally unbounded adversary model is (trivially) secure with respect to computationally bounded adversaries.

Restricted adversarial behavior:. The parameters of the model include questions like whether or not the adversary is "adaptive" and "active" (where these terms are discussed next).

- *Adaptive versus nonadaptive*: The most general type of an adversary considered in the literature is one that may corrupt parties to the protocol while the execution goes on, and does so based on partial information it has gathered so far (cf. Canetti et al. [1996]). A somewhat restricted model, which seems adequate in many settings, postulates that the set of dishonest parties is fixed (arbitrarily) before the execution starts (but this set is, of course, not known to the honest parties). The latter model is called *nonadaptive* as opposed to the *adaptive* adversary discussed first. Although the adaptive model is stronger, the nonadaptive model provides a reasonable level of security in many applications.

- *Active versus passive*: An orthogonal parameter of restriction refers to whether a dishonest party takes active steps to disrupt the execution of the protocol (i.e., sends messages that differ from those specified by the protocol), or merely gathers information (which it may latter share with the other dishonest parties). The latter adversary has been given a variety of names such as *semi-honest*, *passive*, and *honest-but-curious*. This restricted model may be justified in certain settings, and certainly provides a useful methodological locus (cf. Goldreich et al. [1991], Goldreich et al. [1987], Goldreich [1998], and Section 17.9.3). Below we refer to the adversary of the unrestricted model as to *active*; another commonly used name is *malicious*.

Restricted notions of security. One important example is the willingness to tolerate "unfair" protocols in which the execution can be suspended (at any time) by a dishonest party, provided that it is detected doing so. We stress that in case the execution is suspended, the dishonest party does not obtain more information than it could have obtained when not suspending the execution. (What may happen is that the honest parties will not obtain their desired outputs, but rather will detect that the execution was suspended.) We stress that the motivation to this restricted model is the impossibility of obtaining general secure two-party computation in the unrestricted model. For more details, see Section 17.9.1.3.

Upper bounds on the number of dishonest parties. In some models, secure multi-party computation is possible only if a majority of the parties is honest (cf. Ben-Or et al. [1988], Chor and Kushilevitz [1991]). Sometimes even a special majority (e.g., 2/3) is required. General "(resilient) adversarial-structures" have been considered too (cf. Hirt and Maurer [2000]).

17.9.1.2   Example: Multi-Party Protocols with Honest Majority

Here we consider an active, nonadaptive, computationally-bounded adversary, and do not assume the existence of private channels. Our aim is to define multi-party protocols that remain secure provided that the honest parties are in majority. (The reason for requiring a honest majority will be discussed at the end of this subsection.)

Consider any multi-party protocol. We first observe that each party may change its local input before even entering the execution of the protocol. However, this is unavoidable also when the parties utilize a trusted party. Consequently, such an effect of the adversary on the real execution (i.e., modification of its own input prior to entering the actual execution) is not considered a breach of security. In general, whatever cannot be avoided when the parties utilize a trusted party, is not considered a breach of security. We wish secure protocols (in the real model) to suffer only from whatever is unavoidable also when the parties utilize a trusted party. Thus, the basic paradigm underlying the definitions of *secure multi-party computations* amounts to requiring that the only situations that may occur in the real execution of a secure protocol are those that can also occur in a corresponding ideal model (where the parties may employ a trusted party). In other words, the "effective malfunctioning" of parties in secure protocols is restricted to what is postulated in the corresponding ideal model.

When defining secure multi-party protocols with honest majority, we need to pin-point what cannot be avoided in the ideal model (i.e., when the parties utilize a trusted party). This is easy, because the ideal model is very simple. Since we are interested in executions in which the majority of parties are honest, we consider an *ideal model* in which any minority group (of the parties) may collude as follows:

1. First, this dishonest minority shares its original inputs and decides together on replaced inputs to be sent to the trusted party. (The other parties send their respective original inputs to the trusted party.)

2. Upon receiving inputs from all parties, the trusted party determines the corresponding outputs and sends them to the corresponding parties. (We stress that the information sent between the honest parties and the trusted party is not seen by the dishonest colluding minority.)

3. Upon receiving the output-message from the trusted party, each honest party outputs it locally, whereas the dishonest colluding minority may determine

their outputs based on all they know (i.e., their initial inputs and their received outputs).

Note that the foregoing behavior of the minority group is unavoidable in any execution of any protocol (even in presence of trusted parties). This is the reason that the ideal model was defined as above. Now, a *secure multi-party computation with honest majority* is required to emulate this ideal model. That is, the effect of any feasible adversary that controls a minority of the parties in a real execution of the actual protocol, can be essentially simulated by a (different) feasible adversary that controls the corresponding parties in the ideal model. That is:

Definition 17.11 (Secure protocols—a sketch)   Let f be an m-ary functionality and Π be an m-party protocol operating in the real model.

- For a real-model adversary A, controlling some minority of the parties (*and tapping all communication channels*), and an m-sequence $\overline{x}$, we denote by $\text{REAL}_{\Pi,A}(\overline{x})$ the sequence of m outputs resulting from the execution of Π on input $\overline{x}$ under attack of the adversary A.

- For an ideal-model adversary A', controlling some minority of the parties, and an m-sequence $\overline{x}$, we denote by $\text{IDEAL}_{f,A'}(\overline{x})$ the sequence of m outputs resulting from the ideal process described above, on input $\overline{x}$ under attack of the adversary A'.

We say that Π *securely implements* f *with honest majority* if for every feasible real-model adversary A, controlling some minority of the parties, there exists a feasible ideal-model adversary A', controlling the same parties, so that the probability ensembles $\{\text{REAL}_{\Pi,A}(\overline{x})\}_{\overline{x}}$ and $\{\text{IDEAL}_{f,A'}(\overline{x})\}_{\overline{x}}$ are computationally indistinguishable (as in Footnote 9).

Thus, security means that the effect of each minority group in a real execution of a secure protocol is "essentially restricted" to replacing its own local inputs (independently of the local inputs of the majority parties) before the protocol starts, and replacing its own local outputs (depending only on its local inputs and outputs) after the protocol terminates. (We stress that in the real execution the minority parties do obtain additional pieces of information; yet in a secure protocol they gain nothing from these additional pieces of information, because they can actually reproduce those by themselves.)

The fact that Definition 17.11 refers to a model without private channels is due to the fact that our (sketchy) definition of the real-model adversary allowed it to tap the channels, which in turn affects the set of possible ensembles $\{\text{REAL}_{\Pi,A}(\overline{x})\}_{\overline{x}}$.

When defining security in the private-channel model, the real-model adversary is not allowed to tap channels between honest parties, and this again affects the possible ensembles $\{\text{REAL}_{\Pi,A}(\overline{x})\}_{\overline{x}}$. On the other hand, when we wish to define security with respect to passive adversaries, both the scope of the real-model adversaries and the scope of the ideal-model adversaries changes. In the real-model execution, all parties follow the protocol but the adversary may alter the output of the dishonest parties arbitrarily depending on all their intermediate internal states (during the execution). In the corresponding ideal-model, the adversary is not allowed to modify the *inputs* of dishonest parties (in Step 1), but is allowed to modify their outputs (in Step 3).

We comment that a definition analogous to Definition 17.11 can be presented also in the case that the dishonest parties are not in minority. In fact, such a definition seems more natural, but the problem is that such a definition cannot be satisfied. That is, most natural functionalities do not have a protocol for computing them securely in case at least half of the parties are dishonest and employ an adequate adversarial strategy. This follows from an impossibility result regarding two-party computation, which essentially asserts that there is no way to prevent a party from prematurely suspending the execution [Cleve 1986]. On the other hand, secure multi-party computation with dishonest majority is possible if premature suspension of the execution is not considered a breach of security (see next).

17.9.1.3 Another Example: Two-Party Protocols Allowing Abort

In light of the last paragraph, we now consider multi-party computations in which premature suspension of the execution is not considered a breach of security. For concreteness, we focus on the special case of two-party computations.[27]

Intuitively, in any two-party protocol, each party may suspend the execution at any point in time, and furthermore it may do so as soon as it learns the desired output. Thus, in many cases (but not all [Gordon et al. 2011]), it is possible for one of the parties to obtain the desired output while preventing the other party from fully determining its own output. The same phenomenon occurs even in case the two parties just wish to generate a common random value [Cleve 1986]. Thus, when defining security (w.r.t active adversaries in the two-party setting), we do not consider such premature suspension of the execution a breach of security. Consequently, we consider an ideal model where each of the two parties may "shut down" the trusted (third) party at any point in time. In particular, this may happen

---

27. As in Section 17.9.1.2, we consider a nonadaptive, active, computationally bounded adversary.

after the trusted party has supplied the outcome of the computation to one party but before it has supplied it to the other. That is, an execution in the ideal model proceeds as follows:

1. Each party sends its input to the trusted party, where the dishonest party may replace its input or send no input at all (which can be treated as sending a default value).

2. Upon receiving inputs from both parties, the trusted party determines the corresponding outputs, and sends the first output to the first party.

3. In case the first party is dishonest, it may instruct the trusted party to halt, otherwise it always instructs the trusted party to proceed. If instructed to proceed, the trusted party sends the second output to the second party.

4. Upon receiving the output message from the trusted party, an honest party outputs it locally, whereas a dishonest party may determine its output based on all it knows (i.e., its initial input and its received output).

A *secure two-party computation allowing abort* is required to emulate this ideal model. That is, as in Definition 17.11, security is defined by requiring that for every feasible real-model adversary A, there exists a feasible ideal-model adversary A', controlling the same party, so that the probability ensembles representing the corresponding (real and ideal) executions are computationally indistinguishable. This means that each party's "effective malfunctioning" in a secure protocol is restricted to supplying an initial input of its choice and aborting the computation at any point in time. (Needless to say, the choice of the initial input of each party may *not* depend on the input of the other party.)

We mention that an alternative way of dealing with the problem of premature suspension of execution (i.e., abort) is to restrict our attention to *single-output functionalities*; that is, functionalities in which only one party is supposed to obtain an output. The definition of secure computation of such functionalities can be made identical to Definition 17.11, with the exception that no restriction is made on the set of dishonest parties (and in particular one may consider a single dishonest party in the case of two-party protocols). For further details, see Goldreich [2004, Sec. 7.2.3].

17.9.2   Some Known Results

We next list some of the models for which general secure multi-party computation is known to be attainable (i.e., models in which one can construct secure multi-party protocols for computing any desired functionality). We mention that the first results of this type were obtained by Goldreich, Micali, Wigderson, and Yao [Goldreich et al. 1991, Yao 1986, Goldreich et al. 1987].

- *Assuming the existence of enhanced trapdoor permutations,*[28] secure multi-party computation is possible in the following models (see Goldreich et al. [1991], [1987], Yao [1986], with details in Goldreich [1998], [2004]):
    1. Passive adversary, for any number of dishonest parties (see Goldreich [2004, Sec. 7.3]).
    2. Active adversary that may control only a minority of the parties (see Goldreich [2004, Sec. 7.5.4]).
    3. Active adversary, for any number of bad parties, provided that suspension of execution is not considered a violation of security (i.e., as discussed in Section 17.9.1.3). (See Goldreich [2004, Sec. 7.4 and 7.5.5].)

    In all these cases, the adversary is computationally-bounded and nonadaptive.[29] On the other hand, the adversary may tap the communication lines between honest parties (i.e., we do not assume "private channels" here). The results for active adversaries assume a broadcast channel. Indeed, the latter can be implemented (while tolerating any number of bad parties) using a signature scheme and assuming a public-key infrastructure (or that each party knows the verification key corresponding to each of the other parties).

- Making no computational assumptions and allowing computationally-unbounded adversaries, but *assuming private channels*, secure multi-party computation is possible in the following models (cf. Ben-Or et al. [1988], Chaum et al. [1988]):
    1. Passive adversary that may control only a minority of the parties.
    2. Active adversary that may control only less than one-third of the parties.[30]

    In both cases the adversary may be adaptive (cf. Ben-Or et al. [1988], Canetti et al. [1996]).

---

28. See Goldreich [2004, Appendix C.1].

29. Similar results for (active) *adaptive* adversaries are presented in Canetti et al. [1996] and Damgård and Nielsen [2000].

30. Fault-tolerance can be increased to a regular minority if a broadcast channel exists [Rabin and Ben-Or 1989].

Results for asynchronous communication and arbitrary networks of point-to-point channels were presented in Ben-Or et al. [1993], [1994] and Dolev et al. [1993], respectively.

Note that the implementation of a broadcast channel can be cast as a cryptographic protocol problem (i.e., for the functionality $(v, \lambda, \dots, \lambda) \mapsto (v, v, \dots, v)$, where λ denotes the empty string). Thus, it is not surprising that the results regarding active adversaries either assume the existence of such a channel or require a setting in which the latter can be implemented.

Secure reactive computation.   The foregoing results (easily) extend to a reactive model of computation in which each party interacts with a high-level process (or application). The high-level process supplies each party with a sequence of inputs, one at a time, and expect to receive corresponding outputs from the parties. That is, a reactive system goes through (a possibly unbounded number of) iterations of the following type:

- Parties are given inputs for the current iteration.
- Depending on the current inputs, the parties are supposed to compute outputs for the current iteration. That is, the outputs in iteration j are determined by the inputs of the jth iteration.

A more general formulation allows the outputs of each iteration to depend also on a global state, which is possibly updated in each iteration. The global state may include all inputs and outputs of previous iterations, and may only be partially known to individual parties. (In a secure reactive computation such a global state may be maintained by all parties in a "secret sharing" manner.) For further discussion, see Goldreich [2004, Sec. 7.7.1].

Efficiency considerations.   One important efficiency measure regarding protocols is the number of communication rounds in their execution. The aforementioned results were originally obtained using protocols that use an unbounded number of rounds. In some cases, subsequent works obtained secure constant-round protocols (e.g., for multi-party computations with honest majority [Beaver et al. 1990], and for two-party computations allowing abort [Lindell 2001]). Other important efficiency considerations include the total number of bits sent in the execution of a protocol, and the local computation time. Improving the various efficiency measures has been the focus of considerable research.

17.9.3   Construction Paradigms

We briefly sketch a couple of paradigms used in the construction of secure multi-party protocols. We focus on the construction of secure protocols for the model of computationally bounded and nonadaptive adversaries [Goldreich et al. 1991, Yao 1986, Goldreich et al. 1987]. These constructions proceed in two steps (see details in Goldreich [1998], [2004]). First a secure protocol is presented for the model of passive adversaries (for any number of dishonest parties), and next such a protocol is "compiled" into a protocol that is secure in one of the two models of active adversaries (i.e., either in a model allowing the adversary to control only a minority of the parties or in a model in which premature suspension of the execution is not considered a violation of security). These two steps are presented in the following two corresponding subsections.

Recall that in the model of passive adversaries, all parties follow the prescribed protocol, but at termination the adversary may alter the outputs of the dishonest parties depending on all their intermediate internal states (during the execution). Below, we refer to protocols that are secure in the model of passive (respectively, active) adversaries by the term ***passively secure*** (respectively, ***actively secure***).

17.9.3.1   Passively Secure Computation with Shares

For any $m \geq 2$, suppose that m parties, each having a private input, wish to obtain the value of a predetermined m-argument Boolean function evaluated at their sequence of inputs. Below, we outline a passively secure protocol for achieving this goal. For simplicity, we present the passively secure protocol in the private channel model. We mention that the design of passively secure multi-party protocol for any functionality (allowing different outputs to different parties as well as handling also randomized computations) reduces easily to the aforementioned task.

We assume that the parties hold a circuit for computing the value of the function on inputs of the adequate length, and that the circuit contains only and and not gates. The key idea is to have each party "secretly share" its input with everybody else, and have the parties "secretly transform" shares of the input wires of the circuit into shares of the output wire of the circuit, thus obtaining shares of the output (which allows for the reconstruction of the actual output). The value of each wire in the circuit is shared in a way such that all shares yield the value, whereas lacking even one of the shares keeps the value totally undetermined. That is, we use a simple secret sharing scheme (cf. Shamir [1979]) such that a bit b is shared by a random sequence of m bits that sum-up to b mod 2. First, each party shares each of its input bits with all parties (by secretly sending each party a random value and setting its own share accordingly). Next, all parties jointly scan the circuit from its input wires to the output wire, processing each gate as follows:

- When encountering a gate, the parties already hold shares of the values of the wires entering the gate, and their aim is to obtain shares of the value of the wires exiting the gate.

- For a not-gate this is easy: The first party just flips the value of its share, and all other parties maintain their shares.

- Since an and-gate corresponds to multiplication modulo 2, the parties need to securely compute the following randomized functionality (in which the x_i's denote shares of one entry-wire, the y_i's denote shares of the second entry-wire, the z_i's denote shares of the exit-wire, and the shares indexed by i belongs to Party i):

$$((x_1, y_1), \ldots, (x_m, y_m)) \mapsto (z_1, \ldots, z_m) \qquad (17.1)$$

where

$$\sum_{i=1}^{m} z_i = \left(\sum_{i=1}^{m} x_i\right) \cdot \left(\sum_{i=1}^{m} y_i\right). \qquad (17.2)$$

That is, the z_i's are random subject to Eq. (17.2).

Finally, the parties broadcast their shares of the circuit-output wire, and each party reconstructs the value of the output based on all shares it now holds. Thus, the parties have propagated shares of the input wires into shares of the output wire, by repeatedly conducting privately-secure computation of the m-ary functionality of Equations (17.1) and (17.2). That is, securely evaluating the entire (arbitrary) circuit "reduces" to securely conducting a specific (very simple) multi-party computation. But things get even simpler: The key observation is that

$$\left(\sum_{i=1}^{m} x_i\right) \cdot \left(\sum_{i=1}^{m} y_i\right) = \sum_{i=1}^{m} x_i y_i + \sum_{1 \le i < j \le m} (x_i y_j + x_j y_i). \qquad (17.3)$$

Thus, the m-ary functionality of Equations (17.1) and (17.2) can be computed as follows (where all arithmetic operations are mod 2):

1. Each Party i locally computes $z_{i,i} \stackrel{\text{def}}{=} x_i y_i$.

2. Next, each pair of parties (i.e., Parties i and j) securely compute random shares of $x_i y_j + y_i x_j$. That is, Parties i and j (holding (x_i, y_i) and (x_j, y_j), respectively) need to securely compute the randomized two-party functionality $((x_i, y_i), (x_j, y_j)) \mapsto (z_{i,j}, z_{j,i})$, where the z's are random subject

to $z_{i,j} + z_{j,i} = x_i y_j + y_i x_j$. Equivalently, Party j uniformly selects $z_{j,i} \in \{0, 1\}$, and Parties i and j securely compute the deterministic functionality $((x_i, y_i), (x_j, y_j, z_{j,i})) \mapsto (z_{j,i} + x_i y_j + y_i x_j, \lambda)$, where λ denotes the empty string.

The latter simple two-party computation can be securely implemented using a 1-out-of-4 Oblivious Transfer (see Goldreich and Vainish [1987] and Goldreich [2004, Sec. 7.3.3]), which in turn can be implemented using enhanced trapdoor permutations (see Even et al. [1985], Goldreich [2004, Sec. 7.3.2], and Goldreich and Rothblum [2013]). Loosely speaking, a 1-out-of-k Oblivious Transfer is a protocol enabling one party to obtain one of k secrets held by another party, without the second party learning which secret was obtained by the first party. That is, we refer to the two-party functionality

$$(i, (s_1, \ldots, s_k)) \mapsto (s_i, \lambda). \tag{17.4}$$

Note that any function $f : [k] \times \{0, 1\}^* \to \{0, 1\}^*$ can be privately computed by invoking a 1-out-of-k Oblivious Transfer on inputs i and $(f(1, y), \ldots, f(k, y))$, where i (respectively, y) is the initial input of the first (respectively, second) party.

3. Finally, for every $i = 1, \ldots, m$, summing-up all the $z_{i,j}$'s yields the desired share of Party i.

Hence, we have reduced the passively secure computation of a *general m-party functionality* to the passively secure computation a *specific two-party function over* $[4] \times \{0, 1\}^4$ (i.e., 1-out-of-4 Oblivious Transfer of bit secrets). The foregoing reduction is analogous to a construction that was briefly described in Goldreich et al. [1987]. A detailed description and full proofs appear in Goldreich [1998], [2004].

17.9.3.2 Compilation of Passively Secure Protocols into Actively Secure Ones

Recalling that the protocol constructed in Section 17.9.3.1 works in the private-channel model, we first transform it into a protocol for the standard (wire-tapped) model (by using a public-key encryption scheme). Now, we show how to transform any passively secure protocol into a corresponding actively secure protocol. The communication model in both protocols consists of a single broadcast channel. Note that the messages of the original protocol may be assumed to be sent over a broadcast channel, because the adversary may see them anyhow (by tapping the point-to-point channels), and because a broadcast channel is trivially implementable in the case of passive adversaries. As for the resulting actively secure protocol, the broadcast channel it uses can be implemented via a (authenticated) Byzantine Agreement protocol [Dolev and Strong 1983, Lindell et al. 2002], thus providing an emulation of this model on the standard point-to-point model (in which a broadcast channel does not exist). We mention that authenticated Byzantine Agreement is typically implemented using a signature scheme (and assuming that each party knows the verification key corresponding to each of the other parties).

Turning to the transformation itself, the main idea is to use zero-knowledge proofs (as described in Section 17.5.3) in order to force parties to behave in a way that is consistent with the (passively secure) protocol. Actually, we need to confine each party to a unique consistent behavior (i.e., according to some fixed local input and a sequence of coin tosses), and to guarantee that a party cannot fix its input (and/or its coins) in a way that depends on the inputs of honest parties. Thus, some preliminary steps have to be taken before the step-by-step emulation of the original protocol may start. Specifically, the compiled protocol (which like the original protocol is executed over a broadcast channel) proceeds as follows:

1. *Committing to the local input*: Prior to the emulation of the original protocol, each party commits to its input (using a commitment scheme [Naor 1991]). In addition, using a zero-knowledge proof-of-knowledge [Goldwasser et al. 1989, Bellare and Goldreich 1992, Goldreich et al. 1991], each party also proves that it knows its own input; that is, that it can decommit to the commitment it sent. (These zero-knowledge proof-of-knowledge are conducted sequentially to prevent dishonest parties from setting their inputs in a way that depends on inputs of honest parties.)

2. *Generation of local random tapes*: Next, all parties jointly generate a sequence of random bits for each party such that only this party knows the outcome of the random sequence generated for it, but everybody gets a commitment to this outcome. These sequences will be used as the random inputs (i.e., sequence of coin tosses) for the original protocol. Each bit in the random sequence generated for Party X is determined as the exclusive-or of the outcomes of instances of an (augmented) coin-tossing protocol (see Blum [1982] and Goldreich [2004, Sec. 7.4.3.5]) that Party X plays with each of the other parties. The latter protocol provides the other parties with a commitment to the outcome obtained by Party X.

3. *Effective prevention of premature termination*: In addition, when compiling (the passively secure protocol to an actively secure protocol) *for the model that allows the adversary to control only a minority of the parties*, each party shares its input and random input with all other parties using a "Verifiable Secret Sharing" (VSS) protocol (see Chor et al. [1985] and Goldreich [2004,

Sec. 7.5.5.1]). Loosely speaking, a VSS protocol allows to share a secret in a way that enables each participant to verify that the share it got fits the publicly posted information, which includes (on top of the commitments posted in Steps 1 and 2) commitments to all shares. The use of VSS guarantees that if Party X prematurely suspends the execution, then the honest parties can together reconstruct all Party X's secrets and carry on the execution while playing its role. This step effectively prevents premature termination, and is not needed in a model that does not consider premature termination a breach of security.

4. *Step-by-step emulation of the original protocol*: After all the foregoing preliminary steps are completed, we turn to the main step in which the new protocol emulates the original one. In each step, each party augments the message determined by the original protocol with a zero-knowledge proof that asserts that the message was indeed computed correctly. Recall that the next message (as determined by the original protocol) is a function of the sender's own input, its random input, and the messages it has received so far (where the latter are known to everybody because they were sent over a broadcast channel). Furthermore, the sender's input is determined by its commitment (as sent in Step 1), and its random input is similarly determined (in Step 2). Thus, the next message (as determined by the original protocol) is a function of publicly known strings (i.e., the said commitments as well as the other messages sent over the broadcast channel). Moreover, the assertion that the next message was indeed computed correctly is an NP-assertion, and the sender knows a corresponding NP-witness (i.e., its own input and random input as well as the corresponding decommitment information). Thus, the sender can prove in zero-knowledge (to each of the other parties) that the message it is sending was indeed computed according to the original protocol.

The foregoing compilation was first outlined in Goldreich et al. [1987], [1991]. A detailed description and full proofs appear in Goldreich [1998], [2004].

17.9.4   Concurrent Execution of Protocols

The definitions and results surveyed so far refer to a setting in which, at each time, only a single execution of a cryptographic protocol takes place (or only one execution may be controlled by the adversary). In contrast, in many distributed settings (e.g., the Internet), many executions are taking place concurrently (and several of them may be controlled by the same adversary). Furthermore, it is undesirable (and sometimes even impossible) to coordinate these executions (so to effectively enforce a single-execution setting). Still, the definitions and results obtained in the single-execution setting serve as a good starting point for the study of security in the setting of concurrent executions.

As in the case of stand-alone security, the notion of zero-knowledge provides a good test case for the study of concurrent security. Indeed, in order to demonstrate the security issues arising from concurrent execution of protocols, we consider the concurrent execution of zero-knowledge protocols. Specifically, we consider a party P holding a random (or rather, pseudorandom) function $f: \{0, 1\}^{2n} \rightarrow \{0, 1\}^n$, and willing to participate in the following protocol (with respect to security parameter n).[31] The other party, called A for adversary, is supposed to send P a binary value $v \in \{1, 2\}$ specifying which of the following two cases to execute:

For $v = 1$. Party P uniformly selects $\alpha \in \{0, 1\}^n$, and sends it to A, who is supposed to reply with a pair of n-bit-long strings, denoted (β, γ). Party P checks whether or not $f(\alpha\beta) = \gamma$. In the case where equality holds, P sends A some secret information (e.g., the secret key corresponding to P's public key).

For $v = 2$. Party A is supposed to uniformly select $\alpha \in \{0, 1\}^n$, and sends it to P, which selects uniformly $\beta \in \{0, 1\}^n$ and replies with the pair $(\beta, f(\alpha\beta))$.

Observe that P's strategy (in each case) is zero-knowledge (even with respect to auxiliary-inputs as defined in Definition 17.7): Intuitively, if the adversary A chooses the case $v = 1$, then it is infeasible for A to guess a passing pair (β, γ) with respect to a random α provided by P. Thus, except with negligible probability (when it may get secret information), A does not obtain anything from the interaction. On the other hand, if the adversary A chooses the case $v = 2$, then it obtains a pair that is indistinguishable from a uniformly selected pair of n-bit long strings (because β is selected uniformly by P, and for any α the value $f(\alpha\beta)$ looks random to A). In contrast, if the adversary A can conduct two concurrent executions with P, then it may learn the desired secret information: In one session, A sends $v = 1$ while in the other it sends $v = 2$. Upon receiving P's message, denoted α, in the first session, A sends it as its own message in the second session, obtaining a pair $(\beta, f(\alpha\beta))$ from P's execution of the second session. Now, A sends the pair $(\beta, f(\alpha\beta))$ to the first session of P, and A obtains the desired secret, since this pair passes the check.

---

31. In fact, assuming that P shares a pseudorandom function f with its friends (as explained in Section 17.4.3), the foregoing protocol is an abstraction of a natural "mutual identification" protocol. (The example is adapted from Goldreich and Krawczyk [1996].)

An attack of this type is called a *relay attack*: During such an attack the adversary just invokes two executions of the protocol and relays messages between them (without any modification). However, in general, the adversary in a concurrent setting is not restricted to relay attacks. For example, consider a minor modification to the above protocol so that, in the case $v = 2$, party P replies with (say) the pair $(\beta, f(\overline{\alpha}\beta))$, where $\overline{\alpha} = \alpha \oplus 1^{|\alpha|}$, rather than with $(\beta, f(\alpha\beta))$. The modified strategy P is zero-knowledge and it also withstands a relay attack, but it can be "abused" easily by a more general concurrent attack.

The foregoing example is merely the tip of an iceberg, but it suffices for introducing the main lesson: *An adversary attacking several concurrent executions of the same protocol may be able to cause more damage than by attacking a single execution* (or several sequential executions) of the same protocol. One may say that a protocol is **concurrently secure** if whatever the adversary may obtain by invoking and controlling parties in real concurrent executions of the protocol is also obtainable by a corresponding adversary that controls corresponding parties making concurrent functionality calls to a trusted party (in a corresponding ideal model).[32] More generally, one may consider concurrent executions of many sessions of *several* protocols, and say that a *set of protocols* is concurrently secure if whatever the adversary may obtain by invoking and controlling such real concurrent executions is also obtainable by a corresponding adversary that invokes and controls concurrent calls to a trusted party (in a corresponding ideal model). Consequently, a protocol is said to be **secure with respect to concurrent compositions** if adding this protocol to *any set* of concurrently secure protocols yields a set of concurrently secure protocols.

A much more appealing approach was suggested by Canetti [2001]. Loosely speaking, Canetti suggests to consider a protocol to be secure (called *environmentally secure* (or *universally composable secure* [Canetti 2001])) only if it remains secure when executed within any (feasible) environment. Following the simulation paradigm, we get the following definition:

Definition 17.12   (Environmentally secure protocols [Canetti 2001]—a rough sketch)   Let f be an m-ary functionality and Π be an m-party protocol, and consider the following real and ideal models.

---

32. One specific concern (in such a concurrent setting) is the ability of the adversary to "nontrivially correlate the outputs" of concurrent executions. This ability, called *malleability*, was first investigated by Dolev, Dwork, and Naor [Dolev et al. 2000]. We comment that providing a general definition of what "correlated outputs" means (for arbitrary functionalities) seems very challenging (if at all possible). Indeed the focus of [Dolev et al. 2000] is on several important special cases such as encryption and commitment schemes.

- In the *real model* the adversary controls some of the parties in an execution of Π and all parties can communicate with an arbitrary probabilistic polynomial-time process, which is called an *environment* (and possibly represents other executions of various protocols that are taking place concurrently). Honest parties only communicate with the environment before the execution starts and when it ends; they merely obtain their inputs from the environment and pass their outputs to it. In contrast, dishonest parties may communicate freely with the environment, concurrently to the entire execution of Π.

- In the *ideal model* the (*simulating*) adversary controls the same parties, which use an ideal (*trusted party*) that behaves according to the functionality f (as in Section 17.9.1.2). All parties can communicate with the (*same*) environment (*as in the real model*). Indeed, the dishonest parties may communicate extensively with the environment before and after their single communication with the trusted party.

We say that Π *is an environmentally secure protocol for computing* f if for every probabilistic polynomial-time adversary A in the real model there exists a probabilistic polynomial-time adversary A' controlling the same parties in the ideal model such that no probabilistic polynomial-time environment can distinguish the case in which it is accessed by the parties in the real execution from the case it is accessed by parties in the ideal model.

As hinted above, the environment may account for other executions of various protocols that are taking place concurrently to the main execution being considered. The definition requires that such environments cannot distinguish the real execution from an ideal one. This means that anything that the real adversary (i.e., operating in the real model) gains from the execution and some environment, can be also obtained by an adversary operating in the ideal model and having access to the same environment. Indeed, Canetti proves that environmentally secure protocols are secure with respect to concurrent compositions [Canetti 2001].

It is known is that environmentally secure protocols for any functionality can be constructed for settings in which more than two-thirds of the active parties are honest [Canetti 2001]. This holds unconditionally for the private channel model, and under standard assumptions (e.g., allowing the construction of public-key encryption schemes) for the standard model (i.e., without private channel). The immediate consequence of this result is that general environmentally-secure multiparty computation is possible, provided that more than two-thirds of the parties are honest.

In contrast, general environmentally secure *two-party* computation is not possible (in the standard sense, see, for example, Canetti and Fischlin [2001]).[33] Still, one can salvage general environmentally-secure two-party computation in the following reasonable model: Consider a network that contains servers that are willing to participate (as "helpers," possibly for a payment) in computations initiated by a set of (two or more) users. Now, suppose that two users wishing to conduct a secure computation can agree on a set of servers so that each user believes that more than two-thirds of the servers (in this set) are honest. Then, with the active participation of this set of servers, the two users can compute any functionality in an environmentally secure manner.

Other reasonable models where general environmentally secure *two-party* computation is possible include the common random string (CRS) model [Canetti et al. 2002] and variants of the public-key infrastructure (PKI) model [Barak et al. 2004]. In the CRS model, all parties have access to a universal random string (of length related to the security parameter). We stress that the entity trusted to post this universal random string is not required to take part in any execution of any protocol, and that all executions of all protocols may use the same universal random string. The PKI models considered in Barak et al. [2004] require that each party deposits a public key with a trusted center, while proving knowledge of a corresponding private key. This proof may be conducted in zero-knowledge during special epochs in which no other activity takes place.

17.9.5 Concluding Remarks

In Sections 17.9.1 and 17.9.2 we have mentioned a host of definitions of security and constructions for multi-party protocols (especially for the case of more than two parties). Furthermore, some of these definitions are incomparable to others (i.e., they neither imply the others nor are implies by them), and there seems to be no single definition that may be crowned as the central one.

For example, in Sections 17.9.1.2 and 17.9.1.3, we have presented two alternative definitions of "secure multi-party protocols," one requiring an honest majority and the other allowing abort. These definitions are incomparable and there is no generic reason to prefer one over the other. Actually, as mentioned in Section 17.9.1.2, one could formulate a natural definition that implies both definitions (i.e., waiving the bound on the number of dishonest parties in Definition 17.11).

---

33. Of course, some specific two-party computations do have environmentally secure protocols. See Canetti [2001] for several important examples (e.g., key exchange).

Indeed, the resulting definition is free of the annoying restrictions that were introduced in each of the two aforementioned definitions; the "only" problem with the resulting definition is that it cannot be satisfied (in general). Thus, for the first time in this chapter, we have reached a situation in which a natural (and general) definition cannot be satisfied, and we are forced to choose between two weaker alternatives, where each of these alternatives carries fundamental disadvantages.

In general, Section 17.9 carries a stronger flavor of compromise (i.e., recognizing inherent limitations and settling for a restricted meaningful goal) than previous sections. In contrast to the impression given in other parts of this chapter, it is now obvious that we cannot get all that we may want (see Section 17.9.4). Instead, we should study the alternatives, and go for the one that best suits our real needs.

Indeed, as stated in Section 17.1.1, the fact that we can define a cryptographic goal does not mean that we can satisfy it as defined. In case we cannot satisfy the initial definition, we should search for relaxations that can be satisfied. These relaxations should be defined in a clear manner so that it would be obvious what they achieve (and what they fail to achieve). Doing so will allow a sound choice of the relaxation to be used in a specific application. This seems to be a good point to end the current chapter.

A good compromise is one in which the most important interests of all parties are satisfied.

—Adv. Klara Goldreich-Ingwer (1912–2004)

References

W. Aiello and J. Håstad. 1987. Perfect zero-knowledge languages can be recognized in two rounds. In *28th IEEE Symposium on Foundations of Computer Science*, pp. 439–448. DOI: 10.1016/0022-0000(91)90006-Q. 442

W. Alexi, B. Chor, O. Goldreich, and C. P. Schnorr. 1988. RSA/Rabin functions: Certain parts are as hard as the whole. *SIAM Journal on Computing*, 17(April): 194–209. DOI: 10.1007/978-1-4419-5906-5_475. 430

B. Barak. 2001. How to go beyond the black-box simulation barrier. In *42nd IEEE Symposium on Foundations of Computer Science*, pp. 106–115. DOI: 10.1109/SFCS.2001.959885. 443, 444, 451

B. Barak. 2002. Constant-round coin-tossing with a man in the middle, or realizing the shared random string model. In *43rd IEEE Symposium on Foundations of Computer Science*, pp. 345–355. DOI: 10.1007/978-1-4419-5906-5_149. 451

B. Barak, R. Canetti, and J. B. Nielsen. 2004. Universally composable protocols with relaxed set-up assumptions. In *45th IEEE Symposium on Foundations of Computer Science*, pp. 186–195. 487

B. Barak and O. Goldreich. 2002. Universal arguments and their applications. In *17th IEEE Conference on Computational Complexity*, pp. 194–203. 444, 445, 446

B. Barak and Y. Lindell. 2004. Strict polynomial-time in simulation and extraction. *SIAM Journal on Computing*, 33(4): 783–818. DOI: 10.1137/S0097539703427975. 444, 445, 446

D. Beaver. 1991a. Foundations of secure interactive computing. In *Crypto91*, Lecture Notes in Computer Science vol. 576, pp. 377–391. Springer. DOI: 10.1007/3-540-46766-1_31. 469

D. Beaver. 1991b. Secure multi-party protocols and zero-knowledge proof systems tolerating a faulty minority. *Journal of Cryptology*, 4: 75–122. DOI: 10.1007/BF00196771. 469

D. Beaver, S. Micali, and P. Rogaway. 1990. The round complexity of secure protocols. In *22nd ACM Symposium on the Theory of Computing*, pp. 503–513. See details in Rogaway [1991]. DOI: 10.1145/100216.100287. 478

M. Bellare, R. Canetti, and H. Krawczyk. 1998a. A modular approach to the design and analysis of authentication and key-exchange protocols. In *30th ACM Symposium on the Theory of Computing*, pp. 419–428. DOI: 10.1145/276698.276854. 471

M. Bellare, A. Desai, D. Pointcheval, and P. Rogaway. 1998b. Relations among notions of security for public-key encryption schemes. In *Crypto98*, Lecture Notes in Computer Science vol. 1462, pp. 26–45. Springer. DOI: 10.1007/BFb0055718.pdf. 460, 461

M. Bellare and O. Goldreich. 1992. On defining proofs of knowledge. In *Crypto92*, Lecture Notes in Computer Science vol. 740, pp. 390–420. Springer. DOI: 10.1007/3-540-48071-4_28.pdf. 445, 482

M. Bellare, R. Impagliazzo, and M. Naor. 1997. Does parallel repetition lower the error in computationally sound protocols? In *38th IEEE Symposium on Foundations of Computer Science*, pp. 374–383. DOI: 10.1109/SFCS.1997.646126. 433

M. Bellare and P. Rogaway. 1993. Random oracles are practical: A paradigm for designing efficient protocols. In *1st Conference on Computer and Communications Security*, ACM, pp. 62–73. DOI: 10.1145/168588.168596. 433

C. H. Bennett, G. Brassard, and J. M. Robert. 1988. Privacy amplification by public discussion. *SIAM Journal on Computing*, 17: 210–229. Preliminary version in *Crypto85*, titled "How to Reduce your Enemy's Information." DOI: 10.1137/0217014. 425

M. Ben-Or, R. Canetti, and O. Goldreich. 1993. Asynchronous secure computation. In *25th ACM Symposium on the Theory of Computing*, pp. 52–61. See details in Canetti [1995]. DOI: 10.1145/167088.167109. 471, 478

M. Ben-Or, O. Goldreich, S. Goldwasser, J. Håstad, J. Kilian, S. Micali, and P. Rogaway. 1990. Everything provable is probable in zero-knowledge. In *Crypto88*, Lecture Notes in Computer Science vol. 403, pp. 37–56. Springer. DOI: 10.1007/0-387-34799-2_4.

M. Ben-Or, S. Goldwasser, and A. Wigderson. 1988. Completeness theorems for non-cryptographic fault-tolerant distributed computation. In *20th ACM Symposium on the Theory of Computing*, pp. 1–10. DOI: 10.1145/62212.62213. 470, 472, 477

M. Ben-Or, B. Kelmer, and T. Rabin. 1994. Asynchronous secure computations with optimal resilience. In *13th ACM Symposium on Principles of Distributed Computing*, pp. 183–192. DOI: 10.1145/197917.198088. 478

M. Blum. 1982. Coin flipping by phone. *IEEE Spring COMPCOM*, pp. 133–137. See also *SIGACT News*, 15(1), 1983. DOI: 10.1145/1008908.1008911. 482

M. Blum, A. De Santis, S. Micali, and G. Persiano. 1991. Non-interactive zero-knowledge proof systems. *SIAM Journal on Computing*, 20(6): 1084–1118. (Considered the journal version of Blum et al. [1988].) 490

M. Blum, P. Feldman, and S. Micali. 1988. Non-interactive zero-knowledge and its applications. In *20th ACM Symposium on the Theory of Computing*, pp. 103–112. See Blum et al. [1991]. DOI: 10.1145/62212.62222. 446, 460, 490

M. Blum and S. Goldwasser. 1984. An efficient probabilistic public-key encryption scheme which hides all partial information. In *Crypto84*, Lecture Notes in Computer Science vol. 196, pp. 289–302. Springer. 459

M. Blum and S. Micali. 1984. How to generate cryptographically strong sequences of pseudo-random bits. *SIAM Journal on Computing*, 13: 850–864. Preliminary version in *23rd FOCS*, 1982. DOI: 10.1137/0213053. 424, 429, 430

G. Brassard, D. Chaum, and C. Crépeau. 1988. Minimum disclosure proofs of knowledge. *Journal of Computer and System Science*, 37(2): 156–189. Preliminary version by Brassard and Crépeau in *27th FOCS*, 1986. DOI: 10.1016/0022-0000(88)90005-0.

G. Brassard and C. Crépeau. 1987. Zero-knowledge simulation of Boolean circuits. In *Crypto86*, Lecture Notes in Computer Science vol. 263, pp. 223–233. Springer. DOI: 10.1007/3-540-47721-7_16.

R. Canetti. 1995. *Studies in Secure Multi-Party Computation and Applications*. Ph.D. Thesis, Department of Computer Science, Weizmann Institute of Science, Rehovot, Israel. Available from http://www.wisdom.weizmann.ac.il/~oded/PS/ran-phd.ps. 469, 489

R. Canetti. 2000. Security and composition of multi-party cryptographic protocols. *Journal of Cryptology*, 13(1): pp. 143–202. DOI: 10.1007/s001459910006. 469, 470

R. Canetti. 2001. Universally composable security: A new paradigm for cryptographic protocols. In *42nd IEEE Symposium on Foundations of Computer Science*, pp. 136–145. Full version (with different title) is available from *Cryptology ePrint Archive*, Report 2000/067. DOI: 10.1109/SFCS.2001.959888. 471, 485, 486, 487

R. Canetti, U. Feige, O. Goldreich, and M. Naor. 1996. Adaptively secure multi-party computation. In *28th ACM Symposium on the Theory of Computing*, pp. 639–648. 472, 477

R. Canetti and M. Fischlin. 2001. Universally composable commitments. In *Crypto01*, Lecture Notes in Computer Science vol. 2139, pp. 19–40. Springer. DOI: 10.1007/3-540-44647-8_2. 487

R. Canetti, O. Goldreich, and S. Halevi. 1998. The random oracle methodology, revisited. In *30th ACM Symposium on the Theory of Computing*, pp. 209–218. DOI: 10.1145/276698.276741. 433

R. Canetti, J. Kilian, E. Petrank, and A. Rosen. 2001. Black-box concurrent zero-knowledge requires $\tilde{\Omega}(\log n)$ rounds. In *33rd ACM Symposium on the Theory of Computing*, pp. 570–579. DOI: 10.1145/380752.380852. 443, 450, 451

R. Canetti and A. Lichtenberg. 2017. Certifying trapdoor permutations, revisited. *Cryptology ePrint Archive*, Report 2017/631. 460

R. Canetti, Y. Lindell, R. Ostrovsky, and A. Sahai. 2002. Universally composable two-party and multi-party secure computation. In *34th ACM Symposium on the Theory of Computing*, pp. 494–503. 487

D. Chaum, C. Crépeau, and I. Damgård. 1988. Multi-party unconditionally secure protocols. In *20th ACM Symposium on the Theory of Computing*, pp. 11–19. DOI: 10.1145/62212 .62214. 470, 477

B. Chor, S. Goldwasser, S. Micali, and B. Awerbuch. 1985. Verifiable secret sharing and achieving simultaneity in the presence of faults. In *26th IEEE Symposium on Foundations of Computer Science*, pp. 383–395. DOI: 10.1109/SFCS.1985.64. 482

B. Chor and E. Kushilevitz. 1991. A zero-one law for Boolean privacy. *SIAM Journal on Discrete Mathematics*, 4: 36–47. DOI: 10.1137/0404004 472

B. Chor and M. O. Rabin. 1987. Achieving independence in logarithmic number of rounds. In *6th ACM Symposium on Principles of Distributed Computing*, pp. 260–268.

R. Cleve. 1986. Limits on the security of coin flips when half the processors are faulty. In *18th ACM Symposium on the Theory of Computing*, pp. 364–369. DOI: 10.1145/12130.12168. 475

I. Damgård. 1987. Collision free hash functions and public key signature schemes. In *EuroCrypt87*, Lecture Notes in Computer Science vol. 304, pp. 203–216. Springer. DOI: 10.1007/3-540-39118-5_19. 467

I. Damgård and J. B. Nielsen. 2000. Improved non-committing encryption schemes based on general complexity assumption. In *Crypto00*, Lecture Notes in Computer Science vol. 1880, pp. 432–450. Springer. DOI: 10.1007/3-540-44598-6_27. 477

A. De Santis, G. Di Crescenzo, R. Ostrovsky, G. Persiano, A. Sahai. 2001. Robust non-interactive zero-knowledge. In *Crypto01*, Lecture Notes in Computer Science vol. 2139, pp. 566–598. Springer. DOI: 10.1007/3-540-44647-8_33. 447

W. Diffie and M. E. Hellman. 1976. New directions in cryptography. *IEEE Transactions on Information Theory*, IT-22, pp. 644–654. DOI: 10.1109/TIT.1976.1055638. 453, 461

D. Dolev, C. Dwork, and M. Naor. 2000. Non-malleable cryptography. *SIAM Journal on Computing*, 30(2): 391–437. Preliminary version in *23rd STOC*, 1991. DOI: 10.1.1.26 .8267. 460, 461, 485

D. Dolev, C. Dwork, O. Waarts, and M. Yung. 1993. Perfectly secure message transmission. *Journal of the ACM*, 40(1): 17–47. DOI: 10.1145/138027.138036. 471, 478

D. Dolev and H. R. Strong. 1983. Authenticated algorithms for Byzantine agreement. *SIAM Journal on Computing*, 12: 656–666. DOI: 10.1137/0212045. 481

C. Dwork, M. Naor, and A. Sahai. 1998. Concurrent zero-knowledge. In *30th ACM Symposium on the Theory of Computing*, pp. 409–418. 450

S. Even, O. Goldreich, and A. Lempel. 1985. A randomized protocol for signing contracts. *Communications of the ACM*, 28(6): 637–647. DOI: 10.1145/3812.3818. 481

U. Feige, D. Lapidot, and A. Shamir. 1999. Multiple non-interactive zero-knowledge proofs under general assumptions. *SIAM Journal on Computing*, 29(1): 1–28. DOI: 10.1137/S0097539792230010. 447, 448, 460

U. Feige and A. Shamir. 1990. Witness indistinguishability and witness hiding protocols. In *22nd ACM Symposium on the Theory of Computing*, pp. 416–426. DOI: 10.1145/100216.100272. 445

A. Fiat and A. Shamir. 1987. How to prove yourself: Practical solution to identification and signature problems. In *Crypto86*, Lecture Notes in Computer Science vol. 263, pp. 186–189. Springer. DOI: 10.1007/3-540-47721-7_12. 445

L. Fortnow. 1987. The complexity of perfect zero-knowledge. In *19th ACM Symposium on the Theory of Computing*, pp. 204–209. DOI: 10.1145/28395.28418. 455, 469

O. Goldreich. 1993. A uniform complexity treatment of encryption and zero-knowledge. *Journal of Cryptology*, 6(1): pp. 21–53. DOI: 10.1007/BF02620230. 455, 469

O. Goldreich. 1998. *Secure Multi-Party Computation*. Unpublished manuscript. Available from the author's web-page (i.e., http://www.wisdom.weizmann.ac.il/~oded/pp.html). 441, 472, 477, 479, 481, 483, 493

O. Goldreich. 2001. *Foundations of Cryptography—Basic Tools*. Cambridge University Press. 417, 418, 420, 423, 424, 428, 430, 431, 432, 433, 436, 439, 443, 444, 446

O. Goldreich. 2004. *Foundations of Cryptography—Basic Applications*. Cambridge University Press. 417, 418, 433, 447, 452, 457, 460, 464, 465, 470, 476, 477, 478, 479, 481, 482, 483

O. Goldreich. 2005. Foundations of cryptography—A primer. *Foundations and Trends in Translated Computer Science*, 1(1): 1–116. DOI: 10.1561/040000000. 413

O. Goldreich. 2006. Concurrent zero-knowledge with timing, revisited. In *Theoretical Computer Science, Essays in Memory of Shimon Even* (O. Goldreich et al., editors.). Springer. 450

O. Goldreich. 2008. *Computational Complexity: A Conceptual Perspective*. Cambridge University Press. 417, 440

O. Goldreich. 2010. On expected probabilistic polynomial-time adversaries: A suggestion for restricted definitions and their benefits. *Journal of Cryptology*, 23(1): 1–36. DOI: 10.1007/s00145-009-9050-5. 445

O. Goldreich, S. Goldwasser, and S. Micali. 1986. How to construct random functions. *Journal of the ACM*, 33(4): 792–807. Preliminary version in *25th FOCS*, 1984. DOI: 10.1145/6490.6503. 431, 432, 464

O. Goldreich and J. Håstad. 1998. On the complexity of interactive proofs with bounded communication. *IPL*, 67(4): 205–214. 442

O. Goldreich and A. Kahan. 1996. How to construct constant-round zero-knowledge proof systems for NP. *Journal of Cryptology*, 9(2): 167–189. DOI: 10.1007/BF00208001. 440

O. Goldreich and H. Krawczyk. 1996. On the composition of zero-knowledge proof systems. *SIAM Journal on Computing*, 25(1): 169–192. DOI: 10.1137/S0097539791220688. 436, 440, 443, 448, 449, 450, 451, 484

O. Goldreich and L. A. Levin. 1989. Hard-core predicates for any one-way function. In *21st ACM Symposium on the Theory of Computing*, pp. 25–32. DOI: 10.1145/73007.73010. 424

O. Goldreich, S. Micali, and A. Wigderson. 1991. Proofs that yield nothing but their validity, or all languages in NP have zero-knowledge proof systems. *Journal of the ACM*, 38(1): 691–729. Preliminary version in *27th FOCS*, 1986. DOI: 10.1145/116825.116852. 416, 437, 438, 472, 477, 479, 482, 483

O. Goldreich, S. Micali, and A. Wigderson. 1987. How to play any mental game—a completeness theorem for protocols with honest majority. In *19th ACM Symposium on the Theory of Computing,* pp. 218–229. See details in Goldreich [1998]. DOI: 10.1145/28395.28420. 441, 472, 477, 479, 481, 483

O. Goldreich and Y. Oren. 1994. Definitions and properties of zero-knowledge proof systems. *Journal of Cryptology*, 7(1): 1–32. DOI: 10.1007/BF00195207. 435, 436

O. Goldreich and R. Rothblum. 2013. Enhancements of trapdoor permutations. *Journal of Cryptology*, 26(3): 484–512. DOI: 10.1007/s00145-012-9131-8. 460, 481

O. Goldreich, A. Sahai, and S. Vadhan. 1998. Honest-verifier statistical zero-knowledge equals general statistical zero-knowledge. In *30th ACM Symposium on the Theory of Computing*, pp. 399–408. DOI: 10.1145/276698.276852. 443

O. Goldreich, S. Vadhan, and A. Wigderson. 2002. On interactive proofs with a laconic prover. *Computational Complexity*, 11: 1–53. DOI: 10.1007/s00037-002-0169-0. 442

O. Goldreich and R. Vainish. 1987. How to solve any protocol problem—an efficiency improvement. In *Crypto87*, Lecture Notes in Computer Science vol. 293, pp. 73–86. Springer. DOI: 10.1007/3-540-48184-2_6. 481

S. Goldwasser and L. A. Levin. 1990. Fair computation of general functions in presence of immoral majority. In *Crypto90*, Lecture Notes in Computer Science vol. 537, pp. 77–93. Springer. 469

S. Goldwasser and S. Micali. 1984. Probabilistic encryption. *Journal of Computer and System Science*, 28(2): 270–299. Preliminary version in *14th STOC*, 1982. DOI: 10.1016/0022-0000(84)90070-9. 427, 428, 455, 456, 459, 469

S. Goldwasser, S. Micali, and C. Rackoff. 1989. The knowledge complexity of interactive proof systems. *SIAM Journal on Computing*, 18: 186–208. Preliminary version in *17th STOC*, 1985. DOI: 10.1137/0218012. 416, 433, 435, 436, 443, 445, 469, 482

S. Goldwasser, S. Micali, and R. L. Rivest. 1988. A digital signature scheme secure against adaptive chosen-message attacks. *SIAM Journal on Computing*, 17(2): 281–308. DOI: 10.1137/0217017. 463, 465

S. W. Golomb. 1967. *Shift Register Sequences*. Holden-Day. (Aegean Park Press, revised edition, 1982.) 427

D. Gordon, C. Hazay, J. Katz, and Y. Lindell. 2011. Complete fairness in secure two-party computation. *Journal of the ACM*, 58(6): 24:1–24:37. DOI: 10.1145/2049697.2049698. 475

I. Haitner, M. Nguyen, S. Ong, O. Reingold, and S. Vadhan. 2009. Statistically hiding commitments and statistical zero-knowledge arguments from any one-way function. *SIAM Journal on Computing*, 39(3): 1153–1218. DOI: 10.1137/080725404. 442

J. Håstad, R. Impagliazzo, L. A. Levin, and M. Luby. 1999. A pseudorandom generator from any one-way function. *SIAM Journal on Computing*, 28(4): 1364–1396. DOI: 10.1137/S0097539793244708. 431, 437

M. Hirt and U. Maurer. 2000. Complete characterization of adversaries tolerable in secure multi-party computation. *Journal of Cryptology*, 13(1): 31–60. 473

R. Impagliazzo, L. A. Levin, and M. Luby. 1989. Pseudorandom generation from one-way functions. In *21st ACM Symposium on the Theory of Computing*, pp. 12–24. DOI: 10.1145/73007.73009. 415

R. Impagliazzo and M. Luby. 1989. One-way functions are essential for complexity based cryptography. In *30th IEEE Symposium on Foundations of Computer Science*, pp. 230–235. DOI: 10.1109/SFCS.1989.63483. 415

J. Katz and M. Yung. 2000. Complete characterization of security notions for probabilistic private-key encryption. In *32nd ACM Symposium on the Theory of Computing*, pp. 245–254. DOI: 10.1145/335305.335335. 460, 461

J. Kilian. 1992. A note on efficient zero-knowledge proofs and arguments. In *24th ACM Symposium on the Theory of Computing*, pp. 723–732. DOI: 10.1145/129712.129782. 442

J. Kilian and E. Petrank. 2001. Concurrent and resettable zero-knowledge in poly-logarithmic rounds. In *33rd ACM Symposium on the Theory of Computing*, pp. 560–569. DOI: 10.1145/380752.380851. 450

D. E. Knuth. 1969. *The Art of Computer Programming*, Vol. 2 (*Seminumerical Algorithms*). Addison-Wesley Publishing Company, Inc., 1969 (first edition) and 1981 (second edition). 427

Y. Lindell. 2001. Parallel coin-tossing and constant-round secure two-party computation. In *Crypto01*. Lecture Notes in Computer Science vol. 2139, pp. 171–189. Springer. DOI: 10.1007/s00145-002-0143-7. 478

Y. Lindell, A. Lysyanskaya, and T. Rabin. 2002. On the composition of authenticated Byzantine agreement. In *34th ACM Symposium on the Theory of Computing*, pp. 514–523. DOI: 10.1145/509907.509982. 481

A. J. Menezes, P. C. van Oorschot, and S. A. Vanstone. 1996. *Handbook of Applied Cryptography*. CRC Press. 418, 467

R. C. Merkle. 1980. Protocols for public key cryptosystems. In *Proceedings of the 1980 Symposium on Security and Privacy*. DOI: 10.1109/SP.1980.10006. 466

S. Micali. 2000. Computationally sound proofs. *SIAM Journal on Computing*, 30(4): 1253–1298. Preliminary version in *35th FOCS*, 1994. DOI: 10.1137/S0097539795284959. 442

S. Micali and P. Rogaway. 1991. Secure computation. In *Crypto91*, Lecture Notes in Computer Science vol. 576, pp. 392–404. Springer. Elaborated working draft available from the authors. DOI: 10.1007/3-540-46766-1_32. 469

M. Naor. 1991. Bit commitment using pseudorandom generators. *Journal of Cryptology*, 4: 151–158. DOI: 10.1007/BF00196774. 437, 440, 482

M. Naor and M. Yung. 1989. Universal one-way hash functions and their cryptographic application. In *21st ACM Symposium on the Theory of Computing*, pp. 33–43. DOI: 10.1145/73007.73011. 465, 467

M. Naor and M. Yung. 1990. Public-key cryptosystems provably secure against chosen ciphertext attacks. In *22nd ACM Symposium on the Theory of Computing*, pp. 427–437. DOI: 10.1.1.26.5883. 460

National Institute for Standards and Technology. 1991. *Digital Signature Standard* (DSS). *Federal Register*, vol. 56, no. 169. 464

R. Ostrovsky and A. Wigderson. 1993. One-way functions are essential for non-trivial zero-knowledge. In *2nd Israel Symposium on Theory of Computing and Systems*, IEEE Comp. Soc. Press, pp. 3–17. DOI: 10.1007/3-540-45539-6_9. 437

M. Prabhakaran, A. Rosen, and A. Sahai. 2002. Concurrent zero-knowledge proofs in logarithmic number of rounds. In *43rd IEEE Symposium on Foundations of Computer Science*, pp. 366–375. 450

M. O. Rabin. 1977. Digitalized signatures. In *Foundations of Secure Computation* (R. A. DeMillo et al. editors), Academic Press. 461, 466

M. O. Rabin. 1979. Digitalized signatures and public key functions as intractable as factoring. MIT/LCS/TR-212. 421, 464

M. O. Rabin. 1981. How to exchange secrets by oblivious transfer. Tech. Memo TR-81, Aiken Computation Laboratory, Harvard U.

T. Rabin and M. Ben-Or. 1989. Verifiable secret sharing and multi-party protocols with honest majority. In *21st ACM Symposium on the Theory of Computing*, pp. 73–85. DOI: 10.1145/73007.73014. 470, 477

R. Richardson and J. Kilian. 1999. On the concurrent composition of zero-knowledge proofs. In *EuroCrypt99*, Lecture Notes in Computer Science vol. 1592, pp. 415–413. Springer. DOI: 10.1007/3-540-48910-X_29. 450

R. Rivest, A. Shamir, and L. Adleman. 1978. A method for obtaining digital signatures and public key cryptosystems. *Communications of the ACM*, 21(Feb.): 120–126. DOI: 10.1145/359340.359342. 421

P. Rogaway. 1991. *The Round Complexity of Secure Protocols*. Ph.D. Thesis, MIT. Available from http://www.cs.ucdavis.edu/~rogaway/papers. 489

J. Rompel. 1990. One-way functions are necessary and sufficient for secure signatures. In *22nd ACM Symposium on the Theory of Computing*, pp. 387–394. DOI: 10.1145/100216 .100269. 465, 467

A. Sahai and S. Vadhan. 2003. A complete promise problem for statistical zero-knowledge. *Journal of the ACM*, 50(2): 1–54. 440

A. Shamir. 1979. How to share a secret. *Communications of the ACM*, 22(Nov.): 612–613. DOI: 10.1145/359168.359176. 479

C. E. Shannon. 1949. Communication theory of secrecy systems. *Bell System Technical Journal*, 28: 656–715. DOI: 10.1002/j.1538-7305.1949.tb00928.x. 453, 521

M. Sipser. 1983. A complexity theoretic approach to randomness. In *15th ACM Symposium on the Theory of Computing*, pp. 330–335. DOI: 10.1145/800061.808762. 425

S. Vadhan. 1999. A study of statistical zero-knowledge proofs. Ph.D. Thesis, Department of Mathematics, MIT. Available from http://www.eecs.harvard.edu/~salil/papers/ phdthesis-abs.html. 444

S. Vadhan. 2004. An unconditional study of computational zero knowledge. In *45th IEEE Symposium on Foundations of Computer Science*, pp. 176–185. 437, 443

A. C. Yao. 1982. Theory and application of trapdoor functions. In *23rd IEEE Symposium on Foundations of Computer Science*, pp. 80–91. 427, 428, 429, 430

A. C. Yao. 1986. How to generate and exchange secrets. In *27th IEEE Symposium on Foundations of Computer Science*, pp. 162–167. DOI: 10.1109/SFCS.1986.25. 477, 479

On the Impact of Cryptography on Complexity Theory

Oded Goldreich

We trace three major directions of research in complexity theory to their origins in the foundations of cryptography. Specifically, we refer to the theory of pseudorandomness (including the various incarnations of this concept), to the study of various forms of probabilistic proof system (including interactive proofs, zero-knowledge proofs, and probabilistically checkable proofs), and to the finer study of reductions (including random self-reducibility, worst-case to average-case reductions, average-case preserving reductions, and black-box reductions).

18.1 The Story

In this essay we discuss the impact that research in the foundations of cryptography has had on developments in complexity theory. In particular, we trace three major research directions in complexity theory to their origins in the foundations of cryptography. These directions are:

1. The theory of pseudorandomness, including the various incarnations of this concept.

2. The study of various forms of probabilistic proof system, including interactive proofs, zero-knowledge proofs, and probabilistically checkable proofs.

3. The finer study of reductions, including random self-reducibility, worst-case to average-case reductions, average-case preserving reductions, and black-box reductions.

In the following subsections, we shall tell the story of how these complexity theoretic studies have emerged from the study of the foundations of cryptography.

In contrast, in Sections 18.2 and 18.3, we shall further discuss two of these three (complexity theoretic) endeavors while ignoring their cryptographic origins. In Section 18.2, we offer a wide perspective on the notion pseudorandom generators, viewing it as general paradigm that includes the general-purpose pseudorandom generator studied in cryptography as a specific (archetypical) incarnation. In Section 18.3, we shall offer a bird's eye view on the aforementioned types of probabilistic proof systems.

18.1.1 Pseudorandomness

The notion of a pseudorandom generator has first emerged in practice, where such candidate generators were used for various sampling tasks. In that context, it was natural to require that the sequences produced by these generators pass various statistical tests (as reviewed at great length by Knuth [1981]). Given the ad hoc nature of the choice of the statistical tests, such an approach fails to yield a robust notion of pseudorandom generators. The inadequacy of this approach is most striking in the cryptographic setting, where the adversary is likely to launch attacks that are not captured by natural statistical tests.

The potential applications of "cryptographically secure" pseudorandom generators in cryptography (e.g., for the construction of a (private-key) stream cipher), led Blum and Micali to propose such a notion and a candidate construction of it [Blum and Micali 1984]. By their definition, a ***pseudorandom generator*** is an *efficient* deterministic algorithm that *stretches* a short random seed into a long sequence that is *unpredictable* by any feasible observer; that is, no feasible algorithm can predict the next bit in the sequence, when given the previous bits, with success probability that is nonnegligibly higher than half (which is obtained by just tossing a coin). We stress that, under this definition, the potential predictor may be stronger than the generator (as long as it is feasible); this reflects the default cryptographic principle by which the adversary may be more powerful than the honest user (i.e., may be willing to invest more resources than are required for proper use of the system that it attacks).

Having other applications in mind, Yao observed that the unpredictability requirement is equivalent to requiring that the output of the generator be *computationally indistinguishable* from a truly random sequence [Yao 1982], where the notion of computational indistinguishability is exactly the one put forward by Goldwasser and Micali [1984]. Recall that Goldwasser and Micali suggested this notion as a pivot of their definition of secure encryptions, while arguing that indistinguishable distributions are equivalent for all practical purposes. Specifically, by their definition, an encryption scheme is secure if the encryptions of any two messages (of the same length) are computationally indistinguishable. Again, the cryptographic origin of this definition mandates that, in the context of pseudorandom generators, the potential distinguisher may be stronger than the generator.

The foregoing notion of a pseudorandom generator implies that *any efficient randomized algorithm maintains its performance when its internal coin tosses are substituted by a sequence generated by a pseudorandom generator*. The fact that these pseudorandom generators can be used in all efficient applications, including applications that are run for more time than the generator itself, identifies them as *general-purpose* constructs, and hence we call them *general-purpose pseudorandom generators*. We mention that such pseudorandom generators exist if and only if one-way functions exist [Håstad et al. 1999].

General-purpose pseudorandom generators are actually the archetypical incarnation of a general paradigm. In general, pseudorandom generators are efficient deterministic procedures that stretch short random seeds into longer "pseudorandom" sequences. Thus, a generic formulation of pseudorandom generators consists of specifying three fundamental aspects: the *stretch measure* of the generators, the class of distinguishers that the generators are supposed to fool (i.e., the algorithms with respect to which the *computational indistinguishability* requirement should hold), and the resources that the generators are allowed to use (i.e., their own *computational complexity*). Other incarnations of this general paradigm are telegraphically reviewed next.

One notable example is provided by pseudorandom generators that suffice for the derandomization of randomized complexity classes such as $\mathcal{BPP}$, which is the application envisioned by Yao [1982]. In such applications after replacing the original random-tape by the output of a generator, one considers a deterministic algorithm that scans all possible seeds of the generator (and invokes the generator on each possible seed). Hence, as observed by Nisan and Wigderson [1994], in such applications, one may allow the generator to run in time that is exponential in its seed length, which is typically much larger than the running time of the distinguishers that one needs to fool. We call such pseudorandom generators *canonical derandomizers*, and note that they can be constructed under seemingly weaker intractability assumption than those required for the construction of general-purpose pseudorandom generators [Nisan and Wigderson 1994, Impagliazzo and Wigderson 1997].

Another famous incarnation of the notion of pseudorandom generators consists of generators that fool bounded-space machines. Such generators can be constructed without relying on any intractability assumption, and their seed length and space complexity is only moderately higher than the space complexity of the algorithms that they fool [Nisan 1992, Nisan and Zuckerman 1996]. Other incarnations of the paradigm refer to passing very restricted tests such as local tests (yielding limited independence generators) or linear tests (yielding small bias generators). We call such pseudorandom generators *special purpose*, and note that such generators of exponential stretch can be constructed unconditionally (see Goldreich [2008, Sec. 8.5]).

To summarize: The theory of pseudorandomness provides a fresh view at the *question of randomness*, which has puzzled thinkers for ages. This theory postulates that a distribution is random (or rather pseudorandom) if it cannot be told apart from the uniform distribution by any efficient procedure. The paradigm, originally associating efficient procedures with polynomial-time algorithms, has been applied also with respect to a variety of limited classes of such distinguishing procedures. Thus, (pseudo)randomness is not an inherent property of an object, but is rather subjective to the observer. At the extreme, this approach says that the question of whether the world is deterministic or allows for some free choice (which may be viewed as sources of randomness) is irrelevant. *What matters is how the world looks to us and to various computationally bounded devices.* That is, if some phenomenon looks random, then we may just treat it as if it were random.

Hence, the theory of pseudorandomness is pivoted at the notion of computational indistinguishability, which in turn was put forward by Goldwasser and Micali, in the context of defining secure encryption schemes [Goldwasser and Micali 1984]. The archetypical incarnation of this theory, yielding the notion of *general-purpose pseudorandom generator*, was derived from the cryptographic setting considered by Blum and Micali [1984], but other incarnations were proposed as well. The latter were either directly or indirectly inspired by the archetypical case.

In Section 18.2 we provide a wide perspective on the theory of pseudorandomness, but refrain from reproducing definitions and results that appear in Section 17.4. Our focus in Section 18.2 will be on aspects that are not covered in Section 17.4. A more detailed treatment of the subject can be found in Goldreich [2008, Chap. 8].

18.1.2 Probabilistic Proof Systems

The glory attributed to the creativity involved in finding proofs makes us forget that it is the less glorified procedure of verification that gives proofs their value. Philosophically speaking, proofs are secondary to the verification procedure; whereas technically speaking, proof systems are defined in terms of their verification procedures.

The notion of a verification procedure presupposes the notion of computation,[1] and furthermore the notion of efficient computation. This implicit dependency is made explicit in the definition of NP-proof systems (giving rise to the class $\mathcal{NP}$), where efficient computation is associated with deterministic polynomial-time algorithms. However, we can gain a lot if we are willing to take a somewhat nontraditional step and allow *probabilistic* verification procedures. In particular:

- Randomized and interactive verification procedures, giving rise to *interactive proof systems*, seem much more powerful than their deterministic counterparts (see Section 18.3.1).

- Such randomized procedures allow the introduction of *zero-knowledge proofs*, which are of great conceptual and practical interest (see Section 18.3.2).

- NP-proofs can be efficiently transformed into a (redundant) form (called a *probabilistically checkable proof*) that offers a trade-off between the number of bit-locations examined in the NP-proof and the confidence in its validity (see Section 18.3.3).

In all these types of probabilistic proof systems, explicit bounds are imposed on the computational resources of the verification procedure, which in turn is personified by the notion of a verifier. Furthermore, in all these proof systems, the verifier is allowed to toss coins and rule by statistical evidence. Thus, *all these proof systems carry a probability of error, yet this probability is explicitly bounded and, furthermore, can be reduced by successive application of the proof system.*

Like in the case of pseudorandom generators, the story of probabilistic proof systems originates in cryptography. It begins with Goldwasser, Micali, and Rackoff, who sought a general setting for their novel notion of zero-knowledge [Goldwasser et al. 1989], which was aimed to capture cryptographic protocols that preserve the secrecy of the inputs of their users. The choice fell on proof systems—as capturing a fundamental activity that takes place in a cryptographic protocol. Motivated by the desire to formulate the most general type of "proofs" that may be used within cryptographic protocols, they introduced the notion of an *interactive proof system* [Goldwasser et al. 1989]. Although the main thrust of their paper is the introduction of a special type of interactive proofs (i.e., ones that are *zero-knowledge*),

---

1. This may explain the historical fact that notions of computation were first *rigorously formulated* in the context of logic.

the possibility that interactive proof systems may be more powerful than NP-proof system has been pointed out in Goldwasser et al. [1989].

Independently of Goldwasser et al. [1989],[2] Babai suggested a different formulation of interactive proofs, which he called *Arthur–Merlin Games* [Babai 1985]. Syntactically, Arthur–Merlin Games are a restricted form of interactive proof systems, yet it was subsequently shown that these restricted systems are as powerful as the general ones [Goldwasser and Sipser 1989]. Babai's motivation was to place a group-theoretic problem, previously placed in $\mathcal{NP}$ under some group-theoretic assumptions, "as close to $\mathcal{NP}$ as possible" without using any assumptions. Interestingly, Babai underestimated the expressive power of interactive proof systems, conjecturing that the class of sets possessing such proof systems (even with an unbounded number of message-exchange rounds) is "very close" to $\mathcal{NP}$.

The first evidence of the surprising power of interactive proofs was given by Goldreich, Micali, and Wigderson, who presented an interactive proof system for Graph Nonisomorphism [Goldreich et al. 1991], a set not known to be in $\mathcal{NP}$. More importantly, their paper has demonstrated the generality and wide applicability of zero-knowledge proofs. Assuming the existence of one-way function, it was shown how to construct zero-knowledge interactive proofs for any set in $\mathcal{NP}$. This result has had a dramatic impact on the design of cryptographic protocols (cf. Goldreich et al. [1987]). In addition, this result has called attention to the then-new notion of interactive proof systems (since zero-knowledge NP-proofs could exist only in a trivial sense [Goldreich and Oren 1994]).

A generalization of interactive proofs to *multi-prover interactive proofs* was suggested by Ben-Or, Goldwasser, Kilian, and Wigderson [Ben-Or et al. 1988]. Again, the main motivation came from zero-knowledge aspects—specifically, introducing multi-prover zero-knowledge proofs for $\mathcal{NP}$ without relying on intractability assumptions. Yet the complexity theoretic prospects of the new class, denoted $\mathcal{MIP}$, have not been ignored. A more appealing, to our taste, formulation of the class $\mathcal{MIP}$ has been presented in Fortnow et al. [1988]. The latter formulation exactly coincides with the formulation now known as *probabilistically checkable proofs* (i.e., $\mathcal{PCP}$).

The cryptographic lens was responsible for yet another development regarding interactive proof system. Motivated by the desire to construct schemes for delgating computation in a relaiable manner, Goldwasser, Kalai, and Rothblum [Goldwasser

---

2. Although both Goldwasser et al. [1989] and Babai [1985] appeared in the same conference (i.e., *17th STOC*, 1985), early versions of Goldwasser et al. [1989] existed in 1982, and were rejected three times from major conferences (i.e., *FOCS83*, *STOC84*, and *FOCS84*).

et al. 2015] introduced the notion of *doubly efficient* interactive proof systems. In such proof systems, originally termed "interactive proofs for muggles" (where "muggles" are nonmagicians in the Harry Potter lingo), the prover should be relatively efficient and the verifier should be super efficient. Specifically, in the context of delegation schemes, the prover should run in time that is polynomially related to the complexity of the delegated computation, whereas the verifier should be much faster than the latter complexity.

Hence, each of the aforementioned four types of probabilistic proof systems was originally proposed in order to address some cryptographic concern. More generally, these works (especially, the first one [Goldwasser et al. 1989]) introduced the idea that a proof system may be probabilistic, and that the resulting probabilistic proof systems yield very meaningful notions that have many practical benefits. We also mention that the cryptographic lens motivated the definition of computationally sound proof systems (a.k.a. argument systems) [Brassard et al. 1988].[3]

In Section 18.3 we provide a very brief introduction to the aforementioned types of probabilistic proof systems. A detailed treatment of the basic definitions and results can be found in Goldreich [2008, Chap. 9], whereas Chapter 24 provides a survey of doubly efficient interactive proof systems.

18.1.3 Finer Study of Reductions

The notions of random self-reducibility, worst-case to average-case reductions, average-case preserving reductions, and black-box reductions emerged naturally from the study of the foundations of cryptography. In this subsection, we briefly trace their emergence.

Random self-reducibility. Although random self-reducibility was used as an algorithmic tool in the design of "index calculus" algorithms [Adleman 1979, Merkle 1979, Pollard 1978] for solving the Discrete Logarithm Problem, its first emergence as a tool for establishing hardness occured in the work of Goldwasser and Micali [1984]. Specifically, they identified random self-reducibility as the King's road to establishing worst-case to average-case reductions, and this road was taken by many subsequent works, most notably by Babai et al. [1993]. Loosely speaking, if solving a problem on any instance x can be reduced to solving the same problem on m random $|x|$-bit-long instances, which need *not* be independently distributed, then

---

3. Furthermore, a cryptographic primitive (i.e., collision resistant hash functions) was combined with PCP systems to yield argument systems with extremely efficient verification procedures [Kilian 1992].

the worst-case hardness of the problem implies that it is hard to solve on at least an $1/3m$ fraction of the domain.[4]

Worst-case to average-case reductions. Goldwasser and Micali [1984] introduced the aforementioned reduction in order to base the security of their proposed encryption scheme on a seemingly reliable (worst-case) intractability assumption. Their encryption scheme consists of encrypting a bit σ by a random element of $\mathbb{Z}_N$ having a Jacobi symbol 1 and quadratic character σ, where N is the product of two primes that are each congruent to 3 mod 4. Recall that under their robust definition of security, which was introduced in Goldwasser and Micali [1984], security was interpreted as the indistinguishably of an encryption of 0 from an encryption of 1. Hence, proving security of their scheme required showing that it is infeasible to distinguish a quadratic residue mod M from a quadratic nonresidue of Jacobi symbol 1 mod M. Indeed, Goldwasser and Micali showed that if the Quadratic Residuosity problem was hard on the worst case, then the foregoing distinguishing task is infeasible. This was shown by reducing the Quadratic Residuosity problem to the distinguishing task, which is equivalent to predicting the quadratic character of random numbers that have Jacobi symbol 1—that is, by showing a worst-case to average-case reduction.

We warn that the foregoing complexity measures are not purely worst case or average case, since they refer to a fixed parameter, which in the foregoing cases in the composite moduli N. In contrast, subsequent complexity theoretic studies of worst-case to average-case reductions do refer to such pure notions (see, e.g., Bogdanov and Trevisan [2006]). In any case, we stress that it was realized from the very beginning of the study of the foundations of cryptography (i.e., from Goldwasser and Micali [1984])[5] that cryptographic applications have to be secure in an average-case sense, and so basing their security of a worst-case intractability assumption (such as $\mathcal{P} \neq \mathcal{NP}$) requires a worst-case to average-case reduction.

Average-case preserving reductions. Relations between different cryptographic primitives are typically proved by reductions that preserve average-case hardness. This thread was also pioneered by Goldwasser and Micali, who showed that a (secure) bit-

---

4. The counter-positive asserts that an efficient algorithm that solves the problem correctly on at least a $1 - (1/3m)$ fraction of the domain yields an efficient algorithm that solve the problem correctly on each instance with probability at least 2/3.

5. Some researchers realized this point before Goldwasser and Micali [1984]. For example, in the late 1970s, Shimon Even realized that NP-hardness of the problem of breaking an encryption scheme does not guarantee its security.

encryption scheme implies a (secure) full-fledged encryption scheme [Goldwasser and Micali 1984]. Shortly after, Blum and Micali showed that the average-case hardness of DLP implies a "hard-core predicate" (of the modular exponentiation function), which in turn implies a pseudorandom generator [Blum and Micali 1984]. (The argument was generalized by Yao [1982].) All these results are proved by a reduction that preserves average-case hardness in an adequate sense. Specifically, the reductions transform a violation of the average-case hardness of the claimed primitive to the violation of the average-case hardness of the given primitive.

A related ("point-wise") notion of preserving average-case hardness is pivotal to Levin's theory of average-case complexity, which was suggested a couple of years later [Levin 1986].[6]

Yao's result by which weakly one-way functions imply (strong) one-way functions [Yao 1982] (see exposition in Goldreich [2008, Sec. 7.1.2]) heralded a line of research known as "hardness amplification" (see, e.g., Impagliazzo et al. [2010]), which is too rich to review here. Still, the "take home message" is that it all started in cryptography.

Black-box reductions. All traditional reductions used in complexity theory (e.g., for establishing NP-hardness) are black-box.[7] In fact, the definition of a Cook reduction refers to an abstract oracle that provides answers to queries regarding the target problem (see, e.g., Goldreich [2008, Sec. 2.2]), and the notion of a Karp reduction is a special case. Although some early expositions of the notion of NP-completeness entertained the possibility that a set $S \in \mathcal{NP}$ may be "NP-complete" if *it holds that $S \in \mathcal{P}$ implies $\mathcal{NP} = \mathcal{P}$*, the standard notion of NP-completeness calls for a reduction. Yet the possibility of showing hardness without presenting a (black-box) reduction re-emerged in the study of the foundations of cryptography.

It began with the work of Impagliazzo and Rudich [1989], who essentially showed that the security of a public-key encryption scheme cannot be reduced to the existence of one-way permutations via a black-box reduction. This result was taken as indication to the impossibility of constructing public-key encryption schemes based on one-way functions. Similarly, the fact that protocols of a certain type cannot be demonstrated to be zero-knowledge using a black-box simulator [Goldreich and Krawczyk 1996] was taken as indication to the nonexistence

---

6. The interested reader may prefer the expositions provided in Goldreich [1997] and 2008, Sec. 10.2.1.

7. Indeed, this follows the notion of Turing reduction used in computability theory (see, e.g., Goldreich [2008, Sec. 1.2.3.6]).

of such zero-knowledge protocols. The latter belief was refuted by Barak [2001] a decade later, and the interpretation of the host of black-box separation results that followed [Impagliazzo and Rudich 1989] is a controversial topic. For a careful examination of the relevant issues, the interested reader is directed to Reingold et al. [2004].

We mention that a natural notion in the context of zero-knowledge is one of a universal simulator, which obtains the code of the verifier (which it simulates) as an auxiliary input. Such a simulator (used by Barak [2001] and subsequent works in cryptography) corresponds to the notion of a "white-box" reduction, which is often considered in complexity theory (e.g., in the context of derandomization; see Impagliazzo et al. [2001], which explicitly discusses the distinction between black-box and white-box reductions as well as the possibility of nonconstructive proofs (of implications)).

18.2 Pseudorandomness: A Wide Computational Perspective

Indistinguishable things are identical.[8]
—G. W. Leibniz (1646–1714)

The second half of this century has witnessed the development of three theories of randomness, a notion which has been puzzling thinkers for ages. The first theory (cf. Cover and Thomas [1991]), initiated by Shannon, is rooted in probability theory and is focused at distributions that are not perfectly random (i.e., are not uniform over a set of strings of adequate length). Shannon's Information Theory characterizes perfect randomness as the extreme case in which the *information contents* is maximized (i.e., the strings contain no redundancy at all). Thus, perfect randomness is associated with a unique distribution: the uniform one. In particular, by definition, one cannot (deterministically) generate such perfect random strings from shorter random seeds.

The second theory (cf. Li and Vitanyi [1993]), initiated by Solomonov, Kolmogorov, and Chaitin, is rooted in computability theory and specifically in the notion of a universal language (equivalently, universal machine or computing device). It measures the complexity of objects in terms of the shortest program (for a fixed universal machine) that generates the object. Like Shannon's theory, Kolmogorov complexity is quantitative and perfect random objects appear as an extreme case. However, in this approach one may say that a single object, rather

---

8. This is Leibniz's *Principle of Identity of Indiscernibles*. Leibniz admits that counterexamples to this principle are conceivable but will not occur in real life because God is much too benevolent.

than a distribution over objects, is perfectly random. Still, Kolmogorov's approach is inherently intractable (i.e., Kolmogorov complexity is uncomputable), and—by definition—one cannot (deterministically) generate strings of high Kolmogorov complexity from short random seeds.

The third theory, initiated by Blum, Goldwasser, Micali, and Yao [Goldwasser and Micali 1984, Blum and Micali 1984, Yao 1982], is rooted in the notion of *efficient computation* and is the focus of this section. This approach is explicitly aimed at providing a notion of randomness that allows for an efficient generation of random strings from shorter random seeds. The heart of this approach is the suggestion to view objects as equal if they cannot be told apart by any efficient procedure. Consequently, a distribution that cannot be efficiently distinguished from the uniform distribution will be considered as being random (or rather called pseudorandom). Thus, randomness is not an "inherent" property of objects (or distributions) but is rather relative to an observer (and its computational abilities). To demonstrate this approach, let us consider the following mental experiment.

Alice and Bob play "head or tail" in one of the following four ways. In each of them, Alice flips an unbiased coin and Bob is asked to guess its outcome *before* the coin hits the floor. The alternative ways differ by the knowledge Bob has before making his guess.

In the first alternative, Bob has to announce his guess before Alice flips the coin. Clearly, in this case Bob wins with probability 1/2.

In the second alternative, Bob has to announce his guess while the coin is spinning in the air. Although the outcome is *determined in principle* by the motion of the coin, Bob does not have accurate information on the motion and thus we believe that also in this case Bob wins with probability 1/2.

The third alternative is similar to the second, except that Bob has at his disposal sophisticated equipment capable of providing accurate *information* on the coin's motion as well as on the environment effecting the outcome. However, Bob cannot process this information in time to improve his guess.

In the fourth alternative, Bob's recording equipment is directly connected to a *powerful computer* programmed to solve the motion equations and output a prediction. It is conceivable that in such a case Bob can substantially improve his guess of the outcome of the coin.

We conclude that the randomness of an event is relative to the information and computing resources at our disposal. Thus, a natural concept of pseudorandomness arises: a distribution is *pseudorandom* if no efficient procedure can distinguish it from the uniform distribution, where efficient procedures are associated with (probabilistic) polynomial-time algorithms. This notion of pseudorandomness is indeed the most fundamental one, yet weaker notions of pseudorandomness arise as well—they refer to indistinguishability by weaker procedures such as space-bounded algorithms, constant-depth circuits, etc.[9]

18.2.1 The General Paradigm

The foregoing discussion has focused at one aspect of the pseudorandomness question—the resources or type of the observer (or potential distinguisher). Another important aspect is whether such pseudorandom sequences can be generated from much shorter ones, and at what cost (or complexity). A natural approach requires the generation process to be efficient, and furthermore to be fixed before the specific observer is determined. Coupled with the aforementioned strong notion of pseudorandomness, this yields the archetypical notion of pseudorandom generators—those operating in (fixed) polynomial time and producing sequences that are indistinguishable from uniform ones by *any* polynomial-time observer. In particular, this means that the distinguisher is allowed more resources than the generator. Such (*general-purpose*) pseudorandom generators (discussed in Section 18.2.2) allow to decrease the randomness complexity of *any efficient application*, and are thus of great relevance to randomized algorithms and cryptography. The term *general purpose* is meant to emphasize the fact that the same generator is good for all efficient applications, including those that consume more resources than the generator itself.

Although general-purpose pseudorandom generators are very appealing, there are important reasons for considering also the opposite relation between the complexities of the generation and distinguishing tasks—that is, allowing the pseudorandom generator to use more resources (e.g., time or space) than the observer it tries to fool. This alternative is natural in the context of derandomization (i.e., converting randomized algorithms to deterministic ones), where the crucial step is replacing the random input of an algorithm by a pseudorandom input, which in turn can be generated based on a much shorter random seed. In particular, when derandomizing a probabilistic polynomial-time algorithm, the observer (to be fooled by the generator) is a fixed algorithm. In this case employing a more complex generator merely means that the complexity of the derived determinis-

---

9. We mention two perspectives on pseudorandomness that are somewhat different than the one presented in this section. Vadhan's treatment [Vadhan 2012] emphasizes the *connections* between a variety of fundamental "pseudorandom objects" that seem very different in nature. The *Pseudorandomness program of the Simons Institute* (run in Jan–May 2017) emphasizes that *pseudorandomness and structure are complementing opposites*. In both cases (especially, in the second), the computational aspect is somewhat de-emphasized. The word "computational" was inserted in the title of this section in order to reemphasize this aspect.

tic algorithm is dominated by the complexity of the generator (rather than by the complexity of the original randomized algorithm). Needless to say, allowing the generator to use more resources than the observer that it tries to fool makes the task of designing pseudorandom generators potentially easier, and enables derandomization results that are not known when using general-purpose pseudorandom generators.

We note that the goal of all types of pseudorandom generators is to allow the generation of "sufficiently random" sequences based on much shorter random seeds; that is, such generators are actually deterministic algorithms that *stretch* their input seeds into much longer pseudoramndom sequences. Our focus is on pseudorandom generators that have significant stretch, since they offer significant saving in the randomness complexity of various applications (and, in some cases, eliminating randomness altogether). Saving on randomness is valuable because many applications are severely limited in their ability to generate or obtain truly random bits. Furthermore, typically, generating truly random bits is significantly more expensive than standard computation steps. Thus, randomness is a computational resource that should be considered on top of time complexity (analogously to the consideration of space complexity).

18.2.1.1 Three Fundamental Aspects
In light of the foregoing, a generic formulation of pseudorandom generators consists of specifying three fundamental aspects: the *stretch measure* of the generators, the class of distinguishers that the generators are supposed to fool (i.e., the algorithms with respect to which the *computational indistinguishability* requirement should hold), and the resources that the generators are allowed to use (i.e., their own *computational complexity*). Let us elaborate.

Stretch function. A necessary requirement from any notion of a pseudorandom generator is that the generator is a *deterministic algorithm* that stretches short strings, called **seeds**, into longer output sequences.[10] Specifically, this algorithm stretches k-bit-long seeds into $\ell(k)$-bit-long outputs, where $\ell(k) > k$. The function $\ell: \mathbb{N} \to \mathbb{N}$ is called the **stretch measure** (or **stretch function**) of the generator. In some settings (e.g., in the case of general-purpose pseudorandom generators), the stretch measure can be amplified.

---

10. Indeed, the seed represents the randomness that is used in the generation of the output sequences; that is, the randomized generation process is decoupled into a deterministic algorithm and a random seed. This decoupling facilitates the study of such processes.

Computational indistinguishability. A necessary requirement from any notion of a pseudorandom generator is that the generator "fools" some nontrivial algorithms. That is, it is required that any algorithm taken from a predetermined class of interest cannot distinguish the output produced by the generator (when the generator is fed with a uniformly chosen seed) from a uniformly chosen sequence. Thus, we consider a class $\mathcal{D}$ of distinguishers (e.g., probabilistic polynomial-time algorithms) and a class $\mathcal{F}$ of (threshold) functions (e.g., reciprocals of positive polynomials), and require that the generator G satisfies the following: For any $D \in \mathcal{D}$, any $f \in \mathcal{F}$, and for all sufficiently large k's, it holds that

$$| \Pr[D(G(U_k)) = 1] - \Pr[D(U_{\ell(k)}) = 1]| < f(k), \qquad (18.1)$$

where U_n denotes the uniform distribution over $\{0, 1\}^n$ and the probability is taken over U_k (respectively, $U_{\ell(k)}$) as well as over the coin tosses of algorithm D in case it is probabilistic. The reader may think of such a distinguisher, D, as of an observer that tries to tell whether the "tested string" is a random output of the generator (i.e., distributed as $G(U_k)$) or is a truly random string (i.e., distributed as $U_{\ell(k)}$). The condition in Eq. (18.1) requires that D cannot make a meaningful decision; that is, ignoring a negligible difference (represented by $f(k)$), D's verdict is the same in both cases.[11] The archetypical choice is that $\mathcal{D}$ is the set of all probabilistic polynomial-time algorithms, and $\mathcal{F}$ is the set of all functions that are the reciprocal of some positive polynomial.

Complexity of generation. This aspect refers to the complexity of the generator itself, when viewed as an algorithm. The archetypical choice is that the generator has to work in polynomial time (i.e., make a number of steps that is polynomial in the length of its input—the seed). Other choices will be discussed as well. We note that placing no computational requirements on the generator (or, alternatively, imposing very mild requirements such as upper-bounding the running-time by a double-exponential function), yields "generators" that can fool any subexponential-size circuit family.[12]

---

11. The class of threshold functions $\mathcal{F}$ should be viewed as determining the class of *noticeable* probabilities (as a function of k). Thus, we require certain functions (i.e., those presented at the l.h.s of Eq. (18.1)) to be smaller than any noticeable function *on all but finitely many integers*. We call the former functions *negligible*. Note that a function may be neither noticeable nor negligible (e.g., it may be smaller than any noticeable function on infinitely many values and yet larger than some noticeable function on infinitely many other values).

12. This fact can be proved via the probabilistic method; see Goldreich [2008, Exer. 8.1].

18.2.1.2   Some Instantiations of the General Paradigm

Two important instantiations of the notion of pseudorandom generators relate to polynomial-time distinguishers.

General-purpose pseudorandom generators.   This incarnation corresponds to the case that the generator itself runs in polynomial time and is required to withstand *any probabilistic polynomial-time distinguisher*, including distinguishers that run for more time than the generator (i.e., Eq. (18.1) holds for all polynomial-time D's and $F = \{1/p : p \in \text{POLY}\}$). Thus, the same generator may be used safely in any efficient application.

This notion is treated in Section 17.4, and we shall further discuss it in Section 18.2.2. Recall that in this case, any pseudorandom generator (of any stretch function, including the minimal $\ell(k) = k + 1$), implies a pseudorandom generator of any desired (polynomial) stretch function [Goldreich 2008, Sec. 8.2.4].

Canonical derandomizers.   In contrast, pseudorandom generators intended for derandomization may run more time than the distinguisher, which is viewed as a fixed circuit having size that is upper-bounded by a fixed polynomial (say, the quadratic polynomial n^2). Specifically, a *canonical derandomizer* is an exponential-time deterministic algorithm that stretches its k-bit-long random seed to an $\ell(k)$-bit-long sequence that fools any quadratic (in ℓ) size circuits (i.e., Eq. (18.1) holds for any circuit D of size $\ell(n)^2$ and $F = \{1/6\}$).

Note that a canonical derandomizer of exponential stretch implies that $\mathcal{BPP} = \mathcal{P}$. To see this, consider an arbitrary probabilistic polynomial-time algorithm, denoted A, that decides $S \in \mathcal{BPP}$, and denote its running time by p. Letting G denote the canonical derandomizer, and $\ell(k) = \exp(\Omega(k))$ denote its stretch, we obtain an algorithm A_G that, on input x, uniformly selects $s \in \{0, 1\}^k$, where $k = O(\log |x|)$ such that $\ell(k) = p(|x|)$, and invokes A on input x and randomness $G(s)$. By the current incarnation of Eq. (18.1), it follows that, for every x, we have $|\Pr[A(x) = 1] - \Pr[A_G(x) = 1]| < 1/6$, since otherwise we obtain a $o(\ell(k)^2)$-size circuit that distinguishes $U_{\ell(k)}$ from $G(U_k)$. Finally, by trying all possible random tapes of A_G, we obtain a deterministic polynomial-time algorithm that decides S (i.e., this algorithm accepts x if and only if the majority of the possible random tapes lead $A_G(x)$ to accept (i.e., iff $\Pr[A_G(x) = 1] > 1/2$)).[13]

Note that if f is computable in exponential time but is hard to approximate (or predict), on the average, by circuits of smaller exponential size (with advantage

---

13. Recall that for every x, either $\Pr[A(x) = 1] \geq 2/3$ or $\Pr[A(x) = 1] \leq 1/3$.

proportional to their size), then $G(s) = (s, f(s))$ constitutes a canonical derandomizer (of minimal stretch). Interestingly, canonical derandomizers of exponential stretch can also be obtained in this case [Nisan and Wigderson 1994], by applying f to an exponential number of $\Omega(k)$-bit-long substrings of the k-bit-long seed that have relatively small pairwise intersections.[14] For further details on canonical derandomizers, the interested reader is referred to Goldreich [2008, Sec. 8.3].

We now turn to a few additional instantiations of the notion of pseudorandom generators. These instantiations refer to more limited classes of distinguishers such as log-space machines, local computations, and linear computations. In the known constructions for each of these cases, each bit in the output of the generator can be computed in time that is polynomial in the seed length.

Fooling space-bounded distinguishers. Here the distinguishers are space-bounded machines that have unidirectional access to the input they examine; actually, we may consider (nonuniform) OBDDs of bounded width.[15] The two main constructions known are at the extremes the relation between the distinguishers' time and space complexities (i.e., the OBDDs' length and width), where in both cases the generator itself has linear space complexity.

1. Using a seed of length $k = O(\log s)^2$, one can fool 2^s-width OBDDs that read $\exp(s)$-many bits (i.e., $\ell(k) = \exp(\sqrt{k})$) [Nisan 1992].

2. Using a seed of length $k = O(\log s)$, one can fool 2^s-width OBDDs that read $\text{poly}(s)$-many bits (i.e., $\ell(k) = \text{poly}(k)$) [Nisan and Zuckerman 1996].

In the first result one should think of s as being logarithmic in the length of the output sequence (i.e., $s = O(\log \ell(k))$), whereas in the second result one should think of s as being a $O(1)$-root of the length of the output sequence (i.e., $s = \ell(k)^{1/O(1)}$). The specific construction of the first generator allows for derandomizing the class $\mathcal{BPL}$ in polylogarithmic space and polynomial time [Nisan 1994]. For further details on space-bounded pseudorandom generators, the interested reader is referred to Goldreich [2008, Sec. 8.4].

---

14. We mention that the construction of Nisan and Wigderson [1994] has also been applied in other settings. One case, which predated Nisan and Wigderson [1994], is that of constant-depth circuits [Nisan 1991]. Another case is information theoretic; this case led to a breakthrough in the study of randomness extractors [Trevisan 2001]. In both these cases, the hard function f can be proved to exist without relying on any intractability assumptions.

15. Ordered binary decision diagrams (OBDD) are branching programs that reads bits of the input in a predetermined order. Their width correspond to an exponential function of the space bound.

Fooling local distinguishers. Here we consider distinguishers that inspect a constant number, denoted t, of bits in the sequence output by the generator, where these bit locations are not *a priori* known. Random sequences that perfectly fool such distinguishers are called t-***wise independent*** (since each sequence of t bits in them is uniformly distributed in $\{0, 1\}^t$). Constructions of t-wise independence generators can achieve stretch $\ell(k) = 2^{k/t}$, and this result extends to sequences over $\Sigma = \{0, 1\}^{k/t}$; for details, see Goldreich [2008, Sec. 8.5.1].

Fooling linear distinguishers. Here we consider distinguishers that inspect a linear combination (over GF(2)) of bits in the sequence output by the generator, where the linear combination is not *a priori* known. Random sequences that fool such distinguishers with a probability gap of ϵ are called ϵ-***biased***. Constructions of ϵ-biased generators can achieve stretch $\ell(k) = \epsilon \cdot \exp(\Omega(k))$; for details, see Goldreich [2008, Sec. 8.5.2].

Fooling hitting tests distinguishers. Last, we consider distinguishers that inspect sequences over $\Sigma = \{0, 1\}^b$. Each such distinguisher is associated with a target set $T \subseteq \Sigma$ of density at least half, and accepts the sequence if at least one of its elements hit the set T. A generator $G : \{0, 1\}^k \to \Sigma^{\ell'(k)}$ is said to pass such a test if the probability that its output is not accepted (i.e., each element in $G(U_k)$ misses T) is at most $\exp(-\Omega(\ell'(k)))$. Such generators can be constructed for $\ell'(k) = \Omega(k - b)$; for details, see Goldreich [2008, Sec. 8.5.3].

18.2.2 General-Purpose Pseudorandom Generators

Randomness is playing an increasingly important role in computation. It is frequently used in the design of sequential, parallel and distributed algorithms, and it is of course central to cryptography. Whereas it is convenient to design such algorithms making free use of randomness, it is also desirable to minimize the usage of randomness in real implementations. Thus, general-purpose pseudorandom generators (as defined in Section 17.4) are a key ingredient in an "algorithmic toolbox"—they provide an automatic compiler of programs written with free usage of randomness into programs that make an economical use of randomness.

18.2.2.1 The Archetypical Application

Recall that "pseudorandom number generators" appeared with the first computers and have been used ever since for generating random choices (or samples) for various applications. However, typical implementations use generators that are not pseudorandom according to our definition. Instead, at best, these generators are shown to pass *some* ad hoc statistical test (cf., Knuth [1981]). We warn that the fact that a "pseudorandom number generator" passes some statistical tests does not mean that it will pass a new test and that it will be good for a future (untested) application. Needless to say, the approach of subjecting the generator to some ad hoc tests fails to provide general results of the form "for *all* practical purposes using the output of the generator is as good as using truly unbiased coin tosses." In contrast, the approach encompassed in the definition of general-purpose pseudorandom generators aims at such generality, and in fact is tailored to obtain it: The notion of computational indistinguishability, which underlines this definition, covers all possible efficient applications and guarantees that for all of them pseudorandom sequences are as good as truly random ones. Indeed, any efficient randomized algorithm maintains its performance when its internal coin tosses are substituted by a sequence generated by a (general purpose) pseudorandom generator. This substitution is spelled out next.

Construction 18.1 (Typical application of pseudorandom generators) Let G be a (*general-purpose*) pseudorandom generator with stretch function $\ell: \mathbb{N} \to \mathbb{N}$. Let A be a probabilistic polynomial-time algorithm, and $\rho: \mathbb{N} \to \mathbb{N}$ denote its randomness complexity. Denote by $A(x, r)$ the output of A on input x and coin tosses sequence $r \in \{0, 1\}^{\rho(|x|)}$. Consider the following randomized algorithm, denoted A_G:

> On input x, set $k = k(|x|)$ to be the smallest integer such that $\ell(k) \geq \rho(|x|)$, uniformly select $s \in \{0, 1\}^k$, and output $A(x, r)$, where r is the $\rho(|x|)$-bit-long prefix of $G(s)$.

That is, $A_G(x, s) = A(x, G'(s))$, where $|s| = k(|x|) = \operatorname{argmin}_i \{\ell(i) \geq \rho(|x|)\}$, and $G'(s)$ is the $\rho(|x|)$-bit-long prefix of $G(s)$.

Thus, using A_G instead of A, the randomness complexity is reduced from ρ to $\ell^{-1} \circ \rho$, while (as stated in Proposition 18.1) it is infeasible to find inputs (i.e., x's) on which the *noticeable behavior* of A_G is different from the one of A (and the nonexistence of such inputs follows in case pseudorandomness holds with respect to polynomial-size circuits).[16] For example, if $\ell(k) = k^2$, then the randomness complexity is reduced from ρ to $\sqrt{\rho}$. We stress that the pseudorandom generator G is *universal*; that is, it can be applied to reduce the randomness complexity of *any* probabilistic polynomial-time algorithm A.

Proposition 18.1 Let A, ρ, and G be as in Construction 18.1, and suppose that $\rho : \mathbb{N} \to \mathbb{N}$ is 1-1. Then, for every pair of probabilistic polynomial-time algorithms, *a finder F* and *a tester*

---

16. That is, the (nonuniform) existential conclusion follows from a nonuniform hypothesis regarding G (i.e., that $G(U_k)$ is indistinguishable from $U_{\ell(k)}$ by any poly(k)-size circuit).

T, every positive polynomial p and all sufficiently long n's

$$\sum_{x \in \{0,1\}^n} \Pr[F(1^n) = x] \cdot \Delta_{A,T}(x) < \frac{1}{p(n)}, \tag{18.2}$$

where $\Delta_{A,T}(x) \stackrel{\text{def}}{=} | \Pr[T(x, A(x, U_{\rho(|x|)})) = 1] - \Pr[T(x, A_G(x, U_{k(|x|)})) = 1]|$, and the probabilities are taken over the U_m's as well as over the internal coin tosses of the algorithms F and T.

Algorithm F represents a potential attempt to find an input x on which the output of A_G is distinguishable from the output of A. This "attempt" may be benign, as in the case that a user employs algorithm A_G on inputs that are generated by some probabilistic polynomial-time application. However, the attempt may also be adversarial, as in the case that a user employs algorithm A_G on inputs that are provided by a potentially malicious party. The potential tester, denoted T, represents the potential use of the output of algorithm A_G, and captures the requirement that this output be as good as a corresponding output produced by A. Thus, T is given x as well as the corresponding output produced either by $A_G(x) \stackrel{\text{def}}{=} A(x, G'(U_{k(|x|)}))$ or by $A(x) = A(x, U_{\rho(|x|)})$, and it is required that T cannot tell the difference. In the case that A is a probabilistic polynomial-time *decision procedure*, this means that it is infeasible to find an x on which A_G decides incorrectly (i.e., differently than A). In the case that A is a *search procedure for some NP-relation*, it is infeasible to find an x on which A_G outputs a wrong solution. For details, see Goldreich [2008, Sec. 8.2.1].

Conclusion. Although Proposition 18.1 refers to standard probabilistic polynomial-time algorithms, a similar construction and analysis applied to any efficient randomized process (i.e., any efficient multi-party computation). Any such process preserves its behavior when replacing its perfect source of randomness (postulated in its analysis) by a pseudorandom sequence (which may be used in the implementation). Thus, given a pseudorandom generator with a large stretch function, *one can significantly reduce the randomness complexity of any efficient application.*

18.2.2.2 Pseudorandom Functions

Pseudorandom generators allow the efficient generation of long pseudorandom sequences from short random seeds (e.g., using k random bits, we can efficiently generate a pseudorandom bit-sequence of length k^2). Pseudorandom functions (defined below) are even more powerful: they allow efficient direct access to a huge pseudorandom sequence (which is infeasible to scan bit by bit). For example, based on k random bits, we define a sequence of length 2^k such that we can efficiently retrieve any desired bit in this sequence while the retrieved bits look random. In other words, pseudorandom functions can replace truly random functions in any efficient application (e.g., most notably in cryptography). That is, pseudorandom functions are indistinguishable from random functions by any efficient procedure that may obtain the function values at arguments of its choice.

Definition 18.1 (Pseudorandom functions [Goldreich et al. 1986]) A *pseudorandom function* (*ensemble*), with length parameters $\ell_D, \ell_R \colon \mathbb{N} \to \mathbb{N}$ (*e.g.*, $\ell_D(k) = k$ *and* $\ell_R(k) = 1$), is a collection of functions $\{F_k\}_{k \in \mathbb{N}}$, where

$$F_k \stackrel{\text{def}}{=} \{f_s \colon \{0,1\}^{\ell_D(k)} \to \{0,1\}^{\ell_R(k)}\}_{s \in \{0,1\}^k},$$

satisfying:

efficient evaluation. There exists an efficient (*deterministic*) algorithm that when given a *seed*, s, and an $\ell_D(|s|)$-bit *argument*, x, returns the $\ell_R(|s|)$-bit long value $f_s(x)$.

(Thus, the seed s is an "effective description" of the function f_s.)

pseudorandomness. For every probabilistic polynomial-time oracle machine M, every positive polynomial p, and all sufficiently large k,

$$\left| \Pr_{s \sim U_k} [M^{f_s}(1^k) = 1] - \Pr_{\rho \sim R_k} [M^{\rho}(1^k) = 1] \right| < \frac{1}{p(k)},$$

where R_k denotes the uniform distribution over all functions mapping $\{0,1\}^{\ell_D(k)}$ to $\{0,1\}^{\ell_R(k)}$ and $M^f(x)$ denotes the computation of M on input x when M's queries are answered by the function f.

Although pseudorandom functions seem stronger than pseudorandom generators, the former can be constructed using the latter (see Section 17.4.3).

We mention two ("noncryptographic") applications of pseudorandom functions to the theory of computation. The first, which originates in Valiant's seminal work on PAC learning [Valiant 1984], is the observation that pseudorandom functions yield concept classes that are infeasible to learn (since a learning algorithm for a concept class consisting of pseudorandom functions would distinguish pseudorandom functions from truly random functions, which cannot be learned at all). The second application is the pivotal role of pseudorandom functions in the "natural proofs" framework of Razborov and Rudich [1997].

18.2.2.3 **The Intellectual Contents of Pseudorandom Generators**

We briefly discuss some intellectual aspects of general-purpose pseudorandom generators. Actually, the first two aspects apply to all incarnations of the notion of a pseudorandom generator.

Behavioristic versus ontological. Our definition of pseudorandom generators is based on the notion of computational indistinguishability. The behavioristic nature of the latter notion is best demonstrated by confronting it with the Kolmogorov–Chaitin approach to randomness. Loosely speaking, a string is *Kolmogorov random* if its length roughly equals the length of the shortest program producing it. This shortest program may be considered the "true explanation" to the phenomenon described by the string. A Kolmogorov-random string is thus a string that does not have a substantially simpler (i.e., shorter) explanation than itself. Considering the simplest explanation of a phenomenon may be viewed as an ontological approach. In contrast, considering the effect of phenomena (on an observer), as underlying the definition of pseudorandomness, is a behavioristic approach. Furthermore, there exist probability distributions that are not uniform (and are not even statistically close to a uniform distribution), but nevertheless are indistinguishable from a uniform distribution by any efficient procedure. Thus, distributions that are ontologically very different are considered equivalent by the behavioristic point of view taken in the definition of pseudorandomness.

A relativistic view of randomness. Pseudorandomness is defined in terms of its observer: In the archetypical case of the general-purpose incarnation, a pseudorandom distribution is one that cannot be told apart from a uniform distribution by any efficient (i.e., polynomial-time) observer. However, the output of such pseudorandom generators can be distinguished from uniform sequences by an exponential-time machine (which is not at our disposal), which just tries all possible seeds (and rules that the sequence is random if and only if it is not in the image of the generator). Furthermore, the mere variety of different incarnations of the notion of computational indistinguishability testifies that pseudorandomness depends on the abilities of the observer. Hence, pseudorandomness is a relative notion.

Randomness and computational difficulty. In the archetypical case of the general-purpose incarnation (and also in the case of canonical derandomizers), pseudorandomness and computational difficulty play dual roles: The definition of pseudorandomness is pivoted at a difficult computational task (i.e., the task of distinguishing pseudorandom sequences from truly random ones). Furthermore, the known constructions of pseudorandom generators rely on conjectures regarding computational difficulty (e.g., the existence of one-way functions in the archetypical case), and this is inevitable: The existence of such pseudorandom generators implies some known intractability conjectures (e.g., the existence of one-way functions).

Randomness and predictability. The connection between pseudorandomness and unpredictability (by efficient procedures) plays an important role in the analysis of several constructions of pseudorandom generators (see Goldreich [2008, Sec. 8.2.5.2], as well as Goldreich [2008, Sec. 8.3.2.2]). We wish to highlight the intuitive appeal of this connection.

18.3 Probabilistic Proof Systems: A Bird's-Eye View

A proof is whatever convinces me.

—Shimon Even (1935–2004)

The glory attributed to the creativity involved in finding proofs makes us forget that it is the less glorified process of verification that *defines* proof systems. The notion of a verification procedure presupposes the notion of computation, and furthermore the notion of efficient computation (because verification, unlike coming up with proofs, is supposed to be easy). Associating the set of valid assertions with a set of objects that have some property, we view a proof system for a set S (e.g., of satisfiable formulae) as a game between an all-powerful prover and an *efficient* verifier: Both receive an input x, and the prover attempts to convince the verifier that $x \in S$. We seek proof systems that are *complete* and *sound*, where completeness means that the prover succeeds for every $x \in S$, and soundness means that *any* prover fails for every $x \notin S$.

When taking the most natural choice of the efficiency requirement, namely, restricting the verifier to be a deterministic polynomial-time machine, we get the definition of the class $\mathcal{NP}$ (rephrased as a proof system): *A set S is in $\mathcal{NP}$ if and only if membership in S can be verified by a deterministic polynomial-time machine when given an alleged proof of polynomial length* (i.e., polynomial in $|x|$).

Relaxing the efficiency requirement, we let the verifier be a *probabilistic* polynomial-time machine. Furthermore, we allowing it to "rule by statistical evidence" and hence to err (with low probability, which is explicitly bounded, and can be reduced via repetitions). This relaxation is not suggested as a substitute to the notion of a mathematical proof, but rather as a practical solution to the problem of verifying mundane assertions (like the fact that on input x, the program P halts with output $P(x)$). As we shall see below, this relaxation turns out to yield enormous advances in computer science.

18.3.1 Interactive Proof Systems

When the verifier is deterministic, we can always assume that the prover simply sends it a single message (the purported "proof"), and based on this message the verifier decides whether to accept or reject the common input x as a member of the target set S. (More extensive interaction does not help here, since the verifier's steps are predictable by the prover.)

When the verifier is probabilistic, *interaction* may add power. We thus consider a (randomized) interaction between the parties. Such an interaction which may be viewed as an "interrogation" of the teacher (prover) by a persistent student (verifier), who asks the teacher "tough" questions in order to be convinced of the correctness of the claim. Interestingly, it turns out that asking "tough" questions is not (significantly) better than asking random questions (even if one cares about the number of rounds [Goldwasser and Sipser 1989]).[17] In any case, since the verifier ought to be efficient (i.e., run in time polynomial in $|x|$), this interaction is bounded to have at most polynomially many rounds. The class $\mathcal{IP}$ (for Interactive Proofs) contains all sets S for which there is a verifier that accepts every $x \in S$ with probability 1 (after interacting with an adequate prover), but rejects any $x \notin S$ with probability at least $1/2$ (no matter what strategy is employed by the prover).

Clearly, $\mathcal{NP} \subseteq \mathcal{IP}$: To prove that x is in an NP-set S, the prover just sends an adequate NP-witness, which the verifier can easily verify. But how can one prove that x is not in $S \in \mathcal{NP}$? That is, when proving that something (i.e., an NP-witness) exists, the prover merely presents it, but how can the prover convince the verifier that something (i.e., an NP-witness) does not exist? A major result asserts that interactive proofs exists for every set in $\mathcal{PSPACE} \supseteq \text{co}\mathcal{NP}$. In fact, we have the following theorem.

Theorem 18.1 [Lund et al. 1992, Shamir 1992]: $\mathcal{IP} = \mathcal{PSPACE}$.

Recalling that it is widely believed that $\mathcal{NP} \neq \mathcal{PSPACE}$, it follows that interactive proofs seem more powerful than standard noninteractive and deterministic proofs (i.e., NP-proofs). In particular, since $\text{co}\mathcal{NP} \subseteq \mathcal{PSPACE}$, Theorem 18.1 implies that there are such interactive proofs for every set in $\text{co}\mathcal{NP}$, whereas some coNP-sets are believed not to have NP-proofs.

---

17. See Section 19.3 for further discussion. The word "significantly" indicates that the known transformation incurs a polynomial overhead in the verification time.

18.3.2   Zero-Knowledge Proof Systems

Here the thrust is not on being able to prove more assertions, but rather on having proofs with additional properties. Randomized and interactive verification procedures as in Section 18.3.1 allow the (meaningful) introduction of *zero-knowledge proofs*, which are proofs that yield nothing beyond their own validity. Such proofs seem counterintuitive and undesirable for educational purposes, but they are very useful in cryptography.

For example, a *zero-knowledge proof* that a certain propositional formula is satisfiable does not reveal a satisfying assignment to the formula nor any partial information regarding such an assignment (e.g., whether the first variable can assume the value true). In general, whatever the verifier can efficiently compute after interacting with a zero-knowledge prover, can be efficiently reconstructed from the assertion itself (without interacting with anyone).

Clearly, any set in $\mathcal{BPP}$ has a zero-knowledge proof, in which the prover says nothing (and the verifier decides by itself). What is surprising is that zero-knowledge proofs seem to exist also for sets that are widely believed not to be in $\mathcal{BPP}$. In particular:

Theorem 18.2   (Goldreich et al. 1991)   Assuming the existence of (*nonuniformly hard*) one-way functions, every set in $\mathcal{NP}$ has a zero-knowledge proof system.

Interestingly, under the same condition any set in $\mathcal{IP}$ has a zero-knowledge proof system [Ben-Or et al. 1990]. On the other hand, for the actual use of zero-knowledge proof systems, it is crucial that the prover strategy asserted in Theorem 18.2 can be implemented in probabilistic polynomial time, when given an NP-witness for the common input. Of course, this zero-knowledge strategy does not consist of just sending the NP-witness; it rather consists of sending "commitments" to many "randomized versions" of the NP-witness and allowing the verifier to inspect few random location in each such randomized witness (by decommitting to the locations selected by the verifier).

18.3.3   Probabilistically Checkable Proof Systems

Let us return to the noninteractive mode, in which the verifier receives a (alleged) written proof. But now we restrict its access to the proof so as to read only a small part of it (which may be randomly selected by it). An excellent analogy is to imagine a referee trying to decide the correctness of a long proof by sampling a few lines of the proof. It seems hopeless to detect a single "bug" unless the entire "proof" is read, but this intuition is valid only for the "natural" way of writing down proofs, and it fails when "robust" formats of proofs are used (and one is willing to settle for statistical evidence).

Such "robust" proof systems are called PCPs (for Probabilistically Checkable Proofs). Loosely speaking, a *PCP system* for a set S consists of a probabilistic polynomial-time verifier having access to an oracle that represents a proof in redundant form, where (as in case of NP-proofs) the length of the proof is polynomial in the length of the input. The verifier accesses only a constant number of the oracle bits, and accepts every $x \in S$ with probability 1 (when given access to an adequate oracle), but rejects any $x \notin S$ with probability at least $1/2$ (no matter to which oracle it is given access).

Theorem 18.3   (The PCP Theorem [Arora and Safra 1998, Arora et al. 1998][18])   Each set in $\mathcal{NP}$ has a PCP system. Furthermore, there exists a polynomial-time procedure for converting any NP-proof to the corresponding PCP-oracle.

Indeed, the proof of the PCP Theorem suggests a way of writing "robust" proofs, in which any bug must "spread" all over.[19] One important application of the PCP Theorem (and its variants) is its connection to the complexity of combinatorial approximation. For example, using the PCP system of Håstad [2001], it follows that it is NP-complete to decide, when given a linear system of equations over GF(2), *whether the fraction of mutually satisfiable equations is greater than* 99% *or smaller than* 51%.

18.3.4   Doubly Efficient Interactive Proof Systems

Turning back to interactive proof systems, recall that their definition does not restrict the complexity of the strategy of the prescribed prover. Indeed, the constructions of Lund et al. [1992] and Shannon [1949] use prover strategies of high complexity. This fact limits the applicability of these proof systems in practice. (Nevertheless, such proof systems may be actually applied when the prover knows something that the verifier does not know, such as an NP-witness to an NP-claim, and when the proof system offers an advantage such as zero-knowledge [Goldwasser et al. 1989, Goldreich et al. 1991].)

In contrast, the definition of *doubly efficient* interactive proof systems *requires the prescribed prover strategy to be implemented in polynomial time and the verifier's strategy to be implemented in almost-linear time*. (We stress that unlike in *argument*

---

18. See also an alternative proof of Dinur [2007].

19. The analogy to error-correcting codes is indeed in place, and the cross fertilization between these two areas has been very significant.

systems [Brassard et al. 1988], the soundness condition holds for all possible cheating strategies, not only for feasible ones.) Restricting the prescribed prover to run in polynomial time implies that such systems may exist only for sets in $\mathcal{BPP}$, whereas a polynomial-time verifier can check membership in such sets by itself. However, restricting the verifier to run in almost-linear time implies that something can be gained by interacting with a more powerful prover, even though the latter is restricted to polynomial time.

The foregoing potential was first demonstrated in Goldwasser et al. [2015], which presents doubly efficient proof systems for any set that has log-space uniform circuits of small depth (e.g., log-space uniform $\mathcal{NC}$). An incomparable recent result of Reingold et al. [2016] provides such (constant-round) proof systems for any set that can be decided in polynomial time and small amount of space (e.g., for all sets in $\mathcal{SC}$). That is, denoting by $\mathrm{TiSp}(T, s)$ the class of sets that can be decided by a (randomized) algorithm that runs in time T while using space s, we have:

Theorem 18.4 (Reingold et al. 2016) For every polynomial p and $s(n) = \sqrt{n}$, each set in $\mathrm{TiSp}(p, s)$ has a (*constant round*) doubly efficient proof system.

Recall that each set having a doubly efficient proof system is in $\mathcal{BPP}$, and note that it is also decidable in almost-linear space.

Acknowledgments

I am grateful to Yuval Ishai for helpful comments.

References

L. M. Adleman. 1979. A subexponential algorithm for the discrete logarithm problem with applications to cryptography. In *20th FOCS*, pp. 55–60. DOI: 10.1109/SFCS.1979.2. 503

S. Arora, C. Lund, R. Motwani, M. Sudan, and M. Szegedy. 1998. Proof verification and intractability of approximation problems. *Journal of the ACM*, 45: 501–555. Preliminary version in *33rd FOCS*, 1992. DOI: 10.1145/278298.278306. 521

S. Arora and S. Safra. 1998. Probabilistic checkable proofs: A new characterization of NP. *Journal of the ACM*, 45: 70–122. Preliminary version in *33rd FOCS*, 1992. DOI: 10.1145/273865.273901. 521

L. Babai. 1985. Trading group theory for randomness. In *17th ACM Symposium on the Theory of Computing*, pp. 421–429. DOI: 10.1145/22145.22192. 502

L. Babai, L. Fortnow, L. Levin, and M. Szegedy. 1991. Checking computations in polylogarithmic time. In *23rd ACM Symposium on the Theory of Computing*, pp. 21–31. DOI: 10.1145/103418.103428. 537

L. Babai, L. Fortnow, N. Nisan, and A. Wigderson. 1993. BPP has subexponential time simulations unless EXPTIME has publishable proofs. *Complexity Theory*, 3: 307–318. DOI: 10.1.1.53.2426. 503

B. Barak. 2001. How to go beyond the black-box simulation barrier. In *42nd IEEE Symposium on Foundations of Computer Science*, pp. 106–115. 506

M. Ben-Or, S. Goldwasser, J. Kilian, and A. Wigderson. 1988. Multi-prover interactive proofs: How to remove intractability. In *20th ACM Symposium on the Theory of Computing*, pp. 113–131. DOI: 10.1145/62212.62223. 502

M. Ben-Or, O. Goldreich, S. Goldwasser, J. Håstad, J. Kilian, S. Micali, and P. Rogaway. 1990. Everything provable is probable in zero-knowledge. In *Crypto88*, Lecture Notes in Computer Science vol. 403, pp. 37–56. Springer. 520

M. Blum and S. Micali. 1984. How to generate cryptographically strong sequences of pseudo-random bits. *SIAM Journal on Computing*, 13(4): 850–864. Preliminary version in *23rd IEEE Symposium on Foundations of Computer Science, 1982*. DOI: /10.1137/0213053. 498, 500, 505, 507

A. Bogdanov and L. Trevisan. 2006. On worst-case to average-case reductions for NP problems. *SIAM Journal on Computing*, 36(4): 1119–1159. Extended abstract in *44th IEEE Symposium on Foundations of Computer Science*, 2003. DOI: 10.1137/S0097539705446974. 504

G. Brassard, D. Chaum, and C. Crépeau. 1988. Minimum disclosure proofs of knowledge. *Journal of Computer and System Science*, 37(2): 156–189. Preliminary version by Brassard and Crépeau in *27th FOCS*, 1986. DOI: 10.1016/0022-0000(88)90005-0. 503, 522

T. M. Cover and G. A. Thomas. 1991. *Elements of Information Theory*. John Wiley & Sons, Inc. 506

I. Dinur. 2007. The PCP theorem by gap amplification. *Journal of the ACM*, 54(3): Art. 12. DOI: 10.1145/1236457.1236459. 521

U. Feige, S. Goldwasser, L. Lovász, S. Safra, and M. Szegedy. 1996. Approximating clique is almost NP-complete. *Journal of the ACM*, 43: 268–292. Preliminary version in *32nd IEEE Symposium on Foundations of Computer Science*, 1991.

L. Fortnow, J. Rompel, and M. Sipser. 1988. On the power of multi-prover interactive protocols. In *3rd IEEE Symposium on Structure in Complexity*, pp. 156–161. See errata in *5th IEEE Symposium on Structure in Complexity*, pp. 318–319, 1990. DOI: 10.1016/0304-3975(94)90251-8. 502

O. Goldreich. 1997. Notes on Levin's theory of average-case complexity. *Electronic Colloquium on Computational Complexity*, TR97-058. 505

O. Goldreich. 1998. *Secure Multi-Party Computation*. Unpublished manuscript. Available from the author's webpage (i.e., http://www.wisdom.weizmann.ac.il/~oded/pp.html). 524

O. Goldreich. 2008. *Computational Complexity: A Conceptual Perspective*. Cambridge University Press. 500, 503, 505, 510, 511, 512, 513, 515, 518

O. Goldreich, S. Goldwasser, and S. Micali. 1986. How to construct random functions. *Journal of the ACM*, 33(4): 792–807. DOI: 10.1145/6490.6503. 516

O. Goldreich and H. Krawczyk. 1996. On the composition of zero-knowledge proof systems. *SIAM Journal on Computing*, 251: 169–192. Preliminary version in *17th ICALP*, 1990. DOI: 10.1137/S0097539791220688. 505

O. Goldreich, S. Micali, and A. Wigderson. 1991. Proofs that yield nothing but their validity, or all languages in NP have zero-knowledge proof systems. *Journal of the ACM*, 38(1): 691–729. Preliminary version in *27th FOCS*, 1986. DOI: 10.1145/116825.116852. 502, 520, 521

O. Goldreich, S. Micali, and A. Wigderson. 1987. How to play any mental game—a completeness theorem for protocols with honest majority. In *19th ACM Symposium on the Theory of Computing,* pp. 218–229. See details in Goldreich [1998]. DOI: 10.1145/28395.28420. 502

O. Goldreich and Y. Oren. 1994. Definitions and properties of zero-knowledge proof systems. *Journal of Cryptology*, 7(1): 1–32. DOI: 10.1007/BF00195207. 502

S. Goldwasser, Y. Kalai, and G. N. Rothblum. 2015. Delegating computation: Interactive proofs for muggles. *Journal of the ACM*, 62(4): Art. 27:1-27:64. Extended abstract in *40th STOC*, pp. 113–122, 2008. DOI: 10.1145/2699436. 503, 522

S. Goldwasser and S. Micali. 1984. Probabilistic encryption. *Journal of Computer and System Science*, 28(2): 270–299. Preliminary version in *14th ACM Symposium on the Theory of Computing*, 1982. DOI: 10.1016/0022-0000(84)90070-9. 498, 500, 503, 504, 505, 507

S. Goldwasser, S. Micali, and C. Rackoff. 1989. The knowledge complexity of interactive proof systems. *SIAM Journal on Computing*, Vol. 18, pp. 186–208. Preliminary version in *17th ACM Symposium on the Theory of Computing*, 1985. Earlier versions date to 1982. DOI: 10.1145/22145.22178. 501, 502, 503, 521

S. Goldwasser and M. Sipser. 1989. Private coins versus public coins in interactive proof systems. *Advances in Computing Research: a research annual*, vol. 5 (Randomness and Computation, S. Micali, editor), pp. 73–90. Extended abstract in *18th ACM Symposium on the Theory of Computing*, 1986. DOI: 10.1145/12130.12137. 502, 519

J. Håstad. 2001. Getting optimal in-approximability results. *Journal of the ACM*, 48: 798–859. Extended abstract in *29th ACM Symposium on the Theory of Computing*, 1997. DOI: 10.1145/502090.502098. 521

J. Håstad, R. Impagliazzo, L. A. Levin, and M. Luby. 1999. A pseudorandom generator from any one-way function. *SIAM Journal on Computing*, 28(4): 1364–1396. Preliminary versions by Impagliazzo et al. in *21st ACM Symposium on the Theory of Computing* (1989) and Håstad in *22nd ACM Symposium on the Theory of Computing* (1990). DOI: 10.1137/S0097539793244708. 499

R. Impagliazzo, V. Kabanets, and A. Wigderson. 2001. In search of an easy witness: Exponential time vs. probabilistic polynomial time. In *16th IEEE Conference on Computational Complexity*, pp. 2–12. DOI: 10.1016/S0022-0000(02)00024-7. 506

R. Impagliazzo, R. Jaiswal, V. Kabanets, and A. Wigderson. 2010. Uniform direct product theorems: Simplified, optimized, and derandomized. *SIAM Journal on Computing*, 39(4): 1637–1665. DOI: 10.1.1.155.1258. 505

R. Impagliazzo and S. Rudich. 1989. Limits on the provable consequences of one-way permutations. In *21st ACM Symposium on the Theory of Computing*, pp. 44–61. Also presented in *CRYPTO'88*. DOI: 10.1145/73007.73012. 505, 506

R. Impagliazzo and A. Wigderson. 1997. P=BPP if E requires exponential circuits: Derandomizing the XOR Lemma. In *29th ACM Symposium on the Theory of Computing*, pp. 220–229. DOI: 10.1145/258533.258590. 499

J. Kilian. 1992. A note on efficient zero-knowledge proofs and arguments. In *24th ACM Symposium on the Theory of Computing*, pp. 723–732. DOI: 10.1145/129712.129782. 503

D. E. Knuth. 1981. *The Art of Computer Programming*, Vol. 2 (*Seminumerical Algorithms*). Addison-Wesley Publishing Company, Inc., 1969 (first edition) and 1981 (second edition). 498, 513

L. A. Levin. 1986. Average case complete problems. *SIAM Journal on Computing*, 15: 285–286. DOI: 10.1007/978-1-4612-4808-8_26. 505

M. Li and P. Vitanyi. 1993. *An Introduction to Kolmogorov Complexity and Its Applications*. Springer Verlag. 506

C. Lund, L. Fortnow, H. Karloff, and N. Nisan. 1992. Algebraic methods for interactive proof systems. *Journal of the ACM*, 39(4): 859–868. Preliminary version in *31st IEEE Symposium on Foundations of Computer Science*, 1990. DOI: 10.1145/146585.146605. 519, 521

R. Merkle. 1979. *Secrecy, Authentication, and Public Key Systems*. Ph.D. dissertation, Department of Electrical Engineering, Stanford University. 503

N. Nisan. 1991. Pseudorandom bits for constant depth circuits. *Combinatorica*, 11(1): 63–70. DOI: /10.1007/BF01375474. 512

N. Nisan. 1992. Pseudorandom generators for space bounded computation. *Combinatorica*, 12(4): 449–461. Preliminary version in *22nd ACM Symposium on the Theory of Computing*, 1990. 500, 512

N. Nisan. 1994. $\mathcal{RL} \subseteq \mathcal{SC}$. *Computational Complexity*, 4: 1–11. Preliminary version in *24th ACM Symposium on the Theory of Computing*, 1992. 512

N. Nisan and A. Wigderson. 1994. Hardness vs randomness. *Journal of Computer and System Science*, 49(2): 149–167. Preliminary version in *29th IEEE Symposium on Foundations of Computer Science*, 1988. DOI: 10.1016/S0022-0000(05)80043-1. 499, 512

N. Nisan and D. Zuckerman. 1996. Randomness is linear in space. *Journal of Computer and System Science*, 52(1): 43–52. Preliminary version in *25th ACM Symposium on the Theory of Computing*, 1993. DOI: 10.1006/jcss.1996.0004. 500, 512

J. Pollard. 1978. Monte Carlo methods for index computations (mod p). *Mathmatics of Computation*, 32: 918–924. DOI: 10.1090/S0025-5718-1978-0491431-9. 503

A.R. Razborov and S. Rudich. 1997. Natural proofs. *Journal of Computer and System Science*, 55(1): 24–35. Preliminary version in *26th ACM Symposium on the Theory of Computing*, 1994. DOI: 10.1006/jcss.1997.1494. 516

O. Reingold, G. Rothblum, and R. Rothblum. 2016. Constant-round interactive proofs for delegating computation. In *48th ACM Symposium on the Theory of Computing*, pp. 49–62. DOI: 10.1145/2897518.2897652. 522

O. Reingold, L. Trevisan, and S. Vadhan. 2004. Notions of reducibility between cryptographic primitives. *1st Theory of Cryptography Conference*, pp. 1–20. DOI: 10.1007/978-3-540-24638-1_1. 506

A. Shamir. 1992. IP = PSPACE. *Journal of the ACM*, 39(4): 869–877. Preliminary version in *31st IEEE Symposium on Foundations of Computer Science*, 1990. DOI: 10.1145/146585.146609. 519

L. Trevisan. 2001. Extractors and pseudorandom generators. *Journal of the ACM*, 48(4): 860–879. Preliminary version in *31st ACM Symposium on the Theory of Computing*, 1999. DOI: 10.1145/502090.502099. 512

S. Vadhan. 2012. *Pseudorandomness*. Foundations and Trends in TCS, vol.7 (1–3), NOW publishers. 508

L. G. Valiant. 1984. A theory of the learnable. *Communications of the ACM*, 27(11): 1134–1142. 516

A. C. Yao. 1982. Theory and application of trapdoor functions. In *23rd IEEE Symposium on Foundations of Computer Science*, pp. 80–91. DOI: 10.1109/SFCS.1982.45. 498, 499, 505, 507

On Some Noncryptographic Works of Goldwasser and Micali

Oded Goldreich

While this book focuses on the contributions of Goldwasser and Micali to cryptography, their contributions to other areas of computer science are immense too. In particular, while the original works reproduced in this book were all motivated by cryptographic considerations and made significant contributions to the foundations of cryptopgraphy, all of them have had a tremendous influence also outside of cryptography. In fact, Chapter 18 traces the influences that these works have had on complexity theory, but the story does not end there.

A different part of the story refers to works of Goldwasser and Micali that are not naturally classified as belonging to cryptography. The current chapter endeavors to briefly review some of these works.[1] For each of the selected works, we shall reproduce the original abstract, and make a few additional comments about the work.

19.1 An $O(\sqrt{|V|} \cdot |E|)$-time Algorithm for Finding Maximum Matching in General Graphs

The work of Micali and Vazirani [1980] still holds the record for the fastest algorithm known for finding a maximum matching in general graphs, which is one of the most classical problems in graph algorithms [Even 1979]. (For a brief historical account of the problem, the interested reader is referred to Micali and Vazirani

---

1. The works of Goldreich and Goldwasser [2000] and Goldwasser, Kalai, and Rothblum [Goldwasser et al. 2015] were omitted from our selection since they are covered by other surveys in this book (see Chapters 21 and 24, respectively).

[1980].) The time bound of this algorithm (i.e., $O(\sqrt{|V|} \cdot |E|)$) matches the bound for the bipartite case [Hopcroft and Karp 1973], which is considerably simpler. The source of difficulty is the complex "blossom structure" introduced by Edmonds [1965]. The abstract of the conference version of Micali and Vazirani [1980] reads as follows:

> In this paper we present an $O(\sqrt{|V|} \cdot |E|)$ algorithm for finding a maximum matching in general graphs. This algorithm works in 'phases'. In each phase a maximal set of disjoint minimum length augmenting paths is found, and the existing matching is increased along these paths.
>
> Our contribution consists in devising a special way of handling blossoms, which enables an $O(|E|)$ implementation of a phase. In each phase, the algorithm grows Breadth First Search trees at all unmatched vertices. When it detects the presence of a blossom, it does not 'shrink' the blossom immediately. Instead, it delays the shrinking in such a way that the first augmenting path found is of minimum length. Furthermore, it achieves the effect of shrinking a blossom by a special labeling procedure which enables it to find an augmenting path through a blossom quickly.

While the original publication [Micali and Vazirani 1980] provided a detailed description of the algorithm, it did not provide its analysis, and the authors' intentions of publishing a full analysis at a later stage never materialized. A full analysis, which is based on new graph-theoretic structural facts and a revised definition of blossoms, has been provided by Vazirani [2014]. Alternative algorithms meeting the same time bound as Micali and Vazirani [1980] have appeared subsequently to it (see, e.g., Gabow [2017]).

19.2 Certifying Almost All Primes Using Elliptic Curves

The work of Goldwasser and Kilian [1999] predated the deterministic primality testers of Agrawal et al. [2004] by almost two decades. As the following abstract states, at the time, primality testing were either randomized or relied on unproven conjectures. The randomized tests place the set of primes in co$\mathcal{RP}$; that is, they always rule that a prime is a prime, but they may rule with small probability that a composite number is a prime. The randomized procedure provided by Goldwasser and Kilian [1999] efficiently generates (efficiently and deterministically verifiable) certificates of primality, which always vouches that a prime number is indeed a prime, for almost all primes. Indeed, on some primes, the procedure may always fail to produce a certificate, but it never generates false "certificates" for composite numbers. In some sense, this work asserts that the set of primes is in "average-case

$\mathcal{RP}$" (or "typical $\mathcal{RP}$"). The abstract of the conference version of Goldwasser and Kilian [1999] reads as follows:

> This paper presents a new probabilistic primality test. Upon termination the test outputs "composite" or "prime", alone with a short proof of correctness, which can be verified in deterministic polynomial time. The test is different from the tests of Miller [M], Solovay-Strassen [SS], and Rabin [R] in that its assertions of primality are certain, rather than being correct with high probability or dependent on an unproven assumption.
>
> The test terminates in expected polynomial time on all but at most an exponentially vanishing fraction of the inputs of length k, for every k. This result implies:
>
> - There exist an infinite set of primes which can be recognized in expected polynomial time.
> - Large certified primes can be generated in expected polynomial time.
>
> Under a very plausible condition on the distribution of primes in "small" intervals, the proposed algorithm can be shown to run in expected polynomial time on every input. This condition is implied by Cramer's conjecture.
>
> The methods employed are from the theory of elliptic cures over finite fields.

The starting point of this work is Pratt's demonstration [Pratt 1975] that the set of primes is in $\mathcal{NP}$—that is, the fact that there exist (efficiently verifiable) certificates of primality, albeit these certificates may not be easy to find. This is the case, because these certificates are defined recursively such that the certificate for a prime P consists of a generator G of $\mathbb{Z}_P^*$ (i.e., a primitive element modulo P), the prime factorization of $P-1$, and certificates for primality for each of its prime factors. The prime factorization is used to verify that G has (multiplicative) order $P-1$ (in $\mathbb{Z}_P^*$), which in turn implies that P must be a prime.

Specifically, a valid certificate has the form $((P_1, e_1, C_1), \ldots, (P_t, e_t, C_t), G)$ such that $P-1 = \prod_{i=1}^{t} P_i^{e_i}$, the order of G in $\mathbb{Z}_P^*$ is $P-1$ (i.e., $G^{P-1} \equiv 1 \pmod{P}$ but $G^{(P-1)/P_i} \not\equiv 1 \pmod{P}$ for each i), and C_i is a certificante for primality of P_i. The validity of this certificate relies on the fact that G may have order $P-1$ in $\mathbb{Z}_P^*$ if and only if P is a prime. More abstractly, primes P yield groups of predetermined order, denoted $\text{ord}(P)$, whereas composite numbers yield groups of a different order (i.e., if P is composite, then $|\mathbb{Z}_P| \neq \text{ord}(P) = P-1$). The problem with generating such certificates is that it calls for factoring $P-1$, which seems hard.

Suppose, instead, that given a prime P and random choices ω, we can define a group $R_{P,\omega}$, of order $\text{ord}(P, \omega) = P \pm o(P)$ such that the function ord and the group operation are easy to compute. If we can efficiently generate (possibly at random) an element of order $\text{ord}(P, \omega)$ in that group, and if for composite P the "order" of the "structure" $R_{P,\omega}$ disagrees with $\text{ord}(P, \omega)$, then the foregoing reasoning would apply here too. The benefit is that, now, generating a certificate for P calls for factoring $\text{ord}(P, \omega)$ rather than factoring $P - 1$, and if $\text{ord}(P, \cdot)$ is random enough then we are in business. Specifically, if $\text{ord}(P, \cdot)$ is uniformly distributed in a sufficiently large interval around P, then we can factor $\text{ord}(P, \cdot)$ often enough, since in such a case with probability at least $\Omega(1/\log P)$, it holds that $\text{ord}(P, \cdot) = 2Q$ for a prime Q. This is essentially what happens when using (suitably) random elliptic curves mod P, and the complication arise because the relevant interval has size $\sqrt{P}$ (rather than, say, $P/\text{poly}(\log P)$).

Hence, the reviewed work asserted that the set of primes is in "average-case $\mathcal{RP}$" (or "typical $\mathcal{RP}$"), and this begged the challenge of showing that the set of primes is actually in $\mathcal{RP}$. The challenge was met by Adleman and Huang [1992]. Fifteen years later, Agrawal, Kayal, and Saxena [Agrawal et al. 2004] showed that the set of primes is actually in $\mathcal{P}$.

19.3 Private Coins versus Public Coins in Interactive Proof Systems

The work of Goldwasser and Sipser [1989] predated the discovery of the vast power of interactive proof systems, and, in particular, the $\mathcal{IP} = \mathcal{PSPACE}$ theorem [Lund et al. 1992, Shamir 1992]. The starting point of [Goldwasser and Sipser 1989] is the fact that Babai [1985] defined Arthur–Merlin games as a restricted form of interactive proof systems, which were defined before by Goldwasser, Micali, and Rackoff [Goldwasser et al. 1989], where the restriction is that the verifier is only allowed to make uniformly selected queries (a.k.a use public coins). This difference is not surprising given that Goldwasser, Micali, and Rackoff sought to capture the most general notion of a proof system (with efficient verification) [Goldwasser et al. 1989], whereas Babai sought a minimal extension of the class $\mathcal{NP}$ (in order to place some specific computational problem in it) [Babai 1985]. Surprisingly, Goldwasser and Sipser [1989] showed that the aforementioned restriction does not weaken the expressive power of the system; put differently, asking random questions is as good as asking cleverly selected questions (i.e., questions that are the result of an arbitrary probabilistic polynomial-time computation, whose coins are not revealed to the prover but may be re-used when examining the prover's answers). The abstract of the conference version of Goldwasser and Kilian [1999] reads as follows:

> An interactive proof system is a method by which one party of unlimited resources, called the *prover*, can convince a party of limited resources,

called the *verifier*, of the truth of a proposition. The verifier may toss coins, ask repeated questions of the prover, and run efficient tests upon the prover's responses before deciding whether to be convinced. This extends the familiar proof system implicit in the notion of NP in that there the verifier may not toss coins or speak, but only listen and verify. Interactive proof systems may not yield proof in the strict mathematical sense: the "proofs" are probabilistic with an exponentially small, though non-zero chance of error.

We consider two notions of interactive proof systems. One, defined by Goldwasser, Micali and Rackoff [Goldwasser et al. 1989] permits the verifier a coin that can be tossed in *private*, i.e., a secret source of randomness. The second, due to Babai, [B] requires that the outcome of the verifier's coin tosses be *public* and thus accessible to the prover.

Our main result is that these two systems are equivalent in power with respect to language recognition.

The notion of interactive proof system may be seen to yield a probabilistic analog to NP much as BPP is the probabilistic analog to P. We define the *probabilistic, nonderministic, polynomial time Turing machine* and show that it is also equivalent in power to these systems.

We stress that the result actually shown is stronger: The authors showed that any r-round interactive proof system can be emulated by an $(r + 3)$-round interactive proof system of the public-coin type. We comment that the mere fact that interactive proof system can be emulated by interactive proof system of the public-coin type follows from the subsequent demonstration that $\mathcal{IP} = \mathcal{PSPACE}$, because the original demonstration actually shows that any set in $\mathcal{PSPACE}$ has a *public-coin* interactive proof system [Lund et al. 1992, Shamir 1992] (whereas $\mathcal{IP} \subseteq \mathcal{PSPACE}$, where $\mathcal{IP}$ denotes the class of sets having (general) interactive proof systems).

The fact that private coins are of no real help came as a surprise, especially in light of the interactive proof system presented around the same time for graph nonisomorphism, since that proof system makes essential use of private coins [Goldreich et al. 1991]. In that proof system, the verifier selects at random one of the two graphs, sends a randomly permuted (or relabeled) version of it to the prover, and accepts if and only if the prover identifies correctly which graph was chosen. In this specific case, the public-coin proof system derived by Goldwasser and Sipser [1989] amounts to proving a lower bound on the size of automorphism group of the graph consisting of both graphs (and an upper bound on the size of automorphism groups of each of the individual graphs).[2]

---

2. An upper bound on the size of automorphism group of a graph G follows by a lower bound on the number of different graphs that are obtained by relabeling the vertices of G.

In general, a key ingredient of the construction of Goldwasser and Sipser [1989] is a public-coin protocol, known as the *lower bound protocol*, that allows one party to prove to another that the size of a set exceeds some given number (provided that the set is in $\mathcal{NP}$).[3] This protocol, which is closely related to a "random selection" protocol, was used extensively in subsequent works.

19.4 An Optimal Randomized Protocol for Synchronous Byzantine Agreement

The work of Feldman and Micali [1997] presents a constant-round randomized Byzantine agreement protocol for a synchronous communication model with private channels. As in Ben-Or et al. [1988b], the private-channel model allows to abstract away intractability assumptions and cryptographic tools, although implementing this clean model on a network of insecure channels does require such assumptions and tools. The protocol improved over a prior protocol of Bracha [1987] that used logarithmically many rounds (and intractability assumptions). The conference version of Feldman and Micali [1997] had no abstract, and the abstract of the journal version reads as follows:

> Broadcasting guarantees the recipient of a message that everyone else has received the same message. This guarantee no longer exists in a setting in which all communication is person-to-person and some of the people involved are untrustworthy: though he may claim to send the same message to everyone, an untrustworthy sender may send different messages to different people. In such a setting, Byzantine agreement offers the "best alternative" to broadcasting. Thus far, however, reaching Byzantine agreement has required either many rounds of communication (i.e., messages had to be sent back and forth a number of times that grew with the size of the network) or the help of some external trusted party.
>
> In this paper, for the standard communication model of synchronous networks in which each pair of processors is connected by a private communication line, we exhibit a protocol that, in probabilistic polynomial time and without relying on any external trusted party, reaches Byzantine agreement in an expected constant number of rounds and in the worst natural fault model. In fact, our protocol successfully tolerates that up to

---

3. In the general case, when claiming a lower bound of N, the prover is confined to an $1/N$ fraction of the original set. Hence, if the set is smaller than N, then the prover may be confined to an empty subset of it.

1/3 of the processors in the network may deviate from their prescribed instructions in an arbitrary way, cooperate with each other, and perform arbitrarily long computations.

Our protocol effectively demonstrates the power of randomization and zero-knowledge computation against errors. Indeed, it proves that "privacy" (a fundamental ingredient of one of our primitives), even when is not a desired goal in itself (as for the Byzantine agreement problem), can be a crucial tool for achieving correctness.

Our protocol also introduces three new primitives—graded broadcast, graded verifiable secret sharing, and oblivious common coin—that are of independent interest and may be effectively used in more practical protocols than ours.

Byzantine agreement, introduced by Pease, Shostak, and Lamport [Pease et al. 1980], is considered the archetypical problem of processor coordination, which is a central theme in distributed computing [Lynch 1996]. Here, we consider randomized protocols for Byzantine agreement in the synchronous model, since those bypass the linear (in the number of parties) lower bounds on the round complexity of deterministic protocols in this model.[4] The protocol of Feldman and Micali [1997] runs for a constant number of rounds and satisfies the following conditions: (1) In *each* possible execution, each of the parties either terminates with the same value v or terminates with failure, and if all honest parties enter with the same value, then v equals this value; and (2) with constant probability, over all possible executions, no party terminates with failure.

We comment that the private channels used by Feldman and Micali [1997] are essential for a constant-round randomized Byzantine agreement protocol in the full-fledged malicious model considered by Feldman and Micali [1997]: In fact, even in weaker (adaptive) models with no private channels, a number of rounds that grows roughly as the square root of the number of parties is necessary [Bar-Joseph and Ben-Or 1998]. On the other hand, the full-fledged without private channels does allow for randomized Byzantine agreement protocols with a sublinear number of rounds [Chor and Coan 1985].[5]

---

4. In the asynchronous model, deterministic protocols face an impossibility result, whereas randomized protocols do exist. But our focus here is on the synchronous model.

5. The models considered in Chor and Coan [1985], Feldman and Micali [1997], and Bar-Joseph and Ben-Or [1998] are *adaptive* in the sense that an external adversary may adaptively select parties to corrupt during the execution of the protocol (and control their actions). In contrast, in *nonadaptive* models, the faulty parties are determine (arbitrarily) before the execution starts. A

19.5 PCPs and the Hardness of Approximating Cliques

The work of Feige, Goldwasser, Lovász, Safra, and Szegedy [Feige et al. 1996] pioneered the study of (what become later known as) "probabilistically checkable proofs" and its relation to the study of approximation problems. A *probabilistically checkable proof system* for a set S is defined via a probabilistic polynomial-time oracle machine, called a *verifier*, that satisfies the following *completeness* and *soundness* conditions: For every $x \in S$ there exists a proof π such that $\Pr[V^\pi(x) = 1] = 1$, whereas for every $x \notin S$ and every π it holds that $\Pr[V^\pi(x) = 1] \leq 1/2$. For functions $r, q : \mathbb{N} \to \mathbb{N}$, we let $\mathcal{PCP}[r, q]$ denote the class of sets that have a (non-adaptive) probabilistically checkable proof system of randomness complexity r and query complexity q. The reviewed work [Feige et al. 1996] shows that $\mathcal{NP} \subseteq \mathcal{PCP}[\widetilde{O}(\log), \widetilde{O}(\log)]$, which is a "scale down" of a prior result [Babai et al. 1991a] asserting that $\mathcal{NEXP} = \mathcal{PCP}[\text{poly}, \text{poly}]$. Feige, Goldwasser, Lovász, Safra, and Szegedy [Feige et al. 1996] also showed that deciding sets in $\mathcal{PCP}[r, q]$ is reducible in $\text{poly}(2^{t \cdot (r+q)})$-time to approximating the largest clique in a $2^{t \cdot (r+q)}$-vertex graph up to a factor of 2^t. The abstract of the conference version of Feige et al. [1996] reads as follows:

> We consider the computational complexity of approximating $\omega(G)$, the size of the largest clique in a graph G. We show that
>
> 1. If there is an approximation algorithm in **P** for $\omega(G)$ within some constant factor, then $\mathbf{NP} \subseteq DTIME(n^{O(\log \log n)})$.
>
> 2. If there is an approximation algorithm in $\widetilde{\mathbf{P}}$ $(= \cup_{k>0} DTIME(n^{\log^k n}))$ for $\omega(G)$ within a factor of $2^{\log^{1-\epsilon} n}$ (for some $\epsilon > 0$), then $\mathbf{NP} \subseteq \widetilde{\mathbf{P}}$.
>
> We conclude that if such approximation procedures exist, then EXPTIME = NEXPTIME and $\mathbf{N\widetilde{P}} = \widetilde{\mathbf{P}}$.
>
> This work uses the theorem of Babai, Fortnow and Lund that NEXP-TIME has multi-prover interactive proofs. For our purpose, we scale down [BFL90]'s protocol to the NP level, and improve its efficiency. Of independent interest is our simpler proof of correctness for the multi-linearity test.

We mention that independently of Feige et al. [1996], Babai, Fortnow, Levin, and Szegedy [Babai et al. 1991b] showed that $\mathcal{NP} = \mathcal{PCP}[O(\log), \text{poly}(\log)]$. Their results were stated in terms of what became later known as PCPs for promixity (cf., e.g., Ben-Sasson et al. [2006]); specifically, they showed a PCP for proximity for NP-complete sets (which encode standard NP-sets) in which the verifier runs in polylogarithmic time.

---

randomized Byzantine agreement protocols with a logarithmic number of rounds was later shown in the non-adaptive malicious model with no private channels [Ben-Or et al. 2006].

Subsequent work of Arora, Lund, Motwani, Safra, Sudan, and Szegedy [Arora and Safra 1998, Arora et al. 1998] resulted in the celebrated PCP theorem asserting that $\mathcal{NP} = \mathcal{PCP}[O(\log), O(1)]$. A vast amount of research followed. Most of it has been directed toward extending and utilizing the *PCP-to-inapproximabilty connection*, often while optimizing some parameter of the PCP system that governs the quality of the said connection. This type of research is the focus of Chapter 22. In addition, much research has been devoted to exploring various aspects of the PCP Theorem and providing various versions of it, while envisioning these systems as being actually applied to verify the correctness of computations. In such settings, the proof length seems a dominant parameter (and the interested reader is referred to Goldreich [2017, Chapter 13]).

We conclude this review with two comments. First, we note that employing the PCP-to-inapproximabilty connection may call for optimizing parameters significantly differently than when seeking to apply the PCP system for actual verification. For example, the PCP-to-clique connection used in Feige et al. [1996] motivated the authors to minimize the value of $r + q$ (using the setting $r(n) = q(n) = \widetilde{O}(\log n)$), whereas the application to actual verification motivated the authors of Babai et al. [1991b] to minimize r first and only then minimize q (using the setting $r(n) = (1 + \epsilon) \cdot \log n$ for arbitrary small constant $\epsilon > 0$, and $q(n) = \text{poly}(\log n)$).[6] Second, we mention that Babai et al. [1991b] and Feige et al. [1996] used the formulation of probabilistically checkable proofs, which was shown by Fortnow, Rompel, and Sipser [Fortnow et al. 1988] to be equivalent to the formulation of multi-prover interactive proofs, which in turn was introduced by Ben-Or, Goldwasser, Kilian, and Wigderson [Ben-Or et al. 1988a]. However, the aforementioned works [Fortnow et al. 1988, Babai et al. 1991b, Feige et al. 1996] refer to these proof systems by the generic term "oracle machine" (which refers to the syntax of the corresponding verifier). The term "probabilistically checkable proofs" was introduced in Arora and Safra [1998], and used ever since, although the term "locally verifiable (or testable) proofs" might have been much more appropriate (cf. Goldreich [2017, Section 13.2.2]).

19.6 Computationally Sound Proofs

The work of Micali [2000] presented the notion of computationally sound proof systems with relatively efficient proving procedures, termed *CS-proofs*. The notion

---

6. The point is that the proof length is closely related to the randomness complexity: Specifically, a PCP of randomness complexity r and query complexity q uses proofs of ("effective") length at most $2^r \cdot q$.

of computationally sound proofs (a.k.a. arguments) was proposed before by Brassard, Chaum, and Crépeau [Brassard et al. 1988], but in CS-proofs it is coupled with a relative-efficiency requirement (which refers to the completeness condition). Specifically, it is required that the complexity of proving valid statements be (polynomially) related to the complexity of determining the validity of the statement by one's own (i.e., without a proof). The abstract of the conference version of Micali [2000] reads as follows:

> This paper put forward a computationally-based notion of proof and explores its implications to computation at large.
>
> In particular, given a random oracle or a suitable cryptographic assumption, we show that every computation possesses a short certificate vouching its correctness, and that under a cryptographic assumption, any program for a NP-complete problem is checkable in polynomial time.
>
> In addition, our work provides the beginnings of a theory of computational complexity that is based on "individual inputs" rather than languages.

The construction presented by Micali [2000] is similar to a previous construction of Kilian [1992], but the fact that (unlike in Brassard et al. [1988] and Kilian [1992]) the notion of computational-soundness and the construction were de-coupled from zero-knowledge aspects helped focus attention on the notion and the construction.

Micali [2000] also highlights the fact that CS-proof remain meaningful even if $\mathcal{P} = \mathcal{NP}$ and/or also when applied to decision problems in $\mathcal{P}$. Indeed, CS-proofs are related to doubly efficient arguments, which are the computationally-sound variant of doubly efficient interactive proof systems, which were introduced a decade and a half later by Goldwasser, Kalai, and Rothblum [Goldwasser et al. 2015].

19.7 Property Testing and its Connection to Learning and Approximation

The work of Goldreich, Goldwasser, and Ron [Goldreich et al. 1998] initiated a general study of property testing, while focusing on testing of graph properties (in the adjacency matrix representation). Property testing emerged, implicitly and before, in the work of Blum, Luby, and Rubinfeld [Blum et al. 1993]. The earlier line of work, focusing on algebraic properties, culminating in the work of Rubinfeld and Sudan [1996], where the approach was abstracted and captured by the notion of a *robust characterization*, which corresponds to a special type of testers (i.e., non-adaptive testers of one-sided error probability). The work of Goldreich, Goldwasser, and Ron [Goldreich et al. 1998] advocated viewing property testing as a new type of computational problems, rather than as a tool toward program checking [Blum and Kannan 1989] (as viewed in Blum et al. [1993]) or toward the construction of PCP systems (as in [Babai et al. 1991a, Babai et al. 1991], and Feige et al. [1996]). The abstract of the conference version of Goldreich et al. [1998] reads as follows:

> We study the question of determining whether an unknown function has a particular property or is ϵ-far from any function with that property. A property testing algorithm is given a sample of the value of the function on instances drawn according to some distribution, and possibly may query the function on instances of its choice.
>
> First, we establish some connections between property testing and problems in learning theory. Next, we focus on testing graph properties, and devise algorithms to test whether a graph has properties such as being k-colorable or having a ρ-clique (clique of density ρ w.r.t the vertex set). Our graph property testing algorithms are probabilistic and make assertions which are correct with high probability, utilizing only poly$(1/\epsilon)$ edge-queries into the graph, where ϵ is the distance parameter. Moreover, the property testing algorithms can be used to efficiently (i.e., in time linear in the number of vertices) construct partitions of the graph which correspond to the property being tested, if it holds for the input graph.

As started in the original abstract, the main results of Goldreich et al. [1998] are testers for a variety of graph partition problems all having query complexity that is independent of the size of the graph (but rather depending only on the proximity parameter).

In general, instances of the testing problems were viewed as descriptions of actual objects—that is, objects that arise from some application. Consequently, the representation of these objects as functions became a nonobvious step, which required justification. For example, in the case of testing graph properties, the starting point is the graph itself, and its representation as a function is an auxiliary conceptual step. In Goldreich et al. [1998] graphs are represented by their adjacency relation (or matrix), which is not overly redundant when dense graphs are concerned, but in some subsequent works other alternatives were considered (see Goldreich [2017], Chapters 9–10).

As hinted upfront, the notion of a tester presented in Goldreich et al. [1998] allows for adaptive queries and two-sided error probability, while viewing non-adaptivity and one-sided error probability as special cases. While the bulk of their work [Goldreich et al. 1998, Sections 5–10] focuses on testing graph properties, the paper also contains general results (see Goldreich et al. [1998, Sections 3–4]) and its definitional treatment (see Goldreich et al. [1998, Section 2]) foresaw some directions that were pursued only in subsequent works. For more details on property testing see a recent textbook [Goldreich 2017].

19.8 Pseudo-Deterministic Algorithms

The starting point of the work of Gat and Goldwasser [2011] is the observation that probabilistic algorithms that solve search problem may output different solutions in different executions. That is, even if on input x the algorithm outputs a correct solution with high probability (say, with probability at least 2/3), it may be that no solution appears as output with significant probability (let alone with probability at least 2/3). Hence, their paper [Gat and Goldwasser 2011] initiates a study of search problems that may be solved in probabilistic polynomial-time by algorithms that, on each input x, output the same solution with probability at least 2/3. The abstract of their paper reads as follows:

> In this paper we introduce a new type of probabilistic search algorithm, which we call the *Bellagio* algorithm: a probabilistic algorithm which is guaranteed to run in expected polynomial time, and to produce a correct and *unique* solution with high probability. We argue the applicability of such algorithms for the problems of verifying delegated computation in a distributed setting, and for generating cryptographic public-parameters and keys in distributed settings. We exhibit several examples of Bellagio algorithms for problems for which no deterministic polynomial time algorithms are known. In particular, we show such algorithms for:
>
> - Finding a unique generator for $\mathbb{Z}_p$, when p is a prime of the form $kq + 1$ for q is prime and $k = \text{polylog}(p)$. The algorithm runs in expected polynomial in $\log p$ time.
>
> - Finding a unique q'th non-residues of $\mathbb{Z}_p$ for any prime divisor q of $p - 1$, extending Lenstra's algorithm for finding unique quadratic non-residue of $\mathbb{Z}_p$. The algorithm runs in expected polynomial time in $\log p$ and q. The tool we use is a new variant of the Adleman-Manders-Miller probabilistic algorithm for taking q-th roots, which outputs a unique solution to the input equations and runs in expected polynomial time in $\log p$ and q.
>
> - Given a multi-variate polynomial $P \neq 0$, find a unique (with high probability) x such that $P(x) \neq 0$. Alternatively you may think of this as producing a unique polynomial time verifiable certificate of inequality of polynomials.

More generally, we show a necessary and sufficient condition for the existence of a Bellagio Algorithm for relation R: R has a Bellagio algorithm if and only if it is deterministically reducible to some decision problem in BPP.

In later works (e.g., Goldwasser and Grossman [2017]) such algorithms were called *pseudodeterministic*, and the solution that they output, with high probability, was called *canonical*.

We stress that although most research in complexity theory refers to decision problems, search problems are at least as important. Recall that search problems are associated with binary relations, $R \subseteq \{0, 1\}^* \times \{0, 1\}^*$, and each element of $R(x) \stackrel{\text{def}}{=} \{y \in \{0, 1\}^* : (x, y) \in R\}$ is called a ***solution to*** x (and if $R(x) = \emptyset$ then $\perp$ is considered the only solution). Saying that R can be solved by a randomized algorithm A means that, for every x that has a solution, it holds that $\Pr[A(x) \in R(x)] \geq 2/3$ (and $\Pr[A(x) = \perp] \geq 2/3$ if $R(x) = \emptyset$). Algorithm A is called ***pseudodeterministic*** if for every x there exists a (***canonical***) solution s_x such that $\Pr[A(x) = s_x] \geq 2/3$.

The foregoing result of Gat and Goldwasser [2011] asserts that R can be solved by a pseudodeterministic polynomial-time algorithm if and only if solving R is deterministically reducible in polynomial time to some *decision problem* in $\mathcal{BPP}$. In contrast, it was shown in Goldreich [2011] that for every R that is recognizable in probabilistic polynomial time, solving R is deterministically reducible in polynomial-time to some *promise problem* in the promise class corresponding to $\mathcal{BPP}$. Hence, the difference between general randomized algorithms and pseudodeterministic algorithms is reflected in the difference between standard complexity classes (which refer to decision problems) and classes of promise problems.

We mention that the study of pseudodeterministic algorithms was recently extended to $\mathcal{RNC}$; in particular, finding perfect matchings in bipartite graphs (a problem known to be in $\mathcal{RNC}$ (but not in $\mathcal{NC}$)) was shown to have a pseudodeterministic NC algorithm [Goldwasser and Grossman 2017].

References

L. M. Adleman and M. Huang. 1992. *Primality Testing and Abelian Varieties Over Finite Fields.* Lecture Notes in Computer Science vol. 1512. Springer. Preliminary version in *19th ACM Symposium on the Theory of Computing*, 1987. 530

M. Agrawal, N. Kayal, and N. Saxena. 2004. PRIMES is in P. *Annals of Mathematics*, 160(2): 781–793. DOI: 10.4007/annals.2004.160.781. 528, 530

S. Arora, C. Lund, R. Motwani, M. Sudan, and M. Szegedy. 1998. Proof verification and intractability of approximation problems. *Journal of the ACM*, 45: 501–555. Preliminary version in *33rd FOCS*, 1992. DOI: 10.1145/278298.278306. 535

S. Arora and S. Safra. 1998. Probabilistic checkable proofs: A new characterization of NP. *Journal of the ACM*, 45: 70–122. Preliminary version in *33rd FOCS*, 1992. DOI: 10.1145/273865.273901. 535

L. Babai. 1985. Trading group theory for randomness. In *17th ACM Symposium on the Theory of Computing*, pp. 421–429. DOI: 10.1145/22145.22192. 530

L. Babai, L. Fortnow, and C. Lund. 1991a. Non-deterministic exponential time has two-prover interactive protocols. *Computational Complexity*, 1(1): 3–40. Preliminary version in *31st FOCS*, 1990. 534, 537

L. Babai, L. Fortnow, L. Levin, and M. Szegedy. 1991b. Checking computations in polylogarithmic time. In *23rd ACM Symposium on the Theory of Computing*, pp. 21–31. DOI: 0.1145/103418.103428. 534, 535

Z. Bar-Joseph and M. Ben-Or. 1998. A tight lower bound for randomized synchronous consensus. In *17th ACM Symposium on Principles of Distributed Computing*, pp. 193–199. DOI: 10.1145/277697.277733. 533

M. Ben-Or, S. Goldwasser, J. Kilian, and A. Wigderson. 1988a. Multi-prover interactive proofs: How to remove intractability. In *20th ACM Symposium on the Theory of Computing*, pp. 113–131. DOI: 10.1145/62212.62223. 535

M. Ben-Or, S. Goldwasser, and A. Wigderson. 1988b. Completeness theorems for non-cryptographic fault-tolerant distributed computation. In *20th ACM Symposium on the Theory of Computing*, pp. 1–10. DOI: 10.1145/62212.62213. 532

M. Ben-Or, E. Pavlov, and V. Vaikuntanathan. 2006. Byzantine agreement in the full-information model in $O(\log n)$ rounds. In *38th ACM Symposium on the Theory of Computing*, pp. 179–186. DOI: 10.1145/1132516.1132543. 534

E. Ben-Sasson, O. Goldreich, P. Harsha, M. Sudan, and S. Vadhan. 2006. Robust PCPs of proximity, shorter PCPs, and applications to coding. *SIAM Journal on Computing*, 36(4): 889–974. Extended abstract in *36th ACM Symposium on the Theory of Computing, 2004*. DOI: 10.1137/S0097539705446810. 534

M. Blum and S. Kannan. 1989. Designing programs that check their work. In *21st ACM Symposium on the Theory of Computing*, pp. 86–97. DOI: 10.1145/73007.73015. 537

M. Blum, M. Luby, and R. Rubinfeld. 1993. Self-testing/correcting with applications to numerical problems. *Journal of Computer and System Science*, 47(3): 549–595. 536, 537

G. Bracha. 1987. An O(log n) expected rounds randomized Byzantine generals protocol. *Journal of the ACM*, 34(4): 910–920. Preliminary version in *17th STOC*, 1985. DOI: 10.1145/31846.42229. 532

G. Brassard, D. Chaum, and C. Crépeau. 1988. Minimum disclosure proofs of knowledge. *Journal of Computer and System Science*, 37(2): 156–189. Preliminary version by Brassard and Crépeau in *27th FOCS*, 1986. DOI: 10.1016/0022-0000(88)90005-0. 536

B. Chor and B. A. Coan. 1985. A simple and efficient randomized Byzantine agreement algorithm. *IEEE Trans. Software Eng.*, 11(6): 531–539. Preliminary version in *4th SRDS*, 1984. DOI: 10.1109/TSE.1985.232245. 533

J. Edmonds. 1965. Paths, trees, and flowers. *Canadian Journal of Mathematics*, 17: 449–467. DOI: 10.1007/978-0-8176-4842-8_26. 528

S. Even. 1979. *Graph Algorithms*. Computer Science Press. Second edition (edited by G. Even), Cambridge University Press, 2011. 527

U. Feige, S. Goldwasser, L. Lovász, S. Safra, and M. Szegedy. 1996. Approximating clique is almost NP-complete. *Journal of the ACM*, 43: 268–292. Preliminary version in *32nd IEEE Symposium on Foundations of Computer Science*, 1991. DOI: 10.1145/226643 .226652. 534, 535, 537

P. Feldman and S. Micali. 1997. An optimal probabilistic protocol for synchronous Byzantine agreement. *SIAM Journal on Computing*, 26(4): 873–933. Preliminary version in *16th ICALP*, 1989. DOI: 10.1007/978-1-4939-2864-4_269. 532, 533

L. Fortnow, J. Rompel, and M. Sipser. 1988. On the power of multi-prover interactive protocols. In *3rd IEEE Symposium on Structure in Complexity*, pp. 156–161. See errata in *5th IEEE Symposium on Structure in Complexity*, pp. 318–319, 1990. DOI: 10.1016/0304-3975(94)90251-8. 535

H. N. Gabow. 2017. The weighted matching approach to maximum cardinality matching. *Fundamenta Informaticae*, 154(1–4): 109–130. 528

E. Gat and S. Goldwasser. 2011. Probabilistic search algorithms with unique answers and their cryptographic applications. In *Electronic Colloquium on Computational Complexity*, TR11-136. 538, 539

O. Goldreich. 2011. In a world of P = BPP. In *Studies in Complexity and Cryptography*, Lecture Notes in Computer Science vol. 6650, pp. 191–232. Springer. DOI: 10.1007/978-3-642-22670-0_20. 539

O. Goldreich. 2017. *Introduction to Property Testing*. Cambridge University Press. 535, 537, 538

O. Goldreich and S. Goldwasser. 2000. On the limits of nonapproximability of lattice problems. *Journal of Computer and System Science*, 60(3): 540–563. Preliminary version in *30th ACM Symposium on the Theory of Computing*, 1998. DOI: 10.1006/jcss.1999.1686. 527

O. Goldreich, S. Goldwasser, and D. Ron. 1998. Property testing and its connection to learning and approximation. *Journal of the ACM*, pp. 653–750. Extended abstract in *37th FOCS*, 1996. DOI: 10.1145/285055.285060. 536, 537

O. Goldreich, S. Micali, and A. Wigderson. 1991. Proofs that yield nothing but their validity, or all languages in NP have zero-knowledge proof systems. *Journal of the ACM*, 38(1): 691–729. Preliminary version in *27th FOCS*, 1986. DOI: 10.1145/116825.116852. 531

S. Goldwasser and O. Grossman. 2017. Bipartite perfect matching in pseudo-deterministic NC. In *44th ICALP*, pp. 87:1–87:13. 539

S. Goldwasser, Y. Kalai, and G. N. Rothblum. 2015. Delegating computation: Interactive proofs for muggles. *Journal of the ACM*, 62(4): 27:1–27:64. Extended abstract in *40th STOC*, pp. 113–122, 2008. DOI: 10.1145/2699436. 527, 536

S. Goldwasser and J. Kilian. 1999. Almost all primes can be quickly certified. *Journal of the ACM*, 46(4): 450–472. Preliminary version in *18th ACM Symposium on the Theory of Computing*, 1986. 528, 529, 530

S. Goldwasser, S. Micali, and C. Rackoff. 1989. The knowledge complexity of interactive proof systems. *SIAM Journal on Computing*, 18: 186–208. Preliminary version in *17th ACM Symposium on the Theory of Computing*, 1985. Earlier versions date to 1982. DOI: 10.1145/22145.22178. 530, 531

S. Goldwasser and M. Sipser. 1989. Private coins versus public coins in interactive proof systems. *Advances in Computing Research: A Research Annual*, vol. 5 (Randomness and Computation, S. Micali, editor), pp. 73–90. Extended abstract in *18th ACM Symposium on the Theory of Computing*, 1986. 530, 531, 532

J. E. Hopcroft and R. M. Karp. 1973. An $n^{5/2}$ algorithm for maximum matchings in bipartite graphs. *SIAM Journal on Computing*, 2(4): 225–231. DOI: 10.1137/0202019. 528

J. Kilian. 1992. A note on efficient zero-knowledge proofs and arguments. In *24th ACM Symposium on the Theory of Computing*, pp. 723–732. DOI: 10.1145/129712.129782. 536

N. Lynch. 1996. *Distributed Algorithms*. Morgan Kaufmann. 533

C. Lund, L. Fortnow, H. Karloff, and N. Nisan. 1992. Algebraic methods for interactive proof systems. *Journal of the ACM*, 39(4): 859–868. Preliminary version in *31st IEEE Symposium on Foundations of Computer Science*. DOI: 10.1145/146585.146605. 530, 531

S. Micali. 2000. Computationally sound proofs. *SIAM Journal on Computing*, 30(4): 1253–1298. Preliminary version in *25th FOCS*, 1994. DOI: 10.1137/S0097539795284959. 535, 536

S. Micali and V. V. Vazirani. 1980. An $O(\sqrt{|V|} \cdot |E|)$ algorithm for finding maximum matching in general graphs. In *21st IEEE Symposium on Foundations of Computer Science*, pp. 17–27. DOI: 10.1109/SFCS.1980.12. 527, 528

M. Pease, R. Shostak, and L. Lamport. 1980. Reaching agreement in the presence of faults. *Journal of the ACM*, 27(2): 228–234. DOI: 10.1145/322186.322188. 533

V. R. Pratt. 1975. Every prime has a succinct certificate. *SIAM Journal on Computing*, 4(3): 214–220. DOI: 10.1137/0204018. 529

R. Rubinfeld and M. Sudan. 1996. Robust characterization of polynomials with applications to program testing. *SIAM Journal on Computing*, 25(2): 252–271. DOI: 10.1137/S0097539793255151. 536

A. Shamir. 1992. IP = PSPACE. *Journal of the ACM*, 39(4): 869–877. Preliminary version in *31st IEEE Symposium on Foundations of Computer Science*, 1990. DOI: 10.1145/146585.146609. 530, 531

V. V. Vazirani. 2014. *A Proof of the MV Matching Algorithm*. Unpublished manuscript, 2014. Available as https://www.cc.gatech.edu/~vazirani/new-proof.pdf. (This is a revision of CoRR abs/1210.4594, 2012.) 528

Fundamentals of Fully Homomorphic Encryption

Zvika Brakerski

A homomorphic encryption scheme is one that allows computing on encrypted data without decrypting it first. In fully homomorphic encryption it is possible to apply *any* efficiently computable function to encrypted data. This chapter provides a survey on the origins, definitions, properties, constructions and uses of fully homomorphic encryption.

20.1 Homomorphic Encryption: Good, Bad, or Ugly?

In the seminal RSA cryptosystem [Rivest et al. 1978], the public key consists of a product of two primes $N = p \cdot q$ as well as an integer e, and the message space is the set of elements in $\mathbb{Z}_N^*$. Encrypting a message m involved simply raising it to the power e and taking the result modulo N, that is, $c = m^e \pmod{N}$. For the purpose of the current discussion we ignore the decryption process. It is not hard to see that the product of two ciphertexts c_1 and c_2 encrypting messages m_1 and m_2 allows us to compute the value $c_1 \cdot c_2 \pmod{N} = (m_1 m_2)^e \pmod{N}$, that is, to compute an encryption of $m_1 \cdot m_2$ without knowledge of the secret private key. Rabin's cryptosystem [Rabin 1979] exhibited similar behavior, where a product of ciphertexts corresponded to an encryption of their respective plaintexts. This behavior can be expressed in formal terms by saying that the ciphertext space and the plaintext space are *homomorphic (multiplicative) groups*. The decryption process defines the homomorphism by mapping a ciphertext to its image plaintext.

Rivest, Adleman, and Dertouzos [Rivest et al. 1978] realized the potential advantage of this property. In a time where complex computations required "buying computing cycles" from a mainframe computer maintained by an external company, one would be exposed to the danger of their private information being revealed to the vendor of computing power. However, if the computation only involves group operations on the input data, then homomorphism will allow the vendor to perform the computation on the ciphertext, rather than the plaintext, so that sensitive data is not revealed on one hand, and the heavy computational load is outsourced to the vendor on the other. Remarkably, 40 years down the line, outsourcing computation gained popularity once again with the introduction of cloud computing. Indeed, privacy in the era of the cloud is one of the most fascinating topics in modern cryptographic research. Naturally, one would like to extend homomorphism beyond group operations, and indeed [Rivest et al. 1978] put forth the question whether there exist encryption schemes that are homomorphic also with respect to *ring* (or field) operations, which would allow to perform arbitrary computation on the input data.

Alas, plain RSA and Rabin's scheme provide a very weak level of security (and indeed today they are referred to as "trapdoor functions" and not as encryption schemes; see for example, Goldreich [2001, Section 2.4.4.2]). The revolutionary work of Goldwasser and Micali [1982] on randomized encryption defined a new notion, *semantic security*, as a standard for encryption security. Since previous schemes, such as the aforementioned plain RSA and Rabin schemes, were not semantically secure, it was up to Goldwasser and Micali to present a different candidate. Indeed, they presented one based on the hardness of the quadratic residuosity problem (QR). The Goldwasser–Micali encryption scheme was again based on $N = pq$ as public key, but now each element in $\mathbb{Z}_N^*$ was only used to encrypt a single bit. Squares (a.k.a. quadratic residues) encrypt 0, and quadratic nonresidues (nonsquares with Jacobi symbol 1) encrypt 1. Note that in such a scheme, as in *any* semantically secure encryption scheme, each message is associated with a super-polynomial number of possible ciphertexts, all decrypting to the same value. Despite this significant conceptual difference, the Goldwasser–Micali encryption scheme still exhibits group homomorphism, since a product of ciphertexts will decrypt to the XOR of the plaintexts. The El Gamal scheme [El Gamal 1984] that followed soon after exhibited similar behavior, even though it was based on the hardness of a different type of problem (related to the discrete logarithm problem). A decade down the line, as *lattice-based* encryption emerged [Ajtai and Dwork 1997, Goldreich et al. 1997, Hoffstein et al. 1998], they also exhibited homomorphic properties, despite being based on a very different mathematical structure.

It turned out that homomorphic encryption (at least for groups) is abundant and one could have speculated that it is even unavoidable. As Rivest et al. [1978] showed, this can have positive implications, since it could lead to private outsourcing of computation. On the other hand, one could speculate that this property only indicates that public-key encryption schemes have too much structure. Perhaps this is a symptom of insecurity?

Consider the following scenario: Alice and Bob are bidding for some goods in an auction. Each one submits their bid in a sealed envelope, implemented using an encryption scheme. Bob is willing to pay y and he knows that Alice's bid x is much lower than y, but he does not know what it is. Bob can see Alice's sealed envelope, in the form of a ciphertext $\mathsf{Enc}(x)$. If the encryption scheme is homomorphic, then Bob can generate an encryption $\mathsf{Enc}(x + 1)$ thus creating the smallest bid to win the auction, even without learning anything about Alice's input. This demonstrates that in some situation we would like a guarantee that it is impossible to perform any alteration of the ciphertext, in particular homomorphism. This property is called *nonmalleability* [Dolev et al. 1991]. One conclusion from this example is that one should not think of homomorphism as intrinsically useful or intrinsically harmful, but rather consider the specific situation.

In this context, we mention that the aforementioned notion of semantic security is equivalent (in the public-key setting) to security under *chosen plaintext attacks* (CPA) where an attacker gets access to the encryption function but no access at all to the decryption function. In many situations one would consider stricter notions where (limited) access to the decryption function is allowed—for example, to model settings where an adversary can send "made up" ciphertexts to the decryptor and observe the decryptor's behavior upon receiving the message. This is formalized via the notion of security under chosen ciphertext attacks (CCA), and it comes in two main flavors. CCA1 is a notion that models a setting where an adversary has access to the decryption function (as oracle) before the it gets hold of the challenge ciphertext it wants to attack. CCA2 allows the adversary to access the decryption oracle even after seeing the target ciphertext (with a nondegeneracy condition that the adversary cannot use this access to decrypt the challenge itself). It is not hard to see that homomorphism (or malleability) contradict CCA2 security. However, homomorphic encryption schemes can be CCA1 secure [Cramer and Shoup 1998].

As explained above, group homomorphic encryption schemes emerged naturally from attempts for constructing public key encryption scheme. However, ring homomorphism seems much harder to construct. Indeed, over 35 years passed until the vision of Rivest et al. [1978] was materialized by Gentry [2009b] in one of the most inspiring works in cryptography in recent years.

20.2 Definition and Basic Properties

Motivated by the application of outsourcing computation, we might not want to restrict ourselves to algebraic terminology. Instead, we can define $\mathcal{F}$-homomorphism with respect to the class of operations $\mathcal{F}$ that can be applied to encrypted data.

Notation-wise, a public-key encryption scheme consists of a (randomized) key generation process, that produces a secret key sk and a public key pk, a (randomized) encryption function Enc and a (deterministic, without loss of generality) decryption function Dec. Throughout this chapter we will consider a plaintext space of binary strings $\{0, 1\}^*$ and an encryption procedure that encrypts the message bits one at a time. Syntactically, encrypting a message x using a public key pk is denoted $\mathsf{Enc}_{\mathsf{pk}}(x)$. Decrypting a ciphertext c is denoted $\mathsf{Dec}_{\mathsf{sk}}(c)$. We can now define $\mathcal{F}$-homomorphism.

Definition 20.1   Let $\mathcal{F}$ be a set of functions in $\{0, 1\}^* \to \{0, 1\}$. A public-key scheme is $\mathcal{F}$-homomorphic if there exists an *evaluation algorithm* Eval s.t. $\mathsf{Dec}_{\mathsf{sk}}(\mathsf{Eval}(f, \mathsf{Enc}_{\mathsf{pk}}(x))) = f(x)$ for all $f \in \mathcal{F}$ and $x \in \{0, 1\}^*$ of appropriate length.

A *fully* homomorphic encryption (FHE) is a homomorphic encryption scheme where $\mathcal{F}$ is the set of all functions (or at least the set of all efficiently computable functions).

That is, encrypting a value x, followed by applying homomorphic evaluation with f, and decrypting the output, should result in the value $f(x)$. This is the minimal requirement for the purpose of private outsourcing. There are a few points that are worth noting about this definition.

The syntax of the homomorphic evaluation procedure. It is simplest to define the homomorphic evaluation procedure as only taking the respective ciphertexts as input. While this is true without loss of generality (as we explain momentarily), in many cases the evaluation procedure also uses the public key of the encryption scheme. Syntactically this can be avoided by redefining the ciphertexts as containing the public key, and thus allowing evaluation using only the ciphertexts, without loss of generality. Still, often for reasons of efficiency and syntactic elegance the Eval procedure takes the public key as an additional parameter.

Furthermore, in many candidates, it is easy to identify a part of the public key that is used for homomorphic evaluation, and a separate part that is used for encryption. It is sometimes convenient to refer to the former as the "evaluation key" of the scheme, thus characterizing a homomorphic encryption scheme as having a secret key sk and *two* public keys pk, evk, one used for encryption and one used for homomorphic evaluation. This is particularly convenient in cases where it is possible to amplify the homomorphic capabilities of the scheme by modifying evk while keeping sk, pk unchanged (e.g. via *bootstrapping*; see Section 20.3).

Representation of functions. The evaluation procedure takes a function $f \in \mathcal{F}$ as input. This means that it is not enough to think about $\mathcal{F}$ as a class of functions, but rather we must consider the representation of these functions. In particular, since Eval needs to be polynomial time computable, the representation of f effects the permitted running time of $\text{Eval}(f, \cdot)$. It is most common to consider the *Boolean circuit model* to represent f.

Homomorphic evaluation needs not preserve form.. We only required above that the evaluated ciphertext (i.e. the ciphertext output by Eval) is decryptable to the correct value. There is no requirement that $c_f = \text{Eval}(f, \text{Enc}_{\text{pk}}(x))$ looks similar to a fresh ciphertext $\text{Enc}_{\text{pk}}(f(x))$. This choice is made in order to capture the minimal meaningful definition for private outsourcing of computation. However, this minimal definition opens the door to a degenerate FHE construction as follows. Consider any secure public-key encryption scheme, and append it with the function $\text{Eval}(f, c)$ that simply outputs the tuple (f, c). Furthermore extend the decryption algorithm to decrypt pairs (f, c) by first decrypting the c component and then applying the f component on the output. This scheme is homomorphic with respect to the above definition, but fails to capture a notion of nontrivial outsourcing.

To avoid this degeneracy, we present two properties that are natural requirements in the context of outsourcing. Neither one of these is captured by the aforementioned degenerate example.

Compactness. If our intent in homomorphic encryption is to delegate the computational complexity of the computing f to a remote server, then it is natural to require that the decryption complexity does not depend on the complexity of the function being evaluated. Formally, adopting the convention that the decryption procedure runs in fixed polynomial time in its input length, it is sufficient to require that the bit-length of the evaluated ciphertext c_f does not depend on the complexity of f (beyond the obvious dependence on the output length).

Function Privacy. In certain situations, it may be important that c_f does not reveal any information about f itself (e.g. when the evaluator uses a proprietary algorithm). Function privacy should hold even with respect to an adversary that has the secret key; that is, the requirement is that even the decryptor cannot learn anything about f from c_f, except for the value $f(x)$. One could consider even stronger notions of function privacy, for example one that considers public keys and ciphertexts that are maliciously generated in attempt to extract more information about f than permitted [Ostrovsky et al. 2014].

Compactness and function privacy are both sought after properties in certain situations, and in others it could make sense to require only one but not necessarily both. More often than not, the term FHE refers to compact FHE, and it is explicitly mentioned where a noncompact scheme is sufficient (e.g. if only function privacy is needed).

It can be shown that a compact FHE scheme implies a (different) FHE scheme which is both compact and function private via a nontrivial transformation (this is implicit in Gentry et al. [2010]).

No additional security requirements.   Our definition of homomorphism above did not make any requirements about security, except that the underlying scheme (without homomorphic evaluation) is secure. Standard notions of security (e.g. semantic security) are only concerned with information leaked by freshly encrypted ciphertexts, and not about ones that are a result of some manipulation such as homomorphic evaluation. Therefore, one might be worried that post-evaluation ciphertexts might be more vulnerable. However, since the evaluation procedure only uses public information, semantic security guarantees that homomorphic evaluation cannot assist in breaching security of the original ciphertexts. This, in turn, also implies that post-evaluation ciphertexts are protected, at least to the extent that it should not be possible to reveal information about the output of the evaluation process that can assist in learning something about the inputs.

We note that while we are guaranteed that c_f cannot reveal any information about x, it is allowed to reveal information about $f(x)$, to the extent that the information revealed is independent of x. For example, if f is the all zero function, then c_f might expose that $f(x) = 0$ (unless we impose stronger guarantees such as function privacy).

Single-hop vs. multi-hop homomorphism.   In the aforementioned definition it is only required that the post-evaluation ciphertext decrypts properly. As we explained above, this does not necessitate that the output ciphertext is structurally similar to a freshly encrypted ciphertext. In particular, it might be the case that it is not possible to re-apply the homomorphic evaluation function to post-evaluated ciphertexts. Schemes that adhere to the basic definition are sometimes referred to as *single-hop homomorphic*—as opposed to *multi-hop homomorphism*, which allows multiple successive applications of homomorphic evaluation. These notions have been studied in Gentry et al. [2010]. Gentry's bootstrapping theorem [Gentry 2009a, 2009b] allows to convert any compact single-hop fully homomorphic encryption into a multi-hop scheme (see more details in Section 20.3).

Leveled fully homomorphic encryption. As explained above, a fully homomorphic encryption scheme is one that can evaluate any input circuit. Unfortunately, in some cases, this goal is not directly achievable, or requires security and functionality overhead. In those cases it is sometimes useful to define the notion of *leveled* FHE, which refers to a *family* of FHE schemes that allow, for any depth bound d, to generate an instance of the FHE scheme that supports the evaluation of depth-d circuits. The parameters of the scheme are allowed to grow polynomially with d, and some definitions are even stricter and require that evk is the only parameter that depends on d and that this dependence is linear. Leveled FHE schemes are by themselves sufficient for some applications, and in most cases can be upgraded to (nonleveled) FHE using Gentry's bootstrapping theorem [Gentry 2009a, 2009b], albeit with efficiency loss and an additional security assumption.[1]

20.3 Bootstrapping and Circular Security

We will now describe one of the most fundamental and useful tools in the construction of fully homomorphic encryption, *the bootstrapping theorem*, introduced in Gentry's seminal work [Gentry 2009a, 2009b]. The bootstrapping theorem is, to date, a necessary component in all FHE candidates. Using the bootstrapping theorem in its strongest form requires introducing an additional hardness assumption concerning the *circular security* of encryption schemes (we will explain this in detail below). It is currently unknown how to relate this additional assumption to standard cryptographic assumptions, thus the use of bootstrapping subjects all known FHE candidates to the additional circularity requirement.

Key Switching. We start by introducing the key-switching technique which is useful for bootstrapping but can also be used in other settings. Perhaps the simplest motivation for key switching is to show that given a (possibly non-homomorphic)

---

1. In early works on FHE, the term "somewhat homomorphic encryption" (SHE) was used to indicate a scheme with homomorphic capabilities against a restricted class of functions (depth bounded). The two terms are sometimes used interchangeably, however in the original SHE scheme [Gentry 2009a, 2009b] the parameters of the scheme grew *exponentially* with d.

scheme with very efficient encryption, and a different homomorphic scheme (possibly with very inefficient, but still polynomial time, encryption), it is possible to create a scheme that inherits the encryption complexity of the former and homomorphic abilities of the latter.

We denote the keys of the nonhomomorphic scheme by (nhsk, nhpk), and its encryption and decryption functions by NHEnc, NHDec. Let (hsk, hpk) denote the secret key and public key of the homomorphic scheme (with encryption and decryption functions Enc, Dec). Consider a ciphertext c that encrypts a plaintext x under the nonhomomorphic scheme, that is, such that $\mathsf{NHDec}_{\mathsf{nhsk}}(c) = x$. Our goal is to apply homomorphic evaluation of some function f—namely, to generate a ciphertext that encrypts the value $f(x) = f(\mathsf{NHDec}_{\mathsf{nhsk}}(c))$. Note that f and c are publicly known and the only unknown in the expression $f(\mathsf{NHDec}_{\mathsf{nhsk}}(c))$ is nhsk. We can thus define an efficiently computable function $\tilde{f}_c(\alpha) = f(\mathsf{NHDec}_{\alpha}(c))$ (we omit the subscript c and write $\tilde{f}$ when it is clear from the context). Thinking of the value $f(x)$ as a function of $\alpha = \mathsf{nhsk}$ instead of as a function of x itself, we can think about *homomorphic evaluation* of the function $\tilde{f}_c$. This means that we no longer care that c is encrypted under a nonhomomorphic scheme, all we care about now is that α, the input to $\tilde{f}_c$, is encrypted under the homomorphic key hpk. That is, if we had a ciphertext $c^* = \mathsf{Enc}_{\mathsf{hpk}}(\alpha)$—that is, a homomorphic encryption of a value α—then we can compute $c_{\tilde{f}} = \mathsf{Eval}(\tilde{f}_c, c^*)$ (note that the syntax here is correct since we are applying Eval on a ciphertext encrypted under the homomorphic key hpk). What can we say about $c_{\tilde{f}}$? As the output of a homomorphic evaluation of a function $\tilde{f}_c$ on a properly encrypted ciphertext c^*, we can say that $c_{\tilde{f}}$ should decrypt under hsk to the value $\tilde{f}_c(\alpha) = f(\mathsf{NHDec}_{\alpha}(c))$. Since c is encrypted (under the nonhomomorphic scheme), this value will be meaningless for almost all values of α, but it will be meaningful for $\alpha = \mathsf{nhsk}$, for which $\tilde{f}_c(\mathsf{nhsk}) = f(x)$.

The conclusion is that if we can provide the auxiliary information $c^* = \mathsf{Enc}_{\mathsf{hpk}}(\mathsf{nhsk})$, i.e. an encryption of the nonhomomorphic secret key under the homomorphic public key, then it would be possible, given f and c, to compute an encryption of the value $f(x)$, thus performing homomorphic evaluation over a ciphertext encrypted using the nonhomomorphic scheme—specifically, to generate a value $c_{\tilde{f}}$ subject to

$$\mathsf{Dec}_{\mathsf{hsk}}(c_{\tilde{f}}) = \mathsf{Dec}_{\mathsf{hsk}}(\mathsf{Eval}(\tilde{f}_c, c^*)) = \tilde{f}_c(\mathsf{Dec}_{\mathsf{hsk}}(c^*)) = \tilde{f}_c(\mathsf{nhsk})$$

$$= f(\mathsf{NHDec}_{\mathsf{nhsk}}(c)) = f(x).$$

The value c^* should be posted publicly alongside the public keys hpk and nhpk of the homomorphic and nonhomomorphic scheme.

It is important to notice that the output ciphertext $c_{\tilde{f}}$ indeed constitutes an encryption of $f(x)$, but under the *homomorphic* key hsk. In fact, what we showed was a *key-switching* technique that allows to take a ciphertext encrypted under a certain encryption scheme, and convert it into a ciphertext encrypted under a different scheme (using the homomorphic properties of the latter). This explains why the secret key nhsk is required for the generation of $c^* = \mathsf{Enc}_{\mathsf{hpk}}(\mathsf{nhsk})$, since otherwise the ability to decrypt $c_{\tilde{f}}$ using hsk would contradict the semantic security of the nonhomomorphic scheme.

We will see next how to extend key switching into bootstrapping, but let us mention that the switching technique by itself is quite useful. For example, the encryption complexity of an FHE schemes might be quite high, or the ciphertexts are long (which is indeed the case in many of the current candidates). With key switching, it is possible to use a quick and cheap encryption procedure (in fact, even symmetric key encryption will do), and defer all FHE related operations to the evaluation phase.

From Key Switching to Bootstrapping.   Let us assume that the homomorphic encryption scheme from above was only single-hop homomorphic. This still allows us to define c^* and compute $c_{\tilde{f}}$. However, this would still leave us stuck at single-hop homomorphism, since $c_{\tilde{f}}$ cannot undergo additional homomorphic evaluation. However, equipped with our knowledge of key switching, we do not give up so easily. We showed that using the appropriate auxiliary input, we can perform homomorphic evaluation even on ciphertexts that on the face of it cannot be evaluated. We know that $\mathsf{Dec}_{\mathsf{hsk}}(c_{\tilde{f}}) = f(x)$, and let us assume we want to apply a function g on top of this value. Then again we can define $\tilde{g}(\alpha) = g(\mathsf{Dec}_\alpha(c_{\tilde{f}}))$ and define an appropriate c^{**} such that $c_{\tilde{g}} = \mathsf{Eval}(\tilde{g}, c^{**})$ decrypts to the right value $g(f(x))$.

What should the new auxiliary information c^{**} be? It needs to be an encryption of the homomorphic secret key hsk, otherwise the evaluation procedure produces a meaningless value. So what we want is $c^{**} = \mathsf{Enc}_{\mathsf{hpk}}(\mathsf{hsk})$—namely, an encryption of the homomorphic secret key under its own public key.[2] Given this value, we can compute $c_{\tilde{g}} = \mathsf{Eval}(\tilde{g}, c^{**})$ as desired, and obtain $c_{\tilde{g}}$ such that

$$\mathsf{Dec}_{\mathsf{hsk}}(c_{\tilde{g}}) = \tilde{g}(\mathsf{hsk}) = g(\mathsf{Dec}_{\mathsf{hsk}}(c_{\tilde{f}})) = g(f(\mathsf{Dec}_{\mathsf{nhsk}}(c))) = g(f(x)).$$

We see that indeed $c_{\tilde{g}}$ decrypts to the desired value, so given c^{**} we can increase the evaluation capacity of our scheme.

---

2. A knowledgeable reader may have noticed a *circularity* issue; we will discuss this aspect shortly.

The critical observation is that c^{**} is in fact much more useful than our previous c^*. While the latter allows to switch a ciphertext from the nonhomomorphic scheme to the homomorphic scheme, and was completely useless afterward, the former allows us to take homomorphic ciphertexts and produce homomorphic ciphertexts. This in particular means that the same c^{**} can be used more than once. Assume that we want to homomorphically evaluate an additional function h on top of $c_{\tilde{g}}$, we observe that this can be done with the same c^{**}—that is, without requiring a new auxiliary information. Specifically, just define $\tilde{h}(\alpha) = h(\mathsf{Dec}_\alpha(c_{\tilde{g}}))$, and set $c_{\tilde{h}} = \mathsf{Eval}(\tilde{h}, c^{**})$. One can verify that $c_{\tilde{h}}$ indeed decrypts to $h(g(f(x)))$. Note that in order for this to apply, we only require that our encryption scheme is single-hop homomorphic. This is since the Eval function is only executed on the input ciphertext c^{**}, which is a freshly encrypted ciphertext and not the result of a previous homomorphic operation. In a sense, we "tricked" the single-hop scheme to perform multi-hop operations by embedding the "real" input inside the function description. At this point we can forget about the initial nonhomomorphic scheme (although, as we explained, this application is also sometimes useful) and just consider the task of amplifying single-hop to multi-hop homomorphism. We see that this is possible given the auxiliary information c^{**}, which should be placed as a part of the public key of the new multi-hop scheme (or more accurately as a part of the evaluation key).

To extract even more out of this technique, we notice that in a multi-hop homomorphic scheme, it is sufficient to only be able to evaluate the NAND gate (or any other universal family of Boolean gates). This is since each Boolean circuit can be written a sequence of such gates, and homomorphic evaluation of the circuit can proceed by evaluating the gates one at a time (in topological order) on the output of their predecessors. Plugging this observation into our construction of a multi-hop scheme, we see that in order to allow the amplification from single-hop to multi-hop, all that is required is that the single hop scheme supports the homomorphic evaluation of functions of the form $\tilde{f}(\alpha) = \tilde{f}_{c_1,c_2}(\alpha) = \mathsf{NAND}\,(\mathsf{Dec}_\alpha(c_1), \mathsf{Dec}_\alpha(c_2))$, where c_1 and c_2 are bit strings interpreted as ciphertexts for the single-hop scheme. Thus, if we can devise a homomorphic encryption scheme (even single-hop) that supports this family of functions (NAND-augmented decryption functions), then this scheme can be amplified into full-fledged (even multi-hop) FHE for all functions, at the cost of adding c^{**} to the evaluation key (evk) of the scheme (recall that evk is the part of the public key that is used for homomorphic evaluation).

Gentry's bootstrapping theorem states exactly this fact: that once we are able to achieve a certain level of homomorphism, then FHE readily follows. However, our discussion so far neglected an important aspect of the above transformation:

whether the addition of c^{**} to the public evaluation key evk of our resulting scheme (and thus revealing it to a potential attacker) preserves the security of the original scheme. At first glance, this seems to be a nonissue, by definition c^{**} is a properly encrypted ciphertext, so the security of the single-hop scheme should guarantee that revealing it to an attacker should do no harm. However, it turns out that standard notions of encryption security are only concerned with hiding messages that can be generated by an adversary (that has the public key). Encrypting a scheme's secret key using its own public key does not fall under this definition. Indeed, almost all proofs showing that encryption schemes are secure under certain assumptions (e.g., factoring) do not extend to showing security for encrypting the secret key, with the exception of schemes designed especially to have this property such as Boneh et al. [2008], Applebaum et al. [2009], and Brakerski and Goldwasser [2010]. Therefore, the bootstrapping theorem requires that the homomorphic scheme to be amplified is *circular secure*—namely, that it is secure even against adversaries that see an encryption of the scheme's secret key under its public key. To be precise, circular security, or more generally the notion of security against key dependent messages (KDM-security) [Black et al. 2002], is a stronger notion where the adversary can adaptively ask for encryptions of messages with some dependence of the secret key. Thus the notion required from bootstrapping is named "weak" circular security.

Theorem 20.1   (Gentry's bootstrapping theorem)   If there exists an encryption scheme that is single-hop homomorphic with respect to NAND-augmented decryption circuits, and is weakly circular secure, then there exists a multi-hop FHE scheme.

A scheme that is single-hop homomorphic with respect to NAND-augmented decryption circuits is called *bootstrappable*.

In particular, the bootstrapping theorem states that if we have a scheme that supports depth bounded homomorphism, and its depth bound is strictly larger than its decryption complexity, then this scheme can be amplified to an FHE (assuming that it is also weakly circular secure). Schemes with such homomorphic capacity can be constructed from standard cryptographic assumptions, such as the learning with errors (LWE) assumption (see Section 20.4). However, it is not known how to prove weak circular security under a standard assumption for any bootstrappable scheme. Furthermore, bootstrapping underlies all known (nonleveled) FHE constructions, so the current state of affairs is that while leveled FHE can be constructed from standard assumptions, nonleveled FHE requires an explicit weak circular security assumption. *This is the only remaining theoretical barrier towards constructing FHE from standard assumptions.*

The Necessity and Plausibility of the Circular Security Requirement. As explained above, it is not known how to prove circular security based on standard assumptions. However, in the proposed constructions, it is not known how to improve the best known attacks using an encryption of the secret key. Thus, as a heuristic, it appears plausible to assume the circular security holds for known FHE candidates. Having said that, recent works [Goyal et al. 2017] show that weak circular security does not necessarily hold for *every* encryption scheme that is secure under standard assumptions. This is done by introducing contrived schemes where the secret key is design so that its encryption provides additional power to the adversary.

Gentry [2009a] proposed a heuristic argument showing that *any* homomorphic encryption scheme supporting high enough evaluation depth should be circular secure. Assume there exists a hash function H such that providing the adversary with $(\tilde{c} = \mathsf{Enc}_{\mathsf{hpk}}(\rho), \sigma = H(\rho) \oplus \mathsf{hsk})$ for a random ρ does not make the scheme insecure. This assumption indeed holds in the random oracle model as shown in Black et al. [2002]. If we had such a function H in the standard model, then it would have been possible to compute $\mathsf{Eval}(\tilde{H}_\sigma, \tilde{c})$ where $\tilde{H}_\sigma(\alpha) = \sigma \oplus H(\alpha)$. Note that the output of this homomorphic evaluation procedure is an encryption of hsk as needed. While we do know that no explicit hash function can perfectly implement the random oracle heuristic in all applications, in some applications it is possible. Gentry's argument suggests that refuting the circular security of FHE might require showing that for this application it is impossible to replace random oracle with *any* hash function.

One seemingly simple way to get around the circular security problem can be devised by considering our original example of converting a nonhomomorphic scheme into a homomorphic one. In that example, there was no circularity problem since hpk is used to encrypt nhsk, that is, we encrypted a secret key of one scheme under the public key of another scheme. This allows the security proof to go through, since we can argue that even if an adversary knows nhsk, it should still not be able to breach the security of hpk, and thus it cannot distinguish whether c^* contains an encryption of nhsk or an encryption of an unrelated message. We could therefore hope that the following trick could work for bootstrapping homomorphic encryption schemes: Rather than having a single $c^{**} = \mathsf{Enc}_{\mathsf{hpk}}(\mathsf{hsk})$, we will generate two homomorphic key pairs $(\mathsf{hsk}_1, \mathsf{hpk}_1)$, $(\mathsf{hsk}_2, \mathsf{hpk}_2)$, and generate two auxiliary ciphertexts $c_1^{**} = \mathsf{Enc}_{\mathsf{hpk}_1}(\mathsf{hsk}_2)$ and $c_2^{**} = \mathsf{Enc}_{\mathsf{hpk}_2}(\mathsf{hsk}_1)$. Then, during homomorphic evaluation we will alternate between using c_1^{**} and c_2^{**} for each hop of the computation. This indeed provides the intended functionality; however, in terms of security we can see that the prior proof outline no longer works. Even if we only reveal hsk_2 to the adversary, it is straightforward to extract hsk_1 by decrypting c_2^{**}, so we cannot rely on the hardness of hpk_1. Indeed, such a 2-cycle is a type of circular security and the same problems arise.

Before giving up completely on the key cycle concept, we notice that the problem only arises because the chain of keys we generate is a closed loop, so that any of the secret keys can be used to recover all other secret keys. We can consider generating d key pairs (hsk_i, hpk_i) and auxiliary information $c_i^{**} = \text{Enc}_{hpk_{i+1}}(hsk_i)$ for $i = 1, \ldots, d - 1$ (note that we *do not* close the loop since we do not provide $\text{Enc}_{hpk_1}(hsk_d)$, and in fact we do not provide any information at all on hsk_d beyond its respective public key). This chain allows us to perform $d - 1$ homomorphic hops, and the resulting scheme can be proven secure based only on the security of the original scheme. Instantiating our hops with NAND-augmented decryption circuits, we can get a leveled FHE for any polynomial depth bound d, where the only parameter of the scheme that depends on d is the scheme's evaluation key evk (which now contains evk_i for all i, as well as all auxiliaries c_i^{**}), and this evaluation key only grows linearly with d. There is no need for circular security to prove security for this leveled scheme.

Theorem 20.2 (Gentry's bootstrapping theorem for leveled FHE) If there exists an encryption scheme which is single-hop homomorphic with respect to NAND-augmented decryption circuits, then there exists a leveled FHE scheme.

20.4 Constructing FHE

We will now explain how to construct homomorphic encryption schemes from the learning with errors (LWE) assumption. The scheme we construct will be bootstrappable so it is possible to apply Gentry's bootstrapping theorem to achieve full FHE.

20.4.1 Learning with Errors: A Primer

The learning with errors (LWE) problem was introduced by Regev [2005] and has had a profound effect on cryptographic literature, often allowing to realize cryptographic primitives that are not known under any other assumption. LWE considers a set of many random linear equations over a set of n variables that will be assigned random values, modulo a global modulus $q \ll n$ (where the meaningful range of parameters ranges from q being polynomial to subexponential in n). The vector of variables is denoted by $\mathbf{t} \in \mathbb{Z}_q^n$ (we set it as a row vector), and the (random) coefficients of the linear equations are represented by a uniform matrix $\mathbf{B} \in \mathbb{Z}_q^{n \times m}$, where

$m = \text{poly}(n)$ is the number of equations.[3] A set of linear equations is solvable even modulo q, so given $(\mathbf{B}, \mathbf{tB})$ it is possible to efficiently find a solution $\mathbf{t}$ to the set of equations. The LWE problem considers slightly perturbed equations, by adding a small noise to each one. Specifically, let χ be a distribution supported only over integers smaller than some bound B.[4] Consider sampling a noise vector $\mathbf{e}$ from χ^m (a noise term for each equation) and setting $\mathbf{b} = \mathbf{tB} + \mathbf{e} \pmod q$. The (decisional) LWE assumption with parameters (n, q, χ) states that for a uniformly sampled $\mathbf{t}$, the pair $(\mathbf{B}, \mathbf{b})$ is indistinguishable from uniform, even when m is allowed to be an arbitrarily large polynomial. Note that information theoretically this distribution is very far from uniform. The distribution χ is often taken to be a discrete Gaussian, but this is immaterial for the purpose of this chapter. For our discussion we can consider setting $q = n^{10}$ and a distribution χ with a bound $B = n$. To further simplify our notation, we will not explicitly write the noise vector $\mathbf{e}$ and instead write $\mathbf{b} \approx \mathbf{tB}$.

We now present a tool that proved extremely useful in LWE-based cryptography. Let $x \in \{0, \ldots, q-1\}$, then x can be represented as a sequence of $\lceil \log q \rceil$ bits as $x = \sum 2^i \cdot x_i$, which can also be written as an inner product $(1, 2, 2^2, \ldots) \cdot (x_0, x_1, \ldots) = \mathbf{g} \cdot \mathbf{x}$. More generally, considering a vector $\mathbf{v} \in \mathbb{Z}_q^n$, one can consider the vector $\mathbf{v}'$ containing a concatenation of the binary representations of all elements of $\mathbf{v}$. The vector $\mathbf{g}$ can thus be generalized to a matrix $\mathbf{G} \in \mathbb{Z}_q^{n \times n \lceil \log q \rceil}$ s.t. $\mathbf{v} = \mathbf{G}\mathbf{v}'$ (the matrix $\mathbf{G}$ is a block diagonal matrix with each block equaling to $\mathbf{g}$). We note that this matrix found additional uses in contexts beyond what is covered in this chapter (see, e.g., Micciancio and Peikert [2012]). It is customary to denote the binary representation of $\mathbf{v}$ by $\mathbf{G}^{-1}(\mathbf{v})$, so that it will hold that $\mathbf{G}\mathbf{G}^{-1}(\mathbf{v}) = \mathbf{v}$. We note that $\mathbf{G}^{-1}$ is not a matrix, but rather a function. This notation can be even further extended to apply to matrices so that $\mathbf{G}^{-1}(\mathbf{V})$ for a matrix $\mathbf{V} \in \mathbb{Z}_q^{n \times m}$ is a matrix in $\{0, 1\}^{n \lceil \log q \rceil \times m}$, whose every column is the binary decomposition of the respective column of $\mathbf{V}$, so again $\mathbf{G}\mathbf{G}^{-1}(\mathbf{V}) = \mathbf{V}$.

20.4.2   A Homomorphic Encryption Scheme Based on LWE

LWE-based homomorphic encryption was constructed in Brakerski and Vaikuntanathan [2011]. We present a later construction due to Gentry et al. [2013] (using notation from the even later Alperin-Sheriff and Peikert [2014]). The public key is

---

3. We note that the standard notation for the LWE problem is using $\mathbf{s}$, $\mathbf{A}$ instead of $\mathbf{t}$, $\mathbf{B}$. However, this notation will be more convenient for us as we will use $\mathbf{s}$, $\mathbf{A}$ to denote different quantities in Section 20.4.2, below.

4. It is sufficient that the distribution is bounded with overwhelming probability.

a matrix $\mathbf{A} = \begin{bmatrix} \mathbf{B} \\ \mathbf{b} \end{bmatrix}$, where $\mathbf{B}$ is uniform and $\mathbf{b} \approx \mathbf{tB}$ for a random $\mathbf{t}$. The secret key is a vector $\mathbf{s} = (-\mathbf{t}, 1)$. Note that it holds that $\mathbf{sA} \approx 0$, but that $\mathbf{A}$ is indistinguishable from uniform assuming LWE. This public key is identical to that of Regev's original LWE-based public-key encryption scheme. However, the ciphertext itself is quite different. The encryption of a message is done in a bit-by-bit manner, where the encryption of each message bit is a *large matrix*.[5] The encryption of a bit $x \in \{0, 1\}$ is the matrix $\mathbf{C} = \mathbf{AR} + x\mathbf{G}$, where $\mathbf{R}$ is a random *binary* matrix (whose dimensions are chosen based on those of $\mathbf{A}$ and $\mathbf{G}$ to ensure syntactic compatibility).

Since $\mathbf{A}$ is indistinguishable from a uniform matrix, the leftover hash lemma guarantees (for properly chosen parameters) that $\mathbf{C}$ is indistinguishable from a completely random matrix, and in particular hides the value of the message x. On the other hand, it holds that

$$\mathbf{sA} = \underbrace{\mathbf{sA}}_{\approx 0} \mathbf{R} + x\mathbf{sG} \approx x\mathbf{sG},$$

and one can verify that x can indeed be recovered out of this value (knowledge of $\mathbf{s}$ is naturally required). It is important to note that it was important to sample $\mathbf{R}$ from a distribution over small values in order to argue that if $\mathbf{sA} \approx 0$ then $\mathbf{sAR} \approx 0$. Multiplying by $\mathbf{R}$ will most likely somewhat increase the amplitude of the output vector, and in the formal analysis we must keep guard that the amplitude of the resulting vector indeed remains small (i.e., $\ll q$).

To show that the scheme is homomorphic, we will show that starting with two ciphertexts $\mathbf{C}_1, \mathbf{C}_2$ such that $\mathbf{sC}_i \approx x_i\mathbf{sG}$, where $x_1, x_2 \in \{0, 1\}$, we can construct a ciphertext $\mathbf{C}'$ such that $\mathbf{sC}' = (1 - x_1 x_2)\mathbf{sG}$, that is, $\mathbf{C}'$ is an encryption of $1 - x_1 x_2 = \text{NAND}(x_1, x_2)$. After doing that, we will explain how this translates to full homomorphism. We will be guided by the following intuitive observation: Since $\mathbf{sC}_i \approx x_i\mathbf{sG}$, then we can think of $\mathbf{C}_i$ as "equivalent" to $x_i\mathbf{G}$ (where the equivalence is expressed by the two being approximately equal under multiplication by $\mathbf{s}$).

To test the validity of this intuition, let us start by trying to implement the negation functionality $x \to (1 - x)$. We can verify that indeed setting $\mathbf{C}' = \mathbf{G} - \mathbf{C}_1$ leads to $\mathbf{sC}' \approx (1 - x_1)\mathbf{sG}$. Now, let us try to implement conjunction $x_1, x_2 \to x_1 x_2$. We notice that $(x_1\mathbf{G}) \cdot \mathbf{G}^{-1}(x_2\mathbf{G}) = x_1 x_2\mathbf{G}$, and indeed letting $\mathbf{C}' = \mathbf{C}_1\mathbf{G}^{-1}(\mathbf{C}_2)$, we get

$$\mathbf{sC}_1\mathbf{G}^{-1}(\mathbf{C}_2) \approx x_1\mathbf{sGG}^{-1}(\mathbf{C}_2) \approx x_1 x_2\mathbf{sG},$$

---

5. In other words, the *information rate* of this scheme is very low and approaches 0 asymptotically. However, since the ciphertext is still polynomial in the key and message sizes, this is an acceptable solution in a purely theoretical world. Discussion of more efficient solutions will follow.

where as before it is important that $\mathbf{G}^{-1}(\mathbf{C}_2)$ is low norm in order to propagate the validity of the $\approx$ symbol. Putting our two observations together, we have that $\mathbf{C}' = \mathbf{G} - \mathbf{C}_1\mathbf{G}^{-1}(\mathbf{C}_2)$ is indeed an encryption of NAND $(x_1, x_2) = 1 - x_1 x_2$. We note that this expression is asymmetric (since $\mathbf{C}_1\mathbf{G}^{-1}(\mathbf{C}_2) \neq \mathbf{C}_2\mathbf{G}^{-1}(\mathbf{C}_1)$) and this asymmetry gives rise to useful properties in terms of efficiency and security [Brakerski and Vaikuntanathan 2014].

Being able to evaluate the NAND function can be extended to evaluating arbitrary Boolean circuit using the universality of NAND, as explained above. However, as we noted, the approximation $\mathbf{sC} \approx x\mathbf{sG}$ becomes worse with every gate being evaluated. This puts a bound on the *maximal depth* supported by the scheme. The depth bound roughly corresponds to $\log(q/B)$, where B is the bound on the LWE noise distribution. Since the depth of the scheme's decryption circuit grows polynomially with $\log n + \log\log q$ (since it essentially computes an inner product of vectors in $\mathbb{Z}_q^n$), one can choose parameters to allow the evaluation of the decryption circuit, and thus make the scheme bootstrappable (subject to a circular security assumption, if a leveled scheme is not sufficient).

20.4.3 Efficiency and Implementations

The GSW scheme presented above imposes a high communication and computation overhead compared to performing the evaluation on unencrypted data, which is naturally an undesirable property. Nevertheless, various optimization methods were introduced that reduce the computational overhead to a level that is useful for some applications [Ducas and Micciancio 2015, Chillotti et al. 2016]. A significant reduction of the communication overhead for GSW-style schemes remains an open problem.

The information rate overhead problem can be solved in an *amortized* manner using schemes that follow the prior Brakerski and Vaikuntanathan [2011] paradigm. Such schemes allow to *batch* multiple messages into a single ciphertext in a way that allows to perform homomorphic operations in parallel on all encrypted messages. The ciphertext size grows only mildly with the total amount of information. This idea goes back to the prior work of Smart and Vercauteren [2010], and was applied to the Brakerski and Vaikuntanathan [2011] paradigm starting in Brakerski et al. [2012]. The most liberal parameter settings allow to reduce the information rate to a constant, but it is currently unclear, even in this setting, whether it is possible to achieve information rate approaching 1 while preserving full homomorphism.

Using either paradigm, the best efficiency is achieved when using variants of the scheme over polynomial rings—that is, with symbolic polynomials replacing integer vectors, and polynomial multiplication (modulo some ambient polynomial) replacing inner product. This allows for both improved computational complexity and improved information rate. Specifically, current implementations are based either on variants of the NTRU encryption scheme [Hoffstein et al. 1998] or on the Ring-LWE assumption [Lyubashevsky et al. 2010, Lyubashevsky et al. 2013].

20.5 Beyond Vanilla FHE

To conclude this chapter, we mention a few uses and extensions of FHE that go beyond the basic functionality.

Multi-Key FHE.   The standard notion of FHE only considers a single user who owns data and wishes this data is processed remotely. A natural extension is the case of multiple users, each with their own individually generated secret key and public key, and with their own data, and they wish to outsource a computation on the aggregation of data from all users. To maintain security, it must be the case that decryption of the evaluated ciphertext requires using *all* user secret keys. This notion is called *multi-key FHE* and was first introduced by Lopez-Alt, Tromer, and Vaikuntanathan [López-Alt et al. 2012]. Their original scheme was based on a variant of the NTRU assumption [Hoffstein et al. 1998]. A scheme with improved properties and relying on the LWE assumption was later introduced by Clear and McGoldrick [2015].

Evaluating Quantum Circuits.   Considering that a major use of FHE is private delegation of computation suggests considering models where the computational power of the evaluator is qualitatively superior to that of the client. One such case is where the evaluator is in possession of a *quantum computer*. In such case, a classical client may wish to delegate a quantum computation to the evaluator. It was recently shown that this can be achieved under similar assumptions to those required from classical FHE [Mahadev 2017].

References

M. Ajtai and C. Dwork. 1997. A public-key cryptosystem with worst-case/average-case equivalence. In F. T. Leighton and P. W. Shor, editors, *Proceedings of the Twenty-Ninth Annual ACM Symposium on the Theory of Computing, El Paso, TX, USA, May 4–6, 1997*, pp. 284–293. ACM. DOI: 10.1145/258533.258604. 544

J. Alperin-Sheriff and C. Peikert. 2014. Faster bootstrapping with polynomial error. In J. A. Garay and R. Gennaro, editors, *Advances in Cryptology–CRYPTO 2014, 34th Annual Cryptology Conference, Santa Barbara, CA, USA, August 17–21, 2014, Proceedings,*

Part I. Lecture Notes in Computer Science, vol. 8616 pp. 297–314. Springer. DOI: 10.1007/978-3-662-44371-2_17. 556

B. Applebaum, D. Cash, C. Peikert, and A. Sahai. 2009. Fast cryptographic primitives and circular-secure encryption based on hard learning problems. In S. Halevi, editor, *Advances in Crytology–CRYPTO 2009, 29th Annual International Crytology Conference, Santa Barbara, CA, USA, August 16–20, 2009, Proceedings.* Lecture Notes in Computer Science vol. 5677, pp. 595–618. Springer. 553

J. Black, P. Rogaway, and T. Shrimpton. 2002. Encryption-scheme security in the presence of key-dependent messages. In K. Nyberg and H. M. Heys, editors, *Selected Areas in Cryptography, 9th Annual International Workshop, SAC 2002, St. John's, Newfoundland, Canada, August 15–16, 2002. Revised Papers*, Lecture Notes in Computer Science vol. 2595, pp. 62–75. Springer. DOI: 10.1007/3-540-36492-7_6. 553, 554

D. Boneh, S. Halevi, M. Hamburg, and R. Ostrovsky. 2008. Circular-secure encryption from decision Diffie–Hellman. In D. A. Wagner, editor, *Advances in Cryptology–CRYPTO 2008, 28th Annual International Cryptology Conference, Santa Barbara, CA, USA, August 17–21, 2008, Proceedings*. Lecture Notes in Computer Science vol. 5157, pp. 108–125. Springer. DOI: 10.1007/978-3-540-85174-5_7. 553

Z. Brakerski and S. Goldwasser. 2010. Circular and leakage resilient public-key encryption under subgroup indistinguishability (or: Quadratic residuosity strikes back). In T. Rabin, editor, *Advances in Crytology–CRYPTO 2010, 30th Annual International Crytology Conference, Santa Barbara, CA, USA, August 15–19, 2010, Proceedings*. Lecture Notes in Computer Science vol. 6223, pp. 1–20. Springer. DOI: 10.1007/978-3-642-14623-7_1. 553

Z. Brakerski, C. Gentry, and V. Vaikuntanathan. 2012. (Leveled) fully homomorphic encryption without bootstrapping. In S. Goldwasser, editor, *Innovations in Theoretical Computer Science '12*, pp. 309–325. ACM. DOI: 10.1145/2090236.2090262. 558

Z. Brakerski and V. Vaikuntanathan. 2011. Efficient fully homomorphic encryption from (standard) LWE. In R. Ostrovsky, editor, *Foundations of Computer Science*, pp. 97–106. IEEE. Full version in https://eprint.iacr.org/2011/344.pdf. DOI: 10.1109/FOCS.2011.12. 556, 558

Z. Brakerski and V. Vaikuntanathan. 2014. Lattice-based FHE as secure as PKE. In M. Naor, editor, *Innovations in Theoretical Computer Science, ITCS'14, Princeton, NJ, USA, January 12–14, 2014*, pp. 1–12. ACM. DOI: 10.1145/2554797.2554799. 558

I. Chillotti, N. Gama, M. Georgieva, and M. Izabachène. 2016. Faster fully homomorphic encryption: Bootstrapping in less than 0.1 seconds. In J. H. Cheon and T. Takagi, editors, *Advances in Cryptology, ASIACRYPT 2016, 22nd International Conference on the Theory and Application of Cryptology and Information Security, Hanoi, Vietnam, December 4–8, 2016, Proceedings, Part I*. Lecture Notes in Computer Science vol. 10031, pp. 3–33. Springer. DOI: 10.1007/978-3-662-53887-6_1. 558

M. Clear and C. McGoldrick. 2015. Multi-identity and multi-key leveled FHE from learning with errors. In R. Gennaro and M. Robshaw, editors, *Advances in Cryptology–CRYPTO 2015, 35th Annual Cryptology Conference, Santa Barbara, CA, USA, August 16–20, 2015,*

Proceedings, Part II. Lecture Notes in Computer Science vol. 9216, pp. 630–656. Springer. DOI: 10.1007/978-3-662-48000-7_31. 559

R. Cramer and V. Shoup. 1998. A practical public key cryptosystem provably secure against adaptive chosen ciphertext attack. In H. Krawczyk, editor, *Advances in Cryptology–CRYPTO '98, 18th Annual International Cryptology Conference, Santa Barbara, CA, USA, August 23–27, 1998, Proceedings*. Lecture Notes in Computer Science vol. 1462, pp. 13–25. Springer. DOI: 10.1007/BFb0055717. 545

D. Dolev, C. Dwork, and M. Naor. 1991. Non-malleable cryptography (extended abstract). In C. Koutsougeras and J. S. Vitter, editors, *Proceedings of the 23rd Annual ACM Symposium on Theory of Computing, May 5–8, 1991, New Orleans, LA, USA*, pp. 542–552. ACM. DOI: 10.1145/103418.103474. 545

L. Ducas and D. Micciancio. 2015. FHEW: Bootstrapping homomorphic encryption in less than a second. In E. Oswald and M. Fischlin, editors, *Advances in Cryptology–EUROCRYPT 2015, 34th Annual International Conference on the Theory and Applications of Cryptographic Techniques, Sofia, Bulgaria, April 26–30, 2015, Proceedings, Part I*, Lecture Notes in Computer Science vol. 9056, pp. 617–640. Springer. DOI: 10.1007/978-3-662-46800-5_24. 558

T. El Gamal. 1984. A public key cryptosystem and a signature scheme based on discrete logarithms. In G. R. Blakley and D. Chaum, editors, *Advances in Cryptology–CRYPTO '84, Santa Barbara, CA, USA, August 19–22, 1984, Proceedings*. Lecture Notes in Computer Science vol. 196, pp. 10–18. Springer. DOI: 10.1007/3-540-39568-7_2. 544

C. Gentry. 2009a. *A Fully Homomorphic Encryption Scheme*. Ph.D. thesis, Stanford University. 549, 554

C. Gentry. 2009b. Fully homomorphic encryption using ideal lattices. In *Proceedings of the 41st Annual ACM Symposium on Theory of Computing, STOC 2009, Bethesda, MD, USA, May 31 to June 2, 2009*, pp. 169–178. DOI: 10.1.1.362.7592. 545, 549

C. Gentry, S. Halevi, and V. Vaikuntanathan. 2010. i-hop homomorphic encryption and rerandomizable yao circuits. In T. Rabin, editor, *Advances in Cryptology–CRYPTO 2010, 30th Annual Cryptology Conference, Santa Barbara, CA, USA, August 15–19, 2010, Proceedings*. Lecture Notes in Computer Science vol. 6223, pp. 155–172. Springer. DOI: 10.1007/978-3-642-14623-7_9. 548, 549

C. Gentry, A. Sahai, and B. Waters. 2013. Homomorphic encryption from learning with errors: Conceptually-simpler, asymptotically-faster, attribute-based. In R. Canetti and J. A. Garay, editors, *Advances in Cryptology–CRYPTO 2013, 33rd Annual Cryptology Conference, Santa Barbara, CA, USA, August 18–22, 2013. Proceedings, Part I*. Lecture Notes in Computer Science vol. 8042, pp. 75–92. Springer. DOI: 10.1007/978-3-642-40041-4_5. 556

O. Goldreich. 2001. *The Foundations of Cryptography: Volume 1, Basic Techniques*. Cambridge University Press. 544

O. Goldreich, S. Goldwasser, and S. Halevi. 1997. Public-key cryptosystems from lattice reduction problems. In B. S. Kaliski Jr., editor, *Advances in Cryptology–CRYPTO '97,*

17th Annual International Cryptology Conference, Santa Barbara, CA, USA, August 17–21, 1997, Proceedings. Lecture Notes in Computer Science vol. 1294, pp. 112–131. Springer. DOI: 10.1007/BFb0052231. 544

S. Goldwasser and S. Micali. 1982. Probabilistic encryption and how to play mental poker keeping secret all partial information. In *Symposium on Theory of Computing '82*, pp. 365–377. ACM. DOI: 10.1145/800070.802212. 544

R. Goyal, V. Koppula, and B. Waters. 2017. Separating semantic and circular security for symmetric-key bit encryption from the learning with errors assumption. In J.-S. Coron and J. B. Nielsen, editors, *Advances in Cryptology–EUROCRYPT 2017, 36th Annual International Conference on the Theory and Applications of Cryptographic Techniques, Paris, France, April 30 to May 4, 2017, Proceedings, Part II*, Lecture Notes in Computer Science vol. 10211, pp. 528–557. DOI: 10.1007/978-3-319-56614-6_18. 554

J. Hoffstein, J. Pipher, and J. H. Silverman. 1998. NTRU: A ring-based public key cryptosystem. In *ANTS-III, Proceedings of the Third International Symposium on Algorithmic Number Theory, June 23–25, 1998*, pp. 267–288. DOI: 10.1007/BFb0054868. 544, 559

A. López-Alt, E. Tromer, and V. Vaikuntanathan. 2012. On-the-fly multiparty computation on the cloud via multikey fully homomorphic encryption. In H. J. Karloff and T. Pitassi, editors, *Proceedings of the 44th Symposium on Theory of Computing Conference, STOC 2012, New York, NY, USA, May 19–22, 2012*, pp. 1219–1234. ACM. DOI: 10.1145/2213977.2214086. 559

V. Lyubashevsky, C. Peikert, and O. Regev. 2010. On ideal lattices and learning with errors over rings. In H. Gilbert, editor, *Advances in Cryptology–EUROCRYPT 2010, 29th Annual International Conference on the Theory and Applications of Cryptographic Techniques, French Riviera, May 30–June 3, 2010. Proceedings.* Lecture Notes in Computer Science vol. 6110, pp. 1–23. Springer. DOI: 10.1007/978-3-642-13190-5_1. 559

V. Lyubashevsky, C. Peikert, and O. Regev. 2013. A toolkit for ring-LWE cryptography. In T. Johansson and P. Q. Nguyen, editors, *Advances in Cryptology–EUROCRYPT 2013, 32nd Annual International Conference on the Theory and Applications of Cryptographic Techniques, Athens, Greece, May 26–30, 2013. Proceedings.* Lecture Notes in Computer Science vol. 7881, pp. 35–54. Springer. DOI: 10.1007/978-3-642-38348-9_3. 559

U. Mahadev. 2017. Classical homomorphic encryption for quantum circuits. *CoRR*, abs/1708.02130. 559

D. Micciancio and C. Peikert. 2012. Trapdoors for lattices: Simpler, tighter, faster, smaller. In D. Pointcheval and T. Johansson, editors, *Advances in Cryptology–EUROCRYPT 2012, 31st Annual International Conference on the Theory and Applications of Cryptographic Techniques, Cambridge, UK, April 15–19, 2012. Proceedings.* Lecture Notes in Computer Science vol. 7237, pp. 700–718. Springer. DOI: 10.1007/978-3-642-29011-4_41. 556

R. Ostrovsky, A. Paskin-Cherniavsky, and B. Paskin-Cherniavsky. 2014. Maliciously circuit-private FHE. In J. A. Garay and R. Gennaro, editors, *Advances in Cryptology–CRYPTO 2014, 34th Annual Cryptology Conference, Santa Barbara, CA, USA, August 17–21,*

2014. Proceedings, Part I. Lecture Notes in Computer Science vol. 8616, pp. 536–553. Springer. DOI: 10.1007/978-3-662-44371-2_30. 548

M. O. Rabin. 1979. Digitalized signatures and public-key functions as intractable as factorization. Technical report, Cambridge, MA, USA. 543

O. Regev. 2005. On lattices, learning with errors, random linear codes, and cryptography. In H. N. Gabow and R. Fagin, editors, *Symposium on Theory of Computing '05*, pp. 84–93. ACM. Full version in Regev [2009]. DOI: 10.1145/1060590.1060603. 555

O. Regev. 2009. On lattices, learning with errors, random linear codes, and cryptography. *Journal of the ACM*, 56(6). DOI: 10.1145/1568318.1568324. 563

R. Rivest, L. Adleman, and M. L. Dertouzos. 1978. On data banks and privacy homomorphisms. In R. A. DeMillo, R. J. Lipton, D. P. Dobkin, and A. K. Jones, editors *Foundations of Secure Computation*, pp. 169–180. Academic Press. 543, 544, 545

R. L. Rivest, A. Shamir, and L. M. Adleman. 1978. A method for obtaining digital signatures and public-key cryptosystems. *Commununications of the ACM*, 21(2):120–126. DOI: 10.1145/359340.359342. 543

N. P. Smart and F. Vercauteren. 2010. Fully homomorphic encryption with relatively small key and ciphertext sizes. In P. Q. Nguyen and D. Pointcheval, editors, *Public Key Cryptography–PKC 2010, 13th International Conference on Practice and Theory in Public Key Cryptography, Paris, France, May 26–28, 2010. Proceedings*. Lecture Notes in Computer Science vol. 6056, pp. 420–443. Springer. DOI: 10.1007/978-3-642-13013-7_25. 558

Interactive Proofs for Lattice Problems

Daniele Micciancio

Interactive proof systems are a central concept in computer science, and have greatly influenced both cryptography and computational complexity theory. In this chapter, we are concerned with interactive proof systems for lattice problems, a specific area of mathematics that has received much attention during the last two decades, both as a powerful tool to construct advanced cryptographic primitives (like fully homomorphic encryption) and as a plausible defense against the threat presented by the possible development of quantum computers. Starting from the pioneering work of Goldreich and Goldwasser on the limits of inapproximability of lattice problems, we describe the main ideas behind (zero-knowledge) interactive proof systems for lattices, and a number of related papers that were either motivated, influenced or inspired by that work.

21.1 Introduction

The work of Goldwasser and Micali on the development of interactive proof systems, the powerful notion of zero-knowledge proof, and the many applications of these notions in cryptography and computational complexity theory are well covered elsewhere in this volume. In this chapter, we focus on interactive proof systems for problems in a specific area of mathematics that also has proved to be very useful in cryptography: the study of computational problems on point lattices. The study of interactive proof systems for lattice problems was pioneered by Goldreich and Goldwasser in their landmark paper "On the Limits of Inapproximability of Lattice Problems." Simple and elegant, this work has influenced, in more or less direct ways, many other subsequent developments in lattice-based cryptography. In this survey, we describe the original proof system of Goldreich and Goldwasser [2000], and a number of related works on (interactive and noninteractive) proofs, computational complexity, and cryptographic applications of lattices. But, first things first, let us begin by recalling the historical context and original motivations behind Goldreich and Goldwasser [2000].

Historical Context.   Lattices are regular arrangements of points in n-dimensional Euclidean space, and they have been extensively used in cryptology since the development of the LLL lattice reduction algorithm [Lenstra et al. 1982], but primarily as a tool for cryptanalysis. A major shift occurred in 1996, when Ajtai discovered a remarkable connection between the worst-case and average-case complexity of lattice problems [Ajtai 2004]. In short, if certain problems related to finding short vectors in arbitrary n-dimensional lattices are computationally hard to approximate within factors polynomial in n, then one-way functions (arguably, the most basic building blocks of cryptography) exist. This discovery supported and motivated the use of lattices not just for cryptanalysis, but also to design secure cryptographic functions, and marked the beginning of modern lattice-based cryptography. Around the same time, developments in computational complexity had also established that the problem of finding the shortest vector in a lattice (the "Shortest Vector Problem," **SVP**) was **NP**-hard (under randomized reductions), even to approximate within small factors [Ajtai 1998, Cai and Nerurkar 1999, Micciancio 2001]. These discoveries opened up a possible avenue of attack toward the grand challenge of basing cryptography on the minimal assumption that **P** is different from **NP**. But a big gap existed between these works: While the one-way function of Ajtai [2004] required the inapproximability of lattice problems within polynomial factors n^c (for some fairly large constant exponent c), the **NP**-hardness results of Ajtai [1998], Cai and Nerurkar [1999], and Micciancio [2001] only provided lower bounds for very small (constant) approximation factors. Some serious obstacle on the way of basing cryptography on **NP**-hard (lattice) problems was already known: A sequence of works [Håstad 1988, Lagarias et al. 1990, Banaszczyk 1993] had shown that the (promise) problems associated to approximating SVP within a factor $O(n)$ was in the class **NP ∩ coNP**, and therefore not NP-hard under the widely believed conjecture that NP ≠ coNP. But it was conceivable that cryptography could be based on smaller approximation factors. In fact, motivated both by computational complexity [Håstad 1988, Lagarias et al. 1990, Banaszczyk 1993, Goldreich and Goldwasser 2000] and concrete security considerations, efforts on improving Ajtai's proof lead to cryptographic functions that are as hard to break as approximating lattice problems within factors essentially as low as n [Cai and Nerurkar 1997, Micciancio 2004, Micciancio and Regev 2007, Gentry et al. 2008, Micciancio and Peikert 2013]. The work of Goldreich and Goldwasser [2000] lowered the factor for which one could conceivably hope to prove NP-hardness even further, by showing that SVP (and the related closest vector problem, **CVP**) is in the complexity class **coAM** for approximation factors $O(\sqrt{n/\log n})$. Under the standard complexity assumption that the polynomial hierarchy does not collapse, this also rules out the possibility of SVP and CVP being NP-hard problems, and this time for approximation factors as low as $O(\sqrt{n/\log n})$. Establishing such limits on the inapproximability of lattice problems was indeed the primary motivation of Goldreich and Goldwasser [2000], as clearly indicated by the title of the paper. Much progress has occurred since the conference presentation of Goldreich and Goldwasser [2000] in 1998, both on the front of lowering the polynomial worst-case inapproximability factors required to build cryptographic functions [Cai and Nerurkar 1997, Micciancio 2004, Micciancio and Regev 2007, Gentry et al. 2008, Micciancio and Peikert 2013] and proving NP-hardness results for the shortest vector problem [Dinur 2002, Khot 2005, Khot 2006, Haviv and Regev 2012, Micciancio 2012]. But the "limits of inapproximability" established in Goldreich and Goldwasser [2000] still stand as the main barrier between worst-case lower bounds, and cryptographically useful assumptions. As far as we know, approximating lattice problems within a factor $O(n^c)$ may be NP-hard for $c < 1/2$, and imply one-way functions and other cryptographic applications for $c > 1/2$.

Overview. While establishing limits of inapproximability of lattice problems is an important goal, the constructions and proof techniques used in Goldreich and Goldwasser [2000] are very interesting on their own. At a technical level, this work gave simple, constant-round interactive proof systems to show that a lattice does not contain short vectors, or vectors close to some target point.

Given a lattice, it is easy to prove that it contains short vectors: as lattice membership can be efficiently checked, just providing the candidate short lattice vector offers a compact, easily verifiable proof that short lattice vectors exist. Similarly, one can prove that a target point is close to a lattice by providing a lattice point close to it. But how can one efficiently verify the optimality of these solutions? Checking optimality of these solutions is the technical problem at the core of Goldreich and Goldwasser [2000]. Since the number of candidate solutions is, in principle, exponentially large, it would seem that optimality cannot be checked without going through the time-consuming process of exhaustively enumerating all possibilities. This problem is addressed in Goldreich and Goldwasser [2000] by resorting to randomness and interaction, the key features of interactive proof systems. Interestingly, the interactive proof systems of Goldreich and Goldwasser [2000] also have the important security property of being (*statistical*) *zero-knowledge*; that is, the verifier does not learn anything interesting from the interaction with the prover, beyond the validity of the assertion being proved.

Beside establishing clear limits on the inapproximability of lattice problems, the work of Goldreich and Goldwasser also raised several natural questions. Is interaction necessary to establish the inapproximability of lattice problems for factors as low as $O(\sqrt{n})$? (Prior to Goldreich and Goldwasser [2000] it was known how to prove that lattices did not have short vectors only for substantially larger approximation factors $O(n)$.) Can statistical zero-knowledge proofs for hard lattice problems be used to design useful cryptographic functions? Can similar proof systems be designed for other lattice problems, beside SVP and CVP? Can the approximation factor be lowered below $O(\sqrt{n/\log n})$?

In the rest of this chapter, first, in Section 21.2 we give some general background about point lattices. Next, in Section 21.3 we provide a description of the interactive proof system of Goldreich and Goldwasser [2000], henceforth referred to as the **GG** proof system. In Sections 21.4 and 21.5 we show how the GG proof system has been adapted and extended to solve many other related problems, like the construction of proof systems with efficient provers, noninteractive zero-knowledge proofs, or (interactive) proof systems for several other lattice problems of interest to cryptography. Finally, in Section 21.6 we describe how the ideas behind GG proof system were instrumental to resolve one of the main questions related the cryptographic applicability of lattice problems. Specifically, Ajtai's work [2004] provided a surjective one-way function (often described as the shortest integer solution, or **SIS**, problem), useful to build collision-resistant hash functions, commitment schemes, and digital signature schemes, but little more. A much wider range of cryptographic applications, starting from public-key encryption, all the way to identity-based and fully homomorphic encryption, was opened up by Regev's landmark proof [Regev 2009] that learning with errors (**LWE**) problem (an injective version of SIS) is also hard on average, based essentially on the same worst-case problems as those used by Ajtai, but with a catch: Regev's proof required quantum computation. This was in part justified in Regev [2009] by the apparent difficulty of making any nontrivial classical (nonquantum) use of an LWE oracle. In a surprising turn of events, Peikert observed that an LWE oracle is precisely what is needed to implement the prover strategy of the GG proof system, and this can be used to provide a classical (nonquantum) proof that LWE and its countless cryptographic applications are secure under the assumption that certain lattice problems are hard to solve in polynomial time [Peikert 2009]. These are only some of the works that were motivated or somehow influenced by [Goldreich and Goldwasser 2000]. Additional references and pointers to related works are provided in the individual sections.

21.2 Background

In this section we recall the definition of the most important parameters associated to a lattice. Each parameter naturally defines a corresponding computational problem: Given a lattice, compute or approximate the value of the parameter. We use column notation for vectors $\mathbf{v} \in \mathbb{R}^d$. For any $p \geq 1$, the ℓ_p norm of a vector $\mathbf{v}$ is $\|\mathbf{v}\|_p = (\sum_i |v_i|^p)^{1/p}$. Of special interest are the ℓ_1 norm $\|\mathbf{v}\|_1 = \sum_i |v_i|$, the ℓ_∞ norm $\|\mathbf{v}\|_\infty = \lim_{p \to \infty} \|\mathbf{v}\|_p = \max_i |v_i|$, and the Euclidean norm (ℓ_2) $\|\mathbf{v}\| = \|\mathbf{v}\|_2 = \sqrt{\sum_i x^2}$. The dot product between two vectors is $\langle \mathbf{x}, \mathbf{y} \rangle = \sum_i x_i \cdot y_i$. We write $\mathcal{B}(\mathbf{c}, r) = \{\mathbf{v}: \|\mathbf{v} - \mathbf{c}\| < r\}$ for the open ball of radius r centered around $\mathbf{c}$.

A *lattice* is the set

$$\Lambda = \left\{ \sum_{i=1}^n \mathbf{b}_i \cdot x_i : x_i \in \mathbb{Z} \right\}$$

of all *integer* linear combinations of n linearly independent vectors $\mathbf{b}_1, \ldots, \mathbf{b}_n \in \mathbb{R}^d$. In this survey we focus on full rank lattices, where $d = n$, and the basis vectors $\mathbf{b}_1, \ldots, \mathbf{b}_n$ are the columns of a square nonsingular matrix $\mathbf{B} = [\mathbf{b}_1, \ldots, \mathbf{b}_n] \in \mathbb{R}^{n \times n}$.

The length of the shortest nonzero vector in a lattice is

$$\lambda_1(\Lambda) = \inf\{\|\mathbf{v}\|: \mathbf{v} \in \Lambda, \mathbf{v} \neq \mathbf{0}\},$$

and it equals the *minimum distance* between any two lattice points. This definition can be generalized to a sequence of n parameters, $\lambda_1, \ldots, \lambda_n$, called the *successive minima* of a lattice, where

$$\lambda_i(\Lambda) = \inf\{r: \operatorname{span}(\Lambda \cap \mathcal{B}(\mathbf{0}, r)) \geq i\}$$

is the radius of the smallest ball (centered around the origin) that contains at least i linearly independent lattice vectors.

The distance of a point $\mathbf{t}$ to a lattice Λ is the distance

$$\operatorname{dist}(\mathbf{t}, \Lambda) = \inf\{\|\mathbf{t} - \mathbf{v}\|: \mathbf{v} \in \Lambda\}$$

between $\mathbf{t}$ and the closest lattice point. The covering radius of a (full rank) lattice Λ is the maximum distance

$$\rho(\Lambda) = \sup\{\operatorname{dist}(\mathbf{t}, \Lambda): \mathbf{t} \in \mathbb{R}^n\}$$

between the lattice and any point in space. (If the lattice is not full rank, then $\mathbf{t}$ is restricted to the linear span of the lattice.) A point $\mathbf{t}$ achieving $\operatorname{dist}(\mathbf{t}, \Lambda) = \rho(\Lambda)$ is called a *deep hole* of the lattice.

All these parameters arise naturally in applications—for example, when lattices are used as codes in Euclidean space. In this setting, the minimum distance λ_1 is related to the error correction capabilities of the code, while the covering radius ρ is the maximum distortion when then lattice is used for vector quantization.

The dual of a lattice Λ is the set

$$\Lambda^* = \{\mathbf{x} : \forall \mathbf{v} \in \Lambda.\langle \mathbf{x}, \mathbf{v} \rangle \in \mathbb{Z}\}$$

of all vectors (in the linear span of the lattice) that have integer scalar product with all lattice vectors. The dual of a lattice is a lattice, and if Λ has basis $\mathbf{B}$, then its dual has basis $\mathbf{B}^{-t}$, the inverse transpose of $\mathbf{B}$. The dual lattice plays an important role in the mathematical and computational study of lattices. For example, Banaszczyk proved the following fundamental "transference theorem," which allows to relate the parameters of a lattice with those of its dual.

Theorem 21.1   (Transference theorem [Banaszczyk 1993])   For any n-dimensional lattice Λ, and its dual Λ^*, we have

$$1 \leq \lambda_1(\Lambda) \cdot \lambda_n(\Lambda^*) \leq n.$$

21.2.1   Worst-Case Lattice Problems

Each lattice parameter defines an associated computational problem: Given a lattice Λ (typically represented by a basis matrix $\mathbf{B}$), compute or approximate the value of the parameter. Typically, there is a lattice vector (or small set of lattice vectors) associated to the optimal value of the parameter, and applications may also require to find such vectors. The two most important computational problems on lattices are the shortest vector problem and the closest vector problem, which correspond to the lattice minimum distance λ_1 and the distance to a given target $\mathbf{t}$, respectively. In complexity theory, the approximate versions of these problems are usually modeled as *promise problems*—that is, the decision task of distinguishing instances where the value of the parameter is small, from those where the parameter is large. The *gap* between small and large values of the parameter captures the slackness of finding *approximate* solutions.

Definition 21.1   For any approximation factor $\gamma \geq 1$, the shortest vector problem (**GapSVP**), given a lattice basis $\mathbf{B}$, asks to distinguish between the following two cases:

- (**yes** instances) $\lambda_1(\mathbf{B}) \leq 1$.
- (**no** instances) $\lambda_1(\mathbf{B}) > \gamma$.

Sometimes the problem is defined to also include a target value d, and the question is to distinguish between $\lambda_1 \leq d$ and $\lambda_1 > \gamma d$. But one can always assume that $d = 1$ by scaling the lattice by a factor d. Usually, the approximation factor γ is a function of the lattice dimension n, and $\gamma(n) = 1$ corresponds to the exact version of the problem—that is, the problem of computing the exact value of λ_1. An algorithm solves **GapSVP** if it accepts all the YES instances, and rejects all the NO instances. For $\gamma > 1$, there is a gap between YES and NO instances: lattices such that $\lambda_1 \in (1, \gamma]$. For instances in this range, any answer is acceptable, making the problem easier. Clearly, the larger the approximation factor γ, the larger the gap between YES and NO instances and the easier the computational problem. Algorithms to solve **GapSVP** typically work by solving the corresponding search problem, denoted **SVP**, which asks to actually finding a lattice vector of length $\|\mathbf{v}\| \leq \gamma \lambda_1$. the closest vector problem is the inhomogeneous version of **SVP** and it is defined analogously.

Definition 21.2 For any approximation factor $\gamma \geq 1$, the closest vector problem (**GapCVP**), given a lattice basis $\mathbf{B}$, and a target vector $\mathbf{t}$, asks to distinguish between the following two cases:

- (YES instances) $\operatorname{dist}(\mathbf{t}, \mathbf{B}) \leq 1$.
- (NO instances) $\operatorname{dist}(\mathbf{t}, \mathbf{B}) > \gamma$.

Finally, the promise problem associated to λ_n is called the Shortest Independent Vectors Problem, and it is defined as follows.

Definition 21.3 For any approximation factor $\gamma \geq 1$, the Shortest Independent Vectors Problem (**GapSIVP**). given an lattice basis $\mathbf{B}$, asks to distinguish between the following two cases (where n is the dimension of the lattice):

- (YES instances) $\lambda_n(\mathbf{B}) \leq 1$.
- (NO instances) $\lambda_n(\mathbf{B}) > \gamma$.

Search versions of these problems are denoted **CVP** and **SIVP**, and ask to find a lattice vector $\mathbf{v} \in \Lambda$ within distance $\operatorname{dist}(\mathbf{v}, \mathbf{t}) \leq \gamma \cdot \operatorname{dist}(\mathbf{t}, \Lambda)$ from the target, or n linearly independent lattice vectors $\mathbf{v}_1, \ldots, \mathbf{v}_n \in \Lambda$ all of length $\|\mathbf{v}_i\| \leq \gamma \lambda_n$. The *bounded distance decoding* problem (**BDD**) is a special version of **CVP**, where the target $\mathbf{t}$ is chosen as a vector at distance $< \lambda_1/2$ from the lattice. The importance of this problem is due to the fact that for any target $\mathbf{t}$ there is at most one lattice vector within distance $\lambda_1/2$ from it. So, the solution to **BDD** is always unique. These are just the most famous computational problems on lattices. Other lattice problems will be introduced when needed.

21.2.2 Average-Case Lattice Problems and Smoothing Parameter

All problems defined so far are usually understood as *worst-case* problems: An algorithm is deemed to solve the problem if it returns the correct answer on any input instance. In other words, the algorithm should be able to solve the hardest (i.e., computationally "worst") instances of the problem. We say that a problem is computationally hard (in the *worst case*) if no such efficient algorithm exists. This is the standard notion of hardness most commonly used in computational complexity—for example, in the theory of **NP**-hardness. The above lattice problems (in particular, **GapSVP** and **SIVP**) provide a complexity foundation for lattice-based cryptography. However, they cannot be directly used in the construction of cryptographic functions. (The inadequacy of worst-case complexity and NP-hardness to build cryptographic functions is well known; for example, see Even and Yacobi [1980] and the historical notes in Goldreich [2006, page 26].) In cryptography, one needs problems that are hard on average, so that when one picks a cryptographic key at random, one can be reasonably confident that that random key is hard to break with high probability. So, lattice-based cryptography usually makes use of the following *average-case* problems.

- The shortest integer solution problem (**SIS**): For integer parameters n, m, q and bound β, given a uniformly random matrix $\mathbf{A} \in \mathbb{Z}_q^{n \times m}$, find a nonzero integer vector $\mathbf{x}$ of length $\|\mathbf{x}\| \leq \beta$ such that $\mathbf{Ax} = 0 \pmod q$. There is also an inhomogeneous version of this problem, which takes as input also a target vector $\mathbf{u}$, and the goal is to find a short $\mathbf{x}$ such that $\mathbf{Ax} = \mathbf{u} \pmod q$.

- The learning with errors problem (**LWE**): For integer parameters n, m, q and bound α, given a uniformly random matrix $\mathbf{A} \in \mathbb{Z}_q^{n \times m}$ and a vector $\mathbf{b} = \mathbf{A}^t \mathbf{s} + \mathbf{e}$, recover $\mathbf{s}$. Here vectors $\mathbf{s}, \mathbf{e}$ are also chosen at random, with $\mathbf{s} \in \mathbb{Z}_q^n$ usually uniform, and $\mathbf{e} \in \mathbb{Z}^m$ chosen with independent small entries with Gaussian-like distribution of magnitude $\approx \alpha q$.[1]

Both problems can be seen as an average-case version of standard lattice problems as follows. For **SIS**, let $\Lambda^\perp(\mathbf{A})$ be the set of all integer vectors $\mathbf{x}$ such that $\mathbf{Ax} = 0 \pmod q$. This set of points turns out to be a lattice, and a basis for it can be easily computed by performing a sequence of elementary integer row operations on $\mathbf{A}$. In fact, $\Lambda^\perp(\mathbf{A})$ is a special type of lattice, which repeats periodically modulo q. This makes $\Lambda^\perp(\mathbf{A})$ particularly convenient for cryptography, which can be implemented using only arithmetic modulo q on bounded-size integers. Then **SIS** corresponds to finding a short vector (of length at most β) in the lattice $\Lambda^\perp(\mathbf{A})$ defined by a randomly chosen $\mathbf{A}$. The bound β is usually set to a small multiple

1. Specifically, each entry e_i is chosen with probability proportional to $\exp(-\pi(e_i/(\alpha q))^2)$. Other variants of this distribution have also been considered.

of the expected minimum distance of $\Lambda^\perp(\mathbf{A})$. So, **SIS** is essentially an average-case version of **SVP**.

In the case of **LWE** the connection is even more direct, as recovering **s** is equivalent to finding a lattice point ($\mathbf{A}^t\mathbf{s}$, in the lattice generated by $\mathbf{A}^t \pmod q$) close to the target **b**. So, **LWE** is an average-case version of **CVP**, using a randomly chosen lattice $\Lambda(\mathbf{A})$ (which, also in this case, is periodic modulo q), and a random target defined by a Gaussian-like error vector **e**. Usually, **LWE** is employed in a setting where the length of **e** is small (with high probability) relative to the minimum distance of the lattice, so that the solution **s** is essentially unique. So, **LWE** is an average-case version of the bounded distance decoding problem, **BDD**.

In summary, the cryptographic problems **SIS** and **LWE** are average-case versions of standard lattice problems, **SVP** and **BDD**. But there is an even deeper connection between **SIS**, **LWE** and lattices. As originally proved in Ajtai [2004] and Regev [2009], for appropriate values of the parameters, solving these problem on the average (even with very small, but non-negligible, probability) is at least as hard as solving **GapSVP** and **SIVP** in the worst case on n dimensional lattices within approximation factors $\gamma = n^{O(1)}$ polynomial in the lattice dimension. As the best known polynomial-time algorithm to solve these problems only achieves approximation factors exponential in the dimension n, inapproximability within polynomial factors is considered a fairly standard assumption in cryptography. Still, as the concrete hardness of the problems (and security of cryptographic applications) depends on γ, determining the smallest values of γ for which inapproximability of **GapSVP** and **SIVP** (in the worst case) implies the average-case hardness of **SIS** and **LWE** has been an important research problem in cryptography. The approximation factor γ for **SIS** has been improved to almost linear $\gamma = \tilde{O}(n)$ in the lattice dimension using Gaussian measures [Micciancio and Regev 2007]. Gaussian distributions are also used in Regev [2009] to select the error vector **e** and prove the average-case hardness of **LWE** based on similar inapproximability factors γ.

Central both to the study of **SIS** and **LWE**, and most advanced applications of lattice-based cryptography, is a quantity, introduced in Micciancio and Regev [2007], called the *smoothing parameter* of a lattice. Due to its importance in lattice-based cryptography, the smoothing parameter has become an important lattice quantity, of much interest to the complexity study of lattices just like λ_1 and λ_n. This parameter and the computational problem of approximating it, is defined in Section 21.5, where we described a "Gaussian" variant of the GG protocol.

Complexity Classes.   In this survey we will classify computational problems on lattices into a number of standard complexity classes, the most important of which is certainly **NP**, the class of languages (or, more generally, promise problems) that admit efficiently verifiable proofs of membership. The class **AM** [Babai 1985, Babai and Moran 1988, Goldwasser and Sipser 1989] generalizes **NP** by allowing the prover and verifier to interact and use randomness. Specifically, in an **AM** (Arthur–Merlin) protocol, the verifier (Arthur) first sends a uniformly chosen random query to the prover, and then the prover (Merlin) replies with a proof. Finally, the verifier decides (deterministically, in polynomial time) to either accept or reject the proof.[2] The acceptance guarantees are probabilistic (over the random choice of the verifier's query), and the proof system is parameterized by a *completeness error* $c \geq 0$ and a *soundness error* $s \geq 0$. The proof system is *complete* if, on input any YES instance, a prover following the protocol makes the verifier accept, except with probability at most c. The proof system is *sound* if, on input any NO instance, no (computationally unbounded, possibly misbehaving) prover can make the verifier accept with probability better than s. For a proof system to be useful, it should satisfy both the soundness and completeness properties for appropriate values of c and s. The completeness and soundness errors are customarily set to $s = c = 1/3$, but the class **AM** is very robust with the respect to the choice of s, c. In particular, any **AM** proof system with total error $s + c < 1 - n^{-O(1)}$ bounded away from 1 can be turned into an **AM** proof system with *perfect completeness* ($c = 0$) and exponentially small soundness error $s = \exp(-n^{O(1)})$, where n is the input size.

coNP and **coAM** are the complementary classes, where proofs are given to show that an input instance does *not* belong to the language. Finally, **SZK** is the class of languages admitting a statistical zero-knowledge proof system—that is, an interactive proof system where the verifier does not learn anything from the proof, except the fact that the assertion being proved in correct.[3] The zero-knowledge property can be defined either with respect to honest verifiers that follow the protocol, or arbitrary (probabilistic polynomial-time) verifiers that may deviate from it. We remark that cryptographic applications usually require the latter notion of zero-knowledge with respect to arbitrary verifiers. However, it turns out that any

---

2. Technically, this is the definition of **AM**2], the class of problems that admit a 2-round protocol. But increasing the number of rounds to any constant $k \geq 2$ does not change the power of these proof systems. So, **AM** can be equivalently defined as the class of problems admitting a constant-round public-coin interactive protocol.

3. The qualifier *statistical* refers to the fact that anything the verifier observes during a protocol run can be efficiently simulated (without interacting with the prover) up to a small statistical error. The weaker notion of *computational* zero-knowledge only requires the simulated view to be *computationally indistinguishable* from a real interaction. In this survey, we are only concerned with statistical zero-knowledge.

honest-verifier **SZK** proof system can be transformed into a proof system achieving statistical zero-knowledge against arbitrary (possibly cheating) verifiers [Goldreich et al. 1998]. So, for simplicity, in this survey we drop the distinction between these two notions. The inclusions **NP** $\subseteq$ **AM** and **coNP** $\subseteq$ **coAM** are trivial. However, it is conjectured that **NP** $\not\subseteq$ **coNP** and even **NP** $\not\subseteq$ **coAM**. So, a standard method to prove that a language is unlikely to be **NP** complete is to show that it belongs to **coNP** or **coAM**. Finally, the class **SZK** is closed under complement [Okamoto 2000], and **SZK** $\subseteq$ **AM** $\cap$ **coAM** [Aiello and Håstad 1991, Fortnow 1989]. Still, **SZK** is not known to be contained in **NP**.

21.3 The GG Proof Systems

Given a lattice **B** and a target vector **t**, proving that **t** is within distance γ from the lattice is easy: just exhibit a lattice vector **Bx** such that $\|\mathbf{Bx} - \mathbf{t}\| \le \gamma$. While finding the lattice vector **Bx** closest to **t** may be hard, once this vector is found, it is easy to verify that **Bx** is close to **t**. In other words, the integer vector **x** serves as an efficiently verifiable *proof*[4] that dist$(\mathbf{t}, \mathbf{B}) \le \gamma$. But how can one prove that this is indeed the optimal, or almost optimal, solution? This requires proving that there is no lattice vector at distance (substantially) smaller than γ from the target **t**. In other words, one has to prove that a smaller ball $\mathcal{B}(\mathbf{t}, r)$ (for some radius $r < \gamma$) contains no vectors from the lattice $\mathcal{L}(\mathbf{B})$.

A simple and elegant solution to this problem is offered by the GG interactive proof system [Goldreich and Goldwasser 2000], which is based on the following idea. First consider the simple (in fact, trivial) case where the target **t** either belongs to the lattice (i.e., it is at distance 0) or it is far from it. In order to demonstrate that **t** is far from the lattice (say, at distance larger than γ) one may proceed as follows:

- The verifier picks a random perturbation vector $\mathbf{r} \in \mathcal{B}(\mathbf{0}, \gamma/2)$ from a ball of radius $\gamma/2$ and a "uniformly" random[5] lattice point $\mathbf{v} \in \mathcal{L}(\mathbf{B})$. It then sends either $\mathbf{v} + \mathbf{r}$ or $\mathbf{t} + \mathbf{v} + \mathbf{r}$ to the prover. Equivalently, one can think of the verifier as sending a vector $\mathbf{u} = b \cdot \mathbf{t} + \mathbf{v} + \mathbf{r} \in \mathcal{B}(\mathbf{v} + b\mathbf{t}, \gamma/2)$ from a ball of radius $\gamma/2$ centered around $\mathbf{v} + b\mathbf{t}$ for a randomly chosen bit $b \in \{0, 1\}$.

---

4. Formally, for the problem to be in **NP**, one should also show that the size of the proof **x** is polynomially related to the size of the problem instance **B**. This is also fairly easy to prove, using known lattice bounds and simple linear algebra.

5. Technically, since a lattice has a countably infinite number of points, one cannot really choose **v** with uniform distribution. We will address this technicality when presenting the actual protocol.

- The prover checks if **u** is closer to $\mathcal{L}(\mathbf{B})$ or $\mathbf{t} + \mathcal{L}(\mathbf{B})$, or, equivalently, which of the two points **u** and $\mathbf{u} - \mathbf{t}$ is closest to the lattice $\mathcal{L}(\mathbf{B})$. In the former case, it sends the bit $b' = 0$ to the verifier. Otherwise, it sends $b' = 1$.

- The verifier checks if the prover correctly guessed the bit b, and accepts the proof if and only if $b' = b$.

Since we want to prove that **t** is *far* from the lattice, YES instances are those for which $\text{dist}(\mathbf{t}, \mathcal{L}(\mathbf{B})) > \gamma$. Notice that, for these instances, the balls $\mathcal{B}(\mathbf{v}, \gamma/2)$ and $\mathcal{B}(\mathbf{v}' + \mathbf{t}, \gamma/2)$ centered around lattice points **v** or their shifts $\mathbf{v}' + \mathbf{t}$ are disjoint. So, the verifier's message **u** uniquely identifies the center $\mathbf{v} + b\mathbf{t}$. In particular, the prover can recover the bit b by checking which of **u** and $\mathbf{u} - \mathbf{t}$ is closest to (in fact, within distance $\gamma/2$ from) the lattice. This shows that the proof system is *complete*. Conversely, for NO instances of our simplified problem, the target **t** belongs to the lattice. So, **v** and $\mathbf{v} + \mathbf{t}$ are both random lattice points, and the two distributions (for $b \in \{0, 1\}$) are essentially identical. It follows that the proof system is *sound*; that is, no prover (no matter how powerful) can determine the value of the bit b with probability better than 1/2. (Here 1/2 is the soundness error, which can be reduced by repeating the basic proof system an appropriate number of times.)

Notice the similarity between the above proof system, and the classic proof systems for quadratic nonresiduocity, or graph nonisomorphism [Goldwasser et al. 1989, Goldreich et al. 1991]. For example, in the case of graph nonisomorphism, the input is a pair of graphs (G_0, G_1) and the prover claims that the two graphs are *not* isomorphic. To this end, the verifier sends an isomorphic copy $G' = \pi(G_b)$ of one of the two graphs (for a random permutation π and random bit $b \in \{0, 1\}$), and the prover is tasked with recovering the bit b. If the graphs are indeed nonisomorphic, the bit b is uniquely identified by G', and the (all-powerful) prover can recover b by testing G' for isomorphism with G_0 and G_1. On the other hand, if the graphs are isomorphic, then the message G' sent by the verifier is distributed independently of the bit b, and no prover can recover b with probability better than 1/2.

In both problems, a prover can always guess b with probability 1/2 by picking $b' \in \{0, 1\}$ uniformly at random. So, the proof system has soundness error 1/2; that is, the verifier cannot hope to catch a cheating prover with probability higher than 1/2. In order to get high confidence about the assertion that **t** is far from the lattice (or that the graphs are not isomorphic), the prover and the verifier will have to repeat the above process a number of times. In general, if the verifier detects a cheating prover with probability δ (i.e., the prover guesses $b' = b$ with probability at most $1 - \delta$), then repeating the basic proof system n/δ times will allow the verifier to catch a cheating prover except with exponentially small probability $2^{-O(n)}$.

Protocol 1: coAM protocol for **GapCVP**
Input: Lattice basis **B**

1. The Verifier selects $b \in \{0, 1\}$ and $\mathbf{r} \in \mathcal{B}(\mathbf{0}, \gamma/2)$ uniformly at random. He then sends $\mathbf{u} = (b\mathbf{t} + \mathbf{r}) \bmod \mathbf{B}$ to the Prover.

2. The Prover checks if $\mathrm{dist}(\mathbf{u}, \mathcal{L}(\mathbf{B})) < \mathrm{dist}(\mathbf{u}, \mathbf{t} + \mathcal{L}(\mathbf{B}))$. If so, he responds with $b' = 0$. Otherwise, he responds with $b' = 1$.

3. The Verifier accepts with $b = b'$.

Figure 21.1 The Goldreich–Goldwasser **coAM** protocol for **GapCVP**. The proof system has perfect completeness and achieves soundness error bounded away from 1 when $\gamma = \Omega(\sqrt{n/\log n})$. The error probability can be made arbitrarily small either by increasing γ or by standard repetition techniques.

The simplified lattice problem, as described above, is not very interesting: membership of **t** in the lattice can be easily checked in polynomial time—for example, by solving the linear system $\mathbf{Bx} = \mathbf{t}$ and checking if the solution **x** has integer coordinates. But the basic idea works also for the (nontrivial) case where the distance of **t** from the lattice is small, though not necessarily 0. This time the two distributions $\mathbf{u} = \mathbf{v} + \mathbf{r}$ and $\mathbf{u} = \mathbf{t} + \mathbf{v} + \mathbf{r}$ are not identical. But if **t** is sufficiently close to the lattice (relative to the size of the perturbation vector **r**), they will still overlap, making it impossible for the prover to always correctly guess the bit b.

In the above informal description we have overlooked some technicalities, most importantly formalizing what it means to choose a lattice point $\mathbf{v} \in \mathcal{L}(\mathbf{B})$ at random. In fact, since $\mathcal{L}(\mathbf{B})$ is a countably infinite set, there is no well-defined uniform probability distribution over it. This problem can be addressed using standard techniques, either by choosing **v** from a sufficiently large (but finite) subset of lattice points, or, even better, by working modulo the lattice.[6] The final proof system is shown in Figure 21.1.

In the above proof system, one can think of the vector **u** as coming from one of two balls: either $\mathcal{B}(\mathbf{t}, \gamma/2)$, for $b = 1$, or $\mathcal{B}(\mathbf{Bx}, \gamma/2)$, for $b = 0$, where **Bx** is the lattice point closest to **t**. (The lattice point **Bx** disappears when reducing **u** modulo **B**.)

If the target is at distance $\|\mathbf{t} - \mathbf{Bx}\| > \gamma$ from the lattice, then these two balls are disjoint, and **u** uniquely determines the bit b. This allows the prover to always guess

6. A standard representative for the equivalence class of a target vector **t** modulo a lattice with basis **B** can be efficiently computed by expressing the target $\mathbf{t} = \mathbf{Bx}$ in terms of the basis vectors, and then reducing its coordinates modulo 1, to bring them in the interval $\mathbf{x} \in [0, 1)^n$.

the bit b and make the verifier accept with probability 1 the target $\mathbf{t}$ is at distance larger than γ from the lattice.

On the other hand, if $\mathbf{t}$ is within distance $\|\mathbf{t} - \mathbf{Bx}\| \leq 1 \leq \gamma$ from the lattice, then the two balls have a nonempty intersection. If the perturbation $\mathbf{r}$ falls in this intersection, the vector $\mathbf{u}$ is equally likely to come from either of the two balls, and the prover will not be able to determine the bit b with better probability than guessing at random. So, evaluating the soundness error of the proof system boils down to estimating the relative volume of the intersection of the two balls. It turns out that, when $\gamma = \Omega(\sqrt{n/\log n})$, this relative intersection is non-negligible, causing the verifier to reject with probability at least $\delta = n^{-\Omega(1)}$. (See Goldreich and Goldwasser [2000, Lemma 3.6].) The probability of the verifier accepting a target within distance 1 from the lattice can be made arbitrarily small either by increasing γ or by repeating the basic proof system a polynomial number of times.

Theorem 21.2   For any $\gamma(n) = \Omega(\sqrt{n/\log n})$, Protocol 1 is a constant-round interactive proof system for the complement of $\mathbf{GapCVP}_\gamma$ with perfect completeness and soundness error $1 - n^{-\Omega(1)}$. In particular, $\mathbf{GapCVP}_\gamma$ is in $\mathbf{coAM}$.

A similar proof system can also be given for the shortest vector problem, $\mathbf{GapSVP}$. As before, proving that a lattice satisfies $\lambda_1(\mathbf{B}) \leq d$ is easy: It is enough to exhibit a nonzero lattice vector of length $\|\mathbf{Bx}\| \leq 1$. The GG proof system can be used to show that a lattice does *not* have short vectors. One method to show this is to resort to transference theorems relating a lattice and its dual. For example, Theorem 21.1 allows to prove that a lattice has no short vectors by exhibiting n-linearly independent vectors $\mathbf{v}_1, \ldots, \mathbf{v}_n \in \Lambda^*$ in the dual lattice of length $\max_i \|\mathbf{v}_i\| \leq n/\lambda_1$. (These vectors certainly exist by the upper bound in Theorem 21.1.) In fact, by the lower bound in Theorem 21.1, these vectors demonstrate that

$$\lambda_1(\Lambda) \geq 1/\lambda_n(\Lambda^*) \geq 1/\max_i \|\mathbf{v}_i\| \geq \lambda_1/n.$$

So, while this does not prove that $\lambda_1 > 1$, it shows that λ_1 is not much smaller than 1, by a factor n. Technically, this proves that $\mathbf{GapSVP}_n$ is in $\mathbf{coNP}$. But what about factors smaller than $O(n)$? For example, factors $\gamma(n) = O(\sqrt{n/\log n})$, as those achieved by the GG proof system for CVP? Can one prove that a lattice has no vectors smaller than $O(\lambda_1/\gamma)$, possibly using interaction? Using similar ideas to the CVP proof system in Figure 21.1, Goldreich and Goldwasser also give an interactive proof system for (the complement of) $\mathbf{GapSVP}$ achieving the same approximation factor $\gamma = O(\sqrt{n/\log n})$ as for $\mathbf{GapCVP}$ [Goldreich and Goldwasser

2000]. We remark that this result for **GapSVP** can also be obtained by combining the **GapCVP** proof system with a "gap-preserving" reduction from **GapSVP**$_\gamma$ to **GapCVP**$_\gamma$ given in Goldreich et al. [1999]. This reduction solves a **GapSVP** instance by making n calls to a **GapCVP** oracle. So, it may not be immediately obvious how to combine it with an interactive proof system for **GapCVP**. This is possible because of some specific properties of the reduction and the proof system. Specifically, when starting from a NO instance of **GapSVP**, the reduction produces only NO instances of **GapCVP**, and on such instances the GG proof system makes the verifier accept with probability 1. (Recall that GG is a proof system with perfect completeness for the *complement* of **GapCVP**.) On the other hand, starting from a YES instance of **GapSVP**, the reduction produces at least one query to a YES instance of **GapCVP**, which the GG verifier will reject with some probability. So, the verifier for (the complement of) **GapSVP** may run the GG verifier on all **GapCVP** instances produced by the reduction, and accept if they all accept. In fact, the main idea behind this reduction, which appeared after the conference presentation of Goldreich and Goldwasser [2000] in 1998, can be traced back to the GG protocol for **GapSVP**. Specifically, the **GapSVP** protocol can be thought of, at least conceptually, as a combination of the **GapCVP** protocol with the **GapSVP** to **GapCVP** reduction, where the n independent **GapCVP** queries produced by the reduction are consolidated into a single one using the Goldreich–Levin hardcore predicate [Goldreich and Levin 1989].

Adapting the **GapCVP** proof system to other lattice problems by reducing them to **GapCVP** has been used to design **coAM** protocols for many other lattice problems of interest to cryptography. Some of these variants of the GG protocol are described in Section 21.5.

Beside offering a useful tool to design **coAM** protocols for many important lattice problems, the results in Goldreich and Goldwasser [2000] also stimulated the search for stronger **coNP** results than those implied by Theorem 21.1. While proving that **GapSVP** and **GapCVP** are in **coNP** for factors $\gamma = O(\sqrt{n/\log n})$ as small as those in Goldreich and Goldwasser [2000] is still an open problem, the gap has been almost completely closed by Aharonov and Regev [2003], [2005] for factor $\gamma(n) = O(\sqrt{n})$ only slightly larger than those of the GG proof system. These works first put the **GapSVP** and **GapCVP** problems in **coQMA** (the quantum analog of **coNP**), and then achieved the same results without the use of quantum computation, putting the problems in **coNP**. We remark that the proofs in Banaszczyk [1993] and Aharonov and Regev [2005] are substantially more complex than Goldreich and Goldwasser [2000], making extensive use of harmonic analysis techniques that have found countless application in lattice-based cryptography.

21.4   **Zero-Knowledge with Efficient Provers**

An important feature of the GG interactive proof systems is that the verifier does not learn essentially anything from the interaction, other than the validity of the assertion being proved. For example, in the case of **CVP**, the verifier learns that the target **t** is far from the lattice, and nothing more. This is so because the verifier already knows the value of the bit b before interacting with the prover. The prover demonstrates he can also recover the bit b from the verifier's message, but does not provide any additional information. More precisely, the protocol in Figure 21.1 shows that the complement of the **GapCVP**$_\gamma$ problem belongs to **SZK**, the class of decision or promise problems that admit a *statistical zero-knowledge* proof system.

Zero-knowledge proof systems, introduced by Goldwasser, Micali, and Rackoff in Goldwasser et al. [1989], are a fundamental building block for cryptography. One of the most direct applications of zero-knowledge is the construction of secure (public-key) identification schemes. In such a scheme, a user picks a public key (used to represent the user's identity) together with a matching secret key. The public key may be stored on a remote server, or even made publicly available. The user can later gain access to the system by demonstrating knowledge of the matching secret key. Using a zero-knowledge proof system, no information about the secret key is actually revealed, so that not even the server can later impersonate the user. Specialized to the lattice setting, the user may pick a hard (solved) instance $(\Lambda, \mathbf{t})$ of the closest vector problem—that is, a random lattice Λ and target vector **t** close to the lattice. The secret key (known only to the user) is a lattice point $\mathbf{v} \in \Lambda$ close to **t**. Proving that **t** is close to Λ is easy enough: Just reveal the nearby lattice point **v**. But, how can the user prove that **t** is close to the lattice without revealing any information about the secret lattice vector **v**?

The class **SZK** of problems with a statistical zero-knowledge proof system is closed under complement; that is, if there is a **SZK** proof system for the set of strings x satisfying some property $P(x)$, then there is a **SZK** proof system for the set of strings satisfying the complementary property $\neg P(x)$. In particular, the GG proof system for showing that a target vector is *far* from a lattice immediately implies also a zero-knowledge proof system to show that a target is *close* to the lattice (at least approximately, within the same approximation factor $\gamma = O(\sqrt{n/\log n})$ achieved in Goldreich and Goldwasser [2000].)

However, the prover strategy, both in the original **SZK** proof system in Goldreich and Goldwasser [2000] and in the one for the complementary problem, is not efficient. In fact, the prover in the GG proof system (see Protocol 1, Step 2) is required to determine, given $\mathbf{u}, \mathbf{t}$ and **B**, if $\text{dist}(\mathbf{u}, \mathcal{L}(\mathbf{B})) < \text{dist}(\mathbf{u}, \mathbf{t} + \mathcal{L}(\mathbf{B}))$ or not, a hard computational task for an arbitrary challenge **u**. (In fact, it is not even clear what information may serve as a secret key to efficiently prove that a lattice point is *far* from a lattice.)

Motivated by the proof systems of Goldreich and Goldwasser [2000] and the cryptographic applicability of lattices [Ajtai 2004], the problem of prover efficiency in statistical zero-knowledge proofs for lattice problems (and more) is investigated in Micciancio and Vadhan [2003]. The main idea of Micciancio and Vadhan [2003] is that implicit in the GG proof system is the construction of a lattice-based *commitment scheme*. A commitment scheme is a cryptographic primitive that allows a sender (the committer) to communicate a value in the digital equivalent of a *sealed envelope*. The envelope hides the committed value, keeping it secret until the commitment/envelope is opened. Still, the commitment is binding: The sender cannot change the content of the commitment after its transmission, and open it to a different value than the one originally selected. The **CVP** instances in the GG proof system provide a bit-commitment scheme as follows: Commitments to the bit b are random samples $\mathbf{u}$ from the ball $\mathcal{B}(b\mathbf{t}, \gamma/2)$ (mod $\mathbf{B}$). The commitment is opened by showing how it was computed, either starting from $\mathcal{B}(\mathbf{0}, \gamma/2)$ or starting from $\mathcal{B}(\mathbf{t}, \gamma/2)$. This commitment scheme has the peculiar property of being binding when the target is far from the lattice, and hiding when it is close.[7] Indeed, if $\mathbf{t}$ is far from the lattice, then the two balls $\mathcal{B}(\mathbf{0}, \gamma/2)$ and $\mathcal{B}(\mathbf{t}, \gamma/2)$ are disjoint, even after reduction modulo $\mathbf{B}$. So, no commitment $\mathbf{u}$ can later be opened both to $b = 0$ and to $b = 1$. On the other hand, if $\mathbf{t}$ is close to the lattice, then the commitment scheme is somehow hiding, because the balls $\mathcal{B}(\mathbf{0}, \gamma/2)$ and $\mathcal{B}(\mathbf{t}, \gamma/2)$ intersect (mod $\mathbf{B}$), and when $\mathbf{u}$ is in the intersection of the two balls it provides no information about the bit b. This is a very weak hiding property, but enough to build stronger commitment schemes and other useful applications. (See Micciancio and Vadhan [2003] for details.)

Using this commitment scheme as a building block, the GG proof system to show that a target $\mathbf{t}$ is far from a lattice Λ can be abstractly described as follows:

1. The verifier picks a random bit $b \in \{0, 1\}$ and sends a commitment to b to the prover.

2. The prover determines if the verifier committed to 0 or 1, and sends b back to the verifier.

3. The verifier checks that the prover correctly guessed b.

---

7. Following Nguyen and Vadhan [2006], these are called "instance dependent commitments."

Clearly, the prover strategy is not efficient because it requires the prover to "break" the hiding property of the commitment scheme. In order to implement the prover strategy efficiently, an alternative use of the same commitment scheme is proposed in Micciancio and Vadhan [2003], leading to the following proof system to show that the target is close to the lattice:

1. The prover sends a random commitment c to the verifier.
2. The verifier send a random bit b to the prover.
3. The prover opens the commitment c to show that it holds the bit b.

The proof system is sound because when the target $\mathbf{t}$ is far from the lattice, the commitment scheme is perfectly binding, and no prover can successfully open the commitment c both to 0 and 1. Since the query $b \in \{0, 1\}$ is chosen at random by the verifier after receiving the commitment c, and the prover can answer at most one of the two questions, the verifier will reject with probability at least 1/2. On the other hand, if $\mathbf{t}$ is close to a lattice point $\mathbf{v}$, as the prover claims, then the prover can open the commitment both ways with some probability, and this probability can be amplified using repetition techniques.[8] Finally, a lattice vector $\mathbf{Bx}$ close to the target $\mathbf{t}$ can be used to efficiently implement the prover strategy. To see this, we show how to compute a commitment to 1, and later open it as a commitment to 0. Recall that a commitment to 1 is computed by choosing a vector $\mathbf{u}$ within distance $\gamma/2$ from the target $\mathbf{t}$, and reducing it modulo the lattice, to produce the commitment $\mathbf{c} = \mathbf{u} \bmod \mathbf{B}$. In order to open $\mathbf{c}$ to 0, the prover will simply pretend that it was chosen starting from a vector $\mathbf{u}' = \mathbf{u} - \mathbf{Bx}$, which is near the origin. In fact, since $\mathbf{t}$ and $\mathbf{Bx}$ are close to each other, the vector $\mathbf{u}$ is also approximately within distance $\gamma/2$ from $\mathbf{Bx}$. So, the difference vector $\mathbf{u}' = \mathbf{u} - \mathbf{Bx}$ is (with some approximation) within distance $\approx \gamma/2$ from the origin, and it can be used to open the commitment $(\mathbf{u} - \mathbf{Bx}) \bmod \mathbf{B} = \mathbf{u} \bmod \mathbf{B} = \mathbf{c}$ as 0. In the simplified (toy) version of the problem considered at the beginning of Section 21.3, where the distance between $\mathbf{t}$ and the lattice is either 0 or larger than γ, we have $\mathbf{Bx} = \mathbf{t}$, and the prover strategy we just described achieves both perfect completeness and perfect zero-knowledge. Of course, in reality, both properties hold only in an approximate sense, due to the approximation $\mathbf{Bx} \approx \mathbf{t}$, and a big part of the effort in Micciancio and Vadhan [2003] goes into analyzing and reducing the error bounds in an efficient manner.

---

8. This has to be done carefully, in two stages, because one needs to reduce both the soundness and completeness error. See Micciancio and Vadhan [2003] for details.

This initial work on interactive proof systems for lattice problems seeded two distinct and quite different developments in complexity theory and cryptography. In cryptography, interactive proofs provided a method for the direct construction of *lattice-based* digital signature schemes. Digital signatures, formally defined in the seminal work of Goldwasser, Micali, and Rivest [Goldwasser et al. 1988], are among the most important and useful cryptographic primitives used in practice, and, at least in principle, they can be constructed from any one-way function [Rompel 1990]. However, using lattice problems like **SIS** simply as a one-way function, and then building a digital signature from it using generic methods, is terribly inefficient. The identification schemes from Micciancio and Vadhan [2003] can be turned into digital signature schemes in a much more direct and efficient way using the Fiat–Shamir heuristics [Fiat and Shamir 1986]. Interactive proofs are also at the core of the construction of lattice-based (one-time) signatures provably secure in the standard model (i.e., without random oracles), first proposed in 2008 in the conference presentation of Lyubashevsky and Micciancio [2018]. Much progress has occurred since then, producing a sequence of more and more efficient lattice-based signature schemes. The most efficient of these schemes (e.g., see Ducas et al. [2013]) are still based on a form of interactive proof system for lattice problems, and achieve excellent performance in practice, competitive with traditional digital signatures based on problems from number theory, but with the added benefit of conjectured security against quantum attacks.

Another important development in cryptography has been the design of *non-interactive zero-knowledge* proof systems for lattice problems [Peikert and Vaikuntanathan 2008]. These are closely related to proof systems for the covering radius and smoothing parameter problems, and they are described in the next section.

On the complexity front, the work of Micciancio and Vadhan [2003] started the investigation of **SZK** proof systems with efficient provers for arbitrary problems in **SZK** ∩ **NP**, not just lattices. Already in Micciancio and Vadhan [2003], a statistical zero-knowledge proof system with efficient prover is presented for the $\mathbf{SD}^{1/2,1}$ problem, a special case of the **SZK**-complete statistical distance problem $\mathbf{SD}^{a,b}$, which asks if two probability distributions (represented by two digital circuits C_0 and C_1) are close (within statistical distance a) or far (at distance b) from each other. Here distance $b = 1$ corresponds to two distributions with disjoint support, putting the problem in **NP**. This problem admits a **SZK** proof system with efficient prover, which uses a sample in the intersection of the two distributions as a witness that the distributions are not disjoint. Unfortunately the resulting problem is no longer known to be complete for **SZK** or even for **SZK** ∩ **NP**. Still, building on Micciancio and Vadhan [2003], and using additional ideas and extensions of the notion of instance dependent commitment, Nguyen and Vadhan [2006] were able to completely resolve the issue of prover efficiency for **SZK**, showing that any problem in **SZK** ∩ **NP** has a statistical zero-knowledge proof system where the prover strategy can be efficiently implemented given just an **NP**-witness for the input string. Another development specific to lattices, but still based on the instance dependent commitments implicit in Goldreich and Goldwasser [2000], is the construction of proof systems for lattice problems (and more) that are zero-knowledge even when multiple instances of the protocol are executed concurrently, under any adversarial schedule [Micciancio et al. 2006].

21.5 Other Lattice Problems

SVP and **CVP** are perhaps the two most famous lattice problems, but there are several other interesting computational problems on lattices, and some are even more directly related to cryptography. The shortest independent vector problem (**SIVP**) is the main worst-case problem underlying both Ajtai's one-way function [Ajtai 2004] and Regev's learning with errors problem [Regev 2009]. The covering radius problem (**GapCRP**) was suggested as a possible way to improve Ajtai's one-way function using "almost-perfect" lattices [Micciancio 2004]. More recently, even tighter connections have been established between lattice-based cryptography and the computational hardness of approximating the smoothing parameter of a lattice [Chung et al. 2013]. In this section we describe how the original GG proof systems for **CVP** and **SVP** have been adapted to establish similar results for all these problems.

The Covering Radius Problem (GapCRP). This is the problem, given a lattice basis Λ, to determine if $\rho(\Lambda) \leq 1$ or $\rho(\Lambda) > \gamma(n)$, where $\rho(\Lambda) = \max_t \operatorname{dist}(\mathbf{t}, \Lambda)$ is the covering radius of the lattice. From a computational perspective, this is a very interesting problem, as it is not even clear if the problem belongs to **NP**. The most natural formulation of the problem involves a quantifier alternation, putting it at the second level of the polynomial hierarchy: $\rho(\Lambda) \leq 1$ if *for all* $\mathbf{x}$, *there exists* a lattice point $\mathbf{v} \in \Lambda$ such that $\|\mathbf{x} - \mathbf{v}\| \leq 1$.

Interestingly, if one allows for a small approximation factor $\gamma = 2$, the problem is in **AM**; that is, it admits a public-coin constant-round interactive proof system [Guruswami et al. 2005]. The proof is based on the following lemma, which allows, probabilistically, to find a point $\mathbf{t}$ far away from the lattice.

Lemma 21.1 (Guruswami et al. 2005, Lemma 4.1) For any lattice Λ, if $\mathbf{t}$ is chosen uniformly at random (modulo Λ) then $\Pr(\operatorname{dist}(\mathbf{t}, \Lambda) \geq \rho(\Lambda)/2) \geq 1/2$.

Protocol 2: AM protocol for **GapCRP$_2$**
Input: Lattice basis **B**

1. The Verifier picks a uniformly random $\mathbf{x} \in \mathbf{B}[0, 1)^n$ and sends it to the prover.
2. The Prover finds a lattice point $\mathbf{v} \in \mathcal{L}(\mathbf{B})$ within distance $\rho(\Lambda(\mathbf{B})) \leq 1$ from $\mathbf{x}$ and sends $\mathbf{v}$ to the verifier.
3. The Verifier accepts if $\|\mathbf{x} - \mathbf{v}\| \leq 1$ and $\mathbf{v} \in \mathcal{L}(\mathbf{B})$.

Figure 21.2 **AM** protocol for the covering radius problem [Guruswami et al. 2005].

In other words, a random point $\mathbf{t}$ may not be as far away from Λ as possible, but it will achieve half that distance with good probability. An interactive proof system to show that the covering radius of a lattice is *small* is easily obtained, and it is shown in Figure 21.2. The verifier simply picks a random target point $\mathbf{t}$, whose distance from the lattice is (with high probability) within a factor 2 from the covering radius, and the prover then shows that $\mathbf{t}$ is close to the lattice by sending a standard **NP** proof for the **CVP** instance $(\mathbf{B}, \mathbf{t})$.

We recall that, differently from **SZK**, the class **AM** is not known to be closed under complement. Notice also that the above proof system is not (statistical) zero-knowledge because it reveals a lattice point close to the (random) target $\mathbf{t}$. In particular, we cannot conclude that **GapCRP$_2$** $\in$ **coAM**. However, the GG **coAM** protocol for **GapCVP** can be easily adapted to **GapCRP** [Guruswami et al. 2005]. The idea is to give a (polynomial-time, nondeterministic) reduction from **GapCRP$_\gamma$** to **GapCVP$_\gamma$**, and then directly invoke the GG proof system for **GapCRP$_\gamma$**. The reduction simply guesses a "deep hole" for the lattice; that is, a target vector $\mathbf{h}$ achieving the maximum distance $\mathrm{dist}(\mathbf{h}, \Lambda) = \rho(\Lambda)$. Clearly, if $\rho(\Lambda) > \gamma$, then there is a point $\mathbf{h}$ such that $\mathrm{dist}(\mathbf{h}, \Lambda) > \gamma$. On the other hand, if $\rho(\Lambda) \leq 1$, then, no matter how the prover chooses $\mathbf{h}$, we have $\mathrm{dist}(\mathbf{h}, \Lambda) \leq 1$.

Then, the prover uses the GG protocol for **GapCVP$_\gamma$** to show that $\mathrm{dist}(\mathbf{t}, \Lambda) > \gamma$. This provides a **coAM** protocol for **GapCRP$_\gamma$** for the same approximation factor $\gamma = O(\sqrt{n/\log n})$ achieved by Goldreich and Goldwasser [2000] for **GapCVP**. The resulting proof system is shown in Figure 21.3.

Finally, while the protocol in Figure 21.2 is not zero-knowledge, it can be turned into a statistical zero-knowledge proof system by letting the prover choose the lattice point $\mathbf{v} \in \mathcal{L}(\mathbf{B})$ at random—say, with a Gaussian-like distribution centered around the target $\mathbf{x}$ and standard deviation above the smoothing parameter of the lattice. In fact, Peikert and Vaikuntanathan [2008] do even more than that: they

Protocol 3: AM protocol for **GapCRP**$_\gamma$
Input: Lattice basis **B**

1. The prover selects a deep hole **h** (with dist(**h**, $\mathcal{L}(\mathbf{B})$) = $\rho(\mathcal{L}(\mathbf{B}))$) and sends it to the verifier.

2. The Verifier selects $b \in \{0, 1\}$ and $\mathbf{r} \in \mathcal{B}(\mathbf{0}, \gamma)$, and sends $\mathbf{u} = (b\mathbf{h} + \mathbf{r}) \bmod \mathbf{B}$ to the Prover.

3. The Prover replies with $b' = 0$ if dist(**u**, $\mathcal{L}(\mathbf{B})$) < dist(**u**, **h** + $\mathcal{L}(\mathbf{B})$), and with $b' = 1$ otherwise.

4. The Verifier accepts with $b = b'$.

Figure 21.3   **coAM** protocol for the covering radius problem [Guruswami et al. 2005].

observe that the only message sent by the verifier is a target point **x** chosen uniformly at random. So, one can think of **x** as a randomly chosen reference string, available to both the prover and the verifier. This results in a *noninteractive* zero-knowledge proof system, a particularly useful type of zero-knowledge proofs introduced in Blum et al. [1988], where, after seeing a common randomly chosen string **x**, the proof consists of a single (random) message sent by the prover to the verifier. In the case of lattice covering radius proof systems, this message is a lattice point **v** chosen with a Gaussian-like probability distribution centered around the reference vector **x**. The protocol is statistical zero-knowledge because the verifier's view of the entire process can be simulated by first choosing **v** as a random vector with Gaussian distribution, and then setting **x** = **v** mod **B**. The properties of the smoothing parameter, described below, ensure that the distribution of the simulated reference string **x** is essentially uniform.[9] Essentially the same protocol can also be used to give non-interactive statistical zero-knowledge proofs for other lattice problems, like **GapSIVP** and the complement of **GapSVP**. Further improvements and variants of this non-interactive zero-knowledge proof system have recently been proposed in Alamati et al. [2018].

The Shortest Independent Vectors Problem (SIVP).   This is the problem of computing n linearly independent lattice vectors $\mathbf{v}_1, \ldots, \mathbf{v}_n \in \mathcal{L}(\mathbf{B})$ of minimal length $\max_i \|\mathbf{v}_i\|$.

---

9. Technically, as described, **x** is uniform over the fundamental parallelepiped defined by the lattice basis **B**. This point can equivalently be represented by its coordinates with respected to the basis **B**, resulting in the uniform distribution over a set $[0, 1)^n$ that does not depend on the problem instance.

In the approximate decision version of this problem, given a basis **B**, the task is to decide if $\lambda_n(\mathbf{B}) \leq 1$ or $\lambda_n(\mathbf{B}) > \gamma(n)$, where $\gamma(n)$ is the approximation factor.

As for the covering radius problem, **GapSIVP**$_\gamma$ also is in **coAM**. This can be shown by giving a nondeterministic[10] reduction from **GapSIVP**$_\gamma$ to **GapCVP**$_\gamma$ and then invoking the GG protocol for **GapCVP**$_\gamma$ [Guruswami et al. 2005]. This time the reduction is more involved, and we only provide a brief sketch here. For details, the reader is referred to the original paper. On input a **GapSIVP** instance **B**, the reduction outputs a polynomial number of **GapCVP** instances $(\mathbf{S}_i, \mathbf{t}_i)$, such that:

- If $\lambda_n(\mathbf{B}) > \gamma$, then for some nondeterministic choice of the reduction, every **GapCVP** instance satisfies $\text{dist}(\mathbf{S}_i, \mathbf{t}_i) > \gamma$.

- If $\lambda_n(\mathbf{B}) \leq 1$, then for every nondeterministic choice of the reduction, some **GapCVP** instance satisfies $\text{dist}(\mathbf{S}_i, \mathbf{t}_i) \leq 1$.

More specifically, the reduction selects an appropriate basis $\mathbf{S} = [\mathbf{s}_1, \dots, \mathbf{s}_n]$ for the lattice, and for every i, the ith **GapCVP** instances is defined by $\mathbf{S}_i = [\mathbf{s}_1, \dots, \mathbf{s}_{n-1}, 2^i \mathbf{s}_n]$ and $\mathbf{t}_i = 2^{i-1}\mathbf{s}_n$. Combining this reduction with the GG proof system for **GapCVP** shows that **GapSIVP**$_\gamma$ is in **coAM** for the same approximation factors $\gamma = O(\sqrt{n/\log n})$ as in Goldreich and Goldwasser [2000].

The Smoothing Parameter Problem (GapSPP).   One last variant of the GG protocol is proposed in Chung et al. [2013] to approximate the smoothing parameter of a lattice. Technically, the smoothing parameter of a lattice $\eta_\epsilon(\Lambda)$ is defined in terms of Gaussian sums over the dual lattice Λ^* [Micciancio and Regev 2007]. But for our purposes, one can think of the smoothing parameters more intuitively as follows. Consider a (continuous) Gaussian distribution[11] D in $\mathbb{R}^n$, scale it by a factor s, and reduce it modulo the lattice. If s is large enough, the resulting distribution $sD \pmod{\Lambda}$ will be close to uniform over $\mathbb{R}^n/\Lambda$. The smoothing parameter $\eta_\epsilon(\Lambda)$ is the smallest $s > 0$ such that the probability density function of $sD \pmod{\Lambda}$ is within a factor $(1 \pm \epsilon)$ from the uniform distribution. Here $\epsilon > 0$ is an accuracy parameter, and it is assumed to be an inverse polynomial function $\epsilon = 1/n^c$ of the lattice dimension.

---

10. This has been extended to a *deterministic* polynomial-time reduction [Micciancio 2008], but only for the search versions of the problems **SIVP**$_\gamma$ and **CVP**$_\gamma$.

11. Here D is a distribution that selects a point $\mathbf{x}$ with probability proportional to $\exp(-\pi \|\mathbf{x}\|^2)$.

The smoothing parameter plays a fundamental role both in the strongest known connections between the average-case and worst-case complexity of lattice problems [Micciancio and Regev 2007], as well as many of their cryptographic applications (e.g., see Gentry et al. [2008] and Micciancio and Peikert [2012]). Understanding the complexity of computing the smoothing parameter of a lattice has therefore become of central importance to lattice-based cryptography. Formally, for any $\epsilon > 0$, **GapSPP**$_\epsilon$ is defined as the problem of determining if a given lattice satisfies $\eta_\epsilon(\Lambda) \leq 1$ or $\eta_\epsilon(\Lambda) > \gamma$. We remark that since the smoothing parameter of a lattice is determined by a summation with infinitely many terms,[12] it is unclear (just as for **GapCRP**) if **GapSPP**$_\epsilon$ is in **NP** or **coNP**.

Chung, Dadush, Liu, and Peikert [Chung et al. 2013] propose a Gaussian variant of the GG protocol, where the perturbation vector **r** is chosen with Gaussian distribution, rather than uniformly in a ball. This Gaussian Goldreich–Goldwasser (or GGG) protocol is shown in Figure 21.4. Interestingly, and perhaps surprisingly, this results in a much tighter analysis of the GG protocol, with approximation factors (for η_ϵ) as small at $2 + o(1)$. The input to the GGG protocol is just a lattice basis **B**, and the protocol approximates the smoothing parameter of the *dual* lattice $\mathcal{L}^*(\mathbf{B})$ within a factor $2 + o(1)$. In this protocol the verifier chooses a perturbation vector **x** with (scaled) Gaussian distribution $2 \cdot D$ and sends **x** mod **B** to the prover. The verifier accepts if the prover correctly recovers the original vector **x**. Since the Gaussian distribution is spherically symmetric, the optimal prover strategy (maximum likelihood decoding) is to return the shortest point in the lattice coset $\mathbf{x} + \mathcal{L}(\mathbf{B})$. So, without loss of generality, we may assume that even a cheating prover will follow the strategy specified in the protocol in Figure 21.4. It is easy to see that the verifier accepts if and only if the perturbation vector **x** falls within the Voronoi cell of the lattice $\mathcal{V}(\Lambda)$—that is, the set of points in $\mathbb{R}^n$ that are closer to the origin than to any other lattice point. In summary, the optimal success probability for any prover equals $D(\mathcal{V}(\Lambda)/2)$, the Gaussian mass of the Voronoi cell of the lattice. (The cell is scaled by a factor $1/2$ because the verifier sampled **x** with distribution $2 \cdot D$.)

The correctness of the GGG protocol is based on the following geometric characterization of the smoothing parameter of a lattice, proved in Chung et al. [2013]: For any lattice Λ with Voronoi cell $\mathcal{V}$ and (dual) smoothing parameter $s = \eta_\epsilon(\Lambda^*)$, the Gaussian mass of the Voronoi cell satisfies $D(2s\mathcal{V}) \geq 1 - \epsilon$ and $D(s\mathcal{V}) \leq 1/(1 + \epsilon)$.

A $\gamma = O(\sqrt{n/\log n})$ approximation for λ_1 (as achieved by the original GG protocol) can be recovered from the GGG protocol of Chung et al. [2013] simply using

---

12. We recall that the technical definition of the smoothing parameter, as given in Micciancio and Regev [2007], involves a summation over all points of the dual lattice.

Protocol 4: AM protocol for **GapSPP**
Input: Lattice basis **B**

1. The Verifier picks $\mathbf{x} \leftarrow 2 \cdot D$ with Gaussian distribution, and sends $\mathbf{x}' = \mathbf{x} \bmod \mathbf{B}$ to the prover

2. The Prover finds the lattice point $\mathbf{v} \in \mathcal{L}(\mathbf{B})$ closest to $\mathbf{x}'$, and sends $\mathbf{x}'' = \mathbf{x}' - \mathbf{v}$ to the verifier.

3. The Verifier accepts if $\mathbf{x}'' = \mathbf{x}$.

Figure 21.4 The Gaussian Goldreich–Goldwasser (GGG) protocol for the smoothing parameter problem **GapSPP** [Chung et al. 2013].

known bounds $\Omega(\log n) \le \lambda_1 \cdot \eta_\epsilon \le O(\sqrt{n})$ (for $\epsilon = n^{1/c}$) relating λ_1 to the smoothing parameter.

Other Norms. Lattice problems are most commonly defined with respect to the ℓ_2 (Euclidean) norm, but it is often interesting and useful to consider the same problems with respect to other norms—for example, ℓ_p norms for any $1 \le p \le \infty$. Lattice problems in the ℓ_2 norm can be reduced to the same problems in ℓ_p with essentially no loss in approximation, using norm embedding techniques [Regev and Rosen 2006]. This is useful to port hardness results for lattice problems in ℓ_2 to similar results in other ℓ_p norms. However, for positive results (e.g., algorithms, or proof systems showing "limits on the hardness of approximation" as those presented in Goldreich and Goldwasser [2000]), going from ℓ_2 to other ℓ_p norms requires reductions in the opposite direction. This is easily achieved using the fact that all ℓ_p norms are within a factor $\sqrt{n}$ from ℓ_2, but only at the cost of worsening the approximation by factors as large as $\sqrt{n}$. This suggests that lattice problems with respect to ℓ_p norms (for $p \ne 2$) may be strictly harder than the corresponding ℓ_2 problems. In fact, historically, hardness for non-Euclidean norms (e.g., with respect to ℓ_∞) has been easier to achieve, or produced stronger results, than ℓ_2 [van Emde Boas 1981, Dinur 2002].

The problem of establishing stronger positive results in norms other than ℓ_2 is addressed by Peikert, who adapts many previous algorithms and proof systems to any ℓ_p norm for $2 < p < \infty$ [Peikert 2008]. In particular, approximating **GapCVP, GapSVP, GapSIVP, GapCRP** in the ℓ_p norm for any $2 < p < \infty$ within a factor $\gamma = O(\sqrt{n})$ is in **coNP**, matching the approximation factors for the ℓ_2 problems proved in Aharonov and Regev [2005]. Peikert also gives algorithms for the **CVP** and **BDD** with preprocessing, and cryptographic functions based on the worst-case hardness of lattice problems in the ℓ_p norm, again matching the best previous results for ℓ_2. Interestingly, the techniques used to prove these results do not seem to apply to the GG protocols, and it was left as an open problem to give **coAM** protocols for **GapSVP** and **GapCVP** in the ℓ_p norm for the same approximation factors $\gamma = O(\sqrt{n/\log n})$ as in Goldreich and Goldwasser [2000].

21.6 LWE and the GapSVP to BDD Reduction

One last development where the use of ideas behind the GG proof system came most unexpected is Peikert's classical (nonquantum) proof of hardness for the learning with errors problem [Peikert 2009], and a related reduction from **GapSVP** to the bounded distance decoding (**BDD**) problem [Lyubashevsky and Micciancio 2009].

Most advanced applications of lattice-based cryptography are based on the Regev's **LWE** problem [Regev 2009]. **LWE** is closely related to the **SIS** problem [Ajtai 2004], via lattice duality, with the main technical difference that **SIS** provides *surjective* one-way functions, while the one-way function associated to **LWE** is *injective*. This technical difference between the two problems is key to the broad applicability of **LWE**, but also results in very different worst-case to average-case reductions. Interestingly, Regev's reduction [Regev 2009] (from worst-case lattice problems to average-case **LWE**) makes essential use of quantum computation. For several years (since the conference presentation of Regev [2009] in 2005) it has been a puzzling open question whether the use of quantum reductions (in the security proof) was essential to the broad range of applications of lattices enabled by the **LWE** problem, or if one could build similar applications under classic (non-quantum) reductions. As we are going to explain, the puzzle was finally resolved using techniques that are closely related to the GG proof system. But first, we need to explain why the use of quantum computation was perceived as necessary to establish the hardness of the **LWE** problem.

As usual in complexity theory, the average-case hardness of **LWE** is established by assuming (for contradiction) that there is an efficient algorithm to solve **LWE**, and then using this algorithm as an oracle to efficiently solve some other lattice problem like **SIVP** or **GapSIVP** which is believed to be intractable. In particular, this requires to generate random **LWE** problem instances $(\mathbf{A}, \mathbf{u})$, feed them to the **LWE** oracle, and then trying to extract some useful information from their solution $\mathbf{v}$. The difficulty of proving hardness results for **LWE** under classic (nonquantum) reductions is well illustrated by Regev [2009], which states:

> . . . it seems to us that the only way to generate inputs to the [LWE] oracle is the following: somehow choose a lattice point $\mathbf{v}$ and let $\mathbf{u} = \mathbf{v} + \mathbf{r}$ for some

perturbation vector **r** of length at most d. Clearly, on input **u** the oracle outputs **v**. But this is useless since we already know **v**!

By contrast, in the quantum setting, the ability to recover **v** from **u** is quite useful: It allows to "uncompute" **v**, something quite nontrivial and useful in the quantum setting because quantum computations are required to be reversible. More precisely, the **LWE** oracle allows to efficiently transform the quantum state $|\mathbf{u}, \mathbf{v}\rangle$ to the state $|\mathbf{u}, \mathbf{0}\rangle$ in a reversible way, a key step in the reduction of Regev [2009]. The main idea behind the GG proof system Goldreich and Goldwasser [2000] is used in Peikert [2009] to make a nontrivial use of the **LWE** oracle, without resorting to quantum computation! The main observation is that the prover in the GG protocol, although not polynomial time, can be efficiently implemented given oracle access to a **BDD** oracle. Since **LWE** is an average-case version of **BDD**, this provides an interesting way to use an **LWE** oracle: Implementing the GG prover, which, combined with the (polynomial time) verifier of the GG proof system, yields a polynomial time algorithm to solve **GapSVP**.

Here we follow [Lyubashevsky and Micciancio 2009], and present the idea in the context of a reduction between (worst-case) **GapSVP** and **BDD** problems.

Theorem 21.3 (Lyubashevsky and Micciancio 2009, Theorem 7.1) For any $\gamma > 2\sqrt{n/\log n}$ there is a polynomial-time (randomized) reduction from **GapSVP**$_\gamma$ to **BDD**.

In the **GapSVP**$_\gamma$ problem, on input a lattice **B**, one needs to determine if $\lambda_1(\mathbf{B}) \leq 1$ or $\lambda_1(\mathbf{B}) > \gamma$. The reduction to **BDD** works as follows:

1. Generate a random point **r** in a ball $\mathcal{B}(\mathbf{0}, r)$ of radius $r = \sqrt{n/\log n}$, and compute $\mathbf{u} = \mathbf{r} \bmod \mathbf{B}$. Notice that this computation defines a lattice point $\mathbf{v} = \mathbf{u} - \mathbf{r}$ within distance $\|\mathbf{r}\| \leq r$ from **u**.

2. Query the **BDD** oracle on input **u**.

3. If the oracle returns the lattice point **v**, then output NO, otherwise output YES.

We will show that the above reduction always rejects NO instances, and it accepts YES instances with some non-negligible probability. The probability of accepting YES instances can be made arbitrarily close to 1 simply by running the reduction a polynomial number of times, and accepting the **GapSVP** input instance if any execution of the reductions produces YES as an answer. The intuition behind the reduction is the following:

- If **B** is a NO instance of **GapSVP**$_\gamma$, then the lattice **B** has a large minimum distance $\lambda_1 > \gamma = 2r$, and (**B**, **u**) is a valid **BDD** instance. So, the **BDD** oracle is required to correctly recover the (unique) lattice point $\mathbf{v} = \mathbf{u} - \mathbf{r}$ within distance r from $\mathbf{u}$, and the algorithm outputs NO.

- On the other hand, if $\mathbf{B}$ is a YES instance, then $\mathbf{B}$ has a short lattice vector $\mathbf{x}$, of length $\|\mathbf{x}\| = \lambda_1 \leq 1$ much smaller than r, and $(\mathbf{B}, \mathbf{u})$ is *not* a valid **BDD** instance. So, the **BDD** oracle can answer arbitrarily, and may seem to provide no useful information. Still, one can show that the **BDD** oracle cannot possibly recover the vector $\mathbf{v}$ all the times, making the reduction output YES with some non-negligible probability. To see this, recall that, by construction, $\mathbf{v}$ is a lattice point within distance r from $\mathbf{u}$. Since $\mathbf{x}$ is a short lattice vector, also $\mathbf{v} + \mathbf{x}$ is a lattice point not too far from $\mathbf{u}$, and (with some probability over the choice of $\mathbf{r}$) the distance between $\mathbf{v} + \mathbf{x}$ and $\mathbf{u}$ will also be bounded by r. Specifically, this happens when $\mathbf{r}$ belongs to the intersection of $\mathcal{B}(\mathbf{0}, r)$ and $\mathcal{B}(\mathbf{x}, r)$, an event of probability p equal to the relative volume of the intersection of two balls of radius r with centers at distance $\|\mathbf{x}\| = \lambda_1 \leq 1$ from each other. As in the analysis of the GG proof system, this probability is $p = 1/n^{O(1)}$ because $r/\|\mathbf{x}\| \geq \sqrt{n/\log n}$. Moreover, since $\mathbf{r}$ was chosen uniformly at random in a ball of radius r, all lattice points within distance r from $\mathbf{u}$ are equally likely, and the two points $\mathbf{v}$ and $\mathbf{v} + \mathbf{x}$ are perfectly indistinguishable to the **BDD** oracle. So, the oracle cannot output $\mathbf{v}$ with probability higher than $1/2$. This proves that the reduction outputs YES with probability at least $p/2$.

Recall that both **SIS** and **LWE** are parameterized by an integer modulus q. Peikert's proof reduces **GapSVP** to **LWE** with exponentially large modulus q. This has been subsequently improved in Brakerski et al. [2013] to a reduction with polynomial modulus q, as typically used in lattice-based cryptography.

21.7   Conclusion

The study of interactive proof systems for lattice problems, initiated by Goldreich and Goldwasser [2000], has proved very useful to understand the complexity of lattices and has influenced the development of lattice-based cryptography in several, sometime unexpected, ways. The main idea behind the GG proof system appears in some form also in other works not covered in this survey, like the correctness analysis of lattice-sieving algorithms [Micciancio and Voulgaris 2010, Ajtai et al. 2001], the first method to solve lattice problems in single-exponential time. Almost twenty years after Goldreich and Goldwasser [2000], this work is still the strongest known barrier to prove **NP**-hardness results for classic lattice problems **GapSVP** and **GapCVP** within approximation factor potentially useful for cryptography. Achieving smaller approximation factors $\gamma = o(\sqrt{n/\log n})$, or showing that for any such factors **GapSVP** and **GapCVP** are **NP**-hard, is one of the most important unsolved problems on the complexity of lattice problems.

Beside their technical contributions to the foundation of modern cryptography and the study of interactive proof systems, Shafi Goldwasser and Silvio Micali had much influence on the development of cryptography also as educators and mentors. Much of what I know about cryptography, I learned it from them, and if I dedicated much of my professional career to the study of the complexity of lattices and the foundation of lattice-based cryptography, it is thanks to Shafi's early interest in the area.

References

D. Aharonov and O. Regev. 2003. A lattice problem in quantum NP. In *44th Symposium on Foundations of Computer Science (FOCS 2003), 11–14 October 2003, Cambridge, MA, USA, Proceedings*, pp. 210–219. IEEE Computer Society. DOI: 10.1109/SFCS.2003 .1238195. 579

D. Aharonov and O. Regev. 2005. Lattice problems in NP intersect coNP. *Journal of the ACM*, 52(5): 749–765. Preliminary version in FOCS 2004. DOI: 10.1145/1089023.1089025. 579, 589

W. Aiello and J. Håstad. 1991. Statistical zero-knowledge languages can be recognized in two rounds. *Journal of Computer and System Sciences*, 42(3): 327–345. DOI: 10.1016/ 0022-0000(91)90006-Q. 575

M. Ajtai. 1998. The shortest vector problem in L2 is NP-hard for randomized reductions (extended abstract). In *Proceedings of STOC '98*, pp. 10–19. ACM. 566

M. Ajtai. 2004. Generating hard instances of lattice problems. *Complexity of Computations and Proofs, Quaderni di Matematica*, 13: 1–32. Preliminary version in STOC 1996. 566, 568, 573, 581, 584, 590

M. Ajtai, R. Kumar, and D. Sivakumar. 2001. A sieve algorithm for the shortest lattice vector problem. In *Proceedings of STOC*, pp. 266–275. ACM. DOI: 10.1145/380752 .380857. 592

N. Alamati, C. Peikert, and N. Stephens-Davidowitz. 2018. New (and old) proof systems for lattice problems. In *Public-Key Cryptography—PKC 2018, 21st IACR International Conference on Practice and Theory of Public-Key Cryptography, Rio de Janeiro, Brazil, March 25–29, 2018, Proceedings, Part II*, Lecture Notes in Computer Science vol. 10770, pp. 619–643. Springer. DOI: 10.1007/978-3-319-76581-5_21. 586

L. Babai. 1985. Trading group theory for randomness. In *Proceedings of the 17th Annual ACM Symposium on Theory of Computing, May 6–8, 1985, Providence, RI, USA*, pp. 421–429. DOI: 10.1145/22145.22192. 574

L. Babai and S. Moran. 1988. Arthur-Merlin games: A randomized proof system, and a hierarchy of complexity classes. *Journal of Computer and System Sciences*, 36(2): 254–276. DOI: 10.1016/0022-0000(88)90028-1. 574

W. Banaszczyk. 1993. New bounds in some transference theorems in the geometry of numbers. *Mathematische Annalen*, 296: 625–635. 566, 570, 579

M. Blum, P. Feldman, and S. Micali. 1988. Non-interactive zero-knowledge and its applications (extended abstract). In *Proceedings of the 20th Annual ACM Symposium on Theory of Computing, May 2–4, 1988, Chicago, Illinois, USA*, pp. 103–112. DOI: 10.1145/62212.62222. 586

Z. Brakerski, A. Langlois, C. Peikert, O. Regev, and D. Stehlé. 2013. Classical hardness of learning with errors. In *Symposium on Theory of Computing Conference, STOC'13, Palo Alto, CA, USA, June 1–4, 2013*, pp. 575–584. ACM. DOI: 10.1145/2488608.2488680. 592

J.-Y. Cai and A. P. Nerurkar. 1997. An improved worst-case to average-case connection for lattice problems (extended abstract). In *Proceedings of FOCS '97*, pp. 468–477. IEEE. 566, 567

J.-Y. Cai and A. P. Nerurkar. 1999. Approximating the SVP to within a factor $(1 + 1/dim^\epsilon)$ is NP-hard under randomized reductions. *Journal of Computer and System Sciences*, 59(2): 221–239. Preliminary version in CCC 1998. 566

K. Chung, D. Dadush, F. Liu, and C. Peikert. 2013. On the lattice smoothing parameter problem. In *Proceedings of the 2013 IEEE Conference on Computational Complexity (CCC)*, Stanford, CA, USA, pp. 230–241. DOI: 10.1109/CCC.2013.31. 584, 587, 588, 589

I. Dinur. 2002. Approximating SVP_∞ to within almost-polynomial factors is NP-hard. *Theoretical Computer Science*, 285(1): 55–71. DOI: 10.1016/S0304-3975(01)00290-0. Preliminary version in CIAC 2000. 567, 589

L. Ducas, A. Durmus, T. Lepoint, and V. Lyubashevsky. 2013. Lattice signatures and bimodal gaussians. In *Advances in Cryptology—CRYPTO 2013, 33rd Annual Cryptology Conference, Santa Barbara, CA, USA, August 18–22, 2013. Proceedings, Part I*. Lecture Notes in Computer Science vol. 8042, pp. 40–56. Springer. DOI: 10.1007/978-3-642-40041-4_3. 583

S. Even and Y. Yacobi. 1980. Cryptocomplexity and NP-completeness. In *Automata, Languages and Programming, 7th Colloquium, Noordweijkerhout, The Netherlands, July 14–18, 1980, Proceedings*. Lecture Notes in Computer Science vol. 85, pp. 195–207. Springer. DOI: 10.1007/3-540-10003-2_71. 572

A. Fiat and A. Shamir. 1986. How to prove yourself: Practical solutions to identification and signature problems. In *Advances in Cryptology—CRYPTO '86, Santa Barbara, CA, USA, 1986, Proceedings*. Lecture Notes in Computer Science vol. 263, pp. 186–194. Springer. DOI: 10.1007/3-540-47721-7_12. 583

L. Fortnow. 1989. The complexity of perfect zero-knowledge. *Advances in Computing Research*, 5: 327–343. 575

C. Gentry, C. Peikert, and V. Vaikuntanathan. 2008. Trapdoors for hard lattices and new cryptographic constructions. In *Proceedings of STOC*, pp. 197–206. ACM. DOI: 10.1145/1374376.1374407. 566, 567, 588

O. Goldreich. 2006. *Foundations of Cryptography: Volume 1.* Cambridge University Press, New York, NY, USA. ISBN 0521035368. 572

O. Goldreich and S. Goldwasser. 2000. On the limits of nonapproximability of lattice problems. *Journal of Computer and System Sciences*, 60(3): 540–563. Preliminary version in STOC'98. DOI: 10.1006/jcss.1999.1686. 565, 566, 567, 568, 575, 578, 579, 580, 581, 584, 585, 587, 589, 590, 591, 592

O. Goldreich and L. A. Levin. 1989. A hard-core predicate for all one-way functions. In *Proceedings of the 21st Annual ACM Symposium on Theory of Computing, May 14–17, 1989, Seattle, WA, USA*, pp. 25–32. DOI: 10.1145/73007.73010. 579

O. Goldreich, S. Micali, and A. Wigderson. 1991. Proofs that yield nothing but their validity for all languages in NP have zero-knowledge proof systems. *Journal of the ACM*, 38(3): 691–729. DOI: 10.1145/116825.116852. 576

O. Goldreich, D. Micciancio, S. Safra, and J.-P. Seifert. 1999. Approximating shortest lattice vectors is not harder than approximating closest lattice vectors. *Information Processing Letters*, 71(2): 55–61. DOI: 10.1016/S0020-0190(99)00083-6. 579

O. Goldreich, A. Sahai, and S. P. Vadhan. 1998. Honest-verifier statistical zero-knowledge equals general statistical zero-knowledge. In *Proceedings of the Thirtieth Annual ACM Symposium on the Theory of Computing, Dallas, TX, USA, May 23–26, 1998*, pp. 399–408. DOI: 10.1145/276698.276852. 575

S. Goldwasser and M. Sipser. 1989. Private coins versus public coins in interactive proof systems. *Advances in Computing Research*, 5: 73–90. 574

S. Goldwasser, S. Micali, and C. Rackoff. 1989. The knowledge complexity of interactive proof systems. *SIAM Journal on Computing*, 18(1): 186–208. DOI: 10.1137/0218012. 576, 580

S. Goldwasser, S. Micali, and R. L. Rivest. 1988. A digital signature scheme secure against adaptive chosen-message attacks. *SIAM Journal on Computing*, 17(2): 281–308. DOI: 10.1137/0217017. 583

V. Guruswami, D. Micciancio, and O. Regev. 2005. The complexity of the covering radius problem. *Computational Complexity*, 14(2): 90–121. Preliminary version in CCC 2004. DOI: 10.1007/s00037-005-0193-y. 584, 585, 586, 587

J. Håstad. 1988. Dual vectors and lower bounds for the nearest lattice point problem. *Combinatorica*, 8: 75–81. 566

I. Haviv and O. Regev. 2012. Tensor-based hardness of the shortest vector problem to within almost polynomial factors. *Theory of Computing*, 8(1): 513–531. DOI: 10.4086/toc .2012.v008a023. 567

S. Khot. 2005. Hardness of approximating the shortest vector problem in lattices. *Journal of the ACM*, 52(5): 789–808. Preliminary version in FOCS 2004. DOI: 10.1145/1089023 .1089027. 567

S. Khot. 2006. Hardness of approximating the shortest vector problem in high Lp norms. *Journal of Computer and System Sciences*, 72(2): 206–219. Preliminary version in FOCS 2003. DOI: 10.1016/j.jcss.2005.07.002. 567

J. C. Lagarias, H. W. Lenstra Jr., and C.-P. Schnorr. 1990. Korkine-Zolotarev bases and successive minima of a lattice and its reciprocal lattice. *Combinatorica*, 10(4): 333–348. 566

A. K. Lenstra, H. W. Lenstra, Jr., and L. Lovász. 1982. Factoring polynomials with rational coefficients. *Mathematische Annalen*, 261: 513–534. 566

V. Lyubashevsky and D. Micciancio. 2009. On bounded distance decoding, unique shortest vectors, and the minimum distance problem. In *Advances in Cryptology–Crypto 2009, 29th Annual International Cryptology Conference, Santa Barbara, CA, USA, August 16–20, 2009. Proceedings*. Lecture Notes in Computer Science vol. 5677, pp. 577–594. Springer. DOI: 10.1007/978-3-642-03356-8_34. 590, 591

V. Lyubashevsky and D. Micciancio. 2018. Asymptotically efficient lattice-based digital signatures. *Journal of Cryptology*, 31(3): 774–797. DOI: 10.1007/s00145-017-9270-z. 583

D. Micciancio. 2001. The shortest vector problem is NP-hard to approximate to within some constant. *SIAM Journal on Computing*, 30(6): 2008–2035. Preliminary version in FOCS 1998. DOI: 10.1137/S0097539700373039. 566

D. Micciancio. 2004. Almost perfect lattices, the covering radius problem, and applications to Ajtai's connection factor. *SIAM Journal on Computing*, 34(1): 118–169. Preliminary version in STOC 2002. DOI: 10.1137/S0097539703433511. 566, 567, 584

D. Micciancio. 2008. Efficient reductions among lattice problems. In *Proceedings of SODA*, pp. 84–93. ACM/SIAM. 587

D. Micciancio. 2012. Inapproximability of the shortest vector problem: Toward a deterministic reduction. *Theory of Computing*, 8(1): 487–512. DOI: 10.4086/toc.2012 .v008a022. 567

D. Micciancio, S. J. Ong, A. Sahai, and S. Vadhan. 2006. Concurrent zero knowledge without complexity assumptions. In S. Halevi and T. Rabin, *Theory of Crytography, Third Theory of Crytography Conference, ICC 2006, New York, NY, USA, March 4–7, 2006. Proceedings*. Lecture Notes in Computer Science vol. 3876, pp. 1–20. Springer. DOI: 10.1007/11681878_1. 584

D. Micciancio and C. Peikert. 2012. Trapdoors for lattices: Simpler, tighter, faster, smaller. In *Advances in Cryptology—EUROCRYPT 2012, 31st Annual International Conference on the Theory and Applications of Cryptographic Techniques, Cambridge, UK, April 15–19, 2012. Proceedings*. Lecture Notes in Computer Science vol. 7237, pp. 700–718. Springer. DOI: 10.1007/978-3-642-29011-4_41. 588

D. Micciancio and C. Peikert. 2013. Hardness of SIS and LWE with small parameters. In *Advances in Cryptology—CRYPTO 2013, 33rd Annual Cryptology Conference, Santa Barbara, CA, USA, August 18–22, 2013. Proceedings. Part I*. Lecture Notes in Computer Science vol. 8042, pp. 21–39. Springer. DOI: 10.1007/978-3-642-40041-4_2. 566, 567

D. Micciancio and O. Regev. 2007. Worst-case to average-case reductions based on Gaussian measure. *SIAM Journal on Computing*, 37(1): 267–302. Preliminary version in FOCS 2004. DOI: 10.1137/S0097539705447360. 566, 567, 573, 587, 588

D. Micciancio and S. Vadhan. 2003. Statistical zero-knowledge proofs with efficient provers: lattice problems and more. In *Advances in Cryptology–Crypto 2003, 23rd Annual International Cryptology Conference, Santa Barbara, CA, USA, August 17–21, 2003. Proceedings*. Lecture Notes in Computer Science vol. 2729, pp. 282–298. Springer. DOI: 10.1007/b11817. 581, 582, 583

D. Micciancio and P. Voulgaris. 2010. Faster exponential time algorithms for the shortest vector problem. In *Proceedings of SODA*, pp. 1468–1480. ACM/SIAM. http://www.siam.org/proceedings/soda/2010/SODA10_119_miccianciod.pdf. 592

M. Nguyen and S. P. Vadhan. 2006. Zero knowledge with efficient provers. In *Proceedings of the 38th Annual ACM Symposium on Theory of Computing, Seattle, WA, USA, May 21–23, 2006*, pp. 287–295. DOI: 10.1145/1132516.1132559. 581, 584

T. Okamoto. 2000. On relationships between statistical zero-knowledge proofs. *Journal of Computer and System Sciences*, 60(1): 47–108. DOI: 10.1006/jcss.1999.1664. 575

C. Peikert. 2008. Limits on the hardness of lattice problems in l_p norms. *Computational Complexity*, 17(2): 300–351. Special Issue on CCC'07. DOI: 10.1007/s00037-008-0251-3. 589

C. Peikert. 2009. Public-key cryptosystems from the worst-case shortest vector problem. In *Proceedings of STOC*, pp. 333–342. DOI: 10.1145/1536414.1536461. 568, 590, 591

C. Peikert and V. Vaikuntanathan. 2008. Noninteractive statistical zero-knowledge proofs for lattice problems. In *Advances in Cryptology–Crypto 2008, 28th Annual International Cryptology Conference, Santa Barbara, CA, USA, August 17–21, 2008. Proceedings*. Lecture Notes in Computer Science vol. 5157, pp. 536–553. Springer. DOI: 10.1007/978-3-540-85174-5_30. 583, 585

O. Regev. 2009. On lattices, learning with errors, random linear codes, and cryptography. *Journal of ACM*, 56(6): 34. Preliminary version in STOC 2005. DOI: 10.1145/1568318.1568324. 568, 573, 584, 590, 591

O. Regev and R. Rosen. 2006. Lattice problems and norm embeddings. In *Proceedings of STOC*, pp. 447–456. ACM. DOI: 10.1145/1132516.1132581. 589

J. Rompel. 1990. One-way functions are necessary and sufficient for secure signatures. In *Proceedings of the 22nd Annual ACM Symposium on Theory of Computing, May 13–17, 1990, Baltimore, MD, USA*, pp. 387–394. DOI: 10.1145/100216.100269. 583

P. van Emde Boas. 1981. Another NP-complete problem and the complexity of computing short vectors in a lattice. Technical Report 81-04, Mathematische Instituut, University of Amsterdam. Available online at URL http://turing.wins.uva.nl/˜peter/. 589

Following a Tangent of Proofs

Johan Håstad

We discuss a sequence of results, many related to various forms of probabilistic proofs. The tangent I follow is that of single-prover interactive proofs, through multi-prover interactive proofs, to probabilistically checkable proofs, and leading to inapproximability results for NP-hard optimization problems.

22.1 Introduction and Notation

The objective of this paper is not to write scientific history in any objective sense, and in fact in several places I omit the fine-grained history and just cite the final publication. The purpose is rather to give an exposition of a sequence of results and ideas that have evolved during my career and that I find beautiful and important. In some instances I try to recall what I felt at the time when the result first appeared. Any such memories should be taken with a grain of salt since it is easy to, hopefully by mistake, adjust memories based on later experiences.

We use standard notation that we mostly introduce as we go or often just hope is self-evident. We use $[n]$ to denote the integers $\{1, 2 \ldots n\}$. Addition is usually over the integers, but sometimes we work modulo 2 or modulo a prime p.

We spend a significant part of the paper discussing proof systems. We have a polynomial-time verifier, usually called V, and an all-powerful prover, usually called P, which share a mathematical statement. The proof system is *complete* if P can always convince V when the statement is correct. It is *sound* if P always fails to convince V when the statement is false. In many situations both P and V can use randomness. In such a situation a proof is perfectly complete if P can make V accept with probability 1. We also consider proof systems where this probability is slightly less than 1. The soundness of such a probabilistic proof system is the maximal probability with which a cheating prover can make the verifier accept any purported proof for an incorrect statement.

In many situations the soundness can be improved by running the verification several times with independent randomness. This results in a small increase in the verifier's use of resources, which, in most situations, is not important.

22.2 The Beginning, IP, ZK, and AM

The concept of an efficient proof was long felt to be captured by NP. A deterministic polynomial-time verifier that checks a written proof. The verifier always accepts a correct proof of a correct statement and never accepts any proof of an incorrect statement. What more could we possibly hope for?

The key insight here is that also efficient algorithms can learn more quickly by asking questions, and in 1985 Goldwasser, Micali, and Rackoff [Goldwasser et al. 1985][1] introduced the notion of an interactive proof. In such a proof a probabilistic prover, P, and a probabilistic polynomial-time verifier, V, share a binary string x and exchange messages. P wants to convince V that $x \in L$ for some predetermined language L. This is an interactive proof system if whenever $x \in L$ is true, P can make V accept with probability at least 2/3, while if $x \notin L$, no matter how P behaves, the probability that V is convinced is at most 1/3.

At almost the same time Babai [1985] produced a similar notion called Arthur–Merlin games. Merlin plays the role of the prover, while Arthur plays the role of the verifier but is more limited. In particular, every message sent by Arthur is a set of random independent coin flips, and the only real computation performed by Arthur is a polynomial-time computation after the interaction is over.

While the motivation of Babai was to make it possible to recognize more languages using the smallest possible extension of NP, an additional motivation of Goldwasser, Micali, and Rackoff [Goldwasser et al. 1985] came from cryptography, and the seminal concept defined was zero-knowledge. This notion captures that P convinces V that $x \in L$ without disclosing any additional information. This is formalized using the notion of a simulator, but as we here focus on language recognition, we refer to Goldwasser et al. [1988] for the details. To get a flavor of zero-knowledge and at the same time see the difference between the two models, let us give a nice protocol, proposed by Goldreich, Micali, and Wigderson [Goldreich et al. 1991].

---

1. With the full version appearing in Goldwasser et al. [1988].

We are given two graphs G_0 and G_1 on n nodes that the prover, P, claims are nonisomorphic. We have the following interactive protocol:

1. The verifier, V, chooses a random bit b and a random permutation, π of $[n]$, and sends $H = \pi(G_b)$ to P.

2. P responds with a bit b'.

3. V accepts iff $b = b'$.

This is a perfectly complete protocol since if G_0 and G_1 are indeed nonisomorphic then H determines the value of b, and since we assume that P is all powerful, it can compute this value and make V always accept.

On the other hand, if G_0 and G_1 are isomorphic, then it is equally likely that a given H is produced with $b = 0$ and $b = 1$. Indeed, if $G_1 = \sigma(G_0)$ then $(0, \pi)$ and $(1, \pi \circ \sigma)$ are equally likely to appear and produce the same H. This implies that, regardless of the strategy of P, the verifier accepts with probability $1/2$. Repeating the protocol t times can make this error probability decrease to 2^{-t}.

This proof of soundness uses in a strong way that the random choices of V remain hidden from P and that there are two different sets of random coins of V that produce the same H. In particular, there is no obvious way to implement this protocol idea in the AM model where Arthur can only send his random coins to Merlin.

It came as a surprise when Goldwasser and Sipser [1986] proved that, not only for this problem, but for any problem, there is no[2] advantage to allowing hidden coins. If there is a polynomial-time general interactive protocol, there is a different protocol that also runs in polynomial time where the verifier simply sends its random coins. Let us denote the set of languages that admit an interactive proof (thus either in the model of Babai [1985] or Goldwasser et al. [1985]) by IP.

We note that IP contains NP and was known at this time to contain some highly structured languages such as graph-nonisomorphism and some group-theoretic problems studied by Babai [1985].

For the above protocol note that, in some intuitive sense, V does not learn anything. When the graphs are nonisomorphic, P only sends a bit that V already knows. This is correct for a verifier that follows the protocol. To get a protocol that remains zero-knowledge even against a verifier that actively tries to extract knowledge is more complicated, and we refer to Goldreich et al. [1991] for details.

---

2. This is in the black-and-white world of polynomial-time verifiers. If we look on a more detailed level of complexity there might be differences.

In the same paper Goldreich, Micali, and Wigderson [Goldreich et al. 1991] proposed a zero-knowledge protocol for the NP-complete problem of three-colorability. In this simple and beautiful protocol the prover knows a correct three-coloring of the graph G and wants to convince a limited verifier that G is three-colorable without giving any extra information.

1. P randomly permutes the colors in the coloring and for each vertex v, chooses a fresh cryptographic key of a "good" encryption scheme, and encrypts the color of this vertex in a separate message. P sends all these encryptions to V.

2. V chooses a random edge, e, and sends to P.

3. P reveals the keys to decrypt the colors of the endpoints of e.

4. V accepts if the two decrypted colors belong to $\{0, 1, 2\}$ and are different.

Clearly this is a perfectly complete interactive proof because when P has a correct three-coloring it simply follows the protocol as described and V always accepts.

Suppose the encryption scheme has the property that once the encryptions are fixed there is only one set of acceptable secret keys. Then the system is also sound. If G is not three-colorable, then for any set of encryptions of P there is some edge whose endpoints do not decrypt to distinct and legal colors and thus the probability that V rejects is at least $1/m$, where m is the number of edges. Repeating the protocol nm times makes it very unlikely that V is fooled. Let us discuss the zero-knowledge property.

The intuitive notion of a good cryptosystem is that before the secret keys are given, any ciphertext looks like random bits. This notion can be made precise and implies that the above verifier does not learn anything, provided that it is computationally bounded. The difference from learning nothing in an information-theoretic way and in a computational way should not be ignored and in order to give information-theoretic zero-knowledge proofs, Ben-Or, Goldwasser, Kilian, and Wigderson [Ben-Or et al. 1988] introduced multi-prover interactive proofs.

22.3 Multi-Prover Interactive Proofs

In a multi-prover interactive proof a single verifier interacts with several all-powerful provers. The only restriction on these provers is that they cannot communicate during the protocol.

An intuitive reason that this can be used to remove cryptographic assumptions can be seen from the above protocol for three-colorability. V can simply ask the two different provers for the colors of the two endpoints. It is not difficult to see that the best the provers can do is to supply the colors of a predetermined coloring. To be more precise, each prover answers a question of the form (v, i) with the color of v in the ith coloring where the two provers in advance have agreed on a sequence of randomly permuted colorings of G. Each prover never answers two questions with the same i. This is a complete, sound, and somewhat zero-knowledge protocol.

We say "somewhat" as, while a V that follows the protocol learns nothing, this simple protocol is not zero-knowledge for a general V. If V asks for all pairs of vertices (adjacent or not) and G has a unique three-coloring, then V can determine which pairs of vertices have the same color and reconstruct the entire coloring.

As is clear from the title of Ben-Or et al. [1988], its main motivation was to eliminate cryptographic assumptions. At this time I did not expect the language recognition power of multi-prover interactive proofs to be much different from that of single-prover interactive proofs, which in its turn I expected to be just slightly above NP.

It is not difficult to see, and was noted by several people at the time, that the maximal probability that the verifier accepts in an interactive proof can be computed in PSPACE and thus any language that admitted such a proof must belong to this class. This seemed, however, to be a crude and preliminary first upper bound on the complexity of IP.

A result by Aiello, Goldwasser, and Håstad [Austrin et al. 2017] gave an oracle A such that IP^A (with an unbounded number of rounds) contained languages outside the polynomial-time hierarchy relative to the same oracle, while Fortnow and Sipser [1988] gave a different oracle, B, for which IP^B (with a polynomial number of rounds) did not contain coNP^B.

My conclusion regarding these two papers was that we would need nonrelativizing techniques to prove that IP is small, while it turned out that we should use nonrelativizing techniques for proving that it is large.

On a personal note, I recall that I felt that introducing multi-prover interactive proofs was somewhat of a "cheat." It seemed like an artificial model that would not say anything interesting about "actual computation." Single-prover interactive proofs seemed to me a reasonable model, and thus a good plan was to work hard and study this class rather than introducing another even more esoteric complexity class adding more questions and confusion than answers. Fortunately, this view was not shared by everybody.

22.4 The True Power of Interaction

The first real glimpse of the amazing power of interactive proofs came in the work of Lund, Fortnow, Karloff, and Nisan [Lund et al. 1992], where it was proved that a prover can convince a verifier of the value of the permanent (over the integers) of a Boolean matrix, which is a #P-hard task [Valiant 1979]. As the argument is not very complicated, let us give it.

The proof goes by having a number of matrices M_i together with numbers a_i, and we let $Per(M_i, a_i)$ be shorthand for a claim by the prover that the permanent of M_i equals a_i. The original statement is then simply $Per(M, a)$ for some $n \times n$ matrix M and number a specified by the prover.

The first step of the verifier is to pick a random prime p and from this moment on consider all equalities modulo this prime p. As the permanent is easy to bound, it is not difficult to see that it is unlikely that an incorrect claim $Per(M, a)$ is turned to a correct claim when it is considered modulo a random prime p of size at least n^2. The two steps of the argument are now as follows:

1. Reduce one statement $Per(M, a)$ where M is an $n \times n$ matrix to n statement $Per(M_i, a_i)$ where each matrix is of dimension $n - 1$.

2. Reduce two statements $Per(M, a)$ and $Per(M', b)$ of dimension n to one statement $Per(M'', c)$ of dimension n.

The first step is easy and follows by taking the expansion along the first row, and the second step is where something interesting happens. The great idea here is to look at the permanent of $tM + (1 - t)M'$ as a polynomial in t. This is of degree n, and the prover can give the $n + 1$ coefficients of this polynomial $P(t)$.

The verifier now checks that $P(0) = b$ and $P(1) = a$, and then picks a random value t_0 modulo p and sets $M'' = t_0 M + (1 - t_0)M'$ and $c = P(t_0)$. Note that an honest prover trying to establish a correct claim has no problem completing these steps. Assume, however, that at least one of the two statements is incorrect. Then $Per(tM + (1 - t)M')$ and $P(t)$ are two different polynomials of degree n. This follows as they take different values for $t = 0$ and/or $t = 1$. As two different polynomials of degree n agree on at most n points, this implies that with probability $1 - n/p$ also (M'', c) is an incorrect claim. To visualize this more clearly, let us give the an example of this combination step.

Suppose we are working modulo $p = 127$ and we have

$$M = \begin{pmatrix} 92 & 45 & 9 \\ 11 & 17 & 81 \\ 65 & 61 & 23 \end{pmatrix}, \qquad M' = \begin{pmatrix} 47 & 41 & 104 \\ 0 & 112 & 13 \\ 87 & 34 & 12 \end{pmatrix},$$

and the current claims are $Per(M, 77)$ and $Per(M', 54)$. To substantiate this, the prover supplies the polynomial

$$P(t) = 54 + 88t + 9t^2 + 53t^3$$

and the verifier checks that $P(0) = 54$, the claimed permanent for M', while $P(1) = 77$ (remember that we are doing calculations modulo 127). The verifier picks the random number $t_0 = 47$, which gives

$$M'' = \begin{pmatrix} 3 & 102 & 84 \\ 9 & 92 & 34 \\ 69 & 33 & 21 \end{pmatrix},$$

and the claim turns into $Per(M'', 31)$, as $P(47) = 31$. Given that we are down to a single matrix, we use an expansion across one row to decrease the dimension.

In the general situation we start with one claim of dimension n, which we reduce to n claims of dimension $n - 1$. By doing the above combination process $n - 1$ times, we are down to a single claim of dimension $n - 1$, which is then expanded to yield $n - 1$ claims of dimension $n - 2$, and so on. Eventually, after $O(n^2)$ combination steps we end up with claims of dimension 1, which are easily checked without the help of the prover.

If the original claim was incorrect and all final claims are correct, then at some step two claims of which at least one is incorrect is reduced to a correct claim. The probability of this happening in a single step is, as discussed above, bounded by n/p. Thus with probability $1 - O(\frac{n^3}{p})$ if we started with an incorrect claim, the final claim will also be incorrect and the prover will be caught cheating. Thus choosing a random prime p of size roughly n^4 gives us a good proof system.

As computing the permanent is #P-hard, the result by Lund et al. [1992] greatly increased the known power of interactive proofs. In particular, this implied that any problem in coNP did admit such a proof. I was at this point in time back in Sweden, which just barely had email, and thus I have little personal insight into the discussions and exchanges of ideas that took place during a hectic period. The next major step was Shamir's classic result [Shamir 1992] that indeed all of PSPACE admitted interactive proofs. The original proof of this result was not very complicated and was simplified even further by Shen [1992] to fit in three pages. In spite of this, let us here give a simplified sketch. It is enough to discuss the generic PSPACE-complete problem, quantified Boolean formulas, abbreviated as QBF.

In QBF, one is given a sequence of quantifiers and then a formula in CNF. One example is

$$\exists x_1 \forall x_2 \exists x_3 \forall x_4 (x_1 \vee x_2 \vee x_3 \vee x_4) \wedge (\bar{x}_1 \vee \bar{x}_2 \vee \bar{x}_3 \vee \bar{x}_4), \tag{22.1}$$

which is a true formula. One way to attack QBF is to think of integers as truth values where zero corresponds to false and any nonzero positive value corresponds to true. With this convention $\exists$ quantifiers turn into sums and $\forall$ into product. Given formula φ, we can write down a polynomial P_φ such that if φ evaluates to true then P_φ is positive and otherwise P_φ takes the value 0. This can be done by replacing $\vee$ with $+$ and $\wedge$ with $\cdot$. Finally, the negation $\bar{x}$ is replaced by $(1 - x)$. We do not require that we can write down P_φ in dense form; it is enough for us that we can evaluate it on any input in polynomial time.

The expression corresponding to (22.1) is then

$$\sum_{x_1=0}^{1} \prod_{x_2=0}^{1} \sum_{x_3=0}^{1} \prod_{x_4=0}^{1} (x_1 + x_2 + x_3 + x_4)(4 - (x_1 + x_2 + x_3 + x_4)), \qquad (22.2)$$

which evaluates to 576, showing the formulas is indeed true. We remark that it might also be convenient to make sure that P_φ never takes values outside 0 and 1, leading to slightly more complicated formulas.

As above when discussing the permanent, it is also here convenient to have all computations take place modulo p for a random prime p chosen by the verifier.

A straightforward evaluation of an expression such as (22.2) takes exponential time, and hence we need the help of a prover. The idea is to think of the expression (22.2) as

$$\sum_{x_1=0}^{1} P(x_1),$$

where P is a polynomial, and ask the prover to supply the integer value of the total expression as well as to give the description of P as a polynomial in the form of its coefficients. The problem to be overcome, however, is that, as defined above, the degree of the polynomial P is exponential. This problem was overcome by Shamir and then in a simpler form by Shen by adding a degree reduction step. We do not here discuss the technique to maintain low degree, but let us still illustrate the method. If the formula to prove is a coNP statement, then we have no problem with the degree and the argument is simple. Consider the formula

$$x_1 \wedge (\bar{x}_1 \vee x_2) \wedge (\bar{x}_2 \vee x_3) \wedge (\bar{x}_1 \vee \bar{x}_3),$$

which we want to prove is a contradiction. One way to prove this is to establish that

$$\sum_{x_1=0}^{1} \sum_{x_2=0}^{1} \sum_{x_3=0}^{1} x_1(1 + x_2 - x_1)(1 + x_3 - x_2)(2 - x_1 - x_3) = 0. \qquad (22.3)$$

The verifier randomly picks the prime $p = 127$ and from now on we consider all computations modulo p. The prover claims that (22.3) equals

$$\sum_{x_1=0}^{1} P_1(x_1),$$

where $P_1(x) = 6x + 117x^2 + 4x^3$. The verifier checks that $P_1(0) + P_1(1) = 0 + 0 = 0$ and then picks the random value $x_1 = 47$. As $P_1(47) = 38$, the verifier now wants to check that

$$\sum_{x_2=0}^{1} \sum_{x_3=0}^{1} 47(81 + x_2)(1 + x_3 - x_2)(82 - x_3) \equiv 38, \qquad (22.4)$$

and the prover claims that this sum is of the form

$$\sum_{x_2=0}^{1} P_2(x_2),$$

where $P_2(x) = 30 + 19x + 86x^2$. The verifier checks that

$$P_2(0) + P_2(1) \equiv 30 + 8 \equiv 38 \bmod 127$$

and picks the random value 61 for x_2 and computes $P_2(61) = 12$. The final verification is now that

$$\sum_{x_3=0}^{1} 47 \cdot 15 \cdot (67 + x_3)(82 - x_3) \equiv 24 + 115 \equiv 12, \qquad (22.5)$$

which the verifier can evaluate on its own and this convinces the verifier that the formula was indeed not satisfiable.

Progress continued to be very fast and within a month Babai, Fortnow, and Lund [Babai et al. 1992] proved that any language in nondeterministic exponential time (NEXP) admitted a multi-prover interactive proof. Hence, the upper bound proved by Fortnow, Rompel, and Sipser [Fortnow et al. 1994], which at first seemed ridiculously high, turned out to be tight.

The proof of Babai et al. [1992] was more complicated than previous proofs but, of course, used the idea of creating suitable polynomials and then picking random inputs over a domain that is significantly larger than the original Boolean domain.

The immense power of randomness combined with interaction was surprising and wonderful, but this, at least as I felt it, did not really add much information about our favorite computational problems. After all, most problems that we care about are close to NP, and the fact that much more difficult problems have efficient interactive proofs seemed to give little information on problems close to NP.

22.5 Inapproximability Enters the Picture

Of course efficient proofs for NEXP do imply efficient proofs for NP, but since the verifier needs to read the entire statement this is an obvious bottleneck. If the statement is, however, coded in a suitable error-correcting form, Babai, Fortnow, Levin, and Szegedy [Babai et al. 1991] established that it is possible to have the verifier run in polylogarithmic time. Another novelty was that, as described in next paragraph, it was more reasonable to think in terms of a written proof fixed before the verification starts.

Of course in any proof system it is possible to write down the strategy of the prover, but in the previously constructed cases there are exponentially many different actions by the verifier resulting in an exponentially large proof if written down. In the down-scaled version the written proof could be made to be of more reasonable size. A written proof also eliminates the need for more than one prover.

Two parameters that are of key interest are the number of bits the verifier reads in the proof, from here on called b, and the number of random bits, r, that the verifier uses. Counting random bits is by tradition, and the total number of different possibilities (which is closely related) for the randomness is probably more fundamental because this notion, as we describe below, relates closely to proof length.

Of course both the number of bits read in the proof and the number of random bits used by the verifier are upper-bounded by the running time, but in many situations tighter bounds can be found. In particular, the verifier can read the input without any problems as this does not contribute to either measure.

The insight that these parameters are crucial and how this connects to approximability of clique was first given in the seminal paper of Feige, Goldwasser, Lovasz, Safra, and Szegedy [Feige et al. 1996]. The connection is not technically difficult, so let us describe it.

We have a verifier that flips r random bits and always reads at most b bits of the proof. We have 2^r different random choices of the verifier to consider, and as the value of each read bit also affects the execution we have a total of at most 2^{r+b} different possible executions of V. We can also note that the proof need be of size at most $b2^{r+b}$, as each execution reads at most b bits and bits that are not read under any execution need not exist.

Let us consider the behavior of this fixed verifier under all possible proofs. We forget what is being proved and the details of the proof, we just think of all possible proofs that are binary strings of length at most $b2^{b+r}$.

Let us now consider a graph G where the vertices are defined by the at most 2^{r+b} different possible executions of the verifier that causes it to accept. We have vertices $v_{c,a}$, where c is the set of coins and thus a string in $\{0, 1\}^r$ and a is the set of bits read in the proof and thus a string in $\{0, 1\}^b$. Note that the locations of the bits read is determined by c and a because given these two strings we can run the verifier and see what happens.

We connect $v_{c,a}$ to $v_{c',a'}$ if the two executions can appear in the same proof. This is possible if and only if any bit position read in both executions is reported to return the same value. Note that many pairs of vertices are connected simply because they read disjoint sets of bits.

On the other hand, if $c = c'$ then for $a \neq a'$ the nodes are not connected. This follows since once the randomness is fixed to be the same in two executions, the same sequence of positions are read and unless one read bit takes different values in the two executions, these executions are identical.

If you consider a clique in this graph and all executions described by the vertices in this clique, then either none of them reads a particular bit of the proof or all executions that read the bit agree on the value. Thus such a clique gives unique values for some of the bits of the proof while the rest are undetermined. Vice versa, if you start with a fixed written proof and look at the set of nodes that are consistent with this proof they form a clique. Thus there is a very close correspondence between cliques in this graph and written proofs. If the size of the clique is t, then the probability that the verifier accepts is $t2^{-r}$. To get strong inapproximability results for clique, one hence needs to construct proof systems with good soundness that use small amounts of randomness and read few bits in the proofs.

The most efficient construction in Feige et al. [1996] uses both r and b of size $O(\log n \log \log n)$, and one conclusion of the paper can be stated as follows.

Theorem 22.1 (Feige et al. 1996)   Suppose that for some $\epsilon > 0$ and constant c it is possible to approximate the size of the largest clique in a graph with n nodes within a factor $2^{(\log n)^{1-\epsilon}}$ using execution time $\exp((\log n)^c)$. Then $\mathrm{NP} \subseteq \cup_d \mathrm{DTIME}(\exp((\log n)^d))$.

In other words, a rather weak approximation algorithm for clique running in quasi-polynomial time implies that all of NP can be done in quasi-polynomial time.

At this time very little was known about efficiently approximating clique. There was no lower bound, and the upper bound of approximability $n/(\log n)^2$ was proved by Boppana and Halldórsson [1992] only subsequent to Feige et al. [1996], although similar bounds were known for the related problem of coloring. I think it is fair to say that we had no idea how well clique could be approximated. A polynomial-time algorithm giving a $\sqrt{n}$-approximation (which we now know is impossible) would not have been considered surprising. A manuscript claiming an efficient $\log n$ approximation would, as far as I can guess and recall, have been greeted with enthusiasm without any immediate suspicions of being flawed.

22.6   PCP-Theorem and Label-Cover

The need for the $\log \log n$ factor in the bounds of Feige et al. [1996] was annoying and needed to be removed but much more was achieved. The stage was set for the PCP-theorem, proved by Arora, Lund, Motwani, Sudan, and Szegedy [Arora et al. 1998] with a very important next-to-last step by Arora and Safra [1998]. Let us state this seminal theorem.

Theorem 22.2   (PCP theorem [Arora et al. 1998])   Any NP-statement has a polynomial-size written proof that can be checked by an efficient verifier that uses $r = O(\log n)$ bits of randomness and which reads $b = O(1)$ bits. It always accepts a correct proof for a correct statement, and for any purported proof of an incorrect statement the probability that it is accepted is at most s. Here $s < 1$ is an absolute constant independent of the input size.

As often in complexity theory there is a tradeoff of the constants involved, and in the PCP theorem, the most important tradeoff is between the number of bits read and the soundness. The first proof of Theorem 22.2 established that for any $b \geq 3$ a soundness $s_b < 1$ is possible where s_b tends to 0 as b tends to infinity. That the latter is true follows from the possibility of checking the proof many times using fresh randomness. This increases r and b by a constant factor but reduces s.

By an additional adjustment of s_b, it is also possible to make the verifier *nonadaptive*, which is the property that the positions read depend only on the randomness of the verifier and not on values of the previous bits read in the proof.

The PCP theorem implied that there is a constant ϵ such that it is NP-hard to approximate clique within n^ϵ (later results by Håstad [1999] established that this is true for any $\epsilon < 1$). More importantly it opened up for inapproximability results for many new families of problems, and as often in computer science, a very popular problem is 3SAT.

Theorem 22.3 (Arora et al. 1998)   There is a constant $s_3 < 1$ such that it is NP-hard to distinguish satisfiable 3CNF formulas from those where any assignment satisfies at most a fraction s_3 of the clauses.

Proof (Sketch) Take an arbitrary language in NP. Using the PCP theorem there is a polynomial size proof checked by a nonadaptive verifier that only reads three bits in the proof. Consider the bits of this proof as variables, and consider all possible random tapes of the verifier. Each random tape determines three positions in the proof to be read, and there is a constant size 3CNF in the variables of these three bits that describes whether the verifier accepts. Take the conjunction of all such local formulas.

A written proof is an assignment to all bits in the proof. If it is a correct proof of a correct statement, the verifier always accepts and hence the corresponding assignment satisfies all the above constraints.

If the statement to be proved is false, then any proof causes the verifier to reject with constant probability and hence any assignment to the proof variables falsifies a constant fraction of the clauses. ∎

The connection described above is very tight and it is not difficult to derive the PCP theorem (Theorem 22.2) from Theorem 22.3; thus the two statements are equivalent.

The unspecified constant (which was extremely close to one in the first proof) in Theorem 22.3 made it unsuitable for getting quantitative results for interesting problems. With the aid of Raz's parallel repetition theorem [Raz 1998] this unspecified constant can be moved into other unknown parameters (i.e., R and L in Theorem 22.4 below). This approach opens up for better quantitative results and to describe this we start by defining the most useful variant of a problem called label-cover.

Definition 22.1 An instance of ***projection label cover*** is given by a bipartite graph with disjoint sets of vertices V and W and edges $E \subseteq V \times W$. For each edge (v, w) there is a projection $\pi_{wv} : [L] \mapsto [R]$. A labeling assigns a label $l_w \in [L]$ for each $w \in W$ and a label $l_v \in [R]$ for each $v \in V$ and satisfies an edge (v, w) iff $\pi_{wv}(l_w) = l_v$.

The following theorem follows from the PCP theorem and Raz parallel repetition theorem [Raz 1998] for two-prover games.

Theorem 22.4 For any $\epsilon > 0$ there exists constants R and L such that it is NP-hard to distinguish the following objects:

- Label cover instances where there is an assignment that satisfies all constraints

- Label cover instances where any assignment only satisfies a fraction at most ϵ of the constraints

In other words, any algorithm A that outputs "satisfiable" on satisfiable instances and "not satisfiable" on instances where the best assignment satisfies only a fraction ϵ of the constraints can be used to solve any problem in NP.

Let us point out that, on the high level, the proof of Theorem 22.4 is what can be expected. One constructs a polynomial-time algorithm B that takes as input a Boolean formula φ and produces an instance I_φ of label cover. If φ is satisfiable, then there is a labeling that satisfies all constraints of I_φ, while if φ is not satisfiable then no assignment can satisfy more than a fraction ϵ of the constraints. The algorithm B is rather complicated, as it relies on the constructions of the PCP theorem, but it is just an explicit and efficient (well, polynomial-time, so efficient in theory) algorithm.

The hardness of label cover gives an efficient proof system for NP. The proof that φ is satisfiable is given by a good labeling of the vertices of I_φ. The verifier can check this labeling by picking a random edge, reading the two labels corresponding to the endpoints of the edge, and checking the constraint given by the corresponding projection π.

This is a very interesting proof system; it reads only two symbols of constant size (corresponding to numbers in $[L]$ and $[R]$ respectively), always accepts a correct proof of a correct statement, and rejects any purported proof of a false statement except with probability ϵ. The integers R and L are of constant size but we prefer to read single bits and to achieve this we need a good code.

22.7 The Long Code and the Standard Written Proof

In order make the proof contain bits, we ask the prover to write down a binary encoding of the labels. Instead of writing a label ℓ the prover writes down a binary string $c(\ell)$ that is a unique but very redundant representation of ℓ. A code that gave the foundations of many results to come was introduced by Bellare, Goldreich, and Sudan [Bellare et al. 1998] and we describe this next. It is called "the long code," and it is the longest possible[3] binary code.

---

3. This assumes that we do not have two positions in the code that are the same for all codewords. In other words for any positions i and j there is an ℓ such that $c(\ell)_i \neq c(\ell)_j$.

To be more precise, to code an element, $x \in [R]$, we provide for each function $f : [R] \mapsto \{0, 1\}$ the value of $f(x)$. From a practical coding perspective this is quite wasteful as it codes d bits as 2^{2^d} bits and in particular it is not likely that mankind will ever write down the full long code of a 10-bit string. From a theory perspective, however, the long code is affordable and extremely useful.

A long code is slightly nonintuitive in that it takes as input a function, and changing notation is useful to bring us to more familiar ground. A function, f, mapping $[R] \mapsto \{0, 1\}$ can be described as an element in $\{0, 1\}^R$ where the ith coordinate is $f(i)$. In this notation a correct long code of an element ℓ is a table $C_\ell : \{0, 1\}^R \mapsto \{0, 1\}$ where $C_\ell(x) = x_\ell$, a fixed coordinate. In view of this perspective, long codes are also referred to as "dictators." This comes from the view of Boolean functions as voting rules, and in these functions only the vote x_ℓ counts.

The standard written proof of a label-cover instance, SWP[4], supplies, for each vertex v or w, the long code of the label. As R and L are constants this only increases the size of the proof by a constant factor.

When thinking about a SWP it is important to think differently when reasoning about completeness and soundness. In the completeness case we can assume that the table corresponding to a vertex v is a correct long code of an element, and in particular of the good label ℓ_v. When discussing soundness, the table corresponding to v can be arbitrary. There is no reason for a cheating prover to make this binary string be the long code of any element. Indeed, if one could assume that this is a correct long code of a label then the soundness proof is usually easy, and the difficulty of the argument is usually to handle tables that have little structure.

There is a general scheme for verifying SWP as a written proof based on the natural way of verifying a good labeling described above. The starting point is by picking a random edge (v, w) with the same distribution as in the label cover and looking at the two tables corresponding to the supposed long codes of the labels for v and w.

The table corresponding to v is described by a Boolean function $f_v : \{0, 1\}^R \mapsto \{0, 1\}$, the table corresponding to w is $g_w : \{0, 1\}^L \mapsto \{0, 1\}$, and we have a mapping $\pi_{wv} : [L] \mapsto [R]$. We are interested in running a local check (sometimes called an "inner test") on (f_v, g_w, π_{wv}). As we focus on such inner tests, thinking of v and w as fixed, we leave out the subscripts of f, g, and π. In the next section we see two such examples, but let us give a general idea of the approach.

---

4. This is a term introduced in Håstad [2001] but not widely used.

As in the proof of Theorem 22.3, we think of each bit in the proof as a variable. In that proof we had a property on three bits, and as any such property can be coded as a 3CNF the acceptance of the overall proof could be written as a conjunction of 3CNFs, and thus as a 3CNF. If we have a more specialized criteria given by a predicate P in the inner test, we get a result for an optimization problem where each constraint is the predicate P applied to a set of variables.

In many situations it turns out that it is possible to make sure that the tables f and g respect negation. This is done by having a table of half the size and using one bit to represent both $f(x)$ and $f(\bar{x})$ where $\bar{x}$ is the bit-wise complement of x. If the latter bit is needed, the read bit is complemented before use. As this mechanism gives the correct answer for a correct long code it does not hurt completeness and is often helpful in analyzing soundness. This mechanism is often referred to as "folding" a long code, and we use it in the tests in next section. One consequence of this folding is that, following the argument in the previous paragraph, we end up with a set of constraints where the predicate P is applied to a set of literals instead of variables. A negated variable corresponds to the case when we need $f(\bar{x})$ and $f(x)$ is the bit that exists in the proof.

22.8 Two Inner Tests

Let us recall the situation. The written proof is SWP and we have selected a random edge (u, w) according to the label-cover instance. We drop indices and we have tables $f : \{0, 1\}^R \mapsto \{0, 1\}$ and $g : \{0, 1\}^L \mapsto \{0, 1\}$ and a projection $\pi : [L] \mapsto [R]$, and we want to test whether f and g are long codes of elements i and j, respectively, such that $\pi(j) = i$. We want a test that (almost) always accepts if this is indeed the case.

In a perfect world, we would like to have a strong converse—that if the test accepts with high probability then the tables are (close to) two consistent long codes. This is often too much to ask for,[5] and by looking at the soundness criteria of Theorem 22.4 we see that this is also not needed. What we need is to be able to extract a coordinate, i, from the table of f and a coordinate, j, from g such that $\pi(j) = i$ happens with probability higher than ϵ (over the choice of a random edge (u, w)). It is important that the extraction of i only depends on f and nothing else and similarly with j and g.

We let these extraction procedures be randomized. This makes it possible to relate the probability that the inner test accepts, conditioned on (u, w) being chosen,

---

5. After all we are going to read very few bits in the tables of f and g.

to the probability that $\pi(j) = i$ conditioned on the same event. Averaging over all edges proves that this probabilistic labeling satisfies a large number of constraints on average, and hence we can conclude that a good labeling exists.

22.8.1   The Test Underlying Max-3Lin-2 Hardness

An instance of Max-3Lin-2 is given by a set of linear equations modulo 2 with three variables in each equation. The task is to find an assignment that satisfies as many equations as possible. An example is given below.

$$
\begin{aligned}
x_1 + x_2 + x_3 &= 1 \\
x_1 + x_4 + x_5 &= 0 \\
x_2 + x_4 + x_5 &= 1 \\
x_1 + x_2 + x_4 &= 0 \\
x_3 + x_4 + x_5 &= 1 \\
x_1 + x_2 + x_5 &= 0
\end{aligned}
$$

It is easy to see, by summing all equations, that it is impossible to satisfy all equations in the example, but there are many ways to satisfy five equations. The goal of this subsection is to give the test behind the following theorem of Håstad.

Theorem 22.5   (Håstad 2001)   For any $\delta, \epsilon > 0$ it is NP-hard to distinguish instances of Max-3Lin-2 where there is an assignment that satisfies at least a fraction $1 - \epsilon$ of the constraints from instances where any assignment only satisfies at most a fraction $(1 + \delta)/2$ of the constraints.

This is essentially a tight theorem in that if you can satisfy all equations then it is possible to find such an assignment by Gaussian elimination. On the other hand, a random assignment satisfies half the equations on average, and thus there is always an assignment that satisfies half the equations independently of the quality of the best solution.

As indicated above, the key to proving Theorem 22.5 is to design an inner test such that:

1. The acceptance criteria is given by the exclusive-or of three bits.

2. The completeness is $1 - \epsilon$.

3. If the test accepts with probability $(1 + \delta)/2$, then there is a way to extract coordinates i from f and j from g such that $Pr[\pi(j) = i]$ is a positive number that only depends on ϵ and δ.

Such a test is as follows:

- Pick a random $x \in \{0, 1\}^R$.

- Pick a random $y \in \{0, 1\}^L$.

- Construct $z \in \{0, 1\}^L$ by setting each z_j, independently, to equal $\mathrm{xor}(y_j, x_{\pi(j)})$ with probability $1 - \epsilon$, and otherwise setting z_j to equal the negation of this value.

- Accept if $g(z) = \mathrm{xor}(g(y), f(x))$.

We first note that the acceptance criteria of the test is indeed, as required, that the exclusive-or of three bits takes a certain value. At first sight it would seem like the condition is always that the exclusive-or of three bits of the proof is zero. This would not make for a very interesting test, because the proof that only consists of zeros would always be accepted. The reason that this is not the case is the mechanism of folding described above. Indeed, for example, if the proof contains the values for $g(\bar{z})$, $g(y)$ and $f(x)$, then the test is that exclusive-or of these three bits is 1. If it contains the values $g(z)$, $g(\bar{y})$, and $f(\bar{x})$, the exclusive or should be zero, and so on.

If f and g are correct long codes of ℓ_1 and ℓ_2, respectively, such that $\pi(\ell_2) = \ell_1$, then the probability of acceptance is exactly $1 - \epsilon$. This follows as in this case $g(z) = z_{\ell_2}$, $g(y) = y_{\ell_2}$, and $f(x) = x_{\ell_1} = x_{\pi(\ell_2)}$ and thus the test accepts if and only if we set $z_{\ell_2} = \mathrm{xor}(y_{\ell_2}, x_{\ell_1})$, which happens with probability $1 - \epsilon$.

Let us discuss soundness. One interesting and, as it turns out, illuminating special case is when both f and g are exclusive-ors of some subset of the variables. Let us look at this.

Suppose that $f(x) = \oplus_{i \in \alpha} x_i$ and $g(y) = \oplus_{j \in \beta} y_j$ for two sets α and β. Define the set $\pi_2(\beta)$ to be the set of all i such that there is an odd number of elements $j \in \beta$ such that $\pi(j) = i$. Thus π_2 is a "Mod 2-projection." It is not very difficult to see that if z_j was defined to always equal $\mathrm{xor}(y_j, x_{\pi(j)})$ then the test would accept with probability 1 iff $\pi_2(\beta) = \alpha$ and otherwise would accept with probability exactly 1/2. The "noise" introduced in the form of flipping z_j with probability ϵ reduces the former probability to $(1 + (1 - 2\epsilon)^{|\beta|})/2$.

Notice in particular that small consistent (with respect to π_2) exclusive-or tables are accepted with high probability. These tables are very far from correct long codes but do suggest a natural way to find a label—namely, to pick a random element from the corresponding set. This gives a probability of at least $\frac{1}{|\beta|}$ of getting consistent labels. This is enough since only small-size β give a large accepting probability.

The careful reader might have noticed that a subtle case is when β and α are empty, which corresponds to the case when both f and g are constant functions. This is indeed a problem for the analysis but cannot occur because of folding that guarantees that f and g are odd functions. In particular, if they are exclusive-ors then the corresponding sets α and β must be of odd size and in particular nonempty.

It turns out that this simple analysis for tables that are exclusive-ors is the basis for the general analysis through the Fourier expansion of the tables involved. We refer to Håstad [2001] for suitable definitions and more details and here only give a brief summary.

In this analysis it turns out that it is more convenient to use $\{-1, 1\}$ for the two Boolean values, as opposed to $\{0, 1\}$. By taking the Fourier expansion of f and g and doing a small and not very difficult calculation, one can show that if the test accepts with probability at least $(1 + \delta)/2$, then

$$\delta \leq \sum_{\beta \subseteq [L]} \hat{f}_{\pi_2(\beta)} \hat{g}_\beta^2 (1 - 2\epsilon)^{|\beta|}. \tag{22.6}$$

By an application of Cauchy–Schwarz, the right-hand side of (22.6) is upper bounded by

$$\left(\sum_\beta \hat{f}_{\pi_2(\beta)}^2 \hat{g}_\beta^2 (1 - 2\epsilon)^{2|\beta|} \right)^{1/2} \left(\sum_\beta \hat{g}_\beta^2 \right)^{1/2} = \left(\sum_\beta \hat{f}_{\pi_2(\beta)}^2 \hat{g}_\beta^2 (1 - 2\epsilon)^{|\beta|} \right)^{1/2}, \tag{22.7}$$

where we used Parseval's identity, which implies that $\sum_\beta \hat{g}_\beta^2 = 1$ for any Boolean function.

Now we can use the tables to define a probabilistic labeling as follows. For a labeling on $[L]$ we pick a set β with probability $\hat{g}_\beta^2$ and then a uniformly random $j \in \beta$. Here we again use Parseval's identity to make sure that this a well-defined probability distribution. Folding implies that any β with $\hat{g}_\beta \neq 0$ is of odd size and hence nonempty.

Similarly, to pick a labeling $[R]$ we pick a set α with probability $\hat{f}_\alpha^2$ and then a random $i \in \alpha$. The probability that these labels are consistent is at least

$$\sum_\beta \hat{f}_{\pi_2(\beta)}^2 \hat{g}_\beta^2 \frac{1}{|\beta|}. \tag{22.8}$$

Since (22.6) and (22.7) imply

$$\sum_\beta \hat{f}_{\pi_2(\beta)}^2 \hat{g}_\beta^2 (1 - 2\epsilon)^{2|\beta|} \geq \delta^2,$$

and using

$$\frac{1}{2\epsilon x} \geq e^{-2\epsilon x} \geq (1 - 2\epsilon)^x$$

for any $x > 0$, it follows that (22.8) is at least $2\delta^2\epsilon$. As stated above, the key is that this probability of getting consistent labels depends only on ϵ and δ and is independent of R and L. This ends the analysis of this inner test.

22.8.2   A Promise Problem Version of SAT

In this final section we study a problem that almost certainly is less fundamental than the problems studied in previous sections. We do feel, however, that it is a cute problem and has the potential to be useful as a starting point in reductions and deserves to be better known. It is a promise problem version of k-SAT.

We are given a k-SAT formula φ and the promise is that there is an assignment that satisfies at least d literals in each clause. The question is for what values of k and d it is possible to find an assignment that satisfies φ in the ordinary sense—that is, makes at least one literal true in each clause. The standard k-SAT problem corresponds to $d = 1$, and in this case we know the problem is NP-hard for any $k \geq 3$ but in P for $k = 2$. This problem was studied by Austrin, Guruswami, and Håstad [Austrin et al. 2017], and it turns out that as long as $d \geq k/2$ we do have an efficient algorithm.

Theorem 22.6   (Austrin et al. 2017)   Given a k-SAT formula φ such that there is an assignment that satisfies at least $k/2$ literals in each clause. Then it is possible to, in polynomial time, find an assignment that satisfies φ.

The interested reader is referred to Austrin et al. [2017] for the full proof of this theorem, but let us point out that the probabilistic algorithm of Papadimitriou [1991] for 2SAT extends to this situation. In this algorithm, one starts with any assignment and creates a random sequence of assignments and within expected $O(n^2)$ time finds a satisfying assignment.

The algorithm takes any clause that is not satisfied by the current assignment and flips a random variable appearing in that clause. Any assignment that satisfies at least d literals in this clause must give different values (compared to the current assignment) to at least d of the k variables appearing in the clause. If $d > k/2$, the number of positions in which the current assignment differs from the good assignment is expected to decrease, whereas if we have equality, there is no change in expectation. This implies that the distance to any assignment that has d true literals in each clause is a random walk that is either unbiased or biased towards zero. Any such walk will, with high probability, hit zero in time $O(n^2)$.

We note that in our case this distance will never go to zero as we will first run into a situation where all clauses are satisfied in which case it is impossible to continue the walk. This does not matter as we have achieved our goal of finding a assignment that satisfies the formula in the usual sense.

There is also a deterministic polynomial-time algorithm based on linear programming, but we refer to Austrin et al. [2017] for a description of this algorithm. Let us turn to the hardness side with the complementary result.

Theorem 22.7 (Austrin et al. 2017)   Suppose φ is a $(2m + 1)$-CNF. Then it is hard to distinguish the case when there is an assignment that satisfies m literals in each clause of φ from the case when φ is not satisfiable.

This theorem is proved by designing a suitable test for the SWP; let us sketch the inner test. We have tables f and g and a projection π. To avoid cumbersome notation we only address the first nontrivial case, which is $m = 2$ and hence considers 5SAT. We want a test with the following properties:

1. The test always reads 5 bits.

2. When the two tables are consistent long codes, it is always the case that at least two of these five bits are true.

3. If it is always the case the at least one bit is true, then we can extract a somewhat consistent labeling from the two tables.

The test consists of three parts, one that only tests f, one that only tests g, and a combined test. The two first tests are analogous and we describe the former, which we call $T(f)$.

- Choose random $x^1, x^2, \ldots x^5$ in $\{0, 1\}^R$ subject to the condition that for all $i \in R$ at least two of the five coordinates x_i^j equal 1.

- Read the five bits $f(x^j)$ for $j = 1, 2 \ldots 5$.

It follows, more or less by definition, that if f is a correct long code of something then at least two of the five bits are always true and we need to consider property 3. We have the following lemma, whose proof we omit. The curious reader might attempt to prove it and otherwise consult Austrin et al. [2017].

Lemma 22.1   If $T(f)$ always sees at least one true bit, then f depends on at most 3 variables.

There is a natural generalization of $T(f)$ to general m, and the number that appears in the lemma corresponding to Lemma 22.1 is $2m - 1$.

The test $C(f, g)$ for checking that f and g are consistent is very much in spirit similar to $T(f)$. The idea is to take all five-tuples of inputs x^1, x^2, y^1, y^2, and y^3 such that for any j at least two of the bits y_j^1, y_j^2, y_j^3, $x_{\pi(j)}^1$, and $x_{\pi(j)}^2$ are true. The verifier reads $f(x^1)$, $f(x^2)$, $g(y^1)$, $g(y^2)$, and $g(y^3)$. It is again easy to see that for consistent long codes at least two of the five bits read are always true.

Using Lemma 22.1 we can establish property 3 for the overall test. Namely, unless there is a pair (i, j) such that g depends on y_j, f depends on x_i and $\pi(j) = i$ one can argue that one of the tests $T(f)$, $T(g)$ and $C(f, g)$ at some point sees five false bits.

We conclude that the probabilistic labeling of taking a random i such that f depends on x_i and random j such that g depends on y_j has at least a probability 1/9 of giving a consistent pair of labels. The reader interested in the details should consult Austrin et al. [2017].

We do not know of a proof of Theorem 22.7 that does not use the PCP theorem, and we find it to be an interesting question whether it has a simple proof that avoids this rather deep theorem.

Of the theorems given in this paper, Theorem 22.7 is a good candidate for being the least important. The original motivation for studying this promise problem version of SAT was that it would be useful as a starting point for further reductions.

It has turned out that Theorem 22.5 is a good starting point for proving inapproximability results. It refers to very simple local equations and says that in the good situation almost all equations are satisfied whereas in the bad situation almost half of these equations are falsified. The hard problem in Theorem 22.7 is a bit different. It says that in the good situation, all clauses have many true literals, while in the bad situation some clause has no true literal. This would seem usable as a starting point when reducing to optimization problems where the worst local situation is the measure of interest. This has happened in a few cases, but not to the extent that was originally hoped.

22.9 Conclusions

The aim of this paper has been to follow a sequence of results that I have really enjoyed. Some of these results are likely to be important cornerstones of computational complexity for the foreseeable future. The power of the simple observation that a nonzero polynomial is likely to be nonzero at a random point still amazes me.

I also find it interesting that some basic definitions, such as multi-prover interactive proofs, were introduced for reasons that later have been dwarfed by their importance in other situations. A conclusion may be that all aspects of natural definitions should be investigated even if we do not immediately have some application in mind.

The fact that it sometimes took me many years to realize the importance of a theorem is also thought provoking when evaluating contemporary research. The hope that one immediately recognizes the merit of great new ideas is taking a rather optimistic view of one's own abilities.

References

S. Arora, C. Lund, R. Motwani, M. Sudan, and M. Szegedy. 1998. Proof verification and intractability of approximation problems. *Journal of the ACM*, 45: 501–555. DOI: 10.1145/278298.278306. 610, 611

S. Arora and S. Safra. 1998. Probabilistic checking of proofs: A new characterization of NP. *Journal of the ACM*, 45: 70–122. 610

P. Austrin, V. Guruswami, and J. Håstad. 2017. $(2 + \epsilon)$-sat is NP-hard. *SIAM Journal on Computing*, 46: 1554–1573. DOI: 10.1137/15M1006507. 603, 618, 619, 620

L. Babai. 1985. Trading group theory for randomness. In *Proceedings of the Seventeenth Annual ACM Symposium on Theory of Computing, STOC '85*, pp. 421–429, New York, NY, USA. ACM. DOI: 10.1145/22145.22192. 600, 601

L. Babai, L. Fortnow, and C. Lund. 1992. Non-deterministic exponential time has two-prover interactive protocols. *Computational Complexity*, 2(4): 374–374. 607

L. Babai, L. Fortnow, L. A. Levin, and M. Szegedy. 1991. Checking computations in polylogarithmic time. In *Proceedings of the 23rd Annual ACM Symposium on Theory of Computing, STOC '91*, pp. 21–32, New York, NY, USA. ACM. DOI: 10.1145/103418 .103428. 608

M. Bellare, O. Goldreich, and M. Sudan. 1998. Free bits, PCPs and non-approximability—towards tight results. *SIAM Journal on Computing*, 27: 804–915. DOI: /10.1137/ S0097539796302531. 612

M. Ben-Or, S. Goldwasser, J. Kilian, and A. Wigderson. 1988. Multiprover interactive proofs. How to remove intractability. In *Proceedings of the 20th Annual ACM Symposium on Theory of Computating, STOC '88*, pp. 113–131, Chicago. ACM. DOI: 10.1145/62212 .62223. 602, 603

R. Boppana and M. Halldórsson. 1992. Approximating maximum independent sets by excluding subgraphs. *BIT*, 32: 180–196. DOI: 10.1007/BF01994876. 609

U. Feige, S. Goldwasser, L. Lovász, S. Safra, and M. Szegedy. 1996. Interactive proofs and the hardness of approximating cliques. *Journal of the ACM*, 43: 268–292. DOI: 10.1145/ 226643.226652. 608, 609, 610

L. Fortnow, J. Rompel, and M. Sipser. 1994. On the power of multi-prover interactive protocols. *Theoretical Computer Science*, 134: 545–557. DOI: 10.1016/0304-3975(94)90251-8. 607

L. Fortnow and M. Sipser. 1988. Are there interactive proofs for co-np languages? *Information Processing Letters*, 28: 249–251. 603

O. Goldreich, S. Micali, and A. Wigderson. 1991. Proofs that yield nothing but their validity, or all languages in NP have zero-knowledge proof systems. *Journal of the ACM*, 38(3): 690–728. DOI: 10.1145/116825.116852. 600, 601, 602

S. Goldwasser, S. Micali, and C. Rackoff. 1985. The knowledge complexity of interactive proof-systems. In *Proceedings of the Seventeenth Annual ACM Symposium on Theory of Computing, STOC '85*, pp. 291–304, New York, NY, USA. ACM. DOI: 10.1145/22145 .22178. 600, 601

S. Goldwasser, S. Micali, and C. Rackoff. 1988. The knowledge complexity of interactive proof-systems. *SIAM Journal on Computing*, pp. 186–208. 600

S. Goldwasser and M. Sipser. 1986. Private coins versus public coins in interactive proof systems. In *Proceedings of the Eighteenth Annual ACM Symposium on Theory of Computing*, pp. 59–68, New York, NY, USA. ACM. DOI: 10.1145/12130.12137. 601

J. Håstad. 1999. Clique is hard to approximate within $n^{1-\epsilon}$. *Acta Mathematica*, 182: 105–142. DOI: 10.1007/BF02392825. 610

J. Håstad. 2001. Some optimal inapproximability results. *Journal of the ACM*, 48: 798–859. DOI: 10.1145/502090.502098. 613, 615, 617

C. Lund, L. Fortnow, H. Karloff, and N. Nisan. 1992. Algebraic methods for interactive proof systems. *Journal of the ACM*, 39: 859–868. DOI: 10.1145/146585.146605. 603, 605

C. H. Papadimitriou. 1991. On selecting a satisfying truth assignment (extended abstract). In *Proceedings of the 32nd Annual Symposium on Foundations of Computer Science*, pp. 163–169, Washington, DC, USA. IEEE Computer Society. DOI: 10.1109/SFCS .1991.185365. 618

R. Raz. 1998. A parallel repetition theorem. *SIAM Journal on Computing*, 27: 763–803. DOI: /10.1137/S0097539795280895. 611

A. Shamir. 1992. IP=PSPACE. *Journal of the ACM*, 39: 869–877. DOI: 10.1145/146585.146609. 605

A. Shen. 1992. IP = PSPACE: Simplified proof. *Journal of the ACM*, 39(4): 878–880. DOI: 10.1145/146585.146613. 605

L. Valiant. 1979. The complexity of computing the permanent. *Theoretical Computer Science*, 8: 189–201. DOI: 10.1016/0304-3975(79)90044-6. 604

A Tutorial on Concurrent Zero-Knowledge

Rafael Pass

In this tutorial, we provide a brief overview of concurrent zero-knowledge and next present a simple proof of the existence of Concurrent Zero-knowledge arguments for $\mathcal{NP}$ based on one-way permutations.

23.1 Introduction

Following the seminal works of Dolev, Dwork, and Naor [Dolev et al. 2000] and Feige and Shamir [1990] from the early 90's, *concurrent security* of cryptographic protocols has been an active area of research. In this tutorial, we focus on concurrent security of *zero-knowledge proof systems*. Zero-knowledge ($\mathcal{ZK}$) proofs, introduced by Goldwasser, Micali, and Rackoff [Goldwasser et al. 1989] are paradoxical constructs that allow one player P (called the Prover) to convince another player V (called the Verifier) of the validity of a mathematical statement $x \in L$, while providing *zero additional knowledge* to the Verifier. This is formalized by requiring the existence of an efficient (i.e., polynomial-time) *simulator Sim* that can indistinguishably emulate the view of any malicious Verifier V^* in its interaction with the Prover P; thus, anything the Verifier V^* learns in a "real" interaction with the Prover, could have been generated by the Verifier "on-its-own," and as a consequence, the Verifier did not learn anything new.

Soon after their conception, zero-knowledge proofs for all of $\mathcal{NP}$ were demonstrated by Goldreich, Micali, and Wigderson [Goldreich et al. 1991]; subsequently, Brassard, Crépeau, and Yung [Brassard et al. 1991], Feige and Shamir [1990], and Goldreich and Kahan [1996] demonstrated the existence of *constant-round zero-knowledge protocols* with negligible soundness error for all of $\mathcal{NP}$.

Beyond being fascinating in their own right, $\mathcal{ZK}$ proofs and arguments (i.e., proofs that only are computationally sound) have numerous cryptographic applications and are one of the most fundamental cryptographic building blocks. As such (and as we shall also discuss below), techniques developed in the context of $\mathcal{ZK}$ often extend to more general types of interactions (most notably, general secure computations [Yao 1986, Goldreich et al. 1987, Ben-Or et al. 1988].)

Concurrent $\mathcal{ZK}$. The notion of *concurrent $\mathcal{ZK}$*, first introduced and achieved by Dwork, Naor, and Sahai [Dwork et al. 2004], considers the execution of zero-knowledge proofs in an asynchronous and concurrent setting. More precisely, we consider a single adversary Verifier that participates in multiple concurrent executions—called *sessions*—of a $\mathcal{ZK}$ proof. The same $\mathcal{ZK}$ protocol is used in all the sessions, but the adversarial Verifier is communicating with multiple *independent* instances of the Prover. At first sight it may seem like every $\mathcal{ZK}$ protocol also remains $\mathcal{ZK}$ in such a setting, but as shown by Feige and Shamir [1990] and Goldreich and Krawczyk [1996], this turns out to be false: There are $\mathcal{ZK}$ arguments that reveal the whole witness being used in the proof if a Verifier performs a coordinated attack on just two simultaneous protocols!

Roughly speaking (following Feige and Shamir [1990]), one can come up with a $\mathcal{ZK}$ protocol where the Verifier can select between two modes of operation: In Mode 1, the Verifier requests to hear a standard $\mathcal{ZK}$ proof of the statement $x \in L$, whereas in Mode 2, the Verifier may instead attempt to prove x to the Prover using the same type of $\mathcal{ZK}$ proof, and if the proof succeeds, the Prover simply reveals the witness w to x (and otherwise aborts). It is not hard to see that such a protocol is $\mathcal{ZK}$ in isolation, assuming L has *unique* witnesses: In Mode 1, this follows by definition, and in Mode 2, this follows from the fact that the Prover only gives the witness w to the Verifier if the Verifier already knows it! (Actually, the $\mathcal{ZK}$ protocol employed needs to be a so-called *proof of knowledge* [Feige and Shamir 1990, Bellare and Goldreich 1992] to ensure that the Verifier must convince the Prover that it actually knows w before the Prover hands it out.) On the other hand, a malicious Verifier participating in two concurrent executions can use Mode 1 in the first session, and Mode 2 in the second session, and then simply forward the Mode 1 proof provided by the Prover in session 1 as its Mode 2 proof in session 2, and thereby get the Prover to reveal the witness in the session 2. So, by participating in two sessions of a $\mathcal{ZK}$ proof, the malicious Verifier learns a witness for x (even thought it may not have known one before the interaction). In fact, by adding a dummy message, one can obtain a protocol that no longer is zero-knowledge even when two instances of the protocol are repeated in *parallel* (i.e., the two instances proceed in a lockstep fashion).

What Makes Concurrent $\mathcal{ZK}$ **Hard?** Of course, the above construction is clearly artificial—it was designed to break down under concurrent executions. One could have hoped that more "natural" constructions of $\mathcal{ZK}$ protocols retain their $\mathcal{ZK}$ property under concurrent sessions. Indeed, the constant-round protocols of Feige and Shamir [1990], and Goldreich and Kahan [1996] are known to preserve their zero-knowledge property under *parallel* composition (i.e., when we have an un-bounded number of parallel sessions) [Feige and Shamir 1990, Goldreich 2002].

However, it is still unknown whether these protocol remain zero-knowledge under *concurrent* executions (where the Verifier may decide the scheduling of the messages in the different sessions). Even though concrete attacks are not known against these protocols, we also do not know how to prove them secure. The problem is that the standard simulation method fails in the concurrent setting. For concreteness, consider the constant-round $\mathcal{ZK}$ protocol of Feige and Shamir [1990] (we are using this protocol as our example as the ideas underlying it will be useful to us in the sequel). Roughly speaking, the protocol for proving a statement $x \in L$ proceeds in two stages:

- In Stage 1, the Verifier samples a *different* statement $\tilde{x}$ and witness $\tilde{w}$ from some hard-on-the average language and next proves to the Prover that it knows a witness to the statement $\tilde{x}$ using a, so-called, *witness hiding* [Feige and Shamir 1990] proof system that does not reveal the witness $\tilde{w}$.

- In Stage 2, the Prover next provides a proof that it either knows a witness for the true statement x, or that it knows a "fake" witness to the other statement $\tilde{x}$; this second stage proof needs to be *witness indistinguishable* [Feige and Shamir 1990] so that it does not reveal whether the Prover is using a witness for x or $\tilde{x}$.

Each of these subprotocols (for Stage 1 and 2) can be implemented in just three communication rounds using Blum's Hamiltonicity protocol [Blum 1986].[1] We will refer to the Stage 1 messages as $(\alpha_1, \alpha_2, \alpha_3)$ and depict them using (single) arrows, and to simply our illustrations, we refer to the whole Stage 2 protocol as α_4 and depict it as a double arrow; see Figure 23.1 for an illustration.

The idea for why this protocol is $\mathcal{ZK}$ is that (a) clearly, the Verifier cannot learn anything from the Stage 1 protocol, as here it is actually the Verifier who provides a proof to the Prover, and (b) since the Verifier first proves to the Prover that is knows a "fake" witness $\tilde{w}$, it can indistinguishably simulate Stage 2 on its own using this

---

1. As we shall see shortly, the reason why we are relying on Blum's protocol as opposed to, say, Goldreich et al. [1987], is that Blum's protocol satisfies a strong proof-of-knowledge property that will simplify the analysis.

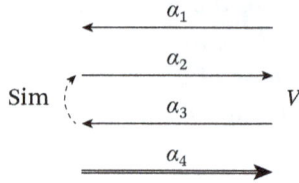

Figure 23.1   A standard $\mathcal{ZK}$ simulation.

fake witness (due to the fact that the Stage 2 protocol is witness indistinguishable). A bit more precisely, to provide the actual simulation, the simulator will need to "extract" out the fake witness from the Stage 1 proof, and can later use this fake witness to complete the simulation of Stage 2.

In more detail, to simulate the view of a malicious Verifier V^*, the simulator honestly emulates the first 3 rounds $(\alpha_1, \alpha_2, \alpha_3)$ of the protocol, and then "rewinds" the Verifier, resending different second messages α_2' until it gets a second accepting third message α_3' from the Verifier in order to extract out the fake witness which can be used to complete the simulation. (Technically, the proof-of-knowledge property of the Stage 1 protocol we here rely on is called "special-soundness" [Cramer et al. 1994]; it stipulates that a valid witness $\tilde{w}$ for $\tilde{x}$ can be computed in polynomial time from any two accepting proof transcripts $(\alpha_1, \alpha_2, \alpha_3)$, $(\alpha_1, \alpha_2', \alpha_3')$ for the statement $\tilde{x}$ with the same first message α_1 but different second messages $\alpha_2 \neq \alpha_2'$. Blum's Hamiltonicity protocol [Blum 1986] satisfies this property.) We refer to the second and third message pair (α_2, α_3) as a ***slot***, and rewinding this slot is the key tool that enables simulation; see Figure 23.1.

This method no longer works in the concurrent setting. More precisely, a concurrent Verifier V^* may *nest* the concurrent sessions—putting session 1 *inside* the slot for session 2, and session 2 inside the slot for session 3, and so on, and may generate its randomness for the different sessions as some function of the prefix of the execution up to this point. Then:

- Simulating the "innermost" session (i.e., session 1) will require running the Verifier twice (just as in the stand-alone simulation).

- Simulating session 2 (which includes session 1 inside it) requires running the simulation of session 1 twice, since every time we rewind session 2, session 1 restarts with new randomness.

- Simulation session 3 (which includes session 2 and 2 inside it) requires running the simulation of session 2 twice (since every time we rewind session

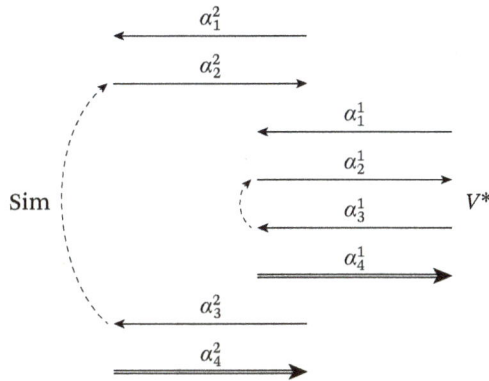

Figure 23.2   A simulation for 2 nested concurrent sessions.

3, session 2 restarts with new randomness), and which in turn requires running the simulation of session 1 *four* times.

- And so on and so forth.

Thus, if we have n sessions, the running time becomes *exponential* in n (and the simulator can no longer be a polynomial-time algorithm). See Figure 23.2 for an illustration for a simulation with just two sessions.

To overcome this exponential blow-up, we instead need to come up with new protocols and analyses. These protocols are significantly harder to construct and analyze than "stand-alone" $\mathcal{ZK}$ protocols [Goldwasser et al. 1989, Goldreich et al. 1991, Feige and Shamir 1990, Goldreich and Kahan 1996].

Benign Schedulings and Set-up Assumptions.   To overcome the above obstacle, the original protocol by Dwork, Naor, and Sahai [Dwork et al. 2004] relied on so-called timing assumptions: Informally speaking, the timing model assumes that every party has a local clock, that all these local clocks are roughly synchronized, and that all parties know a (pessimistic) upper bound Δ on the time it takes to deliver a message on the network. In such a timing model, the Prover can use delays and time-outs to prevent "bad schedulings." Improved Concurrent $\mathcal{ZK}$ protocols in the timing model were presented in Goldreich [2002], and Pass et al. [2010]; the idea behind these works is to identify more expressive classes of schedulings that can be handled and next to use timing contraints to restrict the attacker to those scheduling. For instance, the work of Goldreich [2002] demonstrates that the original constant-round stand-alone $\mathcal{ZK}$ protocol of Goldreich and Kahan [1996] remains

$\mathcal{ZK}$ under the more "benign" schedulings of *parallel composition* and *bounded simultaneity* (where we have only a *constant* number of sessions running at the same time), and next uses timing constraints to ensure that a combination of the simulation techniques used for those special cases of schedulings suffice to get a concurrent $\mathcal{ZK}$ protocol in the timing model. Whereas the protocols of Dwork et al. [2004], and Goldreich [2002] required imposing delays/slowdowns that were longer than the upper bound on the message delivery time, Δ, Pass et al. [2010] showed that the slowdown can be significantly smaller than Δ; moreover, the slowdown can be done adaptively so that only sessions that are slow anyways get "penalized" with delays.

Various other concurrent $\mathcal{ZK}$ protocols were also obtained based on different set-up assumptions (e.g., Dwork and Sahai [1998], Damgård [2000], and Canetti et al. [2000]). In this tutorial, however, our focus will be on the "standard model" without any set-up assumption.

Black-Box Impossibilities.   In the standard model (without any timing assumptions), Canetti, Kilian, Petrank, and Rosen [Canetti et al. 2001] (building on earlier works by Kilian et al. [1998], Rosen [2000], and Goldreich and Krawczyk [1996]) showed that concurrent $\mathcal{ZK}$ protocols for nontrivial languages, with so called "black-box" simulators (i.e., simulators that simply use the Verifier as a black-box but may rewind it), require at least $\tilde{\Omega}(\log n)$ number of communication rounds, where n is the length of the instance being proved; see also Chung et al. [2012] for a simplified (and generalized) analysis of the impossibility result from Canetti et al. [2001]. Thus, if we restrict to black-box $\mathcal{ZK}$, the original constant-round $\mathcal{ZK}$ protocols (e.g., Goldreich and Kahan [1996], and Feige and Shamir [1990]) cannot be concurrently secure (but it is still open whether non-black-box techniques can be used to prove security of them).

Feasibility of Concurrent $\mathcal{ZK}$.   Richardson and Kilian [1999] constructed the first concurrent $\mathcal{ZK}$ argument in the standard model without any set-up assumptions. Their protocol, which uses a black-box simulator, requires $O(n^\epsilon)$ number of rounds; see also the work of Canetti, Goldreich, Goldwasser, and Micali [Canetti et al. 2000] for a somewhat different and more detailed analysis of this protocol. Subsequent works by Kilian and Petrank [2001] and Prabhakaran, Rosen, and Sahai [Prabhakaran et al. 2002.] improved the round complexity to $\tilde{O}(\log n)$; see also Pass et al. [2014] for a simplified and generalized analysis of such more round-efficient concurrent $\mathcal{ZK}$ proofs.

The key idea for overcoming the above-mentioned blow-up in the running-time of the simulator is to construct a protocol with *many sequential **slots***, such that only one of the slots needs to be rewound to ensure that the rest of the session can be simulated. Then, intuitively, the above-mentioned nesting attack can no longer be performed—an attacker would need to nest sessions within *all* of the slots, but since it can only start polynomially many sessions, the nesting depth can never become too big and thus, intuitively, the running time of the simulation remains polynomial. Formalizing this, however, turned out to be quite complex and subtle.

Toward Constant-Round Concurrent $\mathcal{ZK}$**.** The question of whether *constant-round* concurrent $\mathcal{ZK}$ protocols exist still remains an intriguing problem: A breakthrough result in this direction was obtained by Barak in 2001 [Barak 2001]. Barak presented a constant-round $\mathcal{ZK}$ protocol for $\mathcal{NP}$ (based on standard cryptographic hardness assumptions) that remains secure under an *a priori bounded* number of concurrent instances—also known as *bounded concurrency*. More precisely, for any m (polynomial in the security parameter), Barak demonstrates the existence of a $\mathcal{ZK}$ protocol that remains secure as long as the number of concurrent sessions is bounded by m. (On the flipside, however, the communication complexity of his protocol grows linearly with m.) Intriguingly, the black-box impossibility results of Canetti et al. [2001] for constant-round concurrent $\mathcal{ZK}$ actually applies also to bounded concurrency, and indeed Barak develops a new *non-black-box simulation* [Barak 2001] to obtain his result. Note that bounded-concurrent $\mathcal{ZK}$ is different from concurrent $\mathcal{ZK}$ in that for the latter we require the same protocol to be secure under *any* polynomial number of concurrent sessions.

Toward getting a constant-round concurrent $\mathcal{ZK}$ protocol, in Chung et al. [2013a], [2015], the existence of constant-round concurrent $\mathcal{ZK}$ arguments were shown assuming the existence of certain types of "delegation of computation schemes" for $\mathcal{P}$ (as well as standard cryptographic hardness assumptions—namely, collision-resistant hash functions and one-way permutations); additionally, in Chung et al. [2015] it was shown that such delegation schemes can be based on the existence of *indistinguishability obfuscation* (*iO*) [Barak et al. 2001b, Garg et al. 2016] (as well as one-way permutations). Although iO is an extremely intriguing concept in its own right, constructions of iO under standard assumptions are still not known, and thus the question of basing constant-round concurrent $\mathcal{ZK}$ on "standard" assumptions still remains open.

Public Coins vs. Private Coins. Whereas the original ZK protocols of Goldwasser et al. [1989], Goldreich et al. [1991], and Blum [1986] are *public coin*—that is, the

Verifier's messages are its random coin tosses—all of the aforementioned parallel or concurrent $\mathcal{ZK}$ protocols use private coins. Indeed, Goldreich and Krawczyk [1996] showed that only trivial languages can have constant-round public-coin (stand-alone) *black-box* $\mathcal{ZK}$ protocols with negligible soundness error, let alone the question of parallel composition. Their result implies that (unless $\mathcal{NP} \subseteq \mathcal{BPP}$), the constant-round $\mathcal{ZK}$ protocols of, for example, Goldreich et al. [1991], and Blum [1986] with constant soundness error cannot be black-box $\mathcal{ZK}$ under parallel repetition (as this would yield a constant-round black-box $\mathcal{ZK}$ protocol with negligible soundness error). More recently, Pass, Tseng, and Wikström [Pass et al. 2011] showed that *no* public-coin protocol (even those with a polynomial number of rounds) for a nontrivial language can be black-box $\mathcal{ZK}$ under parallel composition.

These black-box barriers can be overcome: Pass, Rosen, and Tseng [Pass et al. 2013] show the existence of a constant-round public-coin $\mathcal{ZK}$ protocol for $\mathcal{NP}$ (with negligible soundness error) that remains secure under (unbounded) parallel composition with a non-black-box simulator (based on standard cryptographic hardness assumptions), and Goyal [2013] demonstrates a (polynomial-round) public-coin protocol that remains secure even under (unbounded) concurrent composition.

Concurrency Beyond $\mathcal{ZK}$: Secure Computation and Black-Box Impossibilites. As one may expect, techniques developed for concurrent $\mathcal{ZK}$ enable reasoning about concurrent security of other types of cryptographic protocols:

- Lindell [2003], Pass and Rosen [2003.], and Pass [2004] show how to extend Barak's simulation technique to develop general secure computation protocols [Yao 1986, Goldreich et al. 1987, Ben-Or et al. 1988] that remain secure under bounded concurrency.

- Canetti et al. [2010] shows how to get general secure computation protocols satisfying a relaxed notion of concurrent "super-polynomial-time" (SPS) security [Pass 2003, Prabhakaran and Sahai 2004, Barak and Sahai 2005, Canetti et al. 2010] based on standard assumptions using simulation techniques similar to those employed by Richardson and Kilian [1999]. It is known that concurrent secure computation satisfying the standard notion of "polynonomial-time-simulation" is impossible [Canetti and Fischlin 2001, Lindell 2004] and thus going for a relaxed notion of security such as SPS is needed here. (See also Goyal et al. [2015] for a protocol with improved round complexity).

But perhaps more surprisingly, techniques developed for establishing the *feasibility* of concurrent $\mathcal{ZK}$ protocols turned out to also be useful for developing *impossibility* results for seemingly unrelated tasks:

- As we showed in Pass [2011], concurrent simulation techniques are important also when trying to show *black-box separations*: Pass [2011] shows that black-box security reductions cannot be used to base the security of several "paradoxical" protocols (such as, e.g., Schnorr's identification scheme, commitment schemes secure against selective openings, Chaum's blind signatures, etc.) on "standard assumptions." As a black-box reduction may invoke multiple (concurrent) sessions of the adversary, dealing with concurrency (and nested sessions) is a key technical challenge in establishing such impossibility results.

And conversely, techniques developed to establish black-box impossibility results for concurrent $\mathcal{ZK}$ turned out to be useful in establishing the feasibility of other primitives:

- In Chung et al. [2013b], it was shown that black-box impossibility results for concurrent $\mathcal{ZK}$ due to Canetti et al. [2001], and Chung et al. [2012] can be used to develop so-called *resettably sound* $\mathcal{ZK}$ protocols [Barak et al. 2001a] based on minimal assumptions.

As we hope to have conveyed, understanding concurrent $\mathcal{ZK}$ is important beyond just $\mathcal{ZK}$—whether it is to study concurrent security of more general secure computations protocols, or to establish black-box impossibility results for other tasks. Furthermore, the question of whether constant-round concurrent $\mathcal{ZK}$ exists is linked to other intriguing open questions in the context of delegation of computation and program obfuscation.

A Simple Concurrent $\mathcal{ZK}$.   Despite improvements, simplifications, and generalizations, the analyses of concurrent $\mathcal{ZK}$ protocols remain very complex and subtle. In the remainder of this tutorial, we aim to present a concurrent $\mathcal{ZK}$ protocol with a simple analysis: We do not try to minimize rounds or assumptions—the protocol requires $O(n^\epsilon)$ rounds (just as the original work by Richardson and Kilian) and relies on the existence of one-way permutations—but our hope is that this analysis may make it feasible to teach the wonders of concurrent $\mathcal{ZK}$ in a graduate class on cryptography.

Our analysis follows simulation techniques from Canetti et al. [2010], and Pass [2011] (and is also closely related to a technique from Deng et al. [2009]) developed for concurrent simulation of more general interaction, but as far as we know, these simulation techniques were not previously brought back to concurrent $\mathcal{ZK}$.

A Personal Note. *$\mathcal{ZK}$ proofs are, in my opinion, one of the deepest, intriguing, and most surprising concepts in computer science. The fact that one can convince someone of the validity of some statement without revealing anything else beyond it, just seems impossible. Yet $\mathcal{ZK}$ proofs enable it! It was this notion that made me fall in love with Cryptography: I had decided to go back to graduate school and Johan Håstad handed me the paper "Resettable Zero-Knowledge" by Canetti, Goldreich, Goldwasser, and Micali [Canetti et al. 2000] and said, "This is a paper by some of my friends; it may be fun." At this point, I had no background in crypto and had never read a research paper. So "fun" it was not. It took me months to get even the most basic understanding of this paper—a core technical component was a detailed analysis of Richardson and Kilian's concurrent zero-knowledge protocol—but, even though I didn't understand the details, I had become obsessed by $\mathcal{ZK}$ and even more so by the notion of concurrent zero-knowledge: How could it be that something gave "zero-knowledge" when executed in isolation, but no longer did so if one provided many concurrent proofs. How can $0 + 0$ not be 0? Over a decade later, I am still as obsessed with this notion, and it is an honor to contribute a piece on concurrent zero-knowledge in this tribute to Shafi's and Silvio's work.*

23.2 Preliminaries

We assume familiarity with probability ensembles, indistinguishability and interactive proofs [Goldwasser et al. 1989], and arguments [Brassard et al. 1988]; recall that in interactive proof, soundness holds with respect to all computationally *unbounded* malicious provers, whereas in an interactive argument, soundness only needs to hold with respect to computationally bounded (i.e., nonuniform polynomial-time) provers.

23.2.1 Black-Box Concurrent Zero-Knowledge

Let (P, V) be an interactive proof/argument for a language L. An m-session *concurrent adversarial verifier* V^* is a probabilistic polynomial-time machine that, on common input x and auxiliary input z, interacts with $m(|x|)$ independent copies—called *sessions*—of some prover $P(x, w)$. There are no restrictions on how V^* schedules the messages among the different sessions, and V^* may choose to abort some sessions but not others. Let View(x, z) be the random variable that denotes the *view* of $V^*(x, z)$ in an interaction with $P(x, w)$ (this includes the random coins of V^* and the messages received by V^*). A *black-box simulator* S is a probabilistic expected polynomial-time machine that is given black-box access to V^* (written as

S^{V^*}). Roughly speaking, we require that for every instance $x \in L$, and every auxiliary input z, the simulator $S^{V^*(x,z)}(x)$ (having only access to $V^*(x,z)$, but *not* the prover $P(x,w)$) can generate the view of $V^*(x,z)$ in an interaction with $P(x,w)$. Since we provide V^* with an auxiliary input, we can without loss of generality restrict our attention to *deterministic* V^* (as V^* can always receive its random coins as auxiliary advice).

Definition 23.1 (Black-box concurrent zero-knowledge [Dwork et al. 2004]) Let (P,V) be an interactive proof/argument for a language $L \in \mathcal{NP}$ with witness relation R_L. (P,V) is *black-box concurrent zero-knowledge* if for all polynomials m, there exists a black-box simulator S_m such that for every common input x and auxiliary input z, and every deterministic m-session concurrent adversary V^*, $S_m^{*(x,z)}(x)$ runs in time polynomial in $|x|$. Furthermore, the following ensembles are computationally indistinguishable:

- $\left\{ \text{View}(x,z) \right\}_{x \in L, w \in R_L(x), z \in \{0,1\}^*}.$
- $\left\{ S_m^{*(x,z)}(x) \right\}_{x \in L, w \in R_L(x), z \in \{0,1\}^*}.$

It is worth noting that the definition of black-box concurrent $\mathcal{ZK}$ allows for a *different* simulator for every polynomial bound m on the number of sessions (whereas the standard definition of black-box $\mathcal{ZK}$ does not need a different simulator for each polynomial that bounds the verifier's running time). The reason for this is that we need to allow the simulator to run in polynomial time in m even just to read all the messages sent by an m-session verifier.

23.2.2 Other Primitives

Witness-Indistinguishable ($\mathcal{WI}$) Proofs [Feige and Shamir 1990]. Roughly speaking, an interactive proof is *witness indistinguishable* if the verifier's view is "independent" of the witness used by the prover for proving the statement.

Definition 23.2 (Witness indistinguishability) Let (P,V) be an interactive proof system for a language $L \in \mathcal{NP}$ with witness relation R_L. We say that (P,V) is *witness indistinguishable ($\mathcal{WI}$)* for R_L if for every probabilistic polynomial-time adversarial V^* and for every two sequences of witnesses $\{w_x^1\}_{x \in L}$ and $\{w_x^2\}_{x \in L}$ satisfying $w_x^1, w_x^2 \in R_L(x)$, the following two probability ensembles are computationally indistinguishable:

- $\left\{ \text{View}_{V^*}^{P(w_x^1)}(x,z) \right\}_{x \in L, z \in \{0,1\}^*}.$
- $\left\{ \text{View}_{V^*}^{P(w_x^2)}(x,z) \right\}_{x \in L, z \in \{0,1\}^*}.$

If, further, the above probability ensembles are identically distributed, we say that (P, V) is *perfectly witness indistinguishable*.

Proofs and Arguments of Knowledge ($\mathcal{POK}$, $\mathcal{AOK}$) [Feige and Shamir 1990, Bellare and Goldreich 1992]. An interactive proof (respectively argument) is a proof (respectively argument) of knowledge if the prover convinces the verifier that it *possesses*, or can *feasibly compute*, a witness for the statement proved. Given two interactive machine, A,B, let $\langle A, B \rangle(x)$ be a random variable denoting the output of B in an interaction with A given the common input x.

Definition 23.3 (Proofs and arguments of knowledge [Bellare and Goldreich 1992]) An interactive protocol (P, V) is a ***proof of knowledge*** (respectively ***argument of knowledge***) of language L with respect to witness relation R_L if (P, V) is an interactive proof (respectively argument) for L, and additionally, there exists a polynomial q, a negligible function v, and a probabilistic oracle machine E, such that for every interactive machine P^* (respectively for every polynomially sized machine P^*) and every $x \in L$, the following holds:

If $\Pr[\langle P^*, V \rangle(x) = 1] > v(|x|)$, then on input x and oracle access to $P^*(x)$, machine E outputs a string from $R_L(x)$ within an expected number of steps bounded by

$$\frac{q(|x|)}{\Pr[\langle P^*, V \rangle(x) = 1] - v(|x|)}.$$

The machine E is called the *knowledge extractor*.

Special-Sound Proofs [Cramer et al. 1994]. Special-sound proofs are proofs of knowledge with a very rigid and useful structure.

Definition 23.4 (Special soundness) A 3-round interactive proof (P, V) for language $L \in \mathcal{NP}$ with witness relation R_L is *special sound* with respect to R_L if:

- (P, V) is public-coin (i.e., the verifier message is its random tape), and the length of the verifier message (also known as the "challenge") on input x is $|x|$.[2]

- There exists a deterministic polynomial-time extraction procedure E such that for any $x \in L$, all $\alpha, \beta, \beta', \gamma, \gamma'$ such that $\beta \neq \beta'$, and (α, β, γ) and $(\alpha, \beta', \gamma')$ are both accepting transcripts of (P, V) on input x, the extractor $E(x, (\alpha, \beta, \gamma), (\alpha, \beta', \gamma'))$ outputs a witness $w \in R_L(x)$ for x.

---

2. For most applications, including ours, it suffices that the length of the challenge is $\omega(\log |x|)$, but for notational simplicity, we simply require the length of the challenge to be $|x|$.

23.2.3 Known Protocols

In our construction of concurrent zero-knowledge arguments we use:

- A $\mathcal{WI}$ special-sound proof for $\mathcal{NP}$; this can be instantiated by a parallel repetition of the Blum's Hamiltonicity protocol [Blum 1986] based on one-way permutations.

- For every $\epsilon > 0$, an $O(n^\epsilon)$-round perfectly $\mathcal{WI}$ argument of knowledge for $\mathcal{NP}$. This can be instantiated with a variant of Blum's Hamiltonicity protocol using an $O(n^\epsilon)$-round perfectly hiding (as opposed to perfectly binding) commitment, which also can be based on one-way permutations [Naor et al. 1998].

Both of these primitives can, for instance, be based on the hardness of the discrete logarithm problem [Goldreich 2001].

23.3 Black-Box Concurrent Zero-Knowledge Arguments of Knowledge

In this section, we prove the following theorem.

Theorem 23.1   For any $\epsilon > 0$, assume the existence of a $\mathcal{WI}$ special-sound proof for $\mathcal{NP}$, and an $O(n^\epsilon)$-round perfectly $\mathcal{WI}$ argument of knowledge for $\mathcal{NP}$. Then, there exists an $O(n^\epsilon)$-round concurrent black-box $\mathcal{ZK}$ argument of knowledge for $\mathcal{NP}$.

23.3.1 The Protocol

Our concurrent $\mathcal{ZK}$ protocol **ConcZKArg** (also used in Pass and Venkitasubramaniam [2008], and Pass et al. [2014]) is a slight variant of the precise $\mathcal{ZK}$ protocol of Micali and Pass [2006], which in turn is a generalization of the Feige–Shamir protocol [Feige and Shamir 1990]. Given a common input statement $x \in \{0, 1\}^n$, a "round-parameter" $k = n^\epsilon$, the protocol for language L proceeds in three stages:

> **Init Stage:** The verifier V picks two random strings $r_1, r_2 \in \{0, 1\}^n$ and sends their images $c_1 = f(r_1)$ and $c_2 = f(r_2)$ under a one-way function f to the prover. Next, V then initiates k repetitions of a $\mathcal{WI}$ special-sound proof of the $\mathcal{NP}$ statement "c_1 or c_2 is in the image set of f" (a witness here would be a pre-image of either c_1 or c_2), and sends the prover P the first messages $(\alpha_1, \ldots, \alpha_k)$ for each of these k instances.

Stage 1: k message exchanges occur in Stage 1. In the jth iteration, the prover P sends $\beta_j \in \{0, 1\}^n$, a random "challenge" for the jth special-sound proof, and V replies with the third message γ_j of the special-sound proof. These k iterations are referred to as slots. A slot is *convincing* if V produces an accepting proof. If there is ever an *unconvincing* slot, P aborts the whole session.

Stage 2: The prover provides a perfectly $\mathcal{WI}$ argument of knowledge of the statement "$x \in L$, or either c_1 or c_2 is in the image set of f."

Completeness and soundness/proof of knowledge follows directly from the proof of Feige and Shamir [Feige and Shamir 1990]; in fact, the protocol is an "instantiation" of theirs. Intuitively, to cheat in the protocol a prover must "know" an inverse to c_1 or c_2 (since Stage 2 is an argument of knowledge), which requires inverting the one-way function f (due to the $\mathcal{WI}$ property of Stage 1). A formal description of protocol ConcZKArg is shown in Figure 23.3.

Protocol ConcZKArg:
Common Input: an instance $x \in \{0, 1\}^n$ of a language L with witness relation R_L.
Auxiliary Input for Prover: a witness w, such that $w \in R_L(x)$.
Init Stage:
    V uniformly chooses $r_1, r_2 \in \{0, 1\}^n$.
    $V \to P$: $c_1 = f(r_1)$ and $c_2 = f(r_2)$ for a one-way function f.
    $V \to P$: the first messages $\alpha_1, \ldots, \alpha_k$ for k $\mathcal{WI}$ special-sound proof of the statement (c_1, c_2) with respect to the witness relation:
$$R_f(c_1, c_2) = \{r : f(r) = c_1 \, or \, f(r) = c_2\}.$$
    Note that V acts as the prover in these special-sound proofs.
Stage 1: For $j = 1$ to k repeat the following slots:
    $P \to V$: The second message (a.k.a. the "challenge") β_j of the jth special-sound proof.
    $V \to P$: The last message (a.k.a. the "response") γ_j of the jth special-sound proof.
Stage 2:
    $P \leftrightarrow V$: a perfectly $\mathcal{WI}$ argument of knowledge from P to V of the statement (c_1, c_2, x) with respect to the witness relation:
$$R_{f \vee L}(c_1, c_2, x) = \{(r, w) : r \in R_f(c_1, c_2) \text{ or } w \in R_L(x)\}.$$

Figure 23.3   Concurrent $\mathcal{ZK}$ argument of knowledge for $\mathcal{NP}$ with round parameter $k(\cdot)$.

23.3.2 The Simulator Algorithm

We will show that the protocol is black-box concurrent $\mathcal{ZK}$ when $k = n^\epsilon$. To simplify notation, let $\tilde{n} = n^{\epsilon/2}$, and thus the number of slots $k = \tilde{n}^2$. We construct a simulator $\boldsymbol{Sim} = \boldsymbol{Sim}^{V^*(x,z)}(x)$ that given as input an instance $x \in L$ and black-box access to $V^*(x, z)$, outputs a view that is statistically close from the "real view" of $V^*(x, z)$ in a multi-session interaction with $P(x, w)$, for any $w \in R_L(x)$.

On a high level, the simulation follows that of Richardson and Kilian [1999]. The simulator simulates the Init Stage and Stage 1 of the protocol by following the honest prover strategy, and attempts to "rewind" one of the slots (i.e., the last two messages of the special-sound proofs provided by V^*). If the simulator manages to successfully rewind some slot (i.e., obtain two accepting responses to the slot), it can use the special-soundness extractor to *extract* a "fake witness" r such that $f(r) = c_1$ or c_2. This fake witness can then be used to simulate Stage 2 of the protocol by straightforward emulation. The crux of the simulation is to provide a method for rewinding slots that ensures the following two properties:

Property 1: Whenever the simulator reaches Stage 2 of the protocol in any of the concurrent sessions, at least one of the slots for that session has been "successfully rewound" (and thus the simulator has a fake witness that can be used to complete Stage 2). We refer to such a session as being *solved*.

Property 2: The rewindings can be done in a way that does not "blow-up" the running-time of the simulation. In particular, to ensure Property 1, the simulator will have to *recursively* rewind the verifier, and will need to carefully select which slot to rewind to ensure to ensure timely termination.

Description of Sim. Given some statement x, let $n = |x|$, and let $m = m(n)$ be an upper bound on the number of concurrent sessions invoked by V^* and $T = T(n)$ be a bound on the total number of messages exchanged to be exchanged with V^*; note that $T = mk = \text{poly}(n)$. Recall that by the definition of black-box simulation, we need only consider deterministic malicious verifiers V^*; therefore, the view of $V^*(x, z)$ is just the transcript of its interaction with the honest prover.

As mentioned above, our simulator Sim starts by honestly simulating the Init Stage and Stage 1 for V^* (i.e., by replying just like the honest prover). We say that a slot (of one of the sessions) "opens" when V^* receives a " challenge" β_j from Sim (i.e., when it receives the first message of the slot), and that the slot "closes" when V^* sends back its response to Sim. Formally, the *opening* of a slot is a partial view v of V^* immediately after which the slot opens. In the sequel, we identify a slot simply by its *opening* (i.e., the partial view after which it opens). Analogously, the *closing* of a slot s is a partial view v immediately after which s closes.

By definition, a slot can never close before opening. But what makes our life complicated is that V^* may send lots of other messages (and start other sessions) before responding to a slot (i.e., it can nest sessions as in Figure 23.2). Thus, we may never see the closing of a slot unless we can simulate all the messages V^* expects to see before closing the slot.

Once a slot closes, we would like to "rewind" it by sending a new slot opening (i.e., a new challenge) and waiting for the slot to close again (so that we can solve the session). But this requires simulating all the messages within the slot again: We do this by *recursively* invoking the simulator. The problem, of course, is that if the recursive depth (i.e., the number of nested recursive calls) becomes large, the running time of the simulation will blow up. Our goal is to ensure that the recursive (i.e., nesting) depth is some *constant D*: This will intuitively ensure that the expected running time will be $\text{poly}(n)^D$ (as the expected number of rewindings for each slot is 1 and there are at most $\text{poly}(n)$ slots).

On a high level, we achieve this goal by carefully selecting which slots to rewind (intuitively, ones that is "light" to simulate). The malicious verifier V^* may abort in the rewinding, in which case we simply rewind the slot again. Furthermore, although the slot was "light" in the initial simulation, V^* may change its scheduling in the rewinding to make the slot "heavy"! Whenever, this happens, we artificially abort the rewinding and restart with a new one. Sim continues rewinding in this fashion until the session gets solved.

More precisely, Sim honestly emulates the Init Stage and Stage 1 for V^* until a slot s closes for which the following property holds:

- Between the time when the slot s opened, and the time that it closed, the *number of other slots* that opened is "small," where "small" will be defined shortly based on the recursive depth of the simulator.

Whenever this happens, Sim rewinds V^* back until the point where s opened, and recursively invokes itself to simulate the messages within the slot s one more time; additionally, if the number of slots s' that V^* opens up in this rewinding (i.e., within slot s) no longer is "small," the rewinding is cancelled. Sim continues rewinding V^* until it gets another accepting closing of the slot s, and can now use the special-soundness extractor to recover a fake witness to use in Stage 2. (We remark that in contrast to the simulation technique of Richardson and Kilian [1999], we do *not* decide what slot to rewind based on the *number of sessions* that start within the slot, but rather, following Deng et al. [2009], Canetti et al. [2010], and Pass [2011], decide what slot to rewind based on the total *number of slots* within the slot (regardless of sessions).)

It remains to specify what "small" means. Note that the recursive depth of the simulation corresponds to the number of "nested rewindings" in the simulation. Recall that we want to make sure that the maximal depth (i.e., maximal number of nested rewindings) becomes a *constant* so that the running time of the simulation stays polynomial. To do this, the definition of "small" will need to vary based on the recursive depth d of the simulation. Given the (partial) view τ of V^*:

- We say that a prefix ρ of τ is d-***good*** if the number of slots that open in τ *after* ρ is less than $\frac{T}{n^d}$ (recall that T is an upper bound on the total number of messages);

- We say that a slot s is d-good in τ if s (i.e, the opening of s) is a d-good prefix of τ. (In other words, a slot s is d-good if the number of new slots that opened since its opening is less than $\frac{T}{n^d}$).

Now, at recursive level d, whenever a slot s closes, we will only rewind it if it is $(d+1)$-good; thus, when we are "deeper" in the recursion (i.e., at a higher recursive depth), we will only rewind slots that have fewer slots inside them (and this ensures that the recursive depth of the simulation is a constant). In more detail, the simulation proceeds as follows:

- On recursive level $d \geq 0$, starting from a view $\mathcal{V}$, Sim honestly emulates the prover strategy for V^*, until a slot s that opened inside the view $\mathcal{V}$ closes *and* the slot is $(d+1)$-good for the current view v. Whenever this happens, it rewinds V^* back to the point when s opened, and invokes itself recursively at level $d+1$ to simulate the slot once more. If the slot closes after this "rewinding," Sim applies the special soundness extractor X to extract a fake witness; if the extractor outputs a valid witness r (to the statement c_1, c_2 currently proved by V^*), the pair (c_1, c_2, r) is stored. If the simulation in the rewinding fails (the condition under which it fails will be defined shortly), Sim simply attempts another rewinding of the slot, and continues doing so until it encounters a closing of the slot.

- At each recursive level $d \geq 1$ (i.e., on all recursive levels except the first one), if V^* aborts in $\mathcal{V}$, or $\mathcal{V}$ is not a d-good prefix of the current view v (i.e., if the number of new openings of slots becomes $\frac{T}{n^d}$), the recursive procedure halts outputting a fail symbol $\perp$ (returning to the earlier recursive call); this ensures that all rewindings are "cut off" if V^* attempts to open more slots in the rewinding.

- Finally, whenever V^* is expecting to hear a Stage 2 proof for session j for a statement (c_1^j, c_2^j, x), Sim checks whether a "fake witness" r for (c_1^j, c_2^j, x) has been extracted; if so, it honestly completes Stage 2 using this witness, and otherwise halts outputting fail.

23.3.3   A Formal Description of Sim

We proceed to a formal description of the procedure Sim, and analyze its running time and success probability. $\text{Sim} = \text{Sim}^{V^*(x,z)}(x)$ starts by invoking the recursively defined procedure SIM (which we assume has oracle access to $V^* = V^*(x, z)$), described in Figure 23.4, on input $(x, 0, \emptyset)$. Let us start by showing that the running time of Sim is bounded in expectation.

PROCEDURE SIM$(x, d, \mathcal{V})$:

On input a statement x, the recursive level d and the partial view $\mathcal{V}$ of V^*, proceeds as follows. Let $v = \mathcal{V}$. Repeat the following:

If $V^*(v)$ is expecting to hear any Init Stage or Stage 1 message, honestly generate it and append it to v.

If $d > 0$ and v is the closing of the slot opened at $\mathcal{V}$, return v.

If $d > 0$ and the partial view v is not d-good, or if $V^*(v)$ aborts (i.e., sends an invalid message or simply terminates), return $\perp$.

If v is the closing of a slot s that opened after $\mathcal{V}$ and that is $(d + 1)$-good for v, repeat:
$$v' = \text{SIM}(x, d + 1, s)$$
until $v' \neq \perp$.

Next, apply the special soundness extractor X on the transcripts corresponding to the special-soundness proofs in the two views v, v'. If X succeeds in finding a witness r for the statement (c_1, c_2) proved, store (c_1, c_2, r).

If $V^*(v)$ is expecting to hear a Stage 2 proof for a statement (c_1, c_2, x), check if a tuple pair (c_1, c_2, r) has been stored. If so, use the "fake witness" r to honestly provide the Stage 2 proof (one message at a time), and append the prover message v; otherwise halt outputting fail.

Finally, if $d = 0$ and $V^*(v)$ aborts (i.e., sends an invalid message or simply terminates), return v.

Figure 23.4   Pseudocode for the recursive simulation strategy employed by Sim.

Proposition 23.1   There exists some polynomial $t(\cdot)$ such that for every $x \in L$, Sim(x) runs in expected time bounded by $t(|x|)$.

Proof   Intuitively, the proposition is based on the following observations:

- The maximal recursive depth is bounded by a constant $D = \lceil \log_{\tilde{n}} T \rceil$, as on level D, SIM returns $\perp$ if it encounters $\frac{T}{\tilde{n}^D} \leq 1$ new slots, so no new recursive calls can be made at level D.

- The expected number of rewindings to solve each slot is 1, as by the *perfect witness indistinguishability* property of Stage 2, the rewinding of a slot is simulated using exactly the same distribution as the original simulation of the slot.

- Since the total number of slots at each recursive level is bounded by T, the expected number of recursive calls at each level is bounded by T, from which we can conclude that expected running time of the simulator is bounded by $\text{poly}(T^D)$.

We proceed to a formal proof. To simplify the analysis, let us consider a slight variant of Sim that never gets "stuck"—instead of ever halting outputting fail, let us assume that Sim has access to a witness w for x, which it can use in Stage 2 if Sim is ever is required to provide a witness for a statement (c_1, c_2, x) for which it has not recovered a fake witness. Clearly this change can only increase Sim's running time.

Note that the recursive depth is bounded by $D = \lceil \log_{\tilde{n}} T \rceil$, which is a constant (since T is polynomial in n and thus also in $\tilde{n}$). Secondly, at each recursive level d, there are at most T possible points from which we can rewind. As we shall argue, from each of these points (i.e., partial views), the expected number of rewindings is bounded by 1. Recall that for every view $\mathcal{V}$, the execution of $\text{SIM}(x, d, \mathcal{V})$, Sim only starts "rewinding" a slot s if (1) the slot s opened after $\mathcal{V}$, (2) the slot s closes in the current view v (which extends $\mathcal{V}$), and (3) the slot s is $(d+1)$-good for v. Furthermore, in each of the rewindings, the simulated view of the adversary on the recursive level $d+1$ (i.e., in the execution of $\text{SIM}(x, d+1, s)$) is *identically distributed* to its view in the execution on level d; note that we here rely on the assumption that Sim never gets "stuck," and the fact that the Stage 2 proof is *perfectly* witness indistinguishable. Thus, the probability that the slot s becomes $(d+1)$-good for some view v' in the recursive call on level $d+1$ (i.e., that the rewinding is successful) is at least the probability that the slot was $(d+1)$-good on level d.[3] Since Sim rewinds the slot until it gets another accepting closings, the expected number of rewindings from each partial view is thus at most 1.

---

3. The probability might actually be larger, since on level d we might also abort if the current view is no longer d-good.

So, for any recursive level d, and any view $\mathcal{V}$, in the execution of $\text{SIM}(x, d, \mathcal{V})$, the expected number of rewindings (i.e., recursive invocations of $\text{SIM}(x, d + 1, \mathcal{V}')$ for some view $\mathcal{V}'$) is bounded by T. It follows using a standard induction that for each recursive level $d \leq D$, and every view $\mathcal{V}$, the expected number of messages sent by $\text{SIM}(x, d, \mathcal{V})$ (and its recursive sub-routine calls) to V^* is bounded by T^{D+1-d}— note that we here rely on the fact that the upper-bound on the expected number of rewindings inside $\text{SIM}(x, d + 1, \mathcal{V}')$ is *independent* of the starting view $\mathcal{V}'$, and thus the expectations can be multiplied. ∎

Let us now argue that Sim generates a view that is statistically close to the real view. First, note that if we consider a variant S̃im of Sim that (1) never halts outputting fail, and (2) always uses the real witnesses for x in Stage 2, then the view output by S̃im is identically distributed to a real view: This directly follows from the fact that S̃im honestly emulates Init Stage, Stage 1 and Stage 2 messages, and only uses rewindings to learn a "fake witness," which is not even used by S̃im.

Next, consider a variant Sim' of Sim that proceeds just as Sim but never fails and instead uses a real witness in Stage 2 for any session for which it fails to extract a fake witness; for all other sessions (i.e., those for which a fake witness is extracted), it still uses the fake witness in Stage 2. It follows directly from the perfect witness indistinguishability property of Stage 2 that the view output by Sim' is identically distributed to the view output by S̃im (and thus also a real view).

Finally, note that Sim and Sim' behave identically except in the event that Sim outputs fail. Below, we show that Sim outputs fail only with negligible probability which concludes the proof of the correctness of the simulation.

Proposition 23.2   There exists a negligible function μ such that for all $x \in L$, the probability that $\text{Sim}(x)$ outputs fail is bounded by $\mu(|x|)$.

Proof   Intuitively, the proposition is based on the following observations:

- Whenever the simulator reaches Stage 2 of some session j, it is the case that $\tilde{n}^2$ slots for that session have closed. Since the maximal recursive depth is some constant D, at least $\tilde{n}^2/D > \tilde{n}$ (for sufficiently large n) of these slots closed in one invokation of SIM on some particular recursive depth $\tilde{d}$.

- As there can be at most a total of $M = \frac{T}{n^{\tilde{d}}}$ slots that opened up in that invokation of SIM (or else SIM would abort returning $\bot$), we are guaranteed that there is at least one slot for session j that has less than $\frac{M}{\tilde{n}}$ slots inside it, and this slot must thus be $(\tilde{d} + 1)$-good and will be rewound.

- Since a slot is rewound until it closes again, we are guaranteed that a witness can be extracted for session j as long as the special-soundness extractor does not fail to extract a witness. But the special-soundness extractor only fails if the challenge (i.e., slot opening) in the two transcript we feed him are the same. This happens with negligible probability as the length of the challenge is n and the expected running time of the simulator is polynomial (as shown in Proposition 23.1).

We proceed to a formal proof. Let us consider the following two events:

- Let E_1 denote the event that Sim is required to provide a Stage 2 proof for some instance (c_1, c_2, x) without having previously "rewound" at least one slot for a proof of (c_1, c_2).

- Let E_2 denote the event that the special soundness extractor X fails to output a valid witness in the execution by Sim.

Note that if neither E_1 nor E_2 happen, there always exists some slot that is rewound for which the special-soundness extractor succeeds, which means that Sim can never fail.

We show below that the these events can happen only with negligible probability, and thus by a union bound, the probability that either of them happens is also negligible, which concludes the proof.

Claim 23.1 For sufficiently large $x \in L$, the probability that E_1 happens in the execution of $\text{Sim}(x)$ is 0.

Proof Assume for contradiction that Sim reaches Stage 2 of some session and is required to provide a proof for (c_1, c_2, x), yet none of the slots for (c_1, c_2) were rewound. Fix some random tape for Sim for which this happens—in the sequel of the proof, we will be considering the execution of Sim with this fixed random tape. Let $\tilde{v}, \tilde{d}$ be the view and recursive level for which this happened. To reach Stage 2, Sim must thus have previously encountered $k = \tilde{n}^2$ slots for (c_1, c_2). These slots may not necessarily have opened on recursive level $\tilde{d}$, but may instead have opened on some earlier recursive level $d < \tilde{d}$—formally, we say that a slot s opened up on recursive level d if the opening of the slot was generated by $\text{SIM}(x, d, v)$ in the execution by Sim (with the fixed random tape), where v is a prefix of $\tilde{v}$. Since the recursive depth of Sim is bounded by some constant $D = \lceil \log_{\tilde{n}} T \rceil$, there nevertheless must exist some recursive level d such that at least $k/D = \tilde{n}^2/D$ of those slots opened on recursive level d. For sufficiently large n, it holds that $\tilde{n}^2/D > \tilde{n}$ and thus there is exists more than $\tilde{n}$ such slots. Additionally, by the recursive construction of the simulator, there exist a *single* partial view v such that all those $\tilde{n}$ slots opened within the execution of $\text{SIM}(x, d, v)$.

Since the total number of slots that can open up during the execution of $\mathrm{SIM}(x, d, v)$ is bounded by $M = \frac{T}{\tilde{n}^d}$ (for $d = 0$, this follows by the definition of T; and for $d > 0$, this follows since by definition of SIM, the simulation at recursive level d is cancelled if more than $\frac{T}{\tilde{n}^d}$ slots open), there exists at least one slot that contains less than $\frac{M}{\tilde{n}} = \frac{T}{\tilde{n}^{d+1}}$ slots; this slot is thus $(d+1)$-good and would have been rewound, which is a contradiction. ∎

Claim 23.2   There exists some negligible function $\mu(\cdot)$, such that for every $x \in L$, the probability that E_2 happens in the execution of $\mathrm{Sim}(x)$ is bounded by $\mu(|x|)$.

Proof   Assume for contradiction that there exists some polynomial $p(\cdot)$ such that E_2 happens in the execution of $\mathrm{Sim}(x)$ with probability $\frac{1}{p(|x|)}$ for infinitely many x. Recall that by Proposition 23.1, the expected running time of Sim is bounded by some polynomial $t(\cdot)$. By the Markov inequality, it follows that the probability that Sim's running time exceeds $t'(|x|) = t(|x|) \cdot 2p(|x|)$ steps is at most $\frac{1}{2p(|x|)}$. Thus, by the union bound, we have that the probability that E_2 happens while Sim takes less than $t'(|x|)$ steps is at least $\frac{1}{2p(|x|)}$ (i.e., inverse polynomial).

Next, note that the special-soundness extractor can only fail to extract a witness if the simulator sent the same verifier challenge in the two views v, v'. Since the length of the verifier challenges is $|x|$, the probability that this happens for any given pair v, v' is $2^{-|x|}$. Consequently, it follows by a union bound that E_2 can happen with probability at most $t'(|x|)2^{-|x|}$ (i.e., with negligible probability) when Sim takes at most $t'(|x|)$ steps, which is a contradiction. ∎

Using Claims 23.1 and 23.2, the proof of the proposition is completed. ∎

23.4 Acknowledgements

I am extremely grateful to Oded Goldreich for his great comments on the presentation of this tutorial. I am also grateful to Naomi Ephraim, Cody Freitag, and Andrew Morgan for their useful feedback. Finally, I am indebted to Alon Rosen for endless hours of discussions about concurrent $\mathcal{ZK}$ in 2004; my understanding of this notion was born out of these discussions.

References

B. Barak. 2001. How to go beyond the black-box simulation barrier. In *42nd FOCS*, pp. 106–115. DOI: 10.1109/SFCS.2001.959885. 629

B. Barak, O. Goldreich, S. Goldwasser, and Y. Lindell. 2001a. Resettably-sound zero-knowledge and its applications. In *42nd FOCS*, pp. 116–125. 631

B. Barak, O. Goldreich, R. Impagliazzo, S. Rudich, A. Sahai, S. Vadhan, and K. Yang. 2001b. On the (im)possibility of obfuscating programs. In *Advances in Cryptology—CRYPTO '01*, pp. 1–18. Springer. 629

B. Barak and A. Sahai. 2005. How to play almost any mental game over the net—concurrent composition via super-polynomial simulation. In *46th FOCS)*, pp. 543–552. DOI: 10.1109/SFCS.2005.43. 630

M. Bellare and O. Goldreich. 1992. On defining proofs of knowledge. In *CRYPTO '92*, pp. 390–420. DOI: 10.1007/3-540-48071-4_28. 624, 634

M. Ben-Or, S. Goldwasser, and A. Wigderson. 1988. Completeness theorems for non-cryptographic fault-tolerant distributed computation. In *20th STOC*, pp. 1–10. DOI: 10.1145/62212.62213. 624, 630

M. Blum. 1986. How to prove a theorem so no one else can claim it. *Proceedings of the International Congress of Mathematicians*, pp. 1444–1451. 625, 626, 629, 630, 635

G. Brassard, D. Chaum, and C. Crépeau. 1988. Minimum disclosure proofs of knowledge. *Journal of Computer and System Sciences*, 37(2): 156–189. 632

G. Brassard, C. Crépeau, and M. Yung. 1991. Constant-round perfect zero-knowledge computationally convincing protocols. *Theoretical Computer Science*, 84(1): 23–52. DOI: 10.1016/0022-0000(88)90005-0. 623

R. Canetti and M. Fischlin. 2001. Universally composable commitments. In *CRYPTO '01*, pp. 19–40. DOI: 10.1007/3-540-44647-8_2. 630

R. Canetti, O. Goldreich, S. Goldwasser, and S. Micali. 2000. Resettable zero-knowledge. In *32nd STOC*, pp. 235–244. DOI: 10.1145/335305.335334. 628, 632

R. Canetti, J. Kilian, E. Petrank, and A. Rosen. 2001. Black-box concurrent zero-knowledge requires $\tilde{\omega}(\log n)$ rounds. In *33rd STOC*, pp. 570–579. DOI: 10.1145/380752.380852. 628, 629, 631

R. Canetti, H. Lin, and R. Pass. 2010. Adaptive hardness and composable security in the plain model from standard assumptions. In *51st FOCS*, pp. 541–550. DOI: 10.1109/FOCS.2010.86. 630, 631, 638

K.-M. Chung, H. Lin, and R. Pass. 2013a. Constant-round concurrent zero knowledge from p-certificates. In *54th FOCS*, pp. 50–59. DOI: 10.1109/FOCS.2013.14. 629

K.-M. Chung, H. Lin, and R. Pass. 2015. Constant-round concurrent zero-knowledge from indistinguishability obfuscation. In *Advances in Cryptology—35th CRYPTO*, pp. 287–307. DOI: 10.1007/978-3-662-47989-6_14. 629

K.-M. Chung, R. Ostrovsky, R. Pass, and I. Visconti. 2013b. Simultaneous resettability from one-way functions. In *54th FOCS*, pp. 60–69. DOI: 10.1109/FOCS.2013.15. 631

K.-M. Chung, R. Pass, and W.-L. D. Tseng. 2012. The knowledge tightness of parallel zero-knowledge. In *Theory of Cryptography—9th Theory of Cryptography Conference, TCC 2012, Taormina, Sicily, Italy, March 19–21, 2012. Proceedings*, pp. 512–529. DOI: 10.1007/978-3-642-28914-9_29. 628, 631

R. Cramer, I. Damgård, and B. Schoenmakers. 1994. Proofs of partial knowledge and simplified design of witness hiding protocols. In *CRYPTO '94*, pp. 174–187. DOI: 10.1007/3-540-48658-5_19. 626, 634

I. Damgård. 2000. Efficient concurrent zero-knowledge in the auxiliary string model. In *EUROCRYPT '00*, pp. 418–430. DOI: 10.1007/3-540-45539-6_30. 628

Y. Deng, V. Goyal, and A. Sahai. 2009. Resolving the simultaneous resettability conjecture and a new non-black-box simulation strategy. In *50th FOCS*, pp. 251–260. DOI: 10.1109/FOCS.2009.59. 631, 638

D. Dolev, C. Dwork, and M. Naor. 2000. Nonmalleable cryptography. *SIAM Journal on Computing*, 30(2): 391–437. DOI: 10.1137/S0097539795291562. 623

C. Dwork, M. Naor, and A. Sahai. 2004. Concurrent zero-knowledge. *Journal of the ACM*, 51(6): 851–898. DOI: 10.1145/1039488.1039489. 624, 627, 628, 633

C. Dwork and A. Sahai. 1998. Concurrent zero-knowledge: Reducing the need for timing constraints. In *CRYPTO '98*, pp. 177–190. DOI: 10.1007/BFb0055746.pdf. 628

U. Feige and A. Shamir. 1990. Witness indistinguishable and witness hiding protocols. In *22nd STOC*, pp. 416–426. DOI: 10.1145/100216.100272. 623, 624, 625, 627, 628, 633, 634, 635, 636

S. Garg, C. Gentry, S. Halevi, M. Raykova, A. Sahai, and B. Waters. 2016. Candidate indistinguishability obfuscation and functional encryption for all circuits. *SIAM Journal on Computing*, 45(3): 882–929. DOI: 10.1137/14095772X. 629

O. Goldreich. 2001. *Foundations of Cryptography—Basic Tools*. Cambridge University Press. 635

O. Goldreich. 2002. Concurrent zero-knowledge with timing, revisited. In *34th STOC*, pp. 332–340. DOI: 10.1007/11685654_2. 625, 627, 628

O. Goldreich and Ariel Kahan. 1996. How to construct constant-round zero-knowledge proof systems for NP. *Journal of Cryptology*, 9(3): 167–190. DOI: 10.1007/BF00208001. 623, 625, 627, 628

O. Goldreich and H. Krawczyk. 1996. On the composition of zero-knowledge proof systems. *SIAM Journal on Computing*, 25(1): 169–192. DOI: 10.1137/S0097539791220688. 624, 628, 630

O. Goldreich, S. Micali, and A. Wigderson. 1987. How to play any mental game. In *19th STOC*, pp. 218–229, New York, NY, USA. ACM. DOI: 0.1145/28395.28420. 624, 625, 630

O. Goldreich, S. Micali, and A. Wigderson. 1991. Proofs that yield nothing but their validity or all languages in NP have zero-knowledge proof systems. *Journal of the ACM*, 38(3): 690–728. DOI: 10.1145/116825.116852. 623, 627, 629, 630

S. Goldwasser, S. Micali, and C. Rackoff. 1989. The knowledge complexity of interactive proof systems. *SIAM Journal on Computing*, 18(1): 186–208. DOI: 10.1137/0218012. 623, 627, 629, 632

V. Goyal. 2013. Non-black-box simulation in the fully concurrent setting. In *45th STOC*, pp. 221–230. 630

V. Goyal, H. Lin, O. Pandey, R. Pass, and A. Sahai. 2015. Round-efficient concurrently composable secure computation via a robust extraction lemma. In *Theory of Cryptography—12th Theory of Cryptography Conference, TCC 2015, Warsaw, Poland, March 23–25, 2015. Proceedings, Part I*, pp. 260–289. 630

J. Kilian and E. Petrank. 2001. Concurrent and resettable zero-knowledge in poly-loalgorithm rounds. In *33rd STOC*, pp. 560–569. DOI: 10.1145/380752.380851. 628

J. Kilian, E. Petrank, and C. Rackoff. 1998. Lower bounds for zero knowledge on the internet. In *39th FOCS*, pp. 484–492. 628

Y. Lindell. 2003. Bounded-concurrent secure two-party computation without setup assumptions. In *35th STOC*, pp. 683–692. DOI: 10.1145/780542.780641. 630

Y. Lindell. 2004. Lower bounds for concurrent self composition. In *TCC '04*, pp. 203–222. DOI: 10.1007/978-3-540-24638-1_12. 630

S. Micali and R. Pass. 2006. Local zero knowledge. In *STOC '06*, pp. 306–315. 635

M. Naor, R. Ostrovsky, R. Venkatesan, and M. Yung. 1998. Perfect zero-knowledge arguments for *NP* using any one-way permutation. *Journal of Cryptology*, 11(2): 87–108. DOI: 10.1007/s001459900037. 635

R. Pass. 2003. Simulation in quasi-polynomial time, and its application to protocol composition. In *EUROCRYPT '03*, pp. 160–176. DOI: 10.1007/3-540-39200-9_10. 630

R. Pass. 2004. Bounded-concurrent secure multi-party computation with a dishonest majority. In *36th STOC*, pp. 232–241. New York, NY, USA. ACM. DOI: 10.1145/1007352.1007393. 630

R. Pass. 2011. Limits of provable security from standard assumptions. In *43rd STOC*, pp. 109–118. DOI: 10.1145/1993636.1993652. 631, 638

R. Pass and A. Rosen. 2003. Bounded-concurrent secure two-party computation in a constant number of rounds. In *44th FOCS*, pp. 404–413. DOI: 10.1109/SFCS.2003.1238214. 630

R. Pass, A. Rosen, and W.-L. D. Tseng. 2013. Public-coin parallel zero-knowledge for NP. *Journal of Cryptology*, 26(1): 1–10. DOI: 10.1007/s00145-011-9110-5. 630

R. Pass, W.-L. D. Tseng, and M. Venkitasubramaniam. 2010. Eye for an eye: Efficient concurrent zero-knowledge in the timing model. In *Theory of Cryptography, 7th Theory of Cryptography Conference, TCC 2010, Zurich, Switzerland, February 9–11, 2010. Proceedings*, pp. 518–534. DOI: 10.1007/978-3-642-11799-2_31. 627, 628

R. Pass, W.-L. D. Tseng, and M. Venkitasubramaniam. 2014. Concurrent zero knowledge, revisited. *Journal of Cryptology*, 27(1): 45–66. DOI: 10.1007/s00145-012-9137-2. 628, 635

R. Pass, W.-L.D. Tseng, and D. Wikström. 2011. On the composition of public-coin zero-knowledge protocols. *SIAM Journal on Computing*, 40(6): 1529–1553. DOI: 10.1137/100811465. 630

R. Pass and M. Venkitasubramaniam. 2008. On constant-round concurrent zero-knowledge. In *TCC '08*, pp. 553–570. 635

M. Prabhakaran, A. Rosen, and A. Sahai. 2002. Concurrent zero knowledge with logarithic round-complexity. In *43rd FOCS*, pp. 366–375. DOI: 10.1109/SFCS.2002.1181961. 628

M. Prabhakaran and A. Sahai. 2004. New notions of security: achieving universal composability without trusted setup. In *36th STOC*, pp. 242–251. DOI: 10.1145/1007352.1007394. 630

R. Richardson and J. Kilian. 1999. On the concurrent composition of zero-knowledge proofs. In *Eurocrypt '99*, pp. 415–432. DOI: 10.1007/3-540-48910-X_29. 628, 630, 637, 638

A. Rosen. 2000. A note on the round-complexity of concurrent zero-knowledge. In *CRYPTO '00*, pp. 451–468. DOI: 10.1007/3-540-44598-6_28. 628

A. C.-C. Yao. 1986. How to generate and exchange secrets (extended abstract). In *27th FOCS*, pp. 162–167. 624, 630

Doubly Efficient Interactive Proofs

Guy Rothblem

A *Doubly Efficient* Interactive Proof (DEIP) allows a polynomial-time prover to convince a verifier, whose computational ability is significantly more restricted, of the validity of complex statements (which are computable in polynomial time). This is achieved by means of an interactive proof, where ideally the verifier's running time is nearly linear in the input length. Soundness of the proof is unconditional; it holds against unbounded cheating provers and does not rely on unproved intractability assumptions. Since their introduction in the work of Goldwasser, Kalai, and Rothblum [Goldwasser et al. 2008], there has been growing interest in DEIPs and their applications. We survey some highlights of this study:

- DEIPs for all bounded-depth (polynomial-size) computations, a protocol due to Goldwasser, Kalai and Rothblum [Goldwasser et al. 2008]

- DEIPs for all bounded-space (polynomial time) computations, a protocol due to Reingold, Rothblum, and Rothblum [Reingold et al. 2016]

We also discuss applications of DEIPS for delegating polynomial-time computations to an untrusted server. This area has seem tremendous activity, spanning theory and implementations. We also discuss complexity-theoretic and cryptographic applications, and conclude by highlighting several central open questions in the area.

24.1 Introduction

Proof systems allow weak verifiers to ascertain the correctness of complex computational statements. For example, to convince a verifier that a given graph contains a k-clique, a prover can supply a proof specifying the vertices in the clique, and this proof can be verified in polynomial time. The power of efficiently verifiable proof systems is a central question in the study of computation. Studying them has led to some of the deepest and most influential insights of the theory of computing, including NP-completeness [Cook 1971, Karp 1972, Levin 1973], zero-knowledge [Goldreich et al. 1991, Goldwasser et al. 1989], the IP = PSPACE theorem [Lund et al. 1992, Shamir 1992], and the PCP theorem [Arora and Safra 1998, Arora et al. 1998].

We focus on the study of *interactive proof systems*, introduced by Goldwasser, Micali, and Rackoff [Goldwasser et al. 1989] and independently by Babai and Moran [1988], which are among the most celebrated achievements of cryptography and complexity theory. An interactive proof system is an interactive protocol between an efficient randomized verifier and an untrusted prover. The prover convinces the verifier of the validity of a computational statement, usually framed as the membership of an input x in a language $\mathcal{L}$. Soundness is unconditional. Namely, if the input is not in the language, then no matter what (unbounded and adaptive) strategy a cheating prover might employ, the verifier should reject with high probability over its own coin tosses. The celebrated IP = PSPACE theorem [Lund et al. 1992, Shamir 1992] showed that interactive proofs are remarkably powerful: a polynomial-time verifier can use them to verify any statement/language that is decidable in polynomial space.

The Complexity of Proving. The vast and rich literature on proof systems focuses primarily (though not exclusively) on intractable computations, such as NP-complete problems, where the proofs can be *verified* in polynomial time. Generating the proof in polynomial time, on the other hand, is implausible. This limits the applicability of such proof systems, both from a theoretical perspective and in their real-world impact.[1] For example, focusing on interactive proofs, the IP = PSPACE protocol places a heavy burden on the honest prover, who needs to perform intractable computations. Indeed, this was unavoidable as the protocol was designed for statements (in PSPACE) that are themselves intractable. If we consider *tractable* computations—that is, languages that can be decided in polynomial time—can we design interactive proofs with an efficient prover where verification is significantly less expensive than deciding the language?

---

1. One notable exception is in the study of zero-knowledge proofs for NP languages, where the honest prover should run in polynomial time given a witness for the statement's validity [Goldreich et al. 1991]. We, however, will focus on the setting where the prover should run in polynomial time without knowing anything more than the verifier about the input.

Doubly Efficient Interactive Proofs. Goldwasser, Kalai, and Rothblum [Goldwasser et al. 2008, 2015] initiated the study of *doubly efficient interactive proofs* (DEIPs).[2] These are interactive proofs for *tractable* languages, where both the honest prover and the verifier run in polynomial time. The verifier should be *super-efficient*; for example, it should run in linear or nearly linear time.[3] In particular, verification requires significantly less resources than it would take to decide the (tractable) language. We emphasize that we still require unconditional soundness against an unbounded cheating prover. With this goal in mind, a burgeoning study considers the following foundational question:

Question 24.1 Which languages have *doubly efficient* interactive proofs? What are the possible complexities (and trade-offs) in terms of number of rounds, communication, and the time required for verification and for proving?

The protocols constructed in earlier works, such as the IP = PSPACE protocol, do not yield doubly efficient interactive proofs (even when they are scaled down to polynomial-time computations).[4] Over the past decade, a sequence of works has made significant progress on this question. In a nutshell, every language that can be decided in polynomial time using a bounded-space Turing machine or a sufficiently uniform bounded-depth circuit (ensemble) has such an interactive proof. The primary goal of this chapter is providing a high-level survey of this progress. The intrigued reader may also refer to the more detailed recent survey by Goldreich [2018].

Outside Our Scope. A literature spanning both theory and practice has considered doubly efficient proof systems in the context of delegating computations reliably. This survey is focused on the study of DEIPs, though we mention some applications in Section 24.1.3. In particular, we do not attempt to survey the literature on *computationally sound* argument systems [Brassard et al. 1988, Kilian 1992, Micali 2000], where soundness is only required to hold against polynomial time cheating

---

2. Early works have also referred to these as "interactive proofs for muggles" or "interactive proofs for delegating computation."

3. We use *nearly linear* to refer to complexity that grows as $O(n^{1+\delta})$ for a small constant $\delta > 0$. In some cases, the actual complexity is in fact quasi-linear, or $O(n \cdot \text{polylog } n)$; we ignore this distinction throughout.

4. For languages decidable in time $T = T(n)$ and space $S = S(n)$, earlier protocols give a prover whose running time grows as $T^{O(S)}$ [Lund et al. 1992, Shamir 1992, Shen 1992]. This is super-polynomial, even for log-space languages.

provers, and is proved under cryptographic assumptions (for a recent work on this topic, see, e.g., Kalai et al. [2014] and the references therein).

24.1.1   DEIPs for Bounded-Depth Computations

The first result we discuss is a doubly efficient public-coin interactive proof for any language computable by an ensemble of (logspace-uniform) Boolean circuits.[5] This protocol is due to Goldwasser, Kalai, and Rothblum [Goldwasser et al. 2015]. The communication complexity and the number of communication rounds are related to the *depth* of the computation; the running time of the verifier is *nearly linear in the input length*, polynomial in the depth, and polylogarithmic in its size; and *the prover's running time is polynomial* (as required for a doubly efficient interactive proof).

Theorem 24.1   (Doubly efficient interactive proofs for bounded depth [Goldwasser et al. 2015]) Let $\mathcal{L}$ be a language that can be computed by a family of $O(\log(n))$-space uniform Boolean circuits of depth $d(n)$ and polynomial size (with fan-in 2). Then $\mathcal{L}$ has a public-coin interactive proof where:

- The prover runs in time $\text{poly}(n)$. The verifier runs in time $(n + d(n)) \cdot \text{polylog}(n)$.
- The number of rounds is $O(d(n) \cdot \log(n))$ and the communication complexity is $d(n) \cdot \text{polylog}(n)$.
- The protocol has perfect completeness and soundness $1/2$.[6]

Several remarks are in order. First, as a primary implication, we conclude that any language in logspace-uniform NC has a doubly efficient IP with polylogarithmic rounds and communication and quasi-linear verification time. Second, it is actually the case that if the verifier has access to a low-degree extension encoding of its input (see Section 24.2.2), then its running time can be reduced to $d(n) \cdot \text{polylog}(n)$ (and, in particular, the running time can be sublinear). Third, the protocol of Theorem 24.1 scales up to super-polynomial circuit ensembles; the communication complexity and verification time scale polylogarithmically with the circuit size (the prover's work scales polynomially with the circuit size). The uniformity requirement can be relaxed to space that is logarithmic in the circuit size. In particular, Theorem

---

5. A circuit ensemble $\{C_n\}_n$ is $s(n)$-space uniform if there exists a Turing machine that on input 1^n runs in space $O(s(n))$ and outputs a description of C_n, the circuit for inputs of length n.

6. Throughout this chapter we focus on interactive proof systems with constant soundness. Soundness can be amplified via parallel or sequential repetition.

24.1 gives an alternative proof of the IP = PSPACE theorem (where the runtime of the honest prover is improved).

A natural question is how can this be done when the verifier cannot even construct the circuit in question (the circuit is larger than the verifier's running time!). This is where the condition on the log-space uniformity of the circuit family comes in. For such circuit families, the circuit has a "short" implicit representation that the verifier can use without ever constructing the entire circuit. We view logspace-uniformity as a relaxed notion of uniformity. In particular, it captures deterministic and nondeterministic logarithmic space uniform computations (the classes L and NL), as well as uniform parallel computing classes. It has also been relaxed in subsequent work [Reingold et al. 2016]. We elaborate on the protocol in Section 24.3.

24.1.2 Constant-Round DEIPs for Bounded-Space Computations

The result of Theorem 24.1 demonstrates that DEIPs can be obtained for a rich class of polynomial-time computation (namely, bounded depth computations). It is known [Goldreich and Håstad 1998] that languages that have interactive proofs with very efficient verifiers can be decided in small space or depth. The space (respectively, depth) required is at most polynomial in the communication and space complexity of the verifier in the interactive proof. While the *time* (respectively, size) needed to decide the language might be exponential in the space (respectively, depth), this still presents an important barrier to the construction of DEIPs. For example, constructing DEIPs for a P-complete problem would require showing that such a problem (and thus also any other polynomial-time problem) can be decided in nearly linear space. Another natural barrier is that any language that has a DEIP must be decidable in (probabilistic) polynomial time, since the decider can simulate the proof system.

Thus, a natural frontier for the study of DEIPs is focusing on languages computable in polynomial time and bounded space. Focusing on nearly linear verification time, can we obtain DEIPs for all languages computable in polynomial time and nearly linear space? Or, alternatively, languages computable in *bounded-polynomial* space? Here and below, by *bounded-polynomial space* we mean space n^σ for some sufficiently small universal constant $\sigma > 0$.

Theorem 24.2   (Doubly efficient interactive proofs for bounded space [Reingold et al. 2016])   Let $\mathcal{L}$ be a language that can be decided in time poly(n) and space $S = S(n)$, and let $\delta \in (0, 1)$ be an arbitrary (fixed) constant. There is a public-coin interactive proof for $\mathcal{L}$ as follows:

- The (honest) prover runs in time poly(n), and the verifier runs in time $(\tilde{O}(n) +$ poly$(S) \cdot n^{\delta})$.

- The number of rounds is $O(1)$ and the communication complexity is poly$(S) \cdot n^{\delta}$.

- The protocol is public coin, with perfect completeness and soundness $1/2$.

Similarly to Theorem 24.1, if the verifier has access to a low-degree extension encoding of its input, then its running time can be reduced to poly$(S) \cdot n^{\delta}$. We elaborate on the protocol in Section 24.4.

The *Round Complexity* of Interactive Proofs. The protocol in Theorem 24.2 uses only a constant number of rounds. In contrast, the Lund et al. [1992] and Shamir [1992] protocol requires poly(S) rounds of communication to prove membership in a language that can be decided in space $S = S(n)$ (and moreover does not yield a DEIP, even for languages in L). Similarly, this is also in contrast to the protocol of Theorem 24.1, where the number of rounds is proportional to the circuit depth (multiplied by a logarithmic factor).

We note that there are several senses in which the result of Theorem 24.2 is tight. The dependence on the space S in the communication or the verification time is tight up to polynomial factors (see above). Also, under reasonable complexity conjectures, no constant-round interactive proof for bounded space computations can have sub-polynomial communication complexity, as this would lead to a super-polynomial AM-speedup for that class of computations (see Reingold et al. [2016], Remark 5.1 in the ECCC version).

An Iterative Construction via Batch Verification. The proof of Theorem 24.2 iteratively constructs a proof system for longer and longer computations. Assume that we already have an interactive proof for verifying Turing machine computations that run in time T and space S; it extends the proof system to verifying computations that run in time $(k \cdot T)$ and space S, for some super-constant integer k. This could easily be reduced to verifying k computations that run in time T, by having the prover send the $k - 1$ intermediate states of the machine. Two simple but ineffective approaches are to either run k instances of the "base" proof system to verify the k computations (which is inefficient) or to check only a small subset of the computations, chosen at random (which drastically increases the success probability of a cheating prover, known as the soundness error). The main ingredient of the proof is therefore a *batch verification theorem* for (certain types of) interactive proofs. This theorem allows for the verification of k computations in a much more efficient way than k independent executions (and while maintaining the soundness error); see Section 24.4 for further details.

24.1.3 Applications and Further Related Work

Delegating Computation. Beyond their importance in the theoretical study of computation, interactive proofs are also motivated by real-world applications, such as delegating computation. As envisioned in Goldwasser et al. [2015], a powerful server can run a computation for a weak client and provide an interactive proof of the output's correctness. The interactive proof should be doubly efficient, so that generating the proof is tractable for the server and verification is feasible for the weak client. Naturally, this scenario focuses on tractable computations that can actually be performed by the server. The interactive proofs of Theorems 24.1 and 24.2 can be used to delegate bounded-depth or bounded-space polynomial-time computations (without making computational assumptions or using cryptographic machinery).

Several works have constructed systems for delegating computations. Cormode, Mitzenmacher, and Thaler [Cormode et al. 2012] gave the first implementation of a delegation system, with a protocol based on Goldwasser et al. [2015]. Other systems based on Goldwasser et al. [2015] include Thaler et al. [2012], Thaler [2013], Vu et al. [2013], Wahby et al. [2017], Zhang et al. [2017], and Wahby et al. [2018]. Indeed, by now there are several different works on this topic using different underlying theoretical results. See Walfish and Blumberg [2013] for a survey on this line of work.

Cryptography and Complexity. Given the fundamental importance of interactive proofs in cryptography and complexity, it should come as no surprise that the new DEIPs described above have implications to a variety of foundational questions, including:

- *Succinct* zero-knowledge proofs from one-way functions for any NP-language whose witnesses can be verified in bounded depth or space. For bounded-space NP relations, the zero-knowledge proofs require only a constant number of rounds. See Goldwasser et al. [2015] and Reingold et al. [2016].

- Sublinear time verification for interactive proofs. In an *interactive proof of proximity* (IPP) [Ergün et al. 2004, Rothblum et al. 2013], the verifier is allowed (sublinear-time) query access to the input, and can verify that the input is "close" to the language. This follows (and is inspired by) the study of property testing [Rubinfeld and Sudan 1996, Goldreich et al. 1998]. Rothblum,

Vadhan, and Wigderson [Rothblum et al. 2013] use DEIPs to construct such Interactive Proof of Proximity (with information-theoretic soundness). Plugging the DEIPs of Theorems 24.1 and 24.2 into their transformation gives IPPs for polynomial-time bounded-space and bounded-depth computations. See Rothblum et al. [2013] and Reingold et al. [2016] for further details.

- Batch verification of UP statements. The study of DEIPs, and in particular the iterative construction behind Theorem 24.2 (see above), has led to a study of interactive proofs for *batch verification* of NP statements. Given k inputs in an NP language, a prover wants to convince a verifier that all k inputs are in the language. The prover, given k witnesses (one for each of the statements) should run in polynomial time. The goal is to design protocols where the communication and verifier work improve over the trivial protocol where the prover sends the k witnesses to the verifier (where the improvement is in terms of the communication and also the verifier's running time). This study has yielded interactive proofs for batch verification of UP languages [Reingold et al. 2016, Reingold et al. 2018]: NP languages where each YES instance has at most one accepting witness. See Section 24.4.1 for an overview of such a protocol.

Further Work on DEIPs.   A recent line of works by Goldreich and Rothblum attempts to construct simpler and more efficient protocols for specific subclasses of bounded-depth and bounded-space computations, as well as for particular structured languages in these classes. The first of these works [Goldreich and Rothblum 2018a] constructs simple DEIPs for a natural subclass of such computations. A different work [Goldreich and Rothblum 2018c] builds on the protocol of Theorem 24.1 to construct *constant-round* DEIPs for AC^0 and NC^1, under certain uniformity constraints. A third work [Goldreich and Rothblum 2018b] constructs a DEIP for counting the number of cliques is a graph, where the prover runs in nearly linear time given an oracle for the problem.

24.1.4   Open Questions

We conclude by briefly outlining central open questions in the study of DEIPs.

The Complexity of *Convincing*.   A foundational question in the study of interactive proofs is whether (or when) the running time of the (honest) prover in an interactive proof can be polynomial in the time required to decide the language (and for what parameters of the proof system—e.g., in terms of the number of rounds, the communication, and the verifier's complexity). We highlight the following challenge:

Question 24.2   Given a language that can be decided by a Turing machine running in time $T = T(n)$ and space $S = S(n)$, is it always possible to construct an interactive proof system, where the (honest) prover runs in $\text{poly}(T)$ time, the communication is $\text{poly}(S, \log T)$, and the verification time is polynomial in the communication and nearly linear in the input length?

For any *constant* $\delta > 0$, the protocol behind Theorem 24.2 has communication and verification time that grow with $\text{poly}(S) \cdot T^{\delta}$. One might hope to answer Question 24.2 in the affirmative by applying this result with $\delta = 1/\log T$. This approach fails because the communication and the number of rounds in that protocol are $\exp(\tilde{O}(1/\delta))$.

Batch Verification for NP.   Does there exist an interactive proof for batch verification of every NP language? We note that known results only apply to UP languages—that is, under the promise that every YES instance has at most a single accepting witness.

Question 24.3   Does there exist, for every NP language L, an interactive proof for verifying that k inputs $x_1, \ldots, x_k$ are all YES instances of L, where the (honest) prover runs in polynomial time given witnesses to the inputs' membership in L, and the communication is much smaller than sending the k witnesses? In particular, can the communication be as small as sending polylog k witnesses?

Doubly Efficient Soundness Amplification.   One approach to resolving both open questions posed above is *doubly efficient soundness amplification* for interactive proofs:

Question 24.4   Given an interactive proof with soundness error ε, where ε might be very close to 1, what are the possible complexities (and trade-offs) for obtaining an interactive proof with soundness error $\max(\varepsilon^k, 1/2)$ (where k is a large positive integer)? What are the overheads in terms of round complexity, communication complexity, prover time, and verifier time?

We note that parallel repetition is known to reduce the soundness error of interactive proofs, but it increases the communication, prover time, and verifier time by a multiplicative factor of $\Omega(k)$ (to reduce the soundness error from ε to ε^k). Is it possible to obtain other/better trade-offs? This question is motivated by the fact that (trivial) interactive proofs with *very large* soundness error are easy to construct. For example, to batch verify k instances of an NP language, the verifier can pick a single instance at random and ask for a witness. This naive protocol has soundness error $(1 - 1/k)$. If we could amplify to constant soudnness without paying a factor of k overhead, we'd get a new NP batching result! Similarly, a naive interactive proof for bounded-space computations can be obtained by repeatedly sending the intermediate state of the (current) computation and recursing randomly on the first or the second half (as chosen by the verifier). The communication is only $(S \cdot \log T)$ and the soundness error is $(1 - 1/T)$.

24.2 Preliminaries

We note that parts of this section are reproduced from Goldwasser et al. [2015] and Reingold et al. [2016]. Parts of Section 24.3 are reproduced from Goldwasser et al. [2015], and parts of Section 24.4 are reproduced from Reingold et al. [2016].

24.2.1 Interactive Proofs

An interactive protocol consists of a pair $(\mathcal{P}, \mathcal{V})$ of interactive Turing machines that are run on a common input x, whose length we denote by $n = |x|$. The first machine, which is deterministic, is called the *prover* and is denoted by $\mathcal{P}$, and the second machine, which is probabilistic, is called the *verifier* and is denoted by $\mathcal{V}$. An execution of the protocol is divided into rounds, where in each round first $\mathcal{P}$ sends a message to $\mathcal{V}$ and then $\mathcal{V}$ sends a message to $\mathcal{P}$. At the end of the interaction $\mathcal{V}$ runs a (deterministic) Turing machine on the communication transcript, the input, and its random coins, and generates an output.

Definition 24.1   (Interactive proof [Goldwasser et al. 1989])   An interactive protocol $(\mathcal{P}, \mathcal{V})$ (as above) is an *interactive proof* (IP) for $\mathcal{L}$ if:

> **Completeness.**   For every $x \in \mathcal{L}$, when $\mathcal{V}$ interacts with $\mathcal{P}$ on common input x, the verifier $\mathcal{V}$ accepts with probability 1.[7]
>
> ε-**Soundness.**   For every $x \notin \mathcal{L}$ and every (computationally unbounded) cheating prover strategy $\tilde{\mathcal{P}}$, the verifier $\mathcal{V}$ accepts when interacting with $\tilde{P}$ with probability at most $\varepsilon(|x|)$, where $\varepsilon = \varepsilon(n)$ is called the soundness error of the proof system. If we do not explicitly note otherwise, the soundness error is taken to be a small constant, say 1/2 (the soundness error can be reduced by sequential or parallel repetition).

---

7. One could allow an error also in the completeness condition. For simplicity, and since all our protocols do not have such an error, we require perfect completeness.

An interactive protocol is public-coin if each message sent by the verifier is a uniformly distributed random string, and at the end of the protocol, $\mathcal{V}$ decides whether to accept or reject as a function of x and the messages it sent (there is no secret randomness).

24.2.2 Polynomials and Low-Degree Extensions

In this section we recall some important facts on multivariate polynomials over finite fields. Throughout this survey we consider fields in which operations can be implemented efficiently (i.e., in polylogarithmic time in the field size). A basic fact, captured by the Schwartz–Zippel lemma is that low degree polynomials cannot have too many roots.

Lemma 24.1 (Schwartz–Zippel lemma)   Let $P : \mathbb{F}^m \to \mathbb{F}$ be a *nonzero* polynomial of total degree d. Then

$$\Pr_{r \in \mathbb{F}^m}[P(r) = 0] \le \frac{d}{|\mathbb{F}|}.$$

An immediate corollary of the Schwartz–Zippel lemma is that two distinct polynomials $P, Q : \mathbb{F}^m \to \mathbb{F}$ of total degree d may agree on at most a $\frac{d}{|\mathbb{F}|}$-fraction of their domain $\mathbb{F}^m$.

Low-Degree Extension.   Let $\mathbb{H}$ be a finite field and $\mathbb{F} \supseteq \mathbb{H}$ a field that contains $\mathbb{H}$. Fix an integer $m \in \mathbb{N}$. A basic fact is that for every function $\phi : \mathbb{H}^m \to \mathbb{F}$, there exists a unique extension of ϕ into a function $\hat{\phi} : \mathbb{F}^m \to \mathbb{F}$ (which agrees with ϕ on $\mathbb{H}^m$; i.e., $\hat{\phi}|_{\mathbb{H}^m} \equiv \phi$), such that $\hat{\phi}$ is an m-variate polynomial of individual degree at most $|\mathbb{H}| - 1$. Moreover, there exists a $2m$-variate polynomial $\hat{\beta} : \mathbb{F}^m \times \mathbb{F}^m \to \mathbb{F}$ that has degree $|\mathbb{H}| - 1$ in each variable, and for every function $\phi : \mathbb{H}^m \to \mathbb{F}$ it holds that

$$\hat{\phi}(z_1, \ldots, z_m) = \sum_{x \in \mathbb{H}^m} \tilde{\beta}(x, z) \cdot \phi(x). \tag{24.1}$$

The function $\tilde{\beta}$ can be evaluated in time $\mathrm{poly}(|\mathbb{H}|, m, \log(|\mathbb{F}|))$ (see, e.g., Proposition 3.2.1 in Rothblum [2009]). The function $\hat{\phi}$ is called the *low-degree extension* of ϕ (with respect to $\mathbb{F}$, $\mathbb{H}$ and m).

24.2.3 The Sum-Check Protocol

Fix a finite field $\mathbb{F}$ and a subset $\mathbb{H} \subseteq \mathbb{F}$. In a sum-check protocol, a (not necessarily efficient) prover takes as input an m-variate polynomial $f : \mathbb{F}^m \to \mathbb{F}$ of degree $\le d$ in each variable (think of d as significantly smaller than $|\mathbb{F}|$). His goal is to convince a verifier that

$$\sum_{z\in H^m} f(z) = \beta,$$

for some constant $\beta \in \mathbb{F}$ known to both of them. The verifier only has oracle access to f, and is given the constant $\beta \in \mathbb{F}$. He is required to be efficient in both its running time and its number of oracle queries. See the exposition in Rothblum [2009, Section 3.2.3]. We denote this protocol (as described in Rothblum [2009]) by $\left(P_{SC}(f), V_{SC}^f(\beta)\right)$.

Theorem 24.3 Let $f : \mathbb{F}^m \to \mathbb{F}$ be an m-variate polynomial of degree at most d in each variable, where $d < |\mathbb{F}|$. The sum-check protocol $\left(P_{SC}(f), V_{SC}^f(\beta)\right)$ satisfies the following properties.

- **Completeness:** If $\sum_{z\in H^m} f(z) = \beta$, then

$$\Pr\left[\left(P_{SC}(f), V_{SC}^f(\beta)\right) = 1\right] = 1.$$

- **Soundness:** If $\sum_{z\in H^m} f(z) \neq \beta$, then for every (unbounded) interactive Turing machine $\tilde{P}$,

$$\Pr\left[\left(\tilde{P}(f), V_{SC}^f(\beta)\right) = 1\right] \leq \frac{md}{|\mathbb{F}|}.$$

- **Complexity:** $P_{SC}(f)$ is an interactive Turing machine, and $V_{SC}^f(\beta)$ is a probabilistic interactive Turing machine with oracle access to $f : \mathbb{F}^m \to \mathbb{F}$. The prover $P_{SC}(f)$ runs in time poly$(|\mathbb{F}|^m)$.[8] The verifier $V_{SC}^f(\beta)$ runs in time $m \cdot d \cdot$ polylog$(|\mathbb{F}|)$, and queries the oracle f at a single point. The number of rounds is $O(m)$, the communication complexity is $O(m \cdot d \cdot \log(|\mathbb{F}|))$, and the total number of bits sent from the verifier to the prover is $O(m \cdot \log |\mathbb{F}|)$. Moreover, this protocol is public-coin.

24.3 DEIPs for Bounded-Depth Computations

In this section we give some details about the protocol behind Theorem 24.1. In a nutshell, our goal is to reduce the verifier's runtime to be proportional to the depth of the circuit C being computed, rather than its size, without increasing the prover's

8. Here we assume the prover's input is a description of the function f, from which f can be computed (on any input) in time poly$(|\mathbb{F}^m|)$.

runtime by too much. Toward this, let C be a depth d arithmetic circuit; that is, the circuit C is composed of addition and multiplication gates with fan-in 2 (say, over the field $\mathbb{GF}[2]$). Assume, without loss of generality, that the circuit is in a layered form, where there are as many layers as the depth of the circuit.[9]

The interactive protocol closely follows the (parallelized) computation of C, layer by layer, from the output layer to the input layer, numbering the layers in increasing order from the top (output) of the circuit to the bottom (input) of the circuit.[10] For each of the circuit layers, the prover computes the low-degree extension (see Section 24.2.2) of the values in that layer's gates. The claim being made by the prover, about the value of the circuit's output gate, is, in particular, also a claim about the value of the output layer's low-degree extension at a particular point. The protocol will "reduce" this claim to claims about the low-degree extensions of lower and lower layers in the circuit (i.e., layers closer to the input layer). Indeed, the claims will be about the values of these low-degree extensions at a single specific point. This culminates in a claim about the value of the low-degree extension of the input layer at a single point. The verifier can check this claim on its own in near-linear time.

An immediate difficulty with this idea is that the verifier cannot compute points in the low-degree extension (of the computation on x) in an intermediate layer i: This is the low-degree extension of the vector of values that the gates in the circuit's ith layer take on input x, and to compute it one needs to actually evaluate C, which we want to avoid! Thus, the value of the point in the low-degree extension of the ith layer will instead be supplied by the prover. Of course, the prover may cheat. Thus, each phase of the protocol lets the verifier reduce verification of a single point in the low-degree extension of an advanced layer in the parallel computation to verification of a single point in the low-degree extension of the previous layer. This process is repeated iteratively (for as many layers as the circuit has), until at the end the verification has been reduced to verifying a single point in the low-degree extension of the lowest circuit layer. As noted above, this lowest layer is simply the input layer, and the verifier can compute the low-degree extension of the input x on its own in nearly linear time.

Going from Layer to Layer.   Given the foregoing outline, the main remaining challenge is reducing verification of a single point in the low degree extension of an ith

---

9. Every circuit can be converted into this format, without increasing its depth. The size is at most squared and space uniformity is preserved up to constant factors.

10. That is, layer 0 is the output layer, and layer d is the input layer.

layer in the circuit, to verification of a single point in the low-degree extension of the previous—that is, the $(i + 1)$th—layer.

The main ingredient used to achieve this is a sum-check protocol (see Section 24.2.3) applied to the gates of layer i. We observe that every point in the low-degree extension (LDE) of layer i is a linear combination, or a weighted sum, of the values of that layer's gates. Each gate in layer i is a function of the values of two gates in layer $i + 1$ (because we assumed that C is a layered circuit with fan-in 2). Thus, we can express the value of each point in the LDE of layer i as a weighted sum, over all gates g in layer i, and over all possible gate pairs (k, ℓ) in layer $(i + 1)$, of a low-degree function of (i) the values of gates k and ℓ, and (ii) a predicate that indicates whether gates k and ℓ are indeed the "children" of gate g. Arithmetizing this entire sum of sums, we run a sum-check protocol to verify the value of one point in the low-degree extension of layer i.

To simplify matters, we assume for now that the verifier has access to (a low-degree extension of) the predicate that says whether a pair of gates (k, ℓ) are the children of gate g. Then (modulo many details) at the end of this sum-check protocol the verifier only needs to verify the values of a pair of points in the LDE of layer $(i + 1)$. This is still not enough, as we need to reduce the verification of a single point in the LDE of layer i to the verification of a *single* point in layer $(i + 1)$ and not of a pair of points. Thus, we use an interactive protocol to reduce verifying two points in the LDE of layer $(i + 1)$ to verifying just one.

We note that rather than assuming that the verifier has access to the low degree extension of the predicate describing the "wiring" of circuit gates, it suffices for the verifier to have access to *any* function that agrees with this predicate on inputs that correspond to circuit gates, so long as the function has bounded degree when viewed as a polynomial over a larger field. Thus, the (central) remaining question is how the verifier gains access to such an extension of the predicates that decide whether circuit gates are connected, without looking at the entire circuit (as the circuit itself is much larger than the verifier's running time). This is where we use the uniformity of the circuit (see below).

The verifier's running time in each of these phases is *polylogarithmic* in the circuit size. In the final phase, computing one point in the low-degree extension of the input requires only nearly linear time, independent of the rest of the circuit. Another important point is that the verifier does not need to remember anything about earlier phases of the verification, at any point in time, it only needs to remember what is being verified about a certain point in the computation. This results in very space-efficient verifiers. The savings in the prover's running time comes (intuitively) from the fact that the prover does not need to arithmetize the *entire* computation, but rather proves statements about one (parallel) computation step at a time.

Utilizing Uniformity. It remains to show how the verifier can compute (a low-degree extension of) a predicate that decides whether circuit gates are connected, without looking at the entire circuit.

To do this, we proceed in two steps. First, we examine low-space computations—for example, uniform log-space Turing machines (deterministic or nondeterministic). A log-space machine can be transformed into an ensemble of Boolean circuits with polylogarithmic depth and polynomial size. We show that in this family of circuits, it is possible to compute the predicate that decides whether circuit gates are connected in polylogarithmic time and constant depth. This computation can itself be arithmetized, which allows the verifier to compute a *low-degree extension* of the predicate (a low-degree function that agrees with the predicate on inputs corresponding to circuit gates) in polylogarithmic time. Thus we obtain an interactive proof with an efficient prover and super-efficient verifier for any L or NL computation. The number of rounds in this protocol is polylogarithmic.

Still, the result above took advantage of the (strong) uniformity of very specific circuits that are constructed from log-space Turing machines. We want to give interactive proofs for general log-space uniform circuits, and not only for log-space languages. How then can a verifier compute even the predicate that decides whether circuit gates in a log-space uniform circuit are connected (let alone its low degree extension)? In general, computing this predicate might require nearly as much time as evaluating the entire circuit. We overcome this obstacle by observing that the verifier does not have to compute this predicate on its own: It can ask the prover to compute the predicate for it! Of course, the prover may cheat, but the verifier can use the above interactive proof for log-space computations to force the prover to *prove* that it computed the (low-degree extensions of) the predicate correctly. This final protocol gives an interactive proof for general log-space uniform circuits with low depth. We note that in more recent work, Goldreich [2018, Chapter 3] employs a different approach, and directly shows how to convert any logspace-uniform circuit ensemble into an ensemble where the circuits' "wiring predicates" can be computed in polylogarithmic time and degree.

Organization. We proceed to elaborate on the main step of the protocol: reducing the verification of coordinates in layer i to layer $i + 1$, where we assume access to an extension for the circuit wiring predicates with sufficiently low degree. We refer to this version as the bare-bones protocol. The curious reader is directed to Goldwasser et al. [2015] or the survey by Goldreich [2018, Section 3.3] for the full details of how the wiring predicates are implemented.

We begin with preliminaries and notations in Section 24.3.1, the protocol is in Section 24.3.2, and a proof of its soundness is in Section 24.3.3.

24.3.1   Setup and Notation

Parameters.   Fix any circuit $C : \{0, 1\}^n \to \{0, 1\}$. We assume the circuit is layered (see below). We denote the maximal width of any layer by S, and the circuit depth by $d \leq S$. Let $\mathbb{H}$ be an extension field of $\mathbb{GF}[2]$ such that

$$\max\{d, \log(S)\} \leq |\mathbb{H}| \leq \text{poly}(d, \log(S)),$$

and let $\mathbb{F}$ be an extension field of $\mathbb{H}$, where

$$|\mathbb{F}| \leq \text{poly}(|\mathbb{H}|).$$

Let m be an integer such that

$$S \leq |\mathbb{H}|^m \leq \text{poly}(S).$$

We associate the integers $\{0, \ldots, S - 1\}$ with the elements in $\mathbb{H}^m$ in a natural (easy-to-compute) way. Finally, let $\delta \in \mathbb{N}$ be a (degree) parameter such that

$$|\mathbb{H}| - 1 \leq \delta < |\mathbb{F}|.$$

Assumptions and Notation.   Note that any Boolean circuit $C : \{0, 1\}^n \to \{0, 1\}$ can be converted into an arithmetic circuit $C : \mathbb{F}^n \to \mathbb{F}$ over the field $\mathbb{F}$, while increasing the size and the depth of the circuit by at most a constant factor. Note that any arithmetic circuit can be converted into a layered arithmetic circuit of fan-in 2, while increasing the size of the circuit by at most a polynomial factor and increasing the depth of the circuit by at most a factor of $O(\log(S))$. We assume for simplicity that the circuit $C : \mathbb{F}^n \to \mathbb{F}$ is a *layered* arithmetic circuit of *fan-in 2* (over the gates $\times$ and $+$ and over the field $\mathbb{F}$) as follows.

A depth-d layered circuit is one where the gates are divided into $(d + 1)$ layers. We think of the 0th layer as the output layer (comprised of the output gate), and of the dth layer as the input layer (composed of the input gates). For a layered circuit, wires can only connect gates in adjacent layers; that is, the output wire of a gate in layer i can only be the input wire for a gate in layer $(i - 1)$.

For simplicity of notation, we also assume that all the layers in C are of the same size, and we assume that the size of each layer is S. We note that any circuit (of size S)

can be transformed into one with exactly S gates in each level, by adding at most S dummy gates (that are the constant zero) to each layer. This increases the size of the circuit by at most a quadratic factor (and does not increase its depth).

Wiring Predicates. For each $0 \leq i \leq d$, we denote the S gates in the ith layer of C by $(g_{i,0}, g_{i,1}, \ldots, g_{i,S-1})$. For each $i \in [d]$, we associate with C two functions

$$\mathrm{add}_i, \mathrm{mult}_i : \{0, 1, \ldots, S-1\}^3 \to \{0, 1\},$$

defined by

$$\mathrm{add}_i(j_1, j_2, j_3) = \begin{cases} 1 & \text{if } g_{i-1,j_1} = g_{i,j_2} + g_{i,j_3} \\ 0 & \text{otherwise} \end{cases} \tag{24.2}$$

and

$$\mathrm{mult}_i(j_1, j_2, j_3) = \begin{cases} 1 & \text{if } g_{i-1,j_1} = g_{i,j_2} \times g_{i,j_3} \\ 0 & \text{otherwise} \end{cases} \tag{24.3}$$

We say that the functions $\{add_i, mult_i\}_{i \in [d]}$ *specify* the circuit C, and we sometimes refer to these as the circuit's *wiring predicates*.

Extensions of Wiring Predicates. For each $i \in [d]$, let

$$\widetilde{\mathrm{add}}_i, \widetilde{\mathrm{mult}}_i : \mathbb{F}^{3m} \to \mathbb{F}$$

be multivariate polynomials of degree at most δ in each variable that extend the functions add_i and mult_i, respectively. Namely, the functions $\widetilde{\mathrm{add}}_i$ and $\widetilde{\mathrm{mult}}_i$ satisfy that for every $z_1, z_2, z_3 \in \mathbb{H}^m$,

$$\widetilde{\mathrm{add}}_i(z_1, z_2, z_3) = \mathrm{add}_i(z_1, z_2, z_3)$$

and

$$\widetilde{\mathrm{mult}}_i(z_1, z_2, z_3) = \mathrm{mult}_i(z_1, z_2, z_3),$$

where we associate the indices in $\{0, \ldots, S-1\}$ with the elements in $\mathbb{H}^m$ in the natural way.

An Important Note. The fact that such functions $\widetilde{\mathrm{add}}_i$ and $\widetilde{\mathrm{mult}}_i$ exist follows from the fact that $\delta \geq |\mathbb{H}| - 1$. In particular, $\widetilde{\mathrm{add}}_i$ (respectively $\widetilde{\mathrm{mult}}_i$) could be the low degree extension of add_i (respectively mult_i), though we will sometimes take them to be different extensions (of slightly higher degree).

We say that the functions $\{\widetilde{\mathrm{add}}_i, \widetilde{\mathrm{mult}}_i\}_{i \in [d]}$ are *extensions of the functions that specify* the circuit C, or extensions of the wiring predicates. Note that unlike the functions $\{add_i, mult_i\}_{i \in [d]}$ that specify C, the extensions $\{\widetilde{add}_i, \widetilde{mult}_i\}_{i \in [d]}$ are not uniquely determined by the circuit C. For $\delta > |\mathbb{H}| - 1$ there are many possible extensions of the functions that specify the circuit C, and $\{\widetilde{add}_i, \widetilde{mult}_i\}_{i \in [d]}$ are *some* such extensions. We will specify $\{\widetilde{add}_i, \widetilde{mult}_i\}$ separately in each implementation of the bare-bones protocol.

Oracle for the Bare-Bones Protocol. We are now ready to specify the oracle $\mathcal{F}$ accessed by the prover and verifier in the bare-bones protocol. This oracle consists of the collection of functions $\{\widetilde{add}_i, \widetilde{mult}_i\}_{i \in [d]}$:

$$\mathcal{F} = \{\widetilde{add}_i, \widetilde{mult}_i\}_{i \in [d]},$$

where the prover and verifier can access $\widetilde{add}_i$ or $\widetilde{mult}_i$ by querying $\mathcal{F}$ with the proper i, a bit specifying add or $mult$, and an input in $(\mathbb{F}^m)^3$.

Circuit Value Vector. For each $0 \leq i \leq d$ we associate a vector $v_i = (v_{i,0}, \ldots, v_{i,S-1}) \in \mathbb{F}^S$ with the ith layer of the circuit C. The vector v_0 is associated with the output layer of the circuit, and the vector v_d is associated with the input layer of the circuit. These vectors are functions of the input $x = (x_1, \ldots, x_n) \in \mathbb{F}^n$ and are defined as follows: For each $0 \leq i \leq d$ we let v_i be the vector that consists of the values of all the gates in the ith layer of the computation of the circuit on input x. So, the vector v_0, which corresponds to the output layer, satisfies $v_0 = (C(x), 0, \ldots, 0) \in \mathbb{F}^S$. Similarly, the vector v_d, which corresponds to the input layer, satisfies $v_d = (x_1, \ldots, x_n, 0, \ldots, 0) \in \mathbb{F}^S$.

For each $0 \leq i \leq d$, let

$$\tilde{V}_i : \mathbb{F}^m \to \mathbb{F}$$

be the low-degree extension of v_i (with respect to $\mathbb{H}, \mathbb{F}, m$). The function $\tilde{V}_i$ is of degree at most $|\mathbb{H}| - 1$ in each of its m variables and can be computed in time $\text{poly}(|\mathbb{F}|^m) = \text{poly}(S)$ (see Section 24.2.2).

24.3.2 The "Bare-Bones" Protocol

In this subsection, we present the bare-bones protocol $(\mathcal{P}_1, \mathcal{V}_1)$ for efficiently verifying that $C(x) = 0$. In this protocol we give both the verifier $\mathcal{V}_1$ and the prover $\mathcal{P}_1$ oracle access to the set of functions

$$\mathcal{F} = \{\widetilde{add}_i, \widetilde{mult}_i\}_{i \in [d]},$$

as defined in Subsection 24.3.1.[11] The prover and verifier also take as input the string $x \in \{0, 1\}^n$.

Protocol Overview. The prover wants to prove that $C(x) = 0$, or equivalently, that $\tilde{V}_0(0, \dots, 0) = 0$. This is done in d phases (where d is the depth of C). In the ith phase ($1 \le i \le d$), the prover reduces the task of proving that $\tilde{V}_{i-1}(z_{i-1}) = r_{i-1}$ to the task of proving that $\tilde{V}_i(z_i) = r_i$, where z_i and r_i are values determined by the protocol (initially $z_0 = (0, \dots, 0)$ and $r_0 = 0$). Finally, after the dth phase, the verifier checks on his own whether $\tilde{V}_d(z_d) = r_d$. Note that $\tilde{V}_d$ is the low-degree extension of the input $x \in \{0, 1\}^n$ (we view x as a vector of length S by padding it with 0's). Computing a single point in the low-degree extension of x can be done in quasi-linear time in the input length (i.e., in time $\tilde{O}(|x|)$). This is the "heaviest" computation run by the verifier. Moreover, if the verifier is given oracle access to the low-degree extension of x, then this only requires a *single* oracle call.

The Bare-Bones Protocol.

  Parameters. We use the parameters defined in Subsection 24.3.1: circuit size S, circuit depth d, input size n, where $n, d \le S$. We also defined there the fields $\mathbb{H}$, $\mathbb{F}$, integers m, m', and a degree parameter δ. The layered arithmetic circuit $C : \mathbb{F}^n \to \mathbb{F}$ is of fan-in 2 (over the gates $+$ and $\times$), of size S, and of depth d.

  Input. The prover and the verifier take as input a string $x \in \mathbb{F}^n$, and are both given oracle access to a set of functions $\mathcal{F} = \{\widetilde{\mathrm{add}}_i, \widetilde{\mathrm{mult}}_i\}_{i \in [d]}$ corresponding to C (as defined in Subsection 24.3.1), where each function in $\mathcal{F}$ is of degree at most δ in each variable.

  The protocol. $(\mathcal{P}_1^{\mathcal{F}}(x), \mathcal{V}_1^{\mathcal{F}}(x))$ The prover needs to prove that $C(x) = 0$, or equivalently, that $\tilde{V}_0(0, \dots, 0) = 0$. This is done in d phases (where d is the depth of C). In the ith phase ($1 \le i \le d$) the prover reduces the task of proving that $\tilde{V}_{i-1}(z_{i-1}) = r_{i-1}$ to the task of proving that $\tilde{V}_i(z_i) = r_i$, where z_i and r_i are values determined by the protocol (initially $z_0 = (0, \dots, 0)$ and $r_0 = 0$). Finally, after the dth phase, the verifier checks on his own that $\tilde{V}_d(z_d) = r_d$.

  In what follows we describe these phases in more detail. In each phase, the communication complexity is $\mathrm{poly}(d, \log S)$, the running time of the prover is at most $\mathrm{poly}(S)$, and the running time of the verifier is $\mathrm{poly}(d, \log S)$.

---

11. We note that the functions in $\mathcal{F}$ could have been given to the prover $\mathcal{P}_1$ as input (say, via their truth tables). We decided to give $\mathcal{P}_1$ oracle access to these functions only for the sake of simplicity of the exposition. Note also that given oracle access to these functions, the prover $\mathcal{P}_1$ can reconstruct the circuit C in time $O(|C|)$.

The *i*th Phase ($1 \leq i \leq d - 1$). In this phase, we reduce the task of proving that

$$\tilde{V}_{i-1}(z_{i-1}) = r_{i-1}$$

to the task of proving that

$$\tilde{V}_i(z_i) = r_i,$$

where $z_i \in \mathbb{F}^m$ is a random value determined by the verifier and r_i is a value determined by the protocol. By Equation (24.1) in Section 24.2.2, for every $z \in \mathbb{F}^m$,

$$\tilde{V}_{i-1}(z) = \sum_{p \in \mathbb{H}^m} \tilde{\beta}(z, p) \cdot \tilde{V}_{i-1}(p),$$

where $\tilde{\beta} : \mathbb{F}^m \times \mathbb{F}^m \to \mathbb{F}$ is a polynomial of size $\mathrm{poly}(|\mathbb{H}|, m)$ and of degree at most $|\mathbb{H}| - 1$ in each variable, that can be computed by a Turing machine that runs in time $\leq \mathrm{poly}(|\mathbb{H}|, m)$.

Notice that for every $p \in \mathbb{H}^m$,

$$\tilde{V}_{i-1}(p) = \sum_{\omega_1, \omega_2 \in \mathbb{H}^m} \widetilde{\mathrm{add}}_i(p, \omega_1, \omega_2) \cdot \left(\tilde{V}_i(\omega_1) + \tilde{V}_i(\omega_2) \right)$$

$$+ \widetilde{\mathrm{mult}}_i(p, \omega_1, \omega_2) \cdot \tilde{V}_i(\omega_1) \cdot \tilde{V}_i(\omega_2).$$

Thus, for every $z \in \mathbb{F}^m$,

$$\tilde{V}_{i-1}(z) = \sum_{p, \omega_1, \omega_2 \in \mathbb{H}^m} \tilde{\beta}(z, p) \cdot \left(\widetilde{\mathrm{add}}_i(p, \omega_1, \omega_2) \cdot \left(\tilde{V}_i(\omega_1) + \tilde{V}_i(\omega_2) \right) \right.$$

$$\left. + \widetilde{\mathrm{mult}}_i(p, \omega_1, \omega_2) \cdot \tilde{V}_i(\omega_1) \cdot \tilde{V}_i(\omega_2) \right).$$

For every $z \in \mathbb{F}^m$, let $f_z : (\mathbb{F}^m)^3 \to \mathbb{F}$ be the function defined by

$$f_z(p, \omega_1, \omega_2) \stackrel{\mathrm{def}}{=} \tilde{\beta}(z, p) \cdot \left(\widetilde{\mathrm{add}}_i(p, \omega_1, \omega_2) \cdot \left(\tilde{V}_i(\omega_1) + \tilde{V}_i(\omega_2) \right) + \widetilde{\mathrm{mult}}_i(p, \omega_1, \omega_2) \right.$$

$$\left. \cdot \tilde{V}_i(\omega_1) \cdot \tilde{V}_i(\omega_2) \right).$$

Equation (24.1), together with the definitions of $\widetilde{\mathrm{add}}_i$, $\widetilde{\mathrm{mult}}_i$, and $\tilde{V}_i$, implies that the function f_z is a $3m$-variate polynomial of degree at most $\delta + |\mathbb{H}| - 1 \leq 2\delta$ in each variable, and can be computed in time of size $\mathrm{poly}(S)$. Note that, for every $z \in \mathbb{F}^m$,

$$\tilde{V}_{i-1}(z) = \sum_{p, \omega_1, \omega_2 \in \mathbb{H}^m} f_z(p, \omega_1, \omega_2).$$

Thus proving that $\tilde{V}_{i-1}(z_{i-1}) = r_{i-1}$ is equivalent to proving that

$$r_{i-1} = \sum_{p, \omega_1, \omega_2 \in \mathbb{H}^m} f_{z_{i-1}}(p, \omega_1, \omega_2).$$

This is done by running the interactive sum-check protocol (see Section 24.2.3).[12]

However, in order to carry out the verification task, the verifier needs to compute on his own the function $f_{z_{i-1}}(p, \omega_1, \omega_2)$, on random inputs $p, \omega_1, \omega_2 \in_R \mathbb{F}^m$ (chosen by the verifier). Recall that the verifier has oracle access to the functions $\widetilde{\mathrm{add}}_i$ and $\widetilde{\mathrm{mult}}_i$. Moreover, computing the function $\tilde{\beta}$ requires time $\mathrm{poly}(|\mathbb{H}|, m) = \mathrm{polylog}(S)$ (see Section 24.2.2). The main computational burden in this verification task is computing $\tilde{V}_i(\omega_1)$ and $\tilde{V}_i(\omega_2)$, which requires time $\mathrm{poly}(S)$ (and thus cannot be computed by our computationally bounded verifier).

In the protocol, the prover $\mathcal{P}_1$ now sends both these values, $\tilde{V}_i(\omega_1)$ and $\tilde{V}_i(\omega_2)$, to the verifier. The verifier $\mathcal{V}_1$ (who knows ω_1 and ω_2) receives two values v_1, v_2 and wants to verify that $\tilde{V}_i(\omega_1) = v_1$ and $\tilde{V}_i(\omega_2) = v_2$.

Thus, so far, using the sum-check protocol, we reduced task of proving that $\tilde{V}_{i-1}(z_{i-1}) = r_{i-1}$ to the task of proving that both $\tilde{V}_i(\omega_1) = v_1$ and $\tilde{V}_i(\omega_2) = v_2$. However, recall that our goal was to reduce the task of proving that $\tilde{V}_{i-1}(z_{i-1}) = r_{i-1}$ to the task of proving a *single* equality of the form $\tilde{V}_i(z_i) = r_i$. Therefore, what remains (in the ith phase) is to reduce the task of proving two equalities of the form $\tilde{V}_i(\omega_1) = v_1$ and $\tilde{V}_i(\omega_2) = v_2$ to the task of proving a single equality of the form $\tilde{V}_i(z_i) = r_i$. This is done via the following (standard) interactive process.

1. Let $t_1, t_2 \in \mathbb{F}$ be two distinct fixed elements known to the prover $\mathcal{P}_1$ and the verifier $\mathcal{V}_1$. Let $\gamma : \mathbb{F} \to \mathbb{F}^m$ be the unique line (i.e., polynomial of degree at most 1) such that $\gamma(t_i) = \omega_i$ for $i \in \{1, 2\}$. It is well known that for any $t_1, t_2, \omega_1, \omega_2$, the conditions $\gamma(t_i) = \omega_i$ determine γ uniquely, and that γ can be computed (by both $\mathcal{P}_1$ and $\mathcal{V}_1$) in time $\mathrm{poly}(|\mathbb{F}|, m)$ and space $O(\log(|\mathbb{F}|) \cdot m)$.

2. The prover $\mathcal{P}_1$ sends the function $\tilde{V}_i \circ \gamma : \mathbb{F} \to \mathbb{F}$ to the verifier $\mathcal{V}_1$. Note that this is a univariate polynomial of degree at most $m \cdot (|\mathbb{H}| - 1)$, since $\tilde{V}_i$ is an m-variate polynomial of individual degree $|\mathbb{H}| - 1$.

3. Upon receiving a function $f : \mathbb{F} \to \mathbb{F}$ from the prover (supposedly, $f = \tilde{V}_i \circ \gamma$), the verifier $\mathcal{V}_1$ checks that f is a polynomial of degree at most $m \cdot (|\mathbb{H}| - 1)$,

---

12. Note that in the interactive sum-check protocol the prover takes the function f_z as input, whereas our prover $\mathcal{P}_1$ does not take f_z as input. This is not a problem since $\mathcal{P}_1$ can compute the function f_z (as a polynomial or as a truth table) using its oracles, in time $\mathrm{poly}(S)$.

and that $f(t_1) = v_1$ and $f(t_2) = v_2$. If these tests pass, then $\mathcal{V}_1$ chooses a random element $t \in \mathbb{F}$ and sends it to $\mathcal{P}_1$.

4. The prover and verifier continue to Phase $i + 1$ with $z_i \stackrel{\text{def}}{=} \gamma(t)$ and $r_i \stackrel{\text{def}}{=} f(t)$.

The Final Verification. After the last (i.e. d-th) verification phase, the verifier $\mathcal{V}_1$ needs to verify on its own that $\tilde{V}_d(z_d) = r_d$. This amounts to computing a single point in the low-degree extension of the input x ($\tilde{V}_d$ is the low degree extension of the input, padded with 0's). As noted above, this can be done in quasi-linear time in the input length n: e.g., see Rothblum [2009, Claim 3.2.2].

24.3.3 Analysis of the Bare-Bones Protocol

Completeness. The perfect completeness follows immediately from the protocol description, as well as the perfect completeness of the sum-check protocol (see Theorem 24.3).

Soundness. For the soundness condition, fix any layered arithmetic circuit $C : \mathbb{F}^n \to \mathbb{F}$, any $x \in \mathbb{F}^n$ such that $C(x) \neq 0$, and any set of functions $\mathcal{F}$ that are low-degree extensions of the functions that specify the circuit C (as defined in Section 24.3.1). Assume that there exists a cheating prover $\mathcal{P}^*$ such that

$$\Pr\left[(\mathcal{P}^{*\mathcal{F}}(x), \mathcal{V}_1^{\mathcal{F}}(x)) = 1\right] = s.$$

Recall that the protocol $(\mathcal{P}_1^{\mathcal{F}}(x), \mathcal{V}_1^{\mathcal{F}}(x))$ consists of d phases. Each phase consists of a sum-check protocol and an additional short interactive protocol. According to our notation, the sum-check protocol requires the values of $\tilde{V}_i(w_1)$ and $\tilde{V}_i(w_2)$ for verification, and the additional interactive protocol reduces the verification of $\tilde{V}_i(w_1) = v_1$ and $\tilde{V}_i(w_2) = v_2$ to the verification of a single equality $\tilde{V}_i(z_i) = r_i$.

For every $0 \leq i \leq d$, let T_i denote the event that indeed $\tilde{V}_i(z_i) = r_i$. Thus, assuming $C(x) \neq 0$ is equivalent to assuming $\neg T_0$. Notice that

$$s \leq \Pr[\neg T_0 \wedge T_d] \leq \Pr[\exists i \in [d] \;\; \text{s.t.} \; \neg T_{i-1} \wedge T_i] \leq \sum_{i=1}^{d} \Pr[\neg T_{i-1} \wedge T_i].$$

For every $i \in [d]$, let E_i denote the event that indeed $\tilde{V}_i(w_1) = v_1$ and $\tilde{V}_i(w_2) = v_2$.[13] Then

$$\Pr[\neg T_{i-1} \wedge T_i] = \Pr[\neg T_{i-1} \wedge T_i \wedge E_i] + \Pr[\neg T_{i-1} \wedge T_i \wedge \neg E_i].$$

---

13. Note that (w_1, v_1) and (w_2, v_2) depend on the phase $i \in [d]$. For the sake of simplicity, this dependence is not captured in our notation.

The soundness property of the interactive sum-check protocol implies that

$$\Pr[\neg T_{i-1} \wedge T_i \wedge E_i] \leq \Pr[\neg T_{i-1} \wedge E_i] \leq \frac{3m \cdot 2\delta}{|\mathbb{F}|} = \frac{6m\delta}{|\mathbb{F}|}.$$

The fact that any two distinct univariate degree t polynomials agree on at most t points implies that

$$\Pr[\neg T_{i-1} \wedge T_i \wedge \neg E_i] \leq \Pr[T_i \wedge \neg E_i] \leq \frac{m(|\mathbb{H}| - 1)}{|\mathbb{F}|} \leq \frac{m\delta}{|\mathbb{F}|}.$$

Thus,

$$\Pr[\neg T_{i-1} \wedge T_i] \leq \frac{6m\delta}{|\mathbb{F}|} + \frac{m\delta}{|\mathbb{F}|} = \frac{7m\delta}{|\mathbb{F}|}.$$

All in all, we get that

$$s \leq \frac{7md\delta}{|\mathbb{F}|}.$$

Taking $\mathbb{F}$ such that $|\mathbb{F}| \geq 700md\delta = \text{poly}(|\mathbb{H}|)$, we get that $s \leq \frac{1}{100}$ as desired.

Complexity. Recall that the bare-bones protocol proceeds in d phases (where d is the depth of C). In the ith phase ($1 \leq i \leq d$) the prover reduces the task of proving that $\tilde{V}_{i-1}(z_{i-1}) = r_{i-1}$ to the task of proving that $\tilde{V}_i(z_i) = r_i$. This is done by running a sum-check protocol and an additional short interactive protocol. Hence, the complexity of the ith phase of the protocol is as follows:

1. The running time of the prover $\mathcal{P}_1$ is $\text{poly}(|\mathbb{F}^m|) = \text{poly}(S)$, both in the sum-check protocol (see Theorem 24.3) and in the proceeding interactive process.

2. The running time of the verifier $\mathcal{V}_1$ (with oracle access to $\mathcal{F}$), both in the sum-check protocol (see Theorem 24.3) and in the subsequent interactive process, is $d \cdot \delta \cdot \log S \cdot \text{polylog}(|\mathbb{F}|)$. So long as $\delta = \text{polylog}(|S|)$ (which is the case in the case in the bare-bones protocol's instantiation), we get that the verifier's running time in this phase of the protocol is $(d \cdot \text{polylog } S)$.

3. The sum-check protocol has communication complexity $\delta \cdot m \cdot \text{polylog } |\mathbb{F}|$ (see Theorem 24.3), and the proceeding interactive process has communication complexity $\delta \cdot \text{polylog}(|\mathbb{F}|)$. Thus, in total, each phase has communication complexity $(\delta \cdot \text{polylog } S)$.

   Moreover, the verifier $\mathcal{V}_1$ is public-coin, and the number of random bits it sends to the prover $\mathcal{P}_1$ in each phase is $O(m \cdot \log |\mathbb{F}|)$. This, together with the fact that the only information that the prover needs to "remember" for the next phase is the values i, z_i, r_i (and does not need to remember any information from previous phases), implies that each message sent by the prover depends only on the preceding $O(m \cdot \log(|\mathbb{F}|)) = O(\log(S))$ random bits sent by the verifier.

4. In each phase, the verifier queries each $\widetilde{\mathrm{add}}_i$ and $\widetilde{\mathrm{mult}}_i$ only at a single location. The verifier's queries to $\widetilde{\mathrm{add}}_i$ and $\widetilde{\mathrm{mult}}_i$ are determined by its (public) coin tosses in the sum-check protocol and are thus also uniformly random (over the verifier's coin tosses).

Finally, the verifier $\mathcal{V}_1$ needs to verify on his own that $\tilde{V}_d(z_d) = r_d$. This can be done in time $n \cdot \mathrm{poly}(|\mathbb{H}|, m) = n \cdot \mathrm{poly}(d, \log(S))$, see the discussion at the end of Section 24.3.2.

24.4 Constant-Round DEIPs for Bounded-Space Computation

In this section we give some details about the protocol behind Theorem 24.2. This protocol is built iteratively: starting with proofs for short bounded-space computations, and building up protocols for increasingly long (complex) bounded-space computations.

An Iterative Construction. Assume we have a "base" interactive proof for verifying the computation of Turing machines that run in time T and space S. We would like to build on this protocol to construct an "augmented" interactive proof for verifying "longer" computations that run in time $k \cdot T$ and space S, where k is an integer (much) larger than 1. The protocol behind Theorem 24.2 employs a series of such augmentation steps iteratively, starting with trivial interactive proofs for short computations and gradually obtaining increasingly powerful interactive proofs for longer and longer computations.

We proceed with a discussion of the augmentation step. We begin with a base protocol, where prover and verifier agree on a (deterministic) Turing machine $\mathcal{M}$, an input $x \in \{0, 1\}^n$, and two configurations $u, v \in \{0, 1\}^S$ (a configuration includes the machine's internal state, the contents of all memory tapes, and the position of the heads). The prover's claim is that after running the machine $\mathcal{M}$ on input x, starting at configuration u and proceeding for T steps, the resulting configuration is v. We augment the base protocol, using it to design a new protocol for verifying longer computations running in time $k \cdot T$.

Consider an augmented claim, where u is the initial configuration, and v is the alleged configuration after $k \cdot T$ steps. The prover's first message in the augmented protocol is $(k-1)$ alleged intermediate configurations

$$(\tilde{w}_T, \tilde{w}_{2T}, \ldots, \tilde{w}_{(k-1)\cdot T}),$$

where $\tilde{w}_t$ is the alleged configuration of the machine $\mathcal{M}$ after t steps (with initial configuration u and on input x).[14] Defining $\tilde{w}_0 = u$ and $\tilde{w}_{(k\cdot T)} = v$, the $k-1$ intermediate configurations sent by the prover specify k "base claims" about T-step computations: For each $j \in [k]$, the prover claims that the machine $\mathcal{M}$, starting from configuration $\tilde{w}_{(j-1)\cdot T}$, and running for T steps, reaches configuration $\tilde{w}_{j\cdot T}$.

In a naive augmentation, the verifier runs the base protocol k times to verify all k base claims. This increases the communication and verification time by a multiplicative factor of k. While the resulting augmented protocol can be used to verify computations that are k times longer then the base protocol, it is also k times more expensive, so we have not made any real progress.

Another naive option is picking just one (or several) of the base claims, and verifying only them. This is less expensive in communication and verification time, but the soundness error grows prohibitively. In particular, suppose that the prover is cheating, and the computation path of length $k \cdot T$ that starts at $\tilde{w}_0$ does not end at $\tilde{w}_{k\cdot T}$. The cheating prover can still generate a sequence $(\tilde{w}_T, \tilde{w}_{2T}, \ldots, \tilde{w}_{(k-1)\cdot T})$ where all but one of the base claims are true. For example, the cheating prover could pick $j^* \in [k]$, set the configurations $(\tilde{w}_T, \ldots, \tilde{w}_{(j^*-1)\cdot T})$ to be the appropriate configurations on a path of length $(j^* - 1) \cdot T$ that starts at $\tilde{w}_0$ (and ends at $\tilde{w}_{(j^*-1)\cdot T}$), and set the configurations $(\tilde{w}_{j^*\cdot T}, \ldots, \tilde{w}_{(k-1)\cdot T})$ to be the appropriate configurations on a path of length $(k - j^*) \cdot T$ that starts at $\tilde{w}_{j^*\cdot T}$ and ends at $\tilde{w}_{k\cdot T}$. Now all of the base claims are true, except for the j^*th (since there could be no path of length T from $\tilde{w}_{(j^*-1)\cdot T}$ to $\tilde{w}_{j^*\cdot T}$). Unless the verifier checks all (or very many) of the base claims, it will fail to detect any cheating.

What we seek is a protocol for verifying the k base claims, but with communication and verification time that is much smaller than running the base protocol k times, and with soundness error that is not much larger than that of the base protocol. Also, the number of rounds should not grow too much (so that we can get interactive proofs with a small number of rounds), and the complexity of the (honest) prover should only grow by a factor of roughly k (so we can get a doubly efficient proof system). We refer to this goal as *"batch verification for interactive proofs."* We

---

14. Here and throughout this section we use tildes to denote potentially corrupted strings that the verifier receives from an untrusted prover.

emphasize that, as described above, it is crucial that if even just one of the claims is false, the verifier should still reject.

At the heart of the proof of Theorem 24.2 is an efficient *batch verification theorem* for a certain class of interactive proofs (so-called *unambiguous* interactive proofs; see below). The remainder of this section is devoted to an overview of key ideas underlying the batch verification theorem. We begin by considering the more modest goal of batching the verification of UP statements (NP statements that have at most one witness), which gives a taste of the ideas and techniques. We then briefly discuss the additional challenges in batching (unambiguous) interactive proof systems.

Unambiguous and Probabilistically Checkable IPs. The batch verification theorem makes use of several new notions for interactive proofs. The first notion captures proof systems where the prover has a unique strategy to convince a verifier (similarly to the unique satisfying assignment of a unique-SAT formula); the moment the prover deviates from the prescribed strategy it will likely fail in convincing the verifier *even when the statement in question is true*. We call this notion an *unambiguous interactive proof*. The second notion can be thought of as an interactive analogue of PCPs. These are interactive proof systems where the verifier only reads a few bits of the input and the transcript when checking the proof. These proofs are called *probabilistically checkable interactive proofs* (PCIPs).[15]

24.4.1 A Warm-Up: Batching the Verification of UP Statements

To illustrate some of the ideas behind the batch verification theorem, we consider the simpler challenge of designing an *interactive* proof system for batching the verification of UP statements. Recall that the complexity class UP (unambiguous nondeterministic polynomial time) is the subclass of NP problems where the nondeterministic Turing machine has at most one accepting path. That is, for a language $\mathcal{L} \in$ UP, and an input $x \in \mathcal{L}$, there is *exactly* one witness to x's membership (and for $x \notin \mathcal{L}$ there are no witnesses). Batching the verification of general NP statements is a fascinating open question.[16]

Consider a UP language $\mathcal{L}$, with witnesses of length $m = m(|x|)$. Our goal is to design an *interactive proof* $(\mathcal{P}^{\mathsf{IP}}, \mathcal{V}^{\mathsf{IP}})$ where, given k inputs $x_1, \ldots, x_k$, the verifier

---

15. A notion that is equivalent to PCIPs, called "Interactive Oracle Proofs," was independently introduced in work of Ben-Sasson et al. [2016c] (see also Ben-Sasson et al. [2016b], Ben-Sasson et al. [2016a]). See Reingold et al. [2016] for further discussion of the relationship between the two works.

16. We note that we do not see a way to deduce a similar theorem for general NP statements by applying the Valiant-Vazirani randomized reduction from NP to UP [Valiant and Vazirani 1986].

accepts only if $\forall j \in [k]$, $x_j \in \mathcal{L}$ (otherwise the verifier rejects with high probability). We also want the prover strategy to be *efficient*: The (honest) prover should run in polynomial time given witnesses to the inputs' membership in $\mathcal{L}$. A sound but naive protocol is for the prover $\mathcal{P}^{\mathsf{IP}}$ to send all k witnesses $w_1, \ldots, w_k$, and for the verifier $\mathcal{V}^{\mathsf{IP}}$ to verify every pair (x_j, w_j). This protocol is sound (indeed, it is an interactive proof system with soundness error 0), but it is very expensive, requiring communication $k \cdot m$ (and k witness verifications). Our goal is to *batch* the verification of these k UP statements via an interactive proof with communication (and verification time) that is (much) smaller than $k \cdot m$. In what follows we show an interactive proof with communication $(\mathrm{polylog}(k, n) \cdot (k + \mathrm{poly}(m)))$.

Theorem 24.4 (Batch verification theorem for UP) Let $\mathcal{L}$ be a language in UP with witnesses of length $m = m(n) = \mathrm{poly}(n)$, and take $k = k(n) \geq 1$. Then, there is an interactive proof that, on input $(x_1, \ldots, x_k) \in \{0, 1\}^{k \cdot n}$, verifies that for every $j \in [k]$, $x_j \in \mathcal{L}$, with perfect completeness, soundness 1/2, and the following complexities:

- The communication complexity is $\mathrm{polylog}(k, n) \cdot (k + \mathrm{poly}(m))$.
- The number of rounds is $\mathrm{polylog}(k)$.
- The running time of the verifier is $\mathrm{polylog}(k, n) \cdot ((k \cdot n) + \mathrm{poly}(m))$.
- The (honest) prover, given witnesses $(w_1, \ldots, w_k) \in \{0, 1\}^{k \cdot m}$ for the inputs' membership in $\mathcal{L}$, runs in time $\mathrm{poly}(k, n)$.

The remainder of this section is devoted to a proof sketch for Theorem 24.4. We note that Reingold, Rothblum, and Rothblum [Reingold et al. 2018] construct an improved protocol, where for any desired constant $\delta > 0$, the batched communication complexity is $k^\delta \cdot \mathrm{poly}(m)$ and the number of rounds is constant.

A Tantalizing (but Flawed) Protocol. We begin by considering a (flawed) attempt to use PCPs in the design of a sound protocol. For this, assume that the language $\mathcal{L} \in \mathsf{UP}$ has a PCP proof system with proofs of length $a = a(n) = \mathrm{poly}(m)$, and a verifier $\mathcal{V}^{\mathsf{PCP}}$ who makes at most $q = q(n) = O(\mathrm{polylog}(a(n)))$ queries. We assume that the PCP verifier is nonadaptive, and its queries depend only on its random coins (as is the case for standard constructions). As $\mathcal{L} \in \mathsf{UP}$, we can assume that for each $x \in \mathcal{L}$, there is a *unique* PCP string $\alpha \in \{0, 1\}^a$ that makes the verifier accept (on input x) with probability 1.[17] We note that this is the main reason we need

---

17. In fact, we can allow more than one PCP string that makes the verifier accept with probability 1. All that we require is that there exist a unique such PCP string α, where given x and a candidate PCP $\alpha' \in \{0, 1\}^a$, we can test in polynomial time whether $\alpha = \alpha'$. This property is satisfied by standard

$\mathcal{L}$ to be a UP language (rather than any language in NP). Using a PCP with the above properties, we wish to design an interactive proof $(\mathcal{P}^{\mathsf{IP}}, \mathcal{V}^{\mathsf{IP}})$ for verifying that $\forall j \in [k], x_j \in \mathcal{L}$.

Consider the following tantalizing (but insecure) protocol. The verifier $\mathcal{V}^{\mathsf{IP}}$ runs $\mathcal{V}^{\mathsf{PCP}}$ to generate k sets of PCP queries for verifying each of the k statements. By the above assumption regarding $\mathcal{V}^{\mathsf{PCP}}$, our verifier $\mathcal{V}^{\mathsf{IP}}$ can use the same random coins for verifying all k statements, and they will issue the same set $S \subset [a]$ of queries. Now $\mathcal{V}^{\mathsf{IP}}$ sends the query set S to the untrusted prover, receives answers for each of the k PCPs, and accepts if and only if for every $j \in [k]$, the answers provided for the jth PCP make $\mathcal{V}^{\mathsf{PCP}}$ accept on input x_j. This requires roughly $O(k \cdot q) = O(k \cdot \mathrm{polylog}(a))$ communication, but it does not guarantee *any* soundness. The problem is that a cheating prover in the interactive proof setting is completely adaptive and can tailor its responses to $\mathcal{V}^{\mathsf{PCP}}$'s queries in an arbitrary manner. Even if $x_{j*} \notin \mathcal{L}$, *after* the cheating (interactive proof) prover sees the queries made by $\mathcal{V}^{\mathsf{PCP}}$, it can tailor answers that make $\mathcal{V}^{\mathsf{PCP}}$ accept. The PCP's soundness is only guaranteed if the entire proof string is fixed in advance, *before* the PCP verifier's queries are made.

Toward Sound Batching. Building on the "tantalizing protocol," we now present our first attempt for a sound batch verification protocol. We assume that the honest prover $\mathcal{P}^{\mathsf{IP}}$ is given as input k witnesses, from which it can construct k PCP proofs, where $\alpha_j \in \{0, 1\}^a$ is a PCP for the jth statement x_j. The protocol proceeds as follows:

1. $\mathcal{P}^{\mathsf{IP}}$ constructs a $k \times a$ matrix A whose rows are the PCP proofs for the k statements:

$$A = \begin{pmatrix} \alpha_1 \\ \alpha_2 \\ \dots \\ \alpha_k \end{pmatrix}.$$

PCP constructions (applied to UP statements), and it comes for free when there is a single fully correct α (as above), so long as q is a constant. We mention that Goldreich and Sudan [2006, Definition 5.6] studied a stronger notion of PCPs, called strong PCPs, in which the rejection probability of the PCP verifier needs to be proportional to the distance of the given PCP from the prescribed PCP.

$\mathcal{P}^{IP}$ computes the parity of A's columns and sends these parities to the verifier. We view this vector of parities (one per column of A) as a "checksum" $chksum = \bigoplus_{j \in [k]} \alpha_j$.

2. $\mathcal{V}^{IP}$ receives a vector $\widetilde{chksum} \in \{0, 1\}^a$. It proceeds to choose a single set of random coins for the PCP verifier $\mathcal{V}^{PCP}$. These coins specify a set $S \subseteq [a]$ of q queries to the k (alleged) PCPs, and $\mathcal{V}^{IP}$ sends S to $\mathcal{P}^{IP}$. (Recall that we assume that the PCP verifier's queries are nonadaptive, and depend only on its random coins.)

3. $\mathcal{P}^{IP}$ receives the set S of coordinates, and for every $j \in [k]$ it sends back the values of the jth PCP (the jth row), restricted to the q entries in S. We view the answers for the jth row as an assignment $\phi_j : S \to \{0, 1\}$.

4. The verifier $\mathcal{V}^{IP}$ runs two tests (and accepts only if they both pass):

   (a) **PCP check.** For every $j \in [k]$, the prover's PCP answers $\{\phi_j(\xi)\}_{\xi \in S}$ make $\mathcal{V}^{PCP}$ accept the input x_j (the same random string, chosen above, is used for all k PCP verifications).

   (b) **Consistency check.** For every query $\xi \in S$, the ξth bit of $\widetilde{chksum}$ indeed equals the parity of the values claimed for the ξth column of A. That is,

$$\forall \xi \in S : \widetilde{chksum}[\xi] = \bigoplus_{j \in [k]} \phi_j(\xi).$$

This batch verification protocol is quite efficient: The communication complexity is only $a + O(k \cdot q)$ bits, a considerable savings over the naive sound protocol that required $k \cdot a$ bits. The verifier $\mathcal{V}^{IP}$ runs in time $O(a + k \cdot |\mathcal{V}^{PCP}|)$, where $|\mathcal{V}^{PCP}|$ is the running time of the PCP verifier. The (honest) prover's running time is $k \cdot \text{poly}(m)$ to construct the k PCPs (from the witnesses), and (given these PCPs) the running time to compute its protocol messages is $O(k \cdot a)$. There are three messages exchanged.

Soundness for Single Deviations. The question, of course, is whether the protocol is sound (completeness follows by construction). Unfortunately, the protocol is not sound in general.[18] However, it *is* sound against an interesting class of cheating

---

18. Consider inputs $x_1, \ldots, x_{k-2} \in \mathcal{L}$ and $x_{k-1} = x_k = x^*$ for some $x^* \notin \mathcal{L}$. Consider a cheating prover that generates the correct PCPs $\alpha_1, \ldots, \alpha_{k-2}$ for $x_1, \ldots, x_{k-2}$, and sends $\widetilde{chksum} = \bigoplus_{j \in [k-2]} \alpha_j$ to the verifier (i.e., the checksum excludes the last two inputs). Once the verifier sends PCP queries S, the prover answers honestly on all but the last two rows. For the latter two rows, it finds some assignment $\widetilde{\phi} : S \to \{0, 1\}$ that satisfies the PCP verifier with respect to input

provers, which we call *single-deviation provers*. For this, we focus on proving soundness when there is only a single $j^* \in [k]$ s.t. $x_{j^*} \notin \mathcal{L}$. In Step 3 (answering the PCP queries), we restrict the cheating prover $\tilde{\mathcal{P}}$ as follows. For every $j \neq j^*$, $\tilde{\mathcal{P}}$ knows the *unique* "correct" PCP $\alpha_j \in \{0, 1\}^a$ (see above) that makes the verifier $\mathcal{V}^{\mathsf{PCP}}$ accept the input x_j with probability 1 (note that α_j, being the unique correct PCP, is fixed in advance before the protocol begins). In Step 3 of the protocol, $\tilde{\mathcal{P}}$ answers all queries to the jth PCP (for $j \neq j^*$) according to α_j. We emphasize that $\tilde{\mathcal{P}}$ is unrestricted in Step 1, it can send an arbitrary $\widetilde{chksum}$, and it can send arbitrary and adaptive answers to the j^*th PCP in Step 3 (after seeing the query set S). In particular, the tantalizing protocol is completely insecure even against single-deviation cheating provers.

We show that the protocol described above *is* sound against single-deviation cheating provers. Suppose that a cheating single-deviation prover $\tilde{\mathcal{P}}$ makes the verifier accept with probability ϵ. We use $\tilde{\mathcal{P}}$ to construct a *fixed* proof $\tilde{\alpha}_{j^*}$ that makes the PCP verifier accept the input $x_{j^*} \notin \mathcal{L}$ with probability ϵ, and conclude that the interactive proof protocol is sound. We derive $\tilde{\alpha}_{j^*}$ from the checksum value $\widetilde{chksum}$ sent by $\tilde{\mathcal{P}}$ in Step 1 (without loss of generality the cheating prover is deterministic and its first message is fixed) by using

$$\tilde{\alpha}_{j^*} = \widetilde{chksum} \oplus \left(\bigoplus_{j \neq j^*} \alpha_j \right).$$

We claim that on input x_{j^*} the PCP verifier $\mathcal{V}^{\mathsf{PCP}}$ will accept $\tilde{\alpha}_{j^*}$ with probability ϵ. To see this, recall that $\tilde{\mathcal{P}}$ answers all queries to rows $j \neq j^*$ according to α_j. Whenever $\tilde{\mathcal{P}}$ makes $\mathcal{V}^{\mathsf{IP}}$ accept, it must pass the consistency check in Step 4(b), and thus it must answer the queries to the j^*th PCP according to $\tilde{\alpha}_{j^*}$. Since it also needs to pass the PCP check in Step 4(a), we conclude that whenever $\tilde{\mathcal{P}}$ makes $\mathcal{V}^{\mathsf{IP}}$ accept, it must also be the case that the PCP answers $\tilde{\alpha}_{j^*}|_S$ make the PCP verifier $\mathcal{V}^{\mathsf{PCP}}$ accept on input x_{j^*}.

Implicit Commitments and Soundness for *d* Deviations.   Reflecting on the soundness of the above protocol, observe that $\widetilde{chksum}$ *implicitly* commits a single-deviation prover to the PCP string $\tilde{\alpha}_{j^*}$ for $x_{j^*} \notin \mathcal{L}$. Once the prover is committed, soundness of the protocol naturally follows from the soundness of the PCP. Of course, $\widetilde{chksum}$ is much too short to include an *explicit* commitment to the k PCP strings (for the k

---

x^* and queries S (this is easy to do given S), and sends $\tilde{\phi}$ as the answer to the PCP queries for rows $k - 1$ and k. The two $\tilde{\phi}$'s cancel out and so the consistency check passes and the verifier accepts.

inputs x_j). Thus, we should not expect soundness against general provers (indeed, it is not clear how to leverage the PCP's soundness against general adaptive provers). Nevertheless, it is not hard to generalize the above protocol to handle d deviations as long as d is not too large.

To extend soundness, in Step 1 of the protocol, we ask the prover to send a "more robust" $O(d \cdot \log k)$-bit checksum for each column of the matrix A, where this checksum has the property that for every $y \in \{0, 1\}^k$ and $z \in \{0, 1\}^{O(d \cdot \log k)}$, there is at most one $y' \in \{0, 1\}^k$ (including y itself) at Hamming distance d or less from y whose checksum equals z. Such a checksum can be constructed using standard techniques from the error-correcting code literature. Putting together these checksums (one per column of A), we get a matrix $chksum \in \{0, 1\}^{O(d \cdot \log k) \times a}$, which $\mathcal{P}^{\mathsf{IP}}$ sends to $\mathcal{V}^{\mathsf{IP}}$. The verifier $\mathcal{V}^{\mathsf{IP}}$ receives a potentially corrupted checksum $\widetilde{chksum} \in \{0, 1\}^{O(d \cdot \log k) \times a}$, and in Step 4(b), it checks that the PCP answers are consistent with this "more robust" checksum. The protocol is unchanged otherwise. Note that this increases the communication to $O((d \cdot \log k \cdot a) + (k \cdot q))$, which remains interesting so long as $d \ll k$.

The new checksum matrix $chksum$ is still not long enough to commit an arbitrary prover to k PCP strings. But intuitively it can implicitly commit a prover as long as it does not deviate on more than d rows. More formally, for every $j \neq j^*$,[19] the cheating prover $\tilde{\mathcal{P}}$ knows the unique PCP α_j. After the verifier specifies the query set S in Step 2, a d-deviation prover $\tilde{\mathcal{P}}$ (adaptively) chooses a set $J^* \subset [k]$ of d of the instances (or rows), and can provide arbitrary answers on queries to those d PCPs. The only restriction is that for every $j \notin J^*$, $\tilde{\mathcal{P}}$ answers the queries to the jth PCP according to the predetermined PCP α_j.

Similarly to the argument for single-deviation prover, it can be shown that the possibly corrupt checksum string $\widetilde{chksum} \in \{0, 1\}^{O(d \cdot \log k) \times a}$ induces an *implicit* commitment to a PCP string $\tilde{\alpha}_{j^*}$ for x_{j^*} (the input that is not in $\mathcal{L}$). In fact, it induces commitments to all the k PCP strings. Of course, this argument only works because we restricted $\tilde{\mathcal{P}}$ to d deviations.

Amplifying Deviations and a $\sqrt{k}$ Overhead. We described a batch verification protocol that is sound for d deviations. We will now show how to exploit it against a general cheating prover (even though the protocol itself sound for such a prover). The key observation is that while even the more robust checksum does not directly induce a commitment to the j^*th PCP, it does tie $\tilde{\mathcal{P}}$'s hands in an important way.

---

19. Recall that we assume that there is exactly one row j^* such that $x_{j^*} \notin \mathcal{L}$ (this assumption is for simplicity and without loss of generality; see Theorem 24.1, below).

In answering PCP queries for the inputs $\{x_j\}_{j \neq j^*}$ *that are in the language,* $\tilde{\mathcal{P}}$ is faced with two hard choices: It can provide answers that are mostly consistent with the correct PCPs (on all but d of the rows), but then soundness against d deviations implies that $\mathcal{V}^{\mathsf{IP}}$ will reject. Alternatively, if $\tilde{\mathcal{P}}$ deviates on d or more rows, then it is sending many answers that are inconsistent with the *unique* correct PCPs, and this is much easier for the verifier to detect (as we show next).

To obtain a sound batching protocol, we add an additional round of communication, where $\mathcal{V}^{\mathsf{IP}}$ picks $O(k/d)$ of the rows at random and asks $\tilde{\mathcal{P}}$ to send those rows' PCPs (in their entirety). If $\tilde{\mathcal{P}}$ deviated from the unique correct PCPs on at least d rows, it is likely that there is some row j that $\mathcal{V}^{\mathsf{IP}}$ requested where $\tilde{\mathcal{P}}$ has deviated. Either $\tilde{\mathcal{P}}$ sends a PCP that is inconsistent with its past answers, or it is forced to send $\tilde{\alpha}_j$ that is not the unique correct PCP for $x_j \in \mathcal{L}$. In either case, $\mathcal{V}^{\mathsf{IP}}$ rejects. To "catch" a cheating prover whenever $\tilde{\alpha}_j$ is not the unique correct PCP, we crucially use the property that for each $x \in \mathcal{L}$, there is a unique correct PCP α, and the verifier can check whether $\tilde{\alpha}_j = \alpha$ in polynomial time (e.g., by extracting the unique accepting UP witness w_j from $\tilde{\alpha}_j$, and then building the PCP proof α from w_j). This is also why our soundness argument applies to UP statement, but does not extend to general NP statements.

The final check adds $O((k/d) \cdot a)$ communication bits (and verification time), and results in a sound protocol for batching UP statements. Setting $d = \sqrt{k}$, we obtain a protocol with $\tilde{O}(\sqrt{k} \cdot a + k \cdot q)$ communication (compared with $k \cdot a$ for the naive protocol).

Here, we use the protocol that is secure against d-deviation provers as a "deviation amplification" protocol. We find it noteworthy that this deviation amplification forces $\tilde{\mathcal{P}}$ to cheat (and get caught!) on inputs *that are in the language*. This is one of the key insights in constructing our batching protocols.

Remark 24.1 (Many inputs not in $\mathcal{L}$) We assumed throughout that there was only a single $j^* \in [k]$ for which $x_{j^*} \notin \mathcal{L}$. More generally, the protocol is sound for any number of inputs that are not in $\mathcal{L}$. Soundness for the general case is shown via a similar argument: If there are less than d inputs that are not in the language, then the above argument goes through in a very similar manner. If there are more than d inputs that are not in the language, then when $\mathcal{V}^{\mathsf{IP}}$ picks $O(k/d)$ statements and checks them explicitly, it will likely "catch" an input that is not in $\mathcal{L}$ and will reject, since the cheating prover cannot supply an accepting PCP for a false statement.

Improving the Dependence on k. Finally, we turn our attention to improving the communication to $(\mathrm{polylog}(k) \cdot (a + k \cdot q))$, as claimed in Theorem 24.4. We begin with the d-deviation protocol. Recall that we can use this protocol to amplify deviations, forcing a cheating $\tilde{\mathcal{P}}$ to send "incorrect" PCP values for at least d rows. As above, $\mathcal{V}^{\text{IP}}$ chooses a random set $J_1 \subset [k]$ of size $O(k/d)$, and we know that with good probability over the choice of J_1 there is at least one row $j \in J_1$ for which either $x_j \notin \mathcal{L}$, or $x_j \in \mathcal{L}$, but $\tilde{\mathcal{P}}$ sent incorrect PCP values: $\exists \xi \in S : \phi_j(\xi) \neq \alpha_j|_\xi$ (where α_j is the unique correct PCP for x_j). Above, $\mathcal{V}^{\text{IP}}$ detected this by asking $\tilde{\mathcal{P}}$ to send the correct PCP for every $j \in J_1$. This guaranteed soundness, but at a cost of $(|J_1| \cdot a)$ communication.

Observe, however, that once $\mathcal{V}^{\text{IP}}$ picks J_1, we are in a familiar situation: We have a relatively large set J_1 of statements, and we would like to detect whether $\tilde{\mathcal{P}}$ is "cheating" on at least one of these statements, but without explicitly sending all $|J_1|$ witnesses. The natural approach is to recurse: Use the deviation amplification protocol to amplify the number of deviations *within* J_1 to at least d rows, pick a smaller set $J_2 \subset J_1$ of size $O(|J_1|/d)$, and recurse again and again until we have a set J_{final} of size $O(d)$ and for some $j \in J_{final}$ we have $x_j \notin \mathcal{L}$ (or the prover deviated from the prescribed protocol PCP for j). At the "base" of this recursion, the prover can send explicit witnesses for each $j \in J_{final}$. Each run of the deviation amplification protocol only requires $O(d \cdot \log(k) \cdot a + k \cdot q)$ communication, so by setting $d = \log k$ we can get a recursion of depth $O(\log k)$ and a total communication cost of $(\text{polylog}(k) \cdot (a + k \cdot q))$ (with $O(\log k)$ rounds). More generally, we could use different values of d to trade off the number of rounds for communication (and in particular to obtain constant-round protocols).

There is a subtlety in the argument outlined above. Namely, in the recursion, *the* UP *language has changed.* The statement we want to verify for each row $j \in J_1$ is that both: (i) The jth input is in the language—that is, $x_j \in \mathcal{L}$ (as before)—and (ii) for S chosen by the verifier and ϕ_j sent by the prover, the correct PCP α_j for x_j satisfies $\phi_j(\xi) = \alpha_j|_\xi$. These two conditions define a new language $\mathcal{L}'$ over triplets (x, S, ϕ), and we want to verify that $\forall j \in J_1, (x_j, S, \phi_j) \in \mathcal{L}'$. First, observe that if $\mathcal{L} \in$ UP then also $\mathcal{L}' \in$ UP. Moreover, we can modify the PCP system for $\mathcal{L}$ to get a PCP system for $\mathcal{L}'$ with only a small loss in the parameters. Note that in further applications of the recursion, we can keep using the same language $\mathcal{L}'$, it is only the set S and values ϕ_j that change. This yields the protocol of Theorem 24.4.

24.4.2 Batching Unambiguous Interactive Proofs

The iterative interactive proof construction of Theorem 24.2 is based on an efficient batch verification theorem for interactive proofs, which builds on the ideas for batch UP verification outlined in Section 24.4.1. Toward this goal, we describe interactive analogues of the building blocks used in the proof of the UP batching theorem. We discuss these new proof system notions in Section 24.4.2.1, and in Section 24.4.2.2 we provide an overview of the batch verification theorem for interactive proofs. See Reingold et al. [2016] for further details.

24.4.2.1   Unambiguous and Probabilistically Checkable Interactive Proofs

In the setting of UP-verification, inputs in the language had a single (PCP) proof string that convinces the verifier. *Unambiguous interactive proofs* are an interactive analogue.

Unambiguous Interactive Proofs (UIPs).   An *unambiguous* interactive proof system for a language $\mathcal{L}$ is specified by a deterministic (honest) prover $\mathcal{P}$, which we call the *prescribed prover*, and a verifier $\mathcal{V}$ (as in any interactive proof system). Suppose that a cheating prover $\tilde{\mathcal{P}}$ follows the protocol in rounds $1, \ldots, i-1$, but "deviates" in round i, sending a message different from the prescribed message that $\mathcal{P}$ would have sent. In an unambiguous interactive proof, we require that for any round i where $\tilde{\mathcal{P}}$ might first deviate, and for any history in rounds $1, \ldots, i-1$ (which is determined by $\mathcal{V}$'s coin tosses and by the prescribed prover strategy), if the prescribed prover would have sent message $\alpha^{(i)}$, but the cheating prover sends a message $\tilde{\alpha}^{(i)} \neq \alpha^{(i)}$, then the verifier will reject with high probability over its coin tosses in subsequent rounds. Note that this requirement also holds *for inputs that are in the language*, whereas the classical notion of an interactive proof does not make any requirement for such inputs. For inputs that are not in the language, the prescribed prover's first message is a special symbol that tells $\mathcal{V}$ to reject. In particular, if $x \notin \mathcal{L}$, but a cheating prover $\tilde{\mathcal{P}}$ tries to convince $\mathcal{V}$ to accept, then $\tilde{\mathcal{P}}$ needs to deviate from $\mathcal{P}$'s strategy in its first message, and the unambiguity property guarantees that with high probability $\mathcal{V}$ will reject. Thus, any unambiguous IP for $\mathcal{L}$ also guarantees the standard notion of soundness. We note that UP proofs correspond to 1-message deterministic UIPs.

Remark 24.2   It may be helpful to consider some examples of protocols that are unambiguous. A prominent example is the classical Sumcheck protocol [Lund et al. 1992]. There, in every round i, the (honest) prover sends the verifier a low-degree polynomial $P^{(i)}$, and the verifier checks the value of $P^{(i)}$ at a random point $\beta^{(i)}$ (we gloss over the details of this check). If a cheating prover sends a low-degree polynomial $\tilde{P}^{(i)} \neq P^{(i)}$, then with high probability over the verifier's choice of $\beta^{(i)}$ we have $\tilde{P}^{(i)}(\beta^{(i)}) \neq P^{(i)}(\beta^{(i)})$, and the verifier will end up rejecting. Building on this property of the sumcheck protocol, we note that the GKR interactive proof [Goldwasser et al.

2015] is also unambiguous. Another well-known example is the interactive proof for Graph Nonisomorphism of Goldreich et al. [1991]. On the other hand, zero-knowledge proofs are *ambiguous* by design: The honest prover is randomized, and there are many messages that it can send that will end up making the verifier accept.

Probabilistically Checkable Interactive Proofs (PCIPs). Analogously to the UP setting, where batch verification used the power of PCPs, we wish to use a notion of probabilistic checking with low query complexity, but for *interactive* proof systems. That is, we use interactive proof systems where the verifier only reads a few bits of the transcript in checking the proof. These are called *probabilistically checkable interactive proofs* (PCIPs).

A PCIP for a language $\mathcal{L}$ is an interactive proof system, where the protocol is partitioned into two phases. In the *communication* phase, the prover and verifier interact for ℓ rounds and generate a transcript (as in a standard interactive proof). Restricting our attention to public-coin protocols, all that the verifier does in this phase is send random strings $\beta_1, \ldots, \beta_\ell$ (one in each of the ℓ rounds). In the *checking* phase, the verifier queries q bits of the messages sent by the prover and accepts or rejects. For the purposes of this survey, in the checking phase we allow the verifier full access to the random strings $\beta_1, \ldots, \beta_\ell$ that it sent in the communication phase (more generally, we could consider only allowing the verifier query access to these strings). The verifier's running time in a PCIP is just the time for the checking phase (generating queries and deciding whether to accept). Thus, in a PCIP, the query complexity and the verifier's runtime can be much smaller than the transcript length. One can think of the prover and verifier as interactively generating a PCP (comprised of the prover's messages), which is then checked by the verifier. Indeed, a one-message PCIP is simply a PCP. For this overview, we assume that the queries do not depend on the input, only on the random coins chosen by the verifier in the communication phase. See Reingold et al. [2016] for formal definitions and further discussions.

Putting the two foregoing notions together, we define *unambiguous PCIPs*, which play a central role in the proof of the batch verification theorem. A subtlety that we mostly ignore in this overview is that full unambiguity cannot be obtained with small query complexity: If a cheating prover $\tilde{\mathcal{P}}$ changes just one bit of the ith message, and the verifier only makes a small number of queries to the message, this change will likely go unnoticed, and unambiguity is lost. There are several ways to reconcile these two notions, and the one most convenient for our purpose is to restrict the family of cheating provers such that every message sent by the cheating prover (as well as by the prescribed prover) is a codeword in a high-distance error-correcting code (the low-degree extension). We refer to this notion as unambiguous PCIP *with respect to encoded provers*. We remark that any unambiguous PCIP *with respect to encoded provers* can be easily transformed into a sound PCIP, by having the verifier run low-degree tests on each message sent by the prover. Thus, we focus our attention on the goal of constructing PCIP *with respect to encoded provers*. See Reingold et al. [2016] for a more complete discussion and formal definitions.

24.4.2.2 Batching Using Unambiguous PCIPs

We are now ready to describe the batch verification protocol for unambiguous PCIPs with respect to encoded provers. Given such a proof system $(\mathcal{P}, \mathcal{V})$ for a language $\mathcal{L}$, we obtain a batched proof system for verifying k instances of $\mathcal{L}$, where the overhead in terms of the communication is sublinear in k. We note that an *inefficient* batch verification theorem for (general) interactive proofs also follows from the IP = PSPACE theorem. However, that batched protocol does not preserve the round complexity or prover efficiency of the base protocols (and is thus not helpful for constructing interactive proofs with efficient provers or small round complexity).

Controlling the Query Complexity. In this overview, we focus on the bounding the communication complexity of the batched PCIP (in particular, the communication will grow by a multiplicative factor that is only polylogarithmic in k). We note, however, that batching will degrade the query complexity and verification time by a multiplicative factor of k. In the iterative construction of Theorem 24.2, this becomes a problem (because we need sublinear query complexity for efficient batching, see below). This can be resolved, however, using a "query reduction" transformation (see the details in Reingold et al. [2016]). Thus, the iterative construction of Theorem 24.2 repeatedly uses a PCIP-batching step, followed by a PCIP-query-reduction step (which also reduces the verifier's runtime), gradually obtaining powerful PCIPs (and interactive proofs) for longer and longer computations. This is similar in spirit to the delicate balancing of parameters in the iterative constructions of Dinur [2007], Reingold [2008], and Reingold et al. [2000] (also abstracted in Goldreich [2011]).

Soundness for *d* Deviations. Let $(\mathcal{P}, \mathcal{V})$ be an unambiguous PCIP for $\mathcal{L}$. Recall that in the UP batching, we began by constructing a sound protocol for provers that only deviate on d of the k inputs. We later use this protocol for "deviation amplification." The ideas translate to the UIP setting, where we use $(\mathcal{P}, \mathcal{V})$ to construct a deviation amplification protocol $(\mathcal{P}_{\text{amplify}}, \mathcal{V}_{\text{amplify}})$. The high level is as follows: The protocol starts with ℓ rounds that correspond to the ℓ communication rounds of the "base" protocol. In each round i, for each $j \in [k]$, let $\alpha_j^{(i)} \in \{0, 1\}^a$ be the message that the (prescribed) "base" prover $\mathcal{P}$ would send on input x_j in round i given randomness $\beta^{(1)}, \ldots, \beta^{(i-1)}$ (which $\mathcal{V}_{\text{amplify}}$ sent in previous rounds). The prover $\mathcal{P}_{\text{amplify}}$ constructs a $k \times a$ matrix $A^{(i)}$, whose rows are the messages $(\alpha_1^{(i)}, \ldots, \alpha_k^{(i)})$, and sends its checksum $chksum^{(i)} \in \{0, 1\}^{O(d \cdot \log k) \times a}$ to the verifier. The verifier receives $\widetilde{chksum}^{(i)}$, and sends random coins $\beta^{(i)}$ as sent by $\mathcal{V}$ in the base protocol (the same random coins are used for all k inputs).

Next, $\mathcal{V}_{\text{amplify}}$ chooses random coins for $\mathcal{V}$'s query/decision phase, sends the queries $S \subset [\ell] \times [a]$ to $\mathcal{P}_{\text{amplify}}$, and receives answers $\{\phi_j : S \to \{0, 1\}\}$ to those queries for each of the k base protocols $j \in [k]$. Now, $\mathcal{V}_{\text{amplify}}$ accepts if and only if (i) $\mathcal{V}$ would have accepted the answers in all k protocols, and (ii) the answers are consistent with the checksums sent in rounds $1, \ldots, \ell$. Note that running these checks requires reading the values in $\{\phi_j\}$ in their entirety ($k \cdot q$ queries), and also making $d \cdot q$ queries into the transcript in rounds $1, \ldots, \ell$ to verify the checksum.

The proof of soundness against a d-deviation cheating prover is similar to the analogous proof for UP batch verification: When a d-deviation prover sends the robust checksum value $\widetilde{chksum}^{(i)}$, it implicitly commits to messages in all k of the protocols. Thus, if $\tilde{\mathcal{P}}$ could get $\mathcal{V}_{\text{amplify}}$ to accept, we could derive a cheating prover for the base protocol, breaking its soundness. We note that it is critically important for this argument that $\tilde{\mathcal{P}}$ sends $\widetilde{chksum}^{(i)}$ (and commits to the messages in round i), before it knows the random coins $\beta^{(i)}$ that will be chosen by the verifier for round i.

Detecting Many Deviations. As in the UP batching, we leverage soundness against d deviations to amplify a cheating prover's deviations from the prescribed strategy, and obtain sound batch verification (without any assumptions on the number of deviations). Here too, a cheating prover $\tilde{\mathcal{P}}$ is faced with a choice. It can deviate from the prescribed strategy on d or fewer of the inputs, but then the verifier will reject with high probability (by soundness against d deviations). So $\tilde{\mathcal{P}}$ may well choose to deviate on more than d of the inputs. Suppose this is the case, and there exists a subset $J^* \subseteq [k]$ of at least d of the statements, such that for every $j \in J^*$, the query answers in ϕ_j are not consistent with the prescribed strategy. The verifier $\mathcal{V}_{\text{amplify}}$ would like to detect this.

Recall that in the UP batch verification, this was simple: The verifier could pick a set J_1 of $O(k/d)$ of the statements, and request the "full proof" for the statements in J_1. Here, however, it is not sufficient to ask $\tilde{\mathcal{P}}$ to send the entire transcript for those statements. To see this, suppose that for $j^* \in (J^* \cap J_1)$, the values in ϕ_{j^*} are not consistent with the prescribed strategy on the chosen random coins $(\beta^{(1)}, \ldots, \beta^{(\ell)})$. Unambiguity of $(\mathcal{P}, \mathcal{V})$ does not guarantee that *every* transcript that is consistent with ϕ_{j^*} makes $\mathcal{V}$ reject (given the fixed coins $(\beta^{(1)}, \dots, \beta^{(\ell)})$). Indeed, since the coins are already fixed, there may well be many possible transcripts that make $\mathcal{V}$ accept and are consistent with ϕ_{j^*}. Thus, if all $\mathcal{V}_{\text{amplify}}$ did was ask $\mathcal{P}_{\text{amplify}}$ to send an accepting transcript consistent with ϕ_{j^*}, then $\tilde{P}$ could find such a transcript, and $\mathcal{V}_{\text{amplify}}$ would not detect that there was a deviation in the j^*th statement.

To make soundness go through, we design an *interactive protocol* $(\mathcal{P}_1, \mathcal{V}_1)$ for verifying that ϕ_{j^*} is consistent with the prescribed strategy on input x_{j^*} and random coins $(\beta^{(1)}, \dots, \beta^{(\ell)})$. We obtain soundness by running this protocol for each statement $j^* \in J_1$. Loosely speaking, the protocol goes as follows. First we ask $\tilde{P}$ to send the entire transcript for that statement, and let $\mathcal{V}_{\text{amplify}}$ verify that this transcript is consistent with ϕ_{j^*} (and makes $\mathcal{V}$ accept). Let $(\tilde{\alpha}^{(1)}, \dots \tilde{\alpha}^{(\ell)})$ be the prover messages in this transcript. Now $\mathcal{V}_1$ simulates $\mathcal{V}$ in ℓ parallel executions of the original PCIP $(\mathcal{P}, \mathcal{V})$. At execution i, the protocol $(\mathcal{P}, \mathcal{V})$ is simulated from round i as a continuation of the ith prefix of the transcript sent by $\tilde{P}$ (namely, assuming that the first $i - 1$ verifier messages were $(\beta^{(1)}, \dots, \beta^{(i-1)})$ and the first i prover messages were $(\tilde{\alpha}^{(1)}, \dots \tilde{\alpha}^{(i)})$). It is important that the verifier uses fresh randomness $(\gamma^{(i)}, \dots, \gamma^{(\ell)})$ for the remaining rounds (the random strings $(\gamma^{(1)}, \dots, \gamma^{(\ell)})$ could be shared among the parallel simulations). Soundness follows, since if the transcript sent by $\tilde{P}$ first deviates from the prescribed proof at round i^*, then, by the definition of unambiguity, $\mathcal{V}$ is likely to reject in the corresponding simulation of $(\mathcal{P}, \mathcal{V})$ using $i = i^*$.

Sound Batch Verification. Building on the consistency-checking protocol $(\mathcal{P}_1, \mathcal{V}_1)$, we construct a batch verification protocol $(\mathcal{P}_{\text{amplify}}, \mathcal{V}_{\text{amplify}})$, where the prover and verifier first run the deviation amplification protocol. Then, $\mathcal{V}_{\text{amplify}}$ picks at random the set J_1 of $O(k/d)$ of the instances, and the prover and verifier run the above protocol $(\mathcal{P}_1, \mathcal{V}_1)$ explicitly on each $j^* \in J_1$. Taking the number of rounds ℓ to be a constant, $(\mathcal{P}_1, \mathcal{V}_1)$ is not much more expensive than $(\mathcal{P}, \mathcal{V})$, and when using $d = \sqrt{k}$, this yields batch verification whose communication only grows by a factor of roughly $\sqrt{k}$.

To improve the dependence on k, we recurse as in the UP batching theorem. $\mathcal{P}_{\text{amplify}}$ and $\mathcal{V}_{\text{amplify}}$ use the protocol $(\mathcal{P}_1, \mathcal{V}_1)$ as a "base protocol," and run the deviation amplification protocol to amplify the number of deviations *within* J_1 to at least d instances (note that $\mathcal{P}_{\text{amplify}}$ and $\mathcal{V}_{\text{amplify}}$ never explicitly run the protocol $(\mathcal{P}_1, \mathcal{V}_1)$). Now $\mathcal{V}_{\text{amplify}}$ picks a smaller set $J_2 \subset J_1$ of size $O(|J_1|/d)$, and the prover and verifier recurse again and again until they obtain a set J_{final} of size $O(d)$ and a protocol $(\mathcal{P}_{\text{final}}, \mathcal{V}_{\text{final}})$ that will w.h.p. reject at least one of the instances in J_{final}. At the "base" of this recursion, the prover and verifier explicitly run the protocol $(\mathcal{P}_{\text{final}}, \mathcal{V}_{\text{final}})$ on every instance in the set J_{final}.

While the complexity of the "base protocol" grows by a factor of ℓ in every level of the recursion, the set of instances under consideration shrinks by a factor of d. Taking $d = k^\tau$ for a constant $0 < \tau \ll 1$, we only have a constant number of levels in the recursion, and the final consistency-checking protocol $(\mathcal{P}_{final}, \mathcal{V}_{final})$ is only roughly $\ell^{O(1/\tau)}$ times more expensive than the base protocol (throughout we think of ℓ as a constant). The resulting protocol $(\mathcal{P}_{amplify}, \mathcal{V}_{amplify})$ has roughly $O(\ell)$ rounds, communication complexity $\text{poly}(\ell) \cdot k^\tau \cdot c$, prover runtime $\text{poly}(\ell) \cdot k \cdot \mathcal{P}\text{time}$ and verifier runtime $\text{poly}(\ell) \cdot k \cdot \mathcal{V}\text{time}$. The query complexity is $(\text{poly}(\ell) \cdot k \cdot q)$.

The soundness error grows linearly with the number of levels in the recursion, yielding $O(\epsilon)$ soundness. For simplicity, we assume here that ϵ is larger than $(1/k^{2\tau})$, so we can take each set $J_m \in \{J_1, \ldots, J_{final}\}$ to be of size $O(\log(1/\epsilon) \cdot |J_{m-1}|/d)$ and still have a constant number of levels in the recursion. The size bound on J_m guarantees that the probability that any set in the sequence $J_1, \ldots, J_{final}$ "misses" the deviating instances is smaller than ϵ.

Acknowledgments

None of this research could have been possible without the creativity, brilliance, and inspiration of Shafi Goldwasser and Silvio Micali. I thank them for laying the foundations for the theoretical study of cryptography and its relationship to complexity theory. This acknowledgement is far too brief to convey my gratitude to Shafi for everything that I have learned from her, for her direct contributions to the study of DEIPs, and for her unwavering support, mentoring, and friendship. Many thanks to my co-authors on works described above, Yael Kalai, Omer Reingold, and Ron Rothblum, for invaluable and treasured collaborations, and for allowing me to include extensive excerpts from our work in this survey. Special thanks to Oded Goldreich for illuminating conversations and collaborations on these topics, for his contributions to the study of doubly efficient interactive proofs, and for reviewing this manuscript.

This project has received funding from the European Research Council (ERC) under the European Union's Horizon 2020 research and innovation programme (grant agreement No. 819702).

References

S. Arora and S. Safra. 1998. Probabilistic checking of proofs: A new characterization of NP. *Journal of the ACM*, 45(1): 70–122. DOI: 10.1145/273865.273901. 650

S. Arora, C. Lund, R. Motwani, M. Sudan, and M. Szegedy. 1998. Proof verification and the hardness of approximation problems. *Journal of the ACM*, 45(3): 501–555. DOI: 10.1145/278298.278306. 650

L. Babai and S. Moran. 1988. Arthur–Merlin games: A randomized proof system, and a hierarchy of complexity classes. *Journal of Computer and System Sciences*, 36(2): 254–276. DOI: 10.1016/0022-0000(88)90028-1. 650

E. Ben-Sasson, A. Chiesa, A. Gabizon, M. Riabzev, and N. Spooner. 2016a. Short interactive oracle proofs with constant query complexity, via composition and sumcheck. Cryptology ePrint Archive, Report 2016/324. http://eprint.iacr.org/. 674

E. Ben-Sasson, A. Chiesa, A. Gabizon, and M. Virza. 2016b. Quasi-linear size zero knowledge from linear-algebraic pcps. In *Theory of Cryptography—13th International Conference, TCC 2016-A, Tel Aviv, Israel, January 10–13, 2016, Proceedings, Part II*, pp. 33–64. DOI: 10.1007/978-3-662-49099-0_2. 674

E. Ben-Sasson, A. Chiesa, and N. Spooner. 2016c. Interactive oracle proofs. Cryptology ePrint Archive, Report 2016/116. http://eprint.iacr.org/. 674

G. Brassard, D. Chaum, and C. Crépeau. 1988. Minimum disclosure proofs of knowledge. *Journal of Computer and System Sciences*, 37(2): 156–189. DOI: 10.1016/0022-0000(88)90005-0. 651

S. A. Cook. 1971. The complexity of theorem-proving procedures. In *Proceedings of the 3rd Annual ACM Symposium on Theory of Computing, May 3–5, 1971, Shaker Heights, Ohio, USA*, pp. 151–158. DOI: 10.1145/800157.805047. 650

G. Cormode, M. Mitzenmacher, and J. Thaler. 2012. Practical verified computation with streaming interactive proofs. In *Innovations in Theoretical Computer Science 2012, Cambridge, MA, USA, January 8–10, 2012*, pp. 90–112. DOI: 10.1145/2090236.2090245. 655

I. Dinur. 2007. The PCP theorem by gap amplification. *Journal of the ACM*, 54(3): 12. DOI: 10.1145/1236457.1236459. 684

F. Ergün, R. Kumar, and R. Rubinfeld. 2004. Fast approximate probabilistically checkable proofs. *Information and Computation*, 189(2): 135–159. 655

O. Goldreich. 2011. Bravely, moderately: A common theme in four recent works. In O. Goldreich, ed., *Studies in Complexity and Cryptography*, volume 6650 of *Lecture Notes in Computer Science*, pp. 373–389. Springer. ISBN 978-3-642-22669-4. DOI: 10.1007/978-3-642-22670-0_26. 684

O. Goldreich. 2018. On doubly-efficient interactive proof systems. *Foundations and Trends in Theoretical Computer Science*, 13(3): 158–246. DOI: 10.1561/0400000084. 651, 663, 664

O. Goldreich and J. Håstad. 1998. On the complexity of interactive proofs with bounded communication. *Information Processing Letters*, 67(4): 205–214. DOI: 10.1016/S0020-0190(98)00116-1. 653

O. Goldreich and G. N. Rothblum. 2018a. Simple doubly-efficient interactive proof systems for locally-characterizable sets. In *9th Innovations in Theoretical Computer Science Conference, ITCS 2018, January 11–14, 2018, Cambridge, MA, USA*, pp. 18:1–18:19. DOI: 10.4230/LIPIcs.ITCS.2018.18. 656

O. Goldreich and G. N. Rothblum. 2018b. Counting t-cliques: Worst-case to average-case reductions and direct interactive proof systems. In *59th IEEE Annual Symposium on Foundations of Computer Science, FOCS 2018, Paris, France, October 7–9, 2018*, pp. 77–88. DOI: 10.1109/FOCS.2018.00017. 656

O. Goldreich and G. N. Rothblum. 2018c. Constant-round interactive proof systems for AC0[2] and NC1. *Electronic Colloquium on Computational Complexity (ECCC)*, 25: 69. https://eccc.weizmann.ac.il/report/2018/069. 656

O. Goldreich and M. Sudan. 2006. Locally testable codes and PCPs of almost-linear length. *Journal of the ACM*, 53(4): 558–655. 676

O. Goldreich, S. Micali, and A. Wigderson. 1991. Proofs that yield nothing but their validity for all languages in NP have zero-knowledge proof systems. *Journal of the ACM*, 38(3): 691–729. DOI: 10.1145/116825.116852. 650, 683

O. Goldreich, S. Goldwasser, and D. Ron. 1998. Property testing and its connection to learning and approximation. *Journal of the ACM*, 45(4): 653–750. DOI: 10.1145/285055.285060. 655

S. Goldwasser, S. Micali, and C. Rackoff. 1989. The knowledge complexity of interactive proof systems. *SIAM Journal on Computing*, 18(1): 186–208. DOI: 10.1137/0218012. 650, 658

S. Goldwasser, Y. T. Kalai, and G. N. Rothblum. 2008. Delegating computation: Interactive proofs for muggles. In *40th Symposium on Theory of Computing, STOC*, pp. 113–122. DOI: 10.1145/1374376.1374396. 649, 651

S. Goldwasser, Y. T. Kalai, and G. N. Rothblum. 2015. Delegating computation: Interactive proofs for muggles. *Journal of the ACM*, 62(4): 27. DOI: 10.1145/2699436. 651, 652, 655, 658, 664, 682, 683

Y. T. Kalai, R. Raz, and R. D. Rothblum. 2014. How to delegate computations: the power of no-signaling proofs. In *Symposium on Theory of Computing, STOC 2014, New York, NY, USA, May 31–June 3, 2014*, pp. 485–494. DOI: 10.1145/2591796.2591809. 652

R. M. Karp. 1972. Reducibility among combinatorial problems. In *Proceedings of a symposium on the Complexity of Computer Computations, held March 20–22, 1972, at the IBM Thomas J. Watson Research Center, Yorktown Heights, New York, USA*, pp. 85–103. http://www.cs.berkeley.edu/%7Eluca/cs172/karp.pdf. 650

J. Kilian. 1992. A note on efficient zero-knowledge proofs and arguments (extended abstract). In *Proceedings of the 24th Annual ACM Symposium on Theory of Computing, May 4–6, 1992, Victoria, British Columbia, Canada*, pp. 723–732. DOI: 10.1145/129712.129782. 651

L. A. Levin. 1973. Universal sequential search problems. *Problems of Information Transmission*, 9(3): 265–266. 650

C. Lund, L. Fortnow, H. J. Karloff, and N. Nisan. 1992. Algebraic methods for interactive proof systems. *Journal of the ACM*, 39(4): 859–868. DOI: 10.1145/146585.146605. 650, 651, 654, 682

S. Micali. 2000. Computationally sound proofs. *SIAM Journal on Computing*, 30(4): 1253–1298. DOI: 10.1137/S0097539795284959. 651

O. Reingold. 2008. Undirected connectivity in log-space. *Journal of the ACM*, 55(4). DOI: 10.1145/1391289.1391291. 684

O. Reingold, S. P. Vadhan, and A. Wigderson. 2000. Entropy waves, the zig-zag graph product, and new constant-degree expanders and extractors. In *41st Annual Symposium on Foundations of Computer Science, FOCS 2000, 12–14 November 2000, Redondo Beach, California, USA*, pp. 3–13. DOI: 10.1109/SFCS.2000.892006. 684

O. Reingold, G. N. Rothblum, and R. D. Rothblum. 2016. Constant-round interactive proofs for delegating computation. In *Proceedings of the 48th Annual ACM SIGACT Symposium on Theory of Computing, STOC 2016, Cambridge, MA, USA, June 18–21, 2016*, pp. 49–62. DOI: 10.1145/2897518.2897652. 649, 653, 654, 655, 656, 658, 674, 682, 683, 684

O. Reingold, G. N. Rothblum, and R. D. Rothblum. 2018. Efficient batch verification for UP. In *33rd Computational Complexity Conference, CCC 2018, June 22–24, 2018, San Diego, CA, USA*, pp. 22:1–22:23. DOI: 10.4230/LIPIcs.CCC.2018.22. 656, 675

G. N. Rothblum. 2009. *Delegating Computation Reliably: Paradigms and Constructions*. Ph.D. thesis, Massachusetts Institute of Technology. 659, 660, 670

G. N. Rothblum, S. P. Vadhan, and A. Wigderson. 2013. Interactive proofs of proximity: Delegating computation in sublinear time. In *45th STOC*, pp. 793–802. DOI: 10.1145/2488608.2488709. 655, 656

R. Rubinfeld and M. Sudan. 1996. Robust characterizations of polynomials with applications to program testing. *SIAM Journal on Computing*, 25(2): 252–271. DOI: 10.1137/S0097539793255151. 655

A. Shamir. 1992. IP = PSPACE. *Journal of the ACM*, 39(4): 869–877. 650, 651, 654

A. Shen. 1992. IP = PSPACE: simplified proof. *Journal of the ACM*, 39(4): 878–880. DOI: 10.1145/146585.146613. 651

J. Thaler. 2013. Time-optimal interactive proofs for circuit evaluation. In *Advances in Cryptology—CRYPTO 2013—33rd Annual Cryptology Conference, Santa Barbara, CA, USA, August 18–22, 2013. Proceedings, Part II*. Lecture Notes in Computer Science 8043, pp. 71–89. Springer. 655

J. Thaler, M. Roberts, M. Mitzenmacher, and H. Pfister. 2012. Verifiable computation with massively parallel interactive proofs. *CoRR*, abs/1202.1350. 655

L. Valiant and V. Vazirani. 1986. NP is as easy as detecting unique solutions. *Theoretical Computer Science*, 47: 85–93. DOI: 10.1016/0304-3975(86)90135-0. 674

V. Vu, S. T. V. Setty, A. J. Blumberg, and M. Walfish. 2013. A hybrid architecture for interactive verifiable computation. In *IEEE Symposium on Security and Privacy*, pp. 223–237. DOI: 10.1109/SP.2013.48. 655

R. S. Wahby, Y. Ji, A. J. Blumberg, A. Shelat, J. Thaler, M. Walfish, and T. Wies. 2017. Full accounting for verifiable outsourcing. In *Proceedings of the 2017 ACM SIGSAC Conference on Computer and Communications Security, CCS 2017, Dallas, TX, USA, October 30–November 3, 2017*, pp. 2071–2086. DOI: 10.1145/3133956.3133984. 655

R. S. Wahby, I. Tzialla, A. Shelat, J. Thaler, and M. Walfish. 2018. Doubly-efficient zksnarks without trusted setup. In *2018 IEEE Symposium on Security and Privacy, SP 2018, Proceedings, May 21–23, 2018, San Francisco, California, USA*, pp. 926–943. DOI: 10.1109/SP.2018.00060. 655

M. Walfish and A. J. Blumberg. 2013. Verifying computations without reexecuting them: From theoretical possibility to near-practicality. *Electronic Colloquium on Computational Complexity (ECCC) TR13–165, 2013*, 20: 165. 655

Y. Zhang, D. Genkin, J. Katz, D. Papadopoulos, and C. Papamanthou. 2017. vsql: Verifying arbitrary SQL queries over dynamic outsourced databases. In *2017 IEEE Symposium on Security and Privacy, SP 2017, San Jose, CA, USA, May 22–26, 2017*, pp. 863–880. DOI: 10.1109/SP.2017.43. 655

Computational Entropy

Salil Vadhan

25.1 Introduction

The foundations of cryptography laid by Shafi Goldwasser and Silvio Micali in the 1980s provided remarkably strong security definitions (e.g., semantic security Goldwasser and Micali [1984]) and amazingly rich cryptographic functionalities (e.g., zero-knowledge proofs Goldwasser et al. [1988]) that could be achieved from precisely stated complexity assumptions (e.g., the quadratic residuosity assumption [Goldwasser and Micali 1984]). This naturally led to an important project of understanding what are the *minimal* complexity assumptions needed to each of the many cryptographic primitives that were emerging.

The pinnacle of success in this effort was to show that a given cryptographic primitive could be based on the existence of mere one-way functions, as defined in the work of Diffie and Hellman [1976] that initiated complexity-based cryptography. The notion of a one-way function is both very general, with many concrete candidates for instantiation, and very simple to state, allowing the candidates to crypt-analyzed more easily. Moreover, almost all primitives in complexity-based cryptography imply the existence of one-way functions [Impagliazzo and Luby 1989], so one-way functions are in some sense the minimal assumption we could hope for.

Remarkably, it was discovered that a wide array of cryptographic primitives could be constructed assuming only the existence one-way functions. These included such powerful objects as chosen-ciphertext-secure symmetric encryption, pseudorandom functions, digital signatures, and zero-knowledge proofs and statistical zero-knowledge arguments for all of **NP** [Goldreich et al. 1986, Goldreich et al. 1991, Håstad et al. 1999, Naor and Yung 1989, Rompel 1990, Naor 1991, Haitner et al. 2009a]. All of these constructions begin by converting the "raw hardness" of a one-way function to one of the following more structured cryptographic primitives: a pseudorandom generator [Blum and Micali 1984, Yao 1982], a universal one-way hash function [Naor and Yung 1989], or a statistically hiding commitment scheme [Brassard et al. 1988].

The goal of this survey is to convey how this conversion from one-wayness to structured hardness is possible, focusing on the cases of constructing pseudorandom generators and statistically hiding commitments. The common answer that has emerged through a series of works is as follows:

1. The security properties of these (and other) cryptographic primitives can be understood in terms of various *computational analogues of entropy*, and in particular how these computational measures of entropy can be very different from real information-theoretic entropy.

2. It can be shown that every one-way function directly exhibits some gaps between real entropy and the various computational entropies.

3. Thus we can construct the desired cryptographic primitives by amplifying and manipulating the entropy gaps in a one-way function, through forms of repetition and hashing.

This viewpoint (of identifying and manipulating computational entropy) was already present in the original constructions of pseudorandom generators, universal one-way hash functions, and statistically hiding commitments from arbitrary one-way functions [Håstad et al. 1999, Rompel 1990, Haitner et al. 2009a], but those constructions were quite complicated and inefficient, making it hard to distinguish the essential ideas from technicalities. Over the past decade, a clearer picture has emerged through the introduction of new, refined notions of computational entropy [Haitner et al. 2009b, Haitner et al. 2013, Haitner et al. 2010, Vadhan and Zheng 2012, Agrawal et al. 2019]. The resulting constructions of pseudorandom generators and statistically hiding commitments from one-way functions are much simpler and more efficient than the original ones, and are based entirely on natural manipulations of computational entropy. The two constructions are "dual" to each other, whereby the construction of pseudorandom generators relies on a form of computational entropy ("pseudoentropy") being larger than the real entropy, while the construction of statistically hiding commitments relies on a form of computational entropy ("accessible entropy") being smaller than the real entropy. Beyond that difference, the two constructions share a common structure, using a very similar sequence of manipulations of real and computational entropy.

In this survey, we will describe the main ideas behind these recent constructions of pseudorandom generators and statistically hiding commitments from one-way functions. We will warm up by "deconstructing" the classic construction of pseudorandom generators from one-way *permutations* [Blum and Micali 1984, Yao 1982, Goldreich and Levin 1989] using the modern language of computational entropy, as it will provide intuition and context for what follows. We will then present the state-of-art construction of pseudorandom generators from general one-way functions, using the computational entropy notions of "conditional KL-hardness" and "next-block pseudoentropy" [Haitner et al. 2013, Vadhan and Zheng 2012]. Finally, we will introduce the dual notion of "next-block accessible entropy" and explain how it is used in constructing statistically hiding commitments from one-way functions in a way that parallels the aforementioned construction of pseudorandom generators [Haitner et al. 2009b].

Beyond the specific constructions covered, we hope that the surveyed notions of computational entropy and the tools for reasoning about them will prove useful elsewhere, for example in some of the other application areas for computational entropy mentioned below.

Other Reading. For general background on the foundations of cryptography and the theory of pseudorandomness, we recommend Goldreich [2019], Goldreich [2008, Ch. 8], and Vadhan [2012]. A more detailed and technical tutorial on the constructions of pseudorandom generators and statistically hiding commitments from one-way functions using computational entropy is given by Haitner and Vadhan [2017]. While we focus on its role in constructions of cryptographic primitives from one-way functions, computational analogues of entropy have been studied from a number of other angles. Yao [1982] introduced a notion of computational entropy for the purposes of studying efficient data compression and error correction. Barak et al. [2003] carry out a systematic study of several different notions of computational entropy (some of which appear here). Forms of computational entropy have also found applications in leakage-resilient cryptography [Dziembowski and Pietrzak 2008], deterministic encryption [Fuller et al. 2015], memory delegation [Chung et al. 2011], and differential privacy [Mironov et al. 2009], and these areas of research have developed the theory of computational entropy in other ways. Recently, Haitner et al. [2018] have introduced a computational analogue of independence for outputs from a 2-party protocol that they use to characterize the 2-party cryptographic primitives whose existence is equivalent to the existence of key agreement protocols.

Acknowledgments. I vividly recall the thrill of learning about the foundations of cryptography from Shafi and Silvio with my fellow graduate students at MIT in the late 1990s. Time and time again, it felt like we were seeing how the seemingly impossible could be achieved. We saw how philosophical and psychological concepts (e.g., knowledge, persuasion, impersonation) could be given convincing mathematical definitions, and cryptographic schemes for controlling these concepts could be constructed based on simple complexity assumptions. Decades later, the desire to better understand how this all could be possible has remained with me, and is a major motivator for the line of research described in this survey. At a more concrete level, much of this work was a direct outgrowth of the line of research that Shafi started me on as her Ph.D. student—namely, the complexity of statistical zero-knowledge proofs [Vadhan 1999]. Attempting to understand the complexity of the prover in statistical zero-knowledge proofs led to a characterization of statistical zero knowledge in terms of "instance-dependent" commitment schemes [Bellare et al. 1990, Itoh et al. 1997, Micciancio and Vadhan 2003, Nguyen and Vadhan 2006, Ong and Vadhan 2007]. The ideas underlying that characterization inspired the construction of statistically hiding commitments from one-way functions [Haitner et al. 2009a], including the use of computational entropies in that work and the subsequent ones discussed in this survey. Thank you, Shafi and Silvio, for creating and leading us to such a beautiful landscape to explore, and for your mentorship and friendship throughout our lives!

I am grateful to Oded Goldreich for his unwavering support and patience for my writing of this survey, and lots of helpful feedback. Thanks also to Hugo Krawczyk, whose encouragement motivated me to write this survey based on my lectures at the 2016 IACR-COST School on Randomness in Cryptography. The writing of this survey was supported by NSF grant CCF-1763299.

25.2 Basic Information-Theoretic Notions

We review a number of information-theoretic notions, before introducing their computational analogues, which will be the main focus of this survey.

Basic Definitions.   We begin with the most intuitive measure of distance between probability distributions:

Definition 25.1   (Statistical difference)   Let X and Y be discrete random variables taking values in a universe $\mathcal{U}$. Then the ***statistical difference*** (a.k.a. ***total variation distance***) between X and Y is

$$d(X, Y) = \max_{T \subseteq \mathcal{U}} |\Pr[X \in T] - \Pr[Y \in T]| \in [0, 1].$$

We say X and Y are *ε-**close*** if $d(X, Y) \leq \varepsilon$.

We will also discuss a number of different measures of entropy:

Definition 25.2 (Entropy measures)   Let X be a discrete random variable. Then:

- The (*Shannon*) *entropy of* X is

$$H(X) = \mathop{E}_{x \xleftarrow{R} X} \left[\log \left(\frac{1}{\Pr[X = x]} \right) \right].$$

- The *min-entropy of* X is

$$H_\infty(X) = \min_x \left[\log \left(\frac{1}{\Pr[X = x]} \right) \right] = \log \left(\frac{1}{\max_x \Pr[X = x]} \right).$$

- The *max-entropy of* X is

$$H_0(X) = \log | \operatorname{Supp}(X) |.$$

Above, and throughout this survey, all logarithms are base 2 (except where explicitly noted otherwise) and $\operatorname{Supp}(X) = \{x : \Pr[X = x] > 0\}$ denotes the support of the random variable X.

$H(X)$ measures the *average* number of bits of randomness in X, while $H_\infty(X)$ and $H_0(X)$ are worst-case lower and upper bounds on $H(X)$. Indeed, we have

$$H_\infty(X) \le H(X) \le H_0(X),$$

with equality if and only if X is uniform on $\operatorname{Supp}(X)$; that is, X is a *flat distribution*.

Extraction and Compression.   The usefulness of min-entropy in theoretical computer science was advocated by Chor and Goldreich [1988]. Specifically, having a random variable with high min-entropy is preferable to having a random variable with high Shannon entropy because high min-entropy can be converted into nearly uniform randomness via extractors:

Definition 25.3 (Randomness extractors Nisan and Zuckerman [1996])   A function $\operatorname{Ext} : \{0, 1\}^n \times \{0, 1\}^d \to \{0, 1\}^m$ is a *strong* (k, ε)*-extractor* if for every random variable X distributed on $\{0, 1\}^n$ with $H_\infty(X) \ge k$, the random variable $(U_d, \operatorname{Ext}(X, U_d))$ is ε-close to (U_d, U_m) where U_d and U_m are uniformly distributed on $\{0, 1\}^d$ and $\{0, 1\}^m$, respectively, and X, U_d, U_m are mutually independent.

Above, and throughout, when the same random variable appears twice in an expression (e.g., the U_d in $(U_d, \operatorname{Ext}(X, U_d))$), they take the same value with probability 1.

Lemma 25.1 (Leftover hash lemma Bennett et al. [1988], Håstad et al. [1999])   For every n, $k \le n$, and $\varepsilon > 2^{-k/2}$, there is a polynomial-time computable strong (k, ε)-extractor

Ext : $\{0, 1\}^n \times \{0, 1\}^d \rightarrow \{0, 1\}^m$ that has output length $m = \lfloor k - 2 \log(1/\varepsilon) \rfloor$ and seed length $d = n$. Specifically, we can take $\text{Ext}(x, h) = h(x)$ where h comes from a 2-universal family of hash functions mapping $\{0, 1\}^n$ to $\{0, 1\}^m$.

Note that the extractors given by the Leftover Hash Lemma extract almost all of the min-entropy out of the source, except for a $2 \log(1/\varepsilon)$ entropy loss, which is necessary for any extractor [Radhakrishnan and Ta-Shma 2000]. The seed length $d = n$, however, is suboptimal, and there is a long line of research on randomness extractors that gives explicit constructions of extractors with seed length depending only logarithmically on n. (See Vadhan [2012, Chapter 6] and the references therein.)

Similarly, having a random variable with low max-entropy is often preferable to having one with low Shannon entropy because low max-entropy allows for "compression".

Lemma 25.2   For every n, $k \leq n$, and $\varepsilon > 0$, there is a polynomial-time computable encoding function $\text{Enc} : \{0, 1\}^n \times \{0, 1\}^d \rightarrow \{0, 1\}^m$ with output length $m = k + \log(1/\varepsilon)$ and seed length $d = n$ such that for every random variable X distributed on $\{0, 1\}^n$ with $H_0(X) \leq k$, there is a (not necessarily efficient) decoding function $\text{Dec} : \{0, 1\}^m \times \{0, 1\}^d \rightarrow \{0, 1\}^n$ such that:

$$\Pr\left[\text{Dec}(\text{Enc}(X, U_d), U_d) = X\right] \geq 1 - \varepsilon.$$

Again we can take $\text{Enc}(x, h) = h(x)$ where h comes from a 2-universal family of hash functions mapping $\{0, 1\}^n$ to $\{0, 1\}^m$.

That is, if the max-entropy is low, then we do not need to reveal much information (just the m bits output by Enc to uniquely determine) to determines x with high probability.

Min-entropy and max-entropy are rather brittle, in that making a small change to the probability distribution can dramatically change the amount of measured entropy. For this reason, it is common to work with "smoothed" forms of these entropies [Renner and Wolf 2005]. Specifically, we consider a random variable X to have **smoothed min-entropy at least** k if X is ε-close to a random variable X' with $H_\infty(X') \geq k$, for a negligible ε. And we consider a random variable X to have **smoothed max-entropy at most** k if X is ε-close to a random variable X' with $H_0(X') \leq k$. Notice that smoothed min-entropy and smoothed max-entropy support randomness extraction and compression, as above, with the smoothing error adding to the error parameter of the randomness extraction or decoding.

Conditional Entropies.   We will also make use of conditional forms of entropy. For Shannon entropy, there is a standard definition:

Definition 25.4   (Conditional entropy)   For jointly distributed discrete random variables (X, Y), the *conditional Shannon entropy* of X given Y is

$$H(X|Y) = E_{y \xleftarrow{R} Y} \left[H\left(X|_{Y=y} \right) \right],$$

where $X|_E$ is the notation we use for conditioning the random variable X on event E.

There are a number of natural ways to define conditional min-entropy and conditional max-entropy, but for the case of min-entropy the following has proved to be particularly convenient in cryptographic applications.

Definition 25.5   (Average min-entropy Dodis et al. [2008])   For jointly distributed discrete random variables (X, Y), the *average min-entropy* of X given Y is

$$H_\infty(X|Y) = \log \left(\frac{1}{E_{y \xleftarrow{R} Y} \left[2^{-H_\infty\left(X|_{Y=y} \right)} \right]} \right).$$

Despite the somewhat complicated definition, average min-entropy has a very natural operational interpretation as measuring the maximum probability of guessing X from Y:

Lemma 25.3   (Guessing min-entropy)   For every pair of jointly distributed discrete random variables (X, Y), the average min-entropy $H_\infty(X|Y)$ equals the *guessing min-entropy* of X given Y, defined as

$$H_{guess}(X|Y) = \log \left(\frac{1}{\max_A \Pr[A(Y) = X]} \right),$$

where the maximum is over all functions A (regardless of computational complexity).

The proof of this lemma follows from observing that $2^{-H_\infty\left(X|_{Y=y} \right)} = \max_x \Pr[X = x|Y = y]$, which is exactly the success probability of an optimal strategy for guessing X given that $Y = y$.

In addition to having this nice operational interpretation, average min-entropy also supports randomness extraction. Indeed, it turns out that every randomness extractor for ordinary min-entropy is also one for average min-entropy with only a small loss in the error parameter:

Lemma 25.4   (Vadhan [2012, Problem 6.8])   Let $\text{Ext} : \{0, 1\}^n \times \{0, 1\}^d \rightarrow \{0, 1\}^m$ be a (k, ε)-extractor for $k \leq n - 1$, and let (X, Y) be any pair of jointly distributed discrete random variables with X taking values in $\{0, 1\}^n$ such that $H_\infty(X|Y) \geq k$. Then $(U_d, \text{Ext}(X, U_d), Y)$ is 3ε-close to (U_d, U_m, Y), where U_d, U_m, and (X, Y) are mutually independent.

The above lemma is proven by showing that on one hand, a (k, ε)-extractor also extracts nearly uniform bits when applied to sources of min-entropy k' slightly smaller than k, and on the other hand, if X has average min-entropy at least k given Y, then $X_{Y=y}$ is very unlikely (over the choice of $y \overset{R}{\leftarrow} Y$) to have min-entropy much smaller than k, In fact, the extractor of the leftover hash lemma can directly be shown to be an extractor for average min-entropy with no loss in the error parameter [Dodis et al. 2008].

Flattening. Although min-entropy and max-entropy are more directly useful in cryptographic applications, many of the results we will discuss will begin by establishing statements involving Shannon entropy. These can converted into statements about (smoothed) min-entropy and max-entropy by taking many independent samples:

Lemma 25.5 (Flattening) Let X be a random variable distributed on $\{0, 1\}^n$, and let X^t consist of t independent samples of X. Then for every $\varepsilon \in (0, 1/2)$, the random variable X^t is ε-close to a random variable X' such that

$$H_\infty(X') \geq t \cdot H(X) - O\left(\sqrt{t \cdot \log(1/\varepsilon)} \cdot n\right) \text{ and}$$

$$H_0(X') \leq t \cdot H(X) + O\left(\sqrt{t \cdot \log(1/\varepsilon)} \cdot n\right).$$

The flattening lemma can be viewed as a quantitative form of the standard "asymptotic equipartition property" in information theory. Various forms of it appear in the literature, including in Håstad et al. [1999]; the tight version above is from Holenstein and Renner [2011].

Note that the Shannon entropy of X^t is exactly $t \cdot H(X)$, which grows linearly with t. The above lemma says that, after some smoothing, the min-entropy and max-entropy of X^t are close to the Shannon entropy of X^t, with a difference that grows only like $\sqrt{t}$. In particular, for $\varepsilon = n^{-\log n}$ and $t = n^2 \cdot \log^3 n$, the smoothed min- and max-entropies are guaranteed to be $t \cdot (H(X) \pm o(1))$. This is referred to as a "flattening" lemma because the only random variables where the Shannon entropy equals the min-entropy or max-entropy are flat random variables (ones that are uniform on their support), whereas X^t is close to a distribution in which the min- and max-entropies are relatively close (i.e., are $o(t)$ away). Flattening also works for jointly distributed random variables (X, Y); see Holenstein and Renner [2011] for a precise statement.

25.3 Basic Computational Notions

We review the standard notions of one-way functions, computational indistinguishability, and pseudorandom generators, highlighting notational choices and conventions we will use throughout this survey.

One-Way Functions.   A one-way function is a function that is easy to compute in the forward direction, but very hard to invert, even on average.

Definition 25.6   (One-way functions Diffie and Hellman [1976])   A function $f : \{0, 1\}^n \to \{0, 1\}^n$ is a *one-way function (OWF)* if:

1. f is computable in time poly(n).

2. For some $s(n) = n^{\omega(1)}$ and $\varepsilon(n) = 1/n^{\omega(1)}$, and all nonuniform algorithms A running in time $s(n)$, we have

$$\Pr\left[A(f(X)) \in f^{-1}(f(X))\right] \leq \varepsilon(n),$$

where the probability is taken over $X \xleftarrow{R} \{0, 1\}^n$ and the coin tosses of A.

Note that the asymptotics are somewhat hidden in the above definition. As usual, the definition actually refers to an infinite family of functions $\{f_n : \{0, 1\}^n \to \{0, 1\}^n\}_{n \in \mathbb{N}}$, one for each value of the security parameter n. Condition 1 means that there should be a single uniform algorithm that can evaluate $f = f_n$ in time poly(n) for all n. On the other hand, we require security to hold even against nonuniform algorithms. We adopt this nonuniform model of security because it simplifies a number of the definitions and proofs, but all of the results we will discuss have uniform-security analogues. The time bound $s(n)$ on the complexity of the nonuniform algorithm A should be interpreted as a bound on both the running time and program size; this is equivalent (up to a polynomial loss) to taking $s(n)$ to be a bound on the size of A as a Boolean circuit.

The security bound $n^{\omega(1)}$ refers to any functions that is asymptotically larger than every polynomial function. It is more common in the literature to state security definitions for cryptographic primitives in the form "for every constant c and every nonuniform algorithm A running in time n^c, the success probability of A in inverting f is at most $1/n^c$ for all sufficiently large n." Definition 25.6 can be shown to be equivalent to such formulations [Bellare 2002]. Note that the functions $s(n)$ and $\varepsilon(n)$ in Definition 25.6 are not necessarily efficiently computable. However, we will ignore that subtlety in this survey, and pretend that they are efficiently computable when it makes the exposition simpler.

Note that we have taken the security parameter n to equal the input and output lengths of the one-way function. When we define other primitives (such as pseudorandom generators below), we will allow their input and output lengths to be polynomially related to the security parameter, rather than equal to the security parameter. This will allow us to have a more fine-grained discussion of the complexity of constructing these primitives from one-way functions, where we will keep the security parameter n equal to the input length of the underlying one-way function.

We stress that Definition 25.6 does not require the function f to be one-to-one, and thus the adversary A succeeds if it finds *any* preimage of its input $f(X)$. Overcoming the challenges introduced by general, many-to-one one-way functions f is a major theme in this survey.

Computational Indistinguishability. The fundamental concept of computational indistinguishability was introduced in the seminal paper of Goldwasser and Micali [1984]. It is the computational analogue of statistical difference (Definition 25.1), obtained by restricting to statistical tests T that are efficiently computable:

Definition 25.7 (Computational indistinguishability Goldwasser and Micali [1984]) Let X and Y be random variables distributed over $\{0, 1\}^m$ for $m = \text{poly}(n)$, where n is a security parameter. We say that X and Y are *computationally indistinguishable*, written $X \stackrel{c}{\equiv} Y$, if for some $s(n) = n^{\omega(1)}$ and $\varepsilon(n) = 1/n^{-\omega(1)}$, and all nonuniform algorithms T running in time $s(n)$, we have

$$|\Pr[T(X) = 1] - \Pr[T(Y) = 1]| \leq \varepsilon(n), \tag{25.1}$$

where the probability is taken over X, Y, and the coin tosses of T. If Y is identically distributed to U_m, the uniform distribution on $\{0, 1\}^m$, then we say that X is *pseudorandom*.

If Inequality (25.1) holds for all (computationally unbounded) functions T (i.e., X and Y are $\varepsilon(n)$-close in statistical difference for some $\varepsilon(n) = n^{-\omega(1)}$), then we say that X and Y are *statistically indistinguishable* and write $X \stackrel{s}{\equiv} Y$.

Computational indistinguishability is the basis of many concepts in modern cryptography, including the fundamental notion of a pseudorandom generator:

Definition 25.8 (Pseudorandom generators Blum and Micali [1984], Yao [1982]) A function $G : \{0, 1\}^{\ell} \to \{0, 1\}^m$, where $\ell, m = \text{poly}(n)$ for a security parameter n, is a *pseudorandom generator (PRG)* if:

1. G is computable in deterministic time $\mathrm{poly}(n)$.

2. $G(U_\ell) \overset{\mathrm{c}}{\equiv} U_m$.

3. $m > \ell$.

We call ℓ the *seed length* of G and m the *output length*.

Note that the above definition only requires that the output length is larger than the seed length by at least one bit ($m > \ell$). Many applications of pseudorandom generators require generating many pseudorandom bits from a short seed ($m \gg \ell$). Fortunately, there is a generic length-expansion technique that converts pseudorandom generators that stretch by one bit into ones that stretch by any desired length (without increasing the seed length) [Goldreich and Micali 1984]. Thus in this survey we will not specify the stretch of the pseudorandom generators.

Pseudorandom Generators from One-Way Functions.   A celebrated result in the foundations of cryptography is that pseudorandom generators can be constructed from any one-way function.

Theorem 25.1   (PRGs from OWFs Håstad et al. [1999])   If there exists a one-way function $f : \{0, 1\}^n \to \{0, 1\}^n$, then there exists a pseudorandom generator $G^f : \{0, 1\}^\ell \to \{0, 1\}^m$.

The original construction of Håstad et al. [1999] proving Theorem 25.1 was quite complex and inefficient. The pseudorandom generator G^f has a seed length of $\ell = \Theta(n^{10})$ and requires evaluating the one-way function at least $q = \Omega(n^{10})$ times. Quantifying these complexity parameters makes sense because the pseudorandom generator construction is a "(fully) black-box" one [Reingold et al. 2004], where the given one-way function is used as an oracle in the algorithm for computing G (so q counts the number of oracle queries), and the security of the construction is proven via a reduction that uses any oracle T that distinguishes $G^f(U_\ell)$ from U_m to invert f with nonnegligible probability. (The reduction also uses an oracle for f and may use nonuniform advice when working in the nonuniform security model, as we are.)

One might think that the large polynomial complexity of the construction does not matter because the "polynomial security" formulations of Definitions 25.6 and 25.8 are invariant to polynomial changes in the security parameter n. For example, G could invoke f on inputs of length $n^{1/10}$ and thereby achieve seed length $\ell = O(n)$. But this does not really change anything. In either case, the problem is that the security of the pseudorandom generator on seed length ℓ is related to the security of the one-way function on inputs of length $\Theta(\ell^{1/10})$, which amounts to an unsatisfactory loss in security. This becomes even more apparent when quantifying the security more finely. For example, even if the one-way function had "optimal" hardness, with security against algorithms running time $s(n) = 2^{cn}$ for a constant $c > 0$ on inputs of length n, we would only be guaranteed that the pseudorandom generator is secure against algorithms running in time $s(n)^{\Theta(1)} = 2^{\Theta(\ell^{1/9})}$, which is very far from the $2^{c'\ell}$ security that we might hope for. Thus it is important to seek more efficient constructions.

25.4 Pseudoentropy

A pseudorandom generator $G : \{0, 1\}^\ell \to \{0, 1\}^m$ with large stretch ($\ell \ll m$) starkly demonstrates the difference between computational and information-theoretic notions. On one hand, the output distribution $G(U_\ell)$ has entropy at most ℓ (since applying a deterministic function cannot increase entropy), but it is computationally indistinguishable from the distribution on $\{0, 1\}^m$ with maximal entropy—namely, U_m. Thus, as an intermediate step toward constructing pseudorandom generators, it is natural to consider a more quantitative measure of the amount of "computational entropy," as done by Håstad et al. [1999] in their proof of Theorem 25.1:

Definition 25.9 (Pseudoentropy Håstad et al. [1999]) Let X be a random variable distributed on strings of length poly(n) for a security parameter n. We say that X has *pseudoentropy at least k* if there exists a random variable X' such that

1. $X' \stackrel{c}{\equiv} X$.

2. $H(X') \geq k$.

If Condition 2 is replaced with $H_\infty(X') \geq k$, then we say that X has *pseudo-min-entropy at least k*.

As discussed above, constructing a pseudorandom generator requires producing an efficiently samplable distribution whose pseudoentropy (and pseudo-min-entropy) is *larger* than its actual entropy. We have formulated the definition of pseudoentropy to only allow for expressing such lower bounds on computational entropy (e.g., "X has pseudoentropy at least k"). Using the same template as a definition of "pseudoentropy at most k" yields a nonuseful definition, since every random variable can be shown to have pseudoentropy at most polylog(n) via a probabilistic argument akin to the one used in Goldreich and Krawczyk [1992]. In Section 25.7, we shall see a different approach that leads to a useful definition of upper bounds on computational entropy.

The Håstad et al. [1999] notion of pseudoentropy is very useful, thanks to the power of computational indistinguishability, which says that two random variables are essentially equivalent for the purposes of any efficient computation on them. In particular, pseudo-min-entropy supports randomness extraction, by any efficiently computable extractor:

Lemma 25.6 Let X be a random variable distributed on strings of length $m = \text{poly}(n)$ for a security parameter n with pseudo-min-entropy at least k, and let $\text{Ext} : \{0, 1\}^m \times \{0, 1\}^d \to \{0, 1\}^{m'}$ be a strong (k, ε)-extractor computable in time $\text{poly}(n)$, with error $\varepsilon = n^{-\omega(1)}$. Then $(U_d, \text{Ext}(X, U_d))$ is pseudorandom.

In particular, using the leftover hash lemma (Lemma 25.1), the pseudoentropy loss $k - m'$ incurred by extraction is only $2 \log(1/\varepsilon)$, which we can take to be any function that is $\omega(\log n)$.

As with the information-theoretic notions, randomness extraction requires pseudo-*min*-entropy rather than plain pseudoentropy. Fortunately, flattening also works in the context of pseudoentropy, and using Lemma 25.5, it can be shown that if X has pseudoentropy at least k, then for any $t = \text{poly}(n)$, the product X^t has pseudo-min-entropy at least $t \cdot k - \sqrt{t} \cdot \tilde{O}(m)$, where m is the bitlength of X.[1]

In light of these facts, the approach of [Håstad et al. 1999] to constructing pseudorandom generators from one-way functions is the following three-step process:

1. **Computational Entropy Gap.** From an arbitrary one-way function, construct an efficiently samplable distribution X that has pseudoentropy at least $\text{H}(X) + \Delta$ for some $\Delta \geq 1/\text{poly}(n)$.

2. **Flattening.** Use flattening to obtain an efficiently samplable distribution whose pseudo-min-entropy is significantly larger than its (smoothed) max-entropy.

3. **Hashing.** Use randomness extraction and hashing (as in Lemma 25.1 and Lemma 25.2) to obtain a generator G whose output distribution is pseudorandom while it is generated using a short seed (and in particular has small max-entropy).

---

1. Here we are using the fact that we have defined computational indistinguishability with respect to nonuniform distinguishers, in order to ensure that $X \stackrel{c}{\equiv} X'$ implies that $X^t \stackrel{c}{\equiv} (X')^t$. The latter implication does not hold in general for uniform distinguishers Goldreich and Meyer [1998]. The implication does hold if X and X' can be sampled in polynomial time, but the constructions we will describe do not seem to have that property for X'. In [Haitner et al. 2013], this is remedied by a more complicated definition, where we require indistinguishability even by distinguishers that have an oracle for sampling from X', but where we also allow X' to depend on the distinguisher.

Unfortunately, the construction of [Håstad et al. 1999] ended up being much more complex and inefficient than this outline suggests. The main reasons are that in Step 1, (a) we do not know the real entropy $H(X)$ of the samplable distribution X, and (b) the entropy gap Δ is quite small (and thus requires more repetitions for flattening to preserve the gap). In Section 25.6 we will see how to avoid these difficulties by using more refined notions of pseudoentropy.

Before proceeding, we define conditional versions of pseudoentropy that will be useful in later sections.

Definition 25.10 (Conditional pseudoentropy Hsiao et al. [2007]) Let (X, Y) be a pair of jointly distributed random variables of total length $\text{poly}(n)$ for a security parameter n. We say that X has **conditional pseudoentropy at least** k given Y if there is a random variable X', jointly distributed with Y, such that:

1. $(X, Y) \stackrel{c}{\equiv} (X', Y)$.

2. $H(X'|Y) \geq k$.

If Condition 2 is replaced with $H_\infty(X'|Y) \geq k$, then we say that X has **pseudo-min-entropy at least** k given Y.

Similarly to the unconditional versions, conditional pseudoentropy supports flattening and randomness extraction by efficiently computable extractors.

25.5 One-Way Permutations to Pseudorandom Generators

In this section, we present the classic construction of pseudorandom generators from one-way *permutations* using the language of computational entropy. Specifically, we will prove the following theorem:

Theorem 25.2 (PRGs from OWPs Blum and Micali [1984], Yao [1982], Goldreich and Levin [1989]) If there exists a one-way permutation $f : \{0, 1\}^n \to \{0, 1\}^n$, then there exists a pseudorandom generator $G^f : \{0, 1\}^\ell \to \{0, 1\}^m$. Moreover, G^f makes $q = 1$ query to f and has seed length $\ell = O(n)$.

Note that this construction is extremely efficient, with only one query to the one-way function and a linear seed length.

Our presentation of the proof of Theorem 25.2 will use more complex concepts than the traditional presentation, in order to set the stage for Section 25.6, where we handle general one-way functions. The construction and security reduction implicit in the proof are actually the same as in the traditional presentation; they are just described using different language.

The first step of the proof is to observe that the definition of one-wayness can be directly related to a computational analogue of guessing entropy, as defined in Lemma 25.3, simply by restricting the guesser A to be efficient:

Definition 25.11 (Guessing pseudoentropy[2] Hsiao et al. [2007])   Let X and Y be jointly distributed random variables of total length poly(n) for a security parameter n. We say that X has **guessing pseudoentropy[2] at least** k given Y if for some $s(n) = n^{\omega(1)}$ and all nonuniform algorithms A running in time $s(n)$, we have

$$\Pr[A(Y) = X] \leq 2^{-k},$$

where the probability is taken over (X, Y) and the coin tosses of A.

If we take $Y = f(X)$ for a one-way function f, then the one-wayness of f implies that the above definition is satisfied for $2^{-k} = n^{-\omega(1)}$:

Lemma 25.7   If $f : \{0, 1\}^n \to \{0, 1\}^n$ is a one-way function, and X is uniformly distributed in $\{0, 1\}^n$, then X has guessing pseudoentropy $\omega(\log n)$ given $f(X)$.

Recall that guessing entropy is equal to average min-entropy in the information-theoretic setting (Lemma 25.3). In the computational setting, however, they are not equivalent; that is, guessing pseudoentropy is *not* in general equal to pseudo-min-entropy. Indeed, if f is a one-to-one one-way function, then X has *negligible* pseudo-min-entropy given $f(X)$, since for every X' such that $H_\infty(X'|f(X))$ is nonnegligible, the efficient test $T(x, y)$ that outputs 1 iff $y = f(x)$ distinguishes $(X, f(X))$ from $(X', f(X))$.

Nevertheless, guessing pseudoentropy does support randomness extraction, not by arbitrary extractors, but ones meeting the following definition, which requires that the extractor is efficiently "list-decodable," in the sense that any test T that distinguishes the output of the extractor (on a fixed but unknown source element x) from uniform can be used to efficiently describe a list of at most 2^k elements that includes x. We will allow this list-decoding to be probabilistic and require it to succeed with some constant probability over its randomness r. Rather than asking the decoder to explicitly write down all 2^k elements of the list, we will index into the list by strings z of length k provided as input to the decoder.

---

2. This was called "unpredictability entropy" by Hsiao et al. [2007], but we use the term *guessing pseudoentropy* to highlight its relationship with *guessing entropy* (which happens to equal average min-entropy).

Definition 25.12   List-decodable extractors Trevisan [2001], Ta-Shma and Zuckerman [2004], Barak et al. [2003], Vadhan [2012].[3] A function $\text{Ext} : \{0, 1\}^n \times \{0, 1\}^d \to \{0, 1\}^m$ is a (t, k, ε)-*list-decodable extractor* if there is a nonuniform time t oracle algorithm $\text{Dec} : \{0, 1\}^k \times \{0, 1\}^\ell \to \{0, 1\}^n$ such that the following holds: for every $x \in \{0, 1\}^n$ and $T : \{0, 1\}^d \times \{0, 1\}^m \to \{0, 1\}$ satisfying $\left|\Pr[T(U_d, \text{Ext}(x, U_d)) = 1] - \Pr[T(U_d, U_m) = 1]\right| > \varepsilon$, we have

$$\Pr_{r \xleftarrow{R} \{0,1\}^\ell} \left[\exists z \in \{0, 1\}^k \ \text{Dec}^T(z, r) = x\right] \geq \frac{1}{2}.$$

It is known that if we remove the time bound on the decoder t (i.e., set $t = \infty$), then list-decodable extractors are equivalent to standard (k, ε) randomness extractors up to an additive $\log(1/\varepsilon) + O(1)$ change in the min-entropy k and a constant factor in the error parameter ε. (See Vadhan [2012, Props. 6.23 and 7.72].)

Our reason for considering list-decodable extractors is that they extract pseudorandom bits from guessing pseudoentropy:

Lemma 25.8   (Extraction from guessing pseudoentropy Ta-Shma and Zuckerman [2004], Hsiao et al. [2007])   Let X and Y be jointly distributed random variables of total length $\text{poly}(n)$ for a security parameter n, and where X has length m. Suppose X has guessing pseudoentropy at least k given Y, and that for every $t = n^{\omega(1)}$, there is an $\varepsilon = n^{-\omega(1)}$ such that $\text{Ext} : \{0, 1\}^m \times \{0, 1\}^d \to \{0, 1\}^{m'}$ is a $(t, k - \log(3/\varepsilon), \varepsilon)$-list-decodable extractor. Then $(U_d, \text{Ext}(X, U_d), Y) \stackrel{c}{\equiv} (U_d, U_m, Y)$.

Proof   By the definition of guessing pseudoentropy, there is an $s = n^{\omega(1)}$ such that for every nonuniform A running in time s,

$$\Pr[A(Y) = X] \leq 2^{-k}.$$

Let $t = \sqrt{s} = n^{\omega(1)}$. By hypothesis, there is an $\varepsilon = n^{-\omega(1)}$ such that Ext is a (t, k', ε)-list-decodable extractor for $k' = k - \log(3/\varepsilon)$. Let $\text{Dec} : \{0, 1\}^{k'} \times \{0, 1\}^\ell \to \{0, 1\}^n$ be as guaranteed by Definition 25.12.

We will show that no nonuniform time t algorithm T can distinguish $(U_d, \text{Ext}(X, U_d), Y)$ and (U_d, U_m, Y) with advantage greater than 2ε. Suppose for contradiction that there is a nonuniform time t algorithm T such that

---

3. This is a variant of definitions that appear in the literature under different names, such as "reconstructive extractors" and "black-box pseudorandom generator constructions." In particular the definition in Vadhan [2012] of "black-box pseudorandom generator constructions" amounts to a definition of *locally* list-decodable extractors, where we only measure the time complexity of computing any one bit of the source string x, rather than all n bits at once.

$$\left| \Pr[T(U_d, \text{Ext}(X, U_d), Y) = 1] - \Pr[T(U_d, U_m, Y) = 1] \right| > 2\varepsilon.$$

Then with probability at least ε over $(x, y) \xleftarrow{R} (X, Y)$, we have

$$\left| \Pr[T(U_d, \text{Ext}(x, U_d), y) = 1] - \Pr[T(U_d, U_m, y) = 1] \right| > \varepsilon.$$

When this event occurs, we have

$$\Pr_{r \xleftarrow{R} \{0,1\}^\ell} \left[\exists z \in \{0, 1\}^{k'} \ \text{Dec}^{T(\cdot, \cdot, y)}(z, r) = x \right] \geq \frac{1}{2}.$$

Therefore, if we define $A(y) = \text{Dec}^{T(\cdot, \cdot, y)}(Z, R)$, where Z and R are both chosen uniformly at random, we have

$$\Pr[A(Y) = X] \geq \varepsilon \cdot \frac{1}{2} \cdot 2^{-k'} > 2^{-k}.$$

Moreover, being obtained from the time t algorithm Dec with an oracle T that is also a time t algorithm, A is a nonuniform algorithm running in time at most $t^2 = s$. This contradicts the guessing pseudoentropy of X given Y. ∎

One of the many interpretations of the celebrated Goldreich–Levin Hardcore Bit Theorem is as providing a list-decodable extractor.

Theorem 25.3 (GL extractor Goldreich and Levin [1989]) For every $\varepsilon > 0$, the function $\text{Ext}(x, r) = \left(\sum_i x_i r_i \right) \mod 2$ is a $(\text{poly}(n, 1/\varepsilon), 2 \log(1/\varepsilon) + O(1), \varepsilon)$-list-decodable extractor.

Note that for any $k = \omega(\log n)$, the GL extractor satisfies the conditions of Lemma 25.8. Indeed, for any $t = n^{\omega(1)}$, if we set $\varepsilon = \max\{1/t^{1/c}, k/4\}$ for a large enough constant c, then Theorem 25.3 ensures that Ext is a $(t, k - \log(3/\varepsilon), \varepsilon)$-list-decodable extractor.

We now can prove Theorem 25.2, constructing a pseudorandom generator from any one-way permutation.

Proof (of Theorem 25.2) Let $f : \{0, 1\}^n \to \{0, 1\}^n$ be a one-way permutation, and let $\text{Ext}(x, r) = \left(\sum_i x_i r_i \right) \mod 2$. Define

$$G^f(x, r) = (r, \text{Ext}(x, r), f(x)).$$

Note that G^f is polynomial-time computable with one query to f, has seed length $\ell = 2n$, and has output length $m = 2n + 1$.

All that remains is to prove the pseudorandomness of $G^f(U_\ell)$. Let X and R be random variables uniformly distributed in $\{0, 1\}^n$, set $Y = f(X)$. By Lemma 25.7, X

has guessing pseudoentropy $\omega(\log n)$ given Y. By Theorem 25.3 and Lemma 25.8, we have

$$G^f(X, R) \equiv (R, \text{Ext}(X, R), Y) \stackrel{c}{\equiv} (R, U_1, Y) \equiv U_{2n+1}. \quad \blacksquare$$

Before moving on to the case of general one-way functions, we revisit the relationship between guessing pseudoentropy and ordinary pseudo-min-entropy. As noted above, the example $Y = f(X)$ for a one-to-one one-way function f shows that X having noticeable guessing pseudoentropy given Y does not in general imply that X has noticeable pseudo-min-entropy given Y. However, it turns out that this implication does hold when X is *short*:

Theorem 25.4 (Guessing pseudoentropy vs. pseudo-min-entropy Zheng [2014], Skórski et al. [2015])   Let (X, Y) be jointly distributed random variables, where X is distributed over strings of length $\ell = O(\log n)$ and Y is distributed over strings of length $\text{poly}(n)$, for a security parameter n. Then for every $k \in [0, \ell]$, the following are equivalent:

1. There is a negligible $\varepsilon = \varepsilon(n)$, such that X has guessing pseudoentropy at least $k - \varepsilon$ given Y.

2. There is a negligible $\varepsilon = \varepsilon(n)$ such that X has pseudo-min-entropy at least $k - \varepsilon$ given Y.[4]

As discussed by Zheng [2014], the case of Boolean X (i.e., $\ell = 1$) amounts to a reinterpretation of (tight) versions of Impagliazzo's Hardcore Theorem [Impagliazzo 1995, Klivans and Servedio 2003, Barak et al. 2009, Sudan et al. 2001]. We also remark that the version of Theorem 25.4 by Skórski, Golovnev, and Pietrzak [Skórski et al. 2015] relaxes the condition that X is short (i.e., $\ell = O(\log n)$) to the pseudoentropy deficiency being small (i.e., $\ell - k = O(\log n)$).

25.6 One-Way Functions to Pseudorandom Generators

We now turn to constructing pseudorandom generators from arbitrary one-way functions. Specifically, we will sketch the most efficient construction to date:

Theorem 25.5 (Improved PRGs from OWFs Haitner et al. [2013], Vadhan and Zheng [2012])   If there exists a one-way function $f : \{0, 1\}^n \to \{0, 1\}^n$, then there exists a pseudo-

---

4. Actually, we can replace Item 2 with the statement that X has pseudo-min-entropy at least k given Y, with no negligible loss, by exploiting the slackness afforded by indistinguishability. Indeed, suppose $(X, Y) \stackrel{c}{\equiv} (X', Y)$ where $H_\infty(X'|Y) \geq k - \varepsilon$. It can be shown that (X', Y) is *statistically* indistinguishable from some (X'', Y) such that $H_\infty(X''|Y) \geq k$. Then (X, Y) is also computationally indistinguishable from (X'', Y), and hence X has pseudo-min-entropy at least k given Y.

random generator $G^f : \{0, 1\}^\ell \to \{0, 1\}^m$ with seed length $\ell = \tilde{O}(n^3)$ that makes $q = \tilde{O}(n^3)$ queries to f.

Pseudoentropy from One-Way Functions. Like the proof of Theorem 25.2 given above, we will begin the proof of Theorem 25.5 by looking for some form of pseudoentropy in an arbitrary one-way function f. Note that the fact that X has guessing pseudoentropy $\omega(\log n)$ given $f(X)$ (Lemma 25.7) holds for every one-way function, regardless of whether or not it is one-to-one. However, when f is many-to-one, this fact may hold for trivial information-theoretic reasons. Indeed, consider any function f that ignores the first half of its input. Then X has average min-entropy at least $n/2$ given $f(X)$, so in particular has guessing pseudoentropy at least $n/2 = \omega(\log n)$ given $f(X)$, regardless of the one-wayness of f.

Thus, we need to replace guessing pseudoentropy with a notion that captures the *gap* between the computational and information-theoretic hardness in X given $f(X)$. To do so, we need to exploit the fact that one-wayness guarantees that it is hard to find *any* preimage of $f(X)$, something that is not captured by guessing pseudoentropy. We will do this by using a computational analogue of KL divergence (a.k.a. relative entropy). We begin with the information-theoretic definition.

Definition 25.13 (KL divergence) Let A and A' be two discrete random variables. The *Kullback–Leibler (KL) divergence from A to A'* is

$$\text{KL}\left(A \| A'\right) = \mathop{\text{E}}_{a \xleftarrow{R} A}\left[\log\left(\frac{\Pr[A = a]}{\Pr[A' = a]}\right)\right].$$

It can be shown that $\text{KL}\left(A \| A'\right) \geq 0$, with equality iff A and A' are identically distributed. Thus KL divergence can be thought of as a measure of "distance" between probability distributions, but note that it is not symmetric and does not satisfy the triangle inequality. Also note that $\text{KL}\left(A \| A'\right)$ is infinite if (and only if) $\text{Supp}(A) \not\subseteq \text{Supp}(A')$.

For intuition about KL divergence, it is useful to consider the case of flat distributions (where A and A' are uniform on their supports). Then, if $\text{Supp}(A) \subseteq \text{Supp}(A')$, $\text{KL}\left(A \| A'\right) = \log(|\text{Supp}(A')|/|\text{Supp}(A)|)$, so $\text{KL}(A \| A')$ measures how densely A is contained in A'. More generally, if A' is flat and A is an arbitrary random variable such that $\text{Supp}(A) \subseteq \text{Supp}(A')$, then $\text{KL}\left(A \| A'\right) = \log |\text{Supp}(A')| - \text{H}(A) = \text{H}(A') - \text{H}(A)$.

We will also refer to a conditional version of KL divergence.

Definition 25.14 (Conditional KL divergence) Let (A, B) and (A', B') be two pairs of discrete random variables. The *Kullback–Leibler (KL) divergence from $A|B$ to $A'|B'$* is

$$\text{KL}\left(A|B\|A'|B'\right) = \mathbb{E}_{b\xleftarrow{R}B}\left[\text{KL}\left(A|_{B=b}\|A'|_{B'=b}\right)\right]$$

$$= \text{KL}\left((A, B)\|(A', B')\right) - \text{KL}\left(B\|B'\right).$$

Note that the dependence of $\text{KL}\left(A|B\|A'|B'\right)$ on (A', B') involves only the family of conditional probability distributions $\{A'|_{B'=b}\}$. In particular, it does not depend on the marginal distribution of B'.

The computational analogue of KL divergence we will use is the following:

Definition 25.15   (Conditional KL-hardness Vadhan and Zheng [2012])   Let (X, Y) be a pair of jointly distributed random variables of total length poly(n), where n is the security parameter. We say that X is Δ-***KL-hard given*** Y iff for some $s(n) = n^{\omega(1)}$ and all nonuniform algorithms A running in time $s(n)$, we have

$$\text{KL}\left(X|Y\|A(Y)|Y\right) \geq \Delta.$$

Equivalently, we require

$$\text{KL}\left((X, Y)\|(A(Y), Y)\right) \geq \Delta.$$

The goal of the adversary A is to minimize the divergence $\text{KL}\left(X|Y\|A(Y)|Y\right)$. To make the divergence small, $A(y)$ should output a distribution that is as close as possible to the conditional distribution $X|_{Y=y}$. That is, the distribution $A(y)$ should contain the distribution $X|_{Y=y}$ as tightly as possible.

A computationally unbounded adversary A can achieve zero divergence by having $A(y)$ be distributed exactly according to the conditional distribution $X|_{Y=y}$. Therefore, X being Δ-KL-hard-to-sample given Y for a nonzero Δ is a statement purely about computational hardness, not information-theoretic hardness. This is in contrast to guessing pseudoentropy, which can be large for purely information-theoretic reasons (as discussed earlier).

We can still show that an arbitrary one-way function gives us KL hardness:

Lemma 25.9   (KL-hardness from one-way functions Vadhan and Zheng [2012])   If $f : \{0, 1\}^n \to \{0, 1\}^n$ is a one-way function and X is uniformly distributed in $\{0, 1\}^n$, then X is $\omega(\log n)$-KL-hard given $f(X)$.

Proof Sketch   Like statistical difference, KL divergence has the property it cannot be increased by applying a function. That is, for all functions T and random variables W and Z, $\text{KL}\left(T(W)\|T(Z)\right) \leq \text{KL}\left(W\|Z\right)$. This fact is known as the *data-processing inequality* for KL divergence. We will apply this inequality with the test $T(x, y)$ that outputs 1 if $y = f(x)$ and 0 otherwise. Specifically, for every adversary A running in time

$s(n) = n^{\omega(1)}$, we have

$$\mathrm{KL}\left((X, f(X))\|(A(f(X)), f(X))\right)$$

$$\geq \mathrm{KL}\left(T(X, f(X))\|T(A(f(X)), f(X))\right) \quad \text{(data-processing inequality)}$$

$$= \log\left(\frac{1}{\Pr[T(A(f(X)), f(X)) = 1]}\right) \quad (\Pr[T(X, f(X)) = 1] = 1)$$

$$= \log\left(\frac{1}{\Pr[A(f(X)) \in f^{-1}(f(X))]}\right) \quad \text{(def of } T)$$

$$= \log(n^{\omega(1)}) \quad \text{(one-wayness of } f)$$

$$= \omega(\log n). \quad\blacksquare$$

Similarly to Theorem 25.4, we can also relate KL-hardness to pseudoentropy when X is short:

Theorem 25.6 (KL-hardness vs. pseudoentropy Vadhan and Zheng [2012]) Let (X, Y) be jointly distributed random variables, where X is distributed over strings of length $\ell = O(\log n)$ and Y is distributed over strings of length poly(n), for a security parameter n. Then for every $\Delta \in [0, \ell - \mathrm{H}(X|Y)]$, the following are equivalent:

1. There is a negligible $\varepsilon = \varepsilon(n)$ such that X is $(\Delta - \varepsilon)$-KL-hard given Y.

2. There is a negligible $\varepsilon = \varepsilon(n)$ such that X has pseudoentropy at least $\mathrm{H}(X|Y) + \Delta - \varepsilon$ given Y.[5]

Note that, as we desired, the KL-hardness quantifies the *gap* between the pseudoentropy and the real entropy $\mathrm{H}(X|Y)$.

However, we cannot directly combine Theorem 25.6 and Lemma 25.9, since the input X to a one-way function is not short. Fortunately, KL-hardness is preserved if we break X up into short blocks:

Lemma 25.10 (Blockwise KL-hardness [Vadhan and Zheng 2012]) Let (X, Y) be a pair of jointly distributed random variables of total length poly(n), where n is the security parameter, and let $X = (X_1, \ldots, X_m)$ be a partition of X into blocks. If X is Δ-KL-hard given Y, then for I uniformly distributed in $\{1, \ldots, m\}$ X_I is (Δ/m)-KL-hard given $(Y, X_1, \ldots, X_{I-1})$.

Proof Sketch Suppose for contradiction that there is an efficient adversary A such that

$$\mathrm{KL}\left((Y, X_1, \ldots, X_I)\|(Y, X_1, \ldots, X_{I-1}, A(Y, X_1, \ldots, X_{I-1}))\right) < \Delta/m.$$

---

5. Similarly to Footnote 4, the negligible loss of ε in Item 2 can be removed.

That is, A samples one block X_I given Y and the previous blocks $X_1, \ldots, X_{I-1}$ with approximately the correct distribution. We now construct an adversary B that uses A iteratively to sample all of X given only Y. Specifically, $B(y)$ defined as follows:

- For $i = 1, \ldots, m$, let $x_i = A(y, x_1, \ldots, x_{i-1})$.

- Output $x = (x_1, \ldots, x_m)$.

Notice that if A achieves divergence zero—that is, $A(y, x_1, \ldots, x_{i-1})$ is always distributed exactly according to the conditional distribution $X_i|_{Y=y, X_1=x_1, \ldots, X_{i-1}=x_{i-1}}$ —then B will also achieve divergence zero, i.e., $B(y)$ is always identically distributed to $X|_{Y=y}$. More generally, it can be shown that the divergence achieved by B equals the sum of the divergences achieved by A over the m blocks. That is,

$$\mathrm{KL}\left(X|Y\|B(Y)|Y\right)$$

$$= \sum_{i=1}^{m} \mathrm{KL}\left(X_i|(Y, X_1, \ldots, X_{i-1})\|A(Y, X_1, \ldots, X_{i-1})|(Y, X_1, \ldots, X_{i-1})\right),$$

$$= m \cdot \mathrm{KL}\left(X_I|(Y, X_1, \ldots, X_{I-1})\|A(Y, X_1, \ldots, X_{I-1})|(Y, X_1, \ldots, X_{I-1})\right),$$

$$< \Delta,$$

contradicting the KL hardness of X given Y. ∎

Combining Lemma 25.10 and Theorem 25.6, we see that if X is Δ-KL-hard given Y and we partition X into m short blocks, then, on average, those blocks will have pseudoentropy larger than their real entropy by Δ/m (given the previous blocks and Y). The latter conclusion can be reinterpreted using the following blockwise notion of pseudoentropy:

Definition 25.16 (Next-block pseudoentropy Haitner et al. [2013]) Let $X = (X_0, X_1, \ldots, X_m)$ be a sequence of random variables distributed on strings of total length poly(n) for a security parameter n. We say that X has *next-block pseudoentropy* at least k if there is a sequence of random variables $(X_0', X_1', \ldots, X_m')$, jointly distributed with X, such that:

1. For each $i = 0, \ldots, m$, $(X_0, X_1, \ldots, X_{i-1}, X_i) \stackrel{c}{\equiv} (X_0, X_1, \ldots, X_{i-1}, X_i')$.

2. $\sum_{i=0}^{m} \mathrm{H}(X_i'|X_0, \ldots, X_{i-1}) \geq k$.

That is, to an "online" adversary that observes the random variables $(X_0, \ldots, X_m)$ in sequence, at each step the next block X_i looks like a "higher entropy" random variable X_i'. For comparison, consider the notion of next-bit *pseudorandomness*, where each of the blocks is of length 1 and $(X_1, \ldots, X_{i-1}, X_i) \stackrel{c}{\equiv} (X_1, \ldots, X_{i-1}, X_i')$ where X_i' is a uniformly random bit independent of $(X_1, \ldots,$

X_{i-1}). As asserted by Yao, next-bit pseudorandomness is equivalent to both the notion of next-bit unpredictability of Blum and Micali [1984] as well as to pseudorandomness of the entire sequence as in Definition 25.7. Next-block pseudoentropy can be thought of as a quantitative generalization of this classic notion, but, importantly, it is *not* generally equivalent to pseudoentropy of the entire sequence as demonstrated by the following theorem and discussion:

Theorem 25.7   (Next-block pseudoentropy from OWFs Vadhan and Zheng [2012])   Let $f : \{0, 1\}^n \to \{0, 1\}^n$ be a one-way function, let X be uniformly distributed in $\{0, 1\}^m$, and let $X = (X_1, \ldots, X_m)$ be a partition of X into blocks of length $O(\log n)$. (For example, we can set $m = n$ and set X_i to be the i'th bit of X.) Then the sequence $(f(X), X_1, \ldots, X_m)$ has next-block pseudoentropy at least $n + \omega(\log n)$.

As discussed earlier, the global pseudoentropy of the random variable $(f(X), X)$ is at most $n + n^{-\omega(1)}$, since the test $T(y, x)$ that checks whether $y = f(x)$ distinguishes $(f(X), X)$ from every distribution of entropy noticeably more than n. Theorem follows combining Lemma 25.9, Lemma 25.10, and Theorem 25.6.

Notice that the amount of next-block pseudoentropy in $(f(X), X)$ is $\omega(\log n)$ bits larger than the number of random bits we need to generate it (choosing a uniformly random X). Thus, if we can extract this pseudoentropy to produce pseudorandomness, we will have a pseudorandom generator. Unfortunately, Theorem 25.7 only guarantees pseudoentropy in the Shannon sense, whereas we need (pseudo-)min-entropy to extract (Lemma 25.6). Thus, we first need to apply flattening (Lemma 25.5).

Flattening Pseudoentropy.   By Theorem 25.7, there are real numbers $k_0, k_1, \ldots,$ $k_m \geq 0$ such that if we let $X_0 = f(X)$ and $X = (X_1, \ldots, X_m)$, we have:

1. $\sum_{i=0}^{m} k_i = n + \omega(\log n)$.
2. X_i has pseudoentropy at least k_i given $X_0, \ldots, X_{i-1}$ for $i = 0, \ldots, m$.

To flatten, we take t independent inputs $X^{(1)}, \ldots, X^{(t)}$ sampled uniformly from $\{0, 1\}^n$ for the one-way function f, define blocks for each by setting $X_0^{(i)} = f(X^{(i)})$ and $(X_1^{(i)}, \ldots, X_m^{(i)}) = X^{(i)}$, and create larger blocks $\tilde{X}_0, \ldots, \tilde{X}_m$ as follows:

- $\tilde{X}_0 = (f(X^{(1)}), f(X^{(2)}), \ldots, f(X^{(t)}))$.
- $\tilde{X}_i = (X_i^{(1)}, X_i^{(2)}, \ldots, X_i^{(t)})$ for $i = 1, \ldots, m$.

Then using Lemma 25.5 (and its generalization to conditional entropy) with $\varepsilon = n^{-\log n}$, it can be shown that for each i, the block $\tilde{X}_i$ has pseudo-min-entropy at least $\tilde{k}_i = t \cdot k_i - O(\sqrt{t} \cdot \log n \cdot \ell_i)$, where ℓ_i is the bit-length of the ith block.

For $t = n^2$, it can be checked that $\sum_i \tilde{k}_i = t \cdot (n + \omega(\log n))$, so the pseudo-min-entropy in the blocks $\tilde{X}_i$ is (significantly) larger than the $t \cdot n$ bits used to generate them. Applying a randomness extractor to each of these larger blocks, we obtain the following pseudorandom generator.

A "Nonuniform" Pseudorandom Generator. The following construction requires knowledge of the entropy thresholds k_i, which may be hard to compute and thus are provided as nonuniform advice to the pseudorandom generator. Later we will see how to remove this nonuniformity.

The seed of our pseudorandom generator consists of the t independent inputs $x^{(1)}, \ldots, x^{(t)}$ to f, and descriptions of universal hash functions $h_0, \ldots, h_m$ where h_i has output length $\tilde{k}_i - \omega(\log n)$, and the output is

$$G^f(x^{(1)}, \ldots, x^{(t)}, h_0, \ldots, h_m) = (h_0, \ldots, h_m, h_0(\tilde{x}_0), \ldots, h_m(\tilde{x}_m)).$$

Pictorially:

		$\tilde{x}_0$	$\tilde{x}_1$	$\cdots$	$\tilde{x}_m$	
		$\parallel$	$\parallel$		$\parallel$	
$x^{(1)} =$		$f(x^{(1)})$	$x_1^{(1)}$	$\cdots$	$x_m^{(1)}$	
$x^{(2)} =$		$f(x^{(2)})$	$x_1^{(2)}$	$\cdots$	$x_m^{(2)}$	
$\vdots$		$\vdots$	$\vdots$	$\vdots$	$\vdots$	
$x^{(t)} =$		$f(x^{(t)})$	$x_1^{(t)}$	$\cdots$	$x_m^{(t)}$	
$\uparrow$		$\downarrow$	$\downarrow$	$\cdots$	$\downarrow$	
seed $\rightarrow$		h_0	h_1	$\cdots$	h_m	$\rightarrow$ output
		$\downarrow$	$\downarrow$	$\cdots$	$\downarrow$	
		$h_0(\tilde{x}_0)$	$h_1(\tilde{x}_1)$	$\cdots$	$h_m(\tilde{x}_m)$	$\rightarrow$ output

It can be proven, following the arguments sketched above, that the output of this generator is indeed pseudorandom and longer than its seed length.

Entropy Equalization. We address the nonuniformity issue above by the following "entropy equalization" technique, which converts any next-block pseudoentropy generator into one where every block has guaranteed to have at least the average amount of pseudoentropy of the blocks in the original generator. It works by concatenating many independent samples of the next-block-pseudoentropy generator, but left-shifted by a random offset from $\{0, 1, \ldots, m\}$, so that each block of the new generator has equal probability of being each of the $m + 1$ blocks of the original generator. We do not use a cyclic shift, but rather drop appropriate parts of the first and last blocks.

Lemma 25.11 (Entropy equalization Haitner et al. [2009b], Haitner et al. [2013]) Let $X = (X_0,$ $\dots, X_m)$ be a random variable distributed on strings of length poly(n), where n is a security parameter. Suppose X has next-block pseudoentropy at least k. For a parameter $u \in \mathbb{N}$, consider the random variable $\hat{X}$ defined as follows:

1. Let $X^{(1)}, \dots, X^{(u)}$ be u independent samples of X, with blocks $X^{(i)} = (X_0^{(i)},$ $\dots, X_m^{(i)})$.

2. Choose $J \xleftarrow{R} \{0, \dots, m\}$.

3. Output

$$
\hat{X} = (\hat{X}_0, \hat{X}_1, \dots, \hat{X}_{(u-1)\cdot(m+1)})
$$

$$
\stackrel{\text{def}}{=} (J, X_J^{(1)}, X_{J+1}^{(1)}, \dots, X_m^{(1)}, X_0^{(2)}, \dots, X_m^{(2)}, \dots X_0^{(u-1)}, \dots,
$$

$$
X_m^{(u-1)}, X_0^{(u)}, \dots, X_{J-1}^{(u)}).
$$

That is, $\hat{X}_0 = J$ and $\hat{X}_i = X_{(J+i+m)\bmod(m+1)}^{(\lfloor (J+i+m)/(m+1) \rfloor)}$ for $i = 1, \dots, (u-1) \cdot (m+1)$.

Then for every $i = 1, \dots, (u-1) \cdot (m+1)$, $\hat{X}_i$ has pseudoentropy at least $k/(m+1)$ given $\hat{X}_0, \dots, \hat{X}_{i-1}$.

As stated above, the left-shifting is not cyclic; we drop J blocks of $X^{(1)}$ and $m + 1 - J$ blocks of $X^{(u)}$. Intuitively, $\hat{X}_i$ has pseudoentropy at least $k/(m+1)$ given the previous blocks because $\hat{X}_i$ is a copy of $X_{(J+i+m)\bmod(m+1)}$ and $(J + i + m) \bmod (m + 1)$ is uniformly distributed in $\{0, \dots, m\}$. Notice that the total next-block pseudoentropy guaranteed in the blocks $\hat{X}_i$ for $i > 1$ is $((t - 1) \cdot (m + 1)) \cdot (k/(m + 1)) = (t - 1) \cdot k$. We generated $\hat{X}$ using t copies of X, which had $t \cdot k$ bits of next-block pseudoentropy, but we lost one copy's worth of pseudoentropy by discarding a prefix of the first copy and a suffix of the last copy.

Applying this to the next-block pseudoentropy generator of Theorem 25.7, with $k = n + \omega(\log n)$, we can take $u = n/\log n$ and have

$$
(u - 1) \cdot k = u \cdot (n + \omega(\log n)) - k = u \cdot (n + \omega(\log n)),
$$

so we still have much more pseudoentropy than the $u \cdot n + \log u$ bits used to generate $\hat{X}$.

Applying the flattening and extraction procedure to this entropy-equalized next-block pseudoentropy generator (rather than to the one of Theorem 25.7), we obtain a uniformly computable pseudorandom generator that makes $q = u \cdot t = O(n^3)$

queries to the one-way functions (with a factor of $t = O(n^2)$ coming from flattening and a factor of $u = O(n)$ from entropy equalization), and has seed length $O(q \cdot n) = O(n^4)$.

To save an extra factor of n in the seed length as claimed in Theorem 25.5, the idea is to show that the repetitions used for entropy equalization need not be independent, and instead randomness can be (adaptively) recycled in a way that is similar to the length expansion for pseudorandom generators. We refer to Vadhan and Zheng [2012] for more details.

25.7   One-Way Functions to Statistically Hiding Commitments

In this section, we describe how another form of computational entropy, *inaccessible entropy*, is used to construct statistically hiding commitment schemes from one-way functions. In doing so, we will highlight the duality between the construction and notions used below and those that were used above for constructing pseudorandom generators.

Commitment Schemes.   Recall that a *commitment scheme* is a two-party protocol between a *sender* S and a *receiver* R. The protocol consists of two phases. In the *commit phase*, the sender takes as input a message m of length poly(n), in addition to both parties receiving the security parameter n. In the *reveal phase*, the sender reveals the message m to the receiver and "proves" that m is the message to which it committed in the first phase, after which the receiver accepts or rejects. Without loss of generality, the sender's proof can consist of the coin tosses r she used in the commit phase, and the receiver simply checks that the transcript of the commit phase is consistent with the behavior of the sender algorithm $S(m; r)$ on message m and coin tosses r.

A commitment scheme has two security requirements. Informally, the *hiding* property requires that the receiver should learn nothing about the message m during the commit phase. The *binding* property requires that after the commit phase, there should be a unique message m that the sender can successfully reveal. Typically, one of these two security properties is statistical (with security against computationally unbounded adversaries), while the other is computational.

Statistically binding commitments can be constructed from any pseudorandom generator [Naor 1991], and hence from any one-way function by Theorem 25.1. Thus, our focus in this section is on the analogous result for statistically hiding commitments:

Theorem 25.8   (Statistically hiding commitments from OWF Haitner et al. [2009a])   If there exists a one-way function, then there exists a statistically hiding commitment scheme.

The original proof of Theorem 25.8 was even more complex than the original proof of Theorem 25.1. Haitner, Reingold, Vadhan, and Wee [Haitner et al. 2009b] gave a much simpler and more conceptual proof using a new computational notion of entropy, called *inaccessible entropy*. That construction actually predated and inspired the more efficient construction of pseudorandom generators from one-way functions given in Section 25.6.

Commitment Schemes and Computational Entropy.   We begin by explaining, at an intuitive level, the relationship between commitment schemes and notions of computational entropy.

A *statistically binding* commitment scheme is very related to pseudorandomness and pseudoentropy. As mentioned above, Naor [1991] exhibited a very efficient construction of statistically binding commitments from any pseudorandom generator. Conversely, consider running a statistically binding commitment protocol on a uniformly random message M, and let T be the transcript of the commit phase. Then the statistical binding property implies that M has negligible real entropy given T (since with all but negligible probability over $t \leftarrow T$, there should be only one message m in the support of $M|_{T=t}$). On the other hand, the computational hiding property implies that M is pseudorandom given T (i.e., $(M, T) \stackrel{c}{\equiv} (U, T)$, where U is a uniformly random message independent of M and T). So the pseudoentropy of M given T is much higher than the real entropy of M given T.

Let us now consider the case of a *statistically hiding* commitment scheme. The statistical hiding property implies that M is statistically close to uniform given T (i.e., $(M, T) \stackrel{s}{\equiv} (U, T)$). On the other hand, the computational binding property says that, from the perspective of a polynomial-time sender, M is effectively determined by T. That is, although M has a lot of real entropy given T, a computationally bounded algorithm cannot "access" this entropy. This motivates the following definition of (*next-block*) *accessible entropy*, which should be thought of as "dual" to (next-block) pseudoentropy (Definition 25.16):

Definition 25.17   (Next-block accessible entropy Haitner et al. [2009b])   Let n be a security parameter, and $Y = (Y_1, \ldots, Y_m)$ be a random variable distributed on strings of length poly(n). We say that Y has *next-block accessible entropy at most* k if the following holds for some $s(n) = n^{\omega(1)}$.

Let $\tilde{G}$ be any nonuniform, probabilistic algorithm running in time $s(n)$ that takes a sequence of uniformly random strings $\tilde{R} = (\tilde{R}_1, \ldots, \tilde{R}_m)$ and outputs a sequence $\tilde{Y} = (\tilde{Y}_1, \ldots, \tilde{Y}_m)$ in an "online fashion" by which we mean that $\tilde{Y}_i = \tilde{G}(\tilde{R}_1, \ldots, \tilde{R}_i)$ depends on only the first i random strings of $\tilde{G}$ for $i = 1, \ldots, m$. Suppose further that $\text{Supp}(\tilde{Y}) \subseteq \text{Supp}(Y)$.

Then we require

$$\sum_{i=1}^{m} \mathrm{H}(\tilde{Y}_i | \tilde{R}_1, \dots, \tilde{R}_{i-1}) \le k.$$

For intuition, think of each individual block Y_i as corresponding to a message being committed to in a statistically hiding commitment scheme, and the prefix $Y_{<i} = (Y_1, \dots, Y_{i-1})$ as the transcript of a commit phase for Y_i. The adversary $\tilde{G}$ is analogous to a sender trying to break the computational binding property of the commitment scheme. $\tilde{G}$ is trying to generate a message $\tilde{Y}_i$ with as much entropy as possible, conditioned on its internal state after the commit phase, which is represented by its prior coin tosses $\tilde{R}_1, \dots, \tilde{R}_{i-1}$. The condition that $\mathrm{Supp}(\tilde{Y}) \subseteq \mathrm{Supp}(Y)$ is analogous to the fact that the reveal phase of a commitment scheme demands that the message revealed is consistent with the transcript of the commit phase. Indeed, the security properties of a statistically hiding commitment scheme can be captured by using a generalization of the definition of accessible entropy to messages in interactive protocols [Haitner et al. 2009b].

(Next-block) accessible entropy differs from (next-block) pseudoentropy in two ways:

1. Accessible entropy is useful as an *upper* bound on computational entropy, and is interesting when it is *smaller* than the real entropy $\mathrm{H}(Y)$. We refer to the gap $\mathrm{H}(Y) - k$ as the *inaccessible entropy* of Y.

2. The accessible entropy adversary $\tilde{G}$ is trying to *generate* the random variables Y_i conditioned on the history rather than recognize them. Note that we take the "history" to not only be the previous blocks $(\tilde{Y}_1, \dots, \tilde{Y}_{i-1})$, but the coin tosses $(\tilde{R}_1, \dots, \tilde{R}_{i-1})$ used by $\tilde{G}$ to generate those blocks. This ensures that the randomness we measure in $\tilde{Y}_i$ comes only from $\tilde{R}_i$, so $\tilde{G}$ really needs to operate in an online fashion. [6]

The proof of Theorem 25.8 begins by showing that every one-way function has next-block inaccessible entropy:

Theorem 25.9 (Inaccessible entropy from OWFs Haitner et al. [2009b]) Let $f : \{0, 1\}^n \to \{0, 1\}^n$ be a one-way function, let X be uniformly distributed in $\{0, 1\}^n$, and let $(Y_1, \dots, Y_m)$

---

6. If we had conditioned only on the prior output blocks $\tilde{Y}_1, \dots, \tilde{Y}_{i-1}$, then an adversary that runs an honest sampling algorithm once for $Y = (Y_1, \dots, Y_m)$ would achieve accessible entropy $\sum_i \mathrm{H}(\tilde{Y}_i | \tilde{Y}_1, \dots, \tilde{Y}_{i-1}) = \sum_i \mathrm{H}(Y_i | Y_1, \dots, Y_{i-1}) = \mathrm{H}(Y)$. Here the entire sequence is determined by $\tilde{R}_1$, the coin tosses for generating Y, but we can get nonzero entropy for blocks 2–m since $\tilde{Y}_1$ will not determine $\tilde{R}_1$ in general.

be a partition of $Y = f(X)$ into blocks of length $O(\log n)$. Then $(Y_1, \ldots, Y_m, X)$ has next-block accessible entropy at most $n - \omega(\log n)$.

Notice that this statement is similar to Theorem 25.7, except that it refers to accessible entropy rather than pseudoentropy, it asserts an upper bound rather than a lower bound on the computational entropy, and that it requires partitioning $f(X)$ rather than X into short blocks.

Given Theorem 25.9, the construction of statistically hiding commitments from one-way functions (Thm. 25.8) follows the same template as what we saw for pseudorandom generators in Section 25.6:

1. An "entropy equalization" step that converts $Y = (Y_1, Y_2, \ldots, Y_{m+1})$ into a random variable $\hat{Y} = (Y_0, Y_2, \ldots, Y_{\hat{m}})$ generator where (a lower bound on) the real entropy in each block conditioned on the prior blocks before it is known, and the total next-block accessible entropy is significantly smaller than the total real entropy. The construction is exactly the same as in Lemma 25.11.

2. A "flattening" step that converts the real Shannon entropy guarantees into real min-entropy. Specifically, after flattening each block will have high (smoothed) min-entropy, while the total next-block accessible entropy is significantly smaller than the total smoothed min-entropy. This construction is again exactly the same as what we saw for pseudorandom generators. Note that we do not claim that the accessible entropy gets converted into accessible *max*-entropy by flattening; the reason is that the adversarial generator need not behave independently across the repetitions of flattening.

3. A "hashing" step that converts the high min-entropy in each block to nearly uniform randomness, and turns the low accessible entropy into a weak binding property (uniquely determining the block with noticeable probability, similar in spirit to Lemma 25.2). The reason that the binding property is weak comes from the fact that we only have a bound on accessible Shannon entropy (as discussed above) and from the fact that an adversarial generator has freedom in how to spread the accessible entropy across the blocks. Moreover, in order to tolerate potentially malicious senders (as is required for binding), it is not enough to directly apply universal hashing, as the sender could then decide on the message/block $\tilde{Y}_i$ after seeing the hash function. Instead, we use (information-theoretic) "interactive hashing" [Naor et al. 1998, Ding et al. 2007], which is designed to address this issue. Constructing full-fledged statistically hiding commitments in this step also utilizes universal one-way

hash functions [Naor and Yung 1989], which can be constructed from one-way functions [Rompel 1990], as well some additional repetitions to amplify the weak binding property. Without universal one-way hash functions, we obtain a non-standard weak binding property, which nevertheless suffices for some applications, such as constructing statistical zero-knowledge arguments for all of **NP**.

For the proof of Theorem 25.9, we recommend the recent work of Agrawal, Chen, Horel, and Vadhan [Agrawal et al. 2019], which gives a new, more modular proof that uses a strengthening of KL-hardness (Definition 25.15), which further illuminates the duality between next-block pseudoentropy and next-block accessible entropy.

References

R. Agrawal, Y.-H. Chen, T. Horel, and S. Vadhan. 2019. Unifying computational entropies via Kullback-Leibler divergence. Technical Report 1902.11202 [cs.CR], arXiv. 694, 722

B. Barak, R. Shaltiel, and A. Wigderson. 2003. Computational analogues of entropy. In S. Arora, K. Jansen, J. D. P. Rolim, and A. Sahai, editors, *Approximation, Randomization, and Combinatorial Optimization: Algorithms and Techniques*, pp. 200–215. Springer. DOI: 10.1007/978-3-540-45198-3_18. 695, 708

B. Barak, M. Hardt, and S. Kale. 2009. The uniform hardcore lemma via approximate Bregman projections. In *Proceedings of the Twentieth Annual ACM-SIAM Symposium on Discrete Algorithms*, SODA '09, pp. 1193–1200. Society for Industrial and Applied Mathematics, Philadelphia. DOI: 10.1137/1.9781611973068.129. 710

M. Bellare. 2002. A note on negligible functions. *Journal of Cryptology*, 15(4): 271–284. DOI: 10.1007/s00145-002-0116-x. 701

M. Bellare, S. Micali, and R. Ostrovsky. 1990. Perfect zero-knowledge in constant rounds. In *Proceedings of the 22nd Annual ACM Symposium on Theory of Computing*, STOC '90, pp. 482–493. ACM, New York. DOI: 10.1145/100216.100283. 696

C. H. Bennett, G. Brassard, and J.-M. Robert. 1988. Privacy amplification by public discussion. *SIAM Journal on Computing*, 17(2): 210–229. Special issue on cryptography. DOI: 10.1137/0217014. 697

M. Blum and S. Micali. 1984. How to generate cryptographically strong sequences of pseudorandom bits. *SIAM Journal on Computing*, 13(4): 850–864. DOI: 10.1137/0213053. 693, 695, 702, 706, 715

G. Brassard, D. Chaum, and C. Crépeau. 1988. Minimum disclosure proofs of knowledge. *Journal of Computer and System Sciences*, 37(2): 156–189. DOI: 10.1016/0022-0000(88)90005-0. 694

B. Chor and O. Goldreich. 1988. Unbiased bits from sources of weak randomness and probabilistic communication complexity. *SIAM Journal on Computing*, 17(2): 230–261. DOI: 10.1137/0217015. 697

K.-M. Chung, Y. T. Kalai, F.-H. Liu, and R. Raz. 2011. Memory delegation. In *Proceedings of the 31st Annual Conference on Advances in Cryptology, CRYPTO '11*, pp. 151–165. Springer-Verlag, Berlin. DOI: 10.1007/978-3-642-22792-9_9. 695

W. Diffie and M. E. Hellman. 1976. New directions in cryptography. *IEEE Transactions on Information Theory*, 22(6): 644–654. DOI: 10.1109/TIT.1976.1055638. 693, 701

Y. Z. Ding, D. Harnik, A. Rosen, and R. Shaltiel. 2007. Constant-round oblivious transfer in the bounded storage model. *Journal of Cryptology*, 20(2): 165–202. DOI: 10.1007/s00145-006-0438-1. 721

Y. Dodis, R. Ostrovsky, L. Reyzin, and A. Smith. 2008. Fuzzy extractors: How to generate strong keys from biometrics and other noisy data. *SIAM Journal of Computing*, 38(1): 97–139. DOI: 10.1137/060651380. 699, 700

S. Dziembowski and K. Pietrzak. 2008. Leakage-resilient cryptography. In *Proceedings of the 2008 49th Annual IEEE Symposium on Foundations of Computer Science*, pp. 293–302. IEEE Computer Society, Washington, DC. DOI: 10.1109/FOCS.2008.56. 695

B. Fuller, A. O'Neill, and L. Reyzin. 2015. A unified approach to deterministic encryption: New constructions and a connection to computational entropy. *Journal of Cryptology*, 28(3): 671–717. DOI: 10.1007/s00145-013-9174-5. 695

O. Goldreich. 2001. *Foundations of Cryptography: Volume 1, Basic Techniques*. Cambridge University Press, Cambridge. 723

O. Goldreich. 2008. *Computational Complexity: A Conceptual Perspective*. Cambridge University Press, Cambridge. 695

O. Goldreich. 2019. On the foundations of cryptography. In *Providing Sound Foundations for Cryptography: On the Work of Shafi Goldwasser and Silvio Micali*, Chapter 17. Association for Computing Machinery and Morgan & Claypool. This volume. 695

O. Goldreich and H. Krawczyk. 1992. Sparse pseudorandom distributions. *Random Structures & Algorithms*, 3(2): 163–174. DOI: 10.1002/rsa.3240030206. 704

O. Goldreich and L. A. Levin. 1989. A hard-core predicate for all one-way functions. In *Proceedings of the 21st Annual ACM Symposium on Theory of Computing*, pp. 25–32. Seattle. DOI: 10.1145/73007.73010. 695, 706, 709

O. Goldreich and B. Meyer. 1998. Computational indistinguishability: Algorithms vs. circuits. *Theoretical Computer Science*, 191(1–2): 215–218. DOI: 10.1016/S0304-3975(97)00162-X. 705

O. Goldreich and S. Micali, 1984. Unpublished manuscript. See Goldreich [2001, Sec. 3.3.2]. 703

O. Goldreich, S. Goldwasser, and S. Micali. 1986. How to construct random functions. *Journal of the ACM*, 33(4): 792–807. DOI: 10.1145/6490.6503. 693

O. Goldreich, S. Micali, and A. Wigderson. 1991. Proofs that yield nothing but their validity or all languages in NP have zero-knowledge proof systems. *Journal of the ACM*, 38(3): 690–728. DOI: 10.1145/116825.116852. 693

S. Goldwasser and S. Micali. 1984. Probabilistic encryption. *Journal of Computer and System Sciences*, 28(2): 270–299. DOI: 10.1016/0022-0000(84)90070-9. 693, 702

S. Goldwasser, S. Micali, and R. L. Rivest. 1988. A digital signature scheme secure against adaptive chosen-message attacks. *SIAM Journal on Computing*, 17(2): 281–308. Preliminary version in *FOCS '84*. DOI: 10.1137/0217017. 693

I. Haitner and S. P. Vadhan. 2017. The many entropies in one-way functions. In Y. Lindell, editor, *Tutorials on the Foundations of Cryptography—Dedicated to Oded Goldreich*, pp. 159–217. Springer. Also posted as *ECCC* TR17-084. DOI: 10.1007/978-3-319-57048-8_4. 695

I. Haitner, M. Nguyen, S. Ong, O. Reingold, and S. Vadhan. 2009a. Statistically hiding commitments and statistical zero-knowledge arguments from any one-way function. *SIAM Journal on Computing*, 39(3): 1153–1218. DOI: 10.1137/080725404. 693, 694, 696, 718

I. Haitner, O. Reingold, S. Vadhan, and H. Wee. 2009b. Inaccessible entropy. In *Proceedings of the 41st Annual ACM Symposium on Theory of Computing*, pp. 611–620. ACM, New York. DOI: 10.1145/1536414.1536497. 694, 695, 717, 719, 720

I. Haitner, T. Holenstein, O. Reingold, S. Vadhan, and H. Wee. 2010. Universal one-way hash functions via inaccessible entropy. In *Proceedings of the 29th Annual International Conference on Theory and Applications of Cryptographic Techniques, EUROCRYPT '10*, pp. 616–637. Springer-Verlag, Berlin. DOI: 10.1007/978-3-642-13190-5_31. 694

I. Haitner, O. Reingold, and S. Vadhan. 2013. Efficiency improvements in constructing pseudorandom generators from one-way functions. *SIAM Journal on Computing*, 42(3): 1405–1430. DOI: 10.1137/100814421. 694, 695, 705, 710, 714, 717

I. Haitner, K. Nissim, E. Omri, R. Shaltiel, and J. Silbak. 2018. Computational two-party correlation: A dichotomy for key-agreement protocols. In *2018 IEEE 59th Annual Symposium on Foundations of Computer Science*, pp. 136–147. DOI: 10.1109/FOCS.2018.00022. 695

J. Håstad, R. Impagliazzo, L. Levin, and M. Luby. 1999. A pseudorandom generator from any one-way function. *SIAM Journal on Computing*, 28(4): 1364–1396. DOI: 10.1137/S0097539793244708. 693, 694, 697, 700, 703, 704, 705, 706

T. Holenstein and R. Renner. 2011. On the randomness of independent experiments. *IEEE Transactions on Information Theory*, 57(4): 1865–1871. DOI: 10.1109/TIT.2011.2110230. 700, 701

C.-Y. Hsiao, C.-J. Lu, and L. Reyzin. 2007. Conditional computational entropy, or toward separating pseudoentropy from compressibility. In M. Naor, editor, *Advances in Cryptology—EUROCRYPT 2007*, pp. 169–186. Springer, Berlin. DOI: 10.1007/978-3-540-72540-4_10. 706, 707, 708

R. Impagliazzo. 1995. Hard-core distributions for somewhat hard problems. In *36th Annual Symposium on Foundations of Computer Science*, pp. 538–545. IEEE, Milwaukee. DOI: 10.1109/SFCS.1995.492584. 710

R. Impagliazzo and M. Luby. 1989. One-way functions are essential for complexity based cryptography. In *Proceedings of the 30th Annual Symposium on Foundations of Computer Science*, pp. 230–235. IEEE Computer Society, Washington, DC. DOI: 10.1109/SFCS .1989.63483. 693

T. Itoh, Y. Ohta, and H. Shizuya. 1997. A language-dependent cryptographic primitive. *Journal of Cryptology*, 10(1): 37–49. DOI: 10.1007/s001459900018. 696

A. R. Klivans and R. A. Servedio. 2003. Boosting and hard-core set construction. *Machine Learning*, 51(3): 217–238. DOI: 10.1023/A:1022949332276. 710

D. Micciancio and S. Vadhan. 2003. Statistical zero-knowledge proofs with efficient provers: Lattice problems and more. In D. Boneh, editor, *Advances in Cryptology—CRYPTO '03*, vol. 2729 of Lecture Notes in Computer Science, pp. 282–298. Springer-Verlag. DOI: 10.1007/978-3-540-45146-4_17. 696

I. Mironov, O. Pandey, O. Reingold, and S. Vadhan. 2009. Computational differential privacy. In S. Halevi, editor, *Advances in Cryptology—CRYPTO '09*, vol. 5677, Lecture Notes in Computer Science, pp. 126–142. Springer-Verlag. DOI: 10.1007/978-3-642-03356-8_8. 695

M. Naor. 1991. Bit commitment using pseudorandomness. *Journal of Cryptology*, 4(2): 151–158. DOI: 10.1007/BF00196774. 693, 718, 719

M. Naor and M. Yung. 1989. Universal one-way hash functions and their cryptographic applications. In *Proceedings of the 21st Annual ACM Symposium on Theory of Computing*, pp. 33–43. ACM, New York. DOI: 10.1145/73007.73011. 693, 694, 722

M. Naor, R. Ostrovsky, R. Venkatesan, and M. Yung. 1998. Perfect zero-knowledge arguments for NP using any one-way permutation. *Journal of Cryptology*, 11(2): 87–108. DOI: 10 .1007/s001459900037. 721

M. Nguyen and S. Vadhan. 2006. Zero knowledge with efficient provers. In *Proceedings of the 38th Annual ACM Symposium on Theory of Computing*, pp. 287–295. DOI: 10.1145/ 1132516.1132559. 696

N. Nisan and D. Zuckerman. 1996. Randomness is linear in space. *Journal of Computer and System Sciences*, 52(1): 43–52. DOI: 10.1006/jcss.1996.0004. 697

S. J. Ong and S. Vadhan. 2007. Zero knowledge and soundness are symmetric. In M. Naor, editor, *Advances in Cryptology—EUROCRYPT '07*, vol. 4515, Lecture Notes in Computer Science, pp. 187–209. Springer-Verlag. DOI: 10.1007/978-3-540-72540-4_11.pdf. 696

J. Radhakrishnan and A. Ta-Shma. 2000. Bounds for dispersers, extractors, and depth-two superconcentrators. *SIAM Journal on Discrete Mathematics*, 13(1): 2–24, (electronic). DOI: 10.1137/S0895480197329508. 698

O. Reingold, L. Trevisan, and S. Vadhan. 2004. Notions of reducibility between cryptographic primitives. In M. Naor, editor, *Proceedings of the First Theory of Cryptography*

Conference, TCC '04, vol. 2951, Lecture Notes in Computer Science, pp. 1–20. Springer-Verlag. DOI: 10.1007/978-3-540-24638-1_1. 703

R. Renner and S. Wolf. 2005. Simple and tight bounds for information reconciliation and privacy amplification. In *Proceedings of the 11th International Conference on Theory and Application of Cryptology and Information Security, ASIACRYPT '05*, pp. 199–216. Springer-Verlag. DOI: 10.1007/11593447_11. 698

J. Rompel. 1990. One-way functions are necessary and sufficient for secure signatures. In *Proceedings of the 22nd Annual ACM Symposium on Theory of Computing*, pp. 387–394. ACM, New York. DOI: 10.1145/100216.100269. 693, 694, 722

M. Skórski, A. Golovnev, and K. Pietrzak. 2015. Condensed unpredictability. In M. M. Halldórsson, K. Iwama, N. Kobayashi, and B. Speckmann, editors, *Automata, Languages, and Programming*, pp. 1046–1057. Springer. DOI: 10.1007/978-3-662-47672-7_85. 710

M. Sudan, L. Trevisan, and S. Vadhan. 2001. Pseudorandom generators without the XOR lemma. *Journal of Computer and System Sciences*, 62: 236–266. 710

A. Ta-Shma and D. Zuckerman. 2004. Extractor codes. *IEEE Transactions on Information Theory*, 50(12): 3015–3025. DOI: 10.1109/TIT.2004.838377. 708

L. Trevisan. 2001. Extractors and pseudorandom generators. *Journal of the ACM*, 48(4): 860–879 (electronic). DOI: 10.1145/502090.502099. 708

S. Vadhan and C. J. Zheng. 2012. Characterizing pseudoentropy and simplifying pseudorandom generator constructions. In *Proceedings of the 44th Annual ACM Symposium on Theory of Computing*, pp. 817–836. ACM, New York. DOI: 10.1145/2213977.2214051. 694, 695, 710, 712, 713, 715, 718

S. P. Vadhan. 1999. *A Study of Statistical Zero-Knowledge Proofs*. Ph.D. thesis, Massachusetts Institute of Technology. 696

S. P. Vadhan. 2012. Pseudorandomness. *Foundations and Trends in Theoretical Computer Science*, 7(1–3): 1–336. DOI: 10.1561/0400000010. 695, 698, 699, 708

A. C. Yao. 1982. Theory and application of trapdoor functions. In *23rd Annual Symposium on Foundations of Computer Science*, pp. 80–91. DOI: 10.1109/SFCS.1982.45. 693, 695, 702, 706

C. J. Zheng. 2014. *A Uniform Min-Max Theorem and Characterizations of Computational Randomness*. Ph.D. thesis, Harvard University. http://nrs.harvard.edu/urn-3:HUL.InstRepos:11745716. 710

A Survey of Leakage-Resilient Cryptography

Yael Tauman Kalai and Leonid Reyzin

In the past 15 years, cryptography has made considerable progress in expanding the adversarial attack model to cover side-channel attacks and has built schemes to provably defend against some of them. This survey covers the main models and results in this so-called leakage-resilient cryptography.

26.1 Introduction

In most theoretical work on cryptography, parties are afforded complete privacy for their local computations. An adversary may, perhaps, be able to obtain a signature on a chosen plaintext or a decryption of a chosen ciphertext, but typically the signing or decryption process itself is assumed to be entirely hidden from the adversary. In particular, the only information correlated with the secret key that the theoretical adversary can obtain is typically confined to well-defined interfaces, such as signing or decrypting. Such an adversary is sometimes called a "black-box" attacker.

Work in modern cryptography—much of it pioneered by Shafi Goldwasser and Silvio Micali—demonstrated that it is possible to provably (based on certain computational complexity assumptions) defend against black-box attackers for large classes of cryptographic tasks, such as pseudorandom generation [Blum and Micali 1982, 1984, Goldreich et al. 1984, 1986], encryption [Goldwasser and Micali 1982, 1984], signatures [Goldwasser et al. 1984, 1988], zero-knowledge proofs [Goldwasser et al. 1985, 1989, 1986, 1991], and secure multi-party computation [Goldreich et al. 1987, Ben-Or et al. 1988].

Real adversaries, unfortunately, do not always respect such clean abstraction boundaries. A variety of successful *side-channel attacks* have demonstrated that information about the secret key and the internal state of a computation can leak out to a determined adversary. These attacks exploit the fact that every cryptographic algorithm is ultimately implemented on a physical device that affects the environment around it in measurable ways. To mention just a few prominent examples, attacks have exploited the time taken by a particular implementation of a cryptographic algorithm [Kocher 1996], the amount of power consumed [Kocher et al. 1999], or the electromagnetic radiation [Agrawal et al. 2003]. So-called *cold boot* attacks [Halderman et al. 2008, Halderman 2009] have been used to recover some fraction of a cryptographic secret key given physical access to a powered-off device. More recent attacks [Lipp et al. 2018, Kocher et al. 2019] allow processes to violate isolation boundaries and read information from other processes on the same machine—even those in secure enclaves [Van Bulck et al. 2018]. In other words, the real adversary may not be black-box.

The emergence of side-channel attacks caused the cryptographic community to re-evaluate the black-box adversary model and to create new adversary models and provably secure designs. This line of work became known as "leakage-resilient cryptography." Shafi Goldwasser and Silvio Micali were again prominent in this effort, both because their past work on black-box security informed models for leakage resilience, and because they themselves proposed models that formalize side-channel leakage and designed leakage-resilient schemes.

In this survey we cover some of the work on leakage-resilient cryptography. It is important to emphasize that our selection is biased toward more theoretical and foundational works. Even among those, our choices are necessarily biased by work we know. The field is vast and rapidly growing: As of Februrary 2019, Google Scholar finds over 400 papers with the phrase "leakage resilient" or "leakage resilience" in the title, and about 2800 with the phrase "leakage resilient" in the paper (98% of them published after 2006).

We do not address the vast literature dealing with adversaries who actively tamper with the memory or computation of the honest parties, rather than merely observe it (see, e.g., [Gennaro et al. 2004, Ishai et al. 2006, Dziembowski et al. 2010, Faust et al. 2011, Liu and Lysyanskaya 2012, Faust et al. 2014a, Jafargholi and Wichs 2015, Faust et al. 2015], and [Dachman-Soled et al. 2015a]), even though it is, of course, connected to the literature on leakage resilience, and often includes leakage resilience as one of its goals.

We apologize in advance to authors whose work we could not include and to readers who will be left to discover other work on their own.

Because leakage-resilient cryptography is a relatively young subset of cryptography, the gap between theory and practice is fairly large. This gap manifests itself in the debates about the practical relevance of theoretical models and the inefficiencies of provably secure constructions. This survey focuses on more theoretical work. An excellent source of more applied research in this field is the Conference on Cryptographic Hardware and Embedded Systems (CHES) and the journal IACR Transactions on Cryptographic Hardware and Embedded Systems (TCHES).

A Bibliographic Note.   For most papers, we cite the conference version. In the few cases we are aware of the journal version, we cite it, as well. Many papers we cite have full versions that were too long to appear in conference proceedings, easily found through an on-line search, more often than not posted on https://eprint.iacr .org. These full versions sometimes correct errors that appeared in the conference version.

26.1.1   Early Works

Early works—such as work on oblivious RAM [Goldreich and Ostrovsky 1996], threshold [Desmedt and Frankel 1990] and proactive [Herzberg et al. 1997] cryptography, and forward [Günther 1990, Bellare and Miner 1999] and intrusion-resilient [Itkis and Reyzin 2002] security—can be thought of, in hindsight, as works on leakage resilience. There are many other examples, too numerous to mention here.

We now elaborate on two particular lines of work. The first of these considers leakage of some of the bits of the secret key. The second one considers leakage during computation.

Leaking Bits from Keys.   Motivated by the problem of key exposure, Canetti et al. [2000], followed by Dodis, Sahai, and Smith [Dodis et al. 2001], proposed an approach of storing a cryptographic key in a redundant form, so that the key remains hidden even when some of the stored bits are leaked to the adversary. They introduced the notion of an "exposure-resilient function" and showed a connection to "all-or-nothing transforms" [Rivest 1997, Boyko 1999]. See Dodis [2000] for a detailed exposition of these results. These results were limited to leakage that consisted of subsets of bits of the stored secret, rather than more general functions of it.

This line of work was generalized by the long sequence of works on *memory leakage*, pioneered by Dziembowski [2006], Di Crescenzo, Lipton, and Walfish [Di Crescenzo et al. 2006], and Akavia, Goldwasser, and Vaikuntanathan [Akavia et al. 2009], who considered *arbitrary* (poly-time computable) partial leakage from memory. We elaborate on these works in Section 26.1.2 and Section 26.2.

Leakage from Computation.   Chari et al. [1999] considered a formal model of attacks in which every bit produced in a computation (i.e., every wire of a circuit) can be measured by the adversary, but each measurement has noise (their model was informed, in particular, by the differential power analysis attacks of Kocher et al. [1999]). Independently, Goubin and Patarin [1999], also concerned about differential power analysis attacks, considered how to keep individual wire values in a smart-card circuit independent of the secret key. Both papers suggested the following countermeasure: represent each bit b by k random bits whose exclusive-or is equal to b (this approach is also known as XOR-secret sharing or Boolean masking). Chari et al. [1999] showed that, given the noisy reading of all k shares of b, the adversary can distinguish $b = 0$ from $b = 1$ only with advantage that is exponentially small in k. They did not, however, show how to compute on shared versions of bits. In contrast, Goubin and Patarin [1999] showed how to compute certain functions using the shared versions of bits, but without a formal model in which to argue security.

Precise models and provable approaches to handling leakage from computation were pioneered by the works of Ishai, Sahai, and Wagner [Ishai et al. 2003] and Micali and Reyzin [2004]. We discuss this line of work in Section 26.1.2 and Section 26.4.

26.1.2   Formalisms of Leakage-Resilient Cryptography

We coarsely divide the works on leakage-resilient cryptography into two strands. The first of these considers leakage from memory, while the second considers leakage during computation.

Memory Leakage.   In most common models of memory leakage, the adversary is usually allowed obtain an *arbitrary* polynomial-time computable but bounded-length leakage on the secret key. The goal is to build cryptographic schemes that remain secure even if this partial information about the secret key is available to the adversary.

Dziembowski [2006] and Di Crescenzo, Lipton, and Walfish [Di Crescenzo et al. 2006] defined the term *bounded retrieval model*, which assumes that the adversary can obtain at most K bits of information about the secret key, for some (absolute, large) value K. The secret key is allowed to be larger than K, as long as the efficiency of the scheme is not negatively affected: The running times of the relevant algorithms should grow only polylogarithmically with K. They constructed leakage-resilient symmetric password and authentication protocols in this model.

Akavia, Goldwasser, and Vaikuntanathan [Akavia et al. 2009] considered arbitrary leakage in the public-key setting. They considered the so-called *bounded memory leakage*, in which the amount of leakage is not an absolute value but rather is expressed as a function of the secret-key size (but growing the key is expensive, because the running times of the relevant algorithms can grow polynomially with the key size). Public-key schemes in the bounded retrieval model of Dziembowski [2006] and Di Crescenzo et al. [2006] were also subsequently constructed [Alwen et al. 2009]. The bounded memory leakage model was later generalized to so-called *auxiliary input leakage* [Dodis et al. 2009]. In this model, leakage is not necessarily bounded in size: the only requirement is the minimum necessary for any security to remain, namely, that the secret should remain computationally hidden even given the leakage. Memory leakage was also generalized to the continual setting [Brakerski et al. 2010, Dodis et al. 2010b], in which the secret key is periodically updated, *without updating the public key*, and it is assumed that there is bounded memory leakage within each time period, but there is no bound on the overall leakage.

We elaborate on this line of work in Section 26.2.

Computation Leakage.   The line of work on leakage from computation considers the situation in which side-channel information comes from the intermediate values created during a computation, rather than only from the secret itself. Sometimes memory leakage models discussed above can also model leakage of intermediate values created during a computation, because these values are just functions of the secret memory. However, this approach to modeling leakage from computation fails whenever secret randomness is used during a computation (though a few papers on memory leakage do model leakage from secret randomness; see Section 26.2 for details).

There are even more important distinctions between the models of memory and computation leakage. Memory leakage models most typically consider one-time leakage (but see Section 26.2.5 for exceptions), while computational leakage models typically consider continual leakage over multiple uses of the secret key, forcing constructions to update the secret memory in order to maintain security. On the other hand, computation leakage models usually place more restrictions on the allowed leakage, such as, for example, assuming that different components of a computation that are separated in space or in time leak independently (i.e., the adversary can obtain separate leakage functions of some intermediate values, but not a joint function of them all), or that some memory does not leak at all. This is in contrast to memory leakage models, which usually allow the leakage to be an arbitrary (bounded) function of the entire secret.

Ishai, Sahai, and Wagner [Ishai et al. 2003] built on the work of Chari et al. [1999] to model leakage from wires of a circuit. In the model of Ishai et al. [2003], the computation is performed by a clocked circuit with a secret state (e.g., a circuit implementing a block cipher with a secret key). The circuit is run repeatedly on various inputs, producing outputs and possibly also updating the state. The adversary is able to provide inputs and observe outputs as well as the exact values of some internal wires during the computation. This model and its variants resulted in a long line of work that we survey in Section 26.4.3.

Micali and Reyzin [2004] gave a more general model of leakage during computation. They modeled computation as proceeding in steps, and allowed the adversary to obtain different side-channel information at each step. Specifically, they described their model in terms of random-access machines (RAMs, which are Turing machines augmented with addressable memory) rather than circuits, although circuit variants of their model were considered later. In this model, an adversary is able to specify a leakage function (from a class of available functions) at each step of the computation. The function is applied to the current state of the computing machine and the output is given to the adversary, who uses this information to specify the function for the next step. In order to enable security against such general attacks, Micali and Reyzin assumed the existence of secure storage that is not given to the leakage function. That is, values can leak when being computed on and being read from or written to memory, but once they are in memory, the leakage function has no access to them. This assumption became known as "only computation leaks information," commonly abbreviated as OCL. This assumption was generalized in later work, as discussed in Sections 26.3 and 26.4 (see, in particular, Section 26.4.1). The power of this assumption comes from enabling constructions that separate computation into two or more components that leak independently, as shown in Dziembowski and Pietrzak [2008] (see Section 26.4.2.2).

We elaborate on leakage from computation in Section 26.4.

26.1.3 Roadmap

In this survey, we address the two strands of works on leakage-resilient cryptography: "leakage from memory" (Section 26.2) and "leakage from computation" (Section 26.4).

We emphasize that this division is not perfect. Some papers consider both memory and computational leakage. In addition, some papers on memory leakage use results on computational leakage, and vice versa. Nevertheless, we feel this division is helpful for systematizing knowledge in this area.

There is yet another category of papers on "leakage-resilient storage". This category lies in between the two categories described above. It considers the problem of storage, rather than computation, and thus considers leakage from memory. However, papers in this category typically restrict the leakage function in the same way as works in the "computational leakage" category do: the stored secret is separated into components, and leakage functions are applied separately to each component, but never jointly to all of them. The works in this category are described in Section 26.3.

We assume that the readers possesses a solid background in cryptography and is familiar with such concepts as CPA-secure encryption, zero-knowledge proofs, and secure multi-party computation. We assume the reader is reasonably comfortable with commonly used tools, such as randomness extractors[1] and pseudorandom generators.[2]

26.2 Memory Leakage

The main goal of works discussed in this section is to build cryptographic schemes that can remain secure even if some partial information about the secret key is available to the adversary. It is important to recall the basic fact that the adversarial inability to recover the full secret key is a necessary, but not a sufficient, condition for the security of a cryptographic construction.

26.2.1 The Models for Memory Leakage

As already mentioned in Section 26.1.2, Dziembowski [2006] and Di Crescenzo, Lipton, and Walfish [Di Crescenzo et al. 2006] considered arbitrary leakage from memory, proposing the *bounded retrieval model*. In this model, the adversary can obtain an arbitrary polynomial-time computable leakage function of the secret key, but the output size of this leakage function is bounded. Security is achieved

---

1. The notion of a seeded randomness extractor, introduced by Nisan and Zuckerman [1996], is defined as follows: A function $\mathsf{Ext}: \{0,1\}^n \times \{0,1\}^d \to \{0,1\}^\ell$ is said to be a (k, ε) extractor if for any random variable X over $\{0,1\}^n$ with min-entropy k, and for a uniformly chosen $r \leftarrow \{0,1\}^d$, it holds that $(r, \mathsf{Ext}(x,r))$ is ε-statistically close to a uniform string over $\{0,1\}^{d+\ell}$.

2. The notion of a cryptographic pseudorandom generator (PRG), introduced in Blum and Micali [1982], Yao [1982], and Blum and Micali [1984], is defined as follows: A function $G: \{0,1\}^k \to \{0,1\}^\ell$ is a PRG if, for a uniform secret s, the output $G(s)$ is computationally indistinguishable from a uniform string over $\{0,1\}^\ell$.

by making the secret key longer than this leakage length bound. While in most cryptographic schemes long secret keys would translate into long running times, this model requires that essentially the only price for increased leakage should be increased secret storage: The running time of the parties should grow only logarithmically with the leakage length bound. In particular, the parties do not need to access the entire long secret key for each operation. We discuss this model and relevant constructions in Section 26.2.4. Initially, works in the bounded retrieval model achieved only symmetric-key cryptographic constructions, because growing the secret key size while maintaining the public key the same presents a challenge.

In the public-key setting, Akavia, Goldwasser, and Vaikuntanathan [Akavia et al. 2009] considered arbitrary leakage from the secret key, defining the term *bounded memory leakage*, also known as *relative memory leakage*. In this model, similarly to the bounded retrieval model, the leakage function is an arbitrary bounded-output-length polynomial-time computable function, but the output length of this function is expressed as function of the key length (or, more generally, of the min-entropy of the key). Typically, the goal is to obtain security even if a large fraction of the secret key (or its min-entropy) is leaked. Unlike the bounded retrieval model, this model does not place any restrictions on running times, and thus increasing key size in order to allow more leakage (in absolute terms) will negatively affect the performance of most constructions. We elaborate on this model in Section 26.2.2.

Shortly after, Dodis, Kalai, and Lovett [Dodis et al. 2009] generalized the notion of bounded leakage to so-called *auxiliary input leakage*. In this model, the leakage function can have *unbounded* output length, and the only restriction is that given the leakage (and the public interface) it is (computationally) hard to find the secret key. This restriction seems to be the minimal necessary to achieve meaningful security, because no security remains if the secret key can be computed from the leakage. We elaborate on this model in Section 26.2.3.

Even though the auxiliary input leakage model seems the strongest possible for one-time leakage, it cannot protect against continual leakage, where the secret key is leaked continually a few bits at a time, since in this case the secret key can eventually leak entirely. To handle leakage over the long term, the continual memory leakage model, defined by Brakerski et al. [2010] and Dodis et al. [2010b], considers the setting in which the secret key is periodically updated, *without updating the public key*, and assumes that there is bounded memory leakage (in the sense of Akavia et al. [2009]) within each time period, but there is no bound on the overall leakage. We elaborate on this line of work in Section 26.2.5.

We emphasize that in all four models mentioned above, each bit of leakage can be an *arbitrary* efficiently computable function of the secret key (with the minimal necessary restriction in the auxiliary input case). This is in contrast to the leakage models that are considered in Sections 26.3 and 26.4, where the leakage functions are restricted in some way (such as OCL, noisy, or low-complexity leakage).

In Sections 26.2.2–26.2.5, we define the foregoing leakage models and show constructions of specific leakage-resilient cryptographic systems. We emphasize that, in most cases, the leakage function is applied only to the *secret key* (and publicly available information, such as the public key), and no leakage occurs during computation. For example, leakage cannot depend on the secret randomness used during a computation. There are a few exceptions, starting from the work of Boyle et al. [2011b] (mentioned in Section 26.2.2, below), which constructs a signature scheme in the bounded memory leakage that is secure even if the leakage is applied to the secret key *and* the randomness used to generate a signature.

In Sections 26.2.2–26.2.5, we focus on constructing non-interactive cryptographic primitives, such as leakage-resilient encryption schemes and signature schemes. In Section 26.2.6 we consider leakage-resilient interactive protocols, which are different from cryptographic schemes discussed in Sections 26.2.2–26.2.5, in that the leakage does not necessarily come from the secret key. Thus, in the setting of interactive protocols, it is more difficult to define security in the presence of leakage, since we have to account for leakage coming not from secret keys, which are meaningless on their own, but from protocol inputs (e.g., witnesses to ZK statements), which carry meaningful private information.

26.2.2 Bounded Memory Leakage

As mentioned above, Akavia, Goldwasswer, and Vaikuntanathan [Akavia et al. 2009] introduced the notion of *bounded memory leakage*. They considered an adversarial model in which the adversary can request a bounded amount of leakage on the secret key, adaptively one bit at a time. Let κ be the length of the secret key sk and let $\alpha \in (0, 1)$ be the allowed leakage fraction. In this model the adversary can make $\alpha\kappa$ oracle queries, where each query consists of a Boolean circuit $C : \{0, 1\}^\kappa \rightarrow \{0, 1\}$ and is answered by $C(\text{sk})$. Each circuit can be chosen based on previous leakage information and other information known to the adversary from the public interface (such as the public key, known signatures, etc.). We note that the size of each circuit is obviously bounded by the running time of the adversary, and hence leakage functions have bounded complexity. If the adversary cannot break the scheme after at most $\alpha\kappa$ such leakage queries, then the scheme is said to be α-leakage-resilient.

As observed in Akavia et al. [2009], any public key encryption scheme that is secure against adversaries running in time $2^{\alpha\kappa}$ is also α-leakage-resilient. Intuitively, this follows from the fact that if one can break the scheme with $L = L(\kappa)$ bits of leakage in time $T = T(\kappa)$, then one can break the scheme without any leakage in time $2^L \cdot T$. This observation was made in the context of Regev's public-key encryption scheme [Regev 2005], but easily extends to any exponentially secure encryption scheme.

Naor and Segev [2009] constructed a public key encryption scheme that is secure against bounded memory leakage under standard *polynomial-time* assumptions. They started with the observation that the circular secure scheme of Boneh et al. [2008] is already leakage-resilient under the DDH assumption. More generally, they showed how to construct a leakage-resilient public key semantically secure encryption from any hash proof system [Cramer and Shoup 2002], thus showing how build leakage-resilient encryption schemes on a variety of assumptions, such as the quadratic residuosity assumption, DDH, and Nth residuosity assumption. Moreover, they prove that the Naor-Yung paradigm [Naor and Yung 1990] is applicable in this setting, and thus obtain leakage-resilient encryption schemes that are CCA2-secure. These schemes are reslient to $1 - o(1)$ leakage rate.

These schemes (as well as schemes in followup work) have the following blueprint: The public key has exponentially many valid secret keys, so that even given the leakage (and the public key), the secret key still has high min-entropy. For example, in the encryption scheme of Boneh et al. [2008], the secret key is $(g_1, g_2, \ldots, g_\ell, s_1, s_2, \ldots, s_\ell)$, where $g_1, g_2, \ldots, g_\ell$ are random generators in a group G of prime order p, and $s_1, s_2, \ldots, s_\ell$ are all randomly chosen in $\mathbb{Z}_p$; the public key is $(g_1, g_2, \ldots, g_\ell, h)$ where $h = g_1^{s_1} \cdot g_2^{s_2} \cdot \ldots \cdot g_\ell^{s_\ell}$. In addition, there is an alternative mode for generating ciphertexts (used only in the proof of security), such that even given the entire secret key one cannot distinguish between an honestly generated ciphertext and one that is generated via the alternative mode. Importantly, if the secret key has sufficient min-entropy then a ciphertext generated via the alternative mode *information theoretically* hides the message.

For example, in the encryption scheme of Boneh et al. [2008], the correct ciphertext corresponding to a message m is of the form $(g_1^r, g_2^r, \ldots, g_\ell^r, (g_1^{s_1} \cdot g_2^{s_2} \cdot \ldots \cdot g_\ell^{s_\ell})^r \cdot m)$ for randomly chosen r in $\mathbb{Z}_p$. In the alternative mode, the ciphertext is generated by $(g_1^{r_1}, g_2^{r_2}, \ldots, g_\ell^{r_\ell}, g_1^{s_1 \cdot r_1} \cdot g_2^{s_2 \cdot r_2} \cdot \ldots \cdot g_\ell^{s_\ell \cdot r_\ell} \cdot m)$, for randomly chosen $r_1, r_2, \ldots, r_\ell$ in $\mathbb{Z}_p$. By DDH, even given the secret key $(g_1, g_2, \ldots, g_\ell, s_1, s_2, \ldots, s_\ell)$, the correct and alternative ciphertexts are indistinguishable. The alternative ciphertext information-theoretically hides the message m, as long as sufficient min-entropy remains in the secret key after leakage, because for fixed $(g_1, g_2, \ldots, g_\ell)$, the mapping from $(s_1, s_2, \ldots, s_\ell, r_1, r_2, \ldots, r_\ell)$ to $g_1^{s_1 \cdot r_1} \cdot g_2^{s_2 \cdot r_2} \cdot \ldots \cdot g_\ell^{s_\ell \cdot r_\ell}$ is a strong randomness extractor when $(r_1, r_2, \ldots, r_\ell)$ is viewed as the seed and $(s_1, s_2, \ldots, s_\ell)$ is viewed as the source. Indeed, it was proven in Naor and Segev [2009] that this scheme is re-silient to $1 - o(1)$ leakage rate, that is, security holds even if all but $o(1)$-fraction of the secret key is leaked.

This blueprint (of analyzing security by showing indistinguishability to a setting where security holds information-theoretically) is used in many followup works, in-cluding constructions of leakage-resilient CCA secure encryption schemes, identity based encryption scheme, pseudorandom functions, and more. See, for example, Faust et al. [2010a], Dodis et al. [2010c], Braverman et al. [2011], Galindo and Vivek [2013a], and Faonio et al. [2015].

We emphasize that leakage-resilient encryption schemes typically assume that the leakage happens *before* the ciphertext is generated, and security is guaranteed only for future ciphertexts. Halevi and Lin [2011], however, considered the model of *after-the-fact leakage*. They formulated the notion of *entropic* leakage-resilient public-key encryption, which captures the intuition that as long as the entropy of the encrypted message is higher than the amount of leakage, the message still has some (pseudo-) entropy left. They show that this notion is realized by the Naor–Segev constructions mentioned above. In order to achieve more traditional CPA security against after-the-fact leakage, they move to a weaker leakage model (the so-called OCL model); we discuss this result and some follow-up work in Section 26.4.2.6, after the OCL model is introduced in Section 26.4.1.

Katz and Vaikuntanathan [2009] showed how to construct a leakage-resilient signature scheme in the bounded memory leakage model. Loosely speaking, their blueprint is somewhat similar to the above: Start with a public verification key pk that has exponentially many secret keys associated with it. In particular, the public verification key contains a hash value $y = h(x)$ and the secret key contains the pre-image x.

Their first observation is that any target-collision-resistant hash function[3] h is leakage resilient. Namely, given $y = h(x)$ and bounded (efficiently computable) leakage $L(x)$ on x, it is hard to invert h on y. The reason is that even given y and $L(x)$, x still has sufficient min-entropy, and thus if an adversary can invert y (given $L(x)$), then with high probability it will output $x' \neq x$ such that $h(x') = h(x)$ and $L(x') = L(x)$. Thus, this adversary can be used to break the target collision resistant property, which gives the adversary even more information (namely, all of x).

Their signature scheme has the property that an adversary that forges a signature must "know" a secret key corresponding to y (which is part of the public key).

---

3. A function h is *target collision resistant* (also known as universal one-way hash function) if given a random element x in the domain it is hard to find $x' \neq x$ such that $h(x) = h(x')$.

This is achieved by having the signature contain an encryption of x, along with a noninteractive zero-knowledge (NIZK) proof that indeed the ciphertext decrypts to a pre-image of y. We note that in order to make the proof go through, one needs to use what is known as a "simulation sound" NIZK [Blum et al. 1988, Sahai 1999]: When using the adversary to break the target collision resistance property, we need to provide this adversary with signatures to messages of its choice, and to ensure that the secret key still has high min-entropy; these signatures will contain a ciphertext that decrypts to 0 (rather than a valid secret key), along with a simulated NIZK. The simulation soundness guarantees that the adversary must still generate a ciphertext that decrypts to a secret key.

All the works mentioned above constructed leakage-resilient schemes based on specific number-theoretic assumptions. Hazay et al. [2013], [2016] construct a leakage-resilient CPA-secure encryption scheme from *any* (not leakage-resilient) CPA-secure encryption scheme. Loosely speaking, Hazay et al. extend the work of Naor and Segev [2009], and construct a leakage-resilient encryption scheme from any *weak hash proof system*. In addition, they show how to build such weak hash proof system from any CPA-secure encryption scheme. However, the leakage rate α in their resulting scheme is quite low. They also construct a leakage-resilient symmetric encryption scheme, weak PRF, and message authentication code from any one-way function. In addition, they extend their results to the after-the-fact leakage model of Halevi and Lin [2011] mentioned above and to the bounded retrieval model (see Section 26.2.4).

We emphasize that in all the schemes mentioned above, the leakage is only a function of the secret key (and publicly available information, such as the corresponding public key). Boyle et al. Boyle et al. [2011b] (and follow-up works) constructed a signature scheme where the leakage can also depend on the randomness used to generate the signatures. This leakage model is somewhat reminiscent of the leakage models considered in Section 26.4, where the leakage occurs during computation. In particular, such leakage-resilient signature scheme must have the property that signatures hide the secret key, even given bounded leakage on the entire state of this computation.

26.2.3 Auxiliary Input Memory Leakage

Shortly after the formalization of bounded memory leakage, Dodis, Kalai, and Lovett [Dodis et al. 2009] formulated the notion of *auxiliary input* memory leakage. The motivation for this model is that in reality side-channel attacks can leak *many* bits about the secret key, more than the length of the secret key. Of course, if the secret key is fully computable from the leakage, all hope is lost. On the other hand, even if many bits are leaked, as long as the secret key is not computable from them, it may still be possible to build a secure cryptographic scheme.

Formally, the *auxiliary input* model considers any (efficiently computable) leakage function f applied to the secret key sk, even one with *long output*, as long as given $f(\text{sk})$, together with other public information, it is computationally (sufficiently) hard to find a valid secret key. Namely, in this model, the adversary can choose an arbitrary leakage function $f : \{0, 1\}^\kappa \to \{0, 1\}^*$ (modelled as a Boolean circuit) to be applied to the entire secret key sk, so long as f is (sufficiently) hard to invert, given all the information known to the adversary, such as the public key. As above, security is required to hold even against adversaries that are given $f(\text{sk})$. This function f can be adaptively chosen based on all the information known to the adversary.

Because this model requires only that the secret key should have computational secrecy given the leakage, it is more general than the bounded memory leakage model of Section 26.2.2, which requires that the secret key should have some information-theoretic uncertainty given the leakage. The auxiliary input leakage model attempts to consider the most general possible leakage that does not trivially break security. This model is inspired by the work of Canetti [1997], which studies cryptography with auxiliary inputs in the context of perfect one-way functions.[4]

In their work, Dodis, Kalai, and Lovett [Dodis et al. 2009] constructed a *symmetric encryption scheme* secure against auxiliary input leakage, as long as the leakage function satisfies the condition that every polynomial size algorithm can invert it with probability at most $2^{-\epsilon n}$ for some constant $\epsilon > 0$, where n is the length of the secret key. In what follows we outline the ideas behind their scheme. The first observation is that constructing a symmetric encryption scheme that is resilient to leakage seems to be much easier than constructing a public key one, since intuitively, one can apply a seeded extractor $\text{Ext} : \{0, 1\}^n \times \{0, 1\}^d \to \{0, 1\}^\ell$ to the (partially leaked) secret key, and use $\text{Ext}(x, r)$ as the secret key, where r is a random seed that is appended to the ciphertext, so that the party decrypting this message could reconstruct the effective secret key $\text{Ext}(x, r)$. We note that this general approach gives only one-time (or bounded-time) security; i.e., security holds only if the adversary is allowed to see only bounded number of ciphertexts. Indeed, if the adversary is given many pairs $(r_i, \text{Ext}(\text{sk}, r_i))$ then he may be able to efficiently reconstruct the

---

4. We note that Goldwasser and Kalai [2005] considered the auxiliary input model in the context of obfuscation. However, they obtained mainly negative results, demonstrating the impossibility of obfuscation with auxiliary input.

secret key sk. However, we can obtain many-time security by adding some "noise," as we explain next.

Specifically, consider the inner product seeded extractor $\mathsf{Ext} : \{0, 1\}^n \times \{0, 1\}^n \to \{0, 1\}$, defined by $\mathsf{Ext}(x, r) = \langle x, r \rangle$. When using this extractor in the approach above, with additional noise, we obtain the following symmetric encryption scheme: To encrypt a message $b \in \{0, 1\}$ using a (partially leaked) secret key sk, choose a random $r \in \{0, 1\}^n$ and let the ciphertext be $(r, \langle \mathsf{sk}, r \rangle \oplus e \oplus b)$, where e is 1 with small probability ϵ and is 0 otherwise. Note that this ciphertext has a decryption error of ϵ. This decryption error is overcome via repetition: Namely, an encryption of $b \in \{0, 1\}$ will consist of many pairs $(r_i, \langle \mathsf{sk}, r_i \rangle \oplus e_i \oplus b)$, where each e_i is sampled independently and is 1 with small probability ϵ and is 0 otherwise. This is indeed a symmetric encryption, and its (many-time) security follows from the assumption that learning parity with noise (LPN) is hard. More importantly, one can argue that even if the secret key is partially leaked (and only has sufficiently high min-entropy), then this encryption remains secure. Intuitively, this follows from the fact that the inner product is an extractor.

Recall, however, that our goal is to prove that security holds given $f(\mathsf{sk})$, for any polynomial-time computable function f that is sufficiently hard-to-invert.[5] This follows from the hard-core predicate theorem of Goldreich and Levin [1989], which asserts that for every one-way function $f : \{0, 1\}^n \to \{0, 1\}^*$, the pair $(r, \langle \mathsf{sk}, r \rangle)$ is computationally indistinguishable from uniform *even given* $f(\mathsf{sk})$.

The foregoing idea was carried over to the public-key setting by Dodis et al. [2010a], who constructed a *public-key* encryption scheme and proved that it is CPA secure against auxiliary inputs under the learning with errors (LWE) assumption. They proved leakage resilience against any sub-exponential hard-to-invert leakage function (i.e., any leakage function such that poly-size circuits can invert it with probability at most 2^{-n^ϵ} for some constant $\epsilon > 0$, where n is the size of the secret key).

They also showed that the BHHO encryption scheme [Boneh et al. 2008], which was proven to be resilient to bounded memory leakage, is in fact CPA secure against such sub-exponentially hard-to-invert auxiliary inputs under the DDH assumption. Recall that the in the BHHO encryption scheme, the secret key is of the form $(g_1, g_2, \ldots, g_\ell, s_1, s_2, \ldots, s_\ell)$, where each g_i is randomly chosen from a group G of prime order p, and each s_i is randomly chosen from $\mathbb{Z}_p$, and the public key is $(g_1, g_2, \ldots, g_\ell, h)$ where $h = g_1^{s_1} \cdot g_2^{s_2} \cdot \ldots \cdot g_\ell^{s_\ell}$. The encryption of a message m is of

---

5. In particular, sk may have no min-entroypy conditioned on $f(\mathsf{sk})$.

the form $(g_1^r, g_2^r, \ldots, g_\ell^r, h^r \cdot m)$. As mentioned in Section 26.2.2, even given the secret key, this cipertext is indistinguishable from an alternative ciphertext of the form $(g_1^{r_1}, g_2^{r_2}, \ldots, g_\ell^{r_\ell}, \prod g_i^{r_i s_i} \cdot m)$, where $r_1, r_2 \ldots, r_\ell$ are all chosen randomly and independently in $\mathbb{Z}_p$. Denoting each $g_i = g^{\alpha_i}$, where g is an (arbitrary) generator of the group G, we note that the (alternative) ciphertext masks m with $g^{\langle r, s \rangle}$, where $r = (r_1, r_2, \ldots, r_\ell)$ and $s = (s_1, s_2, \ldots, s_\ell)$. Thus, the result of Dodis et al. [2010a] is obtained by extending the Goldreich–Levin theorem to provide a hard-core value over large fields.

More generally, Dodis et al. [2010a] proved that these schemes are secure against a richer class of leakage functions—for example, leakage functions that are polynomially hard-to-invert with probability $2^{-\text{polylog}(n)}$ (however, then the corresponding assumptions are the sub-exponential security of LWE/DDH). Following this work, Goldwasser et al. [2010] used a similar approach to argue that the LWE assumption itself is robust to auxiliary inputs.

Brakerski and Goldwasser [2010] showed how to construct a public-key encryption scheme secure against sub-exponentially hard-to-invert leakage, based on the quadratic residuosity (QR) and decisional composite residuosity (DCR) hardness assumptions. Brakerski and Segev [2011] considered the problem of deterministic public-key encryption in the presence of auxiliary leakage and proposed several constructions based on the DDH assumption and subgroup indistinguishability assumptions.

Summary of the Leakage Models Discussed So Far. In Section 26.2.2 we defined bounded memory leakage, where the length of the leakage is bounded *relative* to the length of the secret key, which in turn depends on the security parameter. In Section 26.2.3 we defined the auxiliary input model, where the length of the leakage is arbitrary, but it is required that given this leakage (and other public information), finding the secret key should be hard. Unfortunately, the theoretical restrictions on the leakage function are unsupported by the bitter reality that the key may eventually leak completely over time. While at first glance it may seem impossible to do anything about this problem, as the auxiliary input leakage seems to impose the minimal necessary requirement on the leakage function, two approaches have been proposed to address it. The first is the *bounded retrieval* discussed in Section 26.2.4, and the second is the *continual memory leakage* model discussed in Section 26.2.5.

26.2.4 Bounded Retrieval Model

The bounded retrieval model (BRM), defined by Di Crescenzo, Lipton, and Walfish [Di Crescenzo et al. 2006] and Dziembowski [2006], assumes that there is a bound B

on the overall leakage. However, as opposed to the bounded memory leakage of Section 26.2.2, this bound is thought of as being extremely large, and in particular, can be significantly larger than the security parameter, and longer than the number of steps it takes to decrypt or sign. For security, the minimum requirement is that the secret key must be longer than B (else it could leak entirely); the goal of constructions in this model is to make sure that the efficiency of the system does not degrade with this bound B. That is, the goal of BRM is to protect against large amounts of leakage by making the secret key even larger, while ensuring that this necessary inefficiency in storage is essentially the only inefficiency of the system. This means that for every operation, honest users should have to read only a small portion of the secret (this property is called locality), and their computation and communication should not be much larger than in conventional cryptosystems. To put it differently, the bounded retrieval model studies the same problem as the bounded memory leakage model, but allows the users to increase their secret key size flexibly, so as to protect against large amounts of leakage, *without degrading other efficiency parameters*. This model is motivated by various malware attacks, in which a persistent virus may transmit a large amount of private data to a remote attacker.

As mentioned above, this model preceded the bounded leakage model, and the original work that introduced this model [Di Crescenzo et al. 2006, Dziembowski 2006] constructed leakage-resilient password and authentication protocols. The work of Alwen, Dodis, and Wichs [Alwen et al. 2009] constructed leakage-resilient identification schemes, signature schemes, and authenticated key agreement protocols in this model, and shortly after, Alwene et al. [2010] constructed a leakage-resilient public-key encryption scheme in this model.

Loosely speaking, these schemes are constructed via a generic *leakage-resilience amplification* process. Namely, start with a leakage-resilient primitive in the bounded memory leakage model of Section 26.2.2 (also known as the relative leakage model and use it to construct a B-leakage-resilient primitive in the bounded retrieval model (for an arbitrary value of B).

The naive approach is to artificially inflate the security parameter to be larger than the bound B. This approach clearly does not satisfy the desired efficiency requirements. A better approach is to use *parallel repetition*. For the sake of concreteness, suppose we start with a public key encryption scheme that is secure in the relative leakage model (described in Section 26.2.2). As a first attempt at converting this scheme to the bounded retrieval model, store many secret keys $sk_1, \ldots, sk_N$, together with the corresponding public keys $pk_1, \ldots, pk_N$. To ensure that the ciphertext remains succinct, to encrypt a message m, choose a few random indices

$i_1, \ldots, i_\kappa \in [N]$, secret share the message via a κ-out-of-κ secret sharing scheme (e.g., by choosing κ random messages $m_1, \ldots, m_\kappa$ such that $m = m_1 \oplus \ldots \oplus m_\kappa$), and output $(\mathsf{Enc}_{\mathsf{pk}_{i_1}}(m_1), \ldots, \mathsf{Enc}_{\mathsf{pk}_{i_\kappa}}(m_\kappa))$. Intuitively, even if ϵN bits are leaked, since the adversary does not know ahead of time which indices $i_1, \ldots, i_\kappa$ will be chosen during the ciphertext generation, at least one of the secret keys $\{\mathsf{sk}_{i_j}\}_{j \in [\kappa]}$ is likely to "still have sufficient min-entropy conditioned on the leakage," which in turn seems to imply that security holds. Unfortunately, formalizing this intuition is currently beyond reach, because the leakage can be a complex function of all keys $\mathsf{sk}_1, \ldots, \mathsf{sk}_N$.

Note that the ciphertext is small, independent of the absolute leakage bound B. However, the length of the public key $(\mathsf{pk}_1, \ldots, \mathsf{pk}_N)$ is large (and grows with B). This shortcoming is overcome by using an *identity-based encryption* (IBE) scheme, as opposed to a standard encryption scheme. The public key of the parallel repetition scheme is simply the master public key of the IBE scheme. The secret key is the secret keys corresponding to N fixed IDs $\mathsf{ID}_1, \ldots, \mathsf{ID}_N$.

This scheme satisfies the required efficiency guarantees: the ciphertexts and the public key are succinct (do not grow with B), encryption is efficient, and decryption is efficient given random access to the secret key.

Security. Despite the intuition above, it turns out that this scheme is not necessarily secure. In particular, Alwene et al. [2010] construct an artificial IBE scheme for which this blueprint results in an insecure scheme. Loosely speaking, this IBE scheme has the property that given secret keys of many identities, one can compress these keys to a short "digest" (of size independent of B) such that from this digest one can reconstruct all the compressed secret keys. To get around this problem, Alwene et al. [2010] construct an IBE scheme with an additional special structure, which they call "identity-based hash proof system," and prove the security of the above blueprint if the IBE scheme used is an identity-based hash proof system. They construct such an identity-based hash proof system based on several standard assumptions (such as quadratic residuosity, learning with errors, and bilinear Diffie–Hellman).

We refer the reader to Alwen, Dodis, and Wichs [Alwen et al. 2010] for a fantastic survey on the bounded retrieval model.

26.2.5 Continual Memory Leakage

The continual leakage model considers the setting in which the total leakage is *unbounded* and yet all the parameters of the scheme (including the length of the secret key) are bounded (and depend only on the security parameter). In particular, the leakage can eventually reveal as many bits as there are in the secret key, and we still want to argue security in this case. This seemingly impossible task is achieved by periodically *updating* the secret key, *without changing the public key*. Namely, as is often the case in leakage-resilient schemes, in this setting a public key pk has (exponentially) many secret keys associated with it. The initial secret key is sk_1; it is updated every time period, to sk_2, sk_3, and so on, so that all the secret keys sk_1, sk_2, sk_3 ... correspond to the same public key pk. The security guarantee is that even if the adversary obtains *bounded* leakage on each sk_i (but unbounded leakage overall), the scheme remains secure.

Specifically, in the continual leakage model security holds even given $L_1(sk_1)$, ..., $L_N(sk_N)$, where N is adversarially chosen, and $L_1, \ldots, L_N$ are adversarially chosen functions (represented as circuits) of bounded output length. Of course, for any security to hold, the output length of each L_i must be smaller than $|sk_i|$.

The model was first considered by Brakerski et al. [2010] and Dodis et al. [2010b], who constructed public-key encryption and signature schemes that are secure even when the leakage length in each time period is a constant fraction $|sk_i|$, under the decisional linear assumption in bilinear groups. These works allow no leakage during the key updates.[6]

The encryption scheme (constructed in Brakerski et al. [2010]) is a variant of the BHHO encryption scheme, discussed above. Let the secret key be a random vector $s = (s_1, \ldots, s_\ell) \in \mathbb{Z}_p^\ell$. Let g be a generator of a group G of prime order p. Let $a = (a_1, \ldots, a_\ell)$ be a random element in $\mathbb{Z}_p^\ell$ such that the inner product $\langle a, s \rangle = 0$ modulo p, and the public key be $(g^{a_1}, \ldots, g^{a_\ell})$. To encrypt a bit 0, choose a random $r \in \mathbb{Z}_p$ and output $(g^{a_1 r}, \ldots, g^{a_\ell r})$, and to encrypt the bit 1 output a random element in G^ℓ. Decryption is done by raising the ciphertext to the power of $s = (s_1, \ldots, s_\ell)$ coordinate-wise, multiplying all the coordinates together, and outputting 0 if the resulting product is the identity element of G, and 1 otherwise.

This scheme is resilient to bounded memory leakage, and even to auxiliary input memory leakage, via a similar analysis to the ones outlined in Sections 26.2.2 and 26.2.3, respectively. However, it is not clear how to (efficiently) update the secret key, in order to make this scheme secure against continual memory leakage.

Given a secret key $s = (s_1, \ldots, s_\ell)$ and a public key $(g^{a_1}, \ldots, g^{a_\ell})$, we can efficiently update the secret key by choosing a random $\alpha \in \mathbb{Z}_p$ and setting the updated secret key to be $\alpha s = (\alpha s_1, \ldots, \alpha s_\ell)$. However, this scheme is not secure against con-

---

6. More generally, these works are resilient to logarithmic amount of leakage during key updates. Very loosely speaking, this follows from the fact that such small quantity of leakage can be guessed with nonnegligible probability and thus cannot be of much help to the adversary.

tinual memory leakage, since an adversary can, for example, normalize the secret key by dividing all the coordinates by the first coordinate and leak on this normalized key, which remains unchanged.

To get around this attack, rather than setting the secret key to be $s = (s_1, \ldots, s_\ell)$, set it to be $g^s = (g^{s_1}, \ldots, g^{s_\ell})$. In order to maintain the ability to decrypt we need to rely on a group G with a bilinear map $e : G \times G \to G_T$. To decrypt, pair the ciphertext $(g^{y_1}, \ldots, g^{y_\ell})$ with the secret key $(g^{s_1}, \ldots, g^{s_\ell})$, to obtain $\prod_{i=1}^{\ell} e(g^{y_i}, g^{s_i})$, and output 0 if the value obtained is the identity element of G_T; otherwise output 1. To update the secret key, simply raise the secret key to the power of a random $\alpha \in \mathbb{Z}_p$ (coordinate by coordinate).

One can prove that this scheme is secure against continual leakage under the DDH assumption; however, this assumption is known to be false in groups with bilinear maps. This obstacle is bypassed by either considering an asymmetric map, and relying on the SXDH assumption, or setting the secret key to be a matrix with two rows, and relying on the decisional linear assumption.

To prove security, we rely on the fact that under the SXDH assumption (or the decisional linear assumption), an adversary cannot distinguish between the case that the updates are done as prescribed, and the case that they are done by choosing a fresh random secret s in the kernel of a, and raising it to the power of g; and this indistinguishability holds even given the secret key. Moreover, one can prove that if the key is updated in the alternative way described above, then security holds in the continual memory leakage model.

Leakage During Updates.   Lewko, Lewko, and Waters [Lewko et al. 2011] showed how to achieve constant leakage rate during key updates; the security of their scheme is under the subgroup decision assumption in composite order bilinear groups. This work was improved by Dodis et al. [2011] and modified to achieve leakage-resilient storage (see Section 26.3).

Dachman-Soled et al. [2016] showed a generic way to tolerate leakage during key updates. Specifically, they showed how to use obfuscation to compile any public-key encryption or signature scheme that satisfies a slight strengthening of continual memory leakage (which they refer to as "consecutive" memory leakage) but does not tolerate leakage on key updates, to one that is resilient to continual memory leakage *with leakage on key updates*.

Further Strengthening the Model.   The continual leakage model was further strengthened in different ways. Yuen et al. [2012] considered the *continual auxiliary input leakage* model, in which the leakage per time period is not required to be bounded in length, but rather can be an arbitrary *hard-to-invert* function of the secret key, like the leakage in Section 26.2.3. They construct identity-based encryption which is secure in this model, by applying a modified version of the Goldreich-Levin theorem, together with the ideas from Lewko et al. [2011], of using dual system encryption systems for leakage-resilience.

Malkin et al. [2011] consider continual memory leakage, where leakage can occur also during computations. They present a signature scheme that is resilient to continual leakage, where leakage can occur during the signing process, and thus the leakage is a function of both the secret key and the randomness used to sign a message. We discuss other signature schemes that can handle leakage during the signing process in Section 26.4.2.6.

Dziembowski, Kazana, and Wichs [Dziembowski et al. 2011] consider a combination of continual memory leakage with the bounded retrieval model described in Section 26.2.4, and construct schemes that are resilient against such leakage if the leakage function itself has limited space for its computation (see also Section 26.4.2.4 for more on their model).

26.2.6 Interactive Protocols

So far, we mainly focused on leakage-resilient cryptographic primitives, such as encryption schemes and signature schemes, with the goal of preserving the original security guarantees in the presence of leakage.

In this section, we extend the notion of leakage resilience to the context of *interactive protocols*. The initial works that construct leakage-resilient interactive protocols focused on specific tasks, such as coin tossing [Boyle et al. 2011a], zero-knowledge [Garg et al. 2011, Bitansky et al. 2012], secure message transmission, message authentication, commitment, and oblivious transfer [Bitansky et al. 2012]. These works, as well as followup works, consider the setting where an adversary can obtain arbitrary (bounded) leakage on the entire state of *each* (honest) party during the entire protocol execution.

Boyle et al. [2011a] constructed a coin-tossing protocol with the standard security guarantee upgraded for leakage resilience: Namely, even if the adversary leaks a constant fraction of the state of each (honest) party, she cannot distinguish the output from a random coin toss. In the context of zero-knowledge, it is easy to see that achieving similar leakage resilience under the standard zero-knowledge definition is simply impossible. For example, consider an adversary that leaks ℓ bits of information from the state of the prover by leaking the first ℓ bits of the witness. Clearly, this adversary's view cannot be efficiently simulated (assuming these bits of the witness are hard to compute). Instead, the (concurrent) works of Garg, Jain, and Sahai [Garg et al. 2011] and Bitansky, Canetti, and Halevi [Bitansky et al. 2012] weaken the zero-knowledge condition in the leaky setting, to require that the protocol does not reveal any information beyond the validity of the statement *and the leakage obtained by the adversary*. Defining this formally is nontrivial, as we explain below.

Bitansky, Canetti, and Halevi [Bitansky et al. 2012] presented a *general framework* for expressing security requirements of interactive protocols in the presence of arbitrary (poly-time) leakage. Noting that standard "ideal world" security, where the side-channel adversary does not learn more than the inputs and outputs of the malicious parties, is in general impossible, they defined the notion of *leakage tolerance*, as follows. Consider an adversary who leaks a total of ℓ bits of information from all the (honest) parties. A leakage-tolerant protocol ensures that such an adversary learns at most what can be learned in the *leaky ideal world*, in which the ideal-world adversary also gets ℓ bits of leakage.[7] Thus, a leakage-tolerant protocol is one where the level of security gracefully degrades with the amount of leakage (which may develop over time).

In more detail, they consider a "real world" in which the adversary can get leakage on the entire state of any one party at any time (but cannot get joint leakage on the states of many parties). To account for the security degradation this leakage necessarily causes, they also allow the same amount of leakage in the "ideal world." More specifically, the leaky ideal model they consider is the so-called *individual leakage model*, which allows the ideal world adversary to obtain leakage on the input of each party *separately*, as long as the total number of bits leaked is at most ℓ.

Constructing leakage tolerant protocols is highly nontrivial. Intuitively, the initial difficulty is that we need to simulate the protocol *without knowing* the inputs of the honest parties and then later "explain" the leaked information. As observed in Garg et al. [2011] and Bitansky et al. [2012], this is reminiscent to the difficulty in constructing *adaptively secure* protocols. This connection was formalized in Nielsen et al. [2013].

For example, consider the most basic task of message transmission. Typically, in order to transmit a message m securely, one encrypts m with a secure encryption scheme. However, note that given $\text{Enc}(m; r)$ together with leakage $L(m; r)$, it may be possible to efficiently compute m, even if the amount of leakage is significantly smaller than the length of m. Bitansky, Canetti, and Halevi [Bitansky et al. 2012] observe that if instead of using any secure encryption, one uses a *noncommitting*

---

7. They formalize their notion in the UC framework, but in this survey we focus on the stand-alone setting.

encryption [Canetti etal, 1996], then the message transmission becomes leakage tolerant.[8]

A noncommitting encryption scheme, a concept that was developed for adaptively secure communication, allows one to generate a simulated (equivocal) ciphertext ct *without knowing a corresponding plaintext* and later given any plaintext m generate randomness r that explains this ciphertext—that is, such that ct $=$ Enc$(m; r)$. This ensures that the ciphertex does not leak additional information, beyond what is already leaked by the leakage function. Similar ideas were used in Bitansky et al. [2012] to construct leakage tolerant zero-knowledge, message authentication, commitment, and oblivious transfer protocols. In particular, to construct a leakage-tolerant zero-knowledge protocol, rather than using a standard commitment scheme, they use equivocal commitments [Feige and Shamir 1990].

Ananth, Goyal, and Pandey [Ananth et al. 2014] extend the work of Garg, Jain, and Sahai [Garg et al. 2011] (mentioned above) to the continual leakage setting. Namely, they construct an interactive proof for every language $L \in$ NP, such that any PPT verifier cannot learn a witness corresponding to $x \in L$, even after interacting *many times* with a prover who proves that $x \in L$ (for the *same x*), and even if in each such interaction a constant fraction of the prover's memory is leaked. Their formal requirement is that such an adversary cannot later convince an honest verifier that $x \in L$. Loosely speaking, this is done by encoding the witness using an encoding scheme that is robust to continual leakage.

General Leakage-Resilient MPC. While the works discussed above were for some specific interactive tasks, such as coin tossing and zero-knoweldge, the works Boyle et al. [2013], Boyle et al. [2012] consider the task of constructing arbitrary two-party and multi-party secure computation that remain secure in the face of leakage. Namely, these works consider the setting where during the protocol execution, the state of the honest parties may be partially leaked. Clearly, one cannot hope to achieve "ideal world" security in the face of leakage, since the adversary can leak some of the bits of the input of the honest parties, and obtain information that is not leaked in the ideal world. To deal with this limitation, in Boyle et al. [2013] the ideal-world adversary is allowed to obtain some leakage. The difference between the model of Boyle et al. [2013] and the leakage-tolerant model of Bitansky et al. [2012] discussed above is that Boyle et al. [2013] allows both the real-world and the ideal-

---

8. This observation was previously used in Bitansky et al. [2011], in the context of constructing obfuscation with leaky hardware.

world leakage function to be a joint function of all the inputs, rather than locally computed for each party; in addition, Boyle et al. [2013] allows the leakage length to be arbitrary (but the same in both the real and the ideal world). In contrast, the work of Boyle et al. [2012] does not allow leakage in the ideal world, but allows a leak-free preprocessing stage, where the secret inputs are preprocessed and shared among the parties before the adversary obtains any leakage. We now discuss these works in more detail.

Boyle et al. [2013] define the notion of multi-party protocols that are secure against *adaptive auxiliary information*. In their model, the adversary can corrupt an arbitrary subset of parties and, in addition, can learn arbitrary auxiliary information on the entire states of all honest parties (including their inputs and random coins), in an adaptive manner, throughout the protocol execution. There is no a priori bound on the amount of the auxiliary information that the adversary may be able to learn. Their protocol guarantees that for any amount of information the real-world adversary is able to (adaptively) acquire throughout the protocol, this "same amount" of auxiliary information is given to the ideal-world simulator, thus providing graceful degradation of security.[9]

For any (efficiently computable) functionality they construct a secure (two-party or multi-party) protocol that realizes this functionality securely against malicious adversaries in the presence of adaptive auxiliary input. Their protocols are in the common reference string model, and the security is based on the linear assumption over bilinear groups and on the nth residuosity assumption.

In Boyle et al. [2012], *continual memory leakage* was considered in the MPC setting. This is in contrast to Boyle et al. [2013] and all the other leakage resilient protocols that were mentioned so far, which consider the single execution setting. Boyle et al. [2012] construct multi-party secure computation protocols that achieve standard ideal-world security (where no leakage is allowed in the ideal world) against real-world adversaries that may leak repeatedly from the secret state of each honest player separately, assuming a one-time leak-free preprocessing phase, and assuming the number of parties is large enough (larger than polylog(n), where n is the security parameter).

More specifically, they construct a multi-party computation (MPC) protocol that is secure even if a malicious adversary, in addition to corrupting $1 - \epsilon$ fraction of all parties for an arbitrarily small constant $\epsilon > 0$, can leak information about the

---

9. Note that it is not immediately apparent how to formalize this notion. We refer the reader to Boyle et al. [2013] for details.

secret state of each honest party. This leakage can be continual for an unbounded number of executions of the MPC protocol, computing different functions on the same or different set of inputs.

Interestingly, even though their MPC is secure against continual *memory* leakage, they achieve their result by relying on techniques from the *only computation leaks* (OCL) model (see Section 26.4.1). At a very high level, their basic idea is to run the MPC protocol of Boyle et al. [2013] that is resilient to adaptive auxiliary information, but rather than running the protocol on the underlying function, they run it on an OCL-compiled version of it. Roughly speaking, the OCL version has the property that local leakage does not leak any sensitive information. Therefore, even if all parties have leaked partial information at a certain point in the protocol execution, this leakage corresponds to local leakage in the underlying circuit, and since the underlying circuit is resilient to OCL leakage, no sensitive information is revealed.

This connection between continual memory leakage and the OCL model was further established in the work of Bitansky, Dachman-Soled, and Lin [Bitansky et al. 2014]. Similarly to Boyle et al. [2012], they construct multi-party protocols in the continual leakage setting, but as opposed to requiring a leak-free *input-dependent* preprocessing phase, they only utilize a leak-free *input-independent* preprocessing phase. As a result they can only achieve *leakage tolerance* (as opposed to leakage resilience). However, as opposed to Boyle et al. [2013], where the ideal world leakage is a *joint* function of all the inputs, in this work the real world leakage can be simulated by individually leaking on each party separately in the ideal world, thus giving a stronger security guarantee. Similarly to Boyle et al. [2012], their protocols are resilient to the corruption of $1 - \epsilon$ fraction of all parties for an arbitrarily small constant $\epsilon > 0$, where the number of parties grow with the security parameter.

Very recently, Benhamouda et al. [2018] showed that in the honest-but-curious setting, and assuming the number of parties n is large enough, the GMW compiler Goldreich et al. [1987] implemented with a high-threshold version of the Shamir secret sharing scheme [Shamir 1979] is robust against leakage one-time leakage in the preprocessing model. However, the leakage rate is quite small (roughly, $\frac{O(n)}{|C|}$ where C is the circuit the parties are computing). We refer the reader to Section 26.3 for further details.

26.3 Leakage from Storage

In this section, we consider the following generalization of exposure-resilient functions, mentioned in 26.1.1. Suppose a secret is encoded before being stored in memory; the adversary can repeatedly and adaptively apply a leakage function (from a set of allowed functions) to the encoding. The adversary's goal is to distinguish the stored secret from uniform. Thus, the security requirement for protecting the secret is stronger than in Section 26.2, where some information about the secret is allowed to leak as long as the leakage does not enable the adversary to break the underlying cryptographic scheme (e.g., encryption or signatures). On the other hand, the set of allowed leakage functions, which will depend on the construction, will be generally more restricted than in Section 26.2.

This model, called "leakage-resilient storage," was introduced by Davì, Dziembowski, and Venturi [Davì et al. 2010]. They propose two constructions, both secure only if the leakage is applied a bounded number of times (in their constructions, the encoding is not updated, which makes unbounded leakage impossible to achieve).

The first construction splits the stored secret into two components, and the assumption is that the two components leak independently (i.e., the two components are given to separate leakage functions rather than a single one; this model is known as the OCL model—see Section 26.4.1). Their construction uses a two-source extractor[10] 2-Ext as follows: To hide a secret $s \in \{0, 1\}$, simply choose at random $u, v \in \{0, 1\}^n$ such that 2-Ext$(u, v) = s$, and store the string u in one component and the string v in the other.[11] The secret s is reconstructed by simply evaluating 2-Ext on the two stored strings u and v. This approach has proven quite fruitful, resulting, in particular, in the leakage-resilient encryption and signatures of Dziembowski and Faust [2011] (Section 26.4.2.6) and circuit compilers of Dziembowski and Faust [2012] (Section 26.4.3.4).

The second construction of [Davì et al. 2010] does not require the leakage to be applied to two parts independently; rather, the leakage function is restricted to a limited complexity class. The idea is to use a deterministic extractor, instead of a two-source extractor. While deterministic extractors do not exist in general, Trevisan and Vadhan [2000] constructed, for any polynomial-time bound T, a deterministic extractor for sources that are sampleable in time T (and have sufficient min-entropy). Thus, if the leakage function is restricted to be computable

---

10. A two-source extractor produces an output that is close to uniformly random as long as the two sources are independent and each has sufficient entropy

11. Storing a secret $s \in \{0, 1\}^k$ that consists of many bits can be done in a bit-by-bit manner, but this approach can be secure only against $1/k$-fraction leakage of each component. To improve the leakage bound, we can use a two-source extractor 2-Ext with k-bit outputs. However, it may be hard to choose at random $u, v \in \{0, 1\}^n$ such that 2-Ext$(u, v) = s$, since it may be hard to sample u and v given s. Instead, one can choose at random $u, v \in \{0, 1\}^n$, let 2-Ext$(u, v) = \text{sk}$, encrypt the secret s using the secret key sk, and store (u, sk) in one component and store v in the other.

in some a priori bounded time T (and its output length is also bounded), then one can store a secret s by simply choosing a random $u \in \{0, 1\}$ such that $\mathsf{Ext}(u) = s$, where Ext is a deterministic extractor for T-time sampleableable distributions. Both constructions require no computational assumptions, except on the leakage function.

Protection against continual leakage requires the ability to update the stored secrets. In the OCL model (in which components leak independently), components should be updated before they leak too much information. Akavia, Goldwasser, and Hazay [Akavia et al. 2012] provide such a construction with two components, where the update requires interaction between the components. More generally, they construct a leakage-resilient public-key encryption scheme, where the secret key is stored in two components, and the assumption is that the leakage on each component happens separately (we refer the reader to Section 26.4.2.6 for details). This scheme relies on computational assumptions; in particular it assumes that there exists a group with a bilinear map, for which the linear assumption holds and the bilinear decisional Diffie–Hellman assumption holds.

Eliminating communication during updates presents an additional challenge. This challenge was solved by Dodis et al. [2011] (they also consider extensions to more than two components and allow full compromises of some). In their scheme, the updating of each component happens independently of the other, without the need for communication or synchronization. Technically, this work builds on Lewko et al. [2011]: They encrypt the secret, store the ciphertext in one component and the secret key in the other component, and update both the key and the ciphertext, separately. This work also improves and simplifies the construction of Lewko et al. [2011] for the continual leakage model (see Section 26.2.5). Their scheme assumes the existence of a group with a bilinear map, for which the linear assumption holds.

Faonio and Nielsen [2017] consider the problem of leakage during the encoding process itself, to obtain so-called fully leakage-resilient codes. Leakage during the encoding process means that the secret cannot be completely protected; instead, the requirement is relaxed to leakage-tolerance of Bitansky et al. [2012] (see Section 26.2.6), in which the simulator is allowed to obtain some leakage on the secret.

Benhamouda et al. [2018] consider storage of a secret in n shares produced via additive or high-threshold Shamir secret sharing over a prime field. Assuming each share leaks independently (i.e., in the n-component OCL model), they show that storage remains secure even if each share leaks about a quarter of its bits, for large enough n and field size. While this result requires many independently leaking components, its advantage is that the secret sharing technique is standard, and readily usable in multiparty protocols. They use this result for secure computation (assuming leak-free preprocessing), in which each uncorrupted party can leak, once, a short function of its entire state.

Leakage-resilient storage is often an implicit ingredient in many constructions of leakage-resilient computation, because the master secret must be stored in a leakage-resilient way. Thus, many works discussed in Section 26.4 also provide some form of leakage-resilient storage.

26.4 Leakage from Computation

In this section, we consider leakage models that focus on adversary's access to the entire computation rather than just the secret memory. In general (with some exceptions, noted throughout this section), the goal of works discussed in this section is to protect against continual, rather than one-time, leakage. Thus, some models considered in this section are similar to models considered in Section 26.2.5, and some works could be placed into either section. On the other hand, the classes of leakage discussed in this section are typically more restricted than the classes of leakage discussed in Section 26.2.

The work on leakage from computation can be roughly divided into two categories: constructions of specific cryptographic primitives (Section 26.4.2) and general compilers that work for any cryptographic primitive and, in fact, for any computation (Section 26.4.3). There are, naturally, interactions between the two categories, and general compilation techniques are often applied to specific schemes, as we discuss throughout this section.

The most common leakage models are noisy or probabilistic leakage of each wire introduced in Chari et al. [1999], wire-probing leakage of Ishai et al. [2003], only-computation leaks (OCL) model of Micali and Reyzin [2004], and leakage of limited computational complexity introduced in Faust et al. [2010b]. There is considerable debate as to whether these models correctly capture actual side-channel attacks. Thus, heuristic, rather than fully provable, evaluation approaches are also common, because of the difficulty of capturing actual side-channel attacks with theoretical leakage models. We discuss these briefly in Section 26.4.4.

Because so many constructions are in the only-computation-leaks model, and because this model has slightly different variants and interpretations, we start by giving an overview of this model and its many versions.

26.4.1 The Only Computation Leaks (OCL) Model

The general model of leakage during computation introduced by Micali and Reyzin [2004] (see Section 26.1.2) contains one crucial assumption: the existence of leak-free memory. The model allows for values to be moved to that memory when they are not needed in a computation. Formally, the adversarial leakage function at each step of the computation takes as input the entire state of the Turing machine, including the values on its tapes, except the state of the leak-free memory. It is important to note, however, that leak-free memory does not mean leak-free values, because values in this leak-free memory cannot be used directly; they have to be read from the memory to the working tapes when needed for computation, and written from the working tapes into the leak-free memory when stored. Leakage functions have access to the values when they are on the working tapes and, in particular, during the reading and writing operations. (Recall that in the general model of Micali and Reyzin [2004], leakage functions come from some allowable class, and if the class is sufficiently limited, the adversary doesn't simply see whatever the leakage function sees.) A good analogy is a computer whose CPU, caches, and memory bus leak, but RAM doesn't. Alternatively, one can push the leak-free assumption one level lower in the memory hierarchy, and imagine a computer in which everything leaks except the hard disk. This assumption became known as "Only Computation Leaks Information," commonly abbreviated as OCL. See Section 26.4.2.1 for the first constructions in this model.

Dziembowski and Pietrzak [2008] showed that the following special case of this general OCL model suffices to get strong results. In their model, the state of the computation is broken up into a few (specifically, three) parts. The computation proceeds in steps, and each step uses only some (specifically, two) of the parts. Each step leaks a bounded amount of information (specified by an adversarially chosen polynomial-time leakage function with a bounded output), and the part that is not used does not leak (i.e., is not given to the leakage function). See Section 26.4.2.2 for the first constructions in this model.

As pointed out by Dziembowski and Pietrzak [2008], the restriction on *when* each part leaks is not important for security; what is important, rather, is that the parts leak independently (i.e., any given leakage function does not have access to all of the parts at once), and only a bounded amount of leakage is available at each step of the computation. This independent leakage assumption became commonly used in many subsequent constructions of leakage-resilient cryptographic schemes (Section 26.4.2) and leakage-resilient storage (Section 26.3).

The OCL assumption was also used for the purpose of building general leakage-resilient circuit compilers in the style of Ishai et al. [2003] (see 26.1.2 and 26.4.3.1) rather than specific cryptographic schemes. This line of work, discussed in Sections 26.4.3.4 and 26.4.3.5, assumes that the transformed computation can be broken up into parts that leak independently. Each part can leak an arbitrary (or, depending on the model, any polynomial-time) function of its state, as long as the output size of the function is bounded. Since the leakage function on each component is powerful enough to simulate the inner wires of the component, we do not need to provide the wires explicitly as inputs to the leakage function; it suffices to provide the inputs and the randomness used in each component. Thus, the situation for each component is similar to bounded memory leakage (see Sections 26.2.1 and 26.2.2), and techniques for protection against such leakage are often helpful in this setting.

This line of work can be interpreted in the original OCL model of Micali and Reyzin [2004], in which the CPU leaks and memory does not. Each component corresponds to reading some data from memory, performing the component's work on the CPU, and writing the data back. It can also be interpreted in the circuit model of computation (like the work of Ishai et al. [2003]); the circuit is broken up into separate topologically ordered components, and the leakage function specified by the adversary is limited to working separately on the wires of each component (again, for each component it suffices to give the leakage function only the wires going into it and the randomness generated within it). The latter model is articulated in Goldwasser and Rothblum [2010]. The connection between the models is explained in, for example, Goldwasser and Rothblum [2015, Section 1.2].

Constructions in the OCL model can be also naturally viewed as protocols between two or more stateful parties; the adversary can obtain leakage from each party, but the leakage is independent for each party. Parties can correspond to circuit components in the previous paragraph, with inter-component wires modeled as inter-party communication. More generally, however, each party can be invoked more than once per execution of the protocol, and so there may be fewer parties than components (every invocation of a party corresponds to writing and reading nonleaking memory in the model of Micali and Reyzin [2004] and to a new circuit component in the model of Goldwasser and Rothblum [2010]). The parties are assumed to be able to erase parts of their state that they are no longer using (otherwise the adversary could obtain unbounded leakage about the first invocation by leaking information in subsequent invocations). This model is articulated in Dziembowski and Pietrzak [2008] and Juma and Vahlis [2010] for the two-party setting; the observation that the number of parties can be flexible is made in Dziembowski and Faust [2012]. For some protocols, such as Dziembowski and Pietrzak [2008] and Juma and Vahlis [2010], communication between the parties is fully available to the adversary; for others, such as Dziembowski and Faust [2012], it counts against the adversary's leakage allowance (the adversary can use the leakage function to compute sent messages; received messages are given as input to the leakage function of the receiving party).

Several papers observed that their constructions are secure against a stronger class of leakage functions than just OCL as defined in Micali and Reyzin [2004]: Namely, leakage need not be restricted to computation. The adversary can obtain leakage from any of the parties at any time, repeatedly and adaptively, as long as the amount of leakage is bounded. This bound may be per party, as in Bitansky et al. [2011] and Dziembowski and Faust [2012], or total, as in Goyal et al. [2016]. This view is equivalent to having leakage computed by viruses that have infected all the parties but have limited ability to communicate with each other (virus communication messages correspond to the outputs of the leakage functions); Goyal et al. [2016] call it "bounded-communication leakage" or BCL (note that "communication" here refers not to the computing parties, but to the leakage functions).

This connection between the OCL model and the multi-party protocol model was made more formal and exploited by several works (e.g., Boyle et al. [2012], Bitansky et al. [2014], Damgård et al. [2015], Dachman-Soled et al. [2015b], and Benhamouda et al. [2018]—see Sections 26.2.6, 26.3, and 26.4.3.4).

It should be noted that the leakage functions in the OCL model need not necessarily be limited by the number of output bits, although this is how the limitation on the leakage functions is most commonly stated. What matters, informally, is the amount of useful information contained in the leakage. In particular, if the leakage is noisy, it may be able to hide information even if it's long (see, in particular, Section 26.4.3.5).

26.4.2 Specific Schemes

Because leakage can occur during every computation on a given secret key, the main challenge in most constructions discussed in this section is to evolve the secret key (while securely erasing the previous versions), so that repeated leakage of, for example, one key bit at a time cannot lead the adversary to discover the entire key. In this way, the problems considered in this section are often similar to the problems encountered in the continual memory leakage model discussed in Section 26.2.5. Such key evolution is generally harder to achieve for public-key primitives, because the public key must remain the same as the secret key changes.

Similarly to works on the continual memory leakage model, most works discussed in this section assume that key generation is completely leak-free, and that secure erasure is possible—once erased, values do not leak. However, in contrast to continual memory leakage, most constructions discussed here assume OCL leakage model described in Section 26.4.1.

26.4.2.1 Pseudorandom Generators of Micali and Reyzin [2004]

Micali and Reyzin [2004] showed constructions of leakage-resilient pseudorandom generators out of simpler leakage-resilient building blocks (such as leakage-resilient one-way permutations). These "physical reductions" are analogous to cryptographic reduction based on complexity-theoretic assumptions. This approach makes assumptions on the leakage of the building block as it processes data, but it allows full leakage whenever other code is executed. The reasoning behind this approach is that it may be easier for hardware designers to protect a simple building block.

Specifically, the work of Micali and Reyzin [2004] shows that if the output of a length-preserving one-way function is indistinguishable from random even given the leakage, then the Blum–Micali [Blum and Micali 1984] construction (specifically, iterating the one-way function) with the Goldreich–Levin [Goldreich and Levin 1989] hard-core bit (used as an extractor to "remove" the leakage) is next-bit-unpredictable when the bits are output in reverse order. The same paper also showed that indistinguishability is harder to achieve than unpredictability. Subsequent work on unpredictable generators (which became known as "leakage-resilient stream ciphers") is discussed in Sections 26.4.2.2 and 26.4.2.3.

26.4.2.2 The Power of Only-Computation-Leaks: The Stream Cipher of Dziembowski and Pietrzak [2008]

The remarkable power of the only-computation-leaks (OCL) assumption was demonstrated by Dziembowski and Pietrzak [2008], who built a stream cipher that provably provides leakage resilience based on very mild assumptions. In addition to the OCL assumption, they assume that a bounded number of bits is leaked during an evaluation of two basic cryptographic primitives: a pseudorandom generator and a randomness extractor. They do not make any other restrictions on the leakage function. In fact, like in the model of Micali and Reyzin [2004], the adversary can choose any leakage function to be applied to the currently used portion of the state, as long as it is efficiently computable and its output is not too long. More generally, the leakage function can have arbitrary output length, as long as the secret maintains (pseudo)entropy given the leakage.

The specific use of the OCL assumption in Dziembowski and Pietrzak [2008] is quite simple. The stream cipher proceeds in rounds, outputting a fresh string of pseudorandom bits in each round and evolving its state. The stream cipher state is stored in three variables: two variables M_0 and M_1 that are used and updated in alternate rounds (never together), and the third variable K that is used and updated in every round. The one variable not used in the current round is assumed not to leak (equivalently, is stored in nonleaky memory); formally, it is not given as input to the leakage function. The variable K that is used in every round can be fully public without compromising security.

Dziembowski and Pietrzak also pointed out that in their setting, the OCL assumption can be viewed simply as a restriction on the leakage function. Instead of assuming that some parts of the state do not leak, we can simply assume that a separate leakage function is applied to different parts the state. In other words, different parts of the state leak independently rather than jointly. This view of the OCL assumption was adopted by many subsequent works.

The construction of Dziembowski and Pietrzak [2008] works as follows. Let G be a pseudorandom generator (PRG). The nonsecret variable K is an extractor seed. In each round ℓ, K is used to extract three values from M_i (where $i = \ell \bmod 2$): the stream cipher output bits, a new value for the extractor seed K, and a PRG seed X. M_i is then replaced with $G(X)$. Note that in this construction, the extractor seed that is used for M_i is itself extracted from M_{1-i} in the previous round, using a seed extracted from M_i in the round before, and so on. This technique, introduced in Dziembowski and Pietrzak [2007], is known as alternating extraction. As already shown in Dziembowski and Pietrzak [2007], if M_0 and M_1 start with sufficient entropy, alternating extraction will keep producing uniform values even in the presence of leakage, as long as the leakage function does not get to see M_0 and M_1 simultaneously. Alternating extraction is not enough, however, because it works only until the information-theoretic entropy of M_0 and M_1 is exhausted. To make a stream cipher that outputs more random bits than its seed, Dziembowski and Pietrzak introduce the second ingredient: the PRG, which replaces limited information-theoretic entropy with as much computational entropy as needed. To prove security of the overall scheme, they had to prove that a PRG will work even in the presence of leakage (i.e., when the PRG seed X is not uniform to the adversary). This result, independently also shown in Reingold et al. [2008], became known as the "dense model theorem": It quantifies the amount of entropy in a PRG output given a certain amount of leakage from the PRG seed or computation (see Fuller and Reyzin [2012] for an entropy-based formulation). We note that PRGs secure against specific leakage (rather than the arbitrary bounded leakage of the dense model theorem) have also been considered—for example, Ishai et al. [2003], [2013].

Note that because the stream cipher never needs to output past values, the construction of Dziembowski and Pietrzak [2008] is able to update the secret state in a one-way fashion. This fact allows the construction of Dziembowski and Pietrzak [2008] to be more efficient than the construction of Ishai et al. [2003], which is forced to create fresh randomized representations of the same logical secret state in order to allow for general computations, and thus must use fresh randomness at each iteration and work with a state that is represented via XOR-based secret sharing (also known as masking).

26.4.2.3 More Leakage-Resilient Stream Ciphers

Following the breakthrough result of Dziembowski and Pietrzak [2008], work continued on provably secure leakage-resilient symmetric encryption and pseudorandom objects, such as stream ciphers, pseudorandom functions (PRFs), and pseudorandom permutations (PRPs, also known as block ciphers). A number of results offered various trade-offs between construction complexity, assumptions used, and security achieved. We briefly mention only some of the relevant work.

Pietrzak [2009] simplifies the construction of Dziembowski and Pietrzak [2008] by assuming a stronger underlying primitive (a so-called weak PRF instead of just a pseudorandom generator used in Dziembowski and Pietrzak [2008]).

Standaert et al. [2010] argued that a different leakage model than OCL may be more reflective of real side-channel attacks and may also improve efficiency of constructions. The difficulty in designing a good leakage model is that without sufficient restrictions on the leakage class, the adversarially supplied leakage function can perform a "precomputation" attack, in which the leakage function precomputes the value that the pseudorandom object would output far in the future, thus making the value no longer random-looking when it is finally output. To design a leakage class that is both reflective of reality and prevents these theoretical attacks is a difficult task (OCL is one such design). Standaert et al. suggested not allowing the adversary to choose the leakage function adaptively (as already suggested in Micali and Reyzin [2004]), or employing a random oracle that can be queried by the construction, but not by the leakage function. Both of these leakage models were considered by Yu et al. [2010]; following the discovery by Faust et al. [2012] of a mistake in one of the proofs of Yu et al. [2010], fixes and further improvements were proposed by Yu and Standaert [2013]. The random oracle of Yu et al. [2010] is replaced by a so-called "simulatable leakage" assumption in Standaert et al. [2013], where it is argued that though the assumption may seem strong, it is more realistic than length- or entropy-based restrictions on the leakage function; see Longo et al. [2014] for a discussion on how to break various simulators and Fuller and Hamlin [2015] for connections between simulatable leakage and other leakage-function restrictions.

Leakage-resilient pseudorandom generators "with input" (i.e., whose state can be continually updated by additional input) are considered in Abdalla et al. [2015].

26.4.2.4 Leakage-Resilient Key Evolution

One-way key evolution, which is the main ingredient in leakage-resilient stream ciphers, was considered as a separate primitive by Dziembowski, Kazana, and Wichs [Dziembowski et al. 2011]. Like the authors of Yu et al. [2010], they work in the random oracle model. However, they do not assume that the leakage function cannot evaluate the random oracle; instead, they assume the leakage function is space bounded, and use graph-pebbling problems to protect against such leakage. They show applications of their construction to authentication and to obtaining security against continual leakage in the bounded retrieval model (see Sections 26.2.4 and 26.2.5). Their construction was improved by Smith and Zhang [2013].

26.4.2.5 Leakage-Resilient Block Ciphers, Encryption, and Authentication

A significant stumbling block for achieving efficient leakage-resilient constructions of PRFs, PRPs, and higher-level symmetric primitives, such as encryption and authentication, is the fact that the secret state does not naturally evolve in the mathematical description of the primitive, in contrast to stream ciphers, which naturally evolve their secret state in a one-way fashion. The state does not naturally evolve for PRFs and PRPs because they need to repeatedly produce the same output on the same input. Higher-level primitives, such as encryption and authentication, have multiple participating parties who cannot be assumed to update the state synchronously (in particular, what was encrypted yesterday needs to still be decryptable today).

Such primitives are sometimes called "stateless" in the literature (which is a bit of a misnomer, because they have a secret state—they just don't change it), in contrast to "stateful" stream ciphers discussed above. If such a primitive is used repeatedly with the same secret state, and the leakage class is sufficiently rich, then the adversary will eventually obtain the entire secret state.

General compilers discussed in Section 26.4.3 can be used for any cryptographic primitive and, therefore, can be used to address this challenge. Some works have optimized general compilation techniques for particular symmetric primitives, especially block ciphers. We review these approaches in Sections 26.4.3.2, 26.4.3.5, and 26.4.4. For the remainder of this section, we focus on approaches that have less general applicability. Many of these approaches split the secret key into multiple parts that can evolve even when the secret key remains the same, and thus provide some form of secure storage (see Section 26.3) in such a way that the stored value can be used in the computation by the symmetric primitive.

Dodis and Pietrzak [2010] get around the problem of evolving state for PRFs and PRPs by limiting the leakage class: They consider nonadaptive OCL leakage, in which the adversary must fix the leakage function in advance and keep it the same every time the PRF or PRP is invoked. They construct a PRF and a PRP that are resilient to such nonadaptive OCL leakage without the need for key evolution. They also show generic side-channel attacks on Feistel-based PRP constructions. Faust, Pietrzak, and Schipper [Faust et al. 2012] consider models in which the adversary does not get to choose the leakage function and/or the inputs adaptively, showing that these relaxations lead to more efficient constructions of PRFs and PRPs secure against OCL leakage.

Another way to get around the problem of evolving state is to force all participants to evolve it. In particular, leakage-resilient MACs in which both sides evolve the secret key were considered by Schipper [2010].

Some states can be easily split into multiple evolving components using algebraic techniques (instead of more traditional symmetric primitives), even when the underlying secret (which is never reconstructed) does not evolve. Following ideas from the public-key encryption scheme of Kiltz and Pietrzak [2010] (discussed in Section 26.4.2.6), Martin et al. [2015] use bilinear groups (in the generic group model) to construct a leakage-resilient MAC in the OCL model. The construction splits the secret into two parts multiplicatively and assumes the two parts leak independently. Since their scheme does not allow leakage during verification, it can be seen as a weaker variant of a PRF, with output that is unpredictable rather than pseudorandom. Barwell et al. [2017] demonstrate both a PRF and a MAC that resists leakage during verification using a three-share variant of this construction. Note that bilinear pairings are considerably less efficient than typical block-cipher-based MAC constructions, though they are competitive with public-key schemes.

Andrychowicz, Masny, and Persichetti [Andrychowicz et al. 2015], propose, as an application of their general compiler discussed in 26.4.3.4, a particularly efficient leakage-resilient implementation of interactive secret-key authentication protocol Lapin [Heyse et al. 2012]. The construction splits the secret into two parts that are assumed to leak independently, using the inner-product extractor (see Section 26.3) over large finite fields.

Pereira, Standaert, and Vivek [Pereira et al. 2015] obtain symmetric encryption and MACs by combining a leak-free block cipher in which the key does not evolve with a leaking primitive that evolves its key, emphasizing that the leak-free primitive is more expensive and thus used sparingly. The key of the leak-free block cipher is the master key of the entire scheme, and is used to generate temporary keys for the leaky primitive. The approach of generating temporary keys using a master key is sometimes called re-keying. While Pereira et al. [2015] assume a leak-free primitive for re-keying, some works design leakage-resilient re-keying schemes: At each invocation, such a scheme generates a fresh key for a stream cipher and updates its own state. Re-keying was addressed in theory and practice well before leakage-resilient cryptography was formalized (e.g., Abdalla and Bellare [2000], Kocher [2003]); in the context of leakage-resilience, see Abdalla et al. [2013] and Dziembowski et al. [2016], and references therein. The idea of combining a low-leakage (expensive to implement) primitive with a higher-leakage (inexpensive) one is sometimes called the "leveled leakage setting."

Authenticated symmetric encryption (which protects both secrecy and authenticity of the message against chosen-ciphertext attacks) presents more opportunities for leakage, because, in addition to leakage during computation, the decryption oracle may leak information about how exactly an invalid ciphertext failed to decrypt. This problem was addressed via generic composition of leakage-resilient PRFs, MACs, and symmetric encryption in Barwell et al. [2017], and via the leveled approach (as discussed in the previous paragraph) in a series of works (see Guo et al. [2018] and references therein); some of these works also provide protection in case of poor randomness or nonce generation. One suggestion for implementing the expensive PRF is to use the bilinear-pairings-based PRF construction of Barwell et al. [2017].

It's important to note that there is no consensus on the leakage model for symmetric encryption schemes, because a single bit of leakage about the plaintext trivially breaks the standard indistinguishability notion. Some works (e.g., Barwell et al. [2017]) prohibit leakage during the challenge phase; others (e.g., Pereira et al. [2015] and Guo et al. [2018]) permit it, but provide designs that first hide the plaintext via some operation assumed to leak nothing useful.

26.4.2.6 Leakage-Resilient Public-Key Objects

Micali and Reyzin [2004] construct the first leakage-resilient signature scheme in the OCL model. Specifically, they observe that the following classical stateful signature scheme is already leakage resilient in the OCL model: The public key is the root for a Merkle tree [Merkle 1988] of one-time public keys, where each one-time public key is for Lamport's one-time signature scheme [Lamport 1979]. Leakage resilience in the OCL model is trivial, because the model assumes there is no leakage during key generation, and after key generation, there is no computation on secret values, except to output some of them as part of a signature. The proposed scheme requires an a priori bound on the total number of signatures that will ever be produced and key generation time that is proportional to that bound; it is also stateful.

Faust et al. [2010a] reduce key generation time and remove the a priori bound on the number of signatures by replacing the Merkle tree in the signatures of Micali and Reyzin [2004] with a signature tree. They observe each secret signing key is used at most three times (to sign two leaves and a message), and therefore if the underlying signature scheme is resilient against memory leakage that results from three signatures, the resulting tree-based signature scheme will be leakage resilient in the OCL model. This signature scheme is still stateful, however.

Malkin et al. [2011], building on techniques of Alwen et al. [2009], Katz and Vaikuntanathan [2009], and Brakerski et al. [2010] for memory leakage (see Section 26.2.1), construct signature schemes that resist leakage during the signing process without the OCL assumption.

Kiltz and Pietrzak [2010] construct a leakage-resilient public-key encryption scheme resistant against continual leakage in the OCL model (however, unlike the one-time leakage results discussed in the previous paragraph, in their model no leakage is allowed once the challenge ciphertext is given to the adversary). The main idea of their construction is as follows. Start with ElGamal encryption [ElGamal 1985], but use bilinear groups (i.e., a bilinear pairing operator e that takes two elements of a source group into a single element of a target group) in order to enable multiplicative sharing of the secret key. That is, instead of the usual secret key x, let the secret key be g^x in the source group, where g is the group's generator. The public key is its image in the target group, $X = e(g^x, g)$. Encryption is the usual ElGamal, except the first component is in the source group: An encryptor chooses a random r, outputs g^r, and uses X^r as a symmetric key to encrypt the message. Decryption is done by first computing $e(g^x, g^r) = e(g^x, g)^r = X^r$. To make this scheme leakage resilient, multiplicatively share the secret key g^x into two shares stored in two separate components, and decrypt by working with each share separately within each component and multiplying the results. To obtain security against continual leakage, re-randomize these shares at every decryption. Both decryption and update require a single message between the two components. Note that to obtain security, it is essential for leakage resilience that x is stored in the exponent, because additive secret sharing of x could allow an adversary to obtain sensitive information about x via OCL leakage.

Kiltz and Pietrzak show that this scheme is CCA1-secure in the presence of OCL leakage (i.e., independent leakage from the two shares of the secret key) in the so-called *generic group model*, an idealized model in which group elements are assumed to have random representations that leak only equality information. Galindo et al. [2016] show a software implementation of a variant of this scheme, and then evaluate the implementation to determine whether the amount of leakage is indeed sufficiently small per invocation, as required for security to hold.

Galindo [2013b], Galindo and Vivek [2013a] and Tang et al. [2014] adapt the approach of Kiltz and Pietrzak [2010] to digital signatures, basing their schemes on identity-based encryption (IBE) and signatures schemes of Boneh and Boyen [2011], Boneh et al. [2004], Waters [2005.], and Schnorr [1991]; Wu, Tseng, and Huang [Wu et al. 2016] extend it further to identity-based signatures.

Instead of multiplicative sharing of Kiltz and Pietrzak [2010], Dziembowski and Faust [2011] use the inner-product-based sharing introduced in the leakage-resilient storage work of Davì et al. [2010] (see Section 26.3) to construct CCA2-secure encryption (that handles even post-challenge leakage), identification schemes, and signature schemes in the OCL model. They build on ideas of Davì et al. [2010] and on work in the memory leakage model, such as Naor and Segev [2009] (see Section 26.2.2) and Alwen et al. [2009] (see Section 26.2.4). Their schemes operate in a prime-order group with generators g_1, g_2; the secret key for each scheme is a pair of values x_1, x_2, and the public key is $g^{x_1 x_2}$ (thus ensuring, as in the continual memory leakage model of Section 26.2.5, that there are multiple secret keys for each public key). The secret key is shared into two parts, L and (R_1, R_2) (where L, R_1, R_2 are vectors), so that the inner product of L and R_i is x_i for $i = 1, 2$. The encryption scheme is similar to ElGamal [1985] (and similar to Naor and Segev [2009]), while the identification and signature schemes are based on those of Okamoto [1993] (which were analyzed in the bounded rertrieval model by Alwen et al. [2009]). The most innovative part of this work is a two-message protocol to update the shares L and (R_1, R_2) in a way that ensures security even if the adversary can obtain leakage during the protocol. The protocol requires a leak-free component that samples pairs of values from a fixed, input-independent distribution (this assumption is considerably weaker than the assumption of leak-free updating made in the many works discussed in 26.2.5). The ideas of this work led to a general compiler by Dziembowski and Faust [2012], discussed in Section 26.4.3.4.

Akavia, Goldwasser, and Hazay [Akavia et al. 2012] consider a model very similar to the two-component OCL model of Kiltz and Pietrzak [2010] and Dziembowski and Faust [2011]: There are two parties who hold shares of the secret and communicate over a public channel; the parties' secrets leak independently. In this model they construct CPA-secure public-key encryption and IBE, as well as CCA2-

secure public-key encryption (using the IBE-to-CCA transformation of Boneh et al. [2007]); no post-challenge leakage is allowed. They do not require idealized models or leak-free components. The main idea is to share the master secret key g^α of the Boneh–Boyen [Boneh and Boyen 2004] IBE between the two parties via encryption that is similar to Naor and Segev [2009], with one party holding the secret key and the other holding the ciphertext. Both decryption and share updates are accomplished by a two-party two-message protocol that (again) uses Naor–Segev-like encryption, relying on its homomorphic properties. This scheme can also be used for leakage-resilient storage (see Section 26.3), using the interactive updating protocol to update the stored shares.

Barthe et al. [2018] show how to implement the lattice-based signature scheme of Güneysu, Lyubashevsky, and Pöppelmann [Güneysu et al. 2012] in the wire-probing model of Ishai et al. [2003], using many of the recent advances developed for masking-based circuit transformations (see Section 26.4.3.2), as well as developing additional techniques, such as conversion between masking modulo 2 and modulo a large prime.

We close this section by discussing a few works that address one-time leakage rather than continual leakage discussed above. (Most work addressing one-time leakage is discussed in Section 26.2; we single out the following works for this section because they work in the OCL model.) Halevi and Lin [2011, Section 4], building on their result that the Naor–Segev [Naor and Segev 2009] construction maintains entropic security against memory leakage even if it occurs after the challenge ciphertext is known to the adversary (see Section 26.2.2), show how to build a public encryption scheme in the 2-state OCL model that is CPA-secure for one-time post-challenge leakage. The idea is to store two secret keys separately, use each of them to decrypt a random string, and use the inner product of the two random strings (which is a two-source extractor—see Section 26.3) to decrypt the message. Zhang, Chow, and Cao [Zhang et al. 2015] show how to upgrade this scheme's security to CCA, as well as how to construct IBE schemes by building on techniques from Alwene et al. [2010]. Fujisaki et al. [2015] show a similar upgrade to CCA security as well as security against leakage from the encryptor's randomness.

26.4.3 General Compilers

While Section 26.4.2 discussed specific cryptographic primitives, here we discuss general transformations to achieve leakage resilience for any computation. They are, of course, also applicable to the specific cryptographic goals discussed above, but often less efficient than the specific constructions.

The commonly used paradigm for general leakage-resilient compilers was introduced by Ishai, Sahai, and Wagner [Ishai et al. 2003] (see Section 26.1.2). To recap, they address the situation in which computation is performed by a clocked circuit with a secret state (for example, a circuit implementing a block cipher with a secret key). The circuit is run repeatedly on various inputs, producing outputs and possibly also updating the secret state. They consider adversaries who are able to provide inputs and observe outputs as well as observe some leakage function of the internal wires during the computation. The security goal is to build a circuit in such a way that the adversary learns nothing useful about the secret state from the leakage. The notion of "learning nothing useful" is defined by the existence of a simulator who faithfully simulates the leakage by observing only the input/output behavior. The initial secret state is stored in some specially encoded form and is assumed to be placed into the circuit without any leakage. In order to protect against repeated leakage on multiple inputs, constructions must update the secret state and erase the previous version, similar to constructions in Section 26.4.2.

General compilers achieve this security goal for any computation. The computation itself is specified by a stateful, but not leakage-resilient, circuit C. The goal of a compiler is to create a new circuit C' (and an encoding of the secret state) so that C' computes the same functionality as C and is leakage-resilient in the sense described above.

The specific leakage function considered by Ishai et al. [2003] was wire probing: The adversary could obtain leakage from t wires. We discuss their construction in Section 26.4.3.1. We cover other transformations secure against wire-probing leakage in Section 26.4.3.2.

Following the introduction of general leakage functions in Micali and Reyzin [2004], researchers have considered other types of leakage. A folklore result, attributed to Impagliazzo by Goldwasser and Rothblum [2015, Section 1], is that general leakage-resilient computation is impossible under even a single bit of leakage without some constraint on the leakage function, because of the general impossibility of black-box obfuscation [Barak et al. 2001] (the connection between leakage-resilient computation and obfuscation has been also explored by other works—see, for example, Bitansky et al. [2011]). Thus, some restrictions on the leakage functions, besides the amount of leakage, are necessary.

Transformations secure against a variety of leakage classes are discussed in Sections 26.4.3.3 (leakage of limited complexity), 26.4.3.4 (OCL leakage), and 26.4.3.5 (noisy and noisy OCL leakage).

Before proceeding, we should note the following folklore result (see, e.g., Bitansky et al. [2011, Section 1.1]): to achieve a general compiler secure against some leakage, it often suffices to build a leakage-resilient construction for decryption of a fully homomorphic encryption scheme. The secret state can then be stored encrypted under such a scheme, and all computation and state update can be carried out encrypted until the output is needed.

26.4.3.1 The Compiler of Ishai et al. [2003]

The transformation of Ishai et al. [2003] is similar to the one in Chari et al. [1999]: Each wire carrying a bit b is a replaced by a bundle of $t + 1$ wires carrying the Boolean masking of b—that is, $t + 1$ bits whose exclusive-or is equal to b. The main technical tool is the design of a gadget for the logical AND operation: It takes two wire bundles for bits b_1 and b_2 and outputs a wire bundle for the bit $b_1 \cdot b_2$, in such a way that the adversary cannot learn anything by observing t wires, because the distribution of wire values is t-wise independent. The gadget is made up $\Theta(t^2)$ bit gates and uses $\Theta(t^2)$ random bits.

The secret state is stored encoded in the same way: Each bit b is replaced by $t + 1$ bits that XOR to b. Inputs are encoded and outputs are decoded to the same representation (leakage during encoding and decoding is not a concern, because the adversary is assumed to be able observe inputs and outputs). The encoded secret state is updated (rerandomized) before being stored again, whether the actual secret state changes or not.

As already mentioned, this construction is secure against continual leakage. At its core is a transformation secure against one-time leakage. Specifically, given a stateful circuit C, treat initial state as an additional input and the updated state as an additional output, resulting in a circuit $\tilde{C}$ that has state, but only inputs and outputs. The goal of a one-time-secure (also known as stateless) transformation is to transform $\tilde{C}$ into $\tilde{C}'$ that leaks nothing useful about its input. To enable such a transformation, we will allow $\tilde{C}'$ to receive its input already encoded, and to produce encoded outputs. The stateful C' that is secure against continual leakage is produced by taking $\tilde{C}'$, storing the encoded state in memory registers, and adding input encoding and output decoding.

One-time-secure (stateless) transformations are sometimes interesting on their own. They do not always result in secure transformations against continual leakage, because it is not always possible to update the secret state so that cumulative leakage does not add up to reveal it.

The transformation of Ishai, Sahai, and Wagner [Ishai et al. 2003] achieves perfect security. The authors also show more efficient transformations for large values of t that achieve statistical security, and a derandomized construction that achieves computational security.

26.4.3.2 Improved Compilers for Wire Probing Leakage

Considerable effort has been devoted to improving the compiler of Ishai et al. [2003].

Many subsequent papers improved efficiency of Ishai et al. [2003]. Some papers design special masking-friendly block ciphers (e.g., Piret et al. [2012], Grosso et al. [2015]) or more efficient masking techniques (see, e.g., Groß and Mangard [2017], Goudarzi and Rivain [2017], and Journault and Standaert [2017], and references therein). Some consider automated synthesis and verification of masked circuits for specific computations—see, in particular, Barthe et al. [2015], Barthe et al. [2016], Belaïd et al. [2016], Coron [2018], Bloem et al. [2018], and Belaïd et al. [2018] and references therein (a good overview of this area is given in Barthe et al. [2017, Section 1.2]). Some reduce the amount of randomness used (e.g., Belaïd et al. [2016], Belaïd et al. [2017], Faust et al. [2017]). Some consider both Boolean masking and masking modulo a power of two (see Bettale et al. [2018] and references therein) or a large prime (see Barthe et al. [2018]); the ability to switch between the two gives more efficient implementations. Masking is not the only countermeasure used in this setting—see, for example, Coron et al. [2018] for a randomized table countermeasure and a discussion of other countermeasures used. Even though block cipher constructions are the primary goals of these works, many of them present techniques of general applicability. Some works combine leakage-resilience with resilience to glitches (e.g., Faust et al. [2018]).

Many of the works mentioned above try to optimize not only the circuit size, but also the amount of randomness. Ishai, Sahai, and Wagner [Ishai et al. 2003] showed that if we are willing to settle for computational, rather than information-theoretic security against leakage, then their construction can be fully derandomized (except for an initial random seed) with the help of a leakage-resilient pseudorandom generator that they construct. For the case of perfect security, the randomness complexity is improved from t^2 per gate to $t^{1+\epsilon}$ for the entire circuit in Ishai et al. [2013] and Ananth et al. [2018], with the help of different leakage-resilient (so-called robust) pseudorandom generators (t random bits are necessary according to Ananth et al. [2018]).

A series of works by Balasch et al. (see Balasch et al. [2017] and references therein) considers so-called inner-product masking instead of Boolean masking. It presents both general compilation techniques and applications to AES. This basic idea is similar to Ishai et al. [2003]—replace wires with wire bundles, and gates with gadgets. However, this masking operates on words rather than bits, so, to start with, a "wire" carries b-bit elements of the finite field GF(2^b). Like in Faust et al. [2010b] (see Section 26.4.3.3), the masking operation replaces each such wire with a wire bundle whose inner product with a fixed vector (which is a system parameter) is equal to the wire value. We note that this usage of the inner product operation is different from how the inner product is used in Dziembowski and Faust [2012] (see Section 26.4.3.4), where a wire is represented by two vectors whose dot product is equal to the wire's value, because in Dziembowski and Faust [2012] both vectors are random, while in Balasch et al. [2017] one vector is a fixed parameter. The value of this fixed parameter is of little importance to the theoretical evaluation (as long it has no zero coordinates), but matters to the heuristic security evaluation: In addition to theoretical security evaluation, these and other similar works are evaluated in heuristic evaluation frameworks we discuss in Section 26.4.4.

On the more theoretical side, a number of works considered the problem of leakage rate (i.e., the ratio of leaking wires to total wires in the compiled circuit). Because the circuit size in the construction of Ishai et al. [2003] increases by a factor of t^2 during compilation, the leakage rate is quite low and, in fact, decreases linearly as t increases. If the choice of leaking wires is not completely up to the adversary (for example, each wire leaks with some probability, or not too many wires leak in any particular region of the circuit), then the leakage rate can be improved to a constant [Ajtai 2011, Andrychowicz et al. 2016, Ananth et al. 2018].

26.4.3.3 Compilers for Leakage of Limited Complexity

[Faust et al. 2010b, 2014b] showed two compilers. Both compilers, in addition to the leakage-class restriction, assume the existence of certain leak-free hardware (which is input independent), thus providing a reduction from a simple leak-free piece of hardware to a general leak-free circuit, in the spirit of Micali and Reyzin [2004]. The first compiler provides security against noisy leakage of *every* wire; we discuss it in Section 26.4.3.5. Here we focus on the second compiler of Faust et al., which is secure against a class of leakage functions that cannot decode a linear secret sharing scheme (the specific linear secret sharing scheme determined the class of leakage functions that could be tolerated). In particular, by using the same Boolean masking as used by Ishai et al. [2003], but different AND gadgets, the compiler achieves security against leakage functions in the complexity class AC^0 (i.e., leakage functions computable by unbounded fan-in constant-depth circuits with "and," "or," and "not" gates). It is not practical: to tolerate leakage of λ bits of information per round of execution, the circuit size has to increase by a multiplicative factor of more than λ^{12}. Its theoretical efficiency was been improved in subsequent work [Andrychowicz et al. 2015], using techniques from multi-party computation (in particular, working over large fields and using packed secret sharing), although concrete parameters are not analyzed. It is improved to withstand more leakage, and, in a surprising application, used to construct zero-knowledge PCP by Ishai, Weiss, and Yang [Ishai et al. 2016].

Several subsequent papers improved protection against leakage functions from a restricted complexity class. Rothblum [2012] improved the AC^0-leakage compiler of Faust et al. [2010b] to remove the need for leak-free hardware, but at the cost of adding a computational hardness assumption. This transformation (which builds on the ideas of Goldwasser and Rothblum [2012], [2015] discussed in 26.4.3.4) replaced the leak-free hardware with a leakage-resilient computation, and required changes to the wire-bundle encoding and gate gadgets in order to make simulation possible.

Miles and Viola [2013] proposed a circuit transformation that resists more powerful classes of leakage functions, such as AC^0 augmented with gates that compute any symmetric function (including parity), and, under certain computational assumptions, the class TC^0 (i.e., leakage functions computable by unbounded fan-in constant-depth circuits with "threshold" and "not" gates). Their transformation follows the wire bundles and gadgets approach of prior work, but uses group operations over the alternating group A_5 instead of Boolean masking for sharing each wire (and, of course, completely new gadgets). Miles [Miles 2014] extended this result to leakage functions in NC^1 (all leakage functions computable by polynomial-size logarithmic-depth constant fan-in circuits) under the assumption that $L \neq NC^1$. These compilers, like those of Faust et al. [2010b], require an input-independent leak-free hardware. While precise parameters are not analyzed, they do not seem to be in the realm of practical.

The above work is for continual leakage from stateful circuits. For the more limited case of one-time leakage from circuits without persistent state (see Section 26.4.3.1), Bogdanov et al. [2016] showed that constructions secure against wire-probing leakage of t wires also achieve security against low complexity leakage, where "low-complexity" means low approximate degree of the leakage function. The main technical insight is an equivalence between the notion of low approximate degree of a function and the function's inability to distinguish t-wise indistinguishable distributions (i.e., distributions whose projections on t symbols are identical). This result is similar to the result of Duc et al. [2014] for the connection between wire-probing and noisy leakage (see Section 26.4.3.5). Bogdanov et al. exploit the connection between secure multi-party computation and circuits resilient to wire-probing leakage (observed already in Ishai et al. [2003]) to obtain new constructions of circuits resilient to one-time low-complexity leakage. However, it is not known how to extend their ideas to stateful circuits with security against continual leakage.

26.4.3.4   **Compilers for OCL leakage**

See Section 26.4.1 for a discussion of the "only computation leaks" (OCL) model and its variants.

Two general compilers in the OCL model were shown by Juma and Vahlis [2010] and Goldwasser and Rothblum [2010], using very different approaches.

Juma and Vahlis presented their result in two-component OCL model. One component stores the secret state encrypted under a public key for a fully homomorphic encryption scheme (FHE). The other component stores the FHE secret key. The facts that the two components leak separately and only a bounded amount are used to prove that information about the FHE plaintext is not accessible to the leakage function. In order to evaluate a circuit C, leakage-resilient computation is performed homomorphically under the cover of FHE by the first component; the result is then decrypted with the help of the second component. At the same time, fresh FHE keys are generated to update the state of the second component, and the component's state is re-encrypted under these keys (using decryption under the cover of the FHE) to refresh the ciphertext. The amount of leakage per invocation that this construction can tolerate is logarithmic in the FHE security; the leakage function must be polynomial-time computable. The construction depends on an input-independent leak-free component that produces FHE ciphertexts for a fixed (e.g., all-zero) plaintext.

Goldwasser and Rothblum [2010] divide the computation into many more independently leaking pieces—as many as gates in C. They use a leakage-resilient encryption scheme (with additional properties) as the underlying building block. They replace each wire value of the original circuit C with its ciphertext, and each gate of C with a gadget that takes ciphertexts as inputs and produces ciphertexts as outputs. In order to make the gadget leakage-resilient, they use the encryption scheme of Boneh et al. [2008] and Naor and Segev [2009] (see Section 26.2.2), slightly modified and augmented with (input-indepenent) leak-free hardware. The encryption keys are updated for each iteration. Under the assumption that each gadget leaks independently, the compiled circuit can tolerate a fixed amount of polynomial-time leakage per gadget. Thus, in contrast to circuit compilers described in Section 26.4.3.3 and the result of Juma and Vahlis [2010], the amount of leakage they can tolerate grows with the circuit size.

Dziembowski and Faust [2012] and, independently, Goldwasser and Rothblum [2012], [2015] eliminate the need for computational assumptions in Goldwasser and Rothblum [2010], achieving security against arbitrarily complex (rather than only polynomial-time) leakage functions. Miles and Viola [2013] provide another construction, by observing that their compiler against computationally-bounded leakage also provides security in the OCL model; however, it tolerates less leakage than the constructions of Dziembowski and Faust [2012], Goldwasser and Rothblum [2012], and Goldwasser and Rothblum [2015].

The compiler of Dziembowski and Faust [2012], like prior work, assumes some leak-free hardware. It uses so-called inner-product masking: Each wire is represented by two vectors whose inner-product is equal to the wire value, as in the leakage-resilient storage of Davì et al. [2010] (see Section 26.3). Because the inner product function is a two-source extractor (which means the output is close to uniformly random as long as the two sources are independent and each has sufficient entropy), as long as the two vectors leak independently and not too much, the wire value is well hidden. Gadgets that operate on the vectors are constructed with the help of (input-independent) leak-free hardware. This construction can be viewed in the circuit model, having $2n$ independently leaking components (where n is the number of wires in the original circuit). It can also be viewed as a two-party protocol, where each party keeps one of the two vectors for each wire, and the parties communicate for each gate. The latter view allows for much less leakage. The efficiency of this compiler has been improved by Andrychowicz et al. [2015].

The compiler of Goldwasser and Rothblum [2012], [2015] eliminates not only computational assumptions, but also leak-free hardware, by replacing the computational encryption scheme of Goldwasser and Rothblum [2010] with an information-theoretic one and replacing the leak-free components with leakage-resilient computation. Thus, the only remaining assumption is on the leakage function: that each component leaks independently, and the amount of leakage per component is bounded (it is also assumed, like in previous work, that the compilation itself, which is randomized and places the secret state into the circuit, doesn't leak; this assumption is shown necessary in Damgård et al. [2015]). The number of components is the same as the number of gates in the original circuit.

Bitansky, Dachman-Soled, and Lin [Bitansky et al. 2014] obtain a protocol with a constant number of independently leaking components without computational assumptions or leak-free hardware. The number of parties is estimated to be about 20 in Dachman-Soled et al. [2015b]). Each component is invoked a linear (in the circuit size) number of times. The main idea of the construction is to use the 2-component version of the compiler of Dziembowski and Faust [2012], and replace the leak-free hardware by the leakage-resilient computation of Goldwasser and Rothblum [2012], [2015].

Dachman-Soled, Liu, and Zhou [Dachman-Soled et al. 2015b] reduce the number of components even further—down to the optimal two—without relying on leak-free hardware, but at the cost of very strong computational assumptions. The technical idea behind their construction is to start with a two-component compiler that requires leak-free hardware (such as Juma and Vahlis [2010] or Dziembowski and Faust [2012]) and then replace the leak-free hardware with a leakage-resilient two-party protocol. This protocol is what requires the computational assumption.

For the case of one-time security of stateless circuits (see Section 26.4.3.1), Goyal et al. [2016] build compilers in the 2-component bounded-communication leakage model (which is a generalization of the OCL model; see Section 26.4.1). In this stateless setting, they are able to reduce the assumptions of Dachman-Soled et al. [2015b] and increase efficiency compared to prior constructions, without resorting to leak-free hardware. The technical idea of the construction is a result that shows that protection against leakage functions that simply compute parities of wire values is essentially sufficient. It is not known how to extend this construction to protect against continual leakage in the stateful case.

Genkin, Ishai, and Weiss [Genkin et al. 2017] observe that leakage-resilient stateless circuits make sense as implementation to trusted third parties, in which multiple participants provide inputs and rely on the trusted third party to compute an output. While the party is trusted to compute the output correctly and not leak information deliberately, it may be under a side-channel attack by an adversary. This setting presents its own challenges not present in the usual stateful compilers (in particular, what happens if some participants provide invalidly encoded inputs). Building on the work of Goyal et al. [2016] for stateless compilers and the work of Ishai et al. [2016], they show how these challenges can be overcome.

Most of the papers discussed above focus on the theory feasibility results and do not analyze the practical feasibility of their compilers. Further work is needed to make any of them practical.

On the more applied side, Andrychowicz, Masny, and Persichetti [Andrychowicz et al. 2015] propose a two-component OCL compiler using inner-product masking over large finite fields (and some leak-free components), and apply it to the "Lapin" secret-key authentication protocol [Heyse et al. 2012], producing a working implementation. They evaluate both the concrete leakage-resilient and concrete performance of their proposal, reporting a 30-fold slowdown over the standard version of Lapin for reasonable security parameters.

26.4.3.5 Compilers for Noisy and Noisy OCL Leakage

As already mentioned above, one of the compilers of Faust et al. [2014b] works in a noisy leakage model that is reminiscent of the noisy leakage model of Chari et al. [1999]. Specifically, the assumption is that every wire's value is provided to the adversary, but each one is flipped independently with probability p. The compiler uses the same Boolean masking as Chari et al. [1999] and Ishai et al. [2003], but builds AND gadgets differently. Unfortunately, the compiler is far from practical, requiring at least a million-fold increase in the circuit size even for small security parameters (in particular, to achieve security $2^{-\lambda}$ when the error probability for the leakage of each wire is $p \leq \frac{1}{2}$, the circuit size has to increase by a factor of more than $\max(10^5 \cdot \lambda^2, p^{-12}\lambda/100)$).

Subsequent work considered more general noisy leakage functions, many of them in a variant of the OCL model. In the version of the OCL model used in most works mentioned in 26.4.3.4, the leakage can be an arbitrary polynomial-time function of the relevant portion of the state, but of limited output length. An objection to this model of leakage (raised in multiple forums; e.g., Standaert et al. [2010], [2013]) is that it is both too strong and too weak. It is too strong because in reality, the physical side channels do not compute arbitrary polynomial-time functions, and ensuring protection against arbitrary polynomial-time leakage forces the designs to have unnecessary complexity. It is too weak because real side-channel attacks receive many bits of leakage—typically many more than the amount of secret state.

Addressing these objections, Prouff and Rivain [2013] show a circuit compiler in the OCL model (with a linear number of independently leaking components), where the leakage from each component of the circuit reveals limited information (in the statistical sense of biasing the distribution) about the value being leaked. (Note that the model of power analysis attacks by Chari et al. [1999], discussed in Section 26.1.1, has this property.) Their compiler uses additive secret sharing (also known as masking) for the wires, and gadgets similar to Ishai et al. [2003] and Faust et al. [2014b] for multiplication; it is specialized to block ciphers that consist of s-box and linear operations, following the ideas of Carlet et al. [2012]. It uses some leak-free components. The security model of Prouff and Rivain [2013] is weaker than the model of Ishai et al. [2003]; in particular, it does not provide the adversary with the input-output behavior of the circuit, but only with leakage under random inputs.

Duc, Dziembowski, and Faust [Duc et al. 2014] show a much stronger compiler for the class of leakage functions considered in Prouff and Rivain [2013]. They demonstrate that the original compiler of Ishai et al. [2003], without any leak-free components, and for arbitrary circuits, is also secure against noisy OCL leakage. Moreover, security holds for the strong definition of Ishai et al. [2003], which allows the adversary to probe the input-output behavior of the circuit while obtaining side-channel leakage. They achieve this result by showing equivalence between noisy and wire-probing leakage; this equivalence has been used in subsequent works, as well. Duc, Faust, and Standaert [Duc et al. 2015, 2019] further improve on the result by measuring the "noisiness" of statistical distance via a mutual information metric rather than statistical distance; it is argued that this metric is easier to estimate in practice. The quantitative bounds (relating the amount of noise to the security of the overall scheme) are further improved by Dziembowski, Faust, and Skórski [Dziembowski et al. 2015, 2016]. Andrychowicz, Dziembowski, and Faust [Andrychowicz et al. 2016] and Goudarzi, Joux, and Rivain [Goudarzi et al. 2018] (using techniques from Andrychowicz et al. [2015]) show how to improve the leakage rate and the efficiency of the transformed circuit.

26.4.4   Heuristic Security Evaluation of Leakage-Resilient Constructions

Much effort has also been devoted to understanding the security properties of masking in general and particularly in the context of block ciphers. As already mentioned, the Ishai et al. [2003] compiler is secure against wire probing attacks that do not touch more than t wires. However, most realistic attacks with current technology do not obtain information about only a few wires; instead, they get noisy information about many wires. This kind of leakage is discussed in Section 26.4.3.5, in the simulatability framework of Ishai et al. [2003]. However, simulatability is a very strong requirement, and is often unachievable within realistic efficiency constraints. Thus, researchers have used approaches based on evaluating the best known classes of attack strategies, in order to understand the security of designs for which the simulation proofs either do not exist or do not give meaningful security bounds. These approaches provide weaker security guarantees, because they do not consider all possible adversaries, but rather the best classes of adversaries known today. Nevertheless, they are often very useful for understanding the cost/benefit tradeoffs of various designs, and are used extensively in applied literature.

A prominent heuristic evaluation framework was put forward by Standaert et al. [2009]. A large number of cryptographic designs and side-channel countermeasures have been evaluated in this framework (many of these are referenced in Duc et al. [2015, Section 1]). A comparison between this approach and the more theoretical approach of Dziembowski and Pietrzak [2008] and Pietrzak [2009] (see Sections 26.4.2.2 and 26.4.2.3) is provided in Standaert et al. [2010]. An alternative evaluation framework was proposed in Whitnall and Oswald [2011a], [2011b]. Some works combine provable and heuristic evaluations—see, for example, Duc et al. [2015]. The heuristic evaluation frameworks continue to evolve and mature; see Grosso and Standaert [2018] and references therein.

Barthe et al. [2017] observe that side-channel attackers are often faced with the task of estimating statistical moments of random variables they receive as leakage functions. They therefore propose that the goal of a secure design it to make sure these moments, up to some order, are independent of the secret state of the circuit (the reasoning is that higher-order moments, which may be dependent, are very difficult to estimate). They relate their security goal to the wire-probing leakage of Ishai et al. [2003] and argue that their model is particularly suitable for highly parallel (i.e., hardware rather than software) implementations.

Because of this survey's focus on approaches with a provable security foundation, we do not discuss heuristic evaluation frameworks in more detail, despite their strong impact on applied work.

26.5 Acknowledgements

We are deeply grateful to Shafi and Silvio for the intellectual gems they gave us, for their outstanding professional and personal mentorship, and for nurturing a thriving community of researchers that we are honored to call home.

We are also thankful to the authors of all the papers we surveyed. Many of them were patient enough to explain their results to us and to help put them in context.

We thank Oded Goldreich for a careful reading of our draft and excellent suggestions.

The work of Leonid Reyzin is supported, in part, by the US NSF grant 1422965.

References

M. Abdalla, S. Belaïd, and P.-A. Fouque. 2013. Leakage-resilient symmetric encryption via re-keying. In G. Bertoni and J.-S. Coron, editors, *Cryptographic Hardware and Embedded Systems—CHES 2013*, vol. 8086, Lecture Notes in Computer Science, pp. 471–488. Springer. DOI: 10.1007/978-3-642-40349-1_27. 762

M. Abdalla, S. Belaïd, D. Pointcheval, S. Ruhault, and D. Vergnaud. 2015. Robust pseudo-random number generators with input secure against side-channel attacks. In T. Malkin, V. Kolesnikov, A. B. Lewko, and M. Polychronakis, editors, *ACNS 15: 13th International Conference on Applied Cryptography and Network Security*, vol. 9092, Lecture Notes in Computer Science, pp. 635–654. Springer. DOI: 10.1007/978-3-319-28166-7. 760

M. Abdalla and M. Bellare. 2000. Increasing the lifetime of a key: A comparative analysis of the security of re-keying techniques. In T. Okamoto, editor, *Advances in Cryptology—ASIACRYPT 2000*, vol. 1976, Lecture Notes in Computer Science, pp. 546–559. Springer. DOI: 10.1007/3-540-44448-3_42. 762

D. Agrawal, B. Archambeault, J. R. Rao, and P. Rohatgi. 2003. The EM side-channel(s). In B. S. Kaliski Jr., Ç. K. Koç, and C. Paar, editors, *Cryptographic Hardware and Embedded Systems—CHES 2002*, vol. 2523, Lecture Notes in Computer Science, pp. 29–45. Springer. DOI: 10.1007/3-540-36400-5_4. 728

M. Ajtai. 2011. Secure computation with information leaking to an adversary. In L. Fortnow and S. P. Vadhan, editors, *43rd Annual ACM Symposium on Theory of Computing*, pp. 715–724. ACM Press. 769

A. Akavia, S. Goldwasser, and C. Hazay. 2012. Distributed public key schemes secure against continual leakage. In D. Kowalski and A. Panconesi, editors, *31st ACM Symposium Annual on Principles of Distributed Computing*, pp. 155–164. ACM. DOI: 10.1145/2332432.2332462. 752, 764

A. Akavia, S. Goldwasser, and V. Vaikuntanathan. 2009. Simultaneous hardcore bits and cryptography against memory attacks. In O. Reingold, editor, *TCC 2009: 6th Theory of Cryptography Conference*, vol. 5444, Lecture Notes in Computer Science, pp. 474–495. Springer. DOI: 10.1007/978-3-642-00457-5_28. 730, 731, 734, 735

J. Alwen, Y. Dodis, M. Naor, G. Segev, S. Walfish, and D. Wichs. 2010. Public-key encryption in the bounded-retrieval model. In H. Gilbert, editor, *Advances in Cryptology—EUROCRYPT 2010*, vol. 6110, Lecture Notes in Computer Science, pp. 113–134. Springer. DOI: 10.1007/978-3-642-13190-5_6.pdf. 742, 743, 765

J. Alwen, Y. Dodis, and D. Wichs. 2009. Leakage-resilient public-key cryptography in the bounded-retrieval model. In S. Halevi, editor, *Advances in Cryptology—CRYPTO 2009*, vol. 5677, Lecture Notes in Computer Science, pp. 36–54. Springer. DOI: 10.1007/978-3-642-03356-8_3. 731, 742, 763, 764

J. Alwen, Y. Dodis, and D. Wichs. 2010. Survey: Leakage resilience and the bounded retrieval model. In K. Kurosawa, editor, *ICITS 09: 4th International Conference on Information Theoretic Security*, vol. 5973, Lecture Notes in Computer Science, pp. 1–18. Springer. DOI: 10.1007/978-3-642-14496-7_1. 743

P. Ananth, V. Goyal, and O. Pandey. 2014. Interactive proofs under continual memory leakage. In J. A. Garay and R. Gennaro, editors, *Advances in Cryptology—CRYPTO 2014, Part II*, vol. 8617, Lecture Notes in Computer Science, pp. 164–182. Springer. DOI: 10.1007/978-3-662-44381-1_10. 748

P. Ananth, Y. Ishai, and A. Sahai. 2018. Private circuits: A modular approach. In H. Shacham and A. Boldyreva, editors, *Advances in Cryptology—CRYPTO 2018, Part III*, vol. 10993, Lecture Notes in Computer Science, pp. 427–455. Springer. DOI: 10.1007/978-3-319-96878-0_15. 768, 769

M. Andrychowicz, I. Damgård, S. Dziembowski, S. Faust, and A. Polychroniadou. 2015. Efficient leakage resilient circuit compilers. In K. Nyberg, editor, *Topics in Cryptology—CT-RSA 2015*, vol. 9048, Lecture Notes in Computer Science, pp. 311–329. Springer. DOI: 10.1007/978-3-319-16715-2_1. 769, 772, 775

M. Andrychowicz, S. Dziembowski, and S. Faust. 2016. Circuit compilers with $O(1/\log(n))$ leakage rate. In M. Fischlin and J.-S. Coron, editors, *Advances in Cryptology—EUROCRYPT 2016, Part II*, vol. 9666, Lecture Notes in Computer Science, pp. 586–615. Springer. DOI: 10.1007/978-3-662-49896-5_21. 769, 775

M. Andrychowicz, D. Masny, and E. Persichetti. 2015. Leakage-resilient cryptography over large finite fields: Theory and practice. In T. Malkin, V. Kolesnikov, A. B. Lewko, and M. Polychronakis, editors, *ACNS 15: 13th International Conference on Applied*

Cryptography and Network Security, vol. 9092, Lecture Notes in Computer Science, pp. 655–674. Springer. DOI: 10.1007/978-3-319-28166-7_32. 761, 773

J. Balasch, S. Faust, B. Gierlichs, C. Paglialonga, and F.-X. Standaert. 2017. Consolidating inner product masking. In T. Takagi and T. Peyrin, editors, *Advances in Cryptology—ASIACRYPT 2017, Part I*, vol. 10624, Lecture Notes in Computer Science, pp. 724–754. Springer. DOI: 10.1007/978-3-319-70694-8_25. 768, 769

B. Barak, O. Goldreich, R. Impagliazzo, S, Rudich, A. Sahai, S. P. Vadhan, and K. Yang. 2001. On the (im)possibility of obfuscating programs. In J. Kilian, editor, *Advances in Cryptology—CRYPTO 2001*, vol. 2139, Lecture Notes in Computer Science, pp. 1–18. Springer. 766

G. Barthe, S. Belaïd, F. Dupressoir, P.-A. Fouque, B. Grégoire, and P.-Y. Strub. 2015. Verified proofs of higher-order masking. In E. Oswald and M. Fischlin, editors, *Advances in Cryptology—EUROCRYPT 2015, Part I*, vol. 9056, Lecture Notes in Computer Science, pp. 457–485. Springer. DOI: 10.1007/978-3-662-46800-5_18. 768

G. Barthe, S. Belaïd, F. Dupressoir, P.-A. Fouque, B. Grégoire, P.-Y. Strub, and R. Zucchini. 2016. Strong non-interference and type-directed higher-order masking. In E. R. Weippl, S. Katzenbeisser, C. Kruegel, A. C. Myers, and S. Halevi, editors, *ACM CCS 16: 23rd Conference on Computer and Communications Security*, pp. 116–129. ACM Press. DOI: 10.1145/2976749.2978427. 768

G. Barthe, S. Belaïd, T. Espitau, P.-A. Fouque, B. Grégoire, M. Rossi, and M. Tibouchi. 2018. Masking the GLP lattice-based signature scheme at any order. In J. B. Nielsen and V. Rijmen, editors, *Advances in Cryptology—EUROCRYPT 2018, 37th Annual International Conference on the Theory and Applications of Cryptographic Techniques, Tel Aviv, Israel, April 29–May 3, 2018. Proceedings, Part II*, vol. 10821, Lecture Notes in Computer Science, pp. 354–384. Springer. DOI: 10.1007/978 3-319-78375-8_12. 765, 768

G. Barthe, F. Dupressoir, S. Faust, B. Grégoire, F.-X. Standaert, and P.-Y. Strub. 2017. Parallel implementations of masking schemes and the bounded moment leakage model. In J.-S. Coron and J. B. Nielsen, editors, *Advances in Cryptology—EUROCRYPT 2017, Part I*, vol. 10210, Lecture Notes in Computer Science, pp. 535–566. Springer. DOI: 10.1007/978-3-319-56620-7_19. 768, 775

G. Barwell, D. P. Martin, E. Oswald, and M. Stam. 2017. Authenticated encryption in the face of protocol and side channel leakage. In T. Takagi and T. Peyrin, editors, *Advances in Cryptology—ASIACRYPT 2017, Part I*, vol. 10624, Lecture Notes in Computer Science, pp. 693–723. Springer. DOI: 10.1007/978-3-319-70694-8_24. 761, 762

S. Belaïd, F. Benhamouda, A. Passelègue, E. Prouff, A. Thillard, and D. Vergnaud. 2016. Randomness complexity of private circuits for multiplication. In M. Fischlin and J.-S. Coron, editors, *Advances in Cryptology—EUROCRYPT 2016, Part II*, vol. 9666, Lecture Notes in Computer Science, pp. 616–648. Springer. DOI: 10.1007/978-3-662-49896-5_22. 768

S. Belaïd, F. Benhamouda, A. Passelègue, E. Prouff, A. Thillard, and D. Vergnaud. 2017. Private multiplication over finite fields. In J. Katz and H. Shacham, editors, *Advances in Cryptology—CRYPTO 2017, Part III*, vol. 10403, Lecture Notes in Computer Science, pp. 397–426. Springer. DOI: 10.1007/978-3-319-63697-9_14. 768

S. Belaïd, D. Goudarzi, and M. Rivain. 2018. Tight private circuits: Achieving probing security with the least refreshing. Cryptology ePrint Archive, Report 2018/439. https://eprint .iacr.org/2018/439. DOI: 10.1007/978-3-030-03329-3_12. 768

M. Bellare and S. K. Miner. 1999. A forward-secure digital signature scheme. In M. J. Wiener, editor, *Advances in Cryptology—CRYPTO '99*, vol. 1666, Lecture Notes in Computer Science, pp. 431–448. Springer. DOI: 10.1007/3-540-48405-1_28. 729

M. Ben-Or, S. Goldwasser, and A. Wigderson. 1988. Completeness theorems for non-cryptographic fault-tolerant distributed computation (extended abstract). In *20th Annual ACM Symposium on Theory of Computing*, pp. 1–10. ACM Press. DOI: 10.1145/62212.62213. 727

F. Benhamouda, A. Degwekar, Y. Ishai, and T. Rabin. 2018. On the local leakage resilience of linear secret sharing schemes. In H. Shacham and A. Boldyreva, editors, *Advances in Cryptology—CRYPTO 2018, Part I*, vol. 10991, Lecture Notes in Computer Science, pp. 531–561. Springer. DOI: 10.1007/978-3-319-96884-1_1. 750, 752, 756

L. Bettale, J.-S. Coron, and R. Zeitoun. 2018. Improved high-order conversion from Boolean to arithmetic masking. *IACR Transactions on Cryptography Hardware and Embedded Systems*, 2018(2): 22–45. DOI: 10.13154/tches.v2018.i2.22-45. 768

N. Bitansky, R. Canetti, S. Goldwasser, S. Halevi, Y. T. Kalai, and G. N. Rothblum. 2011. Program obfuscation with leaky hardware. In D. H. Lee and X. Wang, editors, *Advances in Cryptology—ASIACRYPT 2011*, vol. 7073, Lecture Notes in Computer Science, pp. 722–739. Springer. DOI: 10.1007/978-3-642-25385-0_39. 748, 756, 766

N. Bitansky, R. Canetti, and S. Halevi. 2012. Leakage-tolerant interactive protocols. In R. Cramer, editor, *TCC 2012: 9th Theory of Cryptography Conference*, vol. 7194, Lecture Notes in Computer Science, pp. 266–284. Springer. 746, 747, 748, 752

N. Bitansky, D. Dachman-Soled, and H. Lin. 2014. Leakage-tolerant computation with input-independent preprocessing. In J. A. Garay and R. Gennaro, editors, *Advances in Cryptology—CRYPTO 2014, Part II*, vol. 8617, Lecture Notes in Computer Science, pp. 146–163. Springer. DOI: 10.1007/978-3-642-28914-9_15. 750, 756, 772

R. Bloem, H. Groß, R. Iusupov, B. Könighofer, S. Mangard, and J. Winter. 2018. Formal verification of masked hardware implementations in the presence of glitches. In J. B. Nielsen and V. Rijmen, editors, *Advances in Cryptology—EUROCRYPT 2018, Part II*, vol. 10821, Lecture Notes in Computer Science, pp. 321–353. Springer. DOI: 10.1007/978-3-319-78375-8_11. 768

M. Blum, P. Feldman, and S. Micali. 1988. Non-interactive zero-knowledge and its applications (extended abstract). In *20th Annual ACM Symposium on Theory of Computing*, pp. 103–112. ACM Press. DOI: 10.1145/62212.62222. 738

M. Blum and S. Micali. 1982. How to generate cryptographically strong sequences of pseudo random bits. In *23rd Annual Symposium on Foundations of Computer Science*, pp. 112–117. IEEE Computer Society Press. DOI: 10.1109/SFCS.1982.72. 727, 733

M. Blum and S. Micali. 1984. How to generate cryptographically strong sequences of pseudorandom bits. *SIAM Journal on Computing*, 13(4): 850–864. DOI: 10.1137/0213053. 727, 733, 757

A. Bogdanov, Y. Ishai, E. Viola, and C. Williamson. 2016. Bounded indistinguishability and the complexity of recovering secrets. In M. Robshaw and J. Katz, editors, *Advances in Cryptology—CRYPTO 2016, Part III*, vol. 9816, Lecture Notes in Computer Science, pp. 593–618. Springer. DOI: 10.1007/978-3-662-53015-3_21. 768

D. Boneh and X. Boyen. 2004. Secure identity based encryption without random oracles. In M. Franklin, editor, *Advances in Cryptology—CRYPTO 2004*, vol. 3152, Lecture Notes in Computer Science, pp. 443–459. Springer. DOI: 10.1007/978-3-540-28628-8_27. 765

D. Boneh and X. Boyen. 2011. Efficient selective identity-based encryption without random oracles. *Journal of Cryptology*, 24(4): 659–693. DOI: 10.1007/s00145-010-9078-6. 764

D. Boneh, R. Canetti, S. Halevi, and J. Katz. 2007. Chosen-ciphertext security from identity-based encryption. *SIAM Journal of Computing*, 36(5): 1301–1328. 765

D. Boneh, S. Halevi, M. Hamburg, and R. Ostrovsky. 2008. Circular-secure encryption from decision Diffie-Hellman. In D. Wagner, editor, *Advances in Cryptology—CRYPTO 2008*, vol. 5157, Lecture Notes in Computer Science, pp. 108–125. Springer. DOI: 10.1007/978-3-540-85174-5_7. 736, 740, 771

D. Boneh, B. Lynn, and H. Shacham. 2004. Short signatures from the Weil pairing. *Journal of Cryptology*, 17(4): 297–319. DOI: 10.1007/s00145-004-0314-9. 764

V. Boyko. 1999. On the security properties of OAEP as an all-or-nothing transform. In M. J. Wiener, editor, *Advances in Cryptology—CRYPTO'99*, vol. 1666, Lecture Notes in Computer Science, pp. 503–518. Springer. DOI: 10.1007/3-540-48405-1_32. 729

E. Boyle, S. Garg, A. Jain, Y. T. Kalai, and A. Sahai. 2013. Secure computation against adaptive auxiliary information. In R. Canetti and J. A. Garay, editors, *Advances in Cryptology—CRYPTO 2013, Part I*, vol. 8042, Lecture Notes in Computer Science, pp. 316–334. Springer. DOI: 10.1007/978-3-642-40041-4_18. 748, 749, 750

E. Boyle, S. Goldwasser, A. Jain, and Y. T. Kalai. 2012. Multiparty computation secure against continual memory leakage. In H. J. Karloff and T. Pitassi, editors, *44th Annual ACM Symposium on Theory of Computing*, pp. 1235–1254. ACM Press. DOI: 10.1145/2213977.2214087. 748, 749, 750, 756

E. Boyle, S. Goldwasser, and Y. T. Kalai. 2011a. Leakage-resilient coin tossing. In D. Peleg, editor, *Distributed Computing—25th International Symposium, DISC 2011, Rome, Italy, September 20–22, 2011. Proceedings*, vol. 6950, Lecture Notes in Computer Science, pp. 181–196. Springer. DOI: 10.1007/978-3-642-24100-0_16. 746

E. Boyle, G. Segev, and D. Wichs. 2011b. Fully leakage-resilient signatures. In K. G. Paterson, editor, *Advances in Cryptology—EUROCRYPT 2011*, vol. 6632, Lecture Notes in Computer Science, pp. 89–108. Springer. DOI: 10.1007/978-3-642-20465-4_7. 735, 738

Z. Brakerski and S. Goldwasser. 2010. Circular and leakage resilient public-key encryption under subgroup indistinguishability (or: Quadratic residuosity strikes back). In T.

Rabin, editor, *Advances in Cryptology—CRYPTO 2010*, vol. 6223, Lecture Notes in Computer Science, pp. 1–20. Springer. DOI: 10.1007/978-3-642-14623-7_1. 741

Z. Brakerski, Y. T. Kalai, J. Katz, and V. Vaikuntanathan. 2010. Overcoming the hole in the bucket: Public-key cryptography resilient to continual memory leakage. In *51st Annual Symposium on Foundations of Computer Science*, pp. 501–510. IEEE Computer Society Press. DOI: 10.1109/FOCS.2010.55. 731, 734, 744, 763

Z. Brakerski and G. Segev. 2011. Better security for deterministic public-key encryption: The auxiliary-input setting. In P. Rogaway, editor, *Advances in Cryptology—CRYPTO 2011*, vol. 6841, Lecture Notes in Computer Science, pp. 543–560. Springer. DOI: 10.1007/978-3-642-22792-9_31.pdf. 741

M. Braverman, A. Hassidim, and Y. T. Kalai. 2011. Leaky pseudo-entropy functions. In B. Chazelle, editor, *ICS 2011: 2nd Innovations in Computer Science*, pp. 353–366. Tsinghua University Press. 737

R. Canetti. 1997. Towards realizing random oracles: Hash functions that hide all partial information. In B. S. Kaliski Jr., editor, *Advances in Cryptology—CRYPTO'97*, vol. 1294, Lecture Notes in Computer Science, pp. 455–469. Springer. DOI: 10.1007/BFb0052255. 739

R. Canetti, Y. Dodis, S. Halevi, E. Kushilevitz, and A. Sahai. 2000. Exposure-resilient functions and all-or-nothing transforms. In B. Preneel, editor, *Advances in Cryptology—EUROCRYPT 2000*, vol. 1807, Lecture Notes in Computer Science, pp. 453–469. Springer. DOI: 10.1007/3-540-45539-6_33. 729

R. Canetti, U. Feige, O. Goldreich, and M. Naor. 1996. Adaptively secure multi-party computation. In *28th Annual ACM Symposium on Theory of Computing*, pp. 639–648. ACM Press. DOI: 10.1145/237814.238015. 748

C. Carlet, L. Goubin, E. Prouff, M. Quisquater, and M. Rivain. 2012. Higher-order masking schemes for S-boxes. In A. Canteaut, editor, *Fast Software Encryption—FSE 2012*, vol. 7549, Lecture Notes in Computer Science, pp. 366–384. Springer. DOI: 10.1007/978-3-642-34047-5_21. 774

S. Chari, C. S. Jutla, J. R. Rao, and P. Rohatgi. 1999. Towards sound approaches to counteract power-analysis attacks. In M. J. Wiener, editor, *Advances in Cryptology—CRYPTO'99*, vol. 1666, Lecture Notes in Computer Science, pp. 398–412. Springer. DOI: 10.1007/3-540-48405-1_26. 730, 732, 753, 767, 773, 774

J.-S. Coron. 2018. Formal verification of side-channel countermeasures via elementary circuit transformations. In B. Preneel and F. Vercauteren, editors, *ACNS 18: 16th International Conference on Applied Cryptography and Network Security*, vol. 10892, Lecture Notes in Computer Science, pp. 65–82. Springer. DOI: 10.1007/978-3-319-93387-0_4. 768

J.-S. Coron, F. Rondepierre, and R. Zeitoun. 2018. High order masking of look-up tables with common shares. *IACR Transactions on Cryptography Hardware Embedded Systems*, 2018(1): 40–72. 768

R. Cramer and V. Shoup. 2002. Universal hash proofs and a paradigm for adaptive chosen ciphertext secure public-key encryption. In L. R. Knudsen, editor, *Advances in Cryptology—EUROCRYPT 2002*, vol. 2332, Lecture Notes in Computer Science, pp. 45–64. Springer. DOI: 10.1007/3-540-46035-7_4.pdf. 736

D. Dachman-Soled, S. D. Gordon, F.-H. Liu, A. O'Neill, and H.-S. Zhou. 2016. Leakage-resilient public-key encryption from obfuscation. In C.-M. Cheng, K.-M. Chung, G. Persiano, and B.-Y. Yang, editors, *PKC 2016: 19th International Conference on Theory and Practice of Public Key Cryptography, Part II*, vol. 9615, Lecture Notes in Computer Science, pp. 101–128. Springer. DOI: 10.1007/978-3-662-49387-8_5. 745

D. Dachman-Soled, F.-H. Liu, E. Shi, and H.-S. Zhou. 2015a. Locally decodable and updatable non-malleable codes and their applications. In Y. Dodis and J. B. Nielsen, editors, *TCC 2015: 12th Theory of Cryptography Conference, Part I*, vol. 9014, Lecture Notes in Computer Science, pp. 427–450. Springer. 728

D. Dachman-Soled, F.-H. Liu, and H.-S. Zhou. 2015b. Leakage-resilient circuits revisited—optimal number of computing components without leak-free hardware. In E. Oswald and M. Fischlin, editors, *Advances in Cryptology—EUROCRYPT 2015, Part II*, vol. 9057, Lecture Notes in Computer Science, pp. 131–158. Springer. DOI: 10.1007/978-3-662-46803-6_5. 756, 772, 773

I. Damgård, F. Dupuis, and J. B. Nielsen. 2015. On the orthogonal vector problem and the feasibility of unconditionally secure leakage-resilient computation. In A. Lehmann and S. Wolf, editors, *ICITS 15: 8th International Conference on Information Theoretic Security*, vol. 9063, Lecture Notes in Computer Science, pp. 87–104. Springer. DOI: 10.1007/978-3-319-17470-9_6. 756, 772

F. Davì, S. Dziembowski, and D. Venturi. 2010. Leakage-resilient storage. In J. A. Garay and R. De Prisco, editors, *SCN 10: 7th International Conference on Security in Communication Networks*, vol. 6280, Lecture Notes in Computer Science, pp. 121–137. Springer. DOI: 10.1007/978-3-642-15317-4_9. 751, 764, 772

Y. Desmedt and Y. Frankel. 1990. Threshold cryptosystems. In G. Brassard, editor, *Advances in Cryptology—CRYPTO'89*, vol. 435, Lecture Notes in Computer Science, pp. 307–315. Springer. 729

G. Di Crescenzo, R. J. Lipton, and S. Walfish. 2006. Perfectly secure password protocols in the bounded retrieval model. In S. Halevi and T. Rabin, editors, *TCC 2006: 3rd Theory of Cryptography Conference*, vol. 3876, Lecture Notes in Computer Science, pp. 225–244. Springer. DOI: 10.1007/11681878_12. 729, 730, 731, 733, 741, 742

Y. Dodis. 2000. *Exposure-Resilient Cryptography*. Ph.D. thesis, Massachusetts Institute of Technology. 729

Y. Dodis, S. Goldwasser, Y. T. Kalai, C. Peikert, and V. Vaikuntanathan. 2010a. Public-key encryption schemes with auxiliary inputs. In D. Micciancio, editor, *TCC 2010: 7th Theory of Cryptography Conference*, vol. 5978, Lecture Notes in Computer Science, pp. 361–381. Springer. DOI: 10.1007/978-3-642-11799-2_22.pdf. 740, 741

Y. Dodis, K. Haralambiev, A. López-Alt, and D. Wichs. 2010b. Cryptography against continuous memory attacks. In *51st Annual Symposium on Foundations of Computer*

Science, pp. 511–520. IEEE Computer Society Press. DOI: 10.1109/FOCS.2010.56. 731, 734, 744

Y. Dodis, K. Haralambiev, A. López-Alt, and D. Wichs. 2010c. Efficient public-key cryptography in the presence of key leakage. In Masayuki Abe, editor, *Advances in Cryptology—ASIACRYPT 2010*, vol. 6477, Lecture Notes in Computer Science, pp. 613–631. Springer. DOI: 10.1007/978-3-642-17373-8_35. 737

Y. Dodis, Y. T. Kalai, and S. Lovett. 2009. On cryptography with auxiliary input. In M. Mitzenmacher, editor, *41st Annual ACM Symposium on Theory of Computing*, pp. 621–630. ACM Press. DOI: 10.1145/1536414.1536498. 731, 734, 738, 739

Y. Dodis, A. B. Lewko, B. Waters, and D. Wichs. 2011. Storing secrets on continually leaky devices. In R. Ostrovsky, editor, *52nd Annual Symposium on Foundations of Computer Science*, pp. 688–697. IEEE Computer Society Press. DOI: 10.1109/FOCS.2011.35. 745, 752

Y. Dodis and K. Pietrzak. 2010. Leakage-resilient pseudorandom functions and side-channel attacks on Feistel networks. In T. Rabin, editor, *Advances in Cryptology—CRYPTO 2010*, vol. 6223, Lecture Notes in Computer Science, pp. 21–40. Springer. DOI: 10.1007/978-3-642-14623-7_2. 761

Y. Dodis, A. Sahai, and A. Smith. 2001. On perfect and adaptive security in exposure-resilient cryptography. In B. Pfitzmann, editor, *Advances in Cryptology—EUROCRYPT 2001*, vol. 2045, Lecture Notes in Computer Science, pp. 301–324. Springer. DOI: 10.1007/3-540-44987-6_19. 729

A. Duc, S. Dziembowski, and S. Faust. 2014. Unifying leakage models: From probing attacks to noisy leakage. In P. Q. Nguyen and E. Oswald, editors, *Advances in Cryptology—EUROCRYPT 2014*, vol. 8441, Lecture Notes in Computer Science, pp. 423–440. Springer. DOI: 10.1007/978-3-642-55220-5_24. 770, 774

A. Duc, S. Dziembowski, and S. Faust. 2019. Unifying leakage models: From probing attacks to noisy leakage. *Journal of Cryptology*, 32(1): 151–177. 775

A. Duc, S. Faust, and F.-X. Standaert. 2015. Making masking security proofs concrete—or how to evaluate the security of any leaking device. In E. Oswald and M. Fischlin, editors, *Advances in Cryptology—EUROCRYPT 2015, Part I*, vol. 9056, Lecture Notes in Computer Science, pp. 401–429. Springer. DOI: 10.1007/978-3-662-46800-5_16.pdf. 775

S. Dziembowski. 2006. Intrusion-resilience via the bounded-storage model. In S. Halevi and T. Rabin, editors, *TCC 2006: 3rd Theory of Cryptography Conference*, vol. 3876, Lecture Notes in Computer Science, pp. 207–224. Springer. DOI: 10.1007/11681878_11. 729, 730, 731, 733, 741, 742

S. Dziembowski and S. Faust. 2011. Leakage-resilient cryptography from the inner-product extractor. In D. H. Lee and X. Wang, editors, *Advances in Cryptology—ASIACRYPT 2011*, vol. 7073, Lecture Notes in Computer Science, pp. 702–721. Springer. DOI: 10.1007/978-3-642-25385-0_38. 751, 764

S. Dziembowski and S. Faust. 2012. Leakage-resilient circuits without computational assumptions. In R. Cramer, editor, *TCC 2012: 9th Theory of Cryptography Conference*, vol. 7194, Lecture Notes in Computer Science, pp. 230–247. Springer. DOI: 10.1007/978-3-642-28914-9_13. 751, 755, 756, 764, 769, 771, 772, 773

S. Dziembowski, S. Faust, G. Herold, A. Journault, D. Masny, and F.-X. Standaert. 2016. Towards sound fresh re-keying with hard (physical) learning problems. In M. Robshaw and J. Katz, editors, *Advances in Cryptology—CRYPTO 2016, Part II*, vol. 9815, Lecture Notes in Computer Science, pp. 272–301. Springer. DOI: 10.1007/978-3-662-53008-5_10. 762

S. Dziembowski, S. Faust, and M. Skorski. 2015. Noisy leakage revisited. In E. Oswald and M. Fischlin, editors, *Advances in Cryptology—EUROCRYPT 2015, Part II*, vol. 9057, Lecture Notes in Computer Science, pp. 159–188. Springer. DOI: 10.1007/978-3-662-46803-6_6. 775

S. Dziembowski, S. Faust, and M. Skórski. 2016. Optimal amplification of noisy leakages. In E. Kushilevitz and T. Malkin, editors, *TCC 2016-A: 13th Theory of Cryptography Conference, Part II*, vol. 9563, Lecture Notes in Computer Science, pp. 291–318. Springer. DOI: 10.1007/978-3-662-49099-0_11. 775

S. Dziembowski, Tomasz Kazana, and D. Wichs. 2011. Key-evolution schemes resilient to space-bounded leakage. In P. Rogaway, editor, *Advances in Cryptology—CRYPTO 2011*, vol. 6841, Lecture Notes in Computer Science, pp. 335–353. Springer. DOI: 10.1007/978-3-642-22792-9_19. 746, 760

S. Dziembowski and K. Pietrzak. 2007. Intrusion-resilient secret sharing. In *48th Annual Symposium on Foundations of Computer Science*, pp. 227–237. IEEE Computer Society Press. DOI: 10.1109/FOCS.2007.63. 758

S. Dziembowski and K. Pietrzak. 2008. Leakage-resilient cryptography. In *49th Annual Symposium on Foundations of Computer Science*, pp. 293–302. IEEE Computer Society Press. DOI: 10.1109/FOCS.2008.56. 732, 754, 755, 757, 758, 759, 775

S. Dziembowski, K. Pietrzak, and D. Wichs. 2010. Non-malleable codes. In A. C.-C. Yao, editor, *ICS 2010: 1st Innovations in Computer Science*, pp. 434–452. Tsinghua University Press. 728

T. ElGamal. 1985. A public key cryptosystem and a signature scheme based on discrete logarithms. *IEEE Transactions on Information Theory*, 31: 469–472. DOI: 10.1109/TIT.1985.1057074. 763, 764

W. Enck and A. P. Felt, editors. 2018. *27th USENIX Security Symposium, USENIX Security 2018, Baltimore, MD, USA, August 15–17, 2018*. USENIX Association.

A. Faonio and J. B. Nielsen. 2017. Fully leakage-resilient codes. In S. Fehr, editor, *PKC 2017: 20th International Conference on Theory and Practice of Public Key Cryptography, Part I*, vol. 10174, Lecture Notes in Computer Science, pp. 333–358. Springer. DOI: 10.1007/978-3-662-54365-8_14. 752

A. Faonio, J. B. Nielsen, and D. Venturi. 2015. Mind your coins: Fully leakage-resilient signatures with graceful degradation. In M. M. Halldórsson, K. Iwama, N. Kobayashi, and B. Speckmann, editors, *ICALP 2015: 42nd International Colloquium on Automata, Languages and Programming, Part I*, vol. 9134, Lecture Notes in Computer Science, pp. 456–468. Springer. DOI: 10.1007/978-3-662-47672-7_37. 737

S. Faust, V. Grosso, S. M. Del Pozo, C. Paglialonga, and F.-X. Standaert. 2018. Composable masking schemes in the presence of physical defaults & the robust probing model. *IACR Transactions on Cryptographic Hardware and Embedded Systems*, 2018(3): 89–120. DOI: 10.13154/tches.v2018.i3.89-120. 768

S. Faust, E. Kiltz, K. Pietrzak, and G. N. Rothblum. 2010a. Leakage-resilient signatures. In D. Micciancio, editor, *TCC 2010: 7th Theory of Cryptography Conference*, vol. 5978, Lecture Notes in Computer Science, pp. 343–360. Springer. DOI: 10.1007/978-3-642-11799-2_21. 737, 763

S. Faust, P. Mukherjee, J. B. Nielsen, and D. Venturi. 2015. A tamper and leakage resilient von Neumann architecture. In J. Katz, editor, *PKC 2015: 18th International Conference on Theory and Practice of Public Key Cryptography*, vol. 9020, Lecture Notes in Computer Science, pp. 579–603. Springer. DOI: 10.1007/978-3-662-46447-2_26. 728

S. Faust, P. Mukherjee, D. Venturi, and D. Wichs. 2014a. Efficient non-malleable codes and key-derivation for poly-size tampering circuits. In P. Q. Nguyen and E. Oswald, editors, *Advances in Cryptology—EUROCRYPT 2014*, vol. 8441, Lecture Notes in Computer Science, pp. 111–128. Springer. DOI: 10.1007/978-3-642-55220-5_7. 728

S. Faust, C. Paglialonga, and T. Schneider. 2017. Amortizing randomness complexity in private circuits. In T. Takagi and T. Peyrin, editors, *Advances in Cryptology—ASIACRYPT 2017, Part I*, vol. 10624, Lecture Notes in Computer Science, pp. 781–810. Springer. DOI: 10.1007/978-3-319-70694-8_27. 768

S. Faust, K. Pietrzak, and J. Schipper. 2012. Practical leakage-resilient symmetric cryptography. In E. Prouff and P. Schaumont, editors, *Cryptographic Hardware and Embedded Systems—CHES 2012*, vol. 7428, Lecture Notes in Computer Science, pp. 213–232. Springer. DOI: 10.1007/978-3-642-33027-8_13. 759, 761

S. Faust, K. Pietrzak, and D. Venturi. 2011. Tamper-proof circuits: How to trade leakage for tamper-resilience. In L. Aceto, M. Henzinger, and J. Sgall, editors, *ICALP 2011: 38th International Colloquium on Automata, Languages and Programming, Part I*, vol. 6755, Lecture Notes in Computer Science, pp. 391–402. Springer. DOI: 10.1007/978-3-642-22006-7_33. 728

S. Faust, T. Rabin, L. Reyzin, E. Tromer, and V. Vaikuntanathan. 2010b. Protecting circuits from leakage: The computationally-bounded and noisy cases. In H. Gilbert, editor, *Advances in Cryptology—EUROCRYPT 2010*, vol. 6110, Lecture Notes in Computer Science, pp. 135–156. Springer. DOI: 10.1007/978-3-642-13190-5_7. 753, 768, 769, 770

S. Faust, T. Rabin, L. Reyzin, E. Tromer, and V. Vaikuntanathan. 2014b. Protecting circuits from computationally bounded and noisy leakage. *SIAM Journal on Computing*, 43(5): 1564–1614. DOI: 10.1137/120880343. 769, 773, 774

U. Feige and A. Shamir. 1990. Zero knowledge proofs of knowledge in two rounds. In G. Brassard, editor, *Advances in Cryptology—CRYPTO'89*, vol. 435, Lecture Notes in Computer Science, pp. 526–544. Springer. DOI: 10.1007/0-387-34805-0_46. 748

E. Fujisaki, A. Kawachi, R. Nishimaki, K. Tanaka, and K. Yasunaga. 2015. Post-challenge leakage resilient public-key cryptosystem in split state model. *IEICE Transactions*, 98-A(3): 853–862. DOI: 10.1587/transfun.E98.A.853. 765

B. Fuller and A. Hamlin. 2015. Unifying leakage classes: Simulatable leakage and pseudoentropy. In A. Lehmann and S. Wolf, editors, *ICITS 15: 8th International Conference on Information Theoretic Security*, vol. 9063, Lecture Notes in Computer Science, pp. 69–86. Springer. DOI: 10.1007/978-3-319-17470-9_5. 759

B. Fuller and L. Reyzin. 2012. Computational entropy and information leakage. Cryptology ePrint Archive, Report 2012/466. http://eprint.iacr.org/2012/466. 758

D. Galindo, J. Großschädl, Z. Liu, P. K. Vadnala, and S. Vivek. 2016. Implementation of a leakage-resilient elgamal key encapsulation mechanism. *Journal Cryptographic Engineering*, 6(3): 229–238. DOI: 10.1007/s13389-016-0121-x. 764

D. Galindo and S. Vivek. 2013a. A leakage-resilient pairing-based variant of the Schnorr signature scheme. In M. Stam, editor, *14th IMA International Conference on Cryptography and Coding*, vol. 8308, Lecture Notes in Computer Science, pp. 173–192. Springer. DOI: 10.1007/978-3-642-45239-0_11. 737, 764

D. Galindo and S. Vivek. 2013b. A practical leakage-resilient signature scheme in the generic group model. In L. R. Knudsen and H. Wu, editors, *SAC 2012: 19th Annual International Workshop on Selected Areas in Cryptography*, vol. 7707, Lecture Notes in Computer Science, pp. 50–65. Springer. DOI: 10.1007/978-3-642-35999-6_4. 764

S. Garg, A. Jain, and A. Sahai. 2011. Leakage-resilient zero knowledge. In P. Rogaway, editor, *Advances in Cryptology—CRYPTO 2011*, vol. 6841, Lecture Notes in Computer Science, pp. 297–315. Springer. DOI: 10.1007/978-3-642-22792-9_17. 746, 747, 748

D. Genkin, Y. Ishai, and M. Weiss. 2017. How to construct a leakage-resilient (stateless) trusted party. In Y. Kalai and L. Reyzin, editors, *TCC 2017: 15th Theory of Cryptography Conference, Part II*, vol. 10678, Lecture Notes in Computer Science, pp. 209–244. Springer. DOI: 10.1007/978-3-319-70503-3_7. 773

R. Gennaro, A. Lysyanskaya, T. Malkin, S. Micali, and T. Rabin. 2004. Algorithmic tamper-proof (ATP) security: Theoretical foundations for security against hardware tampering. In M. Naor, editor, *TCC 2004: 1st Theory of Cryptography Conference*, vol. 2951, Lecture Notes in Computer Science, pp. 258–277. Springer. DOI: 10.1007/978-3-540-24638-1_15. 728

O. Goldreich, S. Goldwasser, and S. Micali. 1984. On the cryptographic applications of random functions. In G. R. Blakley and D. Chaum, editors, *Advances in Cryptology—CRYPTO'84*, vol. 196, Lecture Notes in Computer Science, pp. 276–288. Springer. 727

O. Goldreich, S. Goldwasser, and S. Micali. 1986. How to construct random functions. *Journal of the ACM*, 33(4): 792–807. DOI: 10.1145/6490.6503. 727

O. Goldreich and L. A. Levin. 1989. A hard-core predicate for all one-way functions. In *21st Annual ACM Symposium on Theory of Computing*, pp. 25–32. ACM Press. DOI: 10.1145/73007.73010. 740, 757

O. Goldreich, S. Micali, and A. Wigderson. 1986. Proofs that yield nothing but their validity and a methodology of cryptographic protocol design (extended abstract). In *27th Annual Symposium on Foundations of Computer Science*, pp. 174–187. IEEE Computer Society Press. DOI: 10.1145/116825.116852. 727

O. Goldreich, S. Micali, and A. Wigderson. 1987. How to play any mental game, or A completeness theorem for protocols with honest majority. In A. Aho, editor, *19th Annual ACM Symposium on Theory of Computing*, pp. 218–229. ACM Press. DOI: 10.1145/28395.28420. 727, 750

O. Goldreich, S. Micali, and A. Wigderson. 1991. Proofs that yield nothing but their validity or all languages in NP have zero-knowledge proof systems. *Journal of the ACM*, 38(3): 691–729. DOI: 10.1145/116825.116852. 727

O. Goldreich and R. Ostrovsky. 1996. Software protection and simulation on oblivious rams. *Journal of the ACM*, 43(3): 431–473. DOI: 10.1145/233551.233553. 729

S. Goldwasser and Y. T. Kalai. 2005. On the impossibility of obfuscation with auxiliary input. In *46th Annual Symposium on Foundations of Computer Science*, pp. 553–562. IEEE Computer Society Press. DOI: 10.1109/SFCS.2005.60. 739

S. Goldwasser, Y. T. Kalai, C. Peikert, and V. Vaikuntanathan. 2010. Robustness of the learning with errors assumption. In A. C.-C. Yao, editor, *ICS 2010: 1st Innovations in Computer Science*, pp. 230–240. Tsinghua University Press. 741

S. Goldwasser and S. Micali. 1982. Probabilistic encryption and how to play mental poker keeping secret all partial information. In *14th Annual ACM Symposium on Theory of Computing*, pp. 365–377. ACM Press. DOI: 10.1145/800070.802212. 727

S. Goldwasser and S. Micali. 1984. Probabilistic encryption. *Journal of Computer and System Sciences*, 28(2): 270–299. DOI: 10.1016/0022-0000(84)90070-9. 727

S. Goldwasser, S. Micali, and C. Rackoff. 1985. The knowledge complexity of interactive proof-systems (extended abstract). In *17th Annual ACM Symposium on Theory of Computing*, pp. 291–304. ACM Press. DOI: 10.1145/22145.22178. 727

S. Goldwasser, S. Micali, and C. Rackoff. 1989. The knowledge complexity of interactive proof systems. *SIAM Journal on Computing*, 18(1): 186–208. DOI: 10.1137/0218012. 727

S. Goldwasser, S. Micali, and R. L. Rivest. 1984. A "paradoxical" solution to the signature problem (abstract) (impromptu talk). In G. R. Blakley and D. Chaum, editors, *Advances in Cryptology—CRYPTO'84*, vol. 196, Lecture Notes in Computer Science, page 467. Springer. 727

S. Goldwasser, S. Micali, and R. L. Rivest. 1988. A digital signature scheme secure against adaptive chosen-message attacks. *SIAM Journal on Computing*, 17(2): 281–308. DOI: 10.1137/0217017. 727

S. Goldwasser and G. N. Rothblum. 2010. Securing computation against continuous leakage. In T. Rabin, editor, *Advances in Cryptology—CRYPTO 2010*, vol. 6223, Lecture Notes in Computer Science, pp. 59–79. Springer. DOI: 10.1007/978-3-642-14623-7_4. 755, 771, 772

S. Goldwasser and G. N. Rothblum. 2012. How to compute in the presence of leakage. In *53rd Annual Symposium on Foundations of Computer Science*, pp. 31–40. IEEE Computer Society Press. 770, 771, 772

S. Goldwasser and G. N. Rothblum. 2015. How to compute in the presence of leakage. *SIAM Journal of Computing*, 44(5): 1480–1549. DOI: 10.1137/130931461. 755, 766, 770, 771, 772

L. Goubin and J. Patarin. 1999. DES and differential power analysis (the "duplication" method). In Ç. K. Koç and C. Paar, editors, *Cryptographic Hardware and Embedded Systems—CHES'99*, vol. 1717, Lecture Notes in Computer Science, pp. 158–172. Springer. DOI: 10.1007/3-540-48059-5_15. 730

D. Goudarzi, A. Joux, and M. Rivain. 2018. How to securely compute with noisy leakage in quasilinear complexity. In T. Peyrin and S. Galbraith, editors, *Advances in Cryptology—ASIACRYPT 2018, Part II*, vol. 11273, Lecture Notes in Computer Science, pp. 547–574. Springer. DOI: 10.1007/978-3-030-03329-3_19. 775

D. Goudarzi and M. Rivain. 2017. How fast can higher-order masking be in software? In J.-S. Coron and J. B. Nielsen, editors, *Advances in Cryptology—EUROCRYPT 2017, Part I*, vol. 10210, Lecture Notes in Computer Science, pp. 567–597. Springer. DOI: 10.1007/978-3-319-56620-7_20. 768

V. Goyal, Y. Ishai, H. K. Maji, A. Sahai, and A. A. Sherstov. 2016. Bounded-communication leakage resilience via parity-resilient circuits. In I. Dinur, editor, *57th Annual Symposium on Foundations of Computer Science*, pp. 1–10. IEEE Computer Society Press. DOI: 10.1109/FOCS.2016.10. 756, 773

H. Groß and S. Mangard. 2017. Reconciling d+1 masking in hardware and software. In W. Fischer and N. Homma, editors, *Cryptographic Hardware and Embedded Systems—CHES 2017*, vol. 10529, Lecture Notes in Computer Science, pp. 115–136. Springer. DOI: 10.1007/978-3-319-66787-4_6. 768

V. Grosso, G. Leurent, F.-X. Standaert, and K. Varici. 2015. LS-designs: Bitslice encryption for efficient masked software implementations. In C. Cid and C. Rechberger, editors, *Fast Software Encryption—FSE 2014*, vol. 8540, Lecture Notes in Computer Science, pp. 18–37. Springer. DOI: 10.1007/978-3-662-46706-0_2. 768

V. Grosso and F.-X. Standaert. 2018. Masking proofs are tight and how to exploit it in security evaluations. In J. B. Nielsen and V. Rijmen, editors, *Advances in Cryptology—EUROCRYPT 2018, Part II*, vol. 10821, Lecture Notes in Computer Science, pp. 385–412. Springer. DOI: 10.1007/978-3-319-78375-8_13. 775

T. Güneysu, V. Lyubashevsky, and T. Pöppelmann. 2012. Practical lattice-based cryptography: A signature scheme for embedded systems. In E. Prouff and P. Schaumont, editors, *Cryptographic Hardware and Embedded Systems—CHES 2012*, vol. 7428, Lecture Notes in Computer Science, pp. 530–547. Springer. DOI: 10.1007/978-3-642-33027-8_31. 765

C. G. Günther. 1990. An identity-based key-exchange protocol. In J.-J. Quisquater and J. Vandewalle, editors, *Advances in Cryptology—EUROCRYPT'89*, vol. 434, Lecture Notes in Computer Science, pp. 29–37. Springer. DOI: 10.1007/3-540-46885-4_5.pdf. 729

C. Guo, O. Pereira, T. Peters, and F.-X. Standaert. 2018. Leakage-resilient authenticated encryption with misuse in the leveled leakage setting: Definitions, separation results, and constructions. Cryptology ePrint Archive, Report 2018/484. https://eprint.iacr.org/2018/484. 762

J. A. Halderman, S. D. Schoen, N. Heninger, W. Clarkson, W. Paul, J. A. Calandrino, A. J. Feldman, J. Appelbaum, and E. W. Felten. 2008. Lest we remember: Cold boot attacks on encryption keys. In P. C. van Oorschot, editor, *Proceedings of the 17th USENIX Security Symposium, July 28–August 1, 2008, San Jose, CA, USA*, pp. 45–60. USENIX Association. 728

J. A. Halderman, S. D. Schoen, N. Heninger, W. Clarkson, W. Paul, J. A. Calandrino, A. J. Feldman, J. Appelbaum, and E. W. Felten. 2009. Lest we remember: Cold-boot attacks on encryption keys. *Communications of the ACM*, 52(5): 91–98. DOI: 10.1145/1506409.1506429. 728

S. Halevi and H. Lin. 2011. After-the-fact leakage in public-key encryption. In Y. Ishai, editor, *TCC 2011: 8th Theory of Cryptography Conference*, vol. 6597, Lecture Notes in Computer Science, pp. 107–124. Springer. DOI: 10.1007/978-3-642-19571-6_8. 737, 738, 765

C. Hazay, A. López-Alt, H. Wee, and D. Wichs. 2013. Leakage-resilient cryptography from minimal assumptions. In T. Johansson and P. Q. Nguyen, editors, *Advances in Cryptology—EUROCRYPT 2013*, vol. 7881, Lecture Notes in Computer Science, pp. 160–176. Springer. DOI: 10.1007/978-3-642-38348-9_10.pdf. 738

C. Hazay, A. López-Alt, H. Wee, and D. Wichs. 2016. Leakage-resilient cryptography from minimal assumptions. *Journal of Cryptology*, 29(3):514–551. DOI: 10.1007/s00145-015-9200-x. 738

A. Herzberg, M. Jakobsson, S. Jarecki, H. Krawczyk, and M. Yung. 1997. Proactive public key and signature systems. In *ACM CCS 97: 4th Conference on Computer and Communications Security*, pp. 100–110. ACM Press. DOI: 10.1145/266420.266442. 729

S. Heyse, E. Kiltz, V. Lyubashevsky, C. Paar, and K. Pietrzak. 2012. Lapin: An efficient authentication protocol based on ring-LPN. In A. Canteaut, editor, *Fast Software Encryption—FSE 2012*, vol. 7549, Lecture Notes in Computer Science, pp. 346–365. Springer. DOI: 10.1007/978-3-642-34047-5_20. 761, 773

Y. Ishai, E. Kushilevitz, X. Li, R. Ostrovsky, M. Prabhakaran, A. Sahai, and D. Zuckerman. 2013. Robust pseudorandom generators. In F. V. Fomin, R. Freivalds, M. Z. Kwiatkowska, and D. Peleg, editors, *ICALP 2013: 40th International Colloquium on Automata, Languages and Programming, Part I*, vol. 7965, Lecture Notes in Computer Science, pp. 576–588. Springer. DOI: 10.1007/978-3-642-39206-1_49. 758, 768

Y. Ishai, M. Prabhakaran, A. Sahai, and D. Wagner. 2006. Private circuits II: Keeping secrets in tamperable circuits. In S. Vaudenay, editor, *Advances in Cryptology—EUROCRYPT 2006*, vol. 4004, Lecture Notes in Computer Science, pp. 308–327. Springer. DOI: 10.1007/11761679_19.pdf. 728

Y. Ishai, A. Sahai, and D. Wagner. 2003. Private circuits: Securing hardware against probing attacks. In D. Boneh, editor, *Advances in Cryptology—CRYPTO 2003*, vol. 2729, Lecture Notes in Computer Science, pp. 463–481. Springer. DOI: 10.1007/978-3-540-45146-4_27. 730, 732, 753, 754, 755, 758, 759, 765, 766, 767, 768, 769, 770, 774, 775, 776

Y. Ishai, M. Weiss, and G. Yang. 2016. Making the best of a leaky situation: Zero-knowledge PCPs from leakage-resilient circuits. In E. Kushilevitz and T. Malkin, editors, *TCC 2016-A: 13th Theory of Cryptography Conference, Part II*, vol. 9563, Lecture Notes in Computer Science, pp. 3–32. Springer. DOI: 10.1007/978-3-662-49099-0_1. 770, 773

G. Itkis and L. Reyzin. 2002. SiBIR: Signer-Base Intrusion-Resilient signatures. In M. Yung, editor, *Advances in Cryptology—CRYPTO 2002*, vol. 2442, Lecture Notes in Computer Science, pp. 499–514. Springer. DOI: 10.1007/3-540-45708-9_32. 729

Z. Jafargholi and D. Wichs. 2015. Tamper detection and continuous non-malleable codes. In Y. Dodis and J. B. Nielsen, editors, *TCC 2015: 12th Theory of Cryptography Conference, Part I*, vol. 9014, Lecture Notes in Computer Science, pp. 451–480. Springer. DOI: 10.1007/978-3-662-46494-6_19. 728

A. Journault and F.-X. Standaert. 2017. Very high order masking: Efficient implementation and security evaluation. In W. Fischer and N. Homma, editors, *Cryptographic Hardware and Embedded Systems—CHES 2017*, vol. 10529, Lecture Notes in Computer Science, pp. 623–643. Springer. DOI: 10.1007/978-3-319-66787-4_30. 768

A. Juma and Y. Vahlis. 2010. Protecting cryptographic keys against continual leakage. In T. Rabin, editor, *Advances in Cryptology—CRYPTO 2010*, vol. 6223, Lecture Notes in Computer Science, pp. 41–58. Springer. DOI: 10.1007/978-3-642-14623-7_3. 755, 771, 773

J. Katz and V. Vaikuntanathan. 2009. Signature schemes with bounded leakage resilience. In M. Matsui, editor, *Advances in Cryptology—ASIACRYPT 2009*, vol. 5912, Lecture Notes in Computer Science, pp. 703–720. Springer. DOI: 10.1007/978-3-642-10366-7_41. 737, 763

E. Kiltz and K. Pietrzak. 2010. Leakage resilient ElGamal encryption. In M. Abe, editor, *Advances in Cryptology—ASIACRYPT 2010*, vol. 6477, Lecture Notes in Computer Science, pp. 595–612. Springer. DOI: 10.1007/978-3-642-17373-8_34.pdf. 761, 763, 764

P. Kocher, J. Horn, A. Fogh, D. Genkin, D. Gruss, W. Haas, M. Hamburg, M. Lipp, S. Mangard, T. Prescher, M. Schwarz, and Y. Yarom. 2019. Spectre attacks: Exploiting speculative execution. In *40th IEEE Symposium on Security and Privacy (S&P'19)*. 728

P. C. Kocher. 1996. Timing attacks on implementations of Diffie-Hellman, RSA, DSS, and other systems. In N. Koblitz, editor, *Advances in Cryptology—CRYPTO'96*, vol. 1109,

Lecture Notes in Computer Science, pp. 104–113. Springer. DOI: 10.1007/3-540-68697-5_9. 728

P. C. Kocher. 2003. Leak-resistant cryptographic indexed key update. U.S. Patent 65539092. 762

P. C. Kocher, J. Jaffe, and B. Jun. 1999. Differential power analysis. In M. J. Wiener, editor, *Advances in Cryptology—CRYPTO'99*, vol. 1666, Lecture Notes in Computer Science, pp. 388–397. Springer. 728, 730

L. Lamport. 1979. Constructing digital signatures from a one-way function. Technical Report SRI-CSL-98, SRI International Computer Science Laboratory. 762

A. B. Lewko, M. Lewko, and B. Waters. 2011. How to leak on key updates. In L. Fortnow and S. P. Vadhan, editors, *43rd Annual ACM Symposium on Theory of Computing*, pp. 725–734. ACM Press. 745, 746, 752

M. Lipp, M. Schwarz, D. Gruss, T. Prescher, W. Haas, A. Fogh, J. Horn, S. Mangard, P. Kocher, D. Genkin, Y. Yarom, and M. Hamburg. 2018. Meltdown: Reading kernel memory from user space. In W. Enck and A. P. Felt, editors, *27th USENIX Security Symposium, USENIX Security 2018, Baltimore, MD, USA, August 15–17, 2018*, pp. 973–990. USENIX Association. 728

F.-H. Liu and A. Lysyanskaya. 2012. Tamper and leakage resilience in the split-state model. In R. Safavi-Naini and R. Canetti, editors, *Advances in Cryptology—CRYPTO 2012*, vol. 7417, Lecture Notes in Computer Science, pp. 517–532. Springer. DOI: 10.1007/978-3-642-32009-5_30. 728

J. Longo, D. P. Martin, E. Oswald, D. Page, M. Stam, and M. Tunstall. 2014. Simulatable leakage: Analysis, pitfalls, and new constructions. In Palash Sarkar and Tetsu Iwata, editors, *Advances in Cryptology—ASIACRYPT 2014, Part I*, vol. 8873, Lecture Notes in Computer Science, pp. 223–242. Springer. DOI: 10.1007/978-3-662-45611-8_12. 759

T. Malkin, I. Teranishi, Y. Vahlis, and M. Yung. 2011. Signatures resilient to continual leakage on memory and computation. In Y. Ishai, editor, *TCC 2011: 8th Theory of Cryptography Conference*, vol. 6597, Lecture Notes in Computer Science, pp. 89–106. Springer. 746, 763

D. P. Martin, E. Oswald, M. Stam, and M. Wójcik. 2015. A leakage resilient MAC. In J. Groth, editor, *15th IMA International Conference on Cryptography and Coding*, vol. 9496, Lecture Notes in Computer Science, pp. 295–310. Springer. DOI: 10.1007/978-3-319-27239-9_18. 761

R. C. Merkle. 1988. A digital signature based on a conventional encryption function. In C. Pomerance, editor, *Advances in Cryptology—CRYPTO'87*, vol. 293, Lecture Notes in Computer Science, pp. 369–378. Springer. DOI: 10.1007/3-540-48184-2_32. 762

S. Micali and L. Reyzin. 2004. Physically observable cryptography (extended abstract). In M. Naor, editor, *TCC 2004: 1st Theory of Cryptography Conference*, vol. 2951, Lecture Notes in Computer Science, pp. 278–296. Springer. DOI: 10.1007/978-3-540-24638-1_16.pdf. 730, 732, 753, 754, 755, 756, 757, 759, 762, 763, 766, 769

E. Miles. 2014. Iterated group products and leakage resilience against NC1. In M. Naor, editor, *ITCS 2014: 5th Conference on Innovations in Theoretical Computer Science*, pp. 261–268. ACM Press. 770

E. Miles and E. Viola. 2013. Shielding circuits with groups. In D. Boneh, T. Roughgarden, and J. Feigenbaum, editors, *45th Annual ACM Symposium on Theory of Computing*, pp. 251–260. ACM Press. DOI: 10.1145/2554797.2554822. 770, 771

M. Naor and G. Segev. 2009. Public-key cryptosystems resilient to key leakage. In S. Halevi, editor, *Advances in Cryptology—CRYPTO 2009*, vol. 5677, Lecture Notes in Computer Science, pp. 18–35. Springer. DOI: 10.1007/978-3-642-03356-8_2. 736, 737, 738, 764, 765, 771

M. Naor and M. Yung. 1990. Public-key cryptosystems provably secure against chosen ciphertext attacks. In *22nd Annual ACM Symposium on Theory of Computing*, pp. 427–437. ACM Press. DOI: 10.1145/100216.100273. 736

J. B. Nielsen, D. Venturi, and A. Zottarel. 2013. On the connection between leakage tolerance and adaptive security. In K. Kurosawa and G. Hanaoka, editors, *PKC 2013: 16th International Conference on Theory and Practice of Public Key Cryptography*, vol. 7778, Lecture Notes in Computer Science, pp. 497–515. Springer. DOI: 10.1007/978-3-642-36362-7_30. 747

N. Nisan and D. Zuckerman. 1996. Randomness is linear in space. *Journal of Computer and System Sciences*, 52(1): 43–52. DOI: 10.1006/jcss.1996.0004. 733

T. Okamoto. 1993. Provably secure and practical identification schemes and corresponding signature schemes. In E. F. Brickell, editor, *Advances in Cryptology—CRYPTO'92*, vol. 740, Lecture Notes in Computer Science, pp. 31–53. Springer. DOI: 10.1007/3-540-48071-4_3. 764

O. Pereira, F.-X. Standaert, and S. Vivek. 2015. Leakage-resilient authentication and encryption from symmetric cryptographic primitives. In I. Ray, N. Li, and C. Kruegel, editors, *ACM CCS 15: 22nd Conference on Computer and Communications Security*, pp. 96–108. ACM Press. DOI: 10.1145/2810103.2813626. 761, 762

K. Pietrzak. 2009. A leakage-resilient mode of operation. In A. Joux, editor, *Advances in Cryptology—EUROCRYPT 2009*, vol. 5479, Lecture Notes in Computer Science, pp. 462–482. Springer. DOI: 10.1007/978-3-642-01001-9_27. 759, 775

G. Piret, T. Roche, and C. Carlet. 2012. PICARO—a block cipher allowing efficient higher-order side-channel resistance. In F. Bao, P. Samarati, and J. Zhou, editors, *ACNS 12: 10th International Conference on Applied Cryptography and Network Security*, vol. 7341, Lecture Notes in Computer Science, pp. 311–328. Springer. DOI: 10.1007/978-3-642-31284-7_19. 768

E. Prouff and M. Rivain. 2013. Masking against side-channel attacks: A formal security proof. In T. Johansson and P. Q. Nguyen, editors, *Advances in Cryptology—EUROCRYPT 2013*, vol. 7881, Lecture Notes in Computer Science, pp. 142–159. Springer. DOI: 10.1007/978-3-642-38348-9_9. 774

O. Regev. 2005. On lattices, learning with errors, random linear codes, and cryptography. In H. N. Gabow and R. Fagin, editors, *37th Annual ACM Symposium on Theory of Computing*, pp. 84–93. ACM Press. DOI: 10.1145/1060590.1060603. 736

O. Reingold, L. Trevisan, M. Tulsiani, and S. P. Vadhan. 2008. Dense subsets of pseudorandom sets. In *49th Annual Symposium on Foundations of Computer Science*, pp. 76–85. IEEE Computer Society Press. DOI: 10.1109/FOCS.2008.38. 758

R. L. Rivest. 1997. All-or-nothing encryption and the package transform. In E. Biham, editor, *Fast Software Encryption—FSE'97*, vol. 1267, Lecture Notes in Computer Science, pp. 210–218. Springer. DOI: 10.1007/BFb0052348.pdf. 729

G. N. Rothblum. 2012. How to compute under AC^0 leakage without secure hardware. In Reihaneh Safavi-Naini and R. Canetti, editors, *Advances in Cryptology—CRYPTO 2012*, vol. 7417, Lecture Notes in Computer Science, pp. 552–569. Springer. DOI: 10.1007/978-3-642-32009-5_32. 770

A. Sahai. 1999. Non-malleable non-interactive zero knowledge and adaptive chosen-ciphertext security. In *40th Annual Symposium on Foundations of Computer Science*, pp. 543–553. IEEE Computer Society Press. 738

J. Schipper. 2010. *Leakage-Resilient Authentication*. Ph.D. thesis, Utrecht University. 761

C.-P. Schnorr. 1991. Efficient signature generation by smart cards. *Journal of Cryptology*, 4(3): 161–174. DOI: 10.1007/BF00196725. 764

A. Shamir. 1979. How to share a secret. *Communications of the Association for Computing Machinery*, 22(11): 612–613. DOI: 10.1145/359168.359176. 750

A. Smith and Y. Zhang. 2013. Near-linear time, leakage-resilient key evolution schemes from expander graphs. Cryptology ePrint Archive, Report 2013/864. http://eprint.iacr.org/2013/864. 760

F.-X. Standaert, T. Malkin, and M. Yung. 2009. A unified framework for the analysis of side-channel key recovery attacks. In A. Joux, editor, *Advances in Cryptology—EUROCRYPT 2009*, vol. 5479, Lecture Notes in Computer Science, pp. 443–461. Springer. DOI: 10.1007/978-3-642-01001-9_26. 775

F.-X. Standaert, O. Pereira, and Y. Yu. 2013. Leakage-resilient symmetric cryptography under empirically verifiable assumptions. In R. Canetti and J. A. Garay, editors, *Advances in Cryptology—CRYPTO 2013, Part I*, vol. 8042, Lecture Notes in Computer Science, pp. 335–352. Springer. DOI: 10.1007/978-3-642-40041-4_19. 759, 774

F.-X. Standaert, O. Pereira, Y. Yu, J.-J. Quisquater, M. Yung, and E. Oswald. 2010. Leakage resilient cryptography in practice. *Information Security and Cryptography*, pp. 99–134. Springer. DOI: 10.1007/978-3-642-14452-3_5. 759, 774, 775

F. Tang, H. Li, Q. Niu, and B. Liang. 2014. Efficient leakage-resilient signature schemes in the generic bilinear group model. In X. Huang and J. Zhou, editors, *Information Security Practice and Experience—10th International Conference, ISPEC 2014, Fuzhou, China, May 5–8, 2014. Proceedings*, vol. 8434, Lecture Notes in Computer Science, pp. 418–432. Springer. DOI: 10.1007/978-3-319-06320-1_31. 764

L. Trevisan and S. P. Vadhan. 2000. Extracting randomness from samplable distributions. In *41st Annual Symposium on Foundations of Computer Science*, pp. 32–42. IEEE Computer Society Press. DOI: 10.1109/SFCS.2000.892063. 751

J. Van Bulck, M. Minkin, O. Weisse, D. Genkin, B. Kasikci, F. Piessens, M. Silberstein, T. F. Wenisch, Y. Yarom, and R. Strackx. 2018. Foreshadow: Extracting the keys to the intel SGX kingdom with transient out-of-order execution. In W. Enck and A. P. Felt, editors. *27th USENIX Security Symposium, USENIX Security 2018, Baltimore, MD, USA, August 15–17, 2018*. pp. 991–1008. USENIX Association. 728

B. R. Waters. 2005. Efficient identity-based encryption without random oracles. In R. Cramer, editor, *Advances in Cryptology—EUROCRYPT 2005*, vol. 3494, Lecture Notes in Computer Science, pp. 114–127. Springer. DOI: 10.1007/11426639_7. 764

C. Whitnall and E. Oswald. 2011a. A comprehensive evaluation of mutual information analysis using a fair evaluation framework. In P. Rogaway, editor, *Advances in Cryptology—CRYPTO 2011*, vol. 6841, Lecture Notes in Computer Science, pp. 316–334. Springer. DOI: 10.1007/978-3-642-22792-9_18. 775

C. Whitnall and E. Oswald. 2011b. A fair evaluation framework for comparing side-channel distinguishers. *Journal of Cryptographic Engineering*, 1(2): 145–160. DOI: 10.1007/s13389-011-0011-1. 775

J.-D. Wu, Y.-M. Tseng, and S.-S. Huang. 2016. Leakage-resilient id-based signature scheme in the generic bilinear group model. *Security and Communication Networks*, 9(17): 3987–4001. DOI: 10.1002/sec.1580. 764

A. C.-C. Yao. 1982. Theory and applications of trapdoor functions (extended abstract). In *23rd Annual Symposium on Foundations of Computer Science*, pp. 80–91. IEEE Computer Society Press. 733

Y. Yu, F.-X. Standaert, O. Pereira, and M. Yung. 2010. Practical leakage-resilient pseudorandom generators. In E. Al-Shaer, A. D. Keromytis, and V. Shmatikov, editors, *ACM CCS 10: 17th Conference on Computer and Communications Security*, pp. 141–151. ACM Press. 759, 760

Y. Yu and F.-X. Standaert. 2013. Practical leakage-resilient pseudorandom objects with minimum public randomness. In E. Dawson, editor, *Topics in Cryptology—CT-RSA 2013*, vol. 7779, Lecture Notes in Computer Science, pp. 223–238. Springer. DOI: 10.1145/1866307.1866324. 759

T. H. Yuen, S. S. M. Chow, Y. Zhang, and S. M. Yiu. 2012. Identity-based encryption resilient to continual auxiliary leakage. In D. Pointcheval and T. Johansson, editors, *Advances in Cryptology—EUROCRYPT 2012*, vol. 7237, Lecture Notes in Computer Science, pp. 117–134. Springer. DOI: 10.1007/978-3-642-29011-4_9. 745

Z. Zhang, S. S. M. Chow, and Z. Cao. 2015. Post-challenge leakage in public-key encryption. *Theoretical Computer Science*, 572: 25–49. DOI: 10.1016/j.tcs.2015.01.010. 765

Editor and Author Biographies

Editor

Oded Goldreich

Oded Goldreich was born on February 4, 1957, in Israel. He received B.A., M.Sc., and D.Sc. degrees in Computer Science at the Technion—Israel Institute of Technology in 1980, 1982 and 1983, respectively. He was a postdoctoral fellow at MIT's Laboratory for Computer Science (1983–1986). Since 1995, he has been on the faculty of the Department of Mathematics and Computer Science of the Weizmann Institute of Science (Israel), where he is the incumbent of the Meyer W. Weisgal Professorial Chair. His current research interests include probabilistic proof systems, property testing, pseudorandomness, and complexity theory at large.

Oded has made numerous contributions to the theory of computation, most notablly to the foundations of cryptography, pseudorandomness, probabilistic proof systems, property testing, and complexity theory at large. He is the author of several books, including *Foundations of Cryptography: Volumes 1 and 2* (2001 and 2004), *Computational Complexity: A Conceptual Perspective* (2008), *P, NP, and NP-Completeness: The Basics of Complexity Theory* (2010), and *Introduction to Property Testing* (2017).

Oded is an associate editor of the journal *Computational Complexity*, and was an editor of *Journal of Cryptology* and *SIAM Journal on Computing*. He has been an invited speaker at various conferences, including the 1994 International Congress of Mathematicians (ICM) and the Crypto '97 conference. He is a Corresponding Fellow of the Bavarian Academy of Sciences and Humanities, a Fellow of the International Association for Cryptologic Research (IACR), and a winner of the 2017 Donald E. Knuth Prize.

Authors

Zvika Brakerski

Zvika Brakerski is a faculty member at the Department of Computer Science and Applied Mathematics of the Weizmann Institute of Science. His research interests lie in foundations of computer science and most of his work is in theory of cryptography.

Zvika completed his Ph.D. at the Weizmann Institute in 2011, advised by Prof. Shafi Goldwasser, and then spent two years as a Simons Postdoctoral Fellow at the Computer Science Department of Stanford University.

Prior to that, he received a joint B.Sc. from the Faculty of Engineering and the School of Computer Science of Tel-Aviv University in 2001, and an M.Sc. from the Faculty of Engineering of Tel-Aviv University in 2002, advised by Prof. Boaz Patt-Shamir.

Johan Håstad

Johan Håstad was born on November 19, 1960, in Sweden. He received a B.Sc. from Stockholm University in 1981, a M.Sc. from Uppsala University in 1984, and a Ph.D. from MIT in 1986 under the supervision of Shafi Goldwasser. Johan was appointed Associate Professor at KTH, the Royal Institute of Technology, in Stockholm, Sweden, in 1988 and advanced to the level of Professor in 1992. He has research interests within several subareas of the theory of algorithms and complexity, but has recently mainly focused on the approximability of NP-hard optimization problems.

Johan Håstad was elected a member of the Swedish Royal Academy of Sciences in 2001. He was an invited speaker at the ICM in 1998 and winner of the ACM Doctoral Dissertation Award in 1986, the Gödel prize in 1994 and 2011, and the Knuth prize in 2018.

Yael Tauman Kalai

Yael Tauman Kalai received her B.A. in mathematics from the Hebrew University in 1997. She received her M.Sc. in Computer Science from the Weizmann Institute in 2001, advised by Professor Adi Shamir. She received her Ph.D. in Computer Science from MIT in 2006, advised by Professor Shafi Goldwasser. Her thesis won the George M. Sprowl award. She was an assistant professor at Georgia Tech (2007–2008), after which she joined Microsoft Research, where she is currently a principal researcher. She is currently also an adjunct professor at MIT.

Yael's research interests include cryptography, probabilistic proof systems, interactive coding, pseudorandomness, and complexity theory at large. Her most known contributions include constructing efficient proof systems and leakage resilient cryptographic schemes. Her research is theoretical in nature, though some of her work is used in practice. For example, her work on ring signatures is used by various cryptocurrencies, and some of her work on leakage resilient cryptography and on delegating computation has been implemented both on software and on hardware.

Yael is an associate editor of the journal *ACM Transactions on Computation Theory* (ToCT). She was an invited speaker at various conferences, including the 2018 International Congress of Mathematicians (ICM) and Crypto 2014.

Daniele Micciancio

Daniele Micciancio was born on November 23, 1971, in Palermo, Italy. He received his B.S. (Laurea/Diploma) in Computer Science from the University of Pisa and Scuola Normale Superiore in 1994, and M.Sc. and Ph.D. degrees in Computer Science from the Massachusetts Institute of Technology (MIT) in 1996 and 1998, respectively. He was a postdoctoral fellow at MIT Laboratory for Computer Science for one year, then joined the faculty of the Computer Science and Engineering department at the University of California at San Diego in 1999, where he has been a full professor since 2009. His current research interests include algorithms and complexity of lattice problems, their cryptographic applications, and computational models for the design and analysis of cryptographic protocols.

Daniele is most known for his contributions to the foundations of lattice-based cryptography, and he is co-author (with Shafi Goldwasser) of the book *Complexity of Lattice Problems: A Cryptographic Perspective*. He is associated editor of *Information and Computation, Journal of Cryptology,* and *SIAM Journal on Computing,* and was an invited speaker at various conferences, including the 2014 Netherland Math Congress (Beeger Lecturer) and Eurocrypt 2019.

Rafael Pass

Rafael Pass was born on November 3, 1976, in Sweden. He obtained his bachelor's in Engineering Physics in 2000 and a master's in Computer Science in 2004, both from the Royal Institute of Technology (KTH) in Sweden. He obtained his Ph.D. in Computer Science from the Massachusetts Institute of Technology (MIT) in 2006. He has been on the faculty of Cornell University since 2006 and joined Cornell Tech in 2013, where he currently is Professor of Computer Science. His research contributions are in the fields of cryptography and its interplay with computational complexity and game theory. Most recently, his research has focused on the theoretical foundations of blockchains.

He is a recipient of the NSF Career Award, the AFOSR Young Investigator Award, the Alfred P. Sloan Fellowship, the Microsoft Faculty Award, the Wallenberg Academy Award, and the Google Faculty Award, and is an author of *A Course in Networks and Markets: Game-Theoretic Models and Reasoning* (MIT Press, 2019).

Before starting research in computer science, Pass worked in the finance industry for J.P. Morgan and PricewaterhouseCoopers, and studied logic and philosophy at the Sorbonne in Paris.

Leonid Reyzin

Leonid Reyzin received his A.B. from Harvard College in 1996 and his Ph.D. from the Massachusetts Institute of Technology in 2001, advised by Professor Silvio Micali. Since receiving his Ph.D., he has been a Professor of Computer Science at Boston University.

Leo Reyzin's research is in cryptography and network security, with work ranging from foundational to applied. In particular, he has made contributions to the development of leakage-resilient cryptography, secure key derivation, authenticated data structures, moderately hard functions, and cryptographic proof systems. The applications of his work have ranged from cryptocurrencies to Internet routing.

Leo Reyzin has held visiting positions at MIT, UCLA, and IST Austria, as well as industry consulting positions. He has served as the program co-chair of the 2018 Theory of Cryptography Conference. His teaching was recognized by Boston University's Neu Family Award for Excellence in Teaching. His research was recognized with the 2014 Applied Networking Research Prize, the 2015 Theory of Cryptography Test of Time Award, and the 2017 Eurocrypt Best Paper Award.

Guy Rothblum

Guy Rothblum is a faculty member at the Department of Computer Science and Applied Mathematics of the Weizmann Institute of Science in Israel. His research interests include cryptography, complexity theory, and societal concerns such as privacy and fairness in algorithms and data analysis. He received his Ph.D. from MIT, where his advisor was Shafi Goldwasser, and his M.Sc. from the Weizmann Institute, where his advisor was Moni Naor. Before joining the faculty at Weizmann, he completed a postdoctoral fellowship at Princeton University and was a researcher at Microsoft Research's Silicon Valley Campus and at Samsung Research America.

Salil Vadhan

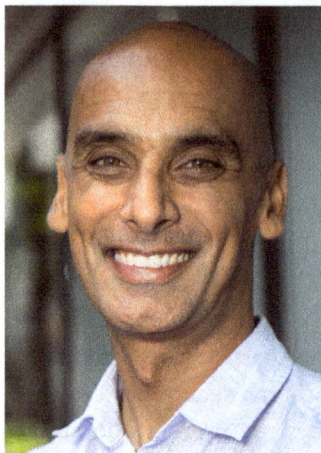

Salil Vadhan is the Vicky Joseph Professor of Computer Science and Applied Mathematics at Harvard University. He received his Ph.D. in Applied Mathematics from MIT in 1999 under the supervision of Shafi Goldwasser, after an undergraduate degree in Mathematics and Computer Science from Harvard University and a year of graduate study in mathematics at Cambridge University. Vadhan was a postdoctoral fellow at MIT and the Institute for Advanced Study before joining the Harvard faculty in 2001. At Harvard, he has served as the Chair of Computer Science, the Director of the Center for Research on Computation and Society, and Lead PI on the large, multidisciplinary "Privacy Tools Project."

Vadhan's research is in computational complexity and cryptography, with specific interests including data privacy, pseudorandomness, and zero-knowledge proofs. His Ph.D. thesis on statistical zero-knowledge proofs received the ACM Doctoral Dissertation Award 2000, and his work on expander graphs with Omer Reingold and Avi Wigderson received a Gödel Prize in 2009. He has also received a Sloan Fellowship, a Guggenheim Fellowship, a Simons Investigator Award, and a Phi Beta Kappa Award for Excellence in Teaching.

www.ingramcontent.com/pod-product-compliance
Lightning Source LLC
Chambersburg PA
CBHW080334220326
41598CB00030B/4504